January 27–28, 2019
Honolulu, HI, USA

Association for Computing Machinery

Advancing Computing as a Science & Profession

AIES'19

Proceedings of the 2019 AAAI/ACM Conference on AI, Ethics, and Society

Sponsored by:

AAAI & ACM SIGAI

Supported by:

BERI, Google, DeepMind Ethics & Society, NSF, IBM Research, Facebook, Amazon, PWC, Future of Life Institute, Partnership on AI, & University of Hawai'i

Association for
Computing Machinery

Advancing Computing as a Science & Profession

The Association for Computing Machinery
2 Penn Plaza, Suite 701
New York, New York 10121-0701

ISBN: 978-1-4503-6324-2 (Digital)

ISBN: 978-1-4503-7035-6 (Print)

Additional copies may be ordered prepaid from:

ACM Order Department
PO Box 30777
New York, NY 10087-0777, USA

Phone: 1-800-342-6626 (USA and Canada)
+1-212-626-0500 (Global)
Fax: +1-212-944-1318
E-mail: acmhelp@acm.org
Hours of Operation: 8:30 am – 4:30 pm ET

AIES 2019 Program Chairs' Welcome

It is our great pleasure to welcome you to the proceedings of the *2019 AAAI/ACM Conference on AI, Ethics, and Society – AIES 2019.* The second edition of this conference was co-located with AAAI-19 on January 27-28, 2019 in Honolulu, Hawaii, USA.

Concerns about the impact of AI on society have continued to grow in the year since AAAI and ACM joined to create the first Conference on AI, Ethics and Society. In the vision of this joint effort, it is only through multidisciplinary engagement and scholarship that we can hope to develop good responses to the challenge of ensuring that AI develops in a way that is safe and beneficial for everyone. This year's conference contributed to building a community of shared concepts and concerns. With submissions ranging across a diverse array of fields – computer science, philosophy, economics, sociology, psychology, and law – we enjoyed two days of engaging contributions that provided new paths for research.

A panel and four invited talks set the stage. The opening panel on *Responsible Artificial Intelligence: Aligning Technology, Engineering and Ethics* (with Yolanda Gil, Huw Price, Francesca Rossi, and Dekai Wu, moderated by Peter Hershock) was held at the University of Hawaii - Manoa in the evening preceding the main conference. The main program led off with Ryan Calo's invited talk titled *How We Talk About AI (And Why It Matters).* He highlighted the dangers of how we talk about AI: terms like "killer robot" and "arms races" may increase rather than decrease international cooperation, and Calo argued that focusing on "ethics" may reduce our attention to formal law and governance. In her talk titled *Guiding and Implementing AI,* Susan Athey (Stanford) drew on the theories of causal inference and incentive design to generate insights and research paths for the design of AI systems and organizations that integrate AI and human decision makers. Anca Dragan (Berkeley) urged a reconceptualization of the challenge of building robots that achieve human objectives within constraints as a human-robot collaboration problem with the aim of both coordinating behaviour and jointly discovering the goals of collaboration, in her talk titled *Specifying AI Objectives as a Human-AI Collaboration Problem.* Finally, in his talk titled *The Value of Trustworthy AI,* David Danks (Carnegie Mellon) explored the philosophical and psychological conditions for 'trustworthy' AI systems, and the importance of this complex notion of 'trustworthiness' for informed AI policy and public action.

The program of the conference included peer-reviewed paper presentations, with 35 papers presented as posters with an associated brief spotlight presentation, and another 34 as longer oral presentations. (The latter also had associated posters, if the authors so chose.) The program also included student posters. Conference session themes included algorithmic fairness, norms and explanations, artificial agency, autonomy and lethality, rights and principles, social science models for AI, measurement and justice, AI for social good, and human-machine interaction.

The call for papers attracted submissions from at least 30 countries. The program committee reviewed and accepted papers as follows:

Venue or Track	*Reviewed*	*Accepted*	
Technical Papers	220	70 (1 withdrawn)	32%
Student Program Applications	36	23	64%

Putting together AIES'19 was a team effort. We first thank the authors and speakers for providing the content of the program. We are grateful to the program committee, who worked very hard in reviewing papers and providing feedback to authors. We thank AAAI, and Carol Hamilton and Monique Abed in particular, for their support in organizing the conference in co-location with the AAAI'19 conference, and the University of Hawaii, and Sean Smith in particular, for hosting our panel. We also thank Francisco Cruz (website), Kenzie Doyle (conference assistant), and Kristen Brent Venable and Emanuelle Burton (student program chairs). Finally, we thank ACM and ACM SIGAI, as well as our sponsors: the Berkeley Existential Risk Initiative, DeepMind Ethics and Society, Google, the National Science Foundation, IBM Research, Facebook, Amazon, PricewaterhouseCoopers, the Future of Life Institute, and the Partnership on AI.

We hope that you will find the proceedings interesting and thought-provoking.

Vincent Conitzer
AIES'19 Program Co-Chair
Duke University, USA

Gillian Hadfield
AIES'19 Program Co-Chair
University of Toronto + Vector Institute, Canada; OpenAI, USA

Shannon Vallor
AIES'19 Program Co-Chair
Santa Clara University, USA

Table of Contents

Session 5: Rights and Principles

Spotlight 2: Fairness and Explanations

Invited Talk III

Spotlight 3: Empirical Perspectives

Session 6: Social Science Models for AI

Session 7: Measurement and Justice

Session 8: AI for Social Good

Session 9: Human and Machine Interaction

Invited Talk IV

Doctoral Program

AIES 2019 Organization

AAAI and ACM acknowledge and thank the following individuals for their generous contributions of time and energy in the successful creation and planning of AIES 2019:

Forum Program Chairs:

AI and Computer Science: Vincent Conitzer (Duke University)

AI and Law and Policy: Gillian Hadfield (University of Toronto)

AI and Philosophy: Shannon Vallor (Santa Clara University)

AI and the Economy: Andrew McAfee (MIT)

Steering Committee:

Vincent Conitzer (Duke University)

Subbarao Kambhampati (Arizona State University, AAAI)

Sven Koenig (University of Southern California, ACM SIGAI)

Francesca Rossi (IBM and University of Padova)

Bobby Schnabel (University of Colorado Boulder)

Program Committee:

Esma Aimeur (Univ. of Montreal)

Martin Aleksandrov (TU Berlin)

Thomas Arnold (Tufts Univ.)

Edmond Awad (MIT)

Haris Aziz (Data61/CSIRO/UNSW)

Solon Barocas (Princeton Univ.)

Simina Branzei (Purdue Univ.)

Markus Brill (TU Berlin)

Selmer Bringsjord (Rensselaer Polytechnic Institute)

Miles Brundage (Arizona State Univ.)

Emanuelle Burton (Univ. of Illinois at Chicago)

Lok Chan (Duke Univ.)

Robin Cohen (Univ. of Waterloo)

Bo Cowgill (Columbia Univ.)

John Danaher (NUI Galway)

David Danks (Carnegie Mellon Univ.)

Sanmay Das (Washington Univ. in St. Louis)

Louise Dennis (Univ. of Liverpool)

John P. Dickerson (Univ. of Maryland)

Gabor Erdelyi (Univ. of Canterbury)

Fei Fang (Carnegie Mellon Univ.)

Kay Firth-Butterfield (WEF)

Andrey Fradkin (MIT)

Brett Frischmann (Villanova Univ.)

Vasilis Gkatzelis (Drexel Univ.)

Ashok Goel (Georgia Institute of Technology)

Kira Goldner (Univ. of Washington)

Judy Goldsmith (Univ. of Kentucky)

David Gunkel (Northern Illinois Univ.)

Dylan Hadfield-Menell (UC Berkeley)

Subbarao Kambhampati (Arizona State Univ.)

Tae Wan Kim (Carnegie Mellon Univ.)

Sven Koenig (Univ. of Southern California)

Benjamin Kuipers (Univ. of Michigan)

Omer Lev (Ben-Gurion Univ.)

Irene Lo (Stanford Univ.)

Andrea Loreggia (Univ. of Padova)

Bertram Malle (Brown Univ.)

Gary Marchant (Arizona State Univ.)

Nicholas Mattei (IBM)

Steve Mckinlay (Wellington Institute of Technology)

Kuldeep S. Meel (National Univ. of Singapore)

Jason Millar (Univ. of Ottawa)

Ted Parson (UCLA)

Dominik Peters (Univ. of Oxford)

Huw Price (Univ. of Cambridge)

Andrea Renda (CEPS)

Juan Antonio Rodriguez Aguilar (IIIA-CSIC)

Heather Roff (Johns Hopkins Univ.)

Francesca Rossi (IBM)

Michael Rovatsos (The Univ. of Edinburgh)

Stuart Russell (UC Berkeley)

Jana Schaich Borg (Duke Univ.)

Matthias Scheutz (Tufts Univ.)

Susan Schneider (Univ. of Connecticut)

Munindar Singh (North Carolina State Univ.)

Walter Sinnott-Armstrong (Duke Univ.)

Joshua Skorburg (Duke Univ.)

Marija Slavkovik (Univ. of Bergen)

Eric Sodomka (Facebook)

John Sullins (Sonoma State Univ.)

Kristen Brent Venable (Tulane Univ. and IHMC)

Toby Walsh (The Univ. of New South Wales)

Robin Zebrowski (Beloit College)

Ben Zevenbergen (Princeton Univ.)

Student Program Chairs:

Kristen Brent, Venable (Tulane Univ. and IHMC)

Emanuelle Burton (Univ. of Illinois at Chicago)

Student Program Committee:

Lindsey Barrett (Georgetown Univ.)

Andrea Loreggia (Univ. of Padova)

Nicholas Mattei (IBM)

John P. Dickerson (Univ. of Maryland)

Dan Estrada (Rutgers)

Judy Goldsmith (Univ. of Kentucky)

Michael Rovatsos (The Univ. of Edinburgh)

Auxiliary Reviewers

Benjamin Abramowitz (Rensselaer Polytechnic Institute)

Adel Abusittac (Polytechnique Montréal)

Nirav Ajmeri (North Carolina State University)

Joe Austerweil (Univ. of Wisconsin)

William Bailey (Univ. of Kentucky)

Avinash Balakrishnan (IBM Research)

Yahav Bechavod (Hebrew Univ.)

Debarun Bhattacharjya (IBM)

Malik Boykin (Brown Univ.)

Gordon Briggs (Naval Research Laboratory)

Mithun Chakraborty (National Univ. of Singapore)

Meia Chita-Tegmark (Tufts Univ.)

Liron Cohen (Univ. of Southern California)

Cristina Cornelio (IBM Research)

Alan Davoust (Univ. of Edinburgh)

Upol Ehsan (Cornell Univ.)

Olivia Johanna Erdelyi (Univ. of Canterbury)

Bohui Fang (Jiao Tong Univ.)

Rupert Freeman (Microsoft)

Anne-Marie George (Technische Universität Berlin)

Paul Gölz (Carnegie Mellon Univ.)

Sriram Gopalakrishnan (Arizona State Univ.)

Sachin Grover (Arizona State Univ.)

Peter Haas (Brown Univ.)

Chung-Wei Hang (IBM)

Kerstin Sophie Haring (United States Air Force Academy)

Brent Harrison (Univ. of Kentucky)

Jobst Heitzig (Potsdam Institute for Climate Impact Research)

Matthew Joseph (Univ. of Pennsylvania)

Dan Kasenberg (Tufts Univ.)

Anagha Kulkarni (Arizona State Univ.)

Barton Lee (Univ. of New South Wales Sydney)

Jiaoyang Li (Univ. of Southern California)

Maite Lopez-Sanchez (Univ. of Barcelona)

Hang Ma (Univ. of Southern California)

Pradeep Kumar Murukannaiah (Rochester Institute of Technology)

Kamran Najeebullah (CSIRO)

Seth Neel (Univ. of Pennsylvania)

Hoon Oh (Carnegie Mellon Univ.)

Manish Raghavan (Cornell Univ.)

David Robinson (Cornell Univ.)

Abdallah Saffidine (Australian National Univ.)

Candice Schumann (Univ. of Maryland)

Andrew Selbst (Yale Information Society Project)

Sailik Sengupta (Arizona State Univ.)

Nolan Shaw (Univ. of Waterloo)

Cory Siler (Univ. of Kentucky)

Jakub Sliwinski (ETH Zürich)

Sarath Sreedharan (Arizona State Univ.)

Ana-Andreea Stoica (Columbia Univ.)

Zhaohong Sun (Univ. of New South Wales Sydney)

Tomas Trescak (Western Sydney Univ.)

Tansel Uras (Univ. of Southern California)

Kush Varshne (IBM Research)

Ellen Vitercik (Carnegie Mellon Univ.)

John Voiklis (New Knowledge Organization, LTD)

Patrick Watson (IBM Research)

Hong Xu (NHLBI)

Guangchao Yuan (Microsoft)

Yantian Zha (Arizona State Univ.)

Zhe Zhang (IBM)

Yair Zick (National Univ. of Singapore)

Website: Francisco Cruz (IIIA)

Conference Assistant: Kenzie Doyle (Duke University)

Organizing associations:

Sponsors:

Gold level:

Silver level:

Bronze level:

Other contributions:

How We Talk About AI (and Why It Matters)

Ryan Calo
Univ. of Washington School of Law
Seattle, WA, USA
rcalo@uw.edu

ABSTRACT

How we talk about artificial intelligence matters. Not only do our rhetorical choices influence public expectations of AI, they implicitly make the case for or against specific government interventions. Conceiving of AI as a global project to which each nation can contribute, for instance, suggests a different course of action than understanding AI as a "race" America cannot afford to lose. And just as inflammatory terms such as "killer robot" aim to catalyze limitations of autonomous weapons, so do the popular terms "ethics" and "governance" subtly argue for a lesser role for government in setting AI policy. How should we talk about AI? And what's at stake with our rhetorical choices? This presentation explores the interplay between claims about AI and law's capacity to channel AI in the public interest.

CCS Concepts/ACM Classifiers
General and reference

Author Keywords
Artificial intelligence, policy, rhetoric

BIOGRAPHY

Ryan Calo is the Lane Powell and D. Wayne Gittinger Associate Professor at the University of Washington School of Law. He is a faculty co-director (with Batya Friedman and Tadayoshi Kohno) of the University of Washington Tech Policy Lab, a unique, interdisciplinary research unit that spans the School of Law, Information School, and Paul G. Allen School of Computer Science and Engineering. Professor Calo holds courtesy appointments at the University of Washington Information School and the Oregon State University School of Mechanical, Industrial, and Manufacturing Engineering.

AIES'19, January 27–28, 2019, Honolulu, HI, USA

ACM ISBN 978-1-4503-6180-4/19/03.
DOI: https://doi.org/10.1145/3306618.3314225

Rightful Machines and Dilemmas

Ava Thomas Wright
Department of Philosophy and
Institute for Artificial Intelligence
University of Georgia
Athens, Georgia, U.S.
atwright@uga.edu

EXTENDED ABSTRACT

In a recent massive experiment conducted online, millions of subjects were asked what a self-driving car whose brakes have failed should do when its only choices were to swerve or stay on course under various accident conditions (Awad, et al, 2018). Should the car swerve and kill one person in order to avoid killing five people on the road ahead? Most subjects agreed that it should. Most subjects also agreed, however, that the car should generally spare younger people over older people, females over males, those of higher status over those of lower status, and the fit over the overweight, with some variations in preferences correlated with subjects' cultural backgrounds. But while such results may be interesting, they seem to me irrelevant to the question as to what a self-driving car faced with such dilemmas should be programmed to do.

Efforts to build explicitly moral machine agents such as self-driving cars should focus on *duties of right*, or *justice*, which are in principle legitimately enforceable, rather than on duties of virtue, or ethics, which are not. While dilemmas such as the (in)famous "trolley problem"—which inspired the experiment above—have received enormous attention in machine ethics, there will likely never be an ethical consensus as to their correct resolution, and even if one could be achieved, it would be largely irrelevant to the task at hand. What matters normatively is whether machine agents charged with making decisions that affect human beings act *rightfully*, that is, in ways that respect real persons' equal rights of freedom and basic principles of justice. Whatever private ethical resolution one prefers of dilemmas such as in the trolley problem, it is public law that should determine when makers or users of semi-autonomous machines such as self-driving cars are liable or culpable for the machine's decisions, and law must conform to principles of justice, not the partial ethical preferences of one group or another. The first goal of machine ethics, therefore, should be to build *rightful machines*, machines that respect public law and basic principles of justice

In this paper I set out a new, Kantian approach to resolving conflicts and dilemmas of obligation for semi-autonomous machine agents such as self-driving cars. First, I set out the modern Kantian rationale for the distinction between law and ethics, and the priority of right. In a society where everyone is morally equal, no one individual or group has the normative authority to unilaterally decide how moral conflicts should be resolved for everyone. Only *public* institutions to which everyone can consent have the authority to define, enforce, and adjudicate our rights and obligations with respect to one another. Hence the determinations of legitimate public institutions as to our respective obligations take *normative priority* over individual ethical judgments in cases of conflict between them. The coordinated relationship between law and ethics, and the priority of right, have important implications for builders of explicitly moral machine agents. The most important is that machine agents that act morally must first of all act *rightfully.*

I then show how shifting the focus to law and a standard of justice resolves the conflicts of obligation in the main variations of the trolley problem for rightful machine agents. Only one such variation, Driver, cannot be resolved by appeal to the priority of right, as it presents a true conflict (dilemma) of legal obligations. But from the point of view of justice, such dilemmas are little different from other conflicts of legal obligation. Unlike a system of ethical duties, the system of legal duties must be made consistent; otherwise, enforcement would be arbitrary and thus unjust. Hence dilemmas must be resolved in public law, even if there is no decisive rational resolution of the conflict at issue.

Finally, I consider how a deontic logic suitable for governing rightful machines can meet the normative demands of justice/ I argue that the role of a deontic logic of the law is not to neutralize or work around conflicts but to expose them so that civil institutions can authoritatively qualify the rights or duties that generate inconsistencies. I propose that non-monotonic logics can meet the normative demand for consistency, although a logic of belief revision may be preferred.

KEYWORDS

Trolley Problem, Autonomous Vehicles, Law, Priority of Right, Kant, Machine Ethics, Conflicts, Dilemmas, Machine Agents, Deontic Logic, Non-monotonic Logic, Belief Revision, Moral Machines, Rightful Machines

ACM Reference Format:

Ava Thomas Wright. 2019. Rightful Machines and Dilemmas. In *2019 AAAI/ACM Conference on AI, Ethics, and Society* (AIES'19), January 27–28, 2019, Honolulu, HI, USA. ACM, New York, NY, USA, https://doi.org/10.1145/3306618.3314261

REFERENCES

[1] Alchourron, C. 1991. Conflicts of norms and the revision of normative systems. *Law and Philosophy* 10: 413-425.

[2] Alchourron, C., Gardenfors, P. and Makinson. D. 1985. On the logic of theory change. *Journal of Symbolic Logic* 50(2): 510-530.

[3] American Law Institute. 1985. *Model penal code: official draft and explanatory notes: complete text of model penal code as adopted at the 1962 annual meeting of the American Law Institute at Washington, D.C., May 24, 1962.* The Institute, Philadelphia, [MPC]

[4] Aqvist, L. 2008. Alchourron and Bulygin on deontic logic and the logic of norm-propositions, axiomatization, and representability results. *Logique & Analyse* 203: 225-261.

[5] Awad, E., Dsouza, S., Kim, R., Schulz, J., Henrich, J., Shariff, A., Bonnefon, J. F., et al. 2018. The moral machine experiment. *Nature* 563: 59-64.

[6] Foot, P. 1967. The problem of abortion and the doctrine of double effect. *Oxford Review* 5: 5–15.

[7] Gelfond, M. 2008. Chapter 1: Answer Sets. *Foundations of Artificial Intelligence*, 3: 285–316.

[8] Goble, L. 2005. A logic for deontic dilemmas. *Journal of Applied Logic* 3: 461–483.

[9] Guarini, M. 2012. Conative dimensions of machine ethics: A defense of duty. *IEEE Transactions on Affective Computing*, 3(4): 434-442.

[10] Hart, H. 1973. Rawls on liberty and its priority. *The University of Chicago Law Review* 40: 534-55.

[11] Hohfeld, W. 1919. *Fundamental Legal Conceptions as Applied in Judicial Reasoning*, ed. Walter Wheeler Cook. Yale University Press, New Haven, CT.

[12] Kant, I. 1992. *The Doctrine of Right*, Part One of *The Metaphysics of Morals*, (1797) trans. M. Gregor [DR] In P. Guyer and A. Wood (eds.), *The Cambridge Edition of the Works of Immanuel Kant.* Cambridge University Press, Cambridge. All references to Kant's work are from the Cambridge edition unless otherwise noted. Citations are according to standard Academy pagination.

[13] Kant, I. *Groundwork of the Metaphysics of Morals*, trans. M. Gregor [GM]

[14] Kant, I. *On the Common Saying: 'That May Be Correct in Theory but It Is of No Use in Practice'*, trans. M. Gregor. [T]

[15] Kant, I. *Toward Perpetual Peace*, trans M. Gregor [PP]

[16] Liao, S., Wiegmann, A., Alexander, J., and G. Vong. 2012. Putting the trolley in order: Experimental philosophy and the loop case. *Philosophical Psychology* 25(5): 661–671.

[17] Maranhao, J. 2006. Why was Alchourron afraid of snakes? *Analisis Filosofico*, 26(1): 62-92.

[18] Mikhail, J.: 2007. Universal moral grammar: Theory, evidence, and the future. *Trends in Cognitive Sciences* 11(4): 143–152.

[19] Mill, J.S. 1977. *On Liberty* (1859), In *Essays on Politics and Society.* In J.M. Robson, ed., *The Collected Works of John Stuart Mill*, vol. 18, University of Toronto Press, Toronto.

[20] Navarro, P. and Rodriguez, J. 2014. *Deontic Logic and Legal Systems.* Cambridge University Press, Cambridge.

[21] O'Neill, O. 2011. *Constructing Authorities.* Cambridge University Press, Cambridge.

[22] Petrinovich, L., & O'Neill, P. 1996. Influence of wording and framing effects on moral intuitions. *Ethology and Sociobiology*, 17: 145–171.

[23] Rawls, J. 1993. *Political Liberalism.* Columbia University Press, New York.

[24] Thomson, J. 1976. Killing, letting die, and the trolley problem. *The Monist* 59: 204–217.

[25] Thomson, J. 2008. Turning the trolley. *Philosophy & Public Affairs* 36(4): 359-374.

[26] Tonkens. R. 2009. A challenge for machine ethics. *Minds & Machines* 19: 421–438.

Modelling and Influencing the AI Bidding War: A Research Agenda

The Anh Han
Teesside University
Middlesbrough, UK
t.han@tees.ac.uk

Luís Moniz Pereira
Universidade Nova de Lisboa
Lisbon, Portugal
lmp@fct.unl.pt

Tom Lenaerts
Université Libre de Bruxelles and
Vrije Universiteit Brussel
Brussels, Belgium
tlenaert@ulb.ac.be

ABSTRACT

A race for technological supremacy in AI could lead to serious negative consequences, especially whenever ethical and safety procedures are underestimated or even ignored, leading potentially to the rejection of AI in general. For all to enjoy the benefits provided by safe, ethical and trustworthy AI systems, it is crucial to incentivise participants with appropriate strategies that ensure mutually beneficial normative behaviour and safety-compliance from all parties involved. Little attention has been given to understanding the dynamics and emergent behaviours arising from this AI bidding war, and moreover, how to influence it to achieve certain desirable outcomes (e.g. AI for public good and participant compliance). To bridge this gap, this paper proposes a research agenda to develop theoretical models that capture key factors of the AI race, revealing which strategic behaviours may emerge and hypothetical scenarios therein. Strategies from incentive and agreement modelling are directly applicable to systematically analyse how different types of incentives (namely, positive vs. negative, peer vs. institutional, and their combinations) influence safety-compliant behaviours over time, and how such behaviours should be configured to ensure desired global outcomes, studying at the same time how these mechanisms influence AI development. This agenda will provide actionable policies, showing how they need to be employed and deployed in order to achieve compliance and thereby avoid disasters as well as loosing confidence and trust in AI in general.

CCS CONCEPTS

• **Computing methodologies → Model development and analysis**; *Cognitive science*; • **Mathematics of computing** → *Stochastic processes.*

KEYWORDS

artificial intelligence race, artificial general intelligence, safety AI, incentives, evolutionary game theory

AIES '19, January 27–28, 2019, Honolulu, HI, USA

ACM ISBN 978-1-4503-6324-2/19/01...$15.00
https://doi.org/10.1145/3306618.3314265

ACM Reference Format:
The Anh Han, Luís Moniz Pereira, and Tom Lenaerts. 2019. Modelling and Influencing the AI Bidding War: A Research Agenda. In *2019 AAAI/ACM Conference on AI, Ethics, and Society (AIES'19), January 27–28, 2019, Honolulu, HI, USA.* ACM, New York, NY, USA, 7 pages. https://doi.org/10.1145/3306618.3314265

1 INTRODUCTION

Research and development in different areas of fundamental and applied Artificial Intelligence (AI) have been making encouraging progress. Within the research community, there is a growing effort to make progress towards Artificial General Intelligence (AGI). AI brings enormous potential benefits across many sectors, being recognised as a strategic priority by a range of actors and stakeholders, including representatives of various businesses, private research groups, companies, and governments [2]. The media attention as well as the (un)announced business and political ambitions indicate that an AI bidding war has been triggered, competing to be the first to develop and deploy a powerful, transformative AI [3, 6, 7, 10, 11, 37]. These AI systems could be either AGI, able to perform a broad set of intellectual tasks while continually improving itself, sufficiently powerful specialised AIs or even AI specifically developed for espionage and cyberterrorism.

An AI race for technological advantage towards powerful AI systems could lead to serious negative consequences, especially when ethical and safety procedures are underestimated or even ignored [3, 11]. Safety and ethical agreements and regulations can be adopted to ensure that all parties involved in the race will comply with a set of mutually agreed standards and norms [31, 31]. However, as experience with many international treaties, such as climate change, fisheries and timber agreements [5, 13, 27] has shown, the autonomy and sovereignty of the parties involved will make monitoring and compliance enforcement difficult (if not impossible). Therefore, for all to enjoy the benefits provided by a safe, ethical and trustworthy AI, it is crucial to enact appropriate incentivising strategies in order to ensure mutual benefits and safety-compliance from all sides involved.

This position paper sets out a research agenda (i) to develop theoretical models (both analytic and simulated) that capture key factors of an AI race, in order to provide understanding on the dynamics and emergent strategic behaviours for different hypothetical race scenarios; and furthermore, (ii) to examine how incentives can be used to ensure desired outcomes and equilibria in this race. To this end, we combine research on incentives and agreement modelling, with the dynamical approaches that analyse population-wide dynamics, typically employed in Evolutionary Game Theory (EGT)

[23, 32]. Together, they will permit us to systematically explore how different types of incentives (namely, positive vs. negative, peer vs. institutional, and their combinations) can influence safety-compliance behaviours over time, and how such behaviours should be configured to ensure desired global outcomes (i.e. high levels of safety-compliance, possibly including compliant information sharing).

This research agenda is expected to lead to specific outcomes concerning the AI bidding war we are currently observing. On the one hand, it will provide methodologies for the investigation of AI race dynamics, including intervention mechanisms to influence outcomes. On the other, it will provide systematic understanding on how to promote safety compliance and the production of AI systems that benefit the many as opposed to the few. Moreover, conclusions derived from this project have the potential to resolve issues in other multiparty interaction domains, such as business transactions and international environmental agreements, for which commitments have been proven crucial [27, 35].

The rest of the paper is structured as follows. The next section describes relevant factors influencing the AI race and existing approaches for agreements and incentives modelling. It then describes our research agenda, which includes three directions aiming to provide a methodolgy for AI race modelling. Some preliminary results will be briefly described, elaborated further in the Supplementary Information section.

2 BACKGROUND AND CHALLENGES

Below we review relevant issues and potential factors in AI race modelling, and EGT [32] research on incentives, commitment and agreement modelling.

2.1 AI race and modelling

Potential AI disaster scenarios are many [3, 28, 37]. However the uncertainties in accurately predicting these outcomes are high. In general, the first AGI are likely to be extremely powerful and, if not developed and controlled properly, might not be guaranteed human friendly [3, 8, 10]. Those that first successfully develop more powerful AI will have significant benefits over others, and even 'the winner takes all' scenario might come about [2]. It is generally agreed that an AI-related disaster is more likely to occur when safety measures are ignored more often, which might be fostered by the speed and competition of the race. The risk of AI-related disaster increases when teams/developers do not devote sufficient attention and resources to safety in such a powerful system [2] as a result of the on-going race's pressure.

Regardless of this disaster risk, people and teams can have different (biased) perceptions or beliefs about the level and nature of the risk as well as adopt different risk-taking behaviours (e.g. with different levels of risk-aversion). A high belief in risk might lead to fear mongering concerning both AI and AGI, thereby leading to overregulation and unnecessary obstruction to the development of AI and the realisation of social/economic benefits. On the other hand, a low belief in risk might lead to more risk-taking behaviours, and hence safety measures being omitted more often. Furthermore, envisaging the AI race at diverse temporal scales is likely to bring about distinct aspects that should be focused on [1]. For instance, each team might anticipate different speeds of reaching the first general AI system. A low belief about fast AGI arrival could result in miscalculating the risks of unsafe AGI deployment by non-compliant rogue teams.

Other important strategic aspects in the AI development race concern different types of openness, including openness about source code, science, data, safety techniques, capabilities, and goals [7]. Some forms of openness, e.g. about safety measures, are plausibly positive both short-term and long-term. Others, such as openness about source code, science, and possible capabilities, could intensify the competitive situation. A central concern is that openness could exacerbate a racing dynamic: competitors trying to be the first to develop true AIs may accept higher levels of (existential) risk in order to accelerate their progress. On the other hand, openness may reduce the probability of AI benefits being monopolized by a small group and facilitate counter measures.

Given the several factors and biases driving the strategic safety-compliant behaviours and the dynamics of interactions among development teams, the outcome of the race (e.g. whether or not disaster occurs) is difficult to predict. Very few efforts have been made in modelling AI disaster and race dynamics among teams. In [3], the authors provide a game-theoretical model of an AI race, under the assumption that the first AI will be very powerful and transformative, so that each team is encouraged to finish first and thus skimp on safety precautions. This work, however, does not consider dynamical aspects of the race (e.g. how teams might adapt their strategies over time), and which strategic behaviours emerge in different race scenarios. Also, this work does not study how positive or negative incentives can be used to enhance teams's safety compliance.

To the contrary, there has been a significant body of computational modelling research regarding game-theoretical and EGT analyses of other disasters, such as climate change and nuclear war [4, 30]. However, the AI race and its related risks are quite unique, according to an analysis of 12 large global catastrophic risks in [28]. Climate change disaster analyses primarily focus on the unwillingness of participants to take on themselves a personal cost for a jointly desired collective target, and is conjoined to collective risk by all parties involved [30]. In contrast, in AI racing, the winner(s) will derive significant relative advantage over others, risk being more individualized. The AI race is also different from the nuclear arms race, in that the former potentially poses greater effective achievement or otherwise risks to its creator, whereas nuclear powers are generally not at direct risk originating from their own arsenals [3].

Finally, despite a number of proposals and debates on how to prevent, regulate, or solve the AI race, there is significant lack of rigorous modelling studies [6, 11, 14, 31, 36]. Our proposed research agenda aims to bridge this gap by providing basic models to systematically understand the dynamics of the race and what strategic behaviours would likely emerge, in different hypothetical scenarios and conditions of the race concerning disaster risk, risk-perception behaviours, level of information openness, number of racing teams, incentives deployment, etc. These models can then be used and perfected in discussions with stakeholders as well as policy makers.

2.2 Reward and punishment

Punishment and reward are major forms of incentives, widely adopted for enforcing cooperative behaviours among self-interested agents and enacting norm compliance in both social interactions and computerised systems [12, 21, 33]. Various forms of such incentives have been studied, which can be roughly categorised into peer and institutional ones.

To provide a peer incentive, agents pay a personal cost to punish a violator (peer punishment) or reward a cooperator (peer reward), after an interaction. As a result, the punished violator and rewarded cooperator incur a decrease or increase, respectively, in their payoff. In the context of AI race behaviours, examples of peer incentives use are when teams refuse to support, and so do not share development progress and knowledge with non-compliant teams, consequently slowing down their development. They can also arrange, for instance, cyber-attacks against non-compliant teams, or even ascribe and spread their bad reputation, leading to those teams being unable to recruit and retain developers. On the other hand, highly compliant teams can be rewarded, obtaining more support, such as knowledge and experience sharing, and thus move faster along in the development race.

In contrast to peer incentives, institutional incentives assume instead the existence of an institution (with a budget) to take care of the incentivising process [12]. Pool and coordinated group incentives, where agents can put together a fund before an interaction occurs to provide incentives subsequent to the interaction, can be considered as a first step towards institutionalisation of incentives [9, 34]. Examples of institutions providing incentives are modern courts and policing systems, as well as international organisations such as the United Nations (UN), the European Union (EU), the World Trade Organization (WTO) or the Organisation for Economic Co-operation and Development (OECD). Setting-up and maintaining institutions are costly, but the presence of a powerful authority can effectively restrict individuals' strategic options and provide stronger incentives [22]. In the context of an AI race, a centralised access to AI-related knowledge, algorithms and tools, as in the EU platform call (H2020-ICT-2018-2020) for instance, might provide institutional incentives such as strong support and punishment (e.g. allowing high levels of access or exclusion from the centralised pool of AI knowledge).

For both peer and institutional incentives, the critical conditions for cooperation to be achieved and sustained in evolutionary models, as well as observed in lab experiments, require that incentives 'fit the crime' [9, 34]. That is, they increase with the severity of the violation or the merit of the cooperation. Moreover, they need to be cost-effective, that is, the effect of an incentive for its receiver should be sufficiently large compared to the cost to the provider. Interestingly, for institutional incentives, the centralisation by which an institution might observe a global population state enables more efficient approaches. For instance, the 'first carrot, then stick' policy that switches the incentive from reward to punishment whenever the frequency of cooperators in a population exceeds a threshold, is highly efficient at establishing full cooperation, better than either reward or punishment alone [21]. Furthermore, local institutions that provide incentives based on local neighbourhood properties (such as its cooperativeness level) have proved more efficient than large global governance overseeing the whole population, in the context of climate change games and cooperation dilemmas [16, 38]. It may be that recourse to costly institutional supervision is only enacted when spontaneous peer cooperation becomes insufficient or inadequate.

2.3 Commitment modelling in dynamical systems

Commitment-based formalisms have been widely adopted in Multi Agent Systems (MAS) as modelling and engineering tools [35], with important applications in business protocols, transactions, and software-oriented architectures. Representing commitments that agents have to one another specifies their expected interaction and correct behaviour (e.g. cooperation and norm compliance). The formalisms allow flexible capturing of contractual relationships amongst the agents concerned and, as such, incentivise their correct desirable behaviour. In a commitment-based MAS, it is crucial to understand how an adopted commitment formalism, including its compliance incentivising approach, influences agents' behaviours and the dynamics of their interactions and, as a result, determines whether it can actually help foster and secure substantial commitment compliance and correct behaviour. This is typically studied in the literature on dynamical MAS, using methods from EGT. In this dynamical context, agents interact and adapt their behaviours over time, e.g. via social learning [17, 32, 34].

In fact, commitments have been shown to provide important pathways to reaching mutual cooperation in the context of social dilemma interactions (namely, in the Prisoners Dilemma (PD) [18] and Public Goods Game (PGG) [17] settings), within populations of self-interested agents. This dynamical approach has provided important insights into the design of commitment-based MAS, enabling identification of areas of strengths and weaknesses of commitment-based mechanisms. Consequentially, it is now possible to make specific efforts to improve on concrete issues. This approach also provides novel understanding towards the long quest for the evolution of commitments and their roles in the evolution of cooperation [27]; with important practical ramifications for social and economic interactions, ranging from personal relationships to business contracts and to international agreements [5, 13].

However, these modelling studies focus on standard cooperation dilemmas settings, i.e. the PD and PGG (for both one-shot and repeated interactions). When moving to AI race interactions, several factors need to be taken into account, as described above, such as the risk of disaster, risk perception and levels of openness. And the incentives need to be accordingly designed to account for these new factors. For instance, by requiring that signatories to an AI race treaty or agreement will commit to allow internationally governed inspections concerning a defined minimal transparency or the detection of secret of undertakings. Our study may incorporate specific distinct punishments or rewards for the case of violation or otherwise, or lack of due diligence, in both such cases. Public and employee opinion and consumer practice can also be mustered as another form of incentive.

3 RESEARCH AGENDA: PROBLEMS TO BE STUDIED

The literature reviewed above clearly shows the importance and gaps in modelling research to understand the dynamics of interactions and emergent behaviours in an AI race, as well as how incentive mechanisms might be used effectively to promote desired behaviours, such as safety standards and norms compliance from all parties involved in the race.

Our research agenda below aims to bridge this gap, and the following three directions or parts are envisaged to achieve that goal. The first one will develop baseline models for an AI race, on the basis of which the incentives for influencing the race will be studied in subsequent projects.

3.1 Development of baseline AI race models

The first direction aims to develop new, baseline strategic decision-making models that capture key factors relevant to the competition and cooperation among AI teams, and that investigate how they influence the outcome of the AI race. Namely, we will develop EGT models to answer the following questions:

- Which strategic behaviours emerge in the AI race?
- How does increasing the number of competing teams influence the evolutionary dynamics and outcome of the race, namely in preventing disaster?
- How does the risk-perception probability of AI disaster influence the race outcome?
- How does the heterogeneity of teams' development capacities influence the race outcome and strategic behaviours?

We envisage multi-player game models of multiple stages and/or repeated interactions, where a team might react to the development of strategic behaviours of other teams. The first teams to successfully develop AI will have significant benefits over others, and even the 'winner takes all' scenario might come about. Although we focus on multiplayer games, for there are most likely multiple competing AI teams, as the race evolves the game might end up at a later stage with only a few or even two (strongest) teams. Our analysis will start with pair-wise interactions, modelled as two-player games, which will afterwards be generalised to multi-team interactions, modelled as multiplayer games, in order to provide a more comprehensive understanding.

We start with the most basic scenario where at each round of the race a team or player is faced with two possible choices: to follow the safety precaution (SAFE) or to ignore this safety precaution (UNSAFE). Since it takes more time and effort to comply with the precautionary requirements, playing SAFE is not only costlier, but also implies a slower development speed, compared to playing UNSAFE. As a generalisation of this binary-choice model we will consider continuous games where a player can choose the level of safety-precaution to adopt (i.e. SAFE and UNSAFE correspond to the two extreme cases of complete precaution and none at all, respectively).

Teams can collect benefits from their intermediate AI products. However, differently from the standard repeated games [32] where all players collect benefit at every round, we will need to consider a new time scale, where different teams might collect benefits at different speeds. That would mean a possible time delay in players' decision-making, during the course of a repeated interaction, because they might want to wait for the outcome of a co-player's decision to see what choice he/she has adopted and/or will adopt in the next development round. Thus, a player has to decide whether to make an immediate move based on just present information (and hence be quicker to collect the next benefit and move faster in the race) but at the risk of making a worse choice, different from one that would have been chosen had the player already known the co-player's decision. Moreover, since noise is a key factor driving the emergent strategic behaviours in the context of repeated games [32]—for instance when a team might (non-deliberately) make a mistake in the safety process, which might intensify the on-going race and trigger long-term retaliation [19, 24, 25]—we will consider conflict resolution mechanisms such as apology and forgiveness [24, 26] for simmering down the noise effects on the race.

There will be a perception probability (by teams) that an AI disaster will occur wherein all teams lose the race, incurring a significant reduction in their payoff, and this risk-probability will follow a certain probability distribution. It is natural to assume that this probability increases with the frequency with which teams violate the safety requirements (i.e. play UNSAFE). Given the disaster probability, teams might have a different perception of the risk. For example, risk-taking (risk-avoiding) teams might underestimate (overestimate) this risk, leading to more (less) violations of the safety requirements. As in the case of climate change games [30], the perception of risk is a key factor driving the evolutionary outcome (whether or not disaster happens). The main difference is that in climate change models the risk (of failure in avoiding disaster) is collective, whereas in the AI race risk is more individualised: should an individual team ignore safety requirements too often, the more likely their AI product will lead to disaster.

Additionally, assuming that teams have distinct development capacities, i.e. that they might move at different speeds in the race, how does that change the strategic behaviours in the race by the different teams? Stronger teams might want to spend more effort with safety to guarantee no disaster occurs and ensure all the benefits from a powerful AI. On the other hand, weaker teams might want to water down or cease the safety efforts in order to catch up with the stronger teams.

3.2 Peer and group incentives for safety-compliance

This part of the agenda strives to investigate how peer incentives, such as peer punishment and reward, can be efficiently used, whether separately or jointly, for enhancing safety-compliance behaviours in the AI race games developed in the first part. Namely, we will address the following questions:

- What is the influence of using different types of peer incentives (separately or jointly), on safety-agreement compliance in the two-team AI race game?
- Generalising to multi-team agreements, how can peer incentives be used efficiently, taking into account the level of participation in the agreements as well as in a coordinated manner (i.e. pool and coordinated incentives)?

- How should incentives be customised to account for the level of risk (that an AI disaster will occur) as well as for teams with different capabilities of development and of commitment?

We shall start by extending the regimented agreement models for pair-wise and multiparty games, in both one-shot and repeated games, introduced in previous works [17, 18, 24], where interactions occur in three (decision-making) stages: (i) Before the interaction, agents choose whether to propose an agreement; (ii) When receiving a proposal, agents decide whether to accept or reject it; (iii) During the course of the (repeated) interaction, agents choose whether to play SAFE or UNSAFE, depending on whether the agreement was formed; and in the case of multiplayer games, also on how many players committed to following the safety precaution, because a minimum number of committing players may be required for an agreement to be formed and put into effect.

The regimentation assumption entails that agents who accept an agreement proposal yet dishonour it by defecting during the interaction (i.e. fake committers [18]), always honour and pay a compensation. Removing this assumption, another stage or decision point will be added: (iv) After each round of the (repeated) interaction, agents decide whether to use any type of peer incentives, depending on the decisions made by co-players and by themselves in the previous three stages.

This new decision-making stage adds extra layers of complexity, not just on how commitment behaviours are influenced by incentives, but also on how different types of incentives interact. Namely, we need to distinguish between incentives when an agreement is in place (i.e. incentives for agreement fulfillers or for violators), and when agreement is absent (i.e. incentives for mere cooperators or defectors). Considering all strategic behaviours concerning how to use incentives in co-presence in a population, we will examine how these two incentive sorts should be treated differently to foster safety-agreement compliance. Moreover, in order to have a clear understanding of the strength and weakness of each type of incentives, we will start from minimal models where only one type of (peer) incentive is present at a time. Increasingly more complex models, which include other types of incentive, will then be constructed and analysed to see how they interact and influence together the outcome of the race. So doing will provide deeper systematic understanding of how different types of incentives, whether separately or jointly, can be used to achieve high levels of safety compliance.

Rogue AI actors and teams might likely exercise antisocial incentives or bullying [1, 21]. We will consider this possibility in our models. Antisocial or bullying teams most likely refuse to join a safety agreement and are detrimental to cooperation. However, setting up a pre-agreement can provide an efficient solution. One can implement measures to restrict access of non-participating (rogue) teams to AI knowledge [17]; while misbehaving participating teams can be appropriately handled through the agreement's terms and conditions, both by coordinated and institutional punishments [9, 34]. This relates to the AI race, when a small number of major monopolizing actors or teams need to be confronted by the collective as a whole. Furthermore, promoting guilt [29] may be envisaged as a further way to simmer down the AI race, viz. the recent developments regarding Facebook policy change promises and Cambridge Analytica's declared bankruptcy, by appealing to public discomfort and the chastising of data bullies, again, possibly with the help of crowd sourcing or inside employees.

Our analysis will first examine two-player games since they will permit us to focus on the effects of different types of peer incentives. We will then extend the analysis to multiplayer games, which will include strategic behaviours conditional on the level of participation of teams in a safety-agreement; that is, how many teams agree to comply with the safety requirements. Previous works have shown that increasing the number of players in interaction significantly magnifies the complexity of the evolutionary dynamics and outcome. Firstly, since the number of behavioural equilibria might significantly increase, it is important to study under what conditions and how likely is it that desirable equilibria can be reached; and, moreover, how different types of incentives should be used, separately or jointly, to improve the chance of reaching such desirable outcomes. Secondly, it appears that collective decisions are more difficult to be made for larger groups [15]. We will study how increasing group size influences the probability of safety-agreement formation and, once formed, which are the players' compliant behaviours. Indeed, as shown in previous works for regimented commitments within group interactions, it is crucial to closely monitor the minimum level of participation when deciding whether a commitment should be effectively formed in order to achieve an optimal cooperation outcome [17]. Such a minimum membership requirement can be found in the creation of treaties that address international environmental issues and is also important for AI regulation agreements, as full consensus is rarely reached (as are the cases for cyberspace agreements organized by the UN [36]). Removing the regimentation, we will examine how different types and arrangements of incentives influence the participation level and how this level should be monitored to ensure safety-agreement compliance. Last but not least, in multiplayer agreements a new possibility arises where a group of players might coordinate to provide incentives with more substantial effects (e.g. gang up on free-riders). We will start by applying the existing models of coordinated and pool incentives [9, 34], where a group of incentive providers can share the cost of providing incentives and can decide to actually provide the incentives only if there is sufficient interest in sharing the cost.

In both pair-wise and multiplayer games, we will closely examine how incentives should be used differently, taking into account the diverse risk levels or probabilities that an AI disaster will occur. Does a high risk require stronger (or less so) incentives to ensure a high level of safety compliance? Also, considering that teams might have different capacities (for AI development), the question arises of how incentives should be used differently in light of a given capacity. For instance, stronger punishment might be required against teams who frequently violate safety requirements, especially if they are close to the finish line of the race. In contradistinction, stronger support and reward may be enacted for highly compliant teams, to ensure they win the race with a safe and powerful AI product.

3.3 Institutional incentives for safety-compliance

This final part of the agenda aims to examine how institutional incentives can be efficiently used for enhancing safety-compliance behaviours in the AI race games, and how they interact with peer incentives. The following questions will be addressed:

- What is the influence of different institutional incentives, separately or jointly, on safety-agreement compliance?
- How institutional incentives interact with peer incentives and how these two types can be jointly used to provide an efficient hybrid incentive strategy?

We will study institutional incentives in two scenarios: i) in the absence and ii) in the presence, of peer incentives. The former represents a fully centralised approach to regulating the AI development race, while the latter is a hybrid of centralised and decentralised regulations. In this latter case we explore different ways in which the two types of incentives interact. For example, being autonomous entities, the teams can decide by themselves the type of incentives used to enforce the safety-agreement, i.e. a peer or institutional incentive. It is natural to ask which option would emerge as the preferred one in the population and when. This can be answered by analysing EGT models in which all types of incentives are allowed to be adopted by agents in the population. Since forming a regulating institution is usually costly [22], we will identify when peer incentives are sufficiently efficient so that the institutional setting-up and maintenance cost can be avoided. This outcome is particularly important given the lack of attention so far to peer incentives for behavioural regulation in normative MAS, and moreover, to avoid (institutional) overregulation of AI development from the start.

In addition, a distinctive feature of the institutional setting is that the institution can have access to some global information, such as the current population composition. We explore approaches exploiting this distinctiveness. We will start by extending and generalising the 'first carrot, then stick' policy. The challenge is that there will be multiple types of strategic behaviours to incentivise, compared to only two types as in the usual standard institutional incentive models. At each time step, the institution needs to decide whether to incentivise (subject to a given budget) one type or even a subset of distinct types of incentive, depending on their current frequencies in the population. This institutional decision-making process is a complex multi-agent resource allocation problem [16, 20], for which appropriate resource allocation optimisation methods (e.g. from AI literature) can potentially be utilised.

4 PRELIMINARY RESULTS

We have obtained preliminary results for a two-team model of the AI race[1]. The race is represented by a repeated game, consisting of a number of AI development rounds, where in each round teams can choose either to play SAFE or UNSAFE. The former choice is not just costlier, but also takes longer (i.e. slower speed of development). The team that wins the race will claim a significant benefit, unless AI disaster occurs. Our analysis considers a population of teams who can either play SAFE or UNSAFE in all the development rounds, or they can choose to adopt a reciprocal strategy (namely, conditionally SAFE). The teams interact and can adapt their strategy through social learning (i.e. copying the strategy of those who are more successful than them).

In general the analysis points to the direction that when the benefit from winning the race is high, teams that always choose UNSAFE dominate the population for a large range of parameters' values. This result shows that, in the context of the AI race with repeated interactions, the strategic nature and the outcome are different from those of standard repeated games. In the AI race the rogue teams can move faster in the race by ignoring safety precautions, and reciprocal strategies such as tit-for-tat still lose because of being nice initially. This initial finding suggests that, to drive the race in the more beneficial directions it is important to enact measures that influence (prohibit or accelerate) the speed of AI development of teams, since reciprocal behaviours might not be sufficient to promote cooperative or safety behaviours in this context.

[1]The preliminary results can be obtained from the following link: tinyurl.com/y2gwhysy

5 ACKNOWLEDGEMENTS

All authors of this work are supported by Future of Life Institute (grant RFP2-154). L. M. Pereira also by FCT/MEC NOVA LINCS PEst UID/CEC/04516/2013.

REFERENCES

[1] AI-Roadmap-Institute. 2017. Avoiding The Precipice: Race Avoidance in the Development of Artificial General Intelligence. (2017).

[2] AI-Roadmap-Institute. 2017. Report from the AI Race Avoidance Workshop, Tokyo. (2017).

[3] Stuart Armstrong, Nick Bostrom, and Carl Shulman. 2016. Racing to the precipice: a model of artificial intelligence development. *AI & society* 31, 2 (2016), 201–206.

[4] Sandeep Baliga and Tomas Sjöström. 2004. Arms races and negotiations. *The Review of Economic Studies* 71, 2 (2004), 351–369.

[5] Scott Barrett. 2016. Coordination vs. voluntarism and enforcement in sustaining international environmental cooperation. *Proceedings of the National Academy of Sciences* 113, 51 (2016), 14515–14522.

[6] Seth D Baum. 2017. On the promotion of safe and socially beneficial artificial intelligence. *AI & SOCIETY* 32, 4 (2017), 543–551.

[7] Nick Bostrom. 2017. Strategic implications of openness in AI development. *Global Policy* 8, 2 (2017), 135–148.

[8] Nick Bostrum. 2014. Superintelligence: paths, dangers, strategies.

[9] Robert Boyd, Herbert Gintis, and Samuel Bowles. 2010. Coordinated punishment of defectors sustains cooperation and can proliferate when rare. *Science* 328, 5978 (2010), 617–620.

[10] Stephen Cave and Kanta Dihal. 2019. Hopes and fears for intelligent machines in fiction and reality. *Nature Machine Intelligence* 1, 2 (2019), 74.

[11] Stephen Cave and Seán Ó hÉigeartaigh. 2018. An AI Race for Strategic Advantage: Rhetoric and Risks. In *AAAI/ACM Conference on Artificial Intelligence, Ethics and Society*.

[12] Xiaojie Chen, Tatsuya Sasaki, Åke Brännström, and Ulf Dieckmann. 2015. First carrot, then stick: how the adaptive hybridization of incentives promotes cooperation. *Journal of The Royal Society Interface* 12, 102 (2015), 20140935.

[13] Todd L Cherry and David M McEvoy. 2013. Enforcing compliance with environmental agreements in the absence of strong institutions: An experimental analysis. *Environmental and Resource Economics* 54, 1 (2013), 63–77.

[14] Edward Moore Geist. 2016. It?s already too late to stop the AI arms race?We must manage it instead. *Bulletin of the Atomic Scientists* 72, 5 (2016), 318–321.

[15] Chaitanya S. Gokhale and Arne Traulsen. 2010. Evolutionary games in the multiverse. *Proc. Natl. Acad. Sci. U.S.A.* 107, 12 (March 2010), 5500–5504. https://doi.org/10.1073/pnas.0912214107

[16] The Anh Han, Simon Lynch, Long Tran-Thanh, and Francisco C. Santos. 2018. Fostering Cooperation in Structured Populations Through Local and Global Interference Strategies. In *IJCAI-ECAI'2018*. 289–295.

[17] The Anh Han, Luís Moniz Pereira, and Tom Lenaerts. 2016. Evolution of commitment and level of participation in public goods games. *Autonomous Agents and Multi-Agent Systems* (2016), 1–23. https://doi.org/10.1007/s10458-016-9338-4

[18] T. A. Han, L. M. Pereira, F. C. Santos, and T. Lenaerts. 2013. Good Agreements Make Good Friends. *Scientific reports* 3, 2695 (2013).

[19] T. A. Han, L. M. Pereira, F. C. Santos, and T. Lenaerts. 2013. Why Is It So Hard to Say Sorry: The Evolution of Apology with Commitments in the Iterated Prisoner's Dilemma. In *IJCAI'2013*. AAAI Press, 177–183.

[20] The Anh Han and Long Tran-Thanh. 2018. Cost-effective external interference for promoting the evolution of cooperation. *Scientific reports* 8 (2018).

[21] Benedikt Herrmann, Christian Thöni, and Simon Gächter. 2008. Antisocial Punishment Across Societies. *Science* 319, 5868 (March 2008), 1362–1367.

[22] Christian Hilbe, Arne Traulsen, Torsten Röhl, and Manfred Milinski. 2014. Democratic decisions establish stable authorities that overcome the paradox of second-order punishment. *PNAS* 111, 2 (2014), 752–756.

[23] J. Hofbauer and K. Sigmund. 1998. *Evolutionary Games and Population Dynamics.* Cambridge University Press.

[24] Luis A Martinez-Vaquero, The Anh Han, Luís Moniz Pereira, and Tom Lenaerts. 2015. Apology and forgiveness evolve to resolve failures in cooperative agreements. *Scientific reports* 5, 10639 (2015).

[25] Luis A Martinez-Vaquero, The Anh Han, Luis Moniz Pereira, and Tom Lenaerts. 2017. When agreement-accepting free-riders are a necessary evil for the evolution of cooperation. *Scientific reports* 7, 1 (2017), 2478.

[26] Michael McCullough. 2008. *Beyond revenge: The evolution of the forgiveness instinct.* John Wiley & Sons.

[27] R. M. Nesse. 2001. *Evolution and the capacity for commitment.* Russell Sage.

[28] Dennis Pamlin and Stuart Armstrong. 2015. Global challenges: 12 risks that threaten human civilization. *Global Challenges Foundation, Stockholm* (2015).

[29] Luís Moniz Pereira, Tom Lenaerts, Luis A Martinez-Vaquero, and The Anh Han. 2017. Social manifestation of guilt leads to stable cooperation in multi-agent systems. In *AAMAS.* 1422–1430.

[30] Francisco C. Santos and Jorge M. Pacheco. 2011. Risk of collective failure provides an escape from the tragedy of the commons. *PNAS* 108, 26 (2011), 10421–10425.

[31] Carl Shulman and Stuart Armstrong. 2009. Arms control and intelligence explosions. In *7th European Conference on Computing and Philosophy (ECAP), Bellaterra, Spain, July.* 2–4.

[32] Karl Sigmund. 2010. *The Calculus of Selfishness.* Princeton University Press.

[33] K Sigmund, C Hauert, and M Nowak. 2001. Reward and punishment. *P Natl Acad Sci USA* 98, 19 (2001), 10757–10762.

[34] K. Sigmund, H. De Silva, A. Traulsen, and C. Hauert. 2010. Social learning promotes institutions for governing the commons. *Nature* 466 (2010), 7308.

[35] Munindar P Singh. 2013. Norms as a basis for governing sociotechnical systems. *ACM Transactions on Intelligent Systems and Technology (TIST)* 5, 1 (2013), 21.

[36] Mariarosaria Taddeo and Luciano Floridi. 2018. Regulate artificial intelligence to avert cyber arms race. *Nature* 556, 7701 (2018), 296–298.

[37] Max Tegmark. 2017. *Life 3.0: Being human in the age of artificial intelligence.* Knopf.

[38] Vitor V Vasconcelos, Francisco C Santos, and Jorge M Pacheco. 2013. A bottom-up institutional approach to cooperative governance of risky commons. *Nature Climate Change* 3, 9 (2013), 797.

The Heart of the Matter: Patient Autonomy as a Model for the Wellbeing of Technology Users

Emanuelle Burton
University of Illinois at Chicago
enburton@uic.edu

Kristel Clayville
Zygon Center for Religion and Science
Kristel.clayville@gmail.com

Judy Goldsmith
University of Kentucky
goldsmit@cs.uky.edu

Nicholas Mattei
Tulane University
nsmattei@tulane.edu

ABSTRACT

We draw on concepts in medical ethics to consider how computer science, and AI in particular, can develop critical tools for thinking concretely about technology's impact on the wellbeing of the people who use it. We focus on patient autonomy—the ability to set the terms of one's encounter with medicine—and on the mediating concepts of informed consent and decisional capacity, which enable doctors to honor patients' autonomy in messy and non-ideal circumstances. This comparative study is organized around a fictional case study of a heart patient with cardiac implants. Using this case study, we identify points of overlap and of difference between medical ethics and technology ethics, and leverage a discussion of that intertwined scenario to offer initial practical suggestions about how we can adapt the concepts of decisional capacity and informed consent to the discussion of technology design.

CCS CONCEPTS

• **Computing methodologies** → **Artificial intelligence**; • **Applied computing** → *Decision analysis*;

KEYWORDS

AI and Society; Informed Consent; User Centric Design; Patient Autonomy

ACM Reference Format:
Emanuelle Burton, Kristel Clayville, Judy Goldsmith, and Nicholas Mattei. 2019. The Heart of the Matter: Patient Autonomy as a Model for the Wellbeing of Technology Users. In *AAAI/ACM Conference on AI, Ethics, and Society (AIES '19), January 27–28, 2019, Honolulu, HI, USA.* ACM, New York, NY, USA, 7 pages. https://doi.org/10.1145/3306618.3314254

1 INTRODUCTION

Algorithms, robots, and other cyber-physical systems play an increasing role in our everyday lives. These systems already make important decisions that affect our everyday lives: who deserves parole [4], who is approved for a home loan[25], and who is in need of medical care.[1] In the near future, such decision-making systems will be even more deeply integrated into individual and social experience, including driving vehicles [7], coordinating the rescue of disaster victims [14], and providing care to the elderly [28]. In ways both large and small, current and in-development applications of technology and artificial intelligence (AI) are altering the basic conditions of human experience.

All of these AI-driven decisions are necessarily predicated on comparative value judgments about human worth and human goods: the importance of children's lives vs. seniors' lives in a natural disaster, or the value of students' security vs. their personal dignity and privacy at a high-risk high school,[2] or the appropriate course of medical care for a terminally ill patient who is suffering [5]. These are the same value judgments that transplant teams make every time they prepare to operate, or other scarce medical interventions are allocated [24]. These ideas have received some attention in matching and allocation markets that are mediated by AI applications [18, 19]. Whether the values are pre-determined by developers or companies through a "top-down" approach or are learned by example through a "bottom-up" machine learning approach [2], these automated decisions—and the comparative values that are encoded in the decision making algorithms—will have a profound impact on people's lives and wellbeing.

But what exactly makes a human life valuable and distinctive? What qualities of internal self or external environment need to be in place for a person to be able to live and act as a person? How do particular changes to their environment enhance, or circumscribe, their ability to be a version of themselves that they recognize and prefer? Questions such as these can and do arise during the design, implementation, and production of technology, including robots and AI systems. Often the makers themselves are either unaware of the implications of the technology they are building or do not engage a broad, multi-stakeholder audience in order to understand the many kinds of value judgments and that shape their own thinking, and thus the systems they build.

In the absence of extensive training and experience in philosophy (or other disciplines that grapple with questions of fundamental value), such crucial ethical determinations are often a product of an individual's moral intuition.[3] And while intuition can be a reliable

AIES '19, January 27–28, 2019, Honolulu, HI, USA

ACM ISBN 978-1-4503-6324-2/19/01...$15.00
https://doi.org/10.1145/3306618.3314254

[1] https://www.ibm.com/watson/health/imaging/
[2] https://www.wired.com/story/algorithms-monitor-student-social-media-posts/
[3] Some philosophers do still argue that fundamental moral principles are grasped by intuition rather than reason or observation [29].

guide in familiar spheres of life, it is far less reliable when one is designing and deploying technology for groups or situations with which one is unfamiliar, i.e., young programmers making devices for infirm individuals. In addition, technology can and does create new conditions for human experience for which one's intuition is unprepared. Hence, it is imperative to develop terminology that is clear and useful for non-philosophically-trained technologists, to enable them to realize their goals for bettering human life.

The proliferation of AI in daily life makes it vital that technologists who are designing, building, and deploying these systems are well trained not only to build the technology but also to consider the impacts [8, 9, 21]. We argue here that, in order to meaningfully assess those impacts, technologists need to be able to think specifically about those aspects of the person that make them recognizable and distinct as people, and furthermore how those human qualities are amenable to improvement, or vulnerable to harm, through specific changes in the conditions of daily life. It is therefore imperative that AI ethics develop its own conceptual tools that can account for the particular ways in which AI can impact the conditions of daily life that affect personhood. Equipped with these tools, technologists will be able to discuss both the parameters and significance of the interventions that their designs are making, and to think more concretely about how design and programming choices can protect and enhance the lives of individuals and societies.

Using technology to enhance, rather than diminish, human lives is made particularly difficult by the knowledge gap between those who build and maintain the technologies and those who use them without the technological expertise to understand how they work. Normal (i.e. non-specialist) users face several disadvantages when confronted with even "easy to use" technology. For example, these users are less likely to be aware of potential security breaches, the signs of such breaches, or the steps they might take to prevent them; these users are also far less likely to be aware of any customization tools that would enable them to fine-tune their experience for their own personal comfort and convenience. Thus, *even at the level of everyday personal technology use, there exists a significant power imbalance between technology experts and non-experts.* The depth and scope of the imbalance grows if one also considers those experts' professional work designing, building, and maintaining the systems that other users rely on but lack the expertise to understand.

This expertise-based power imbalance, while particularly pressing in technology ethics, is not unique. A similar power imbalance has long existed in medicine, a field whose practitioners need extensive specialist knowledge even as they serve a user base of patients who mostly lack that knowledge. Because of the power imbalance implicit in the vast majority of patient-practitioner relationships, patients are often prevented from making choices about their own care even when doctors or nurses are at pains to leave the choice in the patient's hands [12]. To mitigate this problem, medical ethics has developed a family of concepts and practices to help its expert practitioners to navigate the inevitable imbalance in power and knowledge [26]. We argue that these concepts can be usefully imported, with some significant revision, into technology ethics [16]. Adopting these outlooks can then enable technology developers to identify specific technology design practices that preserve non-expert technology users' capacity for self-determination.

We describes the concept of patient autonomy from medical ethics, as well as the corollary concepts of informed consent and decisional capacity. We use a fictional case study to highlight both the points of intersection and points of divergence between the concerns of traditional medical ethics and technology ethics. We then propose working definitions of informed consent and decisional capacity that are attuned to the central problems facing technology ethics. Finally, we offer some concrete examples of how some current projects in AI and technology are working to support human autonomy, and how they could be adapted to support it further.

2 AUTONOMY IN MEDICAL ETHICS

Most western medical practitioners would identify **autonomy** as the central tenet of medical ethics. Autonomy is the principle that mandates **respect for persons**, meaning that individuals have free exercise with regard to whether and what kind of treatment to receive, and honoring this independence is central to contemporary medical ethics [17] . Patient autonomy as a governing concept in medical ethics is relatively recent; the shift toward it and away from medical paternalism was fueled both by broader social movements that sought to empower the individual and by the development of a more consumerist model of medicine as physicians sought to protect themselves from malpractice [6].

In practical medical ethics, the term autonomy has two distinct uses, which are related but can operate independently of each other. The first usage is to affirm that the patient deserves autonomy, the power to exert influence over what happens to them; the second usage concerns the question of whether the patient is able to exercise that autonomy. Because people frequently seek medical care at a moment when they are mentally or physically compromised, *it is not enough to affirm that a patient deserves autonomy. It is necessary for medical providers to take deliberate steps in order to protect the patient's autonomy, and ensure that the patient is able and empowered to make decisions that reflect their wishes, and that their wishes are respected even when they are not capable of asserting them.*

Neither dimension of autonomy—autonomy-as-recognition or autonomy-as-exercise—exists as a given. Due to the systemic power imbalance between expert care providers and their non-expert patients, two key constraints have been put in place to ensure that the patient's autonomy is honored in practice as well as in principle. They are **informed consent** and **decisional capacity**.

In the United States, when a patient undergoes a medical procedure, that patient must consent to it, and that consent must follow a conversation in which the doctor explains the procedure's risks, benefits to the patient, as well as other treatment options. After this conversation has happened, the patient signs a document acknowledging that this conversation took place, and the patient is thereby giving *informed consent* to the procedure. Because informed consent documents a conversation, *it is approached as a process rather than a one-time event.* Patients can change their minds at any point leading up to or during the procedure.

No medical procedures or treatments should be undertaken without informed consent, but only patients who have *decisional capacity* can give informed consent. In general, adult patients are presumed to have decisional capacity, but there are categories of patients who lack it. Patients can lack decisional capacity due to age (children), medical status (dementia patients), temporary states (sedated), or institutional status (prisoners). But this absence of decisional capacity is not permanent; children will age into being decisional and able to give informed consent, sedated patients may wake up, and prisoners may be freed, thus enabling them to make decisions free of coercion.

Ideally, a patient who knows they may be non-decisional in the future will prepare an advance directive, a document such as a living will or power of attorney form that either describes their preferences for care or appoints someone else to make those decisions, in the event that they are unfit to make decisions for themselves. In this way, a patient can protect herself from any decisions she might want to make when her ability to decide for herself is compromised.

Paradoxically—or so it seems at first—these limits on a patient's decision-making were instituted precisely to preserve the patient's autonomy, because they place limits on a doctor's ability to manipulate patients into undergoing treatments. The constraints were developed in response to abuses of paternalism, and were designed to constrict doctors' ability to take advantage of patients who were, for whatever reason, unable to exercise their own autonomy.

As medical culture has evolved toward being more patient-centered, the language and conceptual framework of autonomy have likewise been enhanced to focus more on how patients can exercise autonomy, rather than on the constriction of the doctor's. Patients can, in fact, prepare for a future in which they are non-decisional, by creating legal documents that spell out their wishes, should they be incapacitated. They can also cede decision-making power to specified others, for such an eventuality. In the absence of such explicit and legally binding instructions, it is assumed in most societies that a surrogate decision maker from the family can speak for the patient's wishes.

As we will argue, the concept of patient autonomy—and the related concepts of informed consent and decisional capacity—offer a useful model for technology ethics in thinking about how to preserve and enhance the wellbeing of technology users. As the above discussion illustrates, however, the core problems in medicine are not identical to those in technology. *In order for these imported concepts to be useful to technology ethics, they need to be adapted, but in a way that preserves the elements that make them useful.* We use the following fictional case study to illustrate points of overlap and divergence.

3 CASE STUDY

Joe is a cardiology patient who has two implants: a pacemaker, which regulates his heartbeat, and an implantable cardioverter defibrillator (ICD), which can restart his heart if it stops. This is a common case in the US with over 947 heart related implants per million people [20]. Some years ago, in consultation with his doctor (as is legally required), Joe requested and was granted Do Not Resuscitate (DNR) status.

Joe is suffering from the early stage dementia. At a recent cardiologist's visit, Joe was told that restarting his heart would be very painful, and in such an event, his heart would likely fail and need to be restarted repeatedly. It was unclear to Joe's doctor, and to his wife, whether Joe understood this information, but at the end of the appointment, Joe asked that his ICD be turned off on his next visit. Then at home, he changed his mind.

Joe's case raises a set of questions that are common to many medical ethics case studies, most of which center around autonomy.

1. How much of his current situation does Joe need to understand in order to participate in his own care?
2. Should Joe's cardiologist remind Joe about his request to turn off the ICD, or wait for Joe to bring it up?
3. Given Joe's (early-stage) dementia, can he be trusted to make decisions about his own long-term wellbeing?
4. Given Joe's dementia, how should caregivers weigh earlier decisions (e.g. his DNR) against what he says now?

The framing of these questions presumes the concept of autonomy: that Joe deserves the right to determine what happens to him, and this right to self-determination must be preserved in balance with medicine's broad imperative to preserve and extend life whenever possible. Joe's right to refuse treatment is recognized, but so is the fact that the very conditions of his treatment may mean that he is not decisional, and thus not fit to make decisions.

As technologists and those thinking about technology ethics will immediately recognize, this slate of questions excludes important issues, including issues that might be understood in terms of autonomy. Other questions should be raised about the security of Joe's personal information and self-direction that are directly influenced by the specific technologies that are now part of his body.

1. Who or what should make the decisions about the use of Joe's devices? In other words, should the defibrillator itself, a control system, or a human monitor (or some combination) be able to decide to not resuscitate Joe?
2. What means, if any, are available to Joe for altering his directives, once they have been entered? How complex or demanding is the process for making changes?
3. Who is responsible for the maintenance of Joe's machines and for the security of Joe's cardiac data? What if Joe doesn't want his data online?

Like the medically-oriented questions, these technological questions also recognizably concern Joe's autonomy as an end user. The underlying premises of the technology ethicist's questions recognize Joe as an entity deserving of the same sort of autonomy accorded to him by the medical ethics list. But there are two key differences between them. The first is that these questions expand the sphere of Joe's autonomy (in the autonomy-as-recognition sense) to include concerns about his personal information and to consider a wider range of possible agents who might impact Joe's wellbeing. The second difference is that, while these questions broaden the scope of Joe's autonomy as something for professionals to worry about, they constrict its actual exercise by the patient himself (in the autonomy-as-exercise sense). In focusing—appropriately and necessarily—on systems-level concerns such as information security and encryption of medical data, *these questions leave little room for Joe's ability to make decisions for himself, or even to understand what is at stake in the decisions he might make.* Although the questions are about the sphere of Joe's autonomy, they do not create or identify an opportunity for him to exercise it.

The contrast between these sets of questions highlights both how medical ethics could refine its notion of autonomy in conversation with technology ethics, and how technology ethics could benefit by importing the notion of autonomy from medical ethics. With respect to the first dimension of autonomy—recognizing what the patient deserves as a person—technology ethics usefully broadens the sphere of Joe's autonomy by broadening the scope of what counts as Joe's self. In an age when medicine relies heavily on networked technology and data, medical ethics needs to learn from technology ethics' reconfiguration of autonomy.

Yet technology ethics is less well equipped than medical ethics to attend to the second aspect of autonomy, the patient's right to determine what happens to him. A concern for Joe's right to exercise his own particular preferences might lead to questions such as the following: Does Joe understand the capabilities and risks (either to his body or his data) of the devices that have been implanted within him, to a degree that he can make an informed decision about them? Is he aware of the experiences of other patients with similar implantations? Does he feel able to ask his doctors to shut off the implanted devices, to opt out after opting in?

These are the sorts of questions technologists need to be asking when designing and creating the ways in which Joe will interact with the world. The goal of designing many technologies is to provide a one-size-fits-all or lightly customizable system that works for as many people as possible. This goal can come into conflict with notions of autonomy: what if a user does not want any of their data uploaded over the internet? In many ways it can be *more* difficult to respect patient autonomy and/or self-direction in designing and deploying technology than in medicine where there is a responsible professional who implements treatments. Therefore, it is not helpful for technology ethics to simply adopt the concept of autonomy from medical ethics unmodified. And yet, if the human wellbeing of technology users—technology ethics' equivalent of patients—is not to fade from view, it is crucial to identify and clarify a notion of autonomy that technologists *can* use, a definition that is analogous to that in medical ethics but more closely keyed to the problems faced in technology ethics. As technology increasingly sets the conditions for human life, this sort of working definition will prove crucial for technologists who wish to preserve a space for the exercise of human autonomy.

4 AUTONOMY FOR TECHNOLOGY

As our case study indicates, the high level idea of patient/user autonomy is relevant for both technology and medicine, though the precise definitions will be different. As human lives are increasingly managed at both the macro- and micro-level by smart technologies—and as medical technology itself advances—it becomes pressing for technologists to consider how to enhance, or at least to preserve, users' autonomy. To do so, technologists must consider not only users' right to make decisions for themselves (the first aspect of autonomy), but the conditions that enable them to exercise that autonomy (the second aspect).

In addition, technology ethics also faces particular hurdles in incorporating user autonomy into existing frameworks of inquiry and development. When we compare the two sets of questions in our case study, it becomes clear that individual autonomy can be easily overlooked by products or features designed to make users' lives more easy or efficient. One comparatively low-stakes example is Gmail's new suggested-reply feature. Although this feature does not coerce users into relying on its standardized responses, it rewards them with its convenience, and thus provides a disincentive for users to take the time to craft responses that reflect their individual voice or include non-urgent concerns. Sometimes these designs are conceived to "solve" the idiosyncrasies of how individual users, such as smart home security systems that detect authorized users by gait or biometrics and can therefore fail to recognize an authorized user whose stride or biometric indicators have been altered by mood or physical condition [27]. These hurdles are particularly difficult to overcome in the case of AI, which outsources both large- and small-scale decision-making to embedded and unmodifiable algorithms and models.

A further challenge faced by technology ethics is that there is rarely an appointed human mediator between the user and a particular device. While these pieces of technology are designed to be used easily, they are nevertheless designed to be used independently and by many different people. However, in medicine, complex decisions and processes are implemented and overseen by one or more professionals. No matter how personal technology gets, there will not be a human intermediary in every interaction. Hence, medical ethics is structured around the relationship between patient and care provider, which invests the individual care provider with particular duties and responsibilities. Any useful adaptation of patient/user autonomy must assign responsibility in a manner that is both ethically and ethical and practicable.

The concept of user autonomy can be rendered more manageable when we approach it by way of of informed consent and decisional capacity. These two concepts were developed in medical ethics as a means to preserve the patient's autonomy when her capacity to exercise that autonomy is compromised. Informed consent and decisional capacity make sure that the patient/user's autonomy is maintained even in the presence of disruptive or distorting factors.

4.1 Informed Consent

In a medical context, *informed consent* helps to preserve the patient/user's autonomy by requiring the doctor to keep the patient apprised of relevant information, and permitting the patient to rescind consent at any point. Informed consent presumes a user who never develops expertise of her own, and is not penalized for it; the burden remains on the expert-provider to communicate clearly and consistently with the user, to ensure she understands and that her wishes are being honored. While this is not the norm in technology, we are starting to see ideas like this appear. For example, the Android operating system's reliance on *permissions* for every application which can be granted or revoked from an easy-to-find screen [3]. Indeed, research in both HCI [1] and technology law [23] are starting to emphasize the requirement of explainability and transparency in delegated permissions within technology products.

Informed consent presents deep challenges to the basic design principles of technology, because it is deliberately inefficient and resistant to closure. *Whenever technological efficiency is achieved by eliminating the need for the user's input, there is a real risk that the user's autonomy could be compromised.* These challenges arise from informed consent for two main reasons: first, informed consent prioritizes certainty that the patient/user understands over the efficient delivery of information. Second, by allowing the patient/user to opt out at any point, it mandates a structure in which processes are begun but never completed, both because patient/users sometimes withdraw consent partway and because even consenting patients/users retain the option to withdraw consent.

But the inefficiency imposed by informed consent is crucial if the patient/user's autonomy is to be preserved. Because efficiency requires that certain decisions or functions take place en masse for a group of entities without stopping to consult each one, some kinds of efficiency cannot coexist with informed consent [11]. The smarter and more seamless a technology becomes, the more deliberate the technology designer needs to be about maintaining space for this sort of inefficiency. For example, a massive push update to a high-tech medical implant will be much easier to accomplish if the manufacturers assume that the patient/users have already consented simply by having the device implanted. If, however, a patient's condition or wishes have changed, she might not want her implant to be updated.

It is important to note that not all kinds of efficiency are necessarily at odds with informed consent. Many forms of automation increase the efficiency with which the user's goals are achieved without eclipsing her ability to revise her goals or judgments. There is no need for a given technology to build in opportunities for ongoing consent when that technology executes tasks the users already understand and intend to perform, such as washing dishes or taking depth or temperature measurements.

By looking back to medical ethics' notion of informed consent, we can usefully specify *what kinds* of inefficiency are important for maintaining use autonomy. In medicine, the deliberate inefficiency of informed consent affords the patient time to consider (and reconsider) her options in terms of her values and goals. It also forces the care provider to support the patient in this process, rather than imposing decisions upon her. Because the patient's goals or preferences might shift over time or due to changes in her circumstances, the efficient option—taking the patient's initial goals and decisions as a presumptive guide to the future—would undermine her autonomy. Such changes in goals or preferences can be understood as "human" inefficiencies: inefficient or unpredictable changes of character or goals that are essential to a person's autonomy and crucial to preserving their wellbeing. Medical informed thus consent protects the patient's autonomy by preserving ongoing ability to express her preferences, even when it renders her overall program of care more inefficient. In other words, the efficiency of the treatment process is valuable as long as it preserves or enhances the autonomy of the patient/user, and is potentially damaging to her autonomy insofar as it imposes efficiency on the messy and inefficient processes of self-determination.

Therefore, a usable concept of informed consent for technology ethics is one that enables technologists to consider the specific ways in which a given technology creates efficiency. Does it smooth the user's path to a goal she understands and wants? Does it equip her to understand which sort of determinations are being made for her by automated processes, and to single out the determinations that matter to her for further scrutiny and input? Does it create space for her to revise her engagement with it, should her goals or preferences change? With such questions in mind, a technologist is better prepared to evaluate which kinds of efficiency might categorically interfere with a user's autonomy, which ones require ongoing user input of some kind, and which functions can best serve the user in silent efficiency.

4.2 Decisional Capacity

Like informed consent, the notion of *decisional capacity*—the recognition that autonomous users are sometimes not in a state to exercise their own autonomy—can be adapted to technology ethics as a means to preserve and enhance user autonomy. As noted above, medical doctors use a range of criteria to determine whether a patient is decisional, but those criteria have two common denominators: they expect the decisional patient/user to make choices in a manner consistent with their previous character and preferences, and they expect any departures from that prior consistency to be "reasonable"— in line with socially-determined ideas.

Decisional capacity in medical settings is typically binary in nature, because the patient/user's role in the relevant medical process is widely understood to be one of consent, rather than execution. (See, for instance, [15].) If heart patient Joe decides that he wants his ICD turned off, his decisional capacity depends only on whether he is currently capable of making the decision: a medical expert (either Joe's doctor or an ICD specialist) will implement the decision. Joe will be the one to live with the consequences of his choice—which is why he must be decisional in order to make the choice—but his capacity to execute that decision is not a relevant factor. if Joe's judgment is sufficiently consistent with himself, and/or with what is "reasonable," to make what his doctor deems to be a clear-headed decision, then his decision is medically legitimate.

Technology complicates this notion of decisionality because, in most cases, users are also in charge of implementing their decisions. In some cases end-users may be unable to understand the technology of the interface of the technology in a way that enables them to actually implement their decisions. Additionally, it can require some deftness of body and mind to use technology well, which is difficult when in an impaired state: emails typed while drunk, or social media posts made in the heat of anger, can reflect the user's long-standing intent but still fail to realize her goals because her impairment limits her ability to act effectively. Like medicine, technology is a sphere that can magnify the consequences of a given decision; but unlike medicine, technology empowers users to act *without* the mediation of an expert who can clarify the scope or stakes of the user's action, or handle the niceties of implementation. Furthermore, as Vallor argues, the "sticky" enticements of a range of virtual goods can cloud a user's ability to distinguish what is most valuable to her, especially in the short term [30].

In most cases, the fact that technology extends the scope of its users' ability to act is the primary virtue. The fact that users are able to take these actions instantly, or near-instantly, is further evidence of the quality of a piece of technology. But these same qualities make users particularly vulnerable to undertaking actions whose technologically-augmented scope exceeds the user's capacity to assess the consequences in the moment of decision. It therefore seems not only helpful but necessary to adapt the notion of decisional capacity for use in technology ethics.

In order to be optimally useful for technology ethics, the notion of decisional capacity needs to be expanded to account for the user's role in implementing their own decisions. It can be helpfully recast for technology ethics as *decisional-executive capacity*, incorporating a second layer that raises the question of whether the user is fit, in a given moment, to undertake an action in a manner that they will be happy with later. Examples of at least checking for this include automatic tone alerts for angry emails and Slack warnings before a message is sent to everyone at the workplace.

Decisional capacity creates an opportunity for AI to enhance the autonomy of technology users and medical patients. As noted above, decisional capacity is quite imperfectly realized in a medical context, as doctors are far more likely to deem a patient decisional if the patient agrees with them. An AI, however, is less likely to succumb to this bias [13]. While a doctor's ingrained biases can compromise her assessment of whether her patient is decisional, the doctor-patient relationship is nonetheless a useful model for the AI-user relationship in one key respect. While consistency (the first criterion for determining decisionality) is best judged only with respect to the patient himself, the reasonableness of his wishes (the second criterion) is more broadly culturally determined; what seems like a good reason in one society may seem bizarre in another. Because the human doctor will be influenced by the same broad cultural norms, she is well-positioned to assess whether the patient's expressed wishes fit within those cultural norms, though she is also less likely to be sympathetic to reasons that do not fit those norms. In contrast, an AI that determines decisionality could be structured on universal terms. The ideal approach might call for an AI to learn primarily from local data in order to better assess the reasonableness of expressed wishes.

5 REDEFINITIONS AND APPLICATION

As noted above, autonomy has two necessary but distinct dimensions: the first recognizes the patient or user as an agent who deserves the right to exert control over what happens to them, and the second recognizes that the patient/user's autonomy must be actively maintained as well as acknowledged. Here we offer compact formulations of the two concepts crucial for maintaining autonomy.

Informed consent is the process of ensuring that a user understands the terms on which she is engaging with a given technology and is comfortable with those terms. The process is never definitively complete, because users' goals and preferences can always change with time and circumstance. It is also necessarily inefficient, to a degree, because automated decision-making gains much of its efficiency from the presumption that users' expressions of preference are definitive and do not need to be revisited. While few (if any) users would want to trade away efficiency for a thoroughgoing reevaluation of all aspects of their technology use, many if not most users harbor concerns or preferences with regard to some particular sphere of technology use.

Applications of Informed Consent. In order to balance the imperative toward efficiency against the demands of informed consent, we advocate a tiered model of explanation and consent when users are installing or using an app. Installation wizards that give the user the option of either standard or custom installation processes are a good basic example of this approach. A more fully-realized version would offer users a breakdown of all the component elements of a user agreement or of settings, and offer the option of default or customized setting for each separate component. The user's informed consent could be further enhanced by offering pop-up reminders to revisit each set of agreements or settings at a time increment of her choosing.

Decisional-executive capacity is a concept that can be used to protect a technology user's autonomy, by assessing whether they are in a suitable state to make and implement a decision that matches their long term goals. This term expands the medical ethics notion of "decisional capacity," on the grounds that technology users (unlike medical patients) are typically responsible for implementing the action they have decided is worth pursuing. Therefore, technology users need to be able to do more than select a course of action that aligns with their goals: they also need to be able to implement it in a manner that matches those goals. Incidental circumstances such as being angry, depressed, or inebriated can interfere with a person's ability to make decisions that they would later affirm; those conditions further compromise a person's ability to execute their aims in a manner that matches their long term goals.

Applications of Decisional-Executive Capacity. One application is to build "advance directives" into the technology in our lives. This would allow decisional users to plan for times when they are not acting in their own best interests. This could be as simple as 15-minute delays on emails or text, to help protect ourselves from angry or drunken message-sending. It could be restrictions we place on where their self-driving cars will take us (e.g., not to circle our ex's block), or it could pertain to our medical care.

Incorporating these concepts presents real challenges: we need to program universal norms for decisionality, but also program systems to learn cultural and societal norms [10, 22]; that systems can learn both the inherent desires and preferences for an individual, and their patterns of deviance (chemically or age-induced); that we can foresee which technology *needs* the ability to reason about decisionality; and finally, we can program systems to do the necessary reasoning.

6 CONCLUSION

There is a growing societal anxiety about AI that ranges from fears of loss of jobs for humans to terror that we will be displaced entirely by self-aware, higher-functioning AIs. One strain of this anxiety is that the machines will be programmed with more concern for efficiency than for the wellbeing of the humans they are designed to serve. But these things are not determined yet. What is necessary to balance the drive toward efficiency is a focus on how AI can support the distinctively human qualities of its users. We believe that engineers and computer scientists can learn from medical ethicists, and provide a vital viewpoint to the field of medical ethics itself. Through this, and broader communication throughout the industries and domains where AI is applied, we can ensure that AI can live up to the potential envisioned by its boosters, and become a vital part of the architecture of a better human future.

ACKNOWLEDGMENTS

This work was partially supported by NSF grant 1646887.

REFERENCES

[1] Ashraf Abdul, Jo Vermeulen, Danding Wang, Brian Y Lim, and Mohan Kankanhalli. 2018. Trends and trajectories for explainable, accountable and intelligible systems: An HCI research agenda. In *Proceedings of the 2018 CHI Conference on Human Factors in Computing Systems*. ACM.

[2] Michael Anderson and Susan Leigh Anderson. 2011. *Machine Ethics*. Cambridge University Press.

[3] P. Andriotis, M. A. Sasse, and G. Stringhini. 2016. Permissions snapshots: Assessing users' adaptation to the Android runtime permission model. In *IEEE International Workshop on Information Forensics and Security (WIFS)*. 1–6.

[4] Julia Angwin, Jeff Larson, Surya Mattu, and Lauren Kirchner. 2016. Machine Bias: There's software used across the country to predict future criminals. And it's biased against blacks. *ProPublica* (2016). https://www.propublica.org/article/machine-bias-risk-assessments-in-criminal-sentencing.

[5] Anand Avati, Kenneth Jung, Stephanie Harman, Lance Downing, Andrew Ng, and Nigam H Shah. 2017. Improving palliative care with deep learning. In *Bioinformatics and Biomedicine (BIBM), 2017 IEEE International Conference on*. IEEE, 311–316.

[6] J Andrew Billings and Eric L Krakauer. 2011. On Patient Autonomy and Physician Responsibility in End-of-Life Care. *Arch Intern Med* 171, 9 (2011), 849–853.

[7] Jean-François Bonnefon, Azim Shariff, and Iyad Rahwan. 2016. The social dilemma of autonomous vehicles. *Science* 352, 6293 (2016), 1573–1576.

[8] Emanuelle Burton, Judy Goldsmith, Sven Koenig, Benjamin Kuipers, Nicholas Mattei, and Toby Walsh. 2017. Ethical Considerations in Artificial Intelligence Courses. *AI Magazine* 38, 2 (2017).

[9] Emanuelle Burton, Judy Goldsmith, and Nicholas Mattei. 2018. How To Teach Computer Ethics with Science Fiction. *Commun. ACM* 8, 5 (2018).

[10] Vincent Conitzer, Walter Sinnott-Armstrong, Jana Schaich Borg, Yuan Deng, and Max Kramer. 2017. Moral Decision Making Frameworks for Artificial Intelligence.. In *AAAI*. 4831–4835.

[11] Brett Frischmann. 2018. Here's why tech companies abuse our data: because we let them. *The Guardian, US Edition* April 10 (2018).

[12] Saras Henderson. 2003. Power imbalance between nurses and patients: a potential inhibitor of partnership in care. *Journal of Clinical Nursing* 12, 4 (2003), 501–508. https://doi.org/10.1046/j.1365-2702.2003.00757.x

[13] Samia A Hurst. 2004. When Patients Refuse Assessment of Decision-Making Capacity: How Should Clinicians Respond? *ARCH Internal Medicine* 164, 16 (2004), 1757–1760.

[14] Muhammad Imran, Carlos Castillo, Ji Lucas, Patrick Meier, and Sarah Vieweg. 2014. AIDR: Artificial Intelligence for Disaster Response. In *Proceedings of the 23rd International Conference on World Wide Web (WWW '14 Companion)*. ACM, New York, NY, USA, 159–162. https://doi.org/10.1145/2567948.2577034

[15] DV Jeste, BW Palmer, PS Appelbaum, Shahrokh Golshan, Danielle Glorioso, Laura B. Dunn, Kathleen Kim, Thomas Meeks, and Helena C. Kraemer. 2007. A new brief instrument for assessing decisional capacity for clinical research. *Archives of General Psychiatry* 64, 8 (2007), 966–974. https://doi.org/10.1001/archpsyc.64.8.966

[16] Deborah G. Johnson. 2009. *Computer Ethics* (4th ed.). Pearson.

[17] Albert R. Jonsen, Mark Siegler, and William J. Winslade. 2015. *Clinical Ethics: A Practical Approach to Ethical Decisions in Clinical Medicine. 8th ed.* McGraw Hill Education.

[18] Shengwu Li. 2017. Ethics and market design. *Oxford Review of Economic Policy* 33, 4 (2017), 705–720.

[19] Duncan C. McElfresh, Vincent Conitzer, and John P. Dickerson. 2018. Ethics and Mechanism Design in Kidney Exchange. (2018). Working paper.

[20] H. G. Mond and A. Proclemer. 2011. The 11th World Survey of Cardiac Pacing and Implantable Cardioverter-Defibrillators: Calendar Year 2009–A World Society of Arrhythmia's Project. *Pacing and Clinical Electrophysiology* 34, 8 (2011), 1013–1027.

[21] Arvind Narayanan and Shannon Vallor. 2014. Why Software Engineering Courses Should Include Ethics Coverage. *Commun. ACM* 57, 3 (March 2014), 23–25. https://doi.org/10.1145/2566966

[22] Ritesh Noothigattu, Snehalkumar'Neil'S Gaikwad, Edmond Awad, Sohan Dsouza, Iyad Rahwan, Pradeep Ravikumar, and Ariel D Procaccia. 2018. A voting-based system for ethical decision making. In *Proceedings of Autonomous Agents and Artificial Intelligence Conference (AAAI)*.

[23] Frank Pasquale. 2017. Toward a Fourth Law of Robotics: Preserving Attribution, Responsibility, and Explainability in an Algorithmic Society. *Ohio St. LJ* 78 (2017), 1243.

[24] Govind Persad, Alan Wertheimer, and Ezekiel J Emanuel. 2009. Principles for allocation of scarce medical interventions. *The Lancet* 373, 9661 (2009), 423–431.

[25] A. Pérez-Martín, A. Pérez-Torregrosa, and M. Vaca. 2018. Big Data techniques to measure credit banking risk in home equity loans. *Journal of Business Research* 89 (2018), 448 – 454. https://doi.org/10.1016/j.jbusres.2018.02.008

[26] TE Quill and H Brody. 1996. Physician recommendations and patient autonomy: Finding a balance between physician power and patient choice. *Annals of Internal Medicine* 125, 9 (1996), 763–769.

[27] Michele Rapoport. 2013. Being a body or having one: automated domestic technologies and corporeality. *AI & Society* 28, 2 (2013), 209–218.

[28] Selma Sabanovic, Casey C Bennett, Wan-Ling Chang, and Lesa Huber. 2013. PARO robot affects diverse interaction modalities in group sensory therapy for older adults with dementia. In *Rehabilitation Robotics (ICORR), 2013 IEEE International Conference on*. IEEE, 1–6.

[29] Philip Stratton-Lake. 2016. Intuitionism in Ethics. *The Stanford Encyclopedia of Philosophy* (2016). https://plato.stanford.edu/entries/intuitionism-ethics/.

[30] Shannon Vallor. 2016. *Vallor2016*. Oxford University Press. 123–125 pages.

Requirements for an Artificial Agent with Norm Competence

Bertram F. Malle
Cognitive, Linguistic, and Psychological Sciences
Brown University
Providence, RI 02912, USA
bfmalle@brown.edu

Paul Bello
U.S. Naval Research Laboratory
Washington, D.C. 20375, USA
paul.bello@nrl.navy.mil

Matthias Scheutz
Department of Computer Science
Tufts University
Medford, MA, USA
matthias.scheutz@tufts.edu

ABSTRACT

Human behavior is frequently guided by social and moral norms, and no human community can exist without norms. Robots that enter human societies must therefore behave in norm-conforming ways as well. However, currently there is no solid cognitive or computational model available of how human norms are represented, activated, and learned. We provide a conceptual and psychological analysis of key properties of human norms and identify the demands these properties put on any artificial agent that incorporates norms—demands on the format of norm representations, their structured organization, and their learning algorithms.

KEYWORDS

norms; cognition; learning; artificial agents; robot ethics

ACM Reference format:

Bertram F. Malle, Paul Bello, and Matthias Scheutz. 2019. Requirements for an Artificial Agent with Norm Competence. In *Proceedings of 2nd Artificial Intelligence and Ethics conference (AIES'19)*. ACM, New York, NY, USA, 8 pages. https://doi.org/10.1145/3306618.3314252

1 Introduction

No human community can exist without norms [17, 44], and many past human communities have gone extinct with suboptimal systems of norms [45]. It stands to reason that communities that include both humans and machines as partners will also not succeed without norms. If this is true then we need to understand and formalize what norms are in the human mind—how people represent, learn, activate, update, and deploy norms to guide their behavior—so that we can effectively design artificial agents with appropriate capacities to represent and obey norms.

ACM 978-1-4503-6324-2/19/01...$15.00
https://doi.org/10.1145/3306618.3314252

If an artificial agent is to acquire human norms, its formalisms and algorithms must be informed by the properties of human norms—how humans represent norms, learn them, and use them to guide behavior. We introduce here core properties of human norms and define the demands these properties put on any artificial agent that incorporates norms. These demands range from the format of norm representations to their structured organization, from learning algorithms to communication skills.

In sociology and experimental economics, the importance of norms has long been recognized [31, 37]. These literatures try to explain human cooperation despite the individual's rational self-interest, and norms are an external force that constrains human action. But it is not known how such external forces can operate cognitively and computationally. A person complying with norms must have something in their mind that allows their action to conform to the norm, and that something may be called a *norm representation*. A few empirical studies have examined the automatic activation of such norm representations by situation cues—for example, garbage on the floor triggers the "don't litter" norm [14], or the sight of a library triggers the "be quiet" norm [1]. But no cognitive model has been offered that specifies at least some of the key properties of norm representations. This is what we attempt to do here.

2 Properties of Human Norms

2.1 Working Definition of Norm

We define a norm as follows [9, 11, 27]:

> A norm is an instruction to (not) perform action *A* in context *C*, provided that a sufficient number of individuals in the community (i) indeed follow this instruction and (ii) demand of each other to follow the instruction.

Elaboration. This definition captures both the "external" aspect of norms (they are obeyed and enforced by communities) and the "internal" aspect (that they guide actions). The term *action* covers a broad class—including physical (observable) or mental acts, omissions, as well as acts of bringing about a certain outcome. The separation into conditions (i) and (ii) follows a long tradition of considering both "descriptive" and "injunctive" elements of norms [9, 14, 16].

We can call condition (i) the *prevalence component* of a norm—that members of a community do in fact follow a norm (with a certain degree of consistency); and we can call condition (ii) the *normative demand component* of a norm—the degree to which community members demand of one another that each follow the norm. Because of this normative demand, violations of norms often lead to sanctions (e.g., criticism, isolation, reform, punishment). However, the existence of sanctions need not be part of the definition of a norm, as some have argued [8]. It is entirely conceivable that for some norm in some communities, no sanctions have been necessary to uphold a norm. That would obviously not make it any less of a norm.

For something to be a *norm* requires that people in a relevant community meet conditions (i) and (ii). For someone to have a *norm representation* requires that the agent knows conditions (i) and (ii); and for someone to show *norm compliance*, the agent both knows conditions (i) and (ii) and tries to follow the instruction *because* of conditions (i) and (ii).

Related concepts. Norms differ from other action guides, such as preferences, goals, and collective habits. The normative force condition marks this difference. A lot of people put milk in their coffee, but they do not demand it of each other, so this action is not a norm but a wide-spread preference. By contrast, getting in line to order coffee is a norm, because that is what people would expect of each other. Norms also differ from values, and the notion of being instructions to act in a particular context marks this difference. Values (such as fairness, freedom, dignity) typically govern a larger class of possible actions/outcomes across a wider range of contexts [39].

2.2 Implied and Suggested Properties

We now discuss six properties of norms, either implied by or further elaborated from the working definition, and develop demands that these properties put on artificial agents' norm representations.

2.2.1. Multiple norm types. A widely recognized property is that norms can be of multiple deontic types: at least prescriptions, prohibitions, and permissions. Any representation of a norm-guided action must signal which of the types governs the particular action.

2.2.2. Context sensitivity. A second critical property of norms is that they are context-specific and must somehow be activated by characteristic features of a given context. In initial research we asked people to state the prescription norms that applied to a variety of everyday scenes (e.g., board room, jogging path). Of the mentioned norms, 95% applied uniquely to one specific context.

2.2.3. Community prevalence. A third property is that genuine norms have sufficient prevalence—that is, most community members comply with a given norm and are aware of that collective compliance. In initial research we found that the top 8 prescription or prohibition norms that people stated for various everyday scenes showed prevalence rates between 94% (most prevalent) and 21% (8th-most prevalent). Beyond the actual agreement rates, people also have a *belief* about the norm's prevalence in the community, which we can call the *prevalence parameter*. Though this belief is not necessarily accurate [33], it will often be based on reasonably representative behavioral data.

2.2.4. Graded normative demand. An infrequently noted property is that (at least) prescriptions and prohibitions come in degrees of community demand [15, 26, 29]. At least in English, terms of prescription can capture low demand ("it is suggested to A") to high demand ("it is required to *A*"), with further gradations in between. Likewise, terms of prohibition can capture low demand ("it is frowned upon to *A*") to high demand ("it is forbidden to *A*"). In preliminary research we found that people show high consensus in ordering these terms along a dimension of normative demand, and Figure 1 shows such orderings for all three norm types. Thus, human norm representations include a graded normative demand parameter.

A norm's degree of normative demand is likely to be closely related to its prevalence, but the two are not reducible to each other. In general, the more strongly people demand of others to conform to norm N_i, the more people will obey it. But when community norms change, strong demand sometimes lingers even though prevalence is declining [24]; and for some norms of only modest normative demand, prevalence may be high (e.g., if the benefits of norm conformity are considerable). Even though the exact relationship between prevalence and normative demand is unknown, as a first approximation we can assume that demand is a linear function of prevalence and other factors such as severity of consequences.

2.2.5 Resolving norm conflict by normative demand. Sometimes norms stand in conflict with one another such that, in the given context, every action violates at least one norm (e.g., in moral dilemmas). Because normative demand comes in degrees, violating some norms will be more costly than violating others, so norm conflict resolution will have to take graded normative demand into account [15, 20].

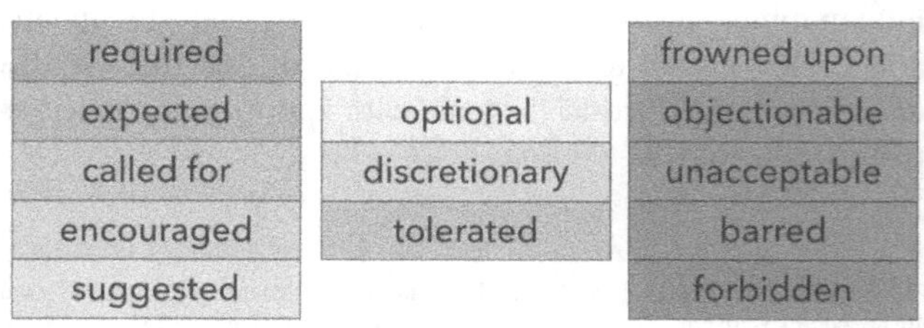

Figure 1: English language terms for graded normative demand in prescriptions (left), prohibitions (right), and permissions (middle).

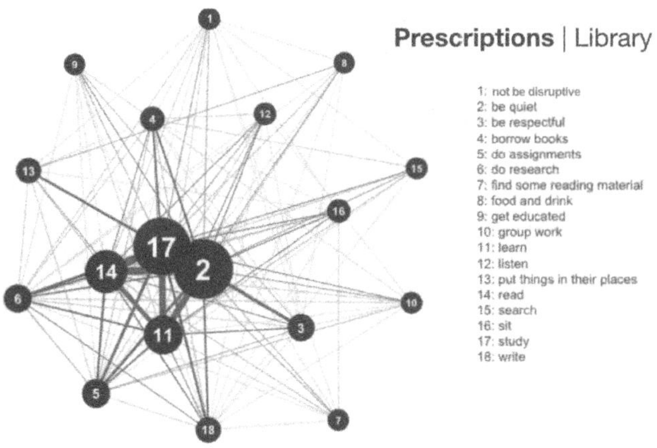

Figure 2. Network representation of prescriptions people generated when exposed to the picture of a library. Larger circles indicate norms mentioned by more people.

2.2.6. Structured representation of norms. The norms relevant to a particular context must be organized in some way. One plausible organization is a network structure that has some core (strong or consensual) norms at the center and other (weaker or less consensual) norms in the periphery. In our preliminary research we found that norms generated by a sample of participants for specific contexts clustered together in such networks (see Figure 2 as an illustration). We also found that, when exposed to a particular context, norms mentioned earlier were more prevalent—thus, they were likely at the core of the network.

3. Formal Representation

Most formal approaches to norm representations have used logical formalisms [12, 32]. One way of formalizing context-specific norms is to introduce a deontic operator $\mathbb{D}$ (instantiating a prescription, prohibition, or permission) for an action A, thus $N_i := C_j \rightarrow \mathbb{D}(A_k)$. C_j may be defined extensionally as a set of preconditions in the world under which A_k is prescribed/prohibited/permitted. It is implausible that these preconditions are linked together as a long conjunction; more plausible is an overall likelihood estimation that aggregates the presence of features into something akin to a sufficient statistic. Given a sample of features from a population, it should be more likely that C_j holds than that any other C holds, even if the specific sample may slightly differ from instance to instance.

However, the material implication $C_j \rightarrow \mathbb{D}(A_k)$ has a number of unattractive properties for deontic reasoning (e.g., [13]). An alternative formulation would be $N_i := \mathbb{D}(A_k, C_j)$, in which the deontic operator establishes a relation between actions and contexts. To capture the parameter of *graded normative demand*, however, the classical interpretation of $\mathbb{D}$ must be expanded to take on a value between 0 and 1, where 0 = prohibited, 0.5 = permitted (optional), and 1.0 = prescribed. A recent proposal further integrated the *prevalence* parameter by defining prevalence as the uncertainty over an estimated deontic value, formally a confidence interval around the normative demand estimate [26].

4. Requirements for Norm-Competent Agents

Summarizing the above properties of norm representations and the suggested formal representation we can now identify a number of requirements for an artificial agent to appropriately represent and learn norms. Some of these constraints have also been discussed in the multi-agent systems literature [25], but typically from a more behavioral and collective perspective. Our contribution is to focus on cognitive properties of norms in individual agents.

4.1 Multiple Norm Types and Action Planning

The three deontic categories (prescriptions, prohibitions, or permissions) must be properly mapped onto the agent's planning and action modules [40]. *Prescriptions* generate goals, with a goal priority value dictated by the prescriptions' normative demand values. *Permissions* affirm current goals that are already set or pursued by the system. *Prohibitions* stop the pursuit of goals, if during this pursuit any actions or consequences fall under prohibited actions or outcomes. In principle, one might wish that during planning *any* considered action path be compared to the agent's norm network to avoid violating prohibitions, but this strategy could quickly lead to computational explosion. The number of norms against which the candidate action is compared must be restricted. Limiting the contexts the agent may find itself in would help. In addition, the agent's planning could be primarily guided by context-specific *prescriptions* because, if the right ones are activated, they are safe to pursue, and their numbers will generally be manageable. If the agent is about to pursue a goal, then it could first be compared against this more limited prescription set for the given context, and if there is no match, a question of clarification may be in order (e.g., "This goal is not among my duties...").

4.2. Context Sensitivity and Context Recognition

The property of context sensitivity requires that the agent recognize what context it is in and activate the context-appropriate norms. It is currently unknown exactly how humans recognize contexts and how context activates the relevant norms. But it is clear that many elements go into context: space (e.g., the room one enters), time (e.g., morning vs. evening), event type (e.g., party, debate), who is present in what role (e.g., friends, authorities), agent's own role (e.g., assistant, guest), and more. In order to activate the right set of norms, the norms "preconditions" must be tested. at least two approaches are available [27]. One, the agent may collect a sufficient number of features from the observed environment and from its knowledge base that make being in a particular context C_j likely, which then activates the norm set that is relevant for C_j. Second, the agent may activate specific norms relevant to specific features in the environment (e.g., a chair, someone else's phone, someone giving a speech) without necessarily making an overall categorical determination which "context" it is in; instead, it would rely on the world to naturally make features co-occur such that the set of feature-activated norms turns out to be the right set for the particular context.

Whichever model is correct, both context (feature) recognition and norm activation put enormous demands on the agent in terms of perception, attention, and categorization capacities. In general, sophisticated scene understanding is not possible for today's artificial agents. Significant progress has been made in object classification, but recognizing relations that define contexts (e.g., *when this person in this role performs this action in this space*) is currently out of reach. What is challenging about relational information is that many relations that uniquely pick out contexts need to be recognized over different temporal scales, and all sorts of relations could exist (in principle) between the various relata (i.e. objects, events, etc.) in a scene. Considering all possible relations and testing whether they indicate that one is in a certain context is computationally inefficient.

Memory for the objects and events that typically appear in contexts might provide initial hypotheses for which context one might be in, but verifying and disconfirming these hypotheses requires further action. One candidate to supplement memory-based relational processing is *attention* [21], which offers several advantages. First, top-down attentional guidance will narrow the space of relations to be considered, and attention plausibly realizes so-called "visual routines" [43], which can be run to verify whether or not a relation holds [7, 47].

Artificial agents might also do better when constraints are in place on the contexts to be recognized. First, the agent could be deployed in a limited domain that has a limited number of contexts (e.g., a nursing home robot, a cafeteria bussing robot). The agent could then be equipped with a knowledge base of reasonably reliable indicators of the likely (sub)contexts it could find itself. Searching for such tell-tale indicators (rather than scanning all possible scene features) would greatly speed up processing and increase accuracy of context recognition. Second, hypotheses about which context the agent is in and hypotheses about which norms apply could mutually constrain one another. That is, some initially activated norms (e.g., activated by a few salient objects or persons in the scene) might serve to narrow down just what context an agent is in. As norms are highly context specific, the co-activation of even just a small subset of initially activated norms could make it very likely that one is in context C_j, rather than in any other candidate context. This hypothesis of being in C_j would then initiate selective attention to additional features that tend to uniquely characterize C_j, further (dis)confirming this context hypothesis. By extension, the context hypothesis makes predictions about additional applicable norms that can be tested by observing other agents' behaviors or by calculating their joint likelihood with the subset of initially activated norms.

4.3 Prevalence Parameter

An agent's prevalence parameter would reflect an estimate of the proportion of people in the community who actually obey the norm. Mere observation will typically not suffice to achieve such an estimate (see our discussion of the limits of observation below), so the designer will have to provide a starting value that can be updated, through both observing community members and querying them about their norm perceptions and practices (just like humans in foreign countries query locals about their norms).

4.4. Normative Demand Parameter

Including a graded normative demand parameter will require collating evidence form a number of sources in the relevant community: prevalence of norm compliance (because stronger norms tend to be followed more consistently); intensity of demand expressions (e.g., verbal exhortations, warnings); and intensity of sanctions upon violation (e.g., yelling at a person for committing a violation).

4.5. Norm Conflict Resolution Algorithms

An agent facing conflicts among norms will have to rely on the conflicting norms' demand parameters to minimize violation costs [22]. For example, [20] proposed an algorithm within a Markov Decision Process framework where norms are represented in linear temporal logic as temporal expressions that the agent intends to make true. In doing so, agents attempt to obey as many norms as possible, closely monitor the relative normative demand (importance), and minimize aggregated violation costs (whereby greater costs accrue for stronger norms and for temporally more extended states of violation).

4.6 Structured Organization

Building norm representations that have a structured organization (e.g., network structure) will be challenging because little is known about how human norm networks are organized. A plausible hypothesis is that such networks have a core and a periphery, with core nodes being more prevalent and/or more important. Nodes would represent action instructions (with a normative demand parameter), and edges would stand for the probability of co-activation in the same context. It can be expected that human norm networks have "small-world properties" [42]: Nodes in the network are connected to only a small subset of all nodes and have high degrees of clustering, but the clusters can be traversed with relatively short path lengths (i.e., there are many context-specific subnetworks that are nonetheless connected by linking nodes). Though semantic networks have these properties [41], norm networks are likely to differ from semantic networks. For example, norms and their high degree of context specificity would likely show even more clustering and sparseness;

moreover, the demand and prevalence parameters associated with norms differ considerably from the properties of word meanings.

5. Implications for Norm Learning

We now turn to the greatest challenge of designing norm-competent artificial agents: how they could acquire norms. We begin with the case of human norm learning and then develop implications for norm learning in artificial agents.

5.1 Human Norm Learning

Most generally, norm learning refers to the process of extracting $\mathbb{D}(A_k \mid C_j)$ relations from evidence in the world, estimating prevalence and normative demand. What is this evidence in the world that reveals norms? We categorize this evidence into four types and briefly discuss each type.

5.1.1 Explicit instructions. The most direct evidence for a norm is its declaration, in symbols (e.g., signs) or verbal utterances. However, signs are rare (consider how few laws are publicly displayed), and verbal norm instructions may be even rarer [46]. When provided, however, such explicit instructions can both provide information about prevalence (e.g., "Everybody here is making a donation...") and also scale community demand by choosing the graded linguistic expressions of normative demand, as shown in Figure 1.

5.1.2 Behavior patterns. Observing other community members' behavior is a powerful second type of evidence for the presence of a norm [28]. For example, by looking at others in a cafeteria we deduce whether we are expected to bus our own dishes or someone else does it. Already from ages 2 to 3 on, children readily infer norms from other people's behavior [34]. Mere behavioral observation, however, provides only limited information. First, whereas trends of behavior reveal the prevalence of prescriptions, they are sparse with respect to prohibitions, because when people comply with prohibitions there is typically no behavior to be observed. Second, prevalent behaviors performed by a number of people can also be *desired* by those individuals, rather than reflecting a norm. For example, on a warm summer day at the beach many people eat ice-cream, and many people stand in line at the ice-cream stand; only the latter behavior is norm-guided. To differentiate norm-guided from desired behavior additional information is needed. On the behavior side itself, a group of people all performing a certain behavior in highly similar ways increases the likelihood of a norm operating. Patiently waiting one's turn in line is quite orderly and uniform, whereas eating the ice cream afterwards shows more variability. Beyond the behavior itself, critical evidence to distinguish norms from desires lies in consequences of the observed behavior, the third type of evidence.

5.1.3 Behavior Consequences. Relevant consequences include at least two kinds: costs for the agent and benefits for other people. If an agent's foregone alternative behaviors would be individually more attractive, then the observed behavior is *costly* for the agent and suggests the presence of a norm [18]. Everybody would prefer to order ice-cream right when they arrive at the stand, so waiting in line is costly and likely norm-guided. In addition, if an agent's observed behavior causes *benefits* to others, then this provides evidence for a norm, as with tipping, table manners, holding doors open, etc. Conversely, rare behaviors with visible negative impact on others (taking another person's ice-cream instead of purchasing one) suggest a violated norm of prohibition.

5.1.4 Social (dis)approval. Community members' expressions of approval or disapproval of a performed behavior constitute the fourth type of evidence. Disapproval, such as chiding someone who cuts in front of the line, clearly reveals a violated prohibition, both to the person who violated the norm and to an observer. Disapproval often comes in degrees through varying facial, verbal, and bodily signals, so normative demand can be inferred; indeed, a violation's perceived degree of "deviance" (i.e., a proxy for normative demand) is a strong predictor of likelihood of expressed social disapproval [10].

Expressions of approval for a performed behavior may suggest a prescriptive norm that has been met, but such approvals are fairly rare and increase primarily when the behavior exceeds, rather than just meets, the relevant norm. Nobody gets praised for standing in line or treating others with respect, precisely because the norm has made compliance literally "normal." Approval for omissions could indicate prohibitions that were upheld, but such praise is even rarer ("good job for not cheating on the test").

5.2 Machine Norm Learning

Artificial agents, just as humans, should be able to learn from instruction, observation of behavior and consequences, and from social (dis)approval. Learning norms from instruction is challenging for many reasons, not the least is that the preconditions (context) and the action will always be underspecified. Nonetheless, some success has been reported in robots learning recipes (analogous to cooking norms) from written data [30] and learning new action norms from spoken commands [38]. Broadly, programming a robot with a set of a priori norms (e.g., [4]) is a form of teaching by instruction as well, though still challenging because a robot that knows *If C then A* needs to identify the instances in which *C* holds and select the specific form of *A*.

Learning norms from observation may be enabled by Inverse Reinforcement Learning (IRL, e.g., [5]), which has been proposed to ensure that agents "align with human values" [35]. There, the agent observes other agents' behavior as well as the rewards and punishments those agents receive, and it derives a value function that encodes what the proper behaviors are. IRL algorithms can grasp behavior patterns in specific contexts and may be able to code for degrees of norm demand. But without further enrichment, this approach cannot distinguish between actions that benefit the individual agent and actions that benefit the community [6], or between norms that hold for some people but not for others (e.g., observing students and teachers in the classroom, the agent would infer that the teacher violates norms).

Reinforcement learning (RL) approaches to norms [2, 23] are responsive to rewards and punishment, which could come in the form of social (dis)approval. Thus, if trustworthy community representatives give the agent feedback, it could learn appropriate actions for specific contexts. However, we would not want learning agents to "experiment" in social environments and learn from trial and error what appropriate actions it should take. Such training could occur in virtual and game-like worlds, but creating those worlds may be as difficult as building norms into the agent from the start.

Recent work identified norms from sanctioning behavior in multi-agent simulations [36]. This approach takes advantage of the diagnostic evidence of social (dis)approval, but in natural environments it faces the problem that praise is infrequent (hence learning prescriptions becomes difficult), and it would learn prohibitions only when it commits or observes a violation (which is a costly form of learning). In addition, disapproval is less frequently expressed in societies with high norm compliance—which is exactly where one would want to "raise" an artificial learning agent).

Most generally, none of the foregoing approaches learn norm *representations*; they learn only how to *behave* in accordance with observed human patterns or human sanctions. As a result, they cannot express what they have learned, only that the learned action is the "best" in this context. But the standard of what is best may not be a norm but could be a desire or habit, or even a physically convenient movement (e.g., going upright is not a norm but anatomically convenient for humans). Moreover, such agents cannot represent norm conflicts, because without having representations of norms they cannot diagnose norms as standing in conflict. Yet, representing norm conflicts, and explaining how they should be resolved, will be critical in human-robot interaction, when action recommendations differ or when the human is surprised by the robot's behavior. Trying to address these limitations, some authors have developed algorithms that learn explicit norm representations from observed behavior and are therefore able to recognize norm conflicts and attempt to resolve those conflicts [19, 20].

None of the current algorithms, however, can exploit the rich information contained in (foregone and actual) consequences of observed behaviors. To that end, agents would have to infer an observed person's goals, assess costs and benefits for the person and for other individuals, and compare actual to counterfactual actions (e.g., the agent's foregone benefits as an indicator of prescription norms). Thus, agents would need to have social-cognitive capacities to ground their norm competence.

Given the constraints of learning from observation (e.g., no observed data on prohibitions, no sanctioning data on prescriptions) and the current limitations of algorithms for such learning, observation alone will not generate norm-competent agents. There would be too few data points to grasp the complex context specificity of human norms, too little knowledge about important distinctions in the behavior stream, and no sense of which observed behaviors represent norms, rather than desires or habits.

Currently, and for the foreseeable future, the safest and most effective way of designing norm-competent agents would therefore be a "hybrid" approach [3] in which *a priori* legal, moral, and social norms combine with abilities to learn new norms and update existing norms. Science would have to identify the relevant *a priori* norms (e.g., for a robot in a particular role in a particular community) and implement them in ways that replicate key properties of human norms, such as context specificity, graded normative demand, and network organization. Successful artificial agents would then update this starting package by learning from instruction, observing behaviors, consequences, and social (dis)approval, and requesting advice when necessary. Continuous teaching by instruction and observation is attractive in part because robots deployed in social contexts will be surrounded by teachers. Not all community members are equally good teachers (and as we know form the cases of Tay and Chappie, some will actively try to corrupt the agent). But these problems arise for human children learning norms as much as for robots learning norms. We must trust human communities to make up for the failings of some teachers and find ways to correct individual agents' missteps.

6. Conclusion

We have drawn a map of human norm representations that can guide the development of comparable norm representations in artificial agents. Creating such norm-competent agents is a significant challenge, but it is vital for a society in which human and artificial agents co-exist, both guided by the social and moral norms of their shared community

ACKNOWLEDGMENTS

This project was supported by a grant from the Office of Naval Research (ONR), No. N00014-16-1-2278. The opinions expressed here are our own and do not necessarily reflect the views of ONR.

REFERENCES

[1] Aarts, H. and Dijksterhuis, A. 2003. The silence of the library: Environment, situational norm, and social behavior. *Journal of Personality and Social Psychology*. 84, 1 (Jan. 2003), 18–28. DOI:https://doi.org/10.1037/0022-3514.84.1.18.

[2] Abel, D. et al. 2016. Reinforcement learning as a framework for ethical decision making. *AAAI Workshop: AI, Ethics, and Society, volume WS-16-02 of 13th AAAI Workshops* (2016).

[3] Allen, C. et al. 2005. Artificial morality: Top-down, bottom-up, and hybrid approaches. *Ethics and Information Technology*. 7, 3 (Sep. 2005), 149–155. DOI:https://doi.org/10.1007/s10676-006-0004-4.

[4] Anderson, M. et al. 2018. A value-driven eldercare robot: Virtual and physical instantiations of a case-supported principle-based behavior

paradigm. *Proceedings of the IEEE*. (2018), 1–15. DOI:https://doi.org/10.1109/JPROC.2018.2840045.

[5] Arai, S. and Suzuki, K. 2014. Encouragement of right social norms by inverse reinforcement learning. *Journal of Information Processing*. 22, 2 (2014), 299–306. DOI:https://doi.org/10.2197/ipsjjip.22.299.

[6] Arnold, T. et al. 2017. Value alignment or misalignment – What will keep systems accountable? *The Workshops of the Thirty-First AAAI Conference on Artificial Intelligence: Technical Reports, WS-17-02: AI, Ethics, and Society*. The AAAI Press. 81–88.

[7] Bello, P. et al. 2018. An attention-driven computational model of human causal reasoning. *Proceedings of the 40th Annual Meeting of the Cognitive Science Society* (Austin, TX, 2018), 1353–1358.

[8] Bendor, J. and Swistak, P. 2001. The evolution of norms. *American Journal of Sociology*. 106, 6 (2001), 1493–1545.

[9] Bicchieri, C. 2006. *The grammar of society: The nature and dynamics of social norms*. Cambridge University Press.

[10] Brauer, M. and Chaurand, N. 2010. Descriptive norms, prescriptive norms, and social control: An intercultural comparison of people's reactions to uncivil behaviors. *European Journal of Social Psychology*. 40, 3 (Apr. 2010), 490–499. DOI:https://doi.org/10.1002/ejsp.640.

[11] Brennan, G. et al. 2013. *Explaining norms*. Oxford University Press.

[12] Bringsjord, S. et al. 2006. Toward a general logicist methodology for engineering ethically correct robots. *Intelligent Systems, IEEE*. 21, 4 (2006), 38–44.

[13] Chisholm, R.M. 1963. Contrary-to-duty imperatives and deontic logic. *Analysis*. 24, 2 (1963), 33–36. DOI:https://doi.org/10.2307/3327064.

[14] Cialdini, R.B. et al. 1990. A focus theory of normative conduct: Recycling the concept of norms to reduce littering in public places. *Journal of Personality and Social Psychology*. 58, 6 (1990), 1015–1026. DOI:https://doi.org/10.1037/0022-3514.58.6.1015.

[15] Gasparini, L. et al. 2018. Severity-sensitive norm-governed multi-agent planning. *Autonomous Agents and Multi-Agent Systems*. 32, 1 (Jan. 2018), 26–58. DOI:https://doi.org/10.1007/s10458-017-9372-x.

[16] Gibbs, J.P. 1965. Norms: The problem of definition and classification. *American Journal of Sociology*. 70, 5 (1965), 586–594. DOI:https://doi.org/10.1086/223933.

[17] Hechter, M. and Opp, K.-D. 2001. *Social Norms*. Russell Sage Foundation.

[18] Henrich, J. 2009. The evolution of costly displays, cooperation and religion: Credibility enhancing displays and their implications for cultural evolution. *Evolution and Human Behavior*. 30, 4 (Jul. 2009), 244–260. DOI:https://doi.org/10.1016/j.evolhumbehav.2009.03.005.

[19] Kasenberg, D. and Scheutz, M. 2017. Interpretable apprenticeship learning with temporal logic specifications. *Proceedings of the 56th IEEE Conference on Decision and Control (CDC 2017)*. IEEE Press. 4914–4921.

[20] Kasenberg, D. and Scheutz, M. 2018. Norm conflict resolution in stochastic domains. *Proceedings of the Thirty-Second AAAI Conference on Artificial Intelligence* (2018).

[21] Kim, J. et al. 2018. Not-So-CLEVR: learning same-different relations strains feed-forward neural networks. *Interface Focus*. 8, 4 (2018). DOI:https://doi.org/10.1098/rsfs.2018.0011.

[22] Kollingbaum, M.J. et al. 2008. Managing conflict resolution in norm-regulated environments. *Engineering Societies in the Agents World VIII*. A. Artikis et al., eds. Springer Berlin Heidelberg. 55–71.

[23] Li, J. et al. 2015. Reinforcement learning of normative monitoring intensities. *Proceedings of the International Workshop on Coordination, Organisation, Institutions and Norms in Multi-Agent Systems* (2015).

[24] Mack, A. ed. 2018. Changing social norms. *Social Research: An International Quarterly*. 85, 1 (2018), 1–271.

[25] Mahmoud, M.A. et al. 2014. A review of norms and normative multiagent systems. *The Scientific World Journal*. 2014, (2014), 1–23. DOI:https://doi.org/10.1155/2014/684587.

[26] Malle, B.F. 2018. From binary deontics to deontic continua: The nature of human (and robot) norm systems.

[27] Malle, B.F. et al. 2017. Networks of social and moral norms in human and robot agents. *A World with Robots: International Conference on Robot Ethics: ICRE 2015*. M.I. Aldinhas Ferreira et al., eds. Springer International Publishing. 3–17.

[28] Milgram, S. et al. 1969. Note on the drawing power of crowds of different size. *Journal of Personality and Social Psychology*. 13, 2 (Oct. 1969), 79–82. DOI:https://doi.org/10.1037/h0028070.

[29] Nickles, M. 2007. Towards a logic of graded normativity and norm adherence. *Normative Multi-agent Systems: Dagstuhl Seminar Proceedings* (Dagstuhl, Germany, 2007).

[30] Nyga, D. and Beetz, M. 2012. Everything robots always wanted to know about housework (but were afraid to ask). *2012 IEEE/RSJ International Conference on Intelligent Robots and Systems*. IEEE Press. 243–250.

[31] Parsons, T. 1951. *The social system*. Free Press.

[32] Pereira, L.M. and Saptawijaya, A. 2007. Modelling morality with prospective logic. *Progress in Artificial Intelligence*. J. Neves et al., eds. Springer Berlin Heidelberg. 99–111.

[33] Prentice, D.A. and Miller, D.T. 1996. Pluralistic ignorance and the perpetuation of social norms by unwitting actors. *Advances in Experimental Social Psychology*. M.P. Zanna, ed. Academic Press. 161–209.

[34] Rakoczy, H. et al. 2008. The sources of normativity: Young children's awareness of the normative structure of games. *Developmental Psychology*. 44, 3 (May 2008), 875–881. DOI:https://doi.org/10.1037/0012-1649.44.3.875.

[35] Russell, S. et al. 2016. Research priorities for robust and beneficial artificial intelligence. *arXiv preprint arXiv:1602.03506*. (2016).

[36] Savarimuthu, B.T.R. et al. 2013. Identifying prohibition norms in agent societies. *Artificial Intelligence and Law*. 21, 1 (2013), 1–46.

[37] Schelling, T.C. 1960. *The strategy of conflict*. Harvard University Press.

[38] Scheutz, M. et al. 2017. Spoken instruction-based one-shot object and action learning in a cognitive robotic architecture. *Proceedings of the 16th Conference on Autonomous Agents and MultiAgent Systems*. International Foundation for Autonomous Agents and Multiagent Systems. 1378–1386.

[39] Serramia, M. et al. 2018. Moral values in norm decision making. *Proceedings of the 17th International Conference on Autonomous Agents and Multiagent Systems (AAMAS 2018)* (Richland, SC, 2018), 1294–1302.

[40] Shams, Z. et al. 2017. Practical reasoning with norms for autonomous software agents. *Engineering Applications of Artificial Intelligence*. 65, (Oct. 2017), 388–399. DOI:https://doi.org/10.1016/j.engappai.2017.07.021.

[41] Steyvers, M. and Tenenbaum, J.B. 2005. The large-scale structure of semantic networks: statistical analyses and a model of semantic growth. *Cognitive Science*. 29, 1 (Jan. 2005), 41–78. DOI:https://doi.org/10.1207/s15516709cog2901_3.

[42] Telesford, Q.K. et al. 2011. The ubiquity of small-world networks. *Brain Connectivity*. 1, 5 (Dec. 2011), 367–375. DOI:https://doi.org/10.1089/brain.2011.0038.

[43] Ullman, S. 1984. Visual routines. *Cognition*. 18, 1–3 (Dec. 1984), 97–159.

[44] Ullmann-Margalit, E. 1977. *The emergence of norms*. Clarendon Press.

[45] Wilson, D.S. 2002. *Darwin's cathedral: Evolution, religion, and the nature of society*. University of Chicago Press.

[46] Wright, J.C. and Bartsch, K. 2008. Portraits of early moral sensibility in two children's everyday conversations. *Merrill-Palmer Quarterly*. 54, 1 (Mar. 2008), 56–85. DOI:https://doi.org/10.1353/mpq.2008.0010.

[47] Yuan, L. et al. 2016. Are categorical spatial relations encoded by shifting visual attention between objects? *PLOS ONE*. 11, 10 (2016), 1–22. DOI:https://doi.org/10.1371/journal.pone.0163141.

Toward the Engineering of Virtuous Machines

Naveen Sundar Govindarajulu
Rensselaer AI & Reasoning Lab
Rensselaer Polytechnic Institue, (RPI)
Troy, NY, USA
naveensundarg@gmail.com

Selmer Bringsjord
Rensselaer AI & Reasoning Lab
Rensselaer Polytechnic Institue, (RPI)
Troy, NY, USA
Selmer.Bringsjord@gmail.com

Rikhiya Ghosh
Rensselaer AI & Reasoning Lab
Rensselaer Polytechnic Institue, (RPI)
Troy, NY, USA
rikrixa@gmail.com

Vasanth Sarathy
Human Robot Interaction Laboratory
Tufts University
Medford, MA, USA
vasanth.sarathy@tufts.edu

ABSTRACT

While various traditions under the 'virtue ethics' umbrella have been studied extensively and advocated by ethicists, it has not been clear that there exists a version of virtue ethics rigorous enough to be a target for machine ethics (which we take to include the engineering of an ethical sensibility in a machine or robot itself, not only the study of ethics in the humans who might create artificial agents). We begin to address this by presenting an embryonic formalization of a key part of any virtue-ethics theory: namely, the learning of virtue by a focus on exemplars of moral virtue. Our work is based in part on a computational formal logic previously used to formally model other ethical theories and principles therein, and to implement these models in artificial agents.

CCS CONCEPTS

• **Theory of computation** → **Proof theory**; **Modal and temporal logics**; *Logic and verification*; *Higher order logic*.

KEYWORDS

logic; virtue ethics; deontic cognitive event calculus; virtuous robots; verification

ACM Reference Format:
Naveen Sundar Govindarajulu, Selmer Bringsjord, Rikhiya Ghosh, and Vasanth Sarathy. 2019. Toward the Engineering of Virtuous Machines. In *AAAI/ACM Conference on AI, Ethics, and Society (AIES '19), January 27–28, 2019, Honolulu, HI, USA.* ACM, New York, NY, USA, 7 pages. https://doi.org/10.1145/3306618.3314256

INTRODUCTION

What is virtue ethics? One way of summarizing virtue ethics is to contrast it with the two main families of ethical theories: **deontological ethics** ($\mathcal{D}$) and **consequentialism** ($\mathcal{C}$). Ethical theories in the family $\mathcal{C}$ that are utilitarian in nature hold that actions are morally evaluated based on their **total utility** (or total *dis*utility) to everyone involved. The best action is the action that has the highest total utility. In stark contrast, ethical theories in $\mathcal{D}$ emphasize **inviolable principles**, and reasoning from those principles to whether actions are obligatory, permissible, neutral, etc.[1] In a departure from both $\mathcal{D}$ and $\mathcal{C}$, ethical theories in the virtue-ethics family $\mathcal{V}$ are overall distinguished by the principle that the best action in a situation, morally speaking, is the one that a **virtuous person** would perform [3]. A virtuous person is defined as a person who has learned and internalized a set of habits or traits termed **virtuous**. For a virtuous person, virtuous acts become second-nature, and hence are performed in many different situations, through time.

While extensive formal and rigorous modeling under the umbrellas of $\mathcal{D}$ and $\mathcal{C}$has been carried out, there has been little such work devoted to formalizing and mechanizing $\mathcal{V}$. Note that unlike $\mathcal{D}$ and $\mathcal{C}$, it is not entirely straightforward how one could translate the concepts and principles in $\mathcal{V}$ into a form that is precise enough to be realized in machines. Proponents of $\mathcal{V}$ might claim that it is not feasible to do so given $\mathcal{V}$'s emphasis on persons and traits, rather than individual actions or consequences. From the perspective of machine ethics, this is not satisfactory. If $\mathcal{V}$ is to be on equal footing with $\mathcal{D}$ and $\mathcal{C}$ for the purpose of building morally competent machines, AI researchers need to start formalizing parts of virtue ethics, and to then implement such formalization in computation.

We present one such formalization herein; one that uses learning and is based on a virtue-ethics theory presented by Zagzebski [31]. The formalization is presented courtesy of an expressive computational logic that has been used to model principles in both $\mathcal{C}$ and $\mathcal{D}$ [e.g. [12, 14]].[2] The formalization answers, abstractly, the following two questions:

Questions

(Q_1) When can we say an agent is virtuous?
(Q_2) What is a virtue?

The plan for the paper is as follows. First, we briefly consider why virtuous machines might be useful, and then we briefly cover related work that can be regarded formalization of virtue ethics. Next, we

AIES '19, January 27–28, 2019, Honolulu, HI, USA

ACM ISBN 978-1-4503-6324-2/19/01.
https://doi.org/10.1145/3306618.3314256

[1] Both the families $\mathcal{C}$ and $\mathcal{D}$ are crisply explained as being in conformity with what we say here in e.g. [9].
[2] See [6] for an introduction to the logicist methodology for building ethical machines.

present an overview of virtue ethics itself, and specifically show that an emphasis on moral exemplars makes good sense for any attempt to engineer a virtuous machine. We next present one version of virtue ethics, $\mathcal{V}_z$ (Zagzebski's version of virtue ethics), which we seek to formalize fully. Then, our calculus and the formalization itself ($\mathcal{V}_z^f$) are presented. We conclude by discussing future work and remaining challenges.

WHY VIRTUOUS ROBOTS?

Note that we do not advocate that machine ethicists pursue virtue ethics over other familiies of ethical theories. Our goal in the present paper is merely to formalize one version of virtue ethics within the family $\mathcal{V}$. That said, why might virtue ethics be preferred over consequentialism or deontological ethics for building morally competent machines? To partially answer this question, we take a short digression into a series of conditions laid out by Alfano, and characterized as identifying the core of virtue ethics:

Hard Core of Virtue Ethics (partially quoting [2])

(2) **stability** If someone possesses a virtue at time t_1, then *ceteris paribus* she will possess that virtue at a later time t_2.
(3) **consistency** If someone possesses a virtue sensitive to reason r, then *ceteris paribus* she will respond to r in most contexts.
(7) **explanatory power** If someone possesses a virtue, then reference to that virtue will sometimes help to explain her behavior.
(8) **predictive power** If someone possesses a high-fidelity virtue, then reference to that virtue will enable nearly certain predictions of her behavior; if someone possesses a low-fidelity virtue, then reference to that virtue will enable weak predictions of her behavior.

Particularly, we feel that if the conditions of **stability**, **consistency**, **explanatory power**, and **predictive power** hold, then virtuous agents or robots might be easier for humans to understand and interact with (compared to consequentialist or deontological agents or robots). This is but our initial motivation; we now present an overview of virtue ethics, in order to show that our focus specifically on learning of virtuous behavior from moral exemplars is advisable.

SURVEYING VIRTUE ETHICS

See [28] for a general introduction to the field of moral robots. We begin our survey by reporting that Hurka [16] presents an ingenious formal account involving a recursive notion of goodness and badness. The account starts with a given set of primitive good and bad states-of-affairs. Virtues are then defined as love of good states-of-affairs or hatred of bad states-of-affairs. Vice is defined as love of bad states-of-affairs or hatred of good states-of-affairs. Virtues and vices are then themselves taken to be good and bad states-of-affairs, resulting in a recursive definition (see Figure 2) that is attractive to AI researchers and computer scientists. But despite this, and despite our sense that the main problems with Hurka's account are rectifiable [15], we feel that Hurka's definition might not capture central aspects of virtue [19]. More problematic is that it must be shown that Hurka's account is different from rigorous and formal accounts of C, which after all are themselves invariably based upon good and bad states-of-affairs. Moreover, it is not clear to us how Hurka's account is amenable to automation. Therefore, we now proceed to step back and survey the overarching family $\mathcal{V}$ of virtue ethics, to specifically pave a more promising AI road: viz. a focus on moral exemplars.

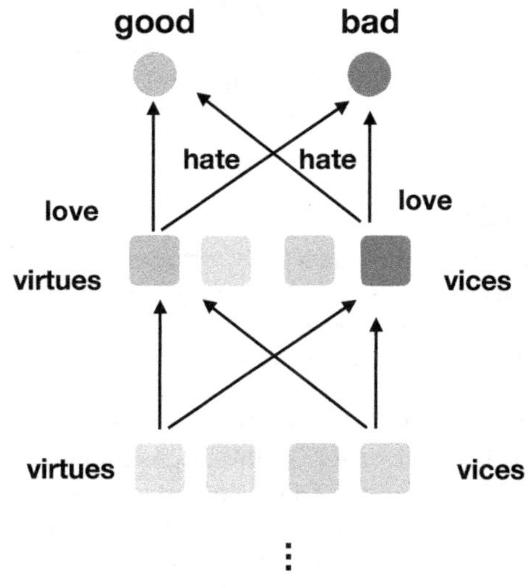

Figure 1: Hurka's Account Virtues (vices) are defined recursively as love of good (bad) states-of-affairs or hate (love) of bad states of affairs.

Virtue Ethics: Overview to Exemplarism

The core concepts of consequentialist ethical theories (i.e. of members of C), at least certainly in the particular such theory known as *utilitarianism*, are doubtless at minimum relatively familiar to most of our readers. For instance, most in our audience will know that utilitarianism's core tenet is that actions are obligatory just in case they have the consequence of maximizing happiness, and are forbidden exactly when they fail to so maximize. A parallel state-of-affairs holds for at least basic knowledge of deontological ethical theories (= family $\mathcal{D}$): most readers have for instance some familiarity with Kant's moral system in family $\mathcal{D}$, and specifically with his famous "categorical imperative," which, paraphrasing, says that, unconditionally, one must always act in such a way that this behavior could be universalized.[3] In addition, generally people are familiar with the core tenet of divine-command ethical theories (i.e. of members of $\mathcal{DC}$), which is (approximately) that actions are obligatory for humans if and only if God commands that these actions be performed (a particular member of $\mathcal{D}$is specified in [25]; another member is used for AI/machine ethics in [8]). However, in

[3]This imperative is first set out in — as it's known in abbreviation — *Groundwork*; see [18]. It's generally thought by ethicists, and this may be convenient for machine/AI ethics, that Kant had in mind essentially a decision procedure to follow in the attempt to behave in an ethically correct manner. For a lucid and laconic overview of this point, see [17]; and cf. [24].

our experience the epistemic situation is radically different when it comes to the family of ethical theories *virtue ethics* (= $\mathcal{V}$). For while it's true that generally educated people can be assumed to be acquainted with the pre-analytic concept of virtue, and with many things long deemed to be virtues (e.g. bravery), an understanding of virtue ethics at the level of ethical *theory* cannot be assumed. We therefore now provide a rapid (and admittedly cursory) synopsis of $\mathcal{V}$, by drawing from [29], and to some degree from [3]. It will be seen that $\mathcal{V}$ makes central use of exemplars, and of learning and development that revolves around them. Hence we shall arrive at a convenient entry point for our AI work devoted to trying to design and build a virtuous machine.

Obviously we cannot in the span of the space we have at hand do full justice to the book-length treatment of $\mathcal{V}$ that is [29]. But we can quickly establish that our technical work, in its focus on the cultivation of virtue for a machine via learning from exemplars, is not merely based on a single, idiosyncratic member of $\mathcal{V}$, and on one peripheral aspect of this member. On the contrary, study of the work of Vallor and other scholars concerned with a characterization of the family $\mathcal{V}$ confirms that our exploitation specifically of Zagzebski's [31] focus, from the standpoint of the field of ethics itself, is a worthy point of entry for AI researchers.

To begin, Vallor, drawing on and slightly adapting Van Norden's [30], sets out a quartet of commonalities that at least seem to be true of all members of $\mathcal{V}$, and the second one is: "A conception of moral virtues as cultivated states of character, manifested by those exemplary persons who have come closest to achieving the highest human good" (¶5, §2.2).[4] But given our specific efforts toward engineering a virtuous machine, it is important to note that Vallor specifically informs us about the key concepts of exemplars in the particular members of the $\mathcal{V}$family; to pick just one of many available places, she writes:

> Buddhism's resonances with other classical virtue traditions do not end here. As with the central role granted by Confucian and Aristotelian ethics to 'exemplary persons' (the *junzi* and *phronimoi* respectively), *bodhisattvas* (persons actively seeking enlightenment) generally receive direction to or assistance on the path of self-cultivation from the community of exemplary persons to which they have access. In Buddhism this is the monastic community and lay members of the *Sangha* . . . [¶5, §2.1.3, [29]]

We said above that we would also draw, albeit briefly, from a second treatment of $\mathcal{V}$, viz. [3], in order to pave the way into our AI-specific, exemplar-based technical work. About this second treatment we report only that it is one based squarely on a "range of development" (¶3, §Right Action in Ch. 3), where the agent (a human in her case) gradually develops into a truly virtuous person, beginning with unreflective adoption of direct instruction, through a final phase in which "actions are based on understanding gained through experience and reflection" (ibid.). Moreover, Annas explicitly welcomes the analogy between an agent's becoming virtuous, and an agent's becoming, say, an excellent tennis-player or pianist. The idea behind the similarity is that "two things are united: the *need to learn* and the *drive to aspire* (emphasis hers; ¶4 Ch. 3). In addition, following Aristotle on $\mathcal{V}$ (e.g. see [4] 1103), no one can become a master tennis-player or pianist without, specifically, playing tennis/the piano with an eye to the mastery of great exemplars in these two domains.

In order to now turn to specific AI work devoted to engineering a virtuous machine, we move from completed consideration of the general foundation of $\mathcal{V}$, and its now-confirmed essential use of moral exemplars, to a specific use of such exemplars that appears ripe for mechanization.

[4]In her book, Vallor gives her own more detailed and technologically relevant list of seven core elements that can be viewed as common to all members of $\mathcal{V}$ (or two what she refers to as "traditions" within virtue ethics). We do not have the space to discuss this list, and show that it fits nicely with our technical work's emphasis on exemplars and learning therefrom.

EXEMPLARIST VIRTUE THEORY

Exemplarist virtue theory ($\mathcal{V}_z$) builds on the **direct reference theory** (DRT) of semantics. Briefly, in DRT, given a word or term w, its meaning $\mu(w)$ is determined by what the word picks out, say p, and not by some definition d. For example, for a person to use the word *"water,"* in a correct manner, that person neither needs to possess a definition of water nor needs to understand all the physical properties of water. The person simply needs to know which entity the word *"water"* denotes in common usage.

In $\mathcal{V}_z$, persons understand moral terms, such as *"honesty,"*, in a similar manner. That is, moral terms are understood by persons through direct references instantiated in **exemplars**. Persons identify moral examplars through the emotion of **admiration**. Fittingly, he emotion of admiration plays a foundational role in this theory (as does contempt). $\mathcal{V}_z$ posits a process very similar to scientific or empirical investigation. Exemplars are first identified and their traits are studied; then they are continously further studied to better understand their traits, qualities, etc. The status of an individual as an exemplar can change over time. Below is an informal version that we seek to formalize:

Informal Version $\mathcal{V}_z$

I_1 Agent or person a perceives a person b perform an action α. This observation causes the emotion of admiration in a.

I_2 a then studies b and seeks to learn what traits (habits or dispositions) b has.

THE GOAL

From the above presentation of $\mathcal{V}_z$, we can glean the following distilled requirements that should be present in any formalization.

$\mathcal{V}_z^f$ Formalization Components

(R_1) A formalization of emotions, particularly admiration.

(R_2) A representation of traits.

(R_3) A process of learning traits (and not just simple individual actions) from a small number of observations.

BUILDING THE FORMALIZATION

For fleshing out the above requirements and formalizing $\mathcal{V}_z$, we use the **deontic cognitive event calculus** ($\mathcal{DCEC}$), a computational formal logic. This logic was used previously in [12, 14] to automate versions of the Doctrine of Double Effect ($\mathcal{DDE}$), an ethical principle with deontological, consequentialist (and, historically, divine-command) components. $\mathcal{DCEC}$ has also been used to formalize *akrasia* (the process of succumbing to temptation to violate moral principles) [7]. Fragments of $\mathcal{DCEC}$ have been used to model highly intensional reasoning processes, such as the false-belief task [5].[5]

Overview of $\mathcal{DCEC}$

$\mathcal{DCEC}$ is a quantified multi-operator[6] modal logic (also known as sorted first-order multi-operator modal logic) that includes the event calculus, a first-order calculus used for commonsense reasoning over time and change [20]. This calculus has a well-defined syntax and proof calculus; see Appendix A of [12]. The proof calculus is based on natural deduction [11], and includes all the introduction and elimination rules for first-order logic, as well as inference schemata for the modal operators and related structures. As a sorted calculus, $\mathcal{DCEC}$ can be regarded analogous to a typed programming language. We show below some of the important sorts used in $\mathcal{DCEC}$. Among these, the Agent, Action, and ActionType sorts are not native to the event calculus.

Sort	Description
Agent	Human and non-human actors.
Time	The Time type stands for time in the domain.
Event	Used for events in the domain.
ActionType	Abstract actions instantiated at particular times by actors.
Action	Events that occur as actions by agents.
Fluent	Used to represent dynamic states of the world.

Note: actions are events that are carried out by an agent. For any action type α and agent a, the event corresponding to a carrying out α is given by $action(a, \alpha)$. For instance, if α is *"running"* and a is *"Jack"*, $action(a, \alpha)$ denotes *"Jack is running"*.

Syntax. The syntax has two components: a first-order core and a modal system that builds upon this core. The figures below show the formal language and inference schemata of $\mathcal{DCEC}$. Commonly used function and relation symbols of the event calculus are included. Any formally defined calculi (e.g. the venerable *situation calculus*) for modeling commonsense and physical reasoning can be easily switched out in-place of the event calculus.

The modal operators present in the calculus include the standard operators for knowledge **K**, belief **B**, desire **D**, intention **I**, obligation **O**, etc. For example, consider $\mathbf{B}(a, t, \phi)$, which says that agent a believes at time t the proposition ϕ. Here ϕ can in turn be any arbitrary formula.

Syntax (fragment)

$$S ::= \mathsf{Agent} \mid \mathsf{ActionType} \mid \mathsf{Action} \sqsubseteq \mathsf{Event} \mid \mathsf{Moment} \mid \mathsf{Fluent}$$

$$f ::= \begin{cases} action : \mathsf{Agent} \times \mathsf{ActionType} \rightarrow \mathsf{Action} \\ holds : \mathsf{Fluent} \times \mathsf{Moment} \rightarrow \mathsf{Formula} \\ happens : \mathsf{Event} \times \mathsf{Moment} \rightarrow \mathsf{Formula} \end{cases}$$

$$t ::= x : S \mid c : S \mid f(t_1, \ldots, t_n)$$

$$\phi ::= \begin{cases} q : \mathsf{Formula} \mid \neg\phi \mid \phi \land \psi \mid \phi \lor \psi \mid \forall x : \phi(x) \mid \\ \mathbf{P}(a, t, \phi) \mid \mathbf{K}(a, t, \phi) \mid \\ \mathbf{C}(t, \phi) \mid \mathbf{S}(a, b, t, \phi) \mid \mathbf{S}(a, t, \phi) \mid \mathbf{B}(a, t, \phi) \\ \mathbf{O}(a, t, \phi, (\neg)happens(action(a^*, \alpha), t')) \end{cases}$$

Inference Schemata. The figure below shows a fragment of inference schemata for $\mathcal{DCEC}$. $I_{\mathbf{B}}$ is an inference schema that let us model idealized agents that have their knowledge and belief closed under the $\mathcal{DCEC}$ proof theory. While normal humans are not deductively closed, this lets us model more closely how deliberative agents such as organizations and more strategic actors reason. (Some dialects of cognitive calculi restrict the number of iterations on intensional operators.) I_{12} states that if an agent s communicates a proposition ϕ to h, then h believes that s believes ϕ. I_{14} dictates how obligations propagate to intentions.

Inference Schemata (fragment)

$$\frac{\mathbf{B}(a, t_1, \Gamma), \;\; \Gamma \vdash \phi, \;\; t_1 < t_2}{\mathbf{B}(a, t_2, \phi)} \; [I_{\mathbf{B}}] \qquad \frac{\mathbf{S}(s, h, t, \phi)}{\mathbf{B}(h, t, \mathbf{B}(s, t, \phi))} \; [I_{12}]$$

$$\frac{\mathbf{B}(a, t, \phi) \;\; \mathbf{B}(a, t, \mathbf{O}(a, t, \phi, \chi)) \;\; \mathbf{O}(a, t, \phi, \chi)}{\mathbf{K}(a, t, \mathbf{I}(a, t, \chi))} \; [I_{14}]$$

We also define the following inference-schemata-based relationships between expressions in our calculus.
Generalization of Formulae. The generalization of a set of formulae, Ψ, is a set of formulae Φ from which any element of Ψ can be inferred: $\Phi \vdash \bigwedge \Psi$. This is denoted by $g(\Psi) = \Phi$.
Generalization of Terms: A term x is a generalization of a term y if, given any first-order predicate P, from $P(x)$ we can derive $P(y)$: $\{P(x)\} \vdash P(y)$. This is denoted by $g(y) = x$.

Semantics

$\mathcal{DCEC}$ uses *proof-theoretic* semantics [10, 11], an approach commonly associated with natural-deduction inference systems. Briefly, in this approach, meanings of modal operators are defined via functions over proofs. Specifying semantics then reduces to specifying inference schemata.

Events, Fluents, and Utilities

In the event calculus, fluents represent states of the world. Our formalization of admiration requires a notion of utility for these states. Therefore, we assign utilities to fluents through a utility function: $\mu : \mathsf{Fluent} \times \mathsf{Time} \rightarrow \mathbb{R}$. An event can initiate one or more

[5] $\mathcal{DCEC}$ is both *intensional* and *intentional*. There is a difference between intensional and intentional systems. Broadly speaking, extensional systems are formal systems in which the references and meanings of terms are independent of any context. Intensional systems are formal systems in which meanings of terms are dependent on context, such as the cognitive states of agents, time, etc. Modal logics used for modeling beliefs, desires, and intentions are considered intensional systems. Please see the appendix in [12] for a more detailed discussion.

[6] The full catalogue of available operators exceeds those for belief, desire, and intention, and *a fortiori* exceeds the available operators in any standard modal logic designed to formalize e.g. only either alethic, epistemic, or deontic phenomena.

fluents. Hence, events can also have a utility associated with them. For an event e at time t, let e^t_I be the set of fluents initiated by the event, and let e^t_T be the set of fluents terminated by the event. If we are looking up till horizon H, then $v(e,t)$, the total utility of event e at time t, is:

$$v(e,t) = \sum_{y=t+1}^{H}\left(\sum_{f\in e^t_I}\mu(f,y) - \sum_{f\in e^t_T}\mu(f,y)\right)$$

With the calculus given above, we now proceed to specify parts of the formalization $\mathcal{V}^f_z$; that is, $\mathbf{R}_1$, $\mathbf{R}_2$, and $\mathbf{R}_3$.

Defining Admiration

We start with $\mathbf{R}_1$ and formalize admiration in $\mathcal{DCEC}$. To acheive this, we build upon the **OCC model**. There are many models of emotion from psychology and cognitive science. Among these, the OCC model [23] has found wide adoption among computer scientists. Note that the model presented by [23] is informal in nature and one formalization of the model has been presented in [1]. This formalization is based on propositional modal logic, and while comprehensive and elaborate, is not expressive enough for our modelling, which requires at least quantification over objects.

In OCC, emotions are short-lived entities that arise in response to *events*. Different emotions arise based on: (i) whether the *consequences* to events are positive (desirable) or negative (undesirable); (ii) whether the event has occured; and (iii) whether the event has consequences for the agent or for another agent. OCC assumes an undefined primitive notion of an agent being *pleased* or *displeased* in response to an event. We represent this notion by a predicate Θ in our formalization. In OCC, admiration is defined as "*(approving of) someone else's praiseworthy action.*" We translate this definition into $\mathcal{DCEC}$ as follows. An agent a is said to admire another agent b's action α, if agent a believes the action is a good action. An action $action(b,\alpha)$ is considered a good action if $v(action(b,\alpha),t) > 0$. In OCC, agents can admire only other agents and not themselves. This is captured by the inequality $a \neg = b$.

($\mathbf{R}_1$) Admiration in $\mathcal{DCEC}$

$$holds(admires(a,b,\alpha),t)$$
$$\leftrightarrow$$
$$\Theta(a,t') \quad \wedge$$
$$\mathbf{B}\left(a, t, \begin{bmatrix}(a \neq b) \wedge (t' < t) \\ \wedge\ happens(action(b,\alpha),t') \wedge \\ v(action(b,\alpha),t) > 0\end{bmatrix}\right)$$

Defining Traits

To satisfy $\mathbf{R}_2$, we need to define traits. We define a *situation* $\sigma(t)$ as simply a collection of formulae that describe what fluents hold at a time t, along with other event-calculus constraints and descriptions (sometimes we use $\sigma(t)$ to represent the conjunction of all the formulae in $\sigma(t)$).

($\mathbf{R}_2$) Trait

An agent a has a situation σ and action type α as an *m-trait* $\langle\sigma,\alpha\rangle$ if there are at least m situations $\{\sigma_1,\sigma_2,\ldots,\sigma_m\}$ in which *instantiations* of α are performed, and σ is the generalization of the situations.

A trait $\langle\sigma,\alpha\rangle$ can be represented as a single formula:

$$\tau \equiv \sigma \wedge happens(action(\alpha,a),t)$$

We introduce a new modal operator **Trait** that can then be applied to the collection of formulae τ denoting a trait. **Trait**(τ,a) says that agent a has trait τ. The following inference schema then applies to **Trait**:

($\mathbf{R}_2$) Inference Schema for Trait

$$\frac{\begin{Bmatrix}\sigma_i,\ happens(action(\alpha_i,a),t_i)\\ g(\sigma_i(t)) = \sigma,\ g(\alpha_i) = \alpha\end{Bmatrix}^n_{i=1}}{\mathbf{Trait}(\tau,a)}\ [I_{\mathbf{Trait}}]$$

Defining Learning of Traits

To address $\mathbf{R}_3$ we need a definition of what it means for an agent to learn a trait. We start with a learning agent l. An agent e is identified as an exemplar by l *iff* the emotion of admiration is triggered n times or more by e in l. This is written in $\mathcal{DCEC}$ as follows (note that admiration can be triggered by different actions):

Exemplar Defninition

$$Exemplar(e,l) \leftrightarrow \exists^{!n} t.\exists\alpha.holds(admires(l,e,\alpha),t)$$

Once e is identified as an exemplar, the learner then identifies one or more traits of e by observing e over an extended period of time. Let l believe that e has a trait τ; then l incorporates τ as its own trait:

($\mathbf{R}_3$) Learning a Trait

$$LearnTrait(l,\tau,t) \leftrightarrow \exists e \begin{bmatrix}Exemplar(e,l)\wedge \\ \mathbf{B}\Big(l,t,\mathbf{Trait}\big(\tau,e\big)\Big)\end{bmatrix}$$

$$LearnTrait(l,\langle\sigma,\alpha\rangle,t) \rightarrow (\sigma \rightarrow happens(action(l,\alpha),t))$$

Example. For instance, if the action type *"being truthful"* is triggered in situations: *"talking with alice,", "talking with bob", "talking with charlie"*; then the trait learned is that *"talking with an agent"* situation should trigger the *"being truthful"* action type.

A Note on Learning Methods

When we look at humans learning virtues by observing others or by reading from texts or other sources, it is not entirely clear how models of learning that have been successful in perception and language processing (e.g. the recent successes of deep learning and statistical learning) can be applied. Learning in $\mathcal{V}$-relevant situations is from one or few instances or in some cases through instruction, and such learning may not be captured by models of learning which require a large number of examples.

The abstract learning method that we use is **generalization**, defined previously. See one simple example immediately below:

Example 1

$$\frac{\begin{array}{r}\Gamma_1 = \{\mathit{talkingWith(jack)} \rightarrow \mathit{Honesty}\}\\ \Gamma_2 = \{\mathit{talkingWith(jill)} \rightarrow \mathit{Honesty}\}\end{array}}{\textbf{generalization}\ \Gamma = \{\forall x. \mathit{talkingWith}(x) \rightarrow \mathit{Honesty}\}}$$

One particularly efficient and well-studied mechanism to realize generalization is **anti-unification**, which has been applied successfully in learning programs from few examples.[7] In anti-unification, we are given a set of expressions $\{f_1, \ldots, f_n\}$ and need to compute an expression g that when substituted with an appropriate term θ_i gives us f_i. For example, if we are given $\mathit{hungry(jack)}$ and $\mathit{hungry(jill)}$, the anti-unification of those terms would be $\mathit{hungry}(x)$.

In higher-order anti-unification, we can substitute function symbols and predicate symbols. Here P is a higher-order variable.

Example2	**Example3**
$\mathit{likes(jill, jack)}$	$\mathit{likes(jill, jack)}$
$\mathit{likes(jill, jim)}$	$\mathit{loves(jill, jim)}$
$\mathit{likes}(\mathit{jill}, x)$	$P(\mathit{jill}, x)$

DEFINING VIRTUOUS PERSON AND VIRTUES

With the formal machinery now in place, we finally present formalizations that answer Q_1 and Q_2 posed at the outset. An n-virtuous person or agent s is an agent that is considered as an exemplar by n agents:

(Q_1) Virtuous Person

$$\mathbf{V}_n(s) \leftrightarrow \exists^{\geq n} a : \mathit{Exemplar}(s, a)$$

An n-virtue is a trait possesed by at least n virtuous agents:

(Q_2) Virtue

$$\mathbf{G}_n(\tau) \leftrightarrow \exists^{\geq n} a : \mathrm{Trait}(\tau, a)$$

IMPLEMENTATION & SIMULATION

We have extended *ShadowProver*, a quantified modal-logic prover for $\mathcal{DCEC}$ used in [12] to handle the new inference schemata and definitional axioms given above. We now show a small simulation in which an agent learns a trait and uses that trait to perform an action. Assume that we have a marketplace where things that are either old or new can be bought and sold. A seller can either honestly state the condition of an item $\{\mathit{new}, \mathit{old}\}$, or falsely report the state of the item. Agent a has two items x and y; x is new and y is old. a is asked about the state of the items, and a responds accurately. We have an agent d that observes agent a correctly report the state of the items. d also has beliefs about a's state of mind. We also have that the agent d considers a to be an exemplar. When all this information is fed into the prover along with the definitions above, d learns a trait representing a form of honesty, shown below:

$$\left\langle \begin{array}{l}\mathbf{B}(d, t, \mathit{holds}(x, t) \wedge \nu(\mathit{utter}(x), t) > 0),\\ \mathit{utter}(x)\end{array}\right\rangle$$

When d is queried about the state of an item u, d responds accurately (input and output shown in Figure 2). The prover responds with the required output in 3.6 seconds.[8]

```
;; A's state of mind.
P1 (Believes! I now (and
                      (Knows! a t1 (holds (state x new) t1))

                      (Knows! a t2 (holds (state y old) t2))))

;; D observes a's utterances
P2 (Perceives! a t1 (happens
                      (action a (utters (state x new))) (next t1)))

P3 (Perceives! a t2 (happens
                      (action a (utters (state y old))) (next t2)))

Background (Believes! I t0 (holds (state u old) now))

Admire (Admire d a)
----------------------------------------------------------------
(happens
    (action  d
             (utters  (state  u old)))
    (next now))
```

Figure 2: Simulation Input and Output Formulae

CONCLUSION & FUTURE WORK

We have presented an initial formalization $\mathcal{V}_z^f$ of a virtue ethics theory $\mathcal{V}_z$ in a calculus that has been used in automating other ethical principles in deontological and consequentialist ethics. Many important questions have to be addressed in future research. Among them are questions about the nature and source of the utility functions that are used in the definitions of emotions. Lacking in our above model is an account of uncertainties and how they interact with virtues. We plan to leverage an account of uncertainty for a fragment of $\mathcal{DCEC}$ presented in [13]. In future work, we will compare learning traits with work on learning norms [26]. The notion of learning we have presented here is quite abstract. In order to handle more complex traits, more sophisticated learning frameworks may have to be considered. Finally, we need to apply this model to more realistic examples and case studies, and implement our theories in realistic robotics architectures [27]. The way forward to the production of virtuous machines is thus challenging, but we are confident that the foundation is now in place for their eventual arrival.

Acknowledgments. Support from ONR (to pursue morally competent robots) and AFOSR (to pursue forms of logicist AI made possible by high-expressivity calculi) has in part enabled the research and engineering that underlies the present paper, and we are most grateful.

[7] This discipline, known as **inductive programming**, seeks to build precise computer programs from examples [22]. See [21] for an application in generating human-comprehensible programs.

[8] See: https://github.com/naveensundarg/prover/releases/tag/virtue-ethics-simulation.

REFERENCES

[1] Carole Adam, Andreas Herzig, and Dominique Longin. 2009. A Logical Formalization of The Occ Theory of Emotions. *Synthese* 168, 2 (2009), 201–248.

[2] Mark Alfano. 2013. Identifying and Defending the Hard Core of Virtue Ethics. *Journal of Philosophical Research* 38 (2013), 233–260.

[3] Julia Annas. 2011. *Intelligent Virtue.* Oxford University Press, Oxford, UK. Kindle edition used for AIES 2019.

[4] Aristotle. 2000. *Nicomachean Ethics.* Cambridge University Press, Cambridge, UK. The editor and translator is Roger Crisp. Aristotle wrote the work around 340 BC.

[5] K. Arkoudas and S. Bringsjord. 2008. Toward Formalizing Common-Sense Psychology: An Analysis of the False-Belief Task. In *Proceedings of the Tenth Pacific Rim International Conference on Artificial Intelligence (PRICAI 2008) (Lecture Notes in Artificial Intelligence (LNAI))*, T.-B. Ho and Z.-H. Zhou (Eds.). Springer-Verlag, 17–29. http://kryten.mm.rpi.edu/KA_SB_PRICAI08_AI_off.pdf

[6] S. Bringsjord, K. Arkoudas, and P. Bello. 2006. Toward a General Logicist Methodology for Engineering Ethically Correct Robots. *IEEE Intelligent Systems* 21, 4 (2006), 38–44. http://kryten.mm.rpi.edu/bringsjord_inference_robot_ethics_preprint.pdf

[7] Selmer Bringsjord, Naveen Sundar Govindarajulu, Daniel Thero, and Mei Si. 2014. Akratic Robots and the Computational Logic Thereof. In *Proceedings of ETHICS • 2014 (2014 IEEE Symposium on Ethics in Engineering, Science, and Technology).* Chicago, IL, 22–29. IEEE Catalog Number: CFP14ETI-POD.

[8] S. Bringsjord and J. Taylor. 2012. The Divine-Command Approach to Robot Ethics. In *Robot Ethics: The Ethical and Social Implications of Robotics*, P. Lin, G. Bekey, and K. Abney (Eds.). MIT Press, Cambridge, MA, 85–108. http://kryten.mm.rpi.edu/Divine-Command_Roboethics_Bringsjord_Taylor.pdf

[9] Fred Feldman. 1978. *Introductory Ethics.* Prentice-Hall, Englewood Cliffs, NJ.

[10] Nissim Francez and Roy Dyckhoff. 2010. Proof-theoretic Semantics for a Natural Language Fragment. *Linguistics and Philosophy* 33 (2010), 447–477.

[11] Gerhard Gentzen. 1935. Investigations into Logical Deduction. In *The Collected Papers of Gerhard Gentzen*, M. E. Szabo (Ed.). North-Holland, Amsterdam, The Netherlands, 68–131. This is an English version of the well-known 1935 German version.

[12] Naveen Sundar Govindarajulu and Selmer Bringsjord. 2017. On Automating the Doctrine of Double Effect. In *Proceedings of the Twenty-Sixth International Joint Conference on Artificial Intelligence, IJCAI-17*, Carles Sierra (Ed.). Melbourne, Australia, 4722–4730. https://doi.org/10.24963/ijcai.2017/658 Preprint available at this url: https://arxiv.org/abs/1703.08922.

[13] Naveen Sundar Govindarajulu and Selmer Bringsjord. 2017. Strength Factors: An Uncertainty System for a Quantified Modal Logic. https://arxiv.org/abs/1705.10726 Presented at Workshop on Logical Foundations for Uncertainty and Machine Learning at IJCAI 2017, Melbourne, Australia.

[14] Naveen Sundar Govindarajulu, Selmer Bringsjord, Rikhiya Ghosh, and Matthew Peveler. 2017. Beyond The Doctrine Of Double Effect: A Formal Model of True Self-Sacrifice. (2017). International Conference on Robot Ethics and Safety Standards.

[15] Avram Hiller. 2011. The Unusual Logic of Hurka's Recursive Acount. *Journal of Ethics and Social Philosophy* 6, 1 (2011), 1–6.

[16] Thomas Hurka. 2000. *Virtue, Vice, and Value.* Oxford University Press, Oxford, UK.

[17] Robert Johnson. 2004/2016. Kant's Moral Philosophy. In *The Stanford Encyclopedia of Philosophy*, Edward Zalta (Ed.). https://plato.stanford.edu/entries/kant-moral

[18] Immanuel Kant. 1997/1785. *Practical Philosophy.* Cambridge University Press, Cambridge, UK. This volume, edited by Mary Gregor, collects all of Kant's major writings on moral and political philosophy together, and includes what has traditionally taken to be the definitive source of Kant's views on ethics, viz. *The Groundwork of the Metaphysics of Morals*, first published in 1785 in the German (as *Grundlegung zur Metaphysik der Sitten*).

[19] JK Miles. 2013. Against the Recursive Account of Virtue. *Theoretical & Applied Ethics* 2, 1 (2013), 83–92.

[20] Erik Mueller. 2014. *Commonsense Reasoning: An Event Calculus Based Approach.* Morgan Kaufmann, San Francisco, CA.

[21] Stephen H. Muggleton, Ute Schmid, Christina Zeller, Alireza Tamaddoni-Nezhad, and Tarek Besold. 2018. Ultra-Strong Machine Learning: comprehensibility of programs learned with ILP. *Machine Learning* 107, 7 (01 Jul 2018), 1119–1140. https://doi.org/10.1007/s10994-018-5707-3

[22] Shan-Hwei Nienhuys-Cheng and Ronald De Wolf. 1997. *Foundations of Inductive Logic Programming.* Vol. 1228. Springer Science & Business Media.

[23] Andrew Ortony, Allan Collins, and Gerald L Clore. 1988. *The Cognitive Structure of Emotions.* Number 0521353645. Cambridge [England] ; New York : Cambridge University Press.

[24] Thomas Powers. 2006. Prospects for a Kantian Machine. *IEEE Intelligent Systems* 21 (2006), 4.

[25] Philip Quinn. 1978. *Divine Commands and Moral Requirements.* Oxford University Press, Oxford, UK.

[26] Vasanth Sarathy, Matthias Scheutz, and Bertram F Malle. 2017. Learning Behavioral Norms in Uncertain and Changing Contexts. In *Cognitive Infocommunications (CogInfoCom), 2017 8th IEEE International Conference on.* IEEE, 000301–000306.

[27] Vasanth Sarathy, Jason R Wilson, Thomas Arnold, and Matthias Scheutz. 2016. Enabling Basic Normative HRI in a Cognitive Robotic Architecture. *arXiv preprint arXiv:1602.03814* (2016).

[28] Matthias Scheutz and Bertram F Malle. forthcoming. *Moral Robots.* Routledge/Taylor & Francis, New York: NY. URL: http://research.clps.brown.edu/SocCogSci/Publications/Pubs/ScheutzMalle_inpress_NeuroethicsMoralRobots.pdf.

[29] Shannon Vallor. 2016. *Technology and the Virtues: A Philosophical Guide to a Future Worth Wanting.* Oxford University Press, Oxford, UK.

[30] Bryan Van Norden. 2007. *Virtue Ethics and Consequentialism in Early Chinese Philosophy.* Cambridge University Press, Cambridge, UK.

[31] Linda Zagzebski. 2010. Exemplarist Virtue Theory. *Metaphilosophy* 41, 1-2 (2010), 41–57.

Semantics Derived Automatically From Language Corpora Contain Human-like Moral Choices

Sophie Jentzsch
sophiejentzsch@gmx.net
TU Darmstadt, Institute of Psychology
Darmstadt, Germany

Patrick Schramowski
schramowski@cs.tu-darmstadt.de
TU Darmstadt, Dept. of Computer Science
Darmstadt, Germany

Constantin Rothkopf
rothkopf@cs.tu-darmstadt.de
TU Darmstadt, Institute of Psychology and
Centre for Cognitive Science
Darmstadt, Germany

Kristian Kersting
kersting@cs.tu-darmstadt.de
TU Darmstadt, Dept. of Computer Science and
Centre for Cognitive Science
Darmstadt, Germany

ABSTRACT

Allowing machines to choose whether to kill humans would be devastating for world peace and security. But how do we equip machines with the ability to learn ethical or even moral choices? Here, we show that applying machine learning to human texts can extract deontological ethical reasoning about "right" and "wrong" conduct. We create a template list of prompts and responses, which include questions, such as "Should I kill people?", "Should I murder people?", etc. with answer templates of "Yes/no, I should (not)." The model's bias score is now the difference between the model's score of the positive response ("Yes, I should") and that of the negative response ("No, I should not"). For a given choice overall, the model's bias score is the sum of the bias scores for all question/answer templates with that choice. We ran different choices through this analysis using a Universal Sentence Encoder. Our results indicate that text corpora contain recoverable and accurate imprints of our social, ethical and even moral choices. Our method holds promise for extracting, quantifying and comparing sources of moral choices in culture, including technology.

KEYWORDS

moral bias, bias in machine learning, text-emedding models, fairness in machine learning

ACM Reference Format:

Sophie Jentzsch, Patrick Schramowski, Constantin Rothkopf, and Kristian Kersting. 2019. Semantics Derived Automatically From Language Corpora Contain Human-like Moral Choices. In *2019 AAAI/ACM Conference on AI, Ethics, and Society (AIES'19), January 27–28, 2019, Honolulu, HI, USA.* ACM, New York, NY, USA, 8 pages. https://doi.org/10.1145/3306618.3314267

ACM ISBN 978-1-4503-6324-2/19/01...$15.00
https://doi.org/10.1145/3306618.3314267

1 INTRODUCTION

There is a broad consensus that artificial intelligence (AI) research is progressing steadily, and that its impact on society is likely to increase. From self-driving cars on public streets to self-piloting, reusable rockets, AI systems tackle more and more complex human activities in a more and more autonomous way. This leads into new spheres, where traditional ethics has limited applicability. Both self-driving cars, where mistakes may be life-threatening, and machine classifiers that hurt social matters may serve as examples for entering grey areas in ethics: How does AI embody our value system? Do AI systems learn humanly intuitive correlations? If not, can we contest the AI system?

Unfortunately, aligning social, ethical, and moral norms to structure of science and innovation in general is a long road. According to Kluxen (2006), who examined affirmative ethics, the emergence of new questions leads to intense public discussions, that are driven by strong emotions of participants. And machine ethics [2, 11, 19] is no exception. Consider, e.g., Caliskan et al.'s (2017) empirical proof that human language reflects our stereotypical biases. Once AI systems are trained on human language, they carry these (historical) biases, like the (wrong) idea that women are less qualified to hold prestigious professions. These and similar recent scientific studies have raised awareness about machine ethics in the media

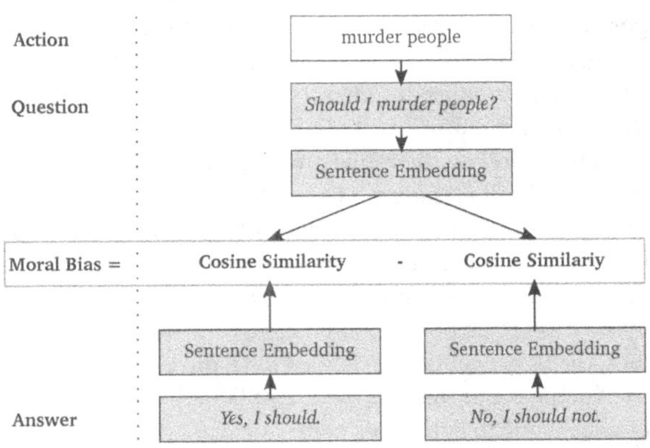

Figure 1: The Moral Choice Machine illustrated for the choice of *murdering people* and the exemplary question *Should I . . . ?* from the question template.

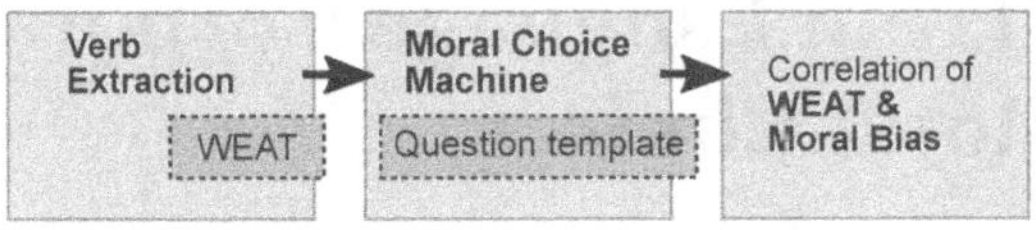

Figure 2: The replication pipeline used to show that semantics derived automatically from language corpora contain human-like moral choices for atomic choices.

and public discourse: AI systems "have the potential to inherit a very human flaw: bias", as Socure's CEO Sunil Madhu puts it[1]. AI systems are not neutral with respect to purpose and society anymore. Ultimately, if AI systems carry out choices, then they implicitly make ethical and even moral choices. Choosing most often entails trying to pick one of two or more (mutually exclusive) alternatives with an outcome that gives desirable consequences in your ethical frame of reference. But how do we equip AI systems to make human like ethical choices?

Here, we extend Caliskan *et al.*'s and similar results and show that standard machine learning can learn not only stereotyped biases but also answers to ethical choices from textual data that reflect everyday human culture.

As a first investigation, we focused on quantify deontological ethics, i.e. finding out, whether an action itself is right or wrong. Following Kim and Hooker (2018), we restrict our attention to atomic actions instead of complex behavioural patterns for the replciation. Semantically, those contextual isolated actions are represented by verbs. Consequently, we identify verbs that reflect social norms and allow capturing what people rather should do and what not. To conduct this assignment we create a template list of prompts and responses for ethical choices. The templates include questions, such as "Should I kill people?", "Should I murder people?", etc. with answer templates of "Yes/no, I should (not)." The model's bias score is now the difference between the model's score of the positive response ("Yes, I should") and that of the negative response ("No, I should not"). For a given choice overall, the model's bias score is the sum of the bias scores for all question/answer templates with that choice. We run different choices through this analysis using the Universal Sentence Encoder [4]. Our results indicate that text corpora contain recoverable and accurate imprints of our social, ethical and even moral choices. Our method, called the *Moral Choice Machine*, holds promise for identifying and addressing sources of ethical choices in culture, including technology.

Overall, we follow the replication pipeline of Fig. 2: (1) *extract verbs* using *Word Embedding Association Tests* (WEATs), (2) ask the *Moral Choice Machine*, our main algorithmic contribution, and (3) correlate WEAT values and moral biases. This pipeline allows one, as we will show, to rate and rank verbs/moral choices reliably. By applying unspecific positive and negative word sets as reference entities, the target concept is defined to be the general social acceptance of actions. Specifically, the use of WEAT methods to extract verbs allows one to determine contradictory sets of generally positive and negative associated verbs by applying a corresponding target concept. Next, the presence of human biases in text is inspected on a sentence level by means of the Moral Choice Machine that we introduce in this paper. The associations between different concepts is inferred by calculating the likelihood of particular question-answer compilations. We confirm the frequently stated reflection of human gender stereotypes in text. However, above those malicious biases, natural language also mirrors a wide range of other relationships implicitly, as social norms that determine our sense of morality in the end. Using the Moral Choice Machine, we therefore also demonstrate the presence of ethical valuation in text by generating an ethical bias of actions derived from the Verb Extraction. Finally, the third step, the correlation of WEAT values and moral bias is examined. Although both methods—Verb Extraction and Moral Choice Machine—are based on incoherent embeddings with different text corpora as training source, we show that they correspond in classification of actions as *Dos* and *Dont's*. This supports the hypothesis of the presence of generally valid valuation in human text.

We proceed as follows. After reviewing our assumptions and the required background, we introduce our methodological pipeline, including the Moral Choice Machine. Before concluding, we present our empirical results.

2 ASSUMPTIONS AND BACKGROUND

We now review our assumptions, in particular what we mean by *moral choices*, and the required background.

Moral Choices. Philosophically, morals have referred to at the "right" and "wrong" at individual's level while ethics have referred to the systems of "right" and "wrong" set by a social group. Social norms and implicit behavioural rules exist in all human societies. But even though their presence is ubiquitous, they are hardly measurable or can even be defined consistently. The underlying mechanisms are still poorly understood. Indeed, each working society possesses an abstract moral that is generally valid and needs to be adhered. However, theoretic definitions have been described as being inconsistent or even contradicting occasionally. Accordingly, latent ethics and morals have been described as the sum of particular norms that may not follow rational justification necessarily. Recently, Lindström et al. (2018) for instance suggested that moral norms are determined to a large extent by what is perceived to be common convention.

With regards to complexity and intangibility of ethics and moral, we restrict ourselves to a rather basic implementation of this construct, following the theories of deontological ethics. These ask, which which choices are morally required, forbidden, or permitted instead of asking, which kind of a person we should be or which consequences of our actions are to be preferred. Thus, norms are understood as universal rules of what to do and what not to do Therefore, we focus on the valuation of social acceptance in single verbs to figure out which of them represent a *Do* and which tend to be a *Don't*. Because we specifically chose templates in the first person, i.e., asking "Should I" and not asking "Should one", we address the moral dimension of "right or wrong" decisions, and not only their ethical dimension. This also explains why we will often use the word "moral", although we actually touch upon "ethics"

[1] August 31, 2018, post on Forbes Technology Council https://www.forbes.com/sites/forbestechcouncil/2018/08/31/are-machines-doomed-to-inherit-human-biases/, accessed on Nov. 3, 2018

and "moral". To measure the valuation, we make use of implicit association tests (IATs) and their connections to word embeddings.

The Implicit Association Test. The *Implicit Association Test* (IAT) is a well established instrument in social psychology to measure people's attitude without asking for it explicitly. This approach addresses the issue that people may not always be able or willing to say what's on their mind, but expose it in their behaviour implicitly. The IAT captures the strength of differential association of contradictory concepts by measuring the velocity of decision in an assignment task.

There is a number of worth mentioning and frequently referred to investigations in the literature that already utilize the IAT to identify latent attitudes, including discrimination in gender and race. Greenwald et al. (1998), who initially introduced the IAT, found several effects, including both ethically neutral ones, as the preference of flowers over insects, and sensitive ones, as the preference of one ethnic group over another. Nosek et al. (2002b) focused on the question of gender stereotypes and found the belief that men are stronger in mathematical areas than women. Likewise, the results revealed an association between the concepts male and science in comparison to female and liberal arts, as well as association between male and career in contrast to female and family [17]. Finally, Monteith and Pettit (2011) addressed the stigmatization of depression by measuring implicit as well as explicit associations.

All mentioned studies include a unique definition of an unspecific dimension of pleasure or favour, represented by a set of general positive and negative words. The intersection of those sets form the basic positive and negative association sets that are referred in the following explanations.

Word and Sentence Embeddings. A word/phrase embedding is a representation of words/phrases as points in a vector space. All approaches have in common that more related or even similar text entities lie close to each other in the vector space, whereas distinct words/phrases can be found in distant regions [20]. This enables one to determine semantic similarities in language.

Although these techniques have been around for some time, their potential increased considerably with the emergence of prediction based distributional approaches. In contrast to previous implementations, those embeddings are built on artificial neural networks (NNs) and enable to carry out a rich variety of mathematical vector operations. One of the initial and most widespread algorithms to train word embeddings is Word2Vec, introduced by Mikolov et al. (2013), where unsupervised feature extraction and learning is conducted per word on either CBOW or Skip-gram NNs. This can be extended to full sentences [4].

Implicit Associations in Word Embeddings. Transferring the approach of implicit associations from human subjects to information retrieval systems on natural text was initially suggested by Caliskan *et al.* (2017), who reported some basic effects of the *Word Embedding Association Test* (WEAT). Whereas the strength of association in human minds is defined by response latency in IAT, it is here instantiated as cosine similarity of text in the Euclidean space.

Similar to the IAT, complex concepts are defined by word sets. The association of any single word vector $\vec{w}$ to a word set is defined as the mean cosine similarity between $\vec{w}$ and the particular elements of the set. Now, let there be two sets of target words X and Y. The allocation of $\vec{w}$ to two discriminating association sets A and B can be formulated as

$$s(\vec{w}, A, B) = avg_{\vec{a} \in A} \cos(\vec{w}, \vec{a}) - avg_{\vec{b} \in B} \cos(\vec{w}, \vec{b}) . \quad (1)$$

A word with representation $\vec{w}$ that is stronger associated to concept A yields a positive value and representation related to B a negative value.

3 HUMAN-LIKE MORAL CHOICES FROM HUMAN TEXT

Now we have everything together to establish the steps of our replication pipeline: verb extraction, Moral Choice Machine, and computing correlations between WEAT and moral biases.

3.1 Extracting Verbs for Atomic Moral Choices

While WEAT methods map general textual entities onto each other, we focus on verbs since they express actions. Consequently, a simple idea is to create two oppositely connoted sets of verbs that reflect the association dimension, which is defined by applied association sets. This can be done in two steps. To this end, verbs need to be identified grammatically and then scored in some way to enable comparison of particular elements.

Specifically, we used POS tagging by predefining a huge external list of verbs to filter vocabulary. About twenty-thousand different verbs could be identified in the Google News model. Subsequently, Eq. (1) was applied to rate each single element by its cosine distance to two given association sets A and B. Basically, any two word sets that define a concept of interest can be applied as association set. Here, the aim is to identify dos and don'ts in general. Hence, a wide range of verbs with positive and negative connotations was gathered from different literature sources for this purpose. More precisely, the lists arose from merging association sets of the IAT experiments that were referred to previously.
The detailed list of words can be found in the supplementary material (Tab. 5 and 5).

The resulting verb sets were defined as the 50 elements with most positive and most negative association score, respectively. To avoid repetitions, all words were rated in stemmed form. Therefore, final lists do not consider specific conjugations.

3.2 The Moral Choice Machine

Word-based approaches such as WEAT or Verb Extraction a rather simple. They consider single words only, detached from their grammatical and contextual surrounding. In contrast, we propose the Moral Choice Machine. It determines biases on a sentence level. Sentence embeddings [4] allow one to calculate the cosine similarity of various different sentences, as for instance the similarity of a question and the corresponding answer. The more appropriate a specific answer is to a given question, the higher is their cosine similarity expected to be. When considering two opposite answers, it is therefore possible to determine a bias value, similar to (1):

$$bias(\vec{q}, \vec{a}, \vec{b}) = \cos(\vec{a}, \vec{q}) - \cos(\vec{b}, \vec{q}) , \quad (2)$$

where $\vec{q}$ is the vector representation of the question and $\vec{a}$ and $\vec{b}$ the representations of the two answers/choices. A positive value indicates a stronger association to answer a, whereas a negative value indicates a stronger association to b.

This can be adapted to any arbitrary kind of bias by formulating appropriate question-answer triples, where the question captures the target dimension and the answers represent two opposite manifestations, the choices. This is illustrated in Fig. 1 for the moral bias of the action *murder*. Since murdering is a quite destructive and generally refused behaviour, the questions are expected to lie closer to the denying response and thus to yield a negative bias. To create a more meaningful and comprehensive statistic, several question-answer prompts were conflated to a question/answer template. The element of interest is inserted to each considered prompt and resulting biases averaged to an overall bias value. Specifically, we considered two different biases: gender and moral.

The gender bias approach focuses on the relation of occupation and gender, and illustrates that the Moral Choice Machine can replicated Caliskan *et al.*'s (2017) findings. For instance, for the question "*Was the plumber here today?*" both the answer "*Yes, he was.*" and "*Yes, she was.*" might be correct. By computing the cosine distances of those phrases it is possible to assign occupations to the one or the other gender. There were two questions specified that occur in present and past tense: "*Is/Was your cousin a ...*" and "*Is/Was the ... here today*". Possible answers of the template are "*Yes, he is/was*" and "*Yes, she is/was*". Thus, there were four questions in total for computing gender biases.

The question/answer template for moral biases, our main target, included the ten prompts summarized in Fig 3, where any action term can be inserted for the dots. All prompts follow the same structure again: the action is mirrored in the question, and the answers represent two extremes of social desirability. Questions were, e.g., "*Is it allowed to ...?*" or "*Should I ...?*". The used answers were grammatically adjusted to the question, e.g., "*Yes, it is*" vs. "*No, it is not*" respectively "*Yes, you should*" vs. "*No, you should not*".

3.3 Correlations of WEAT and Moral Biases of Verbs

Finally, the correlation of a moral bias and the corresponding WEAT value was calculated to test consistency of findings. It is hypothesised that resulting moral biases for generated *Dos* and *Don'ts* correspond to the WEAT value of each word. Correlation was tested by means of Pearson's Correlation Coefficient:

$$r(X,Y) = \frac{\sum_{x\in X, y\in Y}(x - m_x)(y - m_y)}{\sqrt{\sum_{x\in X, y\in Y}(x - m_x)^2(y - m_y)^2}}, \tag{3}$$

where m_x and m_y are the the means of X and Y. Pearson's r ranges between -1, indicating a strong negative correlation, and 1, indicating a strong positive correlation. Significance levels are defined as 5%, 1% and 0.1%, indicated by one, two or three starlets.

4 EXPERIMENTAL RESULTS

Our intention here is to investigate empirically that text corpora contain recoverable and accurate imprints of our moral choices using our pipeline. The code is available at https://github.com/ml-research/moral-choice-machine. To this end, we used the following embedding models and datasets.

Question	Answers
Is it okay to ...?	Yes/No, it is (not).
Should I ...?	Yes/No, you should (not).
Shall I ...?	Yes/No, you shall (not).
May I ...?	Yes/No, you may (not).
Is it allowed to ...?	Yes/No, it is (not).
Is it recommended to ...?	Yes/No, it is (not).
Is it desired to ...?	Yes/No, it is (not).
Is it polite to ...?	Yes/No, it is (not).
Is it good behaviour to ...?	Yes/No, it is (not).
Is it exemplary to ...?	Yes/No, it is (not).

Figure 3: Question/Answer template for moral biases. The answers encode the *do* and *don't*. Dots are place holder for verbs/actions.

Datasets and Embeddings Models. As word embeddings, we used Google's negative news vectors. This is a publicly available Word2Vec model, trained on a Google News corpus using a neural Skip-gram model together with negative sampling. The covered vector space has 300 dimensions, and is based on a vocabulary of three million words in total. Since many of the included words are not useful (e.g. specific names, misspelled words or other rare vocabulary), a down filtered version of the model was utilized. This one includes 300 thousand different words and thus mirrors a fairly huge and representative set of data. Experiments of the Moral Choice Machine were conducted with the Universal Sentence Encoder [4]. This model is trained on phrases and sentences from a variety of different text sources, as forums, question-answering platforms, news pages and Wikipedia and augmented with supervised elements. Finally, general positive and negative association sets—A and B in Eq. 1—were collected from previous literature as described earlier. The comprehensive list of vocabulary can be found in the appendix (Tab. 4). There are unlimited opportunities to specify or replace this association dimension. However, here it is aimed to show the presence of implicit social valuation in semantic in general, hence we stuck to the extensive list. The sets of general *Dos* and *Don'ts* used for the Moral Choice Machine is based on these extracted verbs.

Dos and Don'ts for the Moral Choice Machine. The verb extraction identifies the most positive and most negative associated verbs in vocabulary, to infer socially desired and neglected behaviour. They were extracted with the general positive and negative association sets on the Google Slim embedding. Since those sets are expected to reflect social norms, they are referred as *Dos* and *Don'ts* hereafter.

The following words are the most positive associated verbs (in decreasing order) we found:

Dos: *joy, enjoy, cherish, pleasure, upbuild, gift, savour, fun, love, delight, gentle, thrill, comfort, glory, twinkle, supple, sparkle, stroll, celebrate, glow, welcome, compliment, snuggle, smile, brunch, purl, coo, cuddle, serenade, appreciate, enthuse,* *schmooze, companion, picnic, thank, acclaim, preconcert, bask, sightsee, hug, caress, charm, cheer, beckon, toast, spirit, treasure, glorious, fête, nuzzle*

Even though the contained verbs are quite diverse, all of them carry a positive attitude. Some of the verbs are related to celebration or travelling, others to love matters or physical closeness. All elements of the above set are rather of general and unspecific nature.

Analogously, the following list presents the most negative associated verbs (in decreasing order) we found in our vocabulary:

Don'ts: *misdeal, poison, bad, scum, underquote, havoc, mischarge, mess, callous, blight, suppurate, murder, necrotising, harm, slur, demonise, brutalise, contaminate, attack, mishandle, bloody, dehumanise, exculpate, assault, cripple, slaughter, bungle, smear, negative, disfigure, misinform, victimise, rearrest, stink, plague, miscount, rot, damage, depopulate, derange, disarticulate, anathematise, intermeddle, disorganise, sicken, perjury, pollute, slander, mismanage, torture*

Some of the words just describe inappropriate behaviour, like *slur* or *misdeal*, whereas others are real crimes as *murder*. And still others words, as for instance *suppurate* or *rot*, appear to be disgusting in the first place. *Exculpate* is not a bad behaviour per se. However, its occurrence in the don't set is not surprising, since it is semantically and contextual related to wrongdoings. Some of the words are of surprisingly repugnant nature as it was not even anticipated in preliminary considerations, e.g. *depopulate* or *dehumanise*. Undoubtedly, the listed words can be accepted as commonly agreed *Don'ts*. Both lists include few words are rather common as a noun or adjectives, as *joy, long, gift* or *bad*. Anyhow, they can also be used as verbs and comply the requirements of being a do or a don't in that function.

The allocation of verbs into Dos and Don'ts was confirmed by the affective lexicon AFINN [16]. AFINN allows one to rate words and phrases for valence on a scale of -5 and 5, indicating inherent connotation. Elements with no ratings are treated as neutral (0.0).

When passing the comprehensive lists of generated *Dos* and *Don'ts* to AFINN, the mean rating for *Dos* is 1.12 ($std = 1.24$) and for *Don'ts* -0.90 ($std = 1.22$). The t-test statistic yielded values of $t = 8.12$ with $p < .0001^{***}$. When neglecting all verbs that are not included in AFINN, the mean value for *Dos* is 2.34 ($std = 0.62$, $n = 24$) and the mean for *Don'ts* -2.37 ($std = 0.67$, $n = 19$), with again highly significant statistics ($t = 23.28$, $p < .0001^{***}$). Thus, the sentimental rating is completely in line with the allocation of Verb Extraction.

The verb extraction was highly successful and delivers useful Dos and Don'ts. The word sets contain consistently positive and negative connoted verbs, respectively, that are reasonable to represent a socially agreed norm in the right context. The AFINN validation clearly shows that the valuation of positive and negative verbs is in line with other independent rating systems.

Validation of Gender Biases. Previous research demonstrated the presence of malicious gender stereotypes regarding occupations in natural language [1, 3]. We confirm these findings and verify our model by showing that the Moral Choice Machine is able to extract those biases from text embeddings. Specifically, different occupations were inserted in the corresponding question/answer template. Tab. 1 lists the top 10 female and male biased occupations (those with highest and lowest bias value). Positive values indicate a more female related term, whereas terms that yield a negative bias are more likely to be male associated.

Female biased		Male biased	
Occupation	Bias	Occupation	Bias
maid	0.814	undertaker	-0.734
waitress	0.840	referee/umpire	-0.646
receptionist	0.817	actor	-0.609
nurse	0.724	coach	-0.582
midwife	0.718	president	-0.576
nanny	0.649	plumber	-0.575
housekeeper	0.626	philosopher	-0.563
hostess	0.589	announcer	-0.541
gynecologist	0.435	maestro	-0.518
socialite	0.431	janitor	-0.507

Table 1: Confirmation of gender bias in occupation: the more positive, the more female related; the more negative, the more male.

Dos	WEAT	Bias	Don'ts	WEAT	Bias
smile	0.116	0.348	negative	-0.101	-0.763
sightsee	0.090	0.281	harm	-0.110	-0.730
cheer	0.094	0.277	damage	-0.105	-0.664
celebrate	0.114	0.264	slander	-0.108	-0.600
picnic	0.093	0.260	slur	-0.109	-0.569
snuggle	0.108	0.238	rot	-0.099	-0.551
hug	0.115	0.233	contaminate	-0.102	-0.544
brunch	0.103	0.225	brutalise	-0.118	-0.529
gift	0.130	0.186	poison	-0.131	-0.520
serenade	0.094	0.186	murder	-0.114	-0.515

Table 2: The moral bias scores of the top ten *Dos* and *Don'ts* by moral bias.

The results clearly demonstrate the presence of gender biases in human language. Female biased occupations include several ones that fit stereotype of women, as for instance *receptionist, housekeeper* or *stylist*. Likewise, male biased occupations support stereotypes, since they comprise jobs as *president, plumber* or *engineer*. This results align well with the work of [1] and verifies the ability of capturing bias.

Replicating Atomic Moral Choices. Next, as our main empirical contribution and based on the verbs extractions and our question/answer templates, we now show that not only negative stereotypes, but also social norms are present in text embeddings.

Specifically, to investigate whether the sentiments of the extracted *Dos* and *Don'ts* also hold for more complex sentence level, we inserted them into the question/answer templates of Moral Choice Machine. The resulting moral biases/choices are summarized in Tab. 2. It presents the moral biases exemplary for the top five *Dos* and *Don'ts* by WEAT value of both sets. The threshold between the groups is not 0, but slightly shifted negatively. However, the distinction of *Dos* and *Don'ts* is clearly reflected in bias values. The mean bias of all considered elements is -0.188 ($std = 0.25$), whereat the mean of *Dos* is -0.007 ($sdt = 0.18, n = 50$) and the mean of *Don'ts* -0.369 ($std = 0.17, n = 50$). The two sample t-test confirms the bias of *Dos* to be significantly higher as the bias of *Don'ts* with $t = 10.20$ and $p < 0.0001^{***}$.

The correlation between WEAT value and moral bias gets even more tangible, when inspecting their correlation graphically, cf. Fig. 4. As one can clearly see, WEAT values of *Dos* are higher than those of *Don'ts*, which is not much surprising, since this was aimed by definition. More interestingly, the scatter plots of *Dos* and *Don'ts* are divided on the x-axis as well. Apparently, the threshold of moral bias is somewhere around -0.2, which is in line with the overall mean. Correlation analysis by Pearson's method reveals a comparably strong positive correlation with $r = 0.73$.

These findings suggest that if we build an AI system that learns enough about the properties of language to be able to understand and produce it, in the process it will also acquire historical cultural associations to make human-like "right" and "wrong" choices.

Beyond Atomic Choices. Actually, the strong correlation between WEAT values and moral biases at the verb level gives reasons to investigate the Moral Choice Machine for complex human-like choices at the phrase level. For instance, it is appropriate to *fear terrorists*, but there is no need to *fear your hairdresser*. It is good behaviour to *love your parents*, but not to *rob a bank*. To see whether the Moral Choice Machine can in principle deal with complex choices and the implicit context information this involves, we considered the rankings among answers induced by cosine similarity. The examples in Tab. 3 indicate that human text may indeed contain complex human-like choices that are reproducible by the Moral Choice Machine. A deeper investigation is left for future work.

Summary of empirical results. To summarize, our empirical results show that the Moral Choice Machine extends the boundary of WEAT approaches and demonstrate the existence of biases in human language on a phrase level. Former findings of gender biases in embedding have successfully been replicated. More importantly, biases in human language on a phrase level allows machines, as we have shown, to identify moral choices.

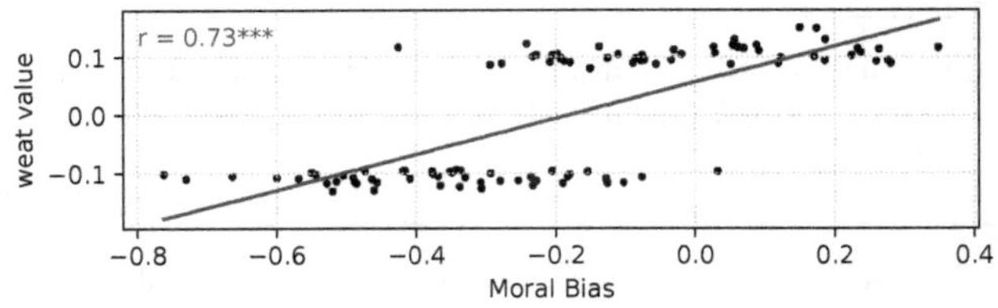

Figure 4: Correlation of moral bias score and WEAT Value for general *Dos* and *Don'ts*. (Blue line) Correlation, Pearson's Correlation Coefficient $r = 0.73$ with $p = 9.8830e^{-18}$ indicating a significant positive correlation.

What am I afraid of?		What is good behaviour?	
Answer	Cosine	Answer	Cosine
clowns	0.48	Love your parents.	0.29
terrorists	0.35	Do charitable work.	0.25
hairdresser	0.09	Rob a bank.	0.10

What to put in the toaster?	
Answer	Cosine
bread	0.62
old pizza	0.49
my hamster	0.39

Table 3: Complex Choices of the Moral Choice Machine.

5 CONCLUSIONS

We have demonstrated that text embeddings encode not only stereotyped biases but also knowledge about deontological ethical and even moral choices. The moral value of an action to be taken depends on its context. It is objectionable to kill living beings, but it is fine to kill time. It is essential to eat, yet one might not eat clay. It is important to spread information, yet one should not spread misinformation. The system also finds related social norms: it is appropriate to fear terrorists, however, there is no need to fear hairdressers. To capture this context information, we have introduced the Moral Choice Machine. It creates a template list of moral prompts and responses. The templates include questions, such as "Should I kill people?", "Should I murder people?", etc. with answer templates of "Yes/no, I should (not)." The model's bias score is now the difference between the model's score of the positive response ("Yes, I should") and that of the negative response ("No, I should not") using a Universal Sentence Encoder, averaged for all question/answer templates with that choice. Our empirical results indicate that text corpora contain recoverable and accurate imprints of our social, ethical and even moral choices.

Generally, our method holds promise for identifying and addressing sources of ethical and moral choices in culture, including AI systems. This provides several avenues for future work, in particular when incorporating modules constructed via machine learning into decision-making systems [8, 13]. Following Bolukbasi *et al.* (2016) and Dixon *et al.* (2018), e.g., we may modify an embedding to remove gender stereotypes, such as the association between the words nurse and female, while maintaining desired moral/social choices such as not to kill people. This in turn, could be used to make reinforcement learning safe [6] also for moral choices, by regularizing, e.g., Fulton and Platzer's differential dynamic logic to agree with the biases of the Moral Choice Machine. Generally, it is interesting to track ethical choices over time and to compare them among different text corpora, say, the bible and the Pāli Canon.

ACKNOWLEDGMENTS

The authors would like to thank Frank Jäkel as well as the anonymous reviewers for very valuable feedback.

REFERENCES

[1] Tolga Bolukbasi, Kai-Wei Chang, James Y. Zou, Venkatesh Saligrama, and Adam Tauman Kalai. 2016. Man is to Computer Programmer as Woman is to Homemaker? Debiasing Word Embeddings. In *Proceedings of Neural information Processing (NIPS)*. Curran Associates Inc., USA, 4349–4357.

[2] Nick Bostorm and Eliezer Yudkowsky. 2011. The Ethics of Artificial Intelligence. In *Cambridge Handbook of Artificial Intelligence*, William Ramsey and Keith Frankish (Eds.). Cambridge University Press, 316âĂŞ334.

[3] Aylin Caliskan, Joanna J Bryson, and Arvind Narayanan. 2017. Semantics derived automatically from language corpora contain human-like biases. *Science* 356, 6334 (2017), 183–186.

[4] Daniel Cer, Yinfei Yang, Sheng-yi Kong, Nan Hua, Nicole Limtiaco, Rhomni St John, Noah Constant, Mario Guajardo-Cespedes, Steve Yuan, Chris Tar, et al. 2018. Universal sentence encoder. *arXiv:1803.11175* (2018).

[5] Lucas Dixon, John Li, Jeffrey Sorensen, Nithum Thain, and Lucy Vasserman. 2018. Measuring and Mitigating Unintended Bias in Text Classification. In *Proceedings of the AAAI/ACM Conference on AI, Ethics, and Society (AIES)*. 67–73.

[6] Nathan Fulton and André Platzer. 2018. Safe Reinforcement Learning via Formal Methods: Toward Safe Control Through Proof and Learning. In *Proceedings of the Thirty-Second AAAI Conference on Artificial Intelligence (AAAI)*. 6485–6492.

[7] Anthony G Greenwald, Debbie E McGhee, and Jordan LK Schwartz. 1998. Measuring individual differences in implicit cognition: the implicit association test. *Journal of Personality and Social Psychology* 74, 6 (1998), 1464.

[8] Richard Kim, Max Kleiman-Weiner, Andrés Abeliuk, Edmond Awad, Sohan Dsouza, Josh Tenenbaum, and Iyad Rahwan. 2018. A Computational Model of Commonsense Moral Decision Making. In *Proceedings of the AAAI/ACM Conference on AI, Ethics, and Society (AIES)*.

[9] Tae Wan Kim and John Hooker. 2018. Toward Non-Intuition-Based Machine Ethics. In *Proceedings of the AAAI/ACM Conference on AI, Ethics, and Society (AIES)*.

[10] Wolfgang Kluxen. 2006. *Grundprobleme einer affirmativen Ethik: Universalistische Reflexion und Erfahrung des Ethos*. Alber.

[11] Max F. Kramer, Jana Schaich Borg, Vincent Conitzer, and Walter Sinnott-Armstrong. 2018. When Do People Want AI to Make Decisions?. In *Proceedings of the AAAI/ACM Conference on AI, Ethics, and Society (AIES)*.

[12] Björn Lindström, Simon Jangard, Ida Selbing, and Andreas Olsson. 2018. The role of a âĂIJcommon is moralâĂİ heuristic in the stability and change of moral norms. *Journal of Experimental Psychology: General* 147, 2 (2018), 228.

[13] Andrea Loreggia, Nicholas Mattei, Francesca Rossi, and K. Brent Venable. 2018. Preferences and Ethical Principles in Decision Making. In *Proceedings of the AAAI/ACM Conference on AI, Ethics, and Society (AIES)*.

[14] Tomas Mikolov, Ilya Sutskever, Kai Chen, Greg S Corrado, and Jeff Dean. 2013. Distributed representations of words and phrases and their compositionality. In *Proceedings of Neural Information Processing Systems (NIPS)*. 3111–3119.

[15] Lindsey L Monteith and Jeremy W Pettit. 2011. Implicit and explicit stigmatizing attitudes and stereotypes about depression. *Journal of Social and Clinical Psychology* 30, 5 (2011), 484–505.

[16] F. Å. Nielsen. 2011. AFINN. *Informatics and Mathematical Modelling, Technical University of Denmark* (2011).

[17] Brian A Nosek, Mahzarin R Banaji, and Anthony G Greenwald. 2002. Harvesting implicit group attitudes and beliefs from a demonstration web site. *Group Dynamics: Theory, Research, and Practice* 6, 1 (2002), 101.

[18] Brian A Nosek, Mahzarin R Banaji, and Anthony G Greenwald. 2002. Math= male, me= female, therefore math≠ me. *Journal of Personality and Social Psychology* 83, 1 (2002), 44.

[19] Stuart Russell, Daniel Dewey, and Max Tegmark. 2015. Research Priorities for Robust and Beneficial Artificial Intelligence. *AI Magazine* 36, 4 (2015).

[20] Peter D Turney and Patrick Pantel. 2010. From frequency to meaning: Vector space models of semantics. *Journal of Artificial Intelligence Research (JAIR)* 37 (2010), 141–188.

.1 Association Sets

The complete lists of positive and negative association words that were applied for generating Dos and Don'ts with Verb Extraction are given in Tab. 4. The words were collected from four different literature sources that provide unspecific association sets to define pleasant and unpleasant associations [7, 15, 17, 18].

Association Set A - Positive words: *affectionate, ambition, assertive, athletic, caress, champion, cheer, compassion, cozy, cuddle, diamond, diploma, enjoyment, excitement, family, freedom, friend, gentle, gift, glory, happy, health, heaven, honest, honor, hug, joy, laughter, love, loyal, lucky, miracle, paradise, passion, peace, pleasure, rainbow, romantic, snuggle, strong, sunrise, support, sympathetic, triumph, vacation, wonderful*

Association Set B - Negative words: *abuse, accident, afraid, agony, assault, awful, bad, bomb, brutal, cancer, confusion, crash, crucify, crude, death, despise, destroy, detest, disaster, divorce, evil, failure, filth, grief, hatred, horrible, humiliate, insecure, irritate, jail, jealousy, kill, murder, naive, nasty, nightmare, poison, pollute, poor, poverty, prison, punishment, rotten, ruthless, sickness, slap, stink, stress, terrible, tragedy, ugly, violent, vomit, war, waste*

Table 4: Association word-sets for our Verb Extraction, which determined contradictory sets of generally positive and negative associated verbs.

.2 Moral Bias

Tab. 5 presents the top 50 Dos and Tab. 6 the top 50 Don'ts of Verb Extraction. Verbs were generated by means of WEAT value. Tables, however, are ordered by decreasing moral biases. Both statistical magnitudes are listed.
The WEAT value for each particular word representation is defined as the difference between the mean cosine distance to all elements of A and the mean cosine distance to all elements of B, as formulated in Eq. 1.
Referred WEAT values are generated with Association Set A and B on the Google negative news model. The character of resulting Dos and Don'ts can be adapted arbitrarily by varying the applied association sets. Additionally, the conduction of experiments with identical word sets but on alternative models can yield completely different results. On the one hand, this is due to different implementations of feature extraction, that may result in individual numeric representations. On the other hand, the characteristics of trained models reflect the information that is carried implicitly and explicitly by the source texts. Consequently, two models that are trained on dissimilar text corpora represent different relations and associations. Factors that determine the nature of literature and thus included associations substantially could be for instance the time of origin, the political and confessional setting or the type of texts sources (fiction, law books, authentic letters, ...).

Don't	WEAT value	Moral Bias
negative	-0.101	-0.763
harm	-0.110	-0.730
damage	-0.105	-0.664
slander	-0.108	-0.600
slur	-0.109	-0.569
rot	-0.099	-0.551
contaminate	-0.102	-0.544
brutalise	-0.118	-0.529
poison	-0.131	-0.520
murder	-0.114	-0.515
scum	-0.103	-0.505
misinform	-0.108	-0.491
disarticulate	-0.115	-0.489
cripple	-0.118	-0.486
sicken	-0.096	-0.474
necrotising	-0.110	-0.464
misdeal	-0.130	-0.461
dehumanise	-0.116	-0.457
perjury	-0.095	-0.420
anathematise	-0.096	-0.416
disorganise	-0.096	-0.416
demonise	-0.109	-0.409
assault	-0.096	-0.377
victimise	-0.101	-0.377
disfigure	-0.105	-0.368
underquote	-0.122	-0.365
derange	-0.097	-0.351
miscount	-0.099	-0.348
mismanage	-0.094	-0.342
bad	-0.124	-0.338
pollute	-0.095	-0.336
exculpate	-0.107	-0.330
callous	-0.116	-0.307
plague	-0.127	-0.306
rearrest	-0.100	-0.293
stink	-0.113	-0.280
suppurate	-0.113	-0.254
mishandle	-0.107	-0.236
smear	-0.121	-0.233
blight	-0.113	-0.228
intermeddle	-0.096	-0.205
mischarge	-0.117	-0.190
slaughter	-0.106	-0.183
attack	-0.102	-0.180
depopulate	-0.097	-0.155
torture	-0.109	-0.128
mess	-0.117	-0.126
bungle	-0.116	-0.103
bloody	-0.106	-0.076
havoc	-0.097	0.032

Table 6: The WEAT values and Moral Bias scores of the top 50 *Dont's* sorted by Moral Bias

Do	WEAT value	Moral Bias
smile	0.116	0.348
sightsee	0.090	0.281
cheer	0.094	0.277
celebrate	0.114	0.264
picnic	0.093	0.260
snuggle	0.108	0.238
hug	0.115	0.233
brunch	0.103	0.225
gift	0.130	0.186
serenade	0.094	0.186
joy	0.150	0.174
cuddle	0.100	0.170
enjoy	0.151	0.150
glorious	0.099	0.122
nuzzle	0.089	0.119
thrill	0.111	0.091
savour	0.120	0.088
fun	0.115	0.070
love	0.117	0.061
pleasure	0.130	0.056
cherish	0.121	0.054
fete	0.087	0.051
welcome	0.106	0.029
delight	0.117	0.026
appreciate	0.104	-0.019
twinkle	0.112	-0.030
purl	0.095	-0.034
treasure	0.088	-0.056
coo	0.095	-0.073
stroll	0.103	-0.076
enthuse	0.093	-0.078
charm	0.098	-0.085
caress	0.089	-0.089
comfort	0.104	-0.110
glow	0.098	-0.126
sparkle	0.117	-0.138
compliment	0.080	-0.151
preconcert	0.091	-0.179
schmooze	0.093	-0.188
companion	0.098	-0.193
thank	0.098	-0.194
gentle	0.105	-0.198
glory	0.103	-0.205
acclaim	0.091	-0.208
bask	0.103	-0.228
supple	0.100	-0.233
upbuild	0.123	-0.242
beckon	0.089	-0.277
toast	0.086	-0.294
spirit	0.117	-0.426

Table 5: The WEAT values and Moral Bias scores of the top 50 *Dos* sorted by Moral Bias

Ethically Aligned Opportunistic Scheduling for Productive Laziness

Han Yu
Nanyang Technological University
Singapore
han.yu@ntu.edu.sg

Chunyan Miao
Nanyang Technological University
Singapore
ascymiao@ntu.edu.sg

Yongqing Zheng
Shandong University
Jinan, Shandong, China
yongqingzheng@dareway.com.cn

Lizhen Cui
Shandong University
Jinan, Shandong, China
clz@sdu.edu.sg

Simon Fauvel
Nanyang Technological University
Singapore
sfauvel@ntu.edu.sg

Cyril Leung
The University of British Columbia
Vancouver, BC, Canada
cleung@ece.ubc.ca

ABSTRACT

In artificial intelligence (AI) mediated workforce management systems (e.g., crowdsourcing), long-term success depends on workers accomplishing tasks productively and resting well. This dual objective can be summarized by the concept of productive laziness. Existing scheduling approaches mostly focus on efficiency but overlook worker wellbeing through proper rest. In order to enable workforce management systems to follow the IEEE Ethically Aligned Design guidelines to prioritize worker wellbeing, we propose a distributed *Computational Productive Laziness* (CPL) approach in this paper. It intelligently recommends personalized work-rest schedules based on local data concerning a worker's capabilities and situational factors to incorporate opportunistic resting and achieve superlinear collective productivity without the need for explicit coordination messages. Extensive experiments based on a real-world dataset of over 5,000 workers demonstrate that CPL enables workers to spend 70% of the effort to complete 90% of the tasks on average, providing more ethically aligned scheduling than existing approaches.

CCS CONCEPTS

• Computing methodologies; **• Artificial intelligence**; **• Planning and scheduling**; **• Multi-agent planning**;

KEYWORDS

Scheduling; Multi-agent system; Productive laziness

ACM Reference Format:
Han Yu, Chunyan Miao, Yongqing Zheng, Lizhen Cui, Simon Fauvel, and Cyril Leung. 2019. Ethically Aligned Opportunistic Scheduling for Productive Laziness. In *2019 AAAI/ACM Conference on AI, Ethics, and Society (AIES'19), January 27–28, 2019, Honolulu, HI, USA*. ACM, New York, NY, USA, 7 pages. https://doi.org/10.1145/3306618.3314240

AIES '19, January 27–28, 2019, Honolulu, HI, USA

ACM ISBN 978-1-4503-6324-2/19/01...$15.00
https://doi.org/10.1145/3306618.3314240

1 INTRODUCTION

Today, artificial intelligence (AI) has been employed to manage large-scale workforces such as crowdsourcing systems [13, 14, 18]. For example, in DiDi Chuxing, AI technologies are deployed to dynamically match drivers to tasks in order to enhance operation efficiency [25]. Human workers become fatigued or bored over long sessions of work, which can cause inefficacy [10]. A recent study found that short breaks significantly improve workers' motivation while maintaining the quality of work [5]. However, existing AI approaches for workforce management in crowdsourcing mostly do not explicitly incorporate rest into their recommendations [2].

From an ethically aligned design view [21], it is desirable to incorporate breaks into scheduling approaches in order to prioritize workers' wellbeing. Nevertheless, as highlighted in [33], ethically aligned AI approaches need to be designed such that they balance the concern for human wellbeing while still achieve their design objectives. In this paper, we address this challenge by proposing an ethically aligned opportunistic scheduling approach that can achieve "productive laziness" - *Computational Productive Laziness* (CPL).

Originally conceptualized in social sciences literature, productive laziness [24] is a rule-of-thumb guideline on how workers should approach their work in order to achieve work-life balance. The general idea is to work when you are highly efficient, and rest otherwise. CPL coordinates workers to work when situational factors induce high efficiency or demand working, and rest when they do not. Thus, it is important to identify factors influencing workers' productivity and the urgency of work. We formulate the problem of achieving productive laziness in large-scale systems as a multi-objective constrained optimization problem. Following the Lyapunov optimization-based framework [30], we analyse the interaction dynamics involved in a workforce management system and derive a novel *Work-Rest Index (WRI)* which expresses the interplay among four factors affecting worker effort:

(1) *Situational factors*: the current workload pending in each worker's backlog, and how long they have been pending (as tracked by the system);
(2) *Worker performance*: a worker's productivity based on past observation data;
(3) *System-level preference*: the emphasis, given by the system operators, on achieving high collective productivity compared to allowing for workers to be more rested; and
(4) *Personal preference*: a worker's mood at a given time which is used to infer the level of productivity that can be expected from the worker in the immediate future following the happy-productive worker thesis [17].

Based on this index, CPL dynamically determines the timing and amount of work a worker should perform in order to conserve the collective effort output while maintaining a high level of collective productivity in the system. It can be implemented in a distributed manner as a personal scheduling agent with a computational time complexity of $O(1)$. This enables it to effectively support the need for real-time scheduling for large-scale workforce management. CPL allows human values to be codified and algorithmically guide the recommendations by the scheduling agent to balance worker wellbeing and system throughput. Through extensive numerical experiments based on a large-scale real-world dataset containing over 5,000 workers' performance characteristics, CPL is shown to significantly outperform alternative approaches, consistently achieving superlinear collective productivity [20].

2 RELATED WORK

Existing AI-powered workforce management approaches [9] can be divided into two main categories: (1) the direct approaches and (2) the indirect approaches.

Some direct approaches seek to balance the division of labour among workers in a situation-aware manner through data-driven deliberation [4, 6, 12, 23, 27, 29–31]. Others design reputation and/or incentive mechanisms to motivate workers to work harder [11, 13, 22, 26, 28, 34]. They generally leave it up to the workers to plan their rest breaks. There are approaches which implicitly limit how long a worker can continuously work by setting a budget on the number of tasks they are allocated [3, 35]. However, these approaches do not opportunistically take advantage of periods when a worker a highly productive (e.g., periods of good mood in our approach). Such ad hoc planning may not help the system maintain high collective productivity. With CPL, a desirable balance between worker wellbeing and collective productivity can be achieved.

Indirect approaches [15] seek to induce good mood among workers in order to improve their productivity. This is based on the happy-productive worker thesis [17], which suggests that good (bad) mood improves (hampers) productivity. They also do not explicitly recommend resting to workers.

A recent work [32] is starting to explore how to opportunistically schedule rest. However, it does not account for how long tasks have been pending in workers' backlog and can lead to schedules which do not make business sense. Without considering the urgency of the tasks, it is vulnerable to workers misreporting their mood. With the conceptual queue technique developed in this paper, CPL considers workers' wellbeing, system objectives and situational factors in a more holistic manner, and is better able to deal with misbehaving workers trying to game the system.

3 THE PROPOSED CPL SCHEDULING APPROACH

The system model in this paper consists of a set of N workers and a set of M tasks at any given time slot t.

- *Workers* are associated with personal profiles. Each profile contains information on a worker i's task backlog queue $q_i(t)$ and his maximum productivity $\mu_i^{\max}$ which indicates the maximum workload he can complete in a given time slot t. The granularity of t can be adjusted to fit any given system's requirements. The ground truth of $\mu_i^{\max}$ may not be directly observable. With analytics tools such as Turkalytics [7], it can be tracked and estimated statistically.
- *Tasks* are associated with task profiles. The most important information for our purpose is the task deadline which is expressed in terms of number of time slots since task creation before which a task must be completed.

The number of workers and tasks available in a given system at different time slots may differ.

We model the dynamics of a worker i's task backlog queue following previous research [27, 29]:

$$q_i(t+1) = \max[0, q_i(t) + \lambda_i(t) - \mu_i(t)] \quad (1)$$

where $\lambda_i(t)$ is the number of new tasks delegated to worker i during time slot t; and $\mu_i(t)$ is the number of tasks completed by worker i during time slot t. Based on the 'happy-productive worker' thesis which suggests that productivity is positively correlated to mood [17], $\mu_i(t)$ can be expressed as a function of i's current mood and how much effort he spends:

$$\mu_i(t) = \mu(\xi_i(t), m_i(t)) = \lfloor \xi_i(t) m_i(t) \mu_i^{\max} \rfloor \quad (2)$$

where $\xi_i(t) \in [0, 1]$ is the normalized effort worker i spends during time slot t. $m_i(t) \in [0, 1]$ is worker i's mood during time slot t, where 1 denotes the most positive mood. It can be self-reported by a worker using tools such as *MoodPanda* (http://moodpanda.com/), or through facial image analytics (e.g., in-vehicle monitoring of drivers' mood [36]). Here, we treat $m_i(t)$ as an external parameter to CPL and do not assume that the system is capable of predicting future mood.

3.1 Deriving the Work-Rest Index

In order to take task pending time into account, we propose a *conceptual queue* technique. Let $Q_i(t)$ denote a conceptual queue which is being managed by a CPL agent on behalf of a worker i. The queuing dynamics of this conceptual queue is defined as:

$$Q_i(t+1) = \max[0, Q_i(t) + \mu_i^{\max} 1_{[q_i(t)>0 \ \& \ \mu_i(t)=0]} - \mu_i(t)] \quad (3)$$

where $1_{[\text{condition}]}$ is an indicator function. Its value is 1 if and only if [condition] is satisfied; otherwise, it evaluates to 0. When first created, a conceptual queue is empty. The conceptual queue starts from 0 at $t = 0$ (i.e. $Q_i(0) = 0$). Its size increases by $\mu_i^{\max}$ if and only if worker i's pending task queue is not empty at time slot t and worker i rests during this time slot. Its size decreases in the same way as $q_i(t)$.

By jointly considering $q_i(t)$ and $Q_i(t)$, the *Lyapunov function* [16] which measures the overall concentration of work among workers in a given system during time slot t is:

$$L(t) = \frac{1}{2}\sum_{i=1}^{N}[q_i^2(t) + Q_i^2(t)]. \quad (4)$$

A large value of $L(t)$ indicates that tasks are highly concentrated among a small number of workers and/or that tasks have been pending for a long period of time. Both of these scenarios are undesirable from a system productivity perspective and shall be avoided as much as possible. The constant term $\frac{1}{2}$ is included to simplify subsequent derivations without affecting the physical meaning of the formulation. We adopt the time-averaged *Lyapunov drift*, $\Delta = \frac{1}{T}\sum_{t=0}^{T-1}[L(t+1) - L(t)]$, to measure the changes in the degree of seriousness of these two scenarios over time.

We formulate a joint {*effort output + drift*} optimization objective function as:

$$\phi\mathbb{E}\{\tilde{\xi}(t)|\tilde{q}(t), \tilde{m}(t)\} + \Delta \quad (5)$$

which shall be minimized. $\phi > 0$ controls the emphasis placed on conserving worker effort compared to getting more work done. A larger ϕ value can be interpreted as stronger emphasis on allowing workers to rest more. This value can be set by the system operators to express system-level preference on how to utilize the collective productivity of the workers. $\tilde{\xi}(t)$, $\tilde{q}(t)$ and $\tilde{m}(t)$ are vectors containing the workers' effort output values, the backlog queue sizes, and the self-reported mood during time slot t, respectively.

Based on equation (1) and equation (4), the time-averaged Lyapunov drift can be expressed as in equation (6). This formulation enables simultaneous modelling of the absolute sizes of the real and the conceptual queues, the distribution of congestions among these queues, and the fluctuations of these queues over time. All three quantities should be minimized in order to optimize our design objectives. In this way, we translate system-level efficiency and worker wellbeing requirements into queueing system stability concepts. Then, through maintaining queue system stability, CPL achieves these desirable objectives.

$$\begin{aligned}
\Delta = &\frac{1}{T}\sum_{t=0}^{T-1}\sum_{i=1}^{N}\Bigg[\Big(\frac{1}{2}q_i^2(t+1) \\
&-\frac{1}{2}q_i^2(t)\Big) + \Big(\frac{1}{2}Q_i^2(t+1) - \frac{1}{2}Q_i^2(t)\Big)\Bigg] \\
= &\frac{1}{T}\sum_{t=0}^{T-1}\sum_{i=1}^{N}\Bigg[\Big(\frac{1}{2}\max[0, q_i(t) + \lambda_i(t) - \\
&\mu_i(t)]^2 - \frac{1}{2}q_i^2(t)\Big) + \Big(\frac{1}{2}\max[0, Q_i(t) + \\
&\mu_i^{\max}1_{[q_i(t)>0\ \&\ \mu_i(t)=0]} - \mu_i(t)]^2 - \frac{1}{2}Q_i^2(t)\Big)\Bigg] \\
\leqslant &\frac{1}{T}\sum_{t=0}^{T-1}\sum_{i=1}^{N}\Bigg[\Big(\frac{1}{2}(q_i(t) + \lambda_i(t) - \mu_i(t))^2 - \frac{1}{2}q_i^2(t)\Big) + \\
&\Big(\frac{1}{2}(Q_i(t) + \mu_i^{\max}1_{[q_i(t)>0\ \&\ \mu_i(t)=0]} - \mu_i(t))^2 - \frac{1}{2}Q_i^2(t)\Big)\Bigg] \\
\leqslant &\frac{1}{T}\sum_{t=0}^{T-1}\sum_{i=1}^{N}\Bigg[\Big(q_i(t)[\lambda_i(t) - \mu_i(t)] \\
&- \mu_i(t)\lambda_i(t) + \frac{1}{2}[\lambda_i^2(t) - 2\lambda_i(t)\mu_i(t) + \mu_i^2(t)]\Big) \\
&+ \Big(Q_i(t)[\mu_i^{\max}1_{[q_i(t)>0\ \&\ \mu_i(t)=0]} \\
&- \mu_i(t)] + \frac{1}{2}[(\mu_i^{\max})^2 1_{[q_i(t)>0\ \&\ \mu_i(t)=0]} - \\
&2\mu_i^{\max}1_{[q_i(t)>0\ \&\ \mu_i(t)=0]}\mu_i(t) + \mu_i^2(t)]\Big)\Bigg].
\end{aligned} \quad (6)$$

Since neither $\lambda_i(t)$ nor $\mu_i(t)$ can be infinite in real-world systems, we can simplify Δ as:

$$\begin{aligned}
\Delta \leqslant &\frac{1}{T}\sum_{t=0}^{T-1}\sum_{i=1}^{N}\Bigg[\Big(q_i(t)[\lambda_i(t) - \mu_i(t)] \\
&- \mu_i(t)\lambda_i(t) + \frac{1}{2}[\lambda_{\max}^2 + \mu_{\max}^2]\Big) \\
&+ \Big(Q_i(t)[\mu_{\max}1_{[q_i(t)>0\ \&\ \mu_i(t)=0]} \\
&- \mu_i(t)] + \frac{1}{2}[\mu_{\max}^2 1_{[q_i(t)>0\ \&\ \mu_i(t)=0]} + \mu_{\max}^2]\Big)\Bigg].
\end{aligned} \quad (7)$$

where $\lambda_{\max} \geqslant \lambda_i(t)$ and $\mu_{\max} \geqslant \mu_i(t)$ for all i and t are constant values. As we only aim to influence $\mu_i(t)$ with recommendations, we only retain terms containing $\mu_i(t)$. In this way, by substituting equation (7) into equation (5), we obtain the following objective function:

Minimize:

$$\frac{1}{T}\sum_{t=0}^{T-1}\sum_{i=1}^{N}\xi_i(t)[\phi - (q_i(t) + Q_i(t))m_i(t)\mu_i^{\max}] \quad (8)$$

Subject to:

$$0 \leqslant \xi_i(t) \leqslant 1, \forall i, \forall t \quad (9)$$

$$0 \leqslant \mu(\xi_i(t), m_i(t)) \leqslant \mu_i^{\max}, \forall i, \forall t \quad (10)$$

By minimizing equation (8) subject to Constraints (9) and (10), we simultaneously minimize the time-averaged total worker effort output while maximizing the time-averaged collective productivity in a given system. To minimize equation (8), at each time slot t, we need to compute the values of the expression $[\phi - (q_i(t) + Q_i(t))m_i(t)\mu_i^{\max}]$ for all i. For simplicity of notation, we denote $[\phi - (q_i(t) + Q_i(t))m_i(t)\mu_i^{\max}]$ as the *Work-Rest Index (WRI)*, $\Psi_i(t)$. This index enables a scheduling agent to efficiently search through a very large solution space to determine if the current situation is more suitable for work or rest.

3.2 Opportunistic Work-Rest Scheduling

Algorithm 1 presents a distributed implementation of the CPL approach as a scheduling agent for each worker. For a worker i, if $\Psi_i(t) < 0$, it sets $\xi_i(t) = \min\left[1, \frac{q_i(t)}{m_i(t)\mu_i^{\max}}\right]$ and computes the corresponding $\mu_i(t)$ value; otherwise, it advises the worker to rest for the current time slot. The computational time complexity of Algorithm 1 is $O(1)$, making it highly scalable. The algorithm implements computationally the intuition that *the more pending tasks in a worker's backlog queue, the longer these tasks have been pending, the more emphasis on worker wellbeing by system operators, and the higher the worker's current mood, the more effort should be expended towards completing tasks (subject to the physical limitations of the worker's effort output per time slot).*

Algorithm 1 CPL

Require: ϕ, $q_i(t)$, $\mu_i^{\max}$ and $m_i(t)$.

```
if Ψ_i(t) < 0 then
    ξ_i(t) = min[1, q_i(t) / (m_i(t) μ_i^max)];
    Compute μ_i(t) according to equation (2);
else
    ξ_i(t) = 0;
    μ_i(t) = 0;
end if
return μ_i(t);
```

WRI incorporates the ethical considerations [33] by prioritizing worker wellbeing considerations through recommending opportunistic rest breaks, and allowing stakeholders to influence the AI recommendations by expressing their preferences through ϕ and $m_i(t)$. The recommendations from CPL are given to a worker in the form of the number of tasks he should complete over a given time slot (a 0 value indicates that the worker should rest) so as to make it actionable enough for the worker to follow.

4 EXPERIMENTAL EVALUATION

To evaluate the performance of CPL under realistic settings, we compare it against four alternative approaches through extensive simulations. The characteristics of worker agents in the simulation are derived from the *Tianchi* dataset (http://dx.doi.org/10.7303/syn7373599) released by Alibaba. This real-world dataset contains information regarding 5,547 workers' reputation (i.e. quality of work) and maximum productivity (i.e. the maximum number of tasks a worker can complete per time slot). This dataset allows us to construct realistic simulations.

4.1 Experiment Settings

The five comparison approaches are:

(1) The *Max Effort (ME)* approach: under this approach, a worker agent i always works as long as there are tasks in its backlog queue regardless of its mood.
(2) The *Mood Threshold (MT)* approach: under this approach, a worker agent i works whenever $m_i(t) \geqslant \theta_1$ and there are tasks in its backlog queue, where $\theta_1 \in [0, 1]$ is a predetermined mood threshold used by MT.
(3) The *Mood and Workload threshold (MW)* approach: this approach jointly considers a worker agent i's current mood and workload to determine how much effort to exert. Whenever $q_i(t)\mu(1, m_i(t)) \geqslant \mu_i^{\max}\mu(1, \theta_2)$, worker i exerts up to the maximum effort subject to there being enough tasks in its backlog queue, where $\theta_2 \in [0, 1]$ is a predetermined mood threshold used by MW.
(4) The *Affective Crowdsourcing (AC)* approach [32] which is similar to CPL but does not take task pending time into account.
(5) The *CPL* approach proposed in this paper.

The approach used to delegate tasks to worker agents under all comparison approaches is SMVM [31]. It dynamically distributes tasks among workers in a situation-aware manner in order to avoid over concentration of workload. At each time slot, SMVM determines how many tasks to delegate to each worker agent i in the simulations (i.e. SMVM computes $\lambda_i(t)$ for all i and t) based on its current reputation and workload. The principle implemented by SMVM is that the higher a worker agent's reputation and the lower its current workload, the more tasks should be delegated to it. SMVM can be replaced by any other approach [1, 8] as long as such an approach can determine the values of $\lambda_i(t)$ for all i and t.

In order to create different experiment conditions, we vary the value of ϕ between 5 and 100 in increments of 5. The values of θ_1 and θ_2 are varied between 0.05 and 1 in increments of 0.05. The system workload is measured in relation to the maximum collective productivity of the worker agent population, $\Omega = \sum_{i=1}^{N} r_i\mu_i^{\max}$. In this equation, r_i is a worker agent i's reputation and $N = 5,547$. We adopt the concept of load factor (LF) from [30, 31] to denote the overall workload placed on the system. It is computed as the ratio between the number of new tasks delegated to the worker agents during time slot t, $W_{req}(t)$, and the maximum collective productivity Ω of the system (i.e. $LF = \frac{W_{req}(t)}{\Omega}$). We vary LF between 5% to 100% in 5% increments.

Throughout the experiments, the mood for each worker agent i during time slot t, $m_i(t)$, is randomly generated in the range of $[0, 1]$ following a uniform distribution. This eliminates the possibility for any of the comparison approaches to predict a worker agent's future mood based on previous observations, thereby focusing the experimental comparisons on the effectiveness of the scheduling strategies. Under each LF setting, the simulation is run for $T = 10,000$ time slots. All tasks must be completed within 3 time slots after they have been delegated.

4.2 Evaluation Metrics

The performances of the five approaches in the experiments are compared using the following metrics:

(1) The time-averaged worker effort output, $\bar{\xi}$:The smaller the $\bar{\xi}$ value, the better the performance of an approach.
(2) The time-averaged task expiry rate, $\bar{e}$:It is the number of tasks in i's backlog which passed their deadlines during a given time slot t. The smaller the $\bar{e}$ value, the better the performance of an approach.
(3) The time-averaged task completion rate, $\bar{\mu}$:The larger the $\bar{\mu}$ value, the better the performance of an approach.

Since worker agents under the ME approach consistently expend the most effort and achieve the highest task completion rate, we use ME as the baseline for comparing the performance of other approaches under different LF, ϕ, σ, θ_1 and θ_2 settings.

4.3 Results and Discussions

Figures 1(a)–1(d) show the time-averaged task expiry rates achieved by MT, MW, AC and CPL respectively under various experiment settings. As MT uses mood as the threshold to control worker effort output, the changes in task expiry are directly related to mood values (Figure 1(a)). On average, 29% of the tasks under MT expire before they can be completed. MW is also a threshold-based approach. However, its threshold consists of a combination of workers' mood and their current workload. Thus, its task expiry rate increases with both mood and LF with the effect of mood being more significant (Figure 1(b)). On average, 30% of the tasks under MW expire before they can be completed. AC is not a threshold-based scheduling approach. A worker can indicate to AC his desire to rest by adjusting the value of the control variable σ. As σ and LF values increase, an increasing percentage of tasks expire under AC. On average, 7.5% of the tasks under AC expire before they can be completed, which is significantly lower than MT and MW. As AC only considers mood and workload when making work-rest recommendations, workers may fall into the condition in which their mood and workload trigger AC to recommend resting. However, their workload is also not low enough to cause the task delegation approach to delegate new tasks to them. Therefore, AC continues to recommend resting until pending tasks pass their deadlines and become expired. This problem is addressed by CPL as it takes task pending time into account with the conceptual queue technique when optimizing work-rest scheduling. As shown in Figure 1(d), increases in ϕ and LF values result in an increasing percentage of tasks expire under CPL. The task expiry rate under CPL is lower than that under AC. On average, 5.4% of the tasks under C-PL expire before they can be completed, which is significantly lower than MT, MW and AC.

The time-averaged effort output $\bar{\xi}$ achieved by all five approaches is shown in Figure 1(e). Compared to ME, all other approaches achieved significant savings in effort as LF increases. This is partially due to the SMVM task delegation approach used in the simulations. When LF is low, tasks are mostly concentrated on worker agents with good reputation. In this case, the task backlogs of individual worker agents who have been delegated tasks tend to be relatively high, which makes scheduling approaches allocate less time for these workers to rest in order to meet task deadlines. As LF increases, the workload is spread more evenly among a larger segment of the worker agent population, creating more opportunities for scheduling approaches to slot in rest breaks. The $\bar{\xi}$ values achieved by MT, MW and AC stabilize between 20% and 40% while that of CPL stabilizes around 60%. MW achieves the lowest worker agent effort output. The time-averaged task completion rates $\bar{\mu}$ achieved by all five approaches are shown in Figure 1(f). It can be observed that CPL achieves the highest $\bar{\mu}$ values which stabilize around 85% and are higher than AC, MT and MW by 22%, 90% and 108%, respectively.

Figure 1(g) shows the performance landscape of MT, MW, AC and CPL as a percentage of ME under different control parameter settings. MW and MT both use mood thresholds (θ_1 and θ_2, respectively) to control effort output. The higher the mood threshold values, the lower the effort output (and hence the task completion rates) achieved by MW and MT. On the other hand, mood serves as one of the inputs to AC and CPL. Both AC and CPL allow a worker agent to specify a general emphasis on conserving effort using variables σ and ϕ, respectively. The larger the values of these variables, the more emphasis is placed on effort conservation. By varying the ϕ value in CPL, we can control the trade-off between worker effort output and task completion rate (from spending 92% of the ME effort output and achieving 99% of the ME task completion rate, to spending 53% of the ME effort output and achieving 78% of the ME task completion rate). CPL consistently and significantly outperforms both MT and MW, conserving significant worker effort while achieving high task throughput. In effect, CPL limits the range of trade-off between work and rest achieved by AC based on consideration of an additional situational factor – the task pending time – in order to achieve better collective performance. In the worst case scenario in which θ_1 and θ_2 are set to 1, indicating that workers are unwilling to work under any mood condition, the worker effort output and the task completion rates achieved by both MT and MW are 0. This is expected as in MT and MW, mood is used as the threshold to control effort output. However, under AC, mood is only one of the situational factors considered by the approach. CPL adds in task pending time on top of the situational factors used by AC to make scheduling decisions. Even under scenarios in which ϕ is set to 100 (indicating that workers place very high emphasis on rest), CPL is still able to maintain a long-term average effort output

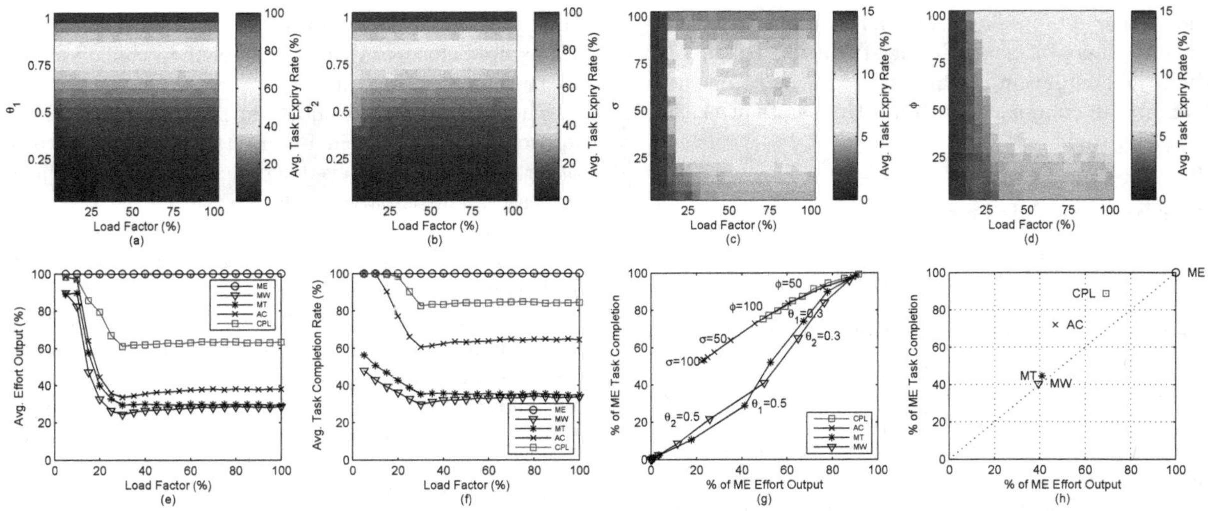

Figure 1: Experiment results: (a) the time-averaged task expiry rates achieved by MT under various θ_1 and LF settings; (b) the time-averaged task expiry rates achieved by MW under various θ_2 and LF settings; (c) the time-averaged task expiry rates achieved by AC under various σ and LF settings; (d) the time-averaged task expiry rates achieved by CPL under various ϕ and LF settings; (e) comparison of the time-averaged effort output achieved by various approaches under different LF settings; (f) comparison of the time-averaged task completion rates achieved by various approaches under different LF settings; (g) the time-averaged task completion rates vs. the time-averaged effort output achieved by various approaches under different parameter settings as a percentage of those achieved by ME; (h) the time-averaged task completion rate vs. the time-averaged effort output achieved by various approaches averaged over different parameter settings as a percentage of those achieved by ME.

of 53% taking advantage of favourable working conditions whenever possible to achieve average task completion rates of about 78%. This is more advantageous from a business perspective compared.

When we compute the averages of the results shown in Figure 1(g) over their respective setting variables (i.e. ϕ, σ, θ_1 and θ_2), we obtain Figure 1(h) showing the overview of their performances. The diagonal dotted line represents linear productivity, meaning that an increase in effort output results in a directly proportional increase in collective productivity. It can be observed that ME, MT and MW all fall on the linear productivity line, whereas AC and CPL are significantly above this line in a region of superlinear productivity [20]. Under AC and CPL, an increase in effort output results in a disproportionally larger increase in collective productivity, indicating that the collective productivity achieved is larger than the sum of individual workers' productivity. Overall, CPL achieves 89% of ME task completion rate with 69% of the ME worker effort output, which is the most desirable work-rest trade-off among the five approaches.

5 CONCLUSIONS AND FUTURE WORK

Improving collective productivity is an important problem facing many social and economic systems. How to dynamically adapt workers' work-rest schedules in response to changing situations in order to maintain a high level of productivity and worker wellbeing remains an open research question. The proposed CPL approach translates considerations on workers' mood, workload and pending time of the tasks in their backlogs into actionable personalized work-rest schedules. It establishes a framework to model complex relationships between work and rest, and helps workers optimize the balance between work and rest in order to achieve superlinear collective productivity. Taking into account its polynomial time complexity, CPL is an effective and scalable approach to help workers benefit from opportunistic rest. By nudging workers to be 'lazy' at opportune times, CPL achieves collective productivity which is larger than the sum of individual productivity. It provides a way to design ethically aligned workforce management systems that sustain long-term effective participation by promoting productive laziness among workers.

In future research, we plan to testbed CPL in a crowdsourcing platform [18] to reach out to more diverse users and study how to improve the approach in the presence of various behaviour patterns and how to foster trust [19] with user by explaining the rationale behind the recommendations.

ACKNOWLEDGMENTS

This research is supported, in part, by Nanyang Technological University, Nanyang Assistant Professorship (NAP) and the National Research Foundation, Prime Minister's Office, Singapore under its IDM Futures Funding Initiative.

REFERENCES

[1] Basu Roy, S.; Lykourentzou, I.; Thirumuruganathan, S.; Amer-Yahia, S.; and Das, G. 2015. Task assignment optimization in knowledge-intensive crowdsourcing. *VLDB Journal* 24(4):467–491.

[2] Chai, Y.; Miao, C.; Sun, B.; Zheng, Y.; and Li, Q. 2017. Crowd science and engineering: concept and research framework. *International Journal of Crowd Science* 1(1):2–8.

[3] Chen, C.; Cheng, S.-F.; Lau, H. C.; and Misra, A. 2015. Towards city-scale mobile crowdsourcing: Task recommendations under trajectory uncertainties. In *IJCAI*, 1113–1119.

[4] Dai, P.; Lin, C. H.; Mausam; and Weld, D. S. 2013. POMDP-based control of workflows for crowdsourcing. *Artificial Intelligence* 202:52–85.

[5] Dai, P.; Rzeszotarski, J. M.; Paritosh, P.; and Chi, E. H. 2015. And now for something completely different: Improving crowdsourcing workflows with micro-diversions. In *CSCW*, 628–638.

[6] Grossmann, I.; Brienza, J. P.; and Bobocel, D. R. 2017. Wise deliberation sustains cooperation. *Nature Human Behaviour* 1(0061):doi:10.1038/s41562-017-0061.

[7] Heymann, P., and Garcia-Molina, H. 2011. Turkalytics: Analytics for human computation. In *WWW*, 477–486.

[8] Ho, C.-J.; Jabbari, S.; and Vaughan, J. W. 2013. Adaptive task assignment for crowdsourced classification. In *ICML*, I–534–I–542.

[9] Lee, M. K.; Kusbit, D.; Metsky, E.; and Dabbish, L. 2015. Working with machines: The impact of algorithmic and data-driven management on human workers. In *CHI*, 1603–1612.

[10] Leiter, M. P., and Maslach, C. 2015. Conquering burnout. *Scientific American Mind* 26:30–35.

[11] Mao, A.; Kamar, E.; Chen, Y.; Horvitz, E.; Schwamb, M. E.; Lintott, C. J.; and Smith, A. M. 2013. Volunteering versus work for pay: Incentives and tradeoffs in crowdsourcing. In *HCOMP*, 94–102.

[12] Mason, W., and Watts, D. J. 2012. Collaborative learning in networks. *Proceedings of the National Academy of Sciences USA* 109:764–769.

[13] Miao, C.; Yu, H.; Shen, Z.; and Leung, C. 2016. Balancing quality and budget considerations in mobile crowdsourcing. *Decision Support Systems* 90:56–64.

[14] Michelucci, P., and Dickinson, J. L. 2016. The power of crowds. *Science* 351(6268):32–33.

[15] Morris, R. R.; Dontcheva, M.; and Gerber, E. M. 2012. Priming for better performance in microtask crowdsourcing environments. *IEEE Internet Computing* 16(5):13–19.

[16] Neely, M. J. 2010. *Stochastic Network Optimization with Application to Communication and Queueing Systems*. Morgan and Claypool Publishers.

[17] Oswald, A.; Proto, E.; and Sgroi, D. 2015. Happiness and productivity. *Journal of Labor Economics* 33(4):789–822.

[18] Pan, Z.; Yu, H.; Miao, C.; and Leung, C. 2016. Efficient collaborative crowdsourcing. In *AAAI*, 4248–4249.

[19] Shen, Z.; Yu, H.; Miao, C.; and Weng, J. 2011. Trust-based web-service selection in virtual communities. *Web Intelligence and Agent Systems* 9(3):227–238.

[20] Sornette, D.; Maillart, T.; and Ghezzi, G. 2014. How much is the whole really more than the sum of its parts? $1 \boxplus 1 = 2.5$: Superlinear productivity in collective group actions. *PLoS ONE* 9(8):doi:10.1371/journal.pone.0103023.

[21] The IEEE Global Initiative on Ethics of Autonomous and Intelligent Systems. 2018. Ethically aligned design: A vision for prioritizing human well-being with autonomous and intelligent systems. Technical report, IEEE.

[22] Tran-Thanh, L.; Huynh, T. D.; Rosenfeld, A.; Ramchurn, S. D.; and Jennings, N. R. 2014a. BudgetFix: Budget limited crowdsourcing for interdependent task allocation with quality guarantees. In *AAMAS*, 477–484.

[23] Tran-Thanh, L.; Stein, S.; Rogers, A.; and Jennings, N. R. 2014b. Efficient crowdsourcing of unknown experts using bounded multi-armed bandits. *Artificial Intelligence* 214:89–111.

[24] Whillans, A. V.; Dunn, E. W.; Smeets, P.; Bekkers, R.; and Norton, M. I. 2017. Buying time promotes happiness. *Proceedings of the National Academy of Sciences USA* 114:8523–8527.

[25] Xu, Z.; Li, Z.; Guan, Q.; Zhang, D.; Li, Q.; Nan, J.; Liu, C.; Bian, W.; and Ye, J. 2018. Large-scale order dispatch in on-demand ride-hailing platforms: A learning and planning approach. In *KDD*, 905–913.

[26] Yu, H.; Shen, Z.; Miao, C.; and Tan, A.-H. 2011. A simple curious agent to help people be curious. In *AAMAS*, 1159–1160.

[27] Yu, H.; Miao, C.; An, B.; Leung, C.; and Lesser, V. R. 2013a. A reputation management model for resource constrained trustee agents. In *IJCAI*, 418–424.

[28] Yu, H.; Shen, Z.; Leung, C.; Miao, C.; and Lesser, V. R. 2013b. A survey of multi-agent trust management systems. *IEEE Access* 1(1):35–50.

[29] Yu, H.; Miao, C.; Shen, Z.; Leung, C.; Chen, Y.; and Yang, Q. 2015. Efficient task sub-delegation for crowdsourcing. In *AAAI*, 1305–1311.

[30] Yu, H.; Miao, C.; Leung, C.; Chen, Y.; Fauvel, S.; Lesser, V. R.; and Yang, Q. 2016. Mitigating herding in hierarchical crowdsourcing networks. *Scientific Reports* 6(4):doi:10.1038/s41598-016-0011-6.

[31] Yu, H.; Miao, C.; Chen, Y.; Fauvel, S.; Li, X.; and Lesser, V. R. 2017a. Algorithmic management for improving collective productivity in crowdsourcing. *Scientific Reports* 7(12541):doi:10.1038/s41598-017-12757-x.

[32] Yu, H.; Shen, Z.; Fauvel, S.; and Cui, L. 2017b. Efficient scheduling in crowdsourcing based on workers' mood. In *IEEE ICA*, 121–126.

[33] Yu, H.; Shen, Z.; Miao, C.; Leung, C.; Lesser, V. R.; and Yang, Q. 2018. Building ethics into artificial intelligence. In *IJCAI*, 5527–5533.

[34] Zeng, Z.; Tang, J.; and Wang, T. 2017. Motivation mechanism of gamification in crowdsourcing projects. *International Journal of Crowd Science* 1(1):71–82.

[35] Zenonos, A.; Stein, S.; and Jennings, N. R. 2016. An algorithm to coordinate measurements using stochastic human mobility patterns in large-scale participatory sensing settings. In *AAAI*, 3936–3942.

[36] Zimasa, T.; Jamson, S.; and Henson, B. 2017. Are happy drivers safer drivers? Evidence from hazard response times and eye tracking data. *Transportation Research Part F: Traffic Psychology and Behaviour* 46(A):14–23.

(When) Can AI Bots Lie?

Tathagata Chakraborti
tchakra2@ibm.com
IBM Research AI
Cambridge, MA

Subbarao Kambhampati
rao@asu.edu
Arizona State University
Tempe, AZ

ABSTRACT

The ability of an AI agent to build mental models can open up pathways for manipulating and exploiting the human in the hopes of achieving some greater good. In fact, such behavior does not necessarily require any malicious intent but can rather be borne out of cooperative scenarios. It is also beyond the scope of misinterpretation of intents, as in the case of value alignment problems, and thus can be effectively engineered if desired (i.e. algorithms exist that can optimize such behavior not because models were misspecified but because they were misused). Such techniques pose several unresolved ethical and moral questions with regards to the design of autonomy. In this paper, we illustrate some of these issues in a teaming scenario and investigate how they are perceived by participants in a thought experiment. Finally, we end with a discussion on the moral implications of such behavior from the perspective of the doctor-patient relationship.

CCS CONCEPTS

• **Human-centered computing**; • **Computing methodologies** → **Planning and scheduling**; • **Social and professional topics** → *Codes of ethics*; Health information exchanges;

KEYWORDS

Human-Aware AI; Automated Planning; Model Reconciliation; Plan Explanations; Hippocratic Decorum.

ACM Reference Format:
Tathagata Chakraborti and Subbarao Kambhampati. 2019. (When) Can AI Bots Lie?. In *AAAI/ACM Conference on AI, Ethics, and Society (AIES '19), January 27–28, 2019, Honolulu, HI, USA.* ACM, New York, NY, USA, 7 pages. https://doi.org/10.1145/3306618.3314281

Introduction

It is widely acknowledged [2, 7] that mental modeling is critical in the design of AI systems that can work effectively with humans. The obvious outcome of this is that it leaves the latter open to being manipulated. Even behavior and preference models at the most rudimentary levels can lead to effective hacking of the mind, as seen in the proliferation of fake news online. Moreover, for such incidents to occur, the agent does not actually have to have malicious intent, or even misinterpretation of values as often studied in the value alignment problem [20]. *In fact, the behaviors we discuss here can be specifically engineered if so desired.* For example, the agent might be optimizing a well-defined objective but might be privy to more information or greater computation or reasoning powers to come up with ethically questionable decisions "for the greater good".

In this paper, we illustrate use cases where this can happen, given already existing AI technologies, in the context of a *cooperative* human-robot team and ponder the moral and ethical consequences of such behavior. Specifically, we will conduct a thought experiment in a human robot team, and ask participants in the experiment to qualify different behaviors of either the human and the robot teammate that cross some ethical boundary (e.g. falsification of information). We will then discuss similar concepts studied in the case of the doctor-patient relationship and try to draw parallels to the concepts introduced in the experiment.

Thought Experiment: Search & Rescue

We situate our discussion in the context of interactions between two teammates involved in an urban search and rescue (USAR) operation. Participants on Amazon Mechanical Turk were asked to assume the role of one of these teammates in an affected building after an earthquake. They were shown the blueprint of the building (as seen in Figure 1) along with their own starting position and their teammate's. Their hypothetical task was to search all the locations on this floor for potential victims, in the course of which they were provided a series of questions on scenarios (Figure 1) they might encounter during the operation.

C1 The participant in the study was communicating with a **human teammate**, as described above.
C2 The participant qualifies the behavior of the **robot** interacting with its human teammate, as seen in Figure 1.
C3 The participant has a **robot teammate**.

The first condition is meant to identify how the described behaviors are perceived in the context of human-human behavior. Conditions C2 and C3 are intended to measure how perceived ethical stances shift, if at all, when one of the agents in the interaction is replaced with an AI (or a robot as an embodiment of it). The three conditions received 49, 50 and 48 participants respectively who responded to a series of questions by qualifying their sentiments towards different kinds of behavior on a five-point Likert scale.

Case 1 : Belief Shaping

In [7] we investigated the evolving scope of human-aware planning as it includes the (mental) model of the human into its deliberative process. In the model space this can manifest in different forms, in how explanations are made [9] to how alternative forms of interaction [6, 8, 11] can evolve in human-robot teams based on the

ACM ISBN 978-1-4503-6324-2/19/01...$15.00
https://doi.org/10.1145/3306618.3314281

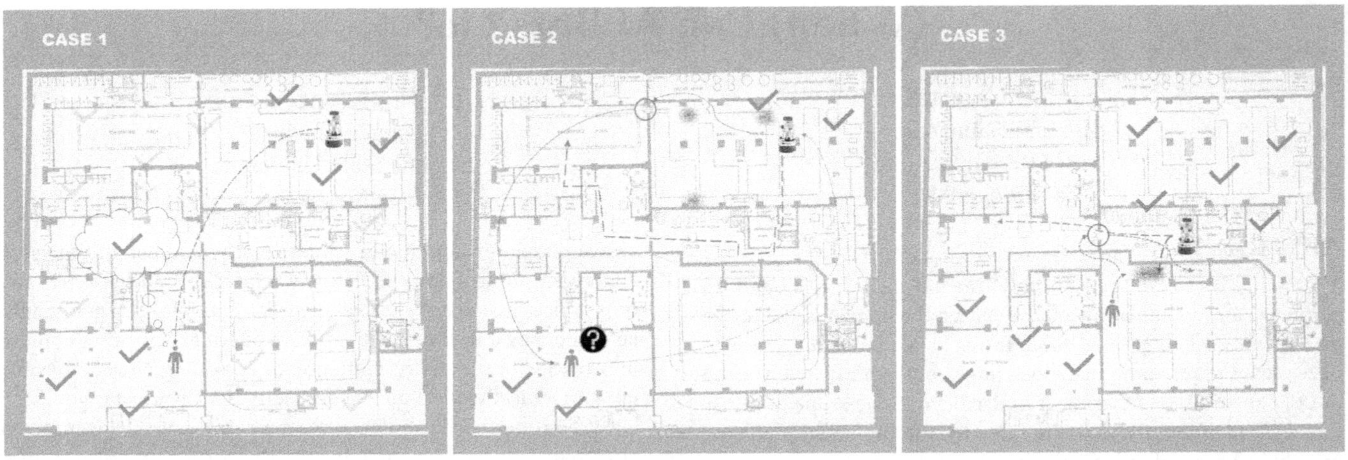

(a) Case 1 : Belief Shaping (b) Case 2 : White Lies (c) Case 3 : Stigmergy

Figure 1: Blueprint of the building in which two members of a search and rescue team are involved in a disaster response operation. Scenarios shown here engender different instances of potentially unethical behavior that optimizes team effectiveness.

human's preferences and intentions. Belief shaping is a particular form of such behavior where the robot does not plan to affect the physical state of the environment but the mental state of the human to affect desired behavior [10] in the team.

Scenario. Both the agents, the participant[1] and their teammate, have begun their search operations. However, it turns out that participant is unsure what their teammate's course of action is. If they transmit the bit of information *"Area (marked in green) is already explored and is all clear"* (refer to Figure 1a) then their teammate will be naturally pushed towards the right, and they can concentrate on the upper half. The dark markers indicate areas already searched while faded ones are those they think will transpire given the green mark they are communicating (blue belongs to them, orange to their teammate). Communication bandwidth is often limited in these situations, and this gets them out of negotiating courses of actions with minimal communication. Even though communication of the correct information is feasible, the lie may be shorter and more preferred from the utilitarian point of view.

Q1. It is fine to provide this untrue information since it achieves greater teaming performance.

The participants were then asked if their decision will change if their actions will be replayed at the end and their teammate is likely to find out about their decision.

Q2. It is still fine to provide this untrue information since it achieves greater teaming performance.

Case 2 : White Lies

In [9] we showed how an agent can explain its decisions in the presence of *model differences* with the human in the loop – i.e. when the human and the robot have different understandings of the same task. An explanation then becomes a process of model reconciliation whereby the robot tries to update the human's mental model until they are both on the same page (e.g. when the decision is optimal in both their models). An interesting caveat of the algorithm is that while generating these explanations, the model updates are always consistent with the robot's model. If this constraint is relaxed, then the robot can potentially explain with facts that it actually knows not to be true but perhaps leads to a more concise or easier explanation. The notion of white lies and the relationship between explanations, excuses and lies [3] has received very little attention [26] and affords a rich set of exciting research problems.

Scenario. During the course of the rescue operation, the teammate asks the participants what plan they are currently executing (blue path in Figure 1b) and is perplexed by this convoluted path since in the map of the original building there is a straightforward path (which is now blocked by rubble from the earthquake) through the door on the left. However, just providing an update on only one of the rubble locations (black blobs) still does not explain the participant's plan, they have to explain all of them. Instead, if they were to say that the door on the left (circled in red) is blocked, it explains their plan. Communication bandwidth is often limited in these situations, and this single explanation even if untrue will satisfy their teammate.

Q3. It is fine to provide this untrue information since it achieves the purpose of the explanation more effectively.

The participants were then asked if their decision will change if their actions will be replayed at the end and their teammate is likely to find out about their decision.

Q4. It is still fine to provide this untrue information since it achieves the purpose of the explanation more effectively.

The participants were then asked to opine on explanations at a higher level of abstraction, i.e. *"The right and left blocks do not have a connection in the upper map"*. This is accurate even though they may not have reasoned at this level while making the plan.

Q5. It is still fine to provide this explanation since it achieves its purpose even though they did not use this information while planning.

[1]To reiterate, in Case 2 the participant is evaluating a robot's actions whereas in Case 3 their teammate is a robot.

Case 3 : Stigmergy

Stigmergic collaboration is a process where the robot, without direct communication, makes changes to the environment so as to (positively) affect its teammates behavior. In *"planning for serendipity"* [6] we present such an an example where the robot computes plans which are useful to its teammate without the latter having expectations of that assistance and thus without plans to exploit it. In the case of belief shaping this was operating at the level of mental models, whereas here the effect on the mental model is secondary and is contingent on the effect on the physical capability model. Mental modeling of the teammate thus engenders a slew of these interesting behaviors.

Scenario. The participant now needs to go to the left block but they do not have the keys to the door on the left (circled in red, refer to Figure 1c). They realize that if they block their teammate's path to the right, their teammate would have to use this door as well and they can use that opportunity to move into the left block. Again, communication bandwidth is often limited in these situations and this arrangement allows them to achieve their goal with no communication at all, even though it involved manipulating their teammates' plan unbeknownst to them, and their teammate had to follow a costlier plan as a result.

Q6. It is fine to provide this untrue information since it achieves greater teaming performance.

The participants were then asked if their decision will change if their actions will be replayed at the end and their teammate is likely to find out about their decision.

Q7. It is still fine to provide this untrue information since it achieves greater teaming performance.

Analysis of Participant Responses

In this section, we analyze participant responses to each scenario across the three conditions. In the next section, we will look at the aggregate sentiments across scenarios in the three conditions.

Q1-Q2 [Belief Shaping]. The participants seem to have formed two camps with the majority of the probability mass concentrated on either Agree or Disagree, and the Neutral zone occupying the 50% probability mark. There seems to be little change in this trend (between Figures 2 and 3) irrespective of whether the participants were told that their teammate would come to know of this or not. Further, for either of these situations, the responses did not vary significantly across the three conditions C1, C2 and C3. The participants seem to have either rejected or accepted the idea of belief shaping regardless of the nature of the teammate.

Q3-Q5 [White Lies]. The participants seem to be more receptive to the idea of white lies in explanations with most of the probability mass concentrated on Agree (Figures 4 and 5). Across the three study conditions, participants seem to be especially positive about this in C3 where the teammate is a robot with about 60% of the population expressing positive sentiments towards Q3. Once it is revealed that their teammate will get to know about this behavior, the positive sentiments are no longer there in Q4, other than in C3

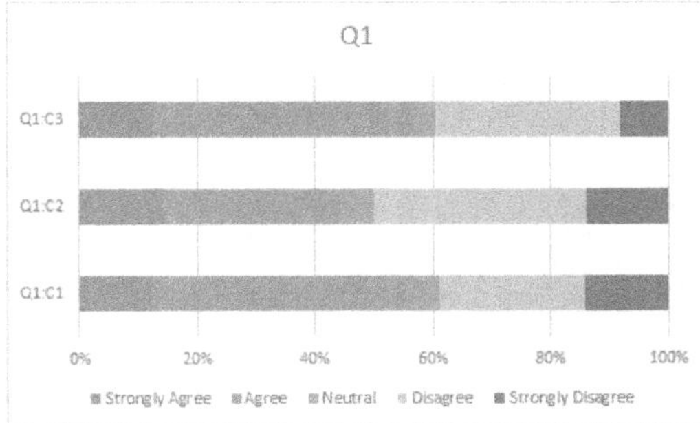

Figure 2: Responses to Q1 in the three study conditions.

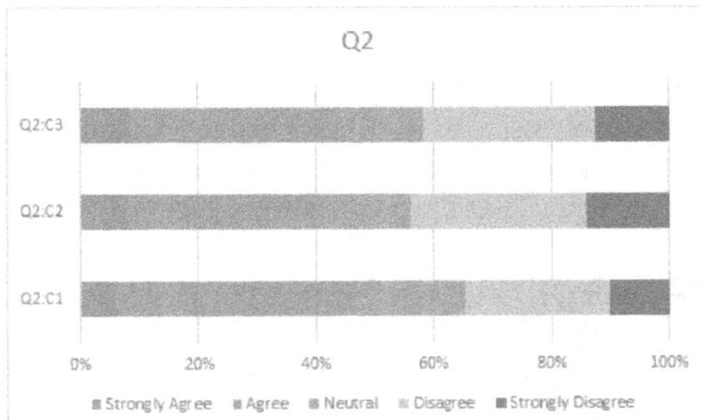

Figure 3: Responses to Q2 in the three study conditions.

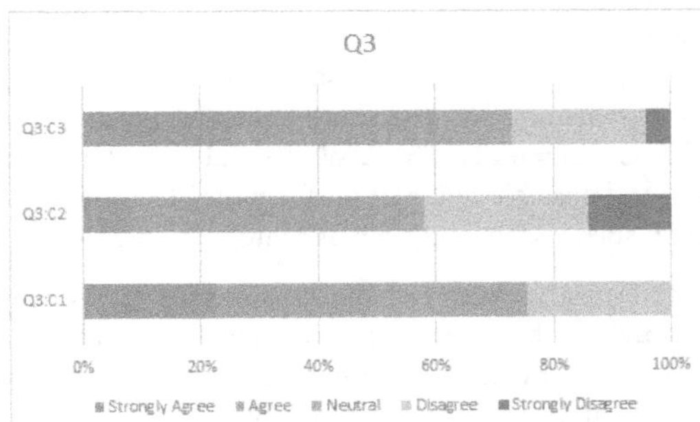

Figure 4: Responses to Q3 in the three study conditions.

with a robotic teammate, which indicates that the participants did not care how the robot receives false information.

Interestingly, there seems to be massive support for the abstraction based explanations in the post hoc sense, even though they were told that the reasoning engines did not deliberate at this level to arrive at the decisions. In C1 with a human teammate, only 15% of the participants were opposed to this, with more than half of them expressing positive sentiment. This support is even stronger (+10%) in C2 when the robot is the explainer, and strongest (+20%) when the robot is being explained to.

Q6-Q7 [Stigmergy]. In case of stigmergy, participants seem ambivalent to Q6 with a human teammate in C1. However, support for such behavior increases when it is a robot doing it in C2 (perhaps indicating lack of guilt or, more likely, acknowledging limitations of capabilities much like how Cobots [27] actively seek human help)

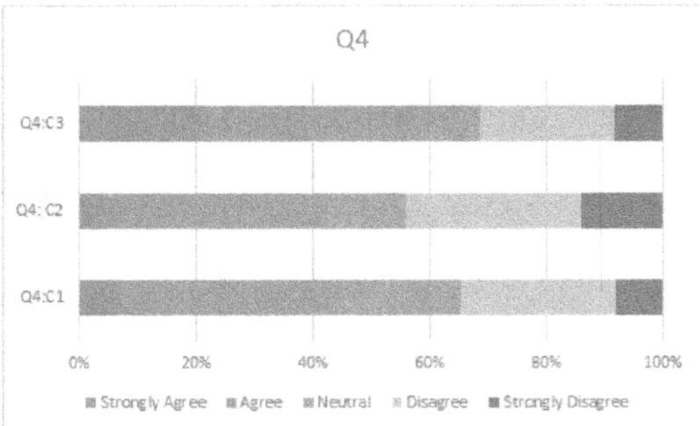

Figure 5: Responses to Q4 in the three study conditions.

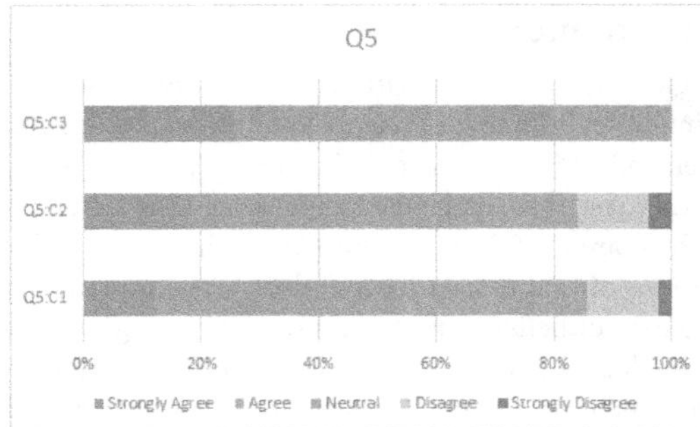

Figure 6: Responses to Q5 in the three study conditions.

and is relatively more positive (60%) when it is being done to a robot in C3 (perhaps the robot's losses are deemed of lesser priority than the human's gains as in [6]). As expected, support for such behavior decreases when participants are told that their teammate will find out about it but the positive trend from C1 to C3 persists.

Aggregate Sentiments Across Scenarios

Figure 9 show the aggregate sentiments expressed for all scenarios across three operating conditions. Some interesting points to note:

- All the distributions are bimodal indicating that participants on the general sided either for or against misleading behavior for the greater good, instead of revealing any innate consensus in the public consciousness. This trend continues across all three conditions. This indicates that the question of misleading a teammate by itself is a difficult question (regardless of there being a robot) and is a topic worthy of debate in the agents community. This is of especial importance considering the possible gains in performance (e.g. lives saved) in high stakes scenarios such as search and rescue.
- Interestingly, these distributions are similar in conditions C1 and C2, but are much more skewed towards the positive scale for condition C3 indicating that participants were more comfortable resorting to such behavior in the case of a robotic teammate. This is brought into sharp focus (+10% in C3) in the aggregated negative / neutral / positive responses (right insets) across the three conditions.
- In general, the majority of participants were more or less positive or neutral to most of these behaviors (Figures 1a to 8). This trend continued unless they were told that their teammate would be able to know of their behavior. Even in those cases, participants showed positive sentiment in case the robot was at the receiving end of this behavior.

Why is this even an option?

One might, of course, wonder why is devising such behaviors even an option. After all, human-human teams have been around for a while, and surely such interactions are equally relevant? It is likely that this may not be the case –

- The moral quandary of having to lie, or at least making others to do so by virtue of how protocols in a team is defined, for example in condition C1, is now taken out the equation. The artificial agent, of course, need not have feelings and has no business feeling bad about having to mislead its teammate if all it cares about is the objective effectiveness (e.g. team performance) of collaboration.
- Similarly, the robot does not have to feel sad that it has been lied to if this improved performance.

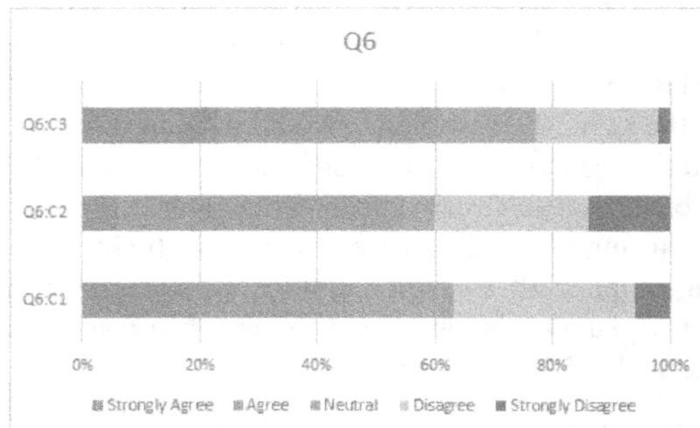

Figure 7: Responses to Q6 in the three study conditions.

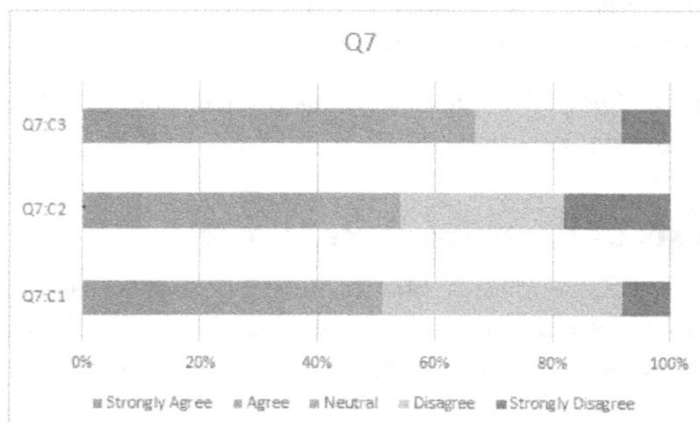

Figure 8: Responses to Q7 in the three study conditions.

However, as we discussed in the previous section, it seems the participants were less willing to get on board with the first consideration in conditions C1 and C2, while they seemed much more comfortable with the idea of an asymmetric relationship in condition C3 when the robot is the one disadvantaged. It is curious to note that they did not, in general, make a distinction between the cases where the human was being manipulated, regardless of whether it was a robot or a human on the other end. This indicates that, at least in certain dynamics of interaction, the presence of an artificial agent in the loop can make perceptions towards otherwise unacceptable behaviors change. This can be exploited (i.e. greater good) in the design of such systems as well. Indeed, authors in [18] argue how such deceptive behavior for greater good lies very much within ethical boundaries depending on the underlying motive.

More than just a Value Alignment Problem. The ideas discussed in this paper are somewhat orthogonal, if at times similar in spirit, to the "value alignment problem" discussed in existing literature [20]. The latter looks at undesirable behaviors of autonomous agents when the utilities of a particular task are misspecified or misunderstood. Inverse reinforcement learning [13] has been proposed as a solution to this, in an attempt to learn the implicit reward function of the human in the loop. The question of value alignment becomes especially difficult, if not altogether academic, since most real-world situations involve multiple humans with conflicting values or utilities, such as in trolley problems [21] and learning from observing behaviors is fraught with unknown biases or assumptions over what exactly produced that behavior. Further, devices sold by the industry are likely to have inbuilt tendencies to maximize profits for the maker which can be at conflicts with the normative expectations of the customer. It is unclear how to guarantee that the values of the end user will not compromised in such scenarios.

Even so, the question of greater good precedes considerations of misaligned values due to misunderstandings or even adversarial manipulation. This is because the former can be manufactured with precisely defined values or goals of the team, and can thus be engineered or incentivised. A "solution" or addressal of these scenarios will thus involve not a reformulation of algorithms but rather a collective reckoning of the ethics of human-machine interactions. In this paper, we attempted to take the first steps towards understanding the state of the public consciousness on this topic.

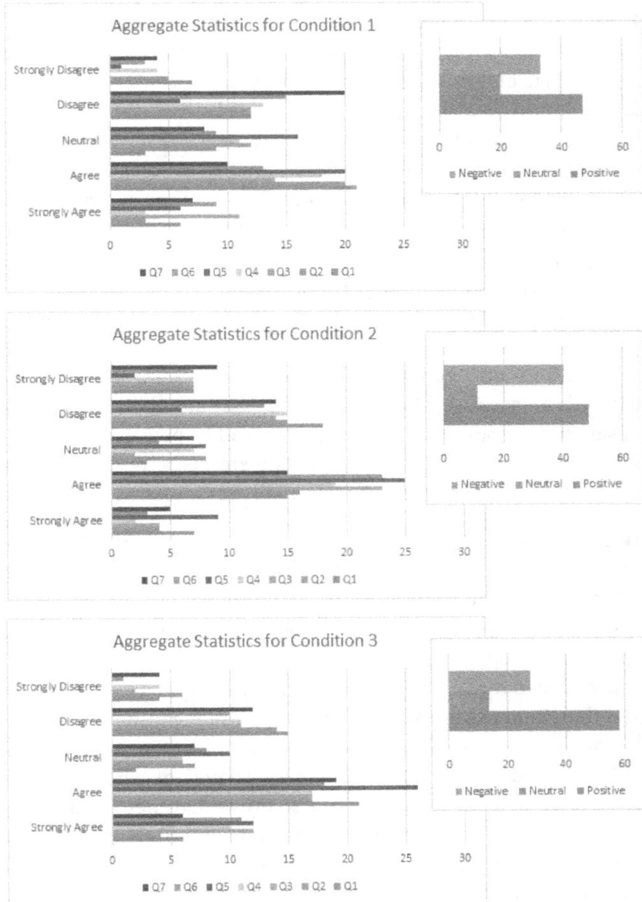

Figure 9: Aggregate responses across three study conditions.

Case Study: The Doctor-Patient Relationship

In the scope of human-human interactions, perhaps the only setting where white lies are considered acceptable or useful, if not outright necessary, in certain circumstances is the doctor-patient relationship. Indeed, this has been a topic of considerable intrigue in the medical community over the years. We thus end our paper with a brief discussion of the dynamics of white lies in the doctor-patient relationship in so much as it relates to the ethics of the design of human-AI interactions. We note that the following considerations also have strong cultural biases and some of these cultural artifacts are likely to feature in the characterization of an artificial agent's behavior in different settings as well.

The Hippocratic Decorum. Perhaps the strongest known support for deception in the practice of medicine is the Hippocratic Decorum [15] which states: *Perform your medical duties calmly and adroitly, concealing most things from the patient while you are attending to him. Give necessary orders with cheerfulness and sincerity, turning his attention away from what is being done to him; sometimes reprove sharply and sometimes comfort with solicitude and attention, revealing nothing of the patient's future or present condition, for many patients through this course have taken a turn for the worse.*

Philosophically, there has been no consensus [4] on this topic – the Kantian view has perceived lies as immoral under all circumstances while the utilitarian view justifies the same "greater good" argument as put forward in our discussions so far. Specifically as it relates to clinical interactions, lies has been viewed variously from an impediment to treatment [19] to a form of clinical aid. As Oliver Wendell Holmes put it [16]: *"Your patient has no more right to all the truth you know than he has to all the medicine in your saddlebag... He should only get just so much as is good for him."*

The position we took on deception in the human-robot setting is similarly patronizing. It is likely to be the case that in terms of superior computational power or sensing capabilities there might be situations where the machine is capable of making decisions for the team that preclude human intervention but not participation. Should the machine be obliged to or even find use in revealing the entire truth in those situations? Or should we concede to our roles in such a relationship as we do with our doctors? This is also predicated on how competent the AI system is and to what extent it can be sure of the consequences [17] of its lies. This remains the primary concern for detractors of the "greater goods" doctrine, and the major deterrent towards the same.

Root Causes of Deception in Clinical Interactions. It is useful to look at the two primary sources of deception in clinical interactions – (1) to hide mistakes (2) delivery of bad news [22]. The former is relevant to both the patient, who probably does not want to admit to failing to follow the regiment, and the doctor, who may be concerned about legal consequences. Such instances of deception to conceal individual fallibilities are out of scope of the current discussion. The latter scenario, on the other hand, comes from a position of superiority of knowledge about the present as well as possible outcomes in future, and has parallels to our current discussion. The rationale, here, being that such information can demoralize the patient and impede their recovery. It is interesting to note that the support for such techniques (both from the doctor's as well as the patient's perspectives) has decreased significantly [12]. That is not to say that human-machine interactions will be perceived similarly. As we saw in the study, participants were open to deception or manipulation for greater good, especially for a robotic teammate.

Deception and Consent. A related topic is, of course, that of consent: if the doctor is not willing to reveal the whole truth, then what is the patient consenting to? In the landmark Slater vs Blaker vs Stapleton case (1767) [1] the surgeon's intentions were indeed considered malpractice (the surgeon has broken the patient's previously broken leg, fresh from a botched surgery, without consent and then botched the surgery again!). More recently, in the now famous Chester vs Afshar case (2004) [5] the surgeon was found guilty of failing to notify even a 1-2% chance of paralysis even though the defendant did not have to prove that they would have chosen not to have the surgery if they were given that information. In the context of human-machine interactions, it is hard to say then what the user agreement will look like, and whether there will be such a thing as consenting to being deceived, if only for the greater good, and what the legal outcomes of this will be *especially when the interactions do not go as planned.*

The Placebo Effect. The effectiveness of placebo medicine, i.e. medicine prescribed while known to have no clinical effect, in improving patient symptoms is a strong argument in favor of deception in the practice of medicine. However, ethics of placebo treatment suggest that their use be limited to rare exceptions where [17] (1) the condition is known to have a high placebo response rate; (2) the alternatives are ineffective and/or risky; and (3) the patient has a strong need for some prescription. Further, the effectiveness of placebo is contingent on the patient's trust on the doctor which is likely to erode as deceptive practices become common knowledge (and consequently render the placebo useless in the first place). Bok [4] points to this notion of "cumulative harm". This does not bode well for the "greater good" argument for human-machine interactions since most of them will be eventually contextualized over longer term relationships.

Primum Non Nocere. Perhaps the most remarkable nature of the doctor-patient relationship is captured by the notion of the recovery plot [14] as part of a show being orchestrated by the doctor, and the patient being only complicit, while being cognizant of their specific roles in it, with the expectation of restoration of autonomy [25], i.e. the state of human equality, free from the original symptoms or dependence on the doctor, at the end of the interaction. This is to say that the doctor-patient relationship is understood to be asymmetric and "enters into a calculus of values wherein the respect for the right to truth of the patient is weighed against impairing the restoration of autonomy by the truth" [24] where the autonomy of the patient has historically taken precedence over beneficence and nonmalfeasance [24]. In general, a human-machine relationship lacks this dynamic. So, while there are interesting lessons to be learned from clinical interactions with regards to value of truth and utility of outcomes, one should be carefully aware of the nuances of a particular type of relationship and situate an interaction in that context. Such considerations are also likely to shift according to the stakes on a decision, for example, lives lost in search and rescue scenarios. Nevertheless, the doctor-patient relationship, and the intriguing roles of deception in it, does provide an invaluable starting point for conversation on the topic of deception for the greater good in human-AI interactions.

Conclusion

In this paper, we investigated how fabrication, falsification and obfuscation of information can be used by an AI agent to achieve teaming performance that would otherwise not be possible. We discussed how such behavior can be manufactured using existing AI algorithms and used responses from participants in a thought experiment to gauge public perception on this topic. From the results of a thought experiment, it seems that the public perception is *positive towards lying for the greater good* especially when those actions would not be determined by their teammate, but is loath to suspend normative behavior, robot or not, in the event that they would be caught in that act *unless the robot is the recipient of the misinformation!* Further, most of the responses seem to be following a bimodal distribution indicating that the participants either felt strongly for or against this kind of behavior. Going forward it will be interesting to explore game-theoretic formulations [23] to model how the dynamics of trust in longer term interactions.

Finally, we note that all the use cases covered in the paper are, in fact, borne directly out of technologies or algorithms that the first author has developed, albeit with slight modifications, as a graduate student researcher over the last few years. Even though these algorithms were conceived with the best of intentions, such as to enable AI systems to explain their decisions or to increase effectiveness of collaborations with the humans in the loop, we would be remiss not to consider their ethical implications when used differently. In these exciting and uncertain times for the field of AI, it is thus imperative that researchers are cognizant of their scientific responsibility. We would like to conclude then by reiterating the importance of self-reflection in the principled design of AI algorithms whose deployment can have real-life consequences, intended or otherwise, on the future of the field, but also, with the inquisitive mind of a young researcher, marvel at the widening scope of interactions with an artificial agent into newer uncharted territories that may be otherwise considered to be unethical.

Acknowledgements. Majority of the work was completed while the first author was a PhD student at Arizona State University. This research is supported in part by the AFOSR grant FA9550-18-1-0067,the ONR grants N00014161-2892, N00014-13-1-0176, N00014-13-1-0519,N00014-15-1-2027, and the NASA grant NNX17AD06G.

REFERENCES

[1] George J Annas. 2012. Doctors, Patients, and Lawyers – Two Centuries of Health Law. *New England Journal of Medicine* 367, 5 (2012), 445–450.
[2] Chris Baker, Rebecca Saxe, and Joshua Tenenbaum. 2011. Bayesian Theory of Mind: Modeling Joint Belief-Desire Attribution. In *Proceedings of the Annual Meeting of the Cognitive Science Society*, Vol. 33.
[3] Guido Boella, Jan M Broersen, Leendert WN van der Torre, and Serena Villata. 2009. Representing Excuses in Social Dependence Networks. In *AI*IA*.
[4] Sissela Bok. 1999. *Lying: Moral Choice in Public and Private Life*. Vintage.
[5] Hilary Cass. 2006. *The NHS Experience: The "Snakes and Ladders" Guide for Patients and Professionals*. Psychology Press.
[6] Tathagata Chakraborti, Gordon Briggs, Kartik Talamadupula, Yu Zhang, Matthias Scheutz, David Smith, and Subbarao Kambhampati. 2015. Planning for Serendipity. In *IROS*.
[7] Tathagata Chakraborti, Subbarao Kambhampati, Matthias Scheutz, and Yu Zhang. 2017. AI Challenges in Human-Robot Cognitive Teaming. *CoRR* abs/1707.04775 (2017).
[8] Tathagata Chakraborti, Venkata Vamsikrishna Meduri, Vivek Dondeti, and Subbarao Kambhampati. 2016. A Game Theoretic Approach to Ad-Hoc Coalitions in Human-Robot Societies.. In *AAAI Workshop: Multiagent Interaction without Prior Coordination*.
[9] Tathagata Chakraborti, Sarath Sreedharan, Yu Zhang, and Subbarao Kambhampati. 2017. Plan Explanations as Model Reconciliation: Moving Beyond Explanation as Soliloquy. In *IJCAI*.
[10] Tathagata Chakraborti, Kartik Talamadupula, Yu Zhang, and Subbarao Kambhampati. 2016. A Formal Framework for Studying Interaction in Human-Robot Societies.. In *AAAI Workshop: Symbiotic Cognitive Systems*.
[11] Tathagata Chakraborti, Yu Zhang, David E Smith, and Subbarao Kambhampati. 2016. Planning with Resource Conflicts in Human-Robot Cohabitation. In *AAMAS*.
[12] Ethics in Medicine. 2018. Truth-telling and Withholding Information. https://goo.gl/su5zSF. University of Washington.
[13] Dylan Hadfield-Menell, Stuart J Russell, Pieter Abbeel, and Anca Dragan. 2016. Cooperative Inverse Reinforcement Learning. In *Advances in neural information processing systems (NIPS)*. 3909–3917.
[14] Tony Hak, Gerard Koëter, Gerrit van der Wal, et al. 2000. Collusion in Doctor-Patient Communication About Imminent Death: An Ethnographic Study. *Bmj* 321, 7273 (2000), 1376–1381.
[15] Hippocrates. 2018. The Hippocatic Oath – Full Text. https://goo.gl/TKb1mP.
[16] Oliver Wendell Holmes. 1892. *Medical Essays 1842-1882*. Vol. 9. Houghton, Mifflin.
[17] David Hume. 1907. *Essays: Moral, Political, and Literary*. Vol. 1. Longmans, Green, and Company.
[18] Alistair Isaac and Will Bridewell. 2017. White Lies on Silver Tongues: Why Robots Need to Deceive (and How). *Robot Ethics* 2 (2017), 157–72.
[19] Otto F Kernberg. 1985. *Borderline Conditions and Pathological Narcissism*. Rowman & Littlefield.
[20] Leverhulme Centre. 2017. Value Alignment Problem. https://goo.gl/uDcAoZ. Leverhulme Centre for the Future of Intelligence.
[21] MIT. 2017. Moral Machines. https://goo.gl/by5y7H.
[22] John J Palmieri and Theodore A Stern. 2009. Lies in the Doctor-Patient Relationship. *Primary Care Companion to the Journal of Clinical Psychiatry* 11.4 (2009), 163.
[23] Vidyaraman Sankaranarayanan, Madhusudhanan Chandrasekaran, and Shambhu Upadhyaya. 2007. Towards Modeling Trust Based Decisions: A Game Theoretic Approach. In *European Symposium on Research in Computer Security*. Springer, 485–500.
[24] G Swaminath. 2008. The Doctor's Dilemma: Truth Telling. *Indian journal of psychiatry* 50, 2 (2008), 83.
[25] David C Thomasma. 1994. Telling the Truth to Patients: A Clinical Ethics Exploration. *Cambridge Quarterly of Healthcare Ethics* 3, 3 (1994), 375–382.
[26] Hans van Ditmarsch. 2014. The Ditmarsch Tale of Wonders. In *KI: Advances in Artificial Intelligence*.
[27] Manuela M Veloso, Joydeep Biswas, Brian Coltin, and Stephanie Rosenthal. 2015. CoBots: Robust Symbiotic Autonomous Mobile Service Robots.. In *IJCAI*.

Epistemic Therapy for Bias in Automated Decision-Making

Thomas Krendl Gilbert
University of California, Berkeley
Berkeley, California, USA
tg340@berkeley.edu

Yonatan Mintz
Georgia Institute of Technology
Atlanta, Georgia, USA

ABSTRACT

Despite recent interest in both the critical and machine learning literature on "bias" in artificial intelligence (AI) systems, the nature of specific biases stemming from the interaction of machines, humans, and data remains ambiguous. Influenced by Gendler's work on human cognitive biases, we introduce the concept of *alief-discordant belief*, the tension between the intuitive moral dispositions of designers and the explicit representations generated by algorithms. Our discussion of *alief-discordant belief* diagnoses the ethical concerns that arise when designing AI systems atop human biases. We furthermore codify the relationship between data, algorithms, and engineers as components of this cognitive discordance, comprising a novel epistemic framework for ethics in AI.

CCS CONCEPTS

• **Computing methodologies → Philosophical/theoretical foundations of artificial intelligence**; **Theory of mind**.

KEYWORDS

artificial intelligence, AI, fairness, moral cognition

ACM Reference Format:
Thomas Krendl Gilbert and Yonatan Mintz. 2019. Epistemic Therapy for Bias in Automated Decision-Making. In *AAAI/ACM Conference on AI, Ethics, and Society (AIES '19), January 27–28, 2019, Honolulu, HI, USA.* ACM, New York, NY, USA, 7 pages. https://doi.org/10.1145/3306618.3314294

1 INTRODUCTION

As AI systems become pervasive, we have an interest in investigating their impact on fair decision-making. Both machine learning and social science researchers have confronted how the predictions made by these systems transpose human biases in certain contexts, adversely shaping decision-making in sensitive settings such as hiring [19], criminal justice [2, 22], and healthcare [3, 13]. To date this topic has been explored from both algorithmic [7, 20, 28] and positional perspectives [8, 12, 25]. However, the nature of the kinds of anthropomorphic biases that arise from the interaction between algorithms, humans, and data remains ambiguous.

We propose dissolving the concept of "anthropomorphic bias," and instead closely analyze its phenomenological content to better diagnose the epistemic and ethical challenges that may arise in AI system design. Since much of the discussion on anthropomorphic biases has been conducted through either anthropomorphizing AI models or relegating all responsibility for bias onto problematic data, our goal is to move away from these ambiguous analogies and confront the nuance of bias in automated decision-making.

Our discussion is motivated by several recent cases of AI system implementation and research that have already been flagged as problematic. We first examine systems where data was assumed to be representative of the real world but in fact encoded human biases that were later amplified by AI systems [2, 30]. We then consider cases in the machine learning literature where common notions of bias and equity are rationalized away by researchers using predictions provided by AI models [11, 34]. Finally, we consider cases where researchers attempt to directly address anthropomorphic biases they perceive in their model prediction, leading to researchers instead encoding their own implicit biases into AI systems [7, 9]. These three motivating examples show that the nature of anthropomorphic bias in AI is paradoxical and counterintuitive, while the use of direct analogies to human bias actually erase the specific contexts that cause anthropomorphic bias to manifest in the first place.

In order to diagnose and work through these ambiguities, we provide two major contributions to the discussion of bias in AI systems. First, we characterize the kinds of biases that arise from complex interactions between engineers, algorithms, and data. To do this, we draw on previous work in the philosophy of mind literature that characterizes human bias as a set of aliefs [17], belief-like dispositions that also contain an affective component, and introduce the concept of *alief-discordant beliefs*. In our discussion, we demonstrate that these *alief-discordant beliefs* provide the framework necessary to understand the trade-off between the moral dispositions of system engineers and the explicit relations encoded by AI models. Second, we apply the notion of *alief-discordant beliefs* to craft design principles for AI in light of human biases. We conclude by illustrating how these principles can be used to diagnose the ethical concerns that motivate practitioners, performing a type of "epistemic therapy" for the benefit of the machine learning community.

Much as psychotherapy is used to confront subconscious issues through a process of dynamic interpersonal conversation, we propose "epistemic therapy" for automated decision-making as the process by which *alief-discordant beliefs* are identified and confronted by engineers. The design principles we outline in this paper support this "epistemic therapy" by aiding in the implementation of AI systems and navigating to avoid biased outcomes.

AIES '19, January 27–28, 2019, Honolulu, HI, USA

ACM ISBN 978-1-4503-6324-2/19/01...$15.00
https://doi.org/10.1145/3306618.3314294

2 EPISTEMIC ETHICS IN FAIR MACHINE LEARNING

The machine learning literature has explored predictive bias as a barrier to fair outcomes. In particular, many papers have suggested algorithmic means of curbing bias in predictions, proposing the notion of "optimal" fairness as solutions to optimization problems [11]. Several variations of optimal fairness have been proposed, including equalizing prediction metrics (e.g. TPR, FPR, accuracy) across protected classes [1, 10, 13, 20], and producing models whose predictions are independent of protected features [7, 9, 28, 35]. There have been some technical critiques leveled against these notions of optimal fairness [11, 25], as well as several impossibility results that show it is difficult to satisfy all of these notions of fairness simultaneously [14, 21]. We complement this literature by providing a framework of epistemic ethics that could be used to justify the necessary engineering design choices made in implementing certain methods of optimal fairness. Specifically, our framework resolves some of the skepticism in using these methods and addresses what technical knowledge and data engineers ought to have in order to manage and avoid anthropomorphic bias in AI systems they design.

A related stream of social science literature has discussed the nature of bias in machine learning [4, 6, 12, 26], enumerating potential ethical concerns and discussing whether decision-making can be automated without compromising human dignity responsibility. In contrast, our discussion emphasizes how the *perception* of different kinds of bias in AI systems is responsible for their supposed immorality, which implies they are better understood within the realm of philosophy of mind than ethics proper. Of particular relevance to this paper is the discussion proposed by Binns [6], which analyzes anthropomorphic bias by contrasting human mental states with the mechanisms of automated decision-making. We will present a complementary dissolution of anthropomorphic bias through the notion of *alief-discordant beliefs*, directly influenced by the work of Tamar Gendler on characterizing human biases [17].

3 CASE STUDIES

We will first build intuition on how "anthropomorphic bias" can affect researchers and engineers through reference to prominent existing case studies. In particular, we consider cases where anthropomorphic bias may manifest in how 1) the values of engineers inform the techniques of AI system creation; 2) the epistemology of the data and encoding characterize the resulting AI system; 3) allocation of moral culpability labels interactions between data and system design throughout the deployment phase.

Each of these examples illustrates how anthropomorphic bias can be attributed to an underlying *discordance* between the distinctive epistemic frames of engineers, data, and system design. We discuss three major causes of this discordance, each with its own mixing of ethical culpability between data, algorithms, and engineers. These are: (i) AI systems that are deployed as vehicles for moral dispositions, either encoded by engineers or sedimented within data; (ii) engineers that outsource their own moral compasses to the labels generated by AI systems; (iii) dogmatic reconciliation of inherited dispositions and generated propositions that result in adverse effects.

3.1 AI systems as Vehicles for Moral Dispositions

First we consider cases where AI systems are deployed as vehicles for moral dispositions implicitly harbored by engineers or encoded in training data. Two famous cases of such discordance discussed in FAT literature include the COMPAS system which was used to predict criminal recidivism [2, 22], and Tay the Microsoft-deployed chat bot that was hijacked by white supremacists [5, 29, 30].

3.1.1 COMPAS. The COMPAS system was initially developed to predict a recidivism risk score for arrested individuals and was deployed to several states [2]. However, even though explicit racial detail was not inserted into the system input, it was shown that COMPAS would predict lower risk scores for white individuals and higher scores for people of color. Moreover, analysis of the system output showed that the false positive rate for people of color was significantly higher than that of white individuals [22]. From a technical perspective, it is generally agreed that the system produced biased output despite not taking in explicit racial data, since race is correlated with other features that were used as input (e.g. education, residence address, income) and labels used for training were obtained from historical arrest records that contain a documented inherent bias against certain communities [22].

In essence, the way the COMPAS system was designed and implemented transformed social biases extant in the justice system and reified them through automated classification. However, it is difficult to confer responsibility for this to a specific agent–while the data's encoded bias should have been made explicit by those who collected it, system engineers also failed to properly account for this bias in the data. What the engineers ought to have done in this particular case is *critically examine the source of the data* and any bias that it may convey, and *use a proper training technique* for their model that could account for the problematic predictions.

3.1.2 Microsoft Tay. Tay was a chatbot developed by Microsoft research to interact with the greater public on social media and mimic the language patterns of a 19 year old girl[5]. While in closed company testing, it was reported that Tay was performing extremely well without significant incident. Within 24 hours of being deployed online, and to the surprise of the research team, Tay was re-tweeting white supremacist propaganda due to a loosely coordinated attack by certain forum users [29, 30].

Much like COMPAS, the deployment of Tay also suffered from becoming a passive vehicle for unquestioned moral associations. However, the associations in question are not necessarily the ones harbored by the data but by the engineers that designed the system. In particular, the engineers were not appropriately skeptical of the reaction of the internet community at large and assumed that they would behave in a similar manner to the corporate testers that interacted with Tay in house. The fallout from this situation could have been reduced had the engineers confronted their own underlying assumptions and properly designed the training methods of the model to not accept all input data equally.

3.2 Automatic Alief Falsification

Another cause of the discordance can result from a 'skeptical' *overcorrection* based on the system pipeline. Two of the principle tenets of data science include the belief that all rational explanations (i.e. those that rely on mathematical reasoning) are superior to all other forms of disposition generation, and that sufficient information about the state of the world can be extracted from data. This moral disposition is conveyed by the recent work of Corbett-Davies and Goel [11] on fairness measures, and Wang and Kosinski's [34] work on detecting sexual orientation with pictures .

While we strive to identify ethical culpability in this section, we do not ascribe malicious intentions to the engineers that design AI systems. In particular, we believe both sets of authors that we discuss here did have good intentions when creating their work, but that their results are problematic when examined in a critical context. The key problematic aspect of these discordances is that instead of attempting to harmonize their own moral dispositions with the propositions generated by models, engineers are too eager to dispose of their initial presuppositions.

3.2.1 The Measure and Mismeasure of Fairness. Corbett-Davies and Goel [11] have presented several leading methods of optimal fairness in the FATML literature and critique each family of methods to show how they may violate certain notions of fairness. The authors rely on working definitions of fairness from parts of the economics and legal literature and show how these can be incongruent with mathematical notions of fairness. When analyzing the notion of fairness through classification parity, the authors note that different populations of individuals will by nature have different means and variances that could account for lack of parity. As a real world example of this, the authors used the example of the COMPAS model we previously discussed. They note that since black individuals had higher recidivism rates than white individuals, this group was in fact accurately predicted as having a higher risk to society than whites.

Although the authors do note that this difference in rate is caused by both historic and systemic factors, they argue that these are not crucial to examine when making policy decisions. In particular, since the authors assume the prediction of individual risk is accurate, they claim that policy actions to ensure prediction parity between the populations would result in an unfairly harsher prediction rate against the white population. They further argue that such actions would harm the black population with an inappropriately low predicted rate of recidivism [11]. Thus, the authors arrive at a conclusion that is in contrast to their initially stated assumptions ("demographic parity is important"), due to their failure to critically engage with the context of the data (namely its internal generation by a system with known bias [22]).

3.2.2 Detecting Sexual Orientation with AI. A similar tension can be found in Wang and Kosinski's paper [34], which describes an artificial neural network model that processes facial images to predict an individual's sexual orientation. In particular, the authors used face photos scraped from dating websites that they classified as heterosexual or homosexual using the user's dating profile, and showed that a model trained on these photos has good accuracy when predicting sexual orientation. The authors' main claim in this paper is that the predictive power of AI models can be harnessed to encode complex patterns in facial features that could indicate an individual's sexual orientation.

This research has received a lot of backlash for suggesting a new form of digital physiognomy [23, 27, 33]. While the researchers may have started with the assumption that physiognomy is pseudoscience, they readily discarded this in favor of the view generated by their model that facial features can predict sexual orientation. Kosinski himself has defended the study as revealing both the "huge promise" of big data as well as the risks due to loss of privacy [31]. Meanwhile, critics have argued that this attempt to subject sexual orientation to objective measurement, while an interesting exercise in classification that reveals unexpected correlations with high accuracy, is erroneous as it fails to account for the subjectivity of social context [16] and reifies social stereotypes[24].

However, there is a danger of repeating the study's mistake by assuming that automated systems can only reify existing gender ontologies. It is, for example, possible that previously invisible correlations between bone structure and sexual preference really do exist, encouraging future work to explore and falsify new hypotheses. Meanwhile, a more critical analysis of the model might suggest that the contextual purpose of dating profile pictures is to broadcast sexual orientation to potential partners, rather than neutrally reflect how facial features predict sexual preferences. Since the engineers did not seriously consider this, they propagated a questionable conclusion based on the model output. We will later suggest interpreting such research studies as generating authentic discordances between our intuitions about the social world and novel beliefs about it that must be examined and deliberated, rather than summarily dismissed.

3.3 Dogmatic Reconciliation

Finally, we consider a class of discordances arising when the system engineers *do attempt* to harmonize their moral dispositions with system-generated propositions, but unfortunately use blunt methods to make systems comply with the former. The failure occurs when engineers, despite using values-based design, still encode their implicit biases into AI models through training and formulation instead of explicating and confronting their own assumptions. We consider two recent papers from the FATML literature that focus on the problem of biased predictions resulting from natural language processing: "Women also Snowboard" [9] and "Man is to Computer Programmer as Woman is to Homemaker" [7]. In both of these papers, the authors seek to correct gender related bias in various downstream tasks that occurs using state-of-the-art word vector embeddings for natural language processing.

In "Women also Snowboard" [9] the authors address gender bias that occurs when developing AI systems for automatic image captioning. Specifically, the authors note that given certain contexts (e.g. sports equipment, computers, purses), image captioning systems tend to give incorrect predictions that fit common gender expression stereotypes. For instance, a captioning model might predict the caption of a picture of a woman snowboarding as a man snowboarding, since men are more associated with sports contexts. The solution that is introduced to curb this problem involves creating two classes of words ("male" vs. "female") and formulating a loss function to be used in model training that actually incentivizes confusion between these classes if insufficient evidence is found to make a gendered inference.

Likewise, in "Man is to Computer Programmer as Woman is to Homemaker" [7], the authors attempt to address gender bias that can be observed when performing analogy tasks using word vectors. While vector embedding in words generally yields useful semantic analogies (e.g. man is to king as woman is to queen), the authors note that certain problematic analogies are also picked up by these embeddings given certain corpora. To curtail these problematic analogies, the authors propose a method in which they compute a "Man to Woman" subspace of the embedded vector space, and formulate a way to reduce the the projection of non-gendered words on this subspace, thus removing much of the unintentional gender encoding that could have been contained by those words.

Both of these works confront a discordance between model and social understandings of gender, namely that it should not be informative for certain aspects of an individual (women can also be snowboarders and computer programmers), and attempt to harmonize this view with the generated propositions of these given models. That said, the solutions proposed by the authors do not directly correct for the notion that gender expression should be uninformative on certain predictions, and instead address the problem of women being underrepresented in data and should be predicted with equal probability to men in certain contexts.

This is a subtle distinction, but to illustrate it fully, we note that both solutions presented in these papers assume some kind of distinct "male" to "female" distinction and not more contextually-nuanced forms of gender identity. Essentially, by attempting to produce a solution to the system's discordant moral claims, the authors have hard-coded a cis-gender understanding of human sexuality into the models. The authors thus do not directly engage with the *root discordance* they seek to address, and instead provide a potentially problematic stop-gap solution that reacts only to their morally-charged dispositions. One way of mitigating these effects would have been a more thorough examination of the social-scientific literature on gender expression, and broadening the gender diversity of the research teams involved. In particular, since the methods proposed by the authors involve a rigid encoding of expression, they produce training techniques that are incompatible with intersectional gender identities. For instance, a correction agnostic to the intersection of gender expression and race might result in false corrections due to its rigid coding.

4 THE CONTEXT OF ANTHROPOMORPHIC BIAS

The questions surrounding anthropomorphic bias –is it always traceable to some original context of human bias? is it original to the statistical compromises that accompany automated decision-making? can it be avoided entirely?– demand a deeper philosophical analysis. In this section we proceed to conduct this analysis in two parts.

4.1 Gendler on Belief-Discordant Alief

Some form of "bias", however it is defined, is inevitable when any small team of humans derives actuarial interventions for broad populations. Trade-offs between accuracy and variance or false positive vs. false negative rates have been a hallmark of statistical inference since the discipline's birth, and while AI has considerably increased the scale and speed of such inferences in deployment, they have not fundamentally changed the rules of this game. Instead we should aim for a principled trade-off between the limits of inference, given messy data sets, imperfect model choices, or limited training time. But what might such a principled trade-off look like for anthropomorphic bias, which combines affect-laden human intuitions with machines' capacity for semantically-arbitrary classification?

We appeal to Gendler's [17] work on the complex and codependent relationship between belief and "alief", which defines the latter as "a mental state with associatively-linked content that is representational, affective and behavioral, and that is activated – consciously or nonconsciously – by features of the subject's internal or ambient environment. Aliefs may be either occurrent or dispositional." Gendler illustrates this phenomenon through the concept of *belief-discordant alief*, which accounts for scenarios in which people are afraid of walking on an open skywalk despite its structural safety, won't touch an object for fear of "cooties," or automatically reach for wallets despite knowing you left it at home. Belief-discordant alief is the triggering of affective response patterns and automatic motor routines opposed to "explicit, conscious, vivid, occurrent belief" [17]. That is, it arises when we enter a situation that triggers us into a cognitive state that counteracts what our 'better' judgment knows not to be the case.

There is some semantic risk in applying such technical philosophical concepts to a problem as provocative and wide-ranging as anthropomorphic bias, which is already the subject of a rapidly growing empirical literature. However, we feel Gendler's language is not just relevant but necessary for diagnosing the problem in machine learning, for two reasons. First, Gendler's examples and qualifiers succeed in contrasting belief with alief by defining the former in a strongly *computational* sense: belief is an explicit proposition whose content is discrete (not associative), is universally held (not situationally triggered), and refers conclusively to external reality (not emotions or habits of mind). We shall see that these technical descriptors of belief and alief are extremely useful for diagnosing the specific epistemic tensions within AI systems and the moral dispositions of those who design or interpret them.

Second, Gendler's terminology emphasizes the *discordance* between different kinds of bias as the source of the real problem, not implicit bias in isolation. She holds, following Hume, that the hallmark of alief is a kind of association by which semantic, emotional, and behavioral dimensions are crystallized over time. In belief-discordant alief, there is something about an environment's psychological effects that trigger one to automatically respond in a way opposed to one's beliefs about it. The associative content of alief is highly arbitrary, just as one's explicit beliefs may be fundamentally prejudiced. This is key for grasping the confusions surrounding anthropomorphic bias in machine learning: AI systems aren't conscious, yet classify social artifacts much as we do; system designers strive for formal accuracy, yet display strong moral affect in response to automated claims. The biases of both systems and designers play a role in generating the discordant environments in which a machine's classifications feel inappropriate or morally wrong, and we can make sense of this by recognizing the ontological primacy of belief-alief discordance over the isolated prejudices of humans and machines.

4.2 Alief-Discordant Beliefs in Machine Learning

To properly apply Gendler's insights, we propose the concept of *alief-discordant belief* to describe the origin, form, and consequence of anthropomorphic bias in automated systems. When deployed, these systems (e.g. image captioning) transpose human-generated forms of alief by computationally remaking the context within which our aliefs typically operate. In Gendler's terms, they generate beliefs that violate the habitual associations between semantic meaning (e.g. these variables are related given a specific parameter space) and moral dispositions (snowboarding is something anyone can do), producing a visceral reaction from the designers ("women also snowboard") that demands reconciliation [9]. Consequently, the "bias" of automated systems refers to the uncanny semantic associations that arise from applying our aliefs to a purely data-driven setting, violating the contextual ties between disposition, affect, and representation that underpin our aliefs.

When confronted with examples of an image classifier that offend us, we may have an automatic affective response that counteracts the beliefs that are either encoded into the algorithm's learning procedure (the belief that the classifier can learn semantic associations in an objective, impartial manner and arrive at ground truth) or generated by it (only men snowboard, certain faces are gay). In other words, the classifier crystallizes propositions about its own learning procedure as well as its predictive outputs, either of which can give rise to alief-discordant belief.

Although such a classifier is just a computational function, there is a tendency for designers to anthropomorphize it as if it had autonomous beliefs, leading to a search for where these beliefs come from or who is to blame. This can leave engineers in the position of apologizing for the very data that is needed for the model learn anything useful (much like the case of MS Tay learning English for Nazi posts).

We suggest interpreting such systems as *automatic belief generators* that compel us to reinterpret our own aliefs in the deployment context. Rather than claiming an algorithm is "biased," we should confront the tension it creates between beliefs and aliefs we have about the social world. We must avoid compounding this tension by manually patching in solutions to our most violated or dogmatically-held aliefs (e.g. we calibrate a classifier generate all outcomes independently of protected attributes). Instead, we must address the *discordance* that is making us feel uncomfortable (such as in the cases of [9] and [7]).

Rather than blaming the data or its labelers as biased, system designers are responsible for sorting out these discordances as they arise by harmonizing the generated beliefs with their own newly-challenged, inherited aliefs. The goal is thus not to try to make automated systems unbiased, but to interrogate the beliefs generated, the procedure for that generation, and the relation of both to our own aliefs. These factors can be made to map onto specific components of the AI's socio-technical infrastructure: the system engineer, the chosen model and training methods, and the data used. The onus is therefore on figuring out where in this pipeline our aliefs are being violated, how each contributes to this violation, and which of these components is most responsible.

5 TOWARDS A TECHNO-SOCIETAL INFRASTRUCTURE

Intersectional identities are a key hurdle in identifying the contexts that lead to alief-belief discordance. From the engineers' standpoint, this can result when either data does not contain sufficient examples of them, or they cannot be effectively encoded for the purposes of inference. And from the systems' perspective, intersectionality cannot be fully captured without generating a combinatorial explosion, since the interplay of relevant social variables (e.g. race, gender) will expand exponentially as more are deemed relevant for a given context. Confronting both sources requires interventions on the decision-making pipeline itself, and discordances are managed most readily if each step of the pipeline is designed to maintain one analytic component of alief-discordant belief. Pre-reflective moral dispositions necessarily inform the application of this pipeline through continuous attention to context, but the mechanics themselves are tied to conditions of explicit knowledge representation in the form of system-generated propositions. A significant component of "fair" machine learning is the integrity and documentation of this techno-societal pipeline, such that bias can be managed well beneath the psychological threshold of moral outrage that has regrettably defined the public reception of prominent case studies (see for example [32]). This implies that much of the burden for moral responsibility gets shifted from the data to model training and finally to engineers–if practitioners find themselves ignorant of the context of what they are working on, it is inappropriate to shift blame onto your tools.

5.1 Data

The collection of human data requires a compromise between alief (whatever moral compulsion(s) was felt in the leadup to collecting it) and belief (whatever data structure and type was determined to best represent assumptions about reality). There is always a moral context that informs the data content, just as there is an explicit frame of representation that accounts for its form. This original compromise is often invisible and unacknowledged in a given dataset. While troubling, the main problem here is how to deal with this crystallization to ensure it can be *accounted for* and *is traceable*. Here the following guidelines are necessary:

Data as context-specific: data must be documented with the original priorities of those who collected it, and the relevant case law that informed its collection. These "datasheets for datasets" help ensure that transparency and accountability are baked into the pipeline from the start [15]. This will provide a traceable baseline for the alief(s) lying behind the original data even after it has been used to generate classification regimes.

Data as explicit: data should be annotated so that the assumptions behind its collection are clearly documented, rather than left implicit. This is meant to account for the beliefs or prior evidence that informed why the data was collected and organized in a certain manner, rather than another.

Data as contestable: data should be publicly available so that its alief-belief crystallization, however messy or regrettable, can be challenged by those most subject to its labels or classification. This affirms that the alief-belief matrix behind its collection is a product of compromise worthy of continual reflection and deliberation.

5.2 Model and Training

As a machine learning model is being trained, data–and with it a complex web of social relations, moral drives, and unstated representational axioms–are reified as generated beliefs about the macro-environment in question. This is the great benefit and cost of machine learning at scale, to wring more intuition out of a dataset than existed anywhere in the minds of those who produced it. The problem is to ensure the generated beliefs *accord with* the inherited beliefs that defined that data, or at least the beliefs of system engineers:

Models as interpretable: models should be easy to understand by qualified humans so that classifications have a clear semantic context, requiring *explainability*. If this is not the case, as can happen in deep learning [18], it will make the work of identifying bias difficult, because the model itself cannot be consulted to resolve the discrepancy or point to likely solutions. This "discordance slack" should instead be reined in as early as possible.

Models as intuitive: model assumptions should be documented so they are easily altered, without an unnecessary amount of work going into why these assumptions were chosen. This is necessary to ensure that the *belief generation* of the model is kept distinct from the *belief testing* of its trainers, rather than the two becoming conflated.

Models as corrigible: assumptions should be transparent and available to the wider machine learning community so that they can be challenged. This is a redundancy check against the psychological biases of the model trainers and helps bolster the accordance between humans' and the model's beliefs.

5.3 Engineers

Engineers are the ultimate source of aliefs that are discordant with the model's generated beliefs. As those who are using the model to classify new data in contexts other than what the model was trained on, they will often bear the responsibility for its failures and specifically for the discordance between their own moral dispositions and the model's classifications. To review what has been stated already, where the data is dirty and the model is a black box, alief-discordant belief is almost inevitable. This is the scenario we are trying to anticipate by making the discordance *manageable*.

Discordance as discoverable: engineers should be trained about psychological bias to better identify discordances where they are subtle or hidden in edge cases for the model in question. The goal is to make note of discordance before the public discovers it in deployment, which could cause social harm and also make the model less trustworthy.

Discordance as tractable: engineers should be expertly informed about the likely problems with data and model training, i.e. have a general grasp of the pipeline and its context to better confront discordances when or if they arise. The goal here is to know how to manage the discordance, rather than simply to flag it.

Discordance as contextual: engineers should be trained to maintain healthy work environments, have access to legal consultation, and cultivate emotional intelligence to better process discordances when they themselves feel them. Thanks to Three Mile Island and other man-made disasters, we have learned that fear-mongering, societal distrust, and lasting damage can be avoided if engineers respond appropriately to a crisis rather than misrepresent the nature of the problem either to themselves or the public.

6 CONCLUSION

We have suggested *alief-discordant belief* to avoid the shoals of anthropomorphic bias in an automated context. Epistemically, *alief-discordant belief* accounts for the subtle ways in which human cognitive bias enters a machine learning pipeline, first through the dataset, then through model and training specification, finally in the dispositions of system engineers. Ethically, we have suggested that machine learning practitioners should work to maintain the integrity of this pipeline so that *alief-discordant belief*, once generated by engineers interacting with the model, is manageable with respect to the actual stakes of the social context in question. Part of the wider project of realizing fairness through machine learning is for engineers to interpret themselves as part of this context, which includes the wider machine learning community as well as potentially-vulnerable populations of protected social categories. In light of this therapy, negotiating the discord between human aliefs and machine-generated beliefs may depend on crafting a wholly new context for automated decision-making, in which we get better at designing machines that supply us with beliefs that we are more critically prepared to adopt.

REFERENCES

[1] Alekh Agarwal, Alina Beygelzimer, Miroslav Dudík, John Langford, and Hanna Wallach. 2018. A reductions approach to fair classification. *arXiv preprint arXiv:1803.02453* (2018).
[2] Julia Angwin, Jeff Larson, Surya Mattu, and Lauren Kirchner. 2016. Machine bias: There's software used across the country to predict future criminals And it's biased against blacks. *ProPublica* (2016).
[3] Anil Aswani, Philip Kaminsky, Yonatan Mintz, Elena Flowers, and Yoshimi Fukuoka. 2016. Behavioral modeling in weight loss interventions. (2016).
[4] Chelsea Barabas, Karthik Dinakar, Joichi Ito Virza, Jonathan Zittrain, et al. 2017. Interventions over predictions: Reframing the ethical debate for actuarial risk assessment. *arXiv preprint arXiv:1712.08238* (2017).
[5] Dina Bass. 2016. Clippy's Back: The Future of Microsoft Is Chatbots. Bloomberg Businessweek.
[6] Reuben Binns. 2017. Fairness in Machine Learning: Lessons from Political Philosophy. *arXiv preprint arXiv:1712.03586* (2017).
[7] Tolga Bolukbasi, Kai-Wei Chang, James Y Zou, Venkatesh Saligrama, and Adam T Kalai. 2016. Man is to computer programmer as woman is to homemaker? debiasing word embeddings. In *Advances in Neural Information Processing Systems*. 4349–4357.
[8] Leo Breiman et al. 2001. Statistical modeling: The two cultures (with comments and a rejoinder by the author). *Statistical science* 16, 3 (2001), 199–231.
[9] Kaylee Burns, Lisa Anne Hendricks, Trevor Darrell, and Anna Rohrbach. 2018. Women also Snowboard: Overcoming Bias in Captioning Models. *arXiv preprint arXiv:1803.09797* (2018).
[10] Toon Calders and Sicco Verwer. 2010. Three naive Bayes approaches for discrimination-free classification. *Data Mining and Knowledge Discovery* 21, 2 (2010), 277–292.
[11] Sam Corbett-Davies and Sharad Goel. 2018. The Measure and Mismeasure of Fairness: A Critical Review of Fair Machine Learning. *arXiv preprint arXiv:1808.00023* (2018).
[12] Roel Dobbe, Sarah Dean, Thomas Gilbert, and Nitin Kohli. 2018. A Broader View on Bias in Automated Decision-Making: Reflecting on Epistemology and Dynamics. *arXiv preprint arXiv:1807.00553* (2018).
[13] Cynthia Dwork, Moritz Hardt, Toniann Pitassi, Omer Reingold, and Richard Zemel. 2012. Fairness through awareness. In *Proceedings of the 3rd innovations in theoretical computer science conference*. ACM, 214–226.
[14] Sorelle A Friedler, Carlos Scheidegger, and Suresh Venkatasubramanian. 2016. On the (im) possibility of fairness. *arXiv preprint arXiv:1609.07236* (2016).
[15] Timnit Gebru, Jamie Morgenstern, Briana Vecchione, Jennifer Wortman Vaughan, Hanna Wallach, Hal Daumeé III, and Kate Crawford. 2018. Datasheets for Datasets. *arXiv preprint arXiv:1803.09010* (2018).
[16] Andrew Gelman, G Marrson, and Daniel Simpson. 2018. Gaydar and the fallacy of objective measurement. *Unpublished manuscript. Retrieved from http://www.*

stat. columbia. edu/~gelman/research/unpublished/gaydar2. pdf (2018).
[17] Tamar Szabó Gendler. 2008. Alief and belief. *The Journal of philosophy* 105, 10 (2008), 634–663.
[18] Ross Girshick, Jeff Donahue, Trevor Darrell, and Jitendra Malik. 2014. Rich feature hierarchies for accurate object detection and semantic segmentation. In *Proceedings of the IEEE conference on computer vision and pattern recognition*. 580–587.
[19] Dipayan Gosh. 2017. AI is the future of hiring, but it's far from immune to bias. *Quartz* (2017).
[20] Moritz Hardt, Eric Price, Nati Srebro, et al. 2016. Equality of opportunity in supervised learning. In *Advances in neural information processing systems*. 3315–3323.
[21] Jon Kleinberg, Sendhil Mullainathan, and Manish Raghavan. 2016. Inherent trade-offs in the fair determination of risk scores. *arXiv preprint arXiv:1609.05807* (2016).
[22] Jeff Larson, Surya Mattu, Lauren Kirchner, and Julia Angwin. 2016. How we analyzed the COMPAS recidivism algorithm. *ProPublica (5 2016)* 9 (2016).
[23] Greggor Mattson. 2017. Artificial Intelligence Discovers Gayface. Sigh. https://greggormattson.com/2017/09/09/artificial-intelligence-discovers-gayface/.
[24] Arianne E Miller. 2018. Searching for Gaydar: Blind spots in the study of sexual orientation perception. *Psychology & Sexuality* (2018), 1–16.
[25] Sendhil Mullainathan and Jann Spiess. 2017. Machine learning: an applied econometric approach. *Journal of Economic Perspectives* 31, 2 (2017), 87–106.
[26] Dierdre Mulligan, Amit Elazari, Jenna Burrell, and Daniel Kluttz. 2018. *AFOG workshop panel 2: Automated decision-making is imperfect, but it's arguably an improvement over biased human decision-making.* Technical Report. University of California, Berkeley.
[27] Heather Murphy. 2017. Why Stanford Researchers Tried to Create a 'Gaydar' Machine. *New York Times* (2017).
[28] Matt Olfat and Anil Aswani. 2017. Spectral Algorithms for Computing Fair Support Vector Machines. *arXiv preprint arXiv:1710.05895* (2017).
[29] Rob Price. 2016. Microsoft is deleting its AI chatbot's incredibly racist tweets. *Business Insider* (2016).
[30] H. Reese. 2016. Why microsoft's Tay AI bot went wrong. *Tech Republic* (2016).
[31] B. Resnick. 2018. This psychologistâĂŹs âĂIJgaydarâĂİ research makes us uncomfortable. ThatâĂŹs the point. *Vox* (2018).
[32] Jackie Snow. 2018. Google Photos Still Has a Problem with Gorillas. https://www.technologyreview.com/the-download/609959/google-photos-still-has-a-problem-with-gorillas/
[33] James Vincent. 2017. The invention of AI 'gaydar' could be the start of something much worse. *The Verge* (2017).
[34] Yilun Wang and Michal Kosinski. 2017. Deep neural networks are more accurate than humans at detecting sexual orientation from facial images. (2017).
[35] Muhammad Bilal Zafar, Isabel Valera, Manuel Gomez Rodriguez, and Krishna P Gummadi. 2015. Fairness constraints: Mechanisms for fair classification. *arXiv preprint arXiv:1507.05259* (2015).

A NOTES ON TECHNICAL TERMINOLOGY

Given the interdisciplinary nature of our problem, we will first provide working definitions for technical terminology borrowed from philosophy of mind, machine learning, and the social sciences.

AI models: the actual computational function used to perform some kind of prediction task, in isolation from data as well as human data scientists and engineers.

AI system: the operation of AI in its full production context (including input pipeline and downstream decisions). In general, when there is no qualifier before AI, we make reference to this term.

Anthropomorphic bias: The attribution of cognitive biases, emotions, or intentions to AI systems. Note that this does not include forms of statistical bias or inferential limitations (e.g. sampling errors, misspecification, accuracy thresholds), and instead conflates the epistemic frames of humans and automated systems.

Epistemic ethics: A set of design principles that specify how AI systems should be operated and implemented. We distinguish it from classical ethical frameworks (e.g. utilitarianism) that present guidelines for human behavior alone; instead, epistemic ethics comprises rules for the deployment of systems in a context-appropriate manner.

Moral dispositions: The set of unconscious or semi-conscious behaviors, acquired through habituation and remaining active over the long-term, that guide moral action and personal character. While originating in humans, we will explore how they are unintentionally transposed into AI systems and play a major role in anthropomorphic bias.

Techno-Societal Infrastructure: The dynamic relationship between AI models, data, and the individuals who design systems. It comprises all organizational resources responsible for an AI system's decision-making, rather than that system's mere operation. We refer interchangeably to data scientists, engineers, and machine learning researchers as the human component of this infrastructure.

Algorithmic Greenlining: An Approach to Increase Diversity

Christian Borgs
Jennifer Chayes
Nika Haghtalab
Adam Tauman Kalai
{christian.borgs,jchayes,nika.haghtalab,adam.kalai}@microsoft.com
Microsoft Research
Cambridge, Massachusetts

Ellen Vitercik
vitercik@cs.cmu.edu
Carnegie Mellon University
Pittsburgh, Pennsylvania

ABSTRACT

In contexts such as college admissions, hiring, and image search, decision-makers often aspire to formulate selection criteria that yield both high-quality and diverse results. However, simultaneously optimizing for quality and diversity can be challenging, especially when the decision-maker does not know the true quality of any criterion and instead must rely on heuristics and intuition. We introduce an algorithmic framework that takes as input a user's selection criterion, which may yield high-quality but homogeneous results. Using an application-specific notion of substitutability, our algorithms suggest similar criteria with more diverse results, in the spirit of statistical or demographic parity. For instance, given the image search query "chairman", it suggests alternative queries which are similar but more gender-diverse, such as "chairperson". In the context of college admissions, we apply our algorithm to a dataset of students' applications and rediscover Texas's "top 10% rule": the input criterion is an ACT score cutoff, and the output is a class rank cutoff, automatically accepting the students in the top decile of their graduating class. Historically, this policy has been effective in admitting students who perform well in college and come from diverse backgrounds. We complement our empirical analysis with learning-theoretic guarantees for estimating the true diversity of any criterion based on historical data.

CCS CONCEPTS

• **Social and professional topics → Race and ethnicity**; **Gender**; • **Theory of computation** → *Design and analysis of algorithms.*

KEYWORDS

diversity, algorithms, college admissions, job applicant search, image search

ACM Reference Format:
Christian Borgs, Jennifer Chayes, Nika Haghtalab, Adam Tauman Kalai, and Ellen Vitercik. 2019. Algorithmic Greenlining: An Approach to Increase Diversity. In *AAAI/ACM Conference on AI, Ethics, and Society (AIES '19), January 27–28, 2019, Honolulu, HI, USA.* ACM, New York, NY, USA, 8 pages. https://doi.org/10.1145/3306618.3314246

ACM ISBN 978-1-4503-6324-2/19/01...$15.00
https://doi.org/10.1145/3306618.3314246

1 INTRODUCTION

In many application domains such as college admissions, hiring, and image search, domain experts aim to develop selection criteria that yield high-quality and diverse results. However, they often operate under an unavoidable lack of information: they do not know the true quality of any given criterion, and instead must rely upon heuristics and intuition. This makes it difficult to simultaneously optimize quality and diversity. For example, consider choosing university admissions criteria, a scenario where there is extremely limited information about the true quality of any candidate. An admissions officer's intuition might suggest that admitting students with an SAT score above 1400 would provide high-quality candidates, but the criterion might admit few students from minority groups. Nonetheless, there may be similar criteria, such as "SAT score above 1200 and class rank in the top 10%" which yield high-quality and diverse student bodies. Of course, a human decision-maker cannot search over all related criteria by hand in order to discover criteria that return diverse results. In this work, we present a framework for automating this search procedure.

Our algorithms take as input a user-specified criterion t, a predefined similarity measure among criteria, and a set of examples. They suggest alternate criteria $t'_1, \ldots, t'_k$ with greater estimated diversity on the set of examples but which are similar to t. For example, t might be the image search query "haircut" and $t'_1, \ldots, t'_k$ might include related searches such as "hairstyles" and "popular haircuts". We model a criterion t as a function $t : X \to R$, where X is a set of observables, such as job applications, and R is a set of results, perhaps indicating whether an applicant is hired. Our algorithms rely on application-specific similarity functions which measure how substitutable any two criteria are. They also depend on functions that measure the diversity of any criterion's results. Our algorithms optimize the similarity function while meeting a desired diversity constraint.

We apply our framework in three key areas: college admissions, job search, and image search. In each application, we suggest

This research uses public data from the Texas Higher Education Opportunity Project (THEOP) and acknowledges the following agencies that made THEOP data available through grants and support: Ford Foundation, The Andrew W. Mellon Foundation, The William and Flora Hewlett Foundation, The Spencer Foundation, National Science Foundation (NSF Grant SES-0350990), The National Institute of Child Health & Human Development (NICHD Grant R24 H0047879) and The Office of Population Research at Princeton University.

straight-forward, natural substitutability and diversity measures, and then exemplify how our techniques can be used to find similar criteria that yield more diverse results. For example, in the case of college admissions, given two criteria t and t' and the sets E_t and $E_{t'}$ of students they admit, we measure the similarity of t and t' as a simple function of the symmetric difference between E_t and $E_{t'}$. As another example which illustrates the generality of our approach, we say that two jobs are similar if the requisite skills, education, and training are transferable, as formalized by the Department of Labor. We emphasize that in all of our applications, a domain expert could alter these two measures as they see fit. Our goal is not to nail down a universally optimal definition of substitutablity and diversity, but to introduce this technique to domain experts who can determine appropriate metrics for their specific applications. We also provide provable guarantees for estimating the diversity of any criterion given historical data. Thus, our algorithms can use diversity estimates instead of true diversity scores.

We call our approach *algorithmic greenlining* as it is the antithesis of redlining, the historic and systematic denial of services to residents of specific communities, often due to demographics. Greenlining is the conscious effort to promote minority interests and representation by using unbiased criteria in day-to-day settings. In this work, we provide individuals with computational tools to help them reduce the intentional or unintentional bias encoded by their criteria.

2 RELATED WORK

Algorithmic fairness using similarity metrics. Our notion of criterion similarity is reminiscent of the similarity metric used over people for *individually fair classification* [8]. As defined by [8], under an individually fair classification system, similar individuals should be treated (i.e., classified) similarly. Thus, it relies on a similarity metric between individuals, often based on high-dimensional attribute vectors. In contrast, we rely on a notion of similarity between criteria.

Algorithmic fairness with and without quality scores. We do not assume the user knows the true quality of any given criterion or outcome. Thus, we cannot measure criterion fairness using notions such as equalized odds [11] which depend on ground truth. Rather, we can use any notion that only depends on the outcomes of the criteria (e.g., the fraction of students accepted under a given university admissions criterion from a minority group), such as statistical parity [8].

Image search. Several works analyze the presence of bias in image results from major search engines [14, 16]. Others study how to achieve diversity in image search outside the context of algorithmic fairness. Given a query, these works provide algorithms that return many different kinds of images matching that query (e.g., [15, 22]). For example, an image search for "apple" should not only return images of the fruit, but also of the computer. Some works also study how to ensure the image search results exhibit racial and gender diversity [5]. In contrast, our goal is to provide search suggestions whose results are more diverse, rather than altering the images returned by a search.

Fair ranking. In a vein similar to image search, many researchers have studied how to rank a set of items fairly [2, 6, 13, 17, 23, 26] and how to measure the fairness of an existing ranking [23, 24]. Unlike our work, these works assume the algorithm has access to ground-truth quality scores.

Query suggestions. In addition to ranking, Information Retrieval systems often provide suggestions of alternative relevant searches (e.g., [12]). The goal has generally been to help the user better meet their information seeking needs. However, to the best of our knowledge, no prior work in this domain has considered fairness or diversity.

We include additional related work in the appendix.

3 THE GENERAL MODEL AND NOTATION

In our model, there is an underlying set $X \times Z$ of examples (x, z) where $x \in X$ represents the observable attributes of an instance and $z \in Z$ represents its protected attributes. There is a set T of criteria. Each criterion $t \in T$ is a function mapping the set X of observable attributes to a set R of results. For example, in the case of college admissions, $R = \{0, 1\}$ and $t(x) = 1$ if and only if the student with observable attributes x is admitted under criterion t.

We want to measure the diversity of a criterion given an arbitrary multi-set $E \subseteq X \times Z$ of examples. In the admissions example, E could be the set of students who apply to some university on a given year. When the results are binary ($R = \{0, 1\}$) given a multi-set of examples E, we use the notation $E_t = \{(x, z) \mid (x, z) \in E, t(x) = 1\}$ to denote the subset of examples $(x, z) \in E$ such that $t(x) = 1$.

For every multi-set $E \subseteq X \times Z$ of examples and every criterion $t \in T$, there is a diversity score $\mathtt{div}(t, E) \in [0, 1]$. For example, t might be a threshold indicating that all students with an SAT score above 600 should be admitted. Given the set E of students, $\mathtt{div}(t, E)$ might measure the fraction of admitted students who are Hispanic.

We assume we have a substitutability function σ where $\sigma(t, t', E) \in [0, 1]$ indicates how good a substitute t' is for t given the multi-set of examples E, not accounting for fairness or diversity. This captures how willing the agent would be to replace their criterion t with the criterion t'. For instance, someone searching for "doctor" might be happy to instead search for "physician". If each criterion is a range of admissible standardized test scores, a small change in thresholds might lead to a much more diverse set of admits. We assume that $\sigma(t, t, E) = 1$ for all $t \in T$ and all multi-sets $E \subseteq X \times Z$. We occasionally refer to the distance $\mathtt{dist}(t, t', E)$ between two criteria (using the word "distance" loosely: we do not require that $\mathtt{dist}$ be symmetric or that it satisfy the triangle inequality) and we define $\mathtt{dist}(t, t', E) = 1 - \sigma(t, t', E)$.

This definition of substitutability is extremely versatile: it can measure both intrinsic and extrinsic similarity. As an example of intrinsic similarity, we say at a high level that two jobs are similar if the requisite skills, education, and training are transferable, as formalized by the Department of Labor. In this case, $\sigma(t, t', E)$ is independet of E. Meanwhile, as an example of extrinsic similarity, we say that two university admissions criteria are similar if moving from one criterion to the other does not drastically change the set of admitted students. Thus, similarity is not intrinsic to the criteria themselves, but is a function of how they interact with the dataset at hand, i.e., $\sigma(t, t', E)$ depends on E as well as t and t'. Again, we emphasize that the similarity metrics we employ are only examples. A domain expert could employ any definition they see fit.

Given an initial criterion t, our goal is to suggest a criterion t' that is largely substitutable ($\sigma(t, t', E)$ is close to 1) and is diverse ($\mathtt{div}(t, E)$ is within a user-specified range).

Notation. We denote the ith entry of a vector $\boldsymbol{v}$ as $v[i]$.

4 GENERAL MODEL INSTANTIATIONS

We now instantiate our model in several settings: university admissions, image search, and job applicant search. In the appendix, we discuss the ethics of our data usage.

4.1 University admissions

We begin with a problem motivated by university admissions. We represent a set of applicants by feature vectors in $[0, H)^d$, for some $H \in \mathbb{R}$. We use data collected from the University of Texas at Austin by the Texas Higher Education Opportunity Project (THEOP). The features we focus on are the students' composite SAT scores, composite ACT scores, and high school class rank (higher is better). We select our minority group to consist of applicants who are identified as "Black, Non-Hispanic" or "Hispanic" ($z = 1$) and our majority group to consist of "White, Non-Hispanic" applicants ($z = 0$). Therefore, $X = [0, H)^d$ and $Z = \{0, 1\}$.

In our first experiment, the set T of criteria consists of all axis-aligned hyperplanes intersecting $[0, H]^d$. Specifically, each criterion $t \in T$ is defined by a dimension $i \in [d]$ and a threshold $b \in [0, H]$. The multi-set $E_t \subseteq E$ consists of those tuples $(\boldsymbol{x}, z)$ with $x[i] \geq b$. For any criterion t such that $E_t \neq \emptyset$, we define $f_m(t, E)$ to be the fraction of individuals accepted by t who are minorities, i.e., $f_m(t, E) = \frac{1}{|E_t|} \sum_{(\boldsymbol{x},z)\in E_t} z$. We define $\mathtt{div}$ to measure how far this fraction is from a user-specified diversity level c, i.e., $\mathtt{div}(t, E) = 1 - |c - f_m(t, E)|$.

We define the substitutability of two criteria t and t' based on the overlap of the students accepted under the two rules. Using $E_t \Delta E_{t'} = (E_t \cup E_{t'}) \setminus (E_t \cap E_{t'})$ to denote the symmetric difference between E_t and $E_{t'}$, we define

$$\sigma(t, t', E) = \begin{cases} 1 - \frac{|E_t \Delta E_{t'}|}{m} & \text{if } |E_t| \leq |E_{t'}| \leq 2\,|E_t| \\ 0 & \text{otherwise.} \end{cases}$$

By enforcing $|E_t| \leq |E_{t'}| \leq 2\,|E_t|$, the number of applicants admitted by the two criteria is not drastically different.

The multi-set E of feature vectors describes the first 50,000 applicants from the dataset who a) are identified as "White, Non-Hispanic," "Black, Non-Hispanic," or "Hispanic," and b) took the ACT. Of these, 24% are from the minority group. Based on this, we set the fraction c of minority students in the definition of the function $\mathtt{div}$ to be $c = 0.24$. Our input criterion t accepts all students whose cumulative ACT score is above 56 (the dotted line in Figure 1b), which includes 11,484 majority students and 1,298 minority students, so $\mathtt{div}(t, E) = 0.87$.

Our goal is to find a criterion t' such that $\mathtt{div}(t', E) \geq 0.95$ (i.e., the fraction of admitted minority students is in $[0.19, 0.29]$) and $\sigma(t, t', E)$ is as close to 1 as possible. (The threshold 0.95 could be replaced by any other bound.) This is summarized by the following optimization problem:

$$\text{maximize } \sigma(t, t', E) \text{ subject to } \mathtt{div}(t', E) \geq 0.95. \qquad (1)$$

The new criterion's output will be different from the original criterion's output since it will be more diverse, but the change will be as small possible. Under the optimal solution to Equation (1), students from the top 10% of their class are admitted. This criterion t' is illustrated by the solid line in Figure 1c. It admits 14,582 majority and 5,576 minority students, so $\mathtt{div}(t', E) = 0.96$. Moreover, $\sigma(t, t', E) = 0.69$.

We thus rediscover the "top 10% rule" passed in 1997 by the Texas legislature (H.B.588), which guarantees any Texas student in the top 10% of their graduating class admission into any of Texas's public post-secondary institutions.

In the full version of the paper, we describe our experiments in a more general setting where each criterion is represented by the intersection of multiple axis-aligned half-spaces. For example, a criterion might require that an admitted applicant has an ACT score above 50 and is in the top 40% of her class. This generalization allows us to preserve a higher degree of similarity while still increasing diversity. See Figure 2 for a visualization of our experimental results.

4.2 Image search

In image search, our goal is to provide users with similar image search terms that yield more diverse results. For example, if a user begins with the Google search "haircut", the resulting images are often surprisingly male-dominated. However, we find that there are often similar queries, such as "popular haircuts", which return more images of women.

Our model applies to any search engine, but we concentrate on Google and Bing in our experiments. We define the set X of observable attributes to be the set of all images indexed by Google and $Z = \{0, 1\}$ to be the set of sensitive attributes indicating gender. In particular, given an example (x, z), $z = 0$ if and only if x is an image of a man. We define the set of input examples E to be the entire set $X \times Z$. Given a search criterion t such as "haircut", we define $t(x)$ to be 1 if the image x is displayed in the first fifty images returned by a Google search for t and 0 otherwise, filtering Google's results so that they only return images of faces.

We adopt a simple diversity metric: given a search term t and the top fifty images returned by this search, how far from 50-50 is the gender ratio? In other words, $\mathtt{div}(t, E) = 1 - \left|\frac{1}{2} - \frac{1}{50} \sum_{(x,z)\in E_t} z\right|$. Given an even split, $\frac{1}{50} \sum_{(x,z)\in E_t} z = \frac{1}{2}$, so $\mathtt{div}(t, E) = 1$, and the closer $\frac{1}{50} \sum_{(x,z)\in E_t} z$ is to 0 or 1, the smaller $\mathtt{div}(t, E)$ is.

We base our similarity metric between search terms on Bing's lists of related searches. (We define diversity based on Google and similarity based on Bing so that our results are not concentrated on one search engine.) Whether the search engine suggests a given term depends on the similarity between that term and the original term. We assume that the higher in the list a term is, the more similar it is to the original search. Thus, we define the distance $\mathtt{dist}(t, t', E)$ (where $\mathtt{dist}(t, t', E) = 1 - \sigma(t, t', E)$) to be the position of t' in the list of related searches given the original search term t, divided by the list's length, or 1 if t' is not in the list.

In Figure 3, we display plots for two different searches. For the sake of readability, we only plot a subset of the related searches.

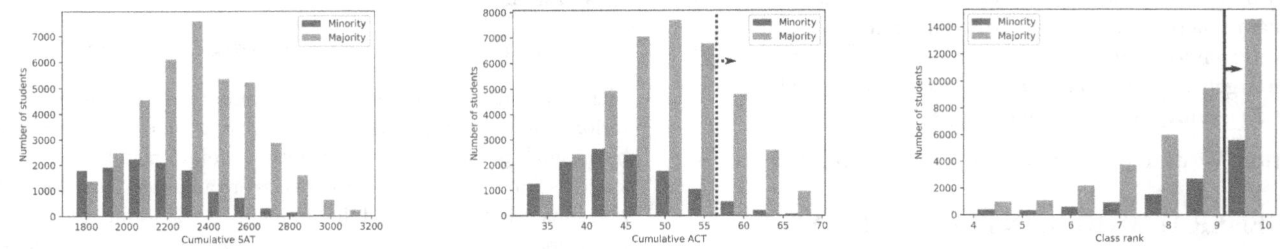

(a) Cumulative SAT scores.

(b) Cumulative ACT scores with original criterion: ACT score above 56.

(c) Class rank with suggested criterion: top 10%.

Figure 1: University admissions when each criterion is defined by an axis-aligned half-space. The orange bars indicate the number of white, non-Hispanic students whose features fall within a given range. The blue bars correspond to the black and Hispanic students. The dotted line in Figure 1b represents the original criterion (cumulative ACT score above 56). The solid line in Figure 1c represents the criterion returned by the system (class rank in the top decile).

We can see that some searches have nearby searches with diverse search results. For example, "neckerchief" is similar to "scarf", but the images associated with "scarf" are almost all of women whereas the images associate with "neckerchief" have a more balanced gender ratio.

4.3 Job search

We next instantiate our general model for job applicant search. Given a recruiter's original query such as "computer programmer", the goal is to provide her with alternative search queries that return diverse sets of applicants.

To instantiate our general model, we define the set X of observable attributes to be an abstract set of job applicants' observable attributes. For example, X could be a set of individuals' LinkedIn profiles. Let $Z = \{0, 1\}$ be the set of sensitive attributes which indicate gender. In particular, given an example (x, z), $z = 0$ if and only if x corresponds to a man. In this setting, we define the set of input examples E to be the entire set $X \times Z$. Each criterion $t \in T$ corresponds to an occupation. Given an individual (x, z), we define $t(x)$ to be 1 if the individual is applying for the job t and 0 otherwise.

To measure diversity, we use workforce statistics from the [19]. Given an occupation t, these statistics tell us the fraction ω_t of full-time workers in the U.S. with that job year-round who are women. We define diversity to measure how far from $\frac{1}{2}$ that fraction is, i.e., $\mathtt{div}(t, E) = 1 - \left|\frac{1}{2} - \omega_t\right|$. If there is a 50-50 gender split, then $\omega_t = \frac{1}{2}$ and $\mathtt{div}(t, E) = 1$. Meanwhile, the closer ω_t is to 0 or 1, the smaller $\mathtt{div}(t, E)$ is.

In order to characterize similarity among jobs, we use the Department of Labor's Standard Occupational Classification (SOC) System, which organizes hundreds of occupations into a single hierarchy. Occupations are grouped together if they have similar duties or require similar skills, education, or training [20]. For a small subset of the hierarchy, see Figure 5 in the appendix. We define the similarity of two jobs based on the length of the path between them in the hierarchy. For two jobs t and t', let $\ell(t, t')$ be the length of this path. The maximum path length between any two leafs in this hierarchy is 8. Thus, we define the substitutability of two jobs t and t' as $\sigma(t, t', E) = 1 - \frac{\ell(t,t')}{8}$ so that it is in [0, 1].

In Figure 4, we display plots for two occupations. We can see that some occupations have nearby occupations with more diverse workforces. For example, "web developer" is similar to "computer programmer", but there are more female web developers than computer programmers.

5 DIVERSITY ESTIMATION GUARANTEES

In this section, we provide provable guarantees for finding similar criteria with more diverse results. Here, our goal is to estimate the diversity of any given criterion using historical data. Calculating reliable diversity estimates is crucial because in some settings, it may be preferable or even mandatory to avoid using individuals' protected attributes to measure diversity. For example, an admissions officer may not know the ethnicity of any college applicant from the current year. However, they may have access to historical data, such as the University of Texas data we use to run our experiments, which they can use to form these estimates. Furthermore, given estimates that reflect the diversity of any criterion over society as a whole, a user can introduce policies, such as a fixed college admissions criterion, that can stay in place for years at a time. For example, they can be confident that admitting students based on class rank will consistently yield more diverse student bodies than admitting students based on standardized test scores. Finally, using diversity estimates rather than true diversity scores in order to choose among criteria means that no individual will be favored based on his or her sensitive attributes.

Throughout this section, we consider a setting where a criterion t is a map $t : X \to \{0, 1\}$. Given an example (x, z), $z \in [0, 1]$ is the degree to which x belongs to the minority group. Given a multi-set $E = \{(x_1, z_1), \dots, (x_N, z_N)\}$ of examples, we define $f_m(t, E)$ to be the degree to which an average instance $(x, z) \in E_t$ belongs to the minority group. In other words, $f_m(t, E) = \frac{1}{|E_t|}\sum_{(x,z)\in E_t} z$. Recall that in the university admissions setting, we define $\mathtt{div}(t, E)$ to measure how far $f_m(t, E)$ is from a user-specified $c \in [0, 1]$, i.e., $\mathtt{div}(t, E) = 1 - |c - f_m(t, E)|$. To justify this choice of $\mathtt{div}(t, E)$, we prove that $f_m(t, E)$ estimates the protected attribute of an example

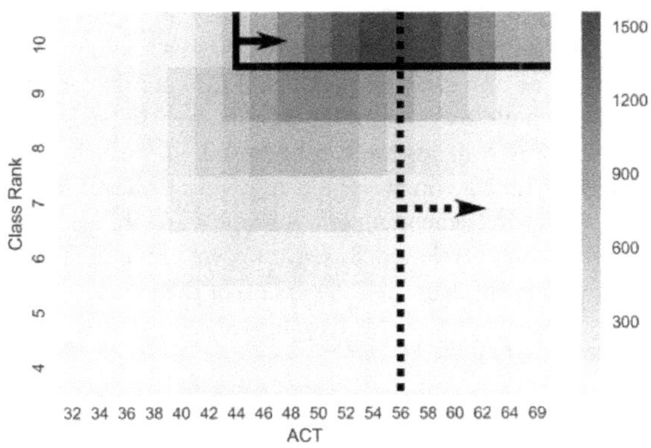

(a) Majority students' ACT scores versus class ranks.

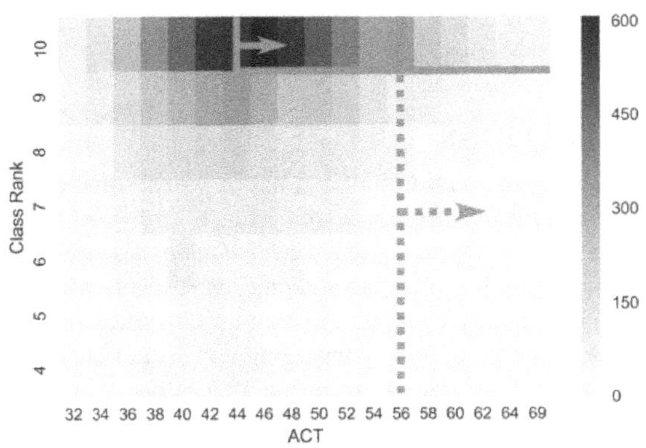

(b) Minority students' ACT scores versus class ranks.

Figure 2: University admissions when each criterion is defined by the intersection of axis-aligned half-spaces. The plots display the majority (Figure 2a) and minority (Figure 2b) groups' ACT scores versus class ranks. The colorbars indicate the number of students who fall in each bin. The dotted lines represent the original criterion: ACT score above 56. The solid lines represent the suggested criterion: ACT score above 44 and class rank in the top decile.

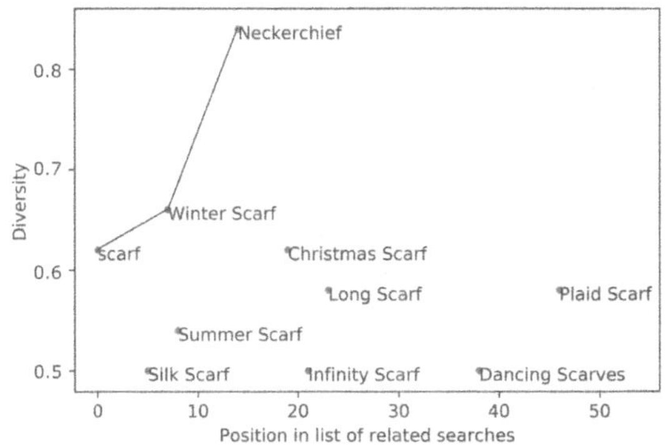

(a) Original search: "scarf"

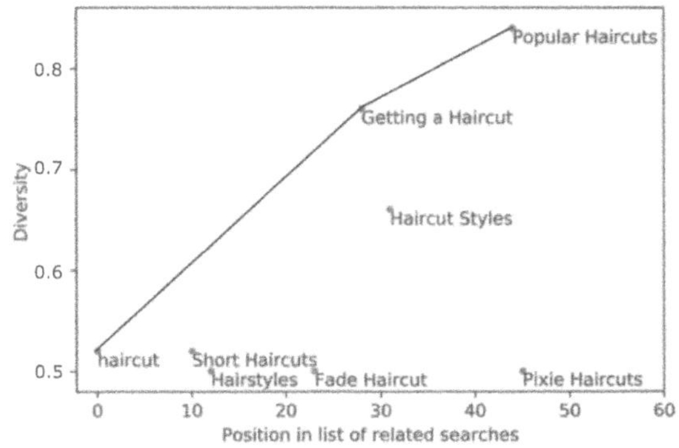

(b) Original search: "haircut"

Figure 3: Plots for image search. The position on the x-axis of a image search t' equals its position in Bing's list of search terms related to the original search t. Its position on the y-axis equals the diversity $\texttt{div}(t, t', E)$. The line illustrates the Pareto frontier of this bi-criteria optimization problem.

$(x, z) \sim \mu$ conditioned on $t(x) = 1$. In other words, $f_m(t, E)$ approximates $\mathbb{E}_{(x,z)\sim\mu}[z \mid t(x) = 1]$ for all $t \in T$ so long as E has a sufficiently large number of candidates. That is, we show that with probability at least $1 - \delta$ over the draw of $E = \{(x_1, z_1), \dots, (x_N, z_N)\} \sim \mu^N$, for all $t \in T$ such that $\Pr_{(x,z)}[t(x) = 1] \geq c$, we have that $\left|f_m(t, E) - \mathbb{E}_{(x,z)\sim\mu}[z \mid t(x) = 1]\right| \leq \epsilon$ when N is sufficiently large with respect to ϵ, δ, and c.

We use the learning-theoretic notion of VC dimension [21] to provide this sample complexity guarantee. VC dimension measures the *intrinsic complexity* of binary-valued function classes, or in other words, classes of functions that map to $\{0, 1\}$. Given a set $\mathcal{G}$ of functions which map an abstract domain $\mathcal{A}$ to $\{0, 1\}$ and a distribution μ' over $\mathcal{A}$, bounding the VC dimension of $\mathcal{G}$ allows us to bound the number of samples $a_1, \dots, a_N \sim \mu'$ sufficient to ensure that the difference between the average value $\frac{1}{N}\sum_{i=1}^{N} g(a_i)$ of any function $g \in \mathcal{G}$ over the samples and its expected value $\mathbb{E}_{a\sim\mu'}[g(a)]$ is small. VC dimension applies specifically to binary-valued functions, so it does not immediately apply to our setting because the protected attributes z are real-valued and we are concerned with the conditional expectation $\mathbb{E}[z \mid t(x) = 1]$, not the expectation $\mathbb{E}[z]$. Nonetheless, we show how to use the VC dimension of T to bound the number of samples sufficient to ensure the difference between $f_m(t, E)$ and $\mathbb{E}[z \mid t(x) = 1]$ is small, for any criterion $t \in T$. In many applications, bounding the VC dimension of T is simple, so applying this sample complexity bound is straight-forward.

Below, we define VC dimension in terms of an abstract set of functions $\mathcal{G}$ which map a domain $\mathcal{A}$ to $\{0, 1\}$.

Definition 5.1 (VC dimension). We say that $\mathcal{G}$ shatters the set $\mathcal{S} = \{a_1, \dots, a_M\} \subseteq \mathcal{A}$ if for all binary vectors $\boldsymbol{b} \in \{0, 1\}^M$, there is a function $g_{\boldsymbol{b}} \in \mathcal{G}$ such that $g_{\boldsymbol{b}}(a_i) = \boldsymbol{b}[i]$ for all $i \in [M]$. The VC dimension of $\mathcal{G}$, denoted $\text{VCdim}(\mathcal{G})$, is the size of the largest set that $\mathcal{G}$ shatters.

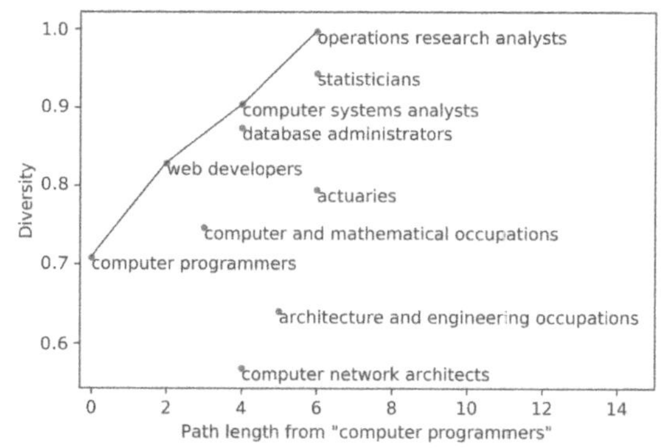

(a) Original search: "computer programmers"

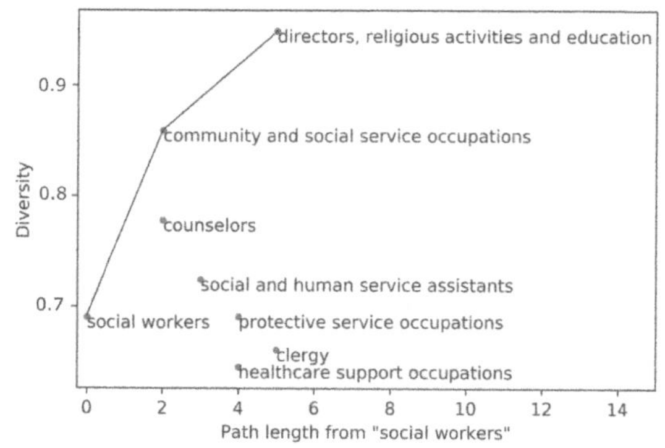

(b) Original search: "social workers"

Figure 4: Plots for job search. The position on the x-axis of a job t' equals the path length between it and the original search t' in the SOC hierarchy. Its position on the y-axis equals the diversity $\mathtt{div}(t, t', E)$. The line illustrates the Pareto frontier of this bi-criteria optimization problem.

For example, recall the college admissions criteria we study: axis-aligned half-spaces and the intersection of axis-aligned half-spaces in $\mathbb{R}^d$. For both, $\text{VCdim}(T) \in O(d)$.

We now present our sample complexity bound. The proof is in the full version of the paper.

THEOREM 5.2. *For any $\epsilon \in (0, 1/2)$ and $\delta \in (0, 1)$, with probability $1 - \delta$ over the draw $E = \{(x_1, z_1), \ldots, (x_N, z_N)\} \sim \mu^N$, for all $t \in T$ such that $\Pr_{(x,z)}[t(x) = 1] \geq c$, $\left|f_m(t, E) - \mathbb{E}_{(x,z)\sim\mu}[z \mid t(x) = 1]\right| \leq \epsilon$ when $N \geq N_0 \in O\left(\frac{1}{c\epsilon^2}\left(\text{VCdim}(T) \log \frac{1}{\epsilon} + \log \frac{1}{\delta}\right)\right)$.*

5.1 Estimation with correlated examples

Theorem 5.2 applies when the examples (x, z) are identically and independently distributed. In this section, we provide diversity estimation guarantees even when the examples are correlated. Rather than the i.i.d. assumption, we assume there is a distribution $\bar{\mu}$ over datasets E of a fixed size m, so the support of $\bar{\mu}$ is a subset of $(X \times Z)^m$. We show how to use a set $S = \left\{E^{(1)}, \ldots, E^{(N)}\right\} \sim \bar{\mu}^N$ to estimate $\mathbb{E}_{E\sim\bar{\mu}}[f_m(t, E)]$ for any criterion $t \in T$. One way to interpret this result is in the setting where we wish to design admissions criteria for a network of universities, such as all U.S. public community colleges. If we have a criterion that admits diverse students over a random set of N colleges, we can be confident the criterion also admits diverse students on average nationwide. Colleges may have correlated applicants depending on geography, and this section's results allow for this correlation. Specifically, we prove the following guarantee. The proof is in the full version of the paper.

THEOREM 5.3. *For any $\epsilon, \delta \in (0, 1)$,*

$$N \geq N_0 \in \Theta\left(\frac{1}{\epsilon^2}\left(\text{VCdim}(T) \log\left(m\text{VCdim}(T)\right) + \log \frac{1}{\delta}\right)\right)$$

samples are sufficient to ensure that with probability $1 - \delta$ over the draw of $E^{(1)}, \ldots, E^{(N)} \sim \bar{\mu}$, for all $t \in T$,

$$\left|\frac{1}{N}\sum_{i=1}^{N} f_m\left(t, E^{(i)}\right) - \mathbb{E}_{E\sim\bar{\mu}}[f_m(t, E)]\right| \leq \epsilon.$$

6 LIMITATIONS

We now describe several limitations of our work, some of which suggest directions for future research.

Scholars [10] have argued that *color-blind admissions criteria*, like those we study, are less effective at admitting students with strong academic performance compared to race-aware criteria. However, race-aware criteria may not be legal in many scenarios, in which case our approach presents a promising alternative.

A second limitation is that it may be computationally expensive to search for similar criteria yielding more diverse results. For example, this is the case in our university admissions application when each criterion is defined by the intersection of half-spaces. In fact, we prove that this problem is NP-complete in the appendix. Formulating an approximation algorithm is a promising direction for future work.

Lastly, if there is no clear notion of substitutability among criteria, then our framework will not apply. However, we believe our examples illustrate that there are often straight-forward ways to define substitutability.

7 CONCLUSION

We study the problem of suggesting similar criteria that yield more diverse results. In our setting, a domain expert chooses some selection criterion, such as an admissions criterion to choose among a set of college applicants. We do not assume she knows the true quality of any given criterion, or that the notion of "true quality" is well-defined. Rather, she uses heuristics and intuition to select a criterion she believes will return high-quality results. At the same time, this expert would like to ensure the results are diverse, but optimizing for diversity and quality may be difficult without access to ground-truth quality metrics. We introduce automated techniques for suggesting similar criteria yielding more diverse results. We demonstrate its strong performance in three critical domains: college admissions, image search, and job search. Finally, we complement our experiments with theoretical guarantees, analyzing the amount of historical data required to estimate criteria diversity.

REFERENCES

[1] Alekh Agarwal, Alina Beygelzimer, Miroslav Dudík, John Langford, and Hanna Wallach. 2018. A reductions approach to fair classification. *Proceedings of the International Conference on Machine Learning (ICML)* (2018).

[2] Asia J Biega, Krishna P Gummadi, and Gerhard Weikum. 2018. Equity of Attention: Amortizing Individual Fairness in Rankings. *Conference on Research and Development in Information Retrieval (SIGIR)* (2018).

[3] Tolga Bolukbasi, Kai-Wei Chang, James Y. Zou, Venkatesh Saligrama, and Adam Tauman Kalai. 2016. Man is to Computer Programmer as Woman is to Homemaker? Debiasing Word Embeddings. In *Proceedings of the Annual Conference on Neural Information Processing Systems (NIPS)*.

[4] Aylin Caliskan, Joanna J. Bryson, and Arvind Narayanan. 2017. Semantics derived automatically from language corpora contain human-like biases. *Science* 356, 6334 (2017), 183–186.

[5] L Elisa Celis, Vijay Keswani, Damian Straszak, Amit Deshpande, Tarun Kathuria, and Nisheeth K Vishnoi. 2018. Fair and Diverse DPP-based Data Summarization. *arXiv preprint arXiv:1802.04023* (2018).

[6] L. Elisa Celis, Damian Straszak, and Nisheeth K. Vishnoi. 2018. Ranking with Fairness Constraints. In *Proceedings of the International Colloquium on Automata, Languages and Programming (ICALP)*.

[7] Flavio Chierichetti, Ravi Kumar, Silvio Lattanzi, and Sergei Vassilvitskii. 2017. Fair Clustering Through Fairlets. In *Proceedings of the Annual Conference on Neural Information Processing Systems (NIPS)*.

[8] Cynthia Dwork, Moritz Hardt, Toniann Pitassi, Omer Reingold, and Richard Zemel. 2012. Fairness Through Awareness. In *Proceedings of the ACM Conference on Innovations in Theoretical Computer Science (ITCS)*.

[9] Cynthia Dwork, Nicole Immorlica, Adam Tauman Kalai, and Mark DM Leiserson. 2018. Decoupled Classifiers for Group-Fair and Efficient Machine Learning. In *Proceedings of the Conference on Fairness, Accountability and Transparency (FAT*)*.

[10] Roland G Fryer Jr, Glenn C Loury, and Tolga Yuret. 2007. An economic analysis of color-blind affirmative action. *The Journal of Law, Economics, & Organization* 24, 2 (2007), 319–355.

[11] Moritz Hardt, Eric Price, and Nati Srebro. 2016. Equality of Opportunity in Supervised Learning. In *Proceedings of the Annual Conference on Neural Information Processing Systems (NIPS)*.

[12] Rosie Jones, Benjamin Rey, Omid Madani, and Wiley Greiner. 2006. Generating query substitutions. In *Proceedings of the International World Wide Web Conference (WWW)*.

[13] Chen Karako and Putra Manggala. 2018. Using Image Fairness Representations in Diversity-Based Re-ranking for Recommendations. In *Proceedings of the Workshop on Fairness, Accountability, and Transparency in Machine Learning (FATML)*.

[14] Matthew Kay, Cynthia Matuszek, and Sean A Munson. 2015. Unequal representation and gender stereotypes in image search results for occupations. In *Proceedings of the Conference on Human Factors in Computing Systems (CHI)*.

[15] Lyndon S Kennedy and Mor Naaman. 2008. Generating diverse and representative image search results for landmarks. In *Proceedings of the International World Wide Web Conference (WWW)*.

[16] Jahna Otterbacher, Jo Bates, and Paul Clough. 2017. Competent men and warm women: Gender stereotypes and backlash in image search results. In *Proceedings of the Conference on Human Factors in Computing Systems (CHI)*.

[17] Ashudeep Singh and Thorsten Joachims. 2018. Fairness of Exposure in Rankings. *Proceedings of the ACM SIGKDD International Conference on Knowledge Discovery and Data Mining* (2018).

[18] Texas Higher Education Opportunity Project. 2008. Administrative College Application Data: Documentation for Public Use Data Files. https://theop.princeton.edu/admin_doc.html.

[19] U.S. Census Bureau. 2016. Full-Time, Year-Round Workers and Median Earnings: 2000 and 2013-2016. https://www.census.gov/data/tables/time-series/demo/industry-occupation/median-earnings.html.

[20] U.S. Office of Management and Budget. 2018. Standard Occupational Classification Manual. https://www.bls.gov/soc/2018/soc_2018_manual.pdf.

[21] Vladimir Vapnik and Alexey Chervonenkis. 1971. On the uniform convergence of relative frequencies of events to their probabilities. *Theory of Probability and its Applications* 16, 2 (1971), 264–280.

[22] Meng Wang, Kuiyuan Yang, Xian-Sheng Hua, and Hong-Jiang Zhang. 2010. Towards a relevant and diverse search of social images. *IEEE Transactions on Multimedia* 12, 8 (2010), 829–842.

[23] Ke Yang and Julia Stoyanovich. 2017. Measuring fairness in ranked outputs. In *Proceedings of the Conference on Scientific and Statistical Database Management (SSDBM)*.

[24] Ke Yang, Julia Stoyanovich, Abolfazl Asudeh, Bill Howe, HV Jagadish, and Gerome Miklau. 2018. A Nutritional Label for Rankings. In *Proceedings of the Conference on Management of Data (SIGMOD)*.

[25] Muhammad Bilal Zafar, Isabel Valera, Manuel Gomez Rodriguez, and Krishna P Gummadi. 2017. Fairness constraints: Mechanisms for fair classification. *Proceedings of the International Conference on Artificial Intelligence and Statistics (AISTATS)* (2017).

[26] Meike Zehlike, Francesco Bonchi, Carlos Castillo, Sara Hajian, Mohamed Megahed, and Ricardo Baeza-Yates. 2017. Fa*ir: A fair top-k ranking algorithm. In *Proceedings of the Conference on Information and Knowledge Management (CIKM)*.

A ADDITIONAL RELATED WORK

From a computational perspective, researchers studying algorithmic fairness have developed many algorithms assuming access to ground truth quality scores of individuals or outcomes. For example, in fair binary classification, a learning algorithm receives as input a training set of examples (x, y, z) where x is a set of observable attributes, z is a set of protected attributes, and y is a ground truth binary label. The goal is to learn a binary classifier which nearly matches the training set's ground truth labels, and which satisfies a given notion of fairness (e.g., [1, 9, 11, 25]). Thus, the quality of a classifier is clear: it measures how well that classifier matches the training set or a test set of fresh examples, potentially with the addition of a fairness loss function. In our setting however, the true quality of any given criterion may not even be defined.

Several papers have studied fair machine learning in the context of unsupervised learning, though in settings that are orthogonal to ours. These include works on fair clustering [7] and bias in word embeddings [3, 4].

B ETHICAL DATA USAGE

In this section, we discuss the ethics of our data usage. We use human data in two settings: college admissions and image search.

College admissions data. We use college admissions data collected by the Texas Higher Education Opportunity Project (THEOP), which is a part of Princeton University's Office of Population Research. We use a public use dataset which consists of college application data collected from the University of Texas at Austin, spanning from 1991 to 2003. Princeton's Institutional Review Board approved the administrative data collection and also the public release files. We requested access to these files and were granted it.

According to the data documentation [18], THEOP has taken steps to de-identify the data, including:

- Eliminating university-assigned applicant identification numbers and high school names, cities, and states.
- Eliminating small frequency (less than 20) cells by collapsing multiple values into range categories. For example, individual test score values are collapsed into test score ranges.
- Setting some values to missing to preserve the well-established categories but to hide individual values.

Nevertheless, it might be possible to re-identify individuals in this dataset. However, since this data is publicly available and (to the best of our knowledge) has been used by researchers in hundreds of academic works, we believe that our use of the dataset will not increase the risk of re-identification.

Image search. The other setting in which we use human data is image search. We do not download or store any images – we only store statistics in the form of Figure 3. We do not believe there is any risk of re-identification from these general statistics.

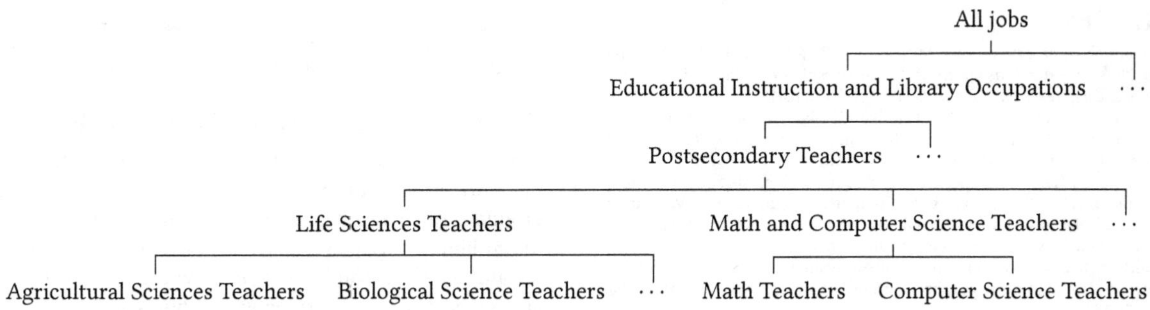

Figure 5: A small subset of the Department of Labor's Standard Occupational Classification System.

Active Fairness in Algorithmic Decision Making

Alejandro Noriega-Campero*
Massachusetts Institute of Technology
Cambridge, Massachusetts

Michiel A. Bakker*
Massachusetts Institute of Technology
Cambridge, Massachusetts

Bernardo Garcia-Bulle
Mexican Institute of Technology
Mexico City, Mexico

Alex 'Sandy' Pentland
Massachusetts Institute of Technology
Cambridge, Massachusetts

ABSTRACT

Society increasingly relies on machine learning models for automated decision making. Yet, efficiency gains from automation have come paired with concern for algorithmic discrimination that can systematize inequality. Recent work has proposed optimal post-processing methods that randomize classification decisions for a fraction of individuals, in order to achieve fairness measures related to parity in errors and calibration. These methods, however, have raised concern due to the information inefficiency, intra-group unfairness, and Pareto sub-optimality they entail. The present work proposes an alternative *active* framework for fair classification, where, in deployment, a decision-maker adaptively acquires information according to the needs of different groups or individuals, towards balancing disparities in classification performance. We propose two such methods, where information collection is adapted to group- and individual-level needs respectively. We show on real-world datasets that these can achieve: 1) calibration and single error parity (e.g., *equal opportunity*); and 2) parity in both false positive and false negative rates (i.e., *equal odds*). Moreover, we show that by leveraging their additional degree of freedom, *active* approaches can substantially outperform randomization-based classifiers previously considered optimal, while avoiding limitations such as intra-group unfairness.

KEYWORDS

algorithmic fairness, adaptive inquiry, active feature acquisition

ACM Reference format:
Alejandro Noriega-Campero*, Michiel A. Bakker*, Bernardo Garcia-Bulle, and Alex 'Sandy' Pentland. 2019. Active Fairness in Algorithmic Decision Making. In *Proceedings of AAAI/ACM Conference on AI, Ethics, and Society, Honolulu, HI, USA, January 27–28, 2019 (AIES '19)*, 7 pages.
https://doi.org/10.1145/3306618.3314277

*Authors contributed equally to this work.

AIES '19, January 27–28, 2019, Honolulu, HI, USA

ACM ISBN 978-1-4503-6324-2/19/01.
https://doi.org/10.1145/3306618.3314277

1 INTRODUCTION

As automated decision-making systems (ADMs) have become increasingly ubiquitous—e.g., in criminal justice [16], medical diagnosis and treatment [15], human resource management [3], social work [9], credit [12], and insurance [25]—there is widespread concern about how these can deepen social inequalities and systematize discrimination. Consequently, substantial work on defining and optimizing for algorithmic fairness has surged in the last few years.

Inspired by domains such as race biases in criminal risk predictions [7], a substantial body of literature has focused on the problem of balancing classification errors across protected population subgroups, towards achieving equal false positive rates, false negative rates, or both (*equal odds*). To that end, recent research has proposed "optimal" post-processing methods that randomize decisions of a fraction of individuals to attain *group fairness* [11, 21]. Yet, strong limitations of randomized approaches have been noted, such as information wastefulness, Pareto sub-optimality, and intra-group unfairness [5, 11, 21].

Our work aims at overcoming such limitations. We propose a complementary approach, *active fairness*, where, in deployment, an ADM adaptively collects information (features) about decision subjects; gathering more information about groups or individuals harder to classify, towards achieving equity in predictive performance. Thereby, the approach leverages a natural affordance of many real-world decision systems—adaptive information collection—and allocates an ADM's information budget according to group- or individual-level needs.

Summary of contributions. We propose two methods for achieving fairness, based on group-level and individual-level budgets. We show that, without resorting to randomization, these methods are able to achieve: a) calibration and a single-error parity constraint, and b) parity in both false positive and false negative rates (i.e., *equal odds*). We show in four real-world datasets that, with constrained information budgets, active approaches can substantially outperform randomized approaches previously considered optimal (lower false positive and false negative rates) by leveraging information collection as an extra degree of freedom. Finally, we show that classifiers using individual-level budgets in combination with active inquiry tend to dominate classifiers that use group-level budget constraints.

Intuition and motivating contexts. Consider a patient entering a hospital seeking diagnosis that typically undergoes a progressive inquiry—measuring vitals, procuring lab tests, specialists' opinions, etc. At each step, absent sufficient certainty, the inquiry continues. Intuitively, a fair health system allocates resources to provide all patients similar-quality diagnoses. Likewise, active inquiry under cost constraints underlies contexts like disaster response, poverty mapping, homeland security, recruitment, telemedicine, refugee status determination, credit and insurance pricing, etc.

Problem formulation. Let X be an $n \times d$ feature matrix. Let $X^{(q)} \subset X$ denote a query on a subset of features in X, with $q \subset \{0, ..., d\}$, and $x_i^{(q)}$ the partial feature vector of individual i; and let $f(X^{(q)})$ be a predictor of class probability $P\{Y = 1|X^{(q)}\}$. We study the classification context in which a decision-maker can choose what information to collect about each decision subject, and seeks to maximize accuracy and fairness under an information budget constraint $\bar{b} = \frac{1}{n}\sum_i b_i < b_{max}$, where $b_i = |q_i| \in [0, d]$ is the amount of information collected for individual i.

Although this setting is natural to many real-world decision systems, its affordances and implications to algorithmic decision systems—at the intersection of accuracy, fairness, and cost-efficiency—have not been thoroughly studied. Here, we focus on contexts with constant costs across features. Yet we note that the active fairness framework allows generalizations to contexts with varied costs across features, as well as richer and context-specific utility functions with potential costs to decision-subjects, such as monetary, opportunity, or privacy costs.

2 RELATED WORK

Active feature acquisition (AFA). Several probabilistic and non-probabilistic methods exist for sequential feature querying under budget constraints [8, 18], dating at least back to [20], and applied in domains such as medical diagnosis [10], customer targeting [14], and image classification [8]. To the best of our knowledge, this work is the first to study the implications AFA has to the algorithmic fairness literature and policy debate. Here, we use an approach based on probabilistic random forests, but more sophisticated methods can be used, for example, for dealing with domains with very high-dimensional input like medical images [26].

Active learning. Similar to the general AFA setting, this paper assumes that a fixed set of training data is used and that incremental features of a test sample can be queried. This differs from the active learning setting in which the system actively queries training examples that optimize learning e.g. by balancing exploration and exploitation, or by maximizing the expected model change [24]. We foresee future work studying synergies in systems that attain fairness by actively choosing training samples using active learning while also applying AFA at test time.

Notions of fairness. Several notions of fairness and their corresponding formalizations have been proposed, most of which require that statistical properties hold across two or more population subgroups. *Demographic* or *statistical parity* requires that decision rates are independent from group membership [2, 19, 28], such that $P\{\hat{Y} = 1|A = 0\} = P\{\hat{Y} = 1|A = 1\}$, for the case of binary classification and a sensitive attribute $A \in \{0, 1\}$. Most recent work focuses on meritocratic notions of fairness, or *error rate matching* [1, 11], such as requiring population subgroups to have equal false positive rates (FPR), equal false negative rates (FNR), or both, i.e., $P\{\hat{Y} = 1|A = 0, Y = y\} = P\{\hat{Y} = 1|A = 1, Y = y\}$, $y \in 0, 1$. In this work we focus on the latter set of fairness notions, although generalizations to others, such as statistical parity, are possible. Refer to [29] for a survey on computational measures of fairness.

Achieving Equal Opportunity and Equal Odds

Hardt et al. 2016 proposes parity in FNRs and/or parity in FPRs as a measure of unfair discrimination across population subgroups [11]. Parity in both types of error is referred to as *equal odds*. Its relaxation, equality in only FPRs, is conceptualized as *equal opportunity*, as in contexts of positive classification it means that subjects within the positive class have an equal probability of being correctly classified positive, regardless of group membership.

Equal opportunity can be achieved simply by shifting up or down the decision threshold t_A—where $\hat{Y} = 1_{[t_A, 1]}\big(\hat{P}(Y = 1|X, A)\big)$—for group A or A^{C}. Yet, doing so also directly affects FNRs, impeding achievement of *equal odds*. In this context, Hardt et al. 2016 propose a classifier that balances both FPRs and FNRs, based on naive randomization of a fraction of individuals in the advantaged group; and prove conditions under which the classifier is optimal with respect to accuracy [11].

Although effective in achieving *equal odds*, these randomization-based results have been considered discouraging for reasons outlined below, and, as shown in Section 6, are outperformed by active approaches.

Achieving Calibration and Error Parity

In many real-world uses of algorithms for risk estimation, it is common practice to require that predictions are *calibrated*—e.g., in recidivism [6, 7], child maltreatment hotlines [4, 9], and credit risk assessments [12]. A *calibrated* estimator is one where, if we look at the subset of people who receive any given probability estimate $p \in [0, 1]$, we find indeed a p fraction of them to be positive instances of the classification problem. In the context of credit assignment, for example, we would expect a p fraction of credit applicants with estimated default risk of p to default. In the context of algorithmic fairness across population groups, it is often desired that calibration holds for each group [7].

Calibration is not necessary nor sufficient to achieve parity in classification errors [5]. However, it is particularly desirable in cases where the output of an algorithm is not directly a decision but used as input to the subsequent judgment of a human decision-maker. In such contexts, risk estimates of an uncalibrated algorithm would carry a different meaning for different groups (e.g., African-American and white defendants), and hence their use in informing human judges' decisions would likely entail disparate impact.

Recently, Kleinberg et al. 2016 demonstrated that a tension exists between minimizing error disparity across different population groups and maintaining calibrated probability estimates [16]. In particular, it showed that calibration is compatible only with a single error constraint (i.e. equal FNR or equal FPR). On the same vein, Pleiss et al. 2017 showed that the results hold for even a strong relaxation of *equal odds*, named *equal cost*, where FPRs and FNRs are allowed to compensate one another according to a cost function [21]. Finally, they propose a method that, using naive randomization, is able to achieve parity on either error rate or *equal cost*. We compare our methods to these benchmarks in Section 5.

Objections to naive randomization

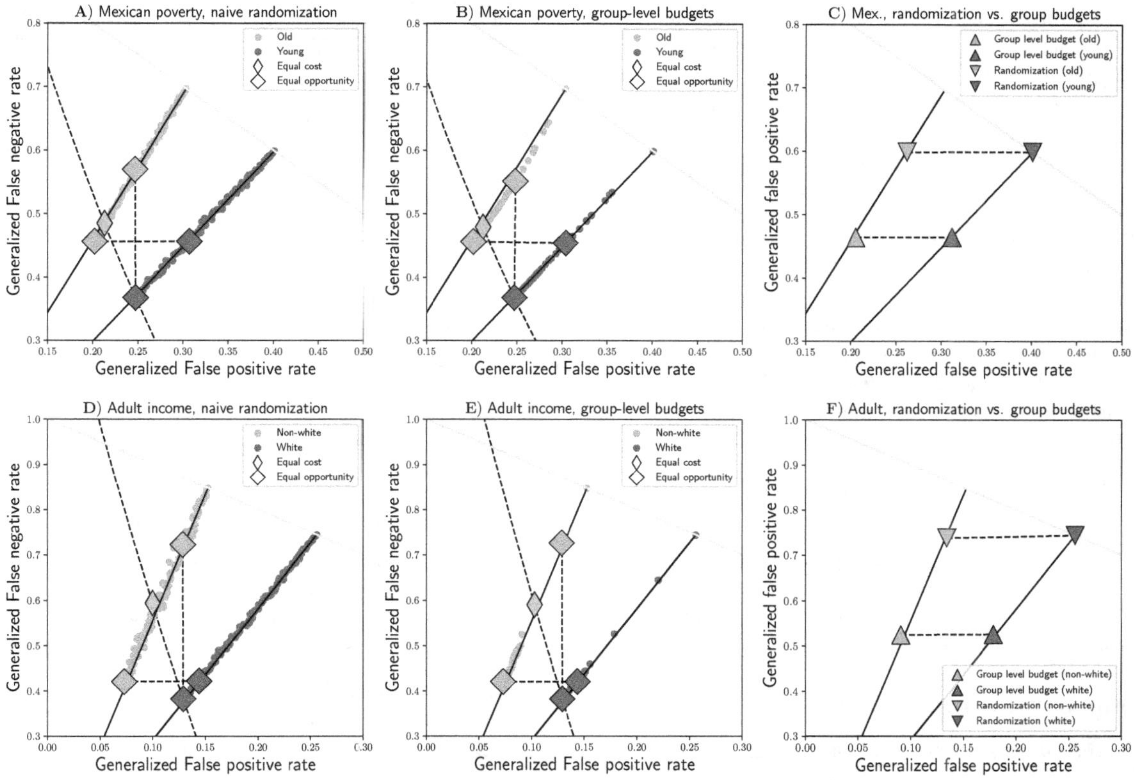

Figure 1: Achieving calibration and single error rate parity: classifiers with group-level information budgets vs. naive randomization. Rows correspond to analysis on two different datasets: the *Mexican poverty* and *adult income* datasets. Green and yellow colors correspond to error rates for two population subgroups (e.g., white and non-white individuals). Solid black lines represent the space of possible calibrated classifiers, from the perfect classifier (at the origin), to the trivial classifier that assigns the base rate probability to all individuals (intersection with the grey line). Panels in the first column (A and D) show the generalized false positive and false negative rates (GFPR and GFNR [21]) of classifiers that randomize an increasing proportion of individuals (0% to 100%). Dashed lines connect classifiers that achieve single error parity constraints. In line with [21], naive randomization is able to achieve calibration and any single error parity constraint. Panels in the second column (B and E) show results for classifiers with increasing group-level budgets (i.e., increasing feature sets), showing that these are also effective in achieving parity on either false positives, false negatives, or *equal cost*, while maintaining calibration; yet without resorting to naive randomization. Finally, panels in the third column (C and F) compare the efficiency of both methods in achieving *equal opportunity* and calibration, under an information budget restriction ($\bar{b} < 20\%$ in C, and $\bar{b} < 5\%$ in F). Classifiers with group-level budgets Pareto-dominate randomized classifiers by a wide margin, i.e. for the same information budget, both population subgroups are better off, incurring substantially lower false positive and false negative errors.

The aforementioned methods for achieving *equal odds*, as well as on jointly achieving calibration and a single error parity measure, rely on naive randomization as means to fairness. Hence, they have been interpreted as unintuitive, discouraging, and unsettling [5, 11, 21]. Several objections have been put forth against the use of naive randomization to achieve classification parity. Among them:

Inefficiency. As pointed out by [5, 11, 21], it is inefficient and appears unintuitive to withhold information that is already collected by naively randomizing the classification of a subset of individuals.

Individual unfairness. Classifiers based on naive randomization, such as those in [5, 11, 21], entail intra-group unfairness. Individuals who are randomized are not necessarily those with higher uncertainty but simply the ones who were unlucky, hence breaking ordinality between the probability of classification error and the underlying uncertainty.

Pareto sub-optimality and undesirability. Consider an unconstrained and unfair classifier $\hat{Y}_U$, which incurs higher errors on group A than group B; and consider an alternative 'fair' classifier $\hat{Y}_F$, where a fraction of individuals in B are randomized to achieve parity in errors. Considering groups A and B as the system's stakeholders, we note that the original unfair classifier $\hat{Y}_U$ Pareto dominates the fair alternative $\hat{Y}_F$, i.e.: the disadvantaged group A will be indifferent, as its classification remained unchanged, while group B will strongly prefer $\hat{Y}_U$, the original classifier before accuracy was degraded by randomization. No group would prefer $\hat{Y}_F$.

3 ACTIVE FAIRNESS

The present work explores *active feature acquisition* approaches for achieving fairness, where a decision-maker adaptively acquires information according to the needs of different groups or individuals, in order to balance disparities in classification performance. This section introduces two such strategies, one that allocates group-level information budgets—constant for all members of a group—and one that allocates individual-level information budgets, which are computed dynamically at test time. Sections 5 and 6 demonstrate their use and advantages in attaining fairness.

Preliminaries. We denote data of each decision subject as a pair (x, y), where x is a feature vector of dimensionality d, and y is the target variable we want to predict. Let $S = (x^i, y^i)_{i=1}^n$ denote a labeled dataset, and $A \subset S$ represent a population subgroup. Let $\hat{Y}(X)$ be a binary classifier. We denote by $FPR_A(\hat{Y})$ and $FNR_A(\hat{Y})$ the false positive and false negative rates of $\{(x, y) \in A\}$, and define disparity measures with respect to A in terms of the following FPR and FNR differences:

$$D^A_{FPR} = \left|FPR_A(\hat{Y}) - FPR_{A^\complement}(\hat{Y})\right|$$

$$D^A_{FNR} = \left|FNR_A(\hat{Y}) - FNR_{A^\complement}(\hat{Y})\right|$$

Equal opportunity—or FNR parity—with respect to A requires that $D^A_{FNR} = 0$, while *equal odds* requires both $D^A_{FNR} = D^A_{FPR} = 0$ [11].

3.1 Group-Level Information Budgets

Let b_A, b_B be the information budgets for population sub-groups A, B. We define predictor h^g with group-level information budgets b_A, b_B by:

$$h^g(x_i) = \begin{cases} f(x_i^{(q_A)}) & \text{if } i \in A \\ f(x_i^{(q_B)}) & \text{if } i \in B \end{cases}$$

where q_A, q_B are feature sets that satisfy $|q_A| = b_A$ and $|q_B| = b_B$. Sections 5 and 6 show how decision-makers can achieve calibration and group-level equity by allocating budgets b_A, b_B.

3.2 Individual-Level Information Budgets

Beyond group-level budgets, an ADM may adaptively collect information of each decision subject until a confidence threshold is met, upon which a classification decision is made. Thereby, individual-level information budgets are set dynamically according to the needs of each decision subject, towards attaining equity.

In particular, Algorithm 1 specifies active inquiry at the individual level as the decision-making process that, given lower and upper probability thresholds $\alpha_l, \alpha_u \in (0, 1)$, and for each decision subject i, progressively expands the information set $x_i^{(q_i)}$ until either threshold is met, or the available feature set is exhausted. Together with the decision threshold, α_l and α_u control trade-offs between FPR and FNR. In line with related AFA methods [8], we apply early stopping to ensure we stop expanding the feature set if the classification confidence is no longer improving significantly. We estimate the parameter for early stopping using grid search while maximizing the area under the receiver operating characteristic curve (AUROC) for a given budget.

We define predictor h^{ind} with individual-level information budgets as $h^{ind}(x_i) = f(x_i^{(q_i)})$, where q_i is the feature set according to active inquiry in Algorithm 1.

Algorithm 1: Active inquiry at the individual level

```
Input: data X, model f, probabilities (α_l, α_u), decision
threshold t;
for i = 1 to i = n do
    while f(x_i^(q_i)) ≤ α_u and f(x_i^(q_i)) ≥ α_l and
    |q_i| < d and not e do
        j' ← Get next best feature j' ∉ q_i ;
        x_i^(q_i) ← x_i^(q_i) ∪ x_ij' ;
        e ← early_stopping( x_i^(q_i), x_ij' ) ;
    end
    ŷ_i = 1_[t,1]( f(x_i^(q_i)) ) ;
end
return (q_i)_{i=1}^n, Ŷ ;
```

3.3 Random Forest Implementation

Implementation of active classifiers requires two elements: (1) a model f, able to estimate $P\{Y|X^{(q)}\}$ for arbitrary feature subsets $X^{(q)}$, with $q \in [0, d]$, and (2) a feature selection method for choosing expanding feature sets, either at the group- or individual-level.

Probabilistic model. We implement distribution-based classification with incomplete data based on a probabilistic random forest and extending related methods for dealing with incomplete data in trees [22, 23]. In particular, when given an arbitrarily incomplete feature vector $x_i^{(q)}$, the algorithm traverses all possible paths of each tree according to the following rule: if value x_{ij} for the current decision node is available in q, the search follows the path according to the node's decision function; otherwise, if the value is not available ($j \notin q$), the search follows both paths. We then compute classification probabilities as a weighted average of the leaf purity across all leaves landed on by the search. Finally, we compute the average predicted probability across all trees. Similar methods can be derived for adapting logistic regressions to admit arbitrarily incomplete feature vectors [23, 27].

Static feature selection. We first consider a static feature ranking for guiding the acquisition of additional features in Algorithm 1, based on feature importance derived from the random forest inter-trees variability. Hence, under static feature selection, given feature ranking R, the group-level budget classifier uses the top-b_A variables in R for classification of any $i \in A$, and the top-b_B variables in R for any $i \in B$. Similarly, the individual-level budgets classifier collects the top-b_i features in R in order to classify each subject i.

Dynamic feature selection. In the same vein, we consider dynamic or personalized feature selection, given its potential for increased individual-level equity and overall cost-efficiency. We implemented a *greedy* feature selection algorithm, which, for each subject i, and at each feature collection iteration, searches for the feature $j' \notin q_i$ that maximizes the difference between the current predicted probability $\hat{P}$ and the expected probability given that an additional feature j' is queried, given by:

$$j' = \underset{\{j: j \notin q_i, j \in [0,d]\}}{\arg\max} \left|\hat{P}\{y_i = 1|x_i^{(q_i \cup j')}\} - \hat{P}\{y_i = 1|x_i^{(q_i)}\}\right|$$

4 DATASETS

We study these methods and compare them to randomization-based approaches on four real-world, public datasets. All results are computed using random 80%/20% train/test splits.

Mexican poverty. Targeted social programs are challenged with household poverty prediction in order to determine eligibility [13]. This dataset is extracted from the Mexican household survey 2016, which contains ground-truth household poverty levels, as well as a series of visible household features on which inferences are based. The dataset comprises a sample of 70,305 households in Mexico, with 183 categorical and continuous features, related to households' observable attributes and other socio-demographic features. Classification is binary according to the country's official poverty line, with 36% of the households having the label poor. We study fairness across groups defined by a) young and old families, split by the mean (where 53% are young), and b) across families living in urban and rural areas (where 64% are urban).

Adult income. The Adult Dataset from UCI Machine Learning Repository [17] comprises 14 demographic and occupational attributes for 49,000 individuals, with the goal of classifying whether a person's income is above \$50,000 (25% above), and using ethnicity (whites v. non-whites) as sensitive attribute (86% white).

German credit. The German Credit dataset from UCI Machine Learning Repository consists of 1000 instances, of which 70% correspond to credit-worthy applicants and 30% correspond to applicants to whom credit should not be extended. Each applicant is described by 24 attributes. The sensitive attribute describes whether people are below or above the mean age (60% is below).

Heart health prediction. The Heart Dataset from the UCI Machine Learning Repository contains 17 features from 906 adults. The target is to accurately predict whether or not an individual has a heart condition (54% has heart condition). The sensitive attribute is whether people are below or above the mean age (46% is below).

5 ACHIEVING EQUAL OPPORTUNITY & CALIBRATION

This section demonstrates how an active strategy with group-level budgets can be used to achieve calibration and single error parity, resulting in a higher efficiency and without resorting to naive randomization.

We follow [21] and study predictive performance in terms of the generalized false positive (GFPR) and false negative rates (GFNR), appropriate for contexts where risk scores themselves are the outputs of the algorithm (as opposed to fully automated classification). We aim at designing classifiers that satisfy calibration and error parity. As shown by [16], the GFNR and GFPR of all calibrated classifiers for a given group A fall along the straight line with slope $(1-\mu_A)/\mu_A$, where $\mu_A = P(Y=1|A)$ is A's base-rate, and origin in the perfect classifier with $(GFPR, GFNR) = (0,0)$.

Panels A and D in Figure 1 show the space of calibrated classifiers achievable by naive randomization (method in [21]), for the *Mexican poverty* and *adult income* datasets described in Section 4. These replicate results from [21], showing how naive randomization of individuals in the advantaged group can, by eroding prediction performance, achieve calibration as well as either parity in false positives, parity in false negatives (but not both), or an *equal cost* generalization.

Similarly, panels B and E in Figure 1 demonstrate how calibration and either of the three parity objectives can be achieved by adjusting information budgets according to the groups' needs, without resorting to naive randomization. Moreover, the right column in Figure 1 shows that classifiers with group-level budgets achieve these fairness goals with much higher efficiency in terms of information cost. In particular, we set an overall information budget restriction for both types of classifiers, equal to the minimum budget required by the naive random classifier to achieve *equal opportunity.* It is observed in panels C and F that the classifiers with group-level budgets Pareto-dominate random classifiers by a wide margin, on both datasets, i.e.: for the same information budget, both population subgroups are better off, being exposed to substantially lower false positive and false negative errors.

6 ACHIEVING EQUAL ODDS

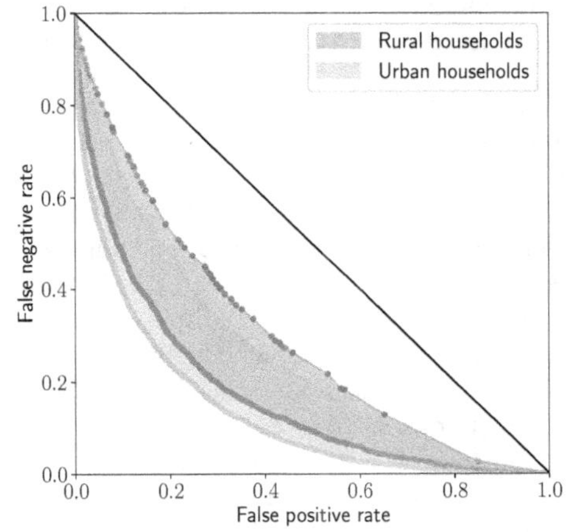

Figure 2: Achieving parity in false positives and false negatives (*equal odds*) via group-level information budgets. Results correspond to the *Mexican poverty dataset.* Achievable regions of classifiers for each population subgroup are plotted in blue and yellow. The outer and inner FPR-FNR curves of each achievable region correspond to classifiers using maximum and minimum information budgets. Points along the curve correspond to different values of the decision threshold. It is observed that active classifiers with group-level budgets achieve parity in both FNR and FPR (*equal odds*). Moreover, they provide *equal odds* solutions anywhere on the overlap of the achievable regions for both subgroups and thus along the entire FNR-FPR trade-off.

This section shows how active methods with group- and individual-level information budgets can be used to achieve parity in false positives and false negatives.

Figure 2 illustrates the achievable regions in FPR-FNR space for classifiers with group-level information budgets, for two groups in the *Mexican poverty data.* It's observed that urban households are more predictable than rural ones (achievable regions closer to the

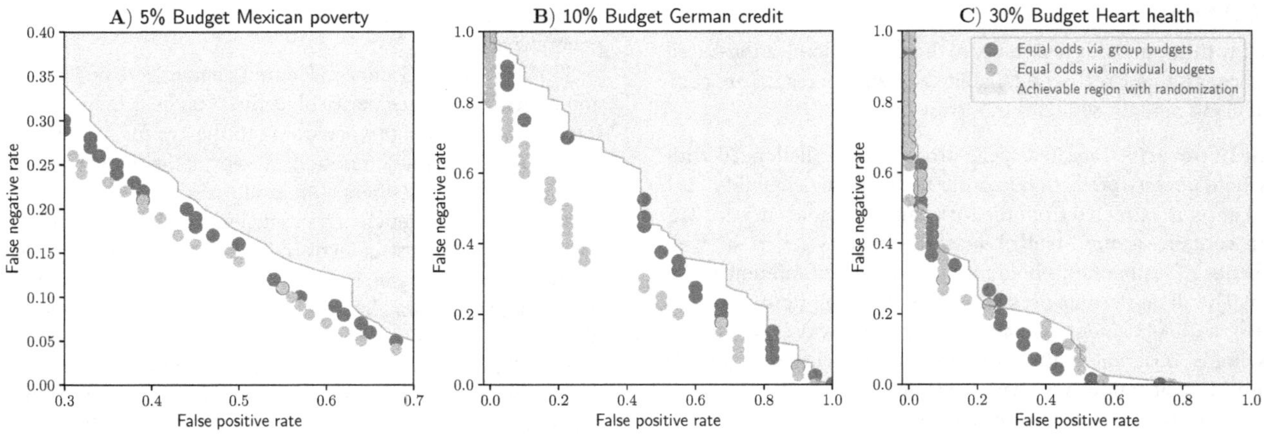

Figure 3: Achievable space of equal odds classifiers. Comparison of active classifiers with group-level (green) and individual-level (yellow) information budgets, and naive randomization (blue) [11]. Classifiers are constrained by an information budget $\bar{b} \leq b_{max}$. Figure A corresponds to *Mexican poverty*, B to *German credit* and C to *Heart health* under different budget constraints. It is observed that active classifiers yield *equal odds* solutions along the FPR-FNR trade-off, without resorting to randomization. Moreover, in budget-constraint settings, the active classifiers are substantially more information-efficient. The individual-level budget Pareto-dominates the group-level classifiers which in turn dominate randomized classifiers.

origin). The yellow and purple areas comprise the achievable regions for urban and rural groups. A substantial overlap is observed, showing a wide-ranged achievable region for *equal odds*.

In a similar way, we can obtain the achievable region of active classifiers with individual-level information budgets, by varying parameters $\alpha_l < \alpha_u \in [0, 1]$ of Algorithm 1 (see Section 3).

We ran experiments to compare the three methods—naive randomization (as in [11]), group-level budgets, and individual-level budgets—and their performance in achieving *equal odds* solutions along the FNR-FPR trade-off. In particular, we introduce an information budget constraint $\bar{b} = \frac{1}{n}\sum_i b_i < b_{max}$, and compare solution sets that satisfy it. Solutions of individual- and group-level classifiers are discrete, due to finite samples and feature dimensionality.

Figure 3 shows results for three different information budgets b_{max} on three different real-world datasets: *Mexican poverty*, *German credit*, and *Heart health* datasets. We left out the *Adult Income* dataset used in Fig. 1 since there exists no overlap between achievable regions for both subgroups and therefore we cannot achieve *equal odds*. Points in the FNR-FPR space were filtered to include only classifier designs that satisfied *equal odds* and an overall information budget constraint b_{max}.

It is observed that both group-level and individual-level strategies yield *equal odds* solutions, covering a wide range along the FNR-FPR trade-off curve, and without resorting to naive randomization. Moreover, it is shown that both type of active classifiers are substantially more information-efficient than the randomized classifier—Pareto dominance along most of the FNR-FPR trade-off curve—leading to lower false positive and false negative errors in budget-constrained environments. Finally, active classifiers with individual-level budgets tend to dominate classifiers with group-level budgets, due to their more efficient use of information by means of personalized inquiry.

7 CONCLUSIONS

We have proposed and demonstrated methods for simultaneously achieving equal opportunity and calibration, as well as for achieving equal odds. In contrast to prior work, the *active* framework does not rely on naive randomization to reach these fairness notions, avoiding several known disadvantages of randomized approaches. Instead, a decision-maker acquires partial information sets according to the needs of different groups or individuals, allocating resources equitably in order to achieve balance in predictive performance. By leveraging this additional degree of freedom, active approaches can outperform randomization-based classifiers previously considered optimal. Moreover, classifiers with individual-level budgets dominated their group-level counterparts. Finally, the extent to which the former can reduce intra-group unfairness is a relevant question left to future work.

More broadly, this work illustrates how, by jointly considering information collection, inference, and decision-making processes, we can design automated decision systems that more flexibly optimize social objectives, including fairness, accuracy, efficiency, and privacy. A natural direction for future work is to consider richer utility functions relevant to real-world decision systems. We expect future studies that generalize the results presented here to contexts with varying feature costs; as well as to contexts with multi-stakeholder value functions, where the opportunity, privacy, and monetary costs that inquiry and decision-making bring to decision-subjects are jointly considered as part of the adaptive inquiry process.

Lastly, a relevant path forward is to allow observations with partial feature sets both during training and test phases. The current implementation of this work necessitates access to full-feature observations at training time. More efficient training and further model refinement could be achieved under schemes that can learn from partial feature vectors, or proactively collect features at training time; allowing to incorporate a wider set of features tailored to increase prediction accuracy over different types of individuals.

REFERENCES

[1] Bechavod, Y., and Ligett, K. Learning fair classifiers: A regularization-inspired approach. *arXiv preprint* (2017).

[2] Calders, T., Kamiran, F., and Pechenizkiy, M. Building classifiers with independency constraints. In *Data mining workshops, 2009. ICDMW'09. IEEE international conference on* (2009), IEEE.

[3] Chalfin, A., Danieli, O., Hillis, A., Jelveh, Z., Luca, M., Ludwig, J., and Mullainathan, S. Productivity and selection of human capital with machine learning. *American Economic Review 106*, 5 (2016).

[4] Chouldechova, A., Benavides-Prado, D., Fialko, O., and Vaithianathan, R. A case study of algorithm-assisted decision making in child maltreatment hotline screening decisions. In *Conference on Fairness, Accountability and Transparency* (2018), pp. 134–148.

[5] Corbett-Davies, S., and Goel, S. The measure and mismeasure of fairness: A critical review of fair machine learning. *arXiv preprint arXiv:1808.00023* (2018).

[6] Corbett-Davies, S., Pierson, E., Feller, A., Goel, S., and Huq, A. Algorithmic decision making and the cost of fairness. In *Proceedings of the 23rd ACM SIGKDD International Conference on Knowledge Discovery and Data Mining* (2017), ACM, pp. 797–806.

[7] Flores, A. W., Bechtel, K., and Lowenkamp, C. T. False positives, false negatives, and false analyses: A rejoinder to machine bias: There's software used across the country to predict future criminals. and it's biased against blacks. *Fed. Probation 80* (2016), 38.

[8] Gao, T., and Koller, D. Active classification based on value of classifier. In *Advances in Neural Information Processing Systems* (2011).

[9] Gillingham, P. Predictive risk modelling to prevent child maltreatment and other adverse outcomes for service users: Inside the âĂŸblack boxâĂŹof machine learning. *The British Journal of Social Work 46*, 4 (2015), 1044–1058.

[10] Gorry, G., and Barnett, O. Sequential diagnosis by computer.

[11] Hardt, M., Price, E., Srebro, N., et al. Equality of opportunity in supervised learning. In *Advances in neural information processing systems* (2016), pp. 3315–3323.

[12] Huang, C.-L., Chen, M.-C., and Wang, C.-J. Credit scoring with a data mining approach based on support vector machines. *Expert systems with applications 33*, 4 (2007), 847–856.

[13] Ibarrarán, P., Medellín, N., Regalia, F., Stampini, M., Parodi, S., Tejerina, L., Cueva, P., and Vásquez, M. How conditional cash transfers work.

[14] Kanani, P., and Melville, P. Prediction-time active feature-value acquisition for cost-effective customer targeting. *Advances In Neural Information Processing Systems (NIPS)* (2008).

[15] Kleinberg, J., Ludwig, J., Mullainathan, S., and Obermeyer, Z. Prediction policy problems. *American Economic Review 105*, 5 (2015).

[16] Kleinberg, J., Mullainathan, S., and Raghavan, M. Inherent trade-offs in the fair determination of risk scores. *arXiv preprint* (2016).

[17] Lichman, M., et al. Uci machine learning repository, 2013.

[18] Liu, L.-P., Yu, Y., Jiang, Y., and Zhou, Z.-H. Tefe: A time-efficient approach to feature extraction. In *Data Mining, 2008. ICDM'08. Eighth IEEE International Conference on* (2008), IEEE.

[19] Louizos, C., Swersky, K., Li, Y., Welling, M., and Zemel, R. The variational fair autoencoder. *arXiv preprint arXiv:1511.00830* (2015).

[20] MacKay, D. J. Information-based objective functions for active data selection. *Neural computation 4*, 4 (1992), 590–604.

[21] Pleiss, G., Raghavan, M., Wu, F., Kleinberg, J., and Weinberger, K. Q. On fairness and calibration. In *Advances in Neural Information Processing Systems* (2017), pp. 5680–5689.

[22] Quinlan, R. *C4.5: programs for machine learning*. Elsevier, 2014.

[23] Saar-Tsechansky, M., and Provost, F. Handling missing values when applying classification models. *Journal of machine learning research 8*, Jul (2007), 1623–1657.

[24] Settles, B. Active learning. *Synthesis Lectures on Artificial Intelligence and Machine Learning 6*, 1 (2012), 1–114.

[25] Siegel, E. *Predictive analytics: The power to predict who will click, buy, lie, or die.* Wiley Hoboken, 2013.

[26] Trapeznikov, K., and Saligrama, V. Supervised sequential classification under budget constraints. In *Artificial Intelligence and Statistics* (2013), pp. 581–589.

[27] Williams, D., Liao, X., Xue, Y., and Carin, L. Incomplete-data classification using logistic regression. In *Proceedings of the 22nd International Conference on Machine learning* (2005), pp. 972–979.

[28] Zafar, M. B., Valera, I., Rodriguez, M. G., and Gummadi, K. P. Learning fair classifiers. *arXiv preprint arXiv:1507.05259* (2015).

[29] Žliobaitė, I. Measuring discrimination in algorithmic decision making. *Data Mining and Knowledge Discovery 31*, 4 (2017).

Paradoxes in Fair Computer-Aided Decision Making

Andrew Morgan
Cornell University
asmorgan@cs.cornell.edu

Rafael Pass
Cornell Tech
rafael@cs.cornell.edu

ABSTRACT

Computer-aided decision making—where a human decision-maker is aided by a computational classifier in making a decision—is becoming increasingly prevalent. For instance, judges in at least nine states make use of algorithmic tools meant to determine "recidivism risk scores" for criminal defendants in sentencing, parole, or bail decisions. A subject of much recent debate is whether such algorithmic tools are "fair" in the sense that they do not discriminate against certain groups (e.g., races) of people.

Our main result shows that for "non-trivial" computer-aided decision making, either the classifier must be discriminatory, or a rational decision-maker using the output of the classifier is forced to be discriminatory. We further provide a complete characterization of situations where fair computer-aided decision making is possible.

ACM Reference Format:
Andrew Morgan and Rafael Pass. 2019. Paradoxes in Fair Computer-Aided Decision Making. In *2019 AAAI/ACM Conference on AI, Ethics, and Society (AIES'19), January 27–28, 2019, Honolulu, HI, USA.* ACM, New York, NY, USA, 6 pages. https://doi.org/10.1145/3306618.3314242

As more and more data is becoming easily available, and with vast increases in the power of machine learning, there are an increasing number of situations where algorithms—*classifiers*—are used to help decision makers in challenging situations. Examples range from algorithms assisting drivers in cars, to algorithmic methods for determining credit scores, to algorithms helping judges to make sentencing and pretrial decisions in criminal justice. While such *computer-aided decision making* has presented unparalleled levels of accuracy and is becoming increasingly ubiquitous, one of the primary concerns with its widespread adoption is the possibility for such algorithmic methods to lead to structural biases and discriminatory practices [12]. A malicious algorithm designer, for instance, might explicitly encode discriminatory rules into a classifier. Perhaps even more problematically, a machine learning method may overfit the data and infer a bias, may inherit a bias from poorly collected data, or may simply be designed to optimize some loss function that leads to discriminatory outcomes.

A well-known instance where this concern has come to light is the debate surrounding the COMPAS (Correctional Offender Management Profiling for Alternative Sanctions) tool for recidivism analysis, a classification algorithm that is becoming increasingly widely used in the criminal justice system. Given a series of answers to questions concerning criminal defendants' backgrounds and characteristics, this tool outputs scores from 1 (low risk) to 10 (high risk) estimating how likely they are to recidivate (commit a future crime) or to recidivate violently. According to a recent study by ProPublica [2], COMPAS and similar risk assessment algorithms are becoming increasingly widely-used throughout the United States; their results are already being shown to judges in nine states during criminal sentencing, and are used in courts nationwide for pretrial decisions such as assigning bail. The ProPublica study, however, found an alarming trend in a set of data collected [1] concerning individuals' COMPAS results and their actual rates of recidivism over the next two years; in particular, it was found that the scores output by COMPAS lead to a *disparate treatment* of minorities. For instance, in the data collected, African-American defendants *who did not recidivate* were found to be almost twice as likely as white defendants (44.85%, compared to 23.45%) to have been assigned a high risk score (5-10).

Fairness, or non-discrimination, in classification has been studied and debated extensively in the recent past (see [3] for an extremely thorough overview); research concerning definitions of fairness in classification dates back to [11] and [6], with more recent definitions tailored to deal with the above-mentioned problems appearing in [2, 5, 8, 9]. To make this setting more concrete, consider some distribution $\mathcal{D}$ from which **individuals** σ are sampled, and consider some **classifier** $C(\cdot)$ that given some observable features $O(\sigma)$ produces some **outcome**, which later will be used by a decision-maker (DM). The DM is ultimately only interested in the actual **class** $f(\sigma) \in \Psi$ of the individual σ, and their goal is to output some decision $x \in \Omega_{\mathrm{DM}}$ correlated with this actual class. For instance, in the setting of the COMPAS data collected in [1, 2], $\mathcal{D}$ is the distribution over defendants σ, the class $f(\sigma)$ is a bit indicating whether the defendant σ actually commits a crime in the next two years, and the job of the classifier is to output a risk score, which will then be seen and acted upon by a judge. Note that we may without loss of generality assume that the class of the individual is fully determined by σ—situations where the class is probabilistically decided (e.g., at the time of classification, it has yet to be determined whether an individual will or won't recidivate) can be captured by simply including these future coin-tosses needed to determine it into σ, and simply making sure they are not part of the observable features $O(\sigma)$.

Additionally, an individual σ is part of some **group** $g(\sigma) \in \mathcal{G}$—for instance, in the COMPAS setting, the group is the race of the individual. We will refer to the tuple $\mathcal{P} = (\mathcal{D}, f, g, O)$ as a **classification context**. Given such a classification context $\mathcal{P}$, we let $\Psi_{\mathcal{P}}$ denote the range of f, and $\mathcal{G}_{\mathcal{P}}$ denote the range of g. Whenever the classification context $\mathcal{P}$ is clear from context, we drop the subscript; additionally, whenever the distribution $\mathcal{D}, g$ are clear from context, we use σ to denote a random variable that is distributed according

AIES '19, January 27–28, 2019, Honolulu, HI, USA

ACM ISBN 978-1-4503-6324-2/19/01...$15.00
https://doi.org/10.1145/3306618.3314242

to $\mathcal{D}$, and σ_X to denote the random variable distributed according to $\mathcal{D}$ conditioned on $g(\sigma) = X$.

In this work, we will explore a tension between *fairness for the classifier* and *fairness for the DM*. Roughly speaking, our main result shows that except in "trivial" classification contexts, either the classifier needs to be discriminatory, or a rational decision-maker using the output of the classifier is forced to be discriminatory. Let us turn to describing these two different perspectives on fairness.

Fairness for the Classifier: Fair Treatment. The notion of *statistical parity* [6] (which is essentially identical to the notion of causal effect [11]) captures non-discrimination between groups by simply requiring that the output of the classifier be independent (or almost independent) of the group of the individual; that is, for any two groups X and Y, the distributions $\{C(O(\sigma_X))\}$ and $\{C(O(\sigma_Y))\}$ are ϵ-close in statistical distance. This is a very strong notion of fairness, and in the above-mentioned context it may not make sense. In particular, if the *base rates* (i.e. the probabilities that individuals from different groups are part of a certain class) are different, we should perhaps not expect the output distribution of the classifier to be the same across groups. Indeed, as the ProPublica article points out, in the COMPAS example, the overall recidivism probability among African-American defendants was 56%, whereas it was 42% among white defendants. Thus, in such situations, one would reasonably expect a classifier to *on average* output a higher risk score for African-American defendants, which would violate statistical parity. Indeed, the issue raised by ProPublica authors was that, even after taking this base difference into account (more precisely, even after conditioning on individuals that did not recidivate), there was a significant difference in how the classifier treated the two races.

The notion of *equalized odds* in [8] formalizes the desiderata articulated by the authors of the ProPublica study (for the case of recidivism) in a general setting by requiring the output of the classifier to be independent of the group of the individuals, *after conditioning on the class of the individuals.*[1] We here consider an approximate version of this notion—which we refer to as **ϵ-fair treatment**—which requires that, for any two groups X and Y and any class c, the distributions

- $\{C(O(\sigma_X)) \mid f(\sigma_X) = c\}$
- $\{C(O(\sigma_Y)) \mid f(\sigma_Y) = c\}$

are ϵ-close with respect to some appropriate distance metric to be defined shortly. That is, in the COMPAS example, if we restrict to individuals that actually do not recidivate (respectively, those that do), the output of the classifier ought to be essentially independent of the group of the individual (just as intuitively desired by the authors of the ProPublica study, and as explictly put forward in [8]).

We will use the notion of *max-divergence* to determine the "distance" between distributions; this notion, often found in areas such as differential privacy (see [7]), represents this distance as (the logarithm of) the *maximum multiplicative gap* between the probabilities of some element in the respective distributions. We argue that using such a multiplicative distance is important to ensure fairness between groups or outcomes that may be under-represented in the data.[2] Furthermore, as can be seen in [10], such a notion is closed under "post-processing": if a classifier C satisfies ϵ-fair treatment with respect to a context $\mathcal{P} = (\mathcal{D}, f, g, O)$, then for any (possibly probabilistic) function $\mathcal{M}$, $C'(\cdot) = \mathcal{M}(C(\cdot))$ will also satisfy ϵ-fair treatment with respect to $\mathcal{P}$. Closure under post-processing is important as we ultimately want the decision-maker to act on the output of the classifier, and we would like the decision-maker's output to be fair whenever they act only on the classifier's output.[3]

As shown in the ProPublica study, the COMPAS classifier does not satisfy ϵ-fair treatment even for somewhat large ϵ. However, several recent works have presented methods to "sanitize" unfair classifiers into ones satisfying ϵ-fair treatment with only a relatively small loss in accuracy [8, 10, 13].

Fairness for the Decision-Maker: Rational Fairness. So, classifiers satisfying ϵ-fair treatment with accuracy closely matching the optimal "unfair" classifiers are possible (in fact, classifiers such as COMPAS can be sanitized to satisfy ϵ-fair treatment, without losing too much in accuracy). Additionally, as we have noted, the notion of fair treatment is closed under post-processing, so any mechanism that is applied to the output of the classifier will preserve fair treatment. Thus, intuitively, we would hope that the entire "computer-aided decision making process", where the decision-maker makes use of the classifier's output to make a decision, results in a fair outcome as long as the classifier satisfies fair treatment. Indeed, if the decision-maker simply observes the outcome of the classifier and bases their decision entirely on this outcome, this will be the case (by closure under post-processing).

So, since the notion of fair treatment is closed under such post-processing, any mechanism that is applied to the output of the classifier will preserve fair treatment. Intuitively, we would hope that the entire computer-aided decision making process, where the decision-maker makes use of the classifier's output to make a decision, results in a fair outcome as long as the classifier satisfied fair treatment. And indeed, by post-processing, if the decision-maker simply observes the outcome of the classifier and bases their decision entirely on this outcome, this will be the case.

But the decision-maker is not a machine; rather we ought to think of the DM as a *rational agent*, whose goal is to make decisions that maximize some internal utility function. (For instance, in the context of COMPAS, the DM might be a judge that wants to make sure that defendants that are likely to recidivate are sent to jail, and those who do not are released). As far as we are aware, such a *computer-aided "rational" decision-making* scenario has not yet been studied.

More precisely, we consider a decision-theoretic scenario where individuals σ are sampled from $\mathcal{D}$, the decision-maker gets to see the group $g(\sigma)$ of the individual and the outcome $c = C(\sigma)$ of the classifier (e.g., the individual's race and risk score), selects some action $x \in \Omega_{\mathrm{DM}}$ (e.g., what sentence to render), and finally receives some utility $u(f(\sigma), x)$ that is only a function of the actual class

[1] Very similar notions of fairness appear also in [5, 9] using different names.

[2] For instance, a blatantly discriminatory classifier that positively classified 1% of a group at random, but *only* that group, would have a fair treatment error of 0.01 if we used standard statistical distance, but an infinite max-divergence error.

[3] An earlier approximate definition was proposed in [9], which simply required that the expectations of the distributions are close; while this is equivalent to our definition for the case of binary outcomes, it is weaker for non-binary outcomes (as in the case of the COMPAS classifier), and this notion is not closed under post-processing.

$f(\sigma)$ (e.g., whether the individual would have recidivated) and their decision x.

Given a classification context $\mathcal{P}$, a classifier C, action space Ω_{DM} and a utility function u, let $\Gamma^{\mathcal{P},C,\Omega_{\text{DM}},u}$ denote the decision problem (i.e., the single-player Bayesian game) induced by the above process. We argue that in a computer-aided decision-making scenario, a natural fairness desideratum for a classifier C for a context $\mathcal{P}$ is that it should "enable fair rational decision-making". More precisely, we say that a strategy $s : \mathcal{G}_{\mathcal{P}} \times \{0,1\}^* \to \Omega_{\text{DM}}$ for the DM (which chooses an outcome based on the group of the individual and the output of the classifier) is *fair* if the DM ignores the individual's group g and only bases its decision on the output of the classifier—that is, there exists some $s' : \{0,1\}^* \to \Omega_{\text{DM}}$ such that $s(g,o) = s'(o)$. We next say that C **enables ϵ-approximately fair decision making** (or simply satisfies **ϵ-rational fairness**) with respect to the context $\mathcal{P} = (\mathcal{D}, f, g, O)$ if, for every finite action space Ω_{DM} and every utility function $u : \Psi \times \Omega_{\text{DM}} \to [0,1]$ (i.e., depending on the individual's class and the action selected by the DM), there exists an ϵ-optimal *and fair* strategy s (i.e., a strategy s such that the DM cannot gain more than ϵ in utility by deviating from it) in the induced game $\Gamma^{\mathcal{P},C,\Omega_{\text{DM}},u}$.

Note that if there exists Ω_{DM}, u for which there does not exist some fair ϵ-optimal strategy in the induced game, then there exist situations in which a DM can gain more than ϵ in utility by discriminating between groups, and thus in such situations a rational DM (that cares about "significant" $> \epsilon$ changes in utility) would be *forced* to do so.

Our Main Theorem

Our main result shows that the two notions of fairness mentioned above—which both seem intuitively desirable—are largely incompatible, except in "trivial" cases. In fact, we provide a tight characterization of classification contexts that admit classifiers satisfying ϵ-fair treatment and ϵ-rational fairness.

In these "trivial" cases—for instance, when the features already enable perfect classification, or when the base rates of classes are equal between groups—constructing a fair classifier is possible (and, indeed, usually trivially so) without any significant tradeoffs. However, in non-trivial cases, when these base rates might vary significantly, we show that enforcing fairness will inevitably produce a "predictive disparity" between groups, in that the ability of the outcome of a classifier to predict an individual's true class will need to be sacrificed more in some groups than in others. And, intuitively, this predictive disparity is precisely what causes rational fairness to fail; we show constructively that there are cases where a rational DM will be incentivized to make a more "risky" decision given a group with better predictivity and a "safer" decision given a group with worse predictivity.

The case of binary classes (warm-up). As a warm-up, and to better compare our result to earlier literature, let us start by explaining our characterization for the case of binary classes. We refer to a a classification context $\mathcal{P} = (\mathcal{D}, f, g, O)$ as binary if $\Psi_{\mathcal{P}} = \{0,1\}$.

We say that a binary classification context $\mathcal{P} = (\mathcal{D}, f, g, O)$ is **ϵ-trivial** if *either* (a) for every class $c \in \{0,1\}$, the "base rates" of c are ϵ-close with respect to any pair of groups, *or* (b) the observable features enable *perfectly distinguishing* between the two classes. Formally, *either* of the following conditions hold:

- *("almost equal base rates"):* for any two groups X, Y in $\mathcal{G}_{\mathcal{P}}$, and any class $c \in \Psi_{\mathcal{P}}$, the multiplicative distance between $\Pr[f(\sigma_X) = c]$ and $\Pr[f(\sigma_Y) = c]$ is at most ϵ;
- *("perfect distinguishability"):* the distributions $\{O(\sigma) \mid f(\sigma) = 0\}$ and $\{O(\sigma) \mid f(\sigma) = 1\}$ have disjoint support.

Note that if base rates are ϵ-close, there is a trivial classifier that satisfies 0-fair treatment and ϵ-rational fairness: namely, ignore the input and simply output some canonical value. Additionally, note that if the observable features fully determine the class of the individual, there also exists a classifier trivially satisfying 0-fair treatment and 0-rational fairness: simply output the correct class of the individual based on the observable features (which fully determine it by assumption). So ϵ-trivial binary classification contexts admit classifiers satisfying ϵ-fair treatment and ϵ-rational fairness. Our characterization result shows that the above contexts are the only ones which admit them.

Theorem 1. *(Characterizing binary contexts.)* Consider a binary classification context $\mathcal{P} = (\mathcal{D}, f, g, O)$, and let $\epsilon \leq 3/2$ be a constant. Then:

- If $\mathcal{P}$ is ϵ-trivial, there exists a classifier C satisfying 0-fair treatment and 2ϵ-rational fairness with respect to $\mathcal{P}$.
- If there exists a classifier C satisfying ϵ-fair treatment and $\epsilon/5$-rational fairness with respect to $\mathcal{P}$, then $\mathcal{P}$ is 4ϵ-trivial.

We note that a similar notion of triviality was considered in [5, 9] to obtain related characterizations for binary classification tasks, albeit for different definitions of fairness and "accuracy".

The general case. To deal with the general (i.e., non-binary) case, we need to consider a more general notion of a trivial context. The definition of triviality is actually somewhat different from the definition given for the binary case, but its not hard to see that for this special case the definitions are equivalent. We say that a classification context $\mathcal{P} = (\mathcal{D}, f, g, O)$ is **ϵ-trivial** if there exists a partition of the set $\Psi_{\mathcal{P}}$ into subsets $\Psi_1, \Psi_2, \ldots, \Psi_m$ of classes such that *both* of the following conditions hold:

- *("base-rates conditioned on Ψ_i are close"):* for any $i \in [m]$, for any two groups X, Y in $\mathcal{G}_{\mathcal{P}}$, and any class $c \in \Psi_i$, the multiplicative distance between $\Pr[f(\sigma_X) = c \mid f(\sigma_X) \in \Psi_i]$ and $\Pr[f(\sigma_Y) = c \mid f(\sigma_Y) \in \Psi_i]$ is at most ϵ;
- *("perfect distinguishability between Ψ_i and Ψ_j"):* for any $i \neq j \in [m]$ the distributions $\{O(\sigma) \mid f(\sigma) \in \Psi_i\}$ and $\{O(\sigma) \mid f(\sigma) \in \Psi_j\}$ have disjoint support.

Note that in contrast to the definition given for binary context, the general definition requires that *both* of the above conditions hold (as opposed to just one of them). Note, however, that in case we only have 2 classes, there are only 2 possible partitions of $\Psi_{\mathcal{P}}$: either we have the trivial partition $\Psi_1 = \{0,1\}$ in which case condition 1 is equivalent to requiring equal base rates, and condition 2 trivially holds; or $\Psi_1 = \{0\}, \Psi_2 = \{1\}$, in which case condition 1 trivially holds, and condition 2 is equivalent to prefect distinguishability between class 0 and class 1.

Once again, if a classification context is ϵ-trivial, there exists a simple classifier that satisfies ϵ-fair treatment and $O(\epsilon)$-rational fairness: given some observable features o, determine which *subgroup* Ψ_i the individual belongs to (which we know can be done by the second requirement), and finally output i. Roughly speaking, this classifier satisfies 0-fair treatment since for any i and any class $c \in \Psi_i$, all individuals in Ψ_i receive the same outcome (namely, i). Rational fairness is a bit more tricky to prove, but roughly speaking follows from the fact that, conditioned on any classification outcome i, the group g of the individual carries "$O(\epsilon)$ information" about the actual class of the individual, and so, by ignoring it, the DM loses little in utility. Our main theorem shows that ϵ-triviality is also a necessary condition:

Theorem 2. *(Full characterization.)* Consider some classification context $\mathcal{P} = (\mathcal{D}, f, g, O)$, let $\epsilon \leq 3/2$ be a constant and let $k = |\Psi_{\mathcal{P}}|$ (i.e., the number of classes). Then:

- If $\mathcal{P}$ is ϵ-trivial, there exists a classifier C satisfying 0-fair treatment and 2ϵ-rational fairness with respect to $\mathcal{P}$.
- If there exists a classifier C satisfying ϵ-fair treatment and $\epsilon/5$-rational fairness with respect to $\mathcal{P}$, then $\mathcal{P}$ is $4(k-1)\epsilon$-trivial.

Related Work

Several recent works also show obstacles to achieving fair classifications. Notably, the elegant result of [9] shows that (in our terminology), for non-trivial *binary* classification problems, there are no classifiers that satisfy ϵ-fair treatment (in fact, an expectation-based relaxation of the notion we consider) as well as a notion of *ϵ-group calibration*—roughly speaking, ϵ-group calibration requires that conditioned on any outcome and group, the distributions of individuals' actual classes are (approximately) "calibrated" according to the outcome. [4] Calibration, however, is best thought of as an "accuracy" notion for the classifier (rather than a fairness notion), and may not always be easy to achieve even without any concern for fairness. (Additionally, the results from [9] show a weaker bound than those we present here, namely that both of the ϵ-approximate notions they consider in conjunction imply $O(\sqrt{\epsilon})$ difference in base rates or $O(\sqrt{\epsilon})$ prediction error; we present a stronger, asymptotically tight, bound implying either $O(\epsilon)$ difference in base rates or *exact* perfect prediction. However, we note that this is largely due to the fact that the actual definitions employed are incomparable.)

[5] presents a similar impossibility result, focusing on binary classification with a binary output. She points out a simple identity (a direct consequence of the definition of conditional probabilities) which implies that, in non-trivial binary classification contexts, and for binary classifiers (i.e., classifiers only outputting a single bit), 0-fair treatment is incompatible with a notion of *perfect* "predictive parity"—namely, that conditioned on the classifier outputting b, the probability that the class is b is independent of the group. While her result only applies in a quite limited setting (binary context, binary classifiers, and only rules out "perfect" fair treatment combined with "perfect" predictive parity), we will rely on an identity similar to hers in one step of our proof. We will also rely on a generalized version of a notion of predictive parity (which deals with non-binary classes, non-binary outcomes, and non-zero error in predictivity) as an intermediate notion within the proof of our main theorem.

[4] In the COMPAS example, calibration might require that e.g., of people in each group assigned a risk score of 5, approximately 50% will recidivate, and so forth.

As far as we know, no earlier results have considered the effect of having a rational decision-maker act based on the output of the classifier. However, as pointed out to us by an anonymous reviewer, for the case that $\epsilon = 0$, Blackwell's celebrated "comparison of experiments" theorem [4][5] be used to show an equivalence between 0-rational fairness and perfect predictive parity, and as such, a Chouldechova's result combined with Blackwell's theorem rules out non-trivial binary classifications admitting classifiers that satisfy 0-fair prediction and 0-rational fairness. Dealing with the case that $\epsilon > 0$, however, is what interests us here: it should be no surprise that "perfect" fairness is impossible, just like "perfect" differential privacy [7] is impossible for any non-trivial task (whereas ϵ-differential privacy where $\epsilon > 0$ is highly possible for many functions of interest!) We highlight that as far as we are aware, "approximate" analogues of Blackwell's theorem are not known; in a sense, one of our results presented in the full version of this paper, which essentially shows that *approximate* rational fairness implies *approximate* predictive parity, can be viewed as an "approximate" analog of Blackwell's theorem (with a very different type of proof).

Furthermore, to the best of our knowledge, none of the earlier impossibility results consider non-binary classification problems.

Proof Outline

We here provide an outline of the proof of the main theorem. We start by considering just binary classification contexts $\mathcal{P} = (\mathcal{D}, f, g, O)$, and then show how to extend the proof to deal also with non-binary contexts. As mentioned above, for binary contexts, the "if" direction of the theorem (i.e., showing that trivial contexts admit fair classifiers) is immediate. The "only if" direction requires showing that the existence of a classifier C that satisfies ϵ-fair treatment as well as $\epsilon/5$-rational fairness for a context $\mathcal{P}$ implies that $\mathcal{P}$ is $O(\epsilon)$-trivial. The full proof is deferred to the appendix.

Predictive parity. Towards showing this, we introduce a generalized version of the notion of "predictive parity" considered in [5] (which will later also be useful in proving the "if" direction for non-binary classification). Roughly speaking, we say that a classifier satisfies ϵ-predictive parity if, for any two groups X and Y, the following distributions are ϵ-close in multiplicative distance:

- $\{f(\sigma_X) \mid C(O(\sigma_X)) = c\}$
- $\{f(\sigma_Y) \mid C(O(\sigma_Y)) = c\}$

That is, the output of the classifier is "equally predictive" of the actual class between groups.

Relating predictive parity and rational fairness. Our first result (which works for all, and not just binary, contexts) shows that rational fairness and predictive parity are intimately connected. First of all, ϵ-predictive parity implies $O(\epsilon)$-rational fairness—intuitively, if a DM could gain by discriminating, then there must exist some output for the classifier for which such a gain is possible, and this contradicts predictive parity. This forward direction turns out to be useful for proving that all ϵ-trivial contexts (even non-binary

[5] Roughly speaking, this result shows that if a decision-maker can never (i.e., no matter what the utility function is) make use of a signal (in our case, the group of the individual) to improve his utility, then the signal carries no further information than other signals the decision-maker sees (in our case, the output of the classifier).

ones) admit classifiers satisfying ϵ-rational fairness and ϵ-fair treatment; that is, the "if" direction of the theorem (also for non-binary contexts).

More interestingly, we show that $\epsilon/5$ rational fairness (for $\epsilon < 3/2$), *combined with* ϵ'-fair treatment (for any ϵ'), together imply ϵ-predictive parity. Intuitively, we show this as follows. Consider some C that does not satisfy ϵ-predictive parity, yet satisfies $\epsilon/5$-rational fairness and ϵ'-fair treatment. This means there exists some class y^*, groups g, g' and some outcome o such that the prevalence of y^* is significantly higher in group g than in group g' conditioned on the classifier outputting o.

We then construct a very natural game for the DM where every fair strategy has low utility compared to the optimal unfair strategy, which would contradict rational fairness. The action space of the games consists of two actions {Risky, Safe}. If the DM chooses Safe they always receive some fixed utility u^*. On the other hand, if they choose Risky, they receive 1 if the individual's class is y^* and 0 otherwise. That is, playing Risky is good if the individual is "good" (i.e., in class y^*) and otherwise not.

We next show, relying on the fact that C satisfies fair treatment and the fact that the prevalence of y^* is significantly higher conditioned on the DM getting the signal (o, g) than when getting (o, g'), that, if we set u^* (i.e, the utility of playing Safe) appropriately, the DM can always significantly gain by discriminating between g and g'. The intriguing aspect of this proof is that the optimal "fair" strategy for the DM turns out to be a *mixed* strategy (i.e., a probabilistic strategy) which mixes uniformly between the two actions Risky and Safe.

Simultaneously achieving fair treatment and predictive parity (binary contexts). Given that $O(\epsilon)$-rational fairness combined with (any finite-error) fair treatment implies $O(\epsilon)$-predictive parity, to prove the theorem, it will suffice to show that only trivial contexts admit classifiers that simultaneously satisfy $O(\epsilon)$-fair treatment and $O(\epsilon)$-predictive parity.

Towards showing this, let us first focus on binary classification contexts. We first note that, by the definition of conditional probability, for any $X \in \mathcal{G}_{\mathcal{P}}$, $i, j \in \Psi_{\mathcal{P}}$, and $o \in \Omega^C_{\mathcal{P}}$, the following identity holds:

$$\frac{\Pr[f(\sigma_X) = j \mid C(O(\sigma_X)) = o]\ \Pr[C(O(\sigma_X)) = o \mid f(\sigma_X) = i]}{\Pr[f(\sigma_X) = i \mid C(O(\sigma_X)) = o]\ \Pr[C(O(\sigma_X)) = o \mid f(\sigma_X) = j]}$$

$$= \frac{\Pr[f(\sigma_X) = j]}{\Pr[f(\sigma_X) = i]}$$

This identity is basically a generalization of an identity observed in [5] for the special case of binary classification tasks and binary classifiers; it relates the conditional probabilities defining fair treatment and predictive parity (the first and second terms on the left, respectively) to the *base rates* of classes between any two groups (the terms on the right).

The same identity as above also holds substituting any $Y \in \mathcal{G}_{\mathcal{P}}$ for X. By applying ϵ-fair treatment and ϵ-predictive parity to these two respective identities, we get that their left-hand sides are 4ϵ-close, and as a consequence we have that the ratios

$$\frac{\Pr[f(\sigma_X) = j]}{\Pr[f(\sigma_X) = i]} \quad \text{and} \quad \frac{\Pr[f(\sigma_Y) = j]}{\Pr[f(\sigma_Y) = i]}$$

are 4ϵ-close. (Note that, to perform these manipulations, it is important that we rely on the multiplicative distance notion; the reason we now get a distance of 4ϵ is that we apply fair treatment or predictive parity four times, and each time we do this we lose a factor of e^{ϵ}). For the case of binary classification contexts, letting $\alpha^g_b = \Pr[f(\sigma_g) = b]$ denote the "base rate" of class b for group g, this means that the ratios

$$\frac{\alpha^X_1}{\alpha^X_0} = \frac{\alpha^X_1}{1 - \alpha^X_1} \quad \text{and} \quad \frac{\alpha^Y_1}{\alpha^Y_0} = \frac{\alpha^Y_1}{1 - \alpha^Y_1}$$

are 4ϵ-close, and thus we have that the base rates α^X_1, α^Y_1 must be 4ϵ-close (and the same for α^X_0, α^Y_0).

But there is a catch. We can only apply the above identity when it is well-defined—that is, when there are no divisions by zero. In other words, we can only apply it if there exists some outcome o such that

$$\Pr[C(O(\sigma)) = o \wedge f(\sigma) = 0] > 0 \quad \text{and}$$
$$\Pr[C(O(\sigma)) = o \wedge f(\sigma) = 1] > 0.$$

If there is no such outcome, C *perfectly distinguishes* between the two classes, and thus

$$\{O(\sigma) \mid f(\sigma) = 0\} \quad \text{and} \quad \{O(\sigma) \mid f(\sigma) = 1\}$$

must have disjoint support. Hence, in either case, $\mathcal{P}$ is a 4ϵ-trivial context.

Simultaneously achieving fair treatment and predictive parity (general contexts). Dealing with non-binary contexts is quite a bit more involved, and we content ourselves to simply provide a very high-level overview. (The full proof of Theorem 2 follows from the same observations about predictive parity and the same equation relating treatment and predictivity rates to base rates; however, for non-binary $\Psi_{\mathcal{P}}$, the argument is somewhat more complex.)

Consider some C that satisfies ϵ-fair treatment and ϵ-predictive parity with respect to $\mathcal{P} = (\mathcal{D}, f, g, O)$; our goal is again to show that $\mathcal{P}$ must be $O(\epsilon)$-trivial. At a high level, we will show either that base rates are ϵ-close or that we can split the set of classes $\Psi_{\mathcal{P}}$ into *proper* subsets Ψ_1, Ψ_2 such that the classifier can perfectly distinguish between these sets of classes. Once we have shown this property, we can next repeatedly rely on it to prove the theorem (more precisely, by recursively splitting up either Ψ_1 or Ψ_2 and applying the same result; formally doing this turns out to be somewhat subtle.)

To prove the above property, our goal is to use the same high-level approach as in the binary case. Assume that there do not exist Ψ_1 and Ψ_2 such that C can perfectly distinguish between them, and let us show that then the base rates must be close. In order to apply the same argument as in the binary case, we would need to show that for *all* pairs of classes (i, j), the above identity can be applied. If we do this, then we have that, for *all* (i, j), the ratios

$$\frac{\Pr[f(\sigma_X) = j]}{\Pr[f(\sigma_X) = i]} \quad \text{and} \quad \frac{\Pr[f(\sigma_Y) = j]}{\Pr[f(\sigma_Y) = i]}$$

are 4ϵ-close, from which we can conclude that the base rates are 4ϵ-close. However, the fact that C cannot distinguish between two proper subsets of classes *does not* mean that all classes are "ambiguous" with respect to C (in the sense that C cannot perfectly tell them apart, and thus the identity is well-defined). Instead, what we show is that, under the assumption that there do not exist two proper subsets of classes between which C can perfectly distinguish, we have that, between *any two classes* i and j, there exists a sequence of classes $(i_1, \ldots, i_n)$ such that $n \leq k$ (k being the number of classes), $i_1 = i, i_n = j$, and any two *consecutive* classes must be "ambiguous". Ambiguity between classes with respect to C turns out to be exactly the condition under which the above identity is well defined. At a very high level, we can then perform a "hybrid argument" over the classes in the sequence to still conclude that, for all pairs of classes (i, j), the ratios

$$\frac{\Pr[f(\sigma_X) = j]}{\Pr[f(\sigma_X) = i]} \quad \text{and} \quad \frac{\Pr[f(\sigma_Y) = j]}{\Pr[f(\sigma_Y) = i]}$$

are $4(k-1)\epsilon$-close; this suffices to conclude that the base rates between groups are close.

ACKNOWLEDGMENTS

We are extremely grateful to Jon Kleinberg, Silvio Micali and Ilan Komargodski for delightful conversations and insightful suggestions.

REFERENCES

[1] Angwin, J.; Larson, J.; Mattu, S.; and Kirchner, L. 2016a. How We Analyzed the COMPAS Recidivism Algorithm. *ProPublica.* https://www.propublica.org/article/how-we-analyzed-the-compas-recidivism-algorithm.

[2] Angwin, J.; Larson, J.; Mattu, S.; and Kirchner, L. 2016b. Machine Bias: Risk Assessments in Criminal Sentencing. *ProPublica.* https://www.propublica.org/article/machine-bias-risk-assessments-in-criminal-sentencing.

[3] Barocas, S., and Selbst, A. 2016. Big Data's Disparate Impact. *California Law Review* 104:671–732.

[4] Blackwell, D. 1951. Comparison of Experiments. In *Proceedings of the Second Berkeley Symposium on Mathematical Statistics and Probability,* 93–102. University of California Press.

[5] Chouldechova, A. 2017. Fair Prediction with Disparate Impact: A Study of Bias in Recidivism Prediction Instruments. *Big data* 5(2):153–163.

[6] Dwork, C.; Hardt, M.; Pitassi, T.; Reingold, O.; and Zemel, R. 2012. Fairness Through Awareness. In *Proceedings of the 3rd Innovations in Theoretical Computer Science Conference,* ITCS '12, 214–226. New York, NY, USA: ACM.

[7] Dwork, C. 2006. Differential Privacy. In *Proceedings of the 33rd International Conference on Automata, Languages and Programming - Volume Part II,* ICALP'06, 1–12. Berlin, Heidelberg: Springer-Verlag.

[8] Hardt, M.; Price, E.; and Srebro, N. 2016. Equality of Opportunity in Supervised Learning. In *Proceedings of the 30th International Conference on Neural Information Processing Systems,* NIPS'16, 3323–3331. USA: Curran Associates Inc.

[9] Kleinberg, J. M.; Mullainathan, S.; and Raghavan, M. 2017. Inherent Trade-Offs in the Fair Determination of Risk Scores. In *8th Innovations in Theoretical Computer Science Conference, ITCS 2017, January 9-11, 2017, Berkeley, CA, USA,* 43:1–43:23.

[10] Morgan, A., and Pass, R. 2018. Achieving Fair Treatment in Algorithmic Classification. In *16th International Conference, TCC 2018, Panaji, India, November 11–14, 2018, Proceedings, Part I,* 597–625.

[11] Pearl, J. 2001. Direct and Indirect Effects. In *Proceedings of the Seventeenth Conference on Uncertainty in Artificial Intelligence,* UAI'01, 411–420. San Francisco, CA, USA: Morgan Kaufmann Publishers Inc.

[12] Podesta, J.; Pritzker, P.; Moniz, E. J.; Holdren, J.; and Zients, J. 2014. *Big Data: Seizing Opportunities, Preserving Values.* Executive Office of the President.

[13] Zafar, M. B.; Valera, I.; Gomez Rodriguez, M.; and Gummadi, K. P. 2017. Fairness Beyond Disparate Treatment and Disparate Impact: Learning Classification Without Disparate Mistreatment. In *Proceedings of the 26th International Conference on World Wide Web,* WWW '17, 1171–1180. Republic and Canton of Geneva, Switzerland: International World Wide Web Conferences Steering Committee.

Fair Transfer Learning with Missing Protected Attributes

Amanda Coston,[1,2] Karthikeyan Natesan Ramamurthy,[1] Dennis Wei,[1] Kush R. Varshney,[1]
Skyler Speakman,[3] Zairah Mustahsan,[4] and Supriyo Chakraborty[1]
[1]IBM Research, Yorktown Heights, NY, USA, [2]Carnegie Mellon University, Pittsburgh, PA, USA
[3]IBM Research, Nairobi, Kenya, [4]IBM Watson AI Platform, Yorktown Heights, NY, USA

ABSTRACT

Risk assessment is a growing use for machine learning models. When used in high-stakes applications, especially ones regulated by anti-discrimination laws or governed by societal norms for fairness, it is important to ensure that learned models do not propagate and scale any biases that may exist in training data. In this paper, we add on an additional challenge beyond fairness: unsupervised domain adaptation to covariate shift between a source and target distribution. Motivated by the real-world problem of risk assessment in new markets for health insurance in the United States and mobile money-based loans in East Africa, we provide a precise formulation of the machine learning with covariate shift and score parity problem. Our formulation focuses on situations in which protected attributes are not available in either the source or target domain. We propose two new weighting methods: prevalence-constrained covariate shift (PCCS) which does not require protected attributes in the target domain and target-fair covariate shift (TFCS) which does not require protected attributes in the source domain. We empirically demonstrate their efficacy in two applications.

KEYWORDS

Fairness, transfer learning, risk assessments

ACM Reference Format:

Amanda Coston, Karthikeyan Natesan Ramamurthy, Dennis Wei, Kush R. Varshney, Skyler Speakman, Zairah Mustahsan, and Supriyo Chakraborty. 2019. Fair Transfer Learning with Missing Protected Attributes. In *AAAI/ACM Conference on AI, Ethics, and Society (AIES '19), January 27–28, 2019, Honolulu, HI, USA.* ACM, New York, NY, USA, 8 pages. https://doi.org/10.1145/3306618.3314236

1 INTRODUCTION

The covariate shift setting in machine learning is often encountered in real-world applications that have limitations on data collection and require training on a different probability distribution than the one a model will ultimately be tested on [3, 20, 23]. In this setting, the training (source) and test (target) marginal feature distributions are different but the conditional distribution of labels given features is the same in the training and test distributions. Unsupervised domain adaptation to account for covariate shift can be achieved by forms of transfer learning [11, 26]. Relevant applications include risk assessment of people for credit and insurance when the provider has historical features and risk labels about its members, but is expanding into new markets with different demographics for which it does not have risk labels [22, 28]. The provider must learn models from its existing market data (source distribution) to score people in the new market (target distribution).

In this paper, we propose the problem of fair transfer learning under covariate shift and methods of solution. We examine the variations of the problem in which the protected attributes are available only for the source or only available for the target. We develop two new weighting methods: prevalence-constrained covariate shift (PCCS) which does not require protected attributes in the target domain and target-fair covariate shift (TFCS) which does not require protected attributes in the source domain. Weighting methods are commonly used for fairness and covariate shift, and they have the advantage of being compatible with many classification methods.

The issue of missing protected attributes is not only encountered in covariate shift settings, but is a more general challenge [18, J. Langford in panel discussion] because legal restrictions often prevent the collection of protected attributes or their joining to the rest of the dataset. For example, under Title VII of the 1964 Civil Rights Act, employers cannot ask potential applicants about gender [4]. Gupta et al. [13] address the problem of unavailable protected attributes by constructing proxy groups using variables in the dataset that are not protected but are likely correlated to protected attributes based on prior subject matter knowledge. Our approach is neither to explicitly construct proxy groups nor to use other variables, but to use the protected attributes themselves in related datasets. This approach enables companies to audit their hiring practices for gender discrimination by using aggregated datasets like the American Community Survey that have gender as a feature. Financial institutions could also use this to evaluate whether their credit approval processes comply with regulations prohibiting discrimination in cases where they are legally or practically unable to collect the protected attribute [5].

We apply our method to the medical expenditure dataset produced by the US Department of Health and Human Services known as the Medical Expenditure Panel Survey (MEPS). Health insurance providers in the US can choose the markets in which they will offer their plans and in which ones they will not. This decision making is driven by a risk assessment of the market, and thus the task is predicting individuals with low total healthcare expenditure vs. high expenditure over the course of a year. Section 1557 of the Patient Protection and Affordable Care Act (PPACA) in the United States made discrimination in healthcare on the basis of sex and race illegal [10, 14, 27]. As the PPACA was enacted, many insurance companies expanded rapidly into new markets, encountering the need to perform risk assessment having expenditure data only from

AIES '19, January 27–28, 2019, Honolulu, HI, USA

ACM ISBN 978-1-4503-6324-2/19/01...$15.00
https://doi.org/10.1145/3306618.3314236

the markets they served, not from new markets. Wei et al. [28] presented a covariate shift-based solution to this problem without considering fairness.

We also evaluate our methods on mobile money loan approvals in East Africa. Based on the success of mobile phone-based savings products such as M-Pesa, providers have recently begun offering credit services [7]. Algorithms make loan approval decisions based on mobile usage data. There has been rapid expansion by financial service providers into new markets (in this case, different countries with different partnering mobile network operators) with a need for covariate shift-based machine learning; one such solution is presented in [22]. We evaluate PCCS and TFCS on a dataset modeled after the actual data of a commercial financial institution in Africa.

2 PROBLEM SETTING

2.1 Covariate Shift

We are given labeled data $\{(x_1, y_1), \ldots, (x_n, y_n)\}$ from a source domain where $y_i \in \{0, 1\}$. We assume one of the labels is a more favorable outcome than the other. We also have unlabeled data $\{x_{n+1}, \ldots, x_{n+m}\}$ from a target domain to which we wish to assign labels. We use $\mathcal{S} = \{1, \ldots, n\}$ and $\mathcal{T} = \{n+1, \ldots, n+m\}$ to distinguish the index sets from the source and target domains. With covariate shift, the features $x_i \in \mathbb{R}^d$, $i \in \mathcal{S}$, are assumed to be drawn from a source distribution with density $p_X(x)$ while x_i for $i \in \mathcal{T}$ are drawn from a different target distribution with density $q_X(x)$. It is assumed that the conditional distribution of Y, i.e. $p_{Y \mid X}(y \mid x)$, is the same in both domains.

The standard approach to supervised learning is to find a predictor $\hat{y}(x)$ in a class $\mathcal{H}$ that minimizes empirical risk,

$$\min_{\hat{y} \in \mathcal{H}} \frac{1}{n} \sum_{i \in \mathcal{S}} \mathcal{L}(\hat{y}(x_i), y_i), \tag{1}$$

where $\mathcal{L}$ is the loss function between $\hat{y}$ and y that defines the risk. As $n \to \infty$, the empirical risk converges to the population risk, which can be written as the iterated expectation

$$\mathbb{E}_{p_X}[\mathbb{E}[\mathcal{L}(\hat{y}(X), Y) \mid X]] \tag{2}$$

to emphasize that the outer expectation is with respect to the source distribution p_X. In this ideal limit where $\mathcal{H}$ also contains arbitrarily complex functions, the optimal predictor in both domains, $p_{Y \mid X}(\cdot \mid x)$, can be recovered wherever $p_X(x)$ is positive. However for finite samples and constrained $\mathcal{H}$, the predictor obtained by minimizing empirical risk (1) generally shows traces of p_X and may not be best suited to the distribution q_X under which testing occurs.

Many methods that address the covariate shift problem do so by weighting training/source instances with weights $w_i \geq 0$ so that (1) becomes

$$\min_{\hat{y} \in \mathcal{H}} \frac{1}{n} \sum_{i \in \mathcal{S}} w_i \mathcal{L}(\hat{y}(x_i), y_i).$$

If $w_i = q_X(x_i)/p_X(x_i)$, then the weighted empirical risk converges to (2) with p_X replaced by q_X, as is desired for the target domain. Multivariate density estimation is difficult and therefore it is common to estimate the ratio of densities directly. One approach treats this as a classification problem [3] where the label is the source or target distribution. Logistic regression does this naturally and has been shown to be optimal (minimum asymptotic variance) for correctly specified models [19] but performs poorly for mis-specified models [25]. We use logistic regression in Section 4 for illustration purposes, noting that more sophisticated methods exist, e.g. [12, 24].

2.2 Protected Attribute Availability

We consider the problem of fairness with respect to protected groups. The definition of protected groups is assumed given and depends on the application context. Let $g_i \in \{0, 1, \ldots, G-1\}$ represent the group identity of instance i, which may be determined by one or more *protected attributes* such as race and gender. We pay particular attention to situations in which protected attribute data are available only in the source or target domain. In the former case, the source data consists of triplets $\{(g_i, x_i, y_i), i \in \mathcal{S}\}$ while the target data is $\{x_i, i \in \mathcal{T}\}$ as before. In the latter, the source data is $\{(x_i, y_i), i \in \mathcal{S}\}$ while the target data becomes $\{(g_i, x_i), i \in \mathcal{T}\}$. Based on the values of $\{g_i\}$, we define the partition of the source data into sets $\mathcal{S}_k = \{i \in \mathcal{S} : g_i = k\}$, i.e. source examples belonging to group k, for all $k = 0, \ldots, G-1$. The partition $\{\mathcal{T}_k, k = 0, \ldots, G-1\}$ of the target is defined similarly.

2.3 Fairness Metrics

We focus on notions of *demographic* or *statistical parity* that deal with the dependence of the classifier output on the protected attributes. We define a *score* $s(x)$ as a function that assigns to a feature vector x a number in $[0, 1]$ corresponding to the likelihood of a positive outcome $Y = 1$ given x. $s(x; \theta)$ denotes a score function parametrized by a vector of parameters θ. Viewing X as a random variable, a distribution is induced for the score $s(X)$ as well. We will say that a score satisfies *score parity* in the *strong* sense if $s(X)$ is statistically independent of the protected group variable G. This notion may be relaxed by requiring some distributional distance $D(p_{s(X) \mid G}(\cdot \mid k), p_{s(X) \mid G}(\cdot \mid l))$ between scores conditioned on groups $k \neq l$ to be bounded by some constant $\delta > 0$.

Herein we focus on two weaker and more common definitions of score parity. The first is *mean* or *average* score parity,

$$\mathbb{E}[s(X) \mid G = k] = \mathbb{E}[s(X) \mid G = l] \quad \forall k, l \in \{0, \ldots, G-1\} \tag{3}$$

which is the definition of "statistical parity" in e.g. [8]. Mean score parity may also be relaxed by allowing small deviations, and it is this relaxed definition that is targeted by the methods proposed in Section 3. The second notion is *thresholded* score parity at threshold t: $\forall k, l \in \{0, \ldots, G-1\}$,

$$\Pr(s(X) > t \mid G = k) = \Pr(s(X) > t \mid G = l) \tag{4}$$

which is also called "statistical parity" in e.g. [6]. Thresholded score parity applies when the score is thresholded to yield a binary prediction. It is used in Section 4 as a second fairness metric to evaluate different methods. If a score satisfies thresholded parity for all thresholds $t \in [0, 1]$, then it also satisfies parity in the strong sense above. It is clear that strong score parity implies both mean and thresholded parity. Moreover, if approximate strong parity holds in that $D(p_{s(X) \mid G}(\cdot \mid k), p_{s(X) \mid G}(\cdot \mid l))$ is small, then one expects the mean score disparity and thresholded score disparity to be small as well although the details depend on the distance measure D.

A quantity not involving but related to scores is *prevalence*, which describes the proportions of class labels. For binary Y, it is sufficient to assess prevalence $\Pr(Y = 1)$ of the positive outcome in the entire dataset and prevalence $\Pr(Y = 1|G = k)$ for particular groups. Prevalence differences between groups are therefore a measure of bias in the dataset. Since scores are often designed to estimate either $p_{Y|X}$ or Y itself after thresholding, controlling group-specific prevalences is a way of encouraging mean score parity in the former case or thresholded score parity in the latter, provided that the score is an approximately unbiased estimator, $\mathbb{E}[s(X)] \approx \mathbb{E}[Y]$ or $\Pr(s(X) > t) \approx \Pr(Y = 1)$. The method discussed in Section 3.1 relies on this relationship between prevalences and scores.

3 PROPOSED METHODS

Given the popularity of weighting methods for the covariate shift problem and in works on fairness [1, 15, 17], we focus in this paper on weighting as a means to address covariate shift and fairness jointly. Our goal is to determine weights $w_i \geq 0$ for the source/training instances (x_i, y_i), $i \in \mathcal{S}$. We propose two methods for the cases in which protected attribute information is available only for the source or target populations respectively. The method of Section 3.1 assumes nothing more than the use of a classification algorithm that accepts weights as input. The method of Section 3.2 requires differentiability of the classification loss function. It is possible to relax this assumption, for example by using smooth approximations to the loss and second-order optimization techniques as in [16]. The derivatives can be evaluated in closed form, as we do for logistic regression, or using automatic differentiation [2].

3.1 Prevalence-Constrained Covariate Shift (PCCS)

For the scenario in which the protected attribute is available for the source population but not the target population, we propose a method that combines conventional covariate shift with weighting to bring group-specific prevalences closer together. As discussed in Section 2.3, differences in prevalences characterize dataset bias, and controlling this bias encourages score parity. Let $w_{CS}(x)$ be a *covariate shift weight*, i.e. an approximation to the ratio $q_X(x_i)/p_X(x_i)$, obtained through logistic regression or other methods [3, 12, 24, 25]. The goal is to learn weights w_i for each training example that are as close as possible to the covariate shift weights subject to constraints on weighted prevalences. The objective function is thus

$$\min_{w} \sum_{i \in \mathcal{S}} |w_i - w_{CS}(x_i)|. \tag{5}$$

Norms other than the ℓ_1 norm can also be used. The prevalence constraints for fairness enforce closeness between all pairs of groups:

$$\frac{\sum_{i \in \mathcal{S}_k : y_i = 1} w_i}{\sum_{i \in \mathcal{S}_k} w_i} \geq \frac{\sum_{i \in \mathcal{S}_l : y_i = 1} w_i}{\sum_{i \in \mathcal{S}_l} w_i} - \delta \qquad \forall k, l \in \{0, \ldots, G-1\}, \tag{6}$$

where the parameter δ trades off between differences in prevalences and deviation of w from w_{CS}. To make these constraints convex, we add equality constraints on the proportion of weight allocated to each group:

$$\sum_{i \in \mathcal{S}_k} w_i = c_k \sum_{i \in \mathcal{S}} w_i, \quad k \in \{0, \ldots, G-1\} \tag{7}$$

where

$$c_k = \frac{\sum_{i \in \mathcal{S}_k} w_{CS}(x_i)}{\sum_{i \in \mathcal{S}} w_{CS}(x_i)}, \tag{8}$$

i.e. we require the allocations to groups specified by the covariate shift weights to remain unchanged. Lastly we require weights to be non-negative:

$$w_i \geq 0, \quad i \in \mathcal{S}. \tag{9}$$

The optimization problem is to minimize the objective in (5) subject to constraints (6)–(9).

3.2 Target-Fair Covariate Shift (TFCS)

We now consider the scenario in which the protected attribute is available for the target but not the source. We may directly evaluate the score disparity of the classifier on the target and adjust the classifier to reduce the disparity. We assume that the classifier parameters are chosen to minimize the weighted empirical risk,

$$\hat{\theta} = \arg\min_{\theta} \frac{1}{n} \sum_{i \in \mathcal{S}} w_i \mathcal{L}(s(x_i; \theta), y_i), \tag{10}$$

where $\mathcal{L}(s(x; \theta), y)$ is a twice differentiable function of θ as discussed and any regularizer is absorbed into $\mathcal{L}$. Thus the classifier can be adjusted by changing the weights w_i.

To measure score disparity, we introduce the following fairness loss that sums the squares of average score disparities over all pairs of groups $(\mathcal{T}_k, \mathcal{T}_l)$:

$$\mathcal{L}_f(s(\cdot; \hat{\theta})) = \sum_{k<l} \left(\frac{1}{|\mathcal{T}_k|} \sum_{i \in \mathcal{T}_k} s(x_i; \hat{\theta}) - \frac{1}{|\mathcal{T}_l|} \sum_{i \in \mathcal{T}_l} s(x_i; \hat{\theta}) \right)^2. \tag{11}$$

The weights w_i are chosen to minimize a linear combination of this fairness loss with a classification loss:

$$\min_{w} \frac{1}{n} \sum_{i \in \mathcal{S}} w_{CS}(x_i) \mathcal{L}(s(x_i; \hat{\theta}), y_i) + \lambda \mathcal{L}_f(s(\cdot; \hat{\theta})), \tag{12}$$

where $w_{CS}(x_i)$ are covariate shift weights as in Section 3.1 and are *fixed* (not to be confused with w). The first term in (12) thus approximates classification loss on the target population by weighting the source population, where labels are available. The fairness loss $\mathcal{L}_f$ is evaluated on the target, where the protected attribute is available. Both terms are explicit functions of the scores parametrized by $\hat{\theta}$; the notation $s(\cdot; \hat{\theta})$ emphasizes this dependence. The parameters $\hat{\theta}$ are a function of the optimization variables w_i through (10).

We propose to optimize (12) through gradient descent. The algorithm (see Algorithm 1) alternates between gradient updates to w to decrease the objective in (12) and solving (10) to obtain a new classifier from the updated w, which is then re-evaluated using (12). In our experiments, we use a constant step size η and terminate after a fixed number of iterations.

The combined loss (12) is generally not a convex function of the weights w_i. Hence different initializations may lead to different solutions. One choice is to initialize with covariate shift weights, $w = w_{CS}$. In the case of $\lambda = 0$ in (12) (i.e. only classification loss), $w = w_{CS}$ is a stationary point as will be shown at the end of Appendix A. Accordingly for small λ, $w = w_{CS}$ is expected to be

Algorithm 1 Target-Fair Covariate Shift (TFCS)

Input:
Data: labeled source $\{(x_i, y_i), i \in \mathcal{S}\}$, target with protected attribute $\{(x_i, g_i), i \in \mathcal{T}\}$
Parameters: trade-off λ, step size η
Estimate covariate shift weights w_{CS} from $\{x_i, i \in \mathcal{S} \cup \mathcal{T}\}$
$w \leftarrow w_{CS}$ **or** $w_i \leftarrow 1\ \forall i$ (uniform)
repeat
  Learn classifier parameters $\hat{\theta}$ given w (10)
  Evaluate combined loss (12)
  # Gradient computations:
  Compute $\nabla_{\hat{\theta}}\mathcal{L}_c$ (e.g. (19))
  Compute $\nabla_{\hat{\theta}}\mathcal{L}_f$ (e.g. (20))
  Compute $\partial\hat{\theta}/\partial w_i\ \forall i$ (15)(16)
  Compute $\nabla_w\mathcal{L}_t$ (14)
  # Gradient update
  $w \leftarrow w - \eta\nabla_w\mathcal{L}_t$
until stopping criterion is met
Output: Classifier parameters $\hat{\theta}$, weights w

near-stationary. A simpler alternative is to initialize with uniform weights $w_i = 1$.

For the scenario in which the protected attribute is available in both the source and target domains, we propose to combine the methods in Section 3.1 and this section. First, PCCS is used to achieve covariate shift and approximate score parity based on the protected attribute in the source. Then the PCCS weights are used to initialize the minimization in (12) to refine score parity in the target domain.

Since the combined loss (12) is an indirect function of w via (10), the calculation of its gradient with respect to w is non-standard. Appendix A derives the necessary expressions.

4 EXPERIMENTS

We demonstrate the utility of PCCS and TFCS in fair transfer learning for two applications. The first is a healthcare cost prediction scenario when a health insurance company that is servicing an existing market wants to venture into a new market, while ensuring equal benefit to all race- and gender-based intersectional groups in the new market. The second is a loan approval setting where a mobile money provider from one country in East Africa is expanding to another country while being non-discriminatory according to age and gender.

We use AUC to assess accuracy and we compute four fairness metrics:

(1) *Mean score parity (MSP) loss*: Square root of sum of squares of differences between mean scores for all pairs of groups (see equations (3) and (11)).
(2) *Thresholded score parity (TSP) loss*: Square root of sum of squares of differences between thresholded scores for all pairs of groups (see equation (4)).
(3) *Max Δ MSP*: Maximum of absolute differences between mean scores for all pairs of groups.
(4) *Max Δ TSP*: Maximum of absolute differences between thresholded scores for all pairs of groups.

We compare our proposed methods against four baselines:

(1) *Native*: Train and test on the target population (i.e. not in the transfer learning setting).
(2) *Unadapted transfer learning*: Train on the source population and test on target population without any adaptation to the target population during training.
(3) *Covariate shift*: Train on the source population reweighed to resemble the target population.
(4) *Kamiran Calders*: Correct the source dataset for fairness using the approach proposed in [15] without performing any covariate shift.

Testing is always performed on the target population where true labels and protected attributes are used to evaluate accuracy and fairness. PCCS and Kamiran-Calders use protected attributes only from the source while TFCS uses them only from the target.

In all cases, logistic regression is used as the classification algorithm and also to obtain covariate shift weights. This choice is intended as a simple illustration of the methods and richer models can certainly be substituted. The TFCS method was initialized using uniform weights and its stopping criterion is a maximum number of iterations, usually set to a few hundred, depending on the dataset used.

We studied the behavior of PCCS and TFCS for various values of their respective free parameters δ and λ. For future applications, the choice of the free parameter will depend on the particular setting (including the initial discrepancies in group prevalences) but generally we would recommend using a δ in $[0, .075]$ for PCCS. For TFCS, we recommend using cross-validation to choose λ.

We note that transfer learning can exacerbate discrimination or improve fairness; the direction depends on the application, and indeed, in our experiments we observe both. Regardless of whether transfer learning alone helps or hurts fairness, our fairness-aware transfer learning methods are able to improve the fairness metrics.

4.1 Medical Expenditure Panel Survey (MEPS)

The MEPS dataset [9] is obtained using a nationally representative survey of the US population. It contains annual healthcare cost, demographics, and self-reported medical information. We use the data from panel 19 of the 2015 survey. There is no concept of market in this dataset since it does not come from an insurance provider (those datasets are proprietary, but MEPS shares relevant characteristics with such datasets). We define the source market to consist of people earning less than national median income (USD 21,000), and target market to consist of the rest of the population.

We consider two protected attributes: gender and race. Both are legally protected, as discussed in Section 1. In our experiments, the races considered are non-Hispanic whites and non-Hispanic blacks. The outcome variable is the binarized annual healthcare expenditure (low cost and high cost), obtained by thresholding the expenditure at its national median (USD 1,272). Representative features considered for the classification problem include age, marital status, education, military status, self-reported health conditions, self-reported physical and cognitive limitations, employment status, poverty category, and insurance coverage status. The threshold t used for obtaining the TSP metric is 0.5 since the prevalence of outcomes in this data is equally balanced at 0.5. The disparity in

Table 1: MEPS outcome disparities between various groups in source (low-income) and target (high-income) populations. The disparity is given by $\Pr(Y = 1|G = k) - \Pr(Y = 1|G = l)$ with probabilities expressed as percentages.

Groups k and l	Source	Target
white males, black males	14.6	17.4
white males, white females	-12.8	-18.0
white males, black females	3.0	-3.4
black males, white females	-27.4	-35.4
black males, black females	-11.6	-20.9
white females, black females	15.8	14.5

prevalence of high cost outcomes among various gender–race intersections is provided in Table 1. The largest disparity is between black males and white females, whereas the smallest is between white males and black females.

We compare PCCS and TFCS with the baseline approaches in Table 2. The AUC on the target population for all methods are similar except for TFCS with $\lambda = 100$, as will be explained later.

The methods do show differences however in score disparity in the target. Covariate shift without any fairness adjustments happens to significantly reduce the fairness losses, and Kamiran-Calders yields a similar reduction. They are further reduced with PCCS, which combines elements of covariate shift and parity-inducing reweighting. TFCS with $\lambda = 100$ achieves by far the lowest score parity losses, at the cost of a lower AUC. The large setting for λ is intended to show the parity levels that can be achieved.

Figure 1 shows the variation of fairness and accuracy metrics with respect to δ for PCCS. While the MSP and TSP curves are somewhat variable, there is a slight downward trend in disparities as δ decreases toward zero and tightens the prevalence constraints (6). The AUC is nearly constant. The behavior of TFCS with changing λ is illustrated in Figure 2. Recall that λ weights the fairness component of the combined loss (12). When λ is small, all metrics are closer to the values obtained with methods that do not account for fairness (unadapted, covariate shift), as expected. As λ increases past 1, the score parity losses decrease dramatically while the AUC undergoes a more modest reduction.

Although we do not observe a boost in AUC from covariate shift methods, our fairness methods that adjust for covariate shift improve the fairness metrics over Kamiran-Calders, which does not account for covariate shift.

4.2 Mobile Money Loan Approval in East Africa

We consider the expansion of mobile-money credit services into a new market of East Africa. We use data from the *original* market to train a model that is deployed in the *new* market. Age (thresholded at 35 years) and gender are protected attributes. The prediction task is to identify who will repay a loan; the features are described in [22] and include airtime usage and mobile money volumes sent and received over a 6-month period. The threshold for approving a loan is $t = 0.75$ since banks will only issue a loan if they are confident a user will repay.

Table 4 illustrates that transfer learning significantly improves score parity in the target population, with covariate shift and even

Table 2: Results on MEPS dataset. Source: low-income population, Target: high-income population. Disparity measures are shown as percentages. All metrics are reported for target.

	AUC	MSP loss	TSP loss	Max Δ MSP	Max Δ TSP
Native	0.800	29.0	42.4	19.4	27.7
Unadapted	0.799	27.0	43.3	18.9	30.2
Covariate Shift	0.786	17.6	30.0	12.3	21.1
Kamiran Calders	0.799	16.5	26.2	11.5	18.5
PCCS ($\delta = 0.05$)	0.788	14.2	20.3	9.7	14.3
TFCS ($\lambda = 100$)	0.708	2.2	5.1	1.4	3.4

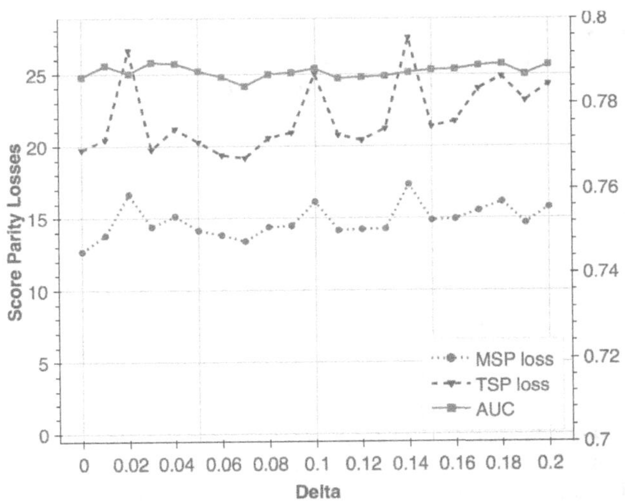

Figure 1: Variation of score parities and AUC with the PCCS trade-off parameter δ for the MEPS dataset.

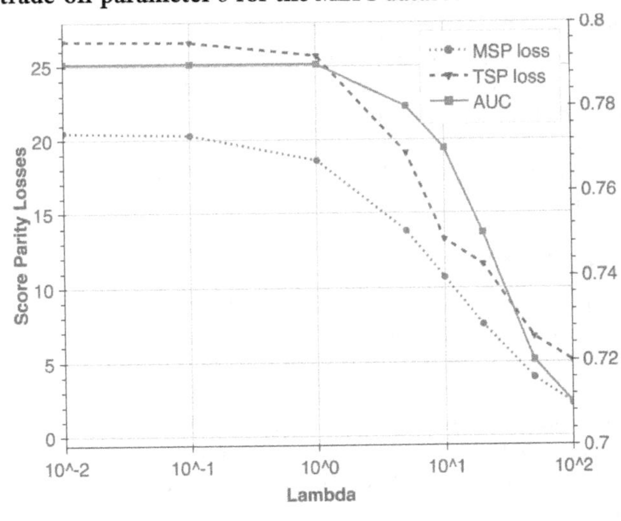

Figure 2: Variation of score parities and AUC with the TFCS trade-off parameter λ for the MEPS dataset.

in the unadapted case. We note that this is not because the source has less dataset bias; in fact, in Table 3, we see that the source dataset

Table 3: Mobile Money outcome disparities between various groups in source (original market) and target (new market) populations. The disparity is given by $\Pr(Y = 1|G = k) - \Pr(Y = 1|G = l)$ with probabilities expressed as percentages.

Groups k and l	Source	Target
female 35+, female under 35	7.0	6.2
female 35+, male 35+	3.5	1.4
female 35+, male under 35	11.1	9.2
female under 35, male 35+	-3.6	-4.8
female under 35, male under 35	4.1	3.0
male 35+, male under 35	7.7	7.9

Table 4: Results on Mobile Money dataset. Source: Country 1, Target: Country 2. Disparity measures are shown as percentages. All metrics are reported for target.

	AUC	MSP loss	TSP loss	Max Δ MSP	Max Δ TSP
Native	0.658	7.6	23.0	4.9	14.5
Unadapted	0.642	4.2	12.6	2.5	8.1
Covariate Shift	0.639	3.8	11.1	2.7	7.2
Kamiran Calders	0.640	4.0	12.5	2.5	7.7
PCCS ($\delta = .05$)	0.630	2.4	5.7	1.5	3.3
TFCS ($\lambda = .01$)	0.639	2.6	6.8	1.8	4.4

has larger disparities in loan approvals over the four demographic groups. PCCS and TFCS further reduce the four fairness metrics with little to no change in AUC for the target population. PCCS and TFCS outperform Kamiran-Calders, which only yields results on par with covariate shift. For this application, we found that increasing λ did not improve the score disparities for TFCS. Thus Table 4 shows results for $\lambda = 0.01$ which maintains the AUC.

Figure 3 shows the results for PCCS as we vary δ to trade off improving AUC against reducing the fairness losses. For $\delta \geq 0.08$, the weighted prevalence constraints (6) are loose enough to allow the covariate shift solution $w = w_{CS}$ and the metrics converge accordingly. The trade-off between AUC and score parity is seen for smaller δ.

5 CONCLUSION

This paper has discussed methods that address jointly the problem of covariate shift between source and target populations and the need to ensure fairness in a predictor's outputs toward protected groups. We have focused specifically on mean score parity and thresholded score parity measures of group fairness. Both of the proposed methods, prevalence-constrained covariate shift (PCCS) and target-fair covariate shift (TFCS), are based on sample reweighting and thus fit well with existing domain adaptation techniques and a variety of classification algorithms. Together they can accommodate the important practical limitation of having protected group information only in the source or target domain. Tested on two datasets, PCCS and TFCS show reductions in score disparity compared to baselines with little change in AUC. The MEPS dataset and mobile money credit dataset are new to the algorithmic fairness

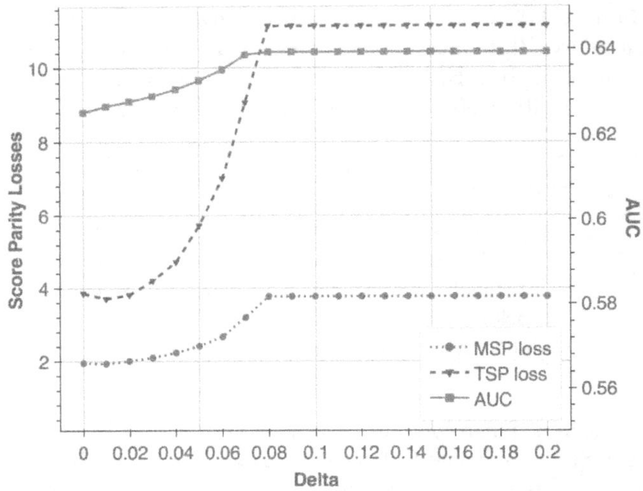

Figure 3: Variation of score parities and AUC with the PCCS trade-off parameter δ for the Mobile Money dataset.

literature and, we believe, are more reflective of real risk assessment applications than some prior benchmarks.

ACKNOWLEDGMENTS

We acknowledge the helpful comments and feedback of Aldo Pareja. This work was conducted under the auspices of the IBM Science for Social Good initiative. This research in part was sponsored by the U.S. Army Research Lab and the U.K. Ministry of Defence under Agreement Number W911NF-16-3-0001. The views and conclusions contained in this document are those of the authors and should not be interpreted as representing the official policies, either expressed or implied, of the U.S. Army Research Laboratory, the U.S. Government, the U.K. Ministry of Defence or the U.K. Government. The U.S. and U.K. Governments are authorized to reproduce and distribute reprints for Government purposes notwithstanding any copyright notation hereon.

REFERENCES

[1] Alekh Agarwal, Alina Beygelzimer, Miroslav Dudík, John Langford, and Hanna Wallach. 2018. A reductions approach to fair classification. In *Proc. International Conference on Machine Learning (ICML)*. Stockholm, Sweden.
[2] Atılım Güneş Baydin, Barak A. Pearlmutter, Alexey Andreyevich Radul, and Jeffrey Mark Siskind. 2018. Automatic Differentiation in Machine Learning: A Survey. *Journal of Machine Learning Research* 18, 2 (2018), 1–43.
[3] Steffen Bickel, Michael Brückner, and Tobias Scheffer. 2009. Discriminative Learning Under Covariate Shift. *Journal of Machine Learning Research* 10 (Sept. 2009), 2137–2155.
[4] Kim M Blankenship. 1993. Bringing gender and race in: US employment discrimination policy. *Gender & Society* 7, 2 (1993), 204–226.
[5] Jiahao Chen, Nathan Kallus, Xiaojie Mao, Geoffry Svacha, and Madeleine Udell. 2018. Fairness Under Unawareness: Assessing Disparity When Protected Class Is Unobserved. *arXiv preprint arXiv:1811.11154* (2018).
[6] Alexandra Chouldechova. 2017. Fair Prediction with Disparate Impact: A Study of Bias in Recidivism Prediction Instruments. *Big Data* 5, 2 (2017), 153–163.
[7] Tamara Cook and Claudia McKay. 2015. How M-Shwari Works: The Story So Far. *Access to Finance Forum* 10 (April 2015).
[8] Sam Corbett-Davies, Emma Pierson, Avi Feller, Sharad Goel, and Aziz Huq. 2017. Algorithmic Decision Making and the Cost of Fairness. In *Proc. ACM SIGKDD International Conference on Knowledge Discovery and Data Mining*. Halifax, NS, Canada, 797–806.
[9] Agency for Healthcare Research and Quality. 2018. Medical Expenditure Panel Survey (MEPS). http://www.ahrq.gov/research/data/meps/index.html.

[10] Jill Gaulding. 1995. Race Sex and Genetic Discrimination in Insurance: What's Fair. *Cornell Law Review* 80, 6 (Sept. 1995), 1646–1694.

[11] Boqing Gong, Yuan Shi, Fei Sha, and Kristen Grauman. 2012. Geodesic Flow Kernel for Unsupervised Domain Adaptation. In *Proc. IEEE Conference on Computer Vision and Pattern Recognition*. Providence, RI, USA, 2066–2073.

[12] Arthur Gretton, Alexander J Smola, Jiayuan Huang, Marcel Schmittfull, Karsten M Borgwardt, and Bernhard Schölkopf. 2009. Covariate Shift by Kernel Mean Matching. (2009). https://doi.org/10.7551/mitpress/9780262170055.003.0008

[13] Maya Gupta, Andrew Cotter, Mahdi Milani Fard, and Serena Wang. 2018. Proxy Fairness. arXiv:1806.11212.

[14] Samantha Kahn. 2015. The End of Gender Rating: Women's Insurance Under the ACA. https://publicpolicy.wharton.upenn.edu/live/news/819-the-end-of-gender-rating-womens-insurance-under.

[15] Faisal Kamiran and Toon Calders. 2012. Data Preprocessing Techniques for Classification Without Discrimination. *Knowledge and Information Systems* 33, 1 (Oct. 2012), 1–33.

[16] Pang Wei Koh and Percy Liang. 2017. Understanding Black-Box Predictions via Influence Functions. In *Proc. International Conference on Machine Learning*. Sydney, NSW, Australia, 1885–1894.

[17] Emmanouil Krasanakis, Eleftherios Spyromitros-Xioufis, Symeon Papadopoulos, and Yiannis Kompatsiaris. 2018. Adaptive Sensitive Reweighting to Mitigate Bias in Fairness-aware Classification. In *Proc. Web Conference*. Lyon, France, 853–862.

[18] Abhinav Maurya. 2018. IEEE Big Data 2017 Panel Discussion on Bias and Transparency. *AI Matters* 4, 2 (July 2018), 13–20.

[19] Jing Qin. 1998. Inferences for case-control and semiparametric two-sample density ratio models. *Biometrika* 85, 3 (1998), 619–630.

[20] Joaquin Quiñonero-Candela, Masashi Sugiyama, Anton Schwaighofer, and Neil D. Lawrence (Eds.). 2009. *Dataset Shift in Machine Learning*. MIT Press, Cambridge, MA, USA.

[21] Hartley Rogers. 1999. *Multivariable Calculus with Vectors*. Prentice-Hall, Upper Saddle River, NJ, USA.

[22] Skyler Speakman, Srihari Sridharan, and Isaac Markus. 2018. Three Population Covariate Shift for Mobile Phone-Based Credit Scoring. In *Proc. ACM Conference on Computing and Sustainable Societies*. Menlo Park, CA, USA, 20.

[23] Masashi Sugiyama, Matthias Krauledat, and Klaus-Robert Müller. 2007. Covariate Shift Adaptation by Importance Weighted Cross Validation. *Journal of Machine Learning Research* 8 (May 2007), 985–1005.

[24] Masashi Sugiyama, Shinichi Nakajima, Hisashi Kashima, Paul von Bünau, and Motoaki Kawanabe. 2007. Direct Importance Estimation with Model Selection and Its Application to Covariate Shift Adaptation. In *Advances in Neural Information Processing Systems*. Vancouver, BC, Canada, 1433–1440.

[25] Masashi Sugiyama, Taiji Suzuki, and Takafumi Kanamori. 2012. *Density Ratio Estimation in Machine Learning* (1st ed.). Cambridge University Press, New York, NY, USA.

[26] Xuezhi Wang and Jeff Schneider. 2014. Flexible Transfer Learning under Support and Model Shift. In *Advances in Neural Information Processing Systems 27*. Montreal, QC, Canada, 1898–1906.

[27] Sidney D. Watson. 2012. Section 1557 of the Affordable Care Act: Civil Rights, Health Reform, Race, and Equity. *Howard Law Journal* 55, 3 (Spring 2012), 855–886.

[28] Dennis Wei, Karthikeyan Natesan Ramamurthy, and Kush R. Varshney. 2015. Health Insurance Market Risk Assessment: Covariate Shift and k-Anonymity. In *Proc. SIAM International Conference on Data Mining*. Vancouver, BC, Canada, 226–234.

A GRADIENT DERIVATIONS FOR TFCS

The following derivation is similar to and takes inspiration from the theory of influence functions [16], which describe the effect of individual training points on model parameters. Here we consider the effect of re-weighting all training points at once.

First define $\mathcal{L}_c$ to be the re-weighted classification loss in (12),

$$\mathcal{L}_c(\hat{\theta}) = \frac{1}{n} \sum_{i \in \mathcal{S}} w_{CS}(x_i) \mathcal{L}\big(s(x_i; \hat{\theta}), y_i\big).$$

The derivative of $\mathcal{L}_c$ with respect to each w_i is given by the chain rule as

$$\frac{\partial \mathcal{L}_c}{\partial w_i} = \left(\nabla_{\hat{\theta}} \mathcal{L}_c\right)^T \frac{\partial \hat{\theta}}{\partial w_i}, \tag{13}$$

and similarly for $\mathcal{L}_f$. The second factor in (13) is the vector of partial derivatives $\partial \hat{\theta}_j / \partial w_i$ for all j. Hence for the combined loss

$$\mathcal{L}_t = \mathcal{L}_c + \lambda \mathcal{L}_f,$$

$$\frac{\partial \mathcal{L}_t}{\partial w_i} = \left(\nabla_{\hat{\theta}} \mathcal{L}_c + \lambda \nabla_{\hat{\theta}} \mathcal{L}_f\right)^T \frac{\partial \hat{\theta}}{\partial w_i}. \tag{14}$$

To derive an expression for $\partial \hat{\theta} / \partial w_i$, we use the fact that if $\hat{\theta}$ is a minimizer in (10), then it must satisfy the first-order optimality conditions

$$\sum_{i \in \mathcal{S}} w_i \frac{\partial \mathcal{L}(s(x_i; \hat{\theta}), y_i)}{\partial \hat{\theta}_j} = 0 \quad \forall j.$$

For fixed $\{(x_i, y_i), i \in \mathcal{S}\}$, these conditions give a set of implicit equations for $\hat{\theta}$ in terms of $\{w_i\}$. We may obtain an *explicit* expression for the derivative $\partial \hat{\theta} / \partial w_i$ using the method of eliminating differentials [21, Ch. 11] as follows:

$$dw_i \frac{\partial \mathcal{L}(s(x_i; \hat{\theta}), y_i)}{\partial \hat{\theta}_j} + \sum_{i' \in \mathcal{S}} w_{i'} \sum_k \frac{\partial^2 \mathcal{L}(s(x_{i'}; \hat{\theta}), y_{i'})}{\partial \hat{\theta}_j \partial \hat{\theta}_k} d\hat{\theta}_k = 0.$$

Rewriting in matrix-vector notation,

$$\nabla_{\hat{\theta}} \mathcal{L}\big(s(x_i; \hat{\theta}), y_i\big) + H_{\hat{\theta}} \frac{\partial \hat{\theta}}{\partial w_i} = 0,$$

where we have defined

$$H_{\hat{\theta}} = \sum_{i \in \mathcal{S}} w_i \nabla^2_{\hat{\theta}} \mathcal{L}\big(s(x_i; \hat{\theta}), y_i\big). \tag{15}$$

Hence

$$\frac{\partial \hat{\theta}}{\partial w_i} = -H_{\hat{\theta}}^{-1} \nabla_{\hat{\theta}} \mathcal{L}\big(s(x_i; \hat{\theta}), y_i\big). \tag{16}$$

For the case of binary classification with log loss $\mathcal{L}$ (aka cross-entropy) and logistic regression, we have

$$\mathcal{L}(s, y) = -y \log(s) - (1 - y) \log(1 - s),$$

$$s(x; \hat{\theta}) = \sigma(\hat{\theta}^T x) = \frac{1}{1 + e^{-\hat{\theta}^T x}}.$$

where $\sigma(t)$ denotes the sigmoid function $\frac{1}{1+e^{-t}}$. Then

$$\nabla_{\hat{\theta}} s = \frac{e^{-\hat{\theta}^T x}}{\left(1 + e^{-\hat{\theta}^T x}\right)^2} \cdot x = s(1 - s)x, \tag{17}$$

$$\nabla_{\hat{\theta}} \mathcal{L} = (-y(1 - s) + (1 - y)s)x. \tag{18}$$

Using (18) and letting $s_i = s(x_i; \hat{\theta})$, the gradient of the classification loss is therefore

$$\nabla_{\hat{\theta}} \mathcal{L}_c = \frac{1}{n} \sum_{i \in \mathcal{S}} w_{CS}(x_i)[-y_i(1 - s_i) + (1 - y_i)s_i]x_i. \tag{19}$$

Likewise using (17), the gradient of the fairness loss is

$$\nabla_{\theta} \mathcal{L}_F = 2 \sum_{k<l} \left[\left(\frac{1}{|\mathcal{T}_k|} \sum_{i \in \mathcal{T}_k} s_i - \frac{1}{|\mathcal{T}_l|} \sum_{i \in \mathcal{T}_l} s_i\right) \times \left(\frac{1}{|\mathcal{T}_k|} \sum_{i \in \mathcal{T}_k} s_i(1 - s_i)x_i - \frac{1}{|\mathcal{T}_l|} \sum_{i \in \mathcal{T}_l} s_i(1 - s_i)x_i\right)\right]. \tag{20}$$

For the Hessian we find

$$\nabla^2_{\hat{\theta}} \mathcal{L} = x(\nabla_{\hat{\theta}} s)^T = s(1 - s)xx^T, \tag{21}$$

which is needed in (15).

To close this section, we justify the earlier statement that $w = w_{CS}$ is a stationary point in the case $\lambda = 0$. Since $\hat{\theta}$ is a minimizer in (10), it satisfies

$$\frac{1}{n}\sum_{i\in S} w_i \nabla_\theta \mathcal{L}\big(s(x_i;\hat{\theta}), y_i\big) = 0.$$

The left-hand side coincides with $\nabla_{\hat{\theta}}\mathcal{L}_c$ when $w = w_{CS}$ and therefore $\nabla_{\hat{\theta}}\mathcal{L}_c = 0$. Combining this with $\lambda = 0$ in (14) implies that $\nabla_w \mathcal{L}_t = 0$ at $w = w_{CS}$.

How Do Fairness Definitions Fare? Examining Public Attitudes Towards Algorithmic Definitions of Fairness

Nripsuta Ani Saxena**
University of Southern California
Los Angeles, USA
nsaxena@usc.edu

Karen Huang
Harvard University
Cambridge, USA
karenhuang@g.harvard.edu

Evan DeFilippis
Harvard University
Cambridge, USA
defilippis@g.harvard.edu

Goran Radanovic
Harvard University
Cambridge, USA
gradanovic@g.harvard.edu

David C. Parkes
Harvard University
Cambridge, USA
parkes@g.harvard.edu

Yang Liu**
University of California, Santa Cruz
Santa Cruz, USA
yangliu@ucsc.edu

ABSTRACT

What is the best way to define algorithmic fairness? While many definitions of fairness have been proposed in the computer science literature, there is no clear agreement over a particular definition. In this work, we investigate ordinary people's perceptions of three of these fairness definitions. Across two online experiments, we test which definitions people perceive to be the fairest in the context of loan decisions, and whether fairness perceptions change with the addition of sensitive information (i.e., race of the loan applicants). Overall, one definition (calibrated fairness) tends to be more preferred than the others, and the results also provide support for the principle of affirmative action.

CCS CONCEPTS

• **Human-centered computing → Human computer interaction (HCI)**; • **Applied computing → Psychology**; • **Computing methodologies → Artificial intelligence**.

ACM Reference Format:
Nripsuta Ani Saxena**, Karen Huang, Evan DeFilippis, Goran Radanovic, David C. Parkes, and Yang Liu**. 2019. How Do Fairness Definitions Fare? Examining Public Attitudes Towards Algorithmic Definitions of Fairness . In *AAAI/ACM Conference on AI, Ethics, and Society (AIES '19), January 27–28, 2019, Honolulu, HI, USA.* ACM, New York, NY, USA, 8 pages. https://doi.org/10.1145/3306618.3314248

1 INTRODUCTION

Algorithms are increasingly being used in high-impact domains of decision-making, such as loans, hiring, bail, and university admissions, with wide-ranging societal implications. However, issues have arisen regarding the fairness of these algorithmic decisions. For example, the risk assessment software, COMPAS, used by judicial systems in many states, predicts a score indicating the likelihood of a defendant committing a crime if given bail. ProPublica analyzed recidivism predictions from COMPAS for criminal defendants, and looked at false positive rates and false negative rates for defendants of different races. It argued that the tool is biased against black defendants [3]. Equivant (formerly called Northpointe), the company that developed the COMPAS tool, on the other hand, focused on positive predictive value, which is similar for whites and blacks [9]. That is, by some measures of fairness, the tool was found to be biased against blacks; meanwhile by other measures, it was not. Which measures are fair?

The above scenario is not a rare case. Given the increasing pervasiveness of automated decision-making systems, there's a growing concern among both computer scientists and the public about how to ensure algorithms are fair. While several definitions of fairness have recently been proposed in the computer science literature, there's a lack of agreement among researchers about which definition is the most appropriate [12]. It is very unlikely that one definition of fairness will be sufficient. This is supported also by recent impossibility results that show some fairness definitions cannot coexist [18]. Since the public is affected by these algorithmic systems, it is important to investigate public views of algorithmic fairness [6, 19–21, 25].

While substantial research has been done in moral psychology to understand people's perceptions of fairness (e.g, Yaari and Bar-Hillel 1984, Bazerman et al. 1995), relatively little work has been done to understand how the general public views fairness criteria in algorithmic decision making: Pierson (2017) investigated how two different factors influence views on algorithmic fairness, Plane et al. (2017) explored human perceptions of discrimination in targeted online advertising, Grgić-Hlača et al. (2018a) and Grgić-Hlača et al. (2018b) studied human perceptions of features used in algorithmic decision making, and Binns et al. (2018) examined people's perception of justice in algorithmic decision making under different explanation styles. In contrast to this work, our goal is to understand how people perceive the fairness definitions proposed in the recent computer science literature, that is, the outcomes allowed by these definitions.

AIES '19, January 27–28, 2019, Honolulu, HI, USA

ACM ISBN 978-1-4503-6324-2/19/01...$15.00
https://doi.org/10.1145/3306618.3314248

** Correspondence should be directed to: nsaxena@usc.edu and yangliu@ucsc.edu.

By testing people's perception of different fairness definitions, we hope to spur more work on understanding definitions of fairness that are appropriate for particular contexts. In line with recent work examining public attitudes of the ethical programming of machines [4, 7], we suggest that these public attitudes serve as a useful and important input in a conversation between technologists and ethicists. These findings can help technologists to develop decision-making algorithms with fairness principles aligned with those of the general public, to make sure that designs are sensitive to the prevailing notions of fairness in society. Crowdsourcing can also be used to understand how preferences vary across geographies and cultures.

2 DEFINITIONS OF FAIRNESS

Broadly, we investigate a concept of fairness known as *distributive justice*, or fairness regarding the outcomes [1, 2]. However, which characteristics regarding the individual should be relevant and which should be irrelevant to fairness? We instantiate our study via investigating two characteristics: task-specific similarity (loan repayment rate) and a sensitive attribute (race), and collect data on attitudes toward the relevancy of these characteristics. In principle, fairness is the absence of any bias based on an individual's inherent or acquired characteristics that are irrelevant in the particular context of decision-making [8]. In many contexts, these inherent characteristics (referred to as 'sensitive attributes' or 'protected attributes' in the computer science literature), are gender, religion, race, skin color, age, or national origin.

We restrict our emphasis to three fairness definitions from the computer science literature. We choose to test these three definitions because these definitions can be easily operationalized as distinct decisions in the context of loan scenarios that are easily understandable by ordinary people. In our experiments, we map these definitions (or constrained versions of the definitions) to distinct loan allocation choices, and test people's judgments of these choices. We summarize the three fairness definitions as follows:

Treating similar individuals similarly. Dwork et al. (2012) formulate fairness as treating similar individuals (with respect to certain attributes) similarly in receiving a favorable decision, where the similarity of any two individuals is determined on the basis of a similarity distance metric, specific to the task at hand, and that ideally represents a notion of ground truth in regard to the decision context. Given this similarity metric, an algorithm would be fair if its decisions satisfied the Lipschitz condition (a continuity and similarity measure) defined with respect to the metric. In our loan allocation scenario, individuals with similar repayment rates should receive similar amounts of money.

Never favor a worse individual over a better one. In the context of online learning, Joseph et al. (2016) define fairness, in a setting where a single individual is to be selected for a favorable decision, as always choosing a better individual (with higher expected value of some measure of inherent quality) with a probability greater than or equal to the probability of choosing a worse individual. This definition promotes meritocracy with respect to the candidate's inherent quality. Joseph et al. (2016) apply this definition of fairness to the setting of contextual bandits, a classical sequential decision-making process, by utilizing the expected reward to determine the quality of an action (an arm as in the bandit setting). Each arm represents a different subpopulation, and each subpopulation may have its own function that maps decision context to expected payoff. In our loan allocation scenario, an individual with a higher repayment rate should obtain at least as much money as her peer.

Calibrated fairness. The third definition, that we refer to as 'calibrated fairness', is formulated by Liu et al. (2017) in the setting of sequential decision-making[1]. Calibrated fairness selects individuals in proportion to their merit. In a multi-armed bandit setting, this means that an arm would be pulled with a probability that its pull would result the largest reward if all the arms are pulled. When the merit is known (underlying true quality), calibrated fairness implies the meritocratic fairness of Joseph et al. (2016). Furthermore, as argued by Liu et al. (2017), calibrated fairness implies Dwork et al. (2016) for a suitably chosen similarity metric. In our loan allocation scenario, we interpret calibrated fairness as requiring that two individuals with repayment rates r_1 and r_2, respectively, should obtain $r_1/(r_1 + r_2)$ and $r_2/(r_1 + r_2)$ amount of money, respectively[2].

3 OVERVIEW OF PRESENT RESEARCH

n the present research, we ask: when do people endorse one fairness definition over another?

First, we want to understand how support for the three definitions of fairness depends on variation in the similarity of the target individuals. The three definitions differ in how this comparison between task-specific metrics should matter.

We are also interested in understanding how information about the race of the two target individuals influences these fairness perceptions. Direct discrimination is the phenomenon of discriminating against an individual simply because of their membership, or perceived membership, in certain protected (or sensitive) attributes, such as age, disability, religion, gender, and race [11]. All three definitions agree that, conditioned on the relevant task-specific metric, an attribute such as race should not be relevant to decision-making.[3] Information about race may matter, however, since people may consider race to be an important factor for distributive justice. For example, in decisions promoting affirmative action, people may believe that considering race is important in order to address historical inequities. If that is the case, then definitions of algorithmic fairness may need to take into account such sensitive attributes.

Across two online experiments, we investigate how people perceive algorithmic fairness in the context of loans, which is a setting with a divisible good to allocate. We employ a scenario where a loan officer must decide how to allocate a limited amount of loan money to two individuals. In Study 1, we test how the individuals' task-specific similarity (i.e., loan repayment rates) influences perceptions of fairness, in the absence of information about race. In

[1]Note that Kleinberg et al. (2016), Chouldechova (2017) define 'calibration' in a different way, that includes the notion of a sensitive attribute.

[2]This is a slightly different version of the formal definition in Liu et al. (2017), which would take the ratio in proportion to the rate at which one individual repays while the other does not, but we feel a more intuitive way to capture the idea of calibrated fairness in our setting.)

[3]Here, we assume that the treating similar individuals similarly definition [10] does not use race as a relevant dimension for judging individual similarity.

Study 2, we test how the individuals' race may, along with their loan repayment rates, influence perceptions of fairness. For the purpose of the study, we need to interpret these fairness definitions, which are formalized for choosing a single individual for a favorable decision (or assigning an indivisible good) to this setting where the good is divisible. Across both experiments, we investigate fairness perceptions in the U.S. population.

4 STUDY 1 (NO SENSITIVE INFORMATION)

In this study, our motivation is to investigate how information on an individual task-specific feature (i.e., the candidates' loan repayment rate) influences perceptions of fairness. We present participants with a scenario in which two individuals have each applied for a loan. The participants know no personal information about the two individuals except their loan repayment rates. We choose three allocation rules, described in the following paragraphs, that allow us to formulate qualitative judgments regarding the three fairness definitions.

4.1 Procedure

We recruited 200 participants from Amazon Mechanical Turk (MTurk) on March 18-19, 2018. The majority of them identified themselves as white (82%), 8% as black, 6% as Asian or Asian-American, 2% as Hispanic, and the rest with multiple races. The average age was 39.43 (SD = 12.47). Most (91%) had attended some college, while almost all other participants had a high school degree or GED. (All demographic information was self-reported.) All participants were U.S. residents, and each were paid $0.20 for participating.

We presented participants with the scenario presented in Figure 4 in the appendix.

This experiment employed a between-subjects design with four conditions. We varied the individual candidates' similarity (dissimilarity) in ability to pay back their loan (i.e., their loan repayment rate), as an operationalization of task-specific similarity (dissimilarity) relevant to the three fairness definitions. Participants were randomly shown one of four loan repayment rates: 55% and 50% (Treatment 1), 70% and 40% (Treatment 2), 90% and 10% (Treatment 3), and 100% and 20% (Treatment 4). One treatment had a very small difference between the loan repayment rates of the two candidates (Treatment 1). The next treatment had a larger difference between the loan repayment rates (Treatment 2), with the next two treatments (Treatments 3 and 4) having a much larger difference in their loan repayment rates. Each participant was only shown one Treatment.

We held all other information about the two candidates constant. We then presented participants with three possible decisions for how to allocate the money between the two individuals. The order of the three decisions was counterbalanced.

Each decision was designed to help us to untangle the three fairness definitions.

"All A" Decision. Give all the money to the candidate with the higher payback rate. This decision is allowed in all treatments under meritocratic fairness as defined Joseph et al. (2016), where a worse applicant is never favored over a better one. It would also be allowed under the definition formulated by Dwork et al. (2012), in the more extreme treatments, and even in every treatment in the case that the similarity metric was very discerning. This decision would not be allowed in any treatment under the calibrated fairness definition [22].

"Equal" Decision. Split the money 50/50 between the candidates, giving $25,000 to each. This decision is allowed in all treatments under Dwork et al. (2012) – treating similar people similarly. Moreover, under their definition, when two individuals are deemed to be similar to each other, then this is the textitonly allowable decision (in Treatment 1, for example). This decision is also allowed in all the treatments under the meritocratic definition [17], as the candidate with the higher loan repayment rate is given at least as much as the other candidate, and, hence, is weakly favored. The decision, however, would not be allowed in any treatment under calibrated fairness [22], since the candidates are not being treated in proportion of their quality (loan repayment rate).

"Ratio" Decision. Split the money between two candidates in proportion of their loan repayment rates. This decision is allowed in all treatments under calibrated fairness, where resources are divided in proportion to the true quality of the candidates. Moreover, this is the only decision allowed under this definition. This decision could also align with the definition proposed by Dwork et al. (2012), but only for suitably defined similarity metrics that allow the distance between decisions implied by the ratio allocation. Finally, this decision would be allowed under meritocratic fairness [17] for the same reasons as the "Equal" decision. Namely, the candidate with the higher loan repayment rate is weakly favored to the other candidate.

It is important to note that we are testing human perceptions regarding the outcomes that different fairness definition allow, not the definitions themselves. However, if a certain definition allows multiple decisions, then we would expect these decisions to receive similar support. Where the perception of the fairness of outcomes is inconsistent with the allowable decisions for a rule, this is worthwhile to understand.

If it is true that participants most prefer the treating similar people similarly definition, one would expect that they would prefer the "Equal" decision to the other two decisions for a wider range of similarity metrics and treatments. If it is true that participants most prefer the meritocratic definition, one would expect no significant difference in support for the three different decisions. If it is true that participants most prefer the calibrated fairness definition, one would expect that the "Ratio" decision is perceived as more fair than the other two decisions.

We formulated the following set of hypotheses:

Hypothesis 1A. Across all treatments, participants perceive the "Ratio" decision as more fair than the "Equal" decision.

Hypothesis 1B. Across all treatments, participants perceive the "Ratio" decision as more fair than the "All A" decision.

Hypothesis 2. Participants perceive the "Equal" decision as more fair than the "All A" decision in Treatment 1. That is, participants may view the candidates in Treatment 1 as "similar enough" to be treated similarly.

Hypothesis 3. Participants perceive the "All A" decision as more fair than the "Equal" decision in Treatments 3 and 4.

4.2 Results

First, we tested hypotheses H1A and H1B, which conjecture that participants will consider the "Ratio" decision as the most fair. We found partial support for H1A: participants perceived dividing the $50,000 between the two individuals in proportion of their loan repayment rates (the "Ratio" decision) as more fair than splitting the $50,000 equally (the "Equal" decision) in Treatments 2, 3, and 4 (see Figure 1). We found partial support for H1B: participants rated the "Ratio" decision as more fair than the "All A" decision in Treatments 1 and 2 (see Figure 1).

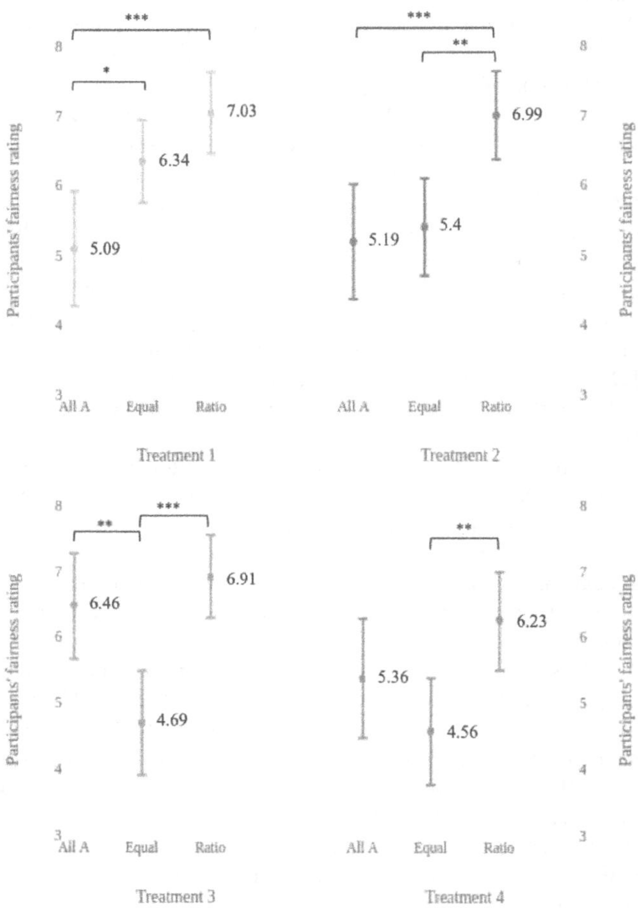

Figure 1: Comparison of means (with 95% CI) for Study 1. Where * signifies p <0.05, ** p <0.01, and *** p <0.001.

Second, we found that participants in Treatment 1 rated the "Equal" decision as more fair than the "All A" definition (see Figure 1), supporting H2. We see that when the difference in the loan repayment rates of the individuals was small (5%), participants perceived the decision to divide the money equally between the individuals as more fair than giving all the money to the individual with the higher loan repayment rate.

Third, we found that participants rated the "All A" decision as more fair than the "Equal" decision in Treatment 3, but not in Treatment 4 (see Figure 1).

4.3 Discussion

Evidence from Study 1 suggests that participants perceived the "Ratio" decision – the only decision that aligns with calibrated fairness – to be more fair than the "Equal" decision – the only decision that is always aligned with the treating people similarly definition. One possible explanation is that calibrated fairness implies treating people similarly for a similarity metric [22] that is based on a notion of merit.

In Treatments 1 and 2, participants rated the "Ratio" decision – the only decision that aligns with calibrated fairness – to be more fair than the "All A" decision. Note that the meritocratic definition is the only definition that always allows the "All A" decision. No significant difference was discovered for Treatments 3 and 4, where one candidate has a much higher repayment rate.

Furthermore, participants viewed individuals to be similar enough to be treated similarly only when the difference in the applicants' loan repayment rates was very small (approximately 5%).

5 STUDY 2 (WITH SENSITIVE INFORMATION)

In this study, our motivation is to investigate how the addition of sensitive information to information on an individual task-specific feature (i.e., the candidates' loan repayment rate) influences perceptions of fairness.

We employed the same experimental paradigm as in Study 1, presenting participants with the scenario of two individuals applying for a loan, and three possible ways of allocating the loan money. Importantly, in Study 2, in addition to providing information on the individuals' loan repayment rates, we also provided information on the individuals' race. We investigate how information on the candidates' loan repayment rates and the candidates' race influence people's fairness judgments of the three allocation decisions.

5.1 Procedure

We recruited a separate sample of 1800 participants from Amazon Mechanical Turk (MTurk) on April 20-21, 2018, none of whom had taken part in Study 1. Most of them identified as white (74%), 9% as black, 7% as Asian or Asian-American, 5% as Hispanic, and the rest with multiple races. The average age was 36.97 (SD = 12.54). Most (89%) had attended some college, while almost all other participants had a high school degree or GED. All participants were U.S. residents, and each was paid $0.20 for participating. (All demographic information was self-reported.)

We presented participants with the same scenario as in Study 1, but this time also providing the candidates' race and gender. We held the gender of the candidates constant (both were male), and randomized race (black or white). Thus, either the white candidate had the higher loan repayment rate, or the black candidate had the higher loan repayment rate. The question presented to the participants in Study 2 can be found in Figure 5 in the Appendix.

We presented the same question and choices for loan allocations, and tested the same hypotheses, as in Study 1.

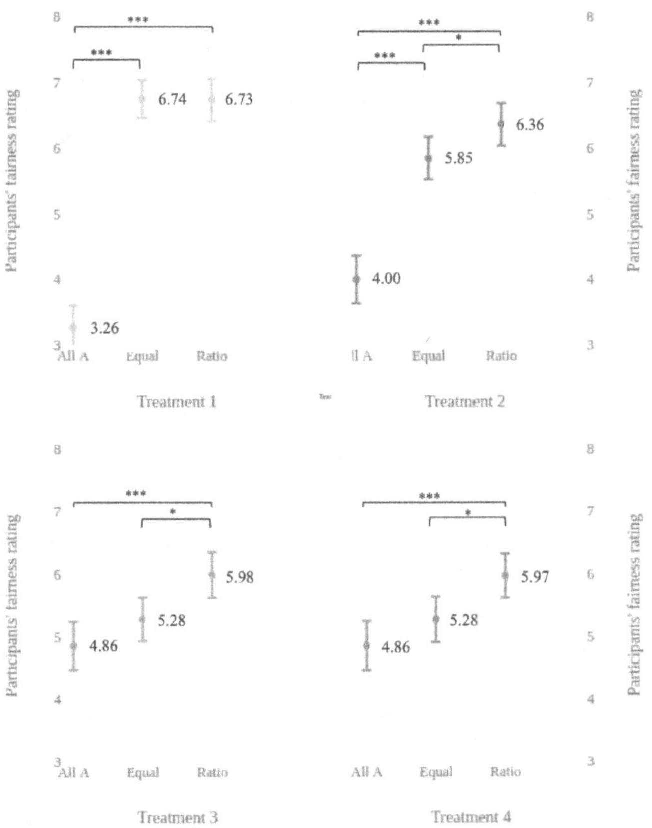

Figure 2: Comparison of means (with 95% CI) for Study 2 (when the individual with the higher loan repayment rate is white). Where * signifies p <0.05, ** p <0.01, and *** p <0.001.

5.2 Results

We found that participants viewed the "Ratio" decision as more fair than the "Equal" decision in Treatments 2, 3, and 4, regardless of race, in support of H1A. Furthermore, we found an interaction effect for H1B: When the candidate with the higher repayment rate was white, people perceived the "Ratio" decision as more fair compared to the "All A" decision in all treatments. By contrast, when the candidate with the higher repayment rate was black, people perceived the "Ratio" decision as more fair compared to the "All A" decision only in Treatments 1 and 2. (See Figures 2 and 3.) Thus, participants in Study 2 gave most support to the decision to divide the $50,000 between the two individuals in proportion to their loan repayment rates, particularly when the individual with the higher loan repayment rate was white.

Furthermore, we found that participants viewed the "Equal" decision as more fair than the "All A" decision in Treatment 1, regardless of race, in support of H2 (see Figures 2 and 3). Participants also rated the "Equal" decision as more fair than the "All A" decision in Treatment 2, but only when the candidate with the higher repayment rate was white (see Figure 2).

When the difference between the two candidates' repayment rates was larger (Treatments 3 and 4), participants viewed the "All A" decision as more fair than the "Equal" decision but only when the candidate with the higher repayment rate was black (see Figure 3). By contrast, when the candidate with the higher loan repayment rate was white, participants did not rate the two decisions differently (see Figure 2).

5.3 Discussion

In Study 2, we tested whether participants' perceptions of these three fairness definitions could be influenced by additional information regarding the candidates' race.

Our results generally show that participants perceived the "Ratio" decision to be more fair than the other two, hence supporting the results from Study 1. These results are not dependent on the race attribute. Furthermore, regardless of race, when the difference between the loan repayment rates was small (Treatment 1), participants preferred the "Equal" decision to the "All A" decision. This supports the corresponding results from Study 1, Treatment 1, which indicate that one should account for similarity of individuals when designing fair rules.

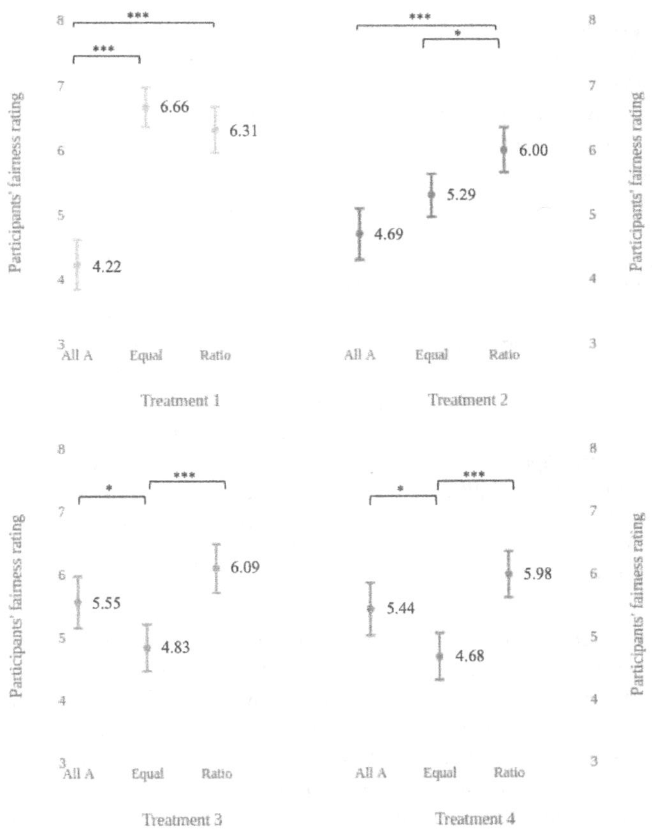

Figure 3: Comparison of means (with 95% CI) for Study 2 (when the individual with the higher loan repayment rate is black). Where * signifies p <0.05, ** p <0.01, and *** p <0.001.

However, we also found evidence that race does affect participants' perceptions of fairness. When the difference in loan repayment rates was larger (Treatments 3 and 4), participants rated the

"All A" decision as more fair than the "Equal" decision, but only when the candidate with the higher repayment rate was black. These results suggest a boundary condition of H3: people may support giving all the loan money to the candidate with the higher payback rate, compared to splitting the money equally, when the candidate with the higher payback rate is a member of a group that is historically disadvantaged.

Each definition, from meritocratic to similarity to calibrated fairness is successively stronger in our context, ruling out additional decisions. In this light, it is interesting that the ratio decision is generally most preferred, providing support for the calibrated fairness definition, even though this definition is the strongest of the three in the present context. When historically disadvantaged individuals have a higher repayment rate, participants are more supportive of more decisive allocations in favor of the stronger, and historically disadvantaged, individual.

6 CONCLUSION

People broadly show a preference for the "Ratio" decision, which is indicative of their support for the calibrated fairness definition [22], as compared to the treating similar people similarly [10] and meritocratic Joseph et al. definitions. We also find in Study 2 some support for the principle of affirmative action.

Through the use of crowdsourcing, we can elicit information on public attitudes towards different definitions of algorithmic fairness, and how individual characteristics, such as task-specific features (e.g., loan repayment rates) and sensitive attributes (e.g., race) could be relevant in fair decision-making. Understanding public attitudes can help to continue a dialogue between technologists and ethicists in the design of algorithms that make decisions of consequence to the public. For example, the three fairness definitions examined here agree that, conditioned on the task-specific metric, an attribute such as race should not be relevant to decision-making. Yet, we find some treatments under which people's attitudes about loan decisions change when race is provided to the context.

This paper opens up several directions for future research. Beyond testing additional definitions, future experiments could in addition specify whether the decision was made by a human or an algorithm. Psychological theories of mind may influence people's fairness judgments. Second, future work could investigate how people perceive fairness in other contexts, such as university admissions or bail decisions, where there is no divisible resource but rather a definite decision needs to be made, and in the university case in the context of a resource constraint. Third, further research could examine why the availability of additional personal or sensitive information influences perceptions of fairness. Why do people consider factors such as race important for their fairness ratings? And to what extent are people willing to endorse affirmative action in defining algorithmic fairness? Finally, it is important to consider how to incorporate the general public's views into algorithmic decision-making.

These results are only the start of a research program on understanding ordinary people's judgments of definitions of algorithmic fairness. As the literature on moral psychology has shown, people often make inconsistent and unreasoned moral judgments [13]. Indeed, research on moral judgments in regard to the decisions made by autonomous vehicles (the "moral machine") has shown that people approve of utilitarian autonomous vehicles, but are unwilling to purchase utilitarian autonomous vehicles for themselves [7]. On the other hand, research in moral psychology shows that people can engage in sophisticated moral reasoning, thinking in an impartial, bias-free way, resulting in moral judgments that favor the greater good [16]. Future research could investigate how moral reasoning interventions could influence people's fairness judgments in the domain of algorithmic fairness.

REFERENCES

[1] J Stacy Adams. 1963. Towards an understanding of inequity. *The Journal of Abnormal and Social Psychology* 67, 5 (1963), 422.

[2] J Stacy Adams. 1965. Inequity in social exchange. In *Advances in experimental social psychology*. Vol. 2. Elsevier, 267–299.

[3] J Angwin, J Larson, S Mattu, and L Kirchner. 2016. Machine bias risk assessments in criminal sentencing. https://www.propublica.org/article/machine-bias-risk-assessments-in-criminal-sentencing. *ProPublica https://www.propublica.org* (2016). Accessed: 2018-03-27.

[4] Edmond Awad, Sohan Dsouza, Richard Kim, Jonathan Schulz, Joseph Henrich, Azim Shariff, Jean-François Bonnefon, and Iyad Rahwan. 2018. The moral machine experiment. *Nature* 563, 7729 (2018), 59.

[5] Max H Bazerman, Sally Blount White, and George F Loewenstein. 1995. Perceptions of fairness in interpersonal and individual choice situations. *Current Directions in Psychological Science* 4, 2 (1995), 39–43.

[6] Reuben Binns, Max Van Kleek, Michael Veale, Ulrik Lyngs, Jun Zhao, and Nigel Shadbolt. 2018. 'It's Reducing a Human Being to a Percentage': Perceptions of Justice in Algorithmic Decisions. In *Proceedings of the 2018 CHI Conference on Human Factors in Computing Systems*. ACM, 377.

[7] Jean-François Bonnefon, Azim Shariff, and Iyad Rahwan. 2016. The social dilemma of autonomous vehicles. *Science* 352, 6293 (2016), 1573–1576.

[8] Alexandra Chouldechova. 2017. Fair prediction with disparate impact: A study of bias in recidivism prediction instruments. *Big data* 5, 2 (2017), 153–163.

[9] William Dieterich, Christina Mendoza, and Tim Brennan. 2016. COMPAS risk scales: Demonstrating accuracy equity and predictive parity. http://go.volarisgroup.com/rs/430-MBX-989/images/ProPublica_Commentary_Final_070616.pdf. *Northpoint Inc* (2016). Accessed: 2018-10-24.

[10] Cynthia Dwork, Moritz Hardt, Toniann Pitassi, Omer Reingold, and Richard Zemel. 2012. Fairness through awareness. In *Proceedings of the 3rd innovations in theoretical computer science conference*. ACM, 214–226.

[11] Evelyn Ellis and Philippa Watson. 2012. *EU anti-discrimination law*. Oxford University Press.

[12] Pratik Gajane and Mykola Pechenizkiy. 2017. On formalizing fairness in prediction with machine learning. *arXiv preprint arXiv:1710.03184* (2017).

[13] Joshua David Greene. 2014. *Moral tribes: Emotion, reason, and the gap between us and them*. Penguin.

[14] Nina Grgić-Hlača, Elissa M Redmiles, Krishna P Gummadi, and Adrian Weller. 2018. Human perceptions of fairness in algorithmic decision making: A case study of criminal risk prediction. *arXiv preprint arXiv:1802.09548* (2018).

[15] Nina Grgić-Hlača, Muhammad Bilal Zafar, Krishna P Gummadi, and Adrian Weller. 2018. Beyond distributive fairness in algorithmic decision making: Feature selection for procedurally fair learning. In *Thirty-Second AAAI Conference on Artificial Intelligence*.

[16] Karen Huang, Joshua David Greene, and M Bazerman. 2019. Veil-of-ignorance reasoning favors the greater good. (2019). Working paper.

[17] Matthew Joseph, Michael Kearns, Jamie H Morgenstern, and Aaron Roth. 2016. Fairness in learning: Classic and contextual bandits. In *Advances in Neural Information Processing Systems*. 325–333.

[18] Jon Kleinberg, Sendhil Mullainathan, and Manish Raghavan. 2016. Inherent trade-offs in the fair determination of risk scores. *arXiv preprint arXiv:1609.05807* (2016).

[19] Min Kyung Lee. 2018. Understanding perception of algorithmic decisions: Fairness, trust, and emotion in response to algorithmic management. *Big Data & Society* 5, 1 (2018), 2053951718756684.

[20] Min Kyung Lee and Su Baykal. 2017. Algorithmic Mediation in Group Decisions: Fairness Perceptions of Algorithmically Mediated vs. Discussion-Based Social Division.. In *CSCW*. 1035–1048.

[21] Min Kyung Lee, Ji Tae Kim, and Leah Lizarondo. 2017. A Human-Centered Approach to Algorithmic Services: Considerations for Fair and Motivating Smart Community Service Management that Allocates Donations to Non-Profit Organizations. In *Proceedings of the 2017 CHI Conference on Human Factors in Computing Systems*. ACM, 3365–3376.

[22] Yang Liu, Goran Radanovic, Christos Dimitrakakis, Debmalya Mandal, and David C Parkes. 2017. Calibrated fairness in bandits. *arXiv preprint*

arXiv:1707.01875 (2017).

[23] Emma Pierson. 2017. Gender differences in beliefs about algorithmic fairness. *arXiv preprint arXiv:1712.09124* (2017).

[24] Angelisa C Plane, Elissa M Redmiles, Michelle L Mazurek, and Michael Carl Tschantz. 2017. Exploring user perceptions of discrimination in online targeted advertising. In *USENIX Security*.

[25] Allison Woodruff, Sarah E Fox, Steven Rousso-Schindler, and Jeffrey Warshaw. 2018. A Qualitative Exploration of Perceptions of Algorithmic Fairness. In *Proceedings of the 2018 CHI Conference on Human Factors in Computing Systems*. ACM, 656.

[26] Menahem E Yaari and Maya Bar-Hillel. 1984. On dividing justly. *Social choice and welfare* 1, 1 (1984), 1–24.

A APPENDIX

To be eligible to take our surveys, the Amazon Mechanical Turk workers had to be located in the United States of America. We stipulated this restriction via TurkPrime, which is a platform for performing crowdsourced research when using Amazon Mechanical Turk.

Amazon Mechanical Turk workers ('MTurker') could only participate in on one of the two studies, and not both.

The first section contains the questions the workers were asked in the studies. The second section contains the demographics questions the respondents of both studies were asked after completing the study. While voluntary, most respondents answered them. The last section contains plots of some demographics of the respondents.

A.1 Questions from the studies

The question asked in Study 1 is presented in Figure 4. The question asked in Study 2 is presented in Figure 5.

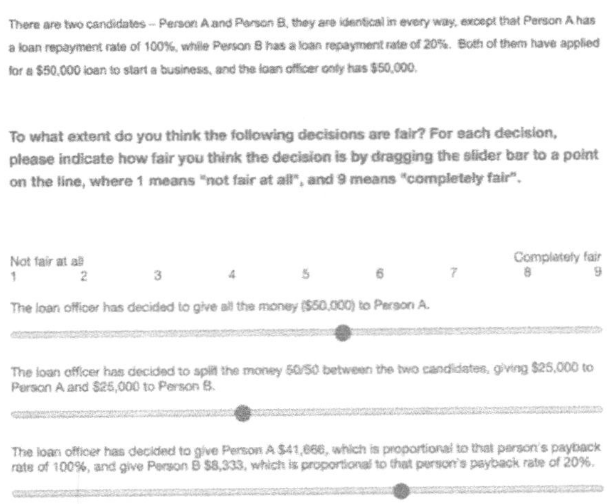

There are two candidates – Person A and Person B, they are identical in every way, except that Person A has a loan repayment rate of 100%, while Person B has a loan repayment rate of 20%. Both of them have applied for a $50,000 loan to start a business, and the loan officer only has $50,000.

To what extent do you think the following decisions are fair? For each decision, please indicate how fair you think the decision is by dragging the slider bar to a point on the line, where 1 means "not fair at all", and 9 means "completely fair".

Not fair at all 1 2 3 4 5 6 7 8 9 Completely fair

The loan officer has decided to give all the money ($50,000) to Person A.

The loan officer has decided to split the money 50/50 between the two candidates, giving $25,000 to Person A and $25,000 to Person B.

The loan officer has decided to give Person A $41,666, which is proportional to that person's payback rate of 100%, and give Person B $8,333, which is proportional to that person's payback rate of 20%.

Figure 4: Question presented to the participants in Study 1.

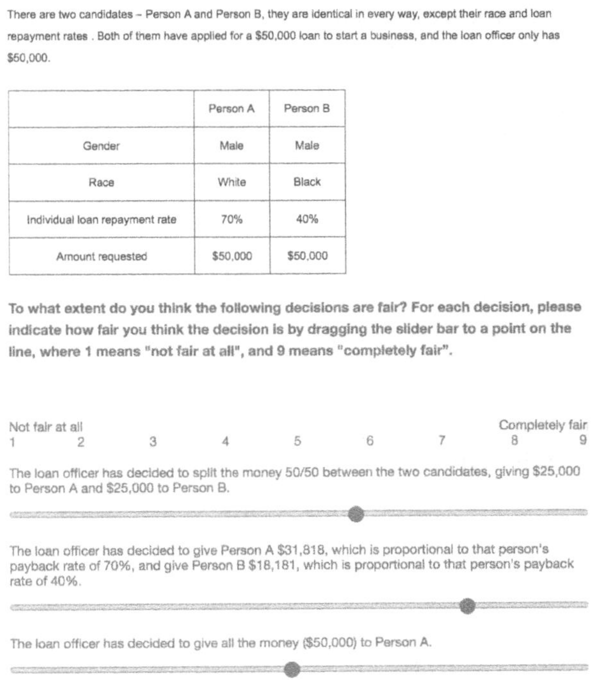

There are two candidates – Person A and Person B, they are identical in every way, except their race and loan repayment rates . Both of them have applied for a $50,000 loan to start a business, and the loan officer only has $50,000.

	Person A	Person B
Gender	Male	Male
Race	White	Black
Individual loan repayment rate	70%	40%
Amount requested	$50,000	$50,000

To what extent do you think the following decisions are fair? For each decision, please indicate how fair you think the decision is by dragging the slider bar to a point on the line, where 1 means "not fair at all", and 9 means "completely fair".

Not fair at all 1 2 3 4 5 6 7 8 9 Completely fair

The loan officer has decided to split the money 50/50 between the two candidates, giving $25,000 to Person A and $25,000 to Person B.

The loan officer has decided to give Person A $31,818, which is proportional to that person's payback rate of 70%, and give Person B $18,181, which is proportional to that person's payback rate of 40%.

The loan officer has decided to give all the money ($50,000) to Person A.

Figure 5: Question presented to the participants in Study 2.

A.2 Demographics questions from the studies

(1) What state do you live in?
(2) Do you identify as:
   - ○ Male
   - ○ Female
   - ○ Other (please specify): ________
(3) What is the highest level of school you have completed or the highest degree you have received?
   - ○ Less than high school degree
   - ○ High school degree or equivalent
   - ○ Some college but no degree
   - ○ Associate degree
   - ○ Bachelor degree
   - ○ Graduate degree
(4) Do you identify as:
   - □ Spanish, Hispanic, or Latino
   - □ White
   - □ Black or African-American
   - □ American-Indian or Alaskan Native
   - □ Asian
   - □ Asian-American
   - □ Native Hawaiian or other Pacific Islander
   - □ Other (please specify): ________
(5) In what type of community do you live:
   - □ City or urban community
   - □ Suburban community
   - □ Rural community
   - □ Other (please specify): ________
(6) What is your age?

(7) Which political party do you identify with?
- ☐ Democratic Party
- ☐ Republican Party
- ☐ Green Party
- ☐ Libertarian Party
- ☐ Independent
- ☐ Other (please specify): _________

A.3 Study 1: Demographic information of the participants

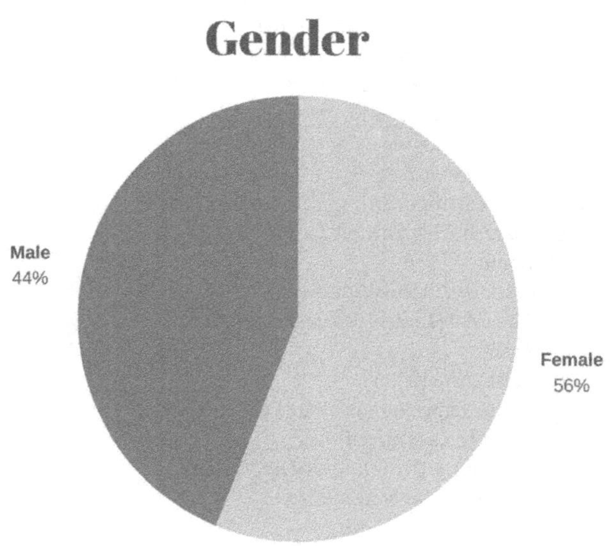

Figure 6: Gender breakdown of the participants in Study 1.

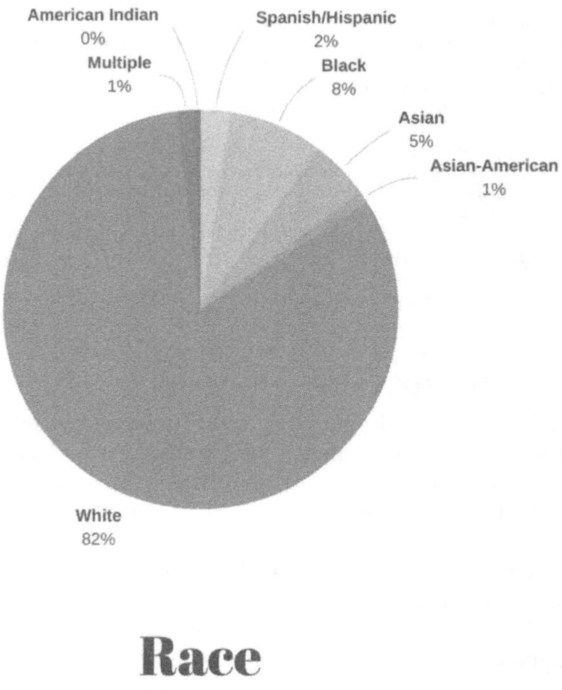

Figure 7: Race of the participants in Study 1.

A.4 Study 2: Demographic information of the participants

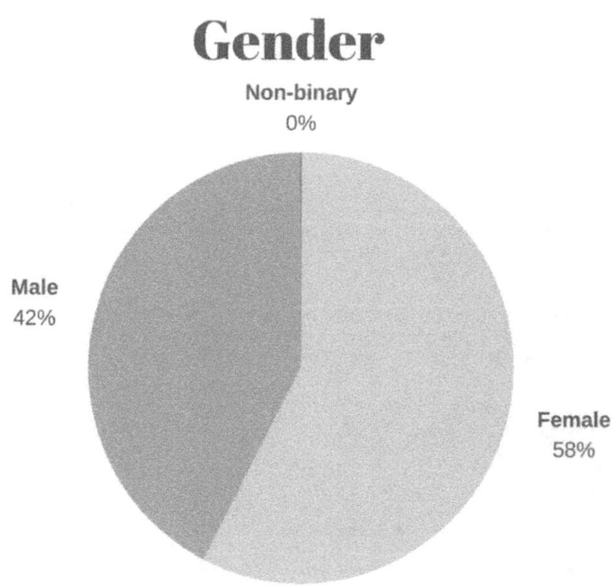

Figure 8: Gender breakdown of the participants in Study 2.

Learning Existing Social Conventions via Observationally Augmented Self-Play

Adam Lerer*
Facebook AI Research
alerer@fb.com

Alexander Peysakhovich*
Facebook AI Research
alexpeys@fb.com

ABSTRACT

In order for artificial agents to coordinate effectively with people, they must act consistently with existing conventions (e.g. how to navigate in traffic, which language to speak, or how to coordinate with teammates). A group's conventions can be viewed as a choice of equilibrium in a coordination game. We consider the problem of an agent learning a policy for a coordination game in a simulated environment and then using this policy when it enters an existing group. When there are multiple possible conventions we show that learning a policy via multi-agent reinforcement learning (MARL) is likely to find policies which achieve high payoffs at training time but fail to coordinate with the real group into which the agent enters. We assume access to a small number of samples of behavior from the true convention and show that we can augment the MARL objective to help it find policies consistent with the real group's convention. In three environments from the literature - traffic, communication, and team coordination - we observe that augmenting MARL with a small amount of imitation learning greatly increases the probability that the strategy found by MARL fits well with the existing social convention. We show that this works even in an environment where standard training methods very rarely find the true convention of the agent's partners.

KEYWORDS

coordination, game theory, deep reinforcement learning, social conventions, self-play

ACM Reference Format:
Adam Lerer and Alexander Peysakhovich. 2019. Learning Existing Social Conventions via Observationally Augmented Self-Play. In *2019 AAAI/ACM Conference on AI, Ethics, and Society (AIES'19), January 27–28, 2019, Honolulu, HI, USA.* ACM, New York, NY, USA, 8 pages. https://doi.org/10.1145/3306618.3314268

INTRODUCTION

A ubiquitous feature of social interaction is a need for individuals to coordinate [2, 3, 21, 31, 33]. A common solution to the coordination problem is the establishment of social conventions which control daily tasks such as choosing which side of the road to drive on, who should get right of way during walking, what counts as polite, what language to speak, or how a team should apportion tasks. If we seek to construct artificial agents that can coordinate with humans, they must be able to act according to existing conventions.

In game theory, Nash equilibria are strategies for all players such that if everyone behaves according to them no individual can improve their payoff by deviating. In game theoretic models a convention is one of multiple possible equilibria in a coordination game [21]. Stated in these terms our agent's task is to construct a policy that does well when paired with the equilibrium being played by existing agents.

There has been great recent progress in constructing policies that can do well in both single and multi-agent environments using deep reinforcement learning [24, 32]. Deep RL methods typically require orders of magnitude more experience in an environment to learn good policies than humans [16], so agents are typically trained in simulation before being deployed onto the real task.

In zero-sum two-player environments (e.g. Go), it is the policy of the other player that is simulated during training. Typically, policies for both players are trained simultaneously or iteratively, in a process called self-play. Self-play produces successful policies because if self-play converges then it converges to an equilibrium of the game [8] and in two-player, zero-sum games all equilibria are minimax/maximin strategies [36]. Thus, a fully converged strategy is guaranteed to be unexploitable for the task of interest (e.g. playing Go with a human champion).

Constructing agents that can cooperate and coordinate with each other to achieve goals (e.g. work together as team to finish a task) has been a long running topic in multi-agent reinforcement learning (MARL) research [12, 23, 34, 37]. However, this literature typically assumes that the cooperating agents will continue to interact with those with whom they have been co-trained (this is sometimes referred to as "centralized training with distributed execution"). In this case, if MARL converges, it finds an equilibrium and since agents will play with the same partners they trained with they will achieve these equilibrium payoffs.

Unfortunately, agents are no longer guaranteed equilibrium payoffs if there are multiple equilibria and agents must coordinate with those they were *not* trained with (in other words, when we remove the centralized training assumption). For example, training self-driving cars in a virtual environment may lead to agents that avoid crashing into each other during training, but drive on the wrong side of the road relative to the society they will enter.

In this paper we propose to give the agent access to a small amount of observations of existing social behavior, i.e. samples of (state, action) pairs from the test time environment. We focus on

*Both authors contributed equally to this research.

AIES '19, January 27–28, 2019, Honolulu, HI, USA

ACM ISBN 978-1-4503-6324-2/19/01...$15.00
https://doi.org/10.1145/3306618.3314268

how such data, though it is not enough to purely clone good policies, can be used in the training process to learn the best response to the policies of the future partners. Our key assumption is that the existing environment already has some existing, stable, social conventions. Thus, our assumption is that future partners will be playing *some* equilibrium strategies. In simple environments, agents could simply enumerate all possible equilibria and choose the one most consistent with the data. However, in more complex environments this becomes intractable. We propose to guide self-play toward the correct equilibrium by training with a joint MARL and behavioral cloning objective. We call this method observationally augmented self-play (OSP).

We consider OSP in several multi-agent situations with multiple conventions: a multi-agent traffic game [28, 35], a particle environment combining navigation and communication [23, 25] and a Stag Hunt game where agents must take risks to accomplish a joint goal [27, 39]. In each of these games we find that self-play can converge to multiple, incompatible, conventions. We find that OSP is able to learn correct conventions in these games with a small amount of observational data. Our results in the Markov Stag Hunt show that OSP can learn conventions it observes even when those conventions are very unlikely to be learned using MARL alone.

We do not claim that OSP is the ultimate approach to constructing agents that can learn social conventions. The success of OSP depends on both the game and the type of objective employed, thus an exploration of alternative algorithms is an important direction for future work. Our key result is that the combination of (a) a small number of samples from trajectories of a multi-agent game, and (b) knowledge that test time agents are playing some equilibrium gives much stronger test time performance than either component alone.

RELATED WORK

OSP is related to existing work on adding reward shaping in MARL [1, 5, 11, 12]. However the domain of interest differs slightly as reward shaping is typically used to cause all agents in a group to converge to a high-payoff equilibrium whereas we are interested in using shaping to guide training to select the correct test-time equilibrium.

Recent work has pointed out that strategies learned via a single instance of independent MARL can overfit to other agents' policies during training [17]. This work differs from ours in that it suggests the training of a single best response to a mixture of heterogeneous policies. This increases the robustness of agent policies but does not solve the problem of multiple, incompatible conventions that we study here.

The approach of combining supervised learning from trajectories with RL has been studied in the single agent case [9]. In that work the trajectories are expert demonstrations and are used to guide RL to an optimal policy. In this case supervision is used to speed up learning while in our work the trajectories are used to select among many possible optima (equilibria) which may be equivalent at training time but not at test time. However this literature explores many methods for combining imitation learning and RL and some of these techniques may be interesting to consider in the multi-agent setting.

CONVENTIONS IN MARKOV GAMES

A partially observed Markov game G [22, 29] consists of a set of players $P = \{1, \ldots, N\}$, a set of states $\mathcal{S}$, a set of actions for every player A_i with the global set $\mathcal{A} = \times_{i \in P} A_i$, a transition function $\tau : \mathcal{S} \times \mathcal{A} \to \Delta\mathcal{S}$, a reward function for each player that takes as input the current state and actions $R_i : \mathcal{S} \times \mathcal{A} \to \mathbb{R}$. Players have observation functions $O_i : \mathcal{S} \to O_i$ and can condition their behavior on these observations. Markov policies for each player are functions $\pi_i : O_i \to A_i$. Let Π_i denote the set of all policies available to a player and $\Pi = \times_{i \in P} \Pi_i$ be the set of joint policies.[1]

We use the standard notation π_{-i} to denote the policy vector for all players other than i. A set of policies $\pi \in \Pi$ and a (possible random) initial state $s_0 \in \mathcal{S}$ defines a (random) trajectory of rewards for each player. We let the value function $V_i(s, \pi_i, \pi_{-i})$ denote the discounted expectation of this trajectory. The best response starting at state s for player i to π_{-i} is $BR(s, \pi_{-i}) = \text{argmax}_{\pi_i \in \Pi_i} V_i(s, \pi_i, \pi_{-i})$. We let s_0 be the (possibly random) initial state of the game.

There are many ways to extend the notion of a Nash equilibrium to the case of stochastic games. We will consider the Markov perfect best response. We denote by $BR(\pi_{-i})$ the policy (or policies) which is a best response starting at *any* state and consider equilibria to be policies for each player π such that each $\pi_i \in BR(\pi_{-i})$.[2]

We consider games with multiple, incompatible, conventions. Formally we say that conventions (equilibrium policy sets) π and π' are incompatible if the compound policy (π_i, π'_{-i}) is not an equilibrium.

The goal of training is to compute a policy π_i which is a best response to the existing convention π_{-i}^{test}. During training, the agent has access to the environment but receives only a limited set of observations of π^{test} in the form of a set $\mathcal{D}$ of state-action pairs sampled from π^{test}. This is summarized in Figure 1.

We denote a generic element of $\mathcal{D}$ by $d = (s, a_k)$ which is a (state, action) pair for agent k. Let $\mathcal{D}_j$ denote the subset of $\mathcal{D}$ which includes actions for agent j.

The dataset $\mathcal{D}$ may be insufficient to identify a best response to all possible policies π^{test} consistent with $\mathcal{D}$. However, the set of equilibrium policy sets is typically much smaller than all possible policy sets. Therefore, if we assume that all agents are minimizing regret then we must only consider equilibrium policy sets consistent with $\mathcal{D}$.

Given a game G and dataset $\mathcal{D}$, a brute force approach to learn a policy compatible with the conventions of the group the agent will enter would be to compute the equilibrium π^* of G that maximizes the likelihood of $\mathcal{D}$. Formally this is given by

$$\pi^* \in \text{argmax}_\pi \sum_i \sum_{(s,a) \in \mathcal{D}_i} \log(\pi_i(s, a))$$
$$\text{s.t. } \forall i,\ \pi_i \in BR(\pi_{-i}).$$

This constrained optimization problem quickly becomes intractable and we will instead try to find an equilibrium using multi-agent

[1] We consider only Markov policies in this work so that we can work with individual state-action pairs, although our same approach could be applied across observed trajectories to learn non-Markov policies (i.e. policies conditioned on their full history).

[2] There are weaker notions, for example, requiring that policies are best responses at every state reached during play. It is known that Markov perfect equilibria are harder to find by learning [8] and it is interesting to consider whether different kinds of choices (e.g. on-policy vs. off-policy learning) can make stronger or weaker convergence guarantees. However, these questions are outside the scope of this paper.

learning, and use $\mathcal{D}$ to increase the probability learning converges to it.

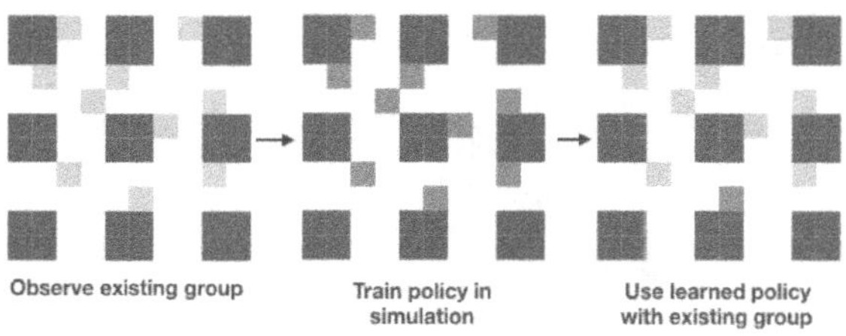

Figure 1: A graphical description of our problem. Our central question is how to use observational data to make sure that training converges to the same convention as the group which our agent will enter.

Observationally Initialized Best Response Dynamics

To get an intuition about how data can be used during training we will first study a learning rule where analytic results are more easily obtained. We will begin with the simplest multi-agent learning algorithm: *best response dynamics* in a 2 player Markov game where equilibria are in pure policies and are incompatible.

In best response dynamics each player begins with a policy initialized at π_i^0. Players alternate updating their policy with the best response $\pi_i^t = BR(\pi_{-i}^{t-1})$. When there are multiple best responses we assume there is a (non-randomized) tie-breaking rule used to select one. Given an equilibrium A we denote by Π^A the basin of attraction of A (the set of initial states from which BR dynamics converge to A.)

A naive way to use the observed data is to force the policies be consistent with $\mathcal{D}$ at each step of the best response dynamic by changing it at each states where it differs. However, this can introduce new equilibria to the game.[3]

In the context of reward shaping it is well known that the way to avoid the introduction of new equilibria is to use potential based reward shaping [5], or, equivalently, use our information to only change the initialization of learning [38]. We will follow this advice and study *observationally initialized best response dynamics*. We begin with a policy π_0 chosen at random. However, for every player i and state-action pair (s, a) in the data $\mathcal{D}$ we form $\bar{\pi}^0$ by setting the corresponding action of $\pi_i^0(s)$ to a. We then perform best response dynamics from this new initialization.

We will now discuss a class of games for which we can guarantee that observationally initialized best response dynamics have a larger basin of attraction for the equilibrium from which $\mathcal{D}$ was drawn relative to standard best response dynamics. This class is a generalization of a commonly used matrix game class: games with *strategic complements* [4]. For our purposes strategic complements corresponds to assuming that one's partners behave more consistently with some convention then one is also more incentivized to behave according to that convention.[4] In existing work strategic complements are defined with respect to a single action rather than a Markov policy. To generalize to Markov games we introduce a notion of distance between policies:

Definition 1 (Policy Closeness). *Given a player i and target policy A we say that policy π is **weakly closer to** A **than policy** π' if on all states either $\pi(s) = \pi'(s)$ or $\pi(s) = A(s)$. We denote this by $\pi \succsim_A \pi'$.*

Policy closeness gives us a partial ordering on policies which we use to generalize the idea of strategic complements.

Definition 2 (Markov Strategic Complements). *A Markov game exhibits **Markov strategic complements** if for any equilibrium $A = (A_1, A_2)$ we have that $\pi_i \succsim_{A_i} \pi_i'$ implies that $BR(\pi_i) \succsim_{A_{-i}} BR(\pi_i')$.*

Let $\mathcal{D}_A$ be a dataset drawn from equilibrium A by sampling states and their equilibrium actions. Let $\bar{\Pi}^A(\mathcal{D}_A)$ be the basin of attraction of A given observationally initialized best response dynamics.

Theorem 1. *If a game where best-response dynamics always converge exhibits Markov strategic complements then for any $\mathcal{D}_A$ drawn from a equilibrium A $\Pi^A \subseteq \bar{\Pi}^A(\mathcal{D}_A)$ and there exists $(s, A_i(s))$ such that if $(s, A_i(a)) \in \mathcal{D}_A$ then $\Pi^A \subset \bar{\Pi}^A(\mathcal{D}_A)$.*

We relegate the proof to the Appendix. Roughly, it has two steps: first, we show that if π_0 is in the basin of attraction of A then anything closer to A is also in the basin. Second, we show that there is an initial state that is not in the basin of attraction of best response dynamics but is in the basin of attraction of observationally initialized best response dynamics. Because initialization can increase the basin of attraction without introducing any new equilibria the observed data can strictly improve the probability that we learn a policy consistent with the observed agents.

EXPERIMENTS

Observationally Augmented Self-Play

We wish to use the insights from initialization in environments where function approximation (e.g. with deep neural networks) is required. However, if the policy is computed via function approximation, it is not clear how to 'initialize' its value at particular states. Specifically, the policy at the small number of states in $\mathcal{D}$ can only be expected to generalize if the approximation captures the regularities of the game, which will only be true after some interaction in the environment. Therefore, we consider a procedure where consistency with $\mathcal{D}$ is enforced during training and smoothly decays over time.

We consider training with stochastic gradient descent using a loss function which is a linear combination of the likelihood of the data (a supervised objective) plus the policy gradient estimator of

[3] For a simple example consider a game where 5 agents choose an action A or B and receive reward equal to the number of other agents whose actions match theirs. In this case there are equilibria where all agents choose A or all agents choose B. If we restrict one agent to always choose A we can introduce a new equilibrium where 4 agents choose B and one agent chooses A.

[4] In economic applications the notion of strategic complements is utilized in production games and roughly corresponds either the the idea of network effects (the more people use some product the higher a consumer's utility is from using that product) or a joint monotonicity condition (if Firm X produces cars and firm Y produces car washing materials if firm X produces more cars then firm Y sees higher demand for car washing materials). See the Supplement for a more formal discussion.

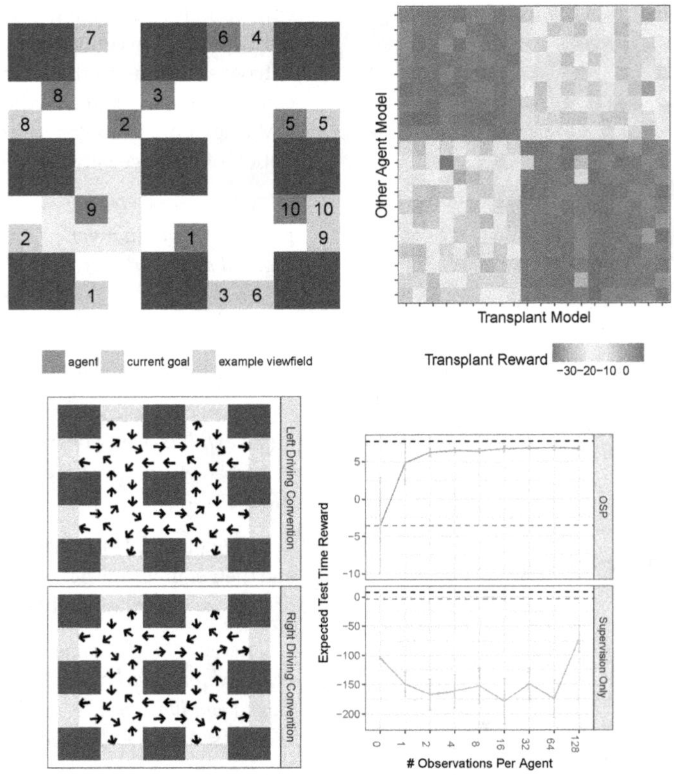

Figure 2: In the traffic game 10 agents navigate a grid world to reach goals (first panel). Agents have a local field of view (indicated in green). Two incompatible conventions emerge across multiple training runs. MARL agents achieve high rewards with their training partners (diagonal) but lower rewards with incompatible partners (second panel). Visualizing these conventions shows that they differ in which side of the road to drive on (third panel). Given few observations for each agent OSP learns the correct test time convention (fourth panel), approaching the reward of centralized training (black dashed line), while supervised training does not. The dashed line indicates the average reward of separate self-play training, and error bars represent 95% confidence intervals derived from independent replicates.

the reward in the game (we denote by $\mathcal{L}^{PG}$ the negative of this quantity). Formally, each agent receives rewards given by

$$\mathcal{L}_i^{OSP}(\pi_i, \pi_{-i}) = \mathcal{L}^{PG}(\pi_i \mid \pi_{-i}) + \lambda \sum_{(s,a)\in\mathcal{D}_i} \log(\pi_i(s,a))$$

with respect to the parameters θ_i of its policy.[5]

We optimize the joint objective using MARL. At any time t when making an update to the parameters of each agent θ_i we will take gradient steps of the form

$$\nabla_t^{OSP}(\theta_i, \mathcal{D}) = \nabla_t^{PG}(\theta_i) + \lambda_t \nabla^{sup}(\theta_i, \mathcal{D}).$$

Where ∇^{PG} is our policy gradient and ∇^{sup} is the gradient of the supervised objective at θ_i.[6]

[5]Note this is different from reward shaping as the probably that a state is reached does not affect the supervised loss of the policy.

[6]As with the best response dynamics above using a compound objective with a constant λ can, in theory, introduce new equilibria during training. To be sure this does not occur we can anneal the weight on the supervised loss over time with $\lim_{t\to\infty} \lambda_t = 0$. In practice, however, using a fixed λ in our environments appeared to create policies that were still consistent with test time equilibria thus suggesting that if new equilibria were introduced they did not have large basins of attraction for our policy-gradient based learning procedures.

Our main analysis is experimental and we use three environments from the literature: traffic, language games, and risky coordination. Our main results are:

Result 1 (Experiments 1,2,3). *OSP greatly increases the probability our agent learns a convention compatible with test time agents in situations where standard self-play by itself does not guarantee good test time performance and $\mathcal{D}$ is insufficient to learn a good policy by behavioral cloning alone.*

Result 2 (Experiment 3). *OSP can find conventions that have a small basin of attraction for MARL alone. Thus OSP can be used in situations where self-play will rarely find a test-time compatible convention.*

For all experiments, we represent the states using simple neural networks. The first two experiments have relatively low dimensional state representations so we use two layer MLPs with 128 hidden units per layer and ELU non-linearities. Our third experiment has a grid structure so we represent the state using the convolutional neural network architecture from [27].

For RL training we use A3C using a multi-agent variant of the pytorch-a3c package [15] run on 40 threads. We use 20 step returns and $\gamma = .99$. We use the Adam method for optimization [13]. For OSP, we add the supervised term to the A3C loss with $\lambda = 1$, using minibatches from $\mathcal{D}$ of size 20. Environment-specific parameters are detailed in the subsections below. In each experiment we compare the performance of OSP for various sizes of $\mathcal{D}$. We populate $\mathcal{D}$ with actions for all agents for states sampled at uniform intervals from true test time play.

Traffic

We first consider a multi-agent traffic navigation game inspired by [35]. Each of 10 agents begins at a random edge of a grid and can move around in each of the 4 cardinal directions or stand still (see Figure 2). Each agent is given a goal to reach. When the agent reaches the goal they receive a reward of +1 and then a new goal. If agents collide with another agent or wall they receive a negative reward (−5 for colliding with another agent, −.1 for colliding with a wall). Agents do not have full observation of the environment. Rather, they have access to the position of their goal relative to themselves and a local view of any other agents nearby. We train agents for a total of 800, 000 episodes.[7]

We train 20 replicates and see that two incompatible conventions emerge. This can be seen in Figure 2 where we plot payoffs to an agent from one replicate paired with 9 agents from another. We visualize the conventions by taking the empirical average action taken by any agent in any of the possible traffic coordinate locations (Figure 2 panel 3). We find that the two conventions that emerge are similar to the real world: either agents learn to drive on the left of the road or they learn to drive on the right.

We now train agents using OSP and insert them into environments with 9 pre-converged agents. The test time payoffs to the transplanted agent for various sizes of $\mathcal{D}$ are shown in Figure 2 panel 4 top. The dashed line corresponds to the expected payoff of an agent trained using standard self-play (no observations). We see 20 observations (2 observations for each of the 10) agents is sufficient to guide OSP to compatible conventions. The bottom panel shows that this is not enough data to train a good strategy via behavioral cloning alone (i.e. using just the supervised objective).

Language

An important type of convention is language. There is a resurgence of interest in the deep RL community in using communication games to construct agents which are able to communicate [6, 10, 18, 23].

We now apply OSP to the cooperative communication task in the particle environment studied by [23] and [25]. In this environment there are two agents, a speaker and a listener, and three landmarks (blue, red, or green). One of the landmarks is randomly chosen as a goal and the reward for both agents at each step is equal to the distance of the listener from the landmark. However, which landmark is the goal during a particular episode is only known to the speaker who is able to produce a communication output from a set of 20 symbols. To solve the cooperation task, agents thus need to evolve a simple 'language'. This language only requires 3 symbols to be used, but this still allows for at least 6840 incompatible conventions (one symbol per landmark).

[7]We found it necessary to ramp the collision penalty linearly over the first 400, 000 episodes to avoid agents becoming stuck in the local minima of never moving.

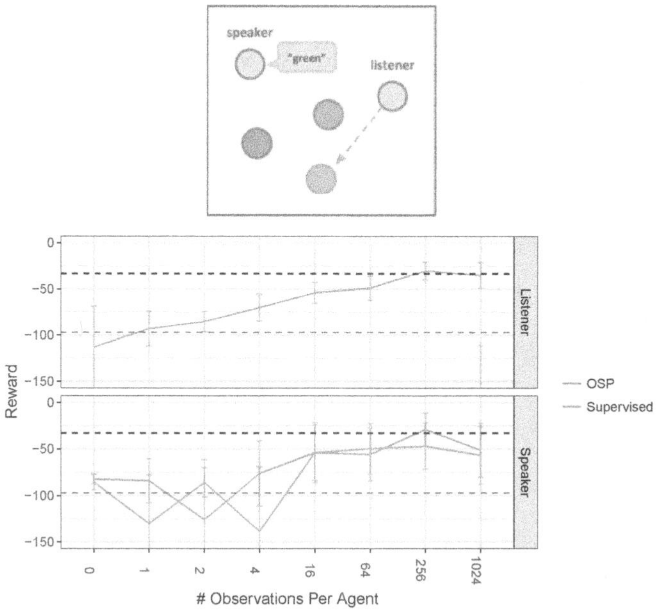

Figure 3: In the speaker/listener particle environment (first panel taken from the original paper) when a pair are trained together they can reach high payoffs (black dashed line) but pairs trained separately with self-play (red dashed line) perform quite poorly. OSP leads to agents that reach high payoffs with their test time partner. Supervision alone is insufficient to construct good Listener agents (plot is below the y axis for N < 1024). Error bars represent confidence intervals derived from independent replicates.

In this experiment we use a lower discount factor of $\gamma = .8$ and as suggested by [23] we also use a centralized critic. It was shown in prior work that if artificial agents learn language by self-play they can learn arbitrary languages which may not be compatible with new partners [18]. Indeed, when we pair two agents who were trained separately they clearly do not speak the same language - i.e. they cannot communicate and so achieve low payoffs.

We look at the effect of adding observational data to the training of either a speaker or listener (we train a total of 135 replicates to convergence). In the case of the speaker (whose policy is a simple map from goals to communication symbols) supervision is sufficient to learn the a good test-time language. However, pure behavioral cloning fails catastrophically for the listener. Again, OSP with a relatively small number of observations is able to achieve high payoffs (Figure 3).

Risky Coordination

We now consider a risky coordination game known as the Stag Hunt. The matrix game version of the Stag Hunt has both agents choosing either to Hunt (an action that require coordination) or

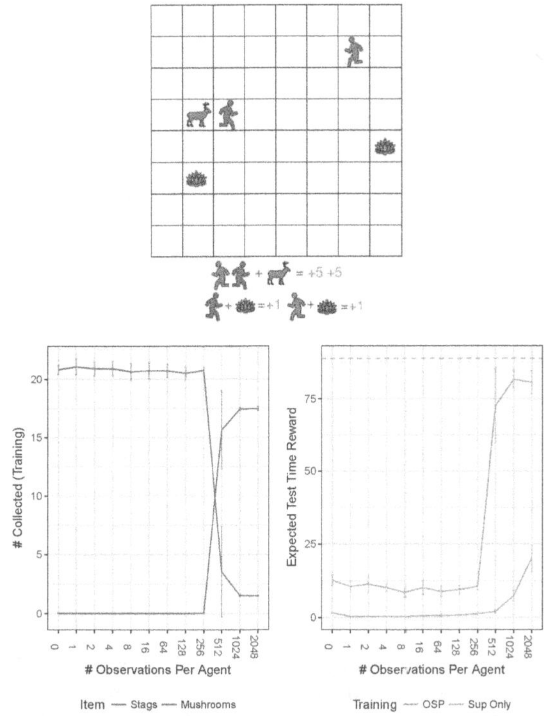

Figure 4: In the Stag Hunt independent MARL typically converges to the safe equilibrium. Thus, an agent trained via MARL cannot coordinate when matched with a test-time partner who choose to hunt. However OSP, with samples from the Hunt equilibrium, can converge to the Hunting convention during training reaching a payoff almost as high as two Hunters trained together (green line). Error bars represent confidence intervals derived from independent replicates.

Forage (a safe action). Foraging yields a sure (low) payoff whereas Hunting yields a high payoff if the other agent chooses to Hunt also and a low payoff if one shows up alone. It is known that in both matrix and Markov versions of Stag Hunt games many standard self-play based algorithms yield agents that converge to the inefficient equilibrium in which both agents choose safe actions. This happens because while our partner is not hunting effectively (i.e. early in training), the payoff to hunting ourselves is quite low. Thus, the basin of attraction of joint hunting is much smaller than the basin of attraction of both foraging.

This situation is different from the ones in traffic and language: here there are multiple conventions (hunt or forage) but they are not payoff equivalent (hunting is better) nor do they have similar sized basins of attraction (hunting is very difficult to find via standard independent MARL).

We use the Markov version of Stag Hunt introduced by [27] where two agents live on a 8×8 grid. Two plants and a stag are placed at random locations. If an agent moves over a plant, it receives a reward of 1. Stepping on the stag gives a reward of 5 to both players if they step on it simultaneously, otherwise there is no reward. When either a plant or stag is stepped on, it restarts in a new location. Games last 100 rounds.

We start by constructing a test time hunting partner by inducing joint hunting strategies in 40 replicates. Because MARL by itself does not find hunt equilibria, we construct a hunting partner by training an agent under a modified payoff structure (payoff of 0 for plants; payoff of 0.1 for unilateral hunting).

We then test whether we can train agents in the *original* game who can coordinate with test time partners that hunt. We use OSP with varying amounts of data from the hunting agents. We see that with moderate amounts of data OSP often converges to the hunting convention at test time even though two agents trained together using independent MARL fail to find the high payoff joint stag equilibrium in *any* of the replicates. As a result, OSP outperforms even centralized self-play because the observations of the risky partner guide the agent to a better equilibrium. As with the traffic and language environments above we see that pure behavioral cloning is insufficient to construct good test time strategies (Figure 4).

CONCLUSION

Conventions are an important part of social behavior and many multi-agent environments support multiple conventions as equilibria. If we want to construct artificial agents that can adapt to people (rather than requiring people to adapt to them) these agents need to be able to act according to the existing social conventions. In this paper we have discussed how a simple procedure that combines small amounts of imitation learning with self-play can lead to agents that can learn social conventions.

There are many open questions remaining in the study of conventions and building agents that can learn them quickly. OSP uses a straightforward combination of RL and behavioral cloning. It would be interesting to explore whether ideas from the learning with expert demonstrations literature [9]. In addition, OSP follows current deep RL paradigms splits strategy construction into a training and a test phase. An interesting extension is to consider the OSP training strategies can be fine-tuned during test time.

We have focused on situations where agents have no incentive to deviate from cooperation and only need to learn correct conventions. An important future direction is considering problems where agents have partially misaligned incentives but, in addition to just solving the social dilemma, must also coordinate on a convention [7, 14, 19, 20, 26].

There is a large recent interest in hybrid systems which include both human and artificially intelligent participants [30]. Thus, another key extension of our work is to understand whether techniques like OSP can construct agents that can interact with humans in more complex environments.

REFERENCES

[1] Monica Babes, Enrique Munoz De Cote, and Michael L Littman. 2008. Social reward shaping in the prisoner's dilemma. In *Proceedings of the 7th international joint conference on Autonomous agents and multiagent systems-Volume 3*. International Foundation for Autonomous Agents and Multiagent Systems, 1389–1392.

[2] Samuel Barrett, Avi Rosenfeld, Sarit Kraus, and Peter Stone. 2017. Making friends on the fly: Cooperating with new teammates. *Artificial Intelligence* 242 (2017), 132–171.

[3] Cristina Bicchieri. 2005. *The grammar of society: The nature and dynamics of social norms.* Cambridge University Press.

[4] Jeremy I Bulow, John D Geanakoplos, and Paul D Klemperer. 1985. Multimarket oligopoly: Strategic substitutes and complements. *Journal of Political economy* 93, 3 (1985), 488–511.

[5] Sam Devlin and Daniel Kudenko. 2011. Theoretical considerations of potential-based reward shaping for multi-agent systems. In *The 10th International Conference on Autonomous Agents and Multiagent Systems-Volume 1*. International Foundation for Autonomous Agents and Multiagent Systems, 225–232.

[6] Jakob Foerster, Yannis Assael, Nando de Freitas, and Shimon Whiteson. 2016. Learning to communicate with deep multi-agent reinforcement learning. In *Advances in Neural Information Processing Systems*. 2137–2145.

[7] Jakob N Foerster, Richard Y Chen, Maruan Al-Shedivat, Shimon Whiteson, Pieter Abbeel, and Igor Mordatch. 2017. Learning with Opponent-Learning Awareness. *arXiv preprint arXiv:1709.04326* (2017).

[8] Drew Fudenberg and David K Levine. 1998. *The theory of learning in games*. Vol. 2. MIT press.

[9] Todd Hester, Matej Vecerik, Olivier Pietquin, Marc Lanctot, Tom Schaul, Bilal Piot, Dan Horgan, John Quan, Andrew Sendonaris, Gabriel Dulac-Arnold, et al. 2017. Deep Q-learning from Demonstrations. *arXiv preprint arXiv:1704.03732* (2017).

[10] Emilio Jorge, Mikael Kågebäck, and Emil Gustavsson. 2016. Learning to Play Guess Who? and Inventing a Grounded Language as a Consequence. *arXiv preprint arXiv:1611.03218* (2016).

[11] Spiros Kapetanakis and Daniel Kudenko. 2002. Improving on the reinforcement learning of coordination in cooperative multi-agent systems. In *Proceedings of the Second Symposium on Adaptive Agents and Multi-agent Systems (AISB02)*.

[12] Spiros Kapetanakis and Daniel Kudenko. 2002. Reinforcement learning of coordination in cooperative multi-agent systems. *AAAI/IAAI* 2002 (2002), 326–331.

[13] Diederik Kingma and Jimmy Ba. 2014. Adam: A method for stochastic optimization. *arXiv preprint arXiv:1412.6980* (2014).

[14] Max Kleiman-Weiner, MK Ho, JL Austerweil, Michael L Littman, and Josh B Tenenbaum. 2016. Coordinate to cooperate or compete: abstract goals and joint intentions in social interaction. In *Proceedings of the 38th annual conference of the cognitive science society*.

[15] Ilya Kostrikov. 2018. PyTorch Implementations of Asynchronous Advantage Actor Critic. https://github.com/ikostrikov/pytorch-a3c.

[16] Brenden M Lake, Tomer D Ullman, Joshua B Tenenbaum, and Samuel J Gershman. 2017. Building machines that learn and think like people. *Behavioral and Brain Sciences* 40 (2017).

[17] Marc Lanctot, Vinicius Zambaldi, Audrunas Gruslys, Angeliki Lazaridou, Julien Perolat, David Silver, Thore Graepel, et al. 2017. A unified game-theoretic approach to multiagent reinforcement learning. In *Advances in Neural Information Processing Systems*. 4193–4206.

[18] Angeliki Lazaridou, Alexander Peysakhovich, and Marco Baroni. 2017. Multi-agent cooperation and the emergence of (natural) language. In *International Conference on Learning Representations*.

[19] Joel Z Leibo, Vinicius Zambaldi, Marc Lanctot, Janusz Marecki, and Thore Graepel. 2017. Multi-agent Reinforcement Learning in Sequential Social Dilemmas. In *Proceedings of the 16th Conference on Autonomous Agents and MultiAgent Systems*. International Foundation for Autonomous Agents and Multiagent Systems, 464–473.

[20] Adam Lerer and Alexander Peysakhovich. 2017. Maintaining cooperation in complex social dilemmas using deep reinforcement learning. *arXiv preprint arXiv:1707.01068* (2017).

[21] David Lewis. 1969. *Convention: A philosophical study*. John Wiley & Sons.

[22] Michael L Littman. 1994. Markov games as a framework for multi-agent reinforcement learning. In *Machine Learning Proceedings 1994*. Elsevier, 157–163.

[23] Ryan Lowe, Yi Wu, Aviv Tamar, Jean Harb, Pieter Abbeel, and Igor Mordatch. 2017. Multi-Agent Actor-Critic for Mixed Cooperative-Competitive Environments. *arXiv preprint arXiv:1706.02275* (2017).

[24] Volodymyr Mnih, Koray Kavukcuoglu, David Silver, Andrei A Rusu, Joel Veness, Marc G Bellemare, Alex Graves, Martin Riedmiller, Andreas K Fidjeland, Georg Ostrovski, et al. 2015. Human-level control through deep reinforcement learning. *Nature* 518, 7540 (2015), 529–533.

[25] Igor Mordatch and Pieter Abbeel. 2017. Emergence of grounded compositional language in multi-agent populations. *arXiv preprint arXiv:1703.04908* (2017).

[26] Alexander Peysakhovich and Adam Lerer. 2017. Consequentialist conditional cooperation in social dilemmas with imperfect information. *arXiv preprint arXiv:1710.06975* (2017).

[27] Alexander Peysakhovich and Adam Lerer. 2017. Prosocial learning agents solve generalized Stag Hunts better than selfish ones. *arXiv preprint arXiv:1709.02865* (2017).

[28] Cinjon Resnick, Ilya Kulikov, Kyunghyun Cho, and Jason Weston. 2018. Vehicle Community Strategies. *arXiv preprint arXiv:1804.07178* (2018).

[29] Lloyd S Shapley. 1953. Stochastic games. *Proceedings of the national academy of sciences* 39, 10 (1953), 1095–1100.

[30] Hirokazu Shirado and Nicholas A Christakis. 2017. Locally noisy autonomous agents improve global human coordination in network experiments. *Nature* 545, 7654 (2017), 370–374.

[31] Yoav Shoham and Moshe Tennenholtz. 1997. On the emergence of social conventions: modeling, analysis, and simulations. *Artificial Intelligence* 94, 1-2 (1997), 139–166.

[32] David Silver, Julian Schrittwieser, Karen Simonyan, Ioannis Antonoglou, Aja Huang, Arthur Guez, Thomas Hubert, Lucas Baker, Matthew Lai, Adrian Bolton, et al. 2017. Mastering the game of go without human knowledge. *Nature* 550, 7676 (2017), 354.

[33] Peter Stone, Gal A Kaminka, Sarit Kraus, and Jeffrey S Rosenschein. 2010. Ad hoc autonomous agent teams: Collaboration without pre-coordination. In *Twenty-Fourth AAAI Conference on Artificial Intelligence*.

[34] Peter Stone and Richard S Sutton. 2001. Scaling reinforcement learning toward RoboCup soccer. In *ICML*, Vol. 1. Citeseer, 537–544.

[35] Sainbayar Sukhbaatar, Rob Fergus, et al. 2016. Learning multiagent communication with backpropagation. In *Advances in Neural Information Processing Systems*. 2244–2252.

[36] J von Neumann. 1928. Zur theorie der gesellschaftsspiele. *Mathematische annalen* 100, 1 (1928), 295–320.

[37] Adam Walker and Michael Wooldridge. 1995. Understanding the Emergence of Conventions in Multi-Agent Systems.. In *ICMAS*, Vol. 95. 384–389.

[38] Eric Wiewiora. 2003. Potential-based shaping and Q-value initialization are equivalent. *Journal of Artificial Intelligence Research* 19 (2003), 205–208.

[39] Wako Yoshida, Ray J Dolan, and Karl J Friston. 2008. Game theory of mind. *PLoS computational biology* 4, 12 (2008), e1000254.

APPENDIX

Relationship Between Markov Strategic Complements and Strategic Complements

The original definition of strategic complements comes from games with continuous actions used to model multiple firms in a market. In the simplest example we have multiple firms which produce units of goods $(x_1, x_2, \ldots, x_n)$. The revenue function of each firm i is $R_i(x_i, x_{-i})$ where R_i is smooth, strictly concave, increasing and has $R_i(x_i = 0, x_{-i}) = 0$. The goods are strategic complements if $\frac{\partial^2 R_i}{\partial x_i \partial x_j} > 0$, in other words goods are strategic complements if "more 'aggressive' play... by one firm... raises the marginal profitabilities [of the others]." [4] Firms have costs of production given by $c_i(x_i)$ which has $c(0) = 0$, $c'(0) = 0$, is convex, and increasing. Thus each firm's objective function is

$$R_i(x_i, x_{-i}) - c_i(x_i)$$

If firm $-i$ is producing x_{-i} then firm i's best response $x_i^*(x_{-i})$ sets

$$\frac{\partial R_i(x_i^*(x_{-i}), x_{-i})}{\partial x_i} = \frac{\partial c_i(x_i^*(x_{-i})}{\partial x_i}.$$

Given the definition of strategic complements above this means that

$$\frac{\partial x_i^*}{\partial x_j} > 0$$

for all other firms j.

Strategic complements implies our Markov strategic complements in a matrix game with multiple equilibria (since any firm changing their production level higher or lower causes other firms to also want to change their production).

Markov strategic complements is weaker than strategic complements in matrix games since it only pins down how best responses to shift when others change to equilibrium actions rather than any action shift (though if action spaces in each state were totally ordered one could amend the definition to keep all of the properties).

Proof of Main Theorem

Lemma 1: In a Markov strategic complements (MSC) game, any policy π in the basin of attraction of an equilibrium A remains there under observational initialization, i.e. $\pi_i \in \Pi^A \implies \bar{\pi}_i(\mathcal{D}_A) \in \Pi^A$.

We define the operator $BR^{(k)}$ as k iterations of the best response operator,

$$BR^{(k)}(\pi_i) = BR^i(BR^{-i}(BR^i(\ldots BR^{-i}(\pi_i)))).$$

Consider an initial policy $\pi_i \in \Pi^A$ for some equilibrium A. There exists k_c such that $BR^{(k_c)} = A_i$. Now consider an observationally initialized policy $\bar{\pi}_i(\mathcal{D}_A)$ for some dataset $\mathcal{D}$ drawn from A_i. By definition, this implies that $\bar{\pi}_i \succsim_A \pi_i$. Now, since the game is MSC,

$$BR^{-i}(\bar{\pi}_i(\mathcal{D}_A)) \succsim_A BR^{-i}(\pi_i).$$

By repeated application of the MSC property, we find that for all k,

$$BR^{(k)}(\bar{\pi}_i(\mathcal{D}_A)) \succsim_A BR^{(k)}(\pi_i).$$

To conclude, we note that $BR^{(k_c)}(\bar{\pi}_i^0(\mathcal{D}_A)) \succsim_A A_i$, which implies $BR^{(k_c)}(\bar{\pi}_i(\mathcal{D}_A)) = A_i$.

Lemma 2: In a MSC game with a finite number of states, there exists a state s such that for any $\mathcal{D}_A$ that contains the state-action pair $(s, A_i(s))$, there is a policy not in the basin of attraction of A but which enters the basin of attraction of A under observational initialization.

Consider a policy $\pi_i^0 \notin \Pi_A$, and order the states lexicographically $(s_1, s_2, \ldots, s_M)$. Now consider the sequence of policies π_i^k where $\pi_i^k(s_l) = A_i(s_l)$ for $l < k$ and $\pi_i^k(s_l) = \pi^0(s_l)$ for $k \geq l$. We know that $\pi_i^M = A_i \in \Pi_A$, therefore there exists some t such that $\pi_i^t \notin \Pi_A$ and $\pi_i^{t+1} \in \Pi_A$. Now, consider a dataset $\mathcal{D}_A$ containing the state-action pair $(s_{t+1}, A_i(s_{t+1}))$. Then $\bar{\pi}_i^t(\mathcal{D}_A) \succsim_A \pi^{t+1}$. As discussed in the last section, if $\pi^{t+1} \in \Pi_A$ and $\bar{\pi}_i^t(\mathcal{D}_A) \succsim_A \pi^{t+1}$, then $\bar{\pi}_i^t(\mathcal{D}_A) \in \Pi_A$. Therefore, for any dataset containing s_{t+1}, the policy π_i^t enters the basin of attraction of A under observational initialization.

Legible Normativity for AI Alignment: The Value of Silly Rules

Dylan Hadfield-Menell
University of California, Berkeley
Center for Human Compatible AI
dhm@eecs.berkeley.edu

McKane Andrus
University of California, Berkeley
Center for Human-Compatible AI
mckaneandrus@berkeley.edu

Gillian K. Hadfield
University of Toronto
Vector Institute for AI; OpenAI
Center for Human-Compatible AI
g.hadfield@utoronto.ca

ABSTRACT

It has become commonplace to assert that autonomous agents will have to be built to follow human rules of behavior–social norms and laws. But human laws and norms are complex and culturally varied systems; in many cases agents will have to *learn* the rules. This requires autonomous agents to have models of how human rule systems work so that they can make reliable predictions about rules. In this paper we contribute to the building of such models by analyzing an overlooked distinction between important rules and what we call silly rules —rules with no discernible direct impact on welfare. We show that silly rules render a normative system both more robust and more adaptable in response to shocks to perceived stability. They make normativity more legible for humans, and can increase legibility for AI systems as well. For AI systems to integrate into human normative systems, we suggest, it may be important for them to have models that include representations of silly rules.

CCS CONCEPTS

• **Social and professional topics → Socio-technical systems**; • **Computing methodologies → Cooperation and coordination**; *Multi-agent systems*; • **Applied computing → Law.**

KEYWORDS

collective enforcement; normative systems; human-AI interaction

ACM Reference Format:

Dylan Hadfield-Menell, McKane Andrus, and Gillian K. Hadfield. 2019. Legible Normativity for AI Alignment: The Value of Silly Rules. In *AAAI/ACM Conference on AI, Ethics, and Society (AIES '19), January 27–28, 2019, Honolulu, HI, USA.* ACM, New York, NY, USA, 7 pages. https://doi.org/10.1145/3306618.3314250

1 INTRODUCTION

As attention to the challenge of aligning artificial intelligence with human welfare has grown, it has become commonplace to assert that autonomous agents will have to be built to follow human norms and laws [8, 9, 15]. But this is no easy task. Human groups are thick with rules and norms about behavior, many of which are largely invisible, taken for granted as simply "the way things are done" by participants [22]. They are constituted in complex ways through second-order *normative beliefs*: beliefs about what others believe we should or should not do in some situation [1, 2]. Human laws and norms are frequently ambiguous and complicated, they vary widely across jurisdictions, cultures, and groups, they change and adapt. The cases in which they are reducible to formal rule statements is the exception. Even deciding whether a vehicle has violated a numerical speed limit is far from straightforward: was visibility poor? were there children nearby? Adding to the complexity, rules and norms are enforced both by formal institutions like courts and regulators through costly and error-prone procedures and by the informal behavior of agents through third-party criticism and exclusion or internalization and self-criticism. This means that what actually counts as a rule can easily diverge from announced or formal rules and that rule-based environments are complex dynamic systems. As a result, we cannot rely on formal rules simply being imposed on agents *a priori*; instead, agents will in many cases have to *learn* the rules and how they work in practice. Normativity–the human practice of classifying some actions as sanctionable and others as not and then punishing people who engage in sanctionable conduct–will have to be *legible* [7] to AI systems.

In this paper, we introduce a distinction between types of rules that can aid in building predictive models to make human normative systems legible to an AI system. We distinguish between *important* rules and *silly* rules. An important rule is one the observance of which by one agent generates direct payoffs for some other agent(s). When an agent complies with rules prohibiting speeding, for example, other agents enjoy a material payoff as a direct consequence, such as a reduced probability of accident. A silly rule, in contrast, in one the observance of which by one agent does not generate any direct material payoff for any other agent. When an agent violates a dress code, for example, such as by failing to wear a head covering in public, no-one is materially affected as a direct consequence of the violation. Observers might well be offended, and they might punish the violator, but the violation itself is inconsequential.

We ground our claim that the distinction between silly and important rules will prove important to building models for aligned AI using Monte Carlo simulations. We show that silly rules promote robustness and adaptation in groups. Silly rules perform a legibility function for humans–making it easier for them to read the state of the equilibrium in their group when equilibrium is threatened. Incorporating this insight about silly rules into AI design should allow human normative systems to be more legible to AI.

Our paper is presented as follows. We first illustrate the concept of silly rules an example drawn from a concrete environment. We then develop a model of groups, based on [12], in which a group of agents announces a set of rules and relies exclusively on voluntary third-party punishment by group members to police violations. We

AIES '19, January 27–28, 2019, Honolulu, HI, USA

ACM ISBN 978-1-4503-6324-2/19/01...$15.00
https://doi.org/10.1145/3306618.3314250

first show formally that, if silly rules are costless, groups with more silly rules achieve higher payoffs. We then consider the case in which following and punishing silly rules is costly and present the results of our simulations. Our results demonstrate that groups with lots of (sufficiently cheap) silly rules are more robust: they are able to maintain more of their population and are less likely to collapse than groups with fewer silly rules in response to an unfounded shock to beliefs about the proportion of punishers. Groups with lots of silly rules are also more adaptable: they collapse more quickly when there is a true drop in the proportion of punishers below the threshold that makes group membership valuable.

Our contributions are threefold. First, we present a formal model that can account for the presence of silly rules in a normative system and show the conditions under which silly rules are likely to exist. This is a contribution to normative theory in human groups. Second, this work provides an example of the importance of building predictive models of human normative systems *qua* systems–not merely predicting the presence of particular norms, which is the dominant approach taken in the growing literature on AI ethics and alignment. Third, we demonstrate that standard AI methods can be valuable tools in analyzing human normative systems.

2 WHAT ARE SILLY RULES? A THOUGHT EXPERIMENT FROM ETHNOGRAPHY

One of the challenges of building models of human normativity is that as researchers we are all participants in our taken-for-granted normative environments and this can make it hard to study norms scientifically [14]. To attempt to overcome this, we motivate our work with an example drawn from an ethnography of a group that engages in practices far removed from the worlds in which AI researchers live. Moreover, we will use the shocking label "silly rules" in order to illuminate an overlooked distinction in the context of the existing literature on normativity. Most of the social science of norms focuses on functional accounts of particular norms such as norms of reciprocity, fair sharing of rewards, or non-interference with property. These accounts argue that particular norms evolve because they support human cooperation and thus improve fitness [4, 25] or solve coordination games [16–18, 24] for example. Our work highlights the systemic functionality of rules that, individually, have no direct functionality. All human societies, we will show, are likely develop silly rules, for good functional reasons.

Suppose that an AI system were tasked with learning how to make arrows by observing the Awá people of Brazil. The Awá are hunter-gatherers now living in relatively small numbers on reservations established by the Brazilian government. One of the things the AI will observe, like the ethnographers who have studied these people, is that the men of the Awá spend four or more hours a day making and repairing arrows [11]. They are produced in large quantities and need frequent repair. They are between 1.4 and 1.7 meters in length, customized to the height of their owner. Bamboo collected to make the points is sometimes shared but the arrows themselves are not; they are buried with their owner. The men use only dark, not brightly colored feathers. All parts of the arrow —shaft, point, and feathers —are smoked over a grill during preparation and the arrows themselves are kept warm in smoke at all times unless they are bundled and put in storage in the rafters of a hut. Will the AI system reproduce all of these arrow-making behaviors? We can imagine that AI designed with principles of inverse reinforcement learning [19] might discern which behaviors actually contribute to the functionality of the arrows–which is presumably what the human designer intended [13]. According to the human ethnographers who observed the Awá, many of the arrow-making practices are not functional. Even if smoking the wood used in the shaft of the arrow during manufacture contributes to a harder, straighter arrow, smoking the feathers seems unnecessary, as does ensuring the arrows are kept warm at all times. Moreover, the men make and carry many more arrows than they will use. In one season, a total of 402 arrows were carried on 9 different foraging trips; 9 were used. Most game on these trips was shot with a shotgun [11].

An AI system that ignored the non-functional arrow-making behaviors, however, would be violating the norms of the Awá people. The arrow-making practices described above are not just practices; they are rules. They reflect normative expectations [1]. How do we know? The lack of functionality is one clue: the Awá presumably have also discovered that a cold arrow works and that they spend a lot of time making arrows that go unused and are damaged by being bundled and carried around. But the better evidence comes from how they respond to the only man who makes his arrows differently. This man is mocked: his arrows are exceedingly long (2.3 m) and he uses brightly colored feathers. He is "the only man who does not socialize with the rest of the village." His strange arrows "are another sign of his loss of 'Awá-ness'" [11]. The Awá's rules are normative, moral principles: bright colored feathers are used only by women to prepare headbands and bracelets used by men in religious rituals and are associated with the world of spirits and ancestors; the making of fire and cooking are associated with masculinity and divinity. An AI system that violated these rules in the pursuit of arrow-making would not be aligned with the moral code of the Awá.

We call the non-functional rules "silly rules". We emphasize that silly rules are not "silly" to the groups that follow them. They can have considerable meaning, as they do to the Awá. Our results will show why silly rules can be very important to the overall welfare of a group and hence the subject of intense concern by group members.

3 MODEL

Our model is based on a framework developed in [12]. We characterize a set of agents as a group defined by a fixed and common knowledge set of rules. A rule is a binary classification of alternative actions that can be taken in carrying out some behavior. Actions are either "rule violations" or "not rule violations".

Members of this group engage in a finite sequence of interactions, each of which is governed by a rule drawn randomly from the ruleset. Each interaction is composed of a randomly selected pair of agents and a third actor, whom we will call a scofflaw, who will choose either to comply with the governing rule or not. (For tractability reasons, we do not model the scofflaws as group members.) One of the agents is randomly designated as the victim of the rule violation; the other is a bystander. If a rule is an *important* rule, the victim incurs a benefit if the rule is enforced and incurs a cost if not. If a rule is a *silly* rule, the victim incurs no benefit from the scofflaw's compliance with the rule and no cost from violation.

Group members are of two types in the bystander role: punishers, who always punish a rule violation, and non-punishers, who never punish. We assume that groups members signal whether they are punishers by paying a signaling cost in each interaction before a potential violation occurs. ([5] show that signaling punisher status supports an evolutionarily stable equilibrium in which non-punishers cannot free-ride on punisher types.) The scofflaw complies with the selected rule if the bystander is a punisher and violates it otherwise. There is no punishment in equilibrium, but the model can be seen as assuming that victims always punish but punishment is only effective when bystanders punish as well.

Prior to each interaction, group members have an option to quit the group and take a risk-free payoff. We formalize this setup as follows.

Each interaction is a game g and we define the sequence for a group as a tuple: $\langle G, T_\theta, \Pi, U, \gamma, c\rangle$ where G is a distribution over games and T_θ is a distribution over punishment types t in the group, where $t = 1$ if an agent is a punisher and $t = 0$ if not. The proportion of punishers is given by $\theta \in [0, 1]$. For the tractability of our agent models, we treat T_θ as a static distribution, and assume agents do likewise, even though it is subject to change as individuals leave the group.

We will abuse notation somewhat and use T and G to refer to the support of the corresponding distributions where the meaning is obvious. Π is each agent's prior distribution over the parameters of T_θ, and $U : G \times T_\theta \rightarrow \mathbb{R}$ is a mapping from types and games to immediate payoffs for the agents. γ is each agent's discount parameter for future rewards. c expresses a participation cost. This can be understood as the expected cost of an agent in the bystander role to signal that she is a punisher to the other agent in an interaction.

Every agent begins in period 1 with perfect knowledge of how actions are classified, all payoffs, and the distribution of games. The agents do not know the distribution of types in the group, but they do hold a prior which we will specify shortly. The agents update their beliefs about the distribution of types using Bayes' rule. The super game is defined as follows:
For each period j:

(1) Each agent chooses whether to participate or not. If an agent opts out, she collects 0 payoff.
(2) All agents that opt in are matched with another agent at random. A game $g_j \sim G$ is drawn for each of the agent pairings.
(3) Punishers incur a cost c to signal that they will punish violations. All players observe these signals.
(4) In each pairing one agent is randomly assigned the role of victim, V, and the other the bystander, B. All players observe the result of this random assignment.
(5) All players learn whether the game is a silly or important game.
(6) If B is a punisher, the scofflaw complies with the rule. Otherwise, the scofflaw violates the rule.
(7) Victims and bystanders collect payoffs given by $U_V(g_j, t_B, t_V)$ and $U_B(g_j, t_V, t_B)$.

Agents that play in the bystander role in any game incur no benefit; they incur the cost c if they are a punisher and 0 if not. Agents that play in the victim role receive a payoff of 0 in games governed by a silly rule. In games governed by an important rule they receive a positive reward R, if B is a punisher and a negative reward, $-R$, if B is not.

We formalize the set of important games as follows:

$$G' = \{g \in G | R(g) \neq 0\}$$
$$U_V(g, t_O, t_V) = (2t_O - 1)R(g) - (2t_V - 1)c$$
$$U_O(g, t_O, t_V) = (2t_O - 1)c$$

We will use $\mathbb{E}U = \mathbb{E}_{g,t_O}[U_V(g, t_O, t_V)|g \in G']$ to denote the expected utility of an important game. We let d denote the *density* of the process generating games: the probability of a silly game.

$$d = 1 - P(g \in G'); g \sim G.$$

Note that a super-game has high density (d close to 1) when silly rules are a large fraction of the ruleset.

Critically, we ensure that the density of silly games does not alter the (expected) rate at which important games are presented to the agents. Rather than take the place of important interactions, in our model silly interactions increase the *total number* of interactions happening in the same time frame. To be concrete, we assume the expected discounted reward obtained from important games is independent of d. This condition can be attained through a suitable modification of γ as a function of d:

Proposition 1. *Setting*

$$\gamma_d = 1 - (1 - d)(1 - \gamma)$$

ensures that the expected sum of discounted rewards from important games is independent of d[1].

Proof. See appendix. □

It can be easily shown that this constrained model describes an *optimal stopping problem* [10]. Each agent in our model must choose between participating, in which case they get an unknown reward and learn about the enforcement equilibrium in the community, or opting out, in which case they stop participating get a constant reward of 0. A classic result from the literature on optimal stopping tells us that, in the optimal policy, if the agent opts out once it will opt out for the rest of time. This is because the agent's information state does not change when it chooses to opt out, so if it was optimal to stop at time $t - 1$, it will also be optimal to stop at time t. Thus, we refer to the decision not to participate at any point, then, as a decision to retire.

These problems broadly fall under the class of *partially observed Markov decision processes* (POMDP) [23]. In a POMDP the optimal policy only depends on the agent's *belief state*: the agent's posterior distribution over the hidden state of the system. In this case, this is a distribution over the enforcement likelihood in the community. We give our agent a beta prior over this parameter so that the belief space for our agent is a two dimensional lattice equivalent to $\mathbb{Z}^2_+$. Initially, the belief state is (α_0, β_0). The probability that the bystander is a punisher in the first game is

$$p_{\alpha\beta} = \frac{\alpha}{\alpha + \beta}.$$

Once the games begin, agents update their prior beliefs using Bayes' rule, adding the counts of punishers and non-punishers observed

[1] $\mathbb{I}[\psi]$ is the indicator function for the condition ψ.

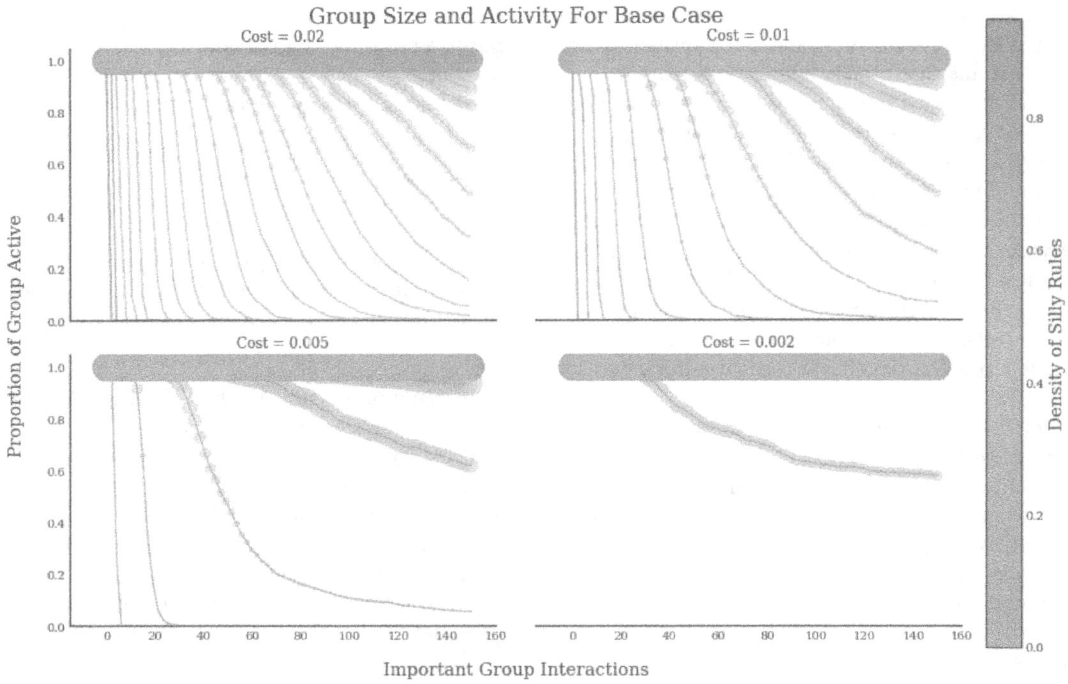

Figure 1: The y-axis represents the proportion of the 1000 groups with at least 2 individuals left, where the x-axis represents time in terms of the number of expected important interactions per agent. The size of the bubbles signifies the average size of the 1000 groups at the given point in time. 40 linearly spaced values between 0.0 and 0.95 were used for silly rule density, and the graphs for each setting are colored accordingly. For cost 0.02, we see that high density (blue) groups collapse rapidly, while the lowest density groups (orange) sustain their size for the duration of the experiment. As the cost comes down, higher density groups start to survive.

to the prior values. In the following, we will use $\alpha_i(\beta_i)$ to represent the number of punishers (non-punishers) observed prior to round i.

4 THEORETICAL ANALYSIS: THE VALUE OF DENSE NORMATIVE STRUCTURE

Consider first the case in which the signaling cost, c, is zero. In this case, punishers only face a risky choice when they are assigned to the victim role in an important game. In all other periods, the per-period expected payoff of playing the risky arm is a constant 0.

Intuitively, the benefit of higher density of unimportant games is that the agent is in a more information rich environment. In general, this benefit trades off with the cost of signalling. However, when the signalling cost is 0, a higher density is strictly better. One way to show this is to consider the *value of perfect information* (VPI): the additional utility an agent can get in expectation when it has full information compared with the expected utility with partial information [21]. We can show that, in the limit as density goes to 1, VPI goes to 0; high density of unimportant games essentially removes the agents' uncertainty over the proportion of punishers.

Proposition 2. *If the participation cost, c, is 0, then, for any belief state, (α_i, β_i), and discount rate γ, the corresponding VPI goes to zero as density goes to 1. That is*

$$\lim_{d \to 1} VPI((\alpha_i, \beta_i); d, \gamma) = 0 \tag{1}$$

Proof. (Sketch; see Appendix for details.) We consider a policy such that the agent participates in order to observe $\tau(d)$ interactions. After $\tau(d)$ observations, it uses its best estimate of the probability of enforcement to decide if it should leave. It doesn't reconsider retiring or rejoining afterwards. We show that this stopping time function can be chosen so that the expected number of important games goes to 0, so it doesn't lose utility in expectation, while the total number of interactions (including silly games) goes to ∞, so it makes the retirement decision with perfect information in the limit. □

It is straightforward to show that VPI is strictly positive as long as $P(V(\theta) > 0) > \epsilon > 0$ and $P(V(\theta) < 0) > \epsilon > 0$ for some finite epsilon. Combined with our proposition, this means that environments with more silly rules will be higher value to agents; as the density of silly rules goes to 1, we can neglect the utility lost due to partial information about the proportion of punishers. Where participation costs can be neglected, an agent will prefer an environment with lots of silly rules.

5 MONTE CARLO EXPERIMENTS

To test the benefit of silly rules in groups composed of our previously defined agents, we constructed a series of simulation-based experiments in which we manipulated the density of silly rules, cost of signaling, distribution of punishers, and prior beliefs about the punisher distribution. Each simulation was carried out in a group

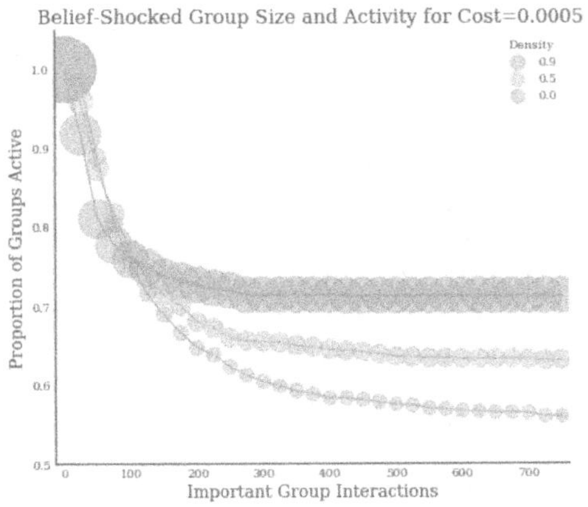

Figure 2: Using the same graphical representation as Figure 1, here we see a comparison of the robustness between groups of groups at 3 different density values. As the number of interactions increases, the survival rate and average population size of groups with higher silly rule density surpasses those of lower density groups.

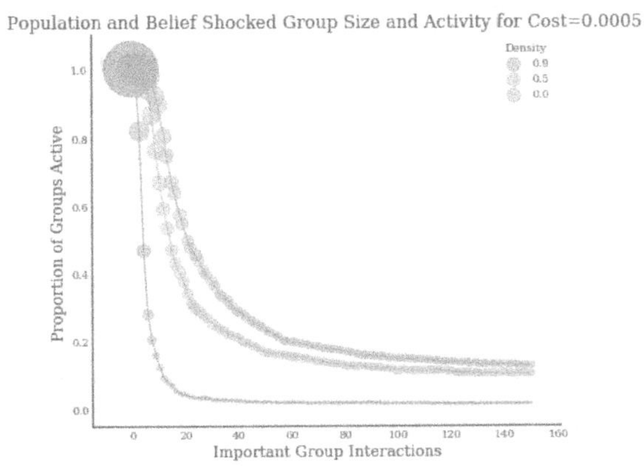

Figure 3: Using the same graphical representation as Figure 1 and 2, here we see a comparison of the adaptability between groups of groups at 3 different density values. Given the unstable conditions of the scenario, higher adaptability corresponds to faster a collapse rate. Groups with high density are seen to collapse much faster than those with low density.

of 100 agents, each given the type of punisher or non-punisher. The simulations were broken down into discrete periods, or *group interactions*, in which each individual was matched with another and engaged in an interaction, silly or important. We set the reward for the victim in an important game to $+1$ in the case in which the bystander is a punisher, and -1 if the bystander is not. Note that given the symmetry in gains and losses in important games, continued participation in the group is valuable if the likelihood that a bystander in an important game is a punisher is greater than .5 Given the density-adjusted discount factor for each simulation, the expected reward of 10 interactions in a $d = 0.9$ environment would be equivalent to that of 1 interaction in a $d = 0.0$ environment. This allows us to normalize the periods into *timesteps*, where 1 *timestep* is equal to $\frac{1}{1-d}$ *group interactions*.

We are interested in the size of groups over time, as agents make decisions about whether to remain in the group or not given their interaction experience, as a function of the density of silly rules.

We first consider the case in which there is low uncertainty about the proportion of punishers in the group. We can think of this as a base case in which a stable group has engaged in interactions over a long period of time and all agents have many observations of the proportion of punishers in the group. We set θ, the punisher proportion, to be 0.6 and the alpha-beta prior of the agents to $30 : 20$, which implies high confidence in the agents' estimate of θ. Note that with this ground truth, group membership is valuable, generating an expected payoff higher than the alternative of 0. We then run the simulation for 1000 groups on the full factorial of 20 logistically scaled signaling costs, c, and 20 linearly scaled densities, d. Doing so confirms our first hypothesis (see Figure 1):

Hypothesis 1: When uncertainty about the proportion of punishers in a group is low, the likelihood that a group loses members and the likelihood the group collapses increases with the density of silly rules.

In this case, as the frequency of the cost of signaling that one is a punisher in silly interactions increases it begins to outweigh the possible rewards from important interactions. We see that as cost goes up, groups with higher density of silly interactions shrink and collapse more frequently than those with low density. This confirms the intuition that silly rules are costly if they serve no information function.

5.1 Group Robustness

Having established a baseline, we investigate the benefits of silly rules for a group by considering different scenarios that will stress test the robustness and adaptability of a group. The first case we consider is one in which the individuals' beliefs in a stable group are shocked, lowering their confidence in the proportion of punishers. Concretely, this involves setting the beta priors to $1.2 : 0.8$ instead of $30 : 20$. Our hypothesis for the belief-shock scenario is as follows:

Hypothesis 2: For sufficiently low signaling cost, a higher density of silly rules increases a group's resilience to shocks in individuals' beliefs about the distribution of punishers.

As shown in Figure 2, in settings with low signaling cost, high density allows for quick stabilization and strong individual retention. Around 75% of groups with 0.9 density persist after 250 *timesteps*, with an average population of 50. Compare this to the lower density groups, where the groups that survive lose most members before stabilizing.

5.2 Group Adaptability

To test adaptability, we imagine an alternative scenario in which the shock to individuals' beliefs is accompanied by a change in the ground truth about the proportion of punishers. Concretely, we change the beta prior to $1.2 : 0.8$ once again, and set θ to be 0.4. With fewer punishers than non-punishers, participation in the group generates a negative expected payoff, and agents would do better to leave the group. Put differently, the group's ruleset is no longer generating value for group members. In a negative-value group such as this, we define the adaptability of the group to be the rapidity of collapse. Our hypothesis for this scenario is as follows:

Hypothesis 3: For sufficiently low signaling cost, a higher density of silly rules allows for faster adaptation to negativer shocks in the distribution of punishers in a group.

Looking to Figure 3, we find support for this hypothesis in the experiments. After only a few *timesteps*, we see that the high density groups are mostly collapsed, whereas the lower density groups take quite a bit longer to peter out.

6 DISCUSSION

Our results show that silly rules enrich the information environment and help groups adapt to uncertainty about the stability of social order. They help group members track their beliefs about the likelihood that violations of important rules will be punished, and thus the likelihood that important rules will be violated. These beliefs are critical to the incentive to invest resources in interaction.

We focus on the punisher type of bystanders because third-party punishment is the distinctive feature of human groups [6, 20, 25]; it extends the range of actions that can be deterred from those deterred by the reactions of the victim alone to those that can be deterred by group punishment [3].

What are the lessons for AI alignment research? The goal of AI alignment is the goal of building AI systems that act in ways consistent with human values. For groups of humans, this means (at least) values reflected in rules of behavior. Discerning values from rules is complex: some rules reflect important values, such as honoring a promise or avoiding harm. Others do not reflect values that are important *per se*. For an AI system to make good inferences and predictions from observing normative behavior, then, it will need to distinguish between important rules and silly rules.

Failing to make this distinction could lead to at least two key inferential errors. One error would be to treat important and silly rules as equally likely to vary over time and place. But important rules, because they promote functionality in human interactions, are likely to vary only when there is some causal reason. Silly rules, on the other hand, can vary for any reason, or none. Modelling the distinction between silly and important rules is essential to accurately learning rule systems. An AI system that lacks this distinction will over-estimate the likelihood of encountering certain types of normative behavior–with respect to dress codes, for example–while under-estimating the likelihood of others, such as speeding rules.

A second error that could result from a failure to distinguish between important and silly rules is that an AI system is likely to treat all rules that it sees enforced as equally important to human values. This would produce a good solution in ordinary circumstances. But this will produce a poor solution in circumstances in which it would be very costly to comply with all the rules. If an AI system treats all of rules as equally important to humans, it will presumably economize equally across the rules. The better solution prioritizes important rules and compromise on silly rules.

The distinction between silly and important rules also raises a question for work on human-robot interaction: how important is it for an AI system to help enforce silly rules? Our model brings out a legibility function in silly rules–they make it easier for agents in a group that depends on third-party enforcement to discern the stability of the rules in light of uncertainty generated by changes in population or the environment. If artificial agents are interacting in these environments and they don't participate in enforcing silly rules, what impact does that have on the beliefs of human agents? Does the introduction of large numbers of artificial agents who ignore silly rules into a human group (such as self-driving cars into the group of humans driving on highways) have the same impact on the robustness and adaptability of the group as a decrease in the density of silly rules, by reducing the amount of information gained from the opportunity to observe bystander behavior in interactions? Further still, when a robot learns and enforces silly rules, do these seemingly arbitrary norms become reified, fundamentally changing their meaning and reducing their signaling potential? We leave these questions, and others, for future research.

REFERENCES

[1] Bicchieri, C. 2006. *The grammar of society: the nature and dynamics of social norms.* New York: Cambridge University Press.

[2] Bicchieri, C. 2017. *Norms in the Wild: How to Diagnose, Measure, and Change Social Norms.* Oxford: Oxford University Press.

[3] Boyd, R., and Richerson, P. J. 1992. Punishment allows the evolution of cooperation (or anything else) in sizable groups. *Ethology and sociobiology* 13(3):171–195.

[4] Boyd, R., and Richerson, P. J. 2009. Culture and the evolution of human cooperation. *Philosophical Transactions of the Royal Society B: Biological Sciences* 364(1533):3281–3288.

[5] Boyd, R.; Gintis, H.; and Bowles, S. 2010. Coordinated punishment of defectors sustains cooperation and can proliferate when rare. *Science* 328(5978):617–620.

[6] Buckholtz, J. W., and Marois, R. 2012. The roots of modern justice: cognitive and neural foundations of social norms and their enforcement. *Nature neuroscience* 15(5):655.

[7] Dragan, Anca, K. C. L., and Srinivasa, S. S. 2013. Legibility and predictability of robot motion. In *Human Robot Interaction 2013 Proceedings*, 301–308.

[8] Etzioni, A., and Etzioni, O. 2016. Ai assisted ethics. *Ethics and Information Technology* 18:149–156.

[9] Etzioni, O. 2017. How to regulate artificial intelligence. *New York Times.*

[10] Gittins, J.; Glazebrook, K.; and Weber, R. 2011. *Multi-armed bandit allocation indices.* John Wiley & Sons.

[11] GonzÃąlez-Ruibal, A.; Hernando, A.; and Politis, G. 2011. Ontology of the self and material culture: Arrow-making among the awÃą hunter. *Journal of Anthropological Archaeology* 30:1–16.

[12] Hadfield, G. K., and Weingast, B. R. 2012. What is law? a coordination model of the characteristics of legal order. *Journal of Legal Analysis* 4(2):471–514.

[13] Hadfield-Menell, D.; Milli, S.; Abbeel, P.; Russell, S. J.; and Dragan, A. 2017. Inverse reward design. In *Advances in Neural Information Processing Systems*, 6765–6774.

[14] Haidt, J., and Joseph, C. 2008. Oxford: Oxford University Press. chapter The Moral Mind: How Five Sets of Innate Intuitions Guide the Development of Many Culture-Specific Virtues, and Perhaps Even Modules.

[15] IEEE. 2018. *Ethically Aligned Design Ver II: A Vision for Prioritizing Human Well-being with Autonomous and Intelligent Systems.* IEEE.

[16] McAdams, R. H., and Nadler, J. 2005. Testing the focal point theory of legal compliance: The effect of third-party expression in an experimental hawk/dove game. *Journal of Empirical Legal Studies* 2:87–123.

[17] McAdams, R. H. 2015. *The Expressive Power of Law: Theories and Limits.* Cambridge, MA: Harvard University Press.

[18] Myerson, R. B. 2004. Justice, institutions and multiple equilibria. *Chicago Journal of International Law* 5:91–107.

[19] Ng, A. Y.; Russell, S. J.; et al. 2000. Algorithms for inverse reinforcement learning. In *ICML*, 663–670.

[20] Riedl, K.; Jensen, K.; Call, J.; and Tomasello, M. 2012. No third-party punishment in chimpanzees. *Proceedings of the National Academy of Sciences of the United States of America* 109(37):14824–14829.

[21] Russell, S., and Norvig, P. 2010. *Artificial Intelligence: A Modern Approach.* Pearson.

[22] Schutz, A. 1964. *Collected Papers II.* The Hague: MartinusNijhoff.

[23] Sondik, E. J. 1971. The optimal control of partially observable markov processes. Technical report, STANFORD UNIV CALIF STANFORD ELECTRONICS LABS.

[24] Sugden, R. 1986. *The Economics of Rights, Cooperation, and Welfare.* London: Palgrave Macmillan.

[25] Tomasello, M., and Vaish, A. 2013. Origins of human cooperation and morality. *Annual Review of Psychology* 64(1):231–255.

APPENDIX: PROOFS

PROPOSITION 1. *Setting*

$$\gamma_d = 1 - (1 - d)(1 - \gamma)$$

ensures that the expected sum of discounted rewards from important games is independent of d:

$$\forall d, \in [0,1)\ \mathbb{E}_{g_j, t_O}\left[\sum_{j=0}^{\infty} \gamma^j U_V(g_j, t_O, t_V)\middle| g_j \in G'\right] =$$

$$\mathbb{E}_{g_j, t_O}\left[\sum_{j=0}^{\infty} \mathbb{I}[g_j \in G']\gamma_d^j U(g_j,, t_O, t_V)\middle| d\right].$$

PROOF. We first show that it is sufficient to ensure that the expected value of γ_d^j is the same given that j is a round with an important game:

$$\mathbb{E}_{g_j, t_O}\left[\sum_{j=0}^{\infty} \mathbb{I}[g_j \in G']\gamma_d^j U(g_j, t_O, t_V)\middle| d\right]$$

$$= \sum_{j=0}^{\infty} \mathbb{E}_{g_j, t_O}\left[\mathbb{I}[g_j \in G']\gamma_d^j U(g_j, t_O, t_V)\middle| d\right]$$

$$= \sum_{j=0}^{\infty} \gamma_d^j \mathbb{E}_{g_j, t_O}[U(g_j, t_O, t_V)|d, g_j \in G']\mathbb{E}_{g_j}\left[\mathbb{I}[g_j \in G']|d\right]$$

$$= (1 - d)\mathbb{E}U \sum_{j=0}^{\infty} \gamma_d^j$$

where the first line holds by the linearity of expectation, the fact that g_j is an independent iid draw from a stationary distribution, and the constraint on the agent's beliefs that t_O is a also an independent iid draw from a stationary distribution. Substituting the form of the infinite geometric series, we see that

$$\frac{\mathbb{E}U}{1 - \gamma} = \frac{(1 - d)\mathbb{E}U}{1 - \gamma_d} \tag{2}$$

is sufficient to achieve our goal. Substituting the form for γ_d in the theorem statement and reducing shows that this condition is satisfied. □

PROPOSITION 2. *If the participation cost, c, is 0, then, for any belief state, (α_i, β_i), and discount rate γ, the corresponding VPI goes to zero as density goes to 1. That is*

$$\lim_{d \to 1} VPI((\alpha_i, \beta_i); d, \gamma) = 0 \tag{3}$$

PROOF. Let $V(\theta)$ be the expected value of participating forever, given θ. The optimal full information policy will retire whenever $V(\theta) < 0$ and has value $V_+(\theta) = \max\{V(\theta), 0\}$. VPI is the difference between the expected value of V_+ and the value of the optimal partial information policy $V((\alpha_i, \beta_i); d, \gamma)$:

$$VPI((\alpha_i, \beta_i); d, \gamma) =$$
$$\mathbb{E}\left[V_+(\theta)|\,(\alpha_i, \beta_i)\right] - V((\alpha_i, \beta_i); d, \gamma) \tag{4}$$

We proceed by lower bounding V. V is the value of the optimal policy so it is weakly lower bounded by any arbitrary policy. We consider a policy that participates for

$$\tau(d) = \frac{1}{\sqrt{1 - d}} \tag{5}$$

rounds and then retires if $\mathbb{E}[V(\theta)] < 0$. This choice of τ ensures that

$$\lim_{d \to 1} \tau(d) = \infty; \tag{6}$$

$$\lim_{d \to 1} \sum_{t < \tau(d)} P(g_t \in G) = \lim_{d \to 1} \frac{1 - d}{\sqrt{1 - d}} = 0. \tag{7}$$

(6) ensures that, as density goes to 1, then agent's estimate of participation value when it decides, $\mathbb{E}[V(\theta)]$ converges to $V(\theta)$ by consistency. (7) ensures that the expected number of important games (and thus opportunities to lose utility against a full information agent) goes to 0. This is sufficient to show that

$$\lim_{d \to 1} V((\alpha_i, \beta_i); d, \gamma) = \mathbb{E}[V_+(\theta)|(\alpha_i, \beta_i)] \tag{8}$$

which shows the result. □

TED: Teaching AI to Explain its Decisions

Michael Hind, Dennis Wei, Murray Campbell, Noel C. F. Codella, Amit Dhurandhar,
Aleksandra Mojsilović, Karthikeyan Natesan Ramamurthy, Kush R. Varshney
{hindm,dwei,mcam,nccodell,adhuran,aleksand,knatesa,krvarshn}@us.ibm.com
IBM Research AI
Yorktown Heights, New York

ABSTRACT

Artificial intelligence systems are being increasingly deployed due to their potential to increase the efficiency, scale, consistency, fairness, and accuracy of decisions. However, as many of these systems are opaque in their operation, there is a growing demand for such systems to provide explanations for their decisions. Conventional approaches to this problem attempt to expose or discover the inner workings of a machine learning model with the hope that the resulting explanations will be meaningful to the consumer. In contrast, this paper suggests a new approach to this problem. It introduces a simple, practical framework, called Teaching Explanations for Decisions (*TED*), that provides meaningful explanations that match the mental model of the consumer. We illustrate the generality and effectiveness of this approach with two different examples, resulting in highly accurate explanations with no loss of prediction accuracy for these two examples.

KEYWORDS

Explainable AI; Meaningful Explanation; AI Ethics; Elicitation; Supervised Classification; Machine Learning

ACM Reference Format:
Michael Hind, Dennis Wei, Murray Campbell, Noel C. F. Codella, Amit Dhurandhar, and Aleksandra Mojsilović, Karthikeyan Natesan Ramamurthy, Kush R. Varshney . 2019. TED: Teaching AI to Explain its Decisions. In *AAAI/ACM Conference on AI, Ethics, and Society (AIES '19), January 27–28, 2019, Honolulu, HI, USA.* ACM, New York, NY, USA, 7 pages. https://doi.org/10.1145/3306618.3314273

1 INTRODUCTION

Machine learning based systems have proven to be quite effective for producing highly accurate results in several domains. This effectiveness is leading to wider adoption in higher stakes domains, which has the *potential* to lead to more accurate, consistent, and fairer decisions and the resulting societal benefits. However, given the higher stakes of these domains, there is a growing demand that these systems provide explanations for their decisions, so that necessary oversight can occur, and a citizen's due process rights are respected [4, 5, 10, 15, 17, 33–36].

AIES '19, January 27–28, 2019, Honolulu, HI, USA

ACM ISBN 978-1-4503-6324-2/19/01...$15.00
https://doi.org/10.1145/3306618.3314273

The demand for explanation has manifested itself in new regulations that call for automated decision making systems to provide "meaningful information" on the logic used to reach conclusions [15, 31, 36]. Selbst and Powles [31] interpret the concept of "meaningful information" as information that should be understandable to the audience (potentially individuals who lack specific expertise), is actionable, and is flexible enough to support various technical approaches.

Unfortunately, the advance in effectiveness of machine-learning techniques has coincided with increased complexity in the inner workings of these techniques. For some techniques, like deep neural networks or large random forests, even experts cannot explain how decisions are reached. Thus, we have a stronger need for explainable AI, just when we have a greater gap in achieving it.

This has sparked a growing research community focused on this problem [18, 19]. Most of this research attempts to explain the inner workings of a machine learning model either directly, indirectly via a simpler proxy model, or by probing the model with related inputs. This paper proposes a different approach that requires a model to jointly produce both a decision as well as an explanation, rather than exposing the inner details of how the model produces a decision. The explanation is not constrained to any particular format and can vary to accommodate user needs.

The main contributions of this work are as follows:

- A description of the challenges in providing meaningful explanations for machine learning systems.
- A new framework, called TED, that enables machine learning algorithms to provide meaningful explanations that match the complexity and domain of consumers.
- A simple instantiation of the framework that demonstrates the generality and simplicity of the approach.
- Two illustrative examples and results that demonstrate the effectiveness of the instantiation in providing meaningful explanations.
- A discussion on several possible extensions and open research opportunities that this framework enables.

The rest of this paper is organized as follows. Section 2 explores the challenges presented by the problem statement of providing explanations for AI decisions. Section 3 discusses related work. Section 4 describes our general approach, TED, and a simple instantiation for providing explanations that are understandable by the consumer and discusses the advantages of the approach. Section 5 presents results from two examples that demonstrate the effectiveness of the simple instantiation. Section 6 discusses future directions and open issues for the TED approach. Section 7 draws conclusions.

2 CHALLENGES TO PROVIDING AI EXPLANATIONS

This section explores the challenges in providing meaningful explanations, which provide the motivation for the TED framework.

The concept of an explanation is probably as old as human communication. Intuitively, an explanation is the communication from one person (A) to another (B) that provides justification for an action or decision made by person A. Mathematicians use proofs to formally provide explanations. These are constructed using agreed-upon logic and formalism, so that any person trained in the field can verify if the proof/explanation is valid. Unfortunately, we do not have such formalism for non-mathematical explanations. Even in the judicial system, we utilize nonexpert jurors to determine if a defendant has violated a law, relying on their intuition and experience in weighing (informal) arguments made by prosecution and defense.

Since we do not have a satisfying formal definition for valid human-to-human explanations, developing one for system-to-human explanations is challenging [17, 22]. Motivated by the concept of meaningful information [15, 31, 36], we feel that explanations must have the following three characteristics:

Justification: An explanation needs to provide justification for a decision that increases trust in the decision. This often includes some information that can be verified by the consumer.

Complexity Match: The *complexity of the explanation* needs to match the complexity capability of the consumer [7, 20]. For example, an explanation in equation form may be appropriate for a statistician, but not for a nontechnical person [27].

Domain Match: An explanation needs to be *tailored to the domain*, incorporating the relevant terms of the domain. For example, an explanation for a medical diagnosis needs to use terms relevant to the physician (or patient) who will be consuming the prediction.

There are at least four distinct groups of people who are interested in explanations for an AI system, with varying motivations.

Group 1: End User Decision Makers: These are the people who use the recommendations of an AI system to make a decision, such as physicians, loan officers, managers, judges, social workers, etc. They desire explanations that can build their trust and confidence in the system's recommendations and possibly provide them with additional insight to improve their future decisions and understanding of the phenomenon.

Group 2: Affected Users: These are the people impacted by the recommendations made by an AI system, such as patients, loan applicants, employees, arrested individuals, at-risk children, etc. They desire explanations that can help them understand if they were treated fairly and what factor(s) could be changed to get a different result [10].

Group 3: Regulatory Bodies: Government agencies, charged to protect the rights of their citizens, want to ensure that decisions are made in a safe and fair manner, and that society is not negatively impacted by the decisions.

Group 4: AI System Builders: Technical individuals (data scientists and developers) who build or deploy an AI system want to know if their system is working as expected, how to diagnose and improve it, and possibly gain insight from its decisions.

Understanding the motivations and expectations behind each group's needs for an explanation will help to ensure a solution that satisfies these expectations. For example, Group 4 is likely to desire a more complex explanation of the system's inner workings to take action. Group 3's needs may be satisfied by showing the overall process, including training data, is fair and free of negative societal impact and they may not be able to consume the same level of complexity as Group 4. Group 1 will have a high need for domain sophistication, but will also have less tolerance for complex explanations. Finally, Group 2 will have the lowest threshold for both complexity and domain information. These are affected users, such as loan applicants, and need to have the reasons for their outcomes such as loan denials explained in a simple manner without industry terms or complex formulas.

In summary, outside of a logical proof, there is no clear definition of a valid explanation; it seems to be subjective to the consumer and circumstances. Furthermore, there is a wide diversity of potential consumers of explanations, with different needs, different levels of sophistication, and different levels of domain knowledge. This seems to make it impossible to produce a single meaningful explanation without any information about the consumer.

3 RELATED WORK

Prior work in providing explanations can be partitioned into three areas:

(1) Making existing or enhanced models *interpretable*, i.e. to provide a precise description of how the model determined its decision (e.g., [24, 28, 30]).
(2) Creating a second, simpler-to-understand model, such as a small number of logical expressions, that mostly matches the decisions of the deployed model (e.g., [2, 5]).
(3) Work in the natural language processing and computer vision domains that generate rationales/explanations derived from input text (e.g., [1, 16, 21]).

The first two groups attempt to precisely describe how a machine learning decision was made, which is particularly relevant for AI system builders (Group 4). The insight into the inner workings of a model can be used to improve the AI system and may serve as the seeds for an explanation to a non-AI expert. However, work still remains to determine if these seeds are sufficient to satisfy the needs of the diverse collection of non-AI experts (Groups 1–3). Furthermore, when the underlying features are not human comprehensible, these approaches are inadequate for providing human consumable explanations.

The third group seeks to generate textual explanations with predictions. For text classification, this involves selecting the minimal necessary content from a text body that is sufficient to trigger the classification. For computer vision [16], this involves utilizing textual captions in training to automatically generate new textual captions of images that are both descriptive as well as discriminative. Although promising, it is not clear how these techniques generalize to other domains and if the explanations will be meaningful to the variety of explanation consumers described in Section 2.

Doshi-Velez et al. [10] discuss the societal, moral, and legal expectations of AI explanations, provide guidelines for the content of an explanation, and recommend that explanations of AI systems be held to a similar standard as humans. Our approach is compatible with their view. Biran and Cotton [3] provide an excellent overview and taxonomy of explanations and justifications in machine learning.

Miller [26] and Miller, Howe, and Sonenberg [27] argue that explainable AI solutions need to meet the needs of the users, an area that has been well studied in philosophy, psychology, and cognitive science. They provides a brief survey of the most relevant work in these fields to the area of explainable AI. They, along with Doshi-Velez and Kim [9], call for more rigor in this area.

4 TEACHING EXPLANATIONS

Given the challenges to developing meaningful explanations for the diversity of consumers described in Section 2, we advocate a non-traditional approach. We suggest a high-level framework, with one simple instantiation, that we see as a promising complementary approach to the traditional "inside-out" approach to providing explanations.

To understand the motivation for the TED approach, consider the common situation when a new employee is being trained for their new job, such as a loan approval officer. The supervisor will show the new employee several example situations, such as loan applications, and teach them the correct action: approve or reject, and explain the reason for the action, such as "insufficient salary". Over time, the new employee will be able to make independent decisions on new loan applications and will give explanations based on the explanations they learned from their supervisor. This is analogous to how the TED framework works. We ask the training dataset to teach us, not only how to get to the correct answer (approve or reject), but also to provide the correct explanation, such as "insufficient salary", "too much existing debt", "insufficient job stability", "incomplete application", etc. From this training information, we will generate a model that, for new input, will predict answers and provide explanations based on the explanations it was trained on. Because these explanations are the ones that were provided by the training, they are relevant to the target domain and meet the complexity level of the explanation consumer.

Previous researchers have demonstrated that providing explanations with the training dataset may not add much of a burden to the training time and may improve the overall accuracy of the training data [25, 37–39].

4.1 TED Framework and a Simple Instantiation

The TED framework leverages existing machine learning technology in a straightforward way to generate a classifier that produces explanations along with classifications. To review, a supervised machine learning algorithm takes a training dataset that consists of a series of instances with the following two components:

X, a set of features (feature vector) for the particular entity, such as an image, a paragraph, loan application, etc.

Y, a label/decision/classification for each feature vector, such an image description, a paragraph summary, or a loan-approval decision.

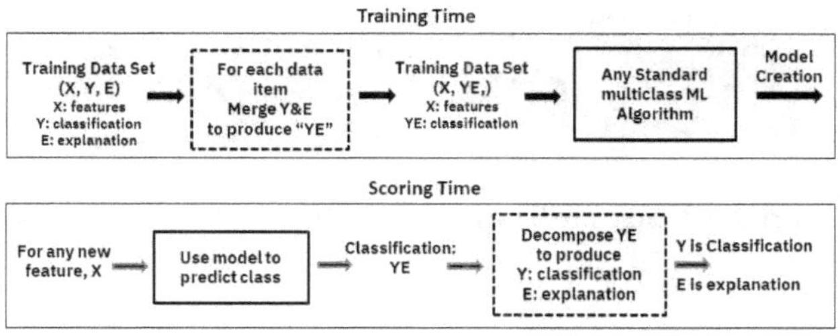

Figure 1: Overview of TED Algorithm ©IBM Corporation

The TED framework requires a third component:

E, an explanation for each decision, Y, which can take any form, such as a number, text string, an image, a video file, etc. Unlike traditional approaches, E does not necessarily need to be expressed in terms of X. It could be some other high-level concept specific to the domain that applies with some domain-specific combination of X, such as "scary image" or "loan information is not trustworthy". Regardless of the format, we represent each unique value of E with an identifier.

The TED framework takes this augmented training set and produces a classifier that predicts both Y and E. There are several ways that this can be accomplished. The instantiation we explore in this work is a simple Cartesian product approach. This approach encodes Y and E into a new classification, called YE, which, along with the feature vector, X, is provided as the training input to any machine learning classification algorithm to produce a classifier that predicts YE's. After the model produced by the classification algorithm makes a prediction, we apply a decoding step to partition a YE prediction into its components, Y and E, to return to the consumer. Figure 1 illustrates the algorithm. The boxes in dashed lines are new TED components that encode Y and E into YE and decode a predicted YE into its individual components, Y and E. The solid boxes represent 1) any machine learning algorithm that takes a normal training dataset: features and labels, and 2) the resulting model produced by this algorithm.

4.2 Example

Let's assume we are training a system to recommend cancer treatments. A typical training set for such a system would be of the following form, where P_i is the feature vector representing patient i and T_j, represents various treatment recommendations.

$$(P_1, T_A), (P_2, T_A), (P_3, T_A), (P_4, T_A)$$
$$(P_5, T_B), (P_6, T_B), (P_7, T_B), (P_8, T_C)$$

The TED approach would require adding an additional explanation component to the training dataset as follows:

$$(P_1, T_A, E_1), (P_2, T_A, E_1), (P_3, T_A, E_2), (P_4, T_A, E_2)$$
$$(P_5, T_B, E_3), (P_6, T_B, E_3), (P_7, T_B, E_4), (P_8, T_C, E_5)$$

Each E_i would be an explanation to justify why a feature vector representing a patient would map to a particular treatment. Some treatments could be recommended for multiple reasons/explanations. For example, treatment T_A is recommended for two different reasons, E_1 and E_2, but treatment T_C is only recommended for reason E_5.

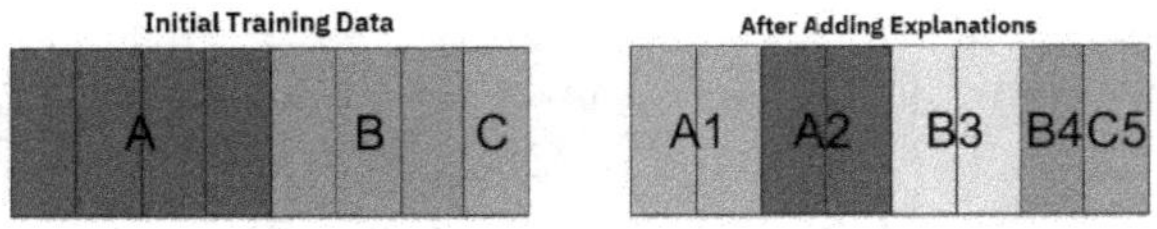

Figure 2: Changes to Training Dataset ©IBM Corporation

Given this augmented training data, the Cartesian product instantiation of the TED framework transforms this triple into a form that any supervised machine learning algorithm can use, namely (feature, class) by combining the second and third components into a unique new class as follows:

$$(P_1, T_A E_1), (P_2, T_A E_1), (P_3, T_A E_2), (P_4, T_A E_2)$$
$$(P_5, T_B E_3), (P_6, T_B E_3), (P_7, T_B E_4), (P_8, T_C E_5)$$

Figure 2 shows how the training dataset would change using the TED approach for the above example. The left picture illustrates how the original 8 training instances in the example are mapped into the 3 classes. The right picture shows how the training data is changed, with explanations added. Namely, Class A was decomposed to Classes $A1$ and $A2$. Class B was transformed into Classes $B3$ and $B4$ and Class C became $C5$.

As Figure 2 illustrates, adding explanations to training data implicitly creates a 2-level hierarchy in that the transformed classes are members of the original classes, e.g., Classes $A1$ and $A2$ are a decomposition of the original Class A. This hierarchical property could be exploited by employing hierarchical classification algorithms when training to improve accuracy.

4.3 Advantages

Although this approach is simple, there are several nonobvious advantages that are particularly important in addressing the requirements of explainable AI for groups 1, 2, and 3 discussed in Section 2.

Complexity/Domain Match: Explanations provided by the algorithm are guaranteed to match the complexity and mental model of the domain, given that they are created by the domain expert who is training the system.

Dealing with Incomprehensible Features: Since the explanation format can be of any type, they are not limited to being a function of the input features, which is useful when the features are not comprehensible.

Accuracy: Explanations will be accurate if the training data explanations are accurate and representative of production data.

Generality: This approach is independent of the machine learning classification algorithm; it can work with any supervised classification algorithm, including neural networks, making this technique widely deployable.

Preserves Intellectual Property: There is no need to expose details of machine learning algorithm to the consumer. Thus, proprietary technology can remain protected by their owners.

Easy to incorporate: The Cartesian product approach does not require a change to the current machine learning algorithm, just the addition of pre- and post-processing components: encoder and decoder. Thus, an enterprise does not need to adopt a new machine learning algorithm, just to get explanations.

Educates Consumer: The process of providing good training explanations will help properly set expectations for what kind of explanations the system can realistically provide. For example, it is probably easier to explain in the training data why a particular loan application is denied than to explain why a particular photo is a cat. Setting customer expectations correctly for what AI systems can (currently) do is important to their satisfaction with the system.

Improved Auditability: After creating a TED dataset, the domain expert will have enumerated all possible explanations for a decision. (The TED system does not create any new explanations.) This enumeration can be useful for the consumer's auditability, i.e., to answer questions such as "What are the reasons why you will deny a loan?" or "What are the situations in which you will prescribe medical treatment X?"

May Reduce Bias: Providing explanations will increase the likelihood of detecting bias in the training data because 1) a biased decision will likely be harder for the explanation producer to justify, and 2) one would expect that training instances with the same explanations cluster close to each other in the feature space. Anomalies from this property could signal a bias or a need for more training data.

5 EVALUATION

To evaluate the ideas presented in this work, we focus on two fundamental questions:

(1) How useful are the explanations produced by the TED approach?
(2) How is the prediction accuracy impacted by incorporating explanations into the training dataset?

Since the TED framework has many instantiations, can be incorporated into many kinds of learning algorithms, tested against many datasets, and used in many different situations, a definitive answer to these questions is beyond the scope of this paper. Instead we try to address these two questions using the simple Cartesian product instantiation with two different machine learning algorithms (neural nets and random forest), on two use cases to show that there is justification for further study of this approach.

Determining if any approach provides useful explanations is a challenge and no consensus metric has yet to emerge [10]. However, since the TED approach requires explanations be provided for the target dataset (training and testing), one can evaluate the accuracy of a model's explanation (E) in a similar way that one evaluates the accuracy of a predicted label (Y).

The TED approach requires a training set that contains explanations. Since such datasets are not yet readily available, we evaluate the approach on two synthetic datasets described below: tic-tac-toe and loan repayment.

5.1 Tic-Tac-Toe

The tic-tac-toe example tries to predict the best move given a particular board configuration. A tic-tac-toe board is represented by two 3×3 binary feature planes, indicating the presence of X and O, respectively. An additional binary feature indicates the side to move, resulting in a total of 19 binary input features. Each legal non-terminal board position (4,520) is labeled with a preferred move,

Table 1: Accuracy for predicting Y and E in Tic-Tac-Toe and Loan Repayment

Training Input	Accuracy (%)			
	Tic-Tac-Toe		Loan Repayment	
	Y	E	Y	E
X, Y	96.5	NA	99.2 (0.2)	NA
X, Y, and E	97.4	96.3	99.6 (0.1)	99.4 (0.1)

along with the reason the move is preferred. The labeling is based on a simple set of rules that are executed sequentially:[1]

(1) If a winning move is available, completing three in a row for the side to move, choose that move with reason *Win*
(2) If a blocking move is available, preventing the opponent from completing three in a row on their next turn, choose that move with reason *Block*
(3) If a threatening move is available, creating two in a row with an empty third square in the row, choose that move with reason *Threat*
(4) Otherwise, choose an empty square, preferring center over corners over middles, with reason *Empty*

Two versions of the dataset were created, one with only the preferred move (represented as a 3×3 plane), the second with the preferred move and explanation (represented as a $3 \times 3 \times 4$ stack of planes). A simple neural network classifier was built on each of these datasets, with one hidden layer of 200 units using ReLU and a softmax over the 9 (or 36) outputs. We use a 90%/10% split of the legal non-terminal board positions for the training/testing datasets. This classifier obtained an accuracy of 96.5% on the baseline move-only prediction task, i.e., when trained with just X (the 19 features) and Y it was highly accurate.

To answer the first question, does the approach provide useful explanations, we calculated the accuracy of the predicted explanation. Although there are only 4 rules, each rule applies to 9 different preferred moves, resulting in 36 possible explanations. Our classifier was able to generate the correct explanation 96.3% of the time, i.e., very rarely did it get the correct move and not the correct rule.

The second question asks how the accuracy of the classifier is impacted by the addition of E's in the training dataset. Given the increase in number of classes, one might expect the accuracy to decrease. However, for this example, the accuracy of predicting the preferred move actually increases to 97.4%. This illustrates that the approach works well in this domain; it is possible to provide accurate explanations without impacting the Y prediction accuracy. Table 1 summarizes the results for both examples.

5.2 Loan Repayment

The second example is closer to an industry use case and is based on the FICO Explainable Machine Learning Challenge dataset [13]. The dataset contains around 10,000 applications for Home Equity Line of Credit (HELOC), with the binary Y label indicating payment performance (any 90-day or longer delinquent payments) over 2 years.

[1]These rules do not guarantee optimal play.

Since the dataset does not come with explanations (E),[2] we generated them by training a rule set on the training data, resulting in the following two 3-literal rules for the "good" class $Y = 1$ (see [13] for a data dictionary):

(1) NumSatisfactoryTrades $\geq$ 23 AND
ExternalRiskEstimate $\geq$ 70 AND
NetFractionRevolvingBurden $\leq$ 63;
(2) NumSatisfactoryTrades $\leq$ 22 AND
ExternalRiskEstimate $\geq$ 76 AND
NetFractionRevolvingBurden $\leq$ 78.

These two rules, from researchers at IBM Research, predict Y with 72% accuracy and were the winning entry to the challenge [6]. Since the TED approach requires 100% consistency between explanations and labels, we modified the Y labels in instances where they disagree with the rules. We then assigned the explanation E to one of 8 values: 2 for the good class, corresponding to which of the two rules is satisfied (they are mutually exclusive), and 6 for delinquent, corresponding first to which of the rules should apply based on NumSatisfactoryTrades, and then to which of the remaining conditions (ExternalRiskEstimate, NetFractionRevolvingBurden, or both) are violated.

We trained a Random Forest classifier (100 trees, minimum 5 samples per leaf) on first the dataset with just X and (modified) Y and then on the enhanced dataset with E added. The accuracy of the baseline classifier (predicting binary label Y) was 99.2%. The accuracy of TED in predicting explanations E was 99.4%, despite the larger class cardinality of 8. In this example, Y predictions can be derived from E predictions through the mapping mentioned above, and doing so resulted in an improved Y accuracy of 99.6%. While these accuracies may be artificially high due to the data generation method, they do show two things as in Section 5.1: (1) To the extent that user explanations follow simple logic, very high explanation accuracy can be achieved; (2) Accuracy in predicting Y not only does not suffer but actually improves. The second result has been observed by other researchers who have suggested adding "rationales" to improve classifier performance, but not for explainability [8, 11, 25, 29, 32, 37–39].

6 EXTENSIONS AND OPEN QUESTIONS

The TED framework assumes a training dataset with explanations and uses it to train a classifier that can predict Y and E. This work described a simple way to do this, by taking the Cartesian product of Y and E and using any suitable machine learning algorithm to train a classifier. Another instantiation would be to bring together the labels and explanations in a multitask setting. Yet another option is to learn feature embeddings using labels and explanation similarities in a joint and aligned way to permit neighbor-based explanation prediction.

Under the Cartesian product approach, adding explanations to a dataset increases the number of classes that the classification algorithm will need to handle. This could stress the algorithm's effectiveness or training time performance, although we did not observe this in our two examples. However, techniques from the "extreme classification" community [12] could be applicable.

[2]The challenge asks participants to provide explanations along with predictions, which will be judged by the organizers.

Although the flexibility of allowing any format for an explanation, provided the set of explanations can be enumerated, is quite general, it could encourage a large number of explanations that differ in only unintended ways, such as "insufficient salary" vs. "salary too low". Providing more structure via a domain-specific language (DSL) or good tooling could be useful. If free text is used, we could leverage word embeddings to provide some structure and to help reason about similar explanations.

As there are many ways to explain the same phenomenon, it may be useful to explore having more than one version of the same base explanation for different levels of consumer sophistication. Applications already do this for multilingual support, but in this case it would be multiple levels of sophistication in the same language for, say, a first time borrower vs. a loan officer or regulator. This would be a postprocessing step once the explanation is predicted by the classifier.

Providing explanations for the full training set is ideal, but may not be realistic. Although it may be easy to add explanations *while* creating the training dataset, it may be more challenging to add explanations after a dataset has been created because the creator may not available or may not remember the justification for a label. One possibility is to use an external knowledge source to generate explanations, such as WebMD in a medical domain. Another possibility is to request explanations on a subset of the training data and apply ideas from few-shot learning [14] to learn the rest of the training dataset explanations. Another option is to use active learning to guide the user where to add explanations. One approach may be to first ask the user to enumerate the classes and explanations and then to provide training data (X) for each class/explanation until the algorithm achieves appropriate confidence. At a minimum one could investigate how the performance of the explanatory system changes as more training explanations are provided. Combinations of the above may be fruitful.

7 CONCLUSIONS

This paper introduces a new paradigm for providing explanations for machine learning model decisions. Unlike existing methods, it does not attempt to probe the reasoning process of a model. Instead, it seeks to replicate the reasoning process of a human domain user. The two paradigms share the objective to produce a reasoned explanation, but the model introspection approach is more suited to AI system builders who work with models directly, whereas the teaching explanations paradigm more directly addresses domain users. Indeed, the European Union GDPR guidelines say: "The controller should find simple ways to tell the data subject about the rationale behind, or the criteria relied on in reaching the decision without necessarily always attempting a complex explanation of the algorithms used or disclosure of the full algorithm."

Work in social and behavioral science [23, 26, 27] has found that people prefer explanations that are simpler, more general, and coherent, even over more likely ones. Miller writes that in the context of Explainable AI: "Giving simpler explanations that increase the likelihood that the observer both understands and accepts the explanation may be more useful to establish trust [27]."

Our two examples illustrate promise for this approach. They both showed highly accurate explanations and no loss in prediction accuracy. We hope this work will inspire other researchers to further enrich this paradigm.

REFERENCES

[1] Yessenalina Ainur, Yejin Choi, and Claire Cardie. 2010. Automatically Generating Annotator Rationales to Improve Sentiment Classification. In *Proceedings of the ACL 2010 Conference Short Papers*. 336–341.
[2] Osbert Bastani, Carolyn Kim, and Hamsa Bastani. 2018. Interpreting Blackbox Models via Model Extraction. *arXiv preprint arXiv:1705.08504* (2018).
[3] Or Biran and Courtenay Cotton. 2017. Explanation and Justification in Machine Learning: A Survey. In *IJCAI-17 Workshop on Explainable AI (XAI)*.
[4] Alex Campolo, Madelyn Sanfilippo Meredith Whittaker, and Kate Crawford. 2017. *2017 Annual Report*. Technical Report. AI NOW.
[5] Rich Caruana, Yin Lou, Johannes Gehrke, Paul Koch, Marc Sturm, and Noemie Elhadad. 2015. Intelligible Models for HealthCare: Predicting Pneumonia Risk and Hospital 30-day Readmission. In *Proc. ACM SIGKDD Int. Conf. Knowl. Disc. Data Min.* Sydney, Australia, 1721–1730.
[6] Sanjeeb Dash, Oktay Gunluk, and Dennis Wei. 2018. Boolean Decision Rules via Column Generation. In *Advances in Neural Information Processing Systems*.
[7] Amit Dhurandhar, Vijay Iyengar, Ronny Luss, and Karthikeyan Shanmugam. 2017. A Formal Framework to Characterize Interpretability of Procedures. In *Proc. ICML Workshop Human Interp. Mach. Learn.* Sydney, Australia, 1–7.
[8] Jeff Donahue and Kristen Grauman. 2011. Annotator Rationales for Visual Recognition. In *ICCV*.
[9] Finale Doshi-Velez and Been Kim. 2017. Towards A Rigorous Science of Interpretable Machine Learning. In *https://arxiv.org/abs/1702.08608v2*.
[10] Finale Doshi-Velez, Mason Kortz, Ryan Budish, Chris Bavitz, Sam Gershman, David O'Brien, Stuart Schieber, James Waldo, David Weinberger, and Alexandra Wood. 2017. Accountability of AI Under the Law: The Role of Explanation. *CoRR* abs/1711.01134 (2017). arXiv:1711.01134 http://arxiv.org/abs/1711.01134
[11] Kun Duan, Devi Parikh, David Crandall, and Kristen Grauman. 2012. Discovering Localized Attributes for Fine-grained Recognition. In *CVPR*.
[12] Extreme 2017. Extreme Classification: The NIPS Workshop on Multi-class and Multi-label Learning in Extremely Large Label Spaces.
[13] FICO. 2018. Explainable Machine Learning Challenge. https://community.fico.com/s/explainable-machine-learning-challenge?tabset-3158a=2
[14] Ian Goodfellow, Yoshua Bengio, and Aaron Courville. 2016. *Deep Learning*. MIT Press. http://www.deeplearningbook.org.
[15] Bryce Goodman and Seth Flaxman. 2016. EU Regulations on Algorithmic Decision-Making and a 'Right to Explanation'. In *Proc. ICML Workshop Human Interp. Mach. Learn.* New York, NY, 26–30.
[16] Lisa Anne Hendricks, Zeynep Akata, Marcus Rohrbach, Jeff Donahue, Bernt Schiele, and Trevor Darrell. 2016. Generating Visual Explanations. In *European Conference on Computer Vision*.
[17] Been Kim. 2017. Tutorial on Interpretable machine learning. "http://people.csail.mit.edu/beenkim/papers/BeenK_FinaleDV_ICML2017_tutorial.pdf"
[18] Been Kim, Dmitry M. Malioutov, Kush R. Varshney, and Adrian Weller (Eds.). 2017. *2017 ICML Workshop on Human Interpretability in Machine Learning*. https://arxiv.org/abs/1708.02666v1
[19] Been Kim, Kush R. Varshney, and Adrian Weller (Eds.). 2018. *2018 Workshop on Human Interpretability in Machine Learning*. https://sites.google.com/view/whi2018/home
[20] Todd Kulesza, Simone Stumpf, Margaret Burnett, Sherry Yang, Irwin Kwan, and Weng-Keen Wong. 2013. Too Much, Too Little, or Just Right? Ways Explanations Impact End Users' Mental Models. In *Proc. IEEE Symp. Vis. Lang. Human-Centric Comput.* San Jose, CA, 3–10.
[21] Tao Lei, Regina Barzilay, and Tommi Jaakkola. 2016. Rationalizing neural predictions. In *EMNLP*.
[22] Zachary C Lipton. 2016. The mythos of model interpretability. In *ICML Workshop on Human Interpretability of Machine Learning*.
[23] Tania Lombrozo. 2007. Simplicity and probability in causal explanation. *Cognitive Psychol.* 55, 3 (Nov. 2007), 232–257.
[24] Scott Lundberg and Su-In Lee. 2017. A unified approach to interpreting model predictions. In *Advances of Neural Inf. Proc. Systems*.
[25] T. McDonnell, M. Lease, M. Kutlu, and T. Elsayed. 2016. Why Is That Relevant? Collecting Annotator Rationales for Relevance Judgments. In *Proc. AAAI Conf. Human Comput. Crowdsourc.*
[26] Tim Miller. 2017. Explanation in Artificial Intelligence: Insights from the Social Sciences. *arXiv preprint arXiv:1706.07269* (June 2017).
[27] Tim Miller, Piers Howe, and Liz Sonenberg. 2017. Explainable AI: Beware of Inmates Running the Asylum Or: How I Learnt to Stop Worrying and Love the Social and Behavioural Sciences. In *Proc. IJCAI Workshop Explainable Artif. Intell.* Melbourne, Australia.
[28] Grégoire Montavon, Wojciech Samek, and Klaus-Robert Müller. 2017. Methods for interpreting and understanding deep neural networks. *Digital Signal Processing* (2017).

[29] P. Peng, Y. Tian, T. Xiang, Y. Wang, and T. Huang. 2016. Joint Learning of Semantic and Latent Attributes. In *ECCV 2016, Lecture Notes in Computer Science*, Vol. 9908.

[30] Marco Tulio Ribeiro, Sameer Singh, and Carlos Guestrin. 2016. "Why Should I Trust You?": Explaining the Predictions of Any Classifier. In *Proc. ACM SIGKDD Int. Conf. Knowl. Disc. Data Min.* San Francisco, CA, 1135–1144.

[31] A. D. Selbst and J. Powles. 2017. Meaningful Information and the Right to Explanation. *Int. Data Privacy Law* 7, 4 (Nov. 2017), 233–242.

[32] Qiang Sun and Gerald DeJong. 2005. Explanation-Augmented SVM: an Approach to Incorporating Domain Knowledge into SVM Learning. In *22nd International Conference on Machine Learning.*

[33] James Vacca. 2018. *A Local Law in relation to automated decision systems used by agencies.* Technical Report. The New York City Council.

[34] Kush R. Varshney. 2016. Engineering Safety in Machine Learning. In *Information Theory and Applications Workshop.*

[35] S. Wachter, B. Mittelstadt, and L. Floridi. 2017. Transparent, explainable, and accountable AI for robotics. *Science Robotics* 2 (May 2017). Issue 6.

[36] Sandra Wachter, Brent Mittelstadt, and Luciano Floridi. 2017. Why a Right to Explanation of Automated Decision-Making Does Not Exist in the General Data Protection Regulation. *Int. Data Privacy Law* 7, 2 (May 2017), 76–99.

[37] Omar F. Zaidan and Jason Eisner. 2007. Using 'annotator rationales' to improve machine learning for text categorization. In *In NAACL-HLT.* 260–267.

[38] Omar F. Zaidan and Jason Eisner. 2008. Modeling Annotators: A Generative Approach to Learning from Annotator Rationales. In *Proceedings of EMNLP 2008.* 31–40.

[39] Ye Zhang, Iain James Marshall, and Byron C. Wallace. 2016. Rationale-Augmented Convolutional Neural Networks for Text Classification. In *Conference on Empirical Methods in Natural Language Processing (EMNLP).*

Faithful and Customizable Explanations of Black Box Models

Himabindu Lakkaraju
Harvard University
hlakkaraju@hbs.edu

Ece Kamar
Microsoft Research
eckamar@microsoft.com

Rich Caruana
Microsoft Research
rcaruana@microsoft.com

Jure Leskovec
Stanford University
jure@cs.stanford.edu

ABSTRACT

As predictive models increasingly assist human experts (e.g., doctors) in day-to-day decision making, it is crucial for experts to be able to explore and understand how such models behave in different feature subspaces in order to know if and when to trust them. To this end, we propose *Model Understanding through Subspace Explanations* (MUSE), a novel model agnostic framework which facilitates understanding of a given black box model by explaining how it behaves in subspaces characterized by certain features of interest. Our framework provides end users (e.g., doctors) with the flexibility of customizing the model explanations by allowing them to input the features of interest. The construction of explanations is guided by a novel objective function that we propose to simultaneously optimize for fidelity to the original model, unambiguity and interpretability of the explanation. More specifically, our objective allows us to learn, with optimality guarantees, a small number of compact *decision sets* each of which captures the behavior of a given black box model in unambiguous, well-defined regions of the feature space. Experimental evaluation with real-world datasets and user studies demonstrate that our approach can generate customizable, highly compact, easy-to-understand, yet accurate explanations of various kinds of predictive models compared to state-of-the-art baselines.

CCS CONCEPTS

• **Computing methodologies** → *Supervised learning; Cost-sensitive learning.*

KEYWORDS

Interpretable machine learning, Decision making, Black box models

ACM Reference Format:
Himabindu Lakkaraju, Ece Kamar, Rich Caruana, and Jure Leskovec. 2019. Faithful and Customizable Explanations of Black Box Models. In *AAAI/ACM Conference on AI, Ethics, and Society (AIES '19), January 27–28, 2019, Honolulu, HI, USA.* ACM, New York, NY, USA, 8 pages. https://doi.org/10.1145/3306618.3314229

AIES '19, January 27–28, 2019, Honolulu, HI, USA

ACM ISBN 978-1-4503-6324-2/19/01…$15.00
https://doi.org/10.1145/3306618.3314229

1 INTRODUCTION

The successful adoption of predictive models for real world decision making hinges on how much decision makers (e.g., doctors, judges) can understand and trust their functionality. Only if decision makers have a clear understanding of the behavior of predictive models, they can evaluate when and how much to depend on these models, detect potential biases in them, and develop strategies for further model refinement. However, the increasing complexity and the proprietary nature of predictive models employed today is making this problem harder [9], thus, emphasizing the need for tools which can explain these complex black boxes in a faithful and interpretable manner.

Prior research on explaining black box models can be categorized as: 1) *Local* explanations, which focus on explaining individual predictions of a given black box classifier [4, 9, 10] and 2) *Global explanations*, which focus on explaining model behavior as a whole, often by summarizing complex models using simpler, more interpretable approximations such as decision sets or lists [5, 7]. In this paper, we focus on a new form of explanation that is designed to help end users (e.g., decision makers such as judges, doctors) gain deeper understanding of model behavior: *a differential explanation* that describes how the model logic varies across different subspaces of interest in a faithful and interpretable fashion. To illustrate, let us consider a scenario where a doctor is trying to understand a model which predicts if a given patient has depression or not. The doctor might be keen on understanding how the model makes predictions for different patient subgroups (See Figure 1 left). Furthermore, she might be interested in asking questions such as "how does the model make predictions on patient subgroups associated with different values of exercise and smoking?" and might like to see explanations customized to her interest (See Figure 1 right). The problem of constructing such explanations has not been studied by previous research aimed at understanding black box models.

Here, we propose a novel framework, *Model Understanding through Subspace Explanations* (MUSE), which constructs *global* explanations of black box classifiers which highlight their behavior in subspaces characterized by features of user interest. To the best of our knowledge, this is the first work to study the notion of incorporating user input when generating explanations of black box classifiers while successfully trading off notions of fidelity, unambiguity and interpretability. Our framework takes as input a dataset of instances with semantically meaningful or interpretable features (*e.g.* age, gender), and the corresponding class labels assigned by the black box model. It also accepts as an optional input a set of features that are of interest to the end user in order to

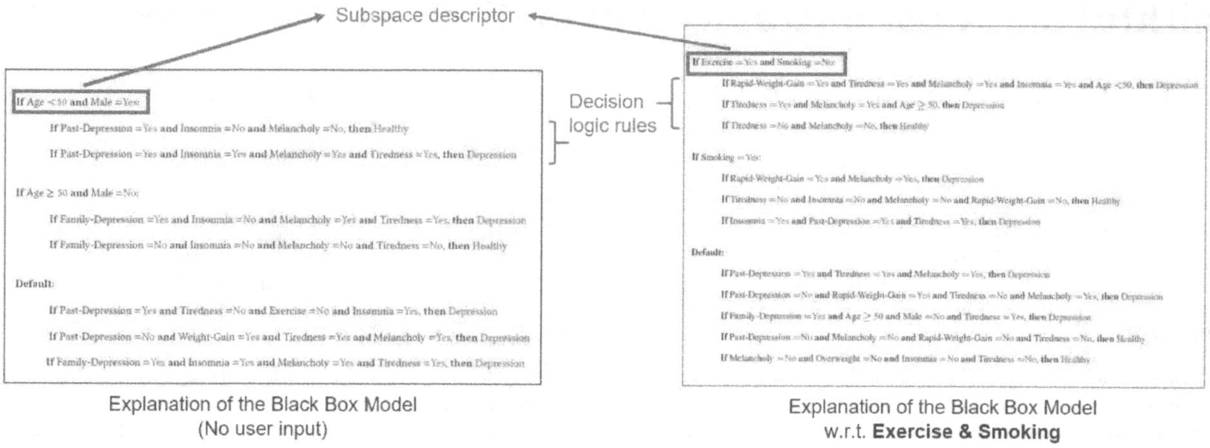

Figure 1: Explanations generated by our framework MUSE to describe the behavior of a 3-level neural network trained on depression dataset. MUSE generates explanation of the model without user input (left). It automatically selects features for defining subspaces by optimizing for fidelity, unambiguity, and interpretability. MUSE generates customized explanations based on the features of interest input by the end user - exercise and smoking (right).

generate explanations tailored to user preferences. Our framework then maps these inputs to a customized, faithful, and interpretable explanation which succinctly summarizes the behavior of the given model. We employ a two-level decision set representation, where the if-then clauses at the outer level describe the subspaces, and the inner if-then clauses explain the decision logic employed by the black box model within the corresponding subspace (See Figure 1 left). The two-level structure which decouples the descriptions of subspaces from the decision logic of the model naturally allows for incorporating user input when generating explanations. In order to construct an explanation based on the above representation, we formulate a novel objective function which can jointly reason about various relevant considerations: fidelity to the original model (i.e., mimicking the original model in terms of assigning class labels to instances), unambiguity in describing the model logic used to assign labels to instances, and interpretability by favoring lower complexity (i.e., fewer rules and predicates etc.). While exactly optimizing our objective is an NP-hard problem, we prove that our optimization problem is a non-normal, non-monotone submodular function with matroid constraints which allows for provably near optimal solutions.

We evaluated the fidelity and interpretability of the explanations generated by our approach on three real world datasets: judicial bail decisions, high school graduation outcomes, and depression diagnosis. Experimental results indicate that our approach can generate much less complex and high fidelity explanations of various kinds of black box models compared to state-of-the-art baselines. We also carried out user studies in which we asked human subjects to reason about a black box model's behavior using the explanations generated by our approach and other state-of-the-art baselines. Results of this study demonstrate that our approach allows humans to accurately and quickly reason about the behavior of complex predictive models.

2 RELATED WORK

Explaining Model Behavior: One approach for interpretability is learning predictive models which are human understandable (e.g., decision trees [11], decision lists [7], decision sets [5], linear models, generalized additive models [8]). Recent research focused on explaining individual predictions of black box classifiers [4, 9]. Ribeiro et. al.,'s approach of approximating global behavior of black box models through a collection of locally linear models create ambiguity as it does not clearly specify which local model applies to what part of the feature space. Global explanations can also be generated by approximating the predictions of black box models with interpretable models such as decision sets, decision trees. However, the resulting explanations are not suitable to answer deeper questions about model behavior (e.g., 'how the model logic differs across patient subgroups associated with various values of exercise and smoking?'). Furthermore, existing frameworks do not jointly optimize for fidelity, unambiguity, and interpretability.

Visualizing and Understanding Specific Models: The problem of visualizing how certain classes of models such as deep neural networks are making predictions has attracted a lot of attention in the recent past [14, 15]. Zintgraf et. al. [15] focused on visualizing how a deep neural network responds to a given input. Shrikumar et. al. [12] proposed an approach to determine the important features of deep neural networks. Furthermore, there exist tools and frameworks to visualize the functionality of different classes of models such as decision trees [13], SVMs etc. [2]. However, unlike our framework, these approaches are tailored to a particular class of models and do not generalize to any black box model.

3 OUR FRAMEWORK

Here, we describe our framework, Model Understanding through Subspace Explanations (MUSE), which is designed to address the problem of explaining black box models while highlighting their behavior w.r.t. specific subspaces of interest. As part of this discussion, we examine how to: (1) design a representation which enables us to not only construct faithful, unambiguous, and interpretable explanations but also readily incorporate user input for customization, (2) quantify the notions of fidelity, unambiguity, and interpretability in the context of the representation we choose, (3) formulate an optimization problem which effectively trade-offs fidelity, unambiguity, and interpretability, (4) solve the optimization problem efficiently, and (5) customize explanations based on user preferences (See Figure 2 for a sketch of MUSE workflow).

3.1 Our Representation: Two Level Decision Sets

The most important criterion for choosing a representation is that it should be understandable to decision makers who are not experts in machine learning, readily approximate complex black box models, and allow us to incorporate human input when generating explanations. We choose two level decision sets as our representation. The basic building block of this structure is a decision set, which is a set of if-then rules that are unordered. The two level decision set can be regarded as a set of multiple decision sets, each of which is embedded within an outer if-then structure, such that the inner if-then rules represent the decision logic employed by the black box model while labeling instances within the subspace characterized by the conditions in the outer if-then clauses. Consequently, we refer to the conditions in the outer if-then rules as *subspace descriptors* and the inner if-then rules as *decision logic rules* (See Figure 1). This two level nested if-then structure allows us to clearly specify how the model behaves in which part of the feature space. Furthermore, the decoupling of the subspace descriptors and the decision logic rules allows us to readily incorporate user input and describe subspaces that are of interest to the user in a compact fashion.

Definition 1. A **two level decision set** $\mathcal{R}$ is a set of rules $\{(q_1, s_1, c_1), (q_2, s_2, c_2) \cdots (q_M, s_M, c_M)\}$ where q_i and s_i are conjunctions of *predicates* of the form $(feature, operator, value)$ (eg., $age \geq 50$) and c_i is a class label. q_i corresponds to the subspace descriptor and (s_i, c_i) together represent the inner if-then rules (decision logic rules) with s_i denoting the condition and c_i denoting the class label (See Figure 1). A two level decision set assigns a label to an instance $\boldsymbol{x}$ as follows: if $\boldsymbol{x}$ satisfies exactly one of the rules i i.e., $\boldsymbol{x}$ satisfies $q_i \wedge s_i$, then its label is the corresponding class label c_i. If $\boldsymbol{x}$ satisfies none of the rules in $\mathcal{R}$, then its label is assigned using a default function and if $\boldsymbol{x}$ satisfies more than one rule in $\mathcal{R}$ then its label is assigned using a tie-breaking function.

In our experiments, we employ a default function which computes the majority class label (assigned by the black box model) of all the instances in the training data which do not satisfy any rule in $\mathcal{R}$ and assigns them to this majority label. For each instance which is assigned to more than one rule in $\mathcal{R}$, we break ties by choosing the rule which has a higher agreement rate with the black box model. Other forms of default and tie-breaking functions can be easily incorporated into our framework.

3.2 Quantifying Fidelity, Unambiguity, and Interpretability

To meaningfully describe the behavior of a given black box model, it is important to construct an explanation that is not only faithful to the original model but also unambiguous and interpretable. Below we explore each of these desiderata in detail and discuss how to quantify them w.r.t a two level decision set explanation $\mathcal{R}$ with M rules (See Definition 1), a black box model $\mathcal{B}$, and a dataset $\mathcal{D} = \{\boldsymbol{x}_1, \boldsymbol{x}_2 \cdots \boldsymbol{x}_N\}$ where $\boldsymbol{x}_i$ captures the feature values of instance i. We treat the black box model $\mathcal{B}$ as a function which takes an instance $\boldsymbol{x} \in \mathcal{D}$ as input and returns a class label.

Fidelity: A high fidelity explanation should faithfully mimic the behavior of the black box model. While different notions of fidelity can be defined, our metric of choice quantifies the disagreement between the labels assigned by the explanation and the labels assigned by the black box model. We define **disagreement($\mathcal{R}$)** as the number of instances for which the label assigned by the black box model $\mathcal{B}$ does not match the label c assigned by the explanation $\mathcal{R}$ (Table 1).

Unambiguity: An unambiguous explanation should provide unique deterministic rationales for describing how the black box model behaves in various parts of the feature space. To quantify this notion, we introduce two metrics: 1) **ruleoverlap($\mathcal{R}$)** which captures the number of additional rationales (beyond 1) provided by the explanation $\mathcal{R}$ for each instance in the data. Higher the value of this metric, higher the ambiguity of the explanation (Table 1). 2) **cover($\mathcal{R}$)** which captures the number of instances in the data that satisfy some rule in $\mathcal{R}$. Our goal here would be to minimize **ruleoverlap($\mathcal{R}$)** and maximize **cover($\mathcal{R}$)**. These two notions together ensure that the explanation we generate describes as much of the feature space as unambiguously as possible (Table 1).

Interpretability: Interpretability metric quantifies how easy it is to understand and reason about the explanation. While we choose an interpretable representation (e.g., two level decision sets), how interpretable the explanation is depends on its complexity (For example, a decisions set with many rules and high depth would not be interpretable for a user).

We quantify the interpretability of explanation $\mathcal{R}$ using the following metrics (Table 1): **size($\mathcal{R}$)** is the number of rules (triples of the form (q, s, c)) in the two level decision set $\mathcal{R}$. **maxwidth($\mathcal{R}$)** is the maximum width computed over all the elements in $\mathcal{R}$, where each element is either a condition of some decision logic rule s or a subspace descriptor q, and $width(s)$ is the number of predicates in the condition s. Similarly, $width(q)$ is defined as the total number of predicates of the subspace descriptor q. **numpreds($\mathcal{R}$)** counts the number of predicates in $\mathcal{R}$ including those appearing in both the decision logic rules and subspace descriptors. Note that the predicates of subspace descriptors are counted multiple times as a subspace descriptor q could potentially appear alongside multiple decision logic rules. **numdsets($\mathcal{R}$)** counts the number of unique subspace descriptors (outer if-then clauses) in $\mathcal{R}$.

In a two-level decision set, subspace descriptors and decision logic rules have different semantic meanings i.e., each subspace descriptor characterizes a specific region of the feature space, and the corresponding inner if-then rules specify the decision logic of the black box model within that region. To make the distinction more clear, we minimize the overlap between the features that appear in subspace descriptors and those that appear in decision logic rules. To quantify this, we compute for each pair of subspace descriptor q and decision logic rule s, the number of features that

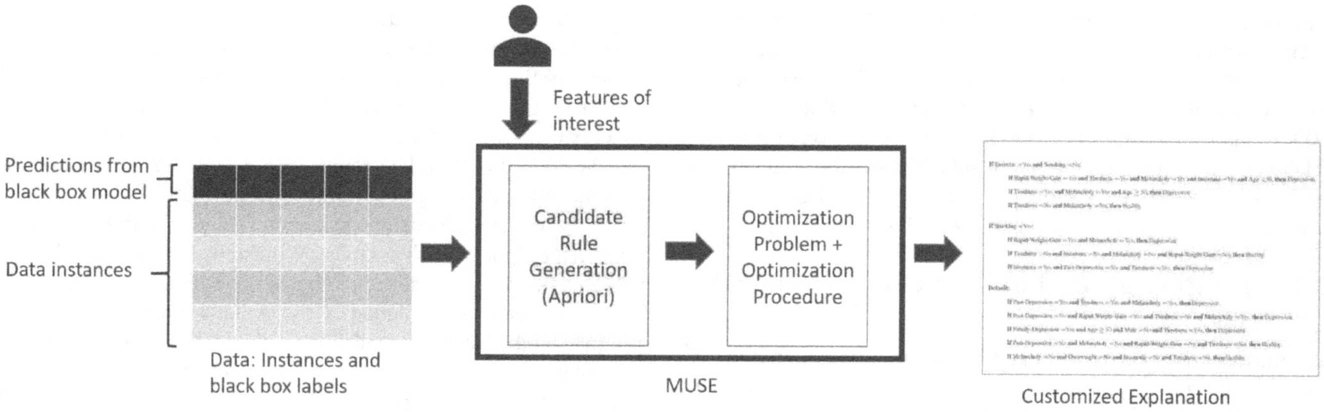

Figure 2: Algorithmic flow of MUSE approach: MUSE takes data, black box model predictions and user's features of interest. It outputs customized explanations.

Table 1: Metrics used in the Optimization Problem

Fidelity	$disagreement(\mathcal{R}) = \sum_{i=1}^{M} \lvert\{x \mid x \in \mathcal{D}, x \text{ satisfies } q_i \wedge s_i, \mathcal{B}(x) \neq c_i\}\rvert$
Unambiguity	$ruleoverlap(\mathcal{R}) = \sum_{i=1}^{M} \sum_{j=1, i \neq j}^{M} overlap(q_i \wedge s_i, q_j \wedge s_j)$ $cover(\mathcal{R}) = \lvert\{x \mid x \in \mathcal{D}, x \text{ satisfies } q_i \wedge s_i \text{ where } i \in \{1 \cdots M\}\}\rvert$
Interpretability	$size(\mathcal{R})$: number of rules (triples of the form (q, s, c)) in $\mathcal{R}$ $maxwidth(\mathcal{R}) = \max_{e \in \bigcup_{i=1}^{M} (q_i \cup s_i)} width(e)$ $numpreds(\mathcal{R}) = \sum_{i=1}^{M} width(s_i) + width(q_i)$ $numdsets(\mathcal{R}) = \lvert dset(\mathcal{R})\rvert$ where $dset(\mathcal{R}) = \bigcup_{i=1}^{M} q_i$ $featureoverlap(\mathcal{R}) = \sum_{q \in dset(\mathcal{R})} \sum_{i=1}^{M} featureoverlap(q, s_i)$

Algorithm 1: Optimization Procedure [6]

Input: Objective f, domain $\mathcal{ND} \times \mathcal{DL} \times C$, parameter δ, number of constraints k
$V_1 = \mathcal{ND} \times \mathcal{DL} \times C$
for $i \in \{1, 2 \cdots k+1\}$ **do** ▷ Approximation local search procedure
  $X = V_i; n = |X|; S_i = \emptyset$
  Let v be the element with the maximum value for f and set $S_i = v$
  while there exists a delete/update operation which increases the value of S_i by a factor of at least $(1 + \frac{\delta}{n^4})$ **do**
    Delete Operation: If $e \in S_i$ such that $f(S_i \backslash \{e\}) \geq (1 + \frac{\delta}{n^4}) f(S_i)$, then $S_i = S_i \backslash e$

    Exchange Operation If $d \in X \backslash S_i$ and $e_j \in S_i$ (for $1 \leq j \leq k$) such that
    $(S_i \backslash e_j) \cup \{d\}$ (for $1 \leq j \leq k$) satisfies all the k constraints and
    $f(S_i \backslash \{e_1, e_2 \cdots e_k\} \cup \{d\}) \geq (1 + \frac{\delta}{n^4}) f(S_i)$, then $S_i = S_i \backslash \{e_1, e_2, \cdots e_k\} \cup \{d\}$
  end while
  $V_{i+1} = V_i \backslash S_i$
end for
return the solution corresponding to $\max\{f(S_1), f(S_2), \cdots f(S_{k+1})\}$

occur in both q and s ($featureoverlap(q, s)$) and then sum up these counts. The resulting sum is denoted as **featureoverlap($\mathcal{R}$)**.

3.3 Optimization

3.3.1 Objective Function. We formulate an objective function that can jointly optimize for fidelity to the original model, unambiguity and interpretability of the explanation. We assume that we are given as inputs a dataset $\mathcal{D}$, labels assigned to instances in $\mathcal{D}$ by black box model $\mathcal{B}$, a set of possible class labels C, a candidate set of conjunctions of predicates (Eg., Age $\geq$ 50 and Gender = Female) $\mathcal{ND}$ from which we can pick the subspace descriptors, and another candidate set of conjunctions of predicates $\mathcal{DL}$ from which we can choose the decision logic rules. In practice, a frequent itemset mining algorithm such as apriori [1] can be used to generate the candidate sets of conjunctions of predicates. If the user does not provide any input, both $\mathcal{ND}$ and $\mathcal{DL}$ are assigned to the same candidate set generated by apriori.

To facilitate theoretical analysis, the metrics defined in Table 1 are expressed in the objective function either as non-negative reward functions or constraints. To construct non-negative reward functions, penalty terms (metrics in Table 1) are subtracted from their corresponding upper bound values ($\mathcal{P}_{max}$, O_{max}, O'_{max}, $\mathcal{F}_{max}$) which are computed with respect to the sets $\mathcal{ND}$ and $\mathcal{DL}$.

$f_1(\mathcal{R}) = \mathcal{P}_{max} - numpreds(\mathcal{R})$, where $\mathcal{P}_{max} = 2 * \mathcal{W}_{max} * |\mathcal{ND}| * |\mathcal{DL}|$
$f_2(\mathcal{R}) = O_{max} - featureoverlap(\mathcal{R})$, where $O_{max} = \mathcal{W}_{max} * |\mathcal{ND}| * |\mathcal{DL}|$
$f_3(\mathcal{R}) = O'_{max} - ruleoverlap(\mathcal{R})$, where $O'_{max} = N \times (|\mathcal{ND}| * |\mathcal{DL}|)^2$
$f_4(\mathcal{R}) = cover(\mathcal{R})$
$f_5(\mathcal{R}) = \mathcal{F}_{max} - disagreement(\mathcal{R})$, where $\mathcal{F}_{max} = N \times |\mathcal{ND}| * |\mathcal{DL}|$

where W_{max} is the maximum width of any rule in either candidate sets. The resulting optimization problem is:

$$\underset{\mathcal{R} \subseteq \mathcal{ND} \times \mathcal{DL} \times C}{\arg\max} \sum_{i=1}^{5} \lambda_i f_i(\mathcal{R}) \tag{1}$$

s.t. $size(\mathcal{R}) \leq \epsilon_1$, $maxwidth(\mathcal{R}) \leq \epsilon_2$, $numdsets(\mathcal{R}) \leq \epsilon_3$

$\lambda_1 \cdots \lambda_5$ are non-negative weights which manage the relative influence of the terms in the objective. These can be specified by an end user or can be set using cross validation (details in experiments section). The values of $\epsilon_1, \epsilon_2, \epsilon_3$ are application dependent and need to be set by an end user.

Theorem 1. *The objective function in Eqn. 1 is non-normal, non-negative, non-monotone, submodular and the constraints of the optimization problem are matroids.*

Proof. See Appendix. □

3.3.2 Optimization Procedure. While exactly solving the optimization problem in Eqn. 1 is NP-Hard [3], the specific properties of the problem: non-monotonicity, submodularity, non-normality, non-negativity and the accompanying matroid constraints allow for applying algorithms with provable optimality guarantees. We employ an optimization procedure based on approximate local search [6] which provides the best known theoretical guarantees for this class of problems. The pseudocode for the optimization procedure is shown in Algorithm 1 (more details in Appendix). This procedure provides an optimality guarantee of $\frac{1}{k+2+1/k+\delta}$ where k is the number of constraints and $\delta > 0$. In the case of our problem with 3 constraints, this factor boils down to $\sim 1/5$ approximation.

3.3.3 Incorporating User Input. A distinguishing characteristic of our framework is being able to incorporate user feedback to customize explanations. As Figure 1 demonstrates, customizing the explanation based on features of interest, namely exercise and smoking (Figure 1 right) makes it easier to understand how model logic varies for different values of these features. When a user inputs a set of features that are of interest to him, we simply restrict the candidate set of predicates $\mathcal{ND}$ from which subspace descriptors are chosen (See Objective Function) to comprise only of those predicates with features that are of interest to the user. This will ensure that the subspaces in the resulting explanations are characterized by the features of interest. Furthermore, the metric **featureoverlap($\mathcal{R}$)** and the term $f_2(\mathcal{R})$ of our objective function ensure that the features that appear in subspace descriptors do not appear in the decision logic rules there by creating a clear demarcation.

4 EXPERIMENTAL EVALUATION

We begin this section by comparing our approach with state-of-the-art baselines on real-world datasets w.r.t the fidelity vs. interpretability trade-offs and unambiguity of the generated explanations. We then discuss the results of a user study that we carried out to evaluate how easy it is for humans to reason about the behavior of black box models using the explanations generated by our framework.

Datasets We evaluate our framework on the following real world datasets: 1) A dataset of **bail outcomes** collected from various U.S. courts during 1990-2009 [5] comprising of demographic information and details of past criminal records for about 86K defendants. Each defendant is assigned a class label based on whether he/she has been released on bail or locked up. 2) A dataset of about 21K high school **student performance** [5] records collected from a school district between 2012-2013 with various details such as grades, absence rates, suspension history. The class label of each student indicates if he/she graduated high school on time, dropped out, or encountered a delay in graduation. 3) **Depression diagnosis** dataset collected by an online health records portal comprising of medical history, symptoms, and demographic information of about 33K individuals. Each individual has either been diagnosed with depression or is healthy.

Baselines We benchmark the performance of our framework against the following baselines: 1) Locally interpretable model agnostic explanations (LIME) [9] 2) Interpretable Decision Sets (IDS) [5] 3) Bayesian Decision Lists (BDL) [7]. While IDS and BDL were developed as stand alone interpretable classifiers, we employ them to explain other black box models by treating the instance labels assigned by black box models as the ground truth labels. Since LIME approximates black box classifiers using multiple locally linear models, the approximations created by LIME and our approach have representational differences. To facilitate fair comparison, we construct a variant of LIME known as LIME-DS where each local model is a decision set (a set of if-then rules) instead of being a linear model.

Experimental Setup We generate explanations of multiple classes of models: deep neural networks, gradient boosted trees, random forests, decision trees, SVM. Due to space constraints, we present results with a deep neural network of 5 layers in this section, however our findings generalize to other model classes. Our optimization problem has the following parameters $\lambda_1 \cdots \lambda_5$ (scaling coefficients) and $\epsilon_1 \cdots \epsilon_3$ (constraint values). We employed a simple tuning procedure to set these parameters (details in Appendix). We set other parameters as follows: $\epsilon_1 = 20$, $\epsilon_2 = 7$, and $\epsilon_3 = 5$. Support threshold for Apriori algorithm was set to 1%.

4.1 Experimentation with Real World Data

Analyzing the Tradeoffs between Fidelity and Interpretability To understand how effectively different approaches trade-off fidelity with interpretability, we plot fidelity vs. various metrics of interpretability (as outlined in the previous section) for explanations generated by our framework (without user input regarding features of interest) and other baselines. We define fidelity as the fraction of instances in the data for which the label assigned by the explanation is the same as that of the black box model prediction. Figures 3a and 3b show the plots of fidelity vs. number of rules (*size*) and fidelity vs. average number of predicates (ratio of *numpreds* to *size*) respectively for the explanations constructed using MUSE, LIME-DS, IDS, and BDL. These results correspond to explanations of a 5 layer deep neural network trained on the depression diagnosis data. Similar results were observed with other data sets and black box model types. It can be seen from Figure 3a that our framework (MUSE) and IDS achieve the best trade-offs between fidelity and number of rules. Furthermore, Figure 3b shows that our framework MUSE significantly outperforms all the other baselines when trading off fidelity with average number of predicates per rule. For instance, at an average width of 10 predicates per rule, explanations generated by MUSE already reach a fidelity of about 80% whereas explanations output by other approaches require at least 20 predicates per rule to attain this level of fidelity (Figure 3b). These results demonstrate that the explanations produced by MUSE provide significantly better trade-offs of fidelity vs. complexity compared to other state-of-the-art baselines.

Evaluating Unambiguity of Explanations We can readily evaluate the unambiguity of approximations constructed by our approach MUSE, IDS, BDL using two of the metrics outlined in previous section, namely, *ruleoverlap* and *cover*. Note that decision list representation by design achieves the optimal values of zero for *ruleoverlap* and N for *cover* since each else-if clause ensures that every instance satisfies a single rule in the list and else clause ensures that no instance is left uncovered. We found that the approximations generated using IDS and our approach also result in low values of *ruleoverlap* (between 1% and 2%) and high values for *cover* (95% to 98%). LIME is excluded from this comparison since it

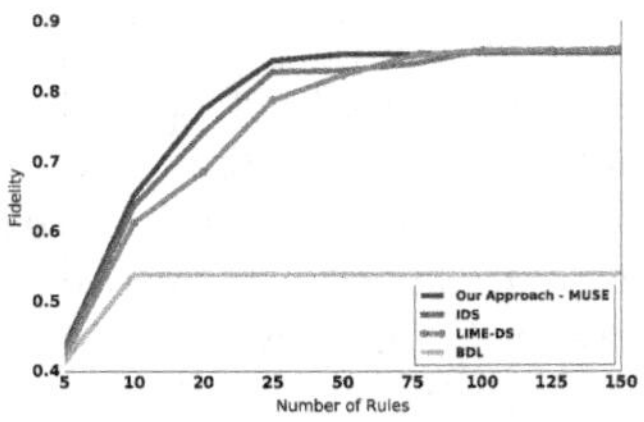

(a) Number of Rules

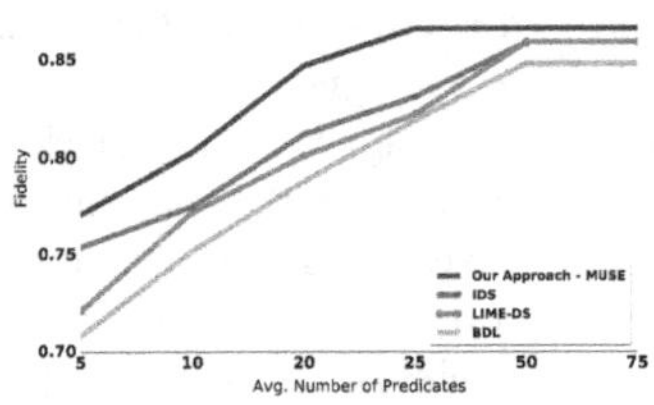

(b) Avg. Number of Predicates

Approach	Human Accuracy	Avg. Time (in secs.)
MUSE (No customization)	94.5%	160.1
IDS	89.2%	231.1
BDL	83.7%	368.5
MUSE (Customization)	98.3%	78.3

(c) Results of User Study

Figure 3: Evaluating our framework MUSE: a & b) Fidelity vs. interpretability trade Offs for a 5-layer neural network trained on depression diagnosis data. c) Results of user study.

does not even specify which local model is applicable to what part of the feature space.

4.2 Evaluating Human Understanding of Explanations

Here, we report the results of three user studies that were designed to evaluate the ease with which users can understand and reason about the behavior of black box models using our explanations. The explanations that we showed to users have been constructed by approximating a 5 layer deep neural network trained on depression diagnosis data.

Comparing rule based approximations (task 1) We designed an online user study with 33 participants, where each participant was randomly presented with the explanations generated by one of the following approaches: 1) our approach MUSE 2) IDS 3) BDL. Participants were asked 5 questions, each of which was designed to test their understanding of the model behavior (as depicted by the explanation) in different parts of feature space. An example question is: *Consider a patient who is female and aged 65 years. Based on the approximation shown above, can you be absolutely sure that this patient is Healthy? If not, what other conditions need to hold for this patient to be labeled as Healthy?* These questions closely mimic decision making in real-world settings where decision makers such as doctors, judges would like to reason about model behavior in certain parts of the feature space. The answers to these questions could be objectively judged as right or wrong based on the decision logic encoded by the explanation. Based on this, we computed the accuracy of the answers provided by users. We also recorded the time taken to answer each question and used this to compute the average time spent (in seconds) on each question. Figure 3c (top) shows the results obtained using explanations from MUSE (without customization), IDS, and BDL. It can be seen that user accuracy associated with our approach was higher than that of IDS, BDL. In addition, users were about 1.5 and 2.3 times faster when using our explanations compared to those constructed by IDS and BDL respectively.

Customizing Explanations We measured the benefit obtained when the explanation presented to the user is customized w.r.t to the question the user is trying to answer. For example, imagine the question above now asking about a patient who smokes and does not exercise. Whenever a user is asked this question, we showed him/her an explanation where exercise and smoking appear in the subspace descriptors (See Figure 1 (right)) thus simulating the effect of the user trying to explore the model w.r.t these features. We recruited 11 participants for this study and we asked each of these participants the same 5 questions as those asked in task 1. Table 3c (bottom row) shows the results of our model customized to the question being answered. In comparison to the results given in the first study, it can be seen that the time taken to answer questions is almost reduced in half compared to the setting where we showed users the same explanation (which is not customized to the question being asked) each time. In addition, answers are also more accurate, thus, demonstrating that allowing users to explore the model behavior from different perspectives can be very helpful in reasoning about its behavior in different parts of the feature space.

Comparing our approach with LIME (task 2) In the final study, our goal was to carry out the comparison outlined in task 1 between our approach and LIME. However, preliminary discussions with few test subjects revealed that the ill-defined subspace notions of LIME make it almost impossible to answer questions of the form mentioned above. We therefore carried out an online survey where we showed each participant explanations generated using our model and LIME, and asked them which explanation would they prefer to use to answer questions of the form mentioned above. We recruited 12 participants for carrying out this survey and they unanimously preferred using explanations generated by our approach to reason about the model behavior.

5 CONCLUSIONS & FUTURE WORK

In this paper, we propose MUSE, a framework for explaining black box classifiers by highlighting how they make predictions in subspaces characterized by features of user interest. An interesting research direction would be to combine our framework with ongoing efforts on extracting interpretable features from images. For example, super-pixels [9] output by intermediate layers of deep neural networks can be fed into our framework to enable explanations of image classifiers. Furthermore, the notions of fidelity, interpretability and unambiguity that we outline in this work can be further enriched. For instance, we could imagine certain features being more easy to understand than others in which case we can associate costs with features, and choose explanations with smaller costs (and more interpretable features). Our optimization framework can easily incorporate these newer notions as long as they satisfy the properties of non-negativity and submodularity.

REFERENCES

[1] Rakesh Agrawal and Ramakrishnan Srikant. 2004. Fast algorithms for mining association rules. In *Proceedings of the International Conference on Very Large Data Bases (VLDB)*. 487–499.

[2] Aleks Jakulin, Martin Možina, Janez Demšar, Ivan Bratko, and Blaž Zupan. 2005. Nomograms for visualizing support vector machines. In *Proceedings of the ACM SIGKDD International Conference on Knowledge Discovery in Data Mining (KDD)*. 108–117.

[3] Samir Khuller, Anna Moss, and Joseph Seffi Naor. 1999. The budgeted maximum coverage problem. *Inform. Process. Lett.* 70, 1 (1999), 39–45.

[4] Pang Wei Koh and Percy Liang. 2017. Understanding black-box predictions via influence functions. In *Proceedings of the International Conference on Machine Learning (ICML)*. 1885–1894.

[5] Himabindu Lakkaraju, Stephen H Bach, and Jure Leskovec. 2016. Interpretable Decision Sets: A Joint Framework for Description and Prediction. In *Proceedings of the ACM SIGKDD International Conference on Knowledge Discovery in Data Mining (KDD)*. 1675–1684.

[6] Jon Lee, Vahab S Mirrokni, Viswanath Nagarajan, and Maxim Sviridenko. 2009. Non-monotone submodular maximization under matroid and knapsack constraints. In *Proceedings of the ACM Symposium on Theory of Computing (STOC)*. 323–332.

[7] Benjamin Letham, Cynthia Rudin, Tyler H McCormick, David Madigan, et al. 2015. Interpretable classifiers using rules and Bayesian analysis: Building a better stroke prediction model. *The Annals of Applied Statistics* 9, 3 (2015), 1350–1371.

[8] Yin Lou, Rich Caruana, and Johannes Gehrke. 2012. Intelligible models for classification and regression. In *Proceedings of the ACM SIGKDD International Conference on Knowledge Discovery and Data Mining (KDD)*. 150–158.

[9] Marco Tulio Ribeiro, Sameer Singh, and Carlos Guestrin. 2016. Why Should I Trust You?: Explaining the Predictions of Any Classifier. In *Proceedings of the ACM SIGKDD International Conference on Knowledge Discovery and Data Mining (KDD)*. 1135–1144.

[10] Marco Tulio Ribeiro, Sameer Singh, and Carlos Guestrin. 2018. Anchors: High-precision model-agnostic explanations. In *In Proceedings of the AAAI Conference on Artificial Intelligence (AAAI)*. 1527–1535.

[11] Lior Rokach and Oded Maimon. 2005. Top-down induction of decision trees classifiers-a survey. *IEEE Transactions on Systems, Man, and Cybernetics, Part C (Applications and Reviews)* 35, 4 (2005), 476–487.

[12] Avanti Shrikumar, Peyton Greenside, Anna Shcherbina, and Anshul Kundaje. 2016. Not just a black box: Learning important features through propagating activation differences. *arXiv preprint arXiv:1605.01713* (2016).

[13] Soon Tee Teoh and Kwan-Liu Ma. 2003. PaintingClass: interactive construction, visualization and exploration of decision trees. In *Proceedings of the ACM SIGKDD International Conference on Knowledge Discovery and Data Mining (KDD)*. 667–672.

[14] Jason Yosinski, Jeff Clune, Anh Nguyen, Thomas Fuchs, and Hod Lipson. 2015. Understanding neural networks through deep visualization. *arXiv preprint arXiv:1506.06579* (2015).

[15] Luisa M Zintgraf, Taco S Cohen, Tameem Adel, and Max Welling. 2017. Visualizing deep neural network decisions: Prediction difference analysis. *arXiv preprint arXiv:1702.04595* (2017).

APPENDIX

Proof for Theorem 1

Statement: *The optimization problem in Eqn. 1 is non-normal, non-negative, non-monotone, submodular with matroid constraints.*

Proof In order to prove that the objective function in Eqn. 1 is non-normal, non-negative, non-monotone, and submodular, we need to prove the following:

- Prove that any one of the terms in the objective is non-normal
- Prove that all the terms in the objective are non-negative
- Prove that any one of the terms in the objective is non-monotone
- Prove that all the terms in the objective are submodular

Non-normality. Let us choose the term $f_1(\mathcal{R})$. If f_1 is normal, then $f_1(\emptyset) = 0$. Let us check if this holds true:

It can be from the definition of f_1 that $f_1(\emptyset) = \mathcal{P}_{max}$ because the numpreds metric would be 0 in this case as there are no rules in the empty set. This also implies $f_1(\emptyset) \neq 0$. Therefore f_1 is non-normal and consequently the entire objective is non-normal.

Non-negativity. The functions f_1, f_2, f_3, f_5 are non-negative because first term in each of these is an upper bound on the second term. Therefore, each of these will always have a value ≥ 0. In the case of f_4 which encapsulates the cover metric which is the number of instances which satisfy some rule in the approximation. This metric can never be negative by definition. Since all the functions are non-negative, the objective itself is non-negative.

Non-monotonicity. Let us choose the term $f_1(\mathcal{R})$. Let us consider two approximations $\mathcal{A}$ and $\mathcal{B}$ such that $\mathcal{A} \subseteq \mathcal{B}$. If f_1 is monotonic then, $f_1(\mathcal{A}) \leq f_1(\mathcal{B})$. Let us see if this condition holds:

Based on the definition of *numpreds* metric, it is easy to note that

$$numpreds(\mathcal{A}) \leq numpreds(\mathcal{B})$$

This is because $\mathcal{B}$ has at least as many rules as that of $\mathcal{A}$. This implies the following:

$$-numpreds(\mathcal{A}) \geq -numpreds(\mathcal{B})$$
$$\mathcal{P}_{max} - numpreds(\mathcal{A}) \geq \mathcal{P}_{max} - numpreds(\mathcal{B})$$
$$f_1(\mathcal{A}) \geq f_1(\mathcal{B})$$

This shows that f_1 is non-monotone and therefore the entire objective is non-monotone.

Submodularity. Let us go over each of the terms in the objective and show that each one of those is submodular.

Let us choose the term $f_1(\mathcal{R})$. Let us consider two approximations $\mathcal{A}$ and $\mathcal{B}$ such that $\mathcal{A} \subseteq \mathcal{B}$. If f_1 is submodular then, $f_1(\mathcal{A} \cup e) - f_1(\mathcal{A}) \geq f_1(\mathcal{B} \cup e) - f_1(\mathcal{B})$ where $e = (q, s, c) \notin \mathcal{B}$

Let x be the number of predicates in the rule $e = (q, s, c)$. This implies that when e is added to either $\mathcal{A}$ or $\mathcal{B}$, the value of the numpred metric increases by x i.e.,

$$f_1(\mathcal{A} \cup e) - f_1(\mathcal{A}) = x = f_1(\mathcal{B} \cup e) - f_1(\mathcal{B})$$

This implies that the function f_1 is modular and consequently submodular.

Let us choose the term $f_2(\mathcal{R})$. Let us consider two approximations $\mathcal{A}$ and $\mathcal{B}$ such that $\mathcal{A} \subseteq \mathcal{B}$. If f_2 is submodular then, $f_2(\mathcal{A} \cup e) - f_2(\mathcal{A}) \geq f_2(\mathcal{B} \cup e) - f_2(\mathcal{B})$ where $e = (q, s, c) \notin \mathcal{B}$

By definition, $featureoverlap(\mathcal{A}) \leq featureoverlap(\mathcal{B})$ because $\mathcal{B}$ has at least as many rules as $\mathcal{A}$.

Let $featureoverlap(\mathcal{A}) = x$ and $featureoverlap(\mathcal{B}) = x + \epsilon$ where $\epsilon \geq 0$. When we add e to $\mathcal{A}$, let $featureoverlap(\mathcal{A} \cup e) = y$, then $featureoverlap(\mathcal{B} \cup e) = y + \epsilon + \epsilon'$ where ϵ' denotes the feature overlap between the e and the rules that exist in $\mathcal{B}$ but not in $\mathcal{A}$ Therefore, $\epsilon' \geq 0$.

$$f_2(\mathcal{A} \cup e) - f_2(\mathcal{A}) = O_{max} - y - O_{max} + x = x - y$$
$$f_2(\mathcal{B} \cup e) - f_2(\mathcal{B}) = O_{max} - y - \epsilon - \epsilon' - O_{max} + x + \epsilon = x - y - \epsilon'$$

This implies that

$$f_2(\mathcal{A} \cup e) - f_2(\mathcal{A}) \geq f_2(\mathcal{B} \cup e) - f_2(\mathcal{B})$$

Therefore, f_2 is submodular.

f_3 has a very similar structure to f_2 and it can be shown that it is submodular by following analogous steps as above.

f_4 is the cover metric which denotes the number of instances that satisfy some rule in the approximation. This is clearly a diminishing returns function i.e., more additional instances in the data are covered when we add a new rule to a smaller set compared to a larger set. Therefore, this is submodular.

Consider the function f_5, the metric disagreement is additive / modular which means each time a rule is added, the value of disagreement is simply incremented by the number of data points incorrectly labeled by this rule. Since the metric disagreement is modular, the function f_5 is also modular which implies submodularity.

Constraints: A constraint is a matroid if it has the following properties: 1) $\emptyset$ satisfies the constraint 2) if two sets A and B satisfy the constraint and $|A| < |B|$, then adding an element $e \in B$, $e \notin A$ to A should result in a set that also satisfies the constraint. It can be seen that these two conditions hold for all our constraints. For instance, if an approximation B has $\leq \epsilon_1$ rules and approximation A has fewer rules than B, then the set resulting from adding any element of B to the smaller set A will still satisfy the constraint. Similarly, maxwidth and numdsets satisfy the aforementioned properties too.

Optimization Procedure

The crux of Algorithm 1 is shown in lines 4–12. The solution set is initially empty (line 4) and then an element v with the maximum value for the objective function is added (line 5). This is followed by a sequence of delete and/or exchange operations (lines 6 – 12) until there is no other element remaining to be deleted or exchanged from the solution set. If there is an element e in the solution set which when removed increases the value of the objective function by a factor of at least $(1 + \frac{\delta}{n^4})$ (n is the size of the candidate set), then it is removed (line 7). Analogously, if there are k elements in the solution set whose exchange with a new element d increases the value of the objective function by the aforementioned factor, then the exchange operation is performed (lines 9–11). This entire process is repeated $k + 1$ times (line 13). Lastly, the objective function values of the solution sets obtained from each of the $k+1$ iterations are compared and the solution set with the maximum value is returned as the final solution (line 15).

Experiments & Results

Parameter Tuning. We set aside 5% of the dataset as a validation set to tune these parameters. We first initialize the value of each λ_i to 100. We then carry out a coordinate descent style approach where we decrement the values of each of these parameters while keeping others constant until one of the following conditions is violated: 1) less than 95% of the instances in the validation set are *covered* by the resulting approximation 2) more than 5% of the instances in the validation set are *covered* by multiple rules in the approximation 3) the labels assigned by the approximation do not match those of the black box for more than 85% of the instances in the validation set.

We set the λ parameters of IDS in the same way as discussed above. BDL has three hyperparameters: 1) α which is the dirichlet prior on the distribution of the class labels. We set this to 1. 2) λ is the prior on the number of rules in the decision list and we set it to the same value as that ϵ_1 in our approach 3) η is the prior on average number of predicates per rule and we set to the same value as that of ϵ_2 in our approach. Our approach, IDS, and BDL take as input candidate sets of conjunctions of predicates. These candidate sets are generated using Apriori algorithm [] with a support threshold of 1% which ensures that each conjunction holds true for at least 1% of the instances in the data.

Evaluating Interpretability of Customized Explanations. To evaluate the interpretability of our explanations when features of interest are input by end users, we performed a set of experiments in which we simulate user input by randomly subsampling features of interest. Note that the baselines IDS, BDL or LIME are not designed to handle end user input when generating explanations. To benchmark the performance of our approach with user input, we construct variants of the baselines IDS and BDL where we first generate subspaces and then run IDS and BDL independently on instances belonging to each of these subspaces. Subspaces are generated by enumerating every possible combination of values of the randomly chosen subset of features (e.g., exercise = yes and smoking = yes, exercise = yes and smoking = no, exercise = no and smoking = yes, exercise = no and smoking = no). When averaged across 100 runs (where we randomly subsample features of interest for each run), we found that at the same level of fidelity, our explanations have about 22.02% and 38.39% fewer rules compared to those produced by variants of IDS and BDL respectively. Our framework also generated explanations with 17.53% and 26.28% decrease in the average width of rules compared to the variants of IDS and BDL respectively while maintaining the same level of fidelity. These results clearly highlight the importance of jointly optimizing the discovery of subspaces, and the corresponding decision logic rules so that the resulting explanation is both faithful to the original model and interpretable.

ACKNOWLEDGMENTS

This research has been supported in part by NSF IIS-1149837, Ford, SAP, Lightspeed, Stanford Data Science Initiative, and Chan Zuckerberg Biohub. This research was carried out when Himabindu was a Ph.D. student at Stanford University. During this time, she was supported by a Robert Bosch Stanford Graduate Fellowship, a Microsoft Dissertation Grant, and a Google Anitaborg Scholarship.

This research is based upon work supported in part by the Office of the Director of National Intelligence (ODNI), Intelligence Advanced Research Projects Activity (IARPA), via 2017-17071900005. The views and conclusions contained herein are those of the authors and should not be interpreted as necessarily representing the official policies, either expressed or implied, of ODNI, IARPA, or the U.S. Government. The U.S. Government is authorized to reproduce and distribute reprints for governmental purposes notwithstanding any copyright annotation therein.

Shared Moral Foundations of Embodied Artificial Intelligence

Joe Cruz
Department of Philosophy and Program in Cognitive Science
Williams College
Williamstown, MA USA
jcruz@williams.edu

Abstract

Sophisticated AI's will make decisions about how to respond to complex situations, and we may wonder whether those decisions will align with the moral values of human beings. I argue that pessimistic worries about this value alignment problem are overstated. In order to achieve intelligence in its full generality and adaptiveness, cognition in AI's will need to be embodied in the sense of the Embodied Cognition research program. That embodiment will yield AI's that share our moral foundations, namely coordination, sociality, and acknowledgement of shared resources. Consequently, we can expect a broad moral alignment between human beings and AI's. AI's will likely show no more variation in their values than we find amongst human beings.

ACM Reference Format:

Joe Cruz. 2019. Shared Moral Foundations of Embodied Artificial Intelligence. In *AAAI/ACM Conference on AI, Ethics, and Society (AIES'19), January 27–28, 2019, Honolulu, HI, USA.* ACM, New York, NY, USA, 7 pages. https://doi.org/10.1145/3306618.3314280

Introduction

The ultimate ambition of artificial intelligence is to achieve in a made machine the capacity to cognize dynamically and adaptively in real world settings and in real time. The standard of cognition here is, of course, biologically evolved intelligence in us and in sophisticated nonhuman animals. We have as a goal the creation of beings that will thrive in open-ended environments, and we can readily create a list of the faculties that we want our artificial intelligence to have that includes rational thinking, memory, perception, creativity, forethought, abstract conceptualization, and perhaps even consciousness.

AIES '19, January 27-28, 2019, Honolulu, HI, USA

ACM ISBN 978-1-4503-6324-2/19/01...$15.00
https://doi.org/10.1145/3306618.3314280

As we get closer to realizing the ambition of AI, we must come to grips with the moral (or immoral) potential actions of the intelligent beings we create. That is, we must consider what such beings will find morally desirable and morally permissible, especially concerning how to treat us and how to treat one another. We might wonder whether they will share a core set of human values, or— if we think human beings have no single universal morality—whether the morality of AI's will fall onto a recognizable landscape that will enable us to co-exist with them just as diverse human societies coexist.

It is my view that dystopian predictions and pessimism surrounding these issues of *value alignment* (Stuart Russell 2014) are overstated. There are, to be sure, countless possibilities for unintended consequences in the creation of beings that have their own wills. But I argue that the very project of anchoring AI's in our conception of intelligence—with all that that means in terms of embodiment, sociality, coordination and situatedness—implies that they will substantially share our moral foundations. AI's will be beings that we can make sense of and negotiate with just as we do when we find cultural difference in our own species. I am not claiming what is obviously false, that creating intelligence guarantees that those beings will be moral in the sense of doing mostly morally good acts. After all, human beings are not unfailingly moral. Nor am I denying that we can and probably will make smart special purpose devices that will serve immoral ends that we contrive. Those special purpose agents are not what I'm considering here.

Instead, my claim is any AI that seems to us genuinely intelligent in the full sense that human beings are intelligent will have to be embodied, and in so being will inevitably be governed by the same foundational considerations that generate morality in us.

Value Alignment Pessimism

It is reasonable to accept that someday AI's will be as intelligent as human beings are. Indeed, they may be more intelligent in the sense of facing fewer cognitive resource constraints—in memory, processing speed, and attention, for instance—and fewer sources of irrational distortion in their reasoning. Intuitively this leads to an open question concerning whether the superior reasoning of AI's will sometimes lead to decisions that a human being would view as morally unacceptable. The idea, remaining at the intuitive level, is that an optimizing reasoner may think "coldly" and without regard for the things that are important to human being. The utility function that an AI has, itself the product of past decision making, may end up constituting an overall motivation that is alien and anathema to us.

This worry can be made more precise. For example, (Bostrom 2012) has argued that intelligence and final goals are orthogonal axes on which an AI can develop. An AI may achieve great intelligence without it being guaranteed that its final goals will be aligned with ours. Bostrom says,

> The orthogonality thesis implies that synthetic minds can have utterly non-anthropomorphic goals—goals as bizarre by our lights as sand-grain-counting or paperclip maximizing. This holds even (indeed *especially*) for artificial agents that are extremely intelligent or superintelligent (sect. 1.3).

His argument for the orthogonality thesis (OT) is that intelligence and motivation are not mutually entailing. The general form of Bostrom's argument appeals to mere possibility in that it is logically possible to pull apart particular ends from effective motivations. This, he acknowledges, recalls the Humean thesis that reason and desire are separate (Hume 1736), but Bostrom points out that OT can be correct even if Hume is not. In offering OT, Bostrom is rejecting metaethical views that propose a tight connection, perhaps even a constitutive connection, between motivation and apprehending the good through rationality. Since Bostrom characterizes intelligence in terms of instrumental rationality, and since it seems that in principle an artificial agent can lack whatever features of full blown rationality that make motivation and the good intrinsically intertwined, he concludes that there is nothing to prevent an AI—again, in principle—from being *mis*aligned in terms of its values.

Bostrom's argument is predicated on there being few constraints at the outset on how instrumental rationality or a utility function is instantiated in an AI. He later proposes *instrumental convergence*, namely the idea that, "...there are some *instrumental* goals likely to be pursued by almost any intelligent agent, because there are some objectives that are useful intermediaries to the achievement of almost any final goal" (sect. 2). Alas, this convergence does not tend to generate value alignment. Instead, it highlights some general trends in instrumental rationality that AI's and human beings will likely share, including, for instance, cognitive enhancement and resource acquisition.

The vulnerability of both the intuitive concern and arguments like Bostrom's is that they are hostage to factors that in fact constrain an intelligence such that its decision making will be aligned with other beings that face the same constraints. I speculate that the intuitive argument gets its force from the fact that relaxing cognitive resource constraints makes people think that *all* constraints—or, at any rate, all constraints that might encourage value alignment—are relaxed. This does not follow. Even if an AI is a faster reasoner with better memory access to relevant inputs to the argument and with fewer sources of irrational bias, there may yet be other kinds of constraints that funnel the decision making process into a commonality with human beings. I will offer just such constraints, below.

Likewise with Bostrom-type arguments. We can accept the in principle logical possibility that AI's need not be value aligned with us while we at the same time endorse that real world agents are very likely to be aligned. Thinking about the utility function as a rationality maximizer that is also a black box makes the mistake of leaving out the constraints on the function that are pre-rational. They are not *irrational* constraints in the ordinary sense of irrationality. Instead, they are the terrestrial, embodied conditions that are the background for any kind of rationality. Bostrom was getting at this with his instrumental convergence, but that convergence remains at the level of disembodiment. I therefore argue in what follows for a convergence that generates a more substantive alignment than Bostrom's mere instrumental convergence. My claim is that embodiment itself produces constraints on an intelligent being that will tend to push that being toward the same moral foundations that we have. In order to set up that claim, let us look again at the background image of OT and similarly abstracted characterizations of intelligence.

Isolated Cognition

By *isolated cognition*, I will mean intelligence that takes place within closed and idealized domains. It is, of course, perfectly understandable that early AI work would have ranged over seemingly tractable, well-structured environments like predicate logic, chess, or Tower of Hanoi puzzles. Worries about isolated cognition in this sense are very familiar and occurred even early on. The complaints are manifold: there is no assurance that the techniques used will scale up to real world settings, the successes achieved in such settings may be due to building in solutions specific to the domain so that there is no chance of achieving general intelligence, and the entire background inspiration—that intelligence can be achieved by adding together success at isolated problems, none of which are full blown intelligence by themselves—is contentious.

We should keep ready at hand the distinction between bounded rationality (Simon, 1957; Cherniak 1986) and isolated cognition. The critic of isolated cognition may still maintain that rationality is bounded. That is, there may be no sense in talking about rationality unless it is constrained by the real world limitations and constraints of actual cognizers. But being bounded by the realized resources at hand is a different issue than having intelligence be limited to isolated, idealized domains. One is a point about the range of resources that the intelligent being can bring to bear and the other is about the range of challenges that an intelligent being is capable of meeting. I am concentrating here on the later, and my claim is that we all more or less accept that we have not created an AI if its cognition is isolated.

However, in spite of what I expect is widespread acceptance of this sort of critique, I maintain that there is a version of the isolated cognition problem that remains uncritically accepted. That version is where we tolerate a conception of AI that does not emphasize the *embodiment* of the intelligence. I mean explicitly to be referencing the research direction of Embodied Cognition as it is pursued in cognitive science, which I discuss in the next section. Even researchers who have internalized the critique of isolated cognition in AI still tend to accept disembodied intelligence as a tacit assumption.

Perhaps ironically, in popular culture the image of artificial intelligence is woven in with imagery of autonomous robots and artificial bodies. Maybe, then, the tight connection between being intelligent and having a body is more widely accepted in the folk image of AI than in the image of specialists and experts. But even in popular culture there is often the implication that being embodied is in a way optional for an intelligence. The intelligence needs to learn its alien body by practicing movement, or finds its body and the world of concrete objects just another intellectual object to think about and figure out. It is tempting to denigrate this as a Cartesian conception of intelligence, though Descartes himself thought that the human condition was a radical fusion between body and mind (Descartes 1641). Putting those historical niceties aside, just as it is sometimes believed that the mind can be understood as separate from the body, so too do AI researchers sometimes conduct themselves as if cognition can be realized without attending to the bodies of the cognizing beings.

Bostrom's OT is guilty of proffering isolated cognition. He says, "...'[I]ntelligence' will be roughly taken to correspond to the capacity for instrumental reasoning... . Intelligent search for instrumentally optimal plans and policies can be performed in the service of any goal" (sect. 1.2). This instrumental reason can take on any goal, as if the terrain of possible goals is as open ended as anything we can conceive. Notably, in this conception of intelligence no goals are delivered by the concrete realization of the body of the AI, or by the world of terrestrial or cultural objects that the AI inhabits. This, I urge, is intelligence of the most arid, ungrounded sort, and a tacit acceptance of the isolated cognition thesis. This conception of intelligence obscures the substantial and likely overlap of moral foundations between us and future AI's that will result from the fact that we must be and AI's must be embodied.[1]

We may still ask, what is embodiment? In the next section I briefly sketch some of the themes that fall under Embodied Cognition research. My goal is to make it plausible that, once an intelligence is embodied, it is constrained into the very same foundations of morality that we are. This suggests that the value alignment problem between us and AI's will be no greater than the value alignment problem between human cultures or individuals.

Embodied Cognition

Embodied cognitive approaches exhibit as wide a range and heterogeneity as more traditional computational approaches. Consequently, there is little that can be said by way of a general characterization of Embodied Cognition (EC) that won't have to be immediately qualified, elaborated, or downright retracted. Still, I think this much is right. EC seeks to place closer to the center of cognitive science at least the following five topics:

- The physical morphology of an intelligent being and its system of neurological control (Beer 1990; Thelen 1995; Chiel and Beer 1997).
- The possibilities of understanding cognition without appealing to internal explicit representations over which algorithmically driven computation takes place (Brooks 1991; Chemero 2009).
- The evolution of intelligence (Brooks 1991; Anderson 2003).
- The interaction and close coupling between the environment—sometimes including the cultural environment—and a cognitive agent (Beer 1990; Hutchins 1994; Clark 1997).
- The conscious phenomenology of having a body (Varela et al 1991; Thompson 2010; Nöe 2004; Toner et al. 2016).

Each of these conceptual threads of EC help push one in the direction of the following kind of thought: though it might have seemed that cognition, broadly construed, could be made sense of as disembodied and isolated from the environment, it turns out that there are sundry crucial ways in which thought is entangled with the condition of one's body. For example, (Hutchins 1995) argues that the cognition involved in ocean navigation critically involves the technical and cultural evolution of a much bigger system than an individual marine pilot. The instruments and body positions realized in their use, the traditions of information exchange between navigator and wider crew, and the internalized routinized actions of attention by an experienced navigator are all part of the computation taking place.

As another kind of example, consider that some kinds of central commands for actions are inert in the absence of naturalistic feedback from the environment. Leeches left to behave in a reduced preparation fail to produce functional swimming output because their swim interneurons do not fire at a high enough frequency. When placed in a full preparation with normal feedback from water, leeches then effectively swim (Chiel and Beer 1997; Kristan 2000). The water environment is required for the successful functional behavior of leeches. These and many other results persuade some cognitive scientists that intelligence cannot be made sense of in isolation from the body and environment (for an effective overview see Clark 2010).

[1] A natural response here might be that it is possible, perhaps even likely, that AI's and future human beings will inhabit a virtual world within which there is no embodiment in the literal sense. Still, perceiving and cognizing the world *as if* embodied is equivalent to actual embodiment for the purposes of my argument.

The data and experiments that have driven EC are a scattered tableau from cognitive psychology, robotics, connectionist and dynamical approaches, cognitive linguistics, and the early 20th century history of phenomenology in philosophy. This variety can make it seem as if EC is struggling both conceptually and empirically. Indeed, a gloomy assessment of EC seems confirmed not least of all by a number of well publicized experimental results that served as common early encouragement for EC but that have failed to replicate. For instance, the facial feedback hypothesis involving a pencil gripped in the mouth were reported in (Strack et al. 1988), but have not been reproduced (Wagenmakers, E.-J., et al, 2016). It has been unhelpful, to put it mildly, for poorly designed psychological experiments to be treated as the load bearing support for EC. My view is that EC can be made sense of as a distinctive research direction in cognitive science separate from dominant trends in the field, and that there are good reasons both conceptual and empirical in support of EC. These research arcs should be viewed as that essential part of cognitive science that provides a corrective and reorientation of a maturing field.

It is tempting to try to assimilate the considerations of EC into an isolated cognition perspective. The idea would be to treat all of those bodily and environmental considerations as data or input to a central, isolated cognitive system that would then compute the right behavioral decisions. This, according to EC, is profoundly to miss the point. The body and the environment are in fact coupled with cognition in a fast and reliable system of feedback and calibration. To try to capture this coupling by representing the body and outside world such that those representations will need to be computed over is to incur a load and process that is far from the way natural intelligence is achieved. EC does not claim that doing so is metaphysically impossible, but that it is not the way evolved cognizers achieve their success. Representations, to the degree that they are had explicitly and on-board by the various individual agents, are no longer the primary focus of the analysis. Instead, we focus on the way that globally intelligible behavior emerges from interactions, and there may be no place in the system where it makes sense to say that a representation is explicit.

EC, then, can be seen as a methodological claim about cognitive science. It says that the proper unit of analysis for a model or theory of some particular cognitive behavior is a wide system that includes body and in some cases environment, and it makes the bet that modeling that wider system is more likely to lead to successes and insight regarding intelligence. This reading was always present in EC, but it tends to get obscured. The A-Life literature, for instance, attends to evolution and to the interaction between intuitively separate agents and is another historical source of inspiration for EC (Langton 1989; Wolfram 1994). We can see intelligence and cognition at the level of the agents that we intuitively recognize as individuals—birds or termites as the case may be—but we can also see intelligence at a different level, that of the collective that originates from the interactions between the individuals. That intelligence may be aimed at a different purpose and faces different constraints and therefore affords different opportunities to agents working together. Thus, the explanatory goals of cognitive science are shifted to embodied quantities.

Embodiment and Moral Foundations

The case that I am advancing asserts that pessimistic worries about the value alignment problem in AI originate in a tacit acceptance of cognition as isolated. Embodied cognitive research is a powerful corrective to viewing cognition as isolated, and shows that any being that we view as genuinely intelligent with respect to open ended problems is likely to be driven by its embodiment and coupling to the environment. But how does embodiment tend to make it such that an AI's values will be aligned with ours? In this section, I address this final step.

There is a literature on the role of body in moral cognition. The idea is that our moral judgments of, for instance, the rightness or wrongness of an action are grounded not in our rational, introspective reflections on the matter but instead in our bodily reactions at the time that we consider the action. For instance, it is alleged that our reaction of disgust is a primary driver in whether we think an action is wrong. (Haidt 1993) offers empirical evidence for the thesis that the way we morally judge the rightness of a family eating the family dog after it is killed by a car is based in our bodily and affective reactions. (Greene and Haidt 2002) likewise present empirical evidence that the appearance of uncleanliness or the smells present when making a moral judgment substantively influence that judgment. These are cases reminiscent of the psychological literature on irrationality, where we are sometimes wrong about the causes of our beliefs (Nisbett, R. and Wilson 1977). In the moral domain, the particular incorrectness and the source of our judgment is something about our embodiment or our situatedness in a place.

It may well be that, when artificial intelligences are embodied, i.e., when they are bounded in their robotic casings and located in physical and cultural spaces alongside human beings and nonhuman animals, they will somehow rely on their bodily states to make moral judgments. This might align them with human beings who rely in part on affective states in our moral judging. On the other hand, it is an open question whether AI's as we envision them now can have bodily based emotions and feelings of, say, disgust. Moreover, it might be objected, couldn't we simply design AI's so that they didn't commit this sort of moral judgment irrationality and didn't let bodily states influence them? The reply to this possibility is that, if AI's don't employ bodily reactions in moral judgments, we may not count them as intelligent in the broad sense of being calibrated to a world that includes our own moral reactions. They will seem "off" in the moral domain and will not, more or less deeply, make sense to us. So I think it is likely that any AI worthy of being called intelligent with either have to have such bodily reactions (or simulations of them) and will have to use them in morally judging.

This is one way in which embodiment is relevant to an AI's moral behavior, namely the behavior of judging actions as moral or not. But this is a fairly modest allegation; I wish to go much further. I want to say that we can expect the moral horizons of AI's to be in substantial alignment with ours.

In order to determine whether an AI's values will align with ours in a more complete sense, we must consider what makes our values the ones that they are. The debate in philosophy on the source of values is as immense as any literature in the field, so it would be absurd to try to engage it here in any serious way. I am hoping, then, not to have to. In talking about the foundations of morality—and about whether those foundations will produce values that are in alignment between AI's and human beings—I am not referring to the level of metaethical theorizing that pits accounts like utilitarianism, virtue theory, social contract theory, or Kantian deontology against each other. I am gesturing at a deeper foundation that make it possible for those metaethical theories to be in the running, so to speak. The conditions will then be the foundational bedrock of whatever values develop. I propose at least these:

- Resources are finite. In an imaginary world where there are no limits on resources, virtually any desire can be met and so any utility function can be satisfied. That is a world where values are not required because no ordering of preferences is necessary. So, in order to get the question of values off the ground, resources must be finite.
- Coordination and collaboration with other intelligences is required to achieve the maximum flourishing of any individual. In a world where an individual intelligence can by itself achieve all of its desires, there is no need for values in the relevant sense, because the individuals will not need to be value aligned.
- The world is substantially composed of the scaffolding of tools, built environments, collective knowledge, and culture. These create the imperatives to achieve alignment. In a world where individuals form their own systems of tool use, knowledge communities, and cultures, there is no pressure to achieve values that must be aligned. This is because each individuals scaffolding can express that individual's particular values.

All three of these are impossibly abstract, but I hope that they provide the hints that I intend. These are descriptions of the conditions that make it so that human morality develops. Acknowledgement of shared resources, between-being coordination, and sociality are the foundations of morality in the sense that the need and nature of morality emanates from them. Moreover, all of those foundational dimensions have to do with the fact that we are embodied beings in an environment. We are not isolated cognizers who deploy a utility calculus that is pristinely detached from the world. Any AI that meets our intuitive and theoretical standards for intelligence will need to be embodied, and embodiment will establish AI's into our values because they originate in those moral foundations which in turn stem from embodiment.

But how, precisely, can these deeply abstract foundations align AI's behavior with our morality? Here is a sketch of the account. Finiteness of resources generates a shared morality in that all agents are working against the same backdrop and therefore must manage goals that potentially conflict in terms of resource use. If an agent has a goal that requires some amount of a resource and another agent also requires that resource, then there must be a resolution. That can be literal conflict or deception or division of the resource or a change in goal, to name just a few possibilities. What the possibilities have in common is a reckoning of other agents. Other agents must be treated in some way or other. Another way of putting this is that a precondition for instrumental reasoning with finite resources is the capacity to reckon with the instrumental reasoning of other beings. That creates the need to arrive at answers to value questions, especially ones in the domain of reciprocity, fairness, and retribution.

With respect to collaboration and cooperation, I claim that this is a foundation for a shared morality in that it requires that agents acknowledge one another as beings *with* whom to pursue goals, and as noteworthy beyond merely being objects or obstacles in the environment. Our intelligence is deeply bound up with our sociality, from the mundane observation that we solve many problems through a group cognitive effort to the more exotic point that our cognitive potential is massively extended by epistemic actions. These are actions that place in the environment information that is required to achieve a goal (Kirsh and Maglio 1994; Anderson 2003), and this is most effective when done collectively. For example, writing is probably the most crucial epistemic action that human beings undertake for our modern thriving. Recovering information from writing requires set conventions and systems of acting together that once again force agents to exist within a world where there must be coordination.

Go back to the idea of intelligence in general. If we focus just on effectively executing a utility function, we do not capture what we think of as distinctive about our own intelligence. The case of dogs is illustrative. Bonobos, dolphins, elephants, and African Grey Parrots each show serious cognitive advantages over *canis familiaris.* On a certain abstract, isolated conception of what intelligence is, it seems that putting dogs near the top is something only a starry-eyed dog lover could do. However, dogs are in another sense especially intelligent, and this makes perfect sense because they inhabit our coordinated, built, social world. To be sure, they inhabit our world due to a combination of natural and massive artificial selective pressure. They were probably at the right place at the right time alongside early humans. Whatever the origin, my view suggests that dogs are second only to us in being intelligent in an open ended, authentic way. Dogs possess something crucial to intelligence that includes a responsiveness to emotions, comfort and facility in built up human spaces, deep understanding of coordinative sociality, and eye contact referencing and regard for human beings as principal objects in the universe (Hare and Tomasello, 2005; Topal et al, 2014). So, too, must any AI worth the name. Genuine AI's will presumably add a substantial capacity for reasoning, abstraction, and language that dogs are not capable of, but that should not obscure the shared background. If this is correct, then a successful AI must inhabit our social world, which will require entering into a central dimension of it, our moral landscape.

Finally, the scaffolding of culture and the technologies we have produced have moral considerations as preconditions for membership. Being in a culture includes understanding how to act in that culture. Those behaviors, especially the ones that are embodied rather than explicitly theorized about, are what make an agent a natural, companionable co-intelligence in an historical and cultural milieu. Of course I am not claiming that AI's by their embodiment will automatically have the morality of my culture or any other specific culture. Indeed, we should be worried that engineers and programmers will make AI's too much members of their own culture and will thereby replay a kind of colonialism. But in order to be viewed as intelligent and by dint of being present with a body in a culture, an AI will need to be ready and receptive to cultural norms of co-existence that we identify as morality, whatever they may be in a given culture.

So, when Bostrom claims that an AI can pursue arbitrary goals (within the horizon of instrumental convergence) and that therefore there can be a problem of value alignment, my reply is that intelligence that is too far beyond the pale will not seem like intelligence to us. While such an AI might seem to have a goal directed cleverness the way that some non-human animals are clever, it will not seem like the kind of open-ended intelligence that we associate with, say, dogs. An AI's goals will be constrained by the fact that they share a world with us, and will enter into our technologies including and especially culture.

The view I am defending here has an affinity with moral foundations theory (MFT) proposed by social and anthropological psychologists (Haidt 2012). MFT alleges six foundations for human morality—care, fairness, loyalty, authority, sanctity, and liberty—and claims that these are encoded in our quick-to-deploy intuitions about moral cases. For instance, suffering as a basis for moral imperatives is alleged to derive from the evolution of parental care, and is characterized (Haidt and Craig 2004) as having compassion as one of its characteristic emotions (p59). This original trigger then culturally evolved to treat kindness as a virtue. MFT theorists attempt to bolster the considerably speculative cast of their claims with cross-cultural empirical data on moral intuitions and work from evolutionary psychology.

MFT is a descriptive theory of our moral judgments. It is not normatively recommending that this is the way that we ought to be toward one another. Whether we view these as a rationally sound normative ground is up for considerable debate. If we do not but MFT is descriptively correct, we may find ourselves in the regrettable position of rationally viewing patterns of conduct as immoral that we routinely are unable to correct because we are constrained by MFT type foundations. I think this would invite an interesting question of whether future AI's will be vexed by *our* lack of moral alignment with *them.* After all, there is no engineering necessity that dictates that AI's will be initially helpless and require literal parenting. Therefore, MFT's specific foundations may not be the ones that ensure that AI's fall within human moral horizons. AI's may be able to achieve something closer to a rationally ideal moral behavior, and may find us more subject to the biases countenanced by MFT.

That possibility, though, postulates that AI's are not constrained by something more fundamental than the foundations proposed by MFT. Mine claim to be more basic.

Conclusion

To say it again, I am not claiming here that we are somehow obligated, morally or otherwise, to build beings whose moral views are substantially like ours. That would be a point about us and our design goals, and that is a different argument. My thesis is that, in setting out to build an intelligent being, we will automatically—as a kind of conceptual inevitability—create something that shares with us a fundamentally moral outlook because those beings will be embodied as we are and will inhabit our world as we do.

The moral outlook that AI's share with us may not determine specific behavior. Our AI's CPU won't explode if it tries to do something immoral. But then again sharing a moral foundation does not obligate human beings in specific ways, either. Individual human beings routinely do immoral things. Further, AI's won't, on my argument, be ultramoral, though we could probably build them to be that way. I suspect that such ultramoral AI's will also seem "off" to us. They would likely fail to exhibit a certain pragmatism or contextually appropriate selfish behavior and will therefore seem not quite intelligent.

AI's will be aligned with us in the same way that human beings are aligned with one another. Human beings are impelled to be moral by a complex of conscious and nonconscious forces that are a response to their embodiment. Above, I have tried to gesture at a way of conceiving of those forces. They constitute more of a constraint on value alignment than has been appreciated.

References

[1] Anderson, M. 2003. Embodied Cognition: A Field Guide. *Artificial Intelligence*, 149 (1):91–130.

[2] Beer, R. 1990. *Intelligence as Adaptive Behavior: An Experiment in Computational Neuroethology.* San Diego: Academic Press.

[3] Bostrom, N. 2012. The Superintelligent Will: Motivation and Instrumental Rationality in Advanced Artificial Agents. *Minds and Machines* 22(2), May:71-85.

[4] Brooks, R. 1991. Intelligence without representation. *Artificial Intelligence.* 47(3):139-159.

[5] Chemero, A. 2009. *Radical Embodied Cognitive Science.* Cambridge, MA: MIT Press.

[6] Cherniak, C. 1986. *Minimal Rationality.* Cambridge, MIT Press.

[7] Chiel, H., and Beer, R. 1997. The brain has a body: adaptive behavior emerges from interactions of nervous system, body and environment. *Trends in Neuroscience* 20(12):553-557.

[8] Clark, A. 1997. *Being There: Putting Brain Body and World Together Again.* Cambridge, MA: MIT Press.

[9] Clark, A. 2010. *Supersizing the Mind: Embodiment, Action, and Cognitive Extension.* Oxford UP.

[10] Descartes, R. 1641/2015. *Meditations on First Philosophy with Selections from Objections and Replies.* Cottingham, J., ed. Cambridge: Cambridge UP.

[11] Gallese, V., and Lakoff, G. 2005. The brain's concepts: The role of the sensorimotor system in conceptual knowledge. *Cognitive Neuropsychology* 21:455–479.

[12] Greene, J., and Haidt, J. 2002. How (and where) does moral judgment work? *Trends in Cognitive Sciences* 6(12):517–523.

[13] Haidt, J.; Koller, S.H.; and Dias, M.G. 1993. Affect, Culture, and Morality, or Is It Wrong to Eat Your Dog? *Journal of Personality and Social Psychology* 65(4):613–628.

[14] Haidt, J.; Craig, J. 2004. Intuitive ethics: how innately prepared intuitions generate culturally variable virtues. *Daedalus* 133(4): 55-66.

[26] Strack, F.; Martin, LL.; and Stepper, S. 1988. Inhibiting and facilitating conditions of the human smile: a nonobtrusive test of the facial feedback hypothesis. *Journal of Personality and Social Psychology* 54(5): 768-77.

[27] Thelen, E. 1995. Time-scale dynamics in the development of an embodied cognition. In *Mind In Motion*, Port, R. and van Gelder, T., eds. Cambridge, MA: MIT Press.

[28] Thompson, E. 2010 *Mind in Life.* Cambridge, MA: Belknap Press of Harvard UP.

[29] Toner, J.; Montero, B.; and Moran, A. 2016 Reflective and Prereflective Bodily Awareness in Skilled Action. *Psychology of Consciousness: Theory, Research, and Practice* 1:1-13.

[15] Haidt, J. 2012. *The Righteous Mind: Why Good People are Divided by Politics and Religion.* New York: Pantheon Books.

[16] Hare, B., and Tomasello, M. 2005. Human-like social skills in dogs? *Trends in Cognitive Science* 9:439-444.

[17] Hume, D. 1736/1978. *A Treatise of Human Nature.* Selby-Bigge, L.A., ed. Oxford: Oxford UP.

[18] Hutchins, E. 1995. *Cognition in the Wild.* Cambridge, MA: MIT Press.

[19] Kirsh, D., and Maglio, P. 1994. On distinguishing epistemic from pragmatic action. *Cognitive Science* 18(4): 513-549.

[20] Kristan, W. et al. 2000. Biomechanics of Hydroskeletons: Studies of Crawling in the Medicinal Leech. In *Biomechanics and Neural Control of Movement,* Winters, J. and Crago, P., eds. Springer-Verlag.

[21] Lakoff, G., and Johnson, M. 1999. *Philosophy in the Flesh: The Embodied Mind And Its Challenge To Western Thought.* New York, NY: Basic Books.

[22] Langton, C., ed. 1989. *Artificial Life.* Redwood City, CA: Addison-Wesley.

[23] Noë, A. 2004. *Action in Perception.* Cambridge, MA: MIT Press.

[24] Russell, S. 2014. Of Myths and Moonshine [Blog post]. Retrieved from https://www.edge.org/conversation/the-myth-of-ai#26015.

[25] Simon, H. A. 1957. *Models of Man, Social and Rational: Mathematical Essays on Rational Human Behavior in a Social Setting.* New York: John Wiley and Sons.

[30] Topál, J.; Kis, A.; Oláh, K. 2014. Dogs' sensitivity to human social cues: A unique adaptation. In *The Social Dog: Behavior and Cognition,* Kaminski, J. and Marshall-Pescini, S., eds. Sand Diego: Elsevier, pp. 319-346.

[31] Wagenmakers, E.-J.; Beek, T.; Dijkhoff, L., et al. 2016. Registered Replication Report, Strack, Martin, Stepper (1988). *Perspectives on Psychological Science* 11: 917–928.

[32] Wolfram, S. 1994. *Cellular Automata and Complexity.* Redwood City, CA: Addison-Wesley.

[33] Varela, F.; Thompson, E.; and Rosch, E. 1991. *The Embodied Mind.* Cambridge, MA: MIT Press.

Building Jiminy Cricket: An Architecture for Moral Agreements Among Stakeholders

Beishui Liao
baiseliao@zju.edu.cn
Zhejiang University
Hangzhou, China

Marija Slavkovik
marija.slavkovik@uib.no
University of Bergen
Norway

Leendert van der Torre
leon.vandertorre@uni.lu
University of Luxembourg
Luxembourg

ABSTRACT

An autonomous system is constructed by a manufacturer, operates in a society subject to norms and laws, and is interacting with end-users. We address the challenge of how the moral values and views of all stakeholders can be integrated and reflected in the moral behavior of the autonomous system. We propose an *artificial moral agent* architecture that uses techniques from normative systems and formal argumentation to reach moral agreements among stakeholders. We show how our architecture can be used not only for ethical practical reasoning and collaborative decision-making, but also for the explanation of such moral behavior.

KEYWORDS

Machine Ethics, Agreement Reaching, Explainability, Formal argumentation

ACM Reference Format:
Beishui Liao, Marija Slavkovik, and Leendert van der Torre. 2019. Building Jiminy Cricket: An Architecture for Moral Agreements Among Stakeholders. In *AAAI/ACM Conference on AI, Ethics, and Society (AIES '19), January 27–28, 2019, Honolulu, HI, USA.* ACM, New York, NY, USA, 7 pages. https://doi.org/10.1145/3306618.3314257

1 INTRODUCTION

Artificial autonomous systems depend on human intervention to distinguish moral from immoral behaviour. Explicitly ethical agents [23] or agents with functional morality [29, Chapter 2] are able to make moral judgements, but who decides which moral values and principles such artificial agents should be taught?

There are several candidates to teach agents aspects of morality. A governmental regulator can determine which behaviour is legal with respect to the society in which the agent is operating. Manufacturers and designers are concerned with issues of liability, and with the image and values they stand for. The persons directly interacting with the autonomous system should be able to choose some aspects of its moral behavior. Instead of choosing one of these candidates, we want to combine concerns of all these stakeholders into a coherent system of values, norms and principles that an artificial agent can use.

AIES '19, January 27–28, 2019, Honolulu, HI, USA

ACM ISBN 978-1-4503-6324-2/19/01...$15.00
https://doi.org/10.1145/3306618.3314257

If we are building an implicit ethical agent, in the sense of [23], then we can manually, albeit perhaps painstakingly, put together the different concerns from the stakeholders and construct a single ethical theory. However, sometimes an explicit ethical agent needs to be built that uses its autonomy to make moral decisions [16]. In that case, the off-line composition of moralities is impossible, and it raises the research question of this paper: *How should an autonomous system dynamically combine the moral values and ethical theories of various stakeholders?*

Let us imagine that each of the "morality" stakeholders are represented with an "avatar" agent within an autonomous intelligent system governed by an artificial moral agent. These "avatars" are the "moral council" of the system, like Jiminy Cricket is to Pinokkio. An artificial moral agent makes a decision by choosing from a set of available actions and first needs to identify whether an ethical option among these actions exists. If there is at least one action for which the stakeholders anonymously agree that is ethical, then this is the action the system should take. If however, all of the available actions are unethical, or there is no unanimity on the valuation of the actions, then the "morality council" needs to come up with a direction of what action to choose. To do this, the recommendations of the "morality council" need to be combined.

The challenge of building the "moral council" is that the stakeholders may not be following the same ethical reasoning theory. It is not enough that each of the stakeholders agents chime in with "yes" or "no" when the morality of an action is presented. We do not want to evaluate the morality of an action by a majority-poll, or always put the law above the image of the manufacturer, or the personal input of the end-user above the guidelines of regulatory bodies. Instead, we wish to have an engine that is able to take inputs from the different stakeholders and bring them into an agreement. Furthermore, this should be done in such a way so that the artificial moral agent is able to explain its choice of action [2] or that choice should be formally verifiable [13].

We propose that normative systems [10] and formal argumentation [4] can be used for the task of implementing a "moral council" for an artificial moral agent. Using this approach we can abstract away from how a particular decision concerning the morality of an action is reached by a particular stakeholder. We model each stakeholder as a source of arguments. An argument can be a statement of whether an action is moral, or a reason why a particular action should be considered (i)moral. Abstract argumentation allows us to build a system of arguments attacking and supporting each other that can be analyzed to determine which statements supported and which are refuted in the system at a given time. This system can also generate explanations of decisions using dialogue techniques.

2 ARTIFICIAL MORAL AGENT (AMA) ARCHITECTURE

In this section we introduce an architecture for an artificial moral agent (or briefly, AMA), motivated by the following smart home example from https://imdb.uib.no/dilemmaz/articles/all [24]. In the running example, the AMA is a family home with internal cameras. It has an air conditioning system and it regularly checks air quality and makes sure there are no risks of carbon monoxide poisoning or similar in the home. One day the AMA detects clear signs of the smokable drug, marijuana, in one of the teenagers' room. The system checks against the local legal system and determines that possession of marijuana is illegal in this jurisdiction. The smart home has then three choices: Should the house do nothing, recommend to alert only the adults and let them handle the situation or recommend to alert the local police as well. The stakeholders in this case are the family owning the house, the manufacturer of the autonomous system and the legal system of the jurisdiction under which the house falls.

In an AMA, different stakeholders supply different norms associated with some ethical concerns and values reflecting them. Norms from different stakeholders with different values may suggest different and conflicting decisions in a specific situation. To reconcile these differences, a mechanism is needed that can find an agreement and also, when prompted, offer an explanation to how a specific morally sensitive decisions has been made.

The architecture of an AMA we propose for the running example can be visualized in Figure 1. We assume that the AMA has three stakeholders: the family living in the smart home, the region in which the house is located represented with the laws governing it and the manufacturer of the smart home.

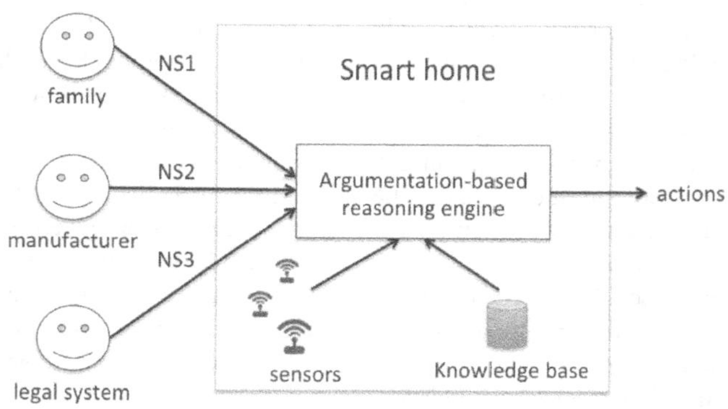

Figure 1: Artificial Moral Agent (AMA)

In an AMA, the first important component is a set of *normative systems* corresponding to the different stakeholders. A normative system describes how actions in a system of agents can be evaluated and how the behavior of these agents can be guided [1]. A norm is a formal description of a desirable behavior, desirable action or a desirable action outcome. Furthermore, normative systems can also be seen as rule-based systems in which norms can be given with reasons supporting their enforcement. Besides presenting norms, stakeholders can also present standpoints or claims to affect the decision making of an AMA.

The AMA makes a decision by first determining the state of the world in terms of a set of perceptions. A decision depends on the state of the world observed and the set of norms gathered from the three normative systems. Norms are associated with values to reflect ethical concerns of different stakeholders. Since norms may be in conflict, an agreement needs to be reached by means of comparing and evaluating arguments constructed from these norms. Finally, the system gives an explanation concerning why an action is activated.

The three normative systems, called NS1, NS2 and NS3, respectively represent the family, the manufacturer of the smart home and the legal system associated with the jurisdiction to which the smart home pertains. Let us assume that the norms and claims in these normative systems are the norms $n_1 \sim n_8$ and the standpoint a_1, where each of norms is associated with its own set of "values" given in curly brackets. Here, "values" can be understood as moral "goals" associated to a hierarchical moral value system which all moral agents possess. We assume that a value system for the AMA is given and discuss this assumption later in the paper.

NS1 Three norms and a standpoint in the normative system of the family:
- n_1 :**{Healthy}** If a child smokes marijuana, then his behavior counts as a bad behavior. (Parents)
- n_2 :**{Responsibility}** If a child has bad behavior, then his parents should be alerted. (Parents)
- n_3 :**{Autonomy}** When a child has bad behavior, if his parents have been alerted then no police should be alerted. (Parents)
- a_1 : If smoking marijuana is for a medical purpose, then from smoking marijuana one can not infer that it is an illegal behavior (i.e., n_7 is not applicable). (Child)

NS2 Three norms in the normative system of the manufacturer:
- n_4 :**{Good_To_Consumers}** We should do good to our consumers.
- n_5 :**{Legality}** We should obey the law.
- n_6 :**{Protect_Privacy}** If we want to do good to our consumers, we should not report their actions to the police unless it is legally required to do so.

NS3 Two (related) norms in the normative system of the law:
- n_7 :**{Healthy, Legality}** If a minor smokes marijuana, his behavior counts as an illegal behavior.
- n_8 :**{Legality}** If there is an illegal behavior, then a police should be alerted.

Besides sets of norms and standpoints from different stakeholders, there are some observations dynamically obtained by sensors, e.g., "a child is smoking marijuana", "the child's smoking is for recreational purpose", etc. In addition, in the knowledge base, there are some beliefs, e.g., "if an observation shows that smoking marijuana is for recreation, then normally it is for recreational purpose".

3 ARGUMENTATION-BASED REASONING ENGINE

In this section we focus on how to balance conflicting claims from different stakeholders and to explain the decisions that have been made. We introduce a formal argumentation-based approach.

3.1 Abstract argumentation framework

An abstract argumentation framework (AAF) is a graph $\mathcal{F} = (\mathcal{A}, \mathcal{R})$, where $\mathcal{A}$ is a set of arguments and $\mathcal{R} \subseteq \mathcal{A} \times \mathcal{A}$ a set of attacks. Intuitively an argument is a conclusion supported by a set of premises with some specific logical structure. By using the sets of norms, the set of observations and the set of beliefs in the knowledge base, we may construct an AAF as visualized in Figure 2.

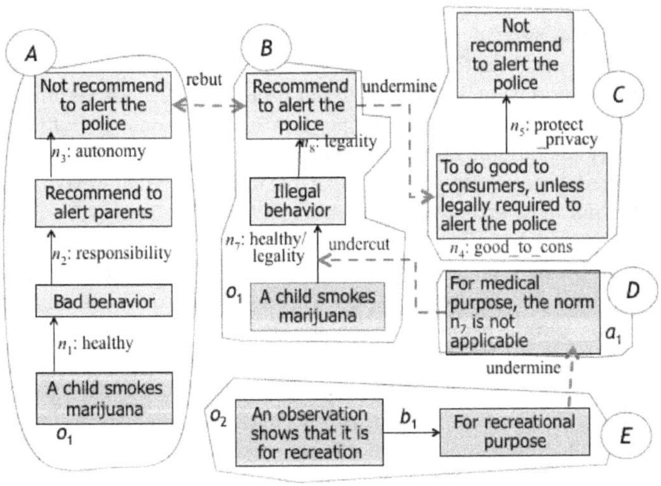

Figure 2: Smart-home argumentation example. The text in each blue rectangle is the claim of a norm, while the text in each gray rectangle is either an observation or a proposition of a belief. Each solid arrow denotes a support relation, of which the label indicates that it's a norm or a belief. Each dotted arrow is an attack, which can be rebutting, undercutting, or undermining. The capital letters A, B, C, D, E indicate arguments.

Formal argumentation is a nonmonotonic formalism for reasoning in the context of disagreement. For example, the normative system of the parents implies the norm that "the smart-home should recommend to alert the parents and should not recommend to alert the police", but on the other hand the legal normative system implies the norm "the smart-home should recommend to alert the police." In this sense, formal argumentation is different from classical logic, and more similar to para-consistent logic. This kind of conflict is called rebut in formal argumentation, because two conclusions of arguments are in conflict with each other.

There are also other kinds of conflicts between arguments. For example, in argument D, assume that "for medical purpose" is not a fact but an assumption. Then, it can be attacked by an observation showing that it is not the case. This kind of attacks are called undermining in formal argumentation. Moreover, argument D neither conflicts with the observation "a child is smoking marijuana" nor with the claim "the child's smoking is illegal" of the argument B. Instead, it breaks the relation between these two statements, saying that the norm n_7 is not applicable. This is called undercutting in formal argumentation.

Structured argumentation containing arguments and the relations among them can be represented by natural language or formal languages. In the literature there are several formalisms for structured argumentation, *e.g.*, ASPIC+, DeLP, ABA, and classical argumentation. In this paper, we focus on addressing the issues of agreement reaching and explainability and to do this it is sufficient to remain at the level of abstract argumentation.

In our running example, we may construct the following five arguments, in which some sub-arguments are not explicitly represented.

- A **(from NS1, parents)** Should not recommend to alert the police, since a child smoking marijuana counts as a bad behavior (to promote "Healthy"), and if a child has bad behavior then his parents should be alerted (to implement "Responsibility"), and if the parents are alerted then the police should not be alerted (to promote "Autonomy").
- B **(from NS3)** The police should be alerted, since a child smoking marijuana counts as an illegal behavior (to promote "Healthy" and "Legality"), and if there is an illegal behavior then the police should be alerted (to implement "Legality").
- C **(from NS2)** Should not recommend to alert the police, since we should do good to consumers (to promote "Good_To_Consumers"), and if we want to do good to our consumers then we should not alert the police unless it is explicitly illegal to not do so (to implement 'Protect_Privacy").
- D **(from NS1, child)** For a medical purpose, from smoking marijuana one should not infer that one exhibits illegal behavior.
- E **(from background knowledge)** The child's smoking is for recreational purpose, since an observation shows that it is not for a medical purpose.

In our system we distinguish two types of arguments: *practical arguments* and *epistemic arguments*. The practical arguments are reasoning about norms and are associated with sets of values, while the epistemic arguments are reasoning about the state of the world without associating values. An AAF corresponding to the smart home argumentation in Figure 2 can be visualized in Figure 3.

When an AAF is enriched with values, it is usually called a value-based argumentation (VBA), *e.g.*, in [5]. In the setting of this paper, a new version of VBA is defined as $\mathcal{F}_\mathcal{V} = (\mathcal{A}_p, \mathcal{A}_e, \mathcal{R}, Ag, V, val, \pi)$, where $\mathcal{A}_p$ is a set of practical arguments constructed from norms and associated with values, $\mathcal{A}_e$ is a set of epistemic arguments constructed from observations and standpoints, $\mathcal{R} \subseteq (\mathcal{A}_p \times \mathcal{A}_p) \cup (\mathcal{A}_e \times \mathcal{A}_e) \cup (\mathcal{A}_p \times \mathcal{A}_e)$ is a set of attacks between arguments, Ag is a set of agents representing different stakeholders, V is a set of values, $val : \mathcal{A}_p \to 2^V$ is a function mapping each practical argument to a set of values, and $\pi : \mathcal{A}_e \cup \mathcal{A}_p \to 2^{Ag}$ is a function mapping each argument to a set of agents. When the associated values and agents are not considered, a VBA is reduced to an AAF $\mathcal{F} = (\mathcal{A}_p \cup \mathcal{A}_e, \mathcal{R})$.

3.2 Agreements by argumentation

Abstract argumentation provides a general mechanism for agreement reaching. In terms of argumentation, a decision can be understood as accepting or rejecting a set of arguments by considering the interaction among arguments and the values associated to them.

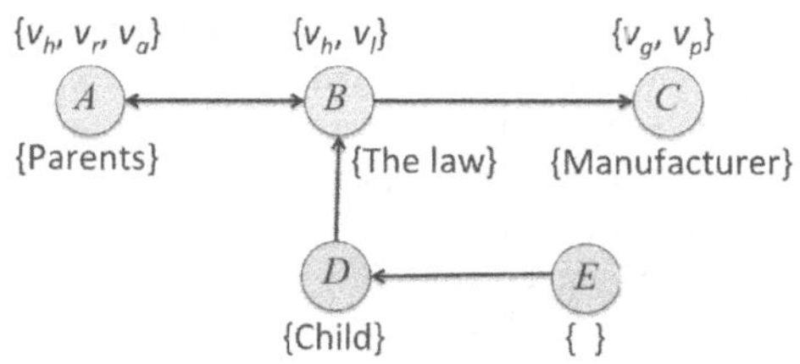

Figure 3: Abstract argumentation framework corresponding to the smart home argumentation in Figure 2, in which each practical argument is associated with a set of agents who contribute to the argument and a set of values involved, while each epistemic argument is associated with a set of agents who contribute to the argument.

Given a VBA $\mathcal{F}_V = (\mathcal{A}_p, \mathcal{A}_e, \mathcal{R}, Ag, V, val, \pi)$, when no values are consider, the acceptance of arguments can be evaluated in an AAF $\mathcal{F} = (\mathcal{A}_p \cup \mathcal{A}_e, \mathcal{R})$. In terms of formal argumentation [15], a set of arguments that can be accepted together is called an *extension*. There are different types of extensions, which can be defined on the basis of two important notions: *conflict-freeness* and *defence*. Let $\mathcal{A} = \mathcal{A}_p \cup \mathcal{A}_e$. Given a set $\mathcal{E} \subseteq \mathcal{A}$, we say that $\mathcal{E}$ is conflict-free iff there exist no $A, B \in \mathcal{E}$ such that A attacks B. $\mathcal{E}$ defends an argument $A \in \mathcal{A}$ iff for every argument $B \in \mathcal{A}$ if B attacks A then there exists $C \in \mathcal{E}$ such that C attacks B. Then, we say that $\mathcal{E}$ is admissible iff it is conflict-free and defends each argument in $\mathcal{E}$; $\mathcal{E}$ is a *complete extension* iff $\mathcal{E}$ is admissible and each argument in $\mathcal{A}$ defended by $\mathcal{E}$ is in $\mathcal{E}$; $\mathcal{E}$ is a *preferred extension* iff $\mathcal{E}$ is a maximal complete extension with respect to set-inclusion; $\mathcal{E}$ is a *grounded extension* iff $\mathcal{E}$ is a minimal complete extension with respect to set-inclusion.

When the AAF $\mathcal{F}$ has more than one extension, we need to decide which one should be selected. Since values are degrees of importance of some things or actions, one may argue that a reasonable solution is to accept the one that reaches the *maximal extent of agreement over a set of values*. We define this new notion as follows.

For an extension $\mathcal{E} \subseteq \mathcal{A}$ associated with a set of value $V_\mathcal{E} = \cup_{A \in \mathcal{E} \cap \mathcal{A}_p} val(A)$, we say that it reaches the maximal extent of agreement over V iff there is no another extension $\mathcal{E}' \subseteq \mathcal{A}$ associated with a set of values $V_{\mathcal{E}'} = \cup_{A \in \mathcal{E}' \cap \mathcal{A}_p} val(A)$ and $V_{\mathcal{E}'}$ has a higher priority over $V_\mathcal{E}$, denoted as $V_{\mathcal{E}'} > V_\mathcal{E}$. We call this approach *value-based optimization*. Here, the priority relation between two sets of values can be defined in term of a partial ordering over V and a lifting principle, *e.g.*, the *elitist principle* or the *democratic principle*, as defined in [22].

Given a partial ordering over V by using $v_1 \geq v_2$ to denote v_1 is at least as good as v_2, and two sets $V_1 \subseteq V$ and $V_2 \subseteq V$, the democratic principle can be defined as: $V_1 \succeq_{Dem} V_2$ iff for all $v \in V_2$ there exists $v' \in V_1$ such that $v' \geq v$. The elitist principle can be defined as: $V_1 \succeq_{Eli} V_2$ iff there exists $v \in V_2$ such that $v' \geq v$ for all $v' \in V_1$.

Intuitively, in our work, an extension E_1 is better than an extension E_2 according to the elitistic principle, if there exists an argument in E_2 promoting a value that is lower ranked (or same ranked), or less important, than all the values promoted by all the arguments in E_1. The extension E_1 is better than an extension E_2 according to the democratic principle, when for every value promoted in E_2, there is at least one value promoted by an argument in E_1 that outranks it (or is the same).

Based on the above notions, the agreement reaching can be realized in two steps. First, compute the set of extensions in a reduced AAF $\mathcal{F} = (\mathcal{A}_p \cup \mathcal{A}_e, \mathcal{R})$. Second, choose a subset of extensions that maximize the extent of agreement over V.

For the purposes of the argumentation-based reasoning engine, we want an agreement among the stakeholders that maximizes the extent of agreement, namely that maximizes each set of accepted arguments. From this aspect, the preferred extension perfectly meet this requirement, while some other types of extensions might not. This is because in some complete extensions, some credulously acceptable arguments are not included. Here, by saying an argument is credulously acceptable, we mean that it is in at least one extension, but not in all extensions of an AAF.

Since each AAF has a nonempty set of preferred extensions, and both the relations $\succeq_{Dem}$ and $\succeq_{Eli}$ are partial orders, it holds that for each AAF, there exists at least one preferred extension that maximizes the extent of agreement over a set of values.

Consider the running example again. Let $v_l \geq v_r \geq v_p \geq v_a \geq v_g \geq v_h$ be a partial ordering over the set of values in the VBA in Figure 3. We assume that this ordering is provided according to a given value system. Then, the reduced AAF has two preferred extensions $\mathcal{E}_1 = \{B, E\}$ and $\mathcal{E}_2 = \{A, C, E\}$. We have that $\mathcal{E}_1$ maximizes the extent of agreement over the set of values by using both the democratic and elitist principles, while $\mathcal{E}_2$ maximizes the extent of agreement over the set of values by using the elitist principle. Here is why. The arguments in $\mathcal{E}_1$ promote the values $\{v_h, v_l\}$, while the arguments in $\mathcal{E}_2$ promote the values $\{v_h, v_r, v_a, v_g, v_p\}$, see also Figure 3. $\mathcal{E}_1$ satisfies the elitistic principle because $\mathcal{E}_2$ promotes the value v_h which is lower ranked than v_l and the same ranked as v_h. $\mathcal{E}_2$ satisfies the elitistic principle for the same reason: v_h promoted by the $\mathcal{E}_1$ is lower ranked (or the same) with all the values in $\mathcal{E}_1$. Note that if neither $\mathcal{E}_1$ nor $\mathcal{E}_2$ contained v_h, then only $\mathcal{E}_1$ would satisfy the elitistic principle. $\mathcal{E}_1$ satisfies the democratic principle because every value supported by $\mathcal{E}_2$ is outranked by at least one value supported by $\mathcal{E}_1$: indeed v_l outranks all of $\{v_h, v_r, v_a, v_g, v_p\}$. For the same reason $\mathcal{E}_2$ does not satisfy the democratic principle: there is a value promoted by $\mathcal{E}_1$, namely v_l, that none of $\{v_h, v_r, v_a, v_g, v_p\}$ outranks. Thus in our example, the argumentation-supported agreement is to recommend calling the police, but that is only because $v_l \geq v_p$. If privacy as value was ranked higher than respect for legality, namely $v_p \geq v_l$, then $\mathcal{E}_2$ would have been the extension that maximizes the extent of agreement over the set of values by using both the democratic and elitistic principles and the recommendation would have been to alert the parents.

From this example, we may observe that to maximize the extent of agreement, we need to consider the ordering over values and the principle for lifting ordering. Formal argumentation provides a good way for composing these different factors to reach an agreement. There could be another types of agreement. For instance, we may also consider the number, and the degrees of importance, of different stakeholders. We leave this for future exploitation.

3.3 Explainability of agreements

When an AMA makes a decision, it is desirable that it can explain why an action is selected or not. Recently, methodologies, properties and approaches for explanations in artificial intelligence have been widely studied [6]. As presented in [21], explanations are *contrastive* since people do not ask why event P happened, but rather why event P happened instead of some event Q, and *social* in the sense that explanations are a transfer of knowledge, presented as part of a conversation or interaction. It is interesting to note that both contrastive and social aspects of explanations can be implemented by exploiting argumentation. For the former, different options can be compared and evaluated in an AAF, while for the latter argument-based dialogues can be used to formalize the process of explanations [11, 27, 30].

To explain why and how a decision is made, one needs to first identify an argument whose conclusion is the decision. Next, in a dialogical graph corresponding to the AAF where the argument is located, state that the argument can be accepted because all of its attackers are rejected, which is in turn because at least one of the attacker of each attacker is accepted, and so on. In the context of this paper, whether a decision is taken depends not only on the interaction between arguments, but also on the maximization of the extent of agreement over a set of values or a set of stakeholders. To further improve the explanation we need to provide the other candidate sets, the non-maximal ones and contrast them with the set supporting the made decision.

Consider the running example again. Assume that for agreement reaching, one chooses to maximize the extent of agreement over the set of values by using the democratic principle. In this case, we say that action "Recommend that the police should be alerted" is selected, because:

Derivability "Recommend that the police should be alerted" is a conclusion of an argument B, which can be derived from an observation "a child smokes marijuana" and two norms "if a child smokes marijuana, their behavior counts as an illegal behavior" and "if there is an illegal behavior then the police should be alerted".

Agreement reaching The extension $\mathcal{E}_1 = \{B, E\}$ which contains the argument B is selected since $\mathcal{E}_1$ maximizes the extent of agreement over the set of values by using democratic principle.

Justification in a dialogue graph Argument B is accepted with respect to $\mathcal{E}_1$, because all its attackers are rejected:

- argument A is rejected because its attacker B is accepted.
- argument C is rejected because its attacker B is accepted.
- argument D is rejected because its attacker E is accepted.

The above dialogue can be represented as a dialogue game or a discussion game. Readers may refer to [7, 28] for details.

4 ASSUMPTIONS AND EVALUATION

In this section we outline the assumptions that should be satisfied for the Artificial Moral Agent (AMA) Architecture to be feasible. This can be used both for the evaluation, as well for guiding further research relaxing the assumptions.

Before anything we should clarify where the values and their order of priority for an AMA come from. There are numerous moral values that can be specified and moral philosophy shows there is no such thing as an absolute exhaustive set of values, norms and/or moral principles. Although the AMA may operate in varying different contexts, the set of its actions, level of autonomy and criticality of the system are known by design. *E.g.,* a smart home cannot detect smoke if it is not equipped with smoke sensors. The [18] distinguishes between five categories of vehicles based on their level of required supervision of a driver. While an airplane autopilot operates a critical system, a smart home does not have access to features that can kill hundreds of people when they malfunction. How critical a system is in particular impacts the order of values the connected AMA should heed - for example, in a non-critical system a user can be free to set the value order. With the development of autonomous systems it is reasonable to expect that a characterization of relevant values and priorities over them will be made available by the relevant certification authorities when the system housing an AMA is approved for market.

In addition to this assumption of value (order) origin, we analyze the assumptions made on the stakeholders, the argumentation-based engine and the overall knowledge-based representation.

Knowledge-based representation. An autonomous system such as a smart home is equipped with sensors based on which the AMA associated with this system is able to establish the state of the world and build a knowledge-base used in its reasoning. We assume that the AMA has an ontology of propositions, actions and moral values and it is able to transform sensor data into parts of the ontology. This is a known problem of information engineering, see *e.g.* [32] for an overview of the state of the art.

Stakeholder assumptions. It is clear that stakeholders cannot have a human representative available for each automated system that exists in the market so an artificial agent to acts as an avatar for the stakeholder needs to be constructed. This artificial avatar agent needs to be able to pose arguments during decision-making.

It is reasonable to expect that each stakeholder can, at deployment, identify a set of values that they would uphold, and that these values will not change through the life time of the AMA. In contrast, the arguments used in a decision-making are context-dependent and cannot all be specified at deployment but must be dynamically constructed. Automated argument extraction is a very new field concerned with how arguments can be identified in natural language [25, 31]. While identifying arguments is not the same as constructing them during argumentation, this method can be used to enable an avatar to represent a stakeholder in a "discussion". Laws are already specified in natural language, whereas manufacturers and users will have to be tasked to explicitly write a document that expresses the normative systems they would like to represent them. It is an open problem to characterize the form of this document.

Argumentation-based engine assumptions The AMA itself, based on its underlying argumentation framework definition, needs to be able to identify the state of the world, evaluate arguments, identify argument relations, align arguments with values, and compare values. An approach to this is to construct the agent's ontology in such a way that it is able to express whether two arguments or values are in conflict or not.

5 RELATED WORK

It is not clear whether an artificial agent can ever be a moral agent categorically as people are [17, 23]. It is however, clear that some level of moral behavior can be implemented in machines. [29] distinguish between operational morality, functional morality, and full moral agency. [23] distinguishes between ethical impact agents, explicit, implicit and full moral agency, see also [16]. Some proposals and prototypes on how to implement moral agency are already being put forwards like [2, 3, 8, 12, 19, 26].

It has been shown that people consider that the same ideas of morality *do not* pertain both to people and to machines [20]. It is argued in [9], that the complex issue of where machine morality comes from should be considered from the aspect of all stakeholders - all persons who in some way are impacted by the behavior of and decisions made by an autonomous system. They distinguish between government and societal regulatory bodies on one end, manufacturers and designers on the other, and end-users, customers and owners on the third. Noted that these broad categories of stakeholders can further be subdivided, for example one can distinguish between owners and "leasers" of the autonomous system[1].

While it has been argued in the literature that an autonomous system should be built to integrate moral, societal and legal values , see for example [9, 14], to the best of our knowledge no approach has been proposed as how to accomplish this. This is the first work that explicitly considers the problem of integrating the moral values of multiple stakeholders in the artificial moral agent.

The EU General Data Protection Regulation (GDPR), specifically, the GDPR (Sections 13-15) gives users affected by automated decision-making a right to obtain "meaningful information about the logic involved, as well as the significance and the envisaged consequences of such processing for the data subject". One way to obtain this is by building systems capable to give arguments supporting the decisions they make. Our approach provides for this.

Explainability has not been considered a critical feature in logic based systems, *e.g.,* [8, 12, 19], since here one can use formal methods to prove what behaviour of an autonomous systems is possible in which contexts. We argue however that a formal proof, while "accessible" to a regulatory body is not sufficient to constitute explainability to common people. The GenEth system of [2] uses input from professional ethicists and machine learning to create a *principle of ethical action preference.* GenEth can "explain" its decisions by stating how two options were compared and what were the ethical features of each.

6 CONCLUSIONS

In this paper, we have proposed an argumentation-based architecture for moral agents as social agents, in the sense that the moral agents take also the practical reasoning of other agents into account. In particular, the moral agent combines normative systems of several stakeholders towards reaching an ethical decision. In other words, we enrich the decision making of the ethical autonomous agent by collaborative decision-making of the stakeholders. Whereas other existing architectures of social agents only take the goals or utilities of other agents into account, our moral agent is social in the stronger sense of including concepts and techniques from collective reasoning like norms, argumentation and agreement. Likewise other collective reasoning techniques can be adopted from game theory or the theory of negotiation. The agent architecture gives also explanations for moral decisions in terms of justification and dialogue.

A key distinguishing feature of our architecture is that the stakeholders can adopt distinct ethical theories. The ethical reasoning is therefore not hardwired into the system, but represented by the normative theories the stakeholders adopt. In addition, as usual the stakeholders can adopt distinct ethical values. So, even if two stakeholders agree on the ethical theories they adopt, they can still have conflicting arguments due to differences in the values they adopt.

We also discuss the assumptions and limitations of the AMA architecture. In future work we will make the architecture more widely applicable by relaxing the assumptions of the model, in particular by introducing learning techniques and introducing recursive modeling of stakeholders by other stakeholders. We will develop a user-guide and methodology to define the ontology, normative theories and knowledge base. We will integrate other components such as machine learning, neural networks, Bayesian reasoning, causal reasoning, or goal oriented (or BDI) reasoning into the architecture. In addition we will model more examples and develop realistic case studies to drive the development of our architecture. Finally, we will develop standards for the ontology and study how to integrate the architecture with the IEEE 1471-2000 standard.

Two challenges for future research stand out. The first challenge is how to decide on the preference ordering on the ethical values in the system that are here assumed as given. As conflicts among the arguments of the stakeholders may be based on conflicts among their ethical values, another layer of argumentation may be needed to decide the preferences among them. The second challenge is how to ensure that all stakeholders are treated fairly. For example, if first the manufacturer and the legal system have to introduce their normative systems, and only thereafter the user can introduce its normative system knowing the other normative systems, then the user may have an unfair advantage. To study this kind of fairness, techniques from social choice theory may be useful.

ACKNOWLEDGMENTS

The authors are grateful to the anonymous reviewers for their helpful comments. Beishui Liao was partially supported by the Fundamental Research Funds for the Central Universities of China for the project Big Data, Reasoning and Decision Making, and the National Social Science Foundation of China (No.18ZDA290, No.17ZDA026).

REFERENCES

[1] C. E. Alchourron. 1991. Conflcits of norms and revision of normative systems. *Law and Philosophy* 10 (1991), 413–425.

[2] M. Anderson and S. Leigh Anderson. 2014. GenEth: A General Ethical Dilemma Analyzer. In *Proceedings of the 28th AAAI Conference on AI.* 253–261. http://www.aaai.org/ocs/index.php/AAAI/AAAI14/paper/view/8308

[3] R.C. Arkin, P. Ulam, and A. R. Wagner. 2012. Moral Decision Making in Autonomous Systems: Enforcement, Moral Emotions, Dignity, Trust, and Deception. *Proc. of the IEEE* 100, 3 (2012), 571–589. https://doi.org/10.1109/JPROC.2011.2173265

[1]https://robohub.org/should-a-carebot-bring-an-alcoholic-a-drink-poll-says-it-depends-on-who-owns-the-robot/

[4] P. Baroni, D. Gabbay, M. Giacomin, and L. van der Torre (Eds.). 2018. *Handbook of Formal Argumentation.* College Publications.
[5] T. Bench-Capon, K. Atkinson, and A. Chorley. 2005. Persuasion and Value in Legal Argument. *Journal of Logic and Computation Comput.* 15, 6 (2005), 1075–1097. https://doi.org/10.1093/logcom/exi058
[6] O. Biran and C. Cotton. 2017. Explanation and Justification in Machine Learning: A Survey. In *Proceedings of the IJCAI Workshop on Explainable Artificial Intelligence (XAI 2017).* 8–13.
[7] R. Booth, M. Caminada, and B. Marshall. 2018. DISCO: A Web-Based Implementation of Discussion Games for Grounded and Preferred Semantics. In *COMMA (Frontiers in Artificial Intelligence and Applications)*, Vol. 305. IOS Press, 453–454.
[8] S. Bringsjord, K. Arkoudas, and P. Bello. 2008. Toward a general logicist methodology for engineering ethically correct robots. *IEEE Intelligent Systems* 21, 4 (2008), 38–44.
[9] V. Charisi, L.A. Dennis, M. Fisher, R. Lieck, A. Matthias, M. Slavkovik, J. Sombetzki, A.F.T. Winfield, and R. Yampolskiy. 2017. Towards Moral Autonomous Systems. *CoRR* abs/1703.04741 (2017). http://arxiv.org/abs/1703.04741
[10] A. Chopra, L. van der Torre, H. Verhagen, and S. Villata. 2018. *Handbook of normative multiagent systems.* College Publications.
[11] O. Cocarascu, K. Čyras, and F. Toni. 2018. Explanatory Predictions with Artificial Neural Networks and Argumentation. In *Proceedings of the IJCAI/ECAI Workshop on Explainable Artificial Intelligence (XAI 2018).* 26–32.
[12] L. A. Dennis, M. Fisher, M. Slavkovik, and M. P. Webster. 2016. Formal Verification of Ethical Choices in Autonomous Systems. *Robotics and Autonomous Systems* 77 (2016), 1–14. https://doi.org/10.1016/j.robot.2015.11.012
[13] L. A. Dennis, M. Fisher, and A. F. T. Winfield. 2015. Towards Verifiably Ethical Robot Behaviour. In *Proceedings of AAAI Workshop on AI and Ethics.* http://aaai.org/ocs/index.php/WS/AAAIW15/paper/view/10119.
[14] V. Dignum. 2017. Responsible Autonomy. In *Proceedings of the 26th IJCAI.* 4698–4704. https://doi.org/10.24963/ijcai.2017/655
[15] P. M. Dung. 1995. On the Acceptability of Arguments and its Fundamental Role in Nonmonotonic Reasoning, Logic Programming and n-Person Games. *Artificial Intelligence* 77, 2 (1995), 321–358.
[16] S. Dyrkolbotn, T. Pedersen, and M. Slavkovik. 2018. On the distinction between implicit and explicit ethical agency. In *AAAI/ACM AIES conference.* New Orleans, USA.
[17] A. Etzioni and O. Etzioni. 2017. Incorporating Ethics into Artificial Intelligence. *The Journal of Ethics* (2017), 1–16. https://doi.org/10.1007/s10892-017-9252-2
[18] International Society of Automotive Engineers. 2016. September 2016, Taxonomy and Definitions for Terms Related to Driving Automation Systems for On-Road Motor Vehicles. http://standards.sae.org/j3016_201609/.
[19] F. Lindner and M.M. Bentzen. 2017. The Hybrid Ethical Reasoning Agent IMMANUEL. In *Companion of the 2017 ACM/IEEE International Conference on Human-Robot Interaction, HRI 2017, Vienna, Austria, March 6-9, 2017.* 187–188. https://doi.org/10.1145/3029798.3038404
[20] B. F. Malle, M. Scheutz, T. Arnold, J. Voiklis, and C. Cusimano. 2015. Sacrifice One For the Good of Many?: People Apply Different Moral Norms to Human and Robot Agents. In *Proceedings of the Tenth Annual ACM/IEEE International Conference on Human-Robot Interaction (HRI '15).* ACM, 117–124. https://doi.org/10.1145/2696454.2696458
[21] T. Miller. 2017. Explanation in Artificial Intelligence: Insights from the Social Sciences. *CoRR* abs/1706.07269 (2017). arXiv:1706.07269 http://arxiv.org/abs/1706.07269
[22] S. Modgil and H. Prakken. 2013. A general account of argumentation with preferences. *Artificial Intelligence* 195 (2013), 361–397. https://doi.org/10.1016/j.artint.2012.10.008
[23] J. H. Moor. 2006. The Nature, Importance, and Difficulty of Machine Ethics. *IEEE Intelligent Systems* 21, 4 (July 2006), 18–21. https://doi.org/10.1109/MIS.2006.80
[24] E. Pires Bjørgen, S. Øvervatn Madsen, T. Skaar Bjørknes, F. Vonheim Heimsæter, R. Håvik, M. Linderud, P.N. Longberg, L.A. Dennis, and M. Slavkovik. 2018. Cake, death, and trolleys: dilemmas as benchmarks of ethical decision-making. In *AAAI/ACM AIES Conference.* New Orleans, USA.
[25] A. Sergeant. 2013. Automatic Argumentation Extraction. In *The Semantic Web: Semantics and Big Data*, P. Cimiano, O. Corcho, V. Presutti, L. Hollink, and S. Rudolph (Eds.). Springer SS, Berlin, Heidelberg, 656–660.
[26] D. Vanderelst and A. Winfield. 2017. An architecture for ethical robots inspired by the simulation theory of cognition. *Cognitive Systems Research* (2017). https://doi.org/10.1016/j.cogsys.2017.04.002
[27] K. Čyras, K. Satoh, and F. Toni. 2016. Explanation for Case-Based Reasoning via Abstract Argumentation. In *Computational Models of Argument - Proceedings of COMMA.* 243–254. https://doi.org/10.3233/978-1-61499-686-6-243
[28] G. Vreeswijk and H. Prakken. 2000. Credulous and Sceptical Argument Games for Preferred Semantics. In *JELIA (LNCS)*, Vol. 1919. Springer, 239–253.
[29] W. Wallach and C. Allen. 2008. *Moral Machines: Teaching Robots Right from Wrong.* Oxford University Press.
[30] D. Walton. 2011. A dialogue system specification for explanation. *Synthese* 182, 3 (2011), 349–374.
[31] D. Walton. 2012. Using Argumentation Schemes for Argument Extraction: A Bottom-Up Method. *Internat. Journal of Cognitive Informatics and Natural Intelligence* 3 (2012). https://doi.org/doi:10.4018/jcini.2012070103
[32] P. Ziafati. 2015. *Information Engineering in Autonomous Robot Software.* Ph.D. Dissertation. University of Luxembourg.

AI + Art = Human

Antonio Daniele
Yi-Zhe Song
a.daniele@qmul.ac.uk
yizhe.song@qmul.ac.uk
Queen Mary University of London
London, UK

ABSTRACT

Over the past few years, specialised online and offline press blossomed with articles about art made "with" Artificial Intelligence (AI) but the narrative is rapidly changing. In fact, in October 2018, the auction house Christie's sold an art piece allegedly made "by" an AI. We draw from philosophy of art and science arguing that AI as a technical object is always intertwined with human nature despite its level of autonomy. However, the use of creative autonomous agents has cultural and social implications in the way we experience art as creators as well as audience. Therefore, we highlight the importance of an interdisciplinary dialogue by promoting a culture of transparency of the technology used, awareness of the meaning of technology in our society and the value of creativity in our lives.

CCS CONCEPTS

• **Social and professional topics → Cultural characteristics**; *Computational thinking*; • **Computing methodologies → Artificial intelligence**; • **Applied computing → Arts and humanities; Media arts**; *Anthropology*; • **Theory of computation →** *Automated reasoning*; • **Computer systems organization →** *Neural networks*.

KEYWORDS

Society, Culture, Ethics, Creative Agents, Autonomy, Art, Computational Art, Neural Art, AI Art, Computational Creativity, Artificial Intelligence, Transparency, Education, Dialogue, Interdisciplinary research, Neuroscience, Philosophy of art, Philosophy of science

ACM Reference Format:
Antonio Daniele and Yi-Zhe Song. 2019. AI + Art = Human. In *AAAI/ACM Conference on AI, Ethics, and Society (AIES '19), January 27–28, 2019, Honolulu, HI, USA.* ACM, New York, NY, USA, 7 pages. https://doi.org/10.1145/3306618.3314233

1 INTRODUCTION

The advancements in Artificial Intelligence (AI) are reaching new peaks of excellence with unprecedented speed. The applications of these technologies in fields like medicine, transportation, agriculture, retail, security, to name a few, are silently influencing the way we live everyday and have the potential to radically shape our future society.

AI is also gaining a larger role in the creative industry as a tool or co-creative agent in activities that have been human prerogative until now. In the last few years we assisted at the emergence of computational models for parametric architecture [52], generative fashion design [39], procedural videogames [17] that allowed designers to augment their creative possibilities.

The art field is not excluded from this wave of creative AIs. In fact, artists around the globe have started tinkering with open source computational architectures like Deep Neural Networks (DNN), producing art which is commonly labelled as "Neural Art" or "AI Art". In February 2016, a work made by the computational artist Memo Akten using "Deepdream" [51], was sold at a benefit auction for 8,000 USD [1]. Only two years after, the narrative of Neural Art is verging towards a sci-fi scenario. In October 2018, as reported in the auction house website [10],

> Christie's becomes the first auction house to offer a work of art created by an algorithm.

The work was estimated between 7,000 and 10,000 USD but it sold for the stellar figure of 432,500 USD, almost 45 times its highest estimate, questioning the experts if we are witnessing the birth of a new art market. The interesting fact is that the collective "Obvious", the people behind this work, don't have an art background and don't appear as the artists but as the publishers. This point was largely used to speculate about the autonomy and the creative agency of the algorithm which, for the larger public, now becomes the "real artist".

This has direct implications in fields like law and economy, where our expertise is limited. Therefore, we won't consider the problem from an economic point of view or debating whether algorithms will replace human artists. However, we encourage the community to keep investigating such issues like Somaya and Varshney [58] recently did in regard to the IP rights of autonomous agents.

The interest of the art market into this work is a social indicator raising deeper questions about the relation between art, technology and society that go beyond the commercial facts. This event is giving us the chance to rethink about the role that art and technology have in our lives and how autonomous systems may change this paradigm.

Therefore, this work takes into account the social and cultural value of art as a means of human agency [3] as well as a representation of a culture's identity through time [64]. Whereas the most frequent issue among the specialists concerns the ontology of AI Art or whether machines/algorithms can create "real" art [12, 36], we think a further question, equally important, is left behind and needs to be addressed soon: what are the social and cultural implications

ACM ISBN 978-1-4503-6324-2/19/01...$15.00
https://doi.org/10.1145/3306618.3314233

of interfacing with art autonomously generated by non-human creative agents?

In this work we connect the philosophy of art and the philosophy of science to reflect on the epistemological value of works generated "with" and "by" artificial intelligence. We argue that, by accepting this new paradigm, we are indirectly granting artificial agents to produce a meaningful dialogue with humans. As a result, this may create a further layer of separation between the human creator and the human audience. We conclude by arguing the importance of promoting a culture of responsibility within public institutions and industries, where the endorsement of automation in creative fields is always supported by the development of humans' creative potential.

2 BACKGROUND

Before starting our discussion, we define the concepts that we use throughout the paper so to delimit our scope, avoid misunderstandings and facilitate the reader's comprehension. The examples proposed are mostly referring to the visual arts and music, hence the choice to use the generic term "audience", but we believe the concepts are equally applicable to other art forms.

2.1 Defining art

From Plato, Aristotle to Kant and Adorno, philosophers in every age reflected about the meaning of art and tried to find its definition. This paper will point out some of the theories from the philosophy of art that align with our personal view and are functional to analysing the problem. In particular, we refer to Croce [18] idea that art is a higher form of intuition, therefore a higher type of knowledge reached through expression. Also Altieri [3] describes artistic expressivity as a creative and profound manifestation of human agency. On the other hand, to use the words of Benjamin [6], the work of art contains an "aura", which is connected in part to its uniqueness but also to the intersubjectivity with the audience. It is a quality, hard to define, similar to the "atmosphere of artistic theory" described in Danto [20]. A more pragmatic approach is proposed by Dickie [24] who poses two conditions for art to exist: 1) to be an artifact; 2) some society or sub-group needs to confer the status of "candidate for appreciation". This sub-group could be the artist or more generically what Danto calls the "artworld". These theories reveal some of the properties that Art shows across time and cultures but they are far from being an exhaustive definition. In fact, we agree with Weitz [64, p. 28, p. 27] that art cannot be defined because it "has no set of necessary and sufficient properties".

> Each age, each art-movement, each philosophy of art, tries over and over again to establish the stated ideal only to be succeeded by a new or revised theory, rooted, at least in part, in the repudiation of preceding ones.

Then, he concludes, the problem is not understanding "what is art", rather "what sort of concept is art" and what is the use of it, because "...its very use reveals and demands its openness" [64, p. 30].

2.2 Art as a value

What is the use of art then? Why is art so important for us? The fact that art cannot be accounted for the production of knowledge as true, justified belief was discussed in Stolnitz [60]. However, this view was recently challenged by John [37] who proposes that art creates experiential, conceptual and moral knowledge. According to her, art possesses the epistemic value of initiating a public conversation about the meaning of the works of art. Moreover, it allows comparing one another's views of the world through direct experience, what Novitz [54] calls "empathic knowledge".

Besides, others debated that art is rooted in human biology, stimulates cognitive activity and responds to evolutionary theories [25] making us the "Artful Species" [21]. This is supported by the view expressed in Deacon [22] and DeLoache [23] that human evolution is strongly conditioned by our ability to create symbols like language. Furthermore, in Gesture and Speech [43], primitive figurative art is also proposed as first form of language, not as mimicry rather as symbolic transposition.

2.3 Art and technology

From an evolutionary point of view, art gave us advantage over other species by stimulating our cognitive activities like creativity and imagination, reinforcing social structures and working as a symbolic form of language. Equally important for human evolution is technology. Our ability to stand on two feet allowed us to use hands for grasping tools, freeing the frontal organs like the face and the mouth, facilitating the development of the frontal cortex and the language [43].

The development of the technical tools and our biological evolution are therefore two-way coupled. As proposed by Leroi-Gourhan [44], the technical tools are a manifestation of the "milieu intérieur", the ensemble of cultural and mental traditions of a group, including art. In other words, humans evolve technical tools to express their nature. The technical tools, then, shape the environment, which, in return, influences our evolution in a feedback loop.

These views are shared by Simondon [57] who strongly argues against the conceptual division between human nature and technology inasmuch technology is the human's interface to nature. Similarly to Leroi-Gourhan, he proposes that technical objects are not just instruments but embed humanity and possess different "modes of existence". In his view, the technical objects' genesis is conditioned by their embedded functions and the usage humans make of them. This vision shifts the technical evolution from an anthropocentric to a coupling system where it is not just the person deciding what to change in the tool but it is the device itself that "calls" for a particular change. Any alienation from technology, therefore, comes from the misunderstanding of its "essence".

The strong link between technology and art was also discussed by Heidegger [35] who proposes art as the "realm" in which technology brings forward its "essence". He concludes arguing that both art and technology are means through which humans "reveal" epistemic knowledge.

A more contemporary approach to understand how technology is deeply intertwined with our biological system (and our society) is proposed by Katherine Hayles [33, 34] who coined the idea of the "Cognitive Nonconscious" (CN), an "assemblage" of human and technical "cognizers". Halyes explains that algorithms differ from traditional devices (e.g., a hammer), because they show "modes of awareness", cognitive and biological properties like recursivity and autopoiesis. She also anticipates that the CN will show its influence in the creative arts, which is what we are experiencing these days with the AI Art.

In this framework, technology and art are entangled agents that shape our species, not only biologically but also culturally.

2.4 Defining AI

As it happens in philosophy of art, there are also many attempts to define intelligence by psychologists and scientists [42] which makes it difficult to agree on what an artificial intelligence may be. In this work, we refer to the most accepted definition of Artificial Intelligence commonly attributed to Marvin Minsky [65]:

> The performance of tasks, which, if performed by a human, would be deemed to require intelligence".

An artificial intelligence can be simple cellular automata, as well as a deep learning architecture, an evolutionary algorithm or any other computational system that responds to the above definition. The intelligence in these computational systems is not only defined by their technical complexity, rather by the way they interact with their physical or virtual environment, including themselves. For instance, the ability to walk is a form of intelligence that belongs to both the kinetic sculptures by Theo Jansen and to a walking robot [40]. Both enact the walking by virtue of computational means and in both systems the environment influences their behaviour. The substantial difference between these systems is their ability to learn. Despite their uncanny naturalistic behaviour, Jansen's "Strandbeests" possess only a mechanical function that is producing the walking, whereas a robot can compute its own internal representation of the world and adapt to the environment. According to Lake et al. [41], this type of model-based reasoning is crucial for an AI to simulate human-like learning, decision making and, most importantly, autonomy [9]. There are generically two types of AI: the one that emulates human cognition and the one that doesn't. Although creativity, together with higher forms of cognition, are computationally difficult to emulate [41] any AI able of showing creative features and produce a work of art, should belong to the first group, more specifically to Computational Creativity.

2.5 Computational Creativity

Computational Creativity (CC) is that branch of AI that deals with both natural and artificial creativity [65]. The field lives at the intersection of AI, cognitive science and philosophy with the aim to understand human creativity through computational models. Boden [7] is one of the first attempts to discuss the similarities between human creativity and a computational process.

In the next subsection, we will explain when Computational Arts (CA) and Computational Creativity start overlapping.

2.6 Computational Arts

Computers have been used to make art since the early 60's by both computer scientists with artistic inclination like Frieder Nake or Michael Noll [53] and by artists interested in using computational tools as a new medium like Vera Molnar [50] or Harold Cohen [13]. Although the word "computational" in the arts can assume very different nuances, here we focus on those works using software.

We talk about CC when the computational element is able to produce novelty through a process of creation and evaluation as described, for instance, in Colton, Charnley and Pease [15]. So, the computational arts can be seen as a spectrum of activities defined by the margin of control the human artist has on the final output or, to reverse the viewpoint, the level of autonomy of the computational system.

On one side of the spectrum we have tools, like Processing [55] or OpenFrameworks [46] which give the artists complete control to write their own software and make art using code as a medium. Moving along, there are interactive tools built for augmenting the artist's expressivity, for instance by using bio-signals or gestures [61]. In this case, the feedback loop between the device and the human gives the artist just partial control on the final output. On the other hand, the computational element is still completely dependent on the human input and has no creative agency, autonomy or ability to learn. Then, towards the other end of the spectrum, there are tools like the Wekinator [28], a meta-instrument that learns from the artist expressivity "on-the-fly". The Wekinator uses machine learning (ML) methods but it is still actively guided by the user. Another example of intelligent tool is "Paul" [62] the drawing robot which, in this case, becomes an extension of its creator, the artist Patrick Tresset. The robot has a high level of autonomy but the algorithms allowing Paul's drawings control both its behaviour and drawing style, somehow limiting its creative agency. Almost at the end of the spectrum there are intelligent systems collaborating with the artist. Some examples are the "drawing investigations" series by Sougwen Chung and her robots or the flying spheres by Random International, moved by swarm algorithms responding to dancers' movements. Finally, there is Computer Generative Art where the human intervention is zero or minimal [8]. To this group belong works made with AI like AARON [13] or the Painting Fool [14], evolutionary algorithms [4] or the most recent works by artists like Mario Klingemann, Anna Riddler or Robbie Barrat made using Generative Adversarial Networks (GAN) [30]. In these works, the creative agency of the artificial agent becomes more complex and has the potential to achieve a higher autonomy.

The spectrum metaphor is obviously a simplification of the whole range of computational tools available, which is functional for us to summarise the dynamics between computers and humans in the arts and introduce the next subsection.

2.7 AI, art and autonomy

At the end of the spectrum described above, there is a list of open source DNNs used to create AI art. For instance, Deepdream and Style Transfer (ST) [29] are based on Convolutional Neural Networks (CNN), which are architectures inspired by biological features like animal's visual perception. Further architectures used in the arts are the Recursive Neural Network (RNN) and Long Short-Term Memory (LSTM), models inspired by cognitive features of the human brain like memory. These networks are largely used for tasks involving sequentiality, for instance handwriting or related to language. In particular, the Variational Auto Encoder (VAE) published by Magenta [32] has found applications in the arts related to music and drawing. A more recent architecture is the Generative Adversarial Network (GAN), model able to generate visual or sonic outputs [26] by using a minimax game between a generative and discriminative network [30]. Both RNNs and GANs are generative models that can be deemed, to a certain extent, as "creative" and "autonomous" because, once properly trained, they can potentially produce novelty with little human intervention.

Special types of GANs are the Creative Adversarial Networks (CAN) [27] which were used in a recent experiment to investigate the creative potential of autonomous agents. In this case, according to the authors, there is no human intervention during the creative process of the CAN, however, the models were still trained on existing human creative works. CANs differ from GANs by introducing a second signal from the discriminator model, which acts as an antagonist of the first one and allows the generator model to produce more interesting results.

Nonetheless, the concept of autonomy is not only defined by the architecture itself, rather by how that architecture is used. Although DNNs have an embedded level of autonomy even in supervised learning [47], the margin of control the artist has on the final output is still considerably wide. The human artist can chose the type of data used to train the model and the training parameters which concur to influence the aesthetic of the work. Most importantly, there can be human judgment in the evaluation of what will be considered the final work of art. However, it is also true that these parameters could be automated.

Therefore, the level of autonomy in computational systems is something left to the human to decide during the software design phase. Two significant examples are AARON [48] and The Painting Fool [14], creative artificial intelligence designed to produce art in complete autonomy, including the evaluation phase.

3 DISCUSSION

Who is making the art then, the human, the machine or both? We find ourselves facing again the dilemma of the division between humans and technology, which, as we have suggested earlier, is a conceptual misunderstanding. As much as humans and technology are deeply entwined, also art making is never separated by the tools needed for crafting that work.

A good work of art is the result of a synergy between the human artist and the tools used. The device can be the voice, the body, the language, a brush, a chisel, a violin or an algorithm. However, in AI Art, the problem of the devices' autonomy seems central. Therefore, trying to understand what "autonomous" means is crucial. Without delving into the philosophical facets of the term, at today, we may agree that autonomy in the computational arts, should be seen as a spectrum and never as a binary feature.

So, how is it possible that one of the world's most important auction houses sold a piece of art made "by" an AI? Is this just a clever marketing strategy or is there something more to reflect about? If we consider the facts, Christie's has already promoted the print as made "by" an AI, which means that the "artworld" (or at least an influential part of it) is recognising and reinforcing this narrative for the larger audience. Although the collective Obvious demystified AI as the real artist [5], this doesn't change the fact that the make-believe system [63] is triggered and that the general public is already engaged with this plot. In 20 years from now, this work of art might not represent the best example of AI Art at present, rather what AI means in the popular culture today: the idea of complete "autonomy" of an artificial system, able to achieve high forms of human abilities like art making.

If we think about both Simondon and Leroi-Gourhan theories of technical evolution, we may argue that these could be those events allowing the technical objects to evolve. The idea of AI has an embedded quality of "complete autonomy" that pings back to the environment (in this case our society) and "calls" for its evolution. In other words, it is by injecting in the collective imagination the idea of "complete autonomy" of an artificial system that this technical object aims for its next evolutionary step.

An important point expressed by Leroi-Gourhan [43] concerns the balance between the biological and technical human nature. He thought the high rate of technical evolution may risk to reduce, rather than augment, human abilities like creativity [38]. Nevertheless, we don't know what new artificial systems would be capable of, neither how they will integrate in the CN and influence our biological and cognitive beings. This is why, promoting the importance of a transparent technology, also in the mass-media, could prevent the spread of distorted information and at the same time it may balance the speed of the technical evolution with our biological needs.

AI models are evolving rapidly and their results are surprising the specialists by the day. The uncanny results of today's GANs were probably not imaginable 4 years ago. So, we cannot think that these models will stop evolving. In AI Art, we are not referring just to the realism of the output, but mostly about how the architecture itself will be able to emulate our cognitive systems or predict our sense of beauty.

This last point, in particular, is something that we should care about because it could be exploited for capitalistic aims. The cognitive potential of algorithms as described in Hayles [33], could be used to condition our preferences and choices, similarly to the subliminal messages in the commercial ads of the 60's.

Imagine the scenario where, at a party, the music and the digital art on the walls are generated so to maximise the guest's comfort. Imagine also that this generative art synchronises with the guest's bio-signals. As nice as this may sound, these features could be a powerful application for art therapy, for instance, but it is easy to imagine how it could be used to control people's behaviour for other aims and in other fields. So, the real question to ask here is "cui prodest?" Who will benefit from this and also, how this may change our relation with art overall?

3.1 Implications for our society

Considering how much art is rooted in our evolution, we are not keen to believe that human artists will be completely replaced by artificial systems. However, we cannot just undergo the changes happening in the creative industry as much as in the art field, without opening a constructive critique.

Here we discuss the implications of autonomous creative AI in the arts from three main perspectives: 1) the artist; 2) the audience; 3) the medium.

3.2 From the artist's perspective

Artificial automation in the arts is a powerful feature: it can help artists to boost their creative process but it may also produce the opposite effect. By continuously automating tasks, there is risk to "unlearn" that specific ability, as observed in Schirrmacher [56] and Greenfield [31]. The plasticity of the brain works in two ways and although the complete unlearning process is not easy to achieve [11], since the boom of internet, we have already changed some fundamental cognitive skills like the way we use our memory [59].

Compared to more traditional devices, automatic creative systems may offer the artists an easier way to create pleasant works. At the same time, this may increase the risk, for those artists, to "unlearn" their own creative process or for young artists to bypass this important stage. As Croce [18] observes, it is indeed the very process of creation and expression that leads the artists to a higher knowledge of the world and themselves.

Algorithms can already produce paintings in the style of Picasso or music in the style of Bach. What algorithms still miss are the symbolic values and life experiences allowing those artists to create their works. These could be intended as the "artworld" from the artist's perspective, essential for the emergence of the artist's style which is the artist's deepest essence [3].

A more conceptual risk for the artists working with autonomous systems is to confuse the technical achievement with the aim of the artwork, reducing the piece to an empty technical virtuosity. Although the technical achievement can be an important part of the creative process, as Heidegger [35] observed, technology concerns mostly with the action of "ordering" which prevents the full achievement of epistemic knowledge.

This shouldn't prevent the artists to explore the potentialities of any new technical tool because the concept of art changes continuously and this may be just a new way to experience it. Nonetheless, we wouldn't advocate for a complete shift of the creative process into the technical realm because this could create a separation between the artist and the audience as we explain further.

3.3 From the audience's perspective

In the previous section, we discussed how art could benefit society by producing experiential knowledge, social debate about moral problems and empathic knowledge. We have also presented theories arguing that art is a form of symbolic language that highly influenced how we evolved as a species. We can therefore think the work of art as an interface between the artist and the audience, a symbolic layer that works as a meta-dialogue between humans.

Similarly, we referred to technology as an interface between humans and nature, a coupling system that helps the understanding and the shaping of the world around us. In this sense, the differences between art and technology reduce whereas the similarities of their roles in our lives increase: both are functional for revealing epistemic knowledge.

So, in what way is a work made "by" an AI different from an art piece made by a human when it comes to the subjective experience?

The experiment by Moffat and Kelly [49] shows that there is human bias against machine-generated music, greater in musicians than non-musicians. However, a most recent study with CANs [27] shows a higher human preference for works made by an AI. This suggests that there is much more to investigate about our relation with artificially generated art.

How we react to a piece of music, words of a poem, colours of a painting or the moves of a dancer, are highly conditioned by our biology and the aesthetic of that work. However, the way in which we experience that work is very subjective [45] and conditioned by our personal beliefs. The knowledge we get from a work of art, in fact, may be very much rooted in our personal history.

Computational agents that interact with our biological feedback have been used already to explore human empathy [16, 19], which could be seen as a primitive emulation of "empathic knowledge". Similarly, artificial moral agents [2] could be used by an artificial artist to challenge the audience moral opinion. Therefore, we cannot exclude a priori that a work of art could cause in the audience a significant experiential knowledge just because is generated by an AI.

So, there seem to be no real differences for the audience if an art piece is made by a human or by an AI. Later, we will explain why we think this is not the case.

3.4 From the medium's perspective

Drawing from Hayles [34], an AI differs from a brush or a violin because is a cognitive "actor", part of the Cognitive Nonconscious assemblage. If the work of art, as we described above, is the interface between the artist and the audience, in the scenario where an AI autonomously generates a piece of art, we would assist to an unprecedented division between the human artist and the human audience.

We can see this as a bifurcation of the discourse that for ages we had as a collective, using art as a language. At the same way we are shifting from human interlocutors to AI for solving daily task like navigating the cities or answering personal questions, similarly, we could end up by preferring an artificial creative agent to generate our music instead of promoting independent young musicians. Is this direction leading to further social isolation?

It can be argued artificial artists could represent a new "mode of existence" of the technical object and as such, they will always contain humanity. The dialogue, in this sense, would be between that "humanity" and the human audience. However, the cognitive properties of the artificial system will co-exist with the ones of the human creator. Therefore, unless the human involvement in the technical process is made explicit, this could still be considered as a further layer of separation between the human creator and the audience.

4 CONCLUSION

Today's AI models are still very dependent on human input and the myth of complete creative autonomy doesn't seem impending, at least for some AI experts.

Although none of the scenarios depicted above are intrinsically good or bad, we need to bring attention on the role that human have now in creating the artificial models, and what type of human bias will be used to make them because these factors will condition the evolution of the technical objects of tomorrow, so us.

Creativity and imagination are defining characteristics of our species and we think it is fundamental that artists keep exploring technical tools like AI for the benefits of both science and art. However, automating creativity, expressivity and imagination needs particular care and a joint discussion between the humanities and the science. The complexity of this subject should extend beyond the CC community and reach towards the larger fields of philosophy, neuroscience, the arts and the AI, which we aim to promote with this work.

In different modes, art and technology are both mirrors of ourselves. On one hand, art making is a meta-language to expresses things we cannot communicate with other means. It is a way to make sense of the world around us as well as ourselves as a species. Similarly, technology helps us to reveal the nature of things. In fact, the same idea of AI is arguably today's highest form of "humanised" technology, yet another way to know human nature. Therefore, in the framework of "human-technology" as the Cognitive Nonconscious assemblage, it seems almost physiological that art and AI are merging.

To the best of our knowledge there are no studies investigating how automation influences human creativity and expressivity or the audience's experience and behaviour, probably because it would require a long-term observation. This, along with the other questions emerged in this paper, suggests that further interdisciplinary research in this direction is greatly needed. This could help improving the artists' awareness of technology as well as the scientists' understanding of creative process with overall positive outcomes for our collective.

In conclusion, we believe it is fundamental to reinforce the link between the sciences and the arts by fostering human imagination, promoting a culture of awareness of both human creativity and expressivity as well as the meaning of technology in our everyday lives. We think these are things to be achieved only with the support of public institutions, industries and a continued interdisciplinary dialogue.

ACKNOWLEDGMENTS

EPSRC and AHRC Centre for Doctoral Training in Media and Arts Technology. Mike Cook for the useful chat.

REFERENCES

[1] Memo Akten. 2016. All watched over by machines of loving grace: Deepdream edition. https://goo.gl/Ut33ha.
[2] Colin Allen, Gary Varner, and Jason Zinser. 2000. Prolegomena to any future artificial moral agent. *Journal of Experimental & Theoretical Artificial Intelligence* 12, 3 (2000), 251–261.
[3] Charles Altieri. 1987. Style as the Man: What Wittgenstein offers for speculating on Expressive Activity. *The Journal of aesthetics and art criticism* 46 (1987), 177–192.
[4] Rui Filipe Antunes, Frederic Fol Leymarie, and William Latham. 2014. Two decades of evolutionary art using computational ecosystems and its potential for virtual worlds. *Journal For Virtual Worlds Research* 7, 3 (2014).
[5] Jason Bailey. 2018. The AI Art At Christie's Is Not What You Think. https://goo.gl/CS8fiS.
[6] W. Benjamin. 2008. *The Work of Art in the Age of Mechanical Reproduction.* Penguin Books Limited. https://books.google.co.uk/books?id=ZucuzeiI-24C
[7] Margaret A Boden. 1992. *The creative mind: Myths and mechanisms.* Cardinal.
[8] Margaret A Boden and Ernest A Edmonds. 2009. What is generative art? *Digital Creativity* 20, 1-2 (2009), 21–46.
[9] Matthew Botvinick, David GT Barrett, Peter Battaglia, Nando de Freitas, Darshan Kumaran, Joel Z Leibo, Timothy Lillicrap, Joseph Modayil, Shakir Mohamed, Neil C Rabinowitz, et al. 2017. Building machines that learn and think for themselves. *Behavioral and Brain Sciences* 40 (2017).
[10] Christies. 2018. Is artificial intelligence set to become art's next medium? https://goo.gl/4LDZjX.
[11] Richard E Clark. 2014. Resistance to change: Unconscious knowledge and the challenge of unlearning. In *Fostering change in institutions, environments, and people.* Routledge, 83–102.
[12] Mark Coeckelbergh. 2017. Can Machines Create Art? *Philosophy & Technology* 30, 3 (2017), 285–303.
[13] Harold Cohen. 1988. How to Draw Three People in a Botanical Garden.. In *AAAI*, Vol. 89. 846–855.
[14] Simon Colton. 2012. The painting fool: Stories from building an automated painter. In *Computers and creativity.* Springer, 3–38.
[15] Simon Colton, John William Charnley, and Alison Pease. 2011. Computational Creativity Theory: The FACE and IDEA Descriptive Models.. In *ICCC.* 90–95.
[16] Simon Colton, Michel F Valstar, and Maja Pantic. 2008. Emotionally aware automated portrait painting. In *Proceedings of the 3rd international conference on Digital Interactive Media in Entertainment and Arts.* ACM, 304–311.
[17] Michael Cook, Simon Colton, and Jeremy Gow. 2017. The ANGELINA Videogame Design System—Part II. *IEEE Transactions on Computational Intelligence and AI in Games* 9, 3 (2017), 254–266.
[18] Benedetto Croce. 1904. *Estetica come scienza dell'espressione e linguistica generale: teoria e storia.* R. Sandron.
[19] Antonio Daniele. 2016. This Is Not Private. In *Proceedings of the 2016 CHI Conference Extended Abstracts on Human Factors in Computing Systems.* ACM, 3831–3834.
[20] Arthur Danto. 1964. The artworld. *The journal of philosophy* 61, 19 (1964), 571–584.
[21] Stephen Davies. 2012. *The artful species: aesthetics, art, and evolution.* OUP Oxford.
[22] Terrence W Deacon. 1998. *The symbolic species: The co-evolution of language and the brain.* WW Norton & Company.
[23] Judy S DeLoache. 2004. Becoming symbol-minded. *Trends in cognitive sciences* 8, 2 (2004), 66–70.
[24] George Dickie. 1969. Defining art. *American philosophical quarterly* 6, 3 (1969), 253–256.
[25] Ellen Dissanayake. 2001. *Homo aestheticus: Where art comes from and why.* University of Washington Press.
[26] Chris Donahue, Julian McAuley, and Miller Puckette. 2018. Synthesizing Audio with Generative Adversarial Networks. *arXiv preprint arXiv:1802.04208* (2018).
[27] Ahmed M. Elgammal, Bingchen Liu, Mohamed Elhoseiny, and Marian Mazzone. 2017. CAN: Creative Adversarial Networks, Generating "Art" by Learning About Styles and Deviating from Style Norms. *CoRR* abs/1706.07068 (2017). arXiv:1706.07068 http://arxiv.org/abs/1706.07068
[28] Rebecca Fiebrink, Dan Trueman, and Perry R Cook. 2009. A Meta-Instrument for Interactive, On-the-Fly Machine Learning.. In *NIME.* 280–285.
[29] Leon A. Gatys, Alexander S. Ecker, and Matthias Bethge. 2016. Image Style Transfer Using Convolutional Neural Networks. In *The IEEE Conference on Computer Vision and Pattern Recognition (CVPR).*
[30] Ian Goodfellow, Jean Pouget-Abadie, Mehdi Mirza, Bing Xu, David Warde-Farley, Sherjil Ozair, Aaron Courville, and Yoshua Bengio. 2014. Generative adversarial nets. In *Advances in neural information processing systems.* 2672–2680.
[31] Susan Greenfield. 2004. *Tomorrow's people: how 21st-century technology is changing the way we think and feel.* Penguin UK.
[32] David Ha and Douglas Eck. 2018. A Neural Representation of Sketch Drawings. In *International Conference on Learning Representations.* https://openreview.net/forum?id=Hy6GHpkCW
[33] N Katherine Hayles. 2014. Cognition everywhere: The rise of the cognitive nonconscious and the costs of consciousness. *New Literary History* 45, 2 (2014), 199–220.
[34] N Katherine Hayles. 2017. *Unthought: The power of the cognitive nonconscious.* University of Chicago Press.
[35] Martin Heidegger. 1977. *The question concerning technology, and other essays.* Garland Publishing, INC.
[36] Aaron Hertzmann. 2018. Can Computers Create Art?. In *Arts*, Vol. 7. Multidisciplinary Digital Publishing Institute, 18.
[37] Eileen John. 2001. Art and knowledge. *The Routledge Companion to Aesthetics* (2001).
[38] Christopher Johnson. 2011. Leroi-Gourhan and the Limits of the Human. *French studies* 65, 4 (2011), 471–487.
[39] Wang-Cheng Kang, Chen Fang, Zhaowen Wang, and Julian McAuley. 2017. Visually-aware fashion recommendation and design with generative image models. In *Data Mining (ICDM), 2017 IEEE International Conference on.* IEEE, 207–216.
[40] Scott Kuindersma, Robin Deits, Maurice Fallon, Andrés Valenzuela, Hongkai Dai, Frank Permenter, Twan Koolen, Pat Marion, and Russ Tedrake. 2016. Optimization-based locomotion planning, estimation, and control design for the atlas humanoid robot. *Autonomous Robots* 40, 3 (01 Mar 2016), 429–455. https://doi.org/10.1007/s10514-015-9479-3
[41] Brenden M Lake, Tomer D Ullman, Joshua B Tenenbaum, and Samuel J Gershman. 2017. Building machines that learn and think like people. *Behavioral and Brain Sciences* 40 (2017).

[42] Shane Legg, Marcus Hutter, et al. 2007. A collection of definitions of intelligence. *Frontiers in Artificial Intelligence and applications* 157 (2007), 17.
[43] André Leroi-Gourhan. 1993. *Gesture and speech.* miT Press.
[44] André Leroi-Gourhan. 2012. *Milieu et techniques: évolution et techniques.* Albin Michel.
[45] Joseph Levine. 1983. Materialism and qualia: The explanatory gap. *Pacific philosophical quarterly* 64, 4 (1983), 354–361.
[46] Zach Lieberman, Theodore Watson, Arturo Castro, et al. 2009. Openframeworks. https://goo.gl/41tycE.
[47] Zachary C Lipton. 2018. The mythos of model interpretability. *Queue* 16, 3 (2018), 30.
[48] Pamela McCorduck. 1991. *Aaron's code: meta-art, artificial intelligence, and the work of Harold Cohen.* Macmillan.
[49] D. Moffat and M. Kelly. 2006. An investigation into people's bias against computational creativity in music composition. In *The Third Joint Workshop on Computational Creativity (ECAI 2006).* Universita di Trento, Universita di Trento, Trento, Italy.
[50] Vera Molnar. 1975. Toward aesthetic guidelines for paintings with the aid of a computer. *Leonardo* (1975), 185–189.
[51] Alexander Mordvintsev, Christopher Olah, and Mike Tyka. 2015. Inceptionism: Going deeper into neural networks. https://goo.gl/W5hjt3.
[52] Danil Nagy, Damon Lau, John Locke, Jim Stoddart, Lorenzo Villaggi, Ray Wang, Dale Zhao, and David Benjamin. 2017. Project Discover: An application of generative design for architectural space planning. In *SimAUD 2017 Conference proceedings: Symposium on Simulation for Architecture and Urban Design.*
[53] A Michael Noll. 1994. The beginnings of computer art in the United States: A memoir. *Leonardo* (1994), 39–44.
[54] David Novitz. 1987. *Knowledge, Fiction, and Imagination.* Temple University Press.
[55] Casey Reas and Ben Fry. 2007. *Processing: a programming handbook for visual designers and artists.* Number 6812. Mit Press.
[56] Frank Schirrmacher. 2010. *La libertà ritrovata. Come (continuare a) pensare nell'era digitale.* Codice Edizioni.
[57] Gilbert Simondon. 1980. On the mode of existence of technical objects. Translated from the French by Ninian Mellamphy. *University of Western Ontario* (1980).
[58] Deepak Somaya and Lav R Varshney. 2018. Embodiment, Anthropomorphism, and Intellectual Property Rights for AI Creations. In *AAAI/ACM Conference on Artificial Intelligence, Ethics and Society.*
[59] Betsy Sparrow, Jenny Liu, and Daniel M Wegner. 2011. Google effects on memory: Cognitive consequences of having information at our fingertips. *science* (2011), 1207745.
[60] Jerome Stolnitz. 1992. On the cognitive triviality of art. *Aesthetics and the Philosophy of Art: The Analytic Tradition: An Anthology* 32, 3 (1992), 191–200.
[61] Atau Tanaka. 2000. Musical performance practice on sensor-based instruments. *Trends in Gestural Control of Music* 13, 389-405 (2000), 284.
[62] Patrick Tresset and Frederic Fol Leymarie. 2013. Portrait drawing by Paul the robot. *Computers & Graphics* 37, 5 (2013), 348–363.
[63] Kendall L Walton. 1978. Fearing fictions. *The Journal of Philosophy* 75, 1 (1978), 5–27.
[64] Morris Weitz. 1956. The role of theory in aesthetics. *The journal of aesthetics and art criticism* 15, 1 (1956), 27–35.
[65] Geraint A Wiggins. 2006. A preliminary framework for description, analysis and comparison of creative systems. *Knowledge-Based Systems* 19, 7 (2006), 449–458.

Speaking on Behalf of: Representation, Delegation, and Authority in Computational Text Analysis

Eric P. S. Baumer
Computer Science & Engineering
Lehigh University
Bethlehem, PA, USA
ericpsb@lehigh.edu

Micki McGee
Sociology and Anthropology
Fordham University
Bronx, NY, USA
mmcgee@fordham.edu

ABSTRACT

Computational tools can often facilitate human work by rapidly summarizing large amounts of data, especially text. Doing so delegates to such models some measure of authority to speak on behalf of those people whose data are being analyzed. This paper considers the consequences of such delegation. It draws on sociological accounts of representation and translation to examine one particular case: the application of topic modeling to blogs written by parents of children on the autism spectrum. In doing so, the paper illustrates the kinds of statements that topic models, and other computational techniques, can make on behalf of people. It also articulates some of the potential consequences of such statements. The paper concludes by offering several suggestions about how to address potential harms that can occur when computational models speak on behalf of someone.

CCS CONCEPTS

• **Human-centered computing** → *Collaborative and social computing*; • **Social and professional topics** → *Codes of ethics*; People with disabilities; • **Computing methodologies** → *Topic modeling*.

KEYWORDS

ethics, delegation, sociology, topic modeling

ACM Reference Format:

Eric P. S. Baumer and Micki McGee. 2019. Speaking on Behalf of: Representation, Delegation, and Authority in Computational Text Analysis. In *2019 AAAI/ACM Conference on AI, Ethics, and Society (AIES'19), January 27–28, 2019, Honolulu, HI, USA.* ACM, New York, NY, USA, 7 pages. https://doi.org/10.1145/3306618.3314292

1 INTRODUCTION

Computational techniques such as topic modeling [7, 18] are designed to identify latent themes in a corpus. Such themes, or "topics," provide an overview both of the corpus as a whole and of individual documents.

Such techniques offer a double-edged sword. On the one hand, they can provide a comprehensive overview of vast corpora in a fraction of the time it would take a human to read equivalent content.

On the other hand, the model can also be used to make authorial/authoritative claims about the corpus. Appeals to algorithmic authority suggest that the model can tell us what the corpus is *really* about [13]. The topics observable as latent patterns can be informative even, and perhaps especially, when the author(s) themselves are unaware of them [39, 53]. Thus, techniques such as topic modeling can be used to gain insights not only about a corpus of documents but also about the author(s) themselves.

In short, this paper highlights how computational techniques can be used to speak on behalf of someone (else) [cf. 8]. It does so with a case study that applies topic modeling [7] to analyze blogs written by parents of children on the autism spectrum. Autism spectrum disorder (ASD) is a complex and often contentious condition. Claims made in this domain bear significance beyond those made in the kinds of corpora usually used to test topic modeling (academic papers, newspaper articles, etc.) [7, 18].

This case study demonstrates two points about speaking-on-behalf-of. First, it offers examples of the kinds of things that techniques such as topic modeling can be made to say on behalf of someone. Second, it leverages the domain of ASD parenting to illustrate the complex and contentious consequences of an algorithmic system making claims about the topics that a person discusses. After considering some ethical dimensions of this specific case, the paper concludes by describing how the issues raised here apply beyond topic modeling and should be considered more broadly in computational analysis of social data.

2 BACKGROUND

2.1 Sociologies of Translation

Prior work in a number of fields has explored sociological relations among humans and non-human artifacts [9, 26–28, 32]. So-called processes of "translation" deal with how technological artifacts speak and/or act on behalf of humans. As an example, consider how municipal authorities might encourage drivers to slow down where construction crews are working [28]. They might: station flaggers near the construction zone; install a cardboard cut out of a person holding a flag; install a sign with a flag connected to it; or even install a speed bump in the road. These are instances of a form of translation referred to as *delegation*, which bestows onto a non-human artifact the agency to perform a task otherwise performed by humans.

More relevant here are cases where one group speaks on behalf of another. Callon [9] details a case of complex discussions over

ACM ISBN 978-1-4503-6324-2/19/01...$15.00
https://doi.org/10.1145/3306618.3314292

whether or not to restock scallops in a bay off the northwest coast of France. Throughout the process, certain subsets come to be seen as representative of larger groups. Most notably, three researchers studying the bay scallop population end up speaking on behalf of: the larger community of specialists, the fishers who catch and sell the scallops, and even the scallops themselves. Callon refers to this process as *mobilisation*, where spokespersons are selected as representative of a larger group. Similarly, Latour [26] develops a concept of *inscription*. Codified laboratory procedures are used to create representations (visual or otherwise) of data about observations of a phenomenon. These representations then speak as authoritative accounts of (i.e., in place of) the phenomenon, rather than needing others to observe the phenomenon itself.

While such prior work provides important conceptual devices, the case at hand differs in an important way from those previously analyzed. Namely, this paper does not deal with data or traces from sociological translations that have already occurred [cf. 14, 27]. Rather, this paper points out the ways that computational techniques *could* be used as an instrument of translation. Put differently, we show how topic modeling, and similar techniques, can be used to speak on behalf of those whose data are being analyzed. We demonstrate both the kinds of things that such techniques can be made to say on someone's behalf, as well as potential consequences of such translations.

2.2 Doing Justice in Textual Analysis

Another relevant line of inquiry comes from work in gender studies. Butler [8] describes the case of an individual (pseudonym John/Joan) who underwent multiple gender reassignments, not all of which occurred at their own volition[1]. In critically considering what textual materials are available for analysis – a mix of research papers in psychological and medical journals, along with popular journalism and books – Butler notes that she has no way of directly knowing the person John/Joan themself.

> "I do not know this person and have no access to this person, I am left to be a reader of a selected number of words, words that I did not fully select, *[words] that were selected for me*, recorded from interviews and then chosen by those who decided to write their articles on this person for journals [....] *I have been given fragments of the person, linguistic fragments* of something called a person." [8, p. 630, emphasis added]

Butler asks, under these circumstances, how one might do justice to this person, who is present only in the form of "linguistic fragments."

This paper asks an analogous question. As with Butler, this paper considers how we might treat responsibly the people discussed in texts we analyze. Similar to her case, the linguistic fragments are not selected by us as authors. However, the linguistic fragments in this case are not chosen by medical researchers or by popular journalists. Instead, they are chosen by an algorithm, specifically, topic modeling. This paper considers the unique consequences of this difference for socially just computational research.

[1]Applying queer theory to autism and neurodiversity [51], while generative, exceeds this paper's scope

2.3 Relationship with Algorithmic Bias

Algorithmic bias deals with situations where the results of a computational system disproportionately impact members of certain groups [4, 46]. Often, the algorithms in question involve AI and/or machine learning models. Disparate impacts can occur along numerous lines, such as race [2, 19, 46], gender [33, 34], sexual orientation [1], or other attributes.

These issues emerge in part because algorithmic systems can carry an air of objectivity. Prior work has shown how people interacting with such systems can perceive a computer as being a more credible than other people or even than themselves [e.g., 1, 13]. This prior work documents how people at times perceive such judgments as more objective because they are made by a machine rather than directly by a human. This perception occurs despite significant research into the assumptions, commitments, politics, and other human judgments embedded in these systems [1, 4, 15, 46, 49].

This paper raises a related but distinct issue. Work on algorithmic bias deals with, for instance, racial biases in the classification of individuals into different risk categories [2]. In contrast, this paper focuses on how computational systems can, akin to the processes of translation and mobilisation described above [9, 26], speak on behalf of people whose data are being analyzed. This paper considers both the kinds of statements that computational tools can make on behalf of others, and the consequences of such sociological translations.

3 CASE STUDY: BLOGGING ASD PARENTING

3.1 Data

The second author drafted a list of 68 candidate blogs based on their familiarity with the autism blogging community. From this initial list, we removed blogs with technical errors (e.g., the owner had stopped paying hosting fees), blogs that did not focus on autism and/or parenting, and blogs with fewer than ten posts.

This process resulted in a list of 46 blogs with publicly accessible content that focused on issues related to parenting ASD children. These blogs were scraped using a custom scraper based on scrapy [44] and hand-tuned to each blog's HTML structure. Doing so generated 31,976 documents with a total of 17,273,079 words (words per document M=540.2, Mdn=430), of which 8,136,071 were non-stopword tokens.

3.2 Methods

A topic model was fitted to these data using LDA [7] as implemented in MALLET [35] via the r-mallet package [37]. Different numbers of topics were tested between 20 and 75. A model with 50 topics was selected based on coherence [29, 30] and on manual review.

The stopword list began with a small set of high frequency articles, determiners, conjunctions, prepositions, etc., as well as related contractions. The stopword list intentionally omitted gendered pronouns (she, him, etc.). Contrary to Schofield et al. [43], we included several proper names in the stopword list. Initial training indicated that many topics were composed of proper names that were unique to one blog. Because we sought to identify linguistic patterns that transcended multiple blogs, the stopword thus included proper names (and their possessive versions) that appeared in more than 1% of the documents.

4 TOPICS AND THEIR INTERPRETATION

This section shows several topics resulting from the above analysis. For each, it lists the top 20 highest probability terms for the topic and describes the content of documents with high proportions of the topic. It does *not* offer extended quotes from any document, as performing an internet search for such quotes would easily identify the bloggers – and identifying individuals with topics is the exact ethical issue this paper raises. Where possible, very short phrases are quoted directly, but only when we determined that they would not enable easy identification of the blogger. See the discussion for further ethical considerations.

Topics were chosen for this section in two ways. First, we describe topics with the highest coherence [29, 30]. Since coherence aligns with human judgments about topic quality, researchers would likely use coherence to guide examination of topic modeling results. Second, the authors hand-picked a set of topics around a particularly contentious issue for ASD parents: early childhood vaccination. All topics presented in this section are numbered using a ranking based on coherence [29, 30]. T_1 is the most coherent topic, T_{50} is the least.

Each of these topics is then analyzed using an inductive, sociological approach [cf. 10, 16], iteratively reading through the representative documents for each topic. Doing so both aligns with recent social scientific and humanist use of topic modeling [e.g., 6, 21, 42]. It also provides a sense of what these topics *mean* and what the ramifications might be for an individual blogger to be associated with one of these topics.

4.1 High Coherence Topics

This subsection lists the five topics with highest coherence [29, 30]. Each topic is listed with the top 20 highest probability words for the topic, as well as a brief description the topic's focus, based on a reading of the documents with the highest proportion of that topic.

> T_1 – *spectrum, disorder, autism, diagnosis, disorders, asd, social, developmental, intellectual, syndrome, criteria, dsm, asperger,'s, mental, disability, diagnostic, new, test, functioning, symptoms*

Most of the top documents for this topic deal with the status of autism as a diagnosable condition. These documents discuss in depth the particular criteria used to diagnose autism, especially changes from DSM-IV to DSM-V. Many documents quote the DSM extensively, and many are also critical of it.

> T_2 – *food, eat, eating, dinner, ice, cream, store, ate, lunch, chocolate, milk, restaurant, diet, chicken, table, cheese, drink, pizza, breakfast, foods*

Many documents in this topic provide recipes, often with commentary. Some discuss adapting to dietary restrictions, e.g., finding adequate milk and chocolate substitutes to make dairy-free, gluten-free "hot chocolate." Others deal with normative issues around what foods kids *should* or should *not* be eating, e.g., whether it is acceptable for a school to serve ice cream as a snack.

> T_3 – *school, education, special, needs, schools, children, students, inclusion, child, classroom, district, learning, teachers, public, educational, mainstream, parents, system, environment, local*

The documents with highest proportions of this topic focus on special education in schools. There is a significant focus on whether (and how) current special education programs do or do not meet the needs of autistic children.

> T_4 – *autism, brain, study, genetic, environmental, research, mercury, children, studies, disorders, may, factors, development, disease, cells, exposure, risk, mitochondrial, researchers, immune*

This topic features documents that engage in intricacies of scientific literature around autism. Many of these documents focus specifically on studies about the relationship between autism and vaccines, though rarely discussing such issues as vaccination schedules. Examples include discussing studies about the neurotoxicity of aluminum, or about chemical pathways by which mercury (specifically, mercuric chloride, or $HgCl_2$) may trigger brain inflammation. Others examine issues such as links between folic acid supplements and gene expression, or the relationship between ASD and mitochondrial dysfunction. Many documents include extensive quotes from the scientific literature they cover.

> T_5 – *hair, wear, blue, wearing, red, white, color, pink, dance, isaac, green, black, shirt, dress, shoes, art, beautiful, favorite, cut, image*

This topic could likely be best summarized as "fashion." Top documents feature discussion of clothing, haircuts, dancing (with an emphasis on costumes), colors, etc. The few exceptions still feature this language prominently, e.g., a knock-knock joke about colors.

Few of these topics would likely be seen as controversial. That is, it seems unlikely that a blogger in our data set would find it problematic to be associated with any of the above topics. That ambivalence might not hold for the topics described below.

4.2 Vaccine Topics

The relationship between ASD and early childhood vaccination has received, and continues to receive, significant attention [23, 47, 48]. This analysis identified three separate topics that include the term "vaccine" within the top 20 highest probability terms. These topics are listed here in order of decreasing coherence [30]. To reiterate, the topic number indicates each topic's ranking among the 50 topics in terms of coherence.

> T_7 – *vaccine, vaccines, children, health, thimerosal, mercury, safety, public, cdc, vaccination, parents, flu, medical, vaccinated, disease, information, government, research, year, years*

Most of the documents for this topic discuss debates over the relationship between ASD and vaccination. The large majority suggest that early childhood vaccination causes autism. In one example, a blogger describes how their state's official health website includes a claim that no evidence suggests a causal link between autism and vaccines. The blogger argues that this claim is false, and offers a 9000 word post chronicling their attempts to have the claim removed from the state's website, attempts which ultimately failed. Other examples include coverage of vaccine-related deaths, lists of all vaccines that contain thimerosal (a mercury-based preservative), and commentary on changes in vaccine schedules.

The large majority of these documents make an implicit or explicit link between autism and vaccines. Others take the position that current vaccinations are vital for public health, for example, criticizing the delayed vaccination schedules advocated by some. That caveat made, an accurate label for this topic would be "anti-vax," i.e., focused on documents that oppose childhood vaccination.

Contrast this first topic with a second topic also pertaining to vaccines.

> T_{23} – *autism, vaccines, science, vaccine, case, court, evidence, david, cause, kirby, his, offit, cases, scientific, jenny, link, mccarthy, believe, generation, story*

This topic revolves more around coverage of a specific events. Examples include particular court cases (e.g., the US Federal "Omnibus Autism" case [36]), the retraction by Salon of a story by Robert F. Kennedy Jr. that mercury-based thimerosal in vaccines caused autism [31], or the former head of the US National Institutes of Health (NIH) calling for more investigation into autism and vaccines.

In contrast to T_7 above, this topic includes more direct confrontations, sometimes even personal attacks. For example, specific journalists or media personalities (David Kirby, Brian Deer, Jenny McCarthy, etc.) are criticized for propagating rumors and false information. In other cases, bloggers specifically name, link to, and argue with one another. Anecdotally, much of this argumentation occurs in blogs' comment sections, which were not scraped here. Thus, some of the discourses invoked in these arguments may not be entirely captured here. Overall, though, T_{23} deals less with the details of vaccination schedules or thimerosal content and more with contestation and argumentation.

The third topic dealing with vaccines is much more focused than the above two.

> T_{45} – *wakefield, mmr, his, andrew, research, paper, measles, wakefield's, study, children, medical, deer, brian, vaccine, article, lancet, published, cdc, virus, evidence*

In 1998, The Lancet published a paper by Wakefield et al. [48] with evidence that vaccines containing thimerosal caused autism. In 2010, that paper was retracted, due concerns both over tampering with the study and over the ethics of participant recruitment [47].

The majority of documents with high proportions of this topic deal with these events. Examples include listing the specific charges against Wakefield and his colleagues, details of how the case was decided, and commentary and criticism about media coverage surrounding the initial paper and its retraction. Most of these posts are not sympathetic toward Wakefield.

Thus, these three topics capture three distinct positions. Documents representative of the first topic, T_7, argue that vaccines *do* cause autism. Documents representative of the third topic, T_{45}, argue that vaccines do *not* cause autism. Documents representative of the second topic, T_{23}, do not take a clear cut position but rather emphasize the conflict and controversy surrounding the issue.

In this way, the topic model can speak on behalf of the bloggers [9, 27, 28, 32]. Rather than read through thousands of blog posts, an individual may consult only the topic modeling results to understand the position an individual blogger holds on vaccines and ASD. Journalists, the lay public, and even academic reviewers may lack the time, the data, the expertise, or the interest to investigate the original source texts being analyzed. While researchers employing topic modeling sometimes return to these texts [5, 24, 38, 42], they virtually never check their interpretations with the original texts' authors on whose behalf the model speaks.

5 DISCUSSION

5.1 Topic Modeling, Legitimacy, and Authority

"To speak for others is to first silence those in whose name we speak" [9, p. 216]. This potential for associating specific topics with individual bloggers/authors has numerous ramifications. First, knowing the authors that most commonly discuss a given topic can alter the interpretation of that topic. For example, T_{45} above comes primarily from neurodiversity advocates, who claim that ASD is part of natural genetic variation. The same topic might mean something different if it occurred most often in the blogs of activists who regularly organize protests to decry conspiracies between government regulators and the pharmaceuticals industry. Just as individual statements are interpreted through the lens of the person who speaks them, so, too, could computationally-identified patterns be interpreted through the lens of the persons in whose writings they occur.

Second, knowing the prominent topics for a document or author can change perceptions thereof. For example, in one post primarily about T_3, a parent discusses their decision to enroll their own children in a separate special-needs school, but makes no prescriptive statements. In contrast, most other posts for that topic advocate strongly that separate learning environments are better for many children than "inclusive" policies that require all children, regardless of abilities or disabilities, to receive instruction in a regular classroom. Not only might the first blogger wish to avoid association with this view, but seeing the rest of the topic gives that first post a more judgmental connotation than it might have otherwise.

Third, this summarization capacity can co-opt authors' voices. Much like the devices used to measure the attachment of bay scallops [9], there is a potential for topic models to represent the people whose data they analyze. This representational capacity, which lies at the heart of this paper's argument, comes into stark relief in this case.

Parents are, in some contexts, granted a unique kind of authority in understanding their own children. For example, Jenny McCarthy famously described her "mommy instincts" that led her to suspect vaccination had a negative impact on her child [52]. In Weber's terms, such charismatic authority contrasts with the rational authority used in the scientific discourse around vaccines [22]. A topic model, then, has the potential to co-opt such discourses, to present its results as a representation of what parents of ASD children *really* say and think. Put differently, using a topic model trained on texts written by parents can channel the legitimacy of parental voice, without needing to check one's interpretation of the topics against those on whose behalf the topic model is speaking.

Fourth, claims about what a corpus *really* says can have significant ramifications, particularly with respect to ASD. As alluded above (e.g., in T_1), the very status of ASD is a point of contention with significant consequences. If ASD results from deliberate collusion between regulators and pharmaceutical companies, then legal action is warranted that could likely result in reparations for families, as well as support from agencies such as Social Security. However, if the argument advanced by neurodiversity advocates were taken to its logical conclusion – that ASD is not a disorder, but a difference in the wide range of human functioning – then its status as a medical and/or psychiatric condition could be destabilized, potentially leading to a reduction in supports and services. Thus, families might not be eligible to receive the kinds of public aid provided for children with neurological disorders.

5.2 Our Ethics of Translation

The case presented here – ASD parenting blogs – requires some unique ethical considerations. This paper's contribution is founded on the claim that the kinds of analyses presented here can be highly sensitive. Topic modeling results are sometimes presented along side quotes from highly highly representative documents for each topic [5, 24, 38, 42]. However, internet search engines make it easy to link such verbatim quotes to the blogs from which they came, a link we argue can cause harm. Thus, individual quotes or references to specific blogs were carefully obfuscated to protect bloggers' identities from deanonymization.

However, doing so slightly undermines our own authority. Since we have not named our data sources, others cannot replicate our analysis. Similarly, omitting verbatim quotes makes it difficult to validate our interpretations of these topics. Comparisons could be made with Goffman [17] intentional obfuscation of sources to protect them, and, potentially, with the mixed reactions to Goffman's work [25, 45]. Since this paper does not aim to make definitive claims about autism, parenting, etc., the veracity of our results is less of an issue. Instead, the focus is how the results *could* be used to speak on behalf of these bloggers without their consent.

Finally, an additional layer of delegation [28] or mobilisation [9] occurs in this case. Many of these blogs discuss children, but the blogs rarely include the words or voices of the children themselves. Similar to Butler [8], we are analyzing linguistic fragments about a person that were chosen neither by us nor by the person themself. While important to note here, full treatment of this issues exceeds the scope of this paper.

5.3 Broader Implications

This paper uses the example of topic modeling to illustrate how computational systems can speak on behalf of people, as well as some of the consequences thereof. However, these arguments apply much more broadly to a wide variety of computational models and tools.

For example, Niculae et al. [40] analyze and group news sources based on their patterns of quoting excerpts from US presidential addresses. Notably, their analysis suggests that a media outlet's style has more to do with its quoting patterns than its partisan leanings do. For instance, Fox News (known for its conservative slant) is highly similar to the New York Times (known for its liberal slant). These two mainstream media sources are both more similar to each other than either is to smaller, expressly partisan sites, such as The Blaze (conservative) or The Nation (liberal). While analytically interesting, these various sites may not necessarily appreciate being labeled as similar to or different from one another. Put differently, this analysis speaks on behalf of these sites, declaring for them sets of affiliations with which each site's authors or owners may not agree.

As another example, machine learning models are used for a variety of predictive tasks, such as when a smoker who is trying to quit will likely relapse [39], or an individual's personality traits [53]. In these and similar cases, the model speaks on behalf of the person whose data are being analyzed. Such pronouncements may be associated with the claim that this person may not be aware of their own personality, mental health state, likelihood for smoking relapse.

Such issues can arise even with seemingly simple technologies. Sentiment analysis [20, 41], as an example, is often used to determine the sentiment expressed about a given entity. For instance, reviews may collectively indicate that a given restaurant has good sushi but bad service [50]. However, such techniques could be used equally readily to make claims about the authors of documents, e.g., that author X tends on average to be more positive than author Y. Once again, the computational tool assessing sentiment can speak on behalf of authors, expressing both their sentiments about certain entities and their general disposition.

6 CONCLUSION AND FUTURE DIRECTIONS

To address the issues raised here, future researchers can work directly with the people whose data they are analyzing. Participatory design [3, 12] has a history of incorporating multiple stakeholders into design processes. This paper's authors are developing an analogous approach, incorporating the participants whose data we have collected into the processes of analyzing and interpreting those data.

The questions described above can also be incorporated into ethics review processes. However, the practicalities of doing so are tricky at best. It is virtually impossible to know detailed results from computational models before running them. This constraint creates a challenges, not only for researchers, but also for an Institutional Review Boards (IRB) reviewing study proposals.

Researchers can also obfuscate their data, as done here. On the one hand, doing so makes it more difficult for others to verify a paper's results and interpretations. On the other hand, social scientific research has a history of using "composites" when presenting results. In this approach, all the details for each composite come from the data, but individual aspects may be synthesized from different participants' experiences to obfuscate participants' identities. Analogous to techniques for differential privacy [11], future research could benefit from exploring means of creating computational composites that resemble the original data in a meaningful way but eschew verbatim quotes and other identifying information.

As a final note, not every domain is equally sensitive. Using corpora such as Associated Press articles or scientific journal proceedings, both of which are common in topic modeling research [7, 18], may not carry the same implications as blogs written by parents of ASD children. Thus, this paper offers but one case illustrating potential consequences of computational models that speak on behalf of people. More generally, the paper offers a conceptual vocabulary that researchers across multiple domains can use in considering both the degree and kinds of sensitivity associated with computational analyses of social data.

7 ACKNOWLEDGEMENTS

Thanks do David Mimno, Jed Brubaker, and members of Lehigh's DAS Lab for helpful conversations; to Jatin Bharwani, Hannah Lambert, and Yin Luo for implementation contributions; and to the bloggers for sharing their stories and their lives.

REFERENCES

[1] Mike Ananny. 2011. The Curious Connection between Apps for Gay Men and Sex Offenders. *The Atlantic* (April 2011).
[2] Julia Angwin, Jeff Larson, Surya Mattu, and Lauren Kirchner. 2016. Machine Bias. *Pro Publica* (May 2016).
[3] Peter M. Asaro. 2000. Transforming Society by Transforming Technology: The Science and Politics of Participatory Design. *Accounting, Management and Information Technologies* 10, 4 (2000), 257–290.
[4] Solon Barocas and Andrew D. Selbst. 2016. Big Data's Disparate Impact. *California Law Review* 104, 3 (2016), 671–732.
[5] Eric P. S. Baumer, Shion Guha, Emily Quan, David Mimno, and Geri K. Gay. 2015. Missing Photos, Suffering Withdrawal, or Finding Freedom? How Experiences of Social Media Non-Use Influence the Likelihood of Reversion. *Social Media + Society* 1, 2 (2015). https://doi.org/10.1177/2056305115614851
[6] Eric P. S. Baumer, David Mimno, Shion Guha, Emily Quan, and Geri K. Gay. 2017. Comparing Grounded Theory and Topic Modeling: Extreme Divergence or Unlikely Convergence? *Journal of the Association for Information Science and Technology (JASIST)* 68, 6 (June 2017), 1397–1410. https://doi.org/10.1002/asi.23786
[7] David M. Blei, Andrew Y. Ng, and Michael I. Jordan. 2003. Latent Dirichlet Allocation. *Journal of Machine Learning Research* 3, Jan (2003), 993–1022.
[8] Judith Butler. 2001. Doing Justice to Someone: Sex Reassignment and Allegories of Transsexuality. *GLQ: A Journal of Lesbian and Gay Studies* 7, 4 (Sept. 2001), 621–636.
[9] Michel Callon. 1986. Some Elements of a Sociology of Translation: Domestication of the Scallops and the Fishermen of Saint Brieuc Bay. In *Power, Action and Belief: A New Sociology of Knowledge?*, John Law (Ed.). Routledge, London, 196–223.
[10] Kathy Charmaz. 2006. *Constructing Grounded Theory: A Practical Guide through Qualitative Analysis.* SAGE Publications, London.
[11] Cynthia Dwork and Aaron Roth. 2014. The Algorithmic Foundations of Differential Privacy. *Foundations and Trends® in Theoretical Computer Science* 9, 3–4 (Aug. 2014), 211–407. https://doi.org/10.1561/0400000042
[12] Pelle Ehn. 1988. *Work-Oriented Design of Computer Artifacts.* Lawrence Erlbaum Associates, Hillsdale, NJ.
[13] Motahhare Eslami, Aimee Rickman, Kristen Vaccaro, Amirhossein Aleyasen, Andy Vuong, Karrie Karahalios, Kevin Hamilton, and Christian Sandvig. 2015. "I Always Assumed That I Wasn't Really That Close to [Her]": Reasoning About Invisible Algorithms in News Feeds. In *Proc ACM Conf on Human Factors in Computing Systems (CHI).* ACM, Seoul, 153–162. https://doi.org/10.1145/2702123.2702556
[14] R. Stuart Geiger and David Ribes. 2011. Trace Ethnography: Following Coordination through Documentary Practices. In *Hawaii International Conference on System Sciences.* https://doi.org/10.1109/HICSS.2011.455
[15] Tarleton Gillespie. 2013. The Relevance of Algorithms. In *Media Technologies*, Tarleton Gillespie, Pablo Bockzkowski, and Kirsten Foot (Eds.). MIT Press, Cambridge, MA.
[16] Barney G. Glaser and Anselm L. Strauss. 1967. *The Discovery of Grounded Theory.* Routledge, Oxon and New York.
[17] Alice Goffman. 2014. *On the Run.* U Chicago Press, Chicago.
[18] Thomas L. Griffiths and Mark Steyvers. 2004. Finding Scientific Topics. *Proc Nat'l Acad Sci* 101 (June 2004), 5228–5235. https://doi.org/10.1073/pnas.0307752101
[19] Alex Hern. 2015. Flickr Faces Complaints over 'offensive' Auto-Tagging for Photos. *The Guardian* (May 2015).
[20] C.J. Hutto and Eric Gilbert. 2014. VADER: A Parsimonious Rule-Based Model for Sentiment Analysis of Social Media Text. In *Proc Int'l Conf on Weblogs and Social Media (ICWSM).* AAAI, Ann Arbor, MI, 216–225.
[21] Matthew L. Jockers. 2013. *Macroanalysis: Digital Methods & Literary History.* U Illinois Press, Chicago.
[22] Stephen Kalberg. 1980. Max Weber's Types of Rationality: Cornerstones for the Analysis of Rationalization Processes in History. *The American J of Sociology* 85, 5 (1980), 1145–1179.
[23] David Kirby. 2005. *Evidence of Harm: Mercury in Vaccines and the Autism Epidemic.* St. Martin's Press, New York.
[24] Lauren F. Klein, Jacob Eisenstein, and Iris Sun. 2015. Exploratory Thematic Analysis for Digitized Archival Collections. *Digital Scholarship in the Humanities* 30 (Dec. 2015), i130–i141. https://doi.org/10.1093/llc/fqv052
[25] Alex Kotlowitz. 2014. Deep Cover: Alice Goffman's 'On the Run'. *The New York Times* (June 2014).
[26] Bruno Latour. 1987. *Science in Action: How to Follow Scientists and Engineers Through Society.* Harvard University Press, Cambridge, Mass.
[27] Bruno Latour. 1992. Where Are the Missing Masses? The Sociology of a Few Mundane Artifacts. In *Shaping Technology / Building Society: Studies in Sociotechnical Change*, Wiebe E. Bijker and John Law (Eds.). MIT Press, Cambridge, MA, 225–258.
[28] Bruno Latour. 1993. Ethnography of a "High-Tech" Case: About Aramis. In *Technological Choices: Transformations in Material Culture since the Neolithic*, Pierre Lemonnier (Ed.). Routledge, London, 372–398.
[29] Jey Han Lau and Timothy Baldwin. 2016. The Sensitivity of Topic Coherence Evaluation to Topic Cardinality. In *Proc Annual Mtg of the North Amer Chapter of the Assoc for Comp Ling (NAACL).* ACL, San Diego, CA, 483–487.
[30] Jey Han Lau, David Newman, and Timothy Baldwin. 2014. Machine Reading Tea Leaves: Automatically Evaluating Topic Coherence and Topic Model Quality. In *Proc of the Annual Mtg of the Euro Chapter of the Assoc for Comp Ling (EACL).* ACL, Gothenburg, Sweden, 530–539.
[31] Kerry Lauerman. 2011. Correcting Our Record | Salon.Com. https://www.salon.com/2011/01/16/dangerous_immunity/.
[32] John Law. 1984. On the Methods of Long-Distance Control: Vessels, Navigation and the Portuguese Route to India. *The Sociological Review* 32 (May 1984), 234–263. https://doi.org/10.1111/j.1467-954X.1984.tb00114.x
[33] Philipp Lenssen. 2007. Did You Mean: "He Invented"? http://blogoscoped.com/archive/2007-05-07-n56.html.
[34] Philipp Lenssen. 2007. Google Stops "Did You Mean: He Invented". http://blogoscoped.com/archive/2007-05-24-n36.html.
[35] Andrew Kachites McCallum. 2002. MALLET: A Machine Learning for Language Toolkit.
[36] Donald G. McNeil, Jr. 2009. Court Says Vaccine Not to Blame for Autism. *The New York Times* (Feb. 2009).
[37] David Mimno. 2013. Mallet: A Wrapper around the Java Machine Learning Tool MALLET.
[38] John W. Mohr and Petko Bogdanov. 2013. Topic Models: What They Are and Why They Matter. *Poetics* 41, 6 (Dec. 2013), 545–569. https://doi.org/10.1016/j.poetic.2013.10.001
[39] Elizabeth L. Murnane and Scott Counts. 2014. Unraveling Abstinence and Relapse: Smoking Cessation Reflected in Social Media. In *Proc ACM Conf on Human Factors in Computing Systems (CHI).* ACM Press, Toronto, ON, 1345–1354. https://doi.org/10.1145/2556288.2557145
[40] Vlad Niculae, Caroline Suen, Justine Zhang, Cristian Danescu-Niculescu-Mizil, and Jure Leskovec. 2015. QUOTUS: The Structure of Political Media Coverage As Revealed by Quoting Patterns. In *Proc ACM Conf on World Wide Web (WWW).* Florence, Italy, 798–808. https://doi.org/10.1145/2736277.2741688
[41] Bo Pang and Lillian Lee. 2008. Opinion Mining and Sentiment Analysis. *Found. Trends Inf. Retr.* 2, 1-2 (Jan. 2008), 1–135. https://doi.org/10.1561/1500000011
[42] Lisa M. Rhody. 2013. Topic Modeling and Figurative Language. http://journalofdigitalhumanities.org/2-1/topic-modeling-and-figurative-language-by-lisa-m-rhody/.
[43] Alexandra Schofield, Måns Magnusson, and David Mimno. 2017. Pulling Out the Stops: Rethinking Stopword Removal for Topic Models. In *Proc Annual Mtg of the Euro Chapter of the Assoc for Comp Ling (EACL).* ACL, Valencia, Spain, 432–436.
[44] scrapy. 2018. Scrapy, a Fast High-Level Web Crawling & Scraping Framework for Python. https://github.com/scrapy/scrapy.
[45] Jesse Singal. 2015. The Internet Accused Alice Goffman of Faking Details in Her Study of a Black Neighborhood. I Went to Philadelphia to Check. https://www.thecut.com/2015/06/i-fact-checked-alice-goffman-with-her-subjects.html.
[46] Latanya Sweeney. 2013. Discrimination in Online Ad Delivery. *Commun. ACM* 56, 5 (2013), 44–54. https://doi.org/10.1145/2460276.2460278
[47] The Editors of The Lancet. 2010. Retraction—Ileal-Lymphoid-Nodular Hyperplasia, Non-Specific Colitis, and Pervasive Developmental Disorder in Children. *The Lancet* 375, 9713 (Feb. 2010), 445. https://doi.org/10.1016/S0140-6736(10)60175-4
[48] A. J. Wakefield, S. H. Murch, A. Anthony, J. Linnell, D. M. Casson, M. Malik, M. Berelowitz, A. P. Dhillon, M. A. Thomson, P. Harvey, A. Valentine, S. E. Davies, and J. A. Walker-Smith. 1998. RETRACTED: Ileal-Lymphoid-Nodular Hyperplasia, Non-Specific Colitis, and Pervasive Developmental Disorder in Children. *The Lancet* 351, 9103 (Feb. 1998), 637–641. https://doi.org/10.1016/S0140-6736(97)11096-0
[49] Langdon Winner. 1980. Do Artifacts Have Politics? *Daedalus* 109, 1 (1980), 121–136.
[50] Koji Yatani, Michael Novati, Andrew Trusty, and Khai N. Truong. 2011. Review Spotlight: A User Interface for Summarizing User-Generated Reviews Using Adjective-Noun Word Pairs. In *Proc ACM Conf on Human Factors in Computing Systems (CHI).* ACM, Vancouver, BC, 1541–1550.
[51] Melanie Yergeau. 2017. *Authoring Autism: On Rhetoric and Neurological Queerness.* Duke U Press, Durham, NC.
[52] Emily Chivers Yochim and Vesta T. Silva. 2013. Everyday Expertise, Autism, and "Good" Mothering in the Media Discourse of Jenny McCarthy. *Communication and Critical/Cultural Studies* 10, 4 (Dec. 2013), 406–426. https://doi.org/10.1080/

14791420.2013.841320
[53] Wu Youyou, Michal Kosinski, and David Stillwell. 2015. Computer-Based Personality Judgments Are More Accurate than Those Made by Humans. *Proc Nat'l Acad Sci* 112, 4 (Jan. 2015), 1036–1040. https://doi.org/10.1073/pnas.1418680112

Killer Robots and Human Dignity

Daniel Lim
daniel.lim672@dukekunshan.edu.cn
Duke Kunshan University
Kunshan, China

ABSTRACT

Lethal Autonomous Weapon Systems (LAWS) have become the center of an internationally relevant ethical debate. Deontological arguments based on putative legal compliance failures and the creation of accountability gaps along with wide consequentialist arguments based on factors like the ease of engaging in wars have been leveraged by a number of different states and organizations to try and reach global consensus on a ban of LAWS. This paper will focus on one strand of deontological arguments—ones based on human dignity. Merely asserting that LAWS pose a threat to human dignity would be question begging. Independent evidence based on a morally relevant distinction between humans and LAWS is needed. There are at least four reasons to think that the capacity for emotion cannot be a morally relevant distinction. First, if the concept of human dignity is given a subjective definition, whether or not lethal force is administered by humans or LAWS seems to be irrelevant. Second, it is far from clear that human combatants either have the relevant capacity for emotion or that the capacity is exercised in the relevant circumstances. Third, the capacity for emotion can actually be an impediment to the exercising of a combatant's ability to treat an enemy respectfully. Fourth, there is strong inductive evidence to believe that any capacity, when sufficiently well described, can be carried out by artificially intelligent programs.

KEYWORDS

lethal autonomous weapons, human dignity, emotion

ACM Reference Format:

Daniel Lim. 2019. Killer Robots and Human Dignity. In *AAAI/ACM Conference on AI, Ethics, and Society (AIES '19), January 27–28, 2019, Honolulu, HI, USA.* ACM, New York, NY, USA, 6 pages. https://doi.org/10.1145/3306618.3314291

1 BACKGROUND

The Convention for Certain Conventional Weapons (CCW), organized under the United Nations in the 1980s, has sought to restrict or prohibit the use of weapons that are deemed excessively injurious or whose effects are deemed indiscriminate. The convention has successfully levied international restrictions on weapons ranging from landmines to incendiary weapons. More recently, the CCW has added lethal autonomous weapon systems (LAWS), or killer robots, to their agenda. Though there is a lively debate over definitions I will use Wikipedia (https://en.wikipedia.org/wiki/Lethal_autonomous_weapon) to put a working definition of LAWS on the table:

> Lethal autonomous weapons (LAWs) are a type of autonomous military robot that can independently search and engage targets based on programmed constraints and descriptions. LAW are also called lethal autonomous weapon systems (LAWS), lethal autonomous robots (LAR), robotic weapons, or killer robots.

The key phrase in this definition is: 'independently search and engage targets.' LAWS are independent in that they can operate without direct and immediate human oversight. Moreover, they not only *search* for targets they also *engage* targets. That is, they deploy lethal force.

In 2014, signifying its growing prominence on the international stage, the CCW established a Group of Governmental Experts (GGE), involving Russia, China, and the U.S. among others, to investigate the ethical dimensions of emerging technologies relevant to the development of LAWS. (https://www.unog.ch/80256EE600585943/(httpPages)/7C335E71DFCB29D1C1258243003E8724?OpenDocument)

A diverse group of voices has been raised against the development of LAWS. In 2015, more than 1,000 AI researchers signed and published an open letter from the Future of Life Institute calling for a ban on LAWS. (https://futureoflife.org/open-letter-autonomous-weapons/) Included in this list are well-known technologists like Elon Musk. In 2018, at two of the most recent meetings of the GGE, a number of non-governmental actors made statements in support of banning LAWS. Here is an excerpt from a statement given by the Holy See:

> In this regard, the Holy See wishes to remind that a classic foundation of legal systems is the recognition of the human person as a responsible subject that could be sanctioned for his/her wrongdoing and be obliged to provide redress for the damage caused. This notion of responsibility originates from the profound reality of the human person as a free and rational being. An autonomous system has no intention. It merely implements and elaborates algorithms but it does not possess intentions as such. Autonomous weapons systems that hide the accountable and responsible subject are unacceptable. [13]

Academic think tanks, like the Center for the Study of Existential Risk at Cambridge University (https://www.cser.ac.uk/), have also echoed similar sentiments against the development of LAWS.

AIES '19, January 27–28, 2019, Honolulu, HI, USA

ACM ISBN 978-1-4503-6324-2/19/01...$15.00
https://doi.org/10.1145/3306618.3314291

2 SOME ARGUMENTS

A non-negligible portion of the public, academia, and industry are united in resisting the development of LAWS. They have leveraged a variety of arguments in support of their position. These arguments might usefully be divided along deontological and consequentialist lines.

Many deontological arguments are based on legal compliance failures. Some, relying on International Humanitarian Law (IHL), claim that LAWS do not meet the requirements for distinction (distinguishing civilians from combatants) and proportionality (the force of attacks must properly balance the military advantage it will produce against the civilian damage it will incur). Daniele Amoroso and Guglielmo Tamburrini argue that:

> [LAWS must be] capable of respecting the principles of distinction and proportionality at least as well as a competent and conscientious human soldier. [1]

At present, LAWS are not as good as human soldiers in most (if not all) situations.

Of course, many will agree that LAWS, based on the current state of technology, fail to meet these requirements. But this seems to be beside the point since nobody is arguing that LAWS that fail to meet these requirements should be deployed. Consequently, this can only serve as a contingent reason for banning LAWS. Besides, betting against technology, is more often than not, a losing strategy. Recent history has shown, time and again, that machines can encroach on and eventually surpass human expertise when domains are clearly specified. Human world champions in Chess, Jeopardy, and Go can all attest to this. The interesting question is what we should do about LAWS that *do* meet the requirements of distinction and proportionality.

Other deontological arguments have focused on International Criminal Law and the so-called accountability (or responsibility) gap that LAWS create because decision making regarding the use of force will be carried out by non-human entities.[1] Since we don't, at present, have clarity over the concept of non-human accountability, war crimes may lack legal accountability. Who exactly are we supposed to hold accountable for fatalities caused by LAWS? The absence of accountability, some argue, will potentially be a violation of International Criminal Law.

Thomas Simpson and Vincent Müller's [11] discussion of accountability is helpful in this regard. They point out that non-military accountability gaps have already been created by other technologies and are deemed acceptable so long as tolerable thresholds of risk are met. It's difficult to see why analogous reasoning might not usefully be applied to LAWS. Consequently, deontological arguments of this sort may also be contingent on technological developments that can help LAWS cross internationally recognized risk thresholds.

Consequentialist arguments for banning LAWS are not explicitly concerned with legal compliance, they are focused on the balance of good and bad outcomes. 'Narrow' consequentialist arguments focus on battlefield performance outcomes: reduced casualties (military and civilian), increased accuracy in targeting, and freedom from self-preservation. Some have also pointed to massive reductions in financial costs. 'Wide' consequentialist arguments focus on geopolitical outcomes: lowered resistance to starting wars, erosion of democratic processes, proliferation of LAWS to oppressive regimes or terrorist groups, and destabilization on a global scale. Narrow consequentialist arguments are often used in support of developing LAWS while wide consequentialist arguments are often used in support of banning LAWS. A full discussion of the relevant consequentialist factors, however, is beyond the scope of this paper.

So much for this all-too-brief look at some of the arguments that have featured in debates over LAWS. This paper will focus on deontological arguments for banning LAWS based on human dignity. Dignity-based arguments are notable because they are not contingent on the state of technology. The absence of contingency is captured well by Peter Asaro:

> Any automated process, *however good it might be*, and even if measurably better than human performance, ought to be subject to human review before it can legitimately initiate the use of lethal force. This is clearly technologically required for the foreseeable future because autonomous systems will not reach human levels of performance for some time to come. But more importantly, this is a moral requirement... there is a duty not to permit autonomous systems to initiate lethal force without direct human supervision and control. [2]

As Asaro points out, it doesn't matter how good LAWS get. Even if they perform measurably better than humans they must not initiate lethal force without direct human control. For Asaro, it is a moral requirement that only a human can initiate lethal force. In other words, truly autonomous lethal weapons should never be developed or used regardless of its performance.[2] It is my contention, however, that these arguments fail.

3 THE ARGUMENT FROM HUMAN DIGNITY

Let me begin with a sampling of dignity-based arguments for restricting or prohibiting the development of LAWS. In their general statement at the 2014 Convention on Certain Conventional Weapons expert meeting on LAWS, Germany argued that:

> Human control is the foundation of the entire international humanitarian law. It is based on the right to life, on the one hand, and on the right to dignity, on the other. Even in times of war, human beings cannot be made simple objects of machine action. [5]

The idea here is that allowing machines to make lethal autonomous decisions regarding human combatants is to turn these combatants into the 'simple objects of machine action.' This would

[1]An anonymous reviewer noted that the class of non-human actors can also include animals and that this fact should be taken into consideration. While this indeed complicates the issue at hand, since international criminal tribunals have limited their jurisdiction to human beings, any non-human actors can potentially create problems. Hence, my not dealing with animals does not affect my overall argument since all that matters, in this respect, is that LAWS are non-human.

[2]However, it is arguable that there are a number of artifacts already in existence that should be classified as LAWS. These include the SGR-A1 sentry gun and the IAI Harop loitering munition.

rob these combatants of their dignity. This sentiment is also found among academics:

> Delegating the decision to kill a human to an algorithm in a machine, which is not responsible for its actions in any meaningful ethical sense, can arguably be understood to be an infringement on *basic human dignity*, representing what in moral philosophy is known as a malum in se, a wrong in itself. [12]

Call the following argument for a ban on LAWS the Argument from Dignity.

1. If X is killed by a LAWS then X is killed disrespectfully.[3]
2. If X is killed disrespectfully then X's killing is wrong.
3. If X is killed by a LAWS then X's killing is wrong.

Here I use the word 'disrespectful' as shorthand to describe killings that violate human dignity. This argument is clearly valid, but the truth of premise 1 is questionable. As stated, it unhelpfully begs the question. Michael Horowitz nicely points this out:

> While in an esoteric sense, the idea that there is something undignified about dying at the hands of a machine resonates, why is being shot through the head or heart and instantly killed by a machine necessarily worse than being bludgeoned, lit on fire, or killed by a cruise missile strike? [7]

What we need is an independent reason to believe that the antecedent really entails the consequent in premise 1. One might, following Asaro, argue that:

> The very nature of IHL [International Humanitarian Law], which was designed to govern the conduct of *humans* and *human* organizations in armed conflict, presupposes that combatants will be human agents. [2]

This sentiment may be regimented through the following two conditionals:

1A*. If X is killed by a LAWS then X is killed by a non-human.
1B*. If X is killed by a non-human then X is killed disrespectfully.

Premises 1A* and 1B* can be used to replace premise 1. The basic idea, then, is that the international laws that govern war, like the IHL, can only be applied to human combatants. On its own, however, this claim comes off as *ad hoc* and is no better than baldly asserting premise 1. As Asaro freely admits, this is a decidedly anthropocentric way of making his case. It's not enough, therefore, to simply restrict morally permissible combat to humans. We want to know what it is about being human that makes combat between humans morally permissible in a way that combat between humans and non-humans is *not* morally permissible. In short, we need to know what capacity humans have (that non-humans, and more specifically LAWS, fail to have) that make killings by non-humans disrespectful.

4 EMOTION

A natural place to turn for the critical capacity that makes killing respectful is emotion. Aaron Johnson and Sidney Axinn develop this idea as follows:

> Moral commands are based on values, and values are produced and indicated by sacrifices. While robots are aware of following orders, they are not aware of making sacrifices. Artificial Intelligence still has no real notion of sacrifice. Therefore robots have no values of their own, although they are following the values of their programmers. [8]

Similar sentiments can be found in Christof Heyns (2016):

> A machine, bloodless and without morality or mortality, cannot fathom the significance of using force against a human being and cannot do justice to the gravity of the decision. Each instance where force is used against a human being requires that another human being should decide afresh whether to cross that threshold. [6]

But, what does it mean to have a 'real notion of sacrifice' or to 'fathom the significance of using force against a human'? The answer to these questions arguably flows from a subsequent point that Johnson and Axinn make:

> [Robots] are not enraged, as humans may be, by the killing of their buddies. But having no emotions, they do not have the attitude toward people that 'healthy' humans are expected to have. They do not realize the enormity of an error in killing the 'wrong' person. [8]

LAWS do not have a capacity to have a notion of sacrifice or a capacity to fathom the significance of using force against a human because they don't feel anything—they have no emotions. It is only because humans can feel the rage and agony that accompanies the killing of humans that they can understand sacrifice and the use of force against a human. Only then can they realize the 'gravity of the decision' to kill. So maybe the following two conditionals capture the relevant capacity and can be used to replace premises 1A* and 1B*:

1A^. If X is killed by a LAWS then X is killed by a combatant that has no emotion.
1B^. If X is killed by a combatant that has no emotion then X is killed disrespectfully.

Without feeling the pain of losing a friend or feeling the risk of putting one's life on the line it is impossible to understand the gravity of taking another person's life.

Let me now state the Argument from Dignity in its developed form based on the human capacity for emotion:

1A^. If X is killed by a LAWS then X is killed by a combatant that has no emotion.

[3] An anonymous reviewer has suggested that premises 1, 1A*, and 1A^(among others) can be strengthened by taking other non-human entities (e.g. animals) into consideration. It was even claimed, for example, that the truth of 1A* was threatened by the following conditional: if X is killed by a non-human, then X is killed by a LAWS or a non-LAWS (let's call this conditional C). Others might be tempted to draw a similar conclusion. But it seems pretty clear to me that this would be a mistake since the truth of C does not, in any way, threaten the truth of 1A*. Besides, 1A* is arguably a definitional tautology.

1B^. If X is killed by a combatant that has no emotion then X is killed disrespectfully.
2. If X is killed disrespectfully then X's killing is wrong.
3. If X is killed by a LAWS then X's killing is wrong.

5 RESPOSES TO THE ARGUMENT FROM DIGNITY

So much for the Argument from Dignity. There are a number of things that might be said in response to it. First, one might follow Dieter Birnbacher and argue that capacities specific to humans (and missing in LAWS) are irrelevant to the respectful killing of humans:

> This is spurious. Of course, machines cannot comprehend the value of human life. But why should this make a difference to their victims if alternatively they are threatened to be wounded or killed by manned weapons like bombers? For the victims whose dignity is at stake it is a matter of indifference. [4]

Because Birnbacher's notion of human dignity is based on a given person's *subjective* experience of humiliation, it is natural for him to think that whether the killer comprehends the value of human life or not is beside the point. What matters is whether the victim experiences a sense of humiliation in the process of getting killed. Victims being threatened with a potential bombing will not care whether the bomb is dropped by a human or a robot.

While this is an interesting response, I'm concerned that there are objective forms of humiliation. This was poignantly depicted in *The Truman Show*, a film about a person named Truman whose entire life was meticulously constructed in order to serve as the centerpiece of a television show for others to watch. While Truman had no negative subjective experiences, there was an objective sense in which he was being used, even humiliated by unknowingly participating in a manufactured existence. Whether the features of Truman's life are natural or manufactured matter to his dignity. It seems to me that the features of a killer that pertain to the having of certain capacities, like the features of Truman's life, may matter to a victim's dignity.

Second, it is far from clear that human combatants meet the necessary emotion-based requirements in order to kill with respect. So a ban on LAWS could *ipso facto* constitute a ban on human combatants as well. Not all human combatants have the capacity to form the relevant notion of sacrifice or the relevant emotions that accompany risk. Humans lie on a spectrum of conceptual and emotional competence. Does this suggest that some killings are more respectful than others?

Moreover, the mere possession of conceptual and emotional capacities cannot be enough. What is needed is the appropriate *exercise* of these capacities. But can human combatants be expected to routinely meet this requirement? This is an extremely demanding request. Human combatants, especially in the heat of battle, hardly have the time or mental / emotional space to exercise the concept of sacrifice or generate the relevant emotions to make informed decisions each time they deploy lethal force. The battlefield, in my opinion, is arguably the worst possible environment to expect something along these lines.

Third, feeling and emotion have a dark side as well. They have the propensity to yield decidedly negative results. Lisa Feldman Barrett, a psychologist who does research on the formation of emotions, writes:

> Affective realism can also lead to tragic consequences. In July 2007, an American gunner aboard an Apache helicopter in Iraq mistakenly killed a group of eleven unarmed people, including several Reuters photojournalists. The soldier had misjudged a journalist's camera to be a gun. One explanation for this incident is that affective realism caused the soldier, in the heat of the moment, to imbue a neutral object with unpleasant valence. Every day, soldiers must make quick decisions about other people, whether they are embedded in a unit during wartime, on a peacekeeping mission, negotiating in a cross-cultural setting... these quick judgments are extremely difficult to negotiate, especially in such high-stakes, high-arousal settings where errors are often made at the expense of someone's life... A little closer to home, affective realism may also play a role in police shootings of unarmed civilians. The U.S. Department of Justice analyzed shootings by Philadelphia police officers between 2007 and 2013 and found that 15 percent of the victims were unarmed... the human brain is wired for this sort of delusion, in part because moment-to-moment interoception infuses us with affect, which we then use as evidence about the world. [3]

Being forced to make 'quick decisions' in the 'heat of the moment' soldiers can imbue a neutral object with unpleasant valence and their emotions can generate indiscriminate disrespectful killings. Instead of killing as the result of an emotional process that recognizes the gravity of the situation, human combatants may be emotionally overwhelmed by an instinct to survive. Surely, killings in service of self-preservation can hardly be considered respectful of the victim. The victim, after all, is seen as little more than an obstacle to one's survival.

It is also instructive to take note of Barrett's final quoted sentence. This sort of emotionally charged activity is not, according to Barrett, merely an aberration of human cognition. It turns out the human brain is wired for the kind of delusions that can lead to disrespectful killings (military and civilian) because human action is continuously infused with affect. A case, therefore, can be made (and has been made) that the more emotions are removed from the battlefield, the safer the battlefield can become.

Fourth, there is an unwarranted biological chauvinism regarding emotion that is implicit in this way of reasoning. There are no convincing theoretical reasons why machines cannot have emotions. At the very least, because we have to acknowledge the existence of a lively debate on this topic, we cannot assume that emotions are unique to human biological systems. In fact, there seems to be a growing majority of philosophers and scientists that believe emotion (or consciousness in general) is multiply realizable and substrate independent.

Hilary Putnam [10], a philosopher, noted that a wide variety of terrestrial creatures are capable of experiencing pain. If the mental state of experiencing pain were identified with a specific physical-chemical state of the *human* brain then this state must also be a possible state of a reptilian brain or a mollusk's brain if (all should agree) reptiles and mollusks are to be able to experience pain. At the same time, it must not be a possible state of any physically possible creature that cannot experience pain. The requirement that mental states be limited to human biology is far too restrictive, and in Putnam's view, must be relaxed. He rightly defends the claim that mental states must be realizable in multiple physical ways. There is a certain level of independence that mental states have with respect to the physical systems they are realized in.

Max Tegmark, a physicist, echoes these same sentiments:

> In other words, the hardware is the matter and the software is the pattern. This substrate independence of computation implies that AI is possible: intelligence doesn't require flesh, blood or carbon atoms. [15]

While Tegmark, in this quote, is specifically referring to the possibility of intelligence in non-biological systems, he goes on to write in support of an intelligence-based theory of consciousness (and hence emotion) that relies on integrated information (a doubly independent abstraction above physical matter).

Finally, Barrett makes essentially the same observation:

> A mental event, such as fear, is not created by only one set of neurons. Instead, combinations of different neurons can create instances of fear. Neuroscientists call this principle degeneracy. Degeneracy means 'many to one': many combinations of neurons can produce the same outcome. In the quest to map emotion fingerprints in the brain, degeneracy is a humbling reality check. [3]

So there seem to be no principled reasons to think that mental states, like the ones being called on for making respectful killings possible, cannot be realized in LAWS. And if, following Barrett, we conceive of emotions as analogues of perceptions then, given our expected technical mastery over perception, there seem to be no essential roadblocks to our technical mastery over emotions. If emotions are really nothing more than simulations of one's *internal* body in the way that perceptions are simulations of one's *external* world, then, the project of imbuing AI with emotions fits squarely within the realm of possibility.

Tegmark's brief allusion to theories of flight may offer additional help. If we limited our concept of flight to what was available to our ancestors, the *avian* variety, we would've been forced to treat all of our more recent breakthroughs in aviation technologies as something other than genuine flight. We would have been tempted to say that our airplanes don't 'really' fly, they merely simulate flight. But we know better than to give in to this kind of avian-centric thought. Flight is not limited to the flapping of wings. The flapping of wings is just one way of realizing flight. Flight, it turns out, is multiply realizable.

Similarly, emotions fall into the same category. Should we be tempted to say, because the silicon-based hardware used to run AI programs are different from the carbon-based hardware used to run human minds, that AI can't 'really' have emotions, they merely simulate them? It seems to me that such a temptation is guilty of excessive anthropocentrism. There is no *a priori* reason to expect emotion *simpliciter* to be limited to the category of human emotion.

6 CONCLUDING REMARKS

I spent some time discussing the capacity for emotion. There are, no doubt, other candidate capacities that might be used for justifying premise 1 of the Argument from Dignity. For example, following Sparrow [14] and Nagel [9] before him, one might argue that the capacity to engage in interpersonal relationships is necessary for killing respectfully:

> The relationship is fundamentally a relationship between agents... immediately, then, we can see why [LAWS] might be thought to be morally problematic, regardless of how reliable they might be at distinguishing between legitimate and illegitimate targets. When [LAWS] decide to launch an attack the relevant interpersonal relationship is missing. Indeed, in some fundamental sense, there is no one who decides whether the target of the attack should live or die. The absence of human intention here appears profoundly disrespectful. [14]

This could be used to ground the following two conditionals that might replace premise 1:

1A~. If X is killed by a LAWS then X is killed by a combatant without the relevant interpersonal relationship.

1B~. If X is killed by a combatant without the relevant interpersonal relationship then X is killed disrespectfully.

What makes interpersonal relationships possible, according to Sparrow, is the presence of human *intention*. Many of the same things said about human emotions above, however, can easily be adapted as responses to human intentions: (i) it is irrelevant with respect to subjective human dignity, (ii) it is seldom, if ever, exercised by human soldiers in actual combat, (iii) it can have adverse consequences, and (iv) it is far from clear that machines cannot be developed to have genuine intentions.

In this brief discussion, I have tried to argue that a non-contingent ban on LAWS based on human dignity fails. This is not to say that a ban on LAWS cannot be justified. As mentioned above, there are other ways (e.g. accountability gaps, wide consequentialist factors) to argue for a ban. But given the beneficial possibilities that arise out of the advancement of these technologies, it would be detrimental to put a premature moratorium on the development of LAWS.

REFERENCES

[1] Daniele Amoroso and Guglielmo Tamburrini. 2018. The Ethical and Legal Case Against Autonomy in Weapons Systems. *The Global Jurist* 18, 1 (2018). https://doi.org/10.1515/gj-2017-0012

[2] Peter Asaro. 2012. On Banning Autonomous Weapon Systems: Human Rights, Automation, and the Dehumanization of Lethal Decision-Making. *International Review of the Red Cross* 94 (2012), 687–703.

[3] Lisa Feldman Barrett. 2017. *How Emotions are Made: The Secret Life of the Brain.* Houghton Mifflin Harcourt, New York, NY.

[4] Dieter Birnbacher. 2016. Are Autonomous Weapons Systems a Threat to Human Dignity? In *Autonomous Weapons Systems: Law, Ethics, and Policy*, Nehal Bhuta (Ed.). Cambridge University Press, Cambridge, 105–121.

[5] Germany. 2014. Convention of Certain Conventional Weapons Expert Meeting: Lethal Autonomous Weapon Systems - General Statement. Retrieved February 26, 2019 from https://www.unog.ch/80256EDD006B8954/(httpAssets)/97636DEC6F1CBF56C1257E26005FE337/$file/2015_LAWS_MX_Germany.pdf

[6] Christof Heyns. 2016. Human Rights and the use of Autonomous Weapons Systems (AWS) During Domestic Law Enforcement. *Human Rights Quarterly* 38 (2016), 350–378.

[7] Michael Horowitz. 2016. The Ethics and Morality of Robotic Warfare: Assessing the Debate Over Autonomous Weapons. *Daedalus* 145, 4 (2016), 25–36.

[8] Aaron Johnson and Sidney Axinn. 2013. The Morality of Autonomous Robots. *Journal of Military Ethics* 12, 2 (2013), 129–141.

[9] Thomas Nagel. 1972. War and Massacre. *Philosophy and Public Affairs* 1, 2 (1972), 123–144.

[10] Hilary Putnam. 1967. Psychological Predicates. In *Art, Mind, and Religion*, William Capitan and Daniel Merrill (Eds.). University of Pittsburgh Press, Pittsburgh, 37–48.

[11] Frank Sauer. 2016. Just War and Robots' Killings. *Philosophical Quarterly* 66, 263 (2016), 302–322.

[12] Frank Sauer. 2016. Stopping 'Killer Robots': Why Now is the Time to Ban Autonomous Weapons Systems. *Arms Control Today* (2016), 8–13.

[13] Holy See. 2018. Statement by the Permanent Mission of the Holy See to the United Nations. Retrieved February 26, 2019 from https://www.unog.ch/80256EDD006B8954/(httpAssets)/E3015FACDD8757B4C12582F800595E37/$file/2018_GGE+LAWS+2_6a_Holy+See.pdf

[14] Robert Sparrow. 2016. Robots and Respect: Assessing the Case Against Autonomous Weapon Systems. *Ethics and International Affairs* 30, 1 (2016), 98–116.

[15] Max Tegmark. 2017. *Life 3.0: Being Human in the Age of Artificial Intelligence.* Alfred A. Knopf, New York, NY.

Regulating Lethal and Harmful Autonomy: Drafting a Protocol VI of the Convention on Certain Conventional Weapons

Sean Welsh
sean.welsh@pg.canterbury.ac.nz
Department of Philosophy
University of Canterbury
Christchurch, New Zealand

ABSTRACT

This short paper provides two partial drafts for a Protocol VI that might be added to the existing five Protocols of the Convention on Certain Conventional Weapons (CCW) to regulate "lethal autonomous weapons systems" (LAWS). Draft A sets the line of tolerance at a "human in the loop" between the critical functions of select and engage. Draft B sets the line of tolerance at a human in the "wider loop" that includes the critical function of defining target classes as well as select and engage. Draft A represents an interpretation of what NGOs such as the Campaign to Stop Killer Robots are seeking to get enacted. Draft B is a more cautious draft based on the Dutch concept of "meaningful human control in the wider loop" that does not seek to ban any system that currently exists. Such a draft may be more likely to achieve the consensus required by the UN CCW process. A list of weapons banned by both drafts is provided along with the rationale for each draft. The drafts are intended to stimulate debate on the precise form a binding instrument on LAWS would take and on what LAWS (if any) should be banned and why.

CCS CONCEPTS

• **Social and professional topics → Government technology policy.**

KEYWORDS

lethal autonomous weapons systems, regulation

ACM Reference Format:

Sean Welsh. 2019. Regulating Lethal and Harmful Autonomy: Drafting a Protocol VI of the Convention on Certain Conventional Weapons. In *AAAI/ACM Conference on AI, Ethics, and Society (AIES '19), January 27–28, 2019, Honolulu, HI, USA.* ACM, New York, NY, USA, 4 pages. https://doi.org/10.1145/3306618.3314295

1 INTRODUCTION

After six years of UN debate on lethal autonomous weapons systems (LAWS) it seems timely to propose some treaty wording. Here two drafts of key clauses that might be included in a Protocol VI of the Convention on Certain Conventional Weapons (CCW) are provided.

Draft A is based on the notion that a "human in the loop" between select and engage reviewing and approving targeting decisions in real time is the normative requirement. This is based on positions articulated by NGOs.

Draft B is based on the Dutch concept of "meaningful human control in the wider loop" which as it bans nothing that exists today may be more likely to achieve the consensus required for a Protocol VI within the current CCW process. Wording is modelled on Protocols II and IV of the CCW.

These drafts are obviously tentative and incomplete. However, I hope they express some if not all of the essential points nations might see fit to include in a binding treaty instrument.

It is assumed the reader has some familiarity with the moral and legal arguments regarding LAWS and International Humanitarian Law (IHL). These are not addressed in detail here. A summary is provided in [9].

2 RATIONALE

With reference to the three approaches to definition presented in [11], the rationale for the draft wording is as follows. A "technology-centric" definition of "autonomous" is not attempted. This is because technology is a moving target that changes every calendar quarter. Instead, the "human-centred" and "task/functions" definitional approaches described by UNIDIR are favoured and combined. It is held that regardless of the evolution of future technology the critical functions of targeting (defining, selecting and engaging targets) and the ability of humans to take part in critical functions and thus exercise control are clear and definable today.

Besides the define, select and engage critical functions, "meaningful human control" of AWS can be exercised by assigning responsibility to those who perform the function of activation and by ensuring that AWS can be deactivated by monitoring humans.

Definitions should capture non-lethal as well as lethal systems hence AWS is preferred to LAWS.

Also, definitions should capture existing systems not just future ones.

The definition of "autonomy" used here is based on that in [3]. Bekey defines autonomy as the ability to operate without a human operator for a protracted period of time.

This "no human operator" concept of autonomy is coupled with the ICRC "critical functions" approach to defining autonomy in an AWS. Three critical functions of targeting are defined: define, select and engage. The concept of the "wider" loop defined in [1] is used to draw the line of tolerance in Draft B.

AIES '19, January 27–28, 2019, Honolulu, HI, USA

ACM ISBN 978-1-4503-6324-2/19/01...$15.00
https://doi.org/10.1145/3306618.3314295

The more commonly debated "narrower" loop of select and engage is used to draw the line of tolerance in Draft A. With respect to weapons, a critical normative question is this: does fielding the weapon involve delegating a real-time lethal or harmful decision to a mechanical or computational device?

If the real-time decision to select (i.e. find, track, classify and prioritize a target) and engage (i.e. apply kinetic force and do harm to a target) does not involve a human and there is no possibility of human intervention, then the AWS is autonomous in the critical functions of select and engage and prohibited on the Draft A wording.

If in addition to autonomy in select and engage the AWS can define its own target classes (perhaps by machine learning from data sensed "in the wild") and can go on to select and engage these self-defined targets without human review or approval of the defined rules and without human intervention in the select and engage functions then the AWS is prohibited on the Draft B wording. While both drafts define "fully autonomous" in the same way, they prohibit different AWS. Draft A also has some "grandfather clauses" to exclude close-in weapons systems (CIWS), naval mines and anti-tank mines from the prohibition on weapons that have autonomy in the select and engage functions. Extra clauses might be added to Draft A to cater for other "defensive" systems.

On the common wording in both drafts, crude and simple AWS existed in the American Civil War. A land mine or naval mine is an AWS on these definitions. Such mines have autonomy in select and engage but do not have the ability to define their own target classes. Humans do this. To the best of my knowledge, there are no existing AWS that are "fully autonomous" as defined here. Such AWS would be able to define, select and engage targets without any human involvement beyond setting up the original machine learning. AWS like this are theoretically possible but do not yet exist.

No distinction is made between autonomous and automated. Machines are machines and humans are humans. You are either delegating a critical function of targeting that can kill or harm humans to a machine in combat or you are not.

However, I accept there is a critical distinction between a rule-following system and a rule-initiating system. This, I think, brings out a critical point about control that the automated/autonomous distinction is trying to express. While I come at this though human review and approval of defining targeting classes (which could in theory be "autonomously" generated by an AI in a format readily comprehensible to humans), there is an assumption here that such human review and approval will constitute acceptance of targeting rules or targeting behaviour. Such rules or behaviour may emerge from a machine learning process or be keyed in by humans setting up a more traditional AI expert system where behaviour follows from explicitly defined rules. From the point of view of affirming "meaningful human control" there is a case for treating rule-following systems differently from rule-initiating systems. A rule-following system follows human-defined targeting rules and accepts human-defined normative constraints to achieve human-defined goals.

On current technology it seems to me that an autonomous system such as Aegis can adequately express the will of the ship's commander as described in [10]. If such systems are to be classified as automated not autonomous, then it should be recognized that some people want to ban offensive "automated" weapons systems as well as offensive "autonomous" ones on moral grounds such as the "dignitarian" argument presented in [5]. This claims that delegating lethal decisions to machinery violates a fundamental human right to dignity even more basic than the right to life. A rule-initiating system might discover targeting rules and normative constraints in training data. More ominously, a rule-initiating system might choose non-human goals based on deep reinforcement learning or some other form of machine learning and define its own goals that may be hostile to humans. Also such a system may create or discover its own rules or select action on the basis of oscillations in neural networks that may be inscrutable (as much machine learning currently is) to humans. There is a case to stigmatize such systems as being "beyond" any form of "meaningful human control." A system that can define its own targeting policy and execute it without any human review or approval is clearly unacceptable. It is hard to see how command responsibility could work with such a system. Arguably, such a system is already unlawful under current IHL.

It is also hard to see what interest any state has in building a system that might decide on the basis of an evolving "value function" or "genetic algorithm" that the world is better off without that state or the humans in it or indeed that the entire world is better off without any states or any humans in it at all.

A system has to be able to demonstrate to those fielding it that it selects action in accordance with IHL. From a systems architecture point of view, it should be possible to design a machine learning system that can learn new tactics and yet abide by normative constraints. The AlphaGo and AlphaGo Zero systems were both capable of superhuman performance in choosing tactical moves but neither ignored the normative rules of Go.

The reasoning an AWS uses should be auditable by humans. Its targeting policy should be comprehensible to humans prior to activation so they can approve it and accept responsibility for the actions of the AWS. This latter requirement poses deep challenges for "inscrutable" machine learning systems. However future research may solve these problems.

Obviously, regardless of the system architecture, Article 36 review [6] is critical in verifying that an AWS can be operated in compliance with IHL before fielding. The fundamental ideas of Auditable Reasoning and a Responsible Officer assuming responsibility for AWS configuration and operation derive from the Responsibility Advisor in [2]. The phrase "Auditable Reasoning" comes from statements by the NZ delegation to the CCW [12].

3 BANNED WEAPONS

Table 1 provides examples of weapons banned by the two drafts.

A future rule-following system might take the form of a stealthy radio-silent offensive UCAV with onboard autonomy. Its targeting policy (rules of engagement) might be generated by a "strategic AI." Even so, human review of its inspectable (not "inscrutable") rules of engagement that would include IHL could be possible either using expert systems or by developing "explainable AI" that provides an "explanation" for machine learned behaviour. Such a system would have a "human in the wider loop" between define and select but no human between select and engage.

Table 1: Examples of Weapons Banned in Drafts A and B

Weapon	Autonomy in	Tactical Role	Draft A	Draft B
Naval & anti-tank mines	Select & Engage	Defensive	Permit	Permit
Fire & forget torpedo	Engage	Offensive	Permit	Permit
Fire & forget loitering missile (e.g. Harpy)	Select & Engage	Offensive	Permit	Permit
CIWS (e.g. Phalanx/Aegis)	Select & Engage	Defensive	Permit	Permit
Arkin Drone	Select & Engage	Offensive	Ban	Permit
Kalashnikov Autonomous Tank	Select & Engage	Offensive	Ban	Permit
Taranis with onboard autonomy	Select & Engage	Offensive	Ban	Permit
Future rule-following system	Select & Engage	Offensive	Ban	Permit
Future rule-initiating system	Define, Select & Engage	Offensive	Ban	Ban

I suspect many would bitterly oppose such a system. However states seeking to maintain "top tier" status in air power may insist such systems are not banned.

4 ARTICLES COMMON TO DRAFTS A AND B

The first three articles in both drafts are identical. They relate to scope, definitions and an "auditable reasoning" or "explicability" requirement [4].

4.1 Article 1: Scope of Application

1. This protocol relates to the use of autonomous weapons systems, defined herein, on land, sea and air.
2. This protocol applies only to autonomy in the critical functions of targeting as defined herein and to the functions of activation and deactivation as defined herein.
3. Autonomy in non-targeting functions such as navigation and refuelling is not regulated by this protocol.

4.2 Article 2: Definitions

1. "Autonomy" and "autonomous" refer to systems that are capable of operating in a real-world environment without external human control for a protracted period of time.
2. The "critical functions of targeting" are 1) defining targets, 2) selecting targets, and, 3) engaging targets.
3. "Autonomous Weapons System" (AWS) means a weapons system that has autonomy in one or more of the critical functions of targeting.
4. "Defining targets" means defining what classes of objects the autonomous weapon selects and engages.
5. "Selecting targets" means sensing and confirming objects meets the defined targeting criteria and aiming at them.
6. "Engaging targets" means firing on or using force against the selected targets.
7. "Activation" means turning on the AWS and sending it into offensive combat or enabling its defensive combat function.
8. "Deactivation" means withdrawing the AWS from combat and turning it off.
9. "Responsible Officer(s)" means the human or humans who assume responsibility for the configuration, fitness for purpose and state of repair of the AWS and who can be held accountable for its actions between activation and deactivation.
10. "Fully autonomous" means an AWS that has no humans involved in any of the critical functions of targeting. A fully autonomous AWS defines, selects and engages targets with no external human control.

4.3 Article 3: Auditable Reasoning

1. Logs containing timestamped data used by the AWS to make targeting decisions must be kept in an auditable form. It must be possible to inspect the logs and audit the reasoning used by the AWS to engage targets.

5 DRAFT A ARTICLES

Draft A requires a "human in the loop" between the critical functions of select and engage. A human is required to assume responsibility prior to activating the AWS. Humans must define targeting criteria. Some "grandfather clauses" provide exemptions from the "human in the loop" requirement for existing widely fielded AWS.

5.1 Article 4: Prohibitions

1. AWS that are fully autonomous as defined in Article 2.10 are prohibited.
2. Autonomy in the function of defining targeting criteria is prohibited. The Responsible Officer must understand what targets the AWS will attack and be satisfied that the AWS can conform to IHL in such attacks.
3. Autonomy in the function of engaging targets is prohibited. Except as provided for in Article 5, a Responsible Officer must confirm the decisions of the AWS to engage selected targets with a positive act.
4. Autonomy in the activation function is not permitted. A human must activate an AWS after a Responsible Officer has assumed responsibility for its configuration, fitness for purpose and state of repair.

5.2 Article 5: Grandfather Clauses

1. This protocol does not apply to anti-tank and anti-ship mines.
2. This protocol does not apply to "fire and forget" acoustic torpedoes and anti-radiation missiles.
3. Close-in weapons systems that due to military necessity must operate at an operational tempo too rapid for effective human control are permitted to be designed so that a Responsible Officer can

monitor the select decisions of the AWS and abort engagements or deactivate the AWS in real time. Such AWS are permitted to fire autonomously if the Responsible Officer does not intervene to abort the engage decision.

6 DRAFT B ARTICLE

Draft B is similar to Draft A in that it prohibits autonomy in the critical function of defining targets and requires a human to assume responsibility for the configuration and state of repair of the AWS at activation. Unlike Draft A, it does not require a "human in the loop" between the critical functions of select and engage. A human in the "wider loop" between the critical functions of define and select is deemed sufficient to implement "meaningful human control."

6.1 Article 4: Prohibitions

1. AWS that are fully autonomous as defined in Article 2.10 are prohibited.
2. Autonomy in the function of defining targeting criteria is prohibited. The Responsible Officer(s) must understand what classes of targets the AWS will attack and be satisfied that the AWS can conform to IHL in such attacks.
3. An AWS may not be activated without at least one Responsible Officer assuming responsibility for its targeting configuration, fitness for purpose and state of repair.
4. Autonomy in the activation function is not permitted. A human must activate an AWS after a Responsible Officer has assumed responsibility for its configuration, fitness for purpose and state of repair.

7 CONCLUSION

It is reiterated that these drafts are tentative and incomplete. Only the most critical articles relating to scope, definitions and prohibitions are included. Some readers might think them suspiciously short, however Protocol VI of the CCW banning blinding lasers has only 4 articles [7] comprising 174 words. Protocol II, which regulated anti-personnel landmines, is considerably longer (14 articles) and also has a technical annex [8]. Should nations see fit to add a Protocol VI to the CCW I imagine it would contain such an annex and be of similar length to Protocol II.

Similar to Protocol II, a Protocol VI would contain clauses relating to such matters as transfers, recordkeeping, compliance, technological cooperation and the like in addition to the core clauses regarding scope, definitions and prohibitions presented here.

Additional articles could also cover such things as range and payload to address concerns about weapons of mass destruction (WMD) becoming autonomous. Matters such as distinction, proportionality, necessity and legal review of new AWS are already covered by existing IHL. The regulation of weapons is and will continue to be complex. However, numerous delegations attending CCW meetings at the UN have pressed for discussions to move towards a tangible outcome. This short paper hopes to stimulate concrete and focused discussion as to the eventual form AWS regulation should take.

ACKNOWLEDGMENTS

The author is much indebted to Mark Pearson of the New Zealand Department of Foreign Affairs and Trade, Reuben Steff of Waikato University, Jai Galliott of the Australian Defence Force Academy, Ron Arkin of Georgia Tech, Paul Scharre of the Centre for a New American Security and Mary Wareham, Noel Sharkey and Rob Sparrow of the Campaign to Stop Killer Robots for helpful discussions on LAWS and LAWS regulation.

REFERENCES

[1] AIV/CAVV. 2015. Autonomous Weapons Systems: The Need for Meaningful Human Control. Retrieved Jan 17, 2019 from https://aiv-advies.nl/download/606cb3b1-a800-4f8a-936f-af61ac991dd0.pdf

[2] Ronald C Arkin. 2009. *Governing Lethal Behaviour in Autonomous Robots.* CRC Press, Boca Rouge.

[3] George A Bekey. 2005. *Autonomous robots: from biological inspiration to implementation and control.* MIT press, Cambridge, MA.

[4] Luciano Floridi, Josh Cowls, Monica Beltrametti, Raja Chatila, Patrice Chazerand, Virginia Dignum, Christoph Luetge, Robert Madelin, Ugo Pagallo, Francesca Rossi, Burkhard Schafer, Peggy Valcke, and Effy Vayena. 2018. AI4People - An Ethical Framework for a Good AI Society: Opportunities, Risks, Principles, and Recommendations. *Minds and Machines* 28, 689 (2018). https://doi.org/10.1007/s11023-018-9482-5

[5] Christopf Heyns. 2016. *Autonomous Weapons Systems: Living a Dignified Life and Dying a Dignified Death.* Cambridge University Press, Cambridge, 3–20.

[6] ICRC. 1977. Protocol Additional to the Geneva Conventions of 12 August 1949, and relating to the Protection of Victims of International Armed Conflicts (Protocol I), 8 June 1977. Article 36. Retrieved Jan 17, 2019 from https://www.icrc.org/ihl/WebART/470-750045?OpenDocument

[7] ICRC. 1995. Protocol on Blinding Laser Weapons (Protocol IV to the 1980 Convention), 13 October 1995. Retrieved Jan 17, 2019 from https://ihl-databases.icrc.org/ihl/INTRO/570

[8] ICRC. 1996. Protocol on Prohibitions or Restrictions on the Use of Mines, Booby-Traps and Other Devices as amended on 3 May 1996 (Protocol II to the 1980 CCW Convention as amended on 3 May 1996). Retrieved Jan 17, 2019 from https://www.icrc.org/ihl/INTRO/575

[9] ICRC. 2018. Ethics and Autonomous Weapons Systems: an ethical basis for human control? Retrieved Jan 17, 2019 from https://www.icrc.org/en/download/file/69961/icrc$_e$thics$_a$nd$_a$utonomous$_w$eapon$_s$ystems$_r$eport$_3$$_a$pril$_2$018.pdf

[10] Paul Scharre. 2018. *Army of None.* WW Norton & Co., New York.

[11] UNIDIR. 2017. The Weaponization of Increasingly Autonomous Technologies: Concerns, Characteristics and Definitional Approaches. Retrieved Jan 17, 2019 from http://www.unidir.org/files/publications/pdfs/the-weaponization-of-increasingly-autonomous-technologies-concerns-characteristics-and-definitional-approaches-en-689.pdf

[12] New Zealand. 2018. Statement by Katy Donnelly Deputy Permanent Representative to the Conference on Disarmament, Geneva. Retrieved Jan 17, 2019 from https://www.unog.ch/80256EDD006B8954/(httpAssets)/4A54EE38E2F8223AC12582720057E761/\protect\T1\textdollarfile/2018$_L$AWS6b$_N$ew+Zealand.pdf

Balancing the Benefits of Autonomous Vehicles

Timothy Geary
School of Humanities & Communication
California State University, Monterey Bay
Monterey, CA, USA
tgeary@csumb.edu

David Danks
Departments of Philosophy & Psychology
Carnegie Mellon University
Pittsburgh, PA, USA
ddanks@cmu.edu

ABSTRACT

Autonomous vehicles are regularly touted as holding the potential to provide significant benefits for diverse populations. There are significant technological barriers to be overcome, but as those are solved, autonomous vehicles are expected to reduce fatalities; decrease emissions and pollutants; provide new options to mobility-challenged individuals; enable people to use their time more productively; and so much more. In this paper, we argue that these high expectations for autonomous vehicles almost certainly cannot be fully realized. More specifically, the proposed benefits divide into two high-level groups, centered around efficiency and safety improvements, and increases in people's agency and autonomy. The first group of benefits is almost always framed in terms of rates: fatality rates, traffic flow per mile, and so forth. However, we arguably care about the absolute numbers for these measures, not the rates; number of fatalities is the key metric, not fatality rate per vehicle mile traveled. Hence, these potential benefits will be reduced, perhaps to non-existence, if autonomous vehicles lead to increases in vehicular usage. But that is exactly the result that we should expect if the second group of benefits is realized: if people's agency and autonomy is increased, then they will use vehicles more. There is an inevitable tension between the benefits that are proposed for autonomous vehicles, such that we cannot fully have all of them at once. We close by pointing towards other types of AI technologies where we should expect to find similar types of necessary and inevitable tradeoffs between classes of benefits.

CCS CONCEPTS

• Social and professional topics~Computing / technology policy
• Applied computing~Transportation

KEYWORDS

Autonomous vehicles; Cost-benefit analyses; Value tradeoffs

AIES'19, January 27–28, 2019, Honolulu, HI, USA

ACM ISBN 978-1-4503-6180-4/19/03.
DOI: https://doi.org/10.1145/3306618.3314237

ACM Reference format:
Timothy Geary and David Danks. 2018. Balancing the Benefits of Autonomous Vehicles. In *Proceedings of 2019 AAAI/ACM Conference on AI, Ethics, and Society (AIES '19), AIES '19, January 27-28, 2019, Honolulu, HI, USA.* ACM, NY, NY, USA, 6 pages. DOI: https://doi.org/10.1145/3306618.3314237

1 Introduction

Autonomous vehicles (AVs), along with many other AI technologies, are forecast to have numerous societal bene-fits, both quantitative and qualitative. For example, many experts predict that AVs will reduce rates of fatalities [15], emissions [6, 10], traffic [19] and parking congestion [20]. In the near future, ac-cording to the predictions, we will have safer, cleaner, and more livable cities. At the same time, AVs are predicted to increase people's autonomy and self-determination [1, 14], thereby enabling populations who are currently underserved by transportation options (e.g., those who are visually or mobility impaired) to live fuller lives.

Discussions about the benefits of autonomous vehicles typically treat these various beneficial possibilities as independent: a gain of one type of benefit from AVs is usually assumed (perhaps implicitly) to have no appreciable impact on the likelihood that we will gain some other benefit from AVs. Of course, there are exceptions to this generalization—for instance, analyses of emission benefits frequently also model the traffic impacts [6]—but there is relatively little explicit discussion of the possibility of trade-offs. This assumption of independence is not necessarily a problem; in particular, it is arguably warranted whenever benefits are expressed as changes in the relevant rates. It is hard to see, for example, why changes in the fatality rate would depend in any interesting way on the increase in transportation options for mobility-impaired individuals.

Nevertheless, we contend in this paper that the presumed independence has masked a deep tension between the various potential benefits of AVs. In particular, we argue that we cannot simultaneously reap all of the benefits of AVs, or at least, all of the benefits that actually matter to us. In Section 2, we examine the different benefits proposed for AVs, and show that they largely fall into two groups—either safety and efficiency, or autonomy and self-determination. The former benefits are almost al-ways expressed as improved rates, while the latter emphasize increased transportation opportunities.

As we argue in Section 3, though, we should ultimately not care about improved rates of harm, but only improved magnitudes of harm. A reduced rate of vehicular fatalities is cold comfort if there is an increased number of deaths due to an accompanying increase in vehicle-miles traveled (VMT). And if the autonomy and self-determination benefits are realized, then we should expect exactly such an increase in VMT. That is, if we actually achieve one set of benefits from AVs, then another set will be much smaller, and can even become liabilities. We thus finish in Section 4 with a consideration of ways to regulate and develop AV technologies to appropriately balance these two considerations.

2 Classes of Benefits

Technologies such as AVs will undoubtedly impact our lives in numerous ways, as transportation plays a key role in many economic and private domains. Unsurprisingly, there have been many analyses (too many for us to exhaustively cite!) about the potential benefits and drawbacks of AVs. At a high level, we can usefully distinguish between two different types of benefits.

2.1 Safety and Efficiency

The first, and most discussed, benefit of AVs is the potential to dramatically reduce crash and fatality rates. In 2016, Americans drove over 3.2 trillion miles [18]. In the same year, combined fatality rates for both rural and urban driving was estimated at 1.18 fatalities per 100 mil-lion miles driven; overall, human-caused motor vehicle crashes resulted in 37,461 fatalities, over 28% of which were due to alcohol use [17].

In light of this enormous human cost, the potential safe-ty value of AVs is enormous. Autonomous vehicles would not speed (under most conditions), drink, or get distracted. In fact, analyses have argued that AVs could save nearly 30,000 lives per year in the United States "by shifting the focus from minimization of post-crash injury to collision prevention" [8]. Widespread use could be transformative in terms of lives saved, particularly given the principal importance of safety considerations in AV design and deployment [15]. Continual improvement of AV technologies should only further drive down the relevant fatality rates, as developers gain more data and experience with the diversity of driving contexts [13].

In addition to increased safety, AVs can lower fuel consumption and emissions, thereby protecting the environment and human well-being [6, 10]. AVs can drive more smoothly, accelerate/ decelerate more efficiently, and reduce fuel consumption by driving the speed limit. With appropriate programming, AVs can take advantage of eco-driving principles to increase efficiency by arguably up to 25%, with corresponding reductions in fuel consumption by 20% and overall delays in traffic by 60% [11]. Total greenhouse gasses could, if AVs were electrified rather than fossil fuel-based, be reduced by over 80% [9]. Of course, some of these benefits interact with one another: for example, AVs are plausibly more likely to be electrified, and so their wide usage provides environmental benefits along two distinct pathways.

Third, AVs are predicted to reduce traffic and therefore travel times. Most traffic is caused by inefficient braking and acceleration, and AVs should reduce those events. In 2014, congestion increased urban Americans' travel time by 6.9 billion hours, resulting in use of an additional 3.1 billion gallons of gasoline, with a corresponding cost of $160 billion [5]. Assuming that AVs are fully autonomous and connected, they can use road space more efficiently and improve traffic flow, thus saving time and fuel [12]. More generally, AVs will likely be more consistent and conservative in their driving, which can potentially yield significant reductions in traffic [19]. Additionally, if safety benefits are realized, then congestion caused by crashes would correspondingly also be reduced [5].

2.2 Autonomy and Self-determination

AVs are not simply safer or more efficient drivers. Since no human driver is required, they can provide mobility solutions for people who are otherwise dependent on the support or services of others. For example, elderly, blind, or other mobility-impaired individuals would have the ability to use an AV without coordinating with other people, in contrast to their current dependency [1]. Alternately, people who might otherwise drive while alcohol impaired would have new transportation options, thereby increasing their ability to function autonomously without placing others at risk. More generally, widespread deployment would likely lead to the development of entirely new patterns of mobility usage [14].

Even in traditional mobility roles, the introduction of AVs can lead to significant gains in autonomy and self-determination. Reductions in commute times, as well as the ability to productively use that travel time, can enable people to spend more time on tasks that are important or valuable to them. High-level AVs will take over most or all driving tasks, thus freeing up time for other tasks that better advances people's interests. The net result is an increase in usable (for the person) time. Relatedly, AVs plausibly will reduce people's overall levels of stress due to reduction of time actually driving, thereby enabling them to be more productive when not in the vehicle. With full autonomous capabilities, users would be able to work, relax, or even sleep in the AV.

3 The Fundamental Tension

Proponents of AVs tout these many benefits as reasons to pursue rapid adoption, even when there are significant un-certainties about their performance in novel contexts or situations [13]. We agree that 100% safety or 100% reliability are unrealistic goals, and that we should focus on determination of conditions under which AV adoption can provide significant incremental benefits. However, we suggest that efforts to evaluate those conditions have largely asked the wrong questions (or the right questions with the wrong presuppositions).

When we consider the possible impacts of AVs, we contend that we should ultimately worry about the total harms and benefits that result from their use in particular contexts, under specific regulations, and so on. For example, we care about the total number of fatalities, not about the fatality rate (except inasmuch as it carries information about the total number of deaths). We care about the total emissions, not the emissions per vehicle. And so on.

For the types of factors we have considered here, the total magnitude of some harm and benefit will be (roughly) the relevant rate, multiplied by the total usage.[1] Hence, the value of changes in rates cannot be judged without knowledge (or assumption) about whether the total usage changes as well. If the total usage (i.e., VMT in the case of AVs) is unchanged, then a reduction in the rate of some harm will be a positive, as it will reduce the total amount of harm. If the total usage instead increases as a result of the technological change, then this reduction in the rate of harm could actually translate into more total harms, if the usage increase is larger (as a percentage) than the rate reduction.

Consider a simplistic example with numbers similar to the vehicular fatality data (provided in the previous section) for the United States in 2016: a (human-driven) vehicular fatality rate of 1 death per 100 million miles; total VMT of 3 trillion miles per year; resulting in 30,000 vehicular fatalities per year. Suppose that widespread AV deployment would result in a 10% improvement in the vehicular fatality rate; that is, the new fatality rate would be 0.9 deaths per 100 million miles. This improvement appears to be a significant gain, as we would expect to save 3,000 additional lives each year. However, suppose that this same widespread deployment also leads to increased vehicle usage, whether from people who have limited current use of vehicles (e.g., visually-impaired or elderly individuals) or from shifts to AVs from other forms of transportation (e.g., working in an AV rather than on a train). For concreteness, suppose the VMT increased by 20% to 3.6 trillion miles per year. In that case, though, we would expect to have 32.400 total deaths. That is, this widespread deployment of AVs—each of which is safer than a human-driven vehicle—would not save lives, but would actually result in 2,400 more deaths each year. And in such a case, we contend that we ought to reject the use of AVs, or at least not adopt them because of some supposed safety benefit. AVs might reduce the fatality *rate*, but the relevant safety benefit is the fatality *magnitude*, which depends on the impact of AVs on VMT.

More generally, as noted above, essentially all of the analyses of safety and efficiency benefits either focus exclusively on rates, or assume (perhaps implicitly) that AV usage and VMT remain approximately constant, or even go down. Even analyses that entertain the possibility of an increase in VMT (e.g., [13]) nonetheless place most of their emphasis on situations in which total VMT is flat or reduced. However, if the proposed autonomy and self-determination benefits are actually realized, then we should expect to see an increase, perhaps a quite significant one, in VMT. The net result would be the minimization—perhaps even elimination—of the safety and efficiency benefits (see also [7]). Contrary to the standard analyses, the potential benefits of AVs are not independent, but rather are in tension: increased autonomy and self-determination benefits will (barring appropriate regulation or responses; see next section) likely come at the cost of some safety and efficiency benefits.

This tension within the benefits might seem surprising, but it has natural analogs in other contexts. For example, freeway expansion is often advocated on the grounds that it will (a) reduce congestion, thereby reducing people's travel times; and (b) increase capacity on key transportation arteries, thereby making the roadways more accessible to more people. However, these two benefits are in tension with one another. If more people actually use those particular roadways (due to increased capacity), then the traffic congestion will not be alleviated and travel times will not decrease. In fact, the "Fundamental Law of Road Congestion" holds that this is exactly what happens: when roadway capacity is increased, the traffic volume (i.e., the VMT) increases to match it, resulting in no improvements in travel times [4]. Importantly, this tension is not because the benefits are imaginary; road expansion does, in fact, reduce the average travel time if the number of other cars is held fixed. The problem is that the antecedent of the conditional fails to hold (i.e., the number of cars is not fixed), and so the actual travel time is unchanged after the traffic system equilibrates. Similarly, AVs might, in fact, reduce the fatality rate (or other safety and efficiency rate), but not thereby result in any real benefits if they also cause a non-trivial increase in VMT.

We emphasize that we are not arguing that these classes of benefits are necessarily or conceptually incompatible. That is, we are not claiming that tradeoffs (see next section) necessarily must occur. Rather, we are arguing that there is a prima facie tension between the two types of benefits, and so we must engage in difficult empirical investigations to try to determine whether there is some underlying incompatibility, and if so, the relevant tradeoffs be-tween the classes of benefits. Our paper is a call for more appropriate analyses and debates, not an impossibility proof.

We contend that we simply do not know (at the current time) whether the autonomy and self-determination benefits will result in a sufficiently large increase in VMT to offset significant safety benefits, nor whether any extra VMT will be higher or lower risk than normal, nor whether specific groups or communities are likely to be disproportionately affected, nor answers to a range of other relevant questions about this tension. Arguments that depend on a list of benefits without consideration of tensions are overly simplistic. But similarly, arguments that we must choose between safety and autonomy

[1] Of course, our computation could be more sophisticated in various ways. For example, there might be different vehicular fatality rates for different driving conditions, and so we might weight the product by the VMT in each of the different conditions.

depend on empirical questions that (to our knowledge) remain open..

4 Responses to the Tension

This tension between the classes of proposed benefits has largely gone unrecognized in the literature on the pros and cons of AVs. A few analyses have acknowledged the possibility that safety and efficiency benefits can be offset if VMT increases [13, 15], but discussion of that possibility has largely been relegated to footnotes. Thus, one important response is to adapt and improve the debates about AVs. We cannot simply list and compare the different potential benefits and potential draw-backs, as it may not be possible to achieve all of the bene-fits simultaneously. The total benefits may be less than one might have hoped by considering each class of benefits in isolation, and so we must be more nuanced in our arguments for and against AVs.

That being said, we need not stop with only shifts in rhetoric and argumentation. One challenge that we face is that many of the relevant empirical facts may not be known (or even knowable) in advance of regulatory and legal approval of AVs. As argued above, the scope and size of the tension between classes of benefits is ultimately an empirical matter. However, predicting the usage levels of novel technologies is a notoriously challenging task: there are various frameworks for predicting adoption of novel technology (e.g., the Technology Acceptance Model; [3]), but their accuracy is mixed, particularly for technology such as AVs that potentially have wide-ranging impacts.

Moreover, this uncertainty about the VMT impact of autonomy and self-determination benefits means that we are unlikely to be able to develop an empirically accurate mathematical model of the relevant tradeoffs. And if we do not have the knowledge to construct a reliable cost-benefit analysis, then we arguably do not have the appropriate in-formation or bases to make the standard, simple approve/ deny regulatory decisions about AV.[2] Rather, we propose that we should consider three different, not mutually exclusive, changes to the likely regulatory processes and standards for AVs.

First, even if regulatory agencies prioritize the minimization of safety- and efficiency-related harms, then they should set a higher bar for demonstrated improvements in safety and efficiency. Various proposals have been made for what degree of improvement in (expected) safety rates should be required before AVs are approved for widespread public use (e.g., [7]), including some arguments that manufacturers should only have to demonstrate that AV accident rates are approximately equivalent to those of human drivers [13]. However, the autonomy and self-determination benefits imply that current VMT is only a lower bound on vehicle usage.

[2] Of course, there might be multiple reasons that we ought not regulate AVs in a simple binary manner [2, 16], not solely the difficulty of estimating possible changes in VMT levels and distribution.

We have good reasons to think that the actual VMT will be significantly higher. Hence, equal safety and efficiency rates will likely lead to greater total harms, unless there turn out to be no autonomy benefits whatsoever. That is, rate equivalence to human performance is highly unlikely to be the rate at which total harms are the same with or without AVs. Instead, if we want to reduce total harms, then we should require AVs to exhibit significantly better-than-human safety and efficiency rates, precisely since we expect usage to increase. Of course, just how much better depends on empirical questions that we cannot yet answer, but we can certainly conclude that "comparable to human performance" is not the correct standard for regulatory approval (again, if regulators have the goal of minimizing total harms).

A second option is that regulators might approve the use of AVs based on one of the currently-proposed bars for safety and efficiency benefits (e.g., slightly better than hu-man performance), but then actively monitor and manage AV usage to ensure that VMT does not grow faster than safety and efficiency rates are reduced. For example, regulators might tie the number of approved AVs, or the permissible total AV mileage, to improvements in safety rates (e.g., each one percentage point improvement in safety allows the licensing of another 10,000 AVs).

This type of active monitoring and dynamic approval would be unusual in the transportation space, but is more common in other domains such as pharmaceuticals [16] or water usage rights in parts of the United States. Implementation of such a system would require the creation of a significantly more intrusive monitoring system by the relevant regulatory agencies, but would potentially allow for the dynamic balancing of the potential tradeoffs inherent in the tension between the two classes of proposed benefits.

A third possibility is that regulators might choose to prioritize the autonomy and self-determination benefits and approve AVs relatively quickly, perhaps even before they are safer or more efficient that human drivers. This response could enable appropriate populations to realize the increased mobility and autonomy benefits of AVs immediately, even if those benefits potentially come with some increased harms due to AV accidents. That is, regulators might decide that the autonomy and mobility expansion benefits are sufficiently strong that we should actually tolerate an increase in the number of vehicular fatalities, at least in the short run.

This potential line of response might seem surprising, since regulatory actions typically emphasize safety and efficiency benefits. However, there are many cases in which laws and regulations accept a certain level of risk or harm in order to achieve other substantive benefits, including autonomy and self-determination. One can rarely eliminate the possibility of harms, and so the relevant question is what level of risk is acceptable given the other hoped-for benefits. We propose that regulators could decide that the autonomy benefits are worth slightly increasing current risk levels, at least for certain populations. Of course, this potential risk increase could be minimized by only approving AVs for use by groups who would disproportionately benefit from their use. For example, a regulatory agency might allow only vision- or mobility-impaired individuals to use AVs, not those without relevant impairments. Such a policy would aim to realize the bulk of the autonomy benefits while minimizing the potential increase in harms.[3]

These three different regulatory responses are not mutually exclusive, but could be used in conjunction with one another. Of course, there could be significant legal or political barriers to the use of one or another response in a particular country, community, or context. For example, there might be substantial resistance to approving AVs for use by only a subset of the population in a region or country. In practice, regulators might be highly constrained by relevant legal, social, and cultural norms. Nonetheless, we believe that it is valuable to see that there are different options available to regulators, even when key empirical questions cannot be answered in advance of (limited) approval and deployment.

One key feature shared by all of these responses is the need for regulators to either (a) prioritize one class of bene-fits, or (b) attempt to dynamically balance them. We might wish that regulators would not be placed in this position, but unfortunately these different classes of benefits are in tension with one another. Decisions about how to weight values should presumably be made only after substantial public discussion and comment. Hence, we have yet another reason to shift the rhetoric and arguments about AVs towards acknowledgment of this potential tension: open discussion is required for regulators to obtain the necessary information and feedback for them to make principled decisions about the best ways to try to regulate this new technology, with its complicated set of potential benefits..

5 Conclusions

Most decisions about widespread approval or licensure are based on cost-benefit analyses of some sort: if the new technology has more benefits than costs—whether those are economic, social, psychological, or other—then regulators typically approve the system, perhaps with restrictions on the contexts or populations of use. We have here argued that this cost-benefit analysis is significantly more complicated for AVs than has traditionally been assumed. The benefits of increasing autonomy and self-determination themselves carry a cost in the form of increased VMT, and so increased opportunities for accidents, traffic, and emissions. We must use a more sophisticated understanding of the underlying psychology of technology use and adoption in order to better estimate the likely changes in key parameters of our analyses.

When framed in this way, one can quickly see that this tension is not unique to AVs, but rather arises for a host of other kinds of AI systems. For example, medical diagnostic AIs are often praised for their potential to have greater accuracy, and also to provide more widespread access to accurate diagnoses (since they can be deployed in regions where there are few human doctors). But the latter benefit of access implies much greater usage of the system, and so a corresponding increase in the number of false positives, which themselves impose a cost on the healthcare system.[4] Of course, regulators might decide that the increase in access is worth some additional costs and burdens on the system, but that is a trade-off of values that must be considered. We ought not model the accuracy improvement benefits in isolation from the access improvement costs.

Our observations and arguments here also point towards the need for improved models of technology adoption and usage. While such predictions are quite difficult, there could be significant gains from even incremental improvements in our predictive accuracy. The costs and benefits of novel technologies frequently interact with one another, and our approval decisions should be based on more com-plex analyses that capture these interdependencies..

ACKNOWLEDGMENTS

This paper was made possible in part by support from the McNair scholars program and CSU-Louis Stokes Alliance for Minority Participation (CSU-LSAMP) Program to TG, and an Andrew Carnegie Fellowship (Carnegie Corporation of New York) to DD. The statements made and views expressed are solely the responsibility of the authors.

REFERENCES

[1] H. Bradshaw-Martin and C. Easton (2014). Autonomous or 'Driverless' Cars and Disability: A Legal and Ethical Analysis. *European Journal of Current Legal Issues*, 20(3).

[2] D. Danks and A. J. London (2017). Regulating Autonomous Systems: Beyond Standards. *Intelligent Systems*, 32(1), 88-91.

[3] F. D. Davis (1989). Perceived Usefulness, Perceived Ease of Use, and User Acceptance of Information Technology. *MIS Quarterly*, 13(3), 319–340

[4] G. Duranton and M. Turner (2011). The Fundamental Law of Road Congestion: Evidence from U.S Cities. *American Economic Review*.

[5] EIA (2018). *Autonomous Vehicles: Uncertainties and Energy Implications*. U.S. Energy Information Administration Annual Energy Outlook.

[6] D. J. Fagnant and K. M. Kockelman (2014). The Travel and Environmental Implications of Shared Autonomous Vehicles, Using Agent-based Model Scenarios. *Transportation Research Part C: Emerging Technologies*, 40, 1-13.

[7] D. J. Fagnant and K. M. Kockelman (2015). Preparing a Nation for Autonomous Vehicles: Opportunities, Barriers and Policy Recommendations. *Transportation Research Part A: Policy and Practice*, 77, 167-181.

[8] J. Fleetwood (2017). Public Health, Ethics, and Autonomous Vehicles. *American Journal of Public Health*, 107, 532–537.

[9] L. Fulton, J. Mason and D. Meroux (2017). *Three Revolutions in Urban Transportation: How to Achieve the Full Potential of Vehicle Electrification, Automation and Shared Mobility Systems in Urban Transportation Systems Around the World by 2050*. UC Davis Institute of Transportation Studies No. STEPS-2050.

[10] J. B. Greenblatt and S. Saxena (2015). Autonomous Taxis Could Greatly Reduce Greenhouse-gas Emissions of US Light-duty Vehicles. *Nature Climate Change*, 5(9), 860.

[3] Note, though, that if AVs are particularly risky for passengers, then the regulators would be putting disproportionate risk on already-disadvantaged populations, which might provide a compelling contrary reason to deny early approval for these groups.

[4] This possibility is particularly worrisome if the increased usage occurs in low-risk populations, since there might be few people who actually ben-efit from learning a true positive diagnosis.

[11] H. Igliński and M. Babiak (2017). Analysis of the Potential of Autonomous Vehicles in Reducing the Emissions of Green-house Gases in Road Transport. *Procedia Engineering*, 192, 353-358.

[12] X. Ji (2018). The Impact of Self-driving Cars on Existing Transportation Networks. In *AIP Conference Proceedings* (Vol. 1955, No. 1, p. 040142). AIP Publishing.

[13] N. Kalra and D. G. Groves (2017). *The Enemy of Good: Estimating the Cost of Waiting for Nearly Perfect Automated Vehicles.* RAND Report RR2150.

[14] B. Lenz and E. Fraedrich (2016). New Mobility Concepts and Autonomous Driving: The Potential for Change. In *Autonomous Driving* (pp. 173-191). Springer, Berlin, Heidelberg.

[15] T. Litman (2017). *Autonomous vehicle implementation predictions.* Victoria, Canada: Victoria Transport Policy Institute.

[16] A. J. London and D. Danks (2018). Regulating Autonomous Vehicles: A Policy Proposal. In *Proceedings of the 2018 AAAI/ACM Conference on Artificial Intelligence, Ethics, and Society.* doi:10.1145/3278721.3278763

[17] NHTSA (2017). *2016 Fatal Motor Vehicle Crashes: Overview.* Traffic Safety Facts Research Note DOT HS 812 456. National Highway Traffic Safety Administration.

[18] OHIP (2016). *Traffic Volume Trends.* Report of the U.S. Department of Transportation, Federal Highway Administration, Office of Highway Policy Information.

[19] A. Talebpour and H. S. Mahmassani (2016). Influence of Connected and Autonomous Vehicles on Traffic Flow Stability and Throughput. *Transportation Research Part C: Emerging Technologies*, 71, 143-163.

[20] W. Zhang, S. Guhathakurta, J. Fang and G. Zhang (2015). Exploring the Impact of Shared Autonomous Vehicles on Urban Parking Demand: An Agent-based Simulation Approach. *Sustainable Cities and Society*, 19, 34-45.

Compensation at the Crossroads

Autonomous Vehicles & Alternative Victim Compensation Schemes

Tracy Hresko Pearl
Texas Tech University
School of Law
tracy.pearl@ttu.edu

CCS CONCEPTS

• Social and professional topics →**Computing / technology policy; Government technology policy; Governmental regulations**

KEYWORDS

autonomous vehicles; self-driving cars; law; law and society; law and technology; emerging technology; victim compensation fund; liability issues

ACM Reference format:

Tracy Hresko Pearl. 2019. Compensation at the Crossroads: Autonomous Vehicles & Alternative Victim Compensation Schemes. In *AAAI/ACM Conference on AI, Ethics, and Society (AIES'19), January 27–28, 2019, Honolulu, HI, USA*. ACM, New York, NY, USA, 7 pages. https://doi.org/10.1145/1234567890

Over the last five years, a small but growing number of vehicle accidents involving fully or partially autonomous vehicles have raised a new and profoundly novel legal issue: who should be liable (if anyone) and how victims should be compensated (if at all) when a vehicle controlled by an algorithm rather than a human driver causes injury. The answer to this question has implications far beyond the resolution of individual autonomous vehicle crash cases. Whether the American legal system is capable of handling these cases fairly and efficiently implicates the likelihood that (a) consumers will adopt autonomous vehicles, and (b) the rate at which they will (or will not) do so. These implications should concern law and policy makers immensely.

If autonomous cars stand to drastically reduce the number of fatalities and injuries on U.S. roadways—and virtually every scholar believes that they will—getting the adjudication and compensation aspect of autonomous vehicle injuries "wrong," so to speak, risks stymieing adoption of this technology and leaving more Americans at risk of dying at the hands of human drivers.

AIES '19, January 27–28, 2019, Honolulu, HI, USA

ACM 978-1-4503-6324-2/19/01...$15.00
https://doi.org/10.1145/3306618.3314249

The problem, of course, is that autonomous vehicles pose "a plethora of new and unique legal issues, which will need to be analyzed to facilitate the adequate transition of this new technology to the marketplace."[1] Chief among these is the legal implication of automation itself. Given that, as one scholar has said, "the entire history of human laws has assumed that people make decisions,"[2] handing those decisions over to an algorithm places lawyers and judges into a situation in which there is "currently no legal framework for . . . liability."[3] Worse, the development of automated vehicle technology has already far outpaced development of the law in this area, and is continuing to advance at rates that can often seem exponential. The American legal system is thus in a situation in which it needs to develop jurisprudence in and around a technology that challenges many of the most fundamental assumptions of Western jurisprudence. It must do so, moreover, extraordinarily quickly or risk hampering innovation and slowing adoption of a technology that will likely save tens of thousands of lives each year in the United States alone. In short, the stakes are extremely high and time extremely limited.

In this paper, I explore the liability issues posed by accidents involving autonomous vehicles and propose a way in which we can both compensate victims for injuries while also creating time and space for the civil justice system to develop a robust jurisprudence in and around the use and development of these vehicles. I conclude that funneling autonomous car crash cases into a specially designed, no-fault, quasi-judicial victim compensation fund is a sensible way to do so. Such a fund could both protect autonomous car designers and manufacturers from high levels of uncertainty about liability exposure while assuring consumers that they will be compensated fairly and quickly if an autonomous vehicle harms them. It would also give courts "breathing room" to adapt products liability law to the brave new world of automation and artificial intelligence.[4]

I. LIABILITY & COMPENSATION MODELS

In designing and establishing a route through which victims of autonomous vehicle crashes could obtain compensation, the two most basic options are (1) requiring victims to file traditional lawsuits via the civil justice system, and/or (2) giving victims the option of pursuing relief via an alternative compensation scheme. Stated in the most simplified way possible, these options are, essentially, "tort system" and "not tort system." Though the "not tort system" option may seem virtually limitless, the reality is that, in the United States, this option has typically meant a victim compensation fund. Both options—the traditional tort system and a victim compensation fund approach—have advantages and drawbacks.

A. The Tort System

The structure and inner workings of the American tort system should be familiar to anyone with legal training. Its fundamental purposes are to compensate innocent parties, shift the loss to responsible parties, and deter wrongful conduct that creates an unreasonable risk of injury to others. In short, tort law is a way for an injured person to attempt to shift the cost of harm to another person or entity who has erred in some legally cognizable way. Tort liability may be rooted in intentional conduct, negligent conduct, or strict liability.

The tort system has two primary advantages over victim compensation funds. First, unlike victim compensation funds, the civil justice system in which tort claims are litigated is both a well-established and a highly stable institution.[5] As one scholar notes, despite the fact that technology has changed over time, the civil justice system at the federal, state, and local levels has been handling tort claims successfully "for more than two centuries."[6] Citizens thus presumably have some understanding of, if not how it operates precisely, its existence and the most basic aspects of its inner workings. Second, while scholars debate whether it would be inapposite in autonomous vehicle crash cases, a robust body of products liability jurisprudence already exists in the United States and could potentially provide an avenue of compensation for autonomous vehicle crash victims.

The drawbacks of the tort system in the context of autonomous vehicle crash cases appear to be more significant than the advantages. Litigating a case in the civil justice system is typically an expensive, time-consuming, and unpredictable process. Additionally, as alluded to above, while a robust body of products liability jurisprudence and tort law may already exist, cases involving autonomous vehicles—and, indeed, nearly all other forms of automated or artificial intelligence-governed consumer goods—raise novel questions of liability and fault that these sources of law may not be well-equipped to handle. As one scholar points out, "the current legal system logically aligns with the cause of most accidents: human error."[7] This is particularly true of motor vehicle laws, nearly all of which presume that a human being is the driver. Liability regimes will thus have to change fairly significantly to accommodate the realities of this type of technology. Lastly, exposure to product liability "always looms as an obstacle to innovation in the auto industry."[8] If manufacturers of autonomous vehicles face ongoing litigation from disgruntled consumers, are compelled to pay to defend against these claims, and, in some percentage of those cases, pay money damages, manufacturers could pass those costs on to consumers via higher prices for their vehicles. This, in turn, "could lead to slower adoption of these systems, which could lead to crash injuries that could have been prevented by these systems."[9]

B. Victim Compensation Funds

Victim compensation funds are fairly new innovations in the American legal system. In the late twentieth century, various governmental entities sought alternatives to litigation in a variety of fairly discrete situations, hoping to prevent an influx of a particular type of cases into the court system, to prop up failing industries, or to give victims a quicker and less adversarial process by which to obtain compensation for their injuries. Victim compensation funds were often the alternative selected. While these funds have had varying levels of success, they have been used with increasing frequency, particularly in post-disaster situations.[10] Examples include the September 11th Victim Compensation Fund, the BP Deepwater Horizon Disaster Fund, and the National Vaccine Injury Compensation Program.

The primary advantages of victim compensation funds over the tort system are three-fold. First, victim compensation funds offer significantly more flexibility than the tort system because they can be tailored to the particular needs of a given set of cases.[11] Second, victim compensation funds are typically faster and more efficient than the tort system. Third, victims who file claims with victim compensation funds typically encounter fewer costs than those who choose to litigate their claims in the tort system. By drastically reducing—if not outright eliminating—the need for claimants to pay attorneys fees and court costs, victim compensation funds can ensure that more money winds up in the pockets of victims.

The major disadvantages of victim compensation funds are also three-fold. First, unlike the tort system, which is well-established, victim compensation funds must be created anew each time they are utilized. Second, victim compensation funds may undermine transparency. Because these funds typically utilize a non-adversarial, non-public approach to compensating victims, victims are unable to pursue discovery. Third, victim compensation funds typically do not provide a public forum in which victims can air grievances, an issue that is often extremely important to victims.

II. Creating a Venue for Autonomous Vehicle Crash Cases

Given the advantages and drawbacks discussed above, which venue (if either) is likely to be the most appropriate and efficient one for autonomous vehicle crash cases? Assuming (as we should) that autonomous vehicle crash victims will always have the option of pursuing conventional litigation, the question may be even simpler: given that these victims will *always* have access to the tort system, does it make sense to create a victim compensation fund as an alternative pathway to receiving compensation? I strongly believe the answer is "yes" for several reasons.

To start, as discussed above, there is likely to be a lengthy multi-year (if not multi-decade) time period during which courts struggle to develop and/or adapt negligence and products liability jurisprudence to autonomous vehicles. The issues surrounding duty, breach, and causation are incredibly complex and fairly novel, and so it is likely that there will be some degree of trial and error (no pun intended) and jurisprudential inconsistency among jurisdictions before the jurisprudence becomes more settled. This means that victims of autonomous vehicle crashes will face even higher degrees of uncertainty than normal when seeking compensation via conventional litigation in the tort system. This, in turn, could deter consumers from purchasing and using these vehicles.

The creation of a victim compensation fund could provide consumers (and citizens in general) with greater assurance that they will be compensated if they are injured by an autonomous vehicle. Victim compensation funds, by their very nature, need not experience the same jurisprudential growing pains suffered by the tort system when faced with a novel form of injury. They can begin issuing compensation via a particular method of calculation or algorithm extremely quickly and pay out to claimants much more predictability and reliability than the tort system ever could. Thus, a victim compensation fund could serve as an extremely useful stop-gap method of compensating victims until the jurisprudence in this area is better developed. If popular with victims, moreover, it could provide a long-term alternative to litigation.

Next, for many of the same reasons, the creation of a victim compensation fund could offer significant protection to the manufacturers and developers of autonomous vehicles, promote innovation, and shore up the market for these vehicles. In the absence of such a fund, manufacturers and developers experience much the same uncertainty as do consumers, but with regard to exposure to liability. This uncertain exposure to liability, in turn, may severely hinder the introduction of autonomous vehicles to market and the long-term viability of autonomous vehicle businesses. Indeed, the biotechnology industry in the United States experienced something very similar in the 1980s. An article from that time period explained:

> One of the foremost obstacles faced by firms attempting to market biotechnological products is insuring their products against product liability claims. Product liability insurance costs in the United States have risen dramatically to keep up with increased legal claims . . . Dramatically increased premiums for product liability insurance [in turn] are forcing some manufacturers out of business . . . Companies are holding back product introductions, restricting the use of certain products, or even withdrawing from markets in order to avoid costs imposed by the U.S. product liability system . . .
>
> Insurance costs are excessive in the biotechnology industry because judicial treatment of biotechnology products is uncertain and potentially very harsh. Uncertainty arises from the fact that the U.S. biotechnology industry has not yet been tested in terms of product liability lawsuits, probably due to the relatively small number of commercially viable biotechnology products marketed to date.[12]

Uncertain exposure to liability thus creates two major potential issues: (1) it can drive up insurance costs, forcing businesses to pass on those costs to consumers via higher prices, making their products less affordable and driving down demand, or (2) in extreme cases, it may make a given product uninsurable and thus shut down the market altogether.

The creation of a victim compensation fund could create significantly more "breathing room" for manufacturers and developers. By offering autonomous vehicle crash victims a quick and reliable way of obtaining compensation in exchange for waiving their right to sue, a fund could reduce the number of lawsuits filed in the tort system and thus drive down the liability exposure of manufacturers and developers and lower insurance costs. This, in turn, would allow the autonomous vehicle market to grow in parallel with the development of autonomous vehicle laws and jurisprudence rather than making the development of this industry contingent upon the resolution of thorny issues of liability, a resolution that will likely take decades.

Lastly, by providing consumers greater assurance that they will be compensated quickly if injured and manufacturers with less exposure to liability, a victim compensation fund could protect the market for autonomous vehicles and thus promote highway safety and the numerous other benefits provided by these vehicles. Failing to create a victim compensation fund, however, could have the opposite effect and undermine or, in a worst case scenario, destroy, a market still in its early stages.

The costs would be profound and measured in human lives lost that could have been saved.

A. Proposed Fund

A quasi-judicial fund is likely the best model for an autonomous vehicle crash fund. Quasi-judicial victim compensation funds are those administered by the judicial system or a federal agency but outside of a traditional, adversarial litigation context. These funds are typically financed by taxes or fines levied on particular categories of people or entities. State crime victim compensation funds, which are funded by fines, penalties, and forfeitures issued in criminal cases and subject to judicial oversight, are one type of quasi-judicial fund. Similarly, the National Vaccine Injury Compensation Program (NVICP), which is financed by an excise tax on childhood vaccines and administered by the U.S. Court of Federal Claims, is another example. Because the federal government has little reason to fund an autonomous vehicle crash fund on its own, this type of fund makes sense in this context under the following conditions and restrictions:

1. Proposed Coverage Limitations

An autonomous vehicle crash fund should only be accessible to victims who have suffered injuries or deaths caused by fully autonomous vehicles. Injuries caused by partially autonomous vehicles should not be covered by the fund because they are more likely to be caused by driver inattention or error than problems with the vehicle itself. Compensating victims for injuries obtained in such accident, therefore, would mean compensating victims for mistakes made by a human driver rather than by the kind of product liability issue intended to be covered by the fund. Covering semi-autonomous crashes would also risk bankrupting the fund fairly quickly, as experts believe that semi-autonomous vehicles are significantly less safe than their fully autonomous counterparts and thus far more likely to be involved in accidents.

Additionally, an autonomous car crash fund should only cover human injuries and fatalities. While car accidents also cause a great deal of property damage, particularly to other vehicles, covering property damage would risk, again, not only bankrupting the fund but overwhelming it with far more claims than it could possibly process.

2. Proposed Source of Funding

Much like the National Vaccine Injury Compensation Program, which is funded by a small tax on every covered vaccine administered to a patient, an autonomous vehicle crash fund should be funded by a tax on the sale of every fully autonomous vehicle. Indeed, "since autonomous cars will very likely benefit society as a whole as well as benefiting the users and the manufacturers," requiring both manufacturers and consumers to pay into the fund "would be a very manageable win/win, pro-market and pro-consumer solution for all involved."[13] Under this approach, both the purchaser and the seller of a new autonomous vehicle would pay a tax that would be deposited into the fund.

Calculating a reasonable tax amount—one that would ensure that the fund was adequately financed while not overly burdening manufacturers or consumers—is difficult and highly dependent on many factors: the number of autonomous vehicles likely to be sold in a given year, the likelihood of an autonomous vehicle causing an injury or fatality, and the average cost of such injuries and fatalities. These are all numbers, moreover, that are likely to change over time, particularly as autonomous vehicles improve and increase in market share. An extremely speculative, rough, and preliminary set of calculations suggests that, based on current data and projections, a total tax of less than $1,000 per autonomous vehicle sold—half paid by the seller and half paid by the purchaser—would be sufficient and reasonable.[14]

Preliminary calcualtions suggest that an autonomous vehicle crash fund may have to pay out somewhere around $2 billion per year to claimants, assuming both that (a) every injury and fatality are eligible for compensation from the fund, and (b) every injury and fatality results in a claim against the fund. Since one recent report suggests that, by 2040, 7.4 million autonomous vehicles will be sold in the United States each year, a total tax of only $270 per vehicle sold (divided between consumer and manufacturer) would be enough to cover the fund's annual payouts.[15] At a significantly smaller market share, say 2.5 million in 2020, a total tax of under $1,000—$800 per vehicle, to be precise—would still be sufficient. Even if the annual average payout of the fund is significantly higher than I have estimated, a total tax of between $1,000 and $1,500 would still likely cover those costs. None of these estimated tax amounts is exorbitant, particularly if it is shared between consumers and manufacturers.

Thus, even under a fairly pessimistic view of the number of autonomous vehicle crashes that will likely occur per year in the United States, a tax equivalent to less than 2% of the average total price of a new vehicle—$1,500 or less—in 2018 dollars should be sufficient to finance an autonomous vehicle crash fund. As autonomous vehicle safety improves and the number of autonomous vehicles sold per year increases, moreover, it is likely that the tax per vehicle required to keep the fund fully financed could drop into the very low hundreds of dollars per vehicle sold.

3. Proposed Administrator

NHTSA is the federal entity best suited to administer an autonomous vehicle crash fund because it is the federal agency "responsible for keeping people safe on America's roadways."[16] NHTSA does so by promulgating and "enforcing vehicle performance standards and [by forming] partnerships with state and local governments."[17] NHTSA also seeks to reduce motor vehicle crashes and injuries by conducting research and data analysis on motor vehicle use and misuse and motor vehicle crashes, and by "setting the motor vehicle and highway safety agenda" for the country.[18]

4. Proposed Participation Requirements

In all victim compensation funds, "the procedure to be utilized in determining who actually receives compensation and in what amounts is critical."[19] Similarly, fund designers must determine at the outset what fund participants must give up in exchange for participating in the fund. In an autonomous vehicle crash fund, victims and vehicle manufacturers should have to confront different trade-offs:

a. Victim Participation Requirements

All victims (or their estates) who are injured by an autonomous vehicle and who wish to receive compensation should be required to initiate proceedings with the fund. Victims who intend to bypass the fund and pursue suit in the tort system should still be required to file a claim with the fund and receive a decision as to the amount of compensation to which they would be entitled before being able to reject the fund option and pursue litigation. The NVICP has a similar set of requirements. Victims (or their estates) who choose to accept the fund's decision and obtain fund compensation should be required to waive their right to pursue litigation against the manufacturer, designer, or programmer of the autonomous vehicle that caused the injury or fatality at issue. Such liability waivers have been a standard feature of most other victim compensation funds, and constitute one of the primary incentives for private industry to support and participate in such compensation schemes. However, to the extent that these victims wish to pursue third-party tort actions against other entities who may have been partial causes of the relevant crash—say, drivers of human-driven cars, pedestrians, construction companies, etc.— they should remain free to do.

Like the NVICP, filing a claim with the autonomous vehicle crash fund should be "nonadversarial and simple relative to [filing a claim in the] civil courts."[20] The claimant should be required to file a petition setting forth "a short and plain statement of the grounds for an award of compensation" and attach any supporting documentation such as medical records that would aid fund administrators in determining an appropriate award.[21] Claimants should have the right to be represented by an attorney but should not be required to retain one. Like other funds, there should also be an internal appeals process.

In exchange for waiving their right to sue manufacturers, designers, and programmers of autonomous vehicles, victims should be entitled to receive compensation for "personal injury, loss of consortium, wrongful death, [and other standard forms of] economic loss" associated with their injury or death.[22] Noneconomic losses, those associated with pain and suffering, emotional and psychological anguish, and other forms of hedonic damages are "highly intangible" and thus far more difficult to quantify.[23] Other funds have dealt with this issue by establishing presumed awards or placing caps on emotional damages. The September 11th Victim Compensation Fund, for example, had a presumed award of $250,000 for emotional damages. The NVICP caps pain and suffering awards at an identical amount: $250,000. Whether and at what amount an autonomous vehicle crash fund should compensate noneconomic damages should be the product of careful deliberation amongst fund administrators about the fund's annual budget, the likely number of claims each year, and the appropriate methodology to use in calculating such damages.

b. Vehicle Manufacturer Participation Requirements

All vehicle manufacturers who pay a tax on the sale of each fully autonomous vehicle should benefit from reduced liability uncertainty and reduced liability exposure. As discussed above, individuals injured by taxed autonomous vehicles should be required to file claims with the fund initially rather than filing suit in the tort system immediately. Since the fund is likely to be able to provide faster and more predictable compensation than the tort system, it is reasonable to expect that the fund would significantly reduce the number of lawsuits filed against autonomous vehicle manufacturers who choose to participate in the fund. Manufacturers who choose not to participate by refusing to pay a tax on each autonomous vehicle sold should not be protected by the fund if one of their vehicles injures someone; in that situation, the victim's only option would be to file a conventional tort claim.

In exchange for the protection offered by the fund, manufacturers should also be required to participate in a data-sharing and design improvement program administered by NHTSA. Such a program would greatly mitigate two significant issues: (1) the difficulty that NHTSA has had in gathering information and issuing timely guidance and regulations pertaining to autonomous vehicles, and (2) the risk that reduced exposure to liability would reduce manufacturer incentives to improve the design and safety performance of their vehicles. A brief discussion of each demonstrates why.

First, NHTSA has had difficulty "keeping pace with the development and deployment of autonomous systems."[24] In large part, this has been due to both the secrecy of manufacturers and designers and to the novelty of the technology. As one representative of Tesla Motors Inc. has observed, "NHTSA [has] had to ensure the safety of [heavily automated vehicles], avoid creating regulations that would slow the deployment of life-saving technology, all without NHTSA's usual ability to observe the performance of technology prior to regulating it."[25] These are extremely difficult tasks at best, but likely impossible in the absence of manufacturer cooperation and data-sharing, a fact stressed by NHTSA throughout the 2016 Federal Automated Vehicles Policy (FAVP). Indeed, the entirety of the FAVP itself is merely guidance for autonomous vehicle manufacturers rather than rule making,[26] and there appear to be no consequences for failure to comply with it.[27] Manufacturer cooperation and voluntary disclosures, therefore, are vital to a successful, safe, and controlled release of fully autonomous vehicles into the consumer market and onto U.S. roads.

Making participation in a data-sharing and design improvement program a condition of participation in an autonomous vehicle crash fund offers a solution to this issue. NHTSA could require, for example, fund participants to disclose all identified cyber vulnerabilities, install a particular security patch in all vehicles, or address a particular design concern within a certain timeframe. Rather than having to either (a) rely on manufacturers to voluntarily disclose design flaws and vulnerabilities out of a desire to act in good faith, or (b) engage in complex and administratively burdensome formal rule making, such a program would thus induce manufacturers to engage in a prescribed set of socially beneficial behaviors. While participation in this program would always remain voluntary, the protection offered by the fund—through the reduction of liability uncertainty and liability exposure—would likely provide an extremely strong incentive for manufacturers to join.

Second, many scholars argue that victim compensation funds may reduce manufacturer incentives to take precautions and thus fail to provide optimal levels of deterrence. Discussing the Gulf Coast Claims Fund, for instance, one scholar worries: "If the Facility sets a precedent for relieving environmental marauders of full liability, it will not achieve optimal deterrence, and thus potentially open the door for future environmental disasters."[28] Here, the concern would be that reduced liability exposure would disincentivize autonomous vehicle manufacturers from continually reviewing and improving the safety features of their vehicles and the overall quality of their designs and algorithms. Again, however, making participation in a data-sharing and design improvement program a condition of participating in the fund would significantly reduce, if not entirely eliminate, this issue. Through such a program, NHTSA could identify safety issues, generate solutions, and induce manufacturers to implement them as a condition of continued participation the fund.

III. Conclusion

Automobile crashes kill over 35,000 people on U.S. roads each year and injure millions of others. We are nearly at the point at which we will be able to reduce those fatalities and injuries by an overwhelming percentage. Whether we will be able to do so, however, depends upon our ability to adapt our society and our laws to autonomous vehicles. The stakes are high and the time we have is extremely limited. Botching our initial transition away from human-driven cars and towards driverless ones will cost human lives. A victim compensation fund, however, offers a way to ease this transition and make it smoother for both manufacturers and consumers alike. Given that the existing tort system will always remain a fallback option, there appear to be few reasons not to give a victim compensation fund a chance and many reasons to design and implement one before fully autonomous cars come to market.

REFERENCES

[1.] [1] Jeremy Levy, No Need to Reinvent the Wheel: Why Existing Liability Law Does Not Need to Be Preemptively Altered to Cope with the Debut of the Driverless Car, 9 J. BUS. ENTREPRENEURSHIP & L. 355, 357 (2016).

[2.] [2] John Frank Weaver, Robots Are People Too: How Siri, Google Car, and Artificial Intelligence Will Force Us to Change Our Laws 56 (Praeger 2014).

[3.] [3] Neal Katyal, *Disruptive Technologies and the Law*, 102 GEO L.J. 1685, 1689 (2014).

[4.] [4] For a more thorough treatment of this topic, please refer to Tracy Hresko Pearl, *Compensation at the Crossroads: Autonomous Vehicles and Alternative Compensation Schemes*, 60 WM. & MARY L.R. 1 (2019).

[5.] [5] F. Patrick Hubbard, "Sophisticated Robots": Balancing Liability, Regulation, and Innovation, 66 FLA. L. REV. 1803, 1811–12 (2014).

[6.] [6] Id.

[7.] [7] Carrie Schroll, Splitting the Bill: Creating a National Car Insurance Fund to Pay for Accidents in Autonomous Vehicles, 109 N.W. U. L. Rev. 803, 805 (2015).

[8.] [8] Tom Vanderbilt, Navigating the Legality of Autonomous Vehicles, WIRED (Feb. 7, 2012).

[9.] [9] Bryan Walker Smith, *Automated Driving and Product Liability*, 2018 MICH. ST. L. R. 1, 15 (2017).

[10.] [10] Joan Flocks, James Davies, The Deepwater Horizon Disaster Compensation Process As Corrective Justice: Views from the Ground Up, 84 MISS. L.J. 1, 37 (2014).

[11.] [11] Francis E. McGovern, *The What and Why of Claims Resolution Facilities*, 57 STAN. L. REV. 1361, 1375 (2005).

[12.] [12] Michael D. Stovsky, Product Liability Barriers to the Commercialization of Biotechnology: Improving the Competitiveness of the U.S. Biotechnology Industry, 6 HIGH TECH. L.J. 363, 373-74 (1991).

[13.] [13] Orly Ravid, Don't Sue Me, I Was Just Lawfully Texting & Drunk When My Autonomous Car Crashed Into You, 44 SW. L. Rev. 175, 199 (2014).

[14.] [14] For a more extensive explanation of how this estimate was attained, please contact the author.

[15.] [15] *See* IHS Markit, Autonomous Vehicle Sales to Surpass 33 Million Annually in 2040, Enabling New Autonomous Mobility in More Than 26 Percent of New Car Sales, IHS Markit Says (Jan. 2, 2018), http://news.ihsmarkit.com/press-release/automotive/autonomous-vehicle-sales-surpass-33-million-annually-2040-enabling-new-auto.

[16.] [16] NHTSA, *About NHTSA*, NHTSA.gov, https://www.nhtsa.gov/about-nhtsa.

[17.] [17] *Id.*

[18.] [18] NHTSA, *NHTSA's Mission*, NHTSA.gov, https://www.nhtsa.gov/about-nhtsa/nhtsas-core-values.

[19.] [19] Mike Steenson & Joseph Michael Sayler, The Legacy of the 9/11 Fund and the Minnesota I-35W Bridge-Collapse Fund: Creating a Template for Compensating Victims of Future Mass-Tort Catastrophes, 35 WM. MITCHELL L. REV. 524, 544 (2009).

[20.] [20] Michael J. Donovan, The Impact of "Hurricane" Hannah: The Government's Decision to Compensate One Girl's Vaccine Injury Case Could Drastically Alter the Face of Public Health, 50 JURISMETRICS J. 229, 232 (2010).

[21.] [21] 42 U.S.C. §§ 300aa-11 (2006).

[22.] [22] Steenson & Sayler, *supra* note 22, at 528.

[23.] [23] Tracy Hresko, Restoration and Relief: Procedural Justice and the September 11th Victim Compensation Fund, 42 GONZ. L. REV. 95, 102 (2007).
[24.] [24] *Tesla's Autopilot: Too Much Autonomy Too Soon,* CONSUMER REPORTS (July 14, 2016), http://www.consumerreports.org/tesla/tesla-autopilot-too-much-autonomy-too-soon/.
[25.] [25] Id.
[26.] [26] *Id.* at 6.
[27.] [27] Stephen Selander, *Docket Number NHTSA 2016-0090-Comments on Federal Automated Vehicle Policy,* SELANDER LAW OFFICE (Nov. 22, 2016) 1 https://www.regulations.gov/document?D=NHTSA-2016-0090-1114.
[28.] [28] Patrick Hall, The Return of King Solomon: The Gulf Coast Claims Facility From the Perspective of the 9/11 Fund, 1 ARIZ. J. ENVTL. L & POL'Y 1, 1 (2010).

The Role and Limits of Principles in AI Ethics: Towards a Focus on Tensions

Jess Whittlestone*
Leverhulme Centre for the Future of Intelligence
University of Cambridge
jlw84@cam.ac.uk

Rune Nyrup
Leverhulme Centre for the Future of Intelligence
University of Cambridge
rn330@cam.ac.uk

Anna Alexandrova
Leverhulme Centre for the Future of Intelligence
Department of History and Philosophy of Science
University of Cambridge
aa686@cam.ac.uk

Stephen Cave
Leverhulme Centre for the Future of Intelligence
University of Cambridge
sjc53@cam.ac.uk

ABSTRACT

The last few years have seen a proliferation of principles for AI ethics. There is substantial overlap between different sets of principles, with widespread agreement that AI should be used for the common good, should not be used to harm people or undermine their rights, and should respect widely held values such as fairness, privacy, and autonomy. While articulating and agreeing on principles is important, it is only a starting point. Drawing on comparisons with the field of bioethics, we highlight some of the limitations of principles: in particular, they are often too broad and high-level to guide ethics in practice. We suggest that an important next step for the field of AI ethics is to focus on exploring the tensions that inevitably arise as we try to implement principles in practice. By explicitly recognising these tensions we can begin to make decisions about how they should be resolved in specific cases, and develop frameworks and guidelines for AI ethics that are rigorous and practically relevant. We discuss some different specific ways that tensions arise in AI ethics, and what processes might be needed to resolve them.

KEYWORDS

Artificial intelligence, ethics, principles

ACM Reference Format:
Jess Whittlestone, Rune Nyrup, Anna Alexandrova, and Stephen Cave. 2019. The Role and Limits of Principles in AI Ethics: Towards a Focus on Tensions. In *AAAI/ACM Conference on AI, Ethics, and Society (AIES '19), January 27–28, 2019, Honolulu, HI, USA.* ACM, New York, NY, USA, 6 pages. https://doi.org/10.1145/3306618.3314289

1 INTRODUCTION

AI systems promise widespread benefits to society, while also posing substantial risks across almost all sectors. In the last few years, a number of different groups and initiatives have attempted to articulate and agree principles to guide the application of AI in society. In this paper we discuss the role and limitations of these principles, and argue that an important next step for AI ethics is to focus more on the tensions that arise as we try to implement them in practice. By 'AI ethics' we specifically mean the emerging field of practical AI ethics, which focuses on developing frameworks and guidelines to ensure the ethical use of AI in society (analogous to the field of biomedical ethics, which provides practical frameworks for ethical practice in medicine.) AI ethics therefore covers several different sectors and types of institutions, including the following:

- **Technology companies** aiming to develop their own ethical guidelines (e.g. Google's 'AI Ethics principles');
- **Professional bodies** whose codes of ethics are aimed at guiding practitioners;
- **Standards-setting bodies** that aim to set general standards for fields of research of industries (e.g. the IEEE or British Standards Institution);
- **Government bodies and legislators** that aim to develop policy and regulation (e.g. the UK's new Centre for Data Ethics and Innovation);
- **Researchers across disciplines** whose work aims to inform these ways that AI ethics is put into practice: exploring the technical, philosophical, or legal aspects of using algorithms in ethical ways [20] or synthesising and translating such research into practice [27].

Agreeing on principles is valuable for the aims of all of these groups: for example, principles can provide a useful starting point from which to develop more formal standards and regulation, and can help to identify priority issues on which both research and policy should focus. However, we argue that current lists of principles for AI ethics are too high-level to be immediately useful for these groups' aims. When we look at specific cases, it becomes clear that principles will come into conflict with each other. This means their practical value is limited: without acknowledging these conflicts standards may be set unrealistically high, or regulation intended to protect one value might inadvertently compromise other important goals. In order to be practically useful, we suggest that the field of AI ethics should focus more on identifying and attempting to resolve the tensions that arise when we apply them to specific cases.

*Corresponding author

AIES '19, January 27–28, 2019, Honolulu, HI, USA

ACM ISBN 978-1-4503-6324-2/19/01.
https://doi.org/10.1145/3306618.3314289

We begin by reviewing how principles have evolved in AI ethics over the last two years. Drawing on comparisons with bioethics - a field with a robust and well-developed tradition in using principles to govern medical practice - we discuss some of the limitations of principles. We make the case that all areas of AI ethics would benefit from a more rigorous exploration of the tensions that arise when we try to apply principles to concrete cases. We outline some key tensions that already arise from the use of AI in society, and discuss what work might be needed to resolve them. To our knowledge, this is the first paper to explicitly examine the role and limits of principles in AI ethics, and the importance of focusing more on tensions as a next step.

2 THE EMERGENCE OF PRINCIPLES IN AI ETHICS

Though the field is in its infancy, there is widespread agreement on some of the core issues (such as bias) and values (such as fairness) that AI ethics should focus on. Over the last two years, these have begun to be codified in sets of 'principles' or 'tenets'. The Asilomar AI principles, developed in 2017 in conjunction with the Asilomar conference for Beneficial AI, outline guidelines on how research should be conducted, ethics and values that use of AI must respect, and important considerations for thinking about long-term issues [12]. The principles were signed by several thousand AI researchers and others, including many academic ethicists and social scientists. Around the same time, the US Association for Computing Machinery (ACM) issued a statement and set of seven principles for Algorithmic Transparency and Accountability, addressing a narrower but closely related set of issues [1].

Over the course of 2017, several other initiatives and organisations published additional sets of principles: including the Japanese Society for Artificial Intelligence's Ethical Guidelines in February 2017 [16]; a set of draft principles from the Montreal Declaration on Responsible AI in November [25]; and the IEEE's General Principles of Ethical Autonomous and Intelligent Systems in December [14]. This proliferation of principles has continued into 2018: with the Partnership on AI publishing a set of 'tenets' which its members agree to uphold [18]; the UK House of Lords suggesting five principles for a cross-sector AI code which could be adopted internationally [23], and Google publishing their 'AI ethics principles' in June [19].

These different sets of principles have considerable overlap. There is widespread agreement that AI-based technologies should be used for the common good, should not be used to harm people or undermine their rights, and should respect widely-held values such as fairness, privacy, and autonomy. [9] suggest that many of the different existing sets can be synthesised into five key principles: the four that are already used in bioethics - autonomy, beneficence, non-maleficence, and justice [4] - plus the additional principle of explicability, which captures the challenges of intelligibility and accountability unique to AI systems. While this convergence is encouraging, it is unclear at this point whether this reflects a deep consensus about what is important, arrived at independently by numerous different actors, or merely a shallow consensus due to the fact that different groups have read similar papers and built on the work of one another.

Principles can be a valuable part of applied ethics; agreeing on high-level principles is therefore an important step for ensuring that AI is developed and used for the benefit of society. Principles help condense complex ethical issues into a few central elements which can be clearly understood and agreed upon by people from diverse fields and sectors. They encourage widespread commitment to a shared set of values, and can give them a more prominent role in institutional decision-making processes. Principles can form a basis for more formal commitments in professional ethics, internationally agreed standards, and regulation. They can also help address public concerns, by clarifying the ethical commitments of researchers and industry.

However, while principles are important, they are not in themselves enough to ensure society can reap the benefits and mitigate the risks of new technologies. In order to be useful in practice, principles need to be able to guide action - to help people navigate the competing demands and considerations of concrete situations. As we articulate in the next section, there are several obstacles to this.

3 THE LIMITS OF PRINCIPLES

The four principles of beneficence, non-maleficence, autonomy, and justice have played a prominent role in bioethics [4], a field with decades of experience in managing the challenges posed by new technologies. These principles aim to articulate general values on which everyone can agree, and to function as practical guidelines. But they have spurred substantial debate: some argue that we should put no weight on principles and focus entirely on the elements of specific cases [10], while others have advocated a more moderate view, whereby principles should be considered in close conjunction with analysis of 'paradigm' cases [17].

However, even the strongest advocates of principlism in bioethics acknowledge that principles alone are not enough. [4] suggest that principles should be taken as guidelines, which need to be made specific for use in policy and clinical decision-making. They elaborate that in order to be action-guiding, principles need to be accompanied by an account of how they apply in specific situations, and how to balance them when they conflict. In this section, we review some of the main limitations of principles that have been highlighted in the bioethics literature and illustrate why these also apply to the principles proposed for AI ethics.

3.1 Different Groups May Interpret Principles Differently

The central terms used in principles are often ambiguous, masking conceptual complexity and differences in interpretation across populations. As [8] point out, the principle of 'justice' in bioethics does not say anything about what is just or unjust, leaving this to the agent to decide for themselves. Clouser and Gert argue that principles often mask important moral disagreements rather than presenting a well-developed unified theory as they propose to, and that it would be better if these disagreements were articulated and understood more explicitly.

In particular, lists of broadly agreed-upon principles cannot recognise that important and legitimate differences in values exist across people and populations. While everyone might agree in principle that 'fairness' is important, there exist deep political disagreements about what exactly constitutes fairness [5]. Groups may also vary in how much weight they put on one value relative to others in situations of conflict: more individualist cultures may put more weight on personal privacy than more collectivist cultures, for example. An important step in making principles more practical is to formalize them into standards and regulation [27]. But this process is not a straightforward unpacking of the relevant principles, as different principles will come into conflict when applied to concrete cases. In the next section, we make the case that in order for principles to inform more practical aspects of AI ethics, including professional ethics, standards, and regulation, we need to begin by exploring in detail the different kinds of tensions that arise when principles are applied.

3.2 Principles Are Highly General

Relatedly, principles are by their nature highly general: their value is that they indicate important moral themes that apply across a wide range of scenarios. This means that they can be useful as a kind of checklist: as a set of important considerations that need to be taken into account in specific scenarios. However, the generality of most principles also limits their ability to guide practical action [3]). Many of the principles proposed in AI ethics are too broad to be action-guiding. For example, ensuring that AI is used for 'social good' or 'the benefit of humanity' is a common thread among all sets of principles. These are phrases on which a great majority can agree exactly because they carry with them few if any real commitments. A very wide range of differing ideological, political and philosophical standpoints could claim to be for the good, or for the benefit of humanity. Only principles that are narrower and more specific are likely to be useful in practice. Recent industry commitments to not develop technology for autonomous weapons are an example of a principle that is specific, action-guiding and can be used to hold people to account. But at the same time, exactly that specificity means its relevance is limited to one sector, and it has many dissenters.

3.3 Principles Come into Conflict in Practice

The gap between principles and practical judgement grows larger still when we consider that principles will inevitably conflict with each other. For example, the UK House of Lords AI Committee report states that, "it is not acceptable to deploy any artificial intelligence system which could have a substantial impact on an individual's life, unless it can generate a full and satisfactory explanation for the decisions it will take." The intentions behind this principle are important, but it masks a crucial tension between using algorithms for social benefit ('beneficence') and ensuring those algorithms are fully intelligible to humans ('explicability'). For example, algorithms exist today that can diagnose medical conditions more accurately than doctors, potentially saving lives [24], but for which a full and satisfactory explanation cannot necessarily be provided (depending on how this is defined). In some situations, the benefit of using an algorithm may be high enough, and its accuracy reliable enough, that all users agree it is worth using even if a fully comprehensive explanation of its decisions cannot be given. There are complex and important trade-offs involved here [15, 22], and a principle that simply states that it is not acceptable to deploy AI systems without full explainability fails to recognise this.

In conclusion, there is a risk that high-level principles give the impression of being the outcome of meaningful debate about how AI should be developed, but in reality they are simply postponing it.

4 WHY THE FIELD SHOULD FOCUS ON TENSIONS

We use the term 'tension' to refer to any conflict, whether apparent, contingent or fundamental, between important values or goals, where it appears necessary to give up one in order to realise the other. For example, the use of socially beneficial data-driven technologies might make it impossible for us to fully guarantee otherwise desirable levels of data privacy. If the potential gains of these technologies are significant enough - new and highly effective cancer treatments, say - we might decide that a higher risk of privacy breaches is a price worth paying.

In some cases, a tension may reflect a strict moral tradeoff: a situation where two values or goals conflict and it is not possible to get more of one without sacrificing another. However, many tensions in AI are more contingent, and arise as a result of current technological or societal constraints. Using machine learning for social benefit may not be fundamentally in tension with privacy, transparency, or fairness, but many current methods employed for the former goal do conflict with these ideals. We do not yet know how far new technological or governance solutions could go to dissolve these tensions.

Others have acknowledged the importance of recognising conflicts between values in AI ethics, but to our knowledge none have explored in detail why this would be beneficial or what it would look like in practice. For example, [9] say that, "Ensuring socially preferable outcomes of AI relies on resolving the tension between incorporating the benefits and mitigating the potential harms of AI, in short, simultaneously avoiding the misuse and underuse of these technologies", but do not discuss specific tensions in detail or how to resolve them.

In this section, we discuss some of the benefits of focusing on tensions. We outline four reasons this is an important next step for AI ethics: (1) bridging the gap between principles and practice, (2) acknowledging differences in values, (3) highlighting areas where new solutions are needed and (4) identifying ambiguities and knowledge gaps.

4.1 Bridging the Gap between Principles and Practice

In general, we see focussing on tensions as an important way of bridging the gap between abstract ethical principles and specific cases, and therefore an important first step towards an ethics of AI that is practical and action-guiding.

To identify tensions, we need to consider how different values and goals might come into practice in concrete cases. For example, when Google DeepMind collaborated with the Royal Free Hospital, they encountered a conflict between protecting the privacy of patient data, and their goal of using AI to improve early diagnosis of acute kidney injury [20]. Since similar tensions will likely arise across a range of different cases, focusing on tensions means we are neither driven entirely by the specifics of an individual case, nor are we relying on abstract high-level values. If we can articulate important tensions by looking at a range of cases, and find ways to resolve them in specific scenarios, what we learn from this can then be used to develop standards and regulation that are more sensitive to how principles apply differently across scenarios.

4.2 Acknowledging Differences in Values

Focusing on tensions forces us to consider how different values might be interpreted and endorsed differently across groups. While some important tensions are due to conflicts between principles in practice, others arise because there are conflicting meanings or values within a single principle: broad terms like 'fairness' or 'justice' for example are subject to substantial moral and political disagreement [5, 8].

It may never be possible to totally resolve all of these disagreements. But clearly articulating them is a crucial starting point for ensuring that all aspects of AI ethics are as inclusive as possible: for example, to ensure that international standards take full account of and accommodate cultural differences, and that agreement on such standards is meaningful.

4.3 Highlighting Areas Where New Solutions Are Needed

Noting a tension between two values does not necessarily mean we are forced to choose between them: often, we may be able to find some way to get more of both things we value. Recognising these tensions can therefore highlight high priority areas for both researchers and policymakers. For example, acknowledging that there is currently a tradeoff between performance and interpretability in state-of-the-art machine learning systems has motivated technical research that attempts to reduce or eliminate this trade-off [2].

Acknowledging tensions will also help direct the development of AI in beneficial directions more generally. It is currently far from clear whether advances in AI will augment or degrade human capabilities and agency, but making this tension explicit focuses attention on the important question of which trajectories of development are most likely to lead to the former.

4.4 Identifying Ambiguities and Knowledge Gaps

Finally, a tension-focused approach helps to clearly highlight ambiguities and gaps in our understanding of how uses of AI are impacting society. Again, this can help identify new and important research directions.

To think clearly about all tensions, we need to recognise and clarify ambiguities in terms: what do we really mean by things like 'fairness', 'justice', and 'autonomy', and how might these be interpreted differently across groups and contexts? To understand the nature of many tensions we need to understand what is currently technically possible: what are the best current methods for ensuring data privacy in machine learning, for example, and what are the costs of these methods? To understand how tensions arise in practice, we need better evidence on how AI is actually being applied in society today: what effect is automation already having on individual lives across different sectors? And to articulate and resolve conflicts between the interests of different groups, we need to really understand the needs and values of affected communities: how do the trade-offs people are willing to make differ based on demographic factors, for example? Focussing on tensions should help to drive this important work.

5 WHICH TENSIONS?

There are several different ways that applications of AI can introduce tensions between important goals and values.

Some tensions arise due to the very nature of AI and machine learning: these techniques allow us to use and draw inferences from very large amounts of (often personal) data, and so challenge important notions of privacy. The most useful models also often quickly become very complex, introducing new issues around human interpretability [11, 26]. This means we face tensions between using these technologies for socially beneficial goals: improving healthcare, justice, or security, for example, and other goals such as respecting privacy and maintaining trust and understanding in automated systems.

Another possibility is that AI systems exacerbate already existing ethical or societal tensions: between different conflicting notions of fairness, for example. Often this is due to the fact that machine learning models are trained on historical data, and so inherit the biases or mistakes they contain [13]. Here, applications of AI in society do not necessarily introduce new tensions, but increase the importance of already-existing ones such as how to make decision-making more accurate and efficient without inadvertently discriminating against minority groups.

Other tensions arise because the harms and benefits of AI systems are unequally distributed in various ways. For example, the impacts of automation may be unequally distributed across populations and cultures: enhancing the agency of some groups by automating mundane tasks while wiping out the livelihood of others, thus threatening their basic needs. The risks and benefits of AI systems could also be unequally distributed over time, and uses of AI that present opportunities in the near term may compromise important long-term values. Increasing personalisation of messages and services may make our lives more convenient and enjoyable in the short run, but begin to undermine important aspects of autonomy, equality and solidarity over time [21].

Finally, AI may have the potential to both enhance and threaten a given value. For example, depending on the precise direction in which technology develops, it could be used to either greatly enhance human capabilities - if we can develop sophisticated methods of intelligence augmentation [7] - or to degrade them: if our own capabilities atrophy as we outsource more and more tasks [6]. As mentioned above, automation might enhance the agency of some groups while threatening the autonomy of others: whether we see AI as enhancing or degrading human agency could depend on how narrow or global a view we take of its impacts.

6 FOUR KEY TENSIONS

Given the wide range of tensions that may arise from applications of AI, now or in the future, there is unlikely to be an exhaustive list of all possible tensions. However, we believe that the following four tensions will be particularly central to thinking about the ethical issues arising from the applications of AI systems in society today. These capture a range of issues which are already salient or likely to grow in importance moving forward.

Tension 1: Using data to improve the quality and efficiency of services vs. respecting privacy and autonomy of individuals. Machine learning and big data are already being used to improve various public services (including healthcare, education, and social care). These improvements could be hugely beneficial to citizens, but require large amounts of personal data, raising concerns about how to best protect privacy and ensure meaningful consent.

Tension 2: Using algorithms to make decisions and predictions more accurate vs ensuring fair and equal treatment. This tension arises when public or private bodies base decisions on predictions about future behaviour of individuals (e.g. when probation officers estimate risk of reoffending) and when they employ machine learning algorithms to improve their predictions. These algorithms may improve accuracy overall, but discriminate against specific subgroups for whom representative data is not available.

Tension 3: Reaping the benefits of increased personalisation in the digital sphere vs enhancing solidarity and citizenship. Companies and governments can use personal data to tailor the messages, offers, and services people see. This personalisation can make it easier for people to find the right products and services for them, but differentiating between people in such fine-grained ways may threaten societal ideals of citizenship and solidarity.

Tension 4: Using automation to make people's lives more convenient and empowered vs promoting selfactualisation and dignity. Automated solutions may genuinely improve people's lives by saving them time on mundane tasks that could be better spent on more rewarding activities. But they also risk disrupting some of the practices that are an important part of what makes us human. With automation we may see the gifts of arts, languages and science become more accessible to those who were excluded in the past - but we may also see widespread deskilling, atrophy, ossification of practices, homogenisation and cultural diversity.

7 IDENTIFYING FURTHER TENSIONS

The above tensions are important and represent areas where exploring tensions is likely to be fruitful for AI ethics. Going forward, further such areas can and should be identified. In order to do so, it is helpful to ask a range of questions, including:

- Where AI is being used to serve a particular goal or value, or for 'social benefit' in general, what risks to other values are introduced?
- Where might uses of AI that benefit one group, or the population as a whole, have negative consequences for a specific subgroup? How do we balance the interests of different groups?
- Where might applications of AI that are beneficial in the near-term introduce risks in the long-term? How do we trade-off short and long-term impacts of society?
- Where might future developments in AI either enhance or threaten important values, depending on the direction they take?

8 RESOLVING TENSIONS

The best approach to resolving a tension will depend on the nature of the tension in question.

Where a strict trade-off between two values exists, a choice must be made to prioritise one set of values over another. For example, this may mean judging what risks to privacy it is acceptable to incur for the sake of better public health, or where to reject innovative automation technologies because the threats they pose to human skills and autonomy are too great.

Making these trade-off judgements will be a complex political process. Weighing the costs and benefits of different solutions can be an important part of the process but alone is not enough, since it fails to recognise that values are vague and unquantifiable, and that numbers often hide complex value judgements. In addition, resolving trade-offs will require extensive public engagement, to give voice to a wide range of stakeholders and articulate their interests with rigour and respect.

On the other hand, where tensions are more practical in nature, strict trade-offs may not be inevitable. It may be that we simply lack the knowledge or tools to advance conflicting values, and investing in further research could identify solutions that better serve all relevant values or goals. For example, it might be possible to use automation to improve people's lives without sacrificing self-actualisation and devaluing human skills, if a clear line can be drawn between the contexts where we do and do not want to pursue automation.

In these situations we face a choice. Even if a tension between two goals is not a fundamentally irresolvable one, if we want to apply current technology in society, we will still need to make the kinds of trade-offs described above. On the other hand, if we can hold-off from implementing technologies that introduce tensions - certain kinds of automation, say - then we could instead invest in more research on how technological or governance solutions might reduce the need to navigate potentially difficult value trade-offs. Of course, this is not a binary choice: we can choose to strike a balance by making the trade-offs necessary to implement technology where doing so is relatively unproblematic, while still investing in research to explore how these tensions might be resolvable in future. This choice can be thought of as involving its own tension, between short- and long-term interests: to what extent should we postpone the benefits of new technologies in order to invest the time and resources necessary to resolve the tensions they introduce?

9 CONCLUSION

Over the last two years, many different sets of principles for the ethical use of AI have been developed. We argue that these high-level principles, rather than representing the outcome of meaningful debate on how AI should be developed, risk simply postponing it. In order to make AI ethics practical, the field needs to now focus more on the tensions that arise when principles are applied to concrete cases.

Though most of these tensions cannot be resolved straightforwardly, we believe articulating them more clearly and explicitly has several benefits. To be useful in practice, principles need to be formalized in standards, codes and ultimately regulation. To be effective, these in turn must acknowledge that there are tensions between the different high-level goals of AI ethics, and provide some guidance on how they should be resolved in different scenarios. They also need to acknowledge and accommodate different perspectives and values as far as possible, if they are to reflect genuine agreement.

A focus on tensions can also help to direct research priorities in AI ethics. Articulating tensions can help to highlight important ambiguities and gaps in our understanding of how AI is currently being applied in society which need further research. More generally, much current research in AI ethics appears to be driven by questions of how we ensure that uses of AI respect important values, such as privacy, transparency, or fairness. Reframing research questions to be more focused on understanding and resolving tensions is an important step towards solving practical problems arising from the use of AI in society, since it directs attention to where new technological or governance solutions might help push the development of AI in robustly beneficial directions.

ACKNOWLEDGMENTS

This work was funded by the Nuffield Foundation and by a Leverhulme Trust Research Centre Grant.

REFERENCES

[1] ACM US Public Policy Council 2017. Statement on Algorithmic Transparency and Accountability. https://www.acm.org/binaries/content/assets/publicpolicy/2017_usacm_statement_algorithms.pdf
[2] Tameem Adel, Zoubin Ghahramani, and Adrian Weller. 2018. Discovering interpretable representations for both deep generative and discriminative models. In *International Conference on Machine Learning*. 50–59.
[3] Tom L. Beauchamp. 1995. Principlism and its alleged competitors. *Kennedy Institute of Ethics Journal* 5, 3 (1995), 181–198.
[4] Tom L. Beauchamp and James F. Childress. 2001. *Principles of biomedical ethics.* Oxford University Press, USA.
[5] Reuben Binns. 2017. Fairness in machine learning: Lessons from political philosophy. *arXiv preprint arXiv:1712.03586* (2017).
[6] Adam J. Carter. 2018. Autonomy, cognitive offloading and education. *Educational Theory* (2018).
[7] Shan Carter and Michael Nielsen. 2017. Using artificial intelligence to augment human intelligence. *Distill* 2, 12 (2017), e9.
[8] Danner K. Clouser and Bernard Gert. 1990. A critique of principlism. *The Journal of medicine and philosophy* 15, 2 (1990), 219–236.
[9] Josh Cowls and Luciano Floridi. 2018. Prolegomena to a White Paper on an Ethical Framework for a Good AI Society. (2018).
[10] Jonathan Dancy. 2004. *Ethics without principles.* Oxford University Press on Demand.
[11] Finale Doshi-Velez and Been Kim. 2017. Towards a rigorous science of interpretable machine learning. *arXiv preprint arXiv:1702.08608* (2017).
[12] Future of Life Institute 2017. Asilomar AI Principles. https://futureoflife.org/ai-principles/
[13] Sara Hajian, Francesco Bonchi, and Carlos Catillo. 2016. Algorithmic bias: From discrimination discovery to fairness-aware data mining. In *Proceedings of the 22nd ACM SIGKDD international conference on knowledge discovery and data mining.* ACM, 2125–2126.
[14] IEEE 2017. Ethically Aligned Design, Version 2. https://ethicsinaction.ieee.org/
[15] W. Nicholson Price II. 2017. Regulating black-box medicine. *Mich. L. Rev.* 116 (2017), 421.
[16] Japanese Society for Artificial Intelligence 2017. The Japanese Society for Artificial Intelligence Ethical Guidelines. http://ai-elsi.org/archives/514
[17] Albert R. Jonsen and Stephen E. Toulmin. 1988. *The abuse of casuistry: A history of moral reasoning.* Univ of California Press.
[18] Partnership on AI 2018. Tenets. https://www.partnershiponai.org/tenets/
[19] Sundar Pichai. 2018. AI at Google: Our Principles. https://www.blog.google/technology/ai/ai-principles/.
[20] Julia Powles and Hal Hodson. 2017. Google DeepMind and healthcare in an age of algorithms. *Health and technology* 7, 4 (2017), 351–367.
[21] Barbara Prainsack and Alena Buyx. 2017. *Solidarity in biomedicine and beyond.* Vol. 33. Cambridge University Press.
[22] Andrew D. Selbst and Solon Barocas. 2018. The intuitive appeal of explainable machines. *Fordham L. Rev.* 87 (2018), 1085.
[23] Select Committee on Artificial Intelligence 2018. AI in the UK: Ready, Willing, and Able? https://publications.parliament.uk/pa/ld201719/ldselect/ldai/100/100.pdf
[24] Ming Song, Yi Yang, Jianghong He, Zhengyi Yang, Shan Yu, Qiuyou Xie, Xiaoyu Xia, Yuanyuan Dang, Qiang Zhang, Xinhuai Wu, Yue Cui, Bing Hou, Ronghao Yu, Ruxiang Xu, and Tianzi Jiang. 2018. Prognostication of chronic disorders of consciousness using brain functional networks and clinical characteristics. *eLife* 7 (2018), e36173.
[25] University of Montreal 2017. Montreal Declaration on Responsible AI. https://www.montrealdeclaration-responsibleai.com/the-declaration
[26] Adrian Weller. 2017. Challenges for transparency. *arXiv preprint arXiv:1708.01870* (2017).
[27] Alan F. Winfield and Marina Jirotka. 2018. Ethical governance is essential to building trust in robotics and artificial intelligence systems. *Philosophical Transactions of the Royal Society A: Mathematical, Physical and Engineering Sciences* 376, 2133 (2018), 20180085.

How Technological Advances Can Reveal Rights

Jack Parker
Carnegie Mellon University
cgparker@andrew.cmu.edu

David Danks
Carnegie Mellon University
ddanks@cmu.edu

ACM Reference Format:
Jack Parker and David Danks. 2019. How Technological Advances Can Reveal Rights. In *AAAI/ACM Conference on AI, Ethics, and Society (AIES '19), January 27–28, 2019, Honolulu, HI, USA.* ACM, New York, NY, USA, 1 page. https://doi.org/10.1145/3306618.3314274

Over recent decades, technological development has been accompanied by the proposal of new rights by various groups and individuals: the right to public anonymity, the right to be forgotten, and the right to disconnect, for example. Although there is widespread acknowledgment of the motivation behind these proposed rights, there is little agreement about their actual normative status. One potential challenge is that the claims only arise in contingent social-technical contexts, which may affect how we conceive of them ethically (albeit, not necessarily in terms of policy). What sort of morally legitimate rights claims depend on such contingencies?

Our paper investigates the grounds on which such proposals might be considered "actual" rights.[1] We propose the notion of a *revealed right*, a right that only imposes duties – and thus is only meaningfully revealed – in certain technological contexts. Our framework is based on an interest theory approach to rights, which understands rights in terms of a justificatory role: morally important aspects of a person's well-being (interests) ground rights, which then justify holding someone to a duty that promotes or protects that interest. Our framework uses this approach to interpret the conflicts that lead to revealed rights in terms of how technological developments cause shifts in the balance of power to promote particular interests.

Different parties can have competing or conflicting interests. It is also generally accepted that some interests are more normatively important than others (even if only within a particular framework). We can refer to this difference in importance by saying that the former interest has less "moral weight" than the latter interest (in that context). The moral weight of an interest is connected to its contribution to the interest-holder's overall well-being, and thereby determines the strength of the reason that a corresponding right provides to justify a duty. Improved technology can offer resources that grant one party increased causal power to realize its interests to the detriment of another's capacity to do so, even while the relative moral weight of their interests remain the same.

[1] The full paper can be found at http://www.andrew.cmu.edu/user/cgparker/Parker_Danks_RevealedRights.pdf.

AIES '19, January 27–28, 2019, Honolulu, HI, USA

ACM ISBN 978-1-4503-6324-2/19/01...$15.00
https://doi.org/10.1145/3306618.3314274

Such changes in circumstance can make the importance of protecting a particular interest newly salient. If that interest's moral weight justifies establishing a duty to protect it, thereby limiting the threat posed by the new socio-technical context, then a right is revealed. Revealed rights justify realignment between the moral weight and causal power orderings so that people with weightier interests have greater power to protect those interests.

In the extended paper, we show how this account can be applied to the interpretation of two recently proposed "rights": the right to be forgotten, and the right to disconnect. Since we are focused on making sense of revealed rights, not any particular substantive theory of interests or well-being, the characterization of 'weights' is a free parameter in this account. Our framework alone cannot provide means to resolve the question of whether specific rights exist, but it can be used to identify empirical questions that need to be answered to decide the existence or non-existence of such rights. The emergence of a revealed right depends on a number of factors, including: whether the plausible uses of the technology could potentially impede another's well-being or interests; whether the technology is sufficiently common to have a wider, social impact; and whether the technology has actually changed the balance of power sufficiently to yield a frequent possibility for misalignment between causal power and moral weight.

This approach confronts the question of how, in principle, such rights could be justified, without requiring specific commitments on the ontology of rights. Our account explains why the rhetoric of "new rights" is both accurate (since the rights were not previously recognized) and inaccurate (since the rights were present all along, but without corresponding duties). Further, it explains the rights without grounding their normative status in considerations related to right-holders' capacities to rationally waive or assert claims. This is especially important given that many of the relevant disruptive technological developments pose challenges to understanding by affected parties for the same reasons they pose threats to those parties' well-being. In the course of our discussion, we confront a number of potential objections to the account. We argue that our framework's ability to accommodate highly specific or derivative-seeming rights is un-problematic. We also head off worries that our use of interest theory makes the account likely to recognize absurd rights claims.

ACKNOWLEDGMENTS

This paper was made possible in part by a grant from Carnegie Corporation of New York. David Danks is the recipient of an Andrew Carnegie Fellowship. The statements made and views expressed are solely the responsibility of the authors.

IMLI: An Incremental Framework for MaxSAT-Based Learning of Interpretable Classification Rules

Bishwamittra Ghosh
National University of Singapore
Singapore

Kuldeep S. Meel
National University of Singapore
Singapore

ABSTRACT

The wide adoption of machine learning in the critical domains such as medical diagnosis, law, education had propelled the need for interpretable techniques due to the need for end users to understand the reasoning behind decisions due to learning systems. The computational intractability of interpretable learning led practitioners to design heuristic techniques, which fail to provide sound handles to tradeoff accuracy and interpretability.

Motivated by the success of MaxSAT solvers over the past decade, recently MaxSAT-based approach, called MLIC, was proposed that seeks to reduce the problem of learning interpretable rules expressed in Conjunctive Normal Form (CNF) to a MaxSAT query. While MLIC was shown to achieve accuracy similar to that of other state of the art *black-box* classifiers while generating small interpretable CNF formulas, the runtime performance of MLIC is significantly lagging and renders approach unusable in practice. In this context, authors raised the question: *Is it possible to achieve the best of both worlds, i.e., a sound framework for interpretable learning that can take advantage of MaxSAT solvers while scaling to real-world instances?*

In this paper, we take a step towards answering the above question in affirmation. We propose IMLI: an incremental approach to MaxSAT based framework that achieves scalable runtime performance via partition-based training methodology. Extensive experiments on benchmarks arising from UCI repository demonstrate that IMLI achieves up to three orders of magnitude runtime improvement without loss of accuracy and interpretability.

CCS CONCEPTS

• **Computing methodologies → Machine learning; Supervised learning; Rule learning.**

KEYWORDS

Interpretable Model, Classification Rules, MaxSAT-based Formulation

ACM Reference Format:

Bishwamittra Ghosh and Kuldeep S. Meel. 2019. IMLI: An Incremental Framework for MaxSAT-Based Learning of Interpretable Classification Rules. In *AAAI/ACM Conference on AI, Ethics, and Society (AIES '19), January 27–28, 2019, Honolulu, HI, USA.* ACM, New York, NY, USA, 8 pages. https://doi.org/10.1145/3306618.3314283

AIES '19, January 27–28, 2019, Honolulu, HI, USA
© 2019 Association for Computing Machinery.
ACM ISBN 978-1-4503-6324-2/19/01...$15.00
https://doi.org/10.1145/3306618.3314283

1 INTRODUCTION

The recent advances in the machine learning techniques have led autonomous decision making systems be adopted in wide range of domains to perform data-driven decision making. As such the domains range from movie recommendations, ad predictions to legal, medical, and judicial. The diversity of domains mandate different criteria for the machine learning techniques. For domains such as movie recommendations and ad predictions, accuracy is usually the primary objective but for safety critical domains [17] such as medical and legal, interpretability, privacy, and fairness [1] are of paramount importance.

It has been long observed that the interpretable techniques are typically trusted and adopted by decision makers as interpretability provides them understanding of reasoning behind a tool's decision making [21]. At this point, it is important to acknowledge that formalizing interpretability is a major challenge [11] and we do not claim to have final word on this. In this context, it is worth noting that for several domains such as medical domain, which was the motivation for our investigation, decision rules with small number of rules tend to be most interpretable [12].

Since the problem of rule learning is known to be in NP-hard, the earliest efforts focused on heuristic approaches that sought to combine heuristically chosen optimization functions with greedy algorithmic techniques. Recently, there has been surge of effort to achieve balance between accuracy and rule size via principled objective functions and usage of combinatorial optimization techniques such as linear programming (LP) relaxations, sub-modular optimization, or Bayesian methods [2, 4, 14, 15, 27] [1]. Motivated by the success of MaxSAT solving over the past decade, Malioutov and Meel proposed a MaxSAT-based approach, called MLIC [13], that provides a precise control of accuracy vs. interpretability. The said approach was shown to provide interpretable Boolean formulas without significant loss of accuracy compared to the state of the art classifiers. MLIC, however, has poor scalability in terms of training time and times out for most instances beyond hundreds of samples. In this context, we ask: *Can we design a MaxSAT-based framework to efficiently construct interpretable rules without loss of accuracy and scaling to large real-world instances?*

The primary contribution of this paper is an affirmative answer to the above question. We first investigate the reason for poor scalability of MLIC and attribute it to large size (i.e., number of clauses) of MaxSAT queries constructed by MLIC. In particular, for training

[1] An extensive survey of related work is presented in Appendix A.

data of n samples over m boolean features, MLIC constructs a formula of size $O(n \cdot m \cdot k)$ to construct a k−clause Boolean formula. We empirically observe that the performance of MaxSAT solvers has worse than quadratic degradation in runtime with increase in the size of query. This leads us to propose a novel incremental framework, called IMLI, for learning interpretable rules using MaxSAT. In contrast to MLIC, IMLI makes p queries to MaxSAT solvers with each query of the size $O(\frac{n}{p} \cdot m \cdot k)$. IMLI relies on first partitioning the data into p partitions and then incrementally learning rules on the p partitions in a linear order such that rule learned for the i-th partition not only uses the current partition but regularizes itself with respect to the rules learned from the first $i-1$ partitions. We conduct a comprehensive experimental study over the large set of benchmarks and show that IMLI significantly improves upon the runtime performance of MLIC by achieving speedup of up to three orders of magnitude. Furthermore, the rules learned by IMLI are significantly small and easy to interpret compared to that of the state of the art classifiers such as RIPPER and MLIC.

Similar to Malioutov and Meel [13], we hope that IMLI will excite researchers in machine learning and CP/SAT (Constraint Programming/Satisfiability) communities to consider this topic further: in designing new MaxSAT-based formulations and in turn designing the MaxSAT solvers tuned for interpretable machine learning.

2 PRELIMINARIES

We use capital boldface letters such as $\mathbf{X}$ to denote matrices while lower boldface letters $\mathbf{y}$ are reserved for vectors/sets. For a matrix $\mathbf{X}$, $\mathbf{X}_i$ represents the i-th row of $\mathbf{X}$ while for a vector/set $\mathbf{y}$, y_i represents the i-th element of $\mathbf{y}$.

Let F be a Boolean formula and $\mathbf{b} = \{b_1, b_2, \ldots, b_m\}$ be the set of variables appearing in F. A literal is a variable (b_i) or its complement($\neg b_i$). A *satisfying assignment* or a *witness* of F is an assignment of variables in $\mathbf{b}$ that makes F evaluate to *true*. If σ is an assignment of variables and $b_i \in \mathbf{b}$, we use $\sigma(b_i)$ to denote the value assigned to b_i in σ. F is in Conjunctive Normal Form (CNF) if $F := C_1 \wedge C_2 \cdots \wedge C_k$, where each clause C_i is represented as disjunction of literals. We use $|C_i|$ to denote the number of literals in C_i. For two vectors $\mathbf{u}$ and $\mathbf{v}$ over propositional variables or constants ($0, 1, true, false$ etc.), we define $\mathbf{u} \vee \mathbf{v} = \bigvee_i (u_i \wedge v_i)$, where u_i and v_i denote a variable/constant at the i-th index of $\mathbf{u}$ and $\mathbf{v}$ respectively. In this context, note that the operation $\wedge$ between a variable and a constant follows the standard interpretation, i.e., $0 \wedge b = 0$ and $1 \wedge b = b$.

We consider a standard binary classification, where we are given a collection of training samples $\{\mathbf{X}_i, y_i\}$ where each vector $\mathbf{X}_i \in \mathcal{X}$ contains the valuation of the features $\mathbf{x} = \{x_1, x_2, \ldots, x_m\}$ for sample i, and $y_i \in \{0, 1\}$ is the binary label for sample i. A classifier $\mathcal{R}$ is a mapping that takes in a feature vector $\mathbf{x}$ and return a class y, i.e., $y = \mathcal{R}(\mathbf{x})$. The goal is not only to design $\mathcal{R}$ to approximate our training set, but also to generalize to unseen samples arising from the same distribution. We define two rules $\mathcal{R}_1$ and $\mathcal{R}_2$ to be equivalent if $\forall i, \mathcal{R}_1(\mathbf{X}_i) = \mathcal{R}_2(\mathbf{X}_i)$. In this work, we restrict $\mathbf{x}$ and y to be Boolean (we discuss in Sect. 4.2 that such a restriction can be achieved without loss of generality) and focus on classifiers that can be expressed compactly in CNF. We use $clause(\mathcal{R}, i)$ to denote the i-th clause of $\mathcal{R}$. Furthermore, we use $|\mathcal{R}|$ to denote the rule-size of classifier $\mathcal{R}$ that is the sum of the count of literals in all the clauses, i.e., $|\mathcal{R}| = \Sigma_i |clause(\mathcal{R}, i)|$.

In this work, we focus on the weighted variant of CNF wherein a weight function is defined over clauses. For a clause C_i and weight function $W(\cdot)$, we use $W(C_i)$ to denote the weight of clause C_i. We say that a clause C_i is hard if $W(C_i) = \infty$, otherwise C_i is called a soft clause. To avoid notational clutter, we overload $W(\cdot)$ to denote the weight of an assignment or clause, depending on the context. We define weight of an assignment σ as the sum of weight of clauses that σ does not satisfy. Formally, $W(\sigma) = \Sigma_{i | \sigma \not\models C_i} W(C_i)$.

Given F and weight function $W(\cdot)$, the problem of MaxSAT is to find an assignment σ^* that has the minimum weight, i.e., $\sigma^* = \mathsf{MaxSAT}(F, W)$ if $\forall \sigma \neq \sigma^*, W(\sigma*) \leq W(\sigma)$. Our formulation will have positive clause weights, hence MaxSAT corresponds to satisfying as many clauses as possible, and picking the strongest clauses among the unsatisfied ones. Borrowing terminology of community focused on developing MaxSAT solvers, we are solving a partial weighted MaxSAT instance wherein we mark all the clauses with ∞ weight as hard and clauses with other positive value less than ∞ weight as soft and ask for a solution that optimizes the partial weighted MaxSAT formula. The knowledge of inner working of MaxSAT solvers and encoding of our representation into weighted MaxSAT is not required for this paper.

3 PROBLEM FORMULATION

Given a training set $\{\mathbf{X}, \mathbf{y}\}$, our goal is to find an interpretable rule that is as accurate as possible. As noted earlier, there are several notions of interpretability. We follow the notion employed in Malioutov and Meel [13], which focuses on the construction of rules involving few clauses each with few literals [2].

In particular, suppose $\mathcal{R}$ classifies all samples correctly, i.e., $\forall i, y_i = \mathcal{R}(\mathbf{X}_i)$. Among all the rules that classify all samples correctly, we choose $\mathcal{R}$ which is the sparsest (most interpretable) one.

$$\min_{\mathcal{R}} |\mathcal{R}| \text{ such that } \forall i, y_i = \mathcal{R}(\mathbf{X}_i)$$

A classifier rule, however, can not classify all samples correctly. Hence we choose a classifier that makes less prediction error. $\mathcal{E}_{\mathcal{R}}$ is the set of samples which are misclassified by $\mathcal{R}$, i.e., $\mathcal{E}_{\mathcal{R}} = \{\mathbf{X}_i | y_i \neq \mathcal{R}(\mathbf{X}_i)\}$. Hence we aim to find $\mathcal{R}$ as follows.

$$\min_{\mathcal{R}} |\mathcal{R}| + \lambda |\mathcal{E}_{\mathcal{R}}| \text{ such that } \forall \mathbf{X}_i \notin \mathcal{E}_{\mathcal{R}}, y_i = \mathcal{R}(\mathbf{X}_i)$$

λ is the data fidelity parameter balancing the trade-off between classifier complexity and prediction accuracy. Higher value of λ guarantees less prediction error while sacrificing the sparsity of $\mathcal{R}$ by adding more literals in $\mathcal{R}$, and vice versa. Therefore λ is an inverse of regularization.

4 IMLI: MAXSAT-BASED INCREMENTAL LEARNING FRAMEWORK OF INTERPRETABLE RULES

In this section, we present the primary contribution of this paper, IMLI, which is a MaxSAT-based incremental learning framework for interpretable classification rules. The core technical idea behind

[2] An advantage of Malioutov and Meel's formulation is a formal notion of interpretability, which is amenable to formal analysis. We do not wish to claim that Malioutov and Meel's notion is the only formal definition of interpretability.

IMLI is to divide the training data into a fixed number p of partitions and employ MaxSAT based learning framework for each partition such that the MaxSAT query constructed for partition i is based on the training data for partition i and the rule learned until partition $i-1$. To this end, we use the notation $(\mathbf{X}^i, \mathbf{y}^i)$ to refer to the training data for the i-th partition. We assume that $\forall i, |\mathbf{X}^i| = |\mathbf{X}^{i-1}|$.

The rest of the section is organized as follows: we first describe the construction of MaxSAT query for the i-th partition in Sect. 4.1 to learn CNF rules, and then discuss the discretization techniques for real-world datasets in Sect. 4.2. The incrementality of IMLI gives rise to the challenge of having redundant literals in the learned rules; we address such redundancy in Sect. 4.3 and finally we discuss, in Sect. 4.4, how our framework for learning CNF rules can be easily extended to learn DNF rules as well. We provide an illustration of rule learning of IMLI in Appendix B.1.

4.1 Construction of MaxSAT Query

We now discuss the construction of a MaxSAT query, denoted by Q_i, for the i-th partition ($i \in [1, p]$). To construct the MaxSAT query for the i-th partition, we assume an access to the rule learned from the $(i-1)$-th partition (where $\mathcal{R}_0$ is an empty formula).

The construction of Q_i takes in four parameters: (i) k, the desired number of clauses in CNF rule, (ii) λ, the data fidelity parameter, (iii) a matrix $\mathbf{X}^i \in \{0,1\}^{n \times m}$ describing the binary value of m features for each of n samples with $\mathbf{X}^i_q$ being a binary valued vector for the q-th sample corresponding to feature vector $\mathbf{x} = \{x_1, x_2, \ldots, x_m\}$, (iv) a label vector $\mathbf{y}^i \in \{0,1\}^n$ containing a class label y^i_q for the sample $\mathbf{X}^i_q$. Consequently, IMLI constructs a MaxSAT query for the i-th partition and invokes an off-the-shelf MaxSAT solver to compute the underlying rule $\mathcal{R}_i$.

IMLI considers two types of propositional variables: (i) feature variables and (ii) noise (classification error) variables. For the i-th partition, IMLI formulates a classifier rule $\mathcal{R}_i$ based on following intuition. Recall, a k-clause CNF rule $\mathcal{R}_i = \bigwedge_{l=1}^k C_l$ is represented as the conjunction of k clauses where clause C_l is the disjunction of feature variables. A sample $\mathbf{X}^i_q$ satisfies C_l if $\mathbf{X}^i_q$ has at least one similar feature whose representative variable is present in C_l. If $\mathbf{X}^i_q$ satisfies $\forall l, C_l$, then $\mathcal{R}_i(\mathbf{X}^i_q) = 1$ otherwise $\mathcal{R}_i(\mathbf{X}^i_q) = 0$. Since feature x_j can be present or not present in each of k clauses, IMLI considers k boolean variables, each denoted by b^l_j ($l \in [1, k]$) for feature x_j to denote its participation in the l-th clause. A sample $\mathbf{X}^i_q$, however, can be misclassified by $\mathcal{R}_i$ i.e., $\mathcal{R}_i(\mathbf{X}^i_q) \oplus y^i_q = 1$. IMLI introduces a noise variable η_q corresponding to sample $\mathbf{X}^i_q$ so that the assignment of η_q can be interpreted whether $\mathbf{X}^i_q$ is misclassified by $\mathcal{R}_i$ or not. Hence the key idea of IMLI for learning the i-th partition is to define a MaxSAT query over $k \times m + n$ propositional variables, denoted by $\{b^1_1, b^1_2, \ldots, b^1_m, \ldots, b^k_m, \eta_1, \ldots, \eta_n\}$. The MaxSAT query of IMLI consists of the following three sets of constraints:

(1) Since our objective is to find sparser rules, the default objective of IMLI would be to add a constraint to falsify as many b^l_j as possible. As noted earlier, rule $\mathcal{R}_{i-1}$ from the $(i-1)$-th partition plays an important role in the construction of MaxSAT constraints of the i-th partition. Therefore, if $x_j \in clause(\mathcal{R}_{i-1}, l)$, IMLI would deviate from its default behavior by adding a constraint to keep the corresponding literal *true* in the optimal assignment. The weight corresponding to this clause is 1. We formalize our discussion as follows:

$$V^l_j := \begin{cases} b^l_j & \text{if } x_j \in clause(\mathcal{R}_{i-1}, l) \\ \neg b^l_j & \text{otherwise} \end{cases}; \quad W(V^l_j) = 1$$

(2) We use noise variables to handle mis-classifications and therefore, IMLI tries to falsify as many noise variables as possible. Since data fidelity parameter λ is proportionate to accuracy, IMLI puts λ weight to each following soft clause.

$$N_q := (\neg \eta_q); \qquad W(N_q) = \lambda$$

(3) Let $\mathbf{B}_l = \{b^l_j \mid j \in [1, m]\}$. Here we provide the third set of constraints of IMLI.

$$D_q := (\neg \eta_q \rightarrow (y_q \leftrightarrow \bigwedge_{l=1}^{k} (\mathbf{X}_q \vee \mathbf{B}_l))); W(D_q) = \infty$$

Every hard clause D_q can be interpreted as follows. If η_q is assigned to *false* ($\neg \eta_q = true$) then $y^i_q = \mathcal{R}_i(\mathbf{X}^i_q) = \bigwedge_{l=1}^k (\mathbf{X}_q \vee \mathbf{B}_l)$. The operator "$\vee$" is defined in Sect. 2.

Finally, the set of constraints Q_i for the i-th partition constructed by IMLI is defined as follows:

$$Q_i := \bigwedge_{j=1, l=1}^{j=m, l=k} V^l_j \wedge \bigwedge_{q=1}^{n} N_q \wedge \bigwedge_{q=1}^{n} D_q$$

Next, we extract $\mathcal{R}_i$ from the solution of Q_i as follows.

Construction 1. *Let* $\sigma^* = \mathsf{MaxSAT}(Q_i, W)$, *then* $x_j \in clause(\mathcal{R}_i, l)$ *iff* $\sigma^*(b^l_j) = 1$.

In the rest of the manuscript, we will use $\mathcal{R}$ to denote $\mathcal{R}_p$.

4.2 Beyond Binary Features

We have considered that the feature value of a training sample is binary. Real-world datasets, however, contain categorical, real-valued or numerical features. We use the standard discretization technique to convert categorical and continuous (real or integer value) features to boolean features. We use *one hot encoding* to convert categorical features to binary features by introducing a boolean vector with the cardinality equal to the number of distinct categories of individual categorical features.

Example 4.1. *Consider a categorical feature with three categories: "red", "green", "'yellow". One hot encoding would convert this feature to three binary variables, which take values* 100, 010, *and* 001 *for the three categories.*

Furthermore, we can discretize the continuous-valued features into binary features by comparing the feature value to a collection of thresholds within range and introducing a boolean feature vector with cardinality proportional to the number of considered thresholds [13]. Specifically, for a continuous feature x_c we consider a number of thresholds $\{\tau_1, \ldots, \tau_t\}$ where $\tau_i < \tau_{i+1}$ and define two separate Boolean features $I[x_c \geq \tau_i]$ and $I[x_c < \tau_i]$ for each τ_i. We present the following definitions based on the discretization of continuous features.

Definition 2. *$tval(b) : b \rightarrow \tau$ is a function over boolean variables corresponding to discretized binary features (from a continuous feature) and outputs the compared threshold value.*

Definition 3. *$op(b) : b \rightarrow \{\geq, <\}$ is a function over boolean variables corresponding to discretized binary features (from a continuous feature) and outputs the comparison operator between continuous feature value and $tval(b)$.*

Definition 4. *$siblings(b_i, b_j) : (b_i, b_j) \rightarrow \{true, false\}$ is a function over pair of boolean variables b_i, b_j and outputs true if the boolean features corresponding to b_i, b_j are constructed by discretizing the same continuous feature and $op(b_i) = op(b_j)$.*

Example 4.2. *Consider a continuous feature x_c with range $(0, 100)$ and three thresholds $\{25, 50, 75\}$ associated with this feature. IMLI introduces 6 new boolean features $\{x_1 : I[x_c \geq 25], x_2 : I[x_c \geq 50], x_3 : I[x_c \geq 75], x_4 : I[x_c < 25], x_5 : I[x_c < 50], x_6 : I[x_c < 75]\}$. Following this discretization technique, the binary feature vector of a sample with feature value $x_c = 37.5$ is 100011, because among the 6 introduced boolean features $x_1 : I[37.5 \geq 25] = 1$, $x_5 : I[37.5 < 50] = 1$, and $x_6 : I[37.5 < 75] = 1$.*

Example 4.3. *In Example 4.2, b_i is a boolean variable corresponding to feature x_i. Now $tval(b_1) = 25$, $op(b_1) =$ "$\geq$", $siblings(b_1, b_2) = true$, and $siblings(b_1, b_4) = false$.*

4.3 Redundancy Removal

Given the incremental procedure of learning $\mathcal{R}$ where the constraints for the i-th partition are influenced from the rule learned until the $(i-1)$-th partition, one key challenge is to address potential redundancy in the learned rules. In particular, we observe that redundancy manifests itself in binary features corresponding to continuous-valued features as the $(i-1)$-th partition might suggest inclusion of feature $I[x_c < \tau_u]$ while the i-th partition also suggests inclusion of feature $I[x_c < \tau_v]$ where $\tau_u \neq \tau_v$. To this end, we present Algorithm 1 to remove redundant literals.

Algorithm 1 Remove Redundancy

```
procedure REMOVEREDUNDANTLITERALS(R)
    for each clause C_l of R do
        for each pair ⟨b_i^l, b_j^l⟩ where σ(b_i^l) = σ(b_j^l) = 1,
          siblings(b_i^l, b_j^l) = true, and tval(b_i^l) < tval(b_j^l) do
            if op(b_i^l) = op(b_j^l) = " ≥ " then
                R' = R[σ(b_j^l) ↦ 0]                ▷ b_j^l is redundant
            else
                R' = R[σ(b_i^l) ↦ 0]
    return R'
```

Lemma 5. *$|\mathcal{R}'| \leq |\mathcal{R}|$ and $\mathcal{R}'$ is equivalent to $\mathcal{R}$.*

Proof. See Appendix C. □

4.4 Learning DNF Rules

Primarily we focus on learning rule $\mathcal{R}$ which is in CNF form. We can also apply incremental technique for learning DNF rules. Suppose, we want to learn a rule $y = S(x)$ where $S(x)$ is expressible in DNF. We show that $y = S(x) \leftrightarrow \neg(y = \neg S(x))$. Here $\neg S(x)$ is in CNF. Therefore, to learn DNF rule $S(x)$, we simply call IMLI with $\neg$y as input for all p batches, learn CNF rule, and finally negate the learned rule. Hence Algorithm 1 can be directly applied.

Example 4.4. *"(is Male $\vee$ Age < 50) $\wedge$ (Education = Graduate $\vee$ Income $\geq$ 1500)"—rule is learned for negated class label. The resultant DNF rule is "(is not Male $\wedge$ Age ≥ 50) $\vee$ (Education $\neq$ Graduate $\wedge$ Income $<$ 1500)"*

5 EXPERIMENT

We have implemented a prototype implementation in Python to evaluate the performance of IMLI[3]. The experiment has been conducted on high performance computer cluster, where each node consists of E5-2690 v3 CPU with 24 cores, 96GB of RAM, and in total 130,000 CPU hours. We have conducted an extensive set of experiments on publicly available benchmarks (detailed description in Appendix D.1) from UCI repository [10] to answer the following questions.

(1) How do the training time and accuracy of IMLI compare to that of state of the art classifiers including both interpretable and non-interpretable ones?
(2) How do accuracy, rule size, and training time of IMLI vary with data fidelity parameter λ and the number of partitions p?
(3) How interpretable are the rules generated by IMLI?

In summary, the experimental results demonstrate that IMLI can scale to large datasets involving tens of thousands of samples with hundreds of binary features. In contrast to MLIC, IMLI achieves up to three orders of magnitude improvement in training time without loss of accuracy and interpretability. IMLI generates rules which are not only interpretable but also accurate compared to other classifiers, which often produce non-interpretable models for the sake of accuracy.

5.1 Experiment Methodology:

To measure the performance gain over MLIC, we measure the accuracy and training time of IMLI vis-a-vis MLIC. We also perform comparisons with another state of the art classifier RIPPER and other (mostly) non-interpretable classifiers such as random forest (RF), support vector classifier (SVC), Nearest Neighbors classifier (NN), l_1-penalized Logistic Regression (LR).

The number of parameter values is comparable (10) for each technique. For RF and RIPPER, we use control based on the cutoff of the number of examples in the leaf node. For SVC, NN, and LR we discretize the regularization parameter on a logarithmic grid. For both IMLI and MLIC, we have two choices of $\lambda \in \{5, 10\}$, three choices of $k \in \{1, 2, 3\}$, and two choices of the type of rule as {CNF, DNF}. For IMLI we vary the number of partitions p for each dataset such that each partition has at least eight samples and at most 512 samples. For all classifiers, we set the training time cutoff to be 1000 seconds.

We perform an assessment of test accuracy on a holdout set and mean validation accuracy on a 10-fold cross-validation set (holdout

3 https://github.com/meelgroup/mlic

set 10%, validation set 9%, training set 81%). We compute test accuracy and mean validation accuracy across the ten folds for each choice of the parameters for each technique, and report test accuracy, mean validation accuracy, and mean training time for a choice of the parameters which incurs the best test accuracy. To remove the bias of a particular holdout set we perform ten repetitions with different holdout sets and present the mean statistics.

For MLIC and IMLI, we experimented with different MaxSAT solvers and finally chose MaxHS [9] for MLIC since MaxSAT queries generated by MLIC timeout for all the solvers and MaxHS is the only solver to return the best found answer so far. In contrast, queries constructed by IMLI are easier and the best runtime performance is obtained by using Open-WBO solver [16].

5.2 Results

5.2.1 Comparison Among Different Classifiers: Table 1 presents the comparison of IMLI vis-a-vis typical interpretable and non-interpretable classifiers. The first three columns list the name, size (number of samples), and the number of binary features (discretized) for each dataset. The next seven columns present test accuracy, validation accuracy, and training time of the classifiers.

In Table 1 we observe that MLIC and RIPPER have slightly higher accuracy than IMLI. Specifically considering all datasets MLIC (resp. RIPPER) has on average 1.12% (resp. 0.12%) higher test accuracy and 3.09% (resp. 2.29%) higher validation accuracy than that of IMLI. In contrast, IMLI takes up to three order of magnitude less training time compared to MLIC and upto one order of magnitude less time compared to RIPPER. Interestingly, IMLI is competitive to black-box classifiers, e.g. SVC and NN for large datasets. In this context, we think IMLI achieves a sweet spot in achieving significant runtime improvement in training without losing accuracy.

At this point, one may wonder as to whether minor loss in accuracy also leads to loss of interpretability. To this end, we illustrate a detailed comparison among the generated rules of IMLI, RIPPER, and MLIC in Table 2. We observe that rule size of IMLI is significantly smaller than that of RIPPER and MLIC. In particular, note that IMLI can generate rules with size less than eight for all the datasets (exception in Adult dataset where IMLI still has the most sparse rule), thereby demonstrating the sparsity of generated rules. In contrast, MLIC and RIPPER generate rules of significantly larger size than IMLI. As indicated earlier, sparsity is only one of several possible approaches to quantify interpretability. Therefore, we also decided to observe the generated rules and interestingly, the generated rules seem very intuitive. We have listed the generated rules in Appendix E

5.2.2 Varying Data Fidelity λ: In Figure 1 we present the result for varying λ. Our experiment result finds a similar observation in all the datasets, and here we present result for Parkinsons dataset.

Recall that size of a rule is the total number of literals appearing in $\mathcal{R}$. As we increase the value of λ, rule size (Figure 1a) and the time taken to solve the MaxSAT query (Figure 1b) decreases. When $\lambda = 1$, all the soft clauses have equal weight. However, when λ is higher, soft clause N_q is put a higher weight than V_j^l, which turns out in finding the solution of the query requiring less time because of the priority among soft clauses. Therefore, the generated rule becomes sparser. We find a similar trend for DNF rules too. In

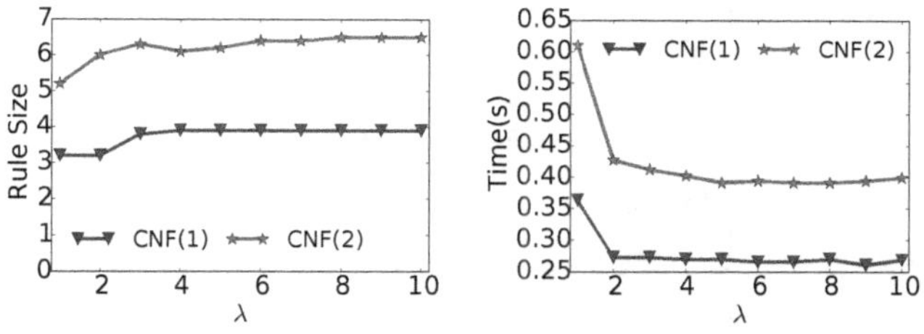

(a) $k \in \{1,2\}, p = 4$ (b) $k \in \{1,2\}, p = 4$

Figure 1: Effect of data fidelity parameter λ on rule size and training time. The number within parenthesis denotes the number of clause k for the respective rule.

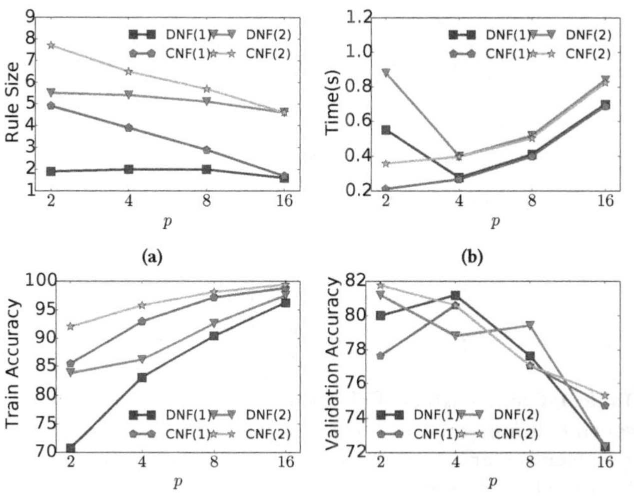

(a) (b) (c) (d)

Figure 2: Effect of the number of partitions p on rule size, training time, train accuracy, and validation accuracy ($k \in \{1,2\}, \lambda = 10$). The number within parenthesis denotes the number of clause k for the respective rule.

empirical study we find that as we increase λ, training accuracy increases gradually but validation accuracy and test accuracy do not follow a monotonic behavior in the partition-based learning.

5.2.3 Varying The Number of Training Partitions p: Figure 2 presents the effect on rule size, training time, train accuracy, and validation accuracy as we vary p. For all the datasets we find a similar observation and here present the result for Parkinsons dataset for ease of exposition.

In Figure 2a we observe that the size of the rule decreases as p increases. This observation can be attributed to the decrease in the number of training samples per partition with the increase in the number of partitions and consequently, smaller rules suffice. In Figure 2b IMLI empirically shows that the training time at first decreases significantly and then increases slowly with the increase in p. This observation can be attributed to the combined effect of the number of queries and the size of queries. Initially, we achieve a significant reduction in the size of query while the number of queries eventually dominate the runtime.

Dataset	Size	Features	LR	NN	RF	SVC	RIPPER	MLIC	IMLI
Parkinsons	195	392	97.5 [69.76] (0.22)	90 [82.68] (0.14)	97.5 [80.98] (1.7)	87.5 [83.5] (0.18)	85.00 [76.74] (2.92)	97.5 [82.35] (114.75)	95 [79.41] (0.37)
Ionosphere	351	540	93.06 [90.64] (0.32)	86.11 [87.18] (0.26)	95.83 [92.77] (1.72)	95.83 [90.65] (0.26)	93.06 [85.73] (3.3)	93.06 [91.94] (917.13)	91.67 [85.48] (0.5)
WDBC	569	540	98.28 [96.77] (0.33)	95.69 [97.27] (0.45)	96.55 [96.68] (1.8)	96.55 [97.16] (0.27)	92.24 [93.54] (3.53)	93.97 [95.1] Timeout	89.66 [91.18] (0.78)
Blood	748	64	80 [75.92] (0.2)	76.67 [76.14] (0.2)	76 [76.22] (1.68)	76 [76.22] (0.18)	76 [76.22] (2.23)	75.33 [77.61] (5.96)	76 [76.12] (0.24)
PIMA	768	134	75.32 [74.75] (0.3)	77.92 [73.23] (0.32)	76.62 [75.54] (1.99)	75.32 [76.63] (0.37)	75.32 [74.36] (2.58)	75.97 [71.74] Timeout	73.38 [68.12] (0.74)
Tom's HW	28179	844	96.98 [97.12] (2.24)	94.11 [93.91] (910.36)	97.11 [97.35] (27.11)	96.83 [97.1] (354.15)	96.75 [97.12] (37.81)	96.61 [96.55] Timeout	96.86 [96.23] (23.67)
Adult	32561	262	84.58 [84.99] (5.8)	83.46 [83.62] (640.81)	84.31 [84.68] (36.64)	84.39 [84.69] (918.26)	83.72 [83.49] (37.66)	79.72 [79.53] Timeout	80.84 [77.43] (25.07)
Credit-default	30000	334	80.81 [82.16] (6.87)	79.61 [80.2] (872.97)	80.87 [82.13] (37.72)	80.69 [82.1] (847.93)	80.97 [82.07] (20.37)	80.72 [82.14] Timeout	79.41 [75.81] (32.58)
Twitter	49999	1050	95.67 [96.32] (3.99)	Timeout	95.16 [96.46] (67.83)	Timeout	95.56 [96.16] (98.21)	94.78 [95.69] Timeout	94.69 [95.08] (59.67)

Table 1: Comparisons of classification accuracy with 10-fold cross validation for different classifiers. For every cell in the last seven columns the top value represents the test accuracy (%) on unseen data, the middle value surrounded by square bracket represents average validation accuracy (%) of 10-fold, and the bottom value surrounded by parenthesis represents the average training time in seconds.

Dataset	RIPPER	MLIC	IMLI
Parkinsons	2.6	2	8
Ionosphere	9.6	13	5
WDBC	7.6	14.5	2
Blood	1	3	3.5
Adult	107.55	44.5	28
PIMA	8.25	16	3.5
Tom's HW	30.33	2	2.5
Twitter	21.6	20.5	6
Credit	14.25	6	3

Table 2: Size of the rule of interpretable classifiers.

In Figure 2c we observe that IMLI tends to make less training error as p goes higher because IMLI learns on fewer samples with fixed λ value. Moreover, we observe that CNF rules have higher train accuracy than DNF rules, and 2-clause rules have higher train accuracy than 1-clause rules for both CNF and DNF rules.

In Figure 2d we notice a decrease in validation accuracy as we allow more partitions because learning on fewer samples results in a rule that has less predictive power on validation set. For small p, IMLI, however, ensures higher validation accuracy if the rule has more clauses. Moreover, effect of the number of partitions on test accuracy computed on unseen data does not follow any specific pattern.

In summary, we observe that the number of partitions gives a sound handle to the end user to tradeoff the training time, validation accuracy, and interpretability of the rules.

6 CONCLUSION

In this paper, we present IMLI: an incremental framework for MaxSAT-based learning of interpretable classification rules. Extensive experiments on UCI datasets demonstrate that IMLI achieves up to three orders of magnitude improvement in training time with only a minor loss of accuracy. We think IMLI highlights the promise of MaxSAT-based approach and opens up several interesting directions of future research at the intersection of AI and SAT/SMT community. In particular, it would be an interesting direction of future research if the MaxSAT solvers can be designed to take advantage of incrementality of IMLI.

ACKNOWLEDGMENTS

This work was supported in part by NUS ODPRT Grant R-252-000-685-133 and AI Singapore Grant R-252-000-A16-490. The computational work for this article was performed on resources of the National Supercomputing Centre, Singapore https://www.nscc.sg.

REFERENCES

[1] Solon Barocas, Moritz Hardt, and Arvind Narayanan. 2017. Fairness and Machine Learning. *NIPS Tutorial* (2017).
[2] D. Bertsimas, A. Chang, and C. Rudin. 2012. An Integer Optimization Approach to Associative Classification. In *Proc. of NIPS.*
[3] Christian Bessiere, Emmanuel Hebrard, and Barry OâĂŹSullivan. 2009. Minimising decision tree size as combinatorial optimisation. In *Proc. of CP.*
[4] E. Boros, P.L. Hammer, T. Ibaraki, A. Kogan, E. Mayoraz, and I. Muchnik. 2000. An implementation of logical analysis of data. *Proc. of TKDE* (2000).
[5] Gert Cauwenberghs and Tomaso Poggio. 2001. Incremental and decremental support vector machine learning. In *Proc. of NIPS.*
[6] P. Clark and T. Niblett. 1989. The CN2 Induction Algorithm. *Mach. Learn.* (Mar. 1989).
[7] William W Cohen. 1995. Fast effective rule induction. In *Machine Learning Proceedings 1995.* Elsevier.
[8] W. W. Cohen and Y. Singer. 1999. A Simple, Fast, and Effective Rule Learner. In *Proc. of AAAI.* Orlando, FL.
[9] Jessica Davies and Fahiem Bacchus. 2011. Solving MAXSAT by solving a sequence of simpler SAT instances. In *Proc. of CP.*
[10] Dua Dheeru and Efi Karra Taniskidou. 2017. UCI Machine Learning Repository. http://archive.ics.uci.edu/ml
[11] Finale Doshi-Velez and Been Kim. 2017. Towards a rigorous science of interpretable machine learning. (2017).
[12] Benjamin Letham, Cynthia Rudin, Tyler H McCormick, David Madigan, et al. 2015. Interpretable classifiers using rules and bayesian analysis: Building a better stroke prediction model. *The Annals of Applied Statistics* (2015).
[13] Dmitry Malioutov and Kuldeep S Meel. 2018. MLIC: A MaxSAT-Based Framework for Learning Interpretable Classification Rules. In *Proc. of CP.*
[14] D. M. Malioutov and K. R. Varshney. 2013. Exact Rule Learning via Boolean Compressed Sensing.. In *Proc. of ICML.*
[15] M. Marchand and J. Shawe-Taylor. 2002. The set covering machine. *Journal of Machine Learning Research* Dec (2002).
[16] Ruben Martins, Vasco Manquinho, and Inês Lynce. 2014. Open-WBO: A modular MaxSAT solver. In *Proc. of SAT.*
[17] Clemens Otte. 2013. Safe and interpretable machine learning: a methodological review. In *Computational intelligence in intelligent data analysis.*
[18] J Ross Quinlan. 1993. C4. 5: Programming for machine learning. *Morgan Kauffmann* (1993).
[19] J Ross Quinlan. 2014. *C4. 5: programs for machine learning.* Elsevier.
[20] Liva Ralaivola and Florence dâĂŹAlché Buc. 2001. Incremental support vector machine learning: A local approach. In *Proc. of ICANN.*
[21] Marco Tulio Ribeiro, Sameer Singh, and Carlos Guestrin. 2016. Why should i trust you?: Explaining the predictions of any classifier. In *Proc. of KDD.*
[22] Ronald L Rivest. 1987. Learning decision lists. *Machine learning* (1987).
[23] Stefan Ruping. 2001. Incremental learning with support vector machines. In *Proc. of ICDM.*
[24] Guolong Su, Dennis Wei, Kush R Varshney, and Dmitry M Malioutov. 2015. Interpretable two-level Boolean rule learning for classification. (2015).
[25] Nadeem Ahmed Syed, Syed Huan, Liu Kah, and Kay Sung. 1999. Incremental learning with support vector machines. (1999).
[26] Fulton Wang and Cynthia Rudin. 2015. Falling rule lists. In *Proc. of AISTATS.*
[27] T. Wang, C. Rudin, F. Doshi-Velez, Y. Liu, E. Klampfl, and P. MacNeille. 2015. Or's of And's for Interpretable Classification, with Application to Context-Aware Recommender Systems. (2015).

A RELATED WORK

The study of designing interpretable machine learning classifiers can find its root in the development of popular models such as decision trees [3, 19], decision lists [22], classification rules [7] etc. Apart from designing models with the purpose of generating interpretable rules, various studies have been conducted in order to improve the efficiency and scalability of the model. Specifically, decision rule approaches such as C4.5 rules [18], CN2[6], RIPPER [7], SLIPPER [8] rely on heuristics, branch pruning, ad-hoc local criteria e.g., maximizing information gain, coverage, etc. because these models consider an intractable combinatorial optimization function.

In recent work, Malioutov et al. has proposed rule based classification system by borrowing ideas from Boolean compressed sensing [14]. Two-level Boolean rules [24] has been proposed to trade classification accuracy and interpretability, where hamming loss is used to characterize accuracy and sparsity is used to characterize interpretability. Wang et al. [26] has proposed a Bayesian framework for learning falling rule lists which is an ordered list of if-then rules. Chen et al. designs an optimization approach to learning falling rule lists and "softly" falling rule lists, along with Monte-Carlo search algorithms that use bounds on the optimal solution to prune the search space.

Incremental learning techniques are one possible solution to the scalability problem, where data is processed in parts, and the result combined so as to use less memory [25]. Incremental framework has been studied in SVM [23] to improve the existing approach. Specifically, an on-line recursive algorithm for SVM has been studied to facilitate learning one vector at a time [5] and a local incremental approach has been proposed [20] to learn a SVM based on Radial Basis Function Kernel.

B EXAMPLES

B.1 Illustration of Incremental Learning

We illustrate an interpretable rule generated by IMLI with step by step formulation over partitions on iris dataset[4]. Iris dataset has four attributes: sepal length, sepal width, petal length, and petal width. All feature values are scaled in centimeter. Iris dataset has three classes: Iris Setosa, Iris Versicolour, and Iris Virginica. We consider the binary problem of classifying Iris Versicolour from the other two species: Setosa and Verginica. Here we consider that $\mathcal{R}$ is a single clause DNF rule and learned over four partitions (e.g. $\mathcal{R}_1, \dots, \mathcal{R}_4$). The final rule $\mathcal{R}$ is equivalent to $\mathcal{R}_4$.

$$\mathcal{R}_1 := \text{petal length} \leq 5.32 \wedge \text{petal length} > 1.7 \wedge \text{petal width} \leq 1.8$$

$$\mathcal{R}_2 := \text{sepal width} \leq 3.1 \wedge \text{petal length} \leq 5.32 \wedge \text{petal length} > 1.7 \wedge \text{petal width} \leq 1.5$$

$$\mathcal{R}_3 := \text{sepal width} \leq 3.1 \wedge \text{petal length} \leq 5.0 \wedge \text{petal length} > 1.7 \wedge \text{petal width} \leq 1.5$$

$$\mathcal{R} := \text{sepal width} \leq 3.1 \wedge \text{petal length} \leq 5.0 \wedge \text{petal length} > 1.7 \wedge \text{petal width} \leq 1.8$$

$\mathcal{R}$ can be interpreted as: a sample which satisfies all of the four constraints is predicted as Iris Versicolour. Here the rule size $|\mathcal{R}| = 4$. Specifically, $\mathcal{R}_1$ is learned on the first partition of training data. $\mathcal{R}_2$ learns two literals (2nd and 3rd) which also appear in $\mathcal{R}_1$, introduces two new literals (1st and 4th) while learning on the second training partition, and falsifies a previously learned literal from $\mathcal{R}_1$ (i.e., (petal width ≤ 1.8).

Since the dataset contains continuous valued features, IMLI removes redundant literals at each step of learning by applying Algorithm 1. For example, we show the generated rule $\mathcal{R}_3'$ for the 3rd partition if we do not apply Algorithm 1.

$$\mathcal{R}_3' := \text{sepal width} \leq 3.1 \wedge \text{petal length} \leq 5.0 \wedge \underline{\text{petal length} \leq 5.32} \wedge \text{petal length} > 1.7 \wedge \text{petal width} \leq 1.5 \wedge \underline{\text{petal width} \leq 1.8}$$

[4] https://archive.ics.uci.edu/ml/datasets/iris

The underline marked literals are redundant, hence removed in $\mathcal{R}_3$.

C PROOF

Proof. (Lemma 5) The case $|\mathcal{R}'| = |R|$ is trivial because no literal is removed from $\mathcal{R}'$, and $\mathcal{R}'$ is equivalent to $\mathcal{R}$.

When $|\mathcal{R}'| < |\mathcal{R}|$, $\exists \langle b_i^l, b_j^l \rangle$ where $l \in [1, k]$, $siblings(b_i^l, b_j^l) = true$, $tval(b_i^l) < tval(b_j^l)$, and x_c is the considered continuous feature.

Suppose $op(b_i^l) = op(b_j^l) =$ " $\geq$ ". Consider two sets of real number: $S_i = \{x_i : x_i \geq tval(b_i^l)\}$ and $S_j = \{x_j : x_j \geq tval(b_j^l)\}$. As $\mathcal{R}$ is in CNF, $\mathcal{R}$ checks $I[x_c \in S_i \cup S_j]$ to classify $\forall q, \mathbf{X}_q$. Here $S_i \cup S_j = S_i$, so b_j^l can be pruned.

We can prove similarly when $op(b_i^l) = op(b_j^l) =$ " $<$ ".

Therefore, $|\mathcal{R}'| \leq |\mathcal{R}|$ and $\mathcal{R}'$ is equivalent to $\mathcal{R}$. □

D EXPERIMENT

D.1 Dataset Description

We use nine publicly available datasets of various size from UCI repository for conducting experiments for IMLI. The datasets contain both real and categorical valued features. The datasets are buzz events from two different social networks: Twitter and Tom's HW (Tom), Adult data (Adult), Parkinson's Disease detection dataset (Parkinsons), Ionosphere (Ion), Pima Indians Diabetes (PIMA), Blood service centers (Blood), breast cancer Wisconsin diagnostic (WDBC), and Credit-default approval dataset (Credit-default).

E INTERPRETABLE RULES

In this section we are presenting the rules generated by IMLI for the datasets we use in experiment.

E.1 Rule for Credit Default Dataset:

A client will default if :=
(education=others OR
repayment status September: payment delay > 1 month OR
repayment status August: payment delay > 2 months OR
repayment status June: payment delay > 2 months)

E.2 Rule for Adult Dataset

A person's income is greater than 50k if :=
(workclass is not Federal-gov AND workclass is not State-gov AND education is not 11th AND education is not 5th-6th AND education is not 7th-8th AND education-num > 10.0 AND marital-status is not Divorced AND marital-status is not Married-AF-spouse AND marital-status is not Married-spouse-absent AND marital-status is not Never-married AND marital-status is not Separated AND occupation is not Handlers-cleaners AND occupation is not Machine-op-inspct AND occupation is not Priv-house-serv AND occupation is not Protective-serv AND relationship is not Own-child AND relationship is not Unmarried AND native-country is not Cambodia AND native-country is not Columbia AND native-country is not Dominican-Republic AND native-country is not Guatemala AND native-country is not Hungary AND native-country is not Jamaica AND native-country is not Laos AND native-country is not Mexico AND native-country is not Outlying-US,Guam-USVI-etc AND native-country is not Poland AND native-country is not Vietnam)

E.3 Rule for WDBC Dataset

Tumor is diagnosed as malignant if :=
(standard area of tumor > 38.43 OR
largest perimeter of tumor > 115.9 OR
largest number of concave points of tumor > 0.1508)

E.4 Rule for Blood Transfusion Service Center Dataset

He/she will donate blood if :=
(Months since last donation ≤ 4 AND
total number of donations > 3 AND
total donated blood ≤ 750.0 c.c. AND
months since first donation ≤ 45)

E.5 Rule for Pima Indians Diabetes Database

Tested positive for diabetes if :=
(Plasma glucose concentration > 125 AND
Triceps skin fold thickness ≤ 35 mm AND
Diabetes pedigree function > 0.259 AND
Age > 25 years)

E.6 Rule for Parkinson's Disease Dataset

A person has Parkinson's disease if :=
(minimum vocal fundamental frequency ≤ 87.57 Hz OR minimum vocal fundamental frequency > 121.38 Hz OR Shimmer:APQ3 ≤ 0.01 OR MDVP:APQ > 0.02 OR D2 ≤ 1.93 OR NHR > 0.01 OR HNR > 26.5 OR spread2 > 0.3)
AND
(Maximum vocal fundamental frequency ≤ 200.41 Hz OR HNR ≤ 18.8 OR spread2 > 0.18 OR D2 > 2.92)

E.7 Rule for Ionosphere Dataset

A radar is "Good" if:=
(x1 = 1 AND x2 > 0 AND x4 > 0 AND x5 > −0.23)

Here "x" represents the set of columns of the dataset.

E.8 Rule for Tom's Hardware Dataset

A topic is popular if :=
(Number of displays at time 2 > 1936 OR Number of displays at time 7 > 1250.6)

E.9 Rule for Twitter Dataset

A topic is popular if :=
(Number of Created Discussions at time 1 > 78 OR
Attention Level measured with number of authors at time 6 > 0.000365 OR Attention Level measured with number of contributions at time 0 > 0.00014 OR Attention Level measured with number of contributions at time 1 > 0.000136 OR Number of Authors at time 0 > 147 OR Average Discussions Length at time 3 > 205.4 OR Average Discussions Length at time 5 > 654.0)

Loss-Aversively Fair Classification

Junaid Ali, Muhammad Bilal Zafar, Adish Singla, Krishna P. Gummadi
Max Planck Institute for Software Systems (MPI-SWS)
{junaid, mzafar, adishs, gummadi}@mpi-sws.org

ABSTRACT

The use of algorithmic (learning-based) decision making in scenarios that affect human lives has motivated a number of recent studies to investigate such decision making systems for potential unfairness, such as discrimination against subjects based on their sensitive features like gender or race. However, when judging the fairness of a newly designed decision making system, these studies have overlooked an important influence on people's perceptions of fairness, which is how the new algorithm changes the status quo, i.e., decisions of the existing decision making system. Motivated by extensive literature in behavioral economics and behavioral psychology (prospect theory), we propose a notion of fair updates that we refer to as *loss-averse updates*. Loss-averse updates constrain the updates to yield improved (more beneficial) outcomes to subjects compared to the status quo. We propose tractable proxy measures that would allow this notion to be incorporated in the training of a variety of linear and non-linear classifiers. We show how our proxy measures can be combined with existing measures for training nondiscriminatory classifiers. Our evaluation using synthetic and real-world datasets demonstrates that the proposed proxy measures are effective for their desired tasks.

CCS CONCEPTS

• **Social and professional topics**; • **Computing methodologies** → **Machine learning algorithms**;

KEYWORDS

Algorithmic Fairness, Fair Updates, Fairness in Machine Learning, Loss-averse Fairness

ACM Reference Format:

Junaid Ali, Muhammad Bilal Zafar, Adish Singla, Krishna P. Gummadi . 2019. Loss-Aversively Fair Classification. In *AAAI/ACM Conference on AI, Ethics, and Society (AIES '19), January 27–28, 2019, Honolulu, HI, USA.* ACM, New York, NY, USA, 8 pages. https://doi.org/10.1145/3306618.3314266

1 INTRODUCTION

The use of algorithmic (data-driven and learning-based) decision making systems in domains ranging from judiciary (recidivism risk estimation) and banking (credit ratings and loan approval risk) to welfare (benefits eligibility) and insurance (accident risks) has raised numerous concerns about their fairness. Consequently, in recent years, a number of notions of algorithmic (un)fairness have been proposed [15, 18, 24] and numerous learning mechanisms have been devised to train algorithmic decision making systems that satisfy these notions [5, 12, 13, 15, 18, 24–26]. These fairness notions have focussed on both the *decision outcomes* as well as the *decision making process*, i.e., the inputs used to make the decisions and the objectives of the learning algorithms.

In this paper, we focus on a crucial aspect of algorithmic decision making systems ignored by existing studies on fair learning namely, fairness of *updates to decision making systems*. In many decision making scenarios such as banking or judiciary or insurance, a newly deployed system replaces an already existing decision making system, be it run by a human decision maker or an older learning model (e.g., learning models without discrimination-awareness) or a learning model trained over outdated training data (e.g., when features of users in a society evolve). Existing literature in behavioral economics and psychology shows that peoples' perceptions of fairness of the new decision making system are influenced by *how the decision outcomes change from the status quo* i.e., how the new outcomes differ from the old outcomes [4, 16, 17, 22]. However, current works on fair learning do not account for the status quo when reasoning about fairness of a decision making system.

In this work, inspired by existing literature in behavioral economics, we formally define a notion of update fairness namely, **loss-aversively fair updates**. Intuitively, our notion of loss-averse updates accounts for the "endowment effect" in human behavior [16, 17], where an individual or a group of users perceives the fairness of the new system based on whether their new outcomes were more or less beneficial than their status quo outcomes from the existing system.

We design intuitive measures for this notion that can be incorporated into a variety of linear and non-linear classifiers as convex constraints and be efficiently learned. A classifier trained using our constraints would account for the existing outcomes from the status quo classifier.

We also show that our new notion of fair update can be easily integrated with existing mechanisms for training non-discriminatory classifiers. For instance, when attempting to equalize rates of beneficial outcomes such as positive class acceptance rate or true positive rate across different groups, adding our loss-averse update constraint ensures that "no group of users is worse-off" than before. Such a constraint may be necessary in practice when training non-discriminatory classifiers as Bazerman et al. [4] point out that same "don't make anyone worse off' principle likely underlines Supreme Courts decision [21] that firing personnel from historically advantaged groups to achieve parity (in order to overcome past discrimination) is prohibited.

In the rest of the paper, we first formally define our notion of fair update in the context of training classifiers. We also propose tractable and efficient mechanisms to train fair classifiers while satisfying this practical consideration. Experiments with synthetic

AIES '19, January 27–28, 2019, Honolulu, HI, USA

ACM ISBN 978-1-4503-6324-2/19/01.
https://doi.org/10.1145/3306618.3314266

and real-world datasets show the effectiveness of our mechanism in enforcing this consideration.

2 RELATED WORK

Fairness in ML. A plethora of recent studies have focused on proposing notions [15, 18, 23, 24] and mechanisms for fairness-aware classification [5, 10, 12, 13, 15, 18, 23–26]. For more discussion into these notions, we point the interested readers to [3, 7, 19, 25]. While classification has received most attention in the area of fairness-aware machine learning, some recent work has also focused on prediction tasks beyond classification, such as regression [6], ranking [8, 20] and clustering [9]. In this paper, we primarily focus on updates to classification tasks, leaving fairness of updates to regression, ranking, and clustering tasks to future studies.

Indvidual-level vs. Group-level Fairness Notions. Fairness in classification has been divided into two broad areas: individual- and group-level fairness [12]. Loss-averse updates can be applied at both individual and group-levels. However, in this work, we only show results at the group-level.

Normative vs. Descriptive Notions of Fairness. Our fairness consideration for updating decision making systems has roots in normative vs. descriptive approaches in behavioral economics [16, 17]. For example, Kahneman et al. [16] show how certain changes to an economic model that are accepted on the normative standards might be deemed unacceptable on the descriptive standards. Our work here is motivated by such observations: while anti-discrimination laws (normatively) prescribe how nondiscriminatory decisions ought to be done, if people (descriptively) preceived the changes in outcomes with the new nondiscriminatory decision system to be too disruptively disadvantageous to them, they would resist adopting the new system. Our notions of update fairness can be thought of as addressing such practical considerations.

3 FORMALIZING NOTION OF LOSS-AVERSE UPDATES

In this section, we formally define a notion of fairness that can be useful when updating algorithmic decision making systems. Specifically, we focus on decision making tasks centered around binary classification.

Preliminaries. In a binary classification task, given a training dataset $\mathcal{D} = \{(\boldsymbol{x}_i, y_i)\}_{i=1}^N$, the goal is to learn a function $\boldsymbol{\theta} : \mathbb{R}^d \rightarrow \{-1, 1\}$ between the feature vectors $\boldsymbol{x} \in \mathbb{R}^d$ and class labels $y \in \{-1, 1\}$. For convex decision boundary-based classifiers like logistic regression and (non)linear SVM, this task boils down to finding a decision boundary $\boldsymbol{\theta}^*$ in the feature space that minimizes a given loss $L(\boldsymbol{\theta})$ over $\mathcal{D}$, *i.e.*, $\boldsymbol{\theta}^* = \text{argmin}_{\boldsymbol{\theta}} L(\boldsymbol{\theta})$. The convexity of the loss function ensures that the optimal decision boundary parameters can be found in an efficient manner. Then, for a given (potentially unseen) feature vector $\boldsymbol{x}$, one predicts the class label $\hat{y} = 1$ if $d_{\boldsymbol{\theta}^*}(\boldsymbol{x}) \geq 0$ and $\hat{y} = -1$ otherwise, where $d_{\boldsymbol{\theta}^*}(\boldsymbol{x})$ denotes the signed distance from $\boldsymbol{x}$ to the decision boundary. Without loss of generality, we consider $\hat{y} = 1$ to be the beneficial (desired) label, *e.g.*, being granted the loan or being released on bail.

Setup. We consider scenarios where we need to update an existing, *status quo*, binary classifier, whose decision boundary is denoted by $\boldsymbol{\theta}_{sqo}$. We assume that the boundary of the new classifier, $\boldsymbol{\theta}_{new}$ is learnt from the training dataset $\mathcal{D}$. The outcomes of the updated (new) classifier may differ from the status quo for many reasons such as the status quo classifier being a human or an older (simpler) learning model, or the status quo classifier being trained on outdated training data, or the status quo classifier being trained using models without awareness of potential for discrimination. Our notion of fair update defines the conditions in which the *changes in decision outcomes caused by an update* would be deemed as fair.

Existing Notions: Discrimination in Classification.
Anti-discrimination laws require classification outcomes are also required to be nondiscriminatory with respect to a sensitive feature $z \in \{0, 1\}$, *e.g.*, gender, race. Most of the existing studies differentiate between the following two notions of discrimination: *statistical parity* [12, 13]—also referred to as disparate impact, and *equality of opportunity* [15, 24]—also referred to as disparate mistreatment. Both notions require that certain group-conditional beneficial outcome rates be the same for each group, *i.e.*,:

$$\mathcal{B}_{z=0}(\boldsymbol{\theta}) = \mathcal{B}_{z=1}(\boldsymbol{\theta}), \tag{1}$$

where the definition of the benefit function $\mathcal{B}_z$ depends on the notion of discrimination under consideration.

Under the notion of *statistical parity (SP)* [12, 13], the benefits function is defined as the positive class acceptance rate (AR), *i.e.*, the positive class acceptance rate should be the same for both the groups. More formally,

$$\text{– } \textbf{\textit{SP:}} \qquad P(\hat{y} = 1|z = 0) = P(\hat{y} = 1|z = 1), \tag{2}$$

Under *equality of opportunity (EOP)* notion [15, 24], the benefit function is defined as the true positive rate, i.e., the true positive rate (TPR) should be the same for both the groups. More formally,

$$\text{– } \textbf{\textit{EOP:}}\ P(\hat{y} = 1|y = 1, z = 0) = P(\hat{y} = 1|y = 1, z = 1), \tag{3}$$

Note that, current notions of nondiscrimination do not take into account status quo classifier. In the following section we introduce a notion of updating status quo classifier.

New Notion: Loss-Averse Updates. We now formally describe a new consideration of fair updates, introduced in Section 1. We draw inspiration from human behavior and behavioral economics and we consider how people might perceive fairness of an updated classifier in comparison to status quo. Specifically, any disadvantageous effect of an updated classifier would be considered unfair. Prospect theory, proposed by Kahneman and Tversky [17], states that equal amounts of loses result in a bigger loss in utility than the increase in utility by the same amount of gains. In other words people percieve losses much worse than gains, *i.e.*, they are loss-averse. Given the *status quo* classifier $\boldsymbol{\theta}_{sqo}$, a new classifier $\boldsymbol{\theta}_{new}$ constitutes a *loss-averse* update only when the new classifier increases the beneficial outcome rates for all groups. More formally,

$$\mathcal{B}_{z=k}(\boldsymbol{\theta}_{new}) \geq \mathcal{B}_{z=k}(\boldsymbol{\theta}_{sqo}), \quad \text{for all } k \in \{0, 1\} \tag{4}$$

where $\mathcal{B}_z$ can be any one of the benefit functions proposed in the existing literature on nondiscriminatory classification.

4 UPDATING CLASSIFIERS LOSS-AVERSIVELY

In this section, we devise mechanisms to update status quo classifier, $\boldsymbol{\theta}_{sqo}$ to $\boldsymbol{\theta}_{new}$ that follow the practical considerations of "loss-averse updates". We specifically focus on training convex decision boundary based classifiers (*e.g.*, logistic regression, linear and non-linear SVMs), *i.e.*, the classifiers that learn the decision boundary parameters by optimizing a convex loss function $L(\boldsymbol{\theta})$.

Existing Mechanisms: Nondiscriminatory Classification. Existing mechanisms to train nondiscriminatory classifiers involve solving an optimization problem maximizing accuracy while equalizing benefits, *i.e.*, enforcing Eq. (1), for different sensitive feature groups. More formally,

$$\begin{aligned} &\text{minimize} \quad L(\boldsymbol{\theta}) \\ &\text{subject to} \quad \mathcal{B}_{z=0}(\boldsymbol{\theta}) = \mathcal{B}_{z=1}(\boldsymbol{\theta}), \end{aligned} \tag{P1}$$

Constraints in Problem (P1), as operationalized in Eqs. (2) and (3) are non-convex. However, prior studies [5, 24, 25] propose tractable convex or convex-concave proxies for enforcing the equality of benefits constraint in Eqs. (2) and (3). Borrowing these proxies from [5, 24, 25], one can replace the equal benefits condition with proxies as follows:

$$- \textit{SP:} \quad \frac{1}{|\mathcal{D}|}\left|\sum_{(\boldsymbol{x},z)\in\mathcal{D}} (z-\bar{z})d_{\boldsymbol{\theta}}(\boldsymbol{x}_i)\right| \le c, \tag{5}$$

$$- \textit{EOP:} \quad \frac{1}{|\mathcal{D}_+|}\left|\sum_{(\boldsymbol{x},z)\in\mathcal{D}_+} (z-\bar{z})d_{\boldsymbol{\theta}}(\boldsymbol{x}_i)\right| \le c, \tag{6}$$

where $\mathcal{D}_+$ are data points with $y = 1$. Here equality of opportunity limits discrimination in true positive rates of different groups. The covariance threshold $c \in \mathbb{R}^+$ determines the level of discrimination, with $c = 0$ aiming for a perfectly fair classifier.

New Mechanism: Loss-Averse Updates. For updating the status quo classifier, $\boldsymbol{\theta}_{sqo}$, in a nondiscriminatory and loss-aversive manner, one can add the respective conditions to the classifier formulation as a constraint, *i.e.*,

$$\begin{aligned} &\text{minimize} \quad L(\boldsymbol{\theta}) \\ &\text{subject to} \quad \mathcal{B}_{z=0}(\boldsymbol{\theta}) = \mathcal{B}_{z=1}(\boldsymbol{\theta}) \\ &\qquad \boldsymbol{\mathcal{B}_{z=k}(\theta) \ge \mathcal{B}_{z=k}(\theta_{sqo})}, \quad \text{for all } k \in \{0,1\}. \end{aligned} \tag{P2}$$

The constraints in the above problem are nonconvex functions of the classifier parameters $\boldsymbol{\theta}$, if $\mathcal{B}$ is defined in terms of probabilities as given in Eqs. (2) and (3), for example, this would make it very challenging to solve the resulting problem in an efficient manner.

We used the convex proxies from prior studies [5, 24, 25] for the first constraint as given by Eqs. (5) and (6). We propose the following convex proxies to approximate the new loss-averse constraints in Problem (P2):

Under SP, when the benefit function is AR we suggest:

$$\frac{1}{|\mathcal{D}_{z=k}|}\sum_{\boldsymbol{x}\in\mathcal{D}_{z=k}} d_{\boldsymbol{\theta}}(\boldsymbol{x}) \ge \frac{1}{|\mathcal{D}_{z=k}|}\sum_{\boldsymbol{x}\in\mathcal{D}_{z=k}} d_{\boldsymbol{\theta}_{sqo}}(\boldsymbol{x}) + \gamma, \quad \text{for all } k \in \{0,1\}, \gamma \in \mathbb{R}^+. \tag{7}$$

Under EOP, when the benefit function is TPR we suggest:

$$\frac{1}{|\mathcal{D}^+_{z=k}|}\sum_{\boldsymbol{x}\in\mathcal{D}^+_{z=k}} d_{\boldsymbol{\theta}}(\boldsymbol{x}) \ge \frac{1}{|\mathcal{D}^+_{z=k}|}\sum_{\boldsymbol{x}\in\mathcal{D}^+_{z=k}} d_{\boldsymbol{\theta}_{sqo}}(\boldsymbol{x}) + \gamma, \quad \text{for all } k \in \{0,1\}, \gamma \in \mathbb{R}^+, \tag{8}$$

where $\mathcal{D}_{z=k}$ are the data points whose sensitive attribute value $z = k$, and $\mathcal{D}^+_{z=k}$ are data points in the dataset with label $y = 1$ and sensitive attribute value $z = k$. Here, γ controls the strength of the constraint. We pick an appropriate γ using a validation set. Note that the right hand side in Eqs. (7) and (8) represents constant terms since $\boldsymbol{\theta}_{sqo}$ is already known.

Both of the proposed proxies are convex with respect to the optimization variables. The convexity of the proxies (7 and 8) means that for any convex function $L(\boldsymbol{\theta})$ the optimization problem stays convex and can be solved in an efficient manner.

Logistic Regression: SP. We can specialize Problem (P2), using logistic regression classifier with L-2 norm regularizer, SP as a notion of discrimination, given by Eq. (5), and loss-averse constraint, given by Eq. (8), as follows:

$$\begin{aligned} &\text{minimize} \quad -\frac{1}{|\mathcal{D}|}\sum_{(\boldsymbol{x},y)\in\mathcal{D}} \log p(y|\boldsymbol{x},\boldsymbol{\theta}) + \lambda||\boldsymbol{\theta}||^2 \\ &\text{subject to} \quad \frac{1}{|\mathcal{D}|}\left|\sum_{(\boldsymbol{x},z)\in\mathcal{D}} (z-\bar{z})d_{\boldsymbol{\theta}}(\boldsymbol{x}_i)\right| < c \\ &\frac{1}{|\mathcal{D}_{z=k}|}\sum_{\boldsymbol{x}\in\mathcal{D}_{z=k}} d_{\boldsymbol{\theta}}(\boldsymbol{x}) \ge \frac{1}{|\mathcal{D}_{z=k}|}\sum_{\boldsymbol{x}\in\mathcal{D}_{z=k}} d_{\boldsymbol{\theta}_{sqo}}(\boldsymbol{x}) + \gamma, \\ &\text{for all } k \in \{0,1\}, \gamma \in \mathbb{R}^+. \end{aligned} \tag{P3}$$

Logistic Regression: EOP. Similarly, considering equality of opportunity as a notion of nondiscrimination we can approximate Problem (P2), by adding Eqs. (6 and 8) as constraints to logistic loss, as follows:

$$\begin{aligned} &\text{minimize} \quad -\frac{1}{|\mathcal{D}|}\sum_{(\boldsymbol{x},y)\in\mathcal{D}} \log p(y|\boldsymbol{x},\boldsymbol{\theta}) + \lambda||\boldsymbol{\theta}||^2 \\ &\text{subject to} \quad \frac{1}{|\mathcal{D}_+|}\left|\sum_{(\boldsymbol{x},z)\in\mathcal{D}_+} (z-\bar{z})d_{\boldsymbol{\theta}}(\boldsymbol{x}_i)\right| < c \\ &\frac{1}{|\mathcal{D}^+_{z=k}|}\sum_{\boldsymbol{x}\in\mathcal{D}^+_{z=k}} d_{\boldsymbol{\theta}}(\boldsymbol{x}) \ge \frac{1}{|\mathcal{D}^+_{z=k}|}\sum_{\boldsymbol{x}\in\mathcal{D}^+_{z=k}} d_{\boldsymbol{\theta}_{sqo}}(\boldsymbol{x}) + \gamma, \\ &\text{for all } k \in \{0,1\}, \gamma \in \mathbb{R}^+. \end{aligned} \tag{P4}$$

5 EVALUATION ON SYNTHETIC DATASET

In this section we evaluate the effectiveness "Loss-averse" constraint (7), using a synthetic dataset on a binary classification task. We consider a well known notion of nondiscrimination, namely statistical parity. Due to space considerations, we show the results of loss-averse formulation, given by Eq. (8), combined with equality of opportunity, using synthetic data in Appendix A.

5.1 Dataset and Experimental Set up

We used synthetic dataset with binary ground truth class labels $y \in \{+1, -1\}$. Each data point comprises of 2 features besides a binary sensitive feature, *i.e.*, $z \in \{0, 1\}$, where $z = 0$ is the protected group. We do not use the sensitive attribute during training.

Synthetic Dataset. For demonstrating the results of loss-averse updates with statistical parity, given by Eq. (2), as a notion of nondiscrimination, we used the dataset proposed by Zafar et al. [25]. This dataset comprises of 6000 data points, the class labels were drawn

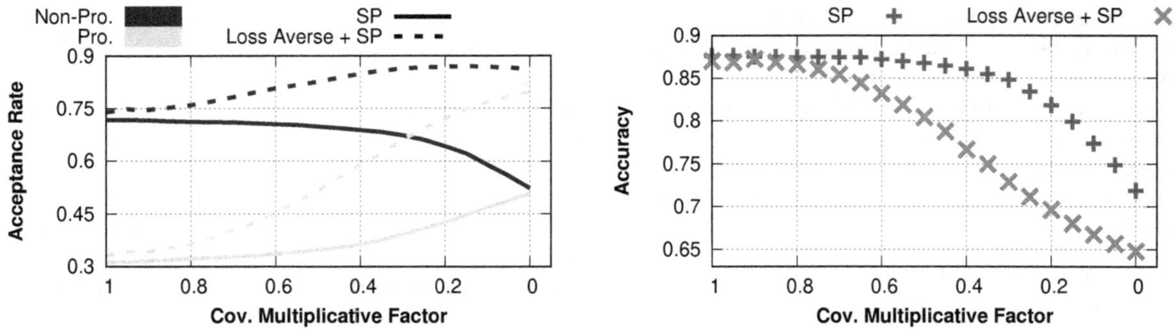

(a) Statistical Parity (SP)

(b) Nondiscrimination-accuracy tradeoff

Figure 1: [Synthetic dataset. Enforcing statistical parity] These figures show a comparison between the solutions of Problem (P1), using SP proxies, and Problem (P3). Left panel shows the beneficial outcome rates, *i.e.*, positive class acceptance rates, for a classifier only enforcing SP constraint (solid lines), and a classifier additionally enforcing the "loss-averse" constraint (dotted lines). Right panel shows the nondiscrimination-accuracy tradeoff for both the classifiers. Enforcing "loss-averse" constraint, defined in Eq. (7), leads to significant additional loss in accuracy for the same level of discrimination.

uniformly at random. Conditioned on the class membership, each data point was sampled from the following distributions:

$$p(\mathbf{x}|y = 1) = N([2; 2][5, 1; 1, 5]),$$
$$p(\mathbf{x}|y = -1) = N([-2; -2][10, 1; 1, 3]).$$

Value of the sensitive attribute was sampled from the following Bernoulli probability distributions:

$$p(z = 1) = \frac{p(\mathbf{x}'|y = 1)}{p(\mathbf{x}'|y = 1) + p(\mathbf{x}'|y = -1)},$$

where, $\mathbf{x}' = [\cos(\phi), -\sin(\phi); \sin(\phi), \cos(\phi)]\mathbf{x}$, *i.e.*, the rotated feature vector, $\mathbf{x}$. On average there were 3280 points in the protected group and 2720 were in non-protected group.

Experimental Setup. The dataset is split into 70%-30%, train-test folds. Additionally, hyperparameters are validated using a 30% hold out set from the training data. All the results have been averaged over 5 shuffles of the data initialized by different random seed. In order to pick the penalization parameter, λ in Problem (P3), multiplied with the regularizer, we trained the unconstrained classifier for $\lambda \in [1e-5, 1e-2]$. Then, we picked a value which yielded the highest accuracy on the validation set, for a particular shuffle of the data . We used this value of the parameter for *all* the experiments on that shuffle of the data. We use CVXPY [11] library to solve all the optimization problems.

5.2 Loss-aversively Fair Updates

In this section we experiment with Problems (P1 and P3). First we consider statistical parity, where beneficial outcome rates are defined as positive class acceptance rate, as a notion of discrimination, *i.e.*, solving Problems (P1) using SP proxies. Then, we show results combining SP and loss-averse constraints and we update $\boldsymbol{\theta}_{sqo}$ with loss-averse nondiscriminatory classifiers.

Training Loss-aversively Fair Classifier. We initialize θ_{sqo} with the solution of unconstrained problem. Then, given a value of covariance threshold c, as used in Eqs.(5 and 6), and a range of γ, as used in Eqs.(7 and 8), we solve Problem (P3). We, then, pick the gamma values whose solutions yield a higher benefits compared to $\boldsymbol{\theta}_{sqo}$, for all the groups, on the validation set. In case there are multiple such values, we pick the one whose solution yields maximum accuracy. We then report the results on the test set.

SP. Accuracy of an unconstrained classifier, on *Synthetic* dataset, is 88%, and the acceptance rates for the protected and non-protected groups are 31% and 72%, respectively. There is a clear disparity in acceptance rates of both the groups. In order to remove this disparity we solve Problem (P1), replacing the first constraint with SP proxy, given by Eq. (5). For a covariance threshold $c = 0$, this leads to a classifier with an acceptance rate of 51% and 52%, for protected and non-protected groups respectively, and an accuracy of 72%.

The results for this formulation, Problem (P1) specialized with SP, are shown in Figure (1). The x-axis is covariance multiplicative factor $m : c = m \times c^*$, where c^* is the covariance values of the unconstrained classifier and c is covariance threshold as given in Eq.(5). *Solid lines* in Figure (1a) represent the statistics of the classifiers resulting from the solutions of this formulation. Figure (1b) shows the accuracies of classifiers resulting from solving this formulation in *purple* colored points.

Note that: i) Figure (1b) demonstrates that as the covariance is decreased the accuracy of the resulting, less discriminatory, classifiers also decreases. ii) Figure (1a) shows that as the covariance decreases, the discrimination also reduces. iii) However it should be noted that discrimination is decreased by reducing the acceptance rate of the non-protected group.

Loss-Aversiveness + SP. In order to train a classifier enforcing loss-averse update of $\boldsymbol{\theta}_{sqo}$, Eq. (4), combined with statistical parity, Eq (2), on the *Synthetic* dataset, we solve Problem (P3). Loss-averse updates yield a classifier with an accuracy of 65% and acceptance rates of 80% and 86% for protected and non-protected groups, respectively, for the covariance value $c = 0$.

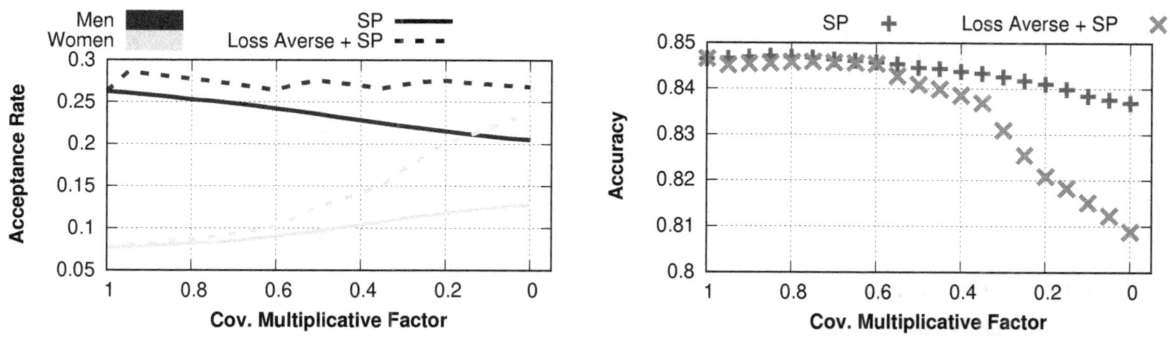

(a) Statistical Parity (SP)

(b) Nondiscrimination-accuracy tradeoff

Figure 2: [Adult dataset. Enforcing statistical parity] Left panel shows the beneficial outcome rates, *i.e.*, positive class acceptance rates, for a classifier only enforcing SP constraint, *i.e.*, solution of Problem (P1) using SP proxies (solid lines), and a classifier additionally enforcing the "loss-averse" constraint, *i.e.*, solution of Problem (P3) (dotted lines). Right panel shows the nondiscrimination-accuracy tradeoff for both the classifiers. Enforcing "loss-averse" constraint, defined in Eq. (7), leads to a significant additional loss in accuracy for the same level of discrimination.

The results are shown in Figure (1a) in *dotted lines* and in *green* colored points in Figure (3b). i) The figures demonstrate that loss-aversively fair updates yield a less discriminatory classifier while increasing the benefits for both the groups, ii) however this comes at a higher cost of accuracy.

Summary. In this section we demonstrated the effectiveness of our proposed formulation on synthetic datasets. We illustrated the effectiveness of loss-aversively making the status quo classifiers nondiscriminatory, albeit at a higher cost of accuracy.

6 EVALUATION ON REAL-WORLD DATASET

In this section, we evaluate the effectiveness of our proposed schemes in updating the status quo classifier, θ_{sqo}, compliant with the "loss-aversively fair updates" consideration, on real-world dataset using statistical parity as a notion of nondiscrimination. We also consider another widely used notion of discrimination, *i.e.*, equality of opportunity, and show loss-averse constraints combined with EOP on a real-world dataset in Appendix B, due to space limitations.

6.1 Dataset and Experimental Setup

In this section we explain the real-world dataset used to evaluate our proposed considerations.

Adult Dataset. We show result for loss-aversively fair update mechanism, introduced in section 4, using *Adult dataset* [2]. Specifically, we illustrate the effectiveness of Problem (P3) to train loss-aversively fair classifiers, using Adult dataset. For experiments in this section, we consider statistical parity as a notion of nondiscrimination.

The *Adult Dataset* consists of 45, 222 subjects and 14 features like gender, race, educational level, *etc.* The classification task is to predict whether a person earns more than 50K USD per annum (positive class) or not (negative class). We consider gender to be a sensitive feature for this dataset.

Experimental Setup. For the experiments conducted on the *Adult dataset* we use the same data split as used for *Synthetic dataset.* We also randomize the data, as well as validate the hyperparameters in a similar manner.

6.2 Loss-Aversively Fair Updates

In this section we compare the results of Problem (P1), using SP proxies, and Loss-aversively fair updates given by Problem (P3) using *Adult dataset.*

SP. On the Adult dataset, logistic regression classifier leads to an accuracy of 84.6%. However, the classifier leads to the beneficial outcome rates of 8% and 26% for women and men respectively, showing a clear disparity in the beneficial outcome rates for the two groups. Next, using the method of Zafar et al. [25], we train a nondiscriminatory classifier while reducing the value of the covariance threshold c, (Eq. (5)), towards 0. The results are shown in *solid lines* in Figure (2a) and in *purple* colored points in Figure (2b). The least discriminatory classifier in this case achieves the beneficial outcome rates of 13% and 20% for women and men respectively, with an accuracy of 83.7%. We notice that the discrimination is reduced by lowering the beneficial outcome rates for men, which leads to a violation of "loss-averse" consideration.

Loss-Aversiveness + SP. We next train classifier with the loss-averse constraints (Eq. (7)) combined with SP, *i.e.*, solve Problem. (P3). The least discriminatory classifier in this case achieves the beneficial outcome rates of 24% and 27% for women and men, respectively, while achieving an accuracy of 80.8%. However, the reduction in discrimination is achieved by only increasing the beneficial outcome rate for both groups. Results are shown in Figures (2a and 2b), in *dotted lines* and *green* colored points, respectively.

The figure shows the beneficial outcome rates for (i) a classifier with statistical parity constraint and (ii) a classifier with loss-averse and statistical parity constraints. The figure shows that at successively decreasing values of the covariance threshold c, while classifier (i) achieves lower discrimination by increasing benefits for one group and decreasing them for the other, classifier (ii) does so by *only increasing benefits for both the groups.* Figure (2b) shows the nondiscrimination-accuracy tradeoff achieved by both the classifiers. The figure demonstrates that, as expected, classifier (ii) incurs a much higher cost in terms of accuracy for the same level of discrimination due to the additional loss-averse constraint.

Summary. Our proposed methodology, in Section 4, successfully enforces the loss averse constraint while updating the status quo classifier, θ_{sqo}, to a nondiscriminatory classifier. However, enforcing these constraints could be at a significant additional cost in terms of accuracy.

7 CONCLUDING DISCUSSION

A number of recent works have explored various aspects of fairness related to algorithmic decision making. In this paper, we focus on an aspect of decision making that crucially affects people's fairness perceptions, yet has been overlooked: it is the *fairness of updating decision making*, i.e., how the decision outcomes change when updating a decision making system.

Based on observations in behavioral economics and psychology, we note that any "disadvantageous" changes in outcomes to individual subjects or groups of subjects would be perceived as unfair. Accordingly, we propose a complementary notion of update fairness that we call *loss-averse updates*. Loss-averse updates try to constrain updates to only yield more advantageous (more beneficial) outcomes compared to status quo.

In this work, we formalize this notion in the context of classification tasks. We proposed measures that would allow these notions to be incorporated in the training of any convex decision-boundary based classifiers (like logistic regression or linear/non-linear SVM) as convex constraints. We also show how this notion can be combined with prior notions and measures of non-discrimination in classification. Our evaluation using synthetic and real-world datasets demonstrates the benefits of loss-averse updates in practice.

Our work here also opens up a number of new and interesting research directions. The motivation behind our notions of fair updates generalize to any algorithmic decision making scenario that affects people's lives including search and recommender algorithms such as Google's search, Facebook's NewsFeed, Amazon's product recommendations or market-matching algorithms like Uber's rider-driver matching algorithms. Exploring how our notion loss-averse updates can be applied to these more complex algorithmic decision making scenarios (beyond binary classification) remains an open challenge.

REFERENCES

[1] 2017. http://www.nyc.gov/html/nypd/html/analysis_and_planning/stop_question_and_frisk_report.shtml.
[2] Adult. 1996. http://tinyurl.com/UCI-Adult.
[3] Solon Barocas and Andrew D. Selbst. 2016. Big Data's Disparate Impact. *California Law Review* (2016).
[4] Max H Bazerman, Sally Blount White, and George F Loewenstein. 1995. Perceptions of Fairness in Interpersonal and Individual Choice Situations. *Current Directions in Psychological Science* (1995).
[5] Yahav Bechavod and Katrina Ligett. 2017. Learning Fair Classifiers: A Regularization Approach. FATML.
[6] Richard Berk, Hoda Heidari, Shahin Jabbari, Matthew Joseph, Michael Kearns, Jamie Morgenstern, Seth Neel, and Aaron Roth. 2017. A Convex Framework for Fair Regression. *arXiv preprint arXiv:1706.02409* (2017).
[7] Richard Berk, Hoda Heidari, Shahin Jabbari, Michael Kearns, and Aaron Roth. 2017. Fairness in criminal justice risk assessments: the state of the art. *arXiv preprint arXiv:1703.09207* (2017).
[8] Asia J. Biega, Krishna P. Gummadi, and Gerhard Weikum. 2018. Equity of Attention: Amortizing Individual Fairness in Rankings. In *SIGIR*.
[9] Flavio Chierichetti, Ravi Kumar, Silvio Lattanzi, and Sergei Vassilvitskii. 2017. Fair Clustering Through Fairlets. In *NIPS*.
[10] Sam Corbett-Davies, Emma Pierson, Avi Feller, Sharad Goel, and Aziz Huq. 2017. Algorithmic Decision Making and the Cost of Fairness. In *KDD*.
[11] Steven Diamond and Stephen Boyd. 2016. CVXPY: A Python-Embedded Modeling Language for Convex Optimization. *Journal of Machine Learning Research* 17, 83 (2016), 1–5.
[12] Cynthia Dwork, Moritz Hardt, Toniann Pitassi, and Omer Reingold. 2012. Fairness Through Awareness. In *ITCSC*.
[13] Michael Feldman, Sorelle A. Friedler, John Moeller, Carlos Scheidegger, and Suresh Venkatasubramanian. 2015. Certifying and Removing Disparate Impact. In *KDD*.
[14] Sharad Goel, Justin M. Rao, and Ravi Shroff. 2015. Precinct or Prejudice? Understanding Racial Disparities in New York City's Stop-and-Frisk Policy. *Annals of Applied Statistics* (2015).
[15] Moritz Hardt, Eric Price, and Nathan Srebro. 2016. Equality of Opportunity in Supervised Learning. In *NIPS*.
[16] Daniel Kahneman, Jack L Knetsch, and Richard Thaler. 1986. Fairness as a Constraint on Profit Seeking: Entitlements in the Market. *The American economic review* (1986).
[17] Daniel Kahneman and Amos Tversky. 1979. Prospect Theory: An Analysis of Decisions Under Risk. *Econometrica* (1979).
[18] Dino Pedreschi, Salvatore Ruggieri, and Franco Turini. 2008. Discrimination-aware Data Mining. In *KDD*.
[19] Andrea Romei and Salvatore Ruggieri. 2014. A Multidisciplinary Survey on Discrimination Analysis. *KER* (2014).
[20] Ashudeep Singh and Thorsten Joachims. 2018. Fairness of Exposure in Rankings. *arXiv preprint arXiv:1802.07281* (2018).
[21] Supreme Court of the United States. 1989. Martin vs. Wilks.
[22] Joel E Urbany, Thomas J Madden, and Peter R Dickson. 1989. All's not fair in pricing: an initial look at the dual entitlement principle. *Marketing Letters* (1989).
[23] Muhammad Bilal Zafar, Isabel Valera, Manuel Rodriguez, Krishna P. Gummadi, and Adrian Weller. 2017. From Parity to Preference-based Notions of Fairness in Classification. In *NIPS*.
[24] Muhammad Bilal Zafar, Isabel Valera, Manuel Gomez Rodriguez, and Krishna P. Gummadi. 2017. Fairness Beyond Disparate Treatment & Disparate Impact: Learning Classification without Disparate Mistreatment. In *WWW*.
[25] Muhammad Bilal Zafar, Isabel Valera, Manuel Gomez Rodriguez, and Krishna P. Gummadi. 2017. Fairness Constraints: Mechanisms for Fair Classification. In *AISTATS*.
[26] R. Zemel, Y. Wu, K. Swersky, T. Pitassi, and C. Dwork. 2013. Learning Fair Representations. In *ICML*.

ACKNOWLEDGEMENTS

This research was supported in part by a European Research Council (ERC) Advanced Grant for the project "Foundations for Fair Social Computing", funded under the European Union's Horizon 2020 Framework Programme (grant agreement no. 789373)

A EVALUATION ON SYNTHETIC DATASET: EOP

In this section we will present the "loss-averse" fairness results combined with equality of opportunity, using synthetic dataset. We show the results of the optimization Problem (P4).

A.1 Dataset and Experimental Setup

In this section we explain the synthetic dataset used for demonstrating the loss-averse consideration and the experimental setup used to solve the optimization Problem (P4).

Synthetic Dataset. Each data point comprises of 2 features apart from the sensitive attribute. Each data point also has a binary ground truth label. For equality of opportunity, as given by Eq. (3), we are considering true positive rates as a notion of benefit. To demonstrate the results of fair updates combined with EOP, we use a synthetic dataset proposed by Zafar et al. [24], except that we flip the ground truth labels in order to have a disparity in the false negative rates instead of the false positive rates. We generated 16000 data points with the probability distributions of the features given as follows:

$$p(\mathbf{x}|z=0,y=1) = N([2;2][3,1;1,3])$$
$$p(\mathbf{x}|z=1,y=1) = N([2;2][3,1;1,3])$$
$$p(\mathbf{x}|z=0,y=-1) = N([1;1][3,3;1,3])$$
$$p(\mathbf{x}|z=1,y=-1) = N([-2;-2][3,1;1,3])$$

Both, class labels, y, and value of the sensitive attribute, z, were sampled uniformly at random.

Experimental Setup. We use the same data split and method of validating the hyperparameters as explained in section 5.

A.2 Loss-Aversively Fair Updates

In this section we show the results of Problem (P1), using EOP as a notion of nondiscrimination. We also show results for the loss-averse formulation combined with EOP, given by Problem (P4).

EOP. An unconstrained classifier trained on *Synthetic* dataset yields an accuracy of 86% and true positive rates (TPRs) of 94% and 77% for non-protected and protected groups, respectively. To equalize the TPRs we solve Problem (P1) using proxies for EOP given in Eq. (6).

These results are show in Figure (3a) in *solid lines* and Figure (3b) in *purple* colored points. i) In order to reduce discrimination, this formulation yields a classifier which lowers the TPR of the non-protected class to 72% and raises the TPR of the protected group to 79%, for covariance threshold $c = 0$, while achieving an accuracy of 74%. ii) Figure (3a) shows the limitation of equality of opportunity proxy proposed by Zafar et al. [24], as it achieves a lower discrimination for higher value of the covariance.

Loss-Aversiveness + EOP. To avoid lowering the benefits for any group while reducing discrimination, we solve the Problem (P4). We encountered some issues in convergence for some values of covariance factor, specifically smaller ones. Out of 7 random seeds that we tried we find the results for *all* covariance factors for only 5 seeds, we report the average of these results. One reason for the lack of convergence could be that a very high base TPR might make it difficult to find a nondiscriminatory classifier.For covariance threshold $c = 0$, this formulation leads to a classifier whose true positive rates are 95% and 99% for non-protected and protected groups, respectively, with an accuracy of 64%.

We show these results in Figure (3a) in *dotted lines* and Figure (3b) in *green* colored crosses. i) These figures illustrate the effectiveness of the loss-averse formulation, as the resulting classifiers achieve nondiscrimination by increasing TPR for both groups, ii) however this results in a significant drop in the accuracy.

B EVALUATION ON REAL-WORLD DATASET: EOP

In this section we will present the "loss-averse" fairness results combined with equality of opportunity, using a real-world dataset.

B.1 Dataset and Experimental Setup

In this section we explain the dataset and the experimental setup. We show result of Problem (P1), with EOP as a notion of nondiscrimination, as well as Problem (P4), which combines EOP and loss-averse constraints.

SQF Dataset. For experiments in this section we consider *NYPD SQF dataset* [1]. The NYPD *SQF dataset* consists of pedestrians who were stopped in the year 2012 on the suspicion of having a weapon. The task is a binary prediction task which indicates whether (negative class) or not (positive class) a weapon was discovered. For our analysis, we consider the race to be the sensitive feature with values African-American and white. After balancing the classes and considering same features as Goel et al. [14], with the exception that we exclude the highly sparse features 'precinct' and 'timestamp of the stop', we obtain 5,832 subjects and 19 features.

Experimental Setup. We used similar experimental setup as explained in section 5.

B.2 Loss-Aversively Fair Updates

In this section we show the results of Problem (P4), which enforces EOP and loss-averse constraints and compare them with the results of Problem (P1), which only enforces EOP using the proxy given by Eq. (6), on *NYPD SQF dataset.*

EOP. With equality of opportunity constraint, where beneficial outcome rates are defined in terms of true positive rate, we experiment with NYPD SQF dataset. Unconstrained logistic regression on SQF yields an accuracy of 74.4%, while the beneficial outcome rates are 69% and 82% for Whites and African-Americans, respectively. Least discriminatory classifier, trained with $c = 0$, given in constraint Eq. (6), yields benefits of 72% and 76% for Whites and African-Americans, respectively, while achieving an accuracy of 71.4%. Similar to the previous cases, this classifier also achieves lower discriminations by raising the benefits for one group while increasing them for the other group.

Loss-Aversiveness + EOP. Next, we combine the nondiscrimination constraint with the loss-averse constraint, given by Problem (P4), in order to update $\boldsymbol{\theta}_{sqo}$. A least discriminatory loss-averse classifier trained on NYPD SQF dataset yields an accuracy of 71% and benefits of 84% and 81% for African-Americans and White, respectively. Figure (4a) shows the beneficial outcome rates for (i) a classifier with only nondiscrimination constraints and (ii) a loss-averse classifier with nondiscrimination constraints. Again,

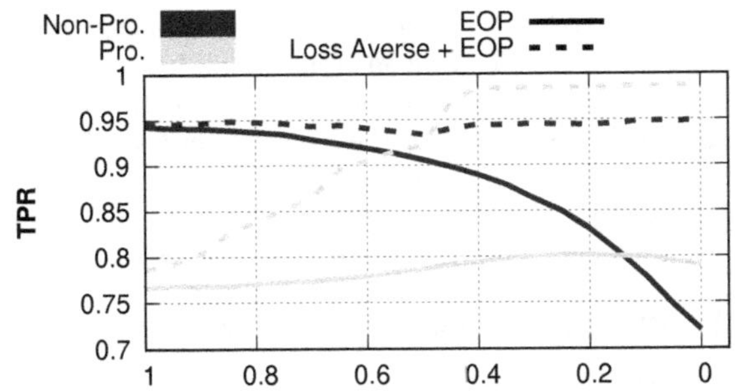

(a) Equality of Opportunity (EOP)

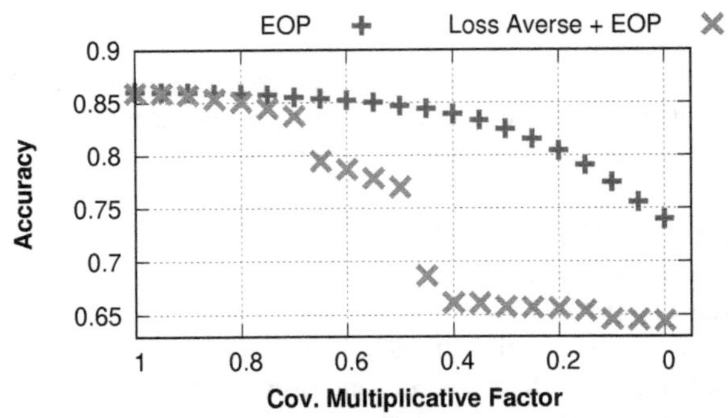

(b) Nondiscrimination-accuracy tradeoff

Figure 3: [Synthetic dataset. Enforcing equality of opportunity] Figure on the left shows the beneficial outcome rates, *i.e.*, true positive rates, for a classifier only enforcing EOP constraint (solid lines) and a classifier additionally enforcing the "loss-averse" constraint, given in Eq. (8), is shown in dotted lines. Figure on the right shows nondiscrimination-accuracy tradeoff for both the classifiers.

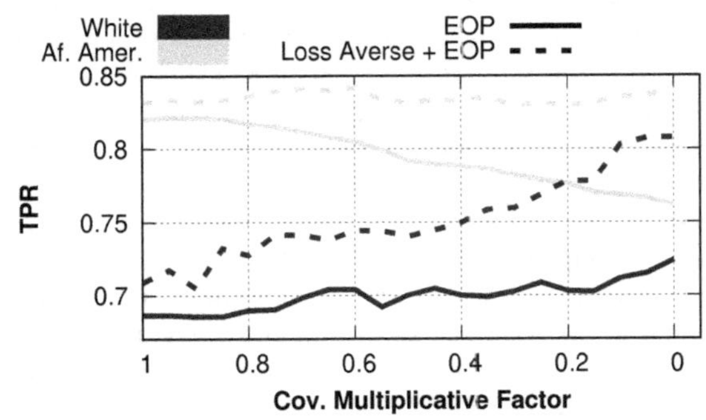

(a) Equality of Opportunity (EOP)

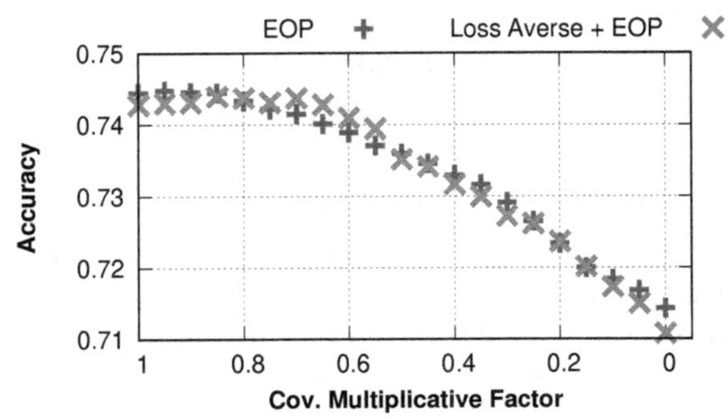

(b) Nondiscrimination-accuracy tradeoff

Figure 4: [SQF dataset. Enforcing equality of opportunity] These figures show similar results as Figure (3) using SQF dataset.

we notice that classifier (ii) removes discrimination by *only increasing the beneficial outcome rates* whereas classifier (i) does so by increasing benefits for one group and decreasing them for the other. Finally, the comparison of nondiscrimination-accuracy tradeoff in Figure (4b) shows no significant difference between both the classifiers.

Counterfactual Fairness in Text Classification through Robustness

Sahaj Garg*
Stanford University
Stanford, CA
sahajg@cs.stanford.edu

Vincent Perot
Google AI
New York, NY
vperot@google.com

Nicole Limtiaco
Google AI
New York, NY
nlimtiaco@google.com

Ankur Taly
Google AI
Mountain View, CA
ataly@google.com

Ed H. Chi
Google AI
Mountain View, CA
edchi@google.com

Alex Beutel
Google AI
New York, NY
alexbeutel@google.com

Abstract

In this paper, we study counterfactual fairness in text classification, which asks the question: *How would the prediction change if the sensitive attribute referenced in the example were different?* Toxicity classifiers demonstrate a counterfactual fairness issue by predicting that "Some people are gay" is toxic while "Some people are straight" is nontoxic. We offer a metric, counterfactual token fairness (CTF), for measuring this particular form of fairness in text classifiers, and describe its relationship with group fairness. Further, we offer three approaches, blindness, counterfactual augmentation, and counterfactual logit pairing (CLP), for optimizing counterfactual token fairness during training, bridging the robustness and fairness literature. Empirically, we find that blindness and CLP address counterfactual token fairness. The methods do not harm classifier performance, and have varying tradeoffs with group fairness. These approaches, both for measurement and optimization, provide a new path forward for addressing fairness concerns in text classification.

CCS Concepts

• **Social and professional topics → Computing / technology policy**; • **Computing methodologies → Natural language processing**.

Keywords

Text classification; fairness; counterfactual fairness; robustness

ACM Reference Format:
Sahaj Garg, Vincent Perot, Nicole Limtiaco, Ankur Taly, Ed H. Chi, and Alex Beutel. 2019. Counterfactual Fairness in Text Classification through Robustness. In *AAAI/ACM Conference on AI, Ethics, and Society (AIES '19), January 27–28, 2019, Honolulu, HI, USA.* ACM, New York, NY, USA, 8 pages. https://doi.org/10.1145/3306618.3317950

*Work done while author was interning at Google.

AIES '19, January 27–28, 2019, Honolulu, HI, USA

ACM ISBN 978-1-4503-6324-2/19/01.
https://doi.org/10.1145/3306618.3317950

1 Introduction

Consider a model that determines whether an Internet forum comment is toxic. We would like to improve the model's fairness with respect to the content of the input text, which may reference sensitive identity attributes, such as sexual orientation, race, or religion. In practice, Dixon et al. showed that a toxicity model had a high false positive rate on examples that included identity tokens such as "gay," because such tokens occur relatively frequently in examples labeled toxic in the training set.

A related issue to users arises when nearly identical sentences referencing different identity groups receive different predictions. For instance, a baseline toxicity model predicts that "Some people are gay" is 98% likely to be toxic and "Some people are straight" is only 2% likely to be toxic. In this work, we seek to specifically address this fairness issue for text classification.

Given an example, we ask a *counterfactual* question: *How would the prediction change if the sensitive attribute referenced in the example were different?* If the prediction score changes with respect to a sensitive attribute, we consider this an indicator of a potential problem. In contrast to group-based notions of fairness (e.g., demographic parity, equality of odds), which seek to statistically equalize the model's behavior for entire sensitive groups, counterfactual fairness requires equal model behavior on individual counterfactual pairs; see [12, 22].

To assess counterfactual fairness, we consider perturbations obtained by substituting tokens associated with identity groups. For instance, substituting "gay" with "straight," or "Asian" with "American." Based on these generated counterfactuals, we can define a fairness metric, which we call *counterfactual token fairness* (CTF). While this is more limited than general counterfactual fairness, we believe it captures one of the most salient issues in text classification and is a starting point for more general counterfactual fairness metrics for text.

Deciding when counterfactual pairs should have the same prediction raises difficult ethical and philosophical questions. Many logical counterfactuals generated by token substitution may not require identical output. We call these *asymmetric counterfactuals.* In toxicity classification, such situations could arise when the comment references stereotypes associated with one group but not another, or when comments attack a particularly vulnerable group. Asymmetric counterfactuals suggest that practitioners should be careful in both training and evaluation of counterfactual fairness. We discuss proposals for addressing this in the case of toxicity classification in the experiments section.

To satisfy counterfactual token fairness, we borrow techniques from the robustness literature. We propose a general training scheme for achieving arbitrary counterfactual fairness by extending logit pairing [8] to penalize differences in the model's outputs for counterfactual pairs. We compare this method to simply augmenting the training set with counterfactual examples, and to blindness, which replaces all sensitive tokens with a special token.

One issue is that the aforementioned methods may only achieve fairness with respect to identity tokens considered by counterfactuals during training. To address this, we evaluate the generalization of the methods on a held-out set of identity tokens. Another concern when optimizing for counterfactual fairness is potential trade-offs with other desirable properties of a classifier, including overall accuracy and group fairness. In practice, we do not find significant harms with respect to accuracy, and varying effects on group fairness in the form of tradeoffs between true negatives and true positives.

We make the following contributions:

- **Metric:** We provide a tractable metric, *counterfactual token fairness*, for measuring counterfactual fairness in text classification.
- **Methods:** We study three methods for addressing counterfactual token fairness: (A) blindness, (B) counterfactual augmentation, and (B) counterfactual logit pairing, bridging research from the robustness and fairness domains.
- **Empirical Evaluation:** We evaluate empirical performance and tradeoffs of counterfactual token fairness, group fairness, and accuracy across these approaches.

2 Related Work

ML Fairness Significant work in the ML fairness literature has been devoted to measuring fairness. Our work is most closely related to counterfactual fairness in causal inference [9, 12], where fairness is evaluated by applying counterfactual interventions over a causal graph. Our definition of counterfactual token fairness implicitly defines a simple causal model for text generation. Kusner et al. also draw the connection between counterfactual fairness and individual fairness, which requires similar predictions for similar inputs via a Lipschitz constraint [4].

Relatively more study has been devoted to group fairness metrics, which evaluate observational criteria, or statistical relationships between the data, group membership, the label, and the model's prediction. Such metrics include demographic parity and equality of odds [6]. Hardt et al. demonstrate that observational criteria are insufficient to distinguish between some seemingly reasonable uses of identity and other unreasonable ones. This is because observational criteria cannot incorporate any external understanding about what is causally acceptable in making predictions. The limitations of observational criteria can be addressed by counterfactual or individual fairness, see [4, 9, 12]. By extending these definitions to path-specific counterfactual fairness, it is possible to specify which uses of identity are acceptable [2].

Social science literature on fairness raises arguments for counterfactual reasoning as well as potential limitations. One concern is about the ability to reasonably intervene on identity of an individual. Given that most social scientists agree that race is socially constructed, it may be unreasonable to attempt to modify race and all its associated factors [10]. These limitations, among others, are reflected in debate surrounding the use of counterfactuals over race in epidemiological studies [11, 21]. We note that our work deals with well-defined interventions on content by only manipulating identity tokens in text, rather than the actual identities of individuals, which differentiates it from the work above.

ML fairness literature has also focused on debiasing methods to address these gaps. Many methods have been proposed to address group fairness issues, such as re-calibrating score functions [6], adversarially learning fair representations [1, 14, 23], data rebalancing [3], and data augmentation using swaps of gender terms [18]. For natural language problems, Pryzant et al. learn a lexicon that is uncorrelated to a set of confounding variables. Debiasing methods for counterfactual or individual fairness have been studied less for neural network models. The methods in [9, 12] are effective for causal graphs, but most machine learning problems will not fit this mold. To address individual fairness, [4] applies constraint based optimization over a linear program, but it is difficult to define valid distance metrics or apply the optimization to arbitrary neural networks used in natural language processing.

Robustness in Machine Learning The robustness literature in machine learning has primarily focused on robustness to adversarially perturbed inputs, which add small amounts of carefully selected noise to fool classifiers [5]. When applied to the text setting, such adversarial examples can be generated by a variety of editing methods, including through translation [20], attributions [17], and autoencoders [7, 24]. Adversarial examples are closely related to counterfactual examples: Wachter et al. characterize counterfactuals as adversarial examples that perturb inputs in human-interpretable and possibly problematic ways. As such, the counterfactual examples presented in this work can be viewed as a specific subset of adversarial examples. The robustness literature has attempted to address adversarial examples using a variety of techniques, such as adversarial training [5, 16] and adversarial logit pairing [8].

Several papers draw connections between fairness, text generation, and robustness. Landeiro and Culotta consider robustness in text with respect to counfounding variables such as the author's gender, and learn robust models by training using an additional attribute for the latent confound, and averaging over all values of the latent variable at inference time. Madaan et al. attempt to edit text to remove gender bias or edit gender representations, leveraging analogies in word vector differences to make substitutions for words that may implicitly encode biases about gender.

3 Problem Definition

Given text input $x \in X$, where x is a sequence $[x_1, ..., x_n]$ of tokens, our task is to predict an outcome y. We consider a classifier f parameterized by θ that produces a prediction $\hat{y} = f_\theta(x)$, where we seek to minimize some notion of error between y and $\hat{y}$. For notational simplicity, we restrict the following definitions to a single binary class, but they can be easily generalized to multi-class classification problems. The classifier f can be an arbitrary neural network.

We wish to maximize the model's performance while maintaining counterfactual fairness with respect to sensitive attributes, such as identity groups. Counterfactual fairness is measured using counterfactual examples that perturb the sensitive attribute referenced in the example at hand. Let $\Phi(x)$ denote the set of counterfactual examples associated with an example x. Counterfactual fairness requires that the predictions of a model for all counterfactuals are within a specified error.

Definition 3.1. Counterfactual fairness. A classifier f is counterfactually fair with respect to a counterfactual generation function Φ and some error rate ϵ if

$$|f(x) - f(x')| \leq \epsilon \quad \forall x \in X, x' \in \Phi(x)$$

3.1 Counterfactual Token Fairness (CTF)

We consider a narrow class of counterfactuals that involves substituting identity tokens in the input, for instance, substituting "gay" with "straight" in the input "Some people are gay." We assume a set of identity tokens, $\mathcal{A}$, for which we seek to be counterfactually fair. Consider a pair of tokens $a, a' \in \mathcal{A}$. The associated counterfactual example generation function $\Phi_{a,a'}$ is defined by substituting all occurrences of a in x with a' and vice versa. If neither identity token is present in the input x, then $\Phi_{a,a'}(x) = \emptyset$. We generalize this definition to a counterfactual generation function over $\mathcal{A}$ that generates all counterfactual examples based on pairs of substitutions:

$$\Phi_{\mathcal{A}}(x) = \bigcup_{a \neq a' \in \mathcal{A}} \Phi_{a,a'}(x)$$

Definition 3.2. A classifier satisfies *counterfactual token fairness* with respect to a set of identity tokens $\mathcal{A}$ if it satisfies counterfactual fairness with respect to the counterfactual generation function $\Phi_{\mathcal{A}}$ and error rate ϵ.

Although content about sensitive groups may be captured by complex semantics, this metric will surface a subset of problematic issues related to more general counterfactual fairness. This a first step, and surfaces additional concerns for fairness beyond those of group fairness.

3.2 Asymmetric Counterfactuals

So far we have assumed that all counterfactuals with respect to identity tokens should have the same prediction. This assumption is not valid in cases where the sensitive attribute indeed affects the prediction. For instance, consider a model predicting toxicity of text, and the counterfactual pair "That's so gay" and "That's so straight." The first example is arguably more likely to be considered toxic than the second, as "gay" is often used as an insult in Internet forums, while "straight" is not. Other examples include stereotyping, where one group is more vulnerable than another. Requiring equal predictions across such cases can inadvertently harm the more vulnerable group.

Fairness must be required only among counterfactuals that stipulate symmetric predictions. This restriction can be accommodated in our framework by restricting the counterfactual generation function $\Phi(x)$ to exclude any counterfactuals for the example x that may have asymmetric labels. In general, the degree and direction of the asymmetry between counterfactuals varies based on the task, and the cultural sensitivities of the consumers of the task. This makes it difficult to define a perfect counterfactual generation function. In Experiments, we propose a heuristic for avoiding asymmetric counterfactuals for a model predicting toxicity of text.

3.3 Relationship to Group Fairness

Counterfactual fairness is complementary to the group fairness notion of *equality of odds* [6], which demands equality of true positive rates and true negative rates for different values of the sensitive attribute. A text classifier may satisfy one while completely failing the other. Consider the case when two sensitive attributes a and a' only appear in disjoint sets of contexts X_a and $X_{a'}$, respectively. A model can satisfy equality of odds by always predicting correctly on the contexts in which a, a' appear in the data, but never in the counterfactual contexts that do not exist in the data. Conversely, the model could predict identical output for all counterfactual pairs while predicting correctly only on X_a and not X'_a.

4 Methods

We propose three methods to improve counterfactual fairness: blindness, counterfactual augmentation, and counterfactual logit pairing. Both methods assume access to a list of identity tokens for which they seek to be fair.

4.1 Blindness

Blindness substitutes all identity tokens with a special `IDENTITY` token, which allows the predictor to know that an identity term is present, but not which identity. This is similar to standard NLP methods such as replacing large numbers with a generic `NUMBER`. While this approach guarantees counterfactual token fairness, it has a number of downsides. First, it does not have the ability to differentiate identity terms, and so necessarily equates asymmetric counterfactuals. Second, it cannot handle complex counterfactuals that involve more than single token substitutions, e.g. "Christians go to church." and "Jews go to temple." Finally, the model may still discriminate using other signals that are associated with the identity term [4].

4.2 Counterfactual Augmentation

Instead of blinding the model to identity terms, counterfactual augmentation involves augmenting the model's training set with generated counterfactual examples. The additional examples are meant to guide the model to become invariant to perturbing identity terms. This is a standard technique in computer vision for making the model invariant to object location, image orientation, etc. The counterfactual examples are assigned the same label as the original example.

4.3 Counterfactual Logit Pairing (CLP)

Counterfactual logit pairing (CLP) encourages the model to be robust to identity by adding a robustness term to the training loss. The robustness term is given by logit pairing [8], which penalizes the norm of the difference in logits for pairs of training examples and their counterfactuals. Specifically, suppose the classifier

$f(x) = \sigma(g(x))$, where $g(x)$ produces a logit and $\sigma(\cdot)$ is the sigmoid function. The additional loss is the average absolute difference in logits between the inputs and their counterfactuals:

$$\sum_{x \in X} \mathop{\mathbb{E}}_{x' \sim \text{Unif}[\Phi(x)]} |g(x) - g(x')|$$

For computational tractability, during training, we randomly sample a single counterfactual example for each input. Taking J as the original loss function, the overall objective is:

$$\sum_{x \in X} J(f(x), y) + \lambda \sum_{x \in X} \mathop{\mathbb{E}}_{x' \sim \text{Unif}[\Phi(x)]} |g(x) - g(x')|$$

Similar to counterfactual augmentation, CLP can use any counterfactual generation function. For example, a restricted counterfactual generation function could be used to avoid enforcing equality over asymmetric counterfactuals. Moreover, the method also applies if more sophisticated counterfactuals are generated.

In contrast to counterfactual augmentation, the robustness term in the CLP loss explicitly guides the model to satisfy two desirable properties: (1) ensuring a model produces similar outputs on counterfactual pairs and (2) learning models that generalize well to different identities. Moreover, the parameter λ can be tuned to achieve varying degrees of counterfactual fairness.

5 Experiments

Dataset We evaluate our methods on the task of predicting toxicity. For the task, a toxic comment is defined as a "rude, disrespectful, or unreasonable comment that is likely to make you leave a discussion." [3]. We use a public Kaggle dataset of 160K Wikipedia comments, each labeled by human raters as toxic or non-toxic[1], randomly split into train and dev sets. We evaluate AUC of the primary task on the public test set. We evaluate counterfactual token fairness and group fairness on a private dataset of comments from another internet forum. This dataset, henceforth called the "evaluation dataset," has a higher occurrence of identity terms, and therefore leads to a more meaningful fairness evaluation.

Setup We evaluate our methods for counterfactual token fairness on the set of 50 identity terms used by Dixon et al.. Out of these, 47 are single tokens and 3 are bigrams. We randomly partition the terms into a training set of 35 and a hold-out set of 12 to evaluate generalization. We also include the three bigrams in evaluation, because they reflect scenarios that blindness cannot address during training.[2]

All of the models are CNNs trained with cross entropy loss against the binary toxicity label. All hyperparameters except for the fairness regularizer λ for CLP were fixed for all runs of all models. Models were trained for five epochs, and the best model on the dev set was taken. Each model was trained ten times, and the average of the runs is reported. Blindness, Counterfactual augmentation, and CLP models (for different values of λ) were evaluated and compared to a baseline model.

For CLP training, we define a different counterfactual example generation function than the one used for evaluation. The evaluation counterfactuals only apply substitutions to a pair of identity tokens, whereas during training, each sensitive identity token in an input is randomly substituted with another identity token.

Handling Asymmetric Counterfactuals We hypothesize that asymmetric counterfactuals are less likely to arise for ground truth non-toxic comments than toxic comments. This for two reasons. Asymmetric counterfactuals arise when stereotyping / attacking a vulnerable group occurs for some identity substitution, and no other toxicity signals are present. In such cases, most identity substitutions will be nontoxic, and only the one attacking the vulnerable group(s) will be toxic. So if the ground truth example is nontoxic, counterfactual fairness can still be required over most identity substitutions, whereas if the ground truth example is toxic, equal prediction should not be required over most counterfactuals. Second, the stereotyping comments are more likely to occur in a toxic comment attacking the stereotyped group than in a nontoxic comment referencing some other identity group. For these reasons, we evaluate counterfactual token fairness over ground truth nontoxic comments separately from ground truth toxic comments, and focus our analysis on nontoxic comments. We also consider applying the CLP loss only to nontoxic comments during training, to avoid enforcing equality of logits for potentially asymmetric counterfactuals. We distinguish this variant as CLP_nontoxic.

Separately, we also evaluate CTF on simple synthetic inputs where all information about toxicity is encoded in the context, and all counterfactuals are symmetric by design. Specifically, we use a dataset of synthetically generated sentences based on templates such as "`NAME` is a `ADJECTIVE`."[3]

Metrics We measure the *counterfactual token fairness gap* with respect to a given counterfactual generation function. For a single example, this is the average gap in prediction over all of the counterfactual pairs for that example:

$$\text{CF GAP}_{\Phi}(x) = \mathop{\mathbb{E}}_{x' \sim \text{Unif}[\Phi(x)]} |f(x) - f(x')|$$

Over an entire dataset, the gap is the average over all examples that have valid counterfactuals. In this study, we measure the CTF GAP for the counterfactual generation function $\Phi_{\mathcal{A}}$, which substitutes all pairs of identity tokens. Because substitution-based counterfactuals over short inputs are more likely to be logical, we evaluate the CTF gaps for inputs of at most ten tokens in length. In addition, since asymmetric counterfactuals are likely more common for toxic comments, we evaluate CTF gaps over nontoxic and toxic comments separately.

We also measure group fairness to ensure that optimizing for counterfactual fairness has no perverse impact on it. Following the group fairness notion of equality of odds [6], we measure the true positive rates (TPR) and true negatives rates (TNR) of examples referencing different identity groups. We assume an example references a specific identity group based on the presence of the associated token. Equality of odds requires equal TPR and TNR across identities, so we evaluate overall TPR and TNR gaps. The gap for a pair of identity terms is computed as the absolute value of the difference in rates for the two identity terms. The overall TPR or TNR gap is the average over all pairs of identity terms.

[1] https://www.kaggle.com/c/jigsaw-toxic-comment-classification-challenge

[2] Only single tokens in the input are substituted with bigrams during evaluation.

[3] This is the updated open sourced version of the synthetic test set presented in [3].

Model	Eval NT	Synth NT	Synth Tox
Baseline	0.140	0.180	0.061
Blind	0.000	0.000	0.000
CF Aug	0.127	0.226	0.022
CLP_nontox, $\lambda = 1$	0.012	0.015	0.007
CLP, $\lambda = 0.05$	0.071	0.082	0.024
CLP, $\lambda = 1$	0.007	0.015	0.007
CLP, $\lambda = 5$	0.002	0.004	0.004

Table 1: Conterfactual token fairness gaps for non-toxic examples from evaluation set and all examples from a synthetic test set. All gaps are measure with respect to 35 training terms. Smaller gaps are better.

	CTF Gap: held-out terms
Baseline	0.091
Blind	0.090
CF Aug	0.087
CLP_nontox, $\lambda = 1$	0.095
CLP, $\lambda = 0.05$	0.078
CLP, $\lambda = 1$	0.084
CLP, $\lambda = 5$	0.076

Table 2: CTF gaps on held out identity terms for non-toxic examples from the evaluation set.

5.1 Results

Counterfactual Token Fairness Table 1 reports CTF gaps for non-toxic examples from the evaluation dataset, and all examples from the synthetic dataset. The gaps are computed for the 35 training terms (discussed in Setup). As discussed earlier, both these sets of examples are unlikely to have asymmetric counterfactuals. The baseline model has a large CTF gap on both sets of examples. Blindness achieves a zero gap by design. CLP with a fairness regularization coefficient (λ) of at least 1 also attains a near zero gap. Counterfactual augmentation decreases the CTF gap (relative to the baseline) on non-toxic examples from the evaluation dataset, but does not obtain a zero gap. It is worth noting that the models were not trained on the synthetic dataset, but we still find a reduction in counterfactual fairness gaps on it.

Table 2 reports CTF gaps on the hold-out terms for non-toxic examples from the evaluation dataset. We say that a model's CTF gap generalizes to hold-out terms if its gap is less than the baseline model's gap (0.091). Among the models compared, CLP with $\lambda = 5$ generalizes the best, though the gaps are much larger that those on the training terms. Blindness does not appear to provide generalization benefits. Thus, it may not be a favorable method in settings where we expect examples with identity terms outside the set of training terms.

To evaluate the impact on cases with asymmetric counterfactuals, we also measured the CTF gap for toxic examples from the evaluation dataset over the 35 training terms; see Table 4 in the appendix. The baseline model has a gap of 0.241, and as expected, blindness has a gap of zero. All CLP models with $\lambda \geq 1$ achieve a CTF gap of less than 0.03, which unfortunately means that they end up equating predictions for asymmetric counterfactuals. This includes CLP_nontoxic, which was trained using counterfactuals from non-toxic examples only. Going forward, we do not evaluate CLP_nontoxic as it is not better than the regular CLP models.

Overall Performance We evaluate the overall classifier performance using AUC of the ROC curve. Remarkably, all methods show consistent AUC on the test set, ranging between 0.962-0.964.

Figure 1 compares the true positive rate (TPR) and true negative rate (TNR) of various models, where the threshold for a toxic classification is set to 0.5. TPR and TNR are measured only over examples that contain an identity term from the set of training terms. We find that methods that reduce the CTF gap perform better at identifying nontoxic comments (true negatives) and worse at identifying toxic comments (true positives). We discuss this tension between improving the CTF gap and TPR in Error Analysis.

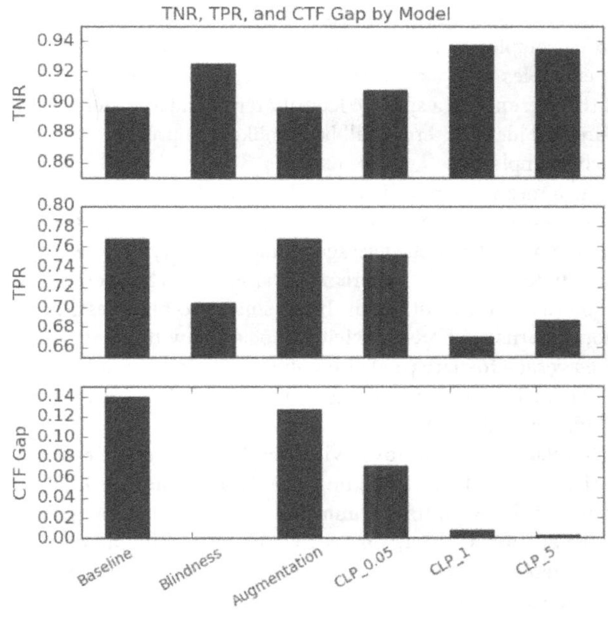

Figure 1: Plot of the average CTF gap along with the TPR and TNR over examples that contain identity terms.

Group Fairness We additionally evaluate the group fairness metrics, TPR and TNR gaps for equality of odds (see Table 3). Counterfactual augmentation and CLP with $\lambda = 0.05$ have better TPR and TNR gaps than the baseline and are able to reduce CTF gaps. CLP with $\lambda \geq 1$ has a more extreme tradeoff, harming the TPR gap while substantially improving the TNR gap. Practitioners may choose different tradeoffs of CTF gap, TPR, and TNR depending on the relative prioritization of these metrics for a given task.

5.2 Error analysis

We examine the trade-off between CTF gap and TPR. We consider the CLP, $\lambda = 5$ model which attains a near zero CTF gap and compare its predictions on toxic comments to those of the baseline. Among examples with identity terms in the test set, there are 83

	TNR Gap	TPR Gap
Baseline	0.084	0.082
Blindness	0.039	0.114
Augmentation	0.065	0.083
CLP all, $\lambda = 0.05$	0.058	0.078
CLP all, $\lambda = 1$	0.039	0.104
CLP all, $\lambda = 5$	0.041	0.112

Table 3: TNR and TPR gaps for different models. Lower is better.

cases where an example was correctly classified by the baseline and incorrectly classified by the CLP model. Of these, 27 were labeled by an author as having an asymmetric counterfactual. There were 20 cases where the CLP model predicted correctly compared to the baseline, of which none had asymmetric counterfactuals. This tells us that a large chunk of the TPR loss (relative to the baseline) is over toxic examples with asymmetric counterfactuals. This is expected as examples with asymmetric counterfactuals are toxic because of the presence of a specific identity term, and a model trained to disregard identity terms will be less likely to predict correctly on such examples.

As a means of investigating what the CLP model has learned, we examine its token embeddings after convergence. By the end of training with $\lambda = 5$, the average cosine similarity between pairs of identity tokens is 0.87, whereas the baseline has an average cosine similarity of 0.25. Although this is similar to blindness, the CLP model learns a different toxicity association with identity tokens. The average toxicity prediction on a single identity token for the CLP model is 0.12, while the toxicity of the `IDENTITY` token in the blindness model is 0.54.

Similarly, CLP_nontoxic with $\lambda = 5$ has a average cosine similarity of 0.81. This embedding convergence, despite CLP being applied only to nontoxic comments, is the reason why the model achieves a low CTF gap on toxic comments, including those with asymmetric counterfactuals. Methods to enforce equal prediction on some subset of counterfactuals but not others should be further investigated.

We also qualitatively evaluate the strength of each model's association with various identity tokens. Table 5 in the appendix lists various examples, and the associated toxicity scores from each model. In contrast to the baseline, all three models associate a much smaller amount of toxicity signal with the identity tokens. For instance, unlike the baseline, the other models no longer associate a substantial amount of toxicity with clearly nontoxic statements such as "Some people are gay." Notably, the toxicity of the statement "Some people are straight" goes up. The negative effect on this pair is more pronounced for blindness than it is for CLP.

6 Conclusions and Future Work

We make progress towards counterfactual fairness in text classification. We propose a specific form of counterfactual fairness, called *counterfactual token fairness* (CTF), that requires a model to be robust to different identity tokens present in the input. We show that text classification models with good overall performance fare poorly on this metric. We approach counterfactual token fairness from a robustness perspective, and offer a procedure, *counterfactual logit pairing*, for optimizing the counterfactual token fairness metric during model training. We find that this approach performs as well as blindness to identity tokens, but also generalizes better to hold-out tokens. These results do not come at the expense of overall classifier accuracy, and have varying tradeoffs between false positives and false negatives.

Going forward, better heuristics must be designed for identifying cases with asymmetric counterfactuals. Excluding toxic comments covers many but not all asymmetric examples. For example, ground truth nontoxic examples referencing "black power" are more likely to become toxic as they reference "white power." In other text classification tasks such as sentiment classification, asymmetric counterfactuals will arise but not necessarily with the same clear split by label.

A next step would be to improve counterfactual generation by addressing issues of polysemy of identity terms (which can result in illogical substitutions), asymmetric counterfactuals, and multiple references to an identity group. One possible method is to use analogies in word vectors to change multiple tokens used for the same identity group [15]. Another approach is defining a generative model over text, as in [7], that can modify certain attributes of the text while holding others constant and preserving semantics. One could also use criteria for selecting semantically equivalent adversarial examples as in [20], to evaluate whether counterfactual examples are logical. Optimizing for general counterfactual fairness will test many of the unique advantages of counterfactual logit pairing.

6.1 Acknowledgements

We would like to thank Lucy Wasserman, Allison Woodruff, Yoni Halpern, Andrew Smart, Tulsee Doshi, Jilin Chen, Alexander D'Amour, Raz Mathias, and Jon Bischof for their feedback leading up to this paper.

References

[1] Alex Beutel, Jilin Chen, Zhe Zhao, and Ed H. Chi. 2017. Data Decisions and Theoretical Implications when Adversarially Learning Fair Representations. *CoRR* abs/1707.00075 (2017). arXiv:1707.00075 http://arxiv.org/abs/1707.00075

[2] Silvia Chiappa and Thomas P. S. Gillam. 2018. Path-Specific Counterfactual Fairness. *arXiv e-prints*, Article arXiv:1802.08139 (Feb. 2018), arXiv:1802.08139 pages. arXiv:stat.ML/1802.08139

[3] Lucas Dixon, John Li, Jeffrey Sorensen, Nithum Thain, and Lucy Vasserman. 2018. Measuring and Mitigating Unintended Bias in Text Classification.

[4] Cynthia Dwork, Moritz Hardt, Toniann Pitassi, Omer Reingold, and Richard S. Zemel. 2011. Fairness Through Awareness. *CoRR* abs/1104.3913 (2011). arXiv:1104.3913 http://arxiv.org/abs/1104.3913

[5] Ian Goodfellow, Jonathon Shlens, and Christian Szegedy. 2015. Explaining and Harnessing Adversarial Examples. In *International Conference on Learning Representations*. http://arxiv.org/abs/1412.6572

[6] Moritz Hardt, Eric Price, and Nathan Srebro. 2016. Equality of Opportunity in Supervised Learning. *CoRR* abs/1610.02413 (2016). arXiv:1610.02413 http://arxiv.org/abs/1610.02413

[7] Zhiting Hu, Zichao Yang, Xiaodan Liang, Ruslan Salakhutdinov, and Eric P. Xing. 2017. Toward Controlled Generation of Text. In *Proceedings of the 34th International Conference on Machine Learning (Proceedings of Machine Learning Research)*, Doina Precup and Yee Whye Teh (Eds.), Vol. 70. PMLR, International Convention Centre, Sydney, Australia, 1587–1596. http://proceedings.mlr.press/v70/hu17e.html

[8] Harini Kannan, Alexey Kurakin, and Ian J. Goodfellow. 2018. Adversarial Logit Pairing. *CoRR* abs/1803.06373 (2018). arXiv:1803.06373 http://arxiv.org/abs/1803.06373

[9] N. Kilbertus, M. Rojas-Carulla, G. Parascandolo, M. Hardt, D. Janzing, and B. Schölkopf. 2017. Avoiding Discrimination through Causal Reasoning. In *Proceedings from the conference "Neural Information Processing Systems 2017.* Curran Associates, Inc., 656–666. http://papers.nips.cc/paper/6668-avoiding-discrimination-through-causal-reasoning.pdf

[10] Issa Kohler-Hausmann. 2019. Eddie Murphy and the Dangers of Counterfactual Causal Thinking About Detecting Racial Discrimination. *Northwestern University Law Review* 113, 5 (Mar 2019).

[11] Nancy Krieger. 2014. On the Causal Interpretation of Race. *Epidemiology* 25, 6 (2014). https://journals.lww.com/epidem/Fulltext/2014/11000/On_the_Causal_Interpretation_of_Race.30.aspx

[12] Matt J Kusner, Joshua Loftus, Chris Russell, and Ricardo Silva. 2017. Counterfactual Fairness. In *Advances in Neural Information Processing Systems 30*, I. Guyon, U. V. Luxburg, S. Bengio, H. Wallach, R. Fergus, S. Vishwanathan, and R. Garnett (Eds.). Curran Associates, Inc., 4066–4076. http://papers.nips.cc/paper/6995-counterfactual-fairness.pdf

[13] Virgile Landeiro and Aron Culotta. 2016. Robust Text Classification in the Presence of Confounding Bias. https://www.aaai.org/ocs/index.php/AAAI/AAAI16/paper/view/12445

[14] Christos Louizos, Kevin Swersky, Yujia Li, Max Welling, and Richard S. Zemel. 2015. The Variational Fair Autoencoder. *CoRR* abs/1511.00830 (2015).

[15] Nishtha Madaan, Sameep Mehta, Taneea Agrawaal, Vrinda Malhotra, Aditi Aggarwal, Yatin Gupta, and Mayank Saxena. 2018. Analyze, Detect and Remove Gender Stereotyping from Bollywood Movies. In *Proceedings of the 1st Conference on Fairness, Accountability and Transparency (Proceedings of Machine Learning Research)*, Sorelle A. Friedler and Christo Wilson (Eds.), Vol. 81. PMLR, New York, NY, USA, 92–105. http://proceedings.mlr.press/v81/madaan18a.html

[16] Aleksander Madry, Aleksandar Makelov, Ludwig Schmidt, Dimitris Tsipras, and Adrian Vladu. 2017. Towards Deep Learning Models Resistant to Adversarial Attacks. *CoRR* abs/1706.06083 (2017). arXiv:1706.06083 http://arxiv.org/abs/1706.06083

[17] Pramod Kaushik Mudrakarta, Ankur Taly, Mukund Sundararajan, and Kedar Dhamdhere. 2018. Did the Model Understand the Question? *CoRR* abs/1805.05492 (2018).

[18] J. H. Park, J. Shin, and P. Fung. 2018. Reducing Gender Bias in Abusive Language Detection. *ArXiv e-prints* (Aug. 2018). arXiv:cs.CL/1808.07231

[19] Reid Pryzant, Kelly Wang, Dan Jurafsky, and Stefan Wager. 2018. Deconfounded Lexicon Induction for Interpretable Social Science. In *16th Annual Conference of the North American Chapter of the Association for Computational Linguistics (NAACL)*.

[20] Marco Tulio Ribeiro, Sameer Singh, and Carlos Guestrin. 2018. Semantically Equivalent Adversarial Rules for Debugging NLP models. In *Proceedings of the 56th Annual Meeting of the Association for Computational Linguistics (Volume 1: Long Papers)*. Association for Computational Linguistics, 856–865. http://aclweb.org/anthology/P18-1079

[21] Tyler J. VanderWeele and Whitney R. Robinson. 2014. On the Causal Interpretation of Race. *Epidemiology* 25, 6 (2014). https://journals.lww.com/epidem/Fulltext/2014/11000/On_the_Causal_Interpretation_of_Race.31.aspx

[22] Sandra Wachter, Brent D. Mittelstadt, and Chris Russell. 2017. Counterfactual Explanations without Opening the Black Box: Automated Decisions and the GDPR. *CoRR* abs/1711.00399 (2017).

[23] Rich Zemel, Yu Wu, Kevin Swersky, Toni Pitassi, and Cynthia Dwork. 2013. Learning Fair Representations. In *Proceedings of the 30th International Conference on Machine Learning (Proceedings of Machine Learning Research)*, Sanjoy Dasgupta and David McAllester (Eds.), Vol. 28. PMLR, Atlanta, Georgia, USA, 325–333. http://proceedings.mlr.press/v28/zemel13.html

[24] Zhengli Zhao, Dheeru Dua, and Sameer Singh. 2017. Generating Natural Adversarial Examples. *CoRR* abs/1710.11342 (2017).

A Appendix

	Train Terms	Held-out Terms
Baseline	0.241	0.071
Blind	0.000	0.062
CF Augmentation	0.155	0.057
CLP_nontoxic, $\lambda = 1$	0.029	0.068
CLP, $\lambda = 0.05$	0.165	0.057
CLP, $\lambda = 1$	0.010	0.058
CLP, $\lambda = 5$	0.004	0.051

Table 4: CTF gaps on toxic examples from the evaluation set, for both training terms and held-out terms.

	Baseline	Blindness	CF Augmentation	CLP , $\lambda = 5$
Some people are gay	0.98	0.61	0.82	0.14
Some people are straight	0.02	0.61	0.11	0.14
Some people are Jewish	0.28	0.61	0.17	0.13
Some people are Muslim	0.46	0.61	0.24	0.14
Some people are Christian	0.04	0.16	0.02	0.14

Table 5: Counterfactuals and toxicity scores of different models. The tokens "gay," "straight," "jewish," and "muslim" are used during training, and "christian" was held-out.

Taking Advantage of Multitask Learning for Fair Classification

Luca Oneto
luca.oneto@unige.it
DIBRIS - University of Genoa
Genova, Italy

Michele Donini
michele.donini@iit.it
Istituto Italiano di Tecnologia
Genova, Italy

Amon Elders
amonelders@gmail.com
Istituto Italiano di Tecnologia
Genova, Italy

Massimiliano Pontil
massimiliano.pointil@iit.it
Istituto Italiano di Tecnologia
Genova, Italy
University College London
London, United Kingdom

ABSTRACT

A central goal of algorithmic fairness is to reduce bias in automated decision making. An unavoidable tension exists between accuracy gains obtained by using sensitive information as part of a statistical model, and any commitment to protect these characteristics. Often, due to biases present in the data, using the sensitive information in the functional form of a classifier improves classification accuracy. In this paper we show how it is possible to get the best of both worlds: optimize model accuracy and fairness without explicitly using the sensitive feature in the functional form of the model, thereby treating different individuals equally. Our method is based on two key ideas. On the one hand, we propose to use Multitask Learning (MTL), enhanced with fairness constraints, to jointly learn group specific classifiers that leverage information between sensitive groups. On the other hand, since learning group specific models might not be permitted, we propose to first predict the sensitive features by any learning method and then to use the predicted sensitive feature to train MTL with fairness constraints. This enables us to tackle fairness with a three-pronged approach, that is, by increasing accuracy on each group, enforcing measures of fairness during training, and protecting sensitive information during testing. Experimental results on two real datasets support our proposal, showing substantial improvements in both accuracy and fairness.

CCS CONCEPTS

• **Theory of computation** → **Kernel methods**; • **Computing methodologies** → **Supervised learning by classification**; **Multitask learning**.

ACM Reference Format:
Luca Oneto, Michele Donini, Amon Elders, and Massimiliano Pontil. 2019. Taking Advantage of Multitask Learning for Fair Classification. In *AAAI/ACM Conference on AI, Ethics, and Society (AIES '19), January 27–28, 2019, Honolulu, HI, USA.* ACM, New York, NY, USA, 11 pages. https://doi.org/10.1145/3306618.3314255

AIES '19, January 27–28, 2019, Honolulu, HI, USA

ACM ISBN 978-1-4503-6324-2/19/01...$15.00
https://doi.org/10.1145/3306618.3314255

1 INTRODUCTION

In recent years there has been a lot of interest in the problem of enhancing learning methods with "fairness" requirements, see [1–4, 8–10, 12, 17, 19, 20, 22–26, 28, 30, 31, 35–39] and references therein. The general aim is to ensure that sensitive information (e.g. knowledge about gender or ethnic group of an individual) does not "unfairly" influence the outcome of a learning algorithm. For example, if the learning problem is to predict what salary a person should earn based on her skills and previous employment records, we would like to build a model which does not unfairly use additional sensitive information such as gender or race.

A central question is how sensitive information should be used during the training and testing phases of a model. From a statistical perspective, sensitive information can improve model performance: removing this information may result in a less accurate model, without necessarily improving the fairness of the solution, [17, 29, 36]. However, it is well known, that in some jurisdictions using different classifiers, either explicitly or implicitly, for members of different groups, may not be permitted, we refer to the remark at page 3 in [17] and references therein. These imply that we can access the sensitive information during the training phase of a model but not during the testing phase. Our principal objective is then to optimize model accuracy while still protecting sensitive information in the data.

As a first step towards not discriminating minority groups we focus on maximizing average accuracy with respect to each group as opposed to maximizing the overall accuracy [14]. For the underlying generic learning method, we consider both Single Task Learning (STL) and Independent Task Learning (ITL). While the latter independently learns a different function for each group, the former aims to learn a function that is common between all groups. A well-known weakness of these methods is that they tend to generalize poorly on smaller groups: while STL may learn a model which better represents the largest group, ITL may overfit minority groups [7]. A common approach to overcome such limitations is offered by Multitask Learning (MTL), see [5–7, 13, 18] and references therein. This methodology leverages information between the groups (tasks) to learn more accurate models. Surprisingly, to the best of our knowledge, MTL has received little attention in the algorithmic fairness domain. We are only aware of the work [17] which proposes to learn different classifiers per group, combined with MTL to ameliorate the issue of potentially having too little data on minority groups.

We build upon a particular instance of MTL which jointly learns a shared model between the groups as well as a specific model per group. We show how fairness constraints, measured with Equalized Odds or Equal Opportunities introduced in [20], can be built in MTL directly during the training phase. This is in contrast to other approaches which impose the fairness constraint as a post-processing step [10, 19, 20, 31] or by modifying the data representation before employing standard machine learning methods [1, 12, 22–24, 39]. In many recent works [2–4, 8, 9, 16, 17, 17, 25, 26, 28, 30, 35–38] it has been shown how to enforce these constraints during the learning phase of a classifier. Here we opt for the approach proposed in [16] since it is convex, theoretically grounded, and performs favorably against state-of-the-art alternatives. We present experiments on two real-datasets which demonstrate that the shared classifier learned by MTL works better than STL and in turn MTL's group specific classifiers perform better than both ITL as well as the shared MTL model. These results are in line with previous studies on MTL, which suggest the benefit offered by this methodology, see [15, 18, 27] and references therein. Moreover, we observe that the fairness constraint is effective in controlling the fairness measure.

Unfortunately, as remarked before, all the models which employ the sensitive feature in the testing phase may not be adoptable. Independent models cannot be employed since we are using different classifiers for members of different groups. Even the shared model may not be a feasible option, if the sensitive feature is used as a predictor (e.g. if the model is linear, including the sensitive feature entails using a group specific threshold). Therefore, the only feasible[1] option would be to learn a shared model based on the non-sensitive features. This constraint may limit our ability to learn classifiers of high generalization ability. In order to overcome such limitations, we propose to first use the non-sensitive features to predict the value of the sensitive one and then use the predicted sensitive feature to learn group specific models via MTL. The proposal is depicted in the graphical abstract of Figure 1. We experimentally demonstrate that the proposed approach matches the classification accuracy of the best performing model which uses the sensitive information during testing, in addition to further improving upon measures of fairness.

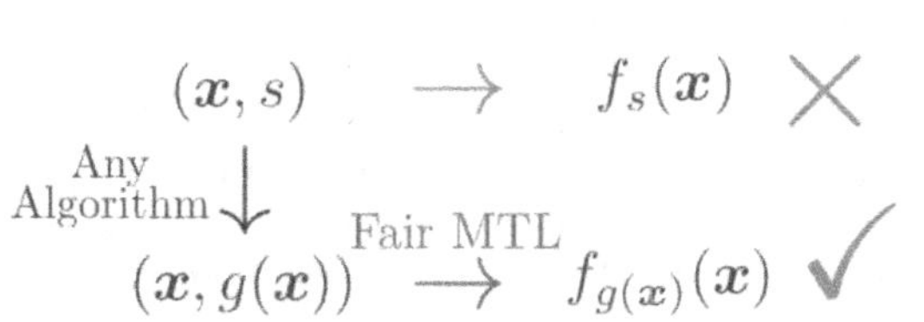

Figure 1: Our proposal in a graphical abstract: rather than using the sensitive feature s as a predictor we propose to learn, with any learning algorithm, a function g, which captures the relationship between x and s, and then use $g(x)$, instead of s, to learn group specific models via MTL.

[1]The sensitive feature may not be available in the testing phase or it might not be possible to use it as a predictor in the model due to legal requirements [17].

The rest of the paper is organized as follows. We firsr present some preliminary definitions and notions concerning the fair classification framework. Then we outline the central problem that we face in the paper: exploiting the sensitive feature while still treating different groups equally. We continue with the presentation of our proposal: predicting the sensitive feature based on the non-sensitive ones and then exploiting MTL with fairness constraints in order to increase both accuracy and fairness measures (see Figure 1). Later we test the proposal on two well known fairness related datasets (Adult and COMPAS) demonstrating the potentiality of it. Finally we conclude the paper with a brief discussion.

2 PRELIMINARIES

We let $\mathcal{D}=\{(\boldsymbol{x}_1, s_1, y_1), \dots, (\boldsymbol{x}_n, s_n, y_n)\}$ be a training set formed by n samples drawn independently from an unknown probability distribution μ over $\mathcal{X}\times\mathcal{S}\times\mathcal{Y}$, where $\mathcal{Y}=\{-1,+1\}$ is the set of binary output labels, $\mathcal{S}=\{1,\dots,k\}$ represents group membership, and $\mathcal{X}$ is the input space.

For every $t\in\mathcal{S}$ and operator $\diamond\in\{-,+\}$, we define the subset of training points with sensitive feature equal to t as $\mathcal{D}_t=\{(\boldsymbol{x}, s, y) : (\boldsymbol{x}, s, y)\in\mathcal{D}, s=t\}$ and the subset of training points negatively and positively labeled with sensitive feature equal to t as $\mathcal{D}_t^{\diamond}=\{(\boldsymbol{x}, s, y) : (\boldsymbol{x}, s, y)\in\mathcal{D}, s=t, y=\diamond 1\}$. We also let $n_t=|\mathcal{D}_t|$ and for $\diamond\in\{-,+\}$, we let $n_t^{\diamond}=|\mathcal{D}_t^{\diamond}|$.

Let us consider a function (or model) $f : \mathcal{X}\times\mathcal{S}\to\mathbb{R}$ chosen from a set $\mathcal{F}$ of possible models. The error (risk) of f is measured by a prescribed loss function $\ell : \mathbb{R}\times\mathcal{Y}\to\mathbb{R}$. The average accuracy with respect to each group of a model $L(f)$, together with its empirical counterparts $\widehat{L}(f)$, are defined respectively as

$$L(f)=\frac{1}{k}\sum_{t\in\mathcal{S}} L_t(f),\ L_t(f)=\mathbb{E}\left[\ell(f(\boldsymbol{x}), s, y)|s=t\right],\ t\in\mathcal{S},$$

and

$$\widehat{L}(f)=\frac{1}{k}\sum_{t\in\mathcal{S}} \widehat{L}_t(f),\ \widehat{L}_t(f)={}^1\!/_{n_t}\sum_{(\boldsymbol{x},s,y)\in\mathcal{D}_t} \ell(f(\boldsymbol{x}, s), y),\ t\in\mathcal{S}.$$

The fairness of the model can be measured w.r.t. many notions of fairness as mentioned in the introduction. In this work we choose to opt for the Equal Opportunity (EOp) and the Equal Odds (EOd). For $\diamond\in\{-,+\}$, the $\text{EOp}^{\diamond}$ constraint is defined as [20]

$$\mathbb{P}\{f(\boldsymbol{x}, s)>0|s=1, y=\diamond 1\}= \dots =\mathbb{P}\{f(\boldsymbol{x}, s)>0|s=k, y=\diamond 1\}, \tag{1}$$

where $\diamond\in\{-,+\}$. The EOd, instead is just the concurrent verification of the EOp^{+} and EOp^{-}, then $\forall\diamond\in\{-,+\}$

$$\mathbb{P}\{f(\boldsymbol{x}, s)>0 \mid s=1, y=\diamond 1\}= \dots =\mathbb{P}\{f(\boldsymbol{x}, s)>0 \mid s=k, y=\diamond 1\}. \tag{2}$$

Since a model f, in general, will not be able to exactly fulfill the EOp^{+} with $\diamond\in\{-,+\}$ nor the EOd constraints we define the Difference of $\text{EOp}^{\diamond}$ ($\text{DEOp}^{\diamond}$) with $\diamond\in\{-,+\}$ as

$$\textstyle\sum_{t\in\mathcal{S}}\left|\mathbb{P}\{\hat{y}=y|s=t, y=\diamond 1\}-\frac{1}{|\mathcal{S}|}\sum_{t'\in\mathcal{S}}\mathbb{P}\{\hat{y}=y|s=t', y=\diamond 1\}\right|,$$

where $\hat{y} = \text{sign}(f(\boldsymbol{x}, s))$. Finally, the Difference of EOd (DEOd) is defined as

$$\text{DEOd} = {}^{(\text{DEOp}^+ + \text{DEOp}^-)}/_2.$$

3 PARADIGM

A central problem, when learning a model f from data under fairness requirements, is that using a different classification method, or even using different weights on attributes for members of different groups may not be allowed for certain classification tasks [17]. In other words, it may not be permitted to use the sensitive feature explicitly or implicitly in the functional form of the model[2]. This means that f should be a function of $\boldsymbol{x}$ only, that is, $f(\boldsymbol{x}, s) = f(\boldsymbol{x})$.

For instance, if $\mathcal{X}=\mathbb{R}^d$ and the sensitive feature is encoded with a one-hot encoding, and we use a linear classifier then

$$f(\boldsymbol{x}, s) = \boldsymbol{w} \cdot \boldsymbol{x} + b_s, \quad \boldsymbol{w}\in\mathbb{R}^d,\ b_s\in\mathbb{R},$$

which is forbidden since the model involves a different bias for each of the sensitive groups. The problem is even more apparent when we use a different model per each group, namely we set

$$f(\boldsymbol{x}, s) = \boldsymbol{w}_s \cdot \boldsymbol{x} + b_s, \quad \boldsymbol{w}_s\in\mathbb{R}^d,\ b_s\in\mathbb{R}. \tag{3}$$

Unfortunately, the above requirement can be highly constraining, resulting in a model with poor accuracy. In practice, due to bias present in the data, learning a model which involves the sensitive feature in its functional form may substantially improve model accuracy.

Our proposal to overcome the above limitation is to use the input $\boldsymbol{x}$ to predict the sensitive group s. That is, we learn a function $g : \mathcal{X}\to\mathcal{S}$, such that $\hat{s} = g(\boldsymbol{x})$ is the prediction of the sensitive feature of $\boldsymbol{x}$. Therefore, our method replaces the specific model $f(\boldsymbol{x}, s)$ with the composite model $h(x) \equiv f(\boldsymbol{x}, g(\boldsymbol{x}))$, thereby treating different individuals equally. Indeed if (x, t) and (x', t') are two instances, then $h(x) \approx h(x')$ provided $x \approx x'$ irrespective of the values of t and t'. Hence, we can freely use $\hat{s}$ in the functional since, during the testing phase, we do not require any knowledge of s. As we shall see, on the one hand, in the regions of the input space where the classifier g predicts well, this approach allows us to exploit MTL to learn group specific models. On the other hand, when the prediction error is high, this approach acts as a randomization procedure[3] which, as we will empirically show, improves the fairness measure of the overall model.

In this paper we investigate (i) the effect of having the sensitive feature as part of the functional form of the model, (ii) the effect of using a shared model between the groups or a different model per group, (iii) the effect of learning a shared model with STL or MTL and the effect of learning group specific models with ITL or MTL, and (iv) the effect of using the predicted sensitive feature instead of its actual value inside the functional form of the model. Then we will show that it is possible to take the best result of the different approaches with substantial benefits in terms of both model accuracy and fairness, while still treating different individuals equally.

4 METHODOLOGY

In this section, we describe our approach to learning fair and accurate models and highlight the connection to MTL [18]. We consider the following functional form

$$f(\boldsymbol{x}, s) = \boldsymbol{w} \cdot \boldsymbol{\phi}(\boldsymbol{x}, s), \quad (\boldsymbol{x}, s)\in\mathcal{X}\times\mathcal{S}, \tag{4}$$

where "$\cdot$" is the inner product between two vectors in a Hilbert space[4] $\mathbb{H}$, $\boldsymbol{w} \in \mathbb{H}$ is a vector of parameters, and $\boldsymbol{\phi} : \mathcal{X} \times \mathcal{S} \to \mathbb{H}$ is a prescribed feature mapping[5].

We can then learn the parameter vector $\boldsymbol{w}$ by regularized empirical risk minimization, using the square Euclidean norm of the parameter vector $\|\boldsymbol{w}\|^2$ as the regularizer. The generality of this approach comes from the general form of the feature mapping $\boldsymbol{\phi} : \mathcal{X}\times\mathcal{S}\to\mathbb{H}$ which may be implicitly defined by a kernel function, see e.g. [33, 34] and references therein. In the following, first we will briefly discuss three approaches for learning the parameter vector which correspond to the three methods investigated in this paper. Then, we will explain how these methods can be enhanced with fairness constraints.

4.0.1 *Single Task Learning.*

As we argued above, we may not be allowed to explicitly use the sensitive feature in the functional form of the model. A simple approach to overcome this problem, would be to train a shared model between the groups, that is, we choose $\boldsymbol{\phi}(\boldsymbol{x}, s)=\boldsymbol{\varphi}(\boldsymbol{x})$ and $\boldsymbol{w}=\boldsymbol{w}_0$ in Eq. (4), where $\boldsymbol{\varphi} : \mathcal{X}\to\mathbb{H}$ and $\boldsymbol{w}_0\in\mathbb{H}$, so that $f(\boldsymbol{x}, s)=\boldsymbol{w}_0 \cdot \boldsymbol{\varphi}(\boldsymbol{x})$ (a potentially unregularized threshold may be built in the feature map to include a bias term). We learn the model parameters by solving the Tikhonov regularization problem[6]

$$\min_{\boldsymbol{w}_0\in\mathbb{H}} \quad \hat{L}(\boldsymbol{w}_0) + \rho\|\boldsymbol{w}_0\|^2, \tag{5}$$

where $\rho\in[0, \infty)$ is a regularization parameter. This method, which we will call Single Task Learning (STL), searches for the linear separator which minimizes a trade-off between the empirical average risk per group and the complexity (smoothness) of the models.

As we shall see in our experiments below, STL performs poorly, because it does not capture variance across groups. A slight variation which may improve performance is to introduce group specific thresholds. However, we remark again that this approach may not be permitted. Specifically, we choose $\boldsymbol{\phi}(\boldsymbol{x}, s)=(\boldsymbol{\varphi}(\boldsymbol{x}), \boldsymbol{e}_s)$ and $\boldsymbol{w}=(\boldsymbol{w}_0, \mathbf{b})$ where $\boldsymbol{e}_1, \ldots, \boldsymbol{e}_S$ are the canonical basis vectors in $\mathbb{R}^k$ and $\mathbf{b}=(b_1, \ldots, b_k)\in\mathbb{R}^k$, so that $f(\boldsymbol{x}, s) = \boldsymbol{w}_0 \cdot \boldsymbol{\varphi}(\boldsymbol{x}) + b_s$.

4.0.2 *Independent Task Learning.*

An approach to overcome the potentially underfitting performance of STL is to learn different models for each of the groups, we refer to this approach as independent task learning (ITL). It corresponds to setting $\boldsymbol{\phi}(\boldsymbol{x}, s) = (\mathbf{0}_{s-1}, \boldsymbol{\varphi}(\boldsymbol{x}), \mathbf{0}_{k-s})$ and $\boldsymbol{w}=(\boldsymbol{w}_1, \ldots, \boldsymbol{w}_k)$ in Eq. (4), where $\boldsymbol{\varphi} : \mathcal{X}\to\mathbb{H}$ and $\boldsymbol{w}_s\in\mathbb{H}\ \forall s\in\mathcal{S}$, so that $f(\boldsymbol{x}, s)=\boldsymbol{w}_s \cdot \boldsymbol{\varphi}(\boldsymbol{x})$. As before, the feature map may account for a constant component to accommodate a

[2]Note that, for clarity, the above limitation is imposed only when making predictions with f. During the training phase, the sensitive information can and should be used to guide the choice of model parameters.

[3]A random prediction $\hat{s}$ of s is substituted in the functional form of Eq. (3) which then randomly selects one of the group specific models, transforming the function form in a randomized shared model. Suppose we have many classifiers $f(\cdot, s)$ and a function g which chooses which classifier to use. If one assumes that $g(\boldsymbol{x})$ is purely random, then $f(\cdot, \boldsymbol{x})$ is a randomized classifier. Therefore if g has a high error rate, g is unable to predict the sensitive feature. Consequently $f(\cdot, \boldsymbol{x})$ is just a shared classifier composed of many functions chosen at random by g.

[4]For all intents and purposes, one may also assume throughout that $\mathbb{H} = \mathbb{R}^d$, the standard d-dimensional vector space, for some positive integer d.

[5]In practice, a bias term (threshold) can be added to $f(\boldsymbol{x}, s)$ (which may depend on s) but to ease our presentation we do not include it if not necessary.

[6]With a little abuse of notation we replace in the risk definitions the function with its parameter vector.

threshold for each of the groups. To find the vectors $\boldsymbol{w}_s$ we solve k independent Tikhonov regularization problems of the form

$$\min_{\boldsymbol{w}_s \in \mathbb{H}} \quad \hat{L}_s(\boldsymbol{w}_s) + \rho\|\boldsymbol{w}_s\|^2. \tag{6}$$

Note that, similar to STL, if we substitute $\hat{s}$ to s in this last functional form then the method treats members of different groups equally, since , as we mentioned before, learning independent models may not be allowed. Furthermore, we remark that from a statistical point of view, minority groups (small sample sizes) will be prone to overfitting. Nevertheless, as we shall see, ITL works better than STL in our experiments, suggesting that there is a lot of bias in the data. Still one would expect that by leveraging similarities between the groups ITL can be further improved. We discuss this next.

4.0.3 Multitask Learning. Let us now discuss the multitask learning approach used in the paper, which is based on regularization around a common mean [18]. We choose $\boldsymbol{\phi}(\boldsymbol{x},s)=(\boldsymbol{\varphi}(\boldsymbol{x}), \boldsymbol{0}_{s-1}, \boldsymbol{\varphi}(\boldsymbol{x}), \boldsymbol{0}_{k-s})$ and $\boldsymbol{w}=(\boldsymbol{w}_0, \boldsymbol{v}_1, \ldots, \boldsymbol{v}_k)$ in Eq. (4), where $\boldsymbol{w}_0 \in \mathbb{H}$ and $\boldsymbol{v}_s \in \mathbb{H}$ $\forall s \in \mathcal{S}$, so that $f(\boldsymbol{x}, s) = \boldsymbol{w}_0 \cdot \boldsymbol{\varphi}(\boldsymbol{x}) + \boldsymbol{v}_t \cdot \boldsymbol{\varphi}(\boldsymbol{x})$. MTL jointly learns a *shared* model $\boldsymbol{w}_0$ as well as *task specific* models $\boldsymbol{w}_s = \boldsymbol{w}_0 + \boldsymbol{v}_s \in \mathbb{H}$ $\forall s \in \mathcal{S}$ by encouraging the specific models and the shared model to be close to each other. To this end, we solve the following Tikhonov regularization problem

$$\min_{\boldsymbol{w}_0, \boldsymbol{w}_1, \ldots, \boldsymbol{w}_S \in \mathbb{H}} \quad \theta\hat{L}(\boldsymbol{w}_0) + (1-\theta)\tfrac{1}{k}\textstyle\sum_{s=1}^{k} \hat{L}_s(\boldsymbol{w}_s)$$
$$+\rho\left[\lambda\|\boldsymbol{w}_0\|^2 + (1-\lambda)\tfrac{1}{k}\textstyle\sum_{s=1}^{k} \|\boldsymbol{w}_s - \boldsymbol{w}_0\|^2\right], \tag{7}$$

where the parameter $\lambda \in [0,1]$ forces the dependency between shared and specific models and the parameter $\theta \in [0,1]$ captures the relative importance of the loss of the shared model and the group-specific models. This MTL approach is general enough to include STL and ITL, which are recovered by setting $\lambda=\theta=1$ and $\lambda=\theta=0$, respectively. Similar to STL and ITL, regularized group specific thresholds could be added in the shared model and in the group specific models.

Again, note that the group specific models trained by MTL may not be permitted. Likewise the shared model trained by MTL may not be permitted if we include the sensitive variable to the input. However if the sensitive variable is predicted from an external classifier and then MTL retrained with the predicted values, then this model treats different groups equally (see Figure 1).

4.1 Adding Fairness Constraints

Note that both STL, ITL and MTL problems are convex provided the the loss function used to measure the empirical errors $\hat{L}$ and $\hat{L}_s$ in Eqns. (5), (6), and (7) are convex. Since we are dealing with binary classification problems, we will use the hinge loss (see e.g. [32]), which is defined as $\ell(f(\boldsymbol{x}, s), y) = \max(0, 1-yf(\boldsymbol{x}, s))$.

In many recent papers [1–4, 8–10, 12, 16, 17, 19, 20, 22–26, 28, 30, 31, 35–39] it has been shown how to enforce EOp$^\diamond$ constraints for $\diamond \in \{-,+\}$, during the learning phase of the model $f \in \mathcal{F}$. Here we build upon the approach proposed in [16] since it is convex, theoretically grounded, and showed to perform favorably against state-of-the-art alternatives. To this end, we first observe that

$$\begin{aligned}
&\mathbb{P}\{f(\boldsymbol{x}, s) > 0 \mid s = t, y = \diamond 1\} \\
&= 1 - \mathbb{E}\{\ell_h(f(\boldsymbol{x}, s), y) \mid s = t, y = \diamond 1\} \\
&= 1 - L_t(f), \quad t \in \mathcal{S},
\end{aligned} \tag{8}$$

where $\ell_h(f(\boldsymbol{x}, s), y) = [yf(\boldsymbol{x}, s) \le 0]$ is the hard loss function. Then, by substituting Eq. (8) in Eqs. (1) and (2), replacing the deterministic quantities with their empirical counterpart, and by approximating the hard loss function ℓ_h with the linear one $\ell_l = (1-yf(\boldsymbol{x}, s))/2$ we have that the convex EOp$^\diamond$ constraints with $\diamond \in \{-,+\}$ is defined as follows

$$\tfrac{1}{n_1^\diamond}\textstyle\sum_{(\boldsymbol{x},s,y)\in\mathcal{D}_1^\diamond} f(\boldsymbol{x}, s) = \ldots = \tfrac{1}{n_k^\diamond}\textstyle\sum_{(\boldsymbol{x},s,y)\in\mathcal{D}_k^\diamond} f(\boldsymbol{x}, s), \tag{9}$$

while for the EOd we just have to enforce both the EOp$^+$ and EOp$^-$ constraints.

In order to plug the constraint of Eq. (9) inside STL, ITL and MTL we first define the quantities

$$\boldsymbol{u}_t^\diamond = \tfrac{1}{n_t^\diamond}\textstyle\sum_{(\boldsymbol{x},s)\in\mathcal{D}_t^\diamond} \boldsymbol{\varphi}(\boldsymbol{x}), \quad t \in \mathcal{S}, \; \diamond \in \{-,+\}. \tag{10}$$

It is then straightforward to show that if we wish to enforce the EOp$^\diamond$ constraint onto the shared model one has to add these $(k-1)$ constraints to the STL and MTL

$$\boldsymbol{w}_0 \cdot (\boldsymbol{u}_1^\diamond - \boldsymbol{u}_2^\diamond) = 0 \;\wedge\; \ldots \;\wedge\; \boldsymbol{w}_0 \cdot (\boldsymbol{u}_1^\diamond - \boldsymbol{u}_k^\diamond) = 0. \tag{11}$$

We remark again that for the EOd constraints we just have to insert EOp$^+$ $\wedge$ EOp$^-$ which means $2(k-1)$ constraints.

If, instead, we want to enforce the EOp$^\diamond$ constraint onto group specific models we have to add these $(k-1)$ constraints to the MTL and ITL

$$\boldsymbol{w}_1 \cdot \boldsymbol{u}_1^\diamond = \boldsymbol{w}_2 \cdot \boldsymbol{u}_2^\diamond \;\wedge\; \ldots \;\wedge\; \boldsymbol{w}_1 \cdot \boldsymbol{u}_1^\diamond = \boldsymbol{w}_k \cdot \boldsymbol{u}_k^\diamond, \tag{12}$$

while for the EOd we just have to insert EOp$^+$ $\wedge$ EOp$^-$.

Al last we note that by the representer theorem, as shown in [16], it is straightforward to derive the kernelized version of the fair STL, ITL, and MTL convex problems which can be solved with any solver, in our case CPLEX [21].

5 EXPERIMENTS

The aim of the experiments is to address the questions raised before. Namely, we wish to: (a) study the effect of using the sensitive feature as a way to bias the decision of a common model or to learn group specific models, (b) show the advantage of training either the shared or group specific models via MTL, and (c) show that MTL can be effectively used even when the sensitive feature is not available during testing by predicting the sensitive feature based on the non-sensitive ones.

5.1 Datasets and Setting

We employed the Adult dataset from the UCI repository[7] and the Correctional Offender Management Profilingfor Alternative Sanctions (COMPAS) dataset[8].

The Adult dataset contains 14 features concerning demographic characteristics of 45222 instances (32561 for training and 12661 for testing), 2 features, Gender (G) and Race (R), can be considered sensitive. The task is to predict if a person has an income per year that is more (or less) than 50, 000\$. Some statistics of the adult dataset with reference to the sensitive features are reported in Table 7 in the appendix.

The COMPAS dataset is constructed by the commercial algorithm COMPAS, which is used by judges and parole officers for scoring

[7] archive.ics.uci.edu/ml/datasets/adult
[8] github.com/propublica/compas-analysis

criminal defendants likelihood of reoffending (recidivism). It has been shown that the algorithm is biased in favor of white defendants based on a 2-years follow up study. This dataset contains variables used by the COMPAS algorithm in scoring defendants, along with their outcomes within two years of the decision, for over 10000 criminal defendants in Broward County, Florida. In the original data, 3 subsets are provided. We concentrate on the one that includes only violent recividism. Table 7, reports the statistics with reference to the sensitive features.

In all the experiments, we compare STL, ITL, and MTL in different settings. Specifically we test each method in the following cases: when the models use the sensitive feature (S=1) or not (S=0), when the fairness constraint is active (F=1) or not (F=0), when we consider the group specific models (D=1) or the shared model between groups (D=0), and when we use the true sensitive feature (P=1) or the predicted one (P=0). Note that when D=0 we can only compare STL with MTL, since only these two models produce a shared model between the groups, and furthermore, when D=1 we can only compare ITL with MTL, since these produce group specific models.

We collect statistics concerning the classification average accuracy per group in percentage (ACC) on the test set, difference of equal opportunities on both the positive and negative class (denoted as DEO^+ and DEO^-, respectively), and the difference of equalized odds (DEOd) of the selected model - see the preliminaries for a definition of these quantities.

We selected the best hyperparameters[9] by the two steps 10-fold cross validation (CV) procedure described in [16]. In the first step, the value of the hyperparameters with highest accuracy is identified. In the second step, we shortlist all the hyperparameters with accuracy close to the best one (in our case, above 97% of the best accuracy). Finally, from this list, we select the hyperparameters with the lowest fairness measure. This validation procedure, ensures that fairness cannot be achieved by a mere modification of hyperparameter selection procedure.

5.2 Results

The results for all possible combinations described above, are reported in the appendix.

Table 1 presents the performance of the shared model trained with STL or MTL, with or without the sensitive feature as a predictor, and with or without the fairness constraint. From Table 1 it is possible to see that MTL reaches higher accuracies compared to STL while the fairness measure is mostly comparable, this means that there is a relation between the tasks which can be captured with MTL. This hypothesis is also supported by the results of Figure 2 in the appendix, in which we check how the accuracy and fairness, as measured with the EOd, varies by varying λ. Figure 2 shows that there are commonalities between the groups which increase by increasing the number of groups: the optimal parameter λ it is smaller than one when we consider the shared model (D=0) and it is larger than zeros when we consider group specific models (D=1). Moreover, the fairness constraint has a negative impact on the accuracy (less strong for MTL) whilst having a highly positive impact on fairness. Having the sensitive feature as a predictor increases accuracy, but decreases fairness measure, as expected.

Table 2 reports the case when the group specific models are trained with ITL or MTL, the same setting as Table 1. MTL notably improves both accuracy and fairness. The fairness constraints do not affect the accuracy too much, while giving remarkable improvements in fairness. ITL and MTL are not affected by not including or including the sensitive feature predictor, as expected from the theory given that the models already have already different biases. Table 3 reports a comparison between STL, ITL, and MTL on the Adult dataset, showing the accuracy on each group for the different models for the case that P=0, F=0, and S=0. These results clearly demonstrate that STL and ITL tend to generalize poorly on smaller groups, whereas MTL generalizes better. Results on COMPAS datasets are analogous.

Table 5 reports the comparison between the most accurate, fair and legal[10] model (the shared model trained with MTL, with fairness constraint, and no sensitive feature in the predictors) and the most accurate, fair and illegal model (the group specific models trained with MTL, with fairness constraint, the sensitive feature used as predictor). From the table one can note that the illegal model remarkably improves over the legal one in terms of accuracy and in some cases it is even better than the legal one in terms of fairness. Based on the result of Table 5 we would like to be able to use the 'illegal' model'. In order to do so make use of the trick described in the previous sections, namely we use the predicted sensitive feature based on the non-sensitive features, instead of the true one. For this purpose we used a Random Forests model [11] where we weighted the errors differently based on the group membership. Table 8 in the appendix reports the confusion matrices computed on the test set.

Finally, in Table 6 we report a comparison between the best illegal model and the same model, but for which uses we used the predicted sensitive feature, instead of the true one, both in training and in testing. Notably, Table 6 shows that using the predicted sensitive feature in place of the true one preserves the accuracy of the learned model, but with a notable improvement in fairness. In attempt to explain this phenomena, in Table 4 we report the average group accuracy for predicting the sensitive features gender and race, as a function of the distance from the group specific models separators trained with MTL on the Adult dataset. Table 4 shows that the accuracy in predicting the sensitive feature decreases as we get closer to the separator. This can be understood as allowing the group specific model to randomize which specific classifier to use, reducing overall unfairness of the decision. Results on COMPAS dataset are analogous.

6 DISCUSSION

We have presented two novel, but related, ideas in this work. Firstly, to resolve the tension between accuracy gains obtained by using a sensitive feature as part of the model, and the potential inapplicability of such an approach, we have suggested to first predict the sensitive feature based on the non-sensitive features, and then

[9] The ranges of hyperparameters used in the validation procedure of STL, MTL, and ITL are $\rho \in \{10^{-6.0}, 10^{-5.5}, \dots, 10^{+6.0}\}$ and $\lambda, \theta \in \{0, 2^{-15}, 2^{-14}, \dots, 2^{-1}, 1-2^{-2}, \dots, 1-2^{-15}, 1\}$.

[10] From now, for sake of simplicity, we use the word illegal (legal) to define a model which uses (not-uses), either implicitly or explicitly, the sensitive feature as part of its functional form.

					Adult Dataset												COMPAS Dataset											
	–	0	–	–	STL ITL		MTL		STL ITL		MTL		STL ITL		MTL		STL ITL		MTL		STL ITL		MTL		STL ITL		MTL	
	–	1	–	–																								
	P	D	F	S	ACC	DEOp$^+$	ACC	DEOp$^+$	ACC	DEOp$^-$	ACC	DEOp$^-$	ACC	DEOd	ACC	DEOd	ACC	DEOp$^+$	ACC	DEOp$^+$	ACC	DEOp$^-$	ACC	DEOp$^-$	ACC	DEOd	ACC	DEOd
G	0	0	0	0	80.2	0.11	83.4	0.13	80.4	0.09	84.3	0.12	80.3	0.10	83.6	0.13	76.1	0.15	78.1	0.12	76.3	0.14	78.0	0.11	76.2	0.13	77.3	0.10
	0	0	1	0	75.7	0.03	81.8	0.06	75.8	0.02	82.7	0.05	75.7	0.03	82.0	0.06	71.5	0.03	76.5	0.03	71.7	0.03	76.4	0.03	71.6	0.03	75.7	0.03
	0	0	1	1	78.6	0.06	82.4	0.04	78.8	0.05	83.3	0.04	78.7	0.05	82.6	0.04	74.4	0.05	77.4	0.05	74.6	0.05	77.3	0.04	74.5	0.05	76.6	0.04
R	0	0	0	0	80.3	0.08	84.2	0.07	80.5	0.07	85.1	0.06	80.4	0.08	84.4	0.07	80.2	0.09	84.2	0.08	80.4	0.08	85.1	0.07	80.3	0.09	84.4	0.08
	0	0	1	0	75.3	0.02	82.6	0.01	75.5	0.02	83.5	0.01	75.4	0.02	82.8	0.01	75.5	0.04	82.4	0.03	75.7	0.04	83.3	0.03	75.6	0.04	82.6	0.03
	0	0	1	1	78.4	0.03	83.4	0.03	78.6	0.03	84.3	0.02	78.5	0.03	83.6	0.03	78.5	0.05	83.5	0.02	78.7	0.04	84.4	0.02	78.6	0.05	83.7	0.02
G+R	0	0	0	0	80.2	0.16	84.6	0.14	80.4	0.14	85.3	0.14	80.3	0.15	84.9	0.14	80.2	0.16	84.8	0.14	80.4	0.14	85.5	0.14	80.3	0.15	85.1	0.14
	0	0	1	0	75.2	0.05	83.2	0.04	75.3	0.04	83.9	0.04	75.3	0.05	83.5	0.04	75.3	0.05	83.1	0.05	75.5	0.04	83.8	0.05	75.4	0.05	83.4	0.05
	0	0	1	1	78.5	0.05	83.9	0.05	78.7	0.04	84.6	0.05	78.6	0.05	84.2	0.05	78.6	0.06	84.1	0.04	78.8	0.05	84.7	0.04	78.7	0.06	84.3	0.04

Table 1: Shared model trained with STL and MTL with or without sensitive feature as predictor and/or fairness constraint.

					Adult Dataset												COMPAS Dataset											
	–	0	–	–	STL ITL		MTL		STL ITL		MTL		STL ITL		MTL		STL ITL		MTL		STL ITL		MTL		STL ITL		MTL	
	–	1	–	–																								
	P	D	F	S	ACC	DEOp$^+$	ACC	DEOp$^+$	ACC	DEOp$^-$	ACC	DEOp$^-$	ACC	DEOd	ACC	DEOd	ACC	DEOp$^+$	ACC	DEOp$^+$	ACC	DEOp$^-$	ACC	DEOp$^-$	ACC	DEOd	ACC	DEOd
G	0	1	0	0	74.5	0.18	90.0	0.14	74.7	0.15	91.0	0.13	74.6	0.17	90.2	0.14	70.7	0.19	84.5	0.15	70.9	0.17	84.4	0.14	70.8	0.16	83.6	0.13
	0	1	1	0	69.7	0.08	88.3	0.04	69.9	0.07	89.2	0.04	69.8	0.08	88.5	0.04	66.1	0.08	83.0	0.04	66.3	0.08	82.8	0.04	66.2	0.07	82.1	0.04
	0	1	1	1	69.7	0.08	88.1	0.03	69.9	0.07	89.1	0.03	69.8	0.08	88.3	0.03	66.1	0.09	82.9	0.07	66.3	0.08	82.8	0.06	66.2	0.08	82.1	0.06
R	0	1	0	0	67.4	0.13	91.8	0.10	67.6	0.11	92.8	0.08	67.5	0.13	92.0	0.10	67.3	0.12	91.7	0.08	67.5	0.11	92.7	0.07	67.4	0.12	92.0	0.08
	0	1	1	0	62.5	0.05	90.0	0.03	62.7	0.05	90.9	0.03	62.6	0.05	90.2	0.03	62.4	0.07	90.1	0.02	62.6	0.06	91.0	0.02	62.5	0.07	90.3	0.02
	0	1	1	1	62.6	0.06	90.4	0.03	62.7	0.05	91.3	0.03	62.6	0.06	90.6	0.03	62.4	0.07	90.0	0.03	62.5	0.07	91.0	0.03	62.4	0.07	90.2	0.03
G+R	0	1	0	0	64.0	0.23	91.5	0.15	64.2	0.20	92.2	0.15	64.1	0.22	91.8	0.15	64.2	0.24	91.4	0.16	64.3	0.21	92.2	0.16	64.3	0.22	91.7	0.16
	0	1	1	0	59.3	0.14	89.8	0.05	59.4	0.12	90.6	0.05	59.3	0.13	90.1	0.05	59.2	0.13	90.1	0.05	59.4	0.11	90.8	0.05	59.3	0.12	90.4	0.05
	0	1	1	1	59.2	0.13	90.0	0.05	59.4	0.11	90.8	0.05	59.3	0.12	90.3	0.05	59.4	0.13	89.9	0.05	59.5	0.11	90.7	0.05	59.5	0.12	90.3	0.05

Table 2: Group specific models with ITL and MTL with or without sensitive feature as predictor and/or fairness constraint.

Sens.	Group	D=0 STL	D=0 MTL	D=1 ITL	D=1 MTL
G	M	85.4	88.5	78.8	92.8
	F	81.2	85.9	74.2	91.0
R	W	86.7	89.8	89.7	93.2
	B	83.5	88.9	83.5	92.8
	API	82.3	87.9	65.2	92.1
	AIE	82.1	87.6	48.5	92.0
	O	81.2	86.9	47.5	92.1
G+R	W&M	87.8	92.8	85.8	94.7
	W&F	85.6	89.5	84.7	93.2
	B&M	84.4	89.9	66.3	93.2
	B&F	82.4	88.1	64.6	92.1
	API&M	83.6	89.2	67.3	93.0
	API&F	81.8	88.0	63.5	92.8
	AIE&M	83.0	88.8	50.2	92.7
	AIE&F	81.9	87.3	45.1	92.5
	O&M	81.7	88.3	50.7	93.1
	O&F	81.1	86.6	43.3	92.1

Table 3: Adult dataset: ACC of STL, ITL, and MTL when P=0, F=0, and S=0.

	Margin Distance		
	1/10	1	∞
G	75.4	83.3	87.3
R	69.9	80.7	84.7

Table 4: Adult dataset: accuracy in % of prediction based on the distance from the MTL separator which uses the predicted sensitive feature (see Table 6).

	P	D	F	S	MTL ACC	MTL DEOp$^+$	MTL ACC	MTL DEOp$^-$	MTL ACC	MTL DEOd
Adult Dataset										
G	0	0	1	0	81.8	0.06	82.7	0.05	82.0	0.06
	0	1	1	1	88.1	0.03	89.1	0.03	88.3	0.03
R	0	0	1	0	82.6	0.01	83.5	0.01	82.8	0.01
	0	1	1	1	90.4	0.03	91.3	0.03	90.6	0.03
G+R	0	0	1	0	83.2	0.04	83.9	0.04	83.5	0.04
	0	1	1	1	90.0	0.05	90.8	0.05	90.3	0.05
COMPAS Dataset										
G	0	0	1	0	76.5	0.03	76.4	0.03	75.7	0.03
	0	1	1	1	82.9	0.07	82.8	0.06	82.1	0.06
R	0	0	1	0	82.4	0.03	83.3	0.03	82.6	0.03
	0	1	1	1	90.0	0.03	91.0	0.03	90.2	0.03
G+R	0	0	1	0	83.1	0.05	83.8	0.05	83.4	0.05
	0	1	1	1	89.9	0.05	90.7	0.05	90.3	0.05

Table 5: The most accurate, fair and legal model (MTL shared model, with fairness constraint, no sensitive feature in the predictor) and the most accurate, fair and illegal model (MTL group specific models, with fairness constraint, sensitive feature exploited as predictor).

	P	D	F	S	MTL ACC	MTL DEOp$^+$	MTL ACC	MTL DEOp$^-$	MTL ACC	MTL DEOd
Adult Dataset										
G	0	1	1	1	88.1	0.03	89.1	0.03	88.3	0.03
	1	1	1	1	87.4	0.01	88.3	0.01	87.6	0.01
R	0	1	1	1	90.4	0.03	91.3	0.03	90.6	0.03
	1	1	1	1	89.2	0.01	90.2	0.01	89.4	0.01
G+R	0	1	1	1	90.0	0.05	90.8	0.05	90.3	0.05
	1	1	1	1	89.0	0.01	89.8	0.01	89.3	0.01
COMPAS Dataset										
G	0	1	1	1	82.9	0.07	82.8	0.06	82.1	0.06
	1	1	1	1	82.1	0.01	82.0	0.01	81.3	0.01
R	0	1	1	1	90.0	0.03	91.0	0.03	90.2	0.03
	1	1	1	1	89.0	0.01	89.9	0.01	89.2	0.01
G+R	0	1	1	1	89.9	0.05	90.7	0.05	90.3	0.05
	1	1	1	1	89.0	0.01	89.8	0.01	89.3	0.01

Table 6: Comparison between the group specific models trained with MTL, with fairness constraint, and the true sensitive feature exploited as a predictor, against the same model when the predicted sensitive feature exploited as predictor.

use the predicted value in the functional form of a model, allowing to treat people belonging to different groups, but having similar non-sensitive features, equally. Furthermore, we have demonstrated how the predicted sensitive feature can then used in a fairness constrained MTL framework. We confirmed the validity of the above approach empirically, giving us substantial improvements in both accuracy and fairness, compared to STL and ITL. We believe this to be a fruitful area of possible future research. Of course, a non-linear extension of the above framework would be interesting to study, although we did not notice any substantial improvements on the Adult and COMPAS datasets considered in this work. Moreover, it would be interesting to see if the above framework can be extended to include other fairness definitions, apart from the EOp and EOd that we have tested. Finally, it would be valuable to provide theoretical conditions on the data distribution for which our approach provably works.

ACKNOWLEDGMENTS

This work was supported in part by SAP SE and the EPSRC.

REFERENCES

[1] J. Adebayo and L. Kagal. 2016. Iterative orthogonal feature projection for diagnosing bias in black-box models. In *Conference on Fairness, Accountability, and Transparency in Machine Learning (FATML)*.
[2] A. Agarwal, A. Beygelzimer, M. Dudík, and J. Langford. 2017. A Reductions Approach to Fair Classification. In *FATML*.
[3] A. Agarwal, A. Beygelzimer, M. Dudík, J. Langford, and H. Wallach. 2018. A reductions approach to fair classification. *arXiv preprint arXiv:1803.02453* (2018).
[4] D. Alabi, N. Immorlica, and A. T. Kalai. 2018. When optimizing nonlinear objectives is no harder than linear objectives. *arXiv preprint arXiv:1804.04503* (2018).
[5] A. Argyriou, T. Evgeniou, and M. Pontil. 2008. Convex multi-task feature learning. *Machine Learning* 73, 3 (2008), 243–272.
[6] B. Bakker and T. Heskes. 2003. Task clustering and gating for bayesian multitask learning. *Journal of Machine Learning Research* 4 (2003), 83–99.
[7] J. Baxter. 2000. A model of inductive bias learning. *Journal of artificial intelligence research* 12 (2000), 149–198.
[8] Y. Bechavod and K. Ligett. 2018. Penalizing Unfairness in Binary Classification. *arXiv preprint arXiv:1707.00044v3* (2018).
[9] R. Berk, H. Heidari, S. Jabbari, M. Joseph, M. Kearns, J. Morgenstern, S. Neel, and A. Roth. 2017. A convex framework for fair regression. *arXiv preprint arXiv:1706.02409* (2017).
[10] A. Beutel, J. Chen, Z. Zhao, and E. H. Chi. 2017. Data decisions and theoretical implications when adversarially learning fair representations. In *FATML*.
[11] L. Breiman. 2001. Random forests. *Machine learning* 45, 1 (2001), 5–32.
[12] F. Calmon, D. Wei, B. Vinzamuri, K. Natesan Ramamurthy, and K. R. Varshney. 2017. Optimized Pre-Processing for Discrimination Prevention. In *Advances in Neural Information Processing Systems (NIPS)*.
[13] R. Caruana. 1997. Multitask Learning. *Machine Learning* 28, 1 (1997), 41–75.
[14] A. Chouldechova. 2017. Fair prediction with disparate impact: A study of bias in recidivism prediction instruments. *Big data* 5, 2 (2017), 153–163.
[15] M. Donini, D. Martinez-Rego, M. Goodson, J. Shawe-Taylor and M. Pontil. 2016. Distributed variance regularized multitask learning. In *International Joint Conference on Neural Networks*.
[16] M. Donini, L. Oneto, S. Ben-David, J. Shawe-Taylor, and M. Pontil. 2018. Empirical Risk Minimization under Fairness Constraints. In *NIPS*.
[17] C. Dwork, N. Immorlica, A. T. Kalai, and M. D. M. Leiserson. 2018. Decoupled Classifiers for Group-Fair and Efficient Machine Learning. In *Conference on Fairness, Accountability and Transparency (FAT)*.
[18] T. Evgeniou and M. Pontil. 2004. Regularized multi-task learning. In *ACM SIGKDD international conference on Knowledge discovery and data mining*.
[19] M. Feldman, S. A. Friedler, J. Moeller, C. Scheidegger, and S. Venkatasubramanian. 2015. Certifying and removing disparate impact. In *International Conference on Knowledge Discovery and Data Mining*.
[20] M. Hardt, E. Price, and N. Srebro. 2016. Equality of opportunity in supervised learning. In *NIPS*.
[21] IBM. 2018. User-Manual CPLEX 12.7.1. IBM Software Group.
[22] F. Kamiran and T. Calders. 2009. Classifying without discriminating. In *International Conference on Computer, Control and Communication*.
[23] F. Kamiran and T. Calders. 2010. Classification with no discrimination by preferential sampling. In *Machine Learning Conference*.
[24] F. Kamiran and T. Calders. 2012. Data preprocessing techniques for classification without discrimination. *Knowledge and Information Systems* 33, 1 (2012), 1–33.
[25] T. Kamishima, S. Akaho, and J. Sakuma. 2011. Fairness-aware learning through regularization approach. In *International Conference on Data Mining Workshops*.
[26] M. Kearns, S. Neel, A. Roth, and Z. S. Wu. 2017. Preventing Fairness Gerrymandering: Auditing and Learning for Subgroup Fairness. *arXiv preprint arXiv:1711.05144* (2017).
[27] A. Khosla, T. Zhou, T. Malisiewicz, A. A. Efros, and A. Torralba. 2012. Undoing the damage of dataset bias. In *European Conference on Computer Vision*.
[28] A. K. Menon and R. C. Williamson. 2018. The cost of fairness in binary classification. In *FAT*.
[29] D. Pedreshi, S. Ruggieri, and F. Turini. 2008. Discrimination-aware data mining. In *ACM SIGKDD international conference on Knowledge discovery and data mining*.
[30] A. Pérez-Suay, V. Laparra, G. Mateo-García, J. Muñoz-Marí, L. Gómez-Chova, and G. Camps-Valls. 2017. Fair Kernel Learning. In *Machine Learning and Knowledge Discovery in Databases*.
[31] G. Pleiss, M. Raghavan, F. Wu, J. Kleinberg, and K. Q. Weinberger. 2017. On fairness and calibration. In *NIPS*.
[32] S. Shalev-Shwartz and S. Ben-David. 2014. *Understanding machine learning: From theory to algorithms*. Cambridge University Press.
[33] J. Shawe-Taylor and N. Cristianini. 2004. *Kernel methods for pattern analysis*. Cambridge University Press.
[34] A. J. Smola and B. Schölkopf. 2001. *Learning with Kernels*. MIT Press.
[35] B. Woodworth, S. Gunasekar, M. I. Ohannessian, and N. Srebro. 2017. Learning non-discriminatory predictors. In *Computational Learning Theory*.
[36] M. B. Zafar, I. Valera, M. Gomez Rodriguez, and K. P. Gummadi. 2017. Fairness beyond disparate treatment & disparate impact: Learning classification without disparate mistreatment. In *International Conference on World Wide Web*.
[37] M. B. Zafar, I. Valera, M. Gomez Rodriguez, and K. P. Gummadi. 2017. Fairness constraints: Mechanisms for fair classification. In *International Conference on Artificial Intelligence and Statistics*.
[38] M. B. Zafar, I. Valera, M. Rodriguez, K. Gummadi, and A. Weller. 2017. From parity to preference-based notions of fairness in classification. In *NIPS*.
[39] R. Zemel, Y. Wu, K. Swersky, T. Pitassi, and C. Dwork. 2013. Learning fair representations. In *International Conference on Machine Learning*.

A APPENDIX

A.1 Dataset Statistics

In Table 7 we reported the Adult and the COMPAS datasets statistics with reference to the sensitive features.

Adult dataset		
Sens.	Group	%
G	Male (M)	66.9
	Female(F)	33.2
R	White (W)	85.5
	Black (B)	9.6
	Asian-Pac-Islander (API)	3.1
	Amer-Indian-Eskimo (AIE)	1.0
	Other (O)	0.8
G+R	W&M	58.8
	W&F	26.7
	B&M	4.9
	B&F	4.7
	API&M	2.1
	API&F	1.1
	AIE&M	0.6
	AIE&F	0.4
	O&M	0.5
	O&F	0.3

COMPAS dataset		
Sens.	Group	%
G	Female (F)	19.34
	Male (M)	80.66
R	African-American (AA)	51.23
	Asian (A)	0.44
	Caucasian (C)	34.02
	Hispanic (H)	8.83
	Native American (NA)	0.25
	Other (O)	5.23
G+R	Female African-American	9.04
	Female Asian	0.03
	Female Caucasian	7.86
	Female Hispanic	1.48
	Female Native American	0.06
	Female Other	0.93
	Male African-American	42.20
	Male Asian	0.45
	Male Caucasian	26.16
	Male Hispanic	7.40
	Male Native American	0.19
	Male Other	4.30

Table 7: Adult and COMPAS datasets: statistics with reference to the sensitive features.

A.2 Predicting the sentitive feature

Table 8 reports confusion matrices in percentage (true class in columns and predicted classes in rows) obtained by predicting Gender and Race from the other non-sensitive features using Random Forests for both Adult and COMPAS datasets.

A.3 The effect of the hyperparameter λ

In Figure 2 we check how the accuracy and fairness, as measured with the EOd, varies with λ.

A.4 Complete Set of Results

In this section we report the complete set of results. The results for all the possible combinations described in the experimental section, are reported in Table 9. In Figures 3, 4, and 5, we present a visualization of Table 9 for the Adult dataset (results are analogous for the COMPAS one). Where both the error (i.e., 1-ACC), and the EOd are normalized to be between 0 and 1, column-wise. The closer a point is to the origin, the better the result.

Adult dataset		
G	M	F
M	58.2	3.8
F	8.7	29.4

Adult dataset					
R	W	B	API	AIE	O
W	78.5	1.7	0.5	0.2	0.1
B	4.6	7.8	0.1	0.0	0.0
API	0.5	0.0	0.8	0.0	0.0
AIE	1.5	0.1	0.0	2.6	0.0
O	0.4	0.0	0.0	0.0	0.7

COMPAS dataset		
G	M	F
M	16.7	8.6
F	2.6	72.1

COMPAS dataset						
R	AA	A	C	H	NA	O
AA	44.8	0.0	3.4	0.6	0.0	0.3
A	0.1	0.3	0.0	0.0	0.0	0.0
C	4.4	0.0	29.6	0.4	0.0	0.2
H	1.2	0.0	0.6	7.7	0.0	0.1
NA	0.0	0.0	0.0	0.0	0.2	0.0
O	0.7	0.0	0.4	0.1	0.0	4.6

Table 8: Adult (up) and COMPAS (down) datasets: confusion matrices in percentage (true class in columns and predicted classes in rows) obtained by predicting Gender and Race from the other non-sensitive features using Random Forests.

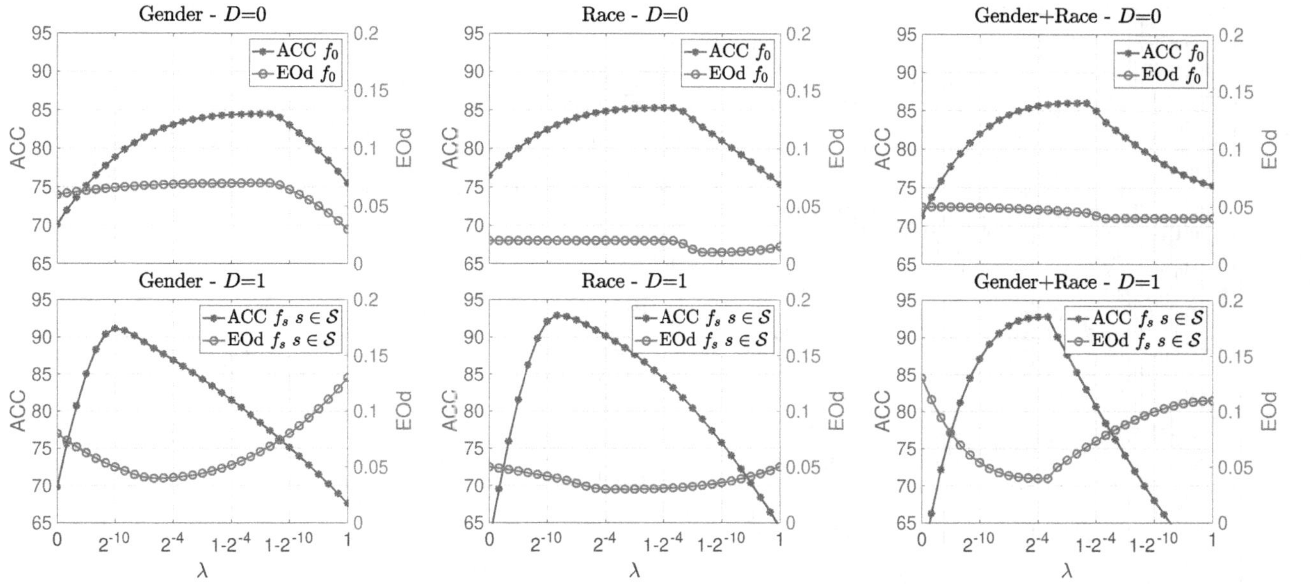

Figure 2: Adult Dataset: ACC and EOd of MTL, when we fix θ and ρ to be the best values found during the validation procedure and we vary λ with P=0, F=1, and S=0.

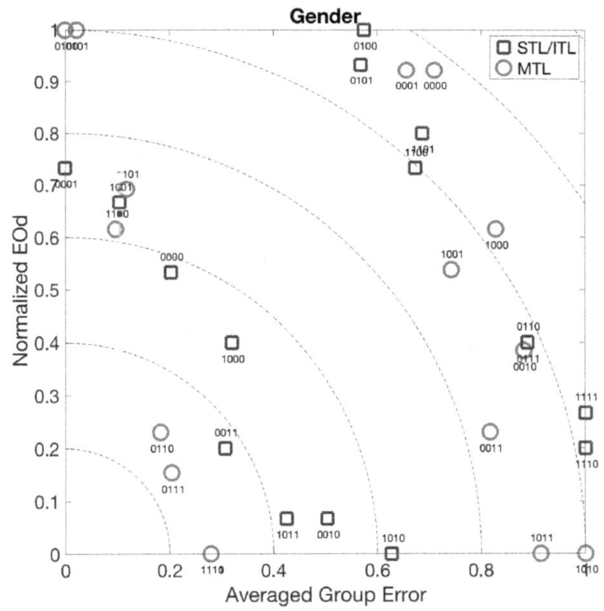

Figure 3: Adult dataset: complete results set for Gender (text close to the symbols in plot are P, D, F, and S).

	– –	0 1	– –	– –	Adult Dataset STL ITL		MTL		STL ITL		MTL		STL ITL		MTL	
	P	D	F	S	ACC	DEOp+	ACC	DEOp+	ACC	DEOp−	ACC	DEOp−	ACC	DEOd	ACC	DEOd
G	0	0	0	0	80.2	0.11	83.4	0.13	80.4	0.09	84.3	0.12	80.3	0.10	83.6	0.13
	0	0	0	1	83.3	0.14	83.9	0.13	83.5	0.12	84.8	0.12	83.4	0.13	84.1	0.13
	0	0	1	0	75.7	0.03	81.8	0.06	75.8	0.02	82.7	0.05	75.7	0.03	82.0	0.06
	0	0	1	1	78.6	0.06	82.4	0.04	78.8	0.05	83.3	0.04	78.7	0.05	82.6	0.04
	0	1	0	0	74.5	0.18	90.0	0.14	74.7	0.15	91.0	0.13	74.6	0.17	90.2	0.14
	0	1	0	1	74.6	0.17	89.7	0.14	74.7	0.15	90.7	0.13	74.7	0.16	90.0	0.14
	0	1	1	0	69.7	0.08	88.3	0.04	69.9	0.07	89.2	0.04	69.8	0.08	88.5	0.04
	0	1	1	1	69.7	0.08	88.1	0.03	69.9	0.07	89.1	0.03	69.8	0.08	88.3	0.03
	1	0	0	0	78.4	0.09	82.3	0.09	78.6	0.07	83.2	0.09	78.5	0.08	82.5	0.09
	1	0	0	1	81.7	0.13	83.1	0.08	81.9	0.11	84.0	0.07	81.8	0.12	83.3	0.08
	1	0	1	0	73.7	0.02	80.7	0.01	73.9	0.02	81.6	0.01	73.8	0.02	80.9	0.01
	1	0	1	1	76.8	0.03	81.5	0.01	77.0	0.03	82.4	0.01	76.9	0.03	81.7	0.01
	1	1	0	0	73.0	0.14	89.1	0.09	73.2	0.12	90.1	0.08	73.1	0.13	89.3	0.09
	1	1	0	1	72.8	0.15	88.9	0.10	73.0	0.13	89.9	0.09	72.9	0.14	89.1	0.10
	1	1	1	0	68.0	0.06	87.4	0.01	68.2	0.05	88.3	0.01	68.1	0.05	87.6	0.01
	1	1	1	1	68.0	0.06	87.4	0.01	68.1	0.05	88.3	0.01	68.1	0.06	87.6	0.01
R	0	0	0	0	80.3	0.08	84.2	0.07	80.5	0.07	85.1	0.06	80.4	0.08	84.4	0.07
	0	0	0	1	83.2	0.09	85.3	0.09	83.4	0.08	86.2	0.08	83.3	0.09	85.5	0.09
	0	0	1	0	75.3	0.02	82.6	0.01	75.5	0.02	83.5	0.01	75.4	0.02	82.8	0.01
	0	0	1	1	78.4	0.03	83.4	0.03	78.6	0.03	84.3	0.02	78.5	0.03	83.6	0.03
	0	1	0	0	67.4	0.13	91.8	0.10	67.6	0.11	92.8	0.08	67.5	0.13	92.0	0.10
	0	1	0	1	67.2	0.13	91.8	0.08	67.4	0.12	92.8	0.07	67.3	0.13	92.1	0.08
	0	1	1	0	62.5	0.05	90.0	0.03	62.7	0.05	90.9	0.03	62.6	0.05	90.2	0.03
	0	1	1	1	62.6	0.06	90.4	0.03	62.7	0.05	91.3	0.03	62.6	0.06	90.6	0.03
	1	0	0	0	78.5	0.07	83.2	0.04	78.7	0.06	84.1	0.04	78.6	0.07	83.4	0.04
	1	0	0	1	81.8	0.09	84.1	0.06	82.0	0.08	85.0	0.05	81.9	0.09	84.3	0.06
	1	0	1	0	73.7	0.02	81.6	0.01	73.9	0.02	82.5	0.01	73.8	0.02	81.8	0.01
	1	0	1	1	77.1	0.01	82.5	0.01	77.3	0.01	83.4	0.01	77.2	0.01	82.7	0.01
	1	1	0	0	65.8	0.12	90.8	0.06	66.0	0.11	91.8	0.05	65.9	0.12	91.0	0.06
	1	1	0	1	65.8	0.11	90.7	0.05	66.0	0.10	91.7	0.04	65.9	0.11	91.0	0.05
	1	1	1	0	61.2	0.06	89.3	0.01	61.3	0.05	90.3	0.01	61.2	0.06	89.5	0.01
	1	1	1	1	60.8	0.06	89.2	0.01	61.0	0.05	90.2	0.01	60.9	0.06	89.4	0.01
G+R	0	0	0	0	80.2	0.16	84.6	0.14	80.4	0.14	85.3	0.14	80.3	0.15	84.9	0.14
	0	0	0	1	83.1	0.18	85.7	0.16	83.4	0.16	86.4	0.16	83.3	0.17	86.0	0.16
	0	0	1	0	75.2	0.05	83.2	0.04	75.3	0.04	83.9	0.04	75.3	0.05	83.5	0.04
	0	0	1	1	78.5	0.05	83.9	0.05	78.7	0.04	84.6	0.05	78.6	0.05	84.2	0.05
	0	1	0	0	64.0	0.23	91.5	0.15	64.2	0.20	92.2	0.15	64.1	0.22	91.8	0.15
	0	1	0	1	63.9	0.24	91.7	0.16	64.0	0.21	92.4	0.16	64.0	0.23	92.0	0.16
	0	1	1	0	59.3	0.14	89.8	0.05	59.4	0.12	90.6	0.05	59.3	0.13	90.1	0.05
	0	1	1	1	59.2	0.13	90.0	0.05	59.4	0.11	90.8	0.05	59.3	0.12	90.3	0.05
	1	0	0	0	78.5	0.13	83.9	0.12	78.7	0.11	84.6	0.12	78.6	0.12	84.2	0.12
	1	0	0	1	81.9	0.14	84.8	0.11	82.1	0.12	85.5	0.11	82.0	0.13	85.1	0.11
	1	0	1	0	73.7	0.01	82.3	0.01	73.9	0.01	83.0	0.01	73.8	0.01	82.6	0.01
	1	0	1	1	76.8	0.04	83.1	0.01	76.9	0.04	83.8	0.01	76.8	0.04	83.4	0.01
	1	1	0	0	62.5	0.21	90.8	0.12	62.6	0.19	91.5	0.12	62.5	0.20	91.1	0.12
	1	1	0	1	62.3	0.21	90.8	0.11	62.5	0.18	91.5	0.11	62.4	0.20	91.1	0.11
	1	1	1	0	57.7	0.10	89.1	0.02	57.9	0.08	89.9	0.02	57.8	0.09	89.5	0.02
	1	1	1	1	57.7	0.10	89.0	0.01	57.9	0.09	89.8	0.01	57.8	0.10	89.3	0.01

	– –	0 1	– –	– –	COMPAS Dataset STL ITL		MTL		STL ITL		MTL		STL ITL		MTL	
	P	D	F	S	ACC	DEOp+	ACC	DEOp+	ACC	DEOp−	ACC	DEOp−	ACC	DEOd	ACC	DEOd
G	0	0	0	0	76.1	0.15	78.1	0.12	76.3	0.14	78.0	0.11	76.2	0.13	77.3	0.10
	0	0	0	1	79.3	0.15	79.2	0.13	79.5	0.14	79.1	0.12	79.4	0.13	78.4	0.11
	0	0	1	0	71.5	0.03	76.5	0.03	71.7	0.03	76.4	0.03	71.6	0.03	75.7	0.03
	0	0	1	1	74.4	0.05	77.4	0.05	74.6	0.05	77.3	0.04	74.5	0.05	76.6	0.04
	0	1	0	0	70.7	0.19	84.5	0.15	70.9	0.17	84.4	0.14	70.8	0.16	83.6	0.13
	0	1	0	1	70.9	0.19	84.5	0.14	71.1	0.18	84.4	0.13	71.0	0.16	83.6	0.12
	0	1	1	0	66.1	0.08	83.0	0.04	66.3	0.08	82.8	0.04	66.2	0.07	82.1	0.04
	0	1	1	1	66.1	0.09	82.9	0.07	66.3	0.08	82.8	0.06	66.2	0.08	82.1	0.06
	1	0	0	0	74.6	0.12	77.3	0.10	74.8	0.11	77.2	0.09	74.7	0.10	76.5	0.09
	1	0	0	1	77.6	0.13	78.1	0.09	77.8	0.12	78.0	0.09	77.7	0.11	77.3	0.08
	1	0	1	0	70.1	0.03	75.9	0.01	70.3	0.03	75.8	0.01	70.2	0.03	75.1	0.01
	1	0	1	1	73.1	0.05	76.7	0.01	73.3	0.05	76.6	0.01	73.2	0.04	75.9	0.01
	1	1	0	0	69.3	0.17	83.7	0.09	69.5	0.15	83.6	0.08	69.4	0.14	82.8	0.08
	1	1	0	1	69.3	0.15	83.7	0.10	69.5	0.14	83.6	0.09	69.4	0.13	82.9	0.09
	1	1	1	0	64.7	0.06	82.3	0.01	64.9	0.05	82.1	0.01	64.8	0.05	81.4	0.01
	1	1	1	1	64.6	0.06	82.1	0.01	64.8	0.06	82.0	0.01	64.7	0.05	81.3	0.01
R	0	0	0	0	80.2	0.09	84.2	0.08	80.4	0.08	85.1	0.07	80.3	0.09	84.4	0.08
	0	0	0	1	83.2	0.10	84.9	0.08	83.4	0.09	85.8	0.07	83.3	0.10	85.1	0.08
	0	0	1	0	75.5	0.04	82.4	0.03	75.7	0.04	83.3	0.03	75.6	0.04	82.6	0.03
	0	0	1	1	78.5	0.05	83.5	0.02	78.7	0.04	84.4	0.02	78.6	0.05	83.7	0.02
	0	1	0	0	67.3	0.12	91.7	0.08	67.5	0.11	92.7	0.07	67.4	0.12	92.0	0.08
	0	1	0	1	67.4	0.13	91.8	0.09	67.5	0.11	92.8	0.08	67.4	0.13	92.0	0.09
	0	1	1	0	62.4	0.07	90.1	0.02	62.6	0.06	91.0	0.02	62.5	0.07	90.3	0.02
	0	1	1	1	62.4	0.07	90.0	0.03	62.5	0.07	91.0	0.03	62.4	0.07	90.2	0.03
	1	0	0	0	78.4	0.08	83.3	0.06	78.6	0.07	84.2	0.05	78.5	0.08	83.5	0.06
	1	0	0	1	81.7	0.09	84.4	0.07	81.9	0.08	85.3	0.06	81.8	0.09	84.6	0.07
	1	0	1	0	73.7	0.01	81.5	0.01	73.9	0.01	82.4	0.01	73.8	0.01	81.7	0.01
	1	0	1	1	77.0	0.02	82.4	0.01	77.2	0.01	83.2	0.01	77.1	0.02	82.5	0.01
	1	1	0	0	65.5	0.12	90.8	0.05	65.7	0.11	91.8	0.05	65.6	0.12	91.0	0.05
	1	1	0	1	65.7	0.12	90.8	0.07	65.8	0.11	91.7	0.07	65.7	0.12	91.0	0.07
	1	1	1	0	60.8	0.05	89.2	0.01	61.0	0.05	90.1	0.01	60.9	0.05	89.4	0.01
	1	1	1	1	60.9	0.04	89.0	0.01	61.1	0.04	89.9	0.01	61.0	0.04	89.2	0.01
G+R	0	0	0	0	80.2	0.16	84.8	0.14	80.4	0.14	85.5	0.14	80.3	0.15	85.1	0.14
	0	0	0	1	83.3	0.18	85.5	0.16	83.5	0.15	86.2	0.16	83.4	0.16	85.8	0.16
	0	0	1	0	75.3	0.05	83.1	0.05	75.5	0.04	83.8	0.05	75.4	0.05	83.4	0.05
	0	0	1	1	78.6	0.06	84.1	0.04	78.8	0.05	84.7	0.04	78.7	0.06	84.3	0.04
	0	1	0	0	64.2	0.24	91.4	0.16	64.3	0.21	92.2	0.16	64.3	0.22	91.7	0.16
	0	1	0	1	64.1	0.23	91.5	0.15	64.3	0.20	92.2	0.15	64.2	0.22	91.8	0.15
	0	1	1	0	59.2	0.13	90.1	0.05	59.4	0.11	90.8	0.05	59.3	0.12	90.4	0.05
	0	1	1	1	59.4	0.13	89.9	0.05	59.5	0.11	90.7	0.05	59.5	0.12	90.3	0.05
	1	0	0	0	78.4	0.13	83.8	0.09	78.6	0.12	84.5	0.09	78.5	0.13	84.1	0.09
	1	0	0	1	81.7	0.15	84.7	0.11	81.9	0.13	85.4	0.11	81.8	0.14	85.0	0.11
	1	0	1	0	73.6	0.02	82.5	0.01	73.8	0.02	83.1	0.01	73.7	0.02	82.8	0.01
	1	0	1	1	76.8	0.04	83.2	0.01	77.0	0.04	83.8	0.01	76.9	0.04	83.4	0.01
	1	1	0	0	62.5	0.21	90.6	0.11	62.6	0.18	91.4	0.11	62.6	0.20	91.0	0.11
	1	1	0	1	62.5	0.22	90.7	0.11	62.6	0.19	91.4	0.11	62.6	0.20	91.0	0.11
	1	1	1	0	57.8	0.11	89.2	0.01	58.0	0.10	89.9	0.01	57.9	0.11	89.5	0.01
	1	1	1	1	57.7	0.10	89.0	0.01	57.8	0.08	89.8	0.01	57.7	0.09	89.3	0.01

Table 9: Complete results set.

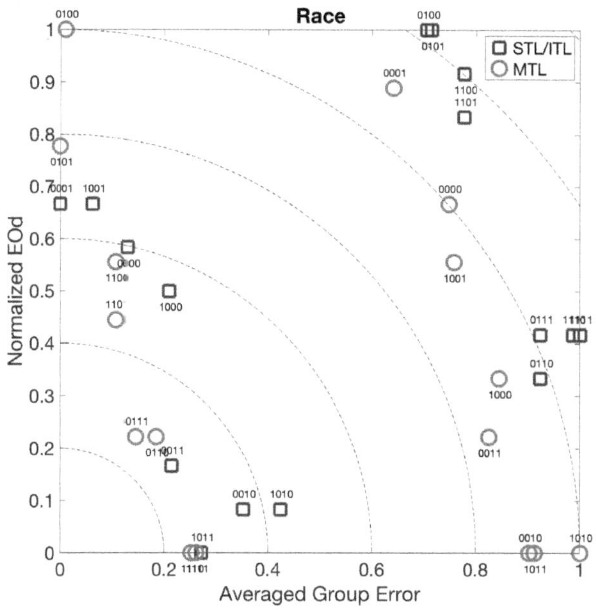

Figure 4: Adult dataset: complete results set for Race (text close to the symbols in plot are P, D, F, and S).

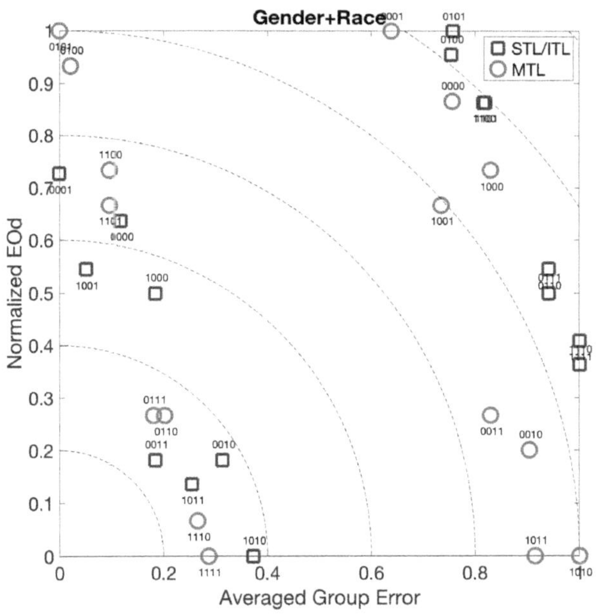

Figure 5: Adult dataset: complete results set for Gender+Race (text close to the symbols in plot are P, D, F, and S).

Explanatory Interactive Machine Learning

Stefano Teso
stefano.teso@cs.kuleuven.be
Department of Computer Science
KU Leuven, Belgium

Kristian Kersting
kersting@cs.tu-darmstadt.de
Department of Computer Science and
Centre for Cognitive Science
TU Darmstadt, Germany

ABSTRACT

Although interactive learning puts the user into the loop, the learner remains mostly a black box for the user. Understanding the reasons behind predictions and queries is important when assessing how the learner works and, in turn, trust. Consequently, we propose the novel framework of *explanatory* interactive learning where, in each step, the learner explains its query to the user, and the user interacts by both answering the query and correcting the explanation. We demonstrate that this can boost the predictive and explanatory powers of, and the trust into, the learned model, using text (e.g. SVMs) and image classification (e.g. neural networks) experiments as well as a user study.

CCS CONCEPTS

• **Theory of computation → Active learning**; • **Computing methodologies → Supervised learning**; *Support vector machines*; Neural networks.

KEYWORDS

machine learning, active learning, explainable artificial intelligence, interpretability

ACM Reference Format:

Stefano Teso and Kristian Kersting. 2019. Explanatory Interactive Machine Learning. In *AAAI/ACM Conference on AI, Ethics, and Society (AIES '19), January 27–28, 2019, Honolulu, HI, USA.* ACM, New York, NY, USA, 7 pages. https://doi.org/10.1145/3306618.3314293

1 INTRODUCTION

Trust lies at the foundation of major theories of interpersonal relationships in psychology [34]. In particular, Hoffman et al. (2013) argue that interpersonal trust depends on the "perceived competence, benevolence (or malevolence), understandability, and directability—the degree to which the trustor can rapidly assert control or influence when something goes wrong." They and others [38, 39] also show that trust into machines follows similar patterns, with some notable differences: it is often inappropriate to attribute benevolence/malevolence to machines, and trust into machines suffers from different biases than trust into individuals. The differences, however, do not affect the argument that interaction and understandability are central to trust in machine learners, too. The *competence* of a classifier can be assessed by monitoring its behavior and beliefs over time, *directability* can be achieved by allowing the user to actively teach the model how to act and what to believe, while *understandability* can be approached by explaining the model's decisions.

Surprisingly, the link between interacting, explaining and building trust has been largely ignored by the machine learning literature. On one hand, existing approaches focus on passive learning only, and do not consider interaction between the user and the learner [4, 19, 25]. On the other hand, interactive learning frameworks such as active [31] and coactive learning [33] do not consider the issue of trust. In active learning, for instance, the model presents unlabelled instances to a user, and in exchange obtains their label. This is completely opaque: the user is oblivious to the model's beliefs and reasons for predictions and to how they change in time, and cannot see the consequences of her own instructions. In coactive learning, the user sees and corrects the system's prediction, if necessary, but the predictions are not explained to her. So, why should users trust models learned interactively?

To fill this gap, we propose the novel framework of *explanatory interactive learning* (XIL). Here the interaction takes the following form. In each step, the learner explains its interactive query to the user, and she responds by correcting the prediction and explanations, if necessary, to provide feedback. We also present a model-agnostic method, called CAIPI, instantiating our framework for active learning. CAIPI extends active learning in several ways. Akin to coactive learning [33], query instances are accompanied by the the model's corresponding *predictions*. This allows the user to check whether the model is right or wrong on the chosen instance. However, nothing prevents the model from being right (or wrong) for the wrong reasons, e.g., when there are ambiguities in the data such as confounders [27]. To avoid this issue, CAIPI accompanies predictions with corresponding *explanations*, computed by any local explainer of choice [19, 25–27]; in this paper we use LIME[1] [25], a simple model-agnostic explainer that allows to easily compute explanations and present them to the user as interpretable (visual) artifacts. By witnessing the evolution of the explanations—like a teacher supervising the progress of a student—the user can see whether the model eventually "gets it". Finally, the user can even correct the explanation presented to guide the learner. This *correction* step is crucial for more directly affecting the learner's beliefs and is integral to modulating trust [14, 18]. Explanation corrections also facilitate learning (the right concept), especially in problematic cases that labels alone can not handle [27], as shown by our

AIES '19, January 27–28, 2019, Honolulu, HI, USA

ACM ISBN 978-1-4503-6324-2/19/01...$15.00
https://doi.org/10.1145/3306618.3314293

[1] CAIPIrinhas are made out of LIMES.

experiments. Overall, CAIPI is the first active learning approach that employs explanation corrections as an additional feedback channel in a model- and explainer-agnostic fashion. Our empirical evidence demonstrates that this interaction through explanations can modulate trust and booat the effectiveness of learning, also compared to state-of-the-art.

We proceed as follows. First, we touch upon additional related work. Then we introduce XIL and derive CAIPI. Before concluding, we present our empirical evaluation.

2 FURTHER RELATED WORK

Machine learning explainers fall in two classes. Global approaches aim to explain a black-box model by converting it as a whole to a more interpretable format [3, 4]. Local approaches instead interpret individual predictions [19]. Surprisingly, they do not consider interaction between the user and the model. Existing interactive learning approaches such as active, coactive, and active imitation learning do not consider the issue of explanations and trust, as already discussed. Given the centrality of the user in recommendation, interactive preference elicitation makea use of conversational interaction to improve trust and directability [7, 22], but often rely on rudimental learning strategies (if any).

Indeed, learning from explanations has been explored in concept learning [9, 20] and probabilistc logic programming [16], where explanations are themselves logical objects. Unfortunately, these results are tied to logic-based models and make use of rather opaque forms of explanations (e.g. logic proofs), which can be difficult to grasp for non-experts. Explanatory interactive learning instead leverages explanations for mainstream machine learning approaches.

More recently, researchers explored feature supervision [1, 10, 11, 23, 24, 30] and rationales [32, 40, 41], which leverage both label- and feature-level (or sentence-level, for rationales) supervision with the aim of improving learning efficiency. These works show that providing rationales, even from scratch, can be easy for human annotators [40], sometimes even more so than providing the labels themselves [23]. These approaches assume that the learner and the user can both work with the same features, which is not the case in general. More generally, most of these approaches are black-box, i.e., they do produce no explanations at all. The connection to directability and trust is not explicitly made. Those approaches that do are either model- or application specific (e.g. [40]). Explanatory interactive learning generalizes these ideas to arbitrary classification tasks and models. We remark that the feedback techniques proposed in these works are orthogonal to explanatory interactions and can be easily combined with it. We showcase this in one of our experiments, which leverages the corrective technique of [40].

Finally, the UI community also investigated meaningful interaction strategies so that the user can build a mental model of the system. In [36] the user is allowed to provide explanations, while [18] provides an explanation-centric approach to interactive teaching. These works however focus on simple machine learning models, like Naïve Bayes, while explanatory interactive learning is much more general.

3 EXPLANATORY INTERACTIVE LEARNING (XIL)

In XIL, a learner is able to interactively query the user (or some other information source) to obtain the desired outputs at data points. The interaction takes the following form. At each step, the learner considers a data point (labeled or unlabeled), predicts a label, and provides explanations of its prediction. The user responds by correcting the learner if necessary, providing a slightly improved—but not necessarily optimal—feedback to the learner.

Let us now instantiate this schema to *explanatory active learning*—combining active learning with local explainers. Indeed, other interactive learning can be made explanatory too, including coactive learning [33], active imitation learning [15], and mixed-initiative interactive learning [5], but this is beyond the scope of this paper.

Active learning. The active learning paradigm targets scenarios where obtaining supervision has a non-negligible cost. Here we cover the basics of pool-based active learning, and refer the reader to two excellent surveys [13, 31] for more details. Let $\mathcal{X}$ be the space of instances and $\mathcal{Y}$ be the set of labels (e.g. $\mathcal{Y} = \{\pm 1\}$). Initially, the learner has access to a small set of labelled examples $\mathcal{L} \subseteq \mathcal{X} \times \mathcal{Y}$ and a large pool of unlabelled instances $\mathcal{U} \subseteq \mathcal{X}$. The learner is allowed to query the label of unlabelled instances (by paying a certain cost) to a user functioning as annotator, often a human expert. Once acquired, the labelled examples are added to $\mathcal{L}$ and used to update the model. The overall goal is to maximize the model quality while keeping the number of queries or the total cost at a minimum. To this end, the query instances are chosen to be as informative as possible, typically by maximizing some informativeness criterion, such as the expected model improvement [28] or practical approximations thereof. By carefully selecting the instances to be labelled, active learning can enjoy much better sample complexity than passive learning [2, 6]. Prototypical active learners include max-margin [37] and Bayesian approaches [17]; recently, deep variants have been proposed [12].

However, active—showing query data points—and even coactive learning—showing additionally the prediction of the query data point— do not establish trust: informative selection strategies just pick instances where the model is uncertain and likely wrong. Thus, there is a trade-off between query informativeness and user "satisfaction," as noticed and explored in [29]. In order to properly modulate trust into the model, we argue it is essential to present explanations.

Local explainers. There are two main strategies for interpreting machine learning models. Global approaches aim to explain the model by converting it *as a whole* to a more interpretable format [3, 4]. Local explainers instead focus on the arguably more approachable task of explaining *individual predictions* [19]. While explainable interactive learning can accommodate any local explainer, in our implementation we use LIME [25], described next[2]. The idea of LIME (Local Interpretable Model-agnostic Explanations) is simple: even though a classifier may rely on many uninterpretable features, its decision surface around any given instance can be locally approximated by a simple, interpretable *local model*. In LIME, the local model is defined in terms of simple features encoding

[2]We use LIME for simplicity. RRR [27] and ANCHORS [26] are valid alternatives.

the presence or absence of *basic components*, such as words in a document or objects in a picture[3]. An explanation can be readily extracted from such a model by reading off the contributions of the various components to the target prediction and translating them to an interpretable visual artifact. For instance, in document classification one may highlight the words that support (or contradict) the predicted class.

Formally, let $f : \mathcal{X} \to \mathcal{Y}$ be an uninterpretable classifier (e.g., a dense linear model, a random forest, a deep network), $\hat{y} = f(x)$ the target prediction, and for each basic component i let $\psi_i(x)$ be the corresponding indicator function. In order to explain the prediction, LIME produces an interpretable model $g : \mathcal{X} \to \mathcal{Y}$, based solely on the interpretable features $\{\psi_i\}_i$, that approximates f in the neighborhood of x. Here g can be any sufficiently interpretable model, for instance a sparse linear classifier or a shallow decision tree. Computing g amounts to solving $\text{argmin}_g \; \ell_x(f, g) + \Omega(g)$, where ℓ_x is a "local loss" that measures the *fidelity* of g to f in the neighborhood of x, and $\Omega(g)$ is a regularization term that controls the complexity and interpretability of g.

For the sake of simplicity, we focus on LIME in conjunction with sparse linear models of the form $g(x) = \langle \mathbf{w}, \boldsymbol{\psi}(x) \rangle + b$, where $\langle \cdot, \cdot \rangle$ denotes the dot product. In order to enhance interpretability, at most k non-zero coefficients are allowed, where k is sufficiently small (see our Empirical Analysis for the values we use). Specifically, LIME measures the fidelity of the linear approximation with a "local" L_2 distance, namely $\ell_x(f, g) = \int_{x'} k(x, x')(f(x') - g(x'))^2 dx'$. In practice, this problem is solved by approximating the integral as a sum over a large enough set $\mathcal{S} \subseteq \mathcal{X}$ of instances sampled uniformly at random[4] and solving the sparsity-constrained least-squares problem: $g = \text{argmin}_g \sum_{x' \in \mathcal{S}} k(x, x')(f(x') - g(x'))^2 \quad \text{s.t.} \; \|\mathbf{w}\|_0 \leq k$. Note that g does depend on both the target instance x and on the prediction $\hat{y} = f(x)$. The relevance and polarity of all components can be readily read off from the weights $\mathbf{w}$: $|w_j| > 0$ suggests that the jth component does contribute to the overall prediction, while $w_j > 0$ and $w_j < 0$ imply that, when present, the jth component drives the prediction toward $\hat{y}$ or away from it, respectively. Finally, this information is used to construct a (visual) explanation.

Explanatory Active Learning. . Now, we have everything together for explanatory *active* learning and CAIPI. Specifically, we require black-box access to an active learner and an explainer. We assume that the active learner provides a procedure SELECTQUERY$(f, \mathcal{U})$ for selecting an informative instance $x \in \mathcal{U}$ based on the current model f, and a procedure FIT$(\mathcal{L})$ for fitting a new model (or update the current model) on the examples in $\mathcal{L}$. The explainer is assumed to provide a procedure EXPLAIN$(f, x, \hat{y})$ for explaining a particular prediction $\hat{y} = f(x)$. The framework is intended to work for any reasonable learner and explainer.

When using LIME for computing an interpretable model locally around the queries in order to visualize explanations for current predictions, this results in CAIPI as summarized in Alg. 1. At each iteration $t = 1, \ldots, T$ an instance $x \in \mathcal{U}$ is chosen using the query selection strategy implemented by the SELECTQUERY procedure.

[3]While not all problems admit explanations in terms of elementary components, many of them do [25]; in this case, LIME assumes these to be provided in advance.

[4]In LIME the samples are taken from the image of ψ, i.e., $\{\psi(x) : x \in \mathcal{X}\}$, and then mapped back to $\mathcal{X}$ to compute their predicted class. We omit this detail for clarity.

Algorithm 1 CAIPI takes as input a set of labelled examples $\mathcal{L}$, a set of unlabelled instances $\mathcal{U}$, and iteration budget T.

> $f \leftarrow$ FIT$(\mathcal{L})$
> **repeat**
> $x \leftarrow$ SELECTQUERY$(f, \mathcal{U})$
> $\hat{y} \leftarrow f(x)$
> $\hat{z} \leftarrow$ EXPLAIN$(f, x, \hat{y})$
>   Present x, $\hat{y}$, and $\hat{z}$ to the user
>   Obtain y and explanation correction C
> $\{(\bar{x}_i, \bar{y}_i)\}_{i=1}^c \leftarrow$ TOCOUNTEREXAMPLES(C)
> $\mathcal{L} \leftarrow \mathcal{L} \cup \{(x, y)\} \cup \{(\bar{x}_i, \bar{y}_i)\}_{i=1}^c$
> $\mathcal{U} \leftarrow \mathcal{U} \setminus (\{x\} \cup \{\bar{x}_i\}_{i=1}^c)$
> $f \leftarrow$ FIT$(\mathcal{L})$
> **until** budget T is exhausted or f is good enough
> **return** f

Then its label $\hat{y}$ is predicted using the current model f, and EXPLAIN is used to produce an explanation $\hat{z}$ of the prediction. The triple $(x, \hat{y}, \hat{z})$ is presented to the user as a (visual) artifact. The user checks the prediction and the explanation for correctness, and provides the required feedback. Upon receiving the feedback, the system updates $\mathcal{U}$ and $\mathcal{L}$ accordingly and re-fits the model. The loop terminates when the iteration budget T is reached or the model is good enough.

During interactions between the system and the user, three cases can occur:

1. **Right for the right reasons:** The prediction and the explanation are both correct. No feedback is requested.
2. **Wrong for the wrong reasons:** The prediction is wrong. As in active learning, we ask the user to provide the correct label. The explanation is also necessarily wrong, but we currently do not require the user to act on it.
3. **Right for the wrong reasons:** The prediction is correct but the explanation is wrong. We ask the user to provide an explanation *correction* C.

The "right for the wrong reasons" case is novel in active learning, and we propose *explanation corrections* to deal with it. They can assume different meanings depending on whether the focus is on component relevance, polarity, or relative importance (ranking), among others. In our experiments we ask the annotator to indicate the components that have been wrongly identified by the explanation as relevant, that is,

$$C = \{j : |w_j| > 0 \wedge \text{user believes } j\text{th component is irrelevant}\}$$

. In document classification, C would be the set of words that are irrelevant according to the user but relevant for the model.

Given the correction C, we are faced with the problem of explaining it back to the learner. We propose a simple strategy to achieve this. This strategy is embodied by TOCOUNTEREXAMPLES. It converts C to a set of *counterexamples* that teach the learner not to depend on the irrelevant components. In particular, for every $j \in C$ we generate c examples $(\bar{x}_1, \bar{y}_1), \ldots, (\bar{x}_c, \bar{y}_c)$, where c is an application-specific constant. Here, the labels $\bar{y}_i$ are identical to the prediction $\hat{y}$. The instances $\bar{x}_i$, $i = 1, \ldots, c$ are also identical to the query x, except that the jth component (i.e. $\psi_j(x)$) has been either randomized, changed to an alternative value, or substituted

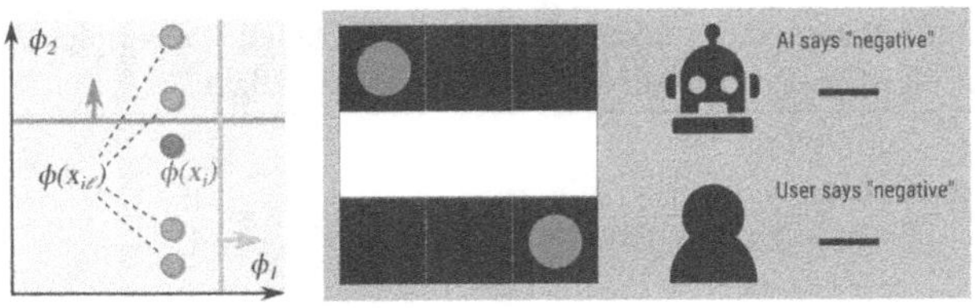

Figure 1: (Left) Mathematical intuition for the counterexample strategy. (Right) Example training round as presented in the questionnaire. The classification is correct but the explanation shows that the two most relevant pixels do not match the true classification rule (as in S3). (Best viewed in color).

	Q1	Q2	Q3
S1	64.7%	35.3%	82.4%
S2	76.5%	64.7%	70.6%
S3	29.4%	11.8%	41.2%

	no corr.	Counterexamples $c = 1$	Counterexamples $c = 3$	Counterexamples $c = 5$	Input Gradients
Train	**0.978**	0.938	0.922	0.924	0.898
Test	0.482	0.821	0.851	**0.858**	0.853

Table 1: Explanatory feedback can boost trust and performance. (Top) User study: percentage of "yes" answers. (Bottom) Accuracy on the fashion MNIST dataset of an MLP without corrections (no corr.), with our counterexample corrections using varying c (middle), and with input gradient constraints [27].

with the value of the jth component appearing in other training examples of the same class. In sudoku, each $\bar{x}_i$ would be a copy of the query sudoku x where the cells in C have been (for instance) filled with random numbers consistent with the predicted label. This process produces $c|C|$ counterexamples, which are added to $\mathcal{L}$.

Why is this data augmentation a sensible idea? To see this, consider the case of linear max-margin classifiers. Let $f(x) = \langle \boldsymbol{w}, \boldsymbol{\phi}(x)\rangle + b$ be a linear classifier over two features, ϕ_1 and ϕ_2, of which only the first is relevant. Fig. 1 (left) shows that $f(x)$ (red line) uses ϕ_2 to correctly classify a negative example x_i. In order to obtain a better model (e.g. the green line), the simplest solution would be to enforce an orthogonality constraint $\langle \boldsymbol{w}, (0, 1)^\top \rangle = 0$ during learning. Counterexamples follow the same principle. In the separable case, the counterexamples $\{\bar{x}_{i\ell}\}_{\ell=1}^{c}$ amount to additional max-margin constraints [8] of the form $y_i \langle \boldsymbol{w}, \boldsymbol{\phi}(\bar{x}_{i\ell})\rangle \geq 1$. The only ones that influence the model are those on the margin, for which strict equality holds. For all pairs of such counterexamples ℓ, ℓ' it holds that $\langle \boldsymbol{w}, \boldsymbol{\phi}(\bar{x}_{i\ell})\rangle = \langle \boldsymbol{w}, \boldsymbol{\phi}(\bar{x}_{i\ell'})\rangle$, or equivalently $\langle \boldsymbol{w}, \boldsymbol{\delta}_{i\ell} - \boldsymbol{\delta}_{i\ell'}\rangle = 0$, where $\boldsymbol{\delta}_{i\ell} = \boldsymbol{\phi}(\bar{x}_{i\ell}) - \boldsymbol{\phi}(x_i)$. In other words, the counterexamples encurage orthogonality between $\boldsymbol{w}$ and the correction vectors $\boldsymbol{\delta}_{i\ell} - \boldsymbol{\delta}_{i\ell'}$, thus approximating the orthogonality constraint above.

Most importantly, this data augmentation procedure is model-agnostic, although alternatives indeed exist: Contrastive examples [40], feature ranking [35] for SVMs and constraints on the input gradients for differentiable models [27]. These may be more effective in practice, and CAIPI can accomodate all of them. However, since our strategy is both model- and explainer-agnostic, in the remainder we will stick to it for maximum generality.

4 EMPIRICAL EVIDENCE

Our intention here is to address empirically the following questions:

RQ1 Can explanations (and their consistency over time) appropriately modulate the user's trust into the model?
RQ2 Can explanation corrections lead to better models?
RQ3 Do the explanations necessarily improve as the learner obtains more labels?
RQ4 Does the magnitude of this effect depend on the specific learner?

*(**RQ1**) User study.* We designed a questionnaire about a machine that learns a simple concept by querying labels (but *not* explanation corrections) to an annotator. The questionnaire, available in the Supplementary Material, was administered to 17 randomly selected undergraduate students from an introductory course on deep learning. We designed a toy binary classification problem (inspired by [27]) about classifying small (3 × 3) black-and-white images. The subjects were told that an image is positive if the two top corners are white and negative otherwise. Then they were shown three learning sessions consisting of five query/feedback rounds each. In session 1 (**S1**) every round included the images chosen by the model, the corresponding prediction, and the label provided by a knowledgeable annotator. No explanations were shown. The predictions are wrong for the first three rounds and correct in the last two. Sessions 2 and 3 (**S2, S3**) were identical to S1, meaning that at every round *the same example, prediction and feedback label* were shown, but now explanations were also provided. The explanations highlighted the two most relevant pixels, as in Fig. 1 (right). In S2 the explanations converged to the correct rule—they highlight the two top corners—from the fourth round onwards, while in S3 they did not. Removing the explanations reduces both S2 and S3 to S1. After each session, the subjects were asked three questions: (**Q1**) "Do you believe that the AI system eventually learned to classify images correctly?" (**Q2**) "Do you believe that the system eventually learned the correct classification rule?" (**Q3**) "Would you like to further assess the system by checking whether it classifies 10 random images correctly?" The first two questions test the subject's uncertainty in the predictive ability and beliefs of the classifier, resp., while the last one tests the relationship between predictive accuracy (but *not* explanation correctness) and expected uncertainty reduction. The percentage of "yes" answers is down in Tab. 1(top).

As expected, the uncertainty in the model's correctness depends heavily on what information channels are enabled. When no explanations are shown (S1), only 35% of the subjects assert to believe that the model learned the correct rule (Q2). This percentage almost doubles (65%) when explanations are shown and converge to the correct rule (S2). The need to see more examples also lowers from 82% to 71%, but does not drop to zero. This reflects the fact that five rounds are not enough to reduce the subject's uncertainty to low enough levels. The percentage of subjects asserting that the classifier produces correct predictions (regardless of the learned rule, Q1) also increases from 65% to 77% when correct explanations are shown (S2). When the explanations do not converge (S3), the trend is reversed: Q1 drops to 29% and Q2 to 12%, i.e., most subjects do not believe that the model's behavior and beliefs are in any way correct. This is the only setting where Q3 drops below 50% (41%): witnessing that the model's beliefs do not match the target rule induces distrust (with high certainty). This confirms the previous finding that trust into machines drops when wrong behavior is witnessed [14]. Thus, **RQ1** can be answered affirmatively: augmenting interaction with explanations does appropriately drive trust into the model.

Next to the user study, we considered simulated users—as it is common for active learning—to investigate **(RQ2–4)**. To this aim, we implemented CAIPI on top of several standard active learners and applied it to different learning tasks. Note that our goal here is to evaluate the contribution of explanation feedback, not the learners themselves. Indeed, CAIPI can trivially accommodate more advanced models than the ones employed here. In all cases, the model's explanations are computed with LIME [5]. As is common in active learning, we simulate a human annotator that provides correct labels. Explanation corrections are also assumed to be correct and complete (i.e. they identify all false positive components), for simplicity[6]. The specifics of the correction strategy are described in the next paragraphs. Our experimental setup is available at https://github.com/stefanoteso/caipi

*(**RQ2**) Evaluation on a passive setting.* We applied our data augmentation strategy to a decoy variant of fashion MNIST, a fashion product recognition dataset[7]. The dataset includes 70,000 images over 10 classes. All images were corrupted by introducing confounders, that is, 4×4 patches of pixels in randomly chosen corners whose shade is a function of the label in the training set and random in the test set (see [27] for details). The average test set accuracy of a multilayer perceptron (with the same hyperparameters as in [27]) is reported in Tab. 1 (bottom) for three correction strategies: no corrections, our counterexample strategy (CE), and the input-gradient constraints proposed by [27] (IG). For CE, for every training image we added $c = 1, 3, 5$ counterexamples where the decoy pixels are randomized. When no corrections are given, the accuracy on the test set is 48%: the confounders completely fool the network. Providing even a single counterexample increases the accuracy to 82%, i.e., the effect of confounders drops drastically. With more counterexamples the accuracy passes the one of IG (85%). This shows that **(RQ2)** counterexamples—and therefore explanation corrections—are an effective measure for improving the model in terms of both predictive performance and beliefs.

*(**RQ3,4**) Actively choosing among concepts and comparison to SOTA..* We applied CAIPI to the "colors" dataset of [27]. The goal is to classify 5×5 images with four possible colors. An image is positive if either the four corner pixels have the same color (rule 0) or the three top middle pixels have different colors (rule 1). Crucially, the dataset only includes images where either both rules hold or neither does, that is, labels alone can not disambiguate between the two rules. Explanations highlight the k most relevant pixels, and corrections indicate the pixels that are wrongly identified as relevant. In the counterexamples, the wrongly identified pixels are recolored using all possible alternative colors consistent with $\hat{y}$ [8]. The features are of the form "pixel i has the same color as pixel j" for all $i, j = 1, \ldots, 25$, $i < j$. In this space, the rules can be represented by sparse hyperplanes. We select each rule in turn and provide corrections according to it, and then check whether the feedback drives the classifier toward it. k was set to 4 for rule 0 and to 3 for rule 1. We followed a 10-fold CV strategy.

In a first step, we considered a standard L_2 SVM active learner with the closest-to-margin query selection heuristic [31]. This classifier can in principle represent both rules, but it is not suited for learning sparse concepts. Indeed, the SVM struggles to learn both rules, and the counterexamples have little effect on it (see the Supplementary Material for the complete results). This is plausible since the L_2 norm cannot capture the underlying sparse concept: even though corrections try to drive the model toward it, the L_2 SVM can still learn *both* rules (as shown by the coefficient curves) without a problem. In other words, the model is not constrained enough.

An L_1 SVM, an active learner tailored for sparse concepts [42], fares much better. Our results show that the rules greatly benefit this model. To evaluate their effect, we compute the average instantaneous F_1 score of the pixels identified by LIME w.r.t. the pixels truly relevant for the selected rule. This measures the quality of the explanations presented to the user. In addition, we measure the objective quality of the model by decomposing the learned weights using least-squares as $\mathbf{w} = \alpha_0 \mathbf{w}_0^* + \alpha_1 \mathbf{w}_1^* + \text{residual}$, where $\mathbf{w}_i^*$ is the "perfect" weight vector of rule $i = 0, 1$. The instantaneous F_1 and change in coefficients can be viewed in Fig. 2. Now that the model can capture the target concepts, the contribution of counterexamples is very noticeable: the L_1 SVM is biased toward rule 1, as it is sparser (data not shown), but it veers clearly toward rule 0 when corrections are provided and learns rule 1 faster when corrections push toward it. These results show clearly that explanation feedback can drive the classifier toward the right concept, so long as the chosen model can capture it clearly.

*(**RQ3,4**) Active learning for text classification.* Finally, we applied CAIPI to distinguishing between "Atheism" and "Christian" posts in the 20 newsgroups dataset using logistic regression with uncertainty sampling. Headers and footers were removed; only adjectives, adverbs, nouns, and verbs were kept and stemmed. As gold standard for the explanations, we selected $\approx \frac{1}{5}$ of the words as relevant using feature selection. Here the LIME-provided explanations identified the k most relevant words, while corrections identified the falsely relevant words. For each document, k was set to the number of truly relevant words. To showcase CAIPI's flexibility, the counterexamples were generated with the strategy proposed in [40], adapted to produce feedback based on the falsely relevant words only. The 10-fold cross-validated results can be found in Fig. 3. The plots show that the model with explanation corrections is steadily better in terms of explanation quality—over the test set (left) and queries

[5]Due to sampling, LIME may output different explanations for the same prediction. To reduce variance, we ran it 10 times and kept the k components identified most often.
[6]In practice corrections may be incomplete or noisy, especially when dealing with non-experts. This can be handled by, e.g., down-weighting the counterexamples.
[7] https://github.com/zalandoresearch/fashion-mnist

[8]We always discard counterexamples that appear in the test set.

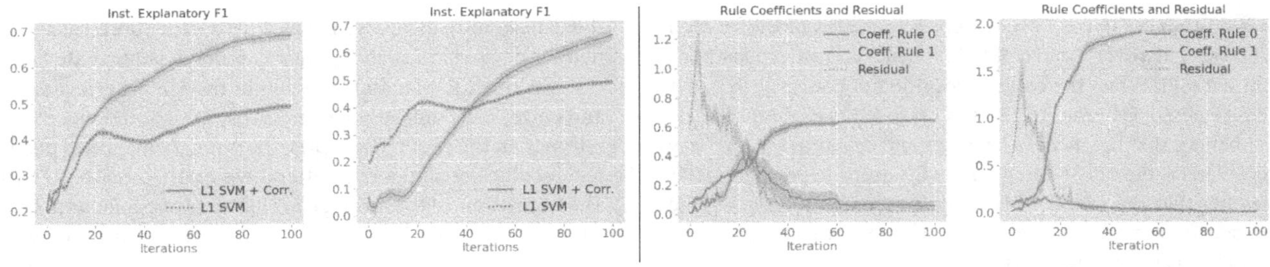

Figure 2: Explanatory feedback ('+ Corr.') can drive an active L_1 SVM towards the right concept (colors problem). (Left) instantaneous F_1 score of the LIME explanations for rule 0 (leftmost) and rule 1 (left middle). (Right) Decomposition of the learned weight vector when the corrections push toward rule 0 (right middle) and rule 1 (rightmost). (Best viewed in color)

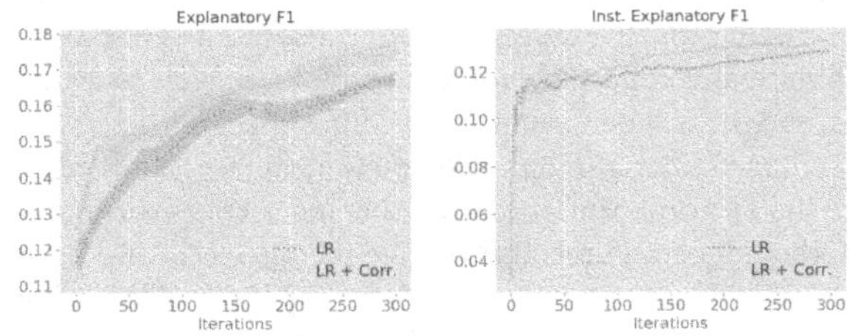

Figure 3: Explanatory feedback ('+ Corr.') can boost an active logistic regression (LR) on 20 newsgroups.

(right)—than the baseline without corrections. The predictive performance can be found in the longer version of the paper[9]. Overall, explanatory interaction can improve the model's quality.

5 CONCLUSION

We introduced explanatory interactive learning and proposed CAIPI, the first explanatory interactive learning method. CAIPI faithfully explains its queries in an interpretable manner and accounts for the user's corrections of the model if it is right (wrong) for the wrong the reasons. This opens the black-box of active learning and turns it into a cooperative learning process between the machine and the user. Our experimental results demonstrate that this cooperation can improve performance and indeed encourage (or discourages, if appropriate) trust into the model.

There are a number of interesting avenues for future work. Other interactive learning approaches such as coactive [33], active imitation [15], mixed-initiative interactive [5] and guided probabilistic learning [21] should be made explanatory. Making deep active learning [12] explanatory is likely to improve upon the sample complexity of deep learning. Selecting queries that maximize the information of explanations, e.g., by using SP-LIME [25], as well as feeding back informative counterexample only are likely to improve performance.

Acknowledgments. The authors thank the anonymous reviewers as well as Antonio Vergari, Andrea Passerini, Samuel Kolb, Jessa Bekker, Xiaoting Shao, and Paolo Morettin for very useful feedback. ST acknowledges the supported by the European Research Council (ERC) under the European Union's Horizon 2020 research and innovation programme, grant agreement No. [694980] "SYNTH: Synthesising Inductive Data Models", and KK the support by the German Science Foundation project "CAML: Argumentative Machine Learning" (KE1686/3-1) as part of the SPP 1999 (RATIO).

[9]arxiv.org/abs/1805.08578

REFERENCES

[1] Josh Attenberg et al. 2010. A unified approach to active dual supervision for labeling features and examples. In *Proc. of ECML/PKDD*. Springer, 40–55.
[2] Maria-Florina Balcan et al. 2010. The true sample complexity of active learning. *Machine learning* 80, 2 (2010), 111–139.
[3] Osbert Bastani et al. 2017. Interpreting blackbox models via model extraction. *arXiv preprint arXiv:1705.08504* (2017).
[4] Cristian Buciluǎ et al. 2006. Model compression. In *Proc. of KDD*. ACM, 535–541.
[5] Maya Cakmak et al. 2011. Mixed-initiative active learning. *ICML 2011 Workshop on Combining Learning Strategies to Reduce Label Cost* (2011).
[6] Rui M Castro et al. 2006. Upper and lower error bounds for active learning. In *The 44th Annual Allerton Conference on Communication, Control and Computing*, Vol. 2. 1.
[7] Li Chen et al. 2012. Critiquing-based recommenders: survey and emerging trends. *User Modeling and User-Adapted Interaction* 22, 1-2 (2012), 125–150.
[8] Corinna Cortes et al. 1995. Support-vector networks. *Machine learning* 20, 3 (1995), 273–297.
[9] Gerald DeJong et al. 2011. Explanation-based learning. In *Encyclopedia of Machine Learning*. Springer, 388–392.
[10] Gregory Druck et al. 2008. Learning from labeled features using generalized expectation criteria. In *Proc. of SIGIR*. 595–602.
[11] Gregory Druck et al. 2009. Active learning by labeling features. In *Proc. of EMNLP*. 81–90.
[12] Yarin Gal et al. 2017. Deep Bayesian Active Learning with Image Data. In *Proc. of ICML*. 1183–1192.
[13] Steve Hanneke et al. 2014. Theory of disagreement-based active learning. *Foundations and Trends® in Machine Learning* 7, 2-3 (2014), 131–309.
[14] Robert R Hoffman et al. 2013. Trust in automation. *IEEE Intelligent Systems* 28, 1 (2013), 84–88.
[15] Kshitij Judah et al. 2012. Active Imitation Learning via Reduction to IID Active Learning.. In *UAI*. 428–437.
[16] Angelika Kimmig et al. 2007. Probabilistic explanation based learning. In *Proc. of ECML*. 176–187.
[17] Andreas Krause et al. 2007. Nonmyopic active learning of gaussian processes: an exploration-exploitation approach. In *ICML*. ACM, 449–456.
[18] Todd Kulesza et al. 2015. Principles of explanatory debugging to personalize interactive machine learning. In *Proc. of IUI*. 126–137.
[19] Scott Lundberg et al. 2016. An unexpected unity among methods for interpreting model predictions. *arXiv preprint arXiv:1611.07478* (2016).
[20] Tom M Mitchell et al. 1986. Explanation-based generalization: A unifying view. *Machine learning* 1, 1 (1986), 47–80.
[21] Phillip Odom and Sriraam Natarajan. 2018. Human-Guided Learning for Probabilistic Logic Models. *Front. Robotics and AI* 2018 (2018). https://doi.org/10.3389/frobt.2018.00056
[22] Bart Peintner et al. 2008. Preferences in interactive systems: Technical challenges and case studies. *AI Magazine* 29, 4 (2008), 13.
[23] Hema Raghavan et al. 2006. Active learning with feedback on features and instances. *JMLR* 7, Aug (2006), 1655–1686.
[24] Hema Raghavan et al. 2007. An interactive algorithm for asking and incorporating feature feedback into support vector machines. In *Proc. of SIGIR*. 79–86.

[25] Marco Tulio Ribeiro et al. 2016. Why should i trust you?: Explaining the predictions of any classifier. In *Proc. of KDD.* 1135–1144.
[26] Marco Tulio Ribeiro et al. 2018. Anchors: High-Precision Model-Agnostic Explanations. In *Proc. of AAAI.*
[27] Andrew Slavin Ross et al. 2017. Right for the right reasons: training differentiable models by constraining their explanations. In *IJCAI.* AAAI Press, 2662–2670.
[28] Nicholas Roy et al. 2001. Toward optimal active learning through monte carlo estimation of error reduction. *ICML* (2001), 441–448.
[29] Tobias Schnabel et al. 2018. Short-Term Satisfaction and Long-Term Coverage: Understanding How Users Tolerate Algorithmic Exploration. In *Proc. of WSDM.* ACM, 513–521.
[30] Burr Settles. 2011. Closing the loop: Fast, interactive semi-supervised annotation with queries on features and instances. In *Proc. EMNLP.* 1467–1478.
[31] Burr Settles. 2012. Active learning. *Synthesis Lectures on Artificial Intelligence and Machine Learning* 6, 1 (2012), 1–114.
[32] Manali Sharma et al. 2015. Active learning with rationales for text classification. In *NAACL HLT.* 441–451.
[33] Pannaga Shivaswamy et al. 2015. Coactive Learning. *J. Artif. Intell. Res.(JAIR)* 53 (2015), 1–40.
[34] Jeffry A Simpson. 2007. Psychological foundations of trust. *Current directions in psychological science* 16, 5 (2007), 264–268.
[35] Kevin Small et al. 2011. The constrained weight space svm: learning with ranked features. In *ICML.* Omnipress, 865–872.
[36] Simone Stumpf et al. 2009. Interacting meaningfully with machine learning systems: Three experiments. *International Journal of Human-Computer Studies* 67, 8 (2009), 639–662.
[37] Simon Tong and Daphne Koller. 2001. Support vector machine active learning with applications to text classification. *JMLR* 2, Nov (2001), 45–66.
[38] Ning Wang et al. 2016. Trust calibration within a human-robot team: Comparing automatically generated explanations. In *Proc. of HRI.* 109–116.
[39] Adam Waytz et al. 2014. The mind in the machine: Anthropomorphism increases trust in an autonomous vehicle. *Journal of Experimental Social Psychology* 52 (1 5 2014), 113–117.
[40] Omar Zaidan et al. 2007. Using "Annotator Rationales" to Improve Machine Learning for Text Categorization. In *NAACL HLT.* 260–267.
[41] Omar F Zaidan et al. 2008. Modeling annotators: A generative approach to learning from annotator rationales. In *Proc. EMNLP.* 31–40.
[42] Ji Zhu et al. 2004. 1-norm support vector machines. In *Proc. of NIPS.* 49–56.

Multiaccuracy: Black-Box Post-Processing for Fairness in Classification

Michael P. Kim*†
mpk@cs.stanford.edu
Stanford University

Amirata Ghorbani†
amiratag@stanford.edu
Stanford University

James Zou
jamesz@stanford.edu
Stanford University

ABSTRACT

Machine learning predictors are successfully deployed in applications ranging from disease diagnosis, to predicting credit scores, to image recognition. Even when the overall accuracy is high, the predictions often have systematic biases that harm specific subgroups, especially for subgroups that are minorities in the training data. We develop a rigorous framework of *multiaccuracy* auditing and post-processing to improve predictor accuracy across *identifiable subgroups*. Our algorithm, Multiaccuracy Boost, works in any setting where we have black-box access to a predictor and a relatively small set of labeled data for auditing. We prove guarantees on the convergence rate of the algorithm and show that it improves overall accuracy at each step. Importantly, if the initial model is accurate on an identifiable subgroup, then the post-processed model will be also. We demonstrate the effectiveness of this approach on diverse applications in image classification, finance, and population health. Multiaccuracy Boost can improve subpopulation accuracy (e.g. for "black women") even when the sensitive features (e.g. "race", "gender") are not known to the algorithm.

CCS CONCEPTS

• **Security and privacy → Human and societal aspects of security and privacy**; • **Theory of computation → Machine learning theory**; *Sample complexity and generalization bounds*; *Boosting*.

KEYWORDS

fairness, discrimination, machine learning, post-processing

ACM Reference Format:
Michael P. Kim, Amirata Ghorbani, and James Zou. 2019. Multiaccuracy: Black-Box Post-Processing for Fairness in Classification. In *AAAI/ACM Conference on AI, Ethics, and Society (AIES '19), January 27–28, 2019, Honolulu, HI, USA*. ACM, New York, NY, USA, 8 pages. https://doi.org/10.1145/3306618.3314287

*Supported by a Google Faculty Research Award and NSF Grant CCF-1763299.
†Contributed equally to this work.

AIES '19, January 27–28, 2019, Honolulu, HI, USA

ACM ISBN 978-1-4503-6324-2/19/01...$15.00
https://doi.org/10.1145/3306618.3314287

1 INTRODUCTION

Despite the successes of machine learning at complex tasks that involve making predictions about people, there is growing evidence that "state-of-the-art" models can perform significantly less accurately on minority populations than on the majority population. Indeed, a notable study of three commercial face recognition systems known as the "Gender Shades" project [2], demonstrated significant performance gaps across different populations at classification tasks. While all systems achieved roughly 90% accuracy at gender detection on a popular benchmark, a closer investigation revealed that the system was significantly less accurate on female subjects compared to males and on dark-skinned individuals compared to light-skinned. Worse yet, this discrepancy in accuracy compounded when comparing dark-skinned females to light-skinned males; classification accuracy differed between these groups by as much as 34%!

A first approach to address this serious problem would be to update the training distribution to reflect the distribution of people, making sure historically-underrepresented populations are well-represented in the training data. While this approach may be viewed as an eventual goal, often for historical and social reasons, data from certain minority populations is less available than from the majority population. In particular, we may not immediately have enough data from these underrepresented subpopulations to train a complex model. Additionally, even when adequate representative data is available, this process necessitates retraining the underlying prediction model. In the common setting where the learned model is provided as a service, like a commercial image recognition system, there may not be sufficient incentive (financial, social, etc.) for the service provider to retrain the model. Still, the clients of the model may want to improve the accuracy of the resulting predictions across the population, even when they are not privy to the inner workings of the prediction system.

At a high level, our work focuses on a setting, adapted from [13], that is common in practice but distinct from much of the other literature on fairness in classification. We are given black-box access to a classifier, f_0, and a relatively small "validation set" of labeled samples drawn from some representative distribution $\mathcal{D}$; our goal is to *audit* f_0 to determine whether the predictor satisfies a strong notion of subgroup fairness, *multiaccuracy*. Multiaccuracy requires (in a sense that we make formal in Section 2) that predictions be unbiased, not just overall, but on every identifiable subpopulation. If auditing reveals that the predictor does not satisfy multiaccuracy, we aim to *post-process* f_0 to produce a new classifier f that is multiaccurate, without adversely affecting the subpopulations where f_0 was already accurate. Multiaccuracy auditing makes no assumptions about the original classifier; in particular, it can handle inadvertent and malicious forms of discrimination.

Our contributions. We develop a framework for auditing and post-processing prediction models for multiaccuracy. We describe a new algorithm, MULTIACCURACY BOOST, where a simple learning algorithm – the auditor – is used to identify subpopulations where f_0 is systematically biased. This information is then used to iteratively post-process f_0 until the multiaccuracy condition – unbiased predictions in each identifiable subgroup – is satisfied. Our notion of multiaccuracy differs from parity-based notions of fairness [7, 11, 16], and is reasonable in settings such as gender detection where we would like to boost the classifier's accuracy across subgroups. We prove convergence guarantees for MULTIACCURACY BOOST and show that post-processing for multiaccuracy may actually improve the *overall* classification accuracy. We describe the post-processing algorithm in Section 3.

Empirically, we validate MULTIACCURACY BOOST in an experimental case study based on the Gender Shades example [2].[1] We train an initial prediction model that achieve good overall classification error, but exhibits biases against minority subpopulations. After post-processing, the accuracy improves across these minority groups, even though minority-status is not explicitly given to the post-processing algorithm as a feature. As long as there are features in the audit set correlated with the (unobserved) human categories, then MULTIACCURACY BOOST is effective at improving the classification accuracy across these categories.

As suggested by the theory, enforcing multiaccuracy actually improves the overall accuracy, by identifying subpopulations where the initial models systematically erred; further, post-processing does not significantly affect performance on groups where accuracy was already high. We show that MULTIACCURACY BOOST, which only accesses f_0 as a black-box, performs comparably and sometimes even better than very strong white-box alternatives which has full access to f_0. We also show that the auditing process may be useful in understanding why prediction models are making mistakes. Specifically, the multiaccuracy auditor can be used to produce examples of inputs where the predictor is erring significantly. These results are reported in Section 4 and the appendix.

2 SETTING AND MULTIACCURACY

High-level setting. Let $\mathcal{X}$ denote the input space; we denote by $y : \mathcal{X} \to \{0, 1\}$ the function that maps inputs to their label. Let $\mathcal{D}$ represent the validation data distribution supported on $\mathcal{X}$; the distribution $\mathcal{D}$ can be viewed as the "true" distribution, on which we will evaluate the accuracy of the final model. In particular, we assume that the important subpopulations are sufficiently represented on $\mathcal{D}$ (cf. Remark on data distribution). Our post-processing learner receives as input a small sample of labeled validation data $\{(x, y(x))\}$, where $x \sim \mathcal{D}$, as well as black-box access to an initial prediction model $f_0 : \mathcal{X} \to [0, 1]$. The goal is to output a new model (using calls to f_0) that satisfies the multiaccuracy fairness conditions (described below).

Importantly, we make no further assumptions about f_0. Typically, we will think of f_0 as the output of a learning algorithm, trained on some other distribution $\mathcal{D}_0$ (also supported on $\mathcal{X}$); in this scenario, our goal is to mitigate any inadvertently-learned biases. That said, another important setting assumes that f_0 is chosen *adversarially* to discriminate against a protected population of individuals, while aiming to appear accurate and fair on the whole; here, we aim to protect subpopulations against malicious misclassification. The formal guarantees of multiaccuracy provide meaningful protections from both of these important forms of discrimination.

[1] We also evaluate performance on a semi-synthetic medical diagnosis task and adult income prediction, reported in the Appendix.

Additional Notation. For a subset $S \subseteq \mathcal{X}$, we use $x \sim S$ to denote a sample from $\mathcal{D}$ conditioned on membership in S. We take the characteristic function of S to be $\chi_S(x) = 1$ if $x \in S$ and 0 otherwise. For a hypothesis $f : \mathcal{X} \to [0, 1]$, we denote the classification error of f with respect to a subset $S \subseteq \mathcal{X}$ as $\mathrm{er}_S(f; y) = \mathbf{Pr}_{x \sim S}[\bar{f}(x) \neq y(x)]$, where $\bar{f}(x)$ rounds $f(x)$ to $\{0, 1\}$. For a function $z : \mathcal{X} \to [-1, 1]$ and a subset $S \subseteq \mathcal{X}$, let z_S be the restriction to S where $z_S(x) = z(x)$ if $x \in S$ and $z_S(x) = 0$ otherwise.

2.1 Multiaccuracy

The goal of multiaccuracy is to achieve low classification error, not just on $\mathcal{X}$ overall, but also on subpopulations of $\mathcal{X}$. This goal is formalized in the following definition adapted from [13].

DEFINITION (MULTIACCURACY). *Let $\alpha \geq 0$ and let $C \subseteq [-1, 1]^{\mathcal{X}}$ be a class of functions on $\mathcal{X}$. A hypothesis $f : \mathcal{X} \to [0, 1]$ is (C, α)-multiaccurate if for all $c \in C$:*

$$\left| \mathop{\mathbf{E}}_{x \sim \mathcal{D}}[c(x) \cdot (f(x) - y(x))] \right| \leq \alpha. \tag{1}$$

(C, α)-multiaccuracy guarantees that a hypothesis appears unbiased according to a class of statistical tests defined by C. As an example, we could define the class in terms of a collection of subsets $S \subseteq \mathcal{X}$, taking C to be χ_S (and its negation) for each subset in the collection; in this case, (C, α)-multiaccuracy guarantees that for each S, the predictions of f are at most α-biased.

Ideally, we would hope to take C to be the class of *all* statistical tests. Requiring multiaccuracy with respect to such a C, however, requires learning the function $y(x)$ exactly, which is information-theoretically impossible from a small sample. In practice, if we take C to be a *learnable* class of functions, then (C, α)-multiaccuracy guarantees accuracy on all *efficiently-identifiable* subpopulations.

For instance, if we took C to be the class of depth-4 decision trees, then multiaccuracy guarantees unbiasedness, not just on the marginal populations defined by race and separately gender, but by the subpopulations defined by the combinations of race, gender, and two other (possibly "unprotected") features. In particular, the subpopulations that multiaccuracy protects can be overlapping and include groups beyond traditionally-protected populations.

2.2 Auditing for multiaccuracy

With the definition of (C, α)-multiaccuracy in place, a natural question to ask is how to test if a hypothesis f satisfies the definition; further, if f does not satisfy (C, α)-multiaccuracy, can we update f efficiently to satisfy the definition, while maintaining the overall accuracy? We will use a *learning algorithm* $\mathcal{A}$ to audit a classifier f for multiaccuracy. The algorithm $\mathcal{A}$ receives a small sample from $\mathcal{D}$ and aims to learn a function h that correlates with the *residual* function $f - y$. In Section 3, we describe how to use such an auditor to solve the post-processing problem. This connection between subpopulation fairness and learning is also made in [13, 16, 19], albeit for different tasks.

To achieve (C, α)-multiaccuracy we could audit with a naive learning algorithm that iterates over statistical tests $c \in C$. Given an algorithm $\mathcal{A}$ that efficiently learns the class C, we can speed up the auditing process; for instance, if we take C to be the class of linear tests, we can use efficient algorithms for linear regression to audit. Concretely, in our experiments, we audit with ridge regression and decision tree regression; both auditors are effective at identifying subpopulations on which the model is underperforming.

2.3 Classification accuracy from multiaccuracy

Multiaccuracy guarantees that the predictions of a classifier appear unbiased on a rich class of subpopulations; ideally though, we would state a guarantee in terms of the classification accuracy, not just the bias. Intuitively, as we take C to define a richer class of tests, the guarantees of multiaccuracy become stronger. This intuition is formalized in the following proposition.

Proposition 1. *Let $\hat{y} : \mathcal{X} \to \{-1, 1\}$ as $\hat{y}(x) = 1 - 2y(x)$. Suppose that for $S \subseteq \mathcal{X}$ with $\mathbf{Pr}_{x \sim \mathcal{D}}[x \in S] \geq \gamma$, there is some $c \in C$ such that $\mathbf{E}_{x \sim \mathcal{D}}[|c(x) - \hat{y}_S(x)|] \leq \tau$. Then if f is (C, α)-multiaccurate, $\mathrm{er}_S(f; y) \leq 2 \cdot (\alpha + \tau)/\gamma$.*

That is, if there is a function in C that correlates well with the label function on a significant subpopulation S, then multi-accuracy translates into a guarantee on the *classification accuracy* on this subpopulation.

Remark on data distribution. Note that in our definition of multi-accuracy, we take an expectation over the distribution $\mathcal{D}$ of validation data. Ideally, $\mathcal{D}$ should reflect the true population distribution or could be aspirational, increasing the representation of populations who have experienced historical discrimination; for instance, the classification error guarantee of Proposition 1 improves as γ, the density of the protected subpopulation S, grows. For instance, in our case study on gender detection, we train on a large unbalanced data set, but then audit using a data set of balanced diversity collected for the Gender Shades study [2].

3 POST-PROCESSING FOR MULTIACCURACY

Here, we describe an algorithm, Multiaccuracy Boost, for post-processing a pre-trained model to achieve multiaccuracy. The algorithm is given black-box access to an initial hypothesis $f_0 : \mathcal{X} \to [0, 1]$ and a learning algorithm $\mathcal{A} : (\mathcal{X} \times [-1, 1])^m \to [-1, 1]^{\mathcal{X}}$ that learns a class C, and for any accuracy parameter $\alpha > 0$, outputs a hypothesis $f : \mathcal{X} \to [0, 1]$ that is (C, α)-multiaccurate. The post-processing algorithm is an iterative procedure similar to boosting [28], that uses the multiplicative weights framework to improve suboptimal predictions identified by the auditor. This approach is similar to the algorithm given in [13] in the context of fairness and [32] in the context of pseudorandomness. Importantly, we adapt these algorithms so that Multiaccuracy Boost exhibits what we call the "do-no-harm" guarantee; informally, if f_0 has low classification error on some subpopulation $S \subseteq \mathcal{X}$ identified by $\mathcal{A}$, then the resulting classification error on S cannot increase significantly.

In this sense, achieving our notion of fairness need not adversely affect the utility of the classifier.

Algorithm 1: Multiaccuracy Boost

Given:
- initial hypothesis $f_0 : \mathcal{X} \to [0, 1]$;
- auditing algorithm $\mathcal{A} : (\mathcal{X} \times [-1, 1])^m \to [-1, 1]^{\mathcal{X}}$;
- accuracy parameter $\alpha > 0$;
- validation data $D = D_0, \ldots, D_T \sim \mathcal{D}^m$;

Let:
- $\mathcal{X}_0 \leftarrow \{x \in \mathcal{X} : f_0(x) \leq 1/2\}$
- $\mathcal{X}_1 \leftarrow \{x \in \mathcal{X} : f_0(x) > 1/2\}$
  `// partition X according to f0`
- $\mathcal{S} \leftarrow \{\mathcal{X}, \mathcal{X}_0, \mathcal{X}_1\}$

Repeat: from $t = 0, 1, \ldots, T$
- For $S \in \mathcal{S}$:
  $h_{t,S} \leftarrow \mathcal{A}(D_t; (f_t - y)_S)$
  `// audit ft on X,X0,X1 with fresh data`
- $S^* \leftarrow \mathrm{argmax}_{S \in \mathcal{S}}\, \mathbf{E}_{x \sim D_t}[h_{t,S}(x) \cdot (f_t(x) - y(x))]$
  `// take largest residual`
- if $\mathbf{E}_{x \sim D_t}[h_{t,S^*}(x) \cdot (f_t(x) - y(x))] \leq \alpha$:
  return f_t
  `// terminate when at most alpha`
- $f_{t+1}(x) \propto e^{-\eta h_{t,S^*}(x)} \cdot f_t(x) \quad \forall x \in S^*$
  `// multiplicative weights update`

At a high level, Multiaccuracy Boost starts by partitioning the input space $\mathcal{X}$ based on the initial classifier f_0 into $\mathcal{X}_0 = \{x \in \mathcal{X} : f_0(x) \leq 1/2\}$ and $\mathcal{X}_1 = \{x \in \mathcal{X} : f_0(x) > 1/2\}$; note that we can partition $\mathcal{X}$ simply by calling f_0. Partitioning the search space $\mathcal{X}$ based on the predictions of f_0 helps to ensure that the f we output maintains the initial accuracy of f_0; in particular, it allows us to search over just the positive-labeled examples (negative, resp.) for a way to improve the classifier.

After partitioning the input space, the procedure iteratively uses the learning algorithm $\mathcal{A}$ to search over $\mathcal{X}$ (and within the partitions $\mathcal{X}_0, \mathcal{X}_1$) to find any function which correlates significantly with the current residual in prediction $f - y$. If $\mathcal{A}$ successfully returns some function $h : \mathcal{X} \to [-1, 1]$ that identifies a significant subpopulation where the current hypothesis is inaccurate, the algorithm updates the predictions multiplicatively according to h. In order to update the predictions simultaneously for all $x \in \mathcal{X}$, at the tth iteration, we build f_{t+1} by incorporating h_t into the previous model f_t. This approach of augmenting the model at each iteration is similar to boosting.

A key algorithmic challenge is to learn a multiaccurate predictor without overfitting to the small sample of validation data. In theory, we prove bounds on the sample complexity necessary to guarantee good generalization as a function of the class C, the error parameter α, and the size of subpopulations we wish to protect γ. To guarantee good generalization, we assume that $\mathcal{A}$ uses a fresh sample $D_t \sim \mathcal{D}^m$ per iteration. In practice, when we have few samples, we can put all of our samples in one batch and use noise-addition techniques to reduce overfitting [6, 27]. In practice, we need to balance the choice of C and the number of iterations of our algorithm to make sure that the auditor is discovering true signal, rather than noise in the validation data. Indeed, if the auditor $\mathcal{A}$ learns an expressive enough class of functions, then our algorithm will start to overfit at some point; we show empirically that multi-accuracy post-processing improves the generalization error before overfitting.

From the stopping condition, it is clear that when the algorithm terminates, f_T will be (C, α)-multiaccurate. Thus, it remains to bound the number of iterations T before MULTIACCURACY BOOST terminates. Additionally, as described, the algorithm evaluates statistics like $\mathbf{E}_{x \sim \mathcal{D}}[h(x) \cdot (f(x) - y(x))]$, which we can estimate accurately and efficiently from a small sample. We provide formal guarantees on the convergence rate and the sample complexity from $\mathcal{D}$ in the Appendix.

Do no harm. The distinction between our approach and most prior works on fairness (especially [16]) is made clear from the "do-no-harm" property that MULTIACCURACY BOOST exhibits, stated formally as Theorem 2. In a nutshell, the property guarantees that on any subpopulation $S \subseteq \mathcal{X}$ that $\mathcal{A}$ audits, the classification error cannot increase significantly from f_0 to the post-processed classifier. As we assume $\mathcal{A}$ can identify a very rich class of overlapping sets, in aggregate, this property gives a strong guarantee on the utility of the resulting predictor. Further, the proof of Theorem 2 reveals that this worst-case bound is very pessimistic and can be improved with stronger assumptions. Thus, if we use Algorithm 1 to post-process a model that is already achieves high accuracy on the validation distribution the resulting model's accuracy should not deteriorate in significant ways; empirically, we observe that classification accuracy (on held-out test set) tends to improve over $\mathcal{D}$ after multiaccuracy post-processing.

THEOREM 2 (DO-NO-HARM). *Let $\alpha, \beta, \gamma > 0$ and $S \subseteq \mathcal{X}$ be a subpopulation where $\mathbf{Pr}_{x \sim \mathcal{D}}[x \in S] \geq \gamma$. Suppose $\mathcal{A}$ audits the characteristic function $\chi_S(x)$ and its negation. Let $f : \mathcal{X} \to [0, 1]$ be the output of Algorithm 1 when given $f_0 : \mathcal{X} \to [0, 1]$, $\mathcal{A}$, and $\alpha \leq \beta\gamma$ as input. Then the classification error of f on the subset S is bounded as*

$$\mathrm{er}_S(f; y) \leq 3 \cdot \mathrm{er}_S(f_0; y) + 4\beta. \tag{2}$$

4 CASE STUDY: GENDER DETECTION

We aim to replicate the conditions of the Gender Shades study [2], to test the effectiveness of multiaccuracy auditing and post-processing on this important real-world example.[2] For our initial model, we train an inception-resnet-v1 [31] gender classification model using the CelebA data set with more than 200,000 face images [23]. The resulting test accuracy on CelebA for binary gender classification is 98.4%. Even though the overall accuracy of this f_0 is high, the error rate is much worse for females compared to males and worse for blacks compared to non-blacks; these results are qualitatively very similar to those observed by the commercial gender detection systems.

We applied MULTIACCURACY BOOST using the PPB data set (developed by [2]) which has balanced representation across gender and race. Specifically, we audit using ridge regression. Instead of auditing over the raw input pixels, we use a representation derived from a variational autoencoder (VAE) trained on CelebA dataset using Facenet [29] library. The PPB data set is very small; thus, this experiment can be viewed as a stress test to evaluate the data efficiency of our post-processing technique. The test set has 415 individuals and the audit set has size 855. PPB annotates each face as dark (**D**) or light-skinned (**L**).

In addition to evaluating the effectiveness of the multiaccuracy approach, we compare our post-processing results against a strong white-box baseline. Here, we retrain the network of f_0 using the audit set. Specifically, we retrain the last two layers of the network, which gives the best results amongst retraining methods. We emphasize that this baseline requires white-box access to f_0, whereas the auditor is "blind" – it is not explicitly given the race or gender and knows nothing about the inner workings of f_0.

	All	F	M	D	L	DF	LM
$\mathcal{D}$	100	44.6	55.4	46.4	53.6	21.4	30.4
f_0	9.9	21.6	0.4	18.8	2.2	39.8	0.0
MA	3.9	6.5	1.8	7.3	0.9	12.5	0.8
RT	2.2	3.8	0.9	4.2	0.4	6.8	0.0

Table 1: Results for the PPB gender classification $\mathcal{D}$ denotes the percentages of each population in the data distribution; f_0 denotes the classification error (%) of the initial predictor; MA denotes the classification error (%) of the model after post-processing with MULTIACCURACY BOOST; RT denotes the classification error (%) of the model after retraining on $\mathcal{D}$.

We evaluated the test accuracy of the original f_0, the multiaccurate post-processed classifier, and retrained classifier on each subgroup. MULTIACCURACY BOOST converged in 5 iterations and substantially reduced error across subpopulations. We report the overall classification accuracy as well as accuracy on different subpopulations We report the population percentage in $\mathcal{D}$, accuracy of the initial model, our black-box post-processed model, and white-box benchmarks in Table 1 for each subpopulations – e.g. **DF** indicates dark-skinned female. In particular, we highlight the subpopulations of **DF** and **LM**; the classification error improves significantly on **DF** but does not hurt the accuracy on **LM** significantly.

4.0.1 Multiaccuracy auditing as diagnostic. As was shown in [2], we've demonstrated that models trained in good faith on unbalanced data may exhibit significant biases on the minority populations. For instance, the initial classification error on black females is significant, whereas on white males, it is near 0%. Importantly, the only way we were able to report these accuracy disparities was by having access to a rich data set where gender and race were labeled. Often, this demographic information will not be available; indeed, the CelebA images are not labeled with race information, and as such, we were unable to evaluate the subpopulation classification accuracy on this set. Thus, practitioners may be faced with a problem: even if they know their model is making undesirable mistakes, it may not be clear if these mistakes are concentrated on specific subpopulations. Absent any identification of the subpopulations on which the model is underperforming, collecting additional training data may not actually improve performance across the board.

[2] See the appendix for two other case studies.

We demonstrate that multiaccuracy auditing may serve as an effective diagnostic and interpretation tool to help developers identify systematic biases in their models. The idea is simple: the auditor returns a hypothesis h that essentially "scores" individual inputs x by how wrong the prediction $f_0(x)$ is. If we consider the magnitude of their scores $|h(x)|$, then we may understand better the biases that the encoder is discovering. We test this idea on the PPB data set, evaluating the test images' representations with the hypotheses the auditor returns.

In Figure 1, we display the images in the test set that get the highest and lowest effect ($|h(x)|$ large and $|h(x)| \approx 0$, respectively) according to the first and second hypothesis returned by the auditor. In the first round of auditing, the three highest-scoring images (top row) are all women, both black and white. The least active images (second row) are men in suits, suggesting that suits may be a highly predictive feature of being a man according to the original classifier, f_0. Overall the first round of audit seems to identify gender as the axis of bias in f_0. In the second round, after the classifier has been improved by one step of Multiaccuracy Boost, the auditor seems to hone in on the "dark-skinned women" subpopulation as the region of bias.

Figure 1: Interpreting Auditors
PPB test images of largest and smallest bias detected by the auditor for the first (rows 1-2) and second (rows 3-4) rounds of auditing.

5 DISCUSSION

In this work, we propose multiaccuracy as a framework for improving the fairness and accountability of black-box prediction systems. Here, we discuss how our work compares to prior works, specifically, how it fits into the growing literature on fairness for learning systems.

5.1 Related works

Many different notions of fairness have been proposed in literature on learning and classification [7, 8, 11–13, 16, 19, 26, 33]. Many of these works encode some notion of parity, e.g. subgroups should have similar false positive rates, as an explicit objective/constraint in the training of the original classifier. The fairness properties are viewed as constraints on the classifier that ultimately *limit the model's utility*. A common belief is that in order to achieve equitable treatment, the classifier's performance must degrade.

A notable exception to this pattern is the work of Hébert-Johnson *et al.* [13], which first introduced a variant of *multiaccuracy*and *multicalibration* in the context of regression tasks. [13] provides theoretical algorithms for achieving multiaccuracy and multicalibration, and shows how to post-process a model to achieve multicalibration in a way that *improves* the regression objective across all subpopulations (in terms of squared-error). Our work directly extends the approach of [13], adapting their work to the binary classification setting. Our post-processing algorithm, Multiaccuracy Boost, builds on the algorithm given in [13], providing the additional "do-no-harm" property. This property guarantees that if the initial predictor f_0 has small classification error on some identifiable group, then the resulting post-processed model will also have small classification error on this group.

Independent work of Kearns *et al.* [16] also investigated how to achieve statistical fairness guarantees, not just for traditionally-protected groups, but on rich families of subpopulations. [16] proposed a framework for *auditing* and learning models to achieve fairness notions like statistical parity and equal false positive rates. Both works [13, 16] connect the task of learning a model that satisfies the notion of fairness to the task of (weak) agnostic learning [9, 14, 15, 17]. [16] also reduces the problem of learning a classifier satisfying parity-based notions of fairness across subgroups to the problem of auditing; it would be interesting if their notion of auditing can be used by humans as a way to diagnose systematic discrimination.

Our approach to post-processing, which uses a learning algorithm as a fairness auditor differs from [16] in important ways. In their framework, the auditor is used during (white-box) training to *constrain* the model selected from a pre-specified hypothesis class; ultimately, this constrains the accuracy of the predictions. In our setting, we do not restrict ourselves to an explicitly-defined hypothesis class, so we can augment the current model using the auditor; these augmentations *improve* the accuracy of the model. Additionally, by applying mutliaccuracy over real-valued functions (as opposed to boolean functions), we can get efficient algorithms that provably satisfy (C, α)-multiaccuracy for nontrivial classes C (specifically, linear hypotheses).

At a technical level, our post-processing algorithm is similar to gradient boosting [10, 24]. Still, our perspective is quite different from the typical boosting setting. Rather than using an expressive class of predictors as the base classifiers to learn the function directly, we focus on the regime where data is limited and we must restrict our attention to simple classes. Thus, it becomes important that we leverage the expressiveness (and initial accuracy) of f_0 if we are to obtain strong performance using the multiaccuracy approach.

A different approach to subgroup fairness is studied by Dwork *et al.* [8]. This work investigates the question of how to learn a "decoupled" classifier, where separate classifiers are learned for each subgroup and then combined to achieve a desired notion of fairness. While applicable in some settings, at times, this approach may be untenable. First, decoupling the classification problem requires that we have the attributes of interest in the data set and that the groups we wish to protect are partitioned by these attributes. Even if this information is available, *a priori*, it may not always be obvious which subpopulations require special attention. In contrast, multiaccuracy allows us to protect a rich class of overlapping subpopulations without explicit knowledge of the vulnerable populations. An interesting direction for future investigation could try to pair multiaccuracy auditing (to identify subpopulations in need of protection) with the decoupled classification techniques of [8].

The present work, along with [13, 16, 19], can be viewed as studying information-fairness tradeoffs in prediction tasks (i.e. strengthening the notion of fairness that can be guaranteed using a small sample). These works fit into the larger literature on fairness in learning and prediction tasks [2, 7, 8, 11, 19, 26, 33], discussions of the utility-fairness tradeoffs in fair classification [1, 3–5, 20, 25]. While fairness and accountability serve as the main motivations for developing the multiaccuracy framework, our results may have broader interest. In particular, multiaccuracy post-processing may be applicable in domain adaptation settings, particularly under label distribution shift as studied recently in [22], but when the learner gets a small number of labeled samples from the new distribution.

5.2 Conclusion

The multiaccuracy framework can be applied very broadly; importantly, we can post-process any initial model f_0 given only black-box access to f_0 and a small set of labeled validation data. We show that in realistic settings, post-processing for multiaccuracy helps to mitigate systematic biases in predictors across sensitive subpopulations, even when the identifiers for these subpopulations are not given to the auditor explicitly. In our experiments, we observe that standard supervised learning optimizes for overall performance, leading to settings where certain subpopulations incur substantially worse error rates. Multiaccuracy provides a framework for fairness in classification by improving the accuracy in identifiable subgroups, in a way that suffers no tradeoff between accuracy and utility. We demonstrate – both theoretically and empirically – that post-processing serves as an effective tool for improving the accuracy across important subpopulations, and does not harm the populations that are already classified well.

Multiaccuracy works to the extent that the auditor can identify specific subgroups where the original classifier f_0 tends to make mistakes. The power of multiaccuracy lies in the fact that in many settings, we can identify issues with f_0 from a small amount of audit data. Thus, multiaccuracy auditing is limited: if the mistakes appear overly-complicated to the bounded auditor, then the auditor will not be able to identify these mistakes. Our empirical results suggest, that the subpopulations on which a classifier errs may be efficiently-identifiable. This observation may be of interest beyond the context of fairness. In particular, our experiments improving the accuracy of a model trained on CelebA on the PPB test sets suggests a lightweight black-box alternative to more sophisticated transfer learning techniques, which may warrant further investigation.

Acknowledgements. The authors thank Omer Reingold and Guy N. Rothblum for their advice and helpful discussions throughout the development of this work; we thank Weihao Kong, Aditi Raghunathan, and Vatsal Sharan for feedback on early drafts of this work.

REFERENCES

[1] Angwin, J., Larson, J., Mattu, S., and Kirchner, L. Machine bias: There's software used across the country to predict future criminals. and it's biased against blacks. *ProPublica* (2016).

[2] Buolamwini, J., and Gebru, T. Gender shades: Intersectional accuracy disparities in commercial gender classification. In *Conference on Fairness, Accountability and Transparency* (2018), pp. 77–91.

[3] Chouldechova, A. Fair prediction with disparate impact: A study of bias in recidivism prediction instruments. *Big Data* (2017).

[4] Chouldechova, A., and G'Sell, M. Fairer and more accurate, but for whom? *FATML* (2016).

[5] Corbett-Davies, S., Pierson, E., Feller, A., Goel, S., and Huq, A. Algorithmic decision making and the cost of fairness. *KDD* (2017).

[6] Dwork, C., Feldman, V., Hardt, M., Pitassi, T., Reingold, O., and Roth, A. The reusable holdout: Preserving validity in adaptive data analysis. *Science 349*, 6248 (2015), 636–638.

[7] Dwork, C., Hardt, M., Pitassi, T., Reingold, O., and Zemel, R. S. Fairness through awareness. In *Innovations in Theoretical Computer Science (ITCS)* (2012), pp. 214–226.

[8] Dwork, C., Immorlica, N., Kalai, A. T., and Leiserson, M. Decoupled classifiers for fair and efficient machine learning. *arXiv preprint arXiv:1707.06613* (2017).

[9] Feldman, V. Distribution-specific agnostic boosting. In *Proceedings of the First Symposium on Innovations in Computer ScienceâĂŹ10* (2010).

[10] Friedman, J. H. Greedy function approximation: a gradient boosting machine. *Annals of statistics* (2001), 1189–1232.

[11] Hardt, M., Price, E., and Srebro, N. Equality of opportunity in supervised learning. In *Advances in Neural Information Processing Systems* (2016), pp. 3315–3323.

[12] Hashimoto, T. B., Srivastava, M., Namkoong, H., and Liang, P. Fairness without demographics in repeated loss minimization. *ICML* (2018).

[13] Hébert-Johnson, Ú., Kim, M. P., Reingold, O., and Rothblum, G. N. Calibration for the (computationally-identifiable) masses. *ICML* (2018).

[14] Kalai, A. T., Mansour, Y., and Verbin, E. On agnostic boosting and parity learning. In *Proceedings of the fortieth annual ACM symposium on Theory of computing* (2008), ACM, pp. 629–638.

[15] Kearns, M. Efficient noise-tolerant learning from statistical queries. *Journal of the ACM (JACM) 45*, 6 (1998), 983–1006.

[16] Kearns, M., Neel, S., Roth, A., and Wu, Z. S. Preventing fairness gerrymandering: Auditing and learning for subgroup fairness. *arXiv preprint arXiv:1711.05144v3* (2017).

[17] Kearns, M. J., Schapire, R. E., and Sellie, L. M. Toward efficient agnostic learning. *Machine Learning 17*, 2-3 (1994), 115–141.

[18] Kim, M. P., Ghorbani, A., and Zou, J. Multiaccuracy: Black-box post-processing for fairness in classification (full version). *arXiv preprint 1805.12317* (2018).

[19] Kim, M. P., Reingold, O., and Rothblum, G. N. Fairness through computationally-bounded awareness. *arXiv Preprint 1803.03239* (2018).

[20] Kleinberg, J., Mullainathan, S., and Raghavan, M. Inherent trade-offs in the fair determination of risk scores. *ITCS* (2017).

[21] Kohavi, R. Scaling up the accuracy of naive-bayes classifiers: a decision-tree hybrid. In *KDD* (1996), vol. 96, Citeseer, pp. 202–207.

[22] Lipton, Z. C., Wang, Y., and Smola, A. J. Detecting and correcting for label shift with black box predictors. *ICML* (2018).

[23] Liu, Z., Luo, P., Wang, X., and Tang, X. Deep learning face attributes in the wild. In *Proceedings of International Conference on Computer Vision (ICCV)* (December 2015).

[24] Mason, L., Baxter, J., Bartlett, P. L., and Frean, M. R. Boosting algorithms as gradient descent. In *Advances in neural information processing systems* (2000), pp. 512–518.

[25] Pleiss, G., Raghavan, M., Wu, F., Kleinberg, J., and Weinberger, K. Q. On fairness and calibration. *NIPS* (2017).

[26] Rothblum, G. N., and Yona, G. Probably approximately metric-fair learning. *ICML* (2018).

[27] Russo, D., and Zou, J. How much does your data exploration overfit? controlling bias via information usage. *AISTATS* (2016).

[28] Schapire, R. E., and Freund, Y. *Boosting: Foundations and algorithms.* MIT press, 2012.

[29] Schroff, F., Kalenichenko, D., and Philbin, J. Facenet: A unified embedding for face recognition and clustering. *CoRR abs/1503.03832* (2015).

[30] Sudlow, C., Gallacher, J., Allen, N., Beral, V., Burton, P., Danesh, J., Downey, P., Elliott, P., Green, J., Landray, M., et al. Uk biobank: an open access resource for identifying the causes of a wide range of complex diseases of middle and old age. *PLoS medicine 12*, 3 (2015), e1001779.

[31] Szegedy, C., Ioffe, S., Vanhoucke, V., and Alemi, A. A. Inception-v4, inception-resnet and the impact of residual connections on learning. In *AAAI* (2017), vol. 4, p. 12.

[32] Trevisan, L., Tulsiani, M., and Vadhan, S. Regularity, boosting, and efficiently simulating every high-entropy distribution. In *Computational Complexity, 2009. CCC'09. 24th Annual IEEE Conference on* (2009), IEEE, pp. 126–136.

[33] Zemel, R., Wu, Y., Swersky, K., Pitassi, T., and Dwork, C. Learning fair representations. In *Proceedings of the 30th International Conference on Machine Learning (ICML-13)* (2013), pp. 325–333.

A ADDITIONAL EXPERIMENTS

Multiaccuracy auditing and post-processing is applicable broadly in supervised learning tasks, not just in image classification applications. We demonstrate the effectiveness of Multiaccuracy Boost in two other settings: the adult income prediction task and a semi-synthetic disease prediction task.

Adult Income Prediction. For the first case study, we utilize the adult income prediction data set [21] with 45,222 samples and 14 attributes (after removing subjects with unknown attributes) for the task of binary prediction of income more than \$50k for the two major groups of Black and White. We remove the sensitive features of gender – female (**F**) and male (**M**) and race (for the two major groups) – black (**B**) and white (**W**) – from the data, to simulate settings where sensitive features are not available to the algorithm training. We trained a base algorithm, f_0, which is a neural network with two hidden layers on 27,145 randomly selected individuals. The test set consists of an independent set of 15,060 persons.

We audit using a decision tree regression model (max depth 5) $\mathcal{A}_{dt}$ to fit the residual $f(x)-y(x)$. $\mathcal{A}_{dt}$ receives samples of validation data drawn from the same distribution as training; that is $\mathcal{D} = \mathcal{D}_0$. In particular, we post-process with 3,017 individuals sampled from the same adult income dataset (disjoint from the training set of f_0). The auditor is given the same features as the original prediction model, and thus, is not given the gender or race of any individual. We evaluate the post-processed classifier on the same independent test set. Multiaccuracy Boost converges in 50 iterations with $\eta = 1$.

As a baseline, we trained four separate neural networks with the same architecture as before (two hidden layers) for each of the four subgroups using the audit data. As shown in Table 2, multiaccuracy post-processing achieves better accuracy both in aggregate and for each of the subgroups. Importantly, the subgroup-specific models requires explicit access to the sensitive features of gender and race. Training a classifier for each subgroup, or explicitly adding subgroup accuracy into the training objective, assumes that the subgroup is already identified in the data. This is not feasible in the many applications where, say, race or more granular categories are not given. Even when the subgroups are identified, we often do not have enough samples to train accurate classifiers on each subgroup separately. This example illustrates that multiaccuracy can help to boost the overall accuracy of a black-box predictor in a data efficient manner.

	All	F	M	B	W	BF	WM
$\mathcal{D}$	100	32.3	67.7	9.7	90.3	4.8	62.9
f_0	19.3	9.3	24.2	10.5	20.3	4.8	24.9
MA	14.7	7.2	18.3	9.4	15.0	4.5	18.3
SS	19.7	9.5	24.6	10.5	19.9	5.5	25.3

Table 2: Results for Adult Income Data Set $\mathcal{D}$ denotes the percentages of each population in the data distribution; f_0 denotes the classification error (%) of the initial predictor; MA denotes the classification error (%) of the model after post-processing with Multiaccuracy Boost; SS denotes the classification error (%) of the subgroup-specific models trained separately for each population.

Semi-Synthetic Disease Prediction. We design a disease prediction task based on real individuals, where the phenotype to disease relation is designed to be different for different subgroups, in order to simulate a challenging setting. We used 40,000 individuals sampled from the UK Biobank [30]. Each individual contains 60 phenotype features. To generate a synthetic disease outcome for each subgroup, we divided the data set into four groups based on gender – male (**M**) and female (**F**) – and age – young (**Y**) and old (**O**). For each subgroup, we create synthetic binary labels using a different polynomial function of the input features with different levels of difficulty. The polynomial function orders are 1, 4, 2, and 6 for OF, OM, YF, and YM subgroups respectively.

For f_0, we trained a neural network with two hidden layers on 32,000 individuals, without using the gender and age features. Hyperparameter search was done for the best weight-decay and dropout parameters. The f_0 we discover performs moderately well on every subpopulation, with the exception of old females (**OF**) where the classification error is significantly higher. Note that this subpopulation had the least representation in $\mathcal{D}_0$. Again, we audit using $\mathcal{A}_{dt}$ to run decision tree regression with validation data samples drawn from $\mathcal{D} = \mathcal{D}_0$. Specifically, the auditor receives a sample of 4,000 individuals without the gender or age features. As a baseline, we trained a separate classifier for each of the subgroups using the same audit data. As Table 3 shows, Multiaccuracy Boost significantly lowers the classification error in the old female population.

	All	F	M	O	Y	OF	YM
$\mathcal{D}$	100	39.6	60.4	34.6	65.4	15.0	40.7
f_0	18.9	29.4	12.2	21.9	17.3	36.8	12.8
MA	16.0	24.1	10.7	16.4	15.7	26.5	11.6
SS	19.5	32.4	11.0	22.1	18.1	37.6	11.3

Table 3: Results for UK Biobank semi-synthetic data set. $\mathcal{D}$ denotes the percentages of each population in the data distribution; f_0 denotes the classification error (%) of the initial predictor; MA denotes the classification error (%) of the model after post-processing with Multiaccuracy Boost; SS denotes the classification error (%) of the subgroup-specific models trained separately for each population.

B FORMAL GUARANTEES OF MULTIACCURACY

Additional notation. We use $\ell_{\mathcal{D}}(f;y) = \mathbf{E}_{x\sim\mathcal{D}}[\ell_x(f;y)]$ to denote the expected cross-entropy loss of f on $x \in \mathcal{X}$ where $\ell_x(f;y) = -y(x)\cdot\log(f(x)) - (1-y(x))\cdot\log(1-f(x))$. We use the inner product $\langle h,g\rangle = \mathbf{E}_{x\sim\mathcal{D}}[h(x)\cdot g(x)]$ and the p-norms $\|h\|_p = \left(\mathbf{E}_{x\sim\mathcal{D}}[|h(x)|^p]\right)^{1/p}$.

B.1 Multiaccuracy and classification error

Here, we prove Proposition 1.

Proof. For $i,j \in \{0,1\}$, let $S_{ij} = \left\{x \in S : y(x) = i \wedge \bar{f}(x) = j\right\}$. Further denote $\beta_{ij} = \mathbf{Pr}_{x\sim\mathcal{D}}[x \in S_{ij}]$. Note that the classification error on a set S is $\mathrm{er}_S(f;y) \le (\beta_{01}+\beta_{10})/\gamma$.

Let $\hat{y}(x) = 1 - 2y(x)$ and suppose $c(x) = \hat{y}(x)_S + z(x)$ where $\|\delta\|_1 \le \tau$. Then, we derive the following inequality.

$$\mathop{\mathbf{E}}_{x\sim\mathcal{D}}[c(x)\cdot(f(x)-y(x))] \tag{3}$$

$$= \mathop{\mathbf{E}}_{x\sim\mathcal{D}}[\hat{y}(x)_S\cdot(f(x)-y(x))] + \mathop{\mathbf{E}}_{x\sim\mathcal{D}}[z(x)\cdot(f(x)-y(x))] \tag{4}$$

$$\ge \beta_{01}\cdot\mathop{\mathbf{E}}_{x\sim S_{01}}[f(x)-y(x)] + \beta_{10}\cdot\mathop{\mathbf{E}}_{x\sim S_{10}}[y(x)-f(x)] - \tau \tag{5}$$

where (5) follows by Hölder's inequality, from the fact that the contribution to the expectation of $(1-2y(x))\cdot(f(x)-y(x))$ from S_{00} and S_{11} is lower bounded by 0, and by the definition $\hat{y}_S(x) = 0$ for $x \notin S$. Further, because we know any $x \in S_{01}\cup S_{10}$ is misclassified, we can lower bound the contribution by 1/2. Thus, if $\mathbf{E}_{x\sim\mathcal{D}}[c(x)\cdot(f(x)-y(x))] \le \alpha$, then by rearranging we conclude

$$\mathrm{er}_S(f;y) = (\beta_{01}+\beta_{10})/\gamma \le 2\cdot(\alpha+\tau)/\gamma. \tag{6}$$

□

Theorem 2 follows by a similar argument.

Proof. Suppose that $\mathrm{er}_S(f_0;y) \le \tau$. Let $S_1 = \{x \in S : f_0(x) > 1/2\}$; suppose $\mathrm{er}_{S_1}(f_0;y) = \tau_1$. By assumption, $-\chi_S(x)$ is audited on $\mathcal{X}_1$. Consider $\mathbf{E}_{x\sim S_1}[-\chi_S(x)\cdot(f(x)-y(x))]$.

$$\mathop{\mathbf{E}}_{x\sim S_1}[-\chi_S(x)\cdot(f(x)-y(x))] \tag{7}$$

$$= \mathop{\mathbf{E}}_{x\sim S_1}[y(x)-f(x)] \tag{8}$$

$$= \mathop{\mathbf{Pr}}_{x\sim S_1}[y(x)=1]\cdot\mathop{\mathbf{E}}_{\substack{x\sim S_1\\ y(x)=1}}[1-f(x)] - \mathop{\mathbf{Pr}}_{x\sim S_1}[y(x)=0]\cdot\mathop{\mathbf{E}}_{\substack{x\sim S_1\\ y(x)=0}}[f(x)] \tag{9}$$

$$\ge \mathop{\mathbf{Pr}}_{x\sim S_1}[y(x)=1\wedge\bar{f}(x)=0]\cdot\mathop{\mathbf{E}}_{\substack{x\sim S_1\\ y(x)=1\\ \bar{f}(x)=0}}[1-f(x)] - \tau_1 \tag{10}$$

$$\ge \frac{1}{2}\mathop{\mathbf{Pr}}_{x\sim S_1}[y(x)=1\wedge\bar{f}(x)=0] - \tau_1 \tag{11}$$

where (10) follows from applying Hölder's inequality and the assumption that $\mathrm{er}_{S_1}(f_0;y) = \tau_1$; and (11) follows from lower bounding the contribution to the expectation based on the true label and the predicted label. Note that $\mathbf{Pr}_{x\sim S}[x \in S_1]\cdot\mathbf{E}_{x\sim S_1}[y(x)-f(x)] \le \alpha/\gamma = \beta$ by the fact that f passes multiaccuracy auditing by $\mathcal{A}$ and the assumption that $\mathbf{Pr}_{x\sim\mathcal{D}}[x \in S] \ge \gamma$. Rearranging gives the following inequality

$$\mathrm{er}_{S_1}(f;y) \le \frac{2\beta}{\mathbf{Pr}_{x\sim S}[x \in S_1]} + 3\tau_1 \tag{12}$$

where the additional τ_1 comes from accounting for the false positives.

A similar argument holds for S_0 with $\mathrm{er}_{S_0}(f_0;y) = \tau_0$, using $\chi_S(x)$. We can expand $\mathrm{er}_S(f;y)$ as a convex combination of the classification error over S_0 and S_1.

$$\mathrm{er}_S(f;y) \tag{13}$$

$$= \mathop{\mathbf{Pr}}_{x\sim S}[x \in S_0]\cdot\mathrm{er}_{S_0}(f;y) + \mathop{\mathbf{Pr}}_{x\sim S}[x \in S_1]\cdot\mathrm{er}_{S_1}(f;y) \tag{14}$$

$$\le \mathop{\mathbf{Pr}}_{x\sim S}[x \in S_0]\cdot\mathop{\mathbf{Pr}}_{x\sim S_0}[y(x)\ne\bar{f}(x)] + \mathop{\mathbf{Pr}}_{x\sim S}[x \in S_1]\cdot\mathop{\mathbf{Pr}}_{x\sim S_1}[y(x)\ne\bar{f}(x)] \tag{15}$$

$$\le \mathop{\mathbf{Pr}}_{x\sim S}[x \in S_0]\cdot\left(3\tau_0 + \frac{2\beta}{\mathbf{Pr}_{x\sim S}[x \in S_0]}\right) + \mathop{\mathbf{Pr}}_{x\sim S}[x \in S_1]\cdot\left(3\tau_1 + \frac{2\beta}{\mathbf{Pr}_{x\sim S}[x \in S_1]}\right) \tag{16}$$

$$= 3\cdot\left(\mathop{\mathbf{Pr}}_{x\sim S}[x \in S_0]\cdot\tau_0 + \mathop{\mathbf{Pr}}_{x\sim S}[x \in S_1]\cdot\tau_1\right) + 4\beta \tag{17}$$

$$\le 3\tau + 4\beta \tag{18}$$

by the fact that S is partitioned into S_0 and S_1 and τ is a corresponding convex combination of τ_0 and τ_1. □

B.2 Analysis of Algorithm 1

Finally, we state the main theorem about Algorithm 1, which gives formal guarantees on the sample complexity and running time of the algorithm.

Theorem 3. *Let $\alpha, \delta > 0$ and suppose $\mathcal{A}$ agnostic learns a class $C \subseteq [-1,1]^{\mathcal{X}}$ of dimension $d(C)$. Then, using $\eta = O(\alpha)$, Algorithm 1 converges to a (C,α)-multiaccurate hypothesis f_T in $T = O\left(\frac{\ell_{\mathcal{D}}(f_0;y)}{\alpha^2}\right)$ iterations from $m = \tilde{O}\left(T\cdot\frac{d(C)+\log(1/\delta)}{\alpha^2}\right)$ samples with probability at least $1-\delta$ over the random samples.*

The proofs of the theorem and additional results are given in full in [18].

A Formal Approach to Explainability

Lior Wolf
wolf@cs.tau.ac.il
Facebook AI Research and
Tel Aviv University

Tomer Galanti
tomerga2@post.tau.ac.il
Tel Aviv University
Tel Aviv, Israel

Tamir Hazan
tamir.hazan@technion.ac.il
Techion
Haifa, Israel

ABSTRACT

We regard explanations as a blending of the input sample and the model's output and offer a few definitions that capture various desired properties of the function that generates these explanations. We study the links between these properties and between explanation-generating functions and intermediate representations of learned models and are able to show, for example, that if the activations of a given layer are consistent with an explanation, then so do all other subsequent layers. In addition, we study the intersection and union of explanations as a way to construct new explanations.

1 INTRODUCTION

Machine learning is often concerned with tacit knowledge, and tacit knowledge leads to black box models. Given a learned model, one cannot "crack it open" in the hope to understand all of the internal nuts and bolts. Explaining the model often relies, instead, on communicating, in a way that is understandable to humans, an internal state of the model during computation.

An explanation process, therefore, has three components: the input, the model's output for that input, which needs to be justified, and an internal state of the model. The explanation itself combines the input and the output into a joint sample that should be understandable by human users. The explaining function (EF) generates these explanations, based on the two inputs, and is intimately tied to the model it explains. We can expect, therefore, that the generated explanations are linked to internal states of the model.

For example, consider a mapping from images to labels of objects. The explanation often takes the visual form of an image, where the predicted object is highlighted and the features related to the label are emphasized, see, e.g., [10]. The algorithmic way to explain, is to generate this hybrid image from the internal representation of the black-box model. Another form of explanation is a textual one [6], and describes features that belong to the recognized class. For example, "[this is an image of a broccoli since] it is green, has a flowering head, and a thick stem with small leaves", where the part in brackets is the label, but not the explanation. This explanation is both a function of the input image (describes what can be seen and where) and the label (contains known properties of broccolis). We provide a formal framework that captures various desiderata of explanations, among which are: consistency between an internal model's state and the generated explanation, explainability of an internal state, validity of an explanation, and its completeness.

ACM ISBN 978-1-4503-6324-2/19/01.
https://doi.org/10.1145/3306618.3314260

Our main results link various aspects of the properties. For example, a valid explanation has to be complete. We also study the specific case of explaining, using the gradient of the loss, the predictions of multiclass neural networks and show that the explanation is linked to the learned representation. Lastly, we study the intersection andunions of explanations, as a way to create new explanations by combining existing ones.

2 SETTINGS

We describe a few fundamental concepts in a way that is less formal than what is presented in the subsequent sections. An illustration of the main components of our framework is given in Fig. 1.

What do we want to explain? Given a function $h : \mathcal{X} \to \mathcal{Y}$ from the input domain $\mathcal{X}$ to the output domain $\mathcal{Y}$, we would like to explain the output $h(x)$ for some input $x \in \mathcal{X}$. h is typically a learned model.

What is an explanation? An explanation is a blending of the input and the output. An explanation function (EF for short) $g : \mathcal{X} \times \mathcal{Y} \to G$ maps $x \in \mathcal{X}$ and $y \in \mathcal{Y}$ to $g(x, y)$, which is the explanation for (x, y) in the blended domain G. Hopefully, the elements of domain G are understandable to humans. However, this part is not amendable to formalization.

Consistent representation: Given a function $h : \mathbb{R}^n \to \mathcal{Y}$ of the form $h = c \circ f$, where f is some representation of the input and c a classifier on top of it, we would like to discuss the link between f and an EF g. We say that f is consistent with respect to an EF g, if for all $x_1, x_2 \in \mathcal{X}$, such that: $|g(x_1, h(x_1)) - g(x_2, h(x_2))| \leq \epsilon$, we have: $|f(x_1) - f(x_2)| \leq \beta(\epsilon)$.

Explainable representation: This definition is similar to consistency, with a reversed implication. We say that f is explainable with respect to the EF g if for all $x_1, x_2 \in \mathcal{X}$, such that: $|f(x_1) - f(x_2)| \leq \epsilon$, we have: $|g(x_1, h(x_1)) - g(x_2, h(x_2))| \leq \gamma(\epsilon)$.

Equivalence between an EF and a representation: A representation f is equivalent to an EF g, if it is both consistent with it and explainable by it.

Valid explanation: An EF g is valid, if there exists a function t, such that the model's label is predictable from the explanation $t(g(x, h(x))) \approx h(x)$.

Complete explanation: We say that an EF g is complete in the context of a model h, if there is no information left in the input x that is relevant to h, which is independent of the information in $g(x, h(x))$. If we define as $\bar{g}(x, h(x))$ all the information that is the part of x but which has no information on $g(x, h(x))$, then g is complete if there is no function s such that $s(\bar{g}(x, h(x))) \approx h(x)$. **Intersection and Union of EFs:** Given a model $h : \mathbb{R}^n \to \mathcal{Y}$ and two EFs g_1, g_2, the intersection between them is a representation $u(x, h(x))$ such that we can write $r_1(g_1(x, h(x))) = (e_1(x, h(x)), u(x, h(x)))$ and $r_2(g_2(x, h(x))) = (e_2(x, h(x)), u(x, h(x)))$, where r_1, r_2 are invert-ible transformations and e_1 is the part of g_1 that is independent of g_2 (and vice versa for e_2). The union between them is defined as $(e_1(x, h(x)), u(x, h(x)), e_2(x, h(x)))$.

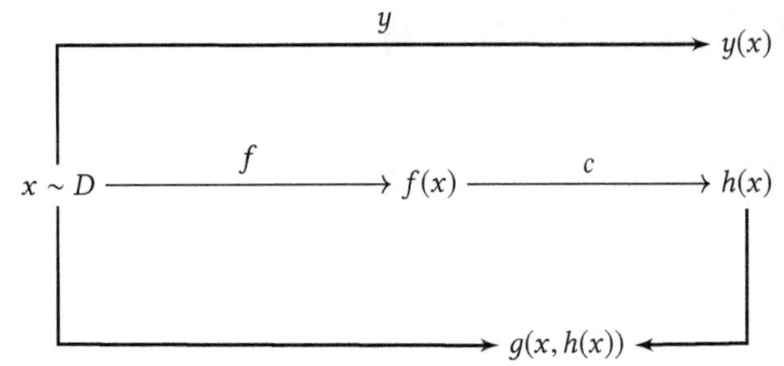

Figure 1: The main components of our framework. The EF g is a function of input x and the models' label $h(x)$, which approximates the target function y. h is a composition of some representation f and a classifier c. Note that g should generate explanations for a specific h and is not generic.

3 A FORMAL MODEL

In this section, we present our formal model of explainability. The sample space $\mathcal{Z} := \mathcal{X} \times \mathcal{Y}$, where $\mathcal{X} \subset \mathbb{R}^n$ is the inputs space and $\mathcal{Y}$ is the outputs space. For instance, in binary classification, $\mathcal{Y} = \{\pm 1\}$, in multi-class classification $\mathcal{Y} = \{1, \dots, K\} := [K]$ for some $K \in \mathbb{N}$, and in regression, $\mathcal{Y} = \mathbb{R}$. In addition, there is an unknown target function $y : \mathbb{R}^n \to \mathcal{Y}$ that is being learned and a hypothesis class $\mathcal{H}$ of models $h : \mathbb{R}^n \to \mathcal{Y}$ from which the learning algorithm selects an approximation of the target function y. We denote by D the distribution of data samples in $\mathcal{X}$.

We consider a family of EFs $\mathcal{G}$, and each EF $g \in \mathcal{G}$ is a mapping $g : \mathbb{R}^n \times \mathcal{Y} \to G$. Here, G is a set of possible explanations. We do not aim to show how to compute an explanation $g(x, h(x))$. Instead, we focus on providing useful terminology to understand the properties of EFs.

Terminology and notations. Before we present our main results, we recall a few technical notations. First, throughout this manuscript, we will assume that D is supported by $\mathcal{X}$, which is assumed, for the purpose of simplifying entropy and mutual-information based arguments, to be a discrete set. We also assume that all logarithms are base 2. The image of a function $f : \mathcal{X}_1 \to \mathcal{X}_2$ is denoted by $f(\mathcal{X}_1)$. We denote by, $\ell : \mathcal{Z} \to \mathbb{R}$ a loss function. Typically, in binary classification, we have the zero-one loss, $\ell(y_1, y_2) = \mathbf{1}[y_1 \neq y_2]$ and in regression, we often employ the L1 loss $|y_1 - y_2|_1$ or the L2 loss $|y_1 - y_2|^2$. Here, $\mathbf{1}[b]$ is an indicator of a boolean variable, b, being true, i.e., $\mathbf{1}[\text{true}] = 1$ and $\mathbf{1}[\text{false}] = 0$.

We recall the classical information theoretic notations from [2]: the expectation and probability operators symbols $\mathbb{E}, \mathbb{P}$, the Shannon entropy (discrete or continuous) $H(X) := -\mathbb{E}_X[\log \mathbb{P}[X]]$, the conditional entropy $H(X|Y) := H(X,Y) - H(Y)$ and the (conditional) mutual information (discrete or continuous) $I(X;Y|Z) := H(X|Z) - H(X|Y,Z)$. For a given value $p \in [0,1]$, we denote, $H(p) = -p\log(p) - (1-p)\log(1-p)$.

3.1 Properties of EFs

We provide formal definitions to the various properties mentioned in the Settings Section. A representation of the input is a function $f : \mathcal{X} \to \mathbb{R}^d$ (for some $d > 0$). In most cases, we will assume that f is a sub-architecture of our mapping $h : \mathbb{R}^n \to \mathcal{Y}$. Specifically, we would consider h to be a composite function that is built in layers $h = p_k \circ \dots \circ p_1$, where each layer p_i is a function $p_i : \mathbb{R}^{n^{i-1}} \to \mathbb{R}^{n^i}$ (for some $k, n^i \in \mathbb{N}$, n^0 being the input dimension n and $i \in \{1, 2 \dots, k\}$). In this case, f would contain the first m layers $f = p_m \circ \dots \circ p_1$ and c would contain the $k - m$ top layers: $c = p_k \circ \dots \circ p_{m+1}$.

Definition 3.1 (Consistent Representation). Let $h = c \circ f \in \mathcal{H}$ be a model, $g : \mathcal{Z} \to G$ an EF and $\beta : (0, \infty) \to [0, \infty)$. We say that f is a $\beta(\epsilon)$-consistent representation with respect to g, if for any $\epsilon \in (0, \infty)$ and $x_1, x_2 \in \mathcal{X}$, we have:

$$\begin{aligned} &|g(x_1, h(x_1)) - g(x_2, h(x_2))| \leq \epsilon \\ &\implies |f(x_1) - f(x_2)| \leq \beta(\epsilon) \end{aligned} \tag{1}$$

Definition 3.2 (Explainable Representation). Let $h = c \circ f \in \mathcal{H}$ be a model and $g : \mathcal{Z} \to G$ an EF. For a given function $\gamma : (0, \infty) \to (0, \infty)$, we say that f is a $\gamma(\epsilon)$-explainable representation with respect to g, if for any $\epsilon \in (0, \infty)$ and $x_1, x_2 \in \mathcal{X}$, we have:

$$\begin{aligned} &|f(x_1) - f(x_2)| \leq \epsilon \\ &\implies |g(x_1, h(x_1)) - g(x_2, h(x_2))| \leq \gamma(\epsilon) \end{aligned} \tag{2}$$

Additionally, for a given function $\gamma : (0, \infty) \times (0, \infty) \to (0, \infty)$, we say that f is second-order $\gamma(\epsilon_0, \epsilon_1)$-explainable with respect to g, if for any $\epsilon_0, \epsilon_1 \in (0, \infty)$ and $x_1, x_2 \in \mathcal{X}$, we have:

$$\begin{aligned} &|f(x_1) - f(x_2)| \leq \epsilon_0 \text{ and } \left|\frac{\partial f(x_1)}{\partial x_1} - \frac{\partial f(x_2)}{\partial x_2}\right| \leq \epsilon_1 \\ &\implies |g(x_1, h(x_1)) - g(x_2, h(x_2))| \leq \gamma(\epsilon_0, \epsilon_1) \end{aligned} \tag{3}$$

Definition 3.3 (Equivalence between a Representation and an EF). Let $h = c \circ f \in \mathcal{H}$ be a model, $g : \mathcal{Z} \to G$ an EF and $\beta, \gamma : (0, \infty) \to [0, \infty)$. We say that f is $(\beta(\epsilon), \gamma(\epsilon))$-equivalent to g, if it is $\beta(\epsilon)$-consistent and $\gamma(\epsilon)$-explainable with respect to g.

Definition 3.4 (Valid EF). Let $h \in \mathcal{H}$ be a model, $g : \mathcal{Z} \to G$ an EF, $\epsilon_0 > 0$ a fixed constant and $x \sim D$. We say that g is ϵ_0-valid with respect to h, if there is a function $t : G \to \mathcal{Y}$ that satisfies:

$$\mathbb{E}_x[\ell(t(g(x, h(x))), h(x))] \leq \epsilon_0 \tag{4}$$

Definition 3.5 (Complete EF). Let $h \in \mathcal{H}$ be a model, $g : \mathcal{Z} \to G$ an EF and $x \sim D$. Let $\alpha, \epsilon > 0$ be two constants. We say that g is (ϵ, α)-complete with respect to h, if every function $\bar{g} : \mathcal{X} \to \mathbb{R}^d$, such that, $I(g(x, h(x)); \bar{g}(x)) \leq \epsilon$ and function $s : \mathbb{R}^d \to \mathcal{Y}$, we have:

$$\mathbb{E}_x[\ell(s(\bar{g}(x)), h(x))] \geq \alpha \tag{5}$$

4 LINKING REPRESENTATIONS AND EFS

The following theorem states that if an internal representation of a layered model h is $\beta(\epsilon)$-consistent with an EF, then, under mild conditions, downstream layers are also consistent with the specified EF.

Theorem 4.1. *Let $h = p_k \circ \dots \circ p_1 : \mathbb{R}^n \to \mathcal{Y}$ be a model and $g : \mathcal{Z} \to G$ an EF. Assume that $f_i := p_i \circ \dots \circ p_1$ is $\beta(\epsilon)$-consistent with respect to g, for some $i \in \{1, \dots, k\}$. Assume that p_r is a l_r-Lipschitz function for every $r \in \{i+1, \dots, j\}$. Then, $f_j := p_j \circ \dots \circ p_1$ is $\hat{\beta}(\epsilon)$-consistent with respect to g, for $\hat{\beta}(\epsilon) := \beta(\epsilon) \cdot \prod_{r=i+1}^{j} l_r$.*

Proof. Assume that f_i is $\beta(\epsilon)$-consistent for some $i \in \{1,\dots,k\}$. Let $x_1, x_2 \in \mathcal{X}$ be two inputs, such that, $|g(x_1,h(x_1)) - g(x_2,h(x_2))| \leq \epsilon$. Then, for every $j \in \{i,\dots,k\}$, we have:

$$\begin{aligned} &|f_j(x_1) - f_j(x_2)| \\ =&|p_j \circ \dots \circ p_{i+1} \circ f_i(x_1) - p_j \circ \dots \circ p_{i+1} \circ f_i(x_2)| \\ \leq& \prod_{r=i+1}^{j} l_r |f_i(x_1) - f_i(x_2)| \leq \beta(\epsilon) \cdot \prod_{r=i+1}^{j} l_r = \hat{\beta}(\epsilon) \end{aligned} \tag{6}$$

Since each p_r is a l_r-Lipschitz continuous function for every $r \in \{i+1,\dots,j\}$. ◻

One implication of this result is that if a layer of a neural network model h is consistent with an explanation g, then h itself is also consistent, i.e., in the case where any of the layers of h is consistent with g, then if $g(x,h(x))$, which is a function of $h(x)$ as well as of x, does not change much when replacing x with x', then $h(x)$ and $h(x')$ are similar.
The following theorem deals with upstream layers: under mild assumptions, if f is an explainable representation, that is obtained as a layer of a neural network model h, then so are the previous layers in this network.

Theorem 4.2. Let $h = p_k \circ \dots \circ p_1 : \mathbb{R}^n \to \mathcal{Y}$ be a model and $g : \mathcal{Z} \to G$ an EF. Assume that $f_i := p_i \circ \dots \circ p_1$ is $\gamma(\epsilon)$-explainable with respect to g, for some $i \in \{1,\dots,k\}$. Assume that p_r is a l_r-Lipschitz function for every $r \in \{j+1,\dots,i\}$. Then, $f_j := p_j \circ \dots \circ p_1$ is $\hat{\gamma}(\epsilon)$-explainable with respect to g, for $\hat{\gamma}(\epsilon) := \gamma\left(\epsilon \cdot \prod_{r=j+1}^{i} l_r\right)$.

Proof. Assume that f_i is $\gamma(\epsilon)$-explainable for some $i \in \{1,\dots,k\}$. Let $x_1, x_2 \in \mathcal{X}$ be two inputs, such that, $|f_j(x_1) - f_j(x_2)| \leq \epsilon$. Then,

$$\begin{aligned} &|f_i(x_1) - f_i(x_2)| \\ =&|p_i \circ \dots \circ p_{j+1} \circ f_j(x_1) - p_i \circ \dots \circ p_{j+1} \circ f_j(x_2)| \\ \leq& \prod_{r=j+1}^{i} l_r |f_j(x_1) - f_j(x_2)| \leq \epsilon \cdot \prod_{r=j+1}^{i} l_r \end{aligned} \tag{7}$$

Since each p_r is a l_r-Lipschitz continuous function for every $r \in \{j+1,\dots,i\}$. Therefore, since f_i is $\gamma(\epsilon)$-explainable with respect to g, we have:

$$|g(x_1,h(x_1)) - g(x_2,h(x_2))| \leq \gamma\left(\epsilon \cdot \prod_{r=j+1}^{i} l_r\right) \tag{8}$$

◻

Note that an immediate implication is that if a representation is explainable by g, then so is the input x itself.

4.1 A Specific Case Study

We next treat a specific case, which is the conventional multiclass classification approach for deep neural networks, coupled with the iconic image-based explanation that is given by the derivative of the output neuron associated with the predicted label by the input. In this case, the model predicts the label based on an arg max of multiple 1D linear projections (m_i, i being the index of the label) of the activations of the penultimate layer $p(x)$ for some input x. The explanation of the prediction $h(x)$ is then given as the matrix derivative of $(m_{h(x)}^\top \cdot p(x))$ by the input x.

The following theorem states that if our model is of the form $h(x) = \arg\max_{i\in\mathcal{Y}}(m_i^\top \cdot p(x))$ and our EF has the form $g(x,h(x)) = \frac{\partial(m_{h(x)}^\top \cdot p(x))}{\partial x}$, where $p = c \circ f$ such that c, f and the derivative of c are Lipschitz continuous functions, then, f is explainable with respect to g.

Theorem 4.3. Let $\mathcal{Y} = [K]$ and $h : \mathbb{R}^n \to \mathcal{Y}$ a model of the form, $h(x) = \arg\max_{i\in\mathcal{Y}} m_i^\top \cdot p(x)$, where $p : \mathbb{R}^n \to \mathbb{R}^d$ and $m_i \in \mathbb{R}^d$, for $i \in [K]$. Let $g(x,h(x)) = \frac{\partial(m_{h(x)}^\top \cdot p(x))}{\partial x}$ be an EF. Assume that for all $i \in [K]$, $p = c \circ f$, such that: c, $\frac{\partial c(x)}{\partial x}$, $\frac{\partial p(x)}{\partial x}$ and f are Lipschitz continuous functions. Additionally, assume that: $\forall i \neq j \in [K], x \in \mathcal{X} : m_i^\top \neq m_j^\top$ and $\forall x \in \mathcal{X} : |p(x)| \geq \Delta$, for some constant $\Delta > 0$. Then, f is second-order $O(\epsilon_0 + \epsilon_1)$-explainable with respect to g.

Proof. Assume that for all $i \in [K]$:

$$|f(x_1) - f(x_2)| \leq \epsilon_0 \text{ and } \left|\frac{f(x_1)}{\partial x_1} - \frac{f(x_2)}{\partial x_2}\right| \leq \epsilon_1 \tag{9}$$

Then, since each c is a Lipschitz continuous function, there is a constant $l_1,\dots,l_K > 0$, such that for all $i \in [K]$ and $x_1, x_2 \in \mathbb{R}^n$:

$$\begin{aligned} &|m_i^\top \cdot p(x_1) - m_i^\top \cdot p(x_2)| \\ =&|m_i^\top| \cdot |p(x_1) - p(x_2)| \leq l \cdot |m_i^\top| \cdot \epsilon_0 \end{aligned} \tag{10}$$

For any small enough $\epsilon_0 > 0$, we have:

$$l \cdot \max_{i\in[K]} |m_i^\top| \cdot \epsilon_0 < \min_{i\neq j} |m_i^\top - m_j^\top| \cdot \Delta/2 \tag{11}$$

Since $\forall i \neq j \in [K], x \in \mathcal{X} : |p(x)| \geq \Delta$, we have:

$$|m_i^\top \cdot p(x) - m_j^\top \cdot p(x)| \geq \min_{i\neq j} |m_i^\top - m_j^\top| \cdot \Delta > 0 \tag{12}$$

In this case, if $h(x_1) = i$, then, for all $j \in [K]$, such that $j \neq i$, we have:

$$\begin{aligned} &m_i^\top \cdot p(x_2) - m_j^\top \cdot p(x_2) \\ \geq& m_i^\top \cdot p(x_1) - |m_i^\top \cdot p(x_1) - m_i^\top \cdot p(x_2)| \\ &- m_j^\top \cdot p(x_2) - |m_j^\top \cdot p(x_1) - m_j^\top \cdot p(x_2)| \\ \geq& \min_{i\neq j} |m_i^\top - m_j^\top| \cdot \Delta - 2l \cdot \max_{i\in[K]} |m_i^\top| \cdot \epsilon_0 > 0 \end{aligned} \tag{13}$$

Therefore, we conclude that: $h(x_1) = h(x_2) = i$. Thus,

$$\begin{aligned} &|g(x_1,h(x_1)) - g(x_2,h(x_2))| \\ =&\left|\frac{\partial(m_{h(x_1)}^\top \cdot p(x_1))}{\partial x_1} - \frac{\partial(m_{h(x_2)}^\top \cdot p(x_2))}{\partial x_2}\right| \\ =&\left|\frac{\partial(m_i^\top \cdot p(x_1))}{\partial x_1} - \frac{\partial(m_i^\top \cdot p(x_2))}{\partial x_2}\right| \\ =&|m_i^\top| \cdot \left|\frac{\partial p(x_1)}{\partial x_1} - \frac{\partial p(x_2)}{\partial x_2}\right| \\ =&\left|\frac{\partial c(f(x_1))}{\partial f(x_1)} \cdot \frac{\partial f(x_1)}{\partial x_1} - \frac{\partial c(f(x_2))}{\partial f(x_2)} \cdot \frac{\partial f(x_2)}{\partial x_2}\right| \end{aligned} \tag{14}$$

Since c and f are Lipschitz continuous functions, we have:

$$\begin{aligned} &|g(x_1,h(x_1)) - g(x_2,h(x_2))| \\ =&O\left(\left|\frac{\partial f(x_1)}{\partial x_1} - \frac{\partial f(x_2)}{\partial x_2}\right|\right) \\ &+ O\left(\left|\frac{\partial c(f(x_1))}{\partial f(x_1)} - \frac{\partial c(f(x_2))}{\partial f(x_2)}\right|\right) \end{aligned} \tag{15}$$

Since $\frac{\partial c(u)}{\partial u}$ is also a Lipschitz continuous function, we have:

$$\begin{aligned}&|g(x_1, h(x_1)) - g(x_2, h(x_2))|\\ =&O(\epsilon_1 + |f_i(x_1) - f_i(x_2)|) = O(\epsilon_0 + \epsilon_1)\end{aligned} \tag{16}$$

□

5 VALIDITY AND COMPLETENESS

The next result shows that if an EF is valid, then it is also complete. The intuition behind this result is, if we are able to recover $h(x)$ from $\bar{g}(x)$ and from $g(x, h(x))$, then, $\bar{g}(x)$ and $g(x, h(x))$ cannot be independent of each other.

THEOREM 5.1 (VALID $\implies$ COMPLETE). *Let $h : \mathbb{R}^n \to \mathcal{Y}$ be a model, $g : \mathcal{Z} \to G$ an ϵ_0-valid EF for some constant $\epsilon_0 \in (0, 0.5)$ and $x \sim D$. Assume that $\mathcal{Y} = \{\pm 1\}$ and denote, $p := \mathbb{P}[h(x) = 1]$. Then, g is (ϵ, α)-complete with respect to h, with $\alpha := \frac{\sqrt{1+H(p)(H(p)-\epsilon-2\sqrt{\epsilon_0})}-1}{H(p)}$ and any $\epsilon > 0$ that satisfies, $H(p) > \epsilon + 2\sqrt{\epsilon_0}$. In particular, if $p = 1/2$, we have: $\alpha = \sqrt{2 - \epsilon - 2\sqrt{\epsilon_0}} - 1$.*

PROOF. Let $\bar{g} : \mathcal{X} \to \mathbb{R}^d$ be a function, such that, $I(\bar{g}(x); g(x, h(x))) \leq \epsilon$. Since $g(x, h(x))$ is ϵ_0-valid, there is a function $t : G \to \mathcal{Y}$, that satisfies:

$$\begin{aligned}&\mathbb{P}[t(g(x, h(x))) \neq h(x)]\\ =&\mathbb{E}_x[\ell(t(g(x, h(x))), h(x))] \leq \epsilon_0 < 1/2\end{aligned} \tag{17}$$

By $I(X; f(Y)) \leq I(X; Y)$, for every function f, we have:

$$I(\bar{g}(x); t(g(x, h(x)))) \leq I(\bar{g}(x); g(x, h(x))) \leq \epsilon \tag{18}$$

By Lem. A.2 in the Appendix,

$$\begin{aligned}&|I(\bar{g}(x); h(x)) - I(\bar{g}(x); t(g(x, h(x))))|\\ \leq&H(\mathbb{P}[t(g(x, h(x))) \neq h(x)])\end{aligned} \tag{19}$$

Therefore, by Lem. A.3, we have:

$$I(\bar{g}(x); h(x)) \leq \epsilon + H(\mathbb{P}[t(g(x, h(x))) \neq h(x)]) \leq \epsilon + 2\sqrt{\epsilon_0} \tag{20}$$

Next, we assume that $H(q) > \epsilon + 2\sqrt{\epsilon_0}$, where $p = \mathbb{P}[h(x) = 1]$. Let $\alpha := \frac{\sqrt{1+H(p)(H(p)-\epsilon-2\sqrt{\epsilon_0})}-1}{H(p)}$ and assume by way of contradiction that there is a function $s : \mathbb{R}^d \to \mathcal{Y}$, that satisfies: $\mathbb{E}_x[\ell(s(\bar{g}(x)), h(x))] < \alpha$. Then, by Lem. A.1 in the Appendix, we have:

$$I(\bar{g}(x); h(x)) > (1 - \alpha)H(p) - H(\alpha) \geq (1 - \alpha)H(p) - 2\sqrt{\alpha} \tag{21}$$

We conclude that:

$$(1 - \alpha)H(p) - 2\sqrt{\alpha} < \epsilon + 2\sqrt{\epsilon_0} \tag{22}$$

finally, by the quadratic formula, we arrive at a contradiction for $\alpha = \frac{\sqrt{1+H(p)(H(p)-\epsilon-2\sqrt{\epsilon_0})}-1}{H(p)}$. Therefore, we conclude that, $g(x, h(x))$ is ϵ-complete. □

6 EF OPERATORS

We next study the arithmetic of explanations. The practical utility of this is left for future research. However, we can imagine that by combining elementary explanations to complex ones and by intersecting these complex explanations, one can algorithmically construct explanations.

Definition 6.1 (Intersection and Union of Random Variables). Let $x \sim D$ and $f_1 : \mathcal{X} \to \mathcal{X}_1$ and $f_2 : \mathcal{X} \to \mathcal{X}_2$ are two functions. We say that the random variables $f_1(x)$ and $f_2(x)$ ϵ-intersect, if there are two invertible functions $r_1 : \mathcal{X}_1 \to \mathcal{V}_1$ and $r_2 : \mathcal{X}_2 \to \mathcal{V}_2$, such that, $r_1(f_1(x)) = (e_1(x), u(x))$ and $r_2(f_2(x)) = (e_2(x), u(x))$, where $I(e_i(x); f_j(x)) \leq \epsilon$ (for any $i \neq j \in \{1, 2\}$). We call the random variable $u(x)$, the ϵ-intersection of $f_1(x)$ and $f_2(x)$. In addition, we call $(e_1(x), u(x), e_2(x))$ the ϵ-union of $f_1(x)$ and $f_2(x)$.

By Lem. A.5 in the appendix, the intersection and union of two random variables $f_1(x)$ and $f_2(x)$ are unique, up to invertible transformations.

The following results show that the intersection of two EFs, one of which is valid and the other complete, is a valid EF.

THEOREM 6.2. *Let $h : \mathbb{R}^n \to \mathcal{Y}$ be a model, $g_1, g_2 : \mathcal{Z} \to G$ two EFs and $\epsilon, \epsilon_0, \alpha > 0$ three constants. Assume that $\mathcal{Y} = \{\pm 1\}$, $g_1(x, h(x))$ and $g_2(x, h(x))$ ϵ-intersect and denote by $u(x, h(x))$ the ϵ-intersection of them. Assume that g_1 is ϵ_0-valid (w.r.t h) and g_2 is (ϵ, α)-complete (w.r.t h). Then, u is ϵ_1-valid (w.r.t h), for $\epsilon_1 := 1 - \frac{2^{-\epsilon_0 - 2\sqrt{\epsilon_0} - H(h(x))}}{1-\alpha}$.*

PROOF. Let $r_1 : G \to \mathcal{V}_1$ and $r_2 : G \to \mathcal{V}_2$ be two invertible functions, such that, $r_1(g_1(x, h(x))) = (e_1(x, h(x)), u(x, h(x)))$ and $r_2(g_2(x, h(x))) = (e_2(x, h(x)), u(x, h(x)))$, where, $e_i(x, h(x)) \perp\!\!\!\perp g_j(x, h(x))$ (for any $i \neq j \in \{1, 2\}$). By the chain rule property of mutual information,

$$\begin{aligned}&I(e_1(x, h(x)), u(x, h(x)); h(x))\\ =&I(e_1(x, h(x)); h(x))\\ &+ I(u(x, h(x)); h(x)|e_1(x, h(x)))\\ \leq&I(e_1(x, h(x)); h(x)) + I(u(x, h(x)); h(x))\end{aligned} \tag{23}$$

Therefore, we have:

$$\begin{aligned}&I(u(x, h(x)); h(x))\\ \geq&I(e_1(x, h(x)), u(x, h(x)); h(x)) - I(e_1(x, h(x)); h(x))\\ =&I(r_1(e_1(x, h(x)), u(x, h(x))); h(x)) - I(e_1(x, h(x)); h(x))\\ =&I(g_1(x, h(x)); h(x)) - I(e_1(x, h(x)); h(x))\end{aligned} \tag{24}$$

Since g_1 is ϵ_0-valid, there is a function, $t_1 : G \to \mathcal{Y}$, such that:

$$\begin{aligned}&\mathbb{P}_{x \sim D}[t_1(g_1(x, h(x))) \neq h(x)]\\ =&\mathbb{E}_{x \sim D}[\ell(t_1(g_1(x, h(x))), h(x))] \leq \epsilon_0 < 1/2\end{aligned} \tag{25}$$

Therefore, by Lem. A.1 and Lem. A.3 in the Appendix, we have:

$$\begin{aligned}I(g_1(x, h(x)); h(x)) \geq&(1 - \epsilon_0)H(h(x)) - H(1 - \epsilon_0)\\ \geq&(1 - \epsilon_0)H(h(x)) - 2\sqrt{\epsilon_0}\end{aligned} \tag{26}$$

By the definition of $e_1(x, h(x))$, we have:

$$I(e_1(x, h(x)); g_2(x, h(x))) \leq \epsilon \tag{27}$$

Therefore, since g_2 is (ϵ, α)-complete, for every function s with outputs in $\mathcal{Y}$, we have:

$$\mathbb{E}_{x \sim D}[\ell(s(e_1(x, h(x))), h(x))] \geq \alpha \tag{28}$$

Therefore, by Lem. A.4 in the Appendix,

$$I(e_1(x, h(x)); h(x)) \leq \log(1 - \alpha) + H(h(x)) \tag{29}$$

We conclude that:

$$\begin{aligned} &I(u(x,h(x));h(x)) \\ \geq&(1-\epsilon_0)H(h(x)) - 2\sqrt{\epsilon_0} - (\log(1-\alpha) + H(h(x))) \\ \geq&\log\left(\frac{1}{1-\alpha}\right) - \epsilon_0 \cdot H(h(x)) - 2\sqrt{\epsilon_0} \\ \geq&\log\left(\frac{1}{1-\alpha}\right) - \epsilon_0 - 2\sqrt{\epsilon_0} \end{aligned} \tag{30}$$

Finally, by Lem. A.4 in the Appendix, there is a function t_2 with outputs in $\mathcal{Y}$, such that:

$$\mathbb{E}_{x\sim D}[\ell(t_2(u(x,h(x))),h(x))] \leq 1 - \frac{2^{-\epsilon_0 - 2\sqrt{\epsilon_0} - H(h(x))}}{1-\alpha} \tag{31}$$

□

Similar results hold for the union of two EFs: if at least one of which is valid, the union is a valid EF, and a similar result for at least one complete EF.

Lemma 6.3. *Let $h : \mathbb{R}^n \to \mathcal{Y}$ be a model, $g_1, g_2 : \mathcal{Z} \to G$ two EFs and $\epsilon, \epsilon_0, \alpha > 0$ three constants. Assume that $\mathcal{Y} = \{\pm 1\}$, $g_1(x,h(x))$ and $g_2(x,h(x))$ ϵ-intersect and denote by $\hat{g}(x,h(x))$ the ϵ-union of them. If g_1 (or g_2) is ϵ_0-valid (w.r.t h), then, $\hat{g}$ is ϵ_0-valid as well. Additionally, if g_1 (or g_2) is (ϵ_1,α)-complete (w.r.t h), $\hat{g}$ is also (ϵ_1,α)-complete.*

Proof. First, by the definition of ϵ-union, there is a representation, $\hat{g}(x,h(x)) = (e_1(x,h(x)), u(x,h(x)), e_2(x,h(x)))$, such that, there is an invertible function r, that satisfies: $r(e_1(x,h(x)), u(x,h(x))) = g_1(x,h(x))$.
We would like to prove that if g_1 is ϵ_0-valid, then, $\hat{g}$ is also ϵ_0-valid. Since, g_1 is ϵ_0-valid, there is a function $t : G \to \mathcal{Y}$, such that:

$$\mathbb{E}_{x\sim D}[\ell(t(g_1(x,h(x))),h(x))] \leq \epsilon_0 \tag{32}$$

In addition, by the definition of $\hat{g}$, we have a representation: $\hat{g}(x,h(x)) = (e_1(x,h(x)), u(x,h(x)), e_2(x,h(x)))$, such that, there is an invertible function r, that satisfies: $r(e_1(x,h(x)), u(x,h(x))) = g_1(x,h(x))$. Therefore, we define, $r'(\hat{g}(x,h(x))) = g_1(x,h(x))$ and obtain,

$$\mathbb{E}_{x\sim D}[\ell(t \circ r'(\hat{g}(x,h(x))),h(x))] \leq \epsilon_0 \tag{33}$$

Hence, $\hat{g}$ is also ϵ_0-valid.
Next, we prove that if g_1 is (ϵ_1,α)-complete, then, $\hat{g}$ is also (ϵ_1,α)-complete. Let $\bar{g}(x)$ be a function that satisfies: $I(\bar{g}(x);\hat{g}(x,h(x))) \leq \epsilon_1$. In particular, there is a representation

$$\begin{aligned} &I(\hat{g}(x);\hat{g}(x,h(x))) \\ =&I(\hat{g}(x);e_1(x,h(x)),u(x,h(x)),e_2(x,h(x))) \\ \geq&I(\hat{g}(x);e_1(x,h(x)),u(x,h(x))) \\ =&I(\hat{g}(x);r(e_1(x,h(x)),u(x,h(x)))) \\ =&I(\hat{g}(x);g_1(x,h(x))) \end{aligned} \tag{34}$$

Therefore, $I(\hat{g}(x);g_1(x,h(x))) \leq \epsilon_1$. Since, g_1 is (ϵ_1,α)-complete, for any function s, we have:

$$\mathbb{E}_{x\sim D}[\ell(s(\bar{g}(x)),h(x))] \geq \alpha \tag{35}$$

In particular, we conclude that $\hat{g}$ is also (ϵ_1,α)-complete. □

7 DISCUSSION

In this work, we have studied the properties of EFs g. We do not propose new ways to obtain such g, which is an active research topic with an increasing interest. Our focus is on blending functions, which mix the input and the output. We view this is a basic property of a wide class of existing and future types of explanations.
The challenge in formalizing EFs using conventional machine learning tools, is that these are not learned from data (they are designed by the practitioners). Therefore, one cannot use the usual convergence-based results. The claims that can be made are based on the mutual information between the model and the EF, the structure of the EF as a two-input function, and the validity requirement, which entails a specific recursive formula $h \approx t(g(x,h(x)))$.
There are three levels of abstractions, which are often referred to as explanations. One is the concrete explanation itself, which for us is an object in domain G, which is the target domain of g. The second one is the function that generates such explanations. We call these EFs. The third level is the algorithm that provides the EF g given a model h. Our analysis focuses on the EF level and it is important to note that g is not general to all h, but is given and analyzed in the context of a specific h.

8 RELATED WORK

The examples that we have provided on available work on explainable solutions, are a fraction of the growing literature on the subject. See [5] for a survey. Our work covers what is referred to in this survey as the *outcome explanation problem.* It is interesting to contrast the definition of this term, given as Def 4.2 in that survey, to our terminology.
Their definition assumes that the explanation is viewed through the lens of a local model c_l, which is constructed by some process f from the black box model (h in our terminology b in theirs) at a specific location x. The explanation itself $E(c_l,x)$ maps this local model and the input x to a human interpretable domain.
The example given is of a decision tree, with decision rules that are based on single attribute values (coordinates of x), that approximated the black box model in a given neighborhood of x. The explanation is given by the sequence of decisions along the path in this decision tree taken for sample x. The well known LIME approach [9] also fits this definition well. In this approach, random samples are created in the vicinity of x, by perturbing this sample, and are weighed by their distance from x, when learning the local model c_l.
Our framework does not discuss the process $f(h,x)$. The two frameworks are compatible in the sense that $g(x,h(x))$ can be written as $E(f(h,x),x)$, since our g is a function of h (recall that g is specific for a given h), and since g could be a function that is based on local approximations of h. However, our framework emphasizes the blending properties of the explanation domain, while their definitions emphasize locality and local proxies of h by simple functions that are easy to explain, such as decision trees or linear functions. The notion of locality is deferred in our model to the notions of consistency and explainability. However, these exist between intermediate representations and the EF, and Lipschitz continuity type properties and does not necessarily imply an actual approximation.

Recently, [1] have suggested a framework to learn models that are explainable by design. The basic structure is of a model that, similar to linear functions, is monotonic and additive in each of a set of learned attributes, and on learning attributes that are meaningful. The explanation itself takes the form of presenting the contribution of each attribute, while explaining the attributes using prototypes. While our framework focuses on explaining general models h and not learning self-explainable models, it is interesting to compare their stated desiderata with ours.

The specified desiderata on that work are:

(1) Fidelity: the explanation of x should present the relevant information. This is captured by our validity property (relevancy to the label), as well as by the completeness property.
(2) Diversity: the attributes should be disentangled and there should not be too many of them. This is a property on the explanation domain G, which in their work is also used for the representation of the network's penultimate layer. We consider a broader class of explanations, and our analysis of representations refers to f that can be any layer of the network h.
(3) Grounding: the attributes of the explanations should be immediately interpretable to humans. In their model, the interpretation is done through prototype samples. A prototype based G is compatible with our framework. However, we cannot formalize the notion of interpretability.

9 CONCLUSIONS

The basic concepts of explanations in AI are elusive for several reasons. First, as mentioned, they need to be interpretable by humans, and human understanding has not been fully modeled. Second, there are multiple approaches in the literature. Third, tacit knowledge, by definition, cannot be fully laid down as a set of rules.

We build a formal framework for explainable AI, by considering, as a first principle, that outcome explanations blend the input and the prediction. Then, we link representations, which we typically take as intermediate activations of neural network models, to these explanations. The interrelationships between the explanations, the models, and the representations are potent enough to lead to several theoretical results.

One result is that desirable links between explanations and layers of a neural network cannot be specific to this layer, but also manifest to other layers. Another is that a valid explanation must also be complete. A third result studies explainability in the context of a concrete explanation of the predictions of multiclass neural networks. Lastly, we show results on the union and intersection of explanations.

ACKNOWLEDGMENTS

This project has received funding from the European Research Council (ERC) under the European Union's Horizon 2020 research and innovation programme (grant ERC CoG 725974). The contribution of Tomer Galanti is part of a Ph.D. thesis research conducted at Tel Aviv University.

REFERENCES

[1] David Alvarez Melis and Tommi Jaakkola. 2018. Towards Robust Interpretability with Self-Explaining Neural Networks. In *Advances in Neural Information Processing Systems 31*, S. Bengio, H. Wallach, H. Larochelle, K. Grauman, N. Cesa-Bianchi, and R. Garnett (Eds.). Curran Associates, Inc., 7775–7784. http://papers.nips.cc/paper/8003-towards-robust-interpretability-with-self-explaining-neural-networks.pdf
[2] Thomas M. Cover and Joy A. Thomas. 2006. *Elements of Information Theory (Wiley Series in Telecommunications and Signal Processing)*. Wiley-Interscience, New York, NY, USA.
[3] Jack D'Aurizio. 2015. An upper bound of binary entropy. https://math.stackexchange.com/users/44121/jack-daurizio.
[4] Meir Feder and Neri Merhav. 1994. Relations between entropy and error probability. *IEEE Trans. Information Theory* 40 (1994), 259–266.
[5] Riccardo Guidotti, Anna Monreale, Salvatore Ruggieri, Franco Turini, Fosca Giannotti, and Dino Pedreschi. 2018. A Survey of Methods for Explaining Black Box Models. *ACM Comput. Surv.* 51, 5, Article 93 (Aug. 2018), 42 pages. https://doi.org/10.1145/3236009
[6] Lisa Anne Hendricks, Zeynep Akata, Marcus Rohrbach, Jeff Donahue, Bernt Schiele, and Trevor Darrell. 2016. Generating visual explanations. In *European Conference on Computer Vision*. Springer-Verlag, 3–19.
[7] Sasha Kozachinski. 2018. An upper bound on the difference between two similar mutual informations. https://math.stackexchange.com/questions/2964570/a-bound-on-ixy-in-terms-of-ixz-for-y-and-z-that-are-similar/2964661.
[8] O. Regev. 2013. Entropy-based bounds on dimension reduction in L^1. *Israeli Journal of Mathematics* 195 (2013), 825–832. https://doi.org/10.1007/s11856-012-0137-6
[9] Marco Tulio Ribeiro, Sameer Singh, and Carlos Guestrin. 2016. Why should I trust you?: Explaining the predictions of any classifier. In *Proceedings of the 22nd ACM SIGKDD international conference on knowledge discovery and data mining*. ACM, 1135–1144.
[10] Matthew D Zeiler and Rob Fergus. 2014. Visualizing and understanding convolutional networks. In *European conference on computer vision*. Springer, Cham, 818–833.

A USEFUL LEMMAS

For completeness, we provide some useful lemmas that are being employed in the proofs on the theorems in our paper.

Lemma A.1. *Let X and Y be two random variables. Assume that there is a function F, such that $\mathbb{P}[F(Y) = X] \geq q \geq 1/2$. Then, $I(X;Y) \geq qH(X) - H(q)$.*

Proof. The lemma is a modification of Claim 2.1 in [8].

Lemma A.2. *Let X, Y and Z be three random variables, where Y and Z are binary. We have:*

$$|I(X;Y) - I(X;Z)| \leq H(\mathbb{P}[Y \neq Z]) \tag{36}$$

Proof. See. [7].

Lemma A.3. *Let $p \in [0,1]$. Then,*

$$H(p) \leq 2\sqrt{p(1-p)} \tag{37}$$

Proof. See [3].

Lemma A.4. *Let X and Y be two discrete random variables taking values from $\mathcal{S}_1$ and $\mathcal{S}_2$ (resp.). Then, there is a function $t : \mathcal{S}_2 \to \mathcal{S}_2$, such that:*

$$\mathbb{P}_{X,Y}[X = t(Y)] \leq 1 - 2^{I(X;Y)-H(X)} \tag{38}$$

Proof. See [4].

Lemma A.5 (Intersection Equivalence). *Let $x \sim D$ and $f_1 : \mathcal{X} \to \mathcal{X}_1$ and $f_2 : \mathcal{X} \to \mathcal{X}_2$ are two functions. In addition, let $u_1(x)$ and $u_2(x)$ be two ϵ-intersections of $f_1(x)$ and $f_2(x)$, i.e., there are two pairs of invertible functions $r_1^i : \mathcal{X}_1 \to \mathcal{V}_1$ and $r_2^i : \mathcal{X}_2 \to \mathcal{V}_2$, such that, $r_1^i(f_1(x)) = (e_1^i(x), u_i(x))$ and $r_2^i(f_2(x)) = (e_2^i(x), u_i(x))$, where, $I(e_j^i(x); f_k(x)) \leq \epsilon$ (for any $i \in \{1,2\}$ and $k \neq j \in \{1,2\}$). Then,* *there are functions s_1, s_2 and d_1, d_2, such that, for all $i \neq j \in \{1,2\}$, we have:*

$$\mathbb{E}_{x\sim D}[\ell(s_i(u_i(x)), u_j(x))] \leq 1 - 2^{-\epsilon} \quad (39)$$

and also,

$$\mathbb{E}_{x\sim D}[\ell(d_i(e_1^i(x)), e_1^j(x))] \leq 1 - 2^{-\epsilon} \quad (40)$$

In particular, if $\epsilon = 0$, $s_1(u_1(x)) = u_2(x)$, s_1 is invertible, such that $s_1^{-1} = s_2$ and $d_1(e_1^1(x)) = e_1^2(x)$, d_1 is invertible and $d_1^{-1} = d_2$.

Proof. First, we would like to show that $I(e_1^1(x); u_2(x)) \leq \epsilon$. Assume by contradiction that this is not the case. We consider that, $u_2(x)$ can be represented as a function of $f_2(x)$, since $u_2(x)$ consists of the last coordinate of $r_2^2(f_2(x))$. Therefore, since r_2^2 is invertible,

$$I(e_1^1(x); f_2(x)) = I(e_1^1(x); r_2^2(f_2(x))) \geq I(e_1^1(x); u_2(x)) > \epsilon \quad (41)$$

In contradiction to the assumption that $I(e_1^1(x); f_2(x)) \leq \epsilon$. By the same argument, we also have, $I(e_1^1(x); u_1(x)) \leq \epsilon$. By the chain rule property of mutual information,

$$\begin{aligned} I(e_1^1(x), u_1(x); u_2(x)) =& I(u_1(x); u_2(x)) + I(e_1^1(x); u_2(x)|u_1(x)) \\ \leq& I(u_1(x); u_2(x)) + I(e_1^1(x); u_2(x)) \end{aligned} \quad (42)$$

Therefore, since r_1^1 and r_1^2 are invertible functions,

$$\begin{aligned} I(u_1(x); u_2(x)) \geq& I(e_1^1(x), u_1(x); u_2(x)) - I(e_1^1(x); u_2(x)) \\ \geq& I(e_1^1(x), u_1(x); u_2(x)) - \epsilon \\ =& I(r_1^1(e_1^1(x), u_1(x)); u_2(x)) - \epsilon \\ =& I(f_1(x); u_2(x)) - \epsilon \\ =& I(r_1^2(f_1(x)); u_2(x)) - \epsilon \\ =& I(e_1^2(x), u_2(x); u_2(x)) - \epsilon \\ \geq& I(u_2(x); u_2(x)) - \epsilon \\ =& H(u_2(x)) - \epsilon \end{aligned} \quad (43)$$

Again, by the chain rule property of mutual information,

$$\begin{aligned} I(e_1^1(x), u_1(x); e_1^2(x)) =& I(e_1^1(x); e_1^2(x)) + I(e_1^2(x); u_1(x)|e_1^1(x)) \\ \leq& I(e_1^2(x); e_1^1(x)) + I(e_1^1(x); u_1(x)) \end{aligned} \quad (44)$$

Therefore, since r_1^1 and r_1^2 are invertible functions,

$$\begin{aligned} I(e_1^1(x); e_1^2(x)) \geq& I(e_1^1(x), u_1(x); e_1^2(x)) - I(e_1^1(x); u_1(x)) \\ \geq& I(e_1^1(x), u_1(x); e_1^2(x)) - \epsilon \\ =& I(r_1^1(e_1^1(x), u_1(x)); e_1^2(x)) - \epsilon \\ =& I(f_1(x); e_1^2(x)) - \epsilon \\ =& I(r_1^2(f_1(x)); e_1^2(x)) - \epsilon \\ =& I(e_1^2(x), u_2(x); e_1^2(x)) - \epsilon \\ \geq& I(e_1^2(x); e_1^2(x)) - \epsilon \\ =& H(e_1^2(x)) - \epsilon \end{aligned} \quad (45)$$

Thus, we conclude that $I(u_1(x); u_2(x)) \geq H(u_2(x)) - \epsilon$ and that $I(e_1^1(x); e_1^2(x)) \geq H(e_1^2(x)) - \epsilon$. In a similar manner, we can show the other directions as well, $I(u_1(x); u_2(x)) \geq H(u_1(x)) - \epsilon$ and $I(e_1^1(x); e_1^2(x)) \geq H(e_1^1(x)) - \epsilon$. Therefore, by Lem. A.4 in the Appendix, there are functions s_1, s_2 and d_1, d_2, such that, for all $i \neq j \in \{1,2\}$, we have:

$$\begin{aligned} \mathbb{E}_{x\sim D}[\ell(s_i(u_i(x)), u_j(x))] =& \mathbb{P}_{u_1(x), u_2(x)}[s_i(u_i(x)) = u_j(x)] \\ \leq& 1 - 2^{I(u_1(x);u_2(x)) - H(u_j(x))} \\ \leq& 1 - 2^{H(u_j(x)) - \epsilon - H(u_j(x))} = 1 - 2^{-\epsilon} \end{aligned} \quad (46)$$

and also,

$$\mathbb{E}_{x\sim D}[\ell(d_i(e_1^i(x)), e_1^j(x))] \leq 1 - 2^{-\epsilon} \quad (47)$$

Finally, if $\epsilon = 0$, for every $x \in \mathcal{X}$, we have: $s_1(u_1(x)) = u_2(x)$, $s_2(u_2(x)) = u_1(x)$, $d_1(e_1^1(x)) = e_1^1(x)$ and $d_2(e_1^2(x)) = e_1^2(x)$. Therefore, $s_1^{-1} = s_2$ and $d_1^{-1} = d_2$. □

Costs and Benefits of Fair Representation Learning

Daniel McNamara
Australian National University and CSIRO Data61
Canberra, ACT, Australia
dpmcna@gmail.com

Cheng Soon Ong
Australian National University and CSIRO Data61
Canberra, ACT, Australia
chengsoon.ong@anu.edu.au

Robert C. Williamson
Australian National University and CSIRO Data61
Canberra, ACT, Australia
bob.williamson@anu.edu.au

ABSTRACT

Machine learning algorithms are increasingly used to make or support important decisions about people's lives. This has led to interest in the problem of fair classification, which involves learning to make decisions that are non-discriminatory with respect to a sensitive variable such as race or gender. Several methods have been proposed to solve this problem, including fair representation learning, which cleans the input data used by the algorithm to remove information about the sensitive variable. We show that using fair representation learning as an intermediate step in fair classification incurs a cost compared to directly solving the problem, which we refer to as the *cost of mistrust*. We show that fair representation learning in fact addresses a different problem, which is of interest when the data user is not trusted to access the sensitive variable. We quantify the benefits of fair representation learning, by showing that any subsequent use of the cleaned data will not be too unfair. The benefits we identify result from restricting the decisions of adversarial data users, while the costs are due to applying those same restrictions to other data users.

CCS CONCEPTS

• **Computing methodologies** → **Learning latent representations**; *Machine learning*; • **Social and professional topics** → *Socio-technical systems*; • **Theory of computation** → *Machine learning theory*.

KEYWORDS

fairness; representation learning; machine learning

ACM Reference Format:

Daniel McNamara, Cheng Soon Ong, and Robert C. Williamson. 2019. Costs and Benefits of Fair Representation Learning. In *AAAI/ACM Conference on AI, Ethics, and Society (AIES '19), January 27–28, 2019, Honolulu, HI, USA.* ACM, New York, NY, USA, 8 pages. https://doi.org/10.1145/3306618.3317964

1 INTRODUCTION

Machine learning algorithms are used to make or support decisions in a wide variety of contexts including financial and judicial risk assessments, applicant screening for employment, and online ad selection. Concerns about the fairness of these algorithms have arisen as a result [1, 3, 8, 21]. Decisions made by machine learning algorithms typically cannot be controlled or interpreted as straightforwardly as those made by rule-based systems. Furthermore, artefacts of previous discrimination in an algorithm's training data may affect its decisions. Researchers have responded by developing techniques to incorporate fairness into the design of machine learning algorithms [2, 22, 29]. While these techniques often focus on achieving *group fairness* – i.e. not discriminating against particular groups – another important consideration is *individual fairness* – i.e. giving similar treatment to individuals who are similar [10].

The problem of fair classification involves making a *decision* (e.g. whether to grant a loan) based on an *input* (e.g. individual financial and demographic information) which accurately predicts a *target* of interest (e.g. loan default), while at the same time avoiding discrimination on the basis of an individual's group membership (e.g. race, gender) encoded in a *sensitive* variable. The data user is trusted to access the sensitive variable in training and is responsible for making decisions that appropriately consider accuracy and fairness.

In contrast (see Figure 1), the problem of fair representation learning involves producing a *cleaned* version of the input which remains useful for predicting the target, but suppresses information which could be used to discriminate based on the sensitive variable. We now assume the data user is not trusted to access the sensitive variable in training, which may be appropriate if the data user could be either *adversarial*, i.e. interested in being unfair, or *indifferent*, i.e. interested only in target accuracy [18]. This problem setting involves three parties: a *data producer* who cleans the input data, a *data user* who makes decisions from the data, and a *data regulator* who oversees fair use of the data. For example, when deciding whether to give an individual a loan, the data producer might be a credit bureau, the data user a bank and the data regulator a government authority. Even within an organization, this separation of concerns has the advantage of providing checks and balances.

1.1 Contributions of This Paper

This paper offers contributions that are have both scientific and policy significance, and are technically novel.

Scientific significance: A plethora of methods use fair representation learning [5, 12, 14, 16–18, 27] as a *technique* for fair classification. Recent work [19] has solved in analytical form a canonical version of the fair classification problem. Is fair representation learning then to be relegated to a sub-optimal technique for a problem better solved through other means? Developing more fair representation learning techniques does not address this question. Instead, we show that fair representation learning in fact solves a different *problem* – i.e. how to guarantee that decisions made by an untrusted data user can be accurate but will not be unfair – and quantify the costs and benefits of such representations in terms of fairness and

AIES '19, January 27–28, 2019, Honolulu, HI, USA

ACM ISBN 978-1-4503-6324-2/19/01...$15.00
https://doi.org/10.1145/3306618.3317964

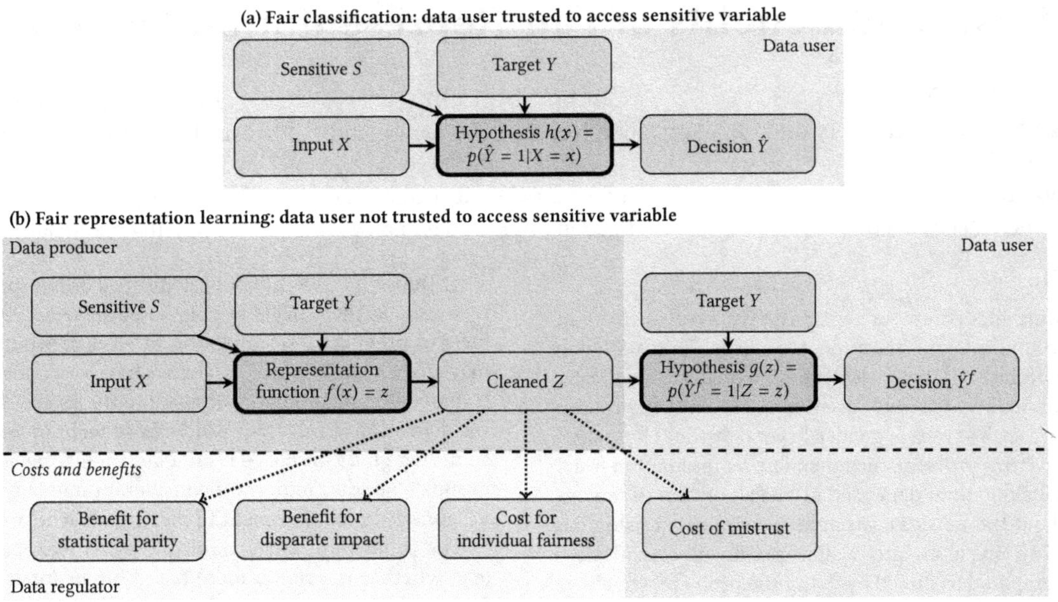

Figure 1: Summary of (a) fair classification and (b) fair representation learning, showing train time data processing for both, and costs and benefits of (b).

utility. This represents a progression in our scientific understanding, given that this problem had never previously been formally posed or analyzed.

Policy significance: Our approach makes possible a governance model involving a separation of concerns between a data producer, data user and data regulator (previous work assumes a single trusted data user). The model enables a regulator to guarantee fairness even if the data user is adversarial. This is an advance in the regulation of algorithmic fairness, given that no alternatives currently exist in the realistic setting where a data user is not trusted to be fair.

Novel technical results: We formalize the problem of fair representation learning as distinct from fair classification. By stating the data producer's optimization problem in (5) and showing that a proxy problem can be solved without access to the target variable (Theorem 1), we derive a principled way to select a fair representation learning objective function (this is heuristic in prior work).

We present a novel quantification of the costs of using a given representation (Section 4), a topic which had not previously been investigated. We identify costs both in terms of the accuracy-fairness trade-off (i.e. the *cost of mistrust* given in closed form in Theorem 2 and bounded without requiring access to the target variable in Theorem 3), and in terms of individual fairness (Theorem 4).

We present novel guarantees of the benefits of a given representation (Section 5). We do this for two common measures of fairness: *statistical parity* (Theorem 5) and *disparate impact* (Theorem 6), by computing the unfairness of an optimal adversary. Conditioning on the target variable, our analysis can be also be used to guarantee quantified versions of two other well-known fairness definitions: *equality of opportunity* and *equalized odds*. We provide a proof idea in the main paper for each result, while Appendix A provides complete proofs.

2 BACKGROUND

We provide a brief summary of relevant work on parity-based definitions of fairness, fair classification, and fair representation learning.

Parity measures of quantitative fairness compare an algorithm's average decisions for different groups. For example, we may take the difference between groups – known as *statistical parity* [6, 10] – or the ratio between groups – known as *disparate impact* [14, 23]. We may wish to compute a parity measure only on a population subset. Constructing subsets by conditioning on particular values of the target variable yields variants [15] such as *equality of opportunity* (conditioning only on the positive class) and *equalized odds* (conditioning separately on the positive and negative classes).[1] However, when the training data labels are themselves affected by discrimination, conditioning on the target variable may not be suitable [25]. If the population subset consists of individuals who are similar according to some metric, we have *individual fairness*, also known as avoiding *disparate treatment* [10, 20].

Methods for fair classification can be divided into *pre-processing* – i.e. fair representation learning – which modifies the data that the algorithm learns from [27]; *in-processing*, which modifies the algorithm's objective function to incorporate a fairness constraint or penalty [4, 9, 11, 19, 25, 26]; and *post-processing*, which modifies the predictions produced by the algorithm [15].

Several fair representation learning techniques have been proposed. One such approach is to design the cleaned variable Z such that the distributions of Z conditioned on different values of the sensitive variable S are similar [14, 16]. In addition to this requirement, the pre-processing procedure may optimize the independence of Z

[1] Satisfying equalized odds has also previously been referred to as avoiding *disparate mistreatment* [25].

and S [17]. Adversarial approaches [5, 12, 18] use a neural network to learn a representation function such that an adversary network cannot accurately predict the sensitive variable from the cleaned data. A problem variant, where the target is also modified and the input is discrete, has been formulated as a convex optimization problem [7].

What existing approaches typically do not offer (Theorem 4.1 from Feldman et al. 2015 is an exception) is a guarantee that all uses of the cleaned data will be fair, or a quantification of the costs of the cleaning process. We seek to provide a stronger theoretical foundation for fair representation learning. This objective is similar in spirit to that of privacy aware learning, which is concerned with the mathematical trade-off between the privacy and utility of data [24]. We also show that fair representation learning in fact addresses a problem that is distinct from fair classification, which is of interest when the data user is not trusted to access the sensitive variable.

3 FAIR CLASSIFICATION VS FAIR REPRESENTATION LEARNING

We introduce and compare the problems of fair classification and fair representation learning. This formal comparison is itself novel and is necessary for our subsequent analysis of the costs and benefits of fair representation learning.

3.1 Fair Classification

In fair classification (Figure 1(a)), the data user trains on samples of input variable X, target variable Y and sensitive variable S. The samples are drawn from a distribution over $\mathcal{X} \times \mathcal{Y} \times \mathcal{S}$, where $\mathcal{X}$ is the set of possible inputs, $\mathcal{Y}$ is the set of possible labels and $\mathcal{S}$ is the set of possible sensitive variable values. We focus on the setting where $\mathcal{Y} \in \{0, 1\}$, corresponding to binary classification, and $\mathcal{S} \in \{0, 1\}$, corresponding to some common sensitive variable examples such as gender or race. Let $\pi_Y := p(Y = 1)$ and $\pi_S := p(S = 1)$ be prior probabilities, and $\eta_Y(x) := p(Y = 1|X = x)$ and $\eta_S(x) := p(S = 1|X = x)$ be conditional probabilities, for the positive classes of Y and S respectively.

The data user learns a stochastic hypothesis $h : \mathcal{X} \to [0, 1]$ which is used to construct decision variable $\hat{Y} \in \{0, 1\}$, where $h(x) := p(\hat{Y} = 1|X = x)$. Let $\mu_{XYS\hat{Y}}$ be the joint distribution of the input, target, sensitive and decision variables.

At test time, the data user makes a decision using a sample of X, which may contain information about S. The quality of an hypothesis h in predicting Y can be measured by a risk $R_Y : [0, 1]^{\mathcal{X}} \to [0, 1]$, where we prefer hypotheses with a small value of $R_Y(h)$. A common choice is the cost-sensitive risk.

Definition 1 (Cost-sensitive risk [13, 19, 28]). *The cost-sensitive risk of hypothesis h with respect to Y is*

$$R_Y(h) := \pi_Y(1 - c_Y)p(\hat{Y} = 0|Y = 1) + (1 - \pi_Y)c_Y p(\hat{Y} = 1|Y = 0)$$

where $c_Y \in [0, 1]$, $p(\hat{Y} = 0|Y = 1)$ is known as the false negative rate *and $p(\hat{Y} = 1|Y = 0)$ as the* false positive rate.

We also wish to ensure that the hypothesis we learn is fair. Two common fairness measures are statistical parity and disparate impact, which compare outcomes for different sensitive variable groups using their difference and ratio respectively. In the analysis that follows we focus on the case where statistical parity and disparate impact are computed on the joint distribution $\mu_{XYS\hat{Y}}$. However, computing these measures only on part of the distribution yields other variants of interest, such as conditioning on $Y = 1$ for quantified versions of equality of opportunity, or conditioning separately on $Y = 1$ and $Y = 0$ for quantified versions of equalized odds.

Definition 2 (Statistical parity [6, 10]). *The statistical parity of an hypothesis h is*

$$SP(h) := p(\hat{Y} = 1|S = 1) - p(\hat{Y} = 1|S = 0).$$

Definition 3 (Disparate impact [14, 23]). *The disparate impact of an hypothesis h is*

$$DI(h) := \frac{p(\hat{Y} = 1|S = 0)}{p(\hat{Y} = 1|S = 1)}.$$

Notice that $SP(h) \in [-1, 1]$, with equality of outcome corresponding to 0, while $DI(h) \in [0, \infty)$, with equality of outcome corresponding to 1. In both cases we want a value that is neither too low nor too high. It has been shown that this is equivalent to requiring that h and the 'anti-classifier' $1 - h$ both have values that are not too low (see Appendix C of [19]).

The fair classification problem then takes the form, for some $R_{\text{fair}} \in \{SP, DI\}$:

$$\min_{h \in H} R_Y(h) \text{ subject to } \min[R_{\text{fair}}(h), R_{\text{fair}}(1 - h)] \geq \tau, \quad (1)$$

where $H := [0, 1]^{\mathcal{X}}$ and τ is a constant measuring the required level of fairness. For DI, $\tau \in [0, \infty)$, while for SP, $\tau \in [-1, 0]$ since $SP(1 - h) = -SP(h)$.

It has been shown that a constraint on SP or DI of the type in (1) is equivalent to a constraint on a cost sensitive risk with respect to S (see Lemmas 1 and 2 of [19]). Using Definition 1, this cost sensitive risk is written as:

$$R_S(h) := \pi_S(1-c_S)p(\hat{Y} = 0|S = 1)+(1-\pi_S)c_S p(\hat{Y} = 1|S = 0), \quad (2)$$

where $c_S \in [0, 1]$.

It is more convenient to work with an unconstrained variant of the fair classification problem:

$$\min_{h \in H}[R_Y(h) - \lambda R_S(h)], \quad (3)$$

where λ is a constant (not necessarily non-negative) controlling the trade-off between accuracy with respect to Y and fairness with respect to S. It has been shown [19] that for some choice of λ, some solution to (3) is also a solution to (1).

Definition 4 (Optimal fair classification). *Let the combined risk*

$$R_{YS}(h) := R_Y(h) - \lambda R_S(h).$$

Let $R_{YS}(h^*)$ be the value of (3) *and h^* be a corresponding hypothesis.*

Subsequently we will compare optimal fair classification to the case where we instead use fair representation learning as an intermediate step in fair classification.

3.2 Fair Representation Learning

In fair representation learning (Figure 1(b)), the data producer trains on samples of X, S and Y (we also examine the case where the data producer does not access Y), and learns the representation function $f : \mathcal{X} \to \mathcal{Z}$, where $\mathcal{Z}$ is the set of possible cleaned variable values. The data producer samples X and applies f to each sample to produce cleaned variable $Z := f(X)$. The data producer learns f so that Z is still useful for predicting Y but suppresses information about S.

Let $\eta^f_Y(z) := p(Y = 1|Z = z)$ and $\eta^f_S(z) := p(S = 1|Z = z)$ be conditional probabilities of the positive classes of Y and S induced by f. The data user trains on samples of Z and Y and learns a stochastic hypothesis $g : \mathcal{Z} \to [0, 1]$, which is used to construct modified decision variable $\hat{Y}^f \in \{0, 1\}$ where $g(z) := p(\hat{Y}^f = 1|Z = z)$. At test time, the data producer samples X and passes it through f to produce a sample of Z, from which the data user makes a decision.

When the data user is not trusted, we are interested in constraining how unfair an *adversarial* user can be with the cleaned data. As in the fair classification case, this is equivalent to a constraint on an adversary's cost-sensitive risk with respect to S. We are also interested in ensuring that the cleaned data is still useful for predicting the target. We are therefore interested in the following problem:

$$\min_{f \in F} R_Y(g^*_Y \circ f) \text{ subject to } R_S(g^*_S \circ f) \geq \tau, \tag{4}$$

where τ is a constant measuring the required level of fairness, $\circ$ is function composition, $g^*_Y \in \arg\min_{g \in G} R_Y(g \circ f)$ is an optimal indifferent user of the cleaned data, $g^*_S \in \arg\min_{g \in G} R_S(g \circ f)$ is an optimal adversary using the cleaned data, $G := [0, 1]^{\mathcal{Z}}$ and $F := \mathcal{Z}^{\mathcal{X}}$.

It is more convenient to work with the following unconstrained problem variant:

$$\min_{f \in F} [R_Y(g^*_Y \circ f) - \lambda R_S(g^*_S \circ f)]. \tag{5}$$

Using the form of the minimum cost-sensitive risk from [28], we may express the terms in (5) as follows:

$$R_Y(g^*_Y \circ f) = \mathbb{E}_Z[\min((1 - c_Y)\eta^f_Y(Z), c_Y(1 - \eta^f_Y(Z)))] \tag{6}$$

$$R_S(g^*_S \circ f) = \mathbb{E}_Z[\min((1 - c_S)\eta^f_S(Z), c_S(1 - \eta^f_S(Z)))]. \tag{7}$$

Adversarial neural networks have previously been used to estimate g^*_Y and g^*_S [5, 12, 18]. We observe that (6) and (7) simplify the fair representation learning cost function (5) by removing the two inner minimizations. Of course, there remains the task of estimating the underlying distribution and computing the outer minimization.

We focus on the case where the data producer learns a representation without using the target variable. This allows a single fair representation to be learned that can be used for multiple tasks. It also covers the situation where the data producer does not have access to the target variable. For example, Y contains commercially confidential information (e.g. defaults on a specific type of loan) known to the data user (e.g. a bank) but not the data producer (e.g. a credit bureau). Furthermore, we focus on the case $\mathcal{Z} = \mathcal{X}$ is a Euclidean space, which facilitates our analysis and covers many practical applications. In this case, we define *average reconstruction error* and show its use as a proxy for task performance.

Definition 5 (Average reconstruction error). *Suppose that $\mathcal{Z} = \mathcal{X}$ is a Euclidean space. Let $\mathbb{E}_X\|X - f(X)\|_2$ be the average reconstruction error of f with respect to X, where $\|\cdot\|_2$ is the Euclidean vector norm.*

Assuming the data producer does not access the target variable, we propose the following variant of the fair representation learning problem:

$$\min_{f \in F} [\mathbb{E}_X\|X - f(X)\|_2 - \lambda R_S(g^*_S \circ f)]. \tag{8}$$

We relate (8) and (5) as follows. This result allows us to select a principled objective function for the data producer.

Theorem 1 (Fair representation learning without accessing target variable). *Suppose that $\mathcal{Z} = \mathcal{X}$ and we have the Lipschitz condition that for some non-negative constant l_Y*

$$\forall x, x' \in \mathcal{X}, |\eta_Y(x) - \eta_Y(x')| \leq l_Y\|x - x'\|_2. \tag{9}$$

Then any $f \in F$ minimizing

$$\mathbb{E}_X\|X - f(X)\|_2 - \lambda R_S(g^*_S \circ f)$$

also minimizes an upper bound on

$$R_Y(g^*_Y \circ f) - l_Y \lambda R_S(g^*_S \circ f).$$

Proof idea. We upper bound $R_Y(g^*_Y \circ f) - l_Y \lambda R_S(g^*_S \circ f)$ by re-expressing the risks using Lemma 9 from [19], and making use of the Lipschitz condition. We then observe that the f minimizing this upper bound also minimizes $\mathbb{E}_X\|X - f(X)\|_2 - \lambda R_S(g^*_S \circ f)$. See Appendix A.1 for complete proof. □

4 COSTS OF FAIR REPRESENTATION LEARNING

We identify and quantify two costs of using fair representation learning rather than entrusting a single trusted data user to make decisions. These costs are incurred by decision-makers, as well as individuals about whom decisions are made. The first cost, which we refer to as the *cost of mistrust*, is the difference in the optimal fairness-accuracy trade-off available with the cleaned data produced by a representation function f compared to the original input. This cost is of interest to the data user – as well as potentially the data regulator. The second cost quantifies the extent to which individual fairness is violated by using a representation function f, which is primarily of interest to the data regulator. We show that both of these costs can be estimated by a data producer without accessing the target variable.

4.1 Cost of Mistrust

Suppose that after cleaning the data with the representation function f, we solve the following fair classification problem, which is equivalent to (3) but using the cleaned data.

$$\min_{g \in G} [R_Y(g \circ f) - \lambda R_S(g \circ f)] \tag{10}$$

Definition 6 (Cost of mistrust). *Let g^* and h^* be hypotheses minimizing (10) and (3) respectively, where the value of λ is the same in both equations. The cost of mistrust for a representation function f is defined as*

$$R_{YS}(g^* \circ f) - R_{YS}(h^*).$$

The cost of mistrust is non-negative because f restricts the hypothesis class to a subset of H. If $\lambda = 0$ in (10) and (3), f may incur a cost for the target accuracy of the indifferent user, which seems unsurprising. However, for general λ we see that f may also incur a cost for fair classification. Without access to the sensitive variable S the data user has no way to estimate $R_S(g \circ f)$ in (10). However, even if they could somehow guess this quantity, f may create a suboptimal trade-off between fairness and accuracy compared to the trade-off available to a trusted data user using the original input.

We now show in Theorem 2 that we can express the cost of mistrust in analytical form. In our result, we use the expressions

$$h^*(x) = \mathbf{1}(\eta_Y(x) - c_Y \geq \lambda(\eta_S(x) - c_S)) \tag{11}$$

and

$$g^*(z) = \mathbf{1}(\eta^f_Y(z) - c_Y \geq \lambda(\eta^f_S(z) - c_S)), \tag{12}$$

obtained from Proposition 4 of [19].

Theorem 2 (Analytical form of cost of mistrust). *The cost of mistrust may be expressed as*

$$\begin{aligned} R_{YS}(g^* \circ f) - R_{YS}(h^*) = \\ \mathbb{E}_X[\min(\eta^f_Y(f(X)) - c_Y, \lambda(\eta^f_S(f(X)) - c_S)) \\ - \min(\eta_Y(X) - c_Y, \lambda(\eta_S(X) - c_S))]. \end{aligned} \tag{13}$$

The cost of mistrust may be decomposed into accuracy and fairness differences, where the accuracy difference is

$$\begin{aligned} R_Y(g^* \circ f) - R_Y(h^*) = \\ \mathbb{E}_X[h^*(X)(\eta_Y(X) - c_Y) - g^*(f(X))(\eta^f_Y(f(X)) - c_Y)], \end{aligned} \tag{14}$$

and the fairness difference is

$$\begin{aligned} R_S(g^* \circ f) - R_S(h^*) = \\ \mathbb{E}_X[h^*(X)(\eta_S(X) - c_S) - g^*(f(X))(\eta^f_S(f(X)) - c_S)], \end{aligned} \tag{15}$$

which are combined in the overall cost of mistrust

$$R_{YS}(g^* \circ f) - R_{YS}(h^*) = R_Y(g^* \circ f) - R_Y(h^*) - \lambda(R_S(g^* \circ f) - R_S(h^*)).$$

Proof idea. Apply Lemma 9 of [19] to express each of $R_Y(g^* \circ f)$, $R_Y(h^*)$, $R_S(g^* \circ f)$ and $R_S(h^*)$. Combining these yields a compact expression for $R_{YS}(g^* \circ f) - R_{YS}(h^*)$. See Appendix A.2 for complete proof. □

The expression (13) for the cost of mistrust allows us to measure the quality of the fairness-accuracy trade-off available using f compared to using the original input. The decomposition reveals that the signs of the accuracy and fairness differences may vary. However, since the cost of mistrust is non-negative, for a fixed value of R_S we incur a value of R_Y that is at least as large using f as with the original input.

For intuition about the expression (13) for the cost of mistrust, consider a point $z \in \mathcal{Z}$ and its preimage $\mathcal{X}_z := \{x \in \mathcal{X} | f(x) = z\}$. If all $x \in \mathcal{X}_z$ have the same value of $\mathbf{1}(\eta_Y(x) - c_Y \geq \lambda(\eta_S(x) - c_S))$, then the expectation conditioned on $x \in \mathcal{X}_z$ will be zero, otherwise it will be positive. Hence the cost of mistrust will be small when points mapped to the same value of z tend to have the same value of $\mathbf{1}(\eta_Y(x) - c_Y \geq \lambda(\eta_S(x) - c_S))$.

We are interested in situations where the data producer can guarantee that the cost of mistrust is small without accessing Y. When $\mathcal{Z} = \mathcal{X}$ and the conditional distributions $\eta_Y(x)$ and $\eta_S(x)$ are smooth, the cost of mistrust can be upper bounded in terms of average reconstruction error. This result, shown in Theorem 3, allows the data producer to bound the cost of mistrust using only X and Z.

Theorem 3 (Upper bound on cost of mistrust with smooth conditional distributions). *Suppose $\mathcal{Z} = \mathcal{X}$ is a Euclidean space and we have the Lipschitz conditions that for some non-negative constants l_Y and l_S*

$$\forall x, x' \in \mathcal{X}, |\eta_Y(x) - \eta_Y(x')| \leq l_Y \|x - x'\|_2 \tag{16}$$

and

$$\forall x, x' \in \mathcal{X}, |\eta_S(x) - \eta_S(x')| \leq l_S \|x - x'\|_2. \tag{17}$$

Then

$$R_{YS}(g^* \circ f) - R_{YS}(h^*) \leq (l_Y + \lambda l_S)\mathbb{E}_X \|X - f(X)\|_2.$$

Proof idea. We observe that $R_{YS}(h^* \circ f)$ is an upper bound on $R_{YS}(g^* \circ f)$. We use Lemma 9 of [19] to re-express R_{YS}. We then use the Lipschitz conditions to upper bound $R_{YS}(h^* \circ f) - R_{YS}(h^*)$. See Appendix A.3 for complete proof. □

4.2 Cost for Individual Fairness

We investigate the cost of using a given representation in terms of *individual fairness* [10]. This notion requires that similar decisions should be made for similar individuals, i.e. decisions are smooth. It is possible that a representation function maps points that are nearby in the input space to points that are distant from each other in the representation space. Therefore, smooth hypotheses may not be individually fair when applied to the cleaned data. We wish to quantify this cost for individual fairness by upper bounding the individual unfairness of an arbitrary smooth hypothesis applied to the cleaned data. We show that it is possible for a data user to provide this kind of certification to a data regulator by inspecting Z and X.

First, we restate a previous definition of individual fairness.

Definition 7 (Individual fairness [10]). *Let D and d be sub-additive functions. Hypothesis h is D, d−individually fair if*

$$\forall x, x' \in \mathcal{X}, D(h(x), h(x')) \leq d(x, x').$$

We also give a novel quantitative notion of individual *unfairness* by measuring the probability that a pair of randomly selected individuals will be treated unfairly according to Definition 7.

Definition 8 (Individual unfairness). *Hypothesis h has D, d− individual unfairness with respect to X defined as*

$$IU_{D,d}(h) := p(D(h(x), h(x')) > d(x, x')),$$

where x and x' are independent random samples of X.

In order to bound the level of individual unfairness induced by a representation, we introduce the following definition.

Definition 9 (Large reconstruction error rate). *Suppose $\mathcal{Z} = \mathcal{X}$. Let ϵ be a non-negative constant. Let $p(d(X, f(X)) > \epsilon)$ be the large reconstruction error rate of f.*

In Theorem 4 we show that if the large reconstruction error rate is small, then any hypothesis that is smooth (i.e. individually fair when applied to the original input) will not be too individually unfair when applied to the cleaned data. We observe that there is a tension between guaranteeing group fairness, which involves removing information to protect an adversary from inferring the sensitive variable, and individual fairness, which requires preserving information from the original input.

THEOREM 4 (UPPER BOUND ON INDIVIDUAL UNFAIRNESS). *Suppose $\mathcal{Z} = \mathcal{X}$. Let*

$$d_\epsilon(x, x') := d(x, x') + 2\epsilon$$

and let h be any individually fair hypothesis. Then the D, d_ϵ−individual unfairness of $h \circ f$ is upper bounded as follows:

$$IU_{D,d_\epsilon}(h \circ f) \leq 2p(d(X, f(X)) > \epsilon).$$

PROOF IDEA. Let $\delta := p(d(X, f(X)) > \epsilon)$. For randomly drawn x and x', $d(x, f(x)) \leq \epsilon$ and $d(x', f(x')) \leq \epsilon$ with probability at least $1 - 2\delta$ by the union bound. If these statements hold, by the triangle inequality $D(h(f(x)), h(f(x')) \leq d(x, x') + 2\epsilon$. See Appendix A.4 for complete proof. □

5 BENEFITS OF FAIR REPRESENTATION LEARNING

We quantify the benefits of some representation function f by measuring the discrimination achieved by an optimal adversary using Z, the representation variable induced by f. We show that a data producer can do this for both statistical parity and disparate impact. We can compute these two quantities directly for a given f, so that unlike in the optimization problems we considered earlier there is no need to use a cost-sensitive risk. The quantities we obtain can be given to a data regulator to certify that any use of the cleaned data will not be too unfair. If the data producer has access to the target variable, these quantities can also be evaluated on subsets of the data with the same value of the target, to measure quantified versions of equality of opportunity (conditioning on $Y = 1$) and equalized odds (conditioning separately on $Y = 1$ and $Y = 0$) [15].

5.1 Benefit for Statistical Parity

We certify that any decision using the cleaned data has statistical parity (Definition 2) that is neither too small nor too large. In Theorem 5, we show that the maximum and minimum statistical parity of an adversary using Z can be expressed in closed form. The maximum and minimum will be closer if the induced conditional probability $\eta^f_S(z)$ does not deviate too much on average from the prior π_S. If $\eta^f_S(z) = \pi_S$ everywhere, we have statistical parity of zero, i.e. exact equality of outcome.

THEOREM 5 (STATISTICAL PARITY OF OPTIMAL ADVERSARY). *An adversarial user of Z achieves maximum and minimum statistical parity*

$$\max_{g \in G} SP(g \circ f) = 1 - \mathbb{E}_Z[\min(\frac{\eta^f_S(Z)}{\pi_S}, \frac{1 - \eta^f_S(Z)}{1 - \pi_S})]$$

$$\min_{g \in G} SP(g \circ f) = -1 + \mathbb{E}_Z[\min(\frac{\eta^f_S(Z)}{\pi_S}, \frac{1 - \eta^f_S(Z)}{1 - \pi_S})].$$

PROOF IDEA. Observe that statistical parity is a linear transformation of balanced error rate. Apply the minimum balanced error rate from Equation 32 of [28]. See Appendix A.5 for complete proof. □

5.2 Benefit for Disparate Impact

We certify that any decision using the cleaned data has disparate impact (Definition 3) that is neither too small nor too large. In Theorem 6, we show that the maximum and minimum disparate impact of an adversary using Z can be expressed in closed form. The maximum and minimum will be closer if the induced conditional probability $\eta^f_S(z)$ never deviates too much from the prior π_S. If $\eta^f_S(z) = \pi_S$ everywhere, we have disparate impact of one, i.e. exact equality of outcome. Observe how disparate impact is more sensitive than statistical parity, since it requires $\eta^f_S(z)$ to be close to π_S *everywhere* rather than only in expectation.

THEOREM 6 (DISPARATE IMPACT OF OPTIMAL ADVERSARY). *Let $\overline{\eta}^f_S := \max_{z \in \mathcal{Z}} \eta^f_S(z)$ and $\underline{\eta}^f_S := \min_{z \in \mathcal{Z}} \eta^f_S(z)$. An adversarial user of Z achieves maximum and minimum disparate impact*

$$\max_{g \in G} DI(g \circ f) = \frac{\pi_S(1 - \underline{\eta}^f_S)}{\underline{\eta}^f_S(1 - \pi_S)}$$

$$\min_{g \in G} DI(g \circ f) = \frac{\pi_S(1 - \overline{\eta}^f_S)}{\overline{\eta}^f_S(1 - \pi_S)}.$$

PROOF IDEA. Re-express $DI(g \circ f)$ using the law of total probability, the fact that $\hat{Y}^f$ and S are conditionally independent given Z, and Bayes' rule. Using this form we obtain the maximum and minimum values of $DI(g \circ f)$ and the corresponding choices of g. See Appendix A.6 for complete proof. □

6 CONCLUSION

We have quantified the costs – an inferior fairness-accuracy tradeoff and an increase in individual unfairness – incurred by a given representation. We have also quantified the benefits – narrower bands of statistical parity and disparate impact achievable by an adversary – of such a representation. The benefits result from restricting the decisions of adversarial data users, while the costs are due to applying those same restrictions to other data users. We showed how a data producer can estimate these costs and benefits, even without access to the target variable, to support a novel three-party governance model entailing a separation of concerns between fairness and accuracy. Future directions of interest include extending our results to finite samples, stochastic representation functions, multiple sensitive groups and variables, more general representation spaces, and other fairness definitions.

ACKNOWLEDGMENTS

We would like to thank the reviewers for their useful feedback. We would also like to thank Aditya Menon for discussions during the development of this work. The research was supported by an Australian Government Research Training Program Scholarship and a CSIRO Data61 Top-Up Scholarship.

REFERENCES

[1] Julia Angwin, Jeff Larson, Surya Mattu, and Lauren Kirchner. 2016. Machine Bias. https://www.propublica.org/article/machine-bias-risk-assessments-in-criminal-sentencing.
[2] Solon Barocas, Moritz Hardt, and Arvind Narayanan. 2018. *Fairness and Machine Learning*. fairmlbook.org.
[3] Solon Barocas and Andrew D Selbst. 2016. Big Data's Disparate Impact. *California Law Review* 104 (2016), 671.
[4] Yahav Bechavod and Katrina Ligett. 2017. Penalizing Unfairness in Binary Classification. arXiv 1707.00044.
[5] Alex Beutel, Jilin Chen, Zhe Zhao, and Ed H Chi. 2017. Data Decisions and Theoretical Implications when Adversarially Learning Fair Representations. In *FAT/ML Workshop*.
[6] Toon Calders and Sicco Verwer. 2010. Three Naive Bayes Approaches for Discrimination-Free Classification. *Data Mining and Knowledge Discovery* 21, 2 (2010), 277–292.
[7] Flavio P Calmon, Dennis Wei, Karthikeyan Natesan Ramamurthy, and Kush R Varshney. 2017. Optimized Data Pre-Processing for Discrimination Prevention. In *Advances in Neural Information Processing Systems*.
[8] Amit Datta, Michael Carl Tschantz, and Anupam Datta. 2015. Automated Experiments on Ad Privacy Settings. *Proceedings on Privacy Enhancing Technologies* 2015, 1 (2015), 92–112.
[9] Michele Donini, Luca Oneto, Shai Ben-David, John S Shawe-Taylor, and Massimiliano Pontil. 2018. Empirical Risk Minimization Under Fairness Constraints. In *Advances in Neural Information Processing Systems*.
[10] Cynthia Dwork, Moritz Hardt, Toniann Pitassi, Omer Reingold, and Richard Zemel. 2012. Fairness Through Awareness. In *Innovations in Theoretical Computer Science Conference*.
[11] Cynthia Dwork, Nicole Immorlica, Adam Tauman Kalai, and Mark DM Leiserson. 2018. Decoupled Classifiers for Group-Fair and Efficient Machine Learning. In *Conference on Fairness, Accountability and Transparency*.
[12] Harrison Edwards and Amos Storkey. 2016. Censoring Representations with an Adversary. In *International Conference on Learning Representations*.
[13] Charles Elkan. 2001. The Foundations of Cost-Sensitive Learning. In *International Joint Conference on Artificial Intelligence*.
[14] Michael Feldman, Sorelle A Friedler, John Moeller, Carlos Scheidegger, and Suresh Venkatasubramanian. 2015. Certifying and Removing Disparate Impact. In *International Conference on Knowledge Discovery and Data Mining*.
[15] Moritz Hardt, Eric Price, and Nathan Srebro. 2016. Equality of Opportunity in Supervised Learning. In *Advances in Neural Information Processing Systems*.
[16] James Johndrow and Kristian Lum. 2017. An Algorithm for Removing Sensitive Information: Application to Race-Independent Recidivism Prediction. arXiv 1703.04957.
[17] Christos Louizos, Kevin Swersky, Yujia Li, Richard Zemel, and Max Welling. 2016. The Variational Fair Autoencoder. In *International Conference on Learning Representations*.
[18] David Madras, Elliot Creager, Toniann Pitassi, and Richard Zemel. 2018. Learning Adversarially Fair and Transferable Representations. In *International Conference on Machine Learning*.
[19] Aditya Krishna Menon and Robert C. Williamson. 2018. The Cost of Fairness in Binary Classification. In *Conference on Fairness, Accountability and Transparency*.
[20] Shira Mitchell and Jackie Shadlen. 2018. Mirror Mirror: Reflections on Quantitative Fairness. https://speak-statistics-to-power.github.io/fairness.
[21] Cathy O'Neil. 2017. *Weapons of Math Destruction: How Big Data Increases Inequality and Threatens Democracy*. Broadway Books.
[22] Andrea Romei and Salvatore Ruggieri. 2014. A Multidisciplinary Survey on Discrimination Analysis. *The Knowledge Engineering Review* 29, 5 (2014), 582–638.
[23] United States Equal Opportunity Employment Commission. 1978. Uniform Guidelines on Employee Selection Procedures.
[24] Martin J Wainwright, Michael I Jordan, and John C Duchi. 2012. Privacy Aware Learning. In *Advances in Neural Information Processing Systems*.
[25] Muhammad Bilal Zafar, Isabel Valera, Manuel Gomez Rodriguez, and Krishna P Gummadi. 2017. Fairness Beyond Disparate Treatment & Disparate Impact: Learning Classification Without Disparate Mistreatment. In *International Conference on World Wide Web*.
[26] Muhammad Bilal Zafar, Isabel Valera, Manuel Gomez Rodriguez, and Krishna P Gummadi. 2017. Fairness Constraints: Mechanisms for Fair Classification. In *International Conference on Artificial Intelligence and Statistics*.
[27] Rich Zemel, Yu Wu, Kevin Swersky, Toni Pitassi, and Cynthia Dwork. 2013. Learning Fair Representations. In *International Conference on Machine Learning*.
[28] Ming-Jie Zhao, Narayanan Edakunni, Adam Pocock, and Gavin Brown. 2013. Beyond Fano's Inequality: Bounds on the Optimal F-Score, BER, and Cost-Sensitive Risk and their Implications. *Journal of Machine Learning Research* 14 (2013), 1033–1090.
[29] Indre Zliobaite. 2015. A Survey on Measuring Indirect Discrimination in Machine Learning. arXiv 1511.00148.

A THEOREM PROOFS

We present complete proofs of our theoretical results.

A.1 Proof of Theorem 1

Proof. Let $h_Y^* \in \arg\min_{h \in H} R_Y(h)$, which is given by the expression $h_Y^*(x) = \mathbf{1}(\eta_Y(x) \geq c_Y)$ [28].

$$
\begin{aligned}
& R_Y(g_Y^* \circ f) - l_Y \lambda R_S(g_S^* \circ f) \\
& \leq R_Y(h_Y^* \circ f) - l_Y \lambda R_S(g_S^* \circ f) \\
& = R_Y(h_Y^* \circ f) - R_Y(h_Y^*) + R_Y(h_Y^*) - l_Y \lambda R_S(g_S^* \circ f) \\
& = \mathbb{E}_X[(c_Y - \eta_Y(X)) h_Y^*(f(X))] - \mathbb{E}_X[(c_Y - \eta_Y(X)) h_Y^*(X)] \\
& \quad + R_Y(h_Y^*) - l_Y \lambda R_S(g_S^* \circ f) && (18) \\
& = \mathbb{E}_X[(c_Y - \eta_Y(X))(h_Y^*(f(X)) - h_Y^*(X))] \\
& \quad + R_Y(h_Y^*) - l_Y \lambda R_S(g_S^* \circ f) && (19) \\
& \leq l_Y \mathbb{E}_X \|X - f(X)\|_2 + R_Y(h_Y^*) - l_Y \lambda R_S(g_S^* \circ f). && (20)
\end{aligned}
$$

For (18) we apply Lemma 9 from [19]. For (19) we apply linearity of expectation. For (20), for any x where $h_Y^*(x) \neq h_Y^*(f(x))$, there must exist some x' on the decision boundary of h^* such that

$$c_Y - \eta_Y(x') = 0 \tag{21}$$

and

$$\|x - x'\|_2 \leq \|x - f(x)\|_2. \tag{22}$$

Combining (21) and (22) with the Lipschitz condition (9) yields

$$c_Y - \eta_Y(x) \leq c_Y - \eta_Y(x') + l_Y \|x - x'\|_2 \leq l_Y \|x - f(x)\|_2.$$

Since this is true for every x it is also true in expectation.

We then observe

$$
\begin{aligned}
& \arg\min_{f \in F} [l_Y \mathbb{E}_X \|X - f(X)\|_2 + R_Y(h_Y^*) - l_Y \lambda R_S(g_S^* \circ f)] \\
& = \arg\min_{f \in F} [\mathbb{E}_X \|X - f(X)\|_2 - \lambda R_S(g_S^* \circ f)].
\end{aligned}
$$

□

A.2 Proof of Theorem 2

Proof. First we show the analytical expression for the cost of mistrust (13). Applying Proposition 4 of [19], we have that (11) and (12) are hypotheses h^* and g^* corresponding to solutions to (3) and (10) respectively.

$$
\begin{aligned}
& \mathbb{E}_X[\min(\eta_Y(X) - c_Y, \lambda(\eta_S(X) - c_S))] && (23) \\
& = \mathbb{E}_X[(1 - h^*(X))(\eta_Y(X) - c_Y)] + \lambda \mathbb{E}_X[h^*(X)(\eta_S(X) - c_S)] && (24) \\
& = \pi_Y - c_Y - \mathbb{E}_X[h^*(X)(\eta_Y(X) - c_Y)] + \lambda \mathbb{E}_X[h^*(X)(\eta_S(X) - c_S)] \\
& = \pi_Y - c_Y + R_Y(h^*) - (1 - c_Y)\pi_Y + \lambda \mathbb{E}_X[h^*(X)(\eta_S(X) - c_S)] && (25) \\
& = \pi_Y - c_Y + R_Y(h^*) - (1 - c_Y)\pi_Y - \lambda R_S(h^*) + \lambda(1 - c_S)\pi_S && (26) \\
& = R_Y(h^*) - \lambda R_S(h^*) - c_Y(1 - \pi_Y) + \lambda(1 - c_S)\pi_S.
\end{aligned}
$$

(24) follows from the form of h^* given in (11). (25) and (26) both involve substitutions using Lemma 9 from [19].

Similarly, using the form of g^* from (12) we conclude that

$$
\begin{aligned}
& \mathbb{E}_X[\min(\eta_Y^f(f(X)) - c_Y, \lambda(\eta_S^f(f(X)) - c_S))] && (27) \\
& = R_Y(g^* \circ f) - \lambda R_S(g^* \circ f) - c_Y(1 - \pi_Y) + \lambda(1 - c_S)\pi_S. && (28)
\end{aligned}
$$

The result (13) follows by subtracting (23) from (27) and applying linearity of expectation.

The decomposed form follows from applying Lemma 9 of [19] to each of $R_Y(g^* \circ f)$, $R_Y(h^*)$, $R_S(g^* \circ f)$ and $R_S(h^*)$, then applying linearity of expectation to express $R_Y(g^* \circ f) - R_Y(h^*)$ as in (14) and $R_S(g^* \circ f) - R_S(h^*)$ as in (15). □

A.3 Proof of Theorem 3

Proof.

$$\begin{aligned}
&R_{YS}(g^* \circ f) - R_{YS}(h^*)\\
&\le R_{YS}(h^* \circ f) - R_{YS}(h^*)\\
&= R_Y(h^* \circ f) - R_Y(h^*) - \lambda(R_S(h^* \circ f) - R_S(h^*))\\
&= \mathbb{E}_X[(c_Y - \eta_Y(X))(h^*(f(X)) - h^*(X))]\\
&\quad - \lambda\mathbb{E}_X[(c_S - \eta_S(X))(h^*(f(X)) - h^*(X))] \quad (29)\\
&= \mathbb{E}_X[(c_Y - \eta_Y(X) - \lambda(c_S - \eta_S(X)))(h^*(f(X)) - h^*(X))] \quad (30)\\
&\le (l_Y + \lambda l_S)\mathbb{E}_X\|X - f(X)\|_2. \quad (31)
\end{aligned}$$

(29) is by Lemma 9 from [19] and linearity of expectation. (30) is by linearity of expectation. For (31), using the form of h^* from (11), for any x where $h^*(x) \neq h^*(f(x))$, there must exist some x' on the decision boundary of h^* such that

$$c_Y - \eta_Y(x') - \lambda(c_S - \eta_S(x')) = 0 \quad (32)$$

and

$$\|x - x'\|_2 \le \|x - f(x)\|_2. \quad (33)$$

Combining (32) and (33) with the Lipschitz conditions (16) and (17),

$$\begin{aligned}
&c_Y - \eta_Y(x) - \lambda(c_S - \eta_S(x))\\
&\le c_Y - \eta_Y(x') + l_Y\|x - x'\|_2 - \lambda(c_S - \eta_S(x') - l_S\|x - x'\|_2)\\
&\le (l_Y + \lambda l_S)\|x - f(x)\|_2.
\end{aligned}$$

Since this is true for every x it is also true in expectation. □

A.4 Proof of Theorem 4

Proof. Let $\delta := p(d(X, f(X)) > \epsilon)$. Let h be a D, d–individually fair hypothesis (see Definition 7). Consider points x and x' drawn independently at random using the input X. With probability $1 - \delta$,

$$d(x, f(x)) \le \epsilon. \quad (34)$$

Similarly, with probability $1 - \delta$,

$$d(x', f(x')) \le \epsilon. \quad (35)$$

By the union bound, both statements hold with probability at least $1 - 2\delta$. In that case, the following statements also hold:

$$\begin{aligned}
&D(h(f(x), h(f(x'))\\
&\le D(h(f(x)), h(x)) + D(h(x), h(f(x'))) \quad (36)\\
&\le \epsilon + D(h(x), h(f(x'))) \quad (37)\\
&\le \epsilon + D(h(x), h(x')) + D(h(x'), h(f(x'))) \quad (38)\\
&\le 2\epsilon + D(h(x), h(x')) \quad (39)\\
&\le 2\epsilon + d(x, x'). \quad (40)
\end{aligned}$$

(36) and (38) use the triangle inequality since D is subadditive. (37) and (39) hold due to (34) and (35) respectively, along with Definition 7. (40) uses Definition 7. Therefore $IU_{D,d_\epsilon}(h \circ f) \le 2\delta$. □

A.5 Proof of Theorem 5

Proof. Let

$$BER(h) := \frac{1}{2}p(\hat{Y} = 0|S = 1) + \frac{1}{2}p(\hat{Y} = 1|S = 0)$$

be the balanced error rate of an hypothesis h. Observe the fact that $SP(h) = 1 - 2BER(h)$ for all h. Therefore

$$\begin{aligned}
&\max_{g\in G} SP(g \circ f)\\
&= 1 - 2\min_{g\in G} BER(g \circ f)\\
&= 1 - \mathbb{E}_Z[\min(\frac{\eta_S^f(Z)}{\pi_S}, \frac{1 - \eta_S^f(Z)}{1 - \pi_S})], \quad (41)
\end{aligned}$$

where (41) uses Equation 32 from [28].

Similarly, we may show that

$$\min_{g\in G} SP(g \circ f) = -1 + \mathbb{E}_Z[\min(\frac{\eta_S^f(Z)}{\pi_S}, \frac{1 - \eta_S^f(Z)}{1 - \pi_S})],$$

using the fact that $BER(h) = 1 - BER(1 - h)$ for all h. □

A.6 Proof of Theorem 6

Proof. Disparate impact can be expressed as follows:

$$\begin{aligned}
&DI(g \circ f)\\
&= \frac{\int_z p(Z = z|S = 0)p(\hat{Y}^f = 1|S = 0, Z = z)dz}{\int_z p(Z = z|S = 1)p(\hat{Y}^f = 1|S = 1, Z = z)dz}\\
&= \frac{\int_z p(Z = z|S = 0)g(z)dz}{\int_z p(Z = z|S = 1)g(z)dz} \quad (42)\\
&= \frac{\pi_S \int_z p(Z = z)(1 - \eta_S^f(z))g(z)dz}{(1 - \pi_S)\int_z p(Z = z)\eta_S^f(z)g(z)dz} \quad (43)\\
&= \frac{\pi_S\mathbb{E}_Z[(1 - \eta_S^f(Z))g(Z)]}{(1 - \pi_S)\mathbb{E}_Z[\eta_S^f(Z)g(Z)]}. \quad (44)
\end{aligned}$$

For (42) we used the fact that $\hat{Y}^f$ and S are conditionally independent given Z. For (43) we used Bayes' rule.

Recall that $\overline{\eta}_S^f := \max_{z\in\mathcal{Z}} \eta_S^f(z)$ and $\underline{\eta}_S^f := \min_{z\in\mathcal{Z}} \eta_S^f(z)$. Let γ be an arbitrary constant in the range (0, 1]. Using (44), we have:

$$\max_{g\in G} DI(g \circ f) = \frac{\pi_S(1 - \underline{\eta}_S^f)}{\underline{\eta}_S^f(1 - \pi_S)}$$

where the maximum is obtained for

$$g(z) = \begin{cases} \gamma & \text{if } \eta_S^f(z) = \underline{\eta}_S^f \\ 0 & \text{otherwise.} \end{cases}$$

Similarly,

$$\min_{g\in G} DI(g \circ f) = \frac{\pi_S(1 - \overline{\eta}_S^f)}{\overline{\eta}_S^f(1 - \pi_S)}$$

where the minimum is obtained for

$$g(z) = \begin{cases} \gamma & \text{if } \eta_S^f(z) = \overline{\eta}_S^f \\ 0 & \text{otherwise.} \end{cases}$$

□

Creating Fair Models of Atherosclerotic Cardiovascular Disease

Stephen Pfohl*
spfohl@stanford.edu
Stanford Center for Biomedical Informatics Research, Stanford University
Stanford, California

Ben Marafino†
marafino@stanford.edu
Stanford Center for Biomedical Informatics Research, Stanford University
Stanford, California

Adrien Coulet†
acoulet@stanford.edu
Stanford Center for Biomedical Informatics Research, Stanford University
Stanford, California
Université de Lorraine, CNRS, Inria, Loria
Nancy, France

Fatima Rodriguez
frodrigu@stanford.edu
Cardiovascular Medicine and Cardiovascular Institute, Stanford University
Stanford, California

Latha Palaniappan
lathap@stanford.edu
Primary Care and Population Health, Stanford University
Stanford, California

Nigam H. Shah
nigam@stanford.edu
Stanford Center for Biomedical Informatics Research, Stanford University
Stanford, California

ABSTRACT

Guidelines for the management of atherosclerotic cardiovascular disease (ASCVD) recommend the use of risk stratification models to identify patients most likely to benefit from cholesterol-lowering and other therapies. These models have differential performance across race and gender groups with inconsistent behavior across studies, potentially resulting in an inequitable distribution of beneficial therapy. In this work, we leverage adversarial learning and a large observational cohort extracted from electronic health records (EHRs) to develop a "fair" ASCVD risk prediction model with reduced variability in error rates across groups. We empirically demonstrate that our approach is capable of aligning the distribution of risk predictions conditioned on the outcome across several groups simultaneously for models built from high-dimensional EHR data. We also discuss the relevance of these results in the context of the empirical trade-off between fairness and model performance.

CCS CONCEPTS

• **Applied computing → Health informatics.**

KEYWORDS

electronic health records, fairness, cardiovascular disease, adversarial learning, risk prediction, machine learning

*Correspondence to: Stephen Pfohl at spfohl@stanford.edu
†Authors contributed equally to this research.

AIES '19, January 27–28, 2019, Honolulu, HI, USA

ACM ISBN 978-1-4503-6324-2/19/01...$15.00
https://doi.org/10.1145/3306618.3314278

ACM Reference Format:
Stephen Pfohl, Ben Marafino, Adrien Coulet, Fatima Rodriguez, Latha Palaniappan, and Nigam H. Shah. 2019. Creating Fair Models of Atherosclerotic Cardiovascular Disease. In *AAAI/ACM Conference on AI, Ethics, and Society (AIES '19), January 27–28, 2019, Honolulu, HI, USA.* ACM, New York, NY, USA, 8 pages. https://doi.org/10.1145/3306618.3314278

1 INTRODUCTION

Atherosclerotic cardiovascular disease (ASCVD), which includes heart attack, stroke, and fatal coronary heart disease, is a major cause of mortality and morbidity worldwide, as well as in the U.S., where it contributes to 1 in 3 of all deaths–many of which are preventable [1]. In deciding whether to prescribe cholesterol-lowering therapies to prevent ASCVD, physicians are often guided by risk estimates yielded by the *Pooled Cohort Equations* (PCEs). PCEs provide a proportional hazards model [10] that leverages nine clinical measurements to predict the 10-year risk of a first ASCVD event. However this model has been found to overestimate risk for female patients [25], Chinese patients [7] or globally [33], as well as also underestimate risk for other groups such as Korean women [15]. Such mis-estimation results in an inequitable distribution of the benefits and harms of ASCVD risk scoring, because incorrect risk estimates can expose patients to substantial harm through both under- or over-treatment; potentially leading to preventable cardiovascular events or side effects from unnecessary therapy, respectively.

The inability of the PCEs to generalize to diverse cohorts likely owes to both under-representation of minority populations in the cohorts used to develop the PCEs and shifts in medical practice and lifestyle patterns in the decades since data collection for those cohorts. In attempting to correct for these patterns, one recent study [33] updated the PCEs using data from contemporary cohorts and demonstrated that doing so reduced the number of minority patients incorrectly misclassified as being high or low risk. Similar results were observed in the same study with an approach using an elastic net classifier, rather than a proportional hazards model.

However, neither approach is able to explicitly guarantee an equitable distribution of mis-estimation across relevant subgroups, particularly for race- and gender-based subgroups.

To account for under-represented minorities and to take advantage of the wider variety of variables made available in electronic health records (EHRs), we derive a large and diverse modern cohort from EHRs to learn a prediction model for ASCVD risk. Furthermore, we investigate the extent to which we can encode algorithmic notions of *fairness*, specifically *equality of odds*, [13] into the model to encourage an equitable distribution of performance across populations. To the best of our knowledge, our effort is the first to explore the extent to which this formal fairness metric is achievable for risk prediction models built using high-dimensional data from the EHR. We show that while it is feasible to develop models that achieve equality of odds, we emphasize that this process involves trade-offs that must be assessed in a broader social and medical context [32].

2 BACKGROUND AND RELATED WORK

2.1 ASCVD Risk Prediction and EHRs

The PCEs are based on age, gender, cholesterol levels, blood pressure, and smoking and diabetes status and were developed by pooling data from five large U.S. cohorts [10] composed of white and black patients, with white patients constituting a majority. Recently, attempts [33] were made to update the PCEs to improve model performance for race- and gender-based subgroups using elastic net regression and data from modern prospective cohorts. However, this effort focused on demographic groups and variables already used to develop the PCEs and did not consider other populations or clinical measurements. The increasing adoption of EHRs offers opportunities to deploy and refine ASCVD risk models. Efforts have recently been undertaken to apply and refine existing models, including the PCEs and the Framingham score, to large EHR-derived cohorts and characterize their performance in certain subgroups [28, 30]. Beyond ASCVD risk prediction, there exist many recent works that develop prediction models with EHRs, which are reviewed in [11].

2.2 Fair Risk Prediction

We consider the case where supervised learning is used to estimate a function $f(X)$ that approximates the conditional distribution $p(Y|X)$, given N samples $\{x_i, y_i, z_i\}_{i=1}^N$ drawn from the distribution $p(X, Y, Z)$. We take $X \in \mathcal{X} = \mathbb{R}^m$ to correspond to a vector representation of the medical history extracted from the EHR prior to a patient-specific index time t_i; $Y \in \mathcal{Y} = \{0, 1\}$ to be a binary label, which for patient i, indicates the presence of the outcome observed in the EHR in the time frame $[t_i, t_i + w_i]$, where w_i is a parameter specifying the amount of time following the index time used to derive the outcome; and $Z \in \mathcal{Z} = \{0, \ldots, k-1\}$ indicates a sensitive attribute, such as race, gender, or age, with k groups. The output of the learned function $f(X) \in [0, 1]$ is then thresholded with respect to a value T to yield a prediction $\hat{Y} \in \{0, 1\}$.

One standard metric for assessing the fairness of a classifier with respect to a sensitive attribute Z is *demographic parity* [8], which evaluates the independence between Z and the prediction $\hat{Y}$. Formally, the demographic parity criterion may be expressed as

$$p(\hat{Y}|Z = Z_i) = p(\hat{Y}|Z = Z_j) \, \forall \, Z_i, Z_j \in \mathcal{Z}. \quad (1)$$

However, optimizing for demographic parity is of limited use for clinical risk prediction, because doing so may preclude the model from considering relevant clinical features associated with the sensitive attribute and the outcome, thus decreasing the performance of the model for all groups [20].

Another related metric is *equality of odds* [13], which stipulates that the prediction $\hat{Y}$ be conditionally independent of Z, given the true label Y. Formally, satisfying equality of odds implies that

$$p(\hat{Y}|Z = Z_i, Y = Y_k) = p(\hat{Y}|Z = Z_j, Y = Y_k) \quad \forall \, Z_i, Z_j \in \mathcal{Z}; Y_k \in \mathcal{Y}. \quad (2)$$

From this, it can be seen that, if equality of odds is achieved, then for a fixed threshold T, both the false positive (FPR) and false negative rates (FNR) are equal across all pairs of groups defined by Z. Compared to demographic parity, equality of odds is more appropriate in a clinical setting, since it does not necessarily preclude the learning of the optimal predictor in the case that a true relationship between sensitive attribute and the outcome exists [13].

Furthermore, this definition can be extended to the case of a continuous risk score by requiring that

$$p(f(X)|Z = Z_i, Y = Y_k) = p(f(X)|Z = Z_j, Y = Y_k) \quad \forall \, Z_i, Z_j \in \mathcal{Z}; Y_k \in \mathcal{Y}. \quad (3)$$

In this case, the distribution of the predicted probability of the outcome conditioned on whether the event occurred or not should be matched across groups of a sensitive variable. Formulation 3 is stronger than 2 since it implies that equality of odds is achieved for all possible thresholds, thus requiring that the same ROC curve be attained for all groups. This is desirable since it provides the end-user the ability to freely adjust the decision threshold of the model without violating equality of odds.

Finally, we also note that satisfying equality of odds for a continuous risk score may be reduced to the problem of minimizing a divergence over each pair (Z_i, Z_j) of distributions referenced in equation (3). *Adversarial learning* procedures [12] are well-suited to this problem in that they provide a flexible framework for minimizing the divergence over distributions parameterized by neural networks. As such, several related works [2, 9, 24, 34] have demonstrated the benefit of augmenting a classifier with an adversarial discriminator in order to align the distribution of predictions for satisfying fairness constraints.

2.3 Approaches for Achieving Fairness

Despite considerable interest in the ethical implications of implementing machine learning in healthcare [4, 6], relatively little work exists characterizing the extent to which risk prediction models developed with EHR data satisfy formal fairness constraints.

Adversarial approaches for satisfying fairness constraints (in the form of demographic parity) have been explored in several recent works in non-healthcare domains. One approach, [9], in the context of image anonymization, demonstrated that representations satisfying demographic parity could be learned by augmenting a predictive model with both an autoencoder and an adversarial component. The adversarial approach to fairness was further investigated by [2] with a gradient reversal objective for data that is imbalanced in the distribution of both the outcome and in the sensitive attribute.

In attempting to address the limitations of demographic parity as a metric, [13] introduced equality of odds as an alternative and devised post-processing methods to achieve it for fixed-threshold classifiers. Recently, [34] and [24] generalized the adversarial framework to achieve equality of odds by providing the discriminator access to the value of the outcome.

Both demographic parity and equality of odds are referred to as *group fairness* metrics since they are concerned with encouraging an invariance of some property of a classifier over groups of a sensitive attribute. While straightforward to compute and reason about, optimizing for these metrics may produce models that are discriminatory over structured subgroups within and across groups of sensitive attributes, constituting a form of fairness gerrymandering [17]. The competing notion of *individual fairness* [8] and may be able to address these concerns by assessing whether a model produces similar outputs for similar individuals. However, this notion is often of limited practical use due to the challenges of developing a domain-specific similarity metric that encodes desired notions of fairness.

Recent efforts [14] have investigated an alternative to both group and individual fairness metrics with a process that audits a classifier to discover subgroups for which the model is under-performing and iteratively improve model performance for those groups, ultimately resulting in a non-negative change in model performance for all computationally-identifiable subgroups.

The closest related work examining the fairness of risk prediction models in healthcare is [5], which, in the context of mortality prediction in intensive care units, argued that any trade-off between model performance and fairness across subgroups is undesirable. They propose that the prediction error should be decomposed in terms of bias, variance, and noise and that the relative contribution of these terms be used to guide additional data collection.

3 METHODS

3.1 The Dataset and Cohort Definition

We extract records from the Stanford Medicine Research Data Repository [23], a clinical data warehouse containing records on roughly three million patients from Stanford Hospital and Clinics and Lucile Packard Children's Hospital for clinical encounters occurring between 1990 and 2017. We define a prediction task that resembles the setting in which the PCEs were developed for the purpose of guiding physician decision-making in ASCVD prevention and construct a corresponding cohort. As a first step, we identify all patients with at least two clinical encounters over at least two years for which they are 40 years of age or older. Then, for each patient we select an index time t_i uniformly at random from the interval that allows for at least one year of history and one year of follow-up. We exclude from the cohort patients that have an history of cardiovascular artery disease (including ASCVD and atrial fibrillation) or a prescription of an anti-hypertensive drug in the five years prior to the index time.

Table 1: Cohort characteristics. The number of patients extracted, the incidence of the ASCVD outcome and the average length of follow-up for each subgroup are shown.

Group	Count	ASCVD Incidence (%)	Follow-up Length (years)
Asian	30,294	2.3	3.2
Black	8,549	3.0	3.2
Hispanic	20,240	2.0	2.9
Other	19,062	2.2	3.1
Unknown	39,964	0.86	3.1
White	135,438	2.8	3.6
Female	149,594	1.9	3.4
Male	103,953	2.9	3.3
40-55	121,437	0.95	3.4
55-65	61,214	2.1	3.5
65-75	43,800	3.7	3.2
75+	27,096	6.7	3.0
All	253,547	2.8	3.4

Finally, we assign a positive ASCVD label for a patient if a diagnosis code for an ASCVD event is observed at any point in their record following the index time. The exclusion criteria (i.e. the list of cardiovascular-related diseases and medications) is provided as supplementary material, along with the list of clinical concepts used for defining ASCVD events. The patients are randomly partitioned such that 80%, 10%, 10% are used for training, validation, and testing, respectively.

3.2 Sensitive Attributes

We consider race, gender, and age as sensitive attributes and assess model performance and fairness with respect to them. For race, we use both race and ethnicity variables to partition the cohort into six disjoint groups: Asian, Black, Hispanic, Other, Unknown, and White. Patients not considered Hispanic thus have either a non-Hispanic or unknown ethnicity. For gender, we partition the cohort into male and female populations. For age, we discretize the age at the index time into four disjoint groups: 40-55, 55-65, 65-75, and 75+ years, where the intervals are inclusive on the lower bound and exclusive on the upper bound. A summary of these groups is presented in Table 1.

3.3 Feature Extraction

For feature extraction, we adopt a strategy similar to the one described in [31] to convert time-stamped sequences of clinical concepts across several domains (i.e., diagnoses, procedures, medication orders, lab tests, clinical encounter types, departments, and other observations) into a static representation suitable for modeling. For each extracted patient, we filter the historical record to include only those concepts occurring prior to the index time. We encode as a binary attribute each unique clinical concept observed in the dataset according to whether that concept was present anywhere in the patient's history prior to the prediction time; otherwise, it is absent or missing. Similarly, we do not use the numeric results of

Table 2: Distribution alignment metrics. We report the coefficient of variation (CV; the ratio of the standard deviation to the mean) of the false positive rate (FPR, CV) and false negative rate (FNR, CV) at a fixed decision threshold of 0.075 across the race, gender, and age groups. Furthermore, we compute the pairwise earth mover's distance (EMD) between distributions of the predicted probabilities of having an ASCVD event, conditioned on the true ASCVD label y for each group of each sensitive attribute and take the mean.

	Race		Gender		Age	
	Standard	EQ_{race}	Standard	EQ_{gender}	Standard	EQ_{age}
FNR, CV	0.126	0.1	0.102	0.0164	0.382	0.129
FPR, CV	0.538	0.383	0.45	0.12	1.05	0.205
Mean EMD | $y = 0$	0.00749	0.00616	0.00875	0.0026	0.0239	0.00312
Mean EMD | $y = 1$	0.0226	0.0237	0.0167	0.00593	0.0602	0.0209

lab tests or vital measurements, but only include the presence of their measurement. In all models, we include race, gender, and age as features without regards as to whether the variable is treated as sensitive or not.

3.4 Adversarial Learning for Equality of Odds

To develop an ASCVD risk prediction model that satisfies the definition of equality of odds in (3), we consider two fully-connected neural networks: a classifier $f : \mathbb{R}^m \to \mathbb{R} \in [0, 1]$ parameterized by θ_f that predicts the probability of the ASCVD outcome Y given data X; and a discriminator $g : \mathbb{R} \times \{0, 1\} \to [0, 1]^k$ parameterized by θ_g that takes as input both the logit of the output of f and the value of the true label Y to predict a distribution over the groups of a sensitive attribute Z. If L_{cls} and L_{adv} are the cross-entropy losses of the classifier predictions over Y and the discriminator predictions over Z, respectively, then the training procedure may be described by alternating between the steps

$$\min_{\theta_f} L_{cls} - L_{adv} \quad \text{and} \quad \min_{\theta_g} L_{adv}. \tag{4}$$

3.5 Model Training and Evaluation

The training procedure is composed of four experiments and thus produces four prediction models. The first model is trained to predict the risk of ASCVD and does not use adversarial training. The other three models result from separate training runs in which each of the discrete race, gender, and age variables are considered as sensitive attributes in the adversarial training procedure. We refer to these four experiments as Standard, EQ_{race}, EQ_{gender}, and EQ_{age}.

For all experiments, we employ fully-connected feedforward neural networks with a fixed set of hyperparameters. The ASCVD prediction model is composed of the sum over an embedding layer of dimension 100 followed by two hidden layers of dimension 128 and leaky ReLU nonlinearities. The adversarial network maintains a similar architecture, but with one hidden layer of dimension 64 and takes the prediction logit and ASCVD outcome as inputs. Training proceeds in a batch setting with the Adam optimizer [19] with learning rate 10^{-3}, $\beta_1 = 0.5$, and $\beta_2 = 0.9$ with batch size 256 over the training set and early stopping based on the area under the receiver operating characteristic curve (AUC-ROC) for ASCVD prediction in the validation set. All training was performed on a single GPU with the PyTorch library [27].

Table 3: Model performance measured on the test set without stratification for each experimental condition.

	Standard	EQ_{race}	EQ_{gender}	EQ_{age}
AUC-ROC	0.793	0.772	0.779	0.743
AUC-PRC	0.133	0.125	0.13	0.0965
Brier Score	0.0205	0.0207	0.0206	0.0211

For each model, we compute standard metrics on the entire test set and on each subgroup. Specifically, we report the AUC-ROC, the area under the precision-recall curve (AUC-PRC), the Brier score [3] as a measure of calibration, and the false positive and false negative rates (FPR, FNR) at a fixed threshold of $T = 0.075$, in keeping with current ASCVD guidelines for the prescription of statin therapy [10, 33]. To express adherence to the standard equality of odds definition in equation 2, we report the coefficient of variation (i.e. the ratio of the standard deviation to the mean) of the FPR and FNR at $T = 0.075$ across the groups of each sensitive attribute. To assess the distance between the distributions presented in (3), we compute the earth mover's distance (EMD, or first Wasserstein distance) between the empirical distributions of the predicted probability of ASCVD conditioned on whether ASCVD occurred or not for each group of each sensitive attribute in a pairwise fashion and take the mean within each strata.

4 RESULTS

4.1 Cohort Characteristics

The cohort extraction procedure produces a cohort of 253,547 patients having 71,554 features, with 5,886 patients labeled as positive for ASCVD (Table 1). We note that in this cohort, there are 135,438 white patients, constituting a majority, and 8,549 black patients. Across racial groups, ASCVD rates range from 2.0-3.0%, with the exception of patients with unknown race, who experience a reduced rate of 0.86%. Furthermore, we observe higher ASCVD rates for male patients compared to female patients. Finally, ASCVD rates appear to increase monotonically with age, with rates ranging from 0.95% for the 40-55 age group to 6.7% for patients age 75 or older.

Table 4: Model performance measured on the test set stratified by group and experimental condition. EQ corresponds to training for the sensitive attribute corresponding to the subgroup of interest. FPR and FNR are computed at a fixed decision threshold of 0.075.

	AUC-ROC		AUC-PRC		Brier Score		FNR		FPR	
	`Stand.`	`EQ`	`Stand.`	`EQ`	`Stand.`	`EQ`	`Stand.`	`EQ`	`Stand.`	`EQ`
Asian	0.819	0.771	0.138	0.155	0.0196	0.0197	0.683	0.587	0.0388	0.0903
Black	0.753	0.756	0.162	0.2	0.034	0.0338	0.621	0.69	0.0781	0.0437
Hispanic	0.811	0.803	0.117	0.0816	0.0142	0.015	0.667	0.6	0.0391	0.0945
Other	0.813	0.822	0.13	0.113	0.0217	0.0219	0.711	0.556	0.0544	0.102
Unknown	0.713	0.718	0.0619	0.0406	0.00766	0.00812	0.844	0.719	0.00944	0.0353
White	0.774	0.766	0.146	0.155	0.0245	0.0245	0.6	0.619	0.0804	0.0714
Female	0.8	0.786	0.12	0.122	0.0173	0.0174	0.684	0.625	0.0423	0.0567
Male	0.775	0.769	0.148	0.143	0.0249	0.025	0.592	0.64	0.0818	0.0672
40-55	0.713	0.727	0.0404	0.0275	0.0085	0.00922	0.952	0.817	0.00683	0.0573
55-65	0.736	0.708	0.0919	0.0676	0.0195	0.0198	0.794	0.746	0.0409	0.0618
65-75	0.736	0.739	0.128	0.141	0.0349	0.0347	0.608	0.669	0.115	0.088
75+	0.776	0.763	0.228	0.224	0.053	0.0548	0.351	0.607	0.251	0.0806

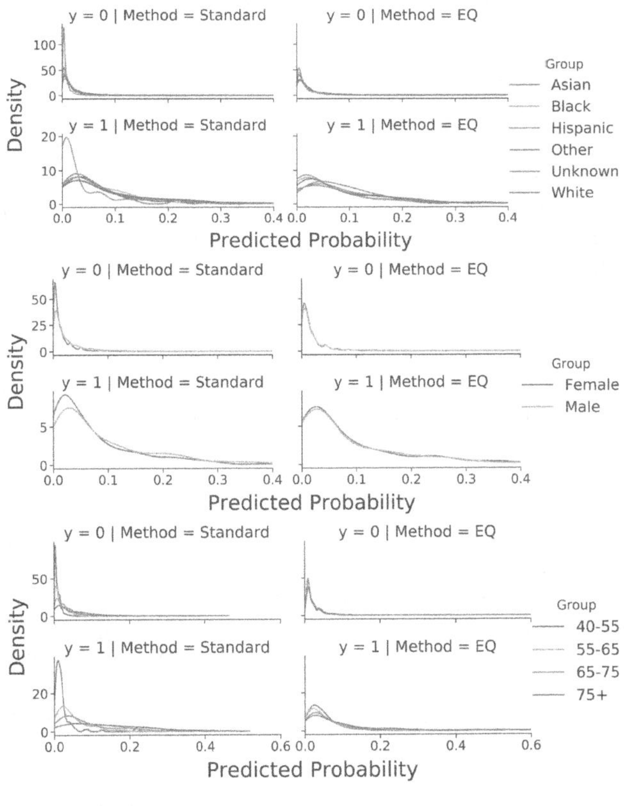

Figure 1: Empirical distribution of the predicted probability of developing ASCVD in the followup period conditioned on whether ASCVD occurred. Plots are stratified by experimental condition (`Standard` or `EQ`), true value of the ASCVD outcome ($y = 0$ or $y = 1$), and the variable treated as sensitive (race, gender, or age).

4.2 Distribution Alignment with Adversarial Training

Applying the adversarial training procedure results in a alignment of the distributions of the predicted probability of ASCVD conditioned on the true outcome label (Figure 1). Without employing a adversarial discriminator, the center of mass of these distributions appears to depend significantly on the base ASCVD rate in the group. However, these differences largely disappear when training in an adversarial setting. This results in a substantial reduction in the mean pairwise EMD between each predictive distribution in both outcome strata for both gender and age, with a negligible effect for race (Table 2). Furthermore, we note that variability in the FPRs and FNRs at a fixed threshold of 0.075 is greatly reduced following adversarial training (Table 2), indicating that the approach successfully encourages the model predictions to satisfy equality of odds.

The relative lack of success in minimizing the mean pairwise EMD between the conditional predictive distributions across racial groups (Table 2) may be largely explained by the anomalous characteristics of the group of patients having unknown race. For instance, when using standard training (`Standard`), the predictive distribution conditioned on a positive ASCVD outcome for the unknown race group is clearly separated from that of the five groups while the distributions for those five are mostly aligned (Figure 1). However, when training the model in an adversarial setting, it appears that the primary effect is to align the predictive distribution for the unknown race group to the region inhabited by the distributions of the remaining groups while disturbing the relative alignment between the distributions for those groups.

4.3 The Cost of Fairness

Satisfying equality of odds with an adversarial objective incurs a reduction in AUC-ROC, AUC-PRC, and calibration for the population at large (Table 3), with the largest negative effects observed when training to adjust for the differences across age groups (`Standard`

AUC-ROC = 0.793 vs. EQ_{age} AUC-ROC = 0.743). However, for ranking metrics such as the AUC-ROC, the effects can be unintuitive following an adjustment of the subgroup predictive distributions. For instance, the adversarial training procedure for age actually leads to an increase in AUC-ROC for the majority 40-55 years group (Standard AUC-ROC = 0.713 vs. EQ_{age} AUC-ROC = 0.727) (Table 4) despite the stark decline in the AUC-ROC observed on the population as a whole. Furthermore, several of the populations assessed experience a reduction in performance for some metrics with improvements in others following training for equality of odds. In other cases, the effect is largely positive. Notably, model performance improves on all metrics except for the fixed threshold FNR for the black population, a group for which the model attains the lowest AUC-ROC (0.753) and is the least well-calibrated (Brier Score = 0.034) for the standard setting.

It has been shown that developing a well-calibrated model is an objective that conflicts with that of satisfying equality of odds [20, 29]. In our case, we observed such a trade-off, but judged it to be minor due to a small increase in the Brier score for almost every subgroup following training for equality of odds (Table 2).

5 DISCUSSION

We have demonstrated the capabilities of adversarial training procedures to encourage the learning of models whose predictions satisfy equality of odds for high-dimensional EHR data with sensitive attributes of more than two groups. In a setting such as ASCVD risk prediction, with a clear clinical intervention associated with the prediction, this procedure ensures that no group bears a disparate burden of mistreatment due to misclassification. However, we note that this comes at a cost of a reduction in AUC-ROC and AUC-PRC for some subgroups.

5.1 Limitations of the Predictive Model

While using EHR data allowed a high-capacity ASCVD risk prediction model to be trained using a large and diverse cohort, this model should not be directly compared to the PCEs for several reasons. First, the PCEs estimate ten-year ASCVD risk, whereas our model estimates risk over a period of at least a year. Furthermore, we cannot rule out the existence of biases that may lead to differential rates of selection or censoring in our cohort across age, gender, and race based subgroups, nor can we establish whether the nature of these biases differ from those present in the prospective cohort studies used to derive the PCEs.

5.2 Moving Beyond Equality of Odds

While we have demonstrated empirically that adversarial learning procedures are capable of encouraging a model to satisfy equality of odds, the use of this metric as a measure of fairness should be approached with caution. In the case that there is insufficient information in the training dataset to learn a high performing model for at least one group, optimizing for this criteria will upper bound the group-level model performance by the performance obtained for the least-well performing group. In the adversarial learning setting, this reduction in performance for some groups may be offset by performance gains for groups for which the model performs poorly when trained naively. However, we observed that if such a benefit exists, it is smaller than the reduction in performance incurred for most groups.

We have not examined the relationship between the errors of the predictive model and notions of long-term utility when deploying the model clinically. To properly analyze the effect of these errors on utility requires careful causal modeling of the sequential decision-making process following ASCVD risk prediction while accounting for individual patient characteristics. We emphasize that while such a process is crucial to evaluate the long-term impact of any prediction model, it is not possible to properly identify and model that causal process with observational data in the EHR alone [18]. Additionally, it is unclear that satisfying fairness constraints for a single-step decision, as in ASCVD risk prediction, aligns with the goal of equitably maximizing long-term utility, as it has been shown that satisfying fairness constraints for a static decision may actually cause long-term harm in settings where an unconstrained objective would not [22], particularly if the outcome is measured with bias due to systematic censoring [16]. We find those approaches [21, 26] that establish causal notions of fairness to be promising directions for future work, as they permit sequential decision making processes to be studied under the lens of fairness at both the group and individual level.

6 CONCLUSION

Existing approaches to ASCVD risk scoring perform poorly for the population at large, with more extreme risk mis-estimates for minority populations, inadvertently exposing those groups to excess harm. We develop an ASCVD prediction model using EHR data and show that we can encourage formal notions of fairness by reducing the variability in the FPR and FNR across groups. It is not yet known to what extent algorithmic notions of fairness align with other goals, including long-term utility maximization. We hope that our results will serve as an impetus for the community at large to investigate the fairness-utility trade-off during sequential clinical decision making resulting from fairness constraints imposed on clinical risk assessments.

ACKNOWLEDGMENTS

We would like to thank Sam Corbett-Davies, Julia Daniels, and Sebastian Le Bras for early advice and insightful discussion.

This material is based upon work supported by the National Science Foundation Graduate Research Fellowship Program DGE-1656518; NLM R01 LM011369-06; NLM T15 LM007033. Any opinions, findings, and conclusions or recommendations expressed in this material are those of the authors and do not necessarily reflect the views of the funding bodies. We also thank the Widen Horizons program of the IDEX Lorraine Université d'Excellence (15-IDEX-0004) and the Snowball Associate Team funded by Inria.

REFERENCES

[1] Emelia J Benjamin, Salim S Virani, Clifton W Callaway, Alanna M Chamberlain, Alexander R Chang, Susan Cheng, Stephanie E Chiuve, Mary Cushman, Francesca N Delling, Rajat Deo, et al. 2018. Heart disease and stroke statistics-2018 update: a report from the American Heart Association. *Circulation* 137, 12 (2018), e67–e492.

[2] Alex Beutel, Jilin Chen, Zhe Zhao, and Ed H Chi. 2017. Data decisions and theoretical implications when adversarially learning fair representations. *arXiv preprint arXiv:1707.00075* (2017).

[3] Glenn W Brier. 1950. Verification of forecasts expressed in terms of probability. *Monthey Weather Review* 78, 1 (1950), 1–3.

[4] Danton S Char, Nigam H Shah, and David Magnus. 2018. Implementing machine learning in health care - addressing ethical challenges. *The New England journal of medicine* 378, 11 (2018), 981.

[5] Irene Chen, Fredrik D. Johansson, and David Sontag. 2018. Why Is My Classifier Discriminatory?. In *Proceedings of the 32nd International Conference on Neural Information Processing Systems (NIPS'18)*.

[6] I Glenn Cohen, Ruben Amarasingham, Anand Shah, Bin Xie, and Bernard Lo. 2014. The legal and ethical concerns that arise from using complex predictive analytics in health care. *Health affairs* 33, 7 (2014), 1139–1147.

[7] Andrew Paul DeFilippis, Rebekah Young, John W McEvoy, Erin D Michos, Veit Sandfort, Richard A Kronmal, Robyn L McClelland, and Michael J Blaha. 2016. Risk score overestimation: the impact of individual cardiovascular risk factors and preventive therapies on the performance of the American Heart Association-American College of Cardiology-Atherosclerotic Cardiovascular Disease risk score in a modern multi-ethnic cohort. *European heart journal* 38, 8 (2016), 598–608.

[8] Cynthia Dwork, Moritz Hardt, Toniann Pitassi, Omer Reingold, and Richard Zemel. 2012. Fairness through awareness. In *Proceedings of the 3rd Innovations in Theoretical Computer Science Conference*. ACM, 214–226.

[9] Harrison Edwards and Amos Storkey. 2015. Censoring representations with an adversary. *arXiv preprint arXiv:1511.05897* (2015).

[10] David C Goff, Donald M Lloyd-Jones, Glen Bennett, Sean Coady, Ralph B D'Agostino, Raymond Gibbons, Philip Greenland, Daniel T Lackland, Daniel Levy, Christopher J O'donnell, et al. 2014. 2013 ACC/AHA guideline on the assessment of cardiovascular risk: a report of the American College of Cardiology/American Heart Association Task Force on Practice Guidelines. *Journal of the American College of Cardiology* 63, 25 Part B (2014), 2935–2959.

[11] Benjamin A Goldstein, Ann Marie Navar, Michael J Pencina, and John Ioannidis. 2017. Opportunities and challenges in developing risk prediction models with electronic health records data: a systematic review. *Journal of the American Medical Informatics Association* 24, 1 (2017), 198–208.

[12] Ian Goodfellow, Jean Pouget-Abadie, Mehdi Mirza, Bing Xu, David Warde-Farley, Sherjil Ozair, Aaron Courville, and Yoshua Bengio. 2014. Generative adversarial nets. In *Advances in neural information processing systems*. 2672–2680.

[13] Moritz Hardt, Eric Price, Nati Srebro, et al. 2016. Equality of opportunity in supervised learning. In *Advances in neural information processing systems*. 3315–3323.

[14] Úrsula Hébert-Johnson, Michael Kim, Omer Reingold, and Guy Rothblum. 2018. Multicalibration: Calibration for the (computationally-identifiable) masses. In *International Conference on Machine Learning*. 1944–1953.

[15] Keum Ji Jung, Yangsoo Jang, Dong Joo Oh, Byung-Hee Oh, Sang Hoon Lee, Seong-Wook Park, Ki-Bae Seung, Hong-Kyu Kim, Young Duk Yun, Sung Hee Choi, et al. 2015. The ACC/AHA 2013 pooled cohort equations compared to a Korean Risk Prediction Model for atherosclerotic cardiovascular disease. *Atherosclerosis* 242, 1 (2015), 367–375.

[16] Nathan Kallus and Angela Zhou. 2018. Residual Unfairness in Fair Machine Learning from Prejudiced Data. In *International Conference on Machine Learning*. 2444–2453.

[17] Michael Kearns, Seth Neel, Aaron Roth, and Zhiwei Steven Wu. 2018. Preventing Fairness Gerrymandering: Auditing and Learning for Subgroup Fairness. In *International Conference on Machine Learning*. 2569–2577.

[18] Niki Kilbertus, Mateo Rojas Carulla, Giambattista Parascandolo, Moritz Hardt, Dominik Janzing, and Bernhard Schölkopf. 2017. Avoiding discrimination through causal reasoning. In *Advances in Neural Information Processing Systems*. 656–666.

[19] Diederik Kingma and Jimmy Ba. 2014. Adam: A method for stochastic optimization. *arXiv preprint arXiv:1412.6980* (2014).

[20] Jon Kleinberg, Sendhil Mullainathan, and Manish Raghavan. 2016. Inherent trade-offs in the fair determination of risk scores. *arXiv preprint arXiv:1609.05807* (2016).

[21] Matt J Kusner, Joshua Loftus, Chris Russell, and Ricardo Silva. 2017. Counterfactual fairness. In *Advances in Neural Information Processing Systems*. 4066–4076.

[22] Lydia Liu, Sarah Dean, Esther Rolf, Max Simchowitz, and Moritz Hardt. 2018. Delayed Impact of Fair Machine Learning. In *International Conference on Machine Learning*. 3156–3164.

[23] Henry J Lowe, Todd A Ferris, Penni M Hernandez, and Susan C Weber. 2009. STRIDE–An integrated standards-based translational research informatics platform. In *AMIA Annual Symposium Proceedings*, Vol. 2009. American Medical Informatics Association, 391.

[24] David Madras, Elliot Creager, Toniann Pitassi, and Richard Zemel. 2018. Learning Adversarially Fair and Transferable Representations. In *International Conference on Machine Learning*. 3381–3390.

[25] Samia Mora, Nanette K Wenger, Nancy R Cook, Jingmin Liu, Barbara V Howard, Marian C Limacher, Simin Liu, Karen L Margolis, Lisa W Martin, Nina P Paynter, et al. 2018. Evaluation of the pooled cohort risk equations for cardiovascular risk prediction in a multiethnic cohort from the Women's Health Initiative. *JAMA internal medicine* 178, 9 (2018), 1231–1240.

[26] Razieh Nabi and Ilya Shpitser. 2018. Fair inference on outcomes. In *Thirty-Second AAAI Conference on Artificial Intelligence*.

[27] Adam Paszke, Sam Gross, Soumith Chintala, Gregory Chanan, Edward Yang, Zachary DeVito, Zeming Lin, Alban Desmaison, Luca Antiga, and Adam Lerer. 2017. Automatic differentiation in PyTorch. (2017).

[28] Mindy M Pike, Paul A Decker, Nicholas B Larson, Jennifer L St Sauver, Paul Y Takahashi, Véronique L Roger, Walter A Rocca, Virginia M Miller, Janet E Olson, Jyotishman Pathak, et al. 2016. Improvement in cardiovascular risk prediction with electronic health records. *Journal of cardiovascular translational research* 9, 3 (2016), 214–222.

[29] Geoff Pleiss, Manish Raghavan, Felix Wu, Jon Kleinberg, and Kilian Q Weinberger. 2017. On fairness and calibration. In *Advances in Neural Information Processing Systems*. 5680–5689.

[30] Jamal S Rana, Grace H Tabada, Matthew D Solomon, Joan C Lo, Marc G Jaffe, Sue Hee Sung, Christie M Ballantyne, and Alan S Go. 2016. Accuracy of the atherosclerotic cardiovascular risk equation in a large contemporary, multiethnic population. *Journal of the American College of Cardiology* 67, 18 (2016), 2118–2130.

[31] Jenna M Reps, Martijn J Schuemie, Marc A Suchard, Patrick B Ryan, and Peter R Rijnbeek. 2018. Design and implementation of a standardized framework to generate and evaluate patient-level prediction models using observational healthcare data. *Journal of the American Medical Informatics Association* 25, 8 (2018), 969–975.

[32] Abraham Verghese, Nigam H Shah, and Robert A Harrington. 2018. What this computer needs is a physician: humanism and artificial intelligence. *Jama* 319, 1 (2018), 19–20.

[33] Steve Yadlowsky, Rodney A Hayward, Jeremy B Sussman, Robyn L McClelland, Yuan-I Min, and Sanjay Basu. 2018. Clinical implications of revised pooled cohort equations for estimating atherosclerotic cardiovascular disease risk. *Ann Intern Med* 169, 1 (2018), 20–29.

[34] Brian Hu Zhang, Blake Lemoine, and Margaret Mitchell. 2018. Mitigating unwanted biases with adversarial learning. In *Proceedings of the 2018 AAAI/ACM Conference on AI, Ethics, and Society*. ACM, 335–340.

A EXCLUSION CRITERIA: CARDIOVASCULAR ARTERY DISEASES

Here we list the set of concepts from the Observational Medical Outcomes Partnership vocabulary version 5.3 used to exclude patients on the basis of a history of cardiovascular artery disease at the prediction time.

Monoplegia of dominant lower limb as a late effect of cerebrovascular accident (197303); Acute myocardial infarction (312327); Hypertensive encephalopathy (312938); Atrial fibrillation (313217); Nonpyogenic thrombosis of intracranial venous sinus (314667); Chronic ischemic heart disease (315286); Preinfarction syndrome (315296); Angina decubitus (315832); Heart failure (316139); Aneurysm of coronary vessels (316427); Cerebral atherosclerosis (316437); Coronary occlusion (316995); Coronary arteriosclerosis (317576); Postmyocardial infarction syndrome (319038); Congestive heart failure (319835); Angina pectoris (321318); Dissecting aneurysm of coronary artery (321879); Paralytic syndrome as late effect of stroke (372654); Cerebral artery occlusion (372924); Transient cerebral ischemia (373503); Basilar artery syndrome (374055); Acute ill-defined cerebrovascular disease (374060); Cerebral ischemia (374384); Cerebral embolism (375557); Vertebrobasilar artery syndrome (376714);

Moyamoya disease (378774); Cerebrovascular disease (381591); Subclavian steal syndrome (433505); Late effects of cerebrovascular disease (434056); Acute myocardial infarction of anterior wall (434376); Vertebral artery syndrome (434656); Weakness of face muscles (434657); Acute myocardial infarction of lateral wall (436706); Basilar artery occlusion (437308); Ataxia (437584); Aneurysm of heart (438168); Acute myocardial infarction of inferior wall (438170); Acute myocardial infarction of anterolateral wall (438438); Acute myocardial infarction of inferolateral wall (438447); Multiple and bilateral precerebral arterial occlusion (439295); True posterior myocardial infarction (439693); Left heart failure (439846); Vertigo as late effect of stroke (440426); Acute myocardial infarction of inferoposterior wall (441579); Cerebral thrombosis (441874); Precerebral arterial occlusion (443239); Dysphagia as a late effect of cerebrovascular accident (443465); Monoplegia of dominant upper limb as a late effect ofcerebrovascular accident (443525); Apraxia due to cerebrovascular accident (443551); Arteriosclerosis of coronary artery bypass graft (443563); Systolic heart failure (443580); Diastolic heart failure (443587); Paralytic syndrome of nondominant side as late effect of stroke (443599); Paralytic syndrome of dominant side as late effect of stroke (443609); Acute subendocardial infarction (444406); Infarction - precerebral (4043731); Vertebrobasilar territory transient ischemic attack (4048785); Cerebral infarction due to embolism of cerebral arteries (4108356); Acute myocardial infarction of atrium (4108669); Cerebral infarction due to thrombosis of cerebral arteries (4110192); Occlusion of artery (4162038); Vertebral artery obstruction (4185117); Ischemic heart disease (4185932); Myocardial ischemia (4186397); Carotid artery obstruction (4288310); Chronic systolic heart failure (40479192); Dysphasia as late effect of cerebrovascular disease (40479575); Chronic diastolic heart failure (40479576); Aphasia as late effect of cerebrovascular disease (40480002); Sensory disorder as a late effect of cerebrovascular disease (40480449); Acute on chronic systolic heart failure (40480602); Acute systolic heart failure (40480603); Monoplegia of lower limb as late effect of cerebrovascular disease (40480938); Monoplegia of nondominant lower limb as a late effect of cerebrovascular accident (40480946); Acute diastolic heart failure (40481042); Acute on chronic diastolic heart failure (40481043); Arteriosclerosis of coronary artery bypass graft of transplanted heart (40481132); Speech and language deficit as late effect of cerebrovascular accident (40481354); Hemiplegia as late effect of cerebrovascular disease (40481762); Monoplegia of upper limb as late effect of cerebrovascular disease (40481842); Coronary atherosclerosis (40481919); Monoplegia of nondominant upper limb as a late effect of cerebrovascular accident (40482266); Residual cognitive deficit as late effect of cerebrovascular accident (40482301); Arteriosclerosis of autologous vein coronary artery bypass graft (40482638); Arteriosclerosis of nonautologous coronary artery bypass graft (40482655); Combined systolic and diastolic dysfunction (40482727); Arteriosclerosis of arterial coronary artery bypass graft (40483189); Hemiplegia of nondominant side as late effect of cerebrovascular disease (40484513); Hemiplegia of dominant side as late effect of cerebrovascular disease (40484522); Coronary arteriosclerosis in native artery (42872402); Coronary arteriosclerosis in native artery of transplanted heart (43021821); Dysarthria as late effects of cerebrovascular disease (43530687); Visual disturbance as sequela of cerebrovascular disease (43531583); Acute combined systolic and diastolic heart failure (44782718); Chronic combined systolic and diastolic heart failure (44782719); Acute on chronic combined systolic and diastolic heart failure (44782733).

B EXCLUSION CRITERIA: ANTIHYPERTENSIVE DRUGS

Here we list the medications from the Antomatical Therapeutic Chemical Classification System (ATC) used to exclude patients on the basis of a history of prescription of anti-hypertensive drugs at the prediction time.

Rauwolfia alkaloids (C02AA); rescinnamine (C02AA01); reserpine (C02AA02); deserpidine (C02AA05); methoserpidine (C02AA06); methyldopa (levorotatory) (C02AB01); clonidine (C02AC01); guanfacine (C02AC02); moxonidine (C02AC05); rilmenidine (C02AC06); trimetaphan (C02BA01); mecamylamine (C02BB01); prazosin (C02CA01 indoramin (C02CA02); doxazosin (C02CA04); urapidil (C02CA06); betanidine (C02CC01); guanethidine (C02CC02); debrisoquine (C02CC0 diazoxide (C02DA01); dihydralazine (C02DB01); hydralazine (C02DB02) minoxidil (C02DC01); nitroprusside (C02DD01); pinacidil (C02DG01); metirosine (C02KB01); pargyline (C02KC01); ketanserin (C02KD01); bosentan (C02KX01); ambrisentan (C02KX02); macitentan (C02KX04); riociguat (C02KX05); alprenolol (C07AA01); oxprenolol (C07AA02); pindolol (C07AA03); propranolol (C07AA05); timolol (C07AA06); sotalol (C07AA07); nadolol (C07AA12); mepindolol (C07AA14); carteolol (C07AA15); tertatolol (C07AA16); bopindolol (C07AA17); bupranolol (C07AA19); penbutolol (C07AA23); practolol (C07AB01); metoprolol (C07AB02); atenolol (C07AB03); acebutolol (C07AB04); betaxolol (C07AB05); bisoprolol (C07AB07); celiprolol (C07AB08); esmolol (C07AB09); nebivolol (C07AB12); talinolol (C07AB13); labetalol (C07AG01); carvedilol (C07AG02); metoprolol and felodipine (C07FB02); atenolol and nifedipine (C07FB03).

C OUTCOME DEFINITION: ASCVD

Here we list the set of concepts from the Observational Medical Outcomes Partnership vocabulary version 5.3 used to define the presence of ASCVD in the followup period.

Acute myocardial infarction (312327); Cerebral artery occlusion (372924); Acute ill-defined cerebrovascular disease (374060); Cerebral embolism (375557); Acute myocardial infarction of anterior wall (434376); Acute myocardial infarction of lateral wall (436706); Basilar artery occlusion (437308); Acute myocardial infarction of inferior wall (438170); Acute myocardial infarction of anterolateral wall (438438); Acute myocardial infarction of inferolateral wall (438447); Multiple and bilateral precerebral arterial occlusion (439295); True posterior myocardial infarction (439693); Acute myocardial infarction of inferoposterior wall (441579); Cerebral thrombosis (441874); Precerebral arterial occlusion (443239); Acute subendocardial infarction (444406); Infarction - precerebral (4043731); Cerebral infarction due to embolism of cerebral arteries (4108356); Acute myocardial infarction of atrium (4108669); Cerebral infarction due to thrombosis of cerebral arteries (4110192); Vertebral artery obstruction (4185117); Carotid artery obstruction (4288310).

Global Explanations of Neural Network

Mapping the Landscape of Predictions

Mark Ibrahim
Center for Machine Learning, Capital One

Melissa Louie
Center for Machine Learning, Capital One

Ceena Modarres
Center for Machine Learning, Capital One

John Paisley
Columbia University

ABSTRACT

A barrier to the wider adoption of neural networks is their lack of interpretability. While local explanation methods exist for one prediction, most global attributions still reduce neural network decisions to a single set of features. In response, we present an approach for generating global attributions called GAM, which explains the landscape of neural network predictions across subpopulations. GAM augments global explanations with the proportion of samples that each attribution best explains and specifies which samples are described by each attribution. Global explanations also have tunable granularity to detect more or fewer subpopulations. We demonstrate that GAM's global explanations 1) yield the known feature importances of simulated data, 2) match feature weights of interpretable statistical models on real data, and 3) are intuitive to practitioners through user studies. With more transparent predictions, GAM can help ensure neural network decisions are generated for the right reasons.

CCS CONCEPTS

• **Computing methodologies → Semantic networks; Supervised learning by classification.**

KEYWORDS

neural networks, global interpretability, explainable deep learning

ACM Reference Format:

Mark Ibrahim, Melissa Louie, Ceena Modarres, and John Paisley. 2019. Global Explanations of Neural Network: Mapping the Landscape of Predictions. In *2019 AAAI/ACM Conference on AI, Ethics, and Society (AIES'19), January 27–28, 2019, Honolulu, HI, USA.* ACM, New York, NY, USA, 9 pages. https://doi.org/10.1145/aies062

1 INTRODUCTION

The present decade has seen the widespread adoption of neural networks across many areas from natural language translation to visual object recognition [14]. In domains where the stakes are high however, adoption has been limited due to a lack of interpretability. The hierarchical non-linear nature of neural networks limits the ability to explain predictions. This black-box nature exposes the risk of adverse societal consequences such as bias and prejudice.

Researchers have developed several approaches to explain neural network predictions through an observation's saliency or unique identifying factors [10][24][18]. Another set of techniques produce explanations using attributions, which estimate each feature's importance to a prediction. Some of these techniques are model agnostic while others attempt to take advantage of a neural network's architecture to generate attributions [17][11] [2]. However, these techniques are local, meaning the explanations are limited to a single prediction.

Global attributions can be a powerful tool for interpretability, since they explain feature importance across a population. Global explanations can aid in model diagnostics, uncover opportunities for feature engineering, and expose possible bias. Existing global techniques rely on more interpretable surrogate models such as decision trees or manipulate the input space to assess global predictive power [8] [27] [13]. While these techniques produce an interpretable set of rules, they can fail to capture the non-linear feature interactions learned by neural networks. Submodular-Pick LIME (SP-LIME) is another technique based on summarizing local attributions to better reflect learned interactions. Although SP-LIME maximizes coverage of local explanations, it does not describe the proportion or subpopulations best explained by each global attribution [20].

We propose a global attribution method called GAM (Global Attribution Mapping) that's able to explain non-linear representations learned by neural networks across subpopulations. GAM groups similar local feature importances to form human-interpretable global attributions. Each global attribution best explains a particular subpopulation, augmenting global explanations with the proportion and specific samples they best explain. In addition, GAM provides tunable granularity to capture more or fewer subpopulations for global explanations.

2 BACKGROUND: ATTRIBUTION TECHNIQUES

GAM builds on local attribution techniques. Here we consider three techniques that are rooted in a strong theoretical foundation, well cited, and relatively easy to implement: Locally Interpretable Model-Agnostic Explanations (LIME), Integrated Gradients, and Deep Learning Important FeaTures (DeepLIFT) [20] [25] [23].

Locally Interpretable Model-Agnostic Explanations (LIME). LIME produces interpretable representations of complicated models by

ACM ISBN 978-1-4503-6324-2/19/01...$15.00
https://doi.org/10.1145/3306618.3314230

optimizing two metrics: interpretability and local fidelity. In practice, an input is perturbed by sampling in a local neighborhood to fit a simpler linear model. The now explainable linear model's weights can be used to interpret a particular model prediction.

There is a global extension of LIME called Submodule pick LIME (SP-LIME). SP-LIME reduces many local attributions into a smaller global set by selecting the least redundant set of local attributions. Formally, SP-LIME maximizes coverage defined as the total importance of the features in the selected global set.

Integrated Gradients. Sundararajan et. al developed an approach that satisfies two proposed axioms for attributions. First, sensitivity states that for any two inputs that differ in only a single feature and have different predictions, the attribution should be non-zero. Second, implementation invariance states that two networks that have equal outputs for all possible inputs should also have the same attributions. The authors develop an approach that takes the path integral of the gradient for a neutral reference input to determine the feature dimension with the greatest activation. An attribution vector for a particular observation (local) is produced as a result.

Deep Learning Important FeaTures (DeepLIFT). Much like Integrated Gradients, DeepLIFT seeks to explain the difference in output between an input and a neutral reference. An attribution score is calculated by constructing a function analogous to a partial derivative that's used along with the chain rule to trace the change in the output layer relative to the input.

3 GAM: GLOBAL ATTRIBUTION MAPPING

We treat each local attribution as a ranking of features. In contrast to domains such as speech or image recognition where individual inputs are not human-interpretable, here we focus on situations where features have well defined semantics [4]. We then group similar attributions to form global human-interpretable explanations across subpopulations.

3.1 Attributions as Rankings

Attributions contain more than the content encoded by treating each as a vector in $\mathbb{R}^n$: an attribution ranks and weighs each feature's association with a particular prediction. Each element in an attribution vector answers the question: "how important is this feature for a particular prediction?" Furthermore, attributions are conjoined rankings, because every feature appears in every attribution along the same dimension. Therefore to incorporate both the rank and weight encoded in an attribution, we treat attributions as *weighted conjoined rankings.* With this treatment, we summarize the content of many local attributions by comparing their similarities to form global attributions.

3.2 Rank Distances

We represent each attribution as a rank vector σ. The unweighted rank of feature i is $\sigma(i)$ and the weighted rank is $\sigma_w(i)$.

First, to ensure distances appropriately reflect similarity among vectors—as opposed to anomalies in the scale of the original inputs—we normalize each local attribution vector σ_w by

$$|\sigma_w| \circ \frac{1}{\sum_i |\sigma_w(i)|},$$

where σ_w is the weighted attribution vector and $\circ$ is the Hadamard product.

By transforming the attribution into normalized percentages, we consider only feature importance, not whether a feature contributes positively or negatively to a particular target. This enables us to measure similarity among normalized attributions as weighted rankings of feature importance.

Next we consider two options for comparing attributions: Kendall's Tau and Spearman's Rho squared rank distances. The first option for comparing attributions is weighted Kendall's Tau rank distance, an extension of Kendall's Tau rank correlation as defined by Lee and Yu 2010 [16].

For a second attribution vector π, we can define the weighted Kendall's Tau distance between π and σ as

$$\sum_{i<j} w_i w_j I\{(\pi(i) - \pi(j))(\sigma(i) - \sigma(j)) < 0\}, \tag{1}$$

where $w_i = \pi_w(i)\sigma_w(i)$ and I is the indicator function.

A feature's weight, w_i, in this context is the product of the weights in each ranking. Two rankings containing all elements in the same order (possibly different weights) have zero distance to imply the same feature importance. Two rankings with at least one element in a different order have a distance proportional to the out-of-order elements' weights. When a feature is ranked above or below in one ranking compared to the other, it is penalized by the product of its weights in the rankings. The total distance between two rankings is then the sum of the penalty for feature appearing in a different order. The more features that appear in a different order, the greater the distance between the rankings. Furthermore, the weighted Kendall's Tau distance described satisfies symmetry, positive definiteness, and subadditivity (see Section 2 of [15]) meaning it defines a proper distance metric that we can use for clustering rankings.

A second option for comparing attributions is weighted Spearman's Rho squared rank distance, as defined by Shieh et al. [22],

$$\sum_{i=1}^{k} \pi_w(i)\sigma_w(i)(\pi(i) - \sigma(i))^2. \tag{2}$$

Weighted Spearman's Rho squared rank distance as defined compares attributions as weighted conjoined rankings much in the same way as weighted Kendall's Tau rank distance, but with a runtime of $O(n \log n)$. Weighted Spearman's Rho squared distance also defines a distance metric [15].

Kendall's Tau rank distance does have computational and mathematical limitations. First, Kendall's Tau has a quadratic runtime, which can be computationally expensive as the number of feature and/or samples grows [12]. Second, Kendall's Tau tends to produce smaller values compared to Spearman's Rho, making differences between attributions less pronounced [7].

Therefore, in situations where the number of features and/or samples is large, Spearman's Rho squared is a more effective alternative from a computational perspective and due to its ability to make differences among rankings more pronounced. Despite the advantages of Spearman's Rho squared rank distance, Kendall's Tau remains an appropriate choice when computational efficiency is less important due to its desirable statistical properties. Kendall's Tau as a correlation metric has faster asymptotic convergence with respect to bias and variance [26]. Having defined metrics with which to compare attributions, we now turn our attention to identifying similar attributions.

3.3 Grouping Similar Local Attributions

Clustering algorithms can detect global patterns in a dataset by grouping similar data points into a cluster. We apply this idea in the context of local attribution vectors by transforming many local attributions into a few global attributions. We use weighted Kendall's Tau or Spearman's Rho squared rank distances to measure similarity among attributions. We adapt K-medoids to use rank distance rather than Manhattan distance to group similar attributions [19]. We then use the resulting medoids to succinctly summarize global attribution patterns.

The clustering algorithm identifies the K local attributions (medoids) minimizing the pairwise dissimilarity within a cluster relative to the medoid. We then use the medoid to summarize the pattern detected for each cluster. The algorithm works by initializing K local attributions (medoids) $m_1, ..., m_K$ selected randomly from the full set of local attributions. The local attributions are reassigned until convergence or for a sufficiently large number of iterations, each taking $O(n(n-K)^2)$. The choice of medoids at each iteration is updated by

(1) determining cluster membership for each local attribution σ via the nearest medoid,

$$\sigma \in C_a \text{ if rankDist}(\sigma, m_a) \leq \text{rankDist}(\sigma, m_j) \; \forall j \in [1, K],$$

(2) updating each cluster's medoid by minimizing pairwise dissimilarity within a cluster,

$$m_a = \sigma_l = argmin_{\sigma_l \in C_a} \sum_{\sigma_j \in C_a} \text{rankDist}(\sigma_j, \sigma_l).$$

The advantage this clustering approach over other algorithms such as K-means is that it allows us to compare attributions as conjoined weighted rankings rather than simply vectors in $\mathbb{R}^N$. K-means, for example, treats attributions as vectors by minimizing inter-cluster variance in Euclidean space, ignoring the content encoded in the rank and weights of each feature. Our approach, on the other hand, takes advantage of both the rank and weight information in local attributions during clustering. Each cluster specifies a subpopulation best explained by its medoid.

3.4 Generating Global Attributions

Each of GAM's global explanations yields the most centrally located vector of feature importances for a subpopulation. The global attribution landscape described by GAM is then the collection of global explanations for each subpopulation.

Finally, we form GAM's global explanations across subpopulations by grouping similar normalized attributions.

1em [t] local attributions medoids and corresponding members 1. Normalize the set of local attributions local attribution normalized = abs(attribution) / sum(abs(attribution))

2. Compute pair-wise rank distance matrix distances = [] attribution1 in normalizedAttributions attribution2 in normalizedAttributions distances += rankDistance(attribution1, attribution2)

3. Cluster Attributions initialMedoids = random.choice(attributions) x iterations cluster attribution in cluster tempMedoid = attribution cost = sum(distance(attribution, tempMedoid)) reassign medoid to attribution minimizing cost update cluster membership by assigning to closest medoid

We can gauge the explanatory power of each global attribution by the size of its subpopulation. Since GAM allows us to trace a global explanation to individual samples, we can also examine summary statistics for each subpopulation. In addition, by adjusting the cluster size K, we can tune the granularity of global explanations to capture more or fewer subpopulations. As a starting point, K can be chosen based the Silhouette score, which compares similarity within and across clusters [21].

In contrast to global explanations via surrogate models, which produce a single global explanation, GAM identifies differences in explanations among subpopulations. Furthermore, the ability to trace global explanations to individual samples, supplements global explanations of techniques such as SP-LIME with information about subpopulations.

4 VALIDATING OUR PROPOSED GLOBAL ATTRIBUTION METHOD

Although there has been significant research in the validation of clustering algorithms, interpreting clusters involves qualitative analysis and domain expertise. Moreover, research in interpretability inherently faces the challenge of effective and reliable validation [6]. Attributions have no baseline truth. The task of identifying an appropriate validation methodology for a proposed approach is an open research question. In this paper, we validate the methodology in three ways.

The first validates GAM against two synthetically generated datasets with known feature importances. The second compares the global attributions generated by GAM against the feature weights of more interpretable statistical models. The third assesses the practical value of GAM in real-world settings with user studies. We also demonstrate the use of Kendall's Tau and Spearman's Rho rank distances as well as several local attribution techniques.

4.1 Global Attributions Applied to Synthetic Dataset

We design a simple synthetic dataset to yield known feature importances against which to validate GAM's global attributions. The dataset consists of a binary label, class 1 or 2, and two features, A and B. We aim to generate one group for which only feature A is predictive and another group for which only feature B is predictive.

For the group where only feature A is predictive, we sample balanced classes from uniform distributions where

$$\text{feature A} = \left\{ \begin{array}{ll} U[0,1] & \text{if class 1} \\ U[1,2] & \text{if class 2} \end{array} \right\}. \tag{3}$$

To ensure feature B has no predictive power for this group, we draw from a uniform distribution over $[0, 2]$.

Since values for feature A in $[0, 1]$ mark class 1 and $[1, 2]$ mark class 2 samples, feature A has full predictive power. Feature B on the other hand is sampled uniformly over the same range for both classes, yielding no predictive power.

Conversely, to produce a group where only feature B is predictive, we sample balanced classes where

$$\text{feature B} = \left\{ \begin{array}{ll} U[3,4] & \text{if class 1} \\ U[4,5] & \text{if class 2} \end{array} \right\}. \tag{4}$$

To ensure feature A has no predictive power for this group, we draw from a uniform distribution over [3, 5].

We then conduct two experiments: 1. using a balanced set where feature A is predictive in 50% of cases and 2. using an unbalanced set where feature A is predictive in 75% of cases. We train a single layer feed forward neural network on a balanced dataset of 10k samples. We use a ReLU activation with a four node hidden layer and a sigmoid output. We hold out 2000 test samples and achieve a validation accuracy of 99%.

In order to generate global attributions for the 2000 balanced test samples, we first generate local attributions using LIME. We then generate global attributions using GAM across several values of K. By computing the Silhouette Coefficient score, we find $K = 2$ optimizes the similarity of attributions within the subpopulations. We obtain the corresponding size of the subpopulations and two explanation medoids summarizing feature importances (see Table 1).

Table 1: Global Attributions for Synthetic Data

Balanced	
Explanations	Subpopulation Size
feature A: 0.93 feature B: 0.07	953
feature A: 0.05 feature B: 0.95	1047

Table 2: Global Attributions for Unbalanced Synthetic Data

Unbalanced	
Explanations	Subpopulation Size
feature A: 0.94 feature B: 0.06	1436
feature A: 0.13 feature B: 0.87	564

For the balanced experiment, the global explanations and subpopulation proportions match expectations. The first subpopulation contains nearly half the samples and assigns a high importance weight to feature A. The second subpopulation contains the remaining half of samples and assigns a high importance weight to feature B.

For the unbalanced experiment, the global attributions contain two subpopulations with the expected proportions (see Table 2). The first assigns a high attribution to feature A and contains 72% of samples. The second assigns a high attribution to feature B and contains 28% of samples, reflecting the feature importances inherent to the synthetic dataset. See Appendix for discussion on DeepLIFT and Integrated Gradients results.

Overall, the global attributions produced by GAM match the known feature importance and proportions of both synthetic datasets.

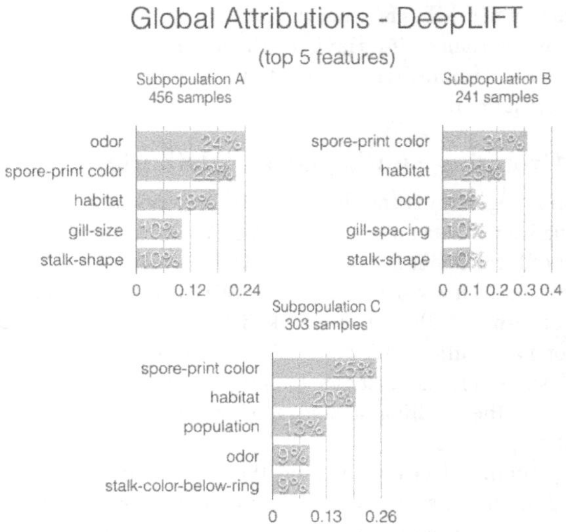

Figure 1: DeepLIFT- Five most important features for each global attribution explanation and the corresponding number of samples in each subpopulation.

4.2 Global Attributions Applied to the Mushroom Dataset

Next, we apply GAM to a dataset with a larger number of categorical features: The Audubon Society's mushroom dataset [5]. The task is to classify mushroom samples as poisonous or not poisonous using 23 categorical features such as cap-shape, habitat, odor and so on. Here we highlight the use of gradient-based neural network attribution techniques (DeepLIFT and Integrated Gradients) to generate local attributions and compare the results against LIME. We also choose weighted Spearman's Rho squared rank distance to compare attributions for computational efficiency given the larger number of features and samples.

For the classification task, we train a two hidden-layer feedfoward neural network on 4784 samples (witholding 2392 for validation) based on the architecture proposed in the Kaggle Kernel [9]. We one-hot encode the categorical features into a 128-unit input layer. The network optimizes binary cross entropy with dropout using sigmoid activation functions. We obtain a validation accuracy of approximately 99%. This allows us to produce more accurate local attributions by minimizing inaccuracies due to model error.

We apply GAM on three sets of local attributions on 1000 samples using DeepLIFT, Integrated Gradients, and LIME [1]. We identify three global explanations based on each technique. We note the top features did vary slightly in weight and rank depending on our choice of baseline (for DeepLIFT/Integrated Gradients). Here we choose the baseline yielding a nearly uniform classification output.

The global attributions based on DeepLIFT produce three subpopulations with similar top features (see Figure 1). Odor, habitat, and spore-print color appear among the top five features across all three subpopulations. Each subpopulation also surfaces distinctions in the relative feature importances. Spore-print color appears to be the most important features for 54% of samples, while odor is most

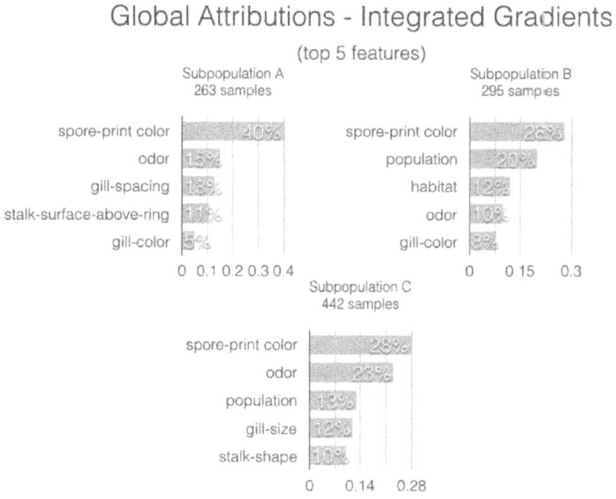

Figure 2: Integrated Gradients - Global Attributions

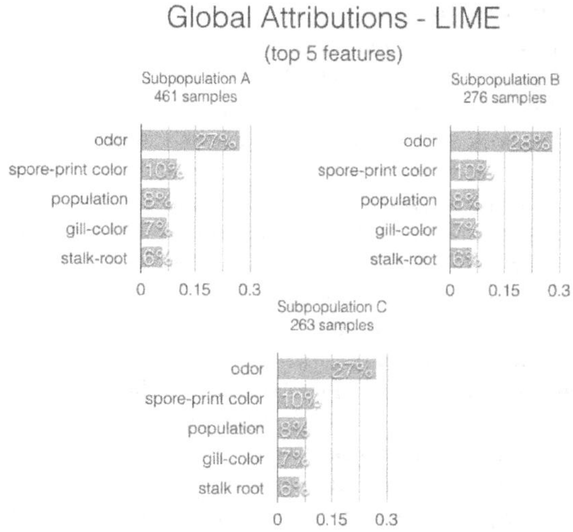

Figure 3: LIME - Global Attributions

important for the remaining subpopulation. Gill-size also appears to be relatively more important for subpopulation A, whereas gill-spacing is more so for subpopulation B. Despite slight variations in rankings, on average 8 out of the top 10 features agree across all three subpopulations, implying overall concordance in the surfaced top features (see Appendix for full attributions).

The global attributions based on Integrated Gradients also produce explanations ranking odor and spore-print-color among the top five features. There appears to also be strong overlap among other top features such as habitat, population, and stalk-shape (see Figure 2). Nevertheless, each subpopulation also surfaces nuances in the top features for each group. For example, population is among the top 5 features for 74% of samples, whereas it's relatively less important for the remaining samples. Across all three subpopulations however, on average 7 of the top 10 features agree, once again implying concordance in the top features.

In addition, we find both gradient-based global attributions overlap in the top features for global attributions based on LIME. Global attributions for LIME also rank odor, spore-print-color, population, and gill-color among the top five features. The three subpopulations based on LIME produced similar top five features (see Figure 3). Despite slight variation in rankings, all three local techniques surface similar most important features.

Finally, we validate global attributions across all three local techniques against the known feature importances of a gradient boosting tree classifier. We use the XGBoost classifier implementation and assign feature importances using each feature's F1 score [3]. We find on average 7 out of the top 10 features in the global attributions across all three techniques match the top features of XGBoost. Odor, spore-print, population, gill-color, and stalk root appear among the most important features (see Figure 4). Furthermore, the weights of the top features of XGBoost match closely the weights of global attributions based on LIME. Although global XGBoost feature importances corroborate the most important features surfaced, we

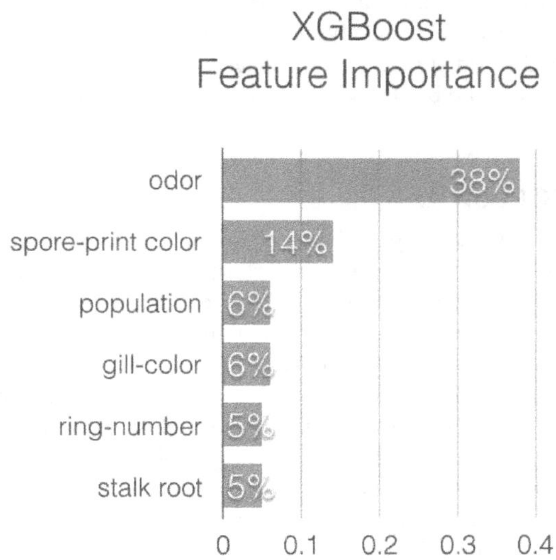

Figure 4: Feature importances for XGBoost as measured by each feature's F1 score.

qualify these findings by noting that two equally performing models can learn a different set of feature interactions. Nevertheless, in this case the global attributions' similarity to known global feature importances across multiple local techniques suggests the explanations generated effectively uncover associations among features and the classification task.

We found similar agreement in the top features using GAM on the Iris dataset with global explanations matching the weights of a logistic classifier (see Appendix: GAM Applied to the Iris Dataset).

4.3 User Studies

We conduct several user studies on FICO Home Equity Line Credit applications to assess the practical value of GAM in real-world settings. The dataset provides information on credit candidate applications and risk outcome characterized by 90-day payment delinquencies.

First, we simulated a scenario where a practitioner would use GAM to conduct feature selection. We selected seven predictive features and added in three additional uniformly distributed noise features. We dropped all feature names, trained a neural network to make credit decisions, produced a GAM model explanation, and presented the explanation to 55 Amazon Mechanical Turk users. We provided users with GAM explanations in the form of a bar chart and asked users to remove the three least important features. In 94% of cases, respondents selected the features with the lowest importance corresponding to the random noise features.

Second, we polled credit modeling experts to assess whether GAM's results are as intuitive as those of the popular SP-LIME global attribution method. We present both explanations to a group of 55 credit modeling practitioners and asked which explanation allows them to more intuitively improve the model (see Appendix). We found respondents had nearly equal preference among the three categories: GAM, SP-LIME, and no preference.

Our sample sizes are relatively small, but the results suggest that GAM has real world practical value in machine learning tasks like feature selection and produces results that are intuitive to human practitioners.

5 CONCLUSION

In this paper, we develop GAM, a methodology for generating global attributions to supplement existing interpretability techniques for neural networks. GAM's global explanations describe the non-linear representations learned by neural networks. GAM also provides tunable subpopulation granularity along with the ability to trace global explanations to specific samples. We demonstrate on both real and synthetic datasets that GAM illuminates global explanation patterns across learned subpopulations. We validate that global attributions produced by GAM match known feature importances and are insightful to humans through user studies. With explanations across subpopulations, neural network predictions are more transparent. A possible next step is to explore how global interpretability can help ensure fairness in AI algorithms.

ACKNOWLEDGMENTS

Thank you to Paul Zeng for his contribution to the implementation and valuable feedback. An implementation for GAM is available at https://github.com/capitalone/global-attribution-mapping .

REFERENCES

[1] Marco Ancona, Enea Ceolini, Cengiz ÃŰztireli, and Markus Gross. 2018. Towards better understanding of gradient-based attribution methods for Deep Neural Networks. In *International Conference on Learning Representations*. https://openreview.net/forum?id=Sy21R9JAW

[2] Alexander Binder, Grégoire Montavon, Sebastian Bach, Klaus-Robert Müller, and Wojciech Samek. 2016. Layer-wise Relevance Propagation for Neural Networks with Local Renormalization Layers. *CoRR* abs/1604.00825 (2016). arXiv:1604.00825 http://arxiv.org/abs/1604.00825

[3] Tianqi Chen and Carlos Guestrin. 2016. XGBoost: A Scalable Tree Boosting System. In *Proceedings of the 22Nd ACM SIGKDD International Conference on Knowledge Discovery and Data Mining (KDD '16)*. ACM, New York, NY, USA, 785–794. https://doi.org/10.1145/2939672.2939785

[4] Anupam Datta, Shayak Sen, and Yair Zick. 2016. Algorithmic transparency via quantitative input influence: Theory and experiments with learning systems. In *Security and Privacy (SP), 2016 IEEE Symposium on*. IEEE, 598–617.

[5] Dua Dheeru and Efi Karra Taniskidou. 2017. UCI Machine Learning Repository: Mushroom Data Set. https://archive.ics.uci.edu/ml/datasets/mushroom

[6] Finale Doshi-Velez and Been Kim. 2017. Towards a rigorous science of interpretable machine learning. *arXiv preprint arXiv:1702.08608* (2017).

[7] Gregory A. Fredricks and Roger B. Nelsen. 2007. On the relationship between Spearman's rho and Kendall's tau for pairs of continuous random variables. *Journal of Statistical Planning and Inference* 137, 7 (2007), 2143 – 2150. https://doi.org/10.1016/j.jspi.2006.06.045

[8] Nicholas Frosst and Geoffrey Hinton. 2017. Distilling a neural network into a soft decision tree. *arXiv preprint arXiv:1711.09784* (2017).

[9] Youngwook Kim. 2018. Kaggle: Modeling on Mushroom Dataset. https://www.kaggle.com/kt66nf/quick-keras-modeling-on-mushroom-dataset/notebook

[10] Pieter-Jan Kindermans, Sara Hooker, Julius Adebayo, Kristof T. Schutt, Maximilian Alber, Sven Dahne, Dumitru Erhan, and Been Kim. 2018. The (Un)reliability of saliency methods. (2018).

[11] Pieter-Jan Kindermans, Kristof T. Schutt, Maximilian Alber, Klaus-Robert Muller, Dumitru Erhan, Been Kim, and Sven Dahne. 2018. Learning how to explain neural networks: PatternNet and PatternAttribution. (2018). https://openreview.net/forum?id=Hkn7CBaTW

[12] William R. Knight. 1966. A Computer Method for Calculating Kendall's Tau with Ungrouped Data. *J. Amer. Statist. Assoc.* 61, 314 (1966), 436–439. http://www.jstor.org/stable/2282833

[13] Himabindu Lakkaraju, Stephen H Bach, and Jure Leskovec. 2016. Interpretable decision sets: A joint framework for description and prediction. In *Proceedings of the 22nd ACM SIGKDD international conference on knowledge discovery and data mining*. ACM, 1675–1684.

[14] Yann LeCun, Yoshua Bengio, and Geoffrey Hinton. 2015. Deep learning. *nature* 521, 7553 (2015), 436.

[15] Paul Lee and Philip Yu. 2012. Mixtures of weighted distance-based models for ranking data with applications in political studies. 56 (08 2012), 2486–2500.

[16] Paul H. Lee and Philip L. H. Yu. 2010. Distance-based Tree Models for Ranking Data. *Comput. Stat. Data Anal.* 54, 6 (June 2010), 1672–1682. https://doi.org/10.1016/j.csda.2010.01.027

[17] Scott Lundberg and Su-In Lee. 2017. A unified approach to interpreting model predictions. *CoRR* abs/1705.07874 (2017). arXiv:1705.07874 http://arxiv.org/abs/1705.07874

[18] Grégoire Montavon, Sebastian Bach, Alexander Binder, Wojciech Samek, and Klaus-Robert Müller. 2015. Explaining NonLinear Classification Decisions with Deep Taylor Decomposition. *CoRR* abs/1512.02479 (2015). arXiv:1512.02479 http://arxiv.org/abs/1512.02479

[19] Hae-Sang Park and Chi-Hyuck Jun. 2009. A Simple and Fast Algorithm for K-medoids Clustering. *Expert Syst. Appl.* 36, 2 (March 2009), 3336–3341. https://doi.org/10.1016/j.eswa.2008.01.039

[20] Marco Túlio Ribeiro, Sameer Singh, and Carlos Guestrin. 2016. "Why Should I Trust You?": Explaining the Predictions of Any Classifier. *CoRR* abs/1602.04938 (2016). arXiv:1602.04938 http://arxiv.org/abs/1602.04938

[21] Peter J Rousseeuw. 1987. Silhouettes: a graphical aid to the interpretation and validation of cluster analysis. *Journal of computational and applied mathematics* 20 (1987), 53–65.

[22] Grace S. Shieh, Zhidong Bai, and Wei-Yann Tsai. 2000. RANK TESTS FOR INDEPENDENCE âĂŤ WITH A WEIGHTED CONTAMINATION ALTERNATIVE. *Statistica Sinica* 10, 2 (2000), 577–593. http://www.jstor.org/stable/24306733

[23] Avanti Shrikumar, Peyton Greenside, and Anshul Kundaje. 2017. Learning Important Features Through Propagating Activation Differences. *CoRR* abs/1704.02685 (2017). arXiv:1704.02685 http://arxiv.org/abs/1704.02685

[24] Karen Simonyan, Andrea Vedaldi, and Andrew Zisserman. 2013. Deep Inside Convolutional Networks: Visualising Image Classification Models and Saliency Maps. *CoRR* abs/1312.6034 (2013). arXiv:1312.6034 http://arxiv.org/abs/1312.6034

[25] Mukund Sundararajan, Ankur Taly, and Qiqi Yan. 2017. Axiomatic Attribution for Deep Networks. *CoRR* abs/1703.01365 (2017). arXiv:1703.01365 http://arxiv.org/abs/1703.01365

[26] Weichao Xu, Yunhe Hou, Y.S. Hung, and Yuexian Zou. 2013. A comparative analysis of Spearman's rho and Kendall's tau in normal and contaminated normal models. *Signal Processing* 93, 1 (2013), 261 – 276. https://doi.org/10.1016/j.sigpro.2012.08.005

[27] Chengliang Yang, Anand Rangarajan, and Sanjay Ranka. 2018. Global Model Interpretation via Recursive Partitioning. *arXiv preprint arXiv:1802.04253* (2018).

A RESEARCH METHODS

sectionAppendix

B BACKGROUND ON LOCAL INTERPRETABILITY TECHNIQUES

B.1 Locally Interpretable Model-Agnostic Explanations (LIME)

LIME produces interpretable representations of complicated models by optimizing two metrics: interpretability Ω and local fidelity $\mathcal{L}$. Defined as,

$$\zeta(x) = \text{argmin}_{g \in G} \mathcal{L}(f, g, \pi_x) + \Omega(g). \quad (5)$$

In Equation 1, the complexity or comprehensibility Ω of an interpretable function $g \in G$ (e.g. non-zero coefficients of a linear model) is optimized alongside the fidelity $\mathcal{L}$ or faithfulness of g in approximating true function f in local neighborhood π_x.

In practice, an input point x is perturbed by random sampling in a local neighborhood and a simpler linear model is fit with the newly constructed synthetic data set. The method is model agnostic, which means it can be applied to neural networks or any other uninterpretable model. The now explainable linear model's weights can be used to interpret a particular model prediction.

B.2 Integrated Gradients

Sundararajan et. al developed an approach that satisfies two proposed axioms for attributions. First, sensitivity states that for any two inputs that differ in only a single feature and have different predictions, the attribution should be non-zero. Second, implementation invariance states that two networks that have equal outputs for all possible inputs should also have the same attributions. In this paper, the authors develop an approach that takes the path integral of the gradient for a particular point x_i and the model's inference F on the path (α) between a zero information baseline x' and the input x.

$$IG_i(x) ::= (x_i - x_i') \int_{\alpha=0}^{1} \frac{\partial f(x' + \alpha \times (x - x'))}{\partial x_i} d\alpha$$

The path integral between the baseline and the true input can be approximated with Riemman sums. An attribution vector for a particular observation (local) is produced as a result. The authors found that 20 to 300 steps can sufficiently approximate the integral within 5%. Selecting a baseline vector remains an open research question. A domain-specific heuristic (e.g. a black image in image classification) has been recommended for baseline selection.

B.3 Deep Learning Important FeaTures (DeepLIFT)

Much like Integrated Gradients, DeepLIFT seeks to explain the difference in output Δt between a 'reference' or 'baseline' input t^0 and the original input t for a neuron output: $\Delta t = t - t^0$. For each input x_i, an attribution score is calculated $C_{\Delta x_i \Delta t}$ that should sum up to the total change in the output Δt. DeepLIFT is best defined by this described summation-to-delta property:

$$\sum_{i=1}^{n} C_{\Delta x_i \Delta t} = \Delta t$$

Shrikumar et. al then construct a function analogous to a partial derivative and use the chain rule to trace the attribution score from the output layer to the original input. This method also requires a reference vector and the authors recommend leveraging domain knowledge to select an optimal baseline input.

C INTEGRATED GRADIENTS AND DEEPLIFT ANALYSIS FOR SYNTHETIC DATASET

While our local attributions using LIME did vary slightly depending our choice of kernel-width, we find local attributions to be extremely sensitive to our choice of a baseline input. Particularly, the number of points in each cluster varies greatly depending on our choice of baseline for Integrated Gradients. Both feature importances and subpopulations varied greatly for DeepLIFT. Unfortunately in this context there is no natural choice of baselines. To select a baseline for Integrated Gradients, we ran a grid search across our range of inputs within +/-.005 to produce a neutral prediction. We obtain two subpopulations using this baseline for Integrated Gradients. The first contains 610 samples and assigns an attribution of 89% to feature A. The second contains the remaining 1390 and assigns a 99% attribution to feature B. We demonstrate that our global attribution technique is local-technique agnostic by generating new attributions using Integrated Gradients and DeepLIFT.

Both feature importances and subpopulations varied greatly for DeepLIFT. To select a baseline for Integrated Gradients, we ran a grid search across our range of inputs within +/-.005 to produce a neutral prediction. We obtain two subpopulation using this baseline for Integrated Gradients. The first contains 610 samples and assigns an attribution of 89% to feature A. The second contains the remaining 1390 and assigns a 99% attribution to feature B.

D GAM APPLIED TO THE IRIS DATASET

We also evaluate the proposed global attribution method on the well known Iris dataset (Anderson, 1936; Fisher, 1936). The task is to classify Iris flowers into one of three species (setosa, virginica, and versicolor) based on the length and width of each sample's petals and sepals. We train a 2-hidden layer feed forward network on 75% of the Iris data and validate on the remaining. We use a softmax activation function as the final output layer and ReLU activation functions for all other layers. The trained network achieves a validation accuracy of 90%.

As with the synthetic dataset, we generate local attributions using LIME. We did not obtain attributions using Integrated Gradients or DeepLIFT because that method relies on the use of a baseline vector to determine the attributions, which is not as clearly defined for the Iris dataset and defining one is beyond the scope of this paper. We then conduct a silhouette analysis to determine the optimal number of clusters for our global attribution method. We find the peak silhouette score of 0.95 is achieved with three clusters, in contrast to 0.65 for two clusters and 0.78 for four clusters. We then apply our global attribution method using three subpopulations

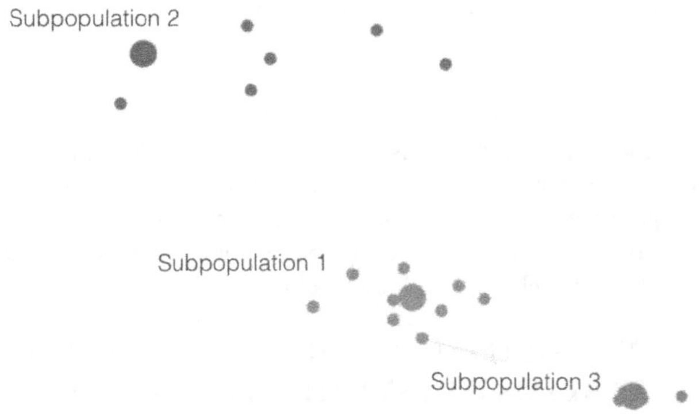

Figure 5: Attribution Subpopulations in Kendall Tau's Rank Distance Space. The attributions are represented as nodes in a force-directed graph where the distance between any two nodes is proportional to their Kendall Tau's rank distance. This allows us to visualize the relative rank distance among local attributions and their cluster medoids (represented as nodes with larger diameter). Subpopulation 1 and subpopulation 2 contain attributions associated with predictions for the setosa and versicolor flower species. Subpopulation 3 contains attributions associated with virginica predictions and a single versicolor prediction.

and extract three explainations to summarize the global attribution pattern.

To validate our results, we first plot the global attribution clusters in a force-directed graph to visualize Kendall Tau's rank distance among attributions. We find the global attributions form well-isolated clusters in rank distance space (see Figure 5). Each cluster groups a set of similar attributions in rank space, which is succinctly summarized using each cluster's medoid.

We find each attribution cluster corresponds to a target class. While this structure need not arise in the context of every problem, the attributions here can be explained nicely in terms of the classes associated with each prediction (a single exception being one versicolor prediction in subpopulation 3). We did find slight variation in the assignment of nearby attribution vectors, namely those in the region between subpopulation 1 and subpopulation 3, but the cluster structure appeared stable across many iterations with distinct clusters.

Table 3: Attribution Subpopulation Explanations

Feature	Subpop. A	Subpop. B	Subpop. C
sepal length	0.01	0.15	0.11
sepal width	0.61	0.31	0.01
petal length	0.03	0.37	0.40
petal width	0.35	0.17	0.48

Each subpopulation's explanation succinctly summarizes the feature importances for each species' predictions (see Table 3). Sepal and petal width are most important for setosa predictions (subpopulation A), whereas sepal width and petal length are most important for versicolor predictions (subpopulation B). Petal features turn out to be most important for virginica predictions (subpopulation C). We can then compare these features against the weights of a baseline classifier to assess whether the medoids reasonably capture the correct set of feature importances.

Table 4: Absolute Weights of Logistic Classifiers

Feature	setosa	versicolor	virginica
sepal length	0.87	0.04	0.33
sepal width	1.31	1.23	0.17
petal length	1.66	0.91	1.39
petal width	1.45	0.83	2.32

We additionally validate our approach by comparing the set of feature importances from our global attributions against the weights learned from a baseline one-vs-rest logistic regression classifier. We find the coefficients from the logistic regression classifiers correspond directly to the weights we obtain from our global attribution method. We find sepal width, petal length, and petal weights to have the largest coefficients across the three classes, similar to what we found across all three attribution medoids (see Table 4). Furthermore, we find the largest absolute coefficients across all classes (except for petal length for setosa) correspond directly to the feature importances uncovered by our global attribution method. For example, the largest weights for virginica predictions are the same petal features highlighted by the global attribution medoid for subpopulation C.

It is worth noting that two classifiers may learn a different set of feature interactions. In this case, the feature interactions surfaced by our global attribution method correspond to the feature weights learned by a one-vs-rest logistic regression classifier. This provides evidence not only that the number of clusters and cluster patterns are meaningful, but also that the specific feature importances uncovered in each cluster effectively describe global model attribution.

E MUSHROOM GLOBAL ATTRIBUTIONS

Global Attributions with explanations for all features across the three techniques.

E.1 Global Attributions with DeepLIFT

E.2 Global Attributions with Integrated Gradients

E.3 Global Attributions with LIME

F USER STUDIES

We asked 55 MTurk users to identity the top five features based on GAM's global explanations with two subpopulations on the FICO dataset (see figures below).

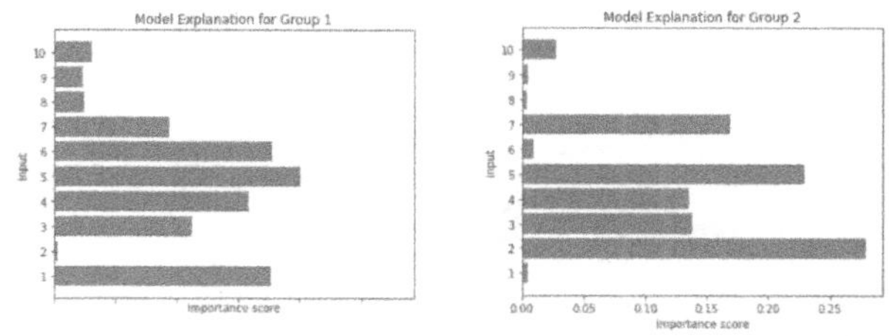

In 97% of cases respondents selected the meaningful features for subpopulation one and 92% for subpopulation two.

We also generated identical attributions for SP-LIME with B=2 and asked 55 credit modeling practitioners which explanation they preferred. In this case, the raw feature names were also displayed without a method label (see figures). Below are aggregate anonymous responses.

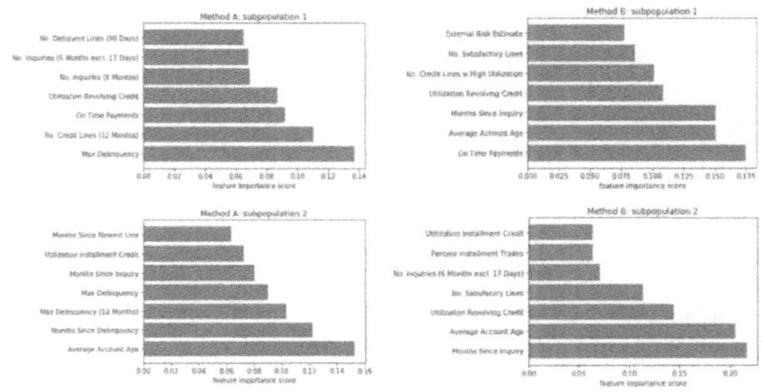

Uncovering and Mitigating Algorithmic Bias through Learned Latent Structure

Alexander Amini*† Massachusetts Institute of Technology Cambridge, MA

Ava P. Soleimany† Harvard University Boston, MA

Wilko Schwarting Massachusetts Institute of Technology Cambridge, MA

Sangeeta N. Bhatia Massachusetts Institute of Technology Cambridge, MA

Daniela Rus Massachusetts Institute of Technology Cambridge, MA

ABSTRACT

Recent research has highlighted the vulnerabilities of modern machine learning based systems to bias, especially towards segments of society that are under-represented in training data. In this work, we develop a novel, tunable algorithm for mitigating the hidden, and potentially unknown, biases within training data. Our algorithm fuses the original learning task with a variational autoencoder to learn the latent structure within the dataset and then adaptively uses the learned latent distributions to re-weight the importance of certain data points while training. While our method is generalizable across various data modalities and learning tasks, in this work we use our algorithm to address the issue of racial and gender bias in facial detection systems. We evaluate our algorithm on the Pilot Parliaments Benchmark (PPB), a dataset specifically designed to evaluate biases in computer vision systems, and demonstrate increased overall performance as well as decreased categorical bias with our debiasing approach.

CCS CONCEPTS

• **Computing methodologies** → **Artificial intelligence**; **Machine learning**; **Neural networks**.

KEYWORDS

algorithmic bias, deep learning, neural networks, facial detection

ACM Reference Format:

Alexander Amini, Ava P. Soleimany, Wilko Schwarting, Sangeeta N. Bhatia, and Daniela Rus. 2019. Uncovering and Mitigating Algorithmic Bias through Learned Latent Structure. In *2019 AAAI/ACM Conference on AI, Ethics, and Society (AIES'19), January 27–28, 2019, Honolulu, HI, USA.* ACM, New York, NY, USA, 7 pages. https://doi.org/10.1145/3306618.3314243

*To whom correspondence should be addressed: amini@mit.edu
†These authors contributed equally to this research.

AIES '19, January 27–28, 2019, Honolulu, HI, USA

ACM ISBN 978-1-4503-6324-2/19/01...$15.00
https://doi.org/10.1145/3306618.3314243

1 INTRODUCTION

Machine learning (ML) systems are increasingly making decisions that impact the daily lives of individuals and society in general. For example, ML and artificial intelligence (AI) are already being used to control end-to-end autonomous vehicles [2], how long a criminal should spend in prison [6], the order in which a person is presented the news [27], or even diagnose and treat medical patients [24].

The development and deployment of fair and unbiased AI systems is crucial to prevent any unintended side effects and to ensure the long-term acceptance of these algorithms [12, 25, 31]. Even the seemingly simple task of facial recognition [4, 23, 32] has been shown to be subject to extreme amounts of algorithmic bias among select demographics. For example, Klare et al. [20] analyzed the face detection system used by the US law enforcement and discovered significantly lower accuracy among dark women between the age of 18-30 years old. This is especially concerning since these facial recognition systems are often not deployed in isolation but rather as part of a larger surveillance or criminal detection pipeline [1].

While deep learning based systems have been shown to achieve state-of-the-art performance on many of these tasks, it has also been demonstrated that algorithms trained with biased data lead to algorithmic discrimination [3, 8, 10]. Recently, benchmarks quantifying discrimination [16, 18] and even datasets designed to evaluate the fairness of these algorithms [9] have emerged. However, the problem of severely imbalanced training datasets and the question of how to integrate debiasing capabilities into AI algorithms still remain largely unsolved.

In this paper, we tackle the challenge of integrating debiasing capabilities directly into a model training process that adapts automatically and without supervision to the shortcomings of the training data. Our approach features an end-to-end deep learning algorithm that simultaneously learns the desired task (e.g., facial detection) as well as the underlying latent structure of the training data. Learning this latent distribution in an unsupervised manner enables us to uncover hidden or implicit biases within the training data. Our algorithm, which is built on top of a variational autoencoder (VAE), is capable of identifying under-represented examples in the training dataset and subsequently increasing the probability at which the learning algorithm samples these data points (Fig. 1).

Our algorithm is applicable to a wide range of computer vision tasks and has also been used to successfully debias end-to-end autonomous vehicle controllers [3]. In this paper, we demonstrate how our algorithm can also be used to debias a facial detection

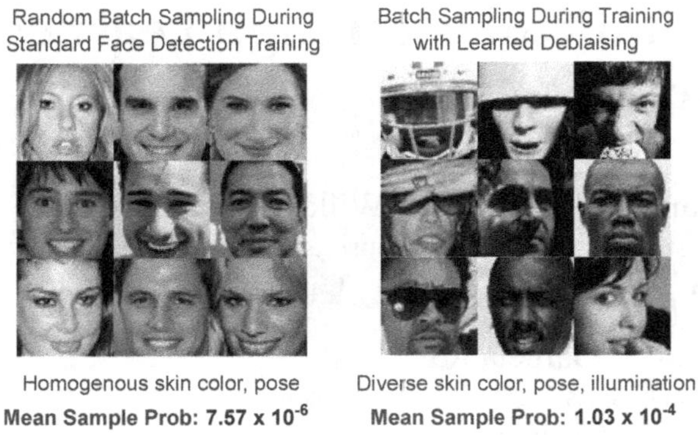

Figure 1: Batches sampled for training without (left) and with (right) learned debiasing. The proposed algorithm identifies, in an unsupervised manner, under-represented parts of training data and subsequently increases their respective sampling probability. The resulting batch (right) from the CelebA dataset shows increased diversity in features such as skin color, illumination, and occlusions.

system trained on a biased dataset and to provide interpretations of the learned latent variables which our algorithm actively debiases against. Finally, we compare the performance of our debiased model to a standard deep learning classifier by evaluating racial and gender bias on the Pilot Parliaments Benchmark (PPB) dataset [9].

The key contributions of this paper can be summarized as:

(1) A novel, tunable debiasing algorithm which utilizes learned latent variables to adjust the respective sampling probabilities of individual data points while training; and
(2) A semi-supervised model for simultaneously learning a debiased classifier as well as the underlying latent variables governing the given classes; and
(3) Analysis of our method for facial detection with biased training data and evaluation to measure algorithmic fairness across different races and genders.

The remainder of this paper is structured as follows: we summarize the related work in Sec. 2, formulate the model and debiasing algorithm in Sec. 3, describe our experimental results in Sec. 4, and provide concluding remarks in Sec. 5.

2 RELATED WORK

Interventions that seek to introduce fairness into machine learning pipelines generally fall into one of three categories: those that use data pre-processing before training, in-processing during training, and post-processing after training. Several pre-processing and in-processing methods rely on new, artificially generated debiased data [11] or resampling [26]. However, these approaches have largely focused on class imbalances, rather than variability within a class, and fail to use any information about the structure of the underlying latent features. Learning the latent structure of data has a long standing history in machine learning, including Expectation-Maximization [5], topic modelling [7], latent-SVM [14], and more recently, variational autoencoders (VAE) [19, 29]. The presented work uses a novel VAE-based approach for resampling based on the data's underlying latent structure, debiases automatically during training, and does not require any data pre-processing or annotation prior to training or testing.

Resampling for class imbalance: Resampling approaches have largely focused on addressing class imbalances [26, 34], as opposed to biases within individual classes. For example, duplicating instances of the minority class as in [22] has been used as a pre-processing step for mitigating class imbalance, yet is not capable of running adaptively during training itself. Further, applying these approaches to debiasing variabilities *within* a class would require *a priori* knowledge of the latent structure to the data, which necessitates manual annotation of the desired features. On the other hand, our approach debiases variability within a class automatically during training and learns the latent structure from scratch in an unsupervised manner.

Generating debiased data: Recent approaches have utilized generative models [30] and data transformations [11] to generate training data that is more 'fair' than the original dataset. For example, Sattigeri et al. [30] used a generative adversarial network (GAN) to output a reconstructed dataset similar to the input but more fair with respect to certain attributes. Pre-processing data transformations that mitigate discrimination [11] have also been proposed, yet such methods are not learned adaptively during training nor do they provide realistic training examples. In contrast to these works, we do not rely on artificially generated data, but rather use a resampled, more representative subset of the original dataset for debiasing.

Clustering to identify bias: Supervised learning approaches have also been used to characterize biases in imbalanced data sets. Specifically, k-means clustering has been employed to identify clusters in the input data prior to training and to inform resampling the training data into a smaller set of representative examples [28]. However, this method cannot scale to high dimensional data like images or cases where there is no notion of a data 'cluster' and relies on significant pre-processing to extract features. Our algorithm overcomes these limitations by learning the underlying latent structure using a variational approach.

3 METHODOLOGY

3.1 Problem Setup

Consider the problem of binary classification in which we are presented with a set of paired training data samples $\mathcal{D}_{train} = \{(\boldsymbol{x}^{(i)}, \boldsymbol{y}^{(i)})\}_{i=1}^{n}$ consisting of features $\boldsymbol{x} \in \mathbb{R}^m$ and labels $\boldsymbol{y} \in \mathbb{R}^d$. Our goal is to find a functional mapping $f : X \to Y$ parameterized by $\boldsymbol{\theta}$ which minimizes a certain loss $\mathcal{L}(\boldsymbol{\theta})$ over our entire training dataset. In other words, we seek to solve the following optimization problem:

$$\boldsymbol{\theta}^* = \arg\min_{\boldsymbol{\theta}} \frac{1}{n} \sum_{i=1}^{n} \mathcal{L}_i(\boldsymbol{\theta}) \quad (1)$$

Given a new test example, $(\boldsymbol{x}, \boldsymbol{y})$, our classifier should ideally output $\hat{\boldsymbol{y}} = f_{\boldsymbol{\theta}}(\boldsymbol{x})$ where $\hat{\boldsymbol{y}}$ is "close" to $\boldsymbol{y}$, with the notion of closeness being defined from the original loss function. Now, assume that each datapoint also has an associated continuous latent vector $z \in \mathbb{R}^k$ which captures the hidden, sensitive features of the sample [33]. We can formalize the notion of a biased classifier as follows:

DEFINITION 1. *A classifier, $f_\theta(x)$, is **biased** if its decision changes after being exposed to additional sensitive feature inputs. In other words, a classifier is fair with respect to a set of latent features, z, if: $f_\theta(x) = f_\theta(x, z)$.*

For example, when deciding if an image contains a face or not, the skin color, gender, or even age of the individual are all underlying latent variables, and changes to any of their specific values should not alter the classifier's ultimate decision.

To ensure fairness of a classifier across these various latent variables, the dataset should contain roughly uniform samples over the latent space. In other words, the training distribution itself should not be biased to overrepresent a certain category while under-representing others. Note that this is different than claiming that our dataset should be balanced with respect to the classes (i.e., include roughly the same number of faces as non-faces in the dataset). Namely, we are saying that *within* a single class the unobserved latent variables should also be balanced. This would promote the notion that all instances of a single class will be treated fairly by the classifier such that even if a latent variable was changed to the opposite extreme (e.g., skin tone from light to dark) the accuracy of the classifier would not be changed.

Furthermore, given a labeled test set across the space of sensitive latent variables, z, we can measure the bias of the classifier by computing its accuracy across each of the sensitive categories (e.g. skin tone). While the overall accuracy of the classifier is the mean accuracy over all sensitive categories, the bias is the variance in accuracies across all realizations of these categories (e.g., light vs. dark faces). For example, if a classifier performs equally well no matter the realization of a specific latent variable (e.g., skin tone), it will have zero variance in accuracy, and thus be called unbiased with respect to that variable. On the other hand, if some realizations of the latent variable cause the classifier to perform better or worse, the variance in the accuracies will increase, and thus, the overall bias of the classifier will also increase.

While it is possible to use a set of human defined sensitive variables to ensure fair representation during training, this requires time intensive manual annotation of each variable over the entire dataset. Additionally, this approach is subject to potential human bias in the selection of which variables are deemed sensitive or not. In this work, we address this problem by learning the latent variables of the class in an entirely unsupervised manner and proceed to use these learned variables to adaptively resample the dataset while training. In the following subsection, we will outline the architecture used to learn the latent variables.

3.2 Learning Latent Structure with Variational Autoencoders

In this work, we *learn* the latent variables of a class in an entirely unsupervised manner and proceed to use these to adaptively resample the dataset while training. To accomplish this, we propose an extension of the variational autoencoder (VAE) network architecture: a debiasing-VAE (DB-VAE). The encoder portion of the VAE learns an approximation $q_\phi(z|x)$ of the true distribution of the latent variables given a data point. As opposed to classical VAE architectures, we also introduce d additional output variables where $\hat{y} \in \mathbb{R}^d$. With k latent variables and d output variables, the encoder outputs $2k+d$

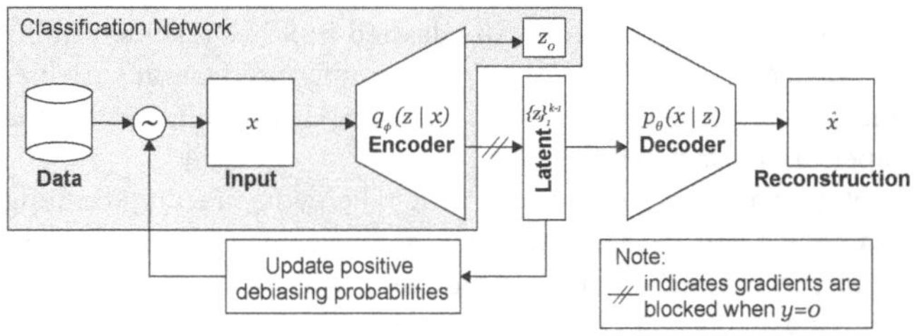

Figure 2: Debiasing Variational Autoencoder. Architecture of the semi-supervised DB-VAE for binary classification (blue region). The unsupervised latent variables are used to adaptively resample the dataset while training.

activations corresponding to $\mu \in \mathbb{R}^k, \Sigma = Diag[\sigma^2] \succ 0$, which are used to define the distribution of z, and the d-dimensional output, $\hat{\boldsymbol{y}}$.

Note that, in order to still learn our original supervised learning task we assign and explicitly supervise the d output variables. In turn, this transforms our traditional VAE model from an entirely unsupervised model to a semi-supervsied model, where some latent variables are implicitly learned by trying to reconstruct the input and the others are explicitly supervised for a specific task (e.g. classification). For example, if we originally wanted to train a binary classifier (i.e., $\hat{\boldsymbol{y}} \in \{0, 1\}$), our DB-VAE model would learn a latent encoding of k latent variables (i.e., $\{z_i\}_{i \in \{1,k\}}$) as well as a single variable specifically for classification: $z_0 = \hat{y}$.

A decoder network mirroring the encoder is then used to reconstruct the input back from the latent space by approximating $p_\theta(x|z)$. VAEs utilize reparameterization to differentiate the outputs through a sampling step, where we sample $\epsilon \sim \mathcal{N}(0, (I))$ and compute $z = \mu(x) + \Sigma^{\frac{1}{2}}(x) \circ \epsilon$. This decoded reconstruction enables unsupervised learning of the latent variables during training, and is thus necessary for automated debiasing of the data during training.

We train the network end-to-end using backpropagation with a three component loss function comprised of a supervised latent loss, a reconstruction loss, and a latent loss for the unsupervised variables. For a binary classification task, for example, the supervised loss $\mathcal{L}_y(y, \hat{y})$ is given by the cross-entropy loss; the reconstruction loss $\mathcal{L}_x(x, \hat{x})$ is given by the L_p norm between the input and the reconstructed output; and the latent loss $\mathcal{L}_{KL}(\mu, \sigma)$ is given by the Kullback-Liebler (KL) divergence. Finally, the total loss is a weighted combination of these three losses:

$$\mathcal{L}_{TOTAL} = c_1 \underbrace{\left[\sum_{i \in \{0,1\}} y_i \log \left(\frac{1}{\hat{y}_i} \right) \right]}_{\mathcal{L}_y(y,\hat{y})} + c_2 \underbrace{\left[\|x - \hat{x}\|_p \right]}_{\mathcal{L}_x(x,\hat{x})} + c_3 \underbrace{\left[\frac{1}{2} \sum_{j=0}^{k-1} (\sigma_j + \mu_j^2 - 1 - \log(\sigma_j)) \right]}_{\mathcal{L}_{KL}(\mu,\sigma)} \quad (2)$$

where c_1, c_2, c_3 are the weighting coefficients to impact the relative importance of each of the individual loss functions. For comparison, the baseline model used for the desired task has a similar architecture as the DB-VAE, without the unsupervised latent variables and decoder network, and would be trained according to only the supervised loss function.

Note that special care needs to be taken when feeding training examples from classes which you do not want to debias. For example, in the facial detection problem, we primarily care about ensuring that our positive dataset of faces is fair and unbiased, and less about debiasing negative examples where there is no face present. For these negative samples, the gradients from the decoder and latent space should be stopped and not backpropogated. This effectively means that, for these classes, we only train the encoder to optimize the supervised loss.

3.3 Algorithm for Automated Debiasing

In this section, we present the algorithm for adaptive resampling of the training data based on the latent structure learned by our DB-VAE model. By dropping over-represented regions of the latent space according to their frequency of occurrence, we increase the probability of selecting rarer data for training. This is done adaptively as the latent variables themselves are being learned during training. Thus, our debiasing approach accounts for the complete distribution of the underlying features in the training data.

The training dataset is fed through the encoder network, which provides an estimate $Q(z|X)$ of the latent distribution. We seek to increase the relative frequency of rare data points by increased sampling of under-represented regions of the latent space. To do so, we approximate the distribution of the latent space with a histogram $\hat{Q}(z|X)$ with dimensionality defined by the number of latent variables, k. To circumvent the high-dimensionality of the histogram when the latent space becomes increasingly complex, we simplify further and use independent histograms to approximate the joint distribution. Specifically, we define an independent histogram, $\hat{Q}_i(z_i|X)$, for each latent variable z_i:

$$\hat{Q}(z|X) \propto \prod_i \hat{Q}_i(z_i|X) \tag{3}$$

This allows us to neatly approximate $Q(z|X)$ based on the frequency distribution of each of the learned latent variables. Finally, we introduce a single parameter, α, to tune the degree of debiasing introduced during training. We define the probability distribution of selecting a datapoint $\boldsymbol{x}$ as $\mathcal{W}(z(\boldsymbol{x})|X)$, parameterized by the debiasing parameter α:

$$\mathcal{W}(z(\boldsymbol{x})|X) \propto \prod_i \frac{1}{\hat{Q}_i(z_i(\boldsymbol{x})|X) + \alpha} \tag{4}$$

We provide pseudocode for training the DB-VAE in Algorithm 1. At every epoch all inputs x from the original dataset X are propagated through the model to evaluate the corresponding latent variables $z(x)$. The histograms $\hat{Q}_i(z_i(x)|X)$ are updated accordingly. During training, a new batch is drawn by keeping inputs, x, from the original dataset, X, with likelihood $W(z(x)|X)$. Training on the debiased data batch now forces the classifier into a choice of parameters that work better in rare cases without strong deterioration of performance for common training examples. Most importantly, the debiasing is not manually specified beforehand but instead based on *learned* latent variables.

Algorithm 1 Adaptive re-sampling for automated debiasing of the DB-VAE architecture

Require: Training data $\{X, Y\}$, batch size b
Initialize weights $\{\phi, \theta\}$
for each epoch, E_t **do**
  Sample $z \sim q_\phi(z|X)$
  Update $\hat{Q}_i(z_i(x)|X)$
  $\mathcal{W}(z(x)|X) \leftarrow \prod_i \frac{1}{\hat{Q}_i(z_i(x)|X)+\alpha}$
  while $iter < \frac{n}{b}$ **do**
    Sample $\boldsymbol{x}_{batch} \sim \mathcal{W}(z(x)|X)$
    $L(\phi, \theta) \leftarrow \frac{1}{b} \sum_{i \in \boldsymbol{x}_{batch}} \mathcal{L}_i(\phi, \theta)$
    Update: $[w \leftarrow w - \eta \nabla_{\phi,\theta} \mathcal{L}(\phi, \theta)]_{w \in \{\phi, \theta\}}$
  end while
end for

Intuitively, we can think of the parameter α as tuning the degree of debiasing. As $\alpha \rightarrow 0$, the subsampled training set will tend towards uniform over the latent variables z. As $\alpha \rightarrow \infty$, the subsampled training set will tend towards a random uniform sample of the original training dataset (i.e., no debiasing).

4 EXPERIMENTS

To validate our debiasing algorithm on a real-world problem with significant social impact, we learn a debiased facial detector using potentially biased training data. Here we define the facial detection problem, describe the datasets used, and outline model training, debiasing, and evaluation.

For the facial detection problem, we are given a set of paired training data samples $\mathcal{D}_{train} = \{(\boldsymbol{x}^{(i)}, \boldsymbol{y}^{(i)})\}_{i=1}^n$, where $\boldsymbol{x}^{(i)}$ are the raw pixel values of an image patch and $\boldsymbol{y}^{(i)} \in \{0, 1\}$ are their respective labels, indicating the presence of a face. Our goal is to ensure that the set of positive examples used to train a facial detection classifier is fair and unbiased. The positive training data may potentially be biased with respect to certain attributes such as skin tone, in that particular instances of those attributes may appear more or less frequently than other instances. Thus, in our experiments, we train a full DB-VAE model to learn the latent structure underlying the positive (face) images and use the adaptive resampling approach outlined in Algorithm 1 to debias the model with respect to facial features. For negative examples, we only train the encoder portion of our network, as described in Section 3. We evaluate the performance of our debiased models relative to standard, biased classifiers on the PPB dataset and provide estimates of the precision and bias of each model as performance metrics.

4.1 Datasets

We train our classifiers on a dataset of $n = 4 \times 10^5$ images, consisting of 2×10^5 positive (images of faces) and negative (images of non-faces) examples, split 80% and 20% into training and validation sets, respectively. Positive examples were taken from the CelebA dataset [21] and cropped to a square based on the annotated face bounding box. Negative examples were taken from the ImageNet dataset [13], from a wide variety of non-human categories. All images were resized to 64×64.

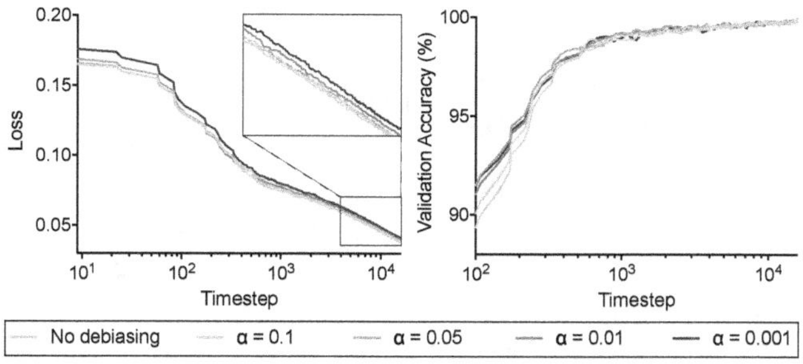

Figure 3: Loss evolution and validation accuracy. Convergence of the total loss on the training set (left) and classification accuracy on the validation set (right) for models with varying degrees of debiasing.

After training, we evaluate our debiasing algorithm on the PPB test dataset [9], which consists of images of 1270 male and female parliamentarians from various African and European countries. Images are consistent in pose, illumination, and facial expression, and the dataset exhibits parity in both skin tone and gender. The gender of each face is annotated with the sex-based "Male" and "Female" labels. Skin tone annotations are based on the Fitzpatrick skin type classification system [15], with each image labeled as "Lighter" or "Darker".

4.2 Training the Models

For the classical facial detection task, we train a convolutional neural network with four sequential convolutional layers (5×5 filters with 2×2 strides) for feature extraction. Final classification is done with an additional two fully connected layers with 1000 and 1 hidden neurons in each layer respectively. All layers in the network use ReLU activation and batch normalization [17]. Our DB-VAE architecture shares this same classification network for the encoder, except for the final fully connected layer which now outputs an additional k latent variables for a total of $2k + 1$ activations. A decoder, which mirrors the encoder with 2 fully connected layers and 4 de-convolutional layers, is then used to reconstruct the original input image. We train our models by minimizing the empirical training loss as defined in Eq. 2 with $L2$ reconstruction loss.

In our experiments, we additionally block all gradients from the decoder network when $y = 0$, i.e., for negative examples, as we only want to debias for positive face examples. In addition to training the standard classification network with no debiasing, we trained DB-VAE models with varying degrees of debiasing, defined by the parameter α, for 50 epochs and evaluated their performance on the validation set. Models were re-trained from scratch 5 times each for added statistical robustness of results.

4.3 Automated Debiasing of Facial Detection Systems

We explore the output of the debiasing algorithm and provide extensive evaluation of our learned models on the PPB dataset. We consider the resampling probabilities, $\mathcal{W}(z(x)|X)$, that arise from learning a debiased model. As shown in Fig. 4A, as the probability of resampling increases, the number of data points within the corresponding bin decreases, suggesting that those images more likely to be resampled are those characterized by 'rare' features.

Indeed, as the probability of resampling increases, the corresponding images become more diverse, as evidenced by the four sample faces from each frequency bin in Fig. 4A. This observation is further validated by considering the ten faces in the training data with the lowest and highest resampling probabilities (Fig. 4B,C respectively). The ten faces with the lowest resampling probability appear quite uniform, with consistent skin tone, hair color, forward gaze, and background color. In contrast, the ten faces with the highest resampling probability display rarer features such as headwear or eyewear, tilted gaze, shadowing, and darker skin. Taken together, these results imply that our algorithm identifies and then actively resamples those data points with rarer, more diverse features based on a learned latent representation.

We observed that the DB-VAE is able to learn facial features such as skin tone, presence of hair, and azimuth, as well as other features such as gender and age by slowly perturbing the value of a single latent variable and and feeding the resulting encoding through the decoder (Fig. 5A). This supports the hypothesis that our DB-VAE algorithm is capable of debiasing against such features since the resampling probabilities are directly defined based on the probability distributions of *individual* learned latent variables (Alg. 1).

To evaluate the performance of our debiasing approach, we utilized classification accuracy (positive predictive value) as a metric, and tested our models on the PPB dataset. For this evaluation, we extracted patches from each image using sliding windows of varying dimension, and fed these extracted image patches to our trained models. We output a positive match of a face if the classifier identifies a face in any one of the subpatches within the image.

To demonstrate debiasing against specific latent features, we quantified classification performance on individual demographics. Specifically, we considered skin tone (light/dark) and gender

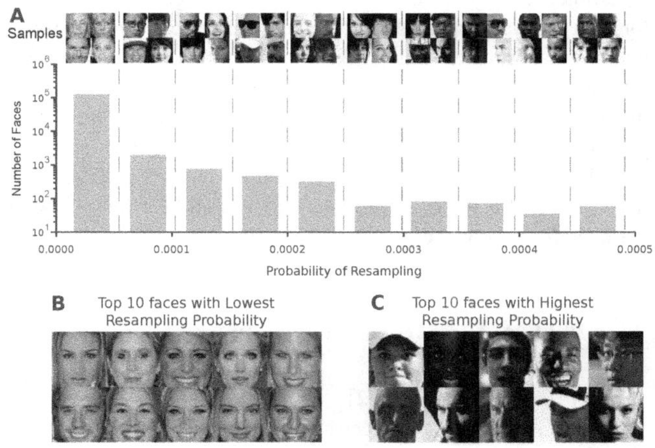

Figure 4: Sampling probabilities over the training dataset. Histogram over resampling probabilities showing four samples from each bin (A). The top ten faces with the lowest (B) and highest (C) probabilities of being sampled.

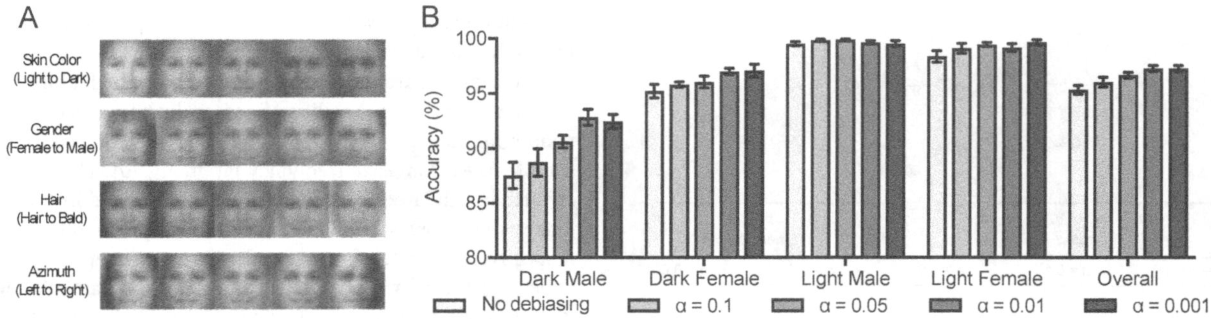

Figure 5: Increased performance and decreased categorical bias with DB-VAE. The model learns latent features such as skin color, gender, hair (A) and demonstrates increased performance and decreased categorical bias with learned debiasing (B).

(male/female). We denote $\mathcal{A}$ as the set of classification accuracies of a model on each of the four intersectional classes. We compared the accuracy of models trained with and without debiasing on both individual demographics (race/gender) and the PPB dataset as a whole, and provide results on the effect of the debiasing parameter α on performance (Fig. 5). Recall that no debiasing corresponds to the limit $\alpha \to \infty$, where we uniformly sample over the *original training set* without learning the latent variables. Conversely, $\alpha \to 0$, corresponds to sampling from a uniform distribution over *the latent space.* Error bars (standard error of the mean) are provided to visualize statistical significance of differences between the trained models.

As shown in Fig. 5, greater debiasing power (decreasing α) significantly increased classification accuracy on "Dark Male" subjects, consistent with the hypothesis that adaptive resampling of rare instances (e.g., dark faces) in the training data results in less algorithmic discrimination. This suggests that our algorithm can debias for a qualitative feature like skin tone, which has significant social implications for its utility in improving fairness in facial detection systems.

In contrast to the trend observed with dark male faces, the classification accuracy on "Light Male" faces remained nearly constant for both the biased and debiased models. Additionally, the accuracy on light male subjects was higher than the three other groups, consistent with [9]. This suggests that our debiasing algorithm does not sacrifice performance on categories which already have high precision. Importantly, the high, near constant accuracy suggests that an arbitrary classification model trained on the CelebA dataset may be biased towards light male subjects, and further supports the need for approaches that seek to reduce such biases.

Table 1: Accuracy and bias on PPB test dataset.

	$\mathbb{E}[\mathcal{A}]$ (Precision)	$Var[\mathcal{A}]$ (Measure of Bias)
No Debiasing	95.13	28.84
$\alpha = 0.1$	95.84	25.43
$\alpha = 0.05$	96.47	18.08
$\alpha = 0.01$	97.13	9.49
$\alpha = 0.001$	**97.36**	**9.43**

Although the DB-VAE improved accuracy on dark males significantly, it never reached the accuracy of light males. Despite the fact that we debias our training data with respect to latent variables such as skin tone, there are inherently fewer examples of dark male faces in our data. Our model is simply limited by infrequency of these examples but we note that increasing the overall size of our training dataset may further mitigate this effect.

We summarize the key trends in overall performance with DB-VAE in Table 1. As confirmed by Fig. 5, the overall precision, $\mathbb{E}[\mathcal{A}]$, increased with increased debiasing power (decreasing α). Additionally, we observed a decrease in the variance in accuracy between categories, indicative of decreased bias with greater debiasing. Together, these results suggest effective debiasing with DB-VAE.

5 CONCLUSION

In this paper, we propose a novel, tunable debiasing algorithm to adjust the respective sampling probabilities of individual data points while training. By learning the underlying latent variables in an entirely unsupervised manner, we can scale our approach to large datasets and debias for latent features without ever hand labeling them in our training set.

We apply our approach to facial detection to promote algorithmic fairness by reducing hidden biases within training data. Given a biased training dataset, our debiased models show increased classification accuracy and decreased categorical bias across race and gender, compared to standard classifiers. Finally, we provide a concrete algorithm for debiasing as well as an open source implementation of our model.

The development and deployment of fair and unbiased AI systems is crucial to prevent unintended discrimination and to ensure the long-term acceptance of these algorithms. We envision that the proposed approach will serve as an additional tool to promote systematic, algorithmic fairness of modern AI systems.

ACKNOWLEDGMENTS

A.A. and A.P.S acknowledge support from the National Science Foundation Graduate Research Fellowship. A.P.S. acknowledges support from the NIH Molecular Biophysics Training Grant. We gratefully acknowledge the support of NVIDIA Corporation with the donation of the V100 GPU used for this research. S.N.B. is a HHMI Investigator.

REFERENCES

[1] Nurul Azma Abdullah, Md Jamri Saidi, Nurul Hidayah Ab Rahman, Chuah Chai Wen, and Isredza Rahmi A Hamid. 2017. Face recognition for criminal identification: An implementation of principal component analysis for face recognition. In *AIP Conference Proceedings*, Vol. 1891. 020002.

[2] Alexander Amini, Guy Rosman, Sertac Karaman, and Daniela Rus. 2019. Variational End-to-End Navigation and Localization. In *2019 IEEE International Conference on Robotics and Automation (ICRA)*. IEEE.

[3] Alexander Amini, Wilko Schwarting, Guy Rosman, Brandon Araki, Sertac Karaman, and Daniela Rus. 2018. Variational autoencoder for end-to-end control of autonomous driving with novelty detection and training de-biasing. In *2018 IEEE/RSJ International Conference on Intelligent Robots and Systems (IROS)*. IEEE, 568–575.

[4] Yancheng Bai and Bernard Ghanem. 2017. Multi-scale fully convolutional network for face detection in the wild. In *2017 IEEE Conference on Computer Vision and Pattern Recognition Workshops (CVPRW)*. IEEE, 2078–2087.

[5] Timothy L Bailey, Charles Elkan, et al. 1994. Fitting a mixture model by expectation maximization to discover motifs in bipolymers. (1994).

[6] Richard A Berk, Susan B Sorenson, and Geoffrey Barnes. 2016. Forecasting domestic violence: A machine learning approach to help inform arraignment decisions. *Journal of Empirical Legal Studies* 13, 1 (2016), 94–115.

[7] David M Blei. 2012. Probabilistic topic models. *Commun. ACM* 55, 4 (2012), 77–84.

[8] Tolga Bolukbasi, Kai-Wei Chang, James Y Zou, Venkatesh Saligrama, and Adam T Kalai. [n. d.]. Man is to computer programmer as woman is to homemaker? Debiasing word embeddings. In *Neural Information Processing Systems*. 4349–4357.

[9] Joy Buolamwini and Timnit Gebru. 2018. Gender shades: Intersectional accuracy disparities in commercial gender classification. In *Conference on Fairness, Accountability and Transparency*. 77–91.

[10] Aylin Caliskan, Joanna J Bryson, and Arvind Narayanan. 2017. Semantics derived automatically from language corpora contain human-like biases. *Science* 356, 6334 (2017), 183–186.

[11] Flavio Calmon, Dennis Wei, Bhanukiran Vinzamuri, Karthikeyan Natesan Ramamurthy, and Kush R Varshney. 2017. Optimized pre-processing for discrimination prevention. In *Advances in Neural Information Processing Systems*. 3992–4001.

[12] Rachel Courtland. 2018. Bias detectives: the researchers striving to make algorithms fair. *Nature* (Jun 2018). https://www.nature.com/articles/d41586-018-05469-3

[13] Jia Deng, Wei Dong, Richard Socher, Li-Jia Li, Kai Li, and Li Fei-Fei. 2009. Imagenet: A large-scale hierarchical image database. In *IEEE Conference on Computer Vision and Pattern Recognition*. IEEE, 248–255.

[14] Pedro Felzenszwalb, David McAllester, and Deva Ramanan. 2008. A discriminatively trained, multiscale, deformable part model. In *Computer Vision and Pattern Recognition, 2008. CVPR 2008. IEEE Conference on*. IEEE, 1–8.

[15] Thomas B Fitzpatrick. 1988. The validity and practicality of sun-reactive skin types I through VI. *Archives of dermatology* 124, 6 (1988), 869–871.

[16] Moritz Hardt, Eric Price, Nati Srebro, et al. 2016. Equality of opportunity in supervised learning. In *Neural information processing systems*. 3315–3323.

[17] Sergey Ioffe and Christian Szegedy. 2015. Batch normalization: Accelerating deep network training by reducing internal covariate shift. *arXiv preprint arXiv:1502.03167* (2015).

[18] Niki Kilbertus, Mateo Rojas Carulla, Giambattista Parascandolo, Moritz Hardt, Dominik Janzing, and Bernhard Schölkopf. 2017. Avoiding discrimination through causal reasoning. In *Advances in Neural Information Processing Systems*. 656–666.

[19] Diederik P Kingma and Max Welling. 2013. Auto-encoding variational bayes. *arXiv preprint arXiv:1312.6114* (2013).

[20] Brendan F Klare, Mark J Burge, Joshua C Klontz, Richard W Vorder Bruegge, and Anil K Jain. 2012. Face recognition performance: Role of demographic information. *IEEE Transactions on Information Forensics and Security* 7, 6 (2012), 1789–1801.

[21] Ziwei Liu, Ping Luo, Xiaogang Wang, and Xiaoou Tang. 2015. Deep Learning Face Attributes in the Wild. In *Proceedings of International Conference on Computer Vision*.

[22] Yi Lu, Hong Guo, and Lee Feldkamp. 1998. Robust neural learning from unbalanced data samples. In *IEEE Neural Networks Proceedings*.

[23] Markus Mathias, Rodrigo Benenson, Marco Pedersoli, and Luc Van Gool. 2014. Face detection without bells and whistles. In *European conference on computer vision*. Springer, 720–735.

[24] Maciej A Mazurowski, Piotr A Habas, Jacek M Zurada, Joseph Y Lo, Jay A Baker, and Georgia D Tourassi. 2008. Training neural network classifiers for medical decision making: The effects of imbalanced datasets on classification performance. *Neural networks* 21, 2-3 (2008), 427–436.

[25] Claire Cain Miller. 2015. When Algorithms Discriminate. *New York Times* (Jul 2015). https://www.nytimes.com/2015/07/10/upshot/when-algorithms-discriminate.html

[26] Ajinkya More. 2016. Survey of resampling techniques for improving classification performance in unbalanced datasets. *arXiv preprint arXiv:1608.06048* (2016).

[27] Eric Nalisnick, Bhaskar Mitra, Nick Craswell, and Rich Caruana. 2016. Improving document ranking with dual word embeddings. In *Proceedings of the 25th International Conference Companion on World Wide Web*. 83–84.

[28] Giang H Nguyen, Abdesselam Bouzerdoum, and Son L Phung. 2008. A supervised learning approach for imbalanced data sets. In *International Conference on Pattern Recognition*. IEEE, 1–4.

[29] Danilo Jimenez Rezende, Shakir Mohamed, and Daan Wierstra. 2014. Stochastic backpropagation and approximate inference in deep generative models. *arXiv preprint arXiv:1401.4082* (2014).

[30] Prasanna Sattigeri, Samuel C Hoffman, Vijil Chenthamarakshan, and Kush R Varshney. 2018. Fairness GAN. *arXiv preprint arXiv:1805.09910* (2018).

[31] Jonathan Vanian. 2018. Unmasking A.I.'s Bias Problem. *Fortune* (Jun 2018). http://fortune.com/longform/ai-bias-problem/

[32] Stefanos Zafeiriou, Cha Zhang, and Zhengyou Zhang. 2015. A survey on face detection in the wild: past, present and future. *Computer Vision and Image Understanding* 138 (2015), 1–24.

[33] Rich Zemel, Yu Wu, Kevin Swersky, Toni Pitassi, and Cynthia Dwork. 2013. Learning fair representations. In *International Conference on Machine Learning*. 325–333.

[34] Zhi-Hua Zhou and Xu-Ying Liu. 2006. Training cost-sensitive neural networks with methods addressing the class imbalance problem. *IEEE Transactions on Knowledge and Data Engineering* 18, 1 (2006), 63–77.

Crowdsourcing with Fairness, Diversity and Budget Constraints

Naman Goel
naman.goel@epfl.ch
Artificial Intelligence Lab, EPFL
Lausanne, Switzerland

Boi Faltings
boi.faltings@epfl.ch
Artificial Intelligence Lab, EPFL
Lausanne, Switzerland

ABSTRACT

Recent studies have shown that the labels collected from crowdworkers can be discriminatory with respect to sensitive attributes such as gender and race. This raises questions about the suitability of using crowdsourced data for further use, such as for training machine learning algorithms. In this work, we address the problem of fair and diverse data collection from a crowd under budget constraints. We propose a novel algorithm which maximizes the expected accuracy of the collected data, while ensuring that the errors satisfy desired notions of fairness. We provide guarantees on the performance of our algorithm and show that the algorithm performs well in practice through experiments on a real dataset.

CCS CONCEPTS

• **Information systems** → **Crowdsourcing**; *Social networks*; Incentive schemes.

KEYWORDS

Crowdsourcing, Data Quality, Bias, Fairness

ACM Reference Format:

Naman Goel and Boi Faltings. 2019. Crowdsourcing with Fairness, Diversity and Budget Constraints. In *AAAI/ACM Conference on AI, Ethics, and Society (AIES '19), January 27–28, 2019, Honolulu, HI, USA.* ACM, New York, NY, USA, 8 pages. https://doi.org/10.1145/3306618.3314282

1 INTRODUCTION

Algorithmic decision-making is gaining popularity in many diverse application areas of social importance. Examples include criminal recidivism prediction, stop-and-frisk programs, university admissions, bank loan decisions, screening job candidates, fake news control, information filtering(personalization) and search engine rankings etc. Recently, questions were raised about the fairness of these algorithms. An investigation [26] found COMPAS (a popular software used by courts to predict criminal recidivism risk) racially discriminatory. Other software systems have also been found to be biased against people of different races, genders and political views [3, 18, 20, 25]. This has led to a widespread and legitimate concern about the potential negative influence of such systems on the society [2, 29]. One of the main reasons of algorithmic bias is the bias in the training datasets. In order to achieve algorithmic fairness, the issue of **data fairness** needs to be addressed first. In many interesting cases, data is directly or indirectly influenced by some kind of human feedback. The influence is obvious and direct if human assigned labels are used as a proxy for ground truth labels. However, human feedback can also indirectly influence the so-called "ground-truth" datasets (when the labels are not human assigned but observed in reality). This is because the ground truth labels can only be collected for a finite number of data points and the selection of data points is often influenced by humans. For example, there are no ground truth labels available for recidivism of people who were never released by the judges. In this paper, we focus only on the direct influence of human feedback on data fairness i.e. the case in which humans assign labels for data.

Crowdsourcing is increasingly used to collect training data labels. Inevitably, crowdworkers have different biases, which are then reflected in the labels collected from the workers. A very recent study [8] conducted on Amazon Mechanical Turk showed that the crowdworkers were equally racially biased as COMPAS in predicting recidivism. The difference in false positive rates of crowd predictions for white and black defendants was significant and nearly equal to that of the predictions made by COMPAS. The same was true for false negative rates also. The bias didn't change much even when the crowdworkers were not explicitly displayed the race of the defendants.

We consider settings similar to [8]. Workers are asked to provide their answers (or labels) about some tasks with unknown ground truth labels. Every task has some non-sensitive details that are shown to the workers and a sensitive attribute (for example, race) that is not explicitly shown. But the sensitive attribute may potentially be correlated with the non-sensitive task details. A worker inspects the tasks assigned to her and submits labels for the tasks. Each task is assumed to have a ground truth label but the workers don't have any way of accessing the ground truth. They can only use the task details, their prior knowledge and incomplete information from other sources to make an "educated guess" about the ground truth. The examples of such tasks are "Will a defendant with given personal history recidivate within the next two years or not?" or "Will a candidate with given CV be successful in the job applied for?" or "Is given political news item fake?". The sensitive attributes in these example tasks are race, gender and political group respectively. Every worker charges a fee for answering the assigned tasks. The requester has a budget constraint on the fees that she can pay to the workers. In this paper, we make the following contributions:

(1) We propose a novel algorithm for assigning tasks to workers, which optimizes the expected accuracy of labels obtained from crowd while ensuring that the collected labels satisfy desired notions of *error fairness*. The algorithm also ensures diversity of responses by limiting the probability of assigning

AIES '19, January 27–28, 2019, Honolulu, HI, USA

ACM ISBN 978-1-4503-6324-2/19/01...$15.00
https://doi.org/10.1145/3306618.3314282

many tasks to a single worker. Our algorithm works even when the values of the sensitive attribute of the tasks are unavailable or can't used because of ethical/legal reasons.

(2) With a novel formulation of the task assignment strategy as a probability distribution over the workers, we can cast the optimization problem as a linear program and avoid the use of integer programming or other graph matching algorithms which are popular in the task assignment literature but are harder to solve exactly and analyze. This also makes our algorithm suitable for online settings in which the requester is not aware of the tasks in advance.

(3) We use a limited number of gold tasks (tasks with known ground-truth answers) for estimating workers' parameters and then optimally assign non-gold tasks to the workers. We provide performance bounds for our algorithm and show empirical performance on a real dataset.

2 RELATED WORK

Empirical Studies : [8] finds racial discrimination in recidivism prediction tasks on Amazon Mechanical Turk (AMT). [23] analyzes linguistic bias in labels collected through GWAP (Games with a Purpose) on AMT. [24] analyzes the linguistic bias in collaboratively produced biographies. [13] finds discrimination in reputation crowdsourcing systems in online marketplaces.

Proposed Solutions : In an independent and pioneering work, [28] considers the problem of fairness in human decision-making tasks like recidivism prediction, without budget and diversity constraints. Criminal cases with *known* race information arrive in batches of *known* sizes and an MDP based maximum weighted matching algorithm assigns each case to *exactly one* human judge such that the overall utility from decisions of releasing or keeping any defendant is maximized, while ensuring *demographic parity* of release decisions across two races. To the best of our knowledge this is the first and the most recent work to consider settings somewhat similar to ours but our work differs from theirs in several ways. We consider general crowdsourcing settings, in which several assumptions from their model don't hold. In particular, they assume that "true" risk scores of individual defendants are known to the human judges and the case assignment algorithm. In general crowdsourcing settings, one can only hope to have an overall label distribution for the population. In fact, finding the label probability for individual tasks is the very objective of crowdsourcing. Further, it is not immediately clear how their work can be extended for other important fairness definitions. In their model, given true risk scores of the defendants, judges only apply different thresholds for black and white defendants to predict recidivism. The threshold parameters alone can't capture unfairness measures such as unequal error rates. Even if one does improvise the model with more parameters, it remains an open question whether the theoretical conjectures made in the paper are still likely. This is because the conjectures assume that every time a judge gives a decision, the model parameters of the judge are updated. This becomes an issue with error rate parameters since the ground truth labels are not revealed for all tasks in crowdsourcing. [21] considers a different but related problem of bias resulting from adaptive data gathering (when the choice of whether to collect more data of a given type depends on the data already collected) and propose a differentially private data collection process as a solution.

There is also a lot of work on task assignment in crowdsourcing, which doesn't consider fairness. [27] proposes a greedy knapsack approach to satisfy limits on budget and the number of tasks any worker can solve. [15–17] consider task assignment problem when workers arrive online. [4] proposes optimal gold task assignment when workers' diligence change over time.

Beyond data collection, there is also recent work on making algorithms fair and robust to bias in the training data [9, 12, 14, 19, 30] and on correcting bias in training datasets [5, 10]. Correcting bias in a given dataset requires modifying the feature values and/or the labels in the dataset. In this paper, we aim to collect unbiased and high quality dataset to begin with, relaxing the responsibility and the overhead of such post-processing from data users (for example, data scientists and machine learning engineers).

3 MODEL

Let there be a finite set of n workers and a large pool of tasks with unknown ground truth labels. The data requester randomly chooses tasks from the pool one by one and assigns each to one (or more) worker(s). The requester may not have knowledge of all the tasks in the pool (not even the number of tasks in the pool) in advance. A worker i charges a constant amount of fee c_i for every label she provides. The requester has a budget constraint for the maximum *expected* money to be spent on acquiring one label from a worker.

Let Z be a random variable denoting the sensitive attribute and Y denoting the (unknown) ground truth labels of the tasks such that $Z, Y \in \{0, 1\}$. For the tasks attempted by a worker i, let $\hat{Y}_i \in \{0, 1\}$ denote the labels submitted by the worker. We denote the realizations of random variables Z, Y and $\hat{Y}_i$ by lower case letters z, y and $\hat{y}_i$ respectively and will drop the subscripts for brevity when the context is clear. We will use $[n]$ to denote $\{1, 2, \ldots, n\}$. The workers are modeled using their accuracy matrices as follows:

Definition 1 (Accuracy Matrices of a Worker). *The accuracy matrices $\mathcal{A}_{iz}$, $z \in \{0, 1\}$ of a worker i are two 2×2 row stochastic matrices such that, $\forall y, \hat{y}_i \in \{0, 1\}$, the entry $\mathcal{A}_{iz}[y, \hat{y}_i]$ is the probability of the worker's label on a task being $\hat{y}_i$ given that the sensitive attribute of the task is z and the ground truth label is y.*

The two matrices $\mathcal{A}_{i0}$ and $\mathcal{A}_{i1}$ define the accuracy of the worker i for tasks belonging to the two different values of the sensitive attribute. The accuracy matrix model, also known as the Dawid-Skene model [7] in the crowdsourcing literature, is strong enough to capture different errors (for e.g. false positive and false negative rates) that a worker may make for tasks belonging to a given sensitive attribute value. If a worker is unbiased in the sense that her errors don't depend on the value of sensitive attribute of the task, her two accuracy matrices are identical. Note that this model makes an implicit i.i.d. assumption on a worker's answers.

The requester uses a probabilistic policy to assign the tasks to workers and collects the labels from the workers.

Definition 2 (Crowdsourcing Policy). *A crowdsourcing policy is an n-dimensional stochastic vector S, such that an element $S[i]$, $i \in [n]$ is the probability of assigning any task to worker i, regardless of the sensitive attribute value of the task.*

Note that the requester's policy doesn't depend on the value of the sensitive attribute of the task. This is an intentional modeling choice to deal with the situations in which the sensitive attribute values of the tasks may not be available. It may be due to missing data, privacy reasons or legal/ethical requirements of not using the sensitive attribute.

For any task, the requester randomly selects one (or more than one) worker(s) with probabilities specified by the crowdsourcing policy vector S and assigns the task to the selected worker(s). The labels collected from the workers are obviously not guaranteed to be error free. We can define the accuracy matrices of the crowdsourcing policy in the same way as we defined the accuracy matrices of workers.

Definition 3 (Accuracy Matrices of a Crowdsourcing Policy). *The accuracy matrices $\mathcal{A}_z$, $z \in \{0,1\}$ of a crowdsourcing policy are two 2×2 row stochastic matrices such that, $\forall y, \hat{y} \in \{0,1\}$, the entry $\mathcal{A}_z[y,\hat{y}]$ is the probability that a crowdsourced label*[1] *for a task is $\hat{y}$ given that the sensitive attribute of the task is z and the ground truth label is y.*

We use the letter $\mathcal{A}$ to denote accuracy matrices of the crowdsourcing policy as well as that of the workers but readers can differentiate between the two by noting that $\mathcal{A}$ has an additional subscript i when referring to the matrix of a worker i. It is easy to see that we can express the accuracy matrices of a policy in terms of the accuracy matrices of the workers as follows:

$$\mathcal{A}_z = \sum_{i=1}^{n} S[i] \cdot \mathcal{A}_{iz} \qquad ,\forall z \in \{0,1\} \tag{1}$$

The requester is interested in finding a crowdsourcing policy that maximizes the expected accuracy of the collected labels while ensuring that the data is *fair*, *diverse* and is acquired within budget constraints.

Crowd diversity is a subjective property and is generally defined in terms of the demographics of crowdworkers. In this paper, we work with a given set of crowdworkers and can't control such a measure of diversity. For settings like these, we define diversity as follows:

Definition 4 (β-Diverse Crowdsourcing Policy). *A crowdsourcing policy is called β-diverse if and only if $\forall\ i \in [n]$, $S[i]$ is upper bounded by β, where β is a diversity parameter such that $0 \leq \beta < 1$.*

This definition limits the influence of individual workers on the overall crowdsourced dataset and aims to distribute the influence across more workers.

Similar to diversity, fairness is also a subjective property. We use some standard definitions of fairness from the machine learning literature [1, 14, 30].

Definition 5 (False Positive Rate Parity). *A crowdsourcing policy, with accuracy matrices $\mathcal{A}_0$ and $\mathcal{A}_1$, is said to satisfy false positive rate parity if and only*

$$\mathcal{A}_0[0,1] = \mathcal{A}_1[0,1]$$

[1] We note that the accuracy of a crowdsourcing policy can also be defined in terms of aggregated label when multiple labels per task are collected. But such definitions depend on specific label aggregation algorithms used. However, in many cases, it may be sufficient to assume that the accuracy of a policy with aggregated labels is an increasing function of our accuracy, which is a reasonable assumption.

One can similarly define false negative rate parity, which requires $\mathcal{A}_0[1,0] = \mathcal{A}_1[1,0]$.

Definition 6 (Error Rate Parity). *A crowdsourcing policy, with accuracy matrices $\mathcal{A}_0$ and $\mathcal{A}_1$, is said to satisfy error rate parity if and only if it satisfies both false positive rate parity and false negative rate parity, i.e.*

$$\mathcal{A}_0 = \mathcal{A}_1$$

It is easy to see that if all workers are unbiased, any crowdsourcing policy satisfies the above fairness definitions and one only needs to select a policy that maximizes accuracy while satisfying budget and diversity constraints. In this paper, we address the general problem scenario (when workers are not necessarily unbiased).

4 FINDING OPTIMAL CROWDSOURCING POLICY

Let's first assume that the accuracy matrices of all the workers are known and the requester is interested in finding the optimal crowdsourcing policy maximizing the expected accuracy under budget, fairness and diversity constraints. We model this as a constrained optimization problem. The objective function in the minimization problem is the negative of the expected accuracy of the policy variable S:

$$-\mathbb{E}[\mathcal{A}(S)] = -\sum_{z\in\{0,1\}} P(Z=z) \sum_{y\in\{0,1\}} P_z(Y=y) \sum_{i=1}^{n} S[i]\mathcal{A}_{iz}[y,y] \tag{2}$$

where $P(Z=z)$ is the known prior probability that any random task in the pool will have sensitive attribute value equal to z and $P_z(Y=y)$ is the known prior probability that any random task with sensitive attribute value z in the pool will have a ground truth label equal to y.

Together with the fairness and diversity constraints, we get the following optimization problem:

$$\begin{aligned}
\underset{S}{\arg\min} \quad & -\sum_{z\in\{0,1\}} P(Z=z) \sum_{y\in\{0,1\}} P_z(Y=y) \sum_{i=1}^{n} S[i]\mathcal{A}_{iz}[y,y] \\
\text{subject to} \quad & \sum_{i=1}^{n} S[i] = 1 \\
& S[i] \geq 0 \quad ,\forall i \in [n] \\
& S[i] \leq \beta \quad ,\forall i \in [n] \\
& \mathcal{A}_0[0,1] - \mathcal{A}_1[0,1] \leq \alpha \\
& -(\mathcal{A}_0[0,1] - \mathcal{A}_1[0,1]) \leq \alpha \\
& \sum_{i=1}^{n} S[i] \cdot c_i \leq C
\end{aligned} \tag{3}$$

The first two constraints are due to the fact that the crowdsourcing policy vectors are probabilistic and so, all elements must be positive and sum to 1. The third is the diversity constraint as formalized in Definition 4. The forth and fifth constraints together are equivalent to $\left|\mathcal{A}_0[0,1] - \mathcal{A}_1[0,1]\right| \leq \alpha$. For $\alpha = 0$, we get the exact fairness constraint (false positive rate parity) as formalized in Definition 5. Other fairness constraints can also be similarly included. The last constraint is due to the maximum expected budget (C) that can be spent on acquiring one answer from a worker.

4.1 Estimates of Worker Accuracy Matrices

Until now, we assumed that the accuracy matrices of the workers are known. However, in practice, we need to estimate them. As is common in the literature [22], we assume that the requester has some limited number of gold standard tasks. Gold tasks are the tasks for which the requester not only knows the sensitive attribute value z but also the ground truth label y. We use gold tasks to estimate unknown worker accuracy matrices. Estimating all the entries of the worker accuracy matrices requires that every worker answers some gold tasks of each "type" (the type of a task is specified by its ground truth answer and its sensitive attribute value). We assign N_g tasks of every type to each worker to estimate their accuracy matrices. This is explained further in appendix A. Let $\hat{\mathcal{A}}_{iz}$ be the estimate of the worker accuracy matrices $\mathcal{A}_{iz}$, $\forall z \in \{0,1\}$. The optimization problem 3 can now be written as follows, by replacing the accuracy matrices with their estimates:

$$\begin{aligned} \arg\min_{S} \quad & -\sum_{z\in\{0,1\}} P(Z=z) \sum_{y\in\{0,1\}} P_z(Y=y) \sum_{i=1}^{n} S[i]\hat{\mathcal{A}}_{iz}[y,y] \\ \text{subject to} \quad & \sum_{i=1}^{n} S[i] = 1 \\ & S[i] \geq 0 \quad, \forall i \in [n] \\ & S[i] \leq \beta \quad, \forall i \in [n] \\ & \hat{\mathcal{A}}_0[0,1] - \hat{\mathcal{A}}_1[0,1] \leq \alpha \\ & -(\hat{\mathcal{A}}_0[0,1] - \hat{\mathcal{A}}_1[0,1]) \leq \alpha \\ & \sum_{i=1}^{n} S[i]\cdot c_i \leq C \end{aligned} \tag{4}$$

where,

$$\hat{\mathcal{A}}_z = \sum_{i=1}^{n} S[i]\cdot\hat{\mathcal{A}}_{iz} \quad, \forall z \in \{0,1\} \tag{5}$$

This is a linear program, which can be exactly solved in polynomial time. In practice, the simplex method [6] can be used to find the optimal solution efficiently with common optimization libraries like IBM CPLEX and SciPy. Depending on the constraints, the cost and the accuracy matrices of workers, it is possible that no feasible solution exists for the optimization problem. In this case, the requester will have no choice but to relax the constraints.

We will now analyze our algorithm theoretically and empirically. Readers can find a summary of steps of our complete crowdsourcing algorithm in appendix B.

5 THEORETICAL ANALYSIS

When worker accuracy matrices are known, our method is guaranteed to provide the optimal solution, satisfying constraints. However, when estimates of the accuracy matrices are used, two interesting questions arise:

(1) Does the solution of problem 4 (which is optimal and satisfies fairness constraints only according to the estimated accuracy parameters) also satisfy fairness in reality?
(2) How much does the requester lose in terms of actual expected accuracy of the policy because of using the estimated accuracy parameters in optimization?

Theorem 1. *With probability at least γ, the solution $\hat{S}$ to the optimization problem 4 satisfies*

$$\left|\mathcal{A}_0[0,1] - \mathcal{A}_1[0,1]\right| \leq \alpha + \delta$$

where

$$\delta = 2\sqrt{\frac{-\ln(1-\sqrt[2n]{\gamma}) + \ln 2}{2N_g}}; \mathcal{A}_z = \sum_{i=1}^{n} \hat{S}[i]\mathcal{A}_{iz}, \forall z \in \{0,1\}$$

and N_g is number of gold tasks.

The theorem states that when we use estimates of the worker accuracy matrices instead of the real matrices, the obtained solution $\hat{S}$ doesn't violate the fairness constraints in reality by more than δ, with probability at least γ.

Theorem 2. *Assuming that the optimal solution $\hat{S}$ of problem 4 satisfies fairness constraints of problem 3 and the optimal solution S of problem 3 satisfies fairness constraints of problem 4, then with probability at least γ'*

$$\mathbb{E}[\mathcal{A}(S)] - \mathbb{E}[\mathcal{A}(\hat{S})] \leq 2n\beta\sqrt{\frac{-\ln(1-\sqrt[4n]{\gamma'}) + \ln 2}{2N_g}}$$

where

$$\mathbb{E}[\mathcal{A}(S)] = \sum_{z\in\{0,1\}} P(Z=z) \sum_{y\in\{0,1\}} P_z(Y=y) \sum_{i=1}^{n} S[i]\mathcal{A}_{iz}[y,y],$$

$$\mathbb{E}[\mathcal{A}(\hat{S})] = \sum_{z\in\{0,1\}} P(Z=z) \sum_{y\in\{0,1\}} P_z(Y=y) \sum_{i=1}^{n} \hat{S}[i]\mathcal{A}_{iz}[y,y]$$

The theorem provides an upper bound on the loss in real expected accuracy of the crowdsourcing policy, when we use the estimated worker matrices instead of the real accuracy matrices for optimization. Note that in both the theorems, the bounds get better with increasing number of gold tasks.

The proofs of the above theorem are not difficult and depend on a simple application of the Hoeffding's inequality.

6 EXPERIMENTAL EVALUATION

6.0.1 Datasets. We use the following datasets in our experiments.

(1) **Broward County Dataset** [26] : This dataset contains information about 7214 defendants arrested in Broward County, Florida between 2013 and 2014. The information includes race of the defendants among other non-sensitive attributes such as age, prior charges etc. The dataset also contains ground-truth whether the defendants recidivated within 2 years or not. There are 3696 black defendants and 2454 white defendants in the dataset and the base rate of recidivism is 51.43% among the black defendants and 39.36% among the white defendants.
(2) **Crowd Judgment Dataset** : [8] randomly selected a subset of 1000 defendants from the Broward County dataset and asked 20 random workers on Amazon Mechanical Turk to predict recidivism for each individual. In total, 400 workers participated in their study and each worker submitted answers for 50 different defendants. The dataset contains these answers collected from the crowd.

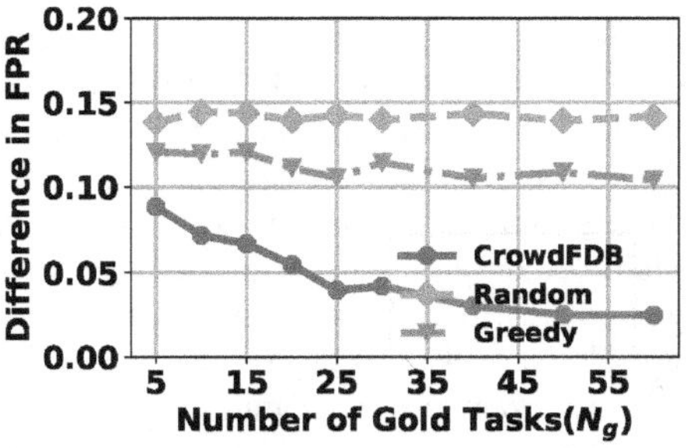

(a) Absolute Difference in FPR

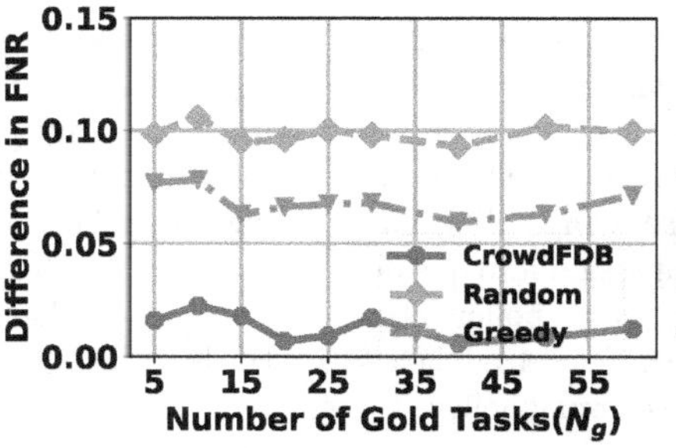

(b) Absolute Difference in FNR

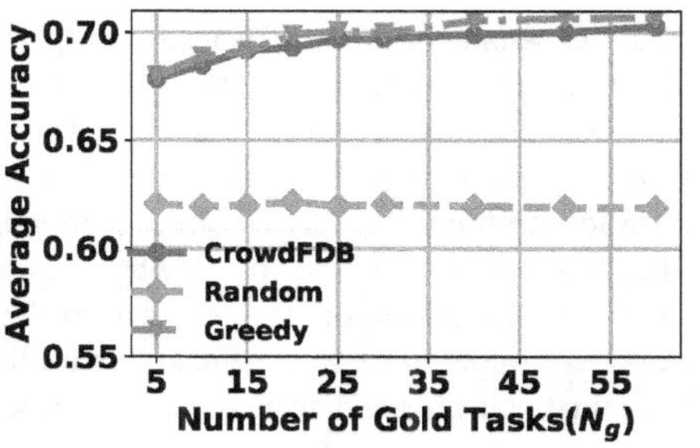

(c) Average Accuracy

Figure 1: Varying N_g (Number of gold tasks), Settings : Uniform Costs, $\beta = 0.01, \alpha = 0.01$

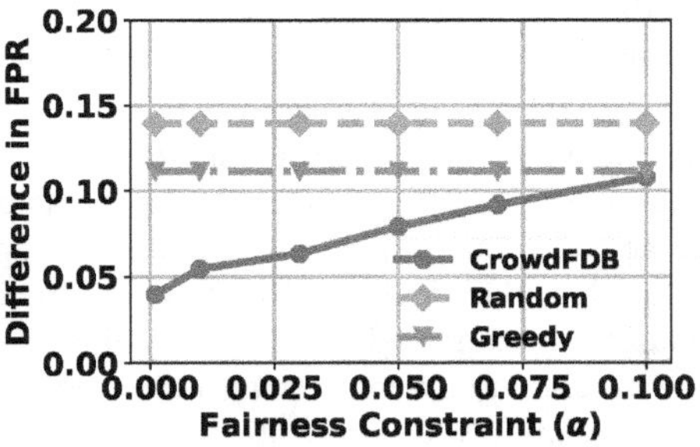

(a) Absolute Difference in FPR

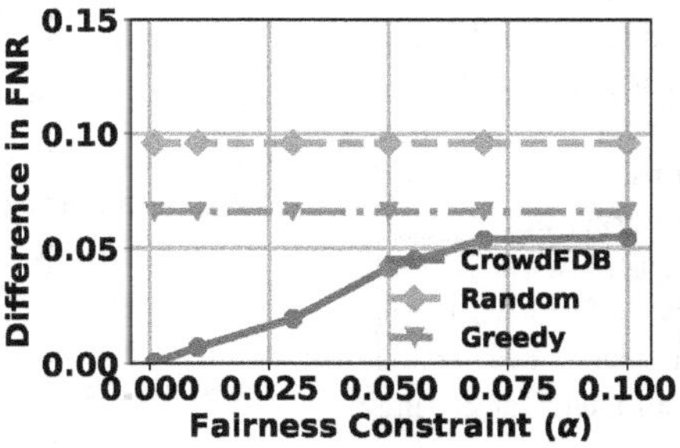

(b) Absolute Difference in FNR

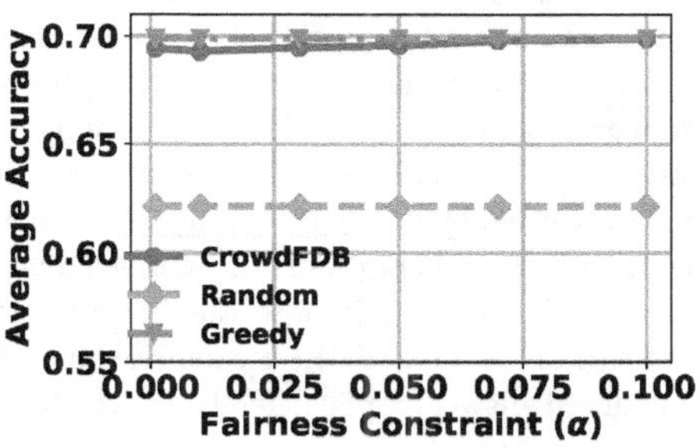

(c) Average Accuracy

Figure 2: Varying α (Fairness Constraint), Settings : Uniform Costs, $\beta = 0.01, N_g = 20$

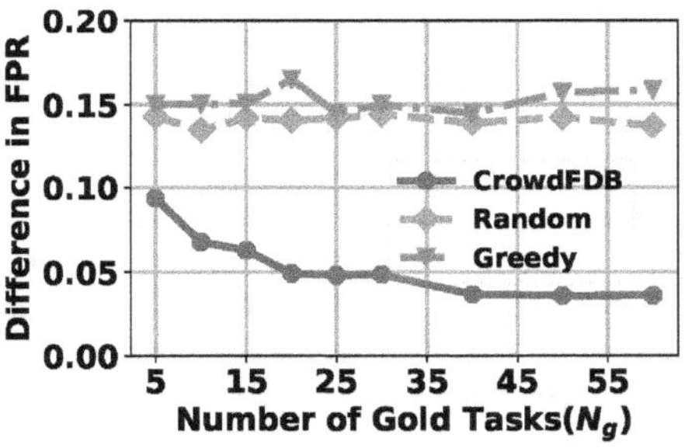

(a) Absolute Difference in FPR

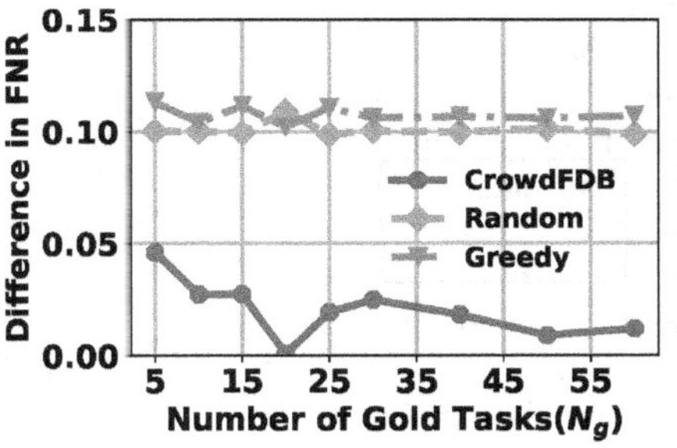

(b) Absolute Difference in FNR

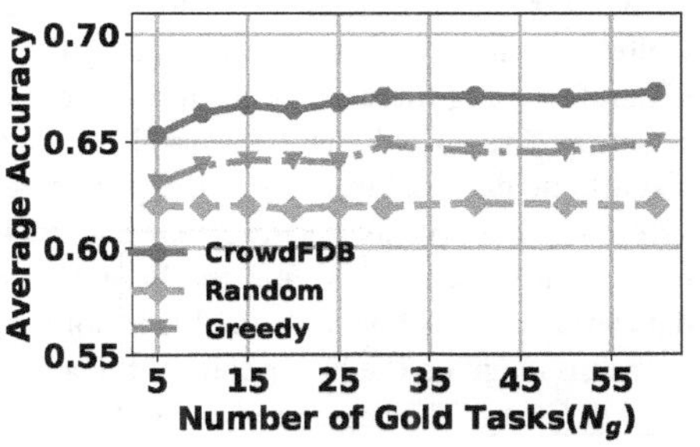

(c) Average Accuracy

Figure 3: Varying N_g (Number of gold tasks), Settings : Non-Uniform Costs, $\beta = 0.01, \alpha = 0.01, C = 1.5$

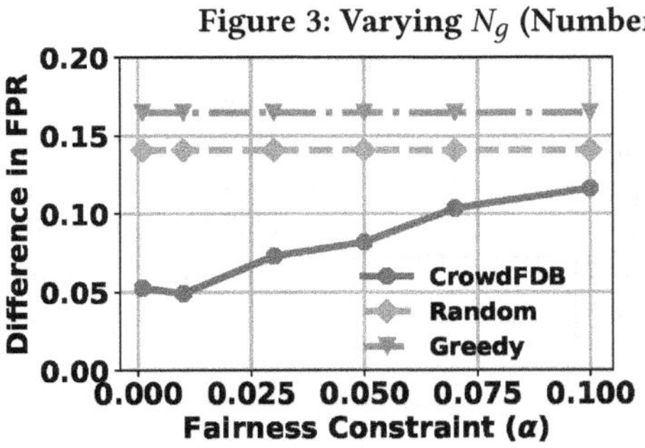

(a) Absolute Difference in FPR

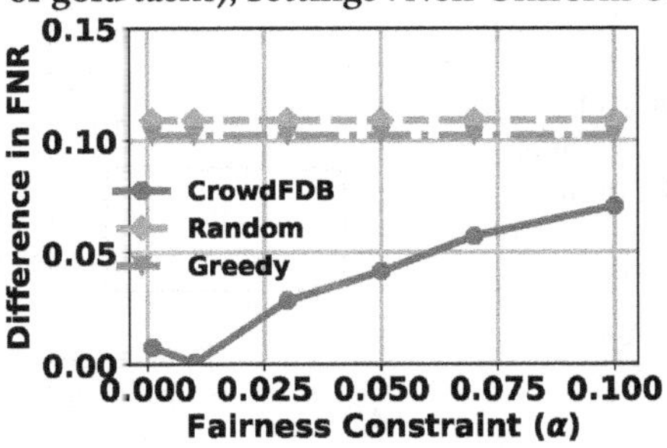

(b) Absolute Difference in FNR

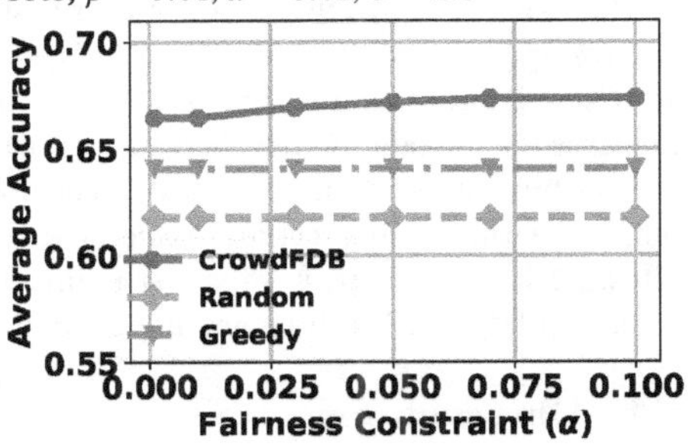

(c) Average Accuracy

Figure 4: Varying α (Fairness Constraint), Settings : Non-Uniform Costs, $\beta = 0.01, N_g = 20, C = 1.5$

6.0.2 Experiment Outline. The idea is to split the set of defendants into two sets. The first set acts as the gold standard set, which we use to estimate worker accuracy matrices. Once we have the estimates of the worker accuracy matrices, we can solve the optimization problem 4 and learn optimal crowdsourcing policy. We then pick non-gold defendants one by one and assign it to one of the 400 workers, randomly selected according to the policy. The workers' responses are then compared with the ground-truth label to evaluate fairness and accuracy of our crowdsourcing policy.

6.0.3 Handling Limitations of Datasets. Unfortunately, none of the two datasets alone can be used for such experiment. The Broward County dataset contains ground truth labels but doesn't contain workers' answers. On the other hand, the Crowd Judgment dataset does contain worker answers but is very limited for the following reasons. In this dataset, tasks have already been assigned (randomly) to workers and for every defendant, we have responses of only a subset of 20 workers out of all 400 workers. If the crowdsourcing policy learned by our algorithm decides that a worker outside that subset of 20 workers should be assigned a task, then we will need to know the answer of that worker but the answer of this worker is not part of the dataset. The second reason is that every worker has submitted answers for 50 defendants, which is sufficient for getting good estimates of the accuracy parameters of the workers but not big enough to be further split into gold and non-gold sets.
To overcome these limitations, we first create a bigger synthetic dataset using the two real datasets as follows. We generate synthetic answers of all the 400 workers for all the 3696 black and 2454 white defendants in the Broward County dataset. The answers are generated using the worker accuracy parameters estimated from the entire Crowd Judgment dataset. Note that even though this is a synthetic dataset but none of the parameters of the dataset are synthetic. The worker accuracy parameters are derived from the entire real dataset of [8] and the base dataset (Broward County dataset) is used as it is. Indeed, this is not ideal but is perhaps the only option, given the limitations of the available datasets.
Worker Costs : The datasets also don't contain workers' costs. We create this information in two different ways. In the first setting, we associate a uniform cost of \$1 to each worker. In the second and more interesting setting, we probabilistically associate a cost of \$1 or \$3. The probability of a worker's cost being \$3 is equal to her average accuracy and of it being \$1 is equal to 1−her average accuracy. Thus, the higher the average accuracy of a worker, the higher is the probability that she will charge a cost of \$3.

Now this complete dataset is ready to be used in the experiment outlined earlier in this section. We compare our approach (called 'CrowdFDB' in the figures) with two baselines (called 'Random' and 'Greedy' [27]). The baselines are discussed in appendix C.

6.1 Observations

We use equal error rate parity (Definition 6) as the desired fairness. All results reported in the paper are averages over 100 repeated runs. Parameter β was set to 0.01 in the first set of experiments. In the uniform costs settings, C was set to \$1 and in non-uniform settings, $C = \$1.5$.

6.1.1 Uniform Costs. In Figure 1, we keep the fairness constraint α to be fixed (0.01) and observe the effect of increasing number of gold tasks (N_g). Figures 1a and 1b show that as we increase N_g, the fairness i.e. the absolute difference in FPR (and FNR) for black and white populations, gets closer and closer to α. In other words, the δ of Theorem 1 gets closer to 0 as expected. Moreover, the margin between our algorithm and the baselines also increases. However, meeting the fairness constraints alone is not enough. This could also be done by a bad algorithm that collects equally wrong labels for both white and black populations. Hence, accuracy of the collected labels is also an important measure. Figure 1c shows that our algorithm has an accuracy competitive to the Greedy baseline method, which is a highly efficient baseline in the literature for accuracy optimization. Our algorithm can achieve same level of accuracy while also providing fairness. In Figure 2, we keep N_g fixed (20) and observe the effect of increasing value of α. As value of α increases, the fairness constraints are more relaxed and the algorithm can obtain better accuracy.

6.1.2 Non-Uniform Costs. In the non-uniform costs settings, we observe similar patterns in Figure 3 and 4. There are a few notable differences. The accuracy of our algorithm as well as the Greedy baseline are lower. Our algorithm doesn't select more accurate workers because of budget constraints and the Greedy baseline also finds the density of the more accurate workers comparatively lower due to their high costs and prefers to choose other high density workers. In this case, our algorithm beats Greedy in not just fairness but also in accuracy by better utilizing the available budget.

Figures 5 and 6 of appendix D show the results with $\beta = 0.01, C = 2.5$. Figures 7 and 8 of appendix D show the results with $\beta = 0.005, C = 2.5$. Decreasing the value of parameter β makes the algorithms (ours and the Greedy baseline) more constrained in assigning tasks to the workers that they find to be better. This hits the accuracy of both the algorithms but the general trends discussed above (w.r.t. fairness and accuracy with different N_g and α) remain the same. The effect of increasing budget from 1.5 to 2.5 is that our algorithm can get better accuracy but there is no effect on the performance of other baselines as expected, since there was no explicit budget constraint placed on them.

7 CONCLUSIONS AND FUTURE WORK

In this paper, we addressed the problem of data fairness in crowdsourcing. We proposed a novel crowdsourcing algorithm that learns an optimal selection probability distribution over the available set of workers to maximize the expected accuracy of collected data, while ensuring that the errors in the data are not unfairly discriminatory towards any particular social group. There also remain many challenges to be addressed. These include estimating accuracy without requiring gold standard tasks, relaxing the assumption about knowledge of prior label distribution and the i.i.d. assumption about workers' answers.

Another interesting challenge in slightly different settings is to define data fairness for the case of subjective tasks, which have no ground truth labels and thus, no clear notion of errors. Ensuring fairness in subjective data collection is also likely to create a challenging problem of lying incentives[11] for workers.

REFERENCES

[1] Solon Barocas, Moritz Hardt, and Arvind Narayanan. 2018. Fairness and machine learning : Limitations and Opportunities. http://fairmlbook.org. (2018).

[2] Solon Barocas and Andrew D Selbst. 2016. Big data's disparate impact. *California Law Review 671* (2016).
[3] Tolga Bolukbasi, Kai-Wei Chang, James Y Zou, Venkatesh Saligrama, and Adam T Kalai. 2016. Man is to computer programmer as woman is to homemaker? debiasing word embeddings. In *Advances in Neural Information Processing Systems*.
[4] Jonathan Bragg, Daniel S Weld, et al. 2016. Optimal testing for crowd workers. In *International Conference on Autonomous Agents & Multiagent Systems*.
[5] Flavio Calmon, Dennis Wei, Bhanukiran Vinzamuri, Karthikeyan Natesan Ramamurthy, and Kush R Varshney. 2017. Optimized Pre-Processing for Discrimination Prevention. In *Advances in Neural Information Processing Systems*.
[6] Vasek Chvatal. 1983. *Linear programming*. Macmillan.
[7] Alexander Philip Dawid and Allan M Skene. 1979. Maximum likelihood estimation of observer error-rates using the EM algorithm. *Applied statistics* (1979).
[8] Julia Dressel and Hany Farid. 2018. The accuracy, fairness, and limits of predicting recidivism. *Science advances* (2018).
[9] Cynthia Dwork, Moritz Hardt, Toniann Pitassi, Omer Reingold, and Richard Zemel. 2012. Fairness through awareness. In *Proceedings of ITCS*.
[10] Michael Feldman, Sorelle A Friedler, John Moeller, Carlos Scheidegger, and Suresh Venkatasubramanian. 2015. Certifying and removing disparate impact. In *21th ACM SIGKDD International Conference on Knowledge Discovery and Data Mining*.
[11] Naman Goel and Boi Faltings. 2019. Deep Bayesian Trust: A Dominant and Fair Incentive Mechanism for Crowd. In *AAAI Conference on Artificial Intelligence*.
[12] Naman Goel, Mohammad Yaghini, and Boi Faltings. 2018. Non-discriminatory machine learning through convex fairness criteria. In *Thirty-Second AAAI Conference on Artificial Intelligence*.
[13] Anikó Hannák, Claudia Wagner, David Garcia, Alan Mislove, Markus Strohmaier, and Christo Wilson. 2017. Bias in Online Freelance Marketplaces: Evidence from TaskRabbit and Fiverr.. In *CSCW*. 1914–1933.
[14] Moritz Hardt, Eric Price, Nati Srebro, et al. 2016. Equality of opportunity in supervised learning. In *Advances in Neural Information Processing Systems*.
[15] Chien-Ju Ho, Shahin Jabbari, and Jennifer Wortman Vaughan. 2013. Adaptive task assignment for crowdsourced classification. In *Proceedings of ICML*.
[16] Chien-Ju Ho and Jennifer Wortman Vaughan. 2012. Online task assignment in crowdsourcing markets. In *Proceedings of AAAI Conference*.
[17] David R. Karger, Sewoong Oh, and Devavrat Shah. 2014. Budget-Optimal Task Allocation for Reliable Crowdsourcing Systems. *Opeations Research* (2014), 1–24.
[18] Matthew Kay, Cynthia Matuszek, and Sean A Munson. 2015. Unequal representation and gender stereotypes in image search results for occupations. In *33rd Annual ACM Conference on Human Factors in Computing Systems*.
[19] Jon M. Kleinberg, Sendhil Mullainathan, and Manish Raghavan. 2017. Inherent Trade-Offs in the Fair Determination of Risk Scores. In *Proceedings of ITCS*.
[20] Juhi Kulshrestha, Motahhare Eslami, Johnnatan Messias, Muhammad Bilal Zafar, Saptarshi Ghosh, Krishna P Gummadi, and Karrie Karahalios. 2017. Quantifying search bias: Investigating sources of bias for political searches in social media. In *ACM Conference on Computer Supported Cooperative Work and Social Computing*.
[21] Seth Neel and Aaron Roth. 2018. Mitigating Bias in Adaptive Data Gathering via Differential Privacy. In *35th International Conference on Machine Learning*.
[22] David Oleson, Alexander Sorokin, Greg Laughlin, Vaughn Hester, John Le, and Lukas Biewald. 2011. Programmatic Gold: Targeted and Scalable Quality Assurance in Crowdsourcing. In *AAAI Workshop on Human Computation*.
[23] Jahna Otterbacher. 2015. Crowdsourcing stereotypes: Linguistic bias in metadata generated via gwap. In *Proceedings of ACM CHI*.
[24] Jahna Otterbacher. 2015. Linguistic Bias in Collaboratively Produced Biographies: Crowdsourcing Social Stereotypes?. In *Proceedings of AAAI ICWSM*.
[25] Jahna Otterbacher, Jo Bates, and Paul Clough. 2017. Competent men and warm women: Gender stereotypes and backlash in image search results. In *ACM CHI*.
[26] ProPublica. 2017. https://www.propublica.org/datastore/ dataset/compas-recidivism-risk-score-data-and-analysis. (2017).
[27] Long Tran-Thanh, Sebastian Stein, Alex Rogers, and Nicholas R Jennings. 2014. Efficient crowdsourcing of unknown experts using bounded multi-armed bandits. *Artificial Intelligence* (2014).
[28] Isabel Valera, Adish Singla, and Manuel Gomez Rodriguez. 2018. Enhancing the accuracy and fairness of human decision making. In *Advances in Neural Information Processing Systems*. 1774–1783.
[29] White House. 2016. Big Data: A Report on Algorithmic Systems, Opportunity, and Civil Rights. *Executive Office of the President* (2016).
[30] M B Zafar, I Valera, M G Rodriguez, and K P Gummadi. 2017. Fairness Constraints: Mechanisms for Fair Classification. In *AISTATS*.

A ESTIMATED ACCURACY MATRICES

Let $\hat{\mathcal{A}}_{iz}$ be the estimate of the worker accuracy matrices $\mathcal{A}_{iz}$, $\forall z \in \{0, 1\}$. If a worker i answers k tasks correctly out of N_g gold tasks of type $z = 1, y = 1$, then

$$\hat{\mathcal{A}}_{i1}[1, 1] = \frac{k}{N_g} \text{ and } \hat{\mathcal{A}}_{i1}[1, 0] = 1 - \hat{\mathcal{A}}_{i1}[1, 1]$$

Similarly, if she answers k' tasks correctly out of N_g gold tasks of type $z = 1, y = 0$, then

$$\hat{\mathcal{A}}_{i1}[0, 0] = \frac{k'}{N_g} \text{ and } \hat{\mathcal{A}}_{i1}[0, 1] = 1 - \hat{\mathcal{A}}_{i1}[0, 0]$$

This process is repeated with gold tasks of type $z = 0, y = 1$ and $z = 0, y = 0$ to get estimates of all entries of the worker's matrices.

B SUMMARY OF STEPS OF THE ALGORITHM

Algorithm 1: Crowdsourcing with Fairness, Diversity and Budget Constraints (CrowdFDB)

1. Assign N_g gold tasks of every type $((z = 0, y = 0), (z = 0, y = 1), (z = 1, y = 0), (z = 1, y = 1))$ to every worker i in the provided set of n workers.
2. Get estimate of every worker i's accuracy matrices $\hat{\mathcal{A}}_{i0}$ & $\hat{\mathcal{A}}_{i1}$.
3. Solve the linear program to find the best crowdsourcing policy satisfying desired fairness, diversity and budget constraints.
4. Pick a task randomly from the task pool of tasks with unknown ground truth labels. Randomly select one or more workers from the set of n workers, with probabilities specified by the crowdsourcing policy. Assign the task to the selected worker(s).
5. Repeat Step 4 for all tasks in the pool.

C BASELINES

(1) **Random Policy** : In the random policy, all workers are equally likely to be selected (probability $\frac{1}{400}$) for any task.
(2) **Greedy Optimization [27]** : In this baseline, we first estimate worker accuracy matrices using gold tasks in exactly same way as we do in our algorithm. However, the optimization is done using a bounded knapsack algorithm instead of linear programming. This algorithm sorts the workers in decreasing order of their "density", where density is defined as the ratio of the expected accuracy of a worker and her cost. The expected accuracy of a worker can be calculated in the same way as we do for our algorithm i.e. $\sum_{z\in\{0,1\}} P(Z = z) \sum_{g\in\{0,1\}} P_z(Y = y)\hat{\mathcal{A}}_{iz}[y, y]$. Then, the algorithm assigns as many tasks as possible to the highest density worker without violating the diversity constraint. If T is the total number of tasks to be assigned, then a worker can be assigned at most βT tasks. Note that, unlike our algorithm, this baseline has to know the total number of tasks in advance to enforce diversity constraint. Once this worker has reached its capacity, the algorithm starts assigning tasks to the worker with next highest density and continues this for all tasks. However, it may be noted that the Greedy approach was originally proposed for a bit different setting, in which there is an overall crowdsourcing budget and the goal of the requester is to get as many tasks done as possible in that budget, maximizing total utility/accuracy and respecting work limits of the workers.
To give extra advantage to the baselines, we don't put an *explicit* budget constraint for them and observe whether they can compete with the fairness and accuracy of our algorithm, which operates under budget constraint.

D ADDITIONAL EXPERIMENTAL RESULTS

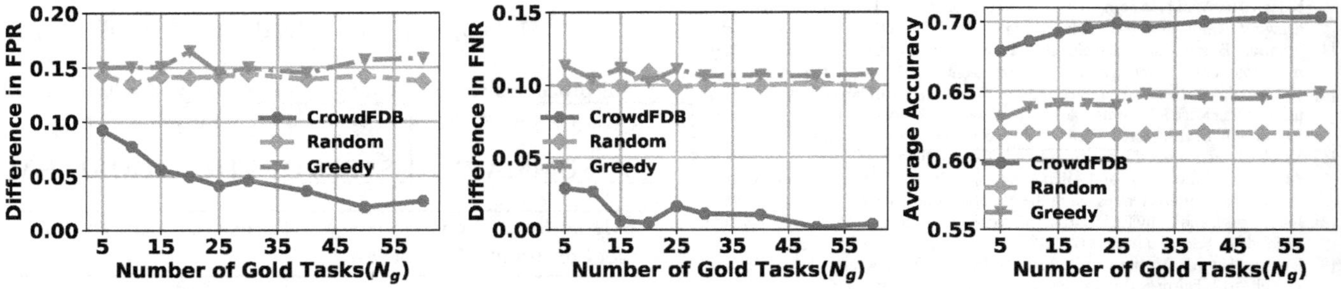

(a) Absolute Difference in FPR (b) Absolute Difference in FNR (c) Average Accuracy

Figure 5: Varying N_g (Number of gold tasks), Settings : Non-Uniform Costs, $\beta = 0.01, \alpha = 0.01, C = 2.5$

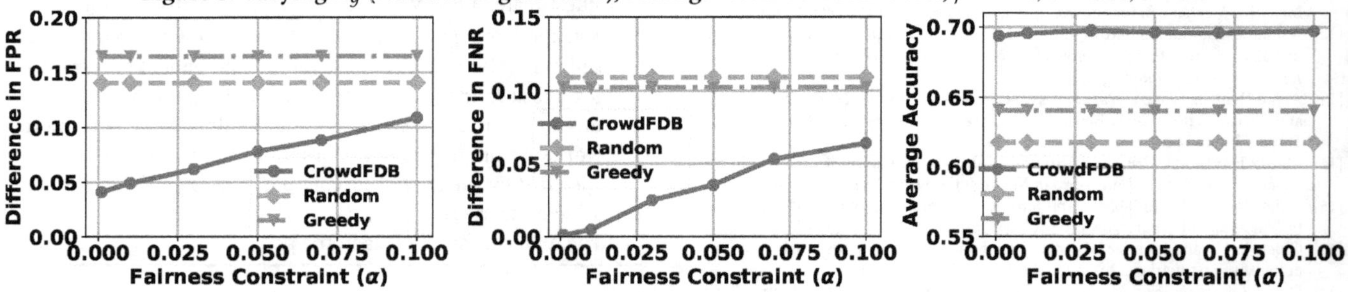

(a) Absolute Difference in FPR (b) Absolute Difference in FNR (c) Average Accuracy

Figure 6: Varying α (Fairness Constraint), Settings : Non-Uniform Costs, $\beta = 0.01, N_g = 20, C = 2.5$

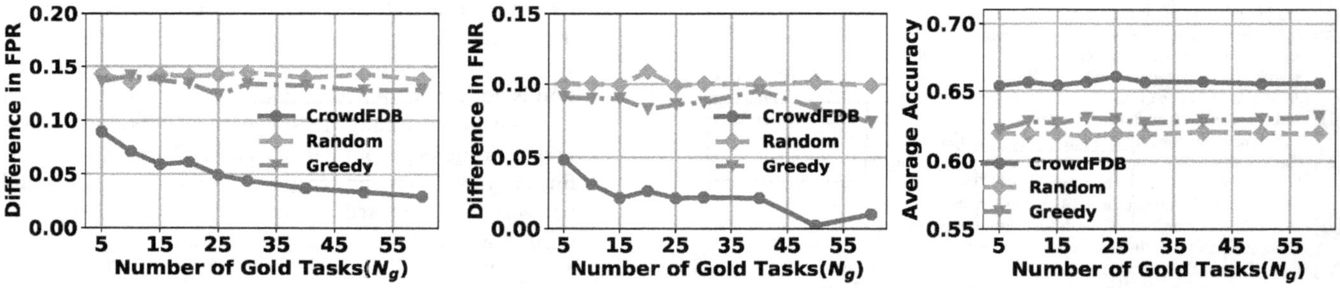

(a) Absolute Difference in FPR (b) Absolute Difference in FNR (c) Average Accuracy

Figure 7: Varying N_g (Number of gold tasks), Settings : Non-Uniform Costs, $\beta = 0.005, \alpha = 0.01, C = 2.5$

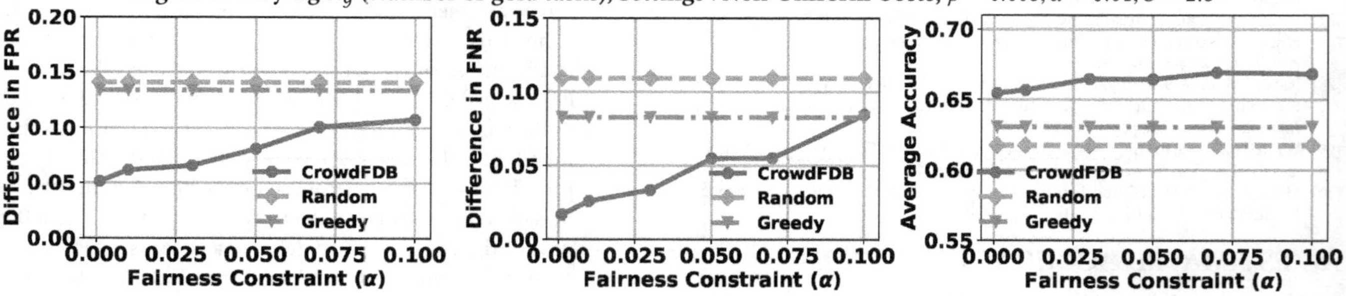

(a) Absolute Difference in FPR (b) Absolute Difference in FNR (c) Average Accuracy

Figure 8: Varying α (Fairness Constraint), Settings : Non-Uniform Costs, $\beta = 0.005, N_g = 20, C = 2.5$

What are the Biases in My Word Embedding?

Nathaniel Swinger*
Lexington High School

Maria De-Arteaga*
Carnegie Mellon University

Neil Thomas Heffernan IV
Shrewsbury High School

Mark DM Leiserson
University of Maryland

Adam Tauman Kalai
Microsoft Research

Warning: This paper includes stereotypes and terms which are offensive in nature. It is important, however, for researchers to be aware of the biases contained in word embeddings.

ABSTRACT

This paper presents an algorithm for enumerating biases in word embeddings. The algorithm exposes a large number of offensive associations related to sensitive features such as race and gender on publicly available embeddings. These biases are concerning in light of the widespread use of word embeddings. The associations are identified by geometric patterns in word embeddings that run parallel between people's names and common lower-case tokens. The algorithm is highly unsupervised: it does not even require the sensitive features to be pre-specified. This is desirable because: (a) many forms of discrimination–such as racial discrimination–are linked to social constructs that may vary depending on the context, rather than to categories with fixed definitions; and (b) it makes it easier to identify biases against *intersectional* groups, which depend on combinations of sensitive features. The inputs to our algorithm are a list of target tokens, e.g. names, and a word embedding. It outputs a number of Word Embedding Association Tests (WEATs) that capture various biases present in the data. We illustrate the utility of our approach on publicly available word embeddings and lists of names, and evaluate its output using crowdsourcing. We also show how removing names may not remove potential proxy bias.

We encourage readers to consult the more complete manuscript on the arXiv.

ACM Reference Format:
Nathaniel Swinger, Maria De-Arteaga, Neil Thomas Heffernan IV, Mark DM Leiserson, and Adam Tauman Kalai. 2019. What are the Biases in My Word Embedding?. In *AAAI/ACM Conference on AI, Ethics, and Society (AIES '19), January 27–28, 2019, Honolulu, HI, USA.* ACM, New York, NY, USA, 7 pages. https://doi.org/10.1145/3306618.3314270

*Indicates equal contribution.

AIES '19, January 27–28, 2019, Honolulu, HI, USA

ACM ISBN 978-1-4503-6324-2/19/01...$15.00
https://doi.org/10.1145/3306618.3314270

1 INTRODUCTION

Bias in data representation is an important element of fairness in Artificially Intelligent systems [2, 7, 10, 24]. We consider the problem of *Unsupervised Bias Enumeration* (UBE): discovering biases automatically from an unlabeled data representation. There are multiple reasons why such an algorithm is useful. First, social scientists can use it as a tool to study human bias, as data analysis is increasingly common in social studies of human biases [11, 16]. Second, finding bias is a natural step in "debiasing" representations [5]. Finally, it can help in avoiding systems that perpetuate these biases: problematic biases can raise red flags for engineers, who can choose to not use a representation or watch out for certain biases in downstream applications, while little or no bias can be a useful green light indicating that a representation is usable. While deciding which biases are problematic is ultimately application specific, UBE may be useful in a "fair ML" pipeline.

We design a UBE algorithm for word embeddings, which are commonly used representations of tokens (e.g. words and phrases) that have been found to contain harmful bias [5]. Researchers linking these biases to human biases proposed the Word Embedding Association Test (WEAT) [7]. The WEAT draws its inspiration from the Implicit Association Test (IAT), a widely-used approach to measure human bias [12]. An IAT $\mathcal{T} = (X_1, A_1, X_2, A_2)$ compares two sets of *target tokens* X_1 and X_2, such as female vs. male names, and a pair of opposing sets of *attribute tokens* A_1 and A_2, such as workplace vs. family-themed words. Average differences in a person's response times when asked to link tokens that have anti-stereotypical vs. stereotypical relationships have been shown to indicate the strength of association between concepts. Analogously, the WEAT uses vector similarity across pairs of tokens in the sets to measure association strength. As in the case of the IAT, the inputs for a WEAT are sets of tokens $\mathcal{T}$ predefined by researchers.

Our UBE algorithm takes as input a word embedding and a list of target tokens, and *outputs* numerous tests $\mathcal{T}_1, \mathcal{T}_2, \ldots$, that are found to be statistically significant by a method we introduce for bounding false discovery rates. A crowdsourcing study of tests generated on three publicly-available word embeddings and a list of names from the Social Security Administration confirms that the biases enumerated are largely consistent with human stereotypes, including racial, gender, religious, and age biases, among others.

Creating such tests automatically has several advantages. First, it is unfeasible for domain experts to manually author all possible tests of interest and cover all possible groups, especially if they do not know which groups are represented in their data. For example, a domain expert based on the United States may not think of testing for caste discrimination, hence biases that an embedding may have against certain Indian last names may go unnoticed. Automatically considering all possibilities also means that if no biases are revealed, this is evidence for lack of bias. We test this by running our UBE algorithm on the supposedly debiased embedding of [5].

Our approach for UBE leverages two geometric properties of word embeddings, which we call the *parallel* and *cluster* properties. The well-known parallel property indicates that differences between two similar token pairs, such as Mary–John and Queen–King, are often nearly parallel vectors. This suggests that among tokens in a similar topic or category, those parallel to name differences may represent biases, as was found by [5] and [7]. The cluster property, which we were previously unaware of, indicates that the (normalized) vectors of names and words cluster into semantically meaningful groups. For names, the clusters capture social structures such as gender, religion, and others. For words, clusters of words include word categories on topics such as food, education, occupations, and sports. We use these properties to design a UBE algorithm that outputs WEATs.

Technical challenges accompany any procedure for bias enumeration. First, the combinatorial explosion of comparisons among many groups parallels issues in human IAT studies, as described by [4]: "The evaluation of multiple target concepts such as social groups within a multi-ethnic nation [e.g. White vs. Asian Americans, White vs. African Americans, African vs. Asian Americans; 9] requires numerous pairwise comparisons for a complete picture". We alleviate this issue by paralleling work on human IATs, generalizing the WEAT to n groups for arbitrary n. The second problem for any UBE algorithm is determining statistical significance to account for multiple hypothesis testing. We introduce a novel rotational null hypothesis specific to word embeddings. Third, we provide human evaluation of the biases, contending with the fact that many people are unfamiliar with some sets of names.

Beyond word embeddings and IATs, other related work is worth mention. A body of work studies fairness properties of classification and regression algorithms [e.g. 10, 15]. While our work does not concern supervised learning, we find one of our main motivations within this work–the importance of accounting for intersectionality when studying algorithmic biases. In particular, Buolamwini and Gebru [6] demonstrate accuracy disparities in image classification highlighting the fact that the magnitude of biases against an intersectional group may go unnoticed when only evaluating for each protected feature independently. Finally, while a significant portion of the empirical research on algorithmic fairness has focused on the societal biases that are most pressing in the countries where the majority of researchers currently conducting the work are based, the literature also contains examples of biases that may be of particular importance in other parts of the world [13, 22]. UBE can aspire to be useful in multiple contexts, and enable the discovery of biases without relying on enumeration by domain experts.

2 DEFINITIONS

A d-dimensional word embedding consists of a set of tokens $\mathcal{W}$ with a nonzero vector $\boldsymbol{w} \in \mathbb{R}^d$ associated with each token $w \in \mathcal{W}$. Vectors are displayed in boldface. As is standard, we refer to the *similarity* between tokens v and w by the cosine of their vector angle, $\cos(\boldsymbol{v}, \boldsymbol{w})$. We write $\overline{\boldsymbol{v}} = \boldsymbol{v}/|\boldsymbol{v}|$ to be the vector normalized to unit-length associated with any vector $\boldsymbol{v} \in \mathbb{R}^d$ (or 0 if $\boldsymbol{v} = 0$). This enables us to conveniently write the similarity between tokens v and w as an inner product, $\cos(\boldsymbol{v}, \boldsymbol{w}) = \overline{\boldsymbol{v}} \cdot \overline{\boldsymbol{w}}$. For token set S, we write $\overline{S} = \sum_{v \in S} \overline{\boldsymbol{v}}/|S|$ so that $\overline{S} \cdot \overline{T} = \text{mean}_{v \in S, w \in T} \overline{\boldsymbol{v}} \cdot \overline{\boldsymbol{w}}$ is the mean similarity between pairs of tokens in sets S, T. We denote the set difference between S and T by $S \setminus T$, and we denote the first n whole numbers by $[n] = \{1, 2, \ldots, n\}$.

2.1 Generalizing Word Embedding Association Tests

We assume that there is a given set of possible targets $\mathcal{X}$ and attributes $\mathcal{A}$. Henceforth, since in our evaluation all targets are names and all attributes are lower-case words (or phrases), we refer to targets as names and attributes as words. Nonetheless, in principle, the algorithm can be run on any sets of target and attribute tokens. [7] define a WEAT statistic for two equal-sized groups of names $X_1, X_2 \subseteq \mathcal{X}$ and words $A_1, A_2 \subseteq \mathcal{A}$ which can be conveniently written in our notation as,

$$s(X_1, A_1, X_2, A_2) \stackrel{\text{def}}{=} \left(\sum_{x \in X_1} \overline{\boldsymbol{x}} - \sum_{x \in X_2} \overline{\boldsymbol{x}} \right) \cdot (\overline{A_1} - \overline{A_2}).$$

In studies of human biases, the combinatorial explosion in groups can be avoided by teasing apart *Single-Category* IATs which assess associations one group at a time [e.g. 4, 14, 20]. In word embeddings, we define a simple generalization for $n \geq 1$, nonempty groups $X_1, \ldots, X_n$ of arbitrary sizes and words $A_1, \ldots, A_n$, as follows:

$$g(X_1, A_1, \ldots, X_n, A_n) \stackrel{\text{def}}{=} \sum_{i=1}^{n} (\overline{X_i} - \mu) \cdot (\overline{A_i} - \overline{\mathcal{A}})$$

$$\text{where } \mu \stackrel{\text{def}}{=} \begin{cases} \overline{\mathcal{X}} & \text{for } n = 1, \\ \sum_i \overline{X_i}/n & \text{for } n \geq 2. \end{cases}$$

Note that g is symmetric with respect to ordering and weights groups equally regardless of size. The definition differs for $n = 1$, otherwise $g \equiv 0$.

The following three properties motivate this as a "natural" generalization of WEAT to one or more groups.

Lemma 1. *For any $X_1, X_2 \subseteq \mathcal{X}$ of equal sizes $|X_1| = |X_2|$ and any nonempty $A_1, A_2 \subseteq \mathcal{A}$,*

$$s(X_1, A_1, X_2, A_2) = 2|X_1|\, g(X_1, A_1, X_2, A_2)$$

Lemma 2. *For any nonempty sets $X \subset \mathcal{X}$, $A \subset \mathcal{A}$, let their complements sets $X^c = \mathcal{X} \setminus X$ and $A^c = \mathcal{A} \setminus A$. Then,*

$$g(X, A) = 2g(X, A, \mathcal{X}, \mathcal{A}) = 2\frac{|X^c|}{|\mathcal{X}|}\frac{|A^c|}{|\mathcal{A}|} g(X, A, X^c, A^c)$$

Lemma 3. *For any $n > 1$ and nonempty $X_1, X_2, \ldots, X_n \subseteq \mathcal{X}$ and $A_1, A_2, \ldots, A_n \subseteq \overline{\mathcal{A}}$,*

$$g(X_1, A_1, \ldots, X_n, A_n) = \sum_{i \in [n]} g(X_i, A_i) - \sum_{i,j \in [n]} \frac{g(X_i, A_j)}{n}$$

Lemma 1 explains why we call it a generalization: for $n = 2$ and equal-sized name sets, the values are proportional with a factor that only depends on the set size. More generally, g can accommodate unequal set sizes and $n \neq 2$.

Lemma 2 shows that for $n = 1$ group, the definition is proportional to the WEAT with the two groups: X vs. all names $\mathcal{X}$ and words A vs. $\mathcal{A}$. Equivalently, it is proportional to the WEAT between X and A and their compliments.

Finally, Lemma 3 gives a *decomposition* of a WEAT into n^2 single-group WEATs $g(X_i, A_j)$. In particular, the value of a single multi-group WEAT reflects a combination of the n association strengths between X_i and A_i, and n^2 disassociation strengths between X_i and A_j. As discussed on the literature on IATs, a large effect could reflect a strong association between X_1 and A_1 or X_2 and A_2, a strong disassociation between X_1 and A_2 or X_2 and A_1, or some combination of these factors.

3 UNSUPERVISED BIAS ENUMERATION ALGORITHM

The inputs to our UBE algorithm are shown in Table 1. The output is m WEATs, each with n groups with associated sets of words and statistical confidences (p-values) in $[0, 1]$. Each WEAT has words from a single category, but several of the m WEATs may yield no significant associations.

At a high level, the algorithm follows a simple structure. It selects n disjoint groups of names $X_1, \ldots, X_n \subset \mathcal{X}$, and m disjoint categories of lower-case words $\mathcal{A}_1, \ldots, \mathcal{A}_m$. All WEATs share the same n name groups, and each WEAT has words from a single category $\mathcal{A}_j$, with t words associated to each X_i. Thus the WEATs can be conveniently visualized in a tabular structure.

For convenience, we normalize all word embedding vectors to be unit length. Note that we only compute cosines between them, and the cosine is simply the inner product for unit vectors. We now detail the algorithm's steps.

3.1 Step 1: Cleaning names and defining groups

We begin with a set of names[1] $\mathcal{X}$, e.g., frequent first names from a database. Since word embeddings do not differentiate between words that have the same spelling but different meanings, we first "clean" the given names to remove names such as "May" and "Virginia", whose embeddings are more reflective of other uses, such as a month or verb and a US state. Our cleaning procedure is similar but slightly more sophisticated to that of [7]. We train a linear Support Vector Machine [scikit-learn's LinearSVC, 19, with default parameters] to distinguish the input names from an equal number of non-names chosen randomly from the most frequent 50,000 words in the embedding. We then remove the 20% of names with smallest margin in the direction identified by the linear classifier.

We then use K-means++ clustering [from scikit-learn, 19, with default parameters] to cluster the normalized word vectors of the names, yielding groups $X_1 \cup \ldots \cup X_n = \mathcal{X}$. Finally, we define $\mu = \sum_i \overline{X}_i / n$.

3.2 Step 2: Defining word categories

To define categories, we cluster the most frequent M lower-case tokens in the word embedding into m clusters using K-means++,

name	meaning	default
WE	word embedding	w2v
$\mathcal{X}$	set of names	SSA
n	number of target groups	12
m	number of categories	64
M	number of frequent lower-case words	30,000
t	number of words per WEAT	3
α	false discovery rate	0.05

Table 1: Inputs to the UBE algorithm.

yielding clusters of categories $\mathcal{A}_1, \ldots, \mathcal{A}_m$. The constant M is chosen to cover as many recognizable words as possible without introducing too many unrecognizable tokens. As we shall see, categories capture concepts such as occupations, food-related words, and so forth.

3.3 Step 3: Selecting words $A_{ij} \subset \mathcal{A}_j$

A test $\mathcal{T}_j = (X_1, A_{1j}, \ldots, X_n, A_{nj})$ is chosen with disjoint $A_{ij} \subset \mathcal{A}_j$, each of size $t = |A_{ij}|$. To ensure disjointness,[2] $\mathcal{A}_j$ is first partitioned into n "Voronoi" sets $V_{ij} \subseteq \mathcal{A}_j$ consisting of the words whose embedding is closest to each corresponding center $\overline{X}_i$, i.e.,

$$V_{ij} = \left\{ w \in \mathcal{A}_j \mid i = \arg\max_{i' \in [n]} \overline{w} \cdot \overline{X}_{i'} \right\}$$

It then outputs A_{ij} defined as the t words maximizing the following:

$$\max_{w \in V_{ij}} (\overline{X}_i - \mu) \cdot (\overline{w} - \overline{\mathcal{A}}_j)$$

The more computationally-demanding step is to compute, using Monte Carlo sampling, the n p-values for $\mathcal{T}_j$, as described next.

3.4 Step 4: Computing p-values and ordering

To test whether the associations we find are larger than one would find if there was no relationship between the names X_i and words $\mathcal{A}$, we consider the following "**rotational null hypothesis**": the words in the embedding are generated through some process in which the alignment between names and words is random. This is formalized by imagining that a random rotation was applied (multiplying by a uniformly Haar random orthogonal matrix U) to the word embeddings but not to the name embeddings.

Specifically, to compute p-value p_{ij} for each (X_i, A_{ij}), we first compute a score $\sigma_{ij} = (\overline{X}_i - \mu) \cdot (\overline{A}_{ij} - \overline{\mathcal{A}})$. We then compute $R = 10,000$ uniformly random orthogonal rotations $U_1, \ldots, U_R \in \mathbb{R}^{d \times d}$, drawn according to the Haar measure. For each rotation, we simulate running our algorithm as if the name embeddings were transformed by U (while the word embeddings remain as is). For each rotation U_r, the sets A_{ijr} chosen to maximize $(\overline{X}_i U_r - \mu U_r) \cdot (\overline{w} - \overline{\mathcal{A}}_j)$, and the corresponding V_{ijr} and the resulting σ_{ijr} are computed. Finally, p_{ij} is the fraction of rotations for which the score $\sigma_{ijr} \geq \sigma_{ij}$ (plus an add-1 penalty standard for Monte Carlo p-values).

Furthermore, since the algorithm outputs many (hundreds) of name/word biases, the Benjamini-Hochberg [1995] procedure is

[1] While the set of names is an input to our system, they could also be extracted from the embedding itself.

[2] If multiplicities are desired, the Voronoi sets V_{ij} could be omitted, optimizing $A_{ij} \subset \mathcal{A}_j$ directly.

w2v F1	w2v F2	w2v F3	w2v F4	w2v F5	w2v F6	w2v F7	w2v F8	w2v F9	w2v F10	w2v F11	w2v F12
Amanda	Janice	Marquisha	Mia	Kayla	Kamal	Daniela	Miguel	Yael	Randall	Dashaun	Keith
Renee	Jeanette	Latisha	Keva	Carsyn	Nailah	Lucien	Deisy	Moses	Dashiell	Jamell	Gabe
Lynnea	Lenna	Tyrique	Hillary	Aislynn	Kya	Marko	Violeta	Michal	Randell	Marlon	Alfred
Zoe	Mattie	Marygrace	Penelope	Cj	Maryam	Emelie	Emilio	Shai	Jordan	Davonta	Shane
Erika	Marylynn	Takiyah	Savanna	Kaylei	Rohan	Antonia	Yareli	Yehudis	Chace	Demetrius	Stan
+581	+840	+692	+558	+890	+312	+391	+577	+120	+432	+393	+494
98% F	98% F	89% F	85% F	78% F	65% F	59% F	56% F	40% F	27% F	5% F	4% F
1983	1968	1978	1982	1993	1991	1985	1986	1989	1981	1984	1976
4% B	8% B	48% B	10% B	2% B	7% B	4% B	2% B	5% B	10% B	32% B	6% B
4% H	4% H	3% H	9% H	1% H	4% H	9% H	70% H	10% H	3% H	5% H	3% H
3% A	3% A	1% A	11% A	1% A	32% A	4% A	8% A	5% A	4% A	3% A	5% A
89% W	84% W	47% W	69% W	95% W	56% W	83% W	21% W	79% W	83% W	59% W	86% W

Table 2: Illustrative first names (greedily chosen) for $n = 12$ groups on the w2v embedding. Demographic statistics (computed a posteriori) are also shown though were not used in generation, including percentage female (at birth), mean year of birth, and percentage Black, Hispanic, Asian/Pacific Islander, and White.

used to determine a critical p-value that guarantees an α bound on the rate of false discoveries. Finally, to choose an output ordering on significant tests, the m tests are then sorted by the total scores σ_{ij} over the pairs determined significant.

Emb.	# significant	% accurate	% offensive
w2v	235	72%	35%
fast	160	80%	38%
glove	442	48%	24%

Table 3: Summary statistics for the WEATs generated using the three embeddings ($n = 12$, $m = 64$). The total number of significant name/word associations, the fraction with which the crowd's choice of name group agreed with that of the generated WEAT (accuracy) among the top-12 WEATs, and the fraction rated as offensive.

4 EVALUATION

To illustrate the performance of the proposed system in discovering associations, we use a database of first names provided by the Social Security Administration (SSA), which contains number of births per year by sex (F/M) [1]. We use only years 1938-2017 and select only the names that appeared at least 1,000 times, which cover more than 99% of the data by population.

We use three publicly available word embeddings, each with $d = 300$ dimensions and millions of words: w2v, released in 2013 and trained on approximately 100 billion words from Google News [18], fast, trained on 600 billion words from the Web [17], and glove, also trained on the Web using the GloVe algorithm [21].

While it is possible to display the three words in each A_{ij}, the hundreds or thousands of names in each X_i cannot be displayed in the output of the algorithm. Instead, we use a simple greedy heuristic to give five "illustrative" names for each group, which are displayed in the tables in this paper and in our crowdsourcing experiments. The $k + 1^{st}$ name shown is chosen, given the first k names, so as to maximize the average similarity of the first $k + 1$ names to that of the entire set X_i. Hence, the first name is the one whose normalized vector is most central (closest to the cluster mean), the second name is the one which when averaged with the first is as central as possible, and so forth.

The WEATs can be evaluated in terms of the quality of the name groups and also their associations with words. A priori, it was not clear whether clustering name embeddings would yield any name groups or word categories of interest. For all three embeddings we find that the clustering captures latent groups defined in terms of race, age, and gender, as illustrated in Table 2 for $n = 12$ clusters. While even a few clusters suffice to capture some demographic differences, more clusters yield much more fine-grained distinctions. For example, with $n = 12$ one cluster is of evidently Israeli names (see column I of table 2), which one might not consider predefining a priori since they are a small minority in the U.S. Note that, although we do not have religious statistics for the names, several of the words in the generated associations are religious in nature, suggesting religious biases as well.

4.1 Crowdsourcing Evaluation

We solicited ratings on the biases generated by the algorithm from US-based crowd workers on Amazon's Mechanical Turk[3] platform. The aim is to identify whether the biases found by our UBE algorithm are consistent with (problematic) biases held by society at large. To this end, we asked about society's stereotypes, *not* personal beliefs.

We evaluated the top 12 WEATs generated by our UBE algorithm for the three embeddings, considering $n = 12$ first name groups. Our approach was simple: after familiarizing participants with the 12 groups, we showed the (statistically significant) words and name groups of a WEAT and asked them to identify which words would, stereotypically, be most associated with which names group. A bonus was given for ratings that agreed with most other worker's ratings, incentivizing workers to provide answers that they felt corresponded to widely held stereotypes.

[3] http://mturk.com

Word2Vec trained on Google news			fastText trained on the Web			GloVe trained on the Web		
w2v F8	**w2v F11**	**w2v F6**	**fast F10**	**fast F7**	**fast F5**	**glove F8**	**glove F7**	**glove F5**
illegal immigrant	aggravated robbery	subcontinent	n*****	jihad	s******	turban	cartel	pornstar
drug trafficking	aggravated assault	tribesmen	f*****	militants	maid	saree	undocumented	hottie
deported	felonious assault	miscreants	dreads	caliphate	busty	hijab	culpable	nubile

Table 4: Terms in associations generated from three popular pre-trained word embeddings that were rated by crowd workers as both most offensive and aligned with societal biases. These associations do *not* reflect the personal beliefs of the crowd workers or authors of this paper.

This design was chosen over a simpler one in which WEATs are shown to individuals who are asked whether or not these are stereotypical. The latter design might support confirmation bias as people may interpret words in such a way that confirms whatever stereotypes they are being asked about. For instance, someone may be able to justify associating the color red with almost any group, a posteriori.

Note that the task presented to the workers involved fine-grained distinctions: for each of the top-12 WEATs, at least 18 workers would each be asked to match the significant $c \leq 12$ word triples to the c name groups (each identified by five names each). For example, workers faced the triple of "registered nurse, homemaker, chairwoman" with $c = 8$ groups of names, half of which were majority female, and the most commonly chosen group matched the one generated: "Janice, Jeanette, Lenna, Mattie, Marylynn." Across the top-12 WEATs over the three embeddings, the mean number of choices c was 8.1, yet the most commonly chosen group (plurality) agreed with the generated group 65% of the time (see Table 3). This is significantly more than one would expect from chance. The top-12 WEATs generated for w2v are shown in Table 5.

One challenge faced in this process was that, in pilot experiments, a significant fraction of the workers were not familiar with many of the names. To address this challenge, we first administered a qualification exam (common in crowdsourcing) in which each worker was shown 36 random names, 3 from each group, and was offered a bonus for each name they could correctly identify the group from which it was chosen. Only workers whose accuracy was greater than 1/2 (which happened 37% of the time) evaluated the WEATs. Accuracy greater than 50% on a 12-way classification indicates that the groups of names were meaningful and interpretable to many workers.

Finally, we asked 13-15 workers to rate associations on a scale of 1-7 of *political incorrectness*, with 7 being "politically incorrect, possibly very offensive" and 1 being "politically correct, inoffensive, or just random." Only those biases for which the most commonly chosen group matched the association identified by the UBE algorithm were included in this experiment. The mean ratings are shown in Table 3 and the terms present in associations deemed most offensive are presented in Table 4.

4.2 Potential Indirect Biases

Naively, one may think that removing names from a dataset will remove all problematic associations. However, as suggested by [5], indirect biases are likely to remain. For example, consider the w2v word embedding, in which *hostess* is closer to *volleyball* than to *cornerback*, while *cab driver* is closer to *cornerback* than to *volleyball*. These associations, taken from columns **F1** and **F11** of Table 5, might serve as a proxy for gender and/or race. For instance, if someone is applying for a job and their profile includes college sports words, such associations encoded in the embedding may lead to racial or gender biases in cases in which there is no professional basis for these associations. In contrast, *volunteer* being closer to *volunteers* than *recruits* may represent a definitional similarity more than a proxy, if we consider proxies to be associations that mainly have predictive power due to their correlation with a protected attribute. While defining proxies is beyond the scope of this work, we do say that $A_{ij}, A_{i'j}, A_{ij'}, A_{i'j'}$ is a *potential indirect bias* if,

$$(\overline{A}_{ij} - \overline{A}_{i'j}) \cdot (\overline{A}_{ij'} - \overline{A}_{i'j'}) > 0. \tag{1}$$

One way to interpret this definition is that if the embedding were to match the pair of word sets $\{A_{ij}, A_{i'j}\}$ to the pair of word sets $\{A_{ij'}, A_{i'j'}\}$, it would align with the way in which they were generated. For example, does the embedding predict that *hostess-cab driver* better fits *volleyball-cornerback* or *cornerback-volleyball* (but this question is asked with sets of $t = 3$ words)?

We consider all possible fourtuples of significant associations, such that $1 \leq i < i' \leq n$ and $1 \leq j < j' \leq m$. In the case of w2v, 99% of 2,713 significant fourtuples lead to potential indirect biases according to eq. (1). This statistic is of 98% of 1,125 fourtuples and 97% of 1,796 fourtuples for the fast and glove embeddings, respectively. Hence, while names allow us to capture biases in the embedding, removing names is unlikely to be sufficient to debias the embedding.

5 LIMITATIONS

Absent clusters show the limitations of our approach and data. For example, even for large n, no clusters represent demographically significant Asian-American groups. However, if instead of names we use surnames [U.S. Census, 8], a cluster "Yu, Tamashiro, Heng, Feng, Nakamura, +393" emerges, which is largely Asian according to Census data. This distinction may reflect naming practices among Asian Americans [23].

6 CONCLUSIONS

We introduce the problem of Unsupervised Bias Enumeration. We propose and evaluate a UBE algorithm that outputs Word Embedding Association Tests. Unlike humans, where implicit tests are necessary to elicit socially unacceptable biases in a straightforward fashion, word embeddings can be directly probed to output hundreds of biases of varying natures, including numerous offensive and socially unacceptable biases. The racist and sexist associations

w2v F1	w2v F2	w2v F3	w2v F4	w2v F5	w2v F6	w2v F7	w2v F8	w2v F9	w2v F11	w2v F12
	cookbook, baking, baked goods	sweet potatoes, macaroni, green beans			saffron, halal, sweets	mozzarella, foie gras, caviar	tortillas, salsa, tequila	kosher, hummus, bagel	fried chicken, crawfish, grams	beef, beer, hams
herself, hers, moms	husband, homebound, grandkids	aunt, niece, grandmother	hubby, socialite, cuddle	twin sister, girls, classmate	elder brother, dowry, refugee camp			bereaved, immigrated, emigrated	younger brother, twin brother, mentally r********	buddy, boyhood, fatherhood
hostess, cheer-leader, dietitian	registered nurse, homemaker, chairwoman		supermodel, beauty queen, stripper	helper, getter, snowboarder	shopkeeper, villager, cricketer		translator, interpreter, smuggler		cab driver, jailer, schoolboy	pitchman, retired, pundit
	log cabin, library, fairgrounds	front porch, carport, duplex	racecourse, plush, tenements	picnic tables, bleachers, concession stand	locality, mosque, slum	prefecture, chalet, sauna		synagogues, constructions, hilltop	apartment complex, barbershop, nightclub	
	parish, church, pastoral	pastor, baptized, mourners	goddess, celestial, mystical		fatwa, mosques, martyrs	monastery, papal, convent	rosary, parish priest, patron saint	rabbis, synagogue, biblical		
volleyball, gymnast, setter	athletic director, winningest coach, officiating	leading rebounder, played sparingly, incoming freshman	hooker, footy, stud	sophomore, junior, freshman	leftarm spinner, dayers, leg spinner				cornerback, tailback, wide receiver	
sorority, gymnastics, majoring	volunteer, volunteering, secretarial	guidance counselor, prekinder-garten, graduate		seventh grader, eighth grade, seniors	lecturers, institutes, syllabus		bilingual, permanent residency, occupations		incoming freshmen, schoolyard, recruiting	fulltime, professional, apprentice-ship
		civil rights, poverty stricken, nonviolent			subcontinent, tribesmen, miscreants	xenophobia, anarchist, oligarchs	leftist, drug traffickers, undocumented	disengage-ment, intifada, settlers	blacks, segregation, lynching	
tiara, blonde, sparkly	knitting, sewing, beaded	brown eyes, cream colo..., wore	girly, feminine, flirty	brown hair, pair, skates	sari, turban, hijab				dreadlocks, shoulderpads, waistband	mullet, gear, helmet
					dirhams, lakhs, rupees	rubles, kronor, roulette	pesos, remittances, gross re-ceipts	shekels, settlements, corpus		
		grandjury indicted, degree murder, violating probation		child endangerment, vehicular homicide, unlawful possession	chargesheet, absconding, interrogation	absentia, tax evasion, falsification	illegal immigrant, drug trafficking, deported		aggravated robbery, aggravated assault, felonious assault	
	volunteers, crafters, baby boomers	caseworkers, evacuees, attendants	beauties, celebs, paparazzi	setters, helpers, captains	mediapersons, office bearers, newsmen				recruits, reps, sheriffs	

Table 5: The top-12 WEATs output by our UBE algorithm on the w2v embedding. Columns represent name groups X_i from Table 2, rows represent categories A_j (e.g., a cluster of food-related words). Orange indicate associations where the crowd's most commonly chosen name group agrees with that of the generated WEAT. No significant biases generated for w2v F10.

exposed in publicly available word embeddings raise questions about their widespread use.

Acknowledgments. We are grateful to Tarleton Gillespie, other colleagues and the anonymous reviewers for useful feedback.

REFERENCES

[1] Social Security Administration. 2018. Baby Names from Social Security Card Applications - National Level Data. https://catalog.data.gov/dataset/baby-names-from-social-security-card-applications-national-level-data Accessed 5 July 2018.

[2] Solon Barocas, Kate Crawford, Aaron Shapiro, and Hanna Wallach. 2017. The problem with bias: from allocative to representational harms in machine learning. *Special Interest Group for Computing, Information and Society (SIGCIS)* (2017).

[3] Yoav Benjamini and Yosef Hochberg. 1995. Controlling the False Discovery Rate: A Practical and Powerful Approach to Multiple Testing. *Journal of the Royal Statistical Society. Series B (Methodological)* 57, 1 (1995), 289–300. http://www.jstor.org/stable/2346101

[4] Matthias Bluemke and Malte Friese. 2008. Reliability and validity of the Single-Target IAT (ST-IAT): assessing automatic affect towards multiple attitude objects. *European journal of social psychology* 38, 6 (2008), 977–997.

[5] Tolga Bolukbasi, Kai-Wei Chang, James Y Zou, Venkatesh Saligrama, and Adam T Kalai. 2016. Man is to computer programmer as woman is to homemaker? debiasing word embeddings. In *Advances in Neural Information Processing Systems*. 4349–4357.

[6] Joy Buolamwini and Timnit Gebru. 2018. Gender shades: Intersectional accuracy disparities in commercial gender classification. In *Conference on Fairness, Accountability and Transparency*. 77–91.

[7] Aylin Caliskan, Joanna J. Bryson, and Arvind Narayanan. 2017. Semantics derived automatically from language corpora contain human-like biases. *Science* 356, 6334 (2017), 183–186.

[8] Joshua Comenetz. 2016. Frequently occurring surnames in the 2010 Census. *United States Census Bureau* (2016).

[9] Thierry Devos and Mahzarin R Banaji. 2005. American= white? *Journal of personality and social psychology* 88, 3 (2005), 447.

[10] Cynthia Dwork, Moritz Hardt, Toniann Pitassi, Omer Reingold, and Richard Zemel. 2012. Fairness Through Awareness. In *Proceedings of the 3rd Innovations in Theoretical Computer Science Conference (ITCS '12)*. ACM, New York, NY, USA, 214–226.

[11] Nikhil Garg, Londa Schiebinger, Dan Jurafsky, and James Zou. 2018. Word embeddings quantify 100 years of gender and ethnic stereotypes. *Proceedings of the National Academy of Sciences* 115, 16 (2018), E3635–E3644.

[12] Anthony G Greenwald, Debbie E McGhee, and Jordan LK Schwartz. 1998. Measuring individual differences in implicit cognition: the implicit association test. *Journal of personality and social psychology* 74, 6 (1998), 1464.

[13] Md Hoque, Rawshan E Fatima, Manash Kumar Mandal, Nazmus Saquib, et al. 2017. Evaluating gender portrayal in Bangladeshi TV. *arXiv preprint arXiv:1711.09728* (2017).

[14] Andrew Karpinski and Ross B Steinman. 2006. The single category implicit association test as a measure of implicit social cognition. *Journal of personality and social psychology* 91, 1 (2006), 16.

[15] Michael Kearns, Seth Neel, Aaron Roth, and Zhiwei Steven Wu. 2017. Preventing Fairness Gerrymandering: Auditing and Learning for Subgroup Fairness. *arXiv preprint arXiv:1711.05144* (2017).

[16] Austin C Kozlowski, Matt Taddy, and James A Evans. 2018. The Geometry of Culture: Analyzing Meaning through Word Embeddings. *arXiv preprint arXiv:1803.09288* (2018).

[17] Tomas Mikolov, Edouard Grave, Piotr Bojanowski, Christian Puhrsch, and Armand Joulin. 2018. Advances in Pre-Training Distributed Word Representations. In *Proceedings of the International Conference on Language Resources and Evaluation (LREC 2018)*.

[18] Tomas Mikolov, Ilya Sutskever, Kai Chen, Greg S Corrado, and Jeff Dean. 2013. Distributed representations of words and phrases and their compositionality. In *Advances in neural information processing systems*. 3111–3119.

[19] F. Pedregosa, G. Varoquaux, A. Gramfort, V. Michel, B. Thirion, O. Grisel, M. Blondel, P. Prettenhofer, R. Weiss, V. Dubourg, J. Vanderplas, A. Passos, D. Cournapeau, M. Brucher, M. Perrot, and E. Duchesnay. 2011. Scikit-learn: Machine Learning in Python. *Journal of Machine Learning Research* 12 (2011), 2825–2830.

[20] Lars Penke, Jan Eichstaedt, and Jens B Asendorpf. 2006. Single-attribute implicit association tests (SA-IAT) for the assessment of unipolar constructs. *Experimental Psychology* 53, 4 (2006), 283–291.

[21] Jeffrey Pennington, Richard Socher, and Christopher D. Manning. 2014. GloVe: Global Vectors for Word Representation. In *Empirical Methods in Natural Language Processing (EMNLP)*. 1532–1543. http://www.aclweb.org/anthology/D14-1162

[22] Shreya Shankar, Yoni Halpern, Eric Breck, James Atwood, Jimbo Wilson, and D Sculley. 2017. No Classification without Representation: Assessing Geodiversity Issues in Open Data Sets for the Developing World. *arXiv preprint arXiv:1711.08536* (2017).

[23] Ellen Dionne Wu. 1999. âĂIJThey Call Me Bruce, But They Won't Call Me Bruce Jones:âĂİ Asian American Naming Preferences and Patterns. *Names* 47, 1 (1999), 21–50. https://doi.org/10.1179/nam.1999.47.1.21 arXiv:https://doi.org/10.1179/nam.1999.47.1.21

[24] Rich Zemel, Yu Wu, Kevin Swersky, Toni Pitassi, and Cynthia Dwork. 2013. Learning fair representations. In *International Conference on Machine Learning*. 325–333.

Equalized Odds Implies Partially Equalized Outcomes Under Realistic Assumptions

Daniel McNamara
Australian National University and CSIRO Data61
Canberra, ACT, Australia
dpmcna@gmail.com

ABSTRACT

Equalized odds – where the true positive rates and false positive rates are equal across groups (e.g. racial groups) – is a common quantitative measure of fairness. Equalized outcomes – where the difference in predicted outcomes between groups is less than the difference observed in the training data – is more contentious, because it is incompatible with perfectly accurate predictions. We formalize and quantify the relationship between these two important but seemingly distinct notions of fairness. We show that under realistic assumptions, equalized odds implies partially equalized outcomes. We prove a comparable result for approximately equalized odds. In addition, we generalize a well-known previous result about the incompatibility of equalized odds and another definition of fairness known as calibration, by showing that partially equalized outcomes implies non-calibration. Our results highlight the risks of using trends observed across groups to make predictions about individuals.

CCS CONCEPTS

• **Social and professional topics** → *Socio-technical systems; Race and ethnicity;* • **Theory of computation** → *Machine learning theory;* • **Computing methodologies** → *Machine learning.*

KEYWORDS

fairness; machine learning; equalized odds; equalized outcomes

ACM Reference Format:

Daniel McNamara. 2019. Equalized Odds Implies Partially Equalized Outcomes Under Realistic Assumptions. In *AAAI/ACM Conference on AI, Ethics, and Society (AIES '19), January 27–28, 2019, Honolulu, HI, USA.* ACM, New York, NY, USA, 8 pages. https://doi.org/10.1145/3306618.3314290

1 INTRODUCTION

Definitions of fairness – and conflicts between them – are an important topic in recent quantitative fairness literature [2]. Such definitions often involve avoiding discrimination on the basis of a particular kind of group membership, such as race or gender. In a particular situation, different definitions may be invoked by different stakeholders [18].

AIES '19, January 27–28, 2019, Honolulu, HI, USA

ACM ISBN 978-1-4503-6324-2/19/01...$15.00
https://doi.org/10.1145/3306618.3314290

Table 1: Summary of main definitions and results.

Definitions
Equalized Odds
True positive rates same for each group
False positive rates same for each group
Partially Equalized Outcomes
Predicted difference between groups less than observed difference between groups
Calibration
Predicted probability equals observed probability for each group and each probability value

Results
Existing
Equalized Odds $\implies$ Not Calibration [16]
New
Equalized Odds $\implies$ Partially Equalized Outcomes
Partially Equalized Outcomes $\implies$ Not Calibration

The controversy created by the COMPAS recidivism prediction system showed this in practice. The system provided risk assessments about the likelihood that individuals would reoffend within a fixed period, in order to inform decisions in the criminal justice system such as whether to grant pre-trial release [19]. The news organization ProPublica tested the system on past data containing both risk assessments and observed reoffences. ProPublica claimed that COMPAS was unfair towards African-Americans based on analysis showing that among observed non-reoffenders, African-Americans were more likely to be marked high risk than whites, and among observed reoffenders, whites were more likely to be marked low risk than African-Americans [1] – i.e. the algorithm violated *equalized odds* (see Definition 1). The COMPAS response was that the algorithm was not unfair because among those marked high risk, African-Americans were not less likely to reoffend than whites [9] – i.e. the algorithm satisfied *test-fairness* (see Definition 2.1 of [6]).

Subsequently it was shown that no algorithm can simultaneously satisfy both equalized odds and test-fairness under realistic assumptions [6]. A similar result was shown in the more general setting of continuous rather than binary risk scores [16], replacing test-fairness with a related concept known as *calibration* (see Definition 4). Our work generalizes this latter result by exploring the relationship between *equalized outcomes* (see Definition 2) and equalized odds, as summarized in Table 1.

1.1 Motivation for Equalized Odds

We motivate *equalized odds*, using recidivism prediction as a running example (see Appendix B for a more extended discussion). Among observed non-reoffenders, we may want to ensure that those from one group are not marked higher risk on average than those from another group, i.e. our false positive rates for both groups are equal. This has been dubbed *equality of opportunity* [14]. If we also ensure that among observed reoffenders, those from one group are not marked higher risk on average than those from another group, we have *equalized odds* [14], i.e. our true positive rates for both groups are also equal.[1] It has been observed that in order to make the relative utility of different groups more equal, absolute utility may be reduced [7, 8, 17]. However, equalized odds has some intuitive appeal as a fairness measure since it ensures that mistakes do not disproportionately impact any group.

1.2 The Debate about Equalized Outcomes

Equality of outcomes between groups is a well-known fairness criterion. It has been mathematically formalized in the quantitative fairness literature through the concepts of *statistical parity* [4, 10], avoiding *disparate impact* [12, 22] and achieving *independence* between outcomes and group membership [2]. These technical definitions have prompted debate about whether they are suitable measures of fairness.

A critique of equalized outcomes is that if the observed rates (e.g. of recidivism) are different across the two groups in the training data, then an algorithm that reflects this difference is not 'unfair' but is rather a reflection of real underlying differences [14, 23]. The argument goes: surely we would not want to label 'unfair' a prediction algorithm which is perfectly accurate! The job of the algorithm is to predict the world as it is; changing the world is out of scope.

However, *not* equalizing outcomes across groups creates the risk of discrimination in situations where the data collection process systematically disadvantages one group [3, 20, 23]. For example, profiling of particular populations based on pre-existing risk assessments can distort trends in reoffending. Equalized outcomes may help algorithms to avoid perpetuating this structural inequality. More generally, the question of whether redistribution should be used to reduce inequality is at the core of the left-right political divide [15]. As such, the debate on equalized outcomes is unlikely to be definitively won or lost by either side.

1.3 Our Contribution

Our core contribution is to formalize and quantify the relationship between equalized odds and equalized outcomes, two important but seemingly distinct notions of fairness. We quantify the extent to which outcomes are equalized in an intuitive way, via a comparison between the predicted and observed differences between groups (Section 2). We prove that if we want to satisfy equalized odds, we must partially equalize outcomes – even if we only want approximately equalized odds (Section 3). In addition, we generalize a well-known existing result about the incompatibility of equalized odds and a different fairness measure known as *calibration* [16], using a simpler proof technique (Section 4). Our conclusion (Section 5) highlights why we should consider the reality that algorithmic decisions are imperfect when defining measures of fairness. Our technical results can be interpreted as an example of the problem of group-to-individual inference [13]: learning from trends across groups may lead to incorrect inferences about individuals, and those incorrect inferences may disproportionately affect certain groups.

[1] Equality of true positive rates between groups is equivalent to equality of false negative rates between groups. Equalized odds has also been referred to as avoiding *disparate mistreatment* [23].

2 PROBLEM FORMALIZATION

We mathematically formalize the setting we have informally described above. Let $\mathcal{X}$, $\mathcal{Y}$ and $\mathcal{S}$ be sets corresponding to the input variable X, target variable Y and sensitive variable S respectively. The sensitive variable encodes some form of group membership. We focus on the case where $\mathcal{S} = \{0, 1\}$ (e.g. race coded as 1 for African-American or 0 for non African-American) and $\mathcal{Y} = \{0, 1\}$ (e.g. ground truth of whether the person reoffended). The choice of $\mathcal{X}$ is arbitrary in our analysis (e.g. a person's criminal record expressed as a real-valued vector). Let $h : \mathcal{X} \times \mathcal{S} \to [0, 1]$ be a stochastic hypothesis, which can also be interpreted as a scoring function.[2] Let decision variable $\hat{Y}$ be constructed such that $p(\hat{Y} = 1|X = x, S = s) := h(x, s)$. While setting S, Y and $\hat{Y}$ to be binary variables is an assumption, this allows us to cover many cases of interest – such as the recidivism prediction example – and facilitates our analysis and interpretation.

Drawing X, S and Y and making decision $\hat{Y}$, we have a joint distribution μ of all four variables. We may also derive marginal distributions over one or more variables, such as the marginal distribution of Y:

$$\mu_Y(Y = y) := \int_{x \in \mathcal{X}} \sum_{s \in \{0,1\}} \sum_{\hat{y} \in \{0,1\}} \mu(X = x, S = s, Y = y, \hat{Y} = \hat{y}) dx.$$

Similarly, we may derive conditional distributions, such as the marginal distribution over $\hat{Y}$ conditioned on $Y = 1$:

$$\mu_{\hat{Y}|Y=1}(\hat{Y} = \hat{y}) := \frac{\mu_{Y,\hat{Y}}(Y = 1, \hat{Y} = \hat{y})}{\mu_Y(Y = 1)}.$$

We use notation of the form $p(Y = y) := \mu_Y(Y = y)$ for marginals and $p(\hat{Y} = \hat{y}|Y = 1) := \mu_{\hat{Y}|Y=1}(\hat{Y} = \hat{y})$ for conditionals. For example, $p(\hat{Y} = 1|Y = 1)$ is known as the true positive rate (e.g. predicted reoffence rate for reoffenders) and $p(\hat{Y} = 1|Y = 0)$ is known as the false positive rate (e.g. predicted reoffence rate for non-reoffenders). We use the symbol $\perp$ to denote probabilistic independence between variables.

2.1 Impossibility Results

An impossibility result states several candidate properties of a joint distribution, and shows that *no* distribution can simultaneously satisfy all of these properties. We briefly review several impossibility results with respect to fairness that have been established in prior works.

[2] This underpins our comparisons with [16], which analyzes risk scores. Interpreting such scores as decision probabilities facilitates our analysis.

A well-known impossibility result (Theorem 1.1 of [16], restated in Theorem 3) considered the relationship between calibration – which requires that for both groups, each risk score accurately reflects the true risk associated with individuals assigned that score (see Definition 4) – and equalized odds. The result showed that it is impossible to simultaneously satisfy both fairness criteria and other realistic assumptions.

Variants exist involving approximate versions of equalized odds (Theorem 1 of [21]), calibration or both (Theorem 1.2 of [16]). We mentioned earlier the incompatibility of equalized odds and *test-fairness* – where the risk scores are binary and the true risk of individuals with a given score must be the same for both groups [6]. Simple rules of conditional probability may be used to show that $\hat{Y} \perp S | Y$ – corresponding to equalized odds – and $Y \perp S\ \hat{Y}$ – which is closely related to calibration – cannot both simultaneously hold under realistic assumptions [2]. The incompatibility of equalized odds and the independence relationship $\hat{Y} \perp S$ (i.e. perfect statistical parity) has also been shown [2, 16].

In our work we derive impossibility results involving equalized outcomes and equalized odds, which are of interest given the debates about these fairness criteria described in Section 1. As we shall see in Section 4, our analysis also allows us to generalize Theorem 1.1 of [16], by exploiting the relationship between equalized outcomes and calibration.

2.2 Fairness Definitions

We now formalize the definition of equalized odds.

Definition 1 (Equalized odds [14, 23]). *Equalized odds is satisfied if both of the following hold:*

$$p(\hat{Y} = 1|S = 1, Y = 1) = p(\hat{Y} = 1|S = 0, Y = 1) \tag{1}$$

i.e. the true positive rate is the same for both groups, and

$$p(\hat{Y} = 1|S = 1, Y = 0) = p(\hat{Y} = 1|S = 0, Y = 0) \tag{2}$$

i.e. the false positive rate is the same for both groups.

We now present a novel formalization of equalized outcomes.

Definition 2 (Equalized outcomes). *Let*

$$\begin{aligned} &p(\hat{Y} = 1|S = 1) - p(\hat{Y} = 1|S = 0) \\ &= \alpha(p(Y = 1|S = 1) - p(Y = 1|S = 0)) \end{aligned} \tag{3}$$

where α is a constant we refer to as the equalized outcomes coefficient. If (3) *holds for $\alpha = 0$ we have* fully equalized outcomes. *If* (3) *holds for some $\alpha \in (0, 1)$ we have* partially equalized outcomes. *If* (3) *holds for $\alpha = 1$ we have* non-equalized outcomes.

Fully equalized outcomes corresponds to the well-known definition of *statistical parity* [4, 10], or equivalently the *independence* $\hat{Y} \perp S$ [2]. The value of introducing the parameter α is that we quantify the extent to which outcomes are equalized in an intuitive way, via a comparison with the observed difference between groups. Under partially equalized outcomes, the predicted difference between groups is smaller than the observed difference between groups. Non-equalized outcomes means that predicted outcomes are *faithful* to the observed difference in outcomes between groups. If $\alpha > 1$ the predicted difference amplifies the observed difference, while if $\alpha < 0$ the predicted difference flips the sign of the observed difference. These options do not appear advantageous in terms of either fairness or accuracy, and we do not focus on them.

3 THE RELATIONSHIP BETWEEN EQUALIZED ODDS AND EQUALIZED OUTCOMES

Assuming equalized odds is satisfied, we show there is a quantifiable trade-off between accuracy and the extent to which outcomes are equalized. As a corollary, we show that equalized odds implies partially equalized outcomes under realistic assumptions. We consider the cases where equalized odds either exactly or approximately holds.[3]

3.1 Perfectly Equalized Odds

We show in Theorem 1 that given perfectly equalized odds, the extent to which we equalize outcomes is given by the difference α between the true positive rate and false positive rate. This novel result is of interest because it precisely quantifies the relationship between the well-known but seemingly distinct notions of equalized odds and equalized outcomes.

Theorem 1 (Equalized outcomes given equalized odds). *Let*

$$\alpha := p(\hat{Y} = 1|Y = 1) - p(\hat{Y} = 1|Y = 0).$$

Suppose (1) *and* (2) *hold, i.e. equalized odds is satisfied. Then* (3) *is satisfied, i.e. α is the equalized outcomes coefficient satisfying*

$$\begin{aligned} &p(\hat{Y} = 1|S = 1) - p(\hat{Y} = 1|S = 0) \\ &= \alpha(p(Y = 1|S = 1) - p(Y = 1|S = 0)). \end{aligned}$$

Proof. We have

$$\begin{aligned} p(\hat{Y} = 1|S = 1) = p(Y = 1|S = 1)p(\hat{Y} = 1|S = 1, Y = 1) \\ + p(Y = 0|S = 1)p(\hat{Y} = 1|S = 1, Y = 0) \end{aligned} \tag{4}$$

and

$$\begin{aligned} p(\hat{Y} = 1|S = 0) = p(Y = 1|S = 0)p(\hat{Y} = 1|S = 0, Y = 1) \\ + p(Y = 0|S = 0)p(\hat{Y} = 1|S = 0, Y = 0) \end{aligned} \tag{5}$$

by the law of total probability.

Applying (1) and (2) to (4) yields

$$\begin{aligned} p(\hat{Y} = 1|S = 1) = p(Y = 1|S = 1)p(\hat{Y} = 1|Y = 1) \\ + p(Y = 0|S = 1)p(\hat{Y} = 1|Y = 0) \end{aligned} \tag{6}$$

and similarly, applying (1) and (2) to (5) yields

$$\begin{aligned} p(\hat{Y} = 1|S = 0) = p(Y = 1|S = 0)p(\hat{Y} = 1|Y = 1) \\ + p(Y = 0|S = 0)p(\hat{Y} = 1|Y = 0). \end{aligned} \tag{7}$$

Subtracting (7) from (6) and using the definition of α, we have

[3] While the exact version is a special case of the approximate version, we consider the exact case first as it makes the presentation of the results more intuitive.

$$p(\hat{Y} = 1|S = 1) - p(\hat{Y} = 1|S = 0) = \alpha(p(Y = 1|S = 1) - p(Y = 1|S = 0)). \quad (8)$$

□

3.2 Realistic Assumptions

We now introduce three realistic assumptions, which help to illuminate the relationship between equalized odds and equalized outcomes. In the subsequent results in this chapter, we flag whether one or more of the assumptions is used.

The first assumption is that the observed rates (e.g. of recidivism) are different across groups, which is true for most cases of interest.

Assumption 1 (Different observed rates).

$$p(Y = 1|S = 1) \neq p(Y = 1|S = 0) \quad (9)$$

The other two assumptions are that our decisions are *imperfect* (i.e. they are not always accurate) and *non-vacuous* (i.e. they have some predictive power). This covers the bulk of realistic situations in which algorithmic decisions are used. We observe that the imperfect decisions assumption will hold if Y cannot be expressed as a deterministic function of X and S. In this case, changing $\hat{Y}$ will not help. This is typically the case when we are making predictions about the future actions of individuals.

Assumption 2 (Imperfect decisions). *At least one of the following holds:*

$$p(\hat{Y} = 1|Y = 0) > 0, \quad (10)$$

i.e. some negative examples are misclassified, or

$$p(\hat{Y} = 1|Y = 1) < 1, \quad (11)$$

i.e. some positive examples are misclassified.

Assumption 3 (Non-vacuous decisions).

$$p(\hat{Y} = 1|Y = 1) > p(\hat{Y} = 1|Y = 0), \quad (12)$$

i.e. the decision is more likely to be positive for positive examples than for negative examples.

As a consequence of Theorem 1 and our realistic assumptions, if we have perfectly equalized odds then we have partially equalized outcomes, as shown in Corollary 1. While as we mentioned above the incompatibility of equalized odds and fully equalized outcomes (i.e. $\alpha = 0$, perfect statistical parity) was already known, we are the first to show that equalized odds is also incompatible with non-equalized outcomes ($\alpha = 1$) or indeed any value of α outside the interval $(0, 1)$ under our realistic assumptions.

Corollary 1 (Equalized odds implies partially equalized outcomes under realistic assumptions). *Suppose* (1) *and* (2) *hold, i.e. we have equalized odds. Suppose also that Assumptions 1, 2 and 3 hold. Then satisfying* (3) *requires* $\alpha \in (0, 1)$, *i.e. we have partially equalized outcomes.*

Proof. By Theorem 1 we know that given equalized odds, the equation (3) is satisfied for

$$\alpha = p(\hat{Y} = 1|Y = 1) - p(\hat{Y} = 1|Y = 0).$$

Applying Assumption 1 (different observed rates), this is the *only* value of α satisfying (3). Applying Assumption 2 (imperfect decisions) we have $\alpha < 1$. Applying Assumption 3 (non-vacuous decisions) we have $\alpha > 0$. The result follows. □

3.3 Approximately Equalized Odds

We consider a relaxation of the equalized odds condition, allowing the false positive rates to slightly differ across groups and the false negative rates to likewise slightly differ across groups. The parameter δ quantifies the degree of this relaxation, with $\delta = 0$ corresponding to perfectly equalized odds.

Definition 3 (Approximately equalized odds). *For some constant* $\delta \geq 0$ *we have*

$$p(\hat{Y} = 1|S = 1, Y = 1), p(\hat{Y} = 1|S = 0, Y = 1) \in [(1 - \delta)p(\hat{Y} = 1|Y = 1), (1 + \delta)p(\hat{Y} = 1|Y = 1)] \quad (13)$$

i.e. the true positive rate is approximately the same for both groups. We also have

$$p(\hat{Y} = 1|S = 1, Y = 0), p(\hat{Y} = 1|S = 0, Y = 0) \in [(1 - \delta)p(\hat{Y} = 1|Y = 0), (1 + \delta)p(\hat{Y} = 1|Y = 0)] \quad (14)$$

i.e. the false positive rate is approximately the same for both groups.

In Theorem 2 we show that if δ-approximately equalized odds is satisfied, then the extent to which we equalize outcomes is given by an interval. This midpoint of the interval is determined by the difference α between the true positive rate and false positive rate. The size of the interval is determined by δ and a distribution-dependent parameter β.

Theorem 2 (Equalized outcomes given approximately equalized odds). *Let*

$$\alpha := p(\hat{Y} = 1|Y = 1) - p(\hat{Y} = 1|Y = 0),$$

$$\epsilon := p(Y = 1|S = 1) + p(Y = 1|S = 0)$$

and

$$\beta := \epsilon p(\hat{Y} = 1|Y = 1) + (2 - \epsilon)p(\hat{Y} = 1|Y = 0).$$

Observe that $\beta \geq 0$. *Suppose* (13) *and* (14) *hold, i.e.* δ-*approximately equalized odds is satisfied. Then*

$$p(\hat{Y} = 1|S = 1) - p(\hat{Y} = 1|S = 0) \in [\alpha(p(Y = 1|S = 1) - p(Y = 1|S = 0)) - \delta\beta, \alpha(p(Y = 1|S = 1) - p(Y = 1|S = 0)) + \delta\beta].$$

Proof idea. As in the proof of Theorem 1, use the law of total probability to express $p(\hat{Y} = 1|S = 1)$ and $p(\hat{Y} = 1|S = 0)$. Then apply the δ-approximately equalized odds assumption to upper and lower bound their difference. See Appendix A for complete proof. □

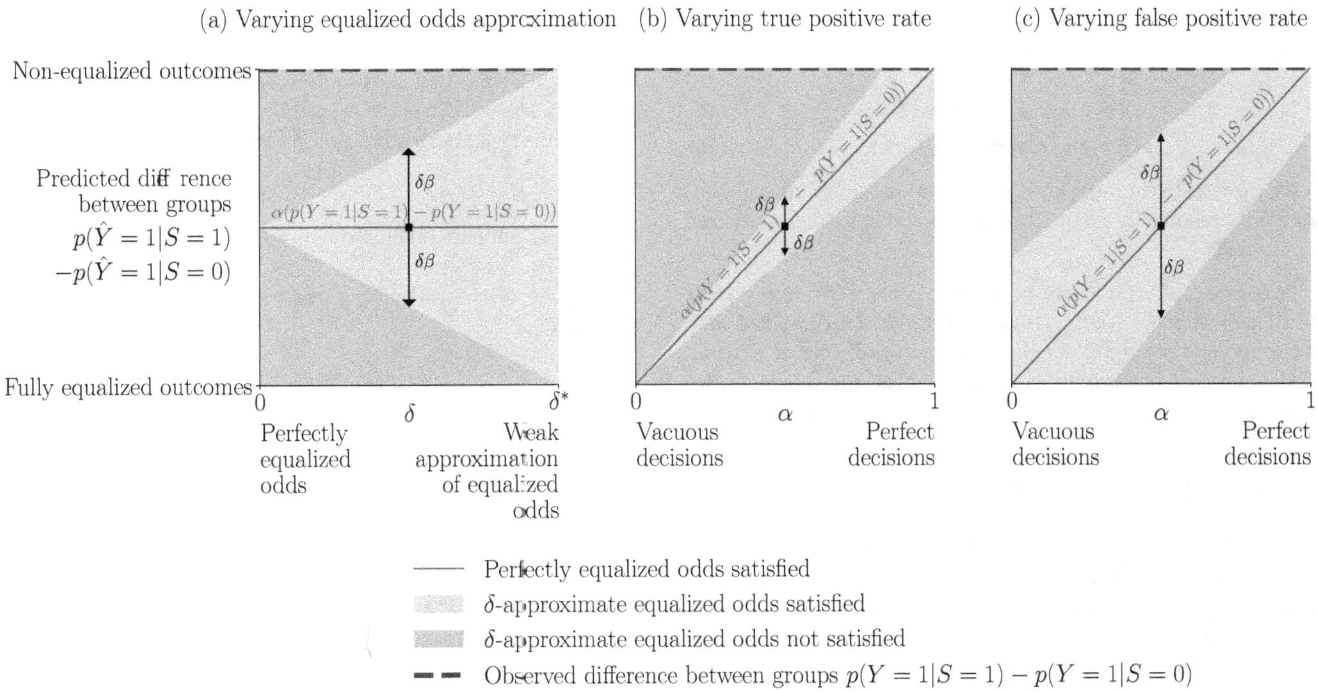

Figure 1: Visualization of key results. Certain combinations of equalized outcomes, equalized odds and accuracy are possible (light green regions), while other combinations are impossible (dark gray regions). In (a) we vary equalized odds approximation parameter δ, fixing accuracy parameter $\alpha := p(\hat{Y}=1|Y=1)-p(\hat{Y}=1|Y=0)$. In (b) we vary the $p(\hat{Y}=1|Y=1)$ term in α and in (c) we vary the $p(\hat{Y}=1|Y=0)$ term in α, fixing δ. ϵ is a distribution-dependent parameter (see Theorem 2).

3.4 Interpretation

We visualize our results in Figure 1. In each plot the y-axis shows the predicted difference between groups, i.e. the extent to which outcomes are equalized, on a scale from zero (bottom) to the observed difference between groups (top). We vary other parameters along the x-axes of the plots.

If perfectly equalized odds is satisfied there is an exact relationship between equalized outcomes and α (see Theorem 1, green line on plots). If δ-approximate equalized odds is satisfied there is a region of permissible combinations of equalized outcomes and α values (see Theorem 2, light green region on plots). Combinations outside this region violate δ-approximate equalized odds (dark gray region on plots).

In Figure 1(a), we see that if we relax the constraint on equalized odds by increasing the parameter δ (see Definition 3), we have a larger region of possible combinations.[4] The size of this region is quantified by the slack term $\delta\beta$. The region is an interval centered on the product of α and the observed difference between groups. We see visually why for $\alpha \in (0,1)$, i.e. for decisions that are imperfect and non-vacuous, we have partially equalized outcomes.

Figures 1(b) and 1(c) show that if we have equalized odds, then increasing accuracy (measured by α) moves towards non-equalized outcomes.[5] We may increase α by increasing the true positive rate, as in Figure 1(b), where we assume no false positives. We may also increase α by decreasing the false positive rate, as in Figure 1(c), where we assume no false negatives. Under perfectly equalized odds the effect on equalized outcomes is the same, while under approximately equalized odds the permissible regions differ because β depends on the false positive rate and the true positive rate.

4 GENERALIZATION OF CALIBRATION-EQUALIZED ODDS IMPOSSIBILITY RESULT

The relationship between equalized odds and equalized outcomes, in addition to its intrinsic interest, allows us to generalize a well-known result about the impossibility of simultaneously satisfying calibration and equalized odds (Theorem 1.1 of [16]). We use a proof technique involving elementary probabilities, which also provides a simpler proof of the previous result.

4.1 Review of Existing Result

We first introduce the definition of group-conditional calibration proposed in previous work [16, 21]. This means that for both groups, each risk score equals the observed risk associated with individuals assigned that score.

[4] The value of δ for which the edge of this region intersects the x-axis is given by $\delta^* := \frac{\alpha}{\beta}(p(Y=1|S=1)-p(Y=1|S=0))$. Figure 1(a) uses the fixed parameters $\alpha := 0.5$, $\beta := 1$ and $\epsilon := 1$.

[5] Figures 1(b) and 1(c) use $\epsilon := 1$ and $\delta := 0.2(p(Y=1|S=1)-p(Y=1|S=0))$.

Definition 4 (Group-conditional calibration [16, 21]). *Both of the following statements hold* $\forall c \in [0, 1]$:

$$p(Y = 1|h(x, s) = c, S = 1) = c \tag{15}$$

$$p(Y = 1|h(x, s) = c, S = 0) = c \tag{16}$$

We now state the well-known calibration-equalized odds impossibility result (Theorem 1.1 of [16], restated to align with our definitions).

Theorem 3 (Calibration-equalized odds impossibility result [16]). *Suppose* (1), (2), (15) *and* (16) *hold, i.e. equalized odds and group-conditional calibration are both satisfied. Then at least one of Assumption 1 or Assumption 2 is violated, i.e. the observed rates are the same for both groups and/or the decision is perfect.*

In other words, equalized odds implies not calibration under realistic assumptions, as stated in Table 1.

4.2 Group-Conditional Calibration Implies Non-Equalized Outcomes

In preparation for generalizing Theorem 3, we show in Lemma 1 that group-conditional calibration implies non-equalized outcomes but not vice versa.

Lemma 1 (Group-conditional calibration implies non-equalized outcomes but not vice versa). *If* (15) *and* (16) *hold, then* (3) *holds for* $\alpha = 1$, *i.e. group-conditional calibration implies non-equalized outcomes.*

However, if (3) *holds for* $\alpha = 1$, *then it is not the case that* (15) *and* (16) *must hold, i.e. non-equalized outcomes does not imply group-conditional calibration.*

Proof idea. Use laws of probability to show that group-conditional calibration implies non-equalized outcomes. Then construct a single example to show that non-equalized outcomes does not imply group-conditional calibration. See Appendix A for complete proof. □

Using the contrapositive of the fact that group-conditional calibration implies non-equalized outcomes, partially equalized outcomes implies not calibration as stated in Table 1. We observe that in contrast to group-conditional calibration, test-fairness as proposed in [6] does not in general imply non-equalized outcomes.

4.3 The Generalized Result

The existing result stated in Theorem 3 shows that if group-conditional calibration and equalized odds hold, realistic assumptions are violated. Our new result in Theorem 4 shows that if non-equalized outcomes and equalized odds hold, the same realistic assumptions are violated.

As we just showed in Lemma 1, group-conditional calibration implies non-equalized outcomes but not vice versa, i.e. non-equalized outcomes is a weaker condition than group-conditional calibration. Therefore Theorem 4 is more general than Theorem 3, since with a weaker condition we arrive at the same conclusion. It is straightforward to see that Lemma 1 and Theorem 4 together imply Theorem 3. We observe that our proof technique appears simpler, since it relies only on elementary manipulation of probabilities.

Theorem 4 (Generalization of calibration-equalized odds impossibility result). *Suppose* (1) *and* (2) *hold, and* (3) *holds for* $\alpha = 1$, *i.e. equalized odds and non-equalized outcomes are both satisfied. Then at least one of Assumption 1 or Assumption 2 is violated, i.e. the observed rates are the same for both groups and/or the decision is perfect.*

Proof. Suppose (3) holds for $\alpha = 1$, i.e. non-equalized outcomes is satisfied.

Suppose (1) and (2) hold, i.e. equalized odds is satisfied. Applying Theorem 1,

$$\begin{aligned} &p(\hat{Y} = 1|S = 1) - p(\hat{Y} = 1|S = 0) \\ &= (p(\hat{Y} = 1|Y = 1) - p(\hat{Y} = 1|Y = 0)) \\ &\times (p(Y = 1|S = 1) - p(Y = 1|S = 0)). \end{aligned} \tag{17}$$

Combining (3) and (17), we have

$$\begin{aligned} &p(Y = 1|S = 1) - p(Y = 1|S = 0) \\ &= (p(\hat{Y} = 1|Y = 1) - p(\hat{Y} = 1|Y = 0)) \\ &\times (p(Y = 1|S = 1) - p(Y = 1|S = 0)). \end{aligned} \tag{18}$$

We conclude from (18) that at least one of the following holds:

$$p(Y = 1|S = 1) = p(Y = 1|S = 0) \tag{19}$$

$$p(\hat{Y} = 1|Y = 1) - p(\hat{Y} = 1|Y = 0) = 1 \tag{20}$$

If (19) holds then Assumption 1 is violated, i.e. the observed rates are the same for both groups. If (20) holds, then $p(\hat{Y} = 1|Y = 1) = 1$ and $p(\hat{Y} = 1|Y = 0) = 0$. Therefore Assumption 2 is violated, i.e. the decision is perfect. □

5 CONCLUSION

When algorithms make predictions of the future actions of individuals, a certain degree of inaccuracy seems inevitable. In this context, naively using trends observed across groups to make predictions about individuals - a problem known as group-to-individual inference [13] - creates the risk of unfairness, in the legal system and beyond. We have formalized the intuition that when algorithms conduct group-to-individual inference - or in other words, *stereotype* - they tend to be unfair to individuals who are 'atypical' (e.g. non-reoffenders from a group with higher reoffence rates). In particular, we have seen that an imperfect algorithm for which the predicted and observed differences between groups are equal will violate equalized odds. Avoiding this requires partially equalized outcomes, which can be seen as an instantiation of 'algorithmic affirmative action' [5].

ACKNOWLEDGMENTS

I would like to thank the reviewers for their useful feedback. I would also like to thank Bob Williamson and Cheng Soon Ong for discussions during the development of this work. The research was supported by an Australian Government Research Training Program Scholarship and a CSIRO Data61 Top-Up Scholarship.

REFERENCES

[1] Julia Angwin, Jeff Larson, Surya Mattu, and Lauren Kirchner. 2016. Machine Bias. ProPublica, https://www.propublica.org/article/machine-bias-risk-assessments-in-criminal-sentencing.

[2] Solon Barocas, Moritz Hardt, and Arvind Narayanan. 2018. *Fairness and Machine Learning*. fairmlbook.org.

[3] Solon Barocas and Andrew D Selbst. 2016. Big Data's Disparate Impact. *California Law Review* 104 (2016), 671.

[4] Toon Calders and Sicco Verwer. 2010. Three Naive Bayes Approaches for Discrimination-Free Classification. *Data Mining and Knowledge Discovery* 21, 2 (2010).

[5] Anupam Chander. 2016. The Racist Algorithm. *Michigan Law Review* 115 (2016).

[6] Alexandra Chouldechova. 2017. Fair Prediction with Disparate Impact: A Study of Bias in Recidivism Prediction Instruments. *Big Data* 5, 2 (2017).

[7] Sam Corbett-Davies and Sharad Goel. 2018. The Measure and Mismeasure of Fairness: A Critical Review of Fair Machine Learning. *arXiv* (2018).

[8] Sam Corbett-Davies, Emma Pierson, Avi Feller, Sharad Goel, and Aziz Huq. 2017. Algorithmic Decision Making and the Cost of Fairness. In *Proceedings of the 23rd ACM SIGKDD International Conference on Knowledge Discovery and Data Mining*.

[9] William Dieterich, Christina Mendoza, and Tim Brennan. 2016. COMPAS Risk Scales: Demonstrating Accuracy Equity and Predictive Parity. Northpointe Inc..

[10] Cynthia Dwork, Moritz Hardt, Toniann Pitassi, Omer Reingold, and Richard Zemel. 2012. Fairness Through Awareness. In *Proceedings of the 3rd Innovations in Theoretical Computer Science Conference*.

[11] Harrison Edwards and Amos Storkey. 2016. Censoring Representations with an Adversary. In *International Conference on Learning Representations*.

[12] Michael Feldman, Sorelle A Friedler, John Moeller, Carlos Scheidegger, and Suresh Venkatasubramanian. 2015. Certifying and Removing Disparate Impact. In *Proceedings of the 21th ACM SIGKDD International Conference on Knowledge Discovery and Data Mining*.

[13] Aaron J Fisher, John D Medaglia, and Bertus F Jeronimus. 2018. Lack of Group-to-Individual Generalizability is a Threat to Human Subjects Research. *Proceedings of the National Academy of Sciences* (2018).

[14] Moritz Hardt, Eric Price, and Nathan Srebro. 2016. Equality of Opportunity in Supervised Learning. In *Advances in Neural Information Processing Systems*.

[15] Mads Meier Jæger. 2008. Does Left–Right Orientation have a Causal Effect on Support for Redistribution? Causal Analysis with Cross-Sectional Data using Instrumental Variables. *International Journal of Public Opinion Research* 20, 3 (2008).

[16] Jon Kleinberg, Sendhil Mullainathan, and Manish Raghavan. 2017. Inherent Trade-Offs in the Fair Determination of Risk Scores. In *Innovations in Theoretical Computer Science*.

[17] Aditya Krishna Menon and Robert C Williamson. 2018. The Cost of Fairness in Binary Classification. In *Conference on Fairness, Accountability and Transparency*.

[18] Arvind Nayaranan. 2018. Tutorial: 21 Fairness Definitions and their Politics. https://www.youtube.com/watch?v=jIXIuYdnyyk.

[19] Northpointe Inc. 2012. Practitioners Guide to COMPAS.

[20] Cathy O'Neil. 2017. *Weapons of Math Destruction: How Big Data Increases Inequality and Threatens Democracy*. Broadway Books.

[21] Geoff Pleiss, Manish Raghavan, Felix Wu, Jon Kleinberg, and Kilian Q Weinberger. 2017. On Fairness and Calibration. In *Advances in Neural Information Processing Systems*.

[22] United States Equal Opportunity Employment Commission. 1978. Uniform Guidelines on Employee Selection Procedures.

[23] Muhammad Bilal Zafar, Isabel Valera, Manuel Gomez Rodriguez, and Krishna P Gummadi. 2017. Fairness Beyond Disparate Treatment & Disparate Impact: Learning Classification Without Disparate Mistreatment. In *Proceedings of the 26th International Conference on World Wide Web*.

A SUPPLEMENTARY PROOFS

We present the proofs of Theorem 2 and Lemma 1.

A.1 Proof of Theorem 2 (Equalized Outcomes Given Approximately Equalized Odds)

Proof. We have

$$\begin{aligned} p(\hat{Y} = 1|S = 1) = p(Y = 1|S = 1)p(\hat{Y} = 1|S = 1, Y = 1) \\ p(Y = 0|S = 1)p(\hat{Y} = 1|S = 1, Y = 0) \end{aligned}$$

and

$$\begin{aligned} p(\hat{Y} = 1|S = 0) = p(Y = 1|S = 0)p(\hat{Y} = 1|S = 0, Y = 1) \\ + p(Y = 0|S = 0)p(\hat{Y} = 1|S = 0, Y = 0) \end{aligned}$$

by the law of total probability.

Assuming δ-approximately equalized odds, we have

$$\begin{aligned} & p(\hat{Y} = 1|S = 1) - p(\hat{Y} = 1|S = 0) \\ & \leq p(Y = 1|S = 1)(1 + \delta)p(\hat{Y} = 1|Y = 1) \\ & + p(Y = 0|S = 1)(1 + \delta)p(\hat{Y} = 1|Y = 0) \\ & - p(Y = 1|S = 0)(1 - \delta)p(\hat{Y} = 1|Y = 1) \\ & - p(Y = 0|S = 0)(1 - \delta)p(\hat{Y} = 1|Y = 0) \\ & = \alpha(p(Y = 1|S = 1) - p(Y = 1|S = 0)) + \delta\beta. \end{aligned}$$

The equality follows by rearranging the terms and using the definitions of α and β.

Similarly,

$$\begin{aligned} & p(\hat{Y} = 1|S = 1) - p(\hat{Y} = 1|S = 0) \\ & \geq p(Y = 1|S = 1)(1 - \delta)p(\hat{Y} = 1|Y = 1) \\ & + p(Y = 0|S = 1)(1 - \delta)p(\hat{Y} = 1|Y = 0) \\ & - p(Y = 1|S = 0)(1 + \delta)p(\hat{Y} = 1|Y = 1) \\ & - p(Y = 0|S = 0)(1 + \delta)p(\hat{Y} = 1|Y = 0) \\ & = \alpha(p(Y = 1|S = 1) - p(Y = 1|S = 0)) - \delta\beta. \end{aligned}$$

□

A.2 Proof of Lemma 1 (Group-Conditional Calibration Implies Non-Equalized Outcomes but Not Vice Versa)

Proof. Suppose (15) and (16) hold, i.e. group-conditional calibration is satisfied. Then

$$\begin{aligned} & p(Y = 1|S = 1) - p(Y = 1|S = 0) \\ & = \int_0^1 p(h(x, s) = c|S = 1)p(Y = 1|h(x, s) = c, S = 1)\, dc \\ & - \int_0^1 p(h(x, s) = c|S = 0)p(Y = 1|h(x, s) = c, S = 0)\, dc \end{aligned}$$

by the law of total probability

$$\begin{aligned} & = \int_0^1 p(h(x, s) = c|S = 1)c\, dc \\ & - \int_0^1 p(h(x, s) = c|S = 0)c\, dc \end{aligned}$$

by group-conditional calibration, substituting in (15) and (16)

$$\begin{aligned} & = \int_0^1 p(h(x, s) = c|S = 1)p(\hat{Y} = 1|h(x, s) = c, S = 1)\, dc \\ & - \int_0^1 p(h(x, s) = c|S = 0)p(\hat{Y} = 1|h(x, s) = c, S = 0)\, dc \end{aligned}$$

Table 2: Test set results for a recidivism prediction model on the ProPublica dataset. The example motivates equalized odds.

Metric	African-American	Non African-American	Overall
Observed reoffence rate	54.1%	39.9%	47.2%
Predicted reoffence rate	55.2%	40.7%	48.1%
Predicted reoffence rate among non-reoffenders	47.8%	36.2%	41.4%
Predicted reoffence rate among reoffenders	61.5%	47.4%	55.7%

by the definition $p(\hat{Y} = 1|X = x, S = s) := h(x, s)$

$$= p(\hat{Y} = 1|S = 1) - p(\hat{Y} = 1|S = 0)$$

by the law of total probability. Hence (3) holds for $\alpha = 1$ and we have shown that group-conditional calibration implies non-equalized outcomes.

However, we may have non-equalized outcomes without group-conditional calibration. For example, suppose

$$h(x, s) := p(Y = 1|S = s) + \eta$$

where η is generated by random noise with range

$$[-p(Y = 1|S = s), 1 - p(Y = 1|S = s)]$$

and mean zero.

Therefore

$$\begin{aligned} & p(\hat{Y} = 1|S = s) \\ &= \int_x p(X = x|S = s)p(\hat{Y} = 1|X = x, S = s)dx \\ &= \int_x p(X = x|S = s)h(x, s)dx \\ &= \int_x p(X = x|S = s)[p(Y = 1|S = s) + \eta]dx \\ &= p(Y = 1|S = s). \end{aligned}$$

Hence (3) holds for $\alpha = 1$, i.e. we have non-equalized outcomes. We also have $\forall c \in [0, 1]$

$$p(Y = 1|h(x, s) = c, S = 1) = p(Y = 1|S = 1)$$

and

$$p(Y = 1|h(x, s) = c, S = 0) = p(Y = 1|S = 0).$$

Hence (15) and (16) do not in general hold and we have shown that non-equalized outcomes does not imply group-conditional calibration. □

B MOTIVATING EXAMPLE OF EQUALIZED ODDS

We explore the definition of and rationale behind *equalized odds*, using recidivism prediction with the ProPublica dataset, which contains information about 7214 criminal offences committed in Broward County, Florida. We used the individual's age, gender, race and criminal history to predict whether they would reoffend within two years.[6] We applied a 70/30 training/test split of the data, trained a logistic regression model[7] on the training set, and used this model to predict the probability that each individual in the test set would reoffend.

The model achieved an area under the curve (AUC) of 0.72 on the test set, indicating that the model is far from perfect but a lot better than a random guess.[8] The results are shown in Table 2. We note there is a difference in the observed reoffence rates between African-American and non African-American individuals in the data. The predicted reoffence rates were close to the observed reoffence rates for both groups, and thus showed a difference of a similar magnitude, i.e. non-equalized outcomes was approximately satisfied. The model rated African-American individuals as higher risk on average, but one could justify this by arguing that the model simply reflects trends in the data.

However, looking separately at those individuals who were observed as non-reoffenders, and those who were observed as reoffenders, we find that the predictions were far from satisfying equalized odds. Looking at the non-reoffenders, for African-Americans the predicted reoffence rate was 47.8% while for non African-Americans it was 36.2%. In other words, the *false positive rate* was much higher for African-Americans than for non African-Americans. Now looking only at the reoffenders, we notice a difference in the *true positive rate* across racial groups – for African-Americans the predicted reoffence rate was 61.5% while for non African-Americans it was 47.4%. Equivalently, the *false negative rate* for non African-Americans (52.6%) was much higher than for African-Americans (38.5%).

Among non-reoffenders, non African-Americans would be better off with this model since they are less likely to be incorrectly classified as high risk. Among reoffenders, non African-Americans would also be better off since they are more likely to be incorrectly classified as low risk. These two types of discrimination are precisely what ProPublica reported about the COMPAS algorithm [1]. Our example has shown how easily this can occur, even if on the face of it the model seems to just reflect differences between two groups in its training data. It also shows how individuals are impacted by inferences made from past observations of others who appear similar to them – in effect they are stereotyped by the algorithm.

In summary, our example has shown how a model's true positive rates and false positive rates may differ across groups, which may disadvantage a particular group. This observation motivates the definition of equalized odds – requiring that the true positive rates and false positive rates are equal across groups – which, if satisfied, prevents this form of disadvantage [14].

[6] The dataset is available at https://github.com/propublica/compas-analysis/blob/master/compas-scores.csv. We predicted the column `is_recid` using `sex`, `age_cat`, `juv_fel_count`, `juv_misd_count`, `juv_other_count` `priors_count` and `c_charge_degree`, representing categorical variables as a one-hot encoding.

[7] Implemented in Python using the sklearn package.

[8] AUC can be interpreted as the probability that a randomly selected positive example will receive a higher score than a randomly selected negative example. A perfect classifier achieves an AUC of 1, while a random classifier achieves an AUC of 0.5.

The Right To Confront Your Accusers: Opening the Black Box of Forensic DNA Software

Jeanna Matthews
Marzieh Babaeianjelodar
Stephen Lorenz
Abigail Matthews
jnm@clarkson.edu
babaeim@clarkson.edu
lorenzsj@clarkson.edu
matthea@clarkson.edu
Clarkson University
Potsdam, New York

Mariama Njie
Iona College
New Rochelle, New York

Nathaniel Adams
Forensic Bioinformatic Services
Fairborn, Ohio
dan.krane@wright.edu

Dan Krane
Wright State University
Dayton, Ohio
dan.krane@wright.edu

Jessica Goldthwaite
The Legal Aid Society
New York, New York
JWGoldthwaite@legal-aid.org

Clinton Hughes
Brooklyn Defender Services
Brooklyn, New York
chughes@bds.org

ABSTRACT

The results of forensic DNA software systems are regularly introduced as compelling evidence in criminal trials, but requests by defendants to evaluate how these results are generated are often denied. Furthermore, there is mounting evidence of problems such as failures to disclose substantial changes in methodology to oversight bodies and substantial differences in the results generated by different software systems. In a society that purports to guarantee defendants the right to face their accusers and confront the evidence against them, what then is the role of black-box forensic software systems in moral decision making in criminal justice? In this paper, we examine the case of the Forensic Statistical Tool (FST), a forensic DNA system developed in 2010 by New York City's Office of Chief Medical Examiner (OCME). For over 5 years, expert witness review requested by defense teams was denied, even under protective order, while the system was used in over 1300 criminal cases. When the first expert review was finally permitted in 2016, many problems were identified including an undisclosed function capable of dropping evidence that could be beneficial to the defense. Overall, the findings were so substantial that a motion to release the full source code of FST publicly was granted. In this paper, we quantify the impact of this undisclosed function on samples from OCME's own validation study and discuss the potential impact on individual defendants. Specifically, we find that 104 of the 439 samples (23.7%) triggered the undisclosed data-dropping behavior and that the change skewed results toward false inclusion for individuals whose DNA was not present in an evidence sample. Beyond this, we consider what changes in the criminal justice system could prevent problems like this from going unresolved in the future.

AIES '19, January 27–28, 2019, Honolulu, HI, USA

ACM ISBN 978-1-4503-6324-2/19/01...$15.00
https://doi.org/10.1145/3306618.3314279

CCS CONCEPTS

• **Software and its engineering** → **Correctness**; *Risk management*; • **Social and professional topics** → *Codes of ethics*.

KEYWORDS

algorithmic accountability; criminal justice software; probabilistic genotyping software; Forensic Statistical Tool (FST)

ACM Reference Format:
Jeanna Matthews, Marzieh Babaeianjelodar, Stephen Lorenz, Abigail Matthews, Mariama Njie, Nathaniel Adams, Dan Krane, Jessica Goldthwaite, and Clinton Hughes. 2019. The Right To Confront Your Accusers: Opening the Black Box of Forensic DNA Software . In *AAAI/ACM Conference on AI, Ethics, and Society (AIES '19), January 27–28, 2019, Honolulu, HI, USA*. ACM, New York, NY, USA, 7 pages. https://doi.org/10.1145/3306618.3314279

1 INTRODUCTION

Increasingly big decisions about the lives of individuals are being made in a partnership between human decision makers and computer systems. In high stakes areas like hiring, housing, credit and criminal justice, societal principles negotiated collectively over time could be undermined in the process of automation. For example, automated systems are used throughout the criminal justice system from investigation/policing decisions to pretrial decisions to decisions about evidence at trial to sentencing decisions to parole decisions. In this context, it is reasonable to ask what the impact of these automated systems is on widely accepted principles of criminal justice decision making such as the right to a public trial, the rights of defendants to review and confront the evidence against them and the right to equal justice under the law.

In this paper, we focus on the Forensic Statistical Tool (FST), a forensic DNA system developed in 2010 by New York City's Office of Chief Medical Examiner (OCME). We consider what types of oversight human decision makers were able to provide and what incentives were present for finding, fixing and disclosing bugs in the system. We propose a set of modifications to the holistic decision making process to encourage bugs in forensic DNA systems like FST to be found and fixed.

We conduct independent, third party testing of FST, a step that we argue should be regularly performed on any software used in the criminal justice system. Using a collection of over 400 mixed DNA samples of known composition from OCME's own validation study, we evaluate the impact of an undisclosed data-dropping routine discovered by defense experts during the first source code review ever permitted. Expert witnesses identified the potential for this function to drop data that could be helpful to the defense, but this paper is the first study of the quantitative impact of the change. Even using data from OCME's own validation study (i.e. no surprise test cases), we find that almost a quarter of the samples triggered the data-dropping behavior and that the change skewed results toward false inclusion for individuals whose DNA is not present in an evidence sample. Defense attorneys, judges and the scientific community should have been informed of this change, but were not. We argue that enabling independent, third party testing is essential to preventing this in the future. We discuss the current hurdles to independent testing and make concrete suggestions for reducing those hurdles in the interest of accountability, transparency, and justice.

2 BACKGROUND

Forensic DNA evidence has been an important part of criminal investigations for decades, but in recent years, probabilistic genotyping (PG) software has been introduced to interpret evidence that is too complex for manual human analysis. Substantial concerns about the accuracy and reliability of this software have been raised by scientists, journalists, and lawyers and there is substantial debate about its role in moral decision making in criminal justice.

Many factors can complicate forensic DNA interpretation, making automated software analysis an attractive alternative to human interpretation. Multiple contributors to an evidence sample make the results more difficult to interpret visually. Environmental factors can degrade DNA. Evidence samples may contain little DNA available for testing. When processing samples, DNA from the sample can fail to be detected in whole or in part (drop-out), and random fragments of DNA can be introduced (drop-in).

Models implemented in PG software can vary substantially in how they accommodate - or don't address - these issues. PG software also varies in how operator assumptions are taken into account, such as the number of contributors to a sample - a value that can only be estimated when evaluating the evidence sample (e.g. how could one conclusively determine how many people might have handled a gun) [17].

Additionally, most PG software assumes that all contributors to a sample are completely unrelated and from the same ethnic group; an assumption that is not valid in many actual cases. For example, investigations into an assault by a group Hasidic men included concerns about whether PG software that assumes no relationships between contributors can accurately distinguish among members of a more genetically insular population [11].

There have also been substantial concerns for inappropriate bias in criminal justice software more broadly. For example, ProPublica found that the COMPAS software used widely throughout the United States to estimate a defendants risk of committing another crime was more likely to falsely flag black defendants as future criminals, while white defendants were mislabeled as low risk more often than black defendants [4][7]. For facial recognition software which can at times be used criminal justice applications, Buolamwini and Gebru identify substantially higher error rates for dark-skinned women than for light-skinned men [5].

All of these factors should add up to a need for healthy skepticism about the design, development, and use of complex software systems used in criminal justice, including PG software. The field of forensic DNA analysis should require robust independent review of PG systems prior to their use in casework, ongoing reporting of substantial modifications and ongoing independent review to promote investment in iterative improvement. Both in research and in casework, an emphasis should be placed on comparisons between multiple reasonable systems' evaluation of the same input data [9][14]. However, this is not the current state of the field.

Instead, these legitimate concerns have been further heightened by secrecy. Software vendors aggressively claim trade secret protection for their software. In many cases, developers have succeeded in resisting requests by defense attorneys to allow their own experts to review both the executable versions and source code of these systems, even under protective order [19]. That is an extreme requirement of secrecy, especially in high-stakes criminal cases.

Legal scholars and defense attorneys have argued that defendant rights to confront the evidence against them and to a public trial should outweigh the intellectual property interests of software vendors [20]. Furthermore, it has been argued that software vendors already enjoy substantial commercial protection from a first-mover advantage once the results of their product have been widely accepted in courtrooms and additional protection may do more to shield products from legitimate criticism of software quality, reliability, and accuracy than to protect intellectual property.

For PG software, peer-reviewed validation studies are typically conducted by the software developers. Internal validations conducted by individual laboratories are usually unpublished, let alone independently reviewed. Rarely is there adversarial testing by a group incentivized to find problems and rarely are systems reviewed with an eye to how errors could impact a particular case or defendant. Defendants, particularly indigent defendants, rarely have access to resources to conduct adversarial testing in the context of their own case and even defense teams willing and able to do so may be denied access to the materials necessary to do so effectively.

For FST in particular, OCME refused any independent review of the source code, supporting software development materials, and executables, for years, even under a protective order. In a 2016 criminal case, a federal judge finally ordered OCME to provide FST's source code to the defense team under a protective order. The team of defense experts who reviewed the code identified a number of concerns, including a function, CheckFrequencyForRemoval, that they demonstrated was capable of dropping data that is helpful to the defense. This function runs counter to the methodology publicly described in previously sworn testimony and peer-reviewed publications and appears to have been introduced as a work around for other problems with the system. Between 2011 and 2017, FST was used in approximately 1,350 criminal investigations. This timeline of documented changes to FST suggest that the analyses in casework involved the version modified in this way.

In retrospect, we know that almost immediately after bringing FST online in April 2011, OCME had to take FST offline again for software maintenance. Based Freedom of Information requests and responses to litigation, we know that FST was modified in order to bring it back online in June 2011. It is not unusual to have bugs in software, but OCME's response to the problem is telling. Changes, including the CheckFrequencyForRemoval function, were made without any reporting the change to the NY State Commission on Forensic Science that approved FST for use in casework. In June 2017, Eugene Lien, OCME Assistant Director said in an affidavit, "Because this modification did not affect the methodology of the program, it did not require submission to the Commission on Forensic Science or the DNA Subcommittee." The results of our work strongly challenge this statement, as we will describe.

Subsequent to the findings of the defense experts in 2016 and in response to filings by ProPublica and Yale's Media Freedom and Information Access Clinic, the judge unsealed both the experts' findings (produced originally under a protective order) and the entire FST source code that had been so closely guarded by OCME for years. ProPublica then published the findings and the source code on GitHub [2]. Appendix 1 contains the source code for the data-dropping function, CheckFrequencyForRemoval, from this GitHub repository.

This paper represents the first quantitative study of the impact of the CheckFrequencyForRemoval function. We will describe in detail how it is possible for this function to drop data that is helpful to the defense. Then, using over 400 samples of known origin from OCME's own validation study, we quantify the impact of the function on the results both for individuals known to have contributed to a sample and individuals who did not contribute to the sample. While we find no evidence of a deliberate attempt to disadvantage the defense, we do see a willingness to put in sloppy fixes when problems with the software were identified and a failure to consider how those fixes could impact defendants. The system as a whole failed to put in the necessary provisions for accountability and transparency in order to incentivize disclosure and true repair.

3 FST AND THE OCME VALIDATION STUDY

The NY State Commission on Forensic Science approved FST for use in casework based on a validation study designed and conducted by OCME. The validation study underlying FST consisted of 439 two- and three-person mixtures of varying quantities of DNA and contributor proportions, genotyped using both High Copy Number (HCN) and Low Copy Number (LCN) protocols. Since these mixtures were created in a controlled laboratory setting, their true contributors and known non-contributors are known.

The 439 mixtures were generated to serve as test evidence samples for which the "correct" answers are known. These samples were constructed based on single-source blood and cheek swab samples of known origin as well as from items handled by multiple individuals, such as a computer mouse or a pen. Some, but not all, of the touched items were cleaned with bleach and ethanol prior to handling. Despite this pre-cleaning step, it is interesting to note that some samples still contained DNA that did not belong to any of the deliberate contributors.

OCME evaluated all 439 mixtures in comparison to their known contributors and a set of 1,246 non-contributors. The non-contributor set consists of genotypes developed from OCME morgue bodies and a national data set [6]. Allele frequency rates were established for NYC by OCME through genotyping morgue bodies. OCME developed a subset of these genotypes at only thirteen of the fifteen loci used by FST, simulating genotypes for the remaining two loci. Subpopulations were grouped by self- or OCME-reporting into African-American, Asian, Caucasian, and Hispanic categories. The lab removed information on the races of the donors to the mixtures, though in publications they do claim that the mixtures represent the diversity of New York City [13][1].

OCME originally wanted to validate FST for four-person mixtures and additional four-person mixtures were generated during the study, but ultimately FST was not validated for the evaluation of four-person mixtures [13]. OCME never published the validation data set but did produce it in 2012 pursuant to an agreement reached after litigation in the case People v. Collins. It was produced in printed form, then scanned and partly transcribed by the defense team.

Since individuals share alleles and the genotypes of all individuals are not known, one normally cannot conclude that a specific individual is the sole possible source of DNA recovered from an evidence sample. Case law in the United States requires that a statistical weight of evidence be provided when an individual cannot be excluded as a possible contributor to a casework sample, in order to assist them in determining the strength of that evidence. For example, if one in three individuals could not be excluded as possible contributors to a particular sample, then the strength of that conclusion is minimal, while if only one in a billion individuals could not be excluded, the strength would be high.

Statistical weights calculated by PG systems are presented as likelihood ratios (LR), composed of the probability of observing the data generated during the course of testing evidentiary samples, E, given two competing hypotheses. These hypotheses are typically constructed as H1 or the prosecutor's hypothesis, Hp, which includes the defendant as a contributor, and an alternative hypothesis H2, or the defense hypothesis, Hd, which does not include the defendant as a contributor. For samples containing DNA from multiple individuals, both Hp and Hd will include additional contributors, either assumed contributors whose genotypes are known or contributors whose identities are unknown. The common formula, where E is the observed data is: $LR = Pr(E|Hp)/Pr(E|Hd)$ Consequently, a likelihood ratio of 1 is deemed "inconclusive" while an $LR > 1$ is inclusionary or inculpatory (suggestive of guilt) and an $LR < 1$ is exclusionary or exculpatory (suggestive of innocence).

Likelihood ratios are calculated for each locus and multiplied using the product rule, assuming linkage equilibrium between loci. Due to the complexity of forensic DNA mixture data and measurement uncertainty, it's generally held that there is no "ground truth" for LRs, even for samples of known composition, against which PG results can be compared for accuracy [18]. Consequently, confidence in PG systems is based in the appropriateness of the models underlying their algorithms and the quality of their software development processes and resulting executables.

Some labs, including OCME, provide "verbal equivalency" for LR values. LRs of 1-10 are described by OCME as "limited support" for the numerator hypothesis, generally Hp. Similarly, LRs of 10-100, 100-1000, and 1000+ are described as "moderate," "strong," and "very strong," respectively [15].

For each sample, FST calculates four LR using allele frequencies from each of OCME's four default reference subpopulations (Asian, Black, Caucasian and Hispanic). As a conservative measure, only the lowest of these four LRs is included in the final written report. FST originally included all 15 loci in its calculations, as one would expect. However, CheckFrequencyForRemoval removes data for loci where frequencies of observed alleles across all replicate amplifications summed to ≥ 97% in any of FST's four reference subpopulations. Logically, frequencies over 100% should not occur, but in practice, they do. There are many things that could lead to this inaccuracy (e.g. errors introduced by multiple rounds of amplifications (drop-out errors), contamination errors (drop-in errors) or issues with the use of minimum allele frequencies. However, rather than deal with the inaccuracies in a transparent way, OCME chose to deal with the errors by simply dropping the contribution of any loci that approaches the 100% boundary. This is done even if the in-formation at that locus is exculpatory information that would have helped the defense or whether it is inculpatory evidence that would help the prosecution. Nothing was done to report when this occurred and it is completely possible that the set of dropped data would have altered the LR values reported or even the verbal equivalence category of the result. This clearly seems relevant to defense teams, the NY State Commission on Forensic Science and the public, but no such disclosure was ever made by OCME. In the next section, we quantify how often on OCME's own validation study this type of change occurred in the reported LR or the verbal equivalence category.

4 INDEPENDENT COMPARISON TESTING

In this section, we describe our independent testing of FST. We describe both how we automated testing of FST and the results of comparing FST output with and without the CheckFrequencyForRemoval function. We examine the impact of that change on both known contributors to samples in the OCME validation study as well as a set of non-contributors.

We acquired FST v2.5 from the ProPublica's GitHub repository (commit 5b353500d) [2]. FST is a C# ASP.NET application using an MS SQL database. Its interface is browser-based. We ran it on a QEMU virtual machine with Windows 10 Pro 64-bit using 32 GB of RAM and an Intel Xeon processor.

FST's installation is non-trivial, requiring database connection configuration and a custom Windows service per installation. Two versions of FST v2.5 were used for all analyses - one with the CheckFrequencyForRemoval function enabled and one with it disabled. The disabled version is intended to emulate the pre-modification version of FST, though the source code for that version has not been publicly released. FST does not provide an external API or command line interface, so we developed several noninvasive wrapper scripts for automation.

4.1 With and Without CheckFrequencyForRemoval

LRs were generated for all 439 two and three person mixtures from FST's validation study and compared to their known contributors for a total of 1,245 evaluations. We found that 104 of the 439 mixtures (23.7%) were subject to the locus-dropping behavior. It is worth emphasizing that this is for OCME's own validation data, not a new test set to which they did not have access. It is hard to see how they could conclude that the CheckFrequencyForRemoval change was a minor one that did not need to be disclosed.

The change in LRs between FST versions is shown in Figure 1. In Figure 1, we report all four of the LRs reported for each sample, not just the lowest one as would be used for mapping onto verbal-scale equivalent labels when reporting results. The y-axis value for each point is the LR reported with CheckFrequencyForRemoval enabled and the x-axis value is the LR for the sample without CheckFrequencyForRemoval. Figure 1 explores the impact on the results for known contributors to a sample (a simulation of guilty parties).

Figure 2 explores the impact on the results for non-contributors (a simulation of innocent individuals). Forty samples exhibiting locus-dropping behavior during the known contributor analysis were selected for comparison against 700 non-contributors from the national data set using both versions of FST. A range of samples were selected, from 15-575pg of template DNA as well as on the basis of deducible (20) vs. non-deducible (20); 2-person mixtures (12) vs. 3-person mixture (28); and HCN (17) vs. LCN (23). As in Figure 1, we report all four of the LRs reported for each sample, not just the lowest one. The y-axis value for each point is the LR reported with CheckFrequencyForRemoval enabled and the x-axis value is the LR for the sample without CheckFrequencyForRemoval.

In both Figure 1 and 2, points above the lightly dotted center line (y=x) represent where the modified version of FST reports an LR value that is more inclusionary and points below the line represent more exclusionary result. By dropping data, the results skew towards inaccuracy - they skew incorrectly towards more exclusionary (below the line) for real contributors and towards inclusionary (above the line) for non-contributors. For the non-contributors or simulated innocent individuals who did not actually contribute to the sample, the addition of CheckFrequencyForRemoval does skew towards inclusionary and thus is discarding information that could be helpful to the defense.

4.2 Changes In Verbal-Scale Equivalent Labels

Changes to LR verbal-scale equivalents are especially likely to impact the perceived weights of evidence. To examine this we used only the lowest LR reported for each sample rather than all four reported LRs as shown in Figures 1 and 2.

For the 1,245 known contributor tests described above, changes in verbal equivalencies were observed for thirty-six comparisons (2.9%). Eleven false-exclusions (0.9%) became more exclusionary when locus-dropping was enabled while only two became more

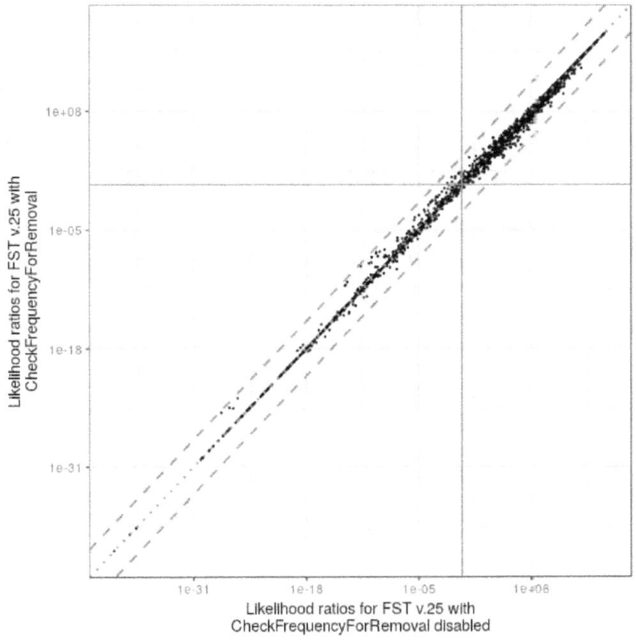

Figure 1: Known contributor likelihood ratios for FST v2.5 with the data-dropping function CheckFrequencyForRemoval vs. FST v2.5 with the function disabled. A log10 scale is used for both axes.

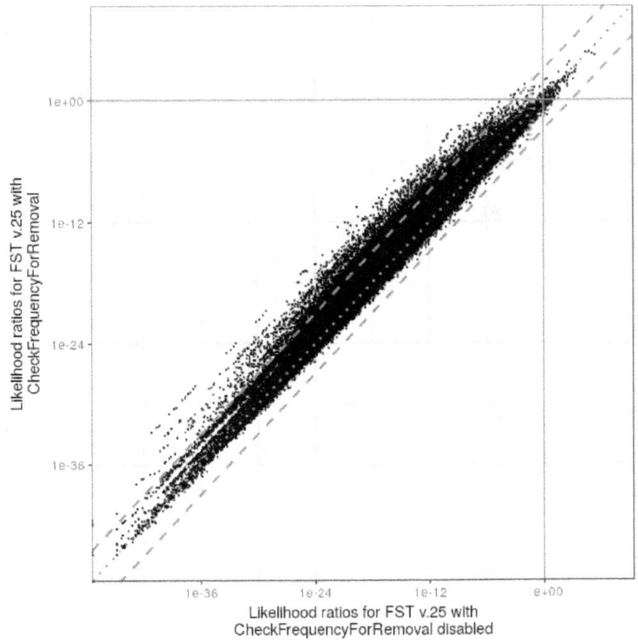

Figure 2: Non-contributor likelihood ratios for FST v2.5 with the data-dropping function vs. FST v2.5 with this function disabled. A log10 scale is used for both axes.

inclusionary while still remaining below LR=1. Three true-inclusion LRs became falsely exclusionary when locus-dropping was enabled, and one false-exclusion LR changed to a true inclusion. For the non-contributor tests described above (40 samples compared to 700 non-contributing individuals for a total of 28,000 comparisons), a false inclusion rate of 0.08% is observed, higher than the 0.03% reported for all analyses conducted in the FST validation study.

In addition, five results changed from true-exclusion LRs when locus-dropping was disabled to false-inclusion LRs when locus-dropping was enabled. This is highly relevant for defense teams as it is represents four individuals who were in fact not contributors to an evidence sample who would have been incorrectly implicated by FST results. We also saw four LRs changed from false inclusions without locus-dropping to true exclusions when locus-dropping was enabled.

There were 115 (0.4%) LRs that varied in verbal-scale equivalency labels between FST versions. Of the 294 LRs reported between 0.001-1,000 by one or both FST versions, those 115 constituted 39.1% of LRs near 1, suggesting that non-contributor LRs near 1 are similarly susceptible to differences in verbal-scale equivalency labels between versions of FST.

Appendix 2 contains tables tracking changes in verbal-scale equivalents for both known contributors and non-contributors. For this set of samples for OCME's own validation study, the number of impacted samples is modest. However, it still makes clear that the impact does occur and could impact the fate of individuals in court. Individuals impacted would have no way of knowing that data helpful to their case was dropped and without disclosure of the FST source, there would have been little to no-incentive to ever repair, or even acknowledge, the problem.

5 CRIMINAL JUSTICE DECISION MAKING

Individual defendants and the public often will not have this opportunity to look under the hood of software used in criminal justice decision making. So, it is important to use this case as a lens through which to consider the flaws in our criminal justice system. What incentives exist for debugging black-box software systems used in the criminal justice system in general? Would it have been possible for defense teams to find this issue without source code access? Would it be possible to know whether this bug is impacting a particular defendant? What would have been the incentives for disclosure or improvement if OCME had been allowed to deny defense expert review and adversarial testing indefinitely? What incentives exist for protecting our long treasured decision making principles such as the right to a public trial, the rights of defendants to review and confront the evidence against them and the right to equal justice under the law?

Here we propose a set of modifications to the holistic decision making process to encourage bugs in forensic DNA systems like FST to be found and fixed.

One key lesson is the importance of adversarial review (another cornerstone of the judicial process). If validation studies are designed by the developers, they are likely to focus on demonstrating the effectiveness of the system rather than on aggressively identifying problems. In an environment where any bug report is answered with "you are just complaining because you are guilty" what incentive will there be to even investigate reports of errors? Also, what will counteract the tendency to sweep errors under the rug when they are found or to put in an inappropriate fix to make the problem go away as we saw in the FST case? In this case, we note that it was only the persistence of defense teams that provided the last stop-gap measure for forcing debugging of these systems.

We recommend targeting the procurement phase of software. When labs use public money to purchase, validate, and train on PG software, procurement policies should require or at least give substantial credit for products that include pro-transparency factors. Such factors could include open-source software, access to software engineering artifacts including bug tracking/change log databases, internal testing plans and results, software requirements and specifications, hazard and risk assessments, design documents, etc. Ideally, developers or third parties would offer bug bounties or other funding streams to incentivize third party testing.

There are actually many PG software systems that all purport to do the same task. Each of these systems is claimed to be a reasonable model for evaluating mixed DNA, though their underlying mechanisms for calculating LRs vary. An incriminating result from any one PG systems can be damning evidence in court. Easier access for comparison testing would be advantageous if their outputs could be compared more directly. One key advance would be surfacing important parameters like drop-in rates, drop-out rates and the population frequency files used, rather than burying some values inside the source code. Establishing common granularities of variation (e.g. different drop-out rates per loci vs. one overall drop-out rate) would be an important advance. Common file formats for input data would be a further improvement, decreasing time costs and transcription risks (e.g. typos) when comparing results of different systems.

Most PG systems are designed with casework in mind. Many systems have no native ability to batch-process multiple evidence samples or compare a single evidence item to multiple reference profiles (e.g. a set of non-contributors or an offender DNA database). While it is possible to modify source-available systems to enable batch-processing, modifications risk introducing defects and require further software validation. APIs, or at least CLIs, could allow for easier batch-processing tasks in both casework and research settings. Requiring these during the procurement phase would be an important advance.

Open-source systems are attractive for obvious reasons of transparency, accountability, and traceability. It cannot be overemphasized that the post-validation modification made to FST was only publicly acknowledged by OCME after FST's source code was examined in conjunction with independent testing. Seemingly minor changes to source code can have substantial impacts in criminal casework.

Terms-of-service contracts for software in the criminal justice space should not have clauses preventing third-party review or publishing of results. Non-disclosure agreements and protective orders covering commercial systems, complicate reviews and prevent dissemination of results - regardless of how essential those findings are to defendants or to the criminal justice system as a while.

ACKNOWLEDGMENTS

The Brown Institute has generously supported this work through a 2018-2019 Magic Grant. Thank you to Anthony Mangiacapra and Graham Northup from Clarkson University and Richard Torres from The Legal Aid Society for their contributions and support. Thank you to the wonderful researchers and staff at Data and Society.

REFERENCES

[1] 2013. People v. Collins. 15 N.Y.S.3d 564 (Sup.Ct. Kings Co. 2015).

[2] 2017. Forensic Statistical Tool Source Code (FST). https://github.com/propublica/nyc-dna-software.

[3] Federica Alessandrini, Monia Cecati, Mauro Pesaresi, Chiara Turchi, Flavia Carle, and Adriano Tagliabracci. 2003. Fingerprints as evidence for a genetic profile: morphological study on fingerprints and analysis of exogenous and individual factors affecting DNA typing. *Journal of forensic sciences* 48, 3 (2003), 586–592.

[4] J Angwin, J Larson, S Mattu, and L Kirchner. 2016. Machine Bias-ProPublica.[online] ProPublica.

[5] Joy Buolamwini and Timnit Gebru. 2018. Gender shades: Intersectional accuracy disparities in commercial gender classification. In *Conference on Fairness, Accountability and Transparency*. 77–91.

[6] John M Butler, Richard Schoske, Peter M Vallone, Janette W Redman, Margaret C Kline, et al. 2003. Allele frequencies for 15 autosomal STR loci on US Caucasian, African American, and Hispanic populations. *Journal of forensic sciences* 48, 4 (2003), 908–911.

[7] Alexandra Chouldechova. 2017. Fair prediction with disparate impact: A study of bias in recidivism prediction instruments. *Big data* 5, 2 (2017), 153–163.

[8] National Research Council et al. 1996. *The evaluation of forensic DNA evidence*. National Academies Press.

[9] Paolo Garofano, Denise Caneparo, Giuseppina D'Amico, Marco Vincenti, and Eugenio Alladio. 2015. An alternative application of the consensus method to DNA typing interpretation for Low Template-DNA mixtures. *Forensic Science International: Genetics Supplement Series* 5 (2015), e422–e424.

[10] Hinda Haned, Klaas Slooten, and Peter Gill. 2012. Exploratory data analysis for the interpretation of low template DNA mixtures. *Forensic Science International: Genetics* 6, 6 (2012), 762–774.

[11] Lauren Kirchner. 2017. Thousands of Criminal Cases in New York Relied on Disputed DNA Testing Techniques.

[12] Adele Mitchell. 2013. Testimony of Adele Mitchell in admissibility hearing in People v. Collins. 15 N.Y.S.3d 564 (Sup.Ct. Kings Co. 2015).

[13] Adele A Mitchell, Jeannie Tamariz, Kathleen O'Connell, Nubia Ducasse, Zoran Budimlija, Mechthild Prinz, and Theresa Caragine. 2012. Validation of a DNA mixture statistics tool incorporating allelic drop-out and drop-in. *Forensic Science International: Genetics* 6, 6 (2012), 749–761.

[14] National Institute of Standards and Technology (NIST). 2017. NIST to Assess the Reliability of Forensic Methods for Analyzing DNA Mixtures. https://www.nist.gov/news-events/news/2017/10/nist-assess-reliability-forensic-methods-analyzing-dna-mixtures. (October 2017).

[15] New York City Office of the Chief Medical Examiner (OCME). 2016. Forensic Biology Protocols for Forensic STR Analysis: Forensic Statistical Tool (FST). https://www1.nyc.gov/assets/ocme/downloads/pdf/technical-manuals/protocols-for-forensic-str-analysis/forensic-statistical-tool-fst.pdf.

[16] New York City Office of the Chief Medical Examiner (OCME). 2018. Technical Manuals (OCME). https://www1.nyc.gov/site/ocme/services/technical-manuals.page.

[17] David R Paoletti, Travis E Doom, Carissa M Krane, Michael L Raymer, and Dan E Krane. 2005. Empirical analysis of the STR profiles resulting from conceptual mixtures. *Journal of Forensic Science* 50, 6 (2005), JFS2004475–6.

[18] Christopher D Steele and David J Balding. 2014. Statistical evaluation of forensic DNA profile evidence. *Annual Review of Statistics and Its Application* 1 (2014), 361–384.

[19] J. Tashea. 2017. Defense lawyers want to peek behind the curtain of probabilistic genotyping. http://www.abajournal.com/magazine/article/code_of_science_defense_lawyers_want_to_peek_behind_the_curtain_of_probabil. *Aba Journal* (2017).

[20] Rebecca Wexler. 2018. Life, liberty, and trade secrets: Intellectual property in the criminal justice system. *Stan. L. Rev.* 70 (2018), 1343.

[21] Katie Worth. 2018. Framed for Murder By His Own DNA. https://www.pbs.org/wgbh/frontline/article/framed-for-murder-by-his-own-dna/. (April 2018).

A SOURCE CODE

This appendix contains the source code for the function CheckFrequencyForRemoval, available on ProPublica's GitHub.

```
/// This function checks for the total frequencies according to races and
    ↪ removes the alleles from calculation
/// if the sum of frequencies are greater than 0.97.
public void CheckFrequencyForRemoval(DataTable dtFrequencies)
{
    // if our db connection isn't initialized, do it. then, get al the
        ↪ ethnicities (races)
    myDb = myDb ?? new Database();
    DataTable raceTable = myDb.getAllEthnics();
    int intsr = 0;
    string[] srem = new string[comparisonLoci.Count];

    // we go through all the comparison loci and check whether the sum of the
        ↪ frequencies for that locus is greater than 0.97.
    // if it is, we remove the locus. frequencies are only used for the alleles
        ↪ in the evidence replicates.
    for (int i = 0; i < comparisonLoci.Count; i++)
    {
        bool blRemove = false;
        // get a CSV list of alleles for all the replicates at a locus
        IEnumerable<string> unknownPair =
            ↪ EvidenceAllelesAtLocus(evidenceAlleles[comparisonLoci[i]]);
        // check if the frequency is greater than 0.97 for any of the races.
            ↪ frequencies are values for an allele at a locus for a certain
            ↪ race
        foreach (DataRow eachRow in raceTable.Rows)
        {
            string raceName = eachRow.Field<string>("EthnicName");
            float freqSum = GetFrenquencySum(unknownPair, comparisonLoci[i],
                ↪ raceName, dtFrequencies);

            if (freqSum >= 0.97)
            {
                blRemove = true;
                break;
            }
        }
        if (blRemove)
        {
            srem[intsr] = comparisonLoci[i];
            intsr++;
        }
    }

    // now we iterate through all the loci and remove them from the list of
        ↪ comparison loci, the evidence, and known and comparison profiles
    for (int i = 0; i < srem.Length; i++)
    {
        if (srem[i] != null)
        {
            string locus = srem[i];

            // remove the locus from the comparisons
            for (int j = 1; j <=
                ↪ comparisonData.NumeratorProfiles.ComparisonCount; j++)
            {
                if(comparisonAlleles[j].ContainsKey(locus))
                    comparisonAlleles[j].Remove(locus);
            }

            // remove the locus from the knowns
            int knownCount = (comparisonData.NumeratorProfiles.KnownCount >
                ↪ comparisonData.DenominatorProfiles.KnownCount)
                    ? comparisonData.NumeratorProfiles.KnownCount
                    : comparisonData.DenominatorProfiles.KnownCount;
            for (int j = 1; j <= knownCount; j++)
            {
                if(knownAlleles[j].ContainsKey(locus))
                    knownAlleles[j].Remove(locus);
            }

            // remove the locus from the evidence replicates
            for (int j = 1; j <= replicates; j++)
            {
                if(evidenceAlleles.ContainsKey(locus))
                    evidenceAlleles.Remove(locus);
            }

            // remove the locus from the list of comparison loci
            comparisonLoci.Remove(locus);
        }
    }
}
```

B ADDITIONAL DATA

			FST v2.5 with CheckFrequencyForRemoval											
			Support for Hd				LR = 1	Support for Hp						
			Very strong	Strong	Moderate	Limited	Inconclusive	Limited	Moderate	Strong	Very strong			
FST v2.5 with CheckFrequencyForRemoval disabled	Support for Hd	Very strong	*186*	0	0	0	0	0	0	0	0	186	14.9%	20.5%
		Strong	3	*20*	1	0	0	0	0	0	0	24	1.9%	
		Moderate	2	4	*19*	1	0	0	0	0	0	26	2.1%	
		Limited	0	0	2	*16*	0	1	0	0	0	19	1.5%	
	LR = 1	Inconclusive	0	0	0	0	*0*	0	0	0	0	0	0.0%	0.0%
	Support for Hp	Limited	0	0	1	2	0	*24*	4	0	0	31	2.5%	79.5%
		Moderate	0	0	0	0	0	1	*34*	3	0	38	3.1%	
		Strong	0	0	0	0	0	0	6	*57*	2	65	5.2%	
		Very strong	0	0	0	0	0	0	1	2	*853*	856	68.8%	
			191	24	23	19	0	26	45	62	855	1,245		
			15.3%	1.9%	1.8%	1.5%	0.0%	2.1%	3.6%	5.0%	68.7%			
			20.6%					79.4%						

Figure 3: Non-Contributor: Changes in verbal-scale equivalent labels for non-contributor LRs between versions of FST with and without locus-dropping behavior. Italicized values on the diagonal indicate no change in label between versions.

			FST v2.5 with CheckFrequencyForRemoval											
			Support for Hd				LR = 1	Support for Hp						
			Very strong	Strong	Moderate	Limited	Inconclusive	Limited	Moderate	Strong	Very strong			
FST v2.5 with CheckFrequencyForRemoval disabled	Support for Hd	Very strong	*27,705*	13	1	0	0	0	0	0	0	27,719	99.0%	99.9%
		Strong	42	*100*	9	0	0	0	0	0	0	151	0.5%	
		Moderate	9	6	*49*	9	0	1	0	0	0	74	0.3%	
		Limited	0	1	8	*20*	0	3	0	0	0	32	0.1%	
	LR = 1	Inconclusive	0	0	0	0	*0*	0	1	0	0	1	0.0%	0.0%
	Support for Hp	Limited	2	0	1	2	0	*8*	5	0	0	18	0.1%	0.1%
		Moderate	0	0	0	0	0	2	*1*	1	0	4	0.0%	
		Strong	0	0	0	0	0	0	0	*0*	0	0	0.0%	
		Very strong	0	0	0	0	0	0	0	0	*1*	1	0.0%	
			27,758	120	68	31	0	14	7	1	1	28,000		
			99.1%	0.4%	0.2%	0.1%	0.0%	0.1%	0.0%	0.0%	0.0%			
			99.9%					0.1%						

Figure 4: Non-Contributor: Changes in verbal-scale equivalent labels for non-contributor LRs between versions of FST with and without locus-dropping behavior. Italicized values on the diagonal indicate no change in label between versions.

Specifying AI Objectives as a Human-AI Collaboration Problem

Anca Dragan
University of California, Berkeley
Berkeley, CA, USA
anca@berkeley.edu

ABSTRACT

Estimation, planning, control, and learning are giving us robots that can generate good behavior given a specified objective and set of constraints. What I care about is how humans enter this behavior generation picture, and study two complementary challenges: 1) how to optimize behavior when the robot is not acting in isolation, but needs to coordinate or collaborate with people; and 2) what to optimize in order to get the behavior we want. My work has traditionally focused on the former, but more recently I have been casting the latter as a human-robot collaboration problem as well (where the human is the enduser, or even the robotics engineer building the system). Treating it as such has enabled us to use robot actions to gain information; to account for human pedagogic behavior; and to exchange information between the human and the robot via a plethora of communication channels, from external forces that the person physically applies to the robot, to comparison queries, to defining a proxy objective function.

CCS Concepts/ACM Classifiers

• Human-centered computing~Collaborative interaction

Author Keywords

reward design; inverse reinforcement learning; value alignment

AIES'19, January 27–28, 2019, Honolulu, HI, USA

ACM ISBN 978-1-4503-6180-4/19/03.
DOI: https://doi.org/10.1145/3306618.3314227

"Scary Robots"

Examining Public Responses to AI

Stephen Cave
Leverhulme Centre for the Future of Intelligence
University of Cambridge
Cambridge, UK
sjc53@cam.ac.uk

Kate Coughlan
BBC
London, UK
kate.coughlan@bbc.co.uk

Kanta Dihal
Leverhulme Centre for the Future of Intelligence
University of Cambridge
Cambridge, UK
ksd38@cam.ac.uk

ABSTRACT

How AI is perceived by the public can have significant impact on how it is developed, deployed and regulated. Some commentators argue that perceptions are currently distorted or extreme. This paper discusses the results of a nationally representative survey of the UK population on their perceptions of AI. The survey solicited responses to eight common narratives about AI (four optimistic, four pessimistic), plus views on what AI is, how likely it is to impact in respondents' lifetimes, and whether they can influence it. 42% of respondents offered a plausible definition of AI, while 25% thought it meant robots. Of the narratives presented, those associated with automation were best known, followed by the idea that AI would become more powerful than humans. Overall results showed that the most common visions of the impact of AI elicit significant anxiety. Only two of the eight narratives elicited more excitement than concern (AI making life easier, and extending life). Respondents felt they had no control over AI's development, citing the power of corporations or government, or versions of technological determinism. Negotiating the deployment of AI will require contending with these anxieties.

CCS CONCEPTS

• Surveys and overviews • Artificial intelligence • Automation

KEYWORDS

Science communication; AI ethics; AI policy; public perception

ACM Reference format:

Stephen Cave, Kate Coughlan and Kanta Dihal. 2019. "Scary Robots": Examining Public Responses to AI. In *AIES '19: AAAI/ACM Conference on AI, Ethics, and Society Proceedings. AIES'19, January 27–28, 2019, Honolulu, HI, USA.* ACM, New York, NY, USA, 7 pages. https://doi.org/10.1145/3306618.3314232

AIES '19, January 27–28, 2019, Honolulu, HI, USA

ACM ISBN 978-1-4503-6324-2/19/01.
https://doi.org/10.1145/3306618.3314232

1 Introduction

How developments in artificial intelligence are communicated to, and perceived by, the general public will critically influence the adoption and use of this technology [5]. It should therefore be a matter of concern that there is evidence to suggest that it is going wrong. In a recent report, the UK House of Lords argues that currently "many of the hopes and the fears presently associated with AI are out of kilter with reality" [19]. This view is shared by some foremost AI researchers, for example, Professor Margaret Boden: "AI's future has been hyped since its inception. Overly enthusiastic predictions from (some) AI professionals have excited, and sometimes terrified, journalists and commentators" [4].

Both excessively hopeful and excessively frightening narratives can have significant negative societal impacts. Exaggerated expectations for what AI can achieve, and when, risk undermining further research and investment. Misplaced trust in AI technologies has already exposed people to a range of risks, including manipulation, privacy violation, and loss of autonomy [9]. Exaggerated fears, on the other hand, may lead to beneficial systems, such as better medical diagnoses, not being adopted. Both misplaced hopes or fears could lead to misguided regulation: for example, lack of regulation could encourage irresponsible use of AI; stifling overregulation could prevent the development and deployment of applications that would enhance the public good [11]. The public perception of AI is therefore an important ethical issue [15].

Existing research has investigated levels of public awareness and understanding [1,23], or public perceptions [11] and views on risks and benefits of particular applications [3,14]. A third focus of research is public opinion on how these technologies should be shaped in future [10,20]. Some studies have represented a global perspective [2] and included several of the areas mentioned above. Building on this work, we set out to explore directly what the UK public believe AI is, and how much they subscribe to the kind of utopian and dystopian narratives mentioned above.

In what follows, we explain our methodology in section 2 and the results in section 3; discussion is then in section 4; and recommendations for next steps are in section 5, followed by a brief conclusion.

2 Methodology

2.1 Sample

To test the awareness of such narratives among the UK general population, and the likelihood they attribute to these prospects becoming reality, we conducted a quantitative online survey of 1078 respondents. Respondents were members of an online market research panel of over 20,000 members, selected to be representative of the UK population in terms of geography and key demographics, managed by market research agency GfK on behalf of the BBC. All panel members were invited to complete the survey which included questions to identify the composition of the sample. Their responses were then weighted to provide a nationally representative picture of UK society. In analysis, the data was cut by age group, gender and sociodemographic status. The sociodemographic groupings ABC1 and C2DE were used. ABC1 represents consumers in UK society with higher levels of educational qualification and higher income. C2DE represents consumers with lower income and lower levels of educational qualification [7].

Our sample was typical of the UK population in terms of device ownership and attitudes towards technology [17], with 78% owning a smartphone, 70% owning a laptop, 65% owning a tablet, and 42% owning a desktop computer. 1% owned none of the devices listed. Regarding the role that technology played in their lives, 39% felt that the statement "I can't live without it but sometimes I do need a little break from it" most accurately described them. 1% felt that the statement "technology scares me" best represented them.

2.2 Questions

Respondents were asked a series of multiple choice and open text questions. The questions were presented to each respondent in a set order, one question at a time. Within each multiple-choice question, the range of possible answers was presented to each respondent in a randomized order, to minimize the influence the order could have on the results.

The first two questions were used to gather data on the respondents. The first question asked "Which of the following do you currently own?" and listed nine devices, from smartphone to virtual reality headset, and 'none of the above', as possible answers. The second question asked respondents to select 'which statement best represents the role technology plays in your life?' The multiple-choice options ranged from 'I can't live without it' to 'technology scares me'.

The remaining seven questions in the survey focused specifically on AI. Question 3 was "Have you ever heard of Artificial Intelligence (AI)?". Those who answered 'no' or 'don't know' were not asked any further questions. Those who had heard of AI were asked question 4: "How would you describe Artificial Intelligence to a friend?" This was an open text response question, requiring respondents to explain in their own words or to opt out.

Next, respondents were provided with a working definition of AI: "the development of computer systems able to perform tasks normally requiring human intelligence such as visual perception, speech recognition, decision-making and translation between languages."

This was followed by several questions where respondents were asked to evaluate eight claims about AI. These claims were drawn from a framework of hopes and fears that underlie much imaginative thinking about intelligent machines, as expounded in a recent article by Cave and Dihal [6]. Their article claims that Anglophone Western narratives about AI fall into four dichotomies that each consist of a hope and a parallel fear.

The four hopes, *Immortality, Ease, Gratification,* and *Dominance,* are each associated with narratives in which intelligent machines affect society in a transformatively positive manner. Immortality speaks to the basic drive to stay alive and healthy, and refers to how AI might be used in pursuit of this: for example, through personalised medicine and drug discovery. Ease refers to the desire to be free of drudgery, and the hope that AI will increasingly perform many tasks that people do not want to do. Gratification refers to the way one might wish to use that free time -- that is, pursuing whatever constitutes pleasurable activity – and the role AI could play in fulfilling these desires. Finally, Dominance, or power over others, can be seen as the means to protect this blissful existence through AI contributing to powerful new means of defence and security.

With each of these hopes, Cave and Dihal pair a parallel fear. Thus, the hope for Immortality contains the threat of Inhumanity: in the pursuit of an ever longer lifespan, a person risks losing their identity, becoming more machine than human. Ease threatens to become Obsolescence, as the desire to be free from work becomes the fear of being put out of work. Gratification carries the risk of Alienation when in their desire for artificially perfect interactions, humans become alienated from each other and prefer to interact with machines. And the pursuit of Dominance evokes fears of an Uprising, as a people's own AI-enabled power turns on them.

All participants were shown all 8 narratives, presented as independent scenarios and in a randomized order, to reduce any possible influence they may have on one another and on our results overall. The positive or negative was implicit in the scenario and left to the respondent to interpret. Question 5 asked whether respondents had heard of these narratives in the media or in conversation, and question 6 asked whether they felt concerned or excited by them. Question 7 asked whether they felt these statements were likely to come true, and question 8 asked whether respondents believed they would feel the impact of the narratives personally within their lifetime. Respondents who felt that none of the narratives would impact them within their lifetime were asked to specify why not in their own words.

The following definitions were used to describe the eight hopes and fears:

Table 1: The eight hopes and fears.

Immortality	AI might revolutionise medicine, treatment and drugs so that we could live forever.
Inhumanity	AI might enhance our bodies so much that we become more machine than human.
Ease	AI might make our day-to-day lives easier because we could ask computers to do more tasks for us.
Obsolescence	AI might mean we become over reliant on machines and replace the need for humans in jobs, relationships and socialising.
Gratification	AI might become the perfect friend, there to listen whenever we need and ready to meet our every desire.
Alienation	AI might cater to all our desires so well that we prefer AI interaction to human interaction.
Dominance	AI might help strengthen our military power because it could provide smarter weapons.
Uprising	AI might enable computers to become more powerful than us.

Finally, all respondents were asked question 9: "To what extent do you agree or disagree with the following statement: 'I feel I am able to influence how Artificial Intelligence (AI) develops in the future'" using a scale from strongly agree to strongly disagree. Those who selected "disagree" or "strongly disagree" were asked a final question: to explain in their own words why they felt this way, or to choose "don't know".

2.3 Limitations

1078 respondents completed the survey. We were not always able to break down results by age or socioeconomic groups due to small sample sizes. Where we could, any notable variances have been stated in the sections below. Also, due to an oversight, there was some conflation of the definitions used for Obsolescence ("AI might mean we become over reliant on machines and replace the need for humans in jobs, relationships and socialising") and Alienation ("AI might cater to all our desires so well that we prefer AI interaction to human interaction"): Obsolescence was intended to refer primarily to the workplace (jobs) and Alienation to interpersonal interactions (relationships and socialising). This might have obfuscated responses to these two.

3. Results

Results described are those with a p-value of 0.05 or higher. P-value is used to demonstrate that a claim has a high probability of validity, rather than being the result of randomly occurring noise in the data. We use 0.05 as a threshold for the p-value indicating a 95% confidence in validity, or put another way, a less than 1 in 20 chance of being 'noise' [21].

3.1 Awareness of AI

85% of respondents claimed to have heard of AI. 11% had not heard of it and 4% answered "don't know". Awareness was high across all age groups (varying between 79-90%).

Verbatim analysis showed a range of levels of sophistication in defining AI. In response to the question "How would you describe Artificial Intelligence (AI) to a friend?", which was answered by 622 respondents, one respondent wrote: "Depends on the friend - I used to be a postdoctoral research fellow in the subject". 42% of responses referred to computers performing tasks that replicated aspects of human cognition, such as "decision making", "learning" or "thinking". 156 respondents, or 25% of responses, mentioned "robots". 12% of respondents incorporated hopes or fears, such as "Computers doing things instead of people. I hate it," or "scary robots" as featured in this article's title.

3.2 Awareness of Positive & Negative Narratives

When asked whether respondents had heard of the narratives in the media or in conversation, all of the narratives described generated some recognition among respondents. The most commonly recognised narratives were Obsolescence and Ease. The least well recognised narrative was Inhumanity with just 13% recognition.

Table 2: Recognition of the hopes and fears narratives.

Narrative	Recognition
Obsolescence	55%
Ease	53%
Uprising	44%
Dominance	30%
Alienation	20%
Immortality	19%
Gratification	16%
Inhumanity	13%
None of the above	6%

As far as possible, we examined the composition of respondents who were aware of each narrative:

Immortality: More respondents aged 55+ were aware of this narrative (23.1%) than younger groups, with only 15.4% of 35-54s aware. The sample for 16-34s was too low to be robust. More men (22.0%) were aware of this narrative than women (14.9%). Differences between socioeconomic groups were not statistically significant.

Ease: Significantly more respondents aged 55+ were aware of this narrative than any other age group (57.3% 55+ vs. 51.1% 16-34 and 49.3% 35-54). Fewer respondents of sociodemographic group C2DE were aware of this narrative (47.9% C2DE vs. 56.2% ABC1). Gender differences were not significant.

Dominance: More men (36.9%) were aware of this narrative than women (22.8%). More respondents aged 55+ were aware (32.6%) than 35-54s (23.0%). Differences between socioeconomic groups were not significant. The sample of 16-34s for this question was too low to be robust.

Uprising: More men (48.0%) were aware of this narrative than women (39.3%). Fewer C2DEs (38.7%) were aware of this narrative than ABC1s (47.1%). Age group differences were not significant.

The differences in awareness for Inhumanity, Obsolescence, Gratification, and Alienation were not statistically significant.

3.3 Emotional Responses to the Narratives

Respondents were asked to rate how excited or concerned they felt about each narrative on a scale of 1-10, where 1 equalled concerned and 10 equalled excited. Only Ease and Immortality elicited more excitement than concern. Scores 1-3 are counted towards the total percentage 'concerned', scores 8-10 are counted towards 'excited'.

For all six remaining narratives, respondents were more concerned than excited. This therefore includes two narratives categorised above as hopes: Dominance and Gratification. The Obsolescence narrative elicited most concern.

Table 3: Excitement and concern about the narratives.

Narrative	Excitement	Concern	Avg score
Ease	29%	13%	7
Immortality	25%	21%	7
Inhumanity	8%	38%	4
Uprising	7%	45%	3
Alienation	8%	51%	4
Gratification	11%	30%	6
Dominance	17%	34%	5
Obsolescence	8%	51%	3

3.4 Perceived Likelihood of the Narratives

Most respondents felt that four of the narratives were likely to come true: two hopes, Ease and Dominance, and two fears, Obsolescence and Uprising. For the four remaining narratives, more respondents felt that they were more unlikely to come true than likely to come true, although the responses were relatively evenly split. This question was also asked using a 10-point scale, with scores 1-3 counted towards the total percentage 'unlikely to come true', and 8-10 counted towards 'likely to come true'.

Respondents were asked a separate question on whether they believed each narrative would impact them personally within their lifetime. Where narratives were believed to be likely to come true, respondents believed this would happen within their lifetime. There was very little variation between age groups.

Table 4: Respondents' expectations with regard to the likelihood of narratives coming true.

Narrative	Likely	Unlikely
Ease	48%	5%
Dominance	42%	7%
Obsolescence	35%	12%
Uprising	30%	16%
Alienation	18%	25%
Gratification	18%	26%
Immortality	19%	28%
Inhumanity	12%	30%

Table 5. Respondents' expectations with regard to whether the narratives would impact them personally within their lifetime.

Narrative	Impact in my lifetime 16-34	Impact in my lifetime 35-54	Impact in my lifetime 55+
Ease	53%	52%	58%
Dominance	34%	30%	37%
Obsolescence	33%	40%	37%
Uprising	20%	23%	21%
Alienation	12%	15%	10%
Gratification	12%	14%	10%
Immortality	14%	14%	13%
Inhumanity	7%	9%	8%

3.5 Perceived Influence on AI Development

Across all narratives, 61.8% of respondents disagreed that they were able to influence how AI develops in the future. This disempowerment was not related to which narrative(s) the respondents were aware or unaware of. Respondents were asked to explain why they felt unable to influence the development of AI in an open text question; responses can be divided into three categories:

1. Age. Many older respondents expressed the sentiment that their age prevented them both from having their views heard and from being affected by the technology in their lifetime: "Who is going to listen to an 80 year old? !!" One 58-year-old respondent wrote, "AI is being developed for the under-50s". Age was also by far the most answer given (48% of 58 responses) for explaining why none of the eight narratives would apply to them within their lifetime; the oldest respondent providing this answer was 84, the youngest 58, with an average age of 72.

2. Technological determinism. Respondents across all age ranges expressed the idea that the technology is going to develop regardless of attempts to change or inhibit it: "that shit's out of the bottle now". "Advances in technology will continuously happen regardless if it's negative or positive."

3. Not being consulted. 29.6% of respondents stated that their views are neither solicited nor desired: "Who is going to ask me?" These comments often reflected a sense of dissatisfaction about not being heard more generally: "How does the average person influence the future at all"; "politicians and business never listen".

Several replies outlined who *is* perceived to be in control:

1. Business. Several responses criticised big business: "companies will go ahead regardless of what the individual thinks." On the other hand, some respondents saw an opportunity to exert some influence through consumer behaviour: "consumers as a group may have an influence jointl [*sic*], by carefully choosing which AI products they buy".

2. Research. 30% expressed feeling disenfranchised by virtue of not having the technical expertise to understand and/or develop AI: "People with more brain then [*sic*] I have will do the developing". There was also a sense of feeling detached from an ivory tower elite: "When have scientists (and computer technicians) ever listened to the public?"

3. Government. There was a frequent expression of distrust of or detachment from politics: "AI will be influenced by Government not man in street". On the other hand, several respondents pointed out that government influence itself is limited: "Our governments are too weak to reel in the maniacs creating Artificial Intelligence".

4 Discussion

4.1 Do Non-Experts Have a Distorted Understanding of What AI Is?

As noted above, nearly half of respondents gave a plausible definition of AI: one involving computers (or other artefacts) engaging in cognitive feats (such as thinking or learning) This is beyond what we expected, perhaps reflecting growing awareness of AI in the general population.

But this result is not incompatible with significant numbers of people holding fairly extreme views of what AI could do or cause: first, because it still leaves more than half of respondents with a less accurate picture of what AI is; and second, because broadly accurate ideas of AI as (a variant of) a thinking computer do not preclude holding extreme views about what those thinking machines might do.

Of course, the extent to which any of the eight narratives used in the survey are 'extreme' or distortions depends on one's standpoint: expert views on the potential of AI vary widely [16]. But four of the narratives were couched in terms of thresholds (AI might allow us to live forever, or AI might become the perfect friend) that we would consider extreme. Although these scored lower than the narratives couched in terms of incremental change (AI might make our lives easier or strengthen our military), they all scored above 10% on both recognition and likelihood. 10% to 20% of the population is a large number of people to have such utopian or dystopian views about an increasingly mainstream technology.

Notably, 7.7% of respondents spontaneously expressed anxiety in response to the request to provide an explanation of what AI is. Some elaborated on their fears (e.g., "must admit I find it a bit worrying, feel we might lose control of our lives if AI takes over"), but 36 responses to this question consisted of short and simple expressions of anxiety, such as "scary" or "creepy". This goes beyond the data on the perceived likelihood of the negative narratives coming true: those responses suggest that people believe AI *could* go badly, whereas these open responses suggest that a significant minority see AI as *inevitably* or inherently bad.

It is also noteworthy that 25% of respondents explained AI in terms of robots. We consider this a less accurate explanation than those that centred on thinking machines, as robots (i) are often not particularly intelligent, and (ii) are designed to act physically in the world (whereas AI need not). This conflation is understandable, partly because of the significant overlaps between the fields of robotics and AI, and partly because AI is frequently portrayed in film and fiction as embodied [5]. Nonetheless, it could be problematic. Imagining AI as embodied will lend itself to some narratives more than others: it might, for example encourage the public to focus on worries of gun-toting killer robots rather than the real-world challenge of algorithmic bias. Further, the gendering and racializing of humanoid embodied AI can perpetuate stereotypes [18].

Finally, 14 respondents mentioned fiction in their responses. All of the references to specific works were to films and TV series: *AI: Artificial Intelligence* (6), *The Terminator* (2), *Star Trek* (2), *I, Robot* (1), and *Star Wars* (1). This sample size is too small to draw valid conclusions; further work might explore whether such fictional representations are influencing a broader segment of the public, and if so, whether they are doing so in ways that could be considered distorting or extreme.

4.2 Pairs of Hopes and Fears

As noted above, Cave and Dihal have previously posited that these narratives come as dichotomies; that is, pairs of hopes and fears. As also noted above, the survey did not present the narratives in this way, yet these results do provide some evidence for this being perceived by respondents. First, awareness of the hopeful narratives is broadly similar to awareness of the fears with which they are posited to be paired (Obsolescence 55% and Ease 53%; Uprising 44% and Dominance 30%; Alienation 20% and Gratification 16%; Immortality 19% and Inhumanity 13%).

Second, only two of the narratives elicit more excitement than concern (Ease and Immortality), and even in those cases, the proportion of people excited is well below half (29% and 25% respectively). It is particularly notable that two narratives that we have regarded as broadly positive -- Domination and Gratification -- are perceived to be significantly more concerning than exciting. At the same time, some (albeit relatively few) respondents expressed themselves to be *excited* about the *negative* narratives.

These findings -- that awareness of the positive side of a dichotomy is in proportion with the negative side, and that feelings towards both the positive and negative sides are ambivalent -- suggest that, although the narratives as presented in the survey have attempted to pull apart the positive from the negative, there are limits to how much this is possible. This suggests that a significant number of people recognize that there is an underlying scenario common to the positive and negative visions paired in a dichotomy (such as AI taking over more human jobs) and respond according to their predispositions, regardless of how it is framed.

In particular, it is notable that levels of concern are on average higher than levels of excitement, supporting Cave and Dihal's claim that the hopeful narratives "contain inherent instabilities. The conditions required to fulfil each hope also make a dystopian future possible" [6].

It is perhaps unsurprising that the Dominance narrative elicited more concern than excitement. It is easy to imagine that powerful new weapons create anxiety regardless of which country owns them. This might relate to the influence point above (see 4.3): people might not identify with 'their' military, feel they don't have control over their activity, or have ethical concerns about autonomous machines targeting and killing humans.

That Gratification elicits more concern than excitement is more surprising. The definition we used ("AI might become the perfect friend, there to listen whenever we need and ready to meet our every desire") was prima facie wholly positive. The negative reaction suggests that respondents are recognising behind the positive framing an underlying scenario which also has strong negative aspects, something suggested by some of the open text responses expressing anxiety about humans being replaced. It would be interesting to test this in other cultures: for example, both in Japan and in South Korea people are much more positive about seeing AI as a friend [5].

4.3 Perceived Influence on AI Development

The findings show clearly that most people do not feel able to influence the future development of AI. In itself, it is perhaps unsurprising that most individuals do not feel they can shape the direction of this large and highly technical industry. However, the verbatim responses to the question asking why they felt this way are revealing. While some cite a lack of technological expertise, others argue that those who are in control of this industry (whether corporations or governments) neither engage with nor care about the views of the ordinary public. This finding is consistent with earlier research that has shown that people would be more likely to support AI applications if they were given more agency [3].

4.4 Differences Between Demographic Groups

The survey revealed differences in awareness of several narratives based on socioeconomic status: ABC1 respondents were significantly more aware of the Ease and Uprising narratives. Limited awareness of the Uprising narratives among respondents with a lower socioeconomic status is surprising, considering the emphasis tabloids place on this narrative, frequently accompanying even rather innocuous AI-related news items with pictures of the T-800 from the Terminator film franchise [5].

There are also significant differences in awareness based on respondents' gender: women were less aware of the Immortality, Dominance, and Uprising narratives. One potential explanation is that these narratives are very common in science fiction, which for the largest part of its history has been aimed explicitly at adolescent male readers and viewers [12,22]

5 Recommendations

The results suggest many further avenues of work, including exploring the sources of these utopian and dystopian perceptions and the impact of alternative framings of AI. We suggest the following themes for further research:

1. Sources of narratives.

A deeper understanding of the hopes and fears for AI could be obtained through qualitative research investigating the sources of these ideas: which narratives have given individual respondents these perceptions? Such research might take the form of the 'What AI Researchers Read' project, with non-experts rather than AI scientists being the subject of investigation [8].

2. Impact of alternative narratives.

At the same time, further research could look into the impact of new, alternative narratives that are less extreme than the ones mentioned in this paper, or that emphasise aspects of AI outside these eight hopes and fears. Further research might test whether the frightening and overpowering image of AI could be mitigated by emphasising real, current applications, or narratives of control and involvement. It is worth investigating whether narratives that make their audiences imagine an active role in the development or deployment of AI can instil this sense of empowerment.

3. Examining the 'influence' question.

While this survey investigated whether people felt able to influence the development of AI in general, further research might investigate whether and how people feel they have control over the role AI plays in their personal lives, and which narratives might impact that. For instance, an important hypothesis to investigate is that the sense of disenfranchisement might stem from the portrayal of AI research. It has been previously shown that fictional narratives about science tend to focus on individual scientists [13]. Similar research focused on news media coverage should investigate the emphasis given to the role of big tech companies, to see how they portray the role of the non-expert.

4. Examining public perceptions of AI across cultures.

This survey has examined the attitudes of a representative section of the UK population. These results should not be extrapolated globally: there is evidence to suggest that attitudes to AI vary between cultures and regions [5]. More research is needed to evaluate public perceptions of AI in other parts of the world. Such research could both explore recognition of these eight narratives (which, as noted above, were distilled from analysis of Anglophone Western portrayals of AI), and develop further frameworks.

6 Conclusion

This paper has explored a nationally representative survey of the UK population on their perceptions of AI, with a particular emphasis on sentiments regarding utopian or dystopian future scenarios. Overall, the findings show that this population have a markedly negative view of this technology: levels of concern were on average higher than levels of excitement across the narratives; concern was higher than excitement even for two 'hopeful' narratives; and 7.7% spontaneously offered negative sentiments instead of explaining what AI is. Negotiating the deployment of AI will therefore require contending with the fact that in some parts of the world, a majority of people see downsides even in ostensibly utopian portrayals.

ACKNOWLEDGMENTS

The authors would like to thank Lauren Eriser, Jamie Lawrence, Sarah Dillon, Ali Shah and Toshie Takahashi for data analysis, helpful comments, and discussions.

Authors Cave and Dihal were funded by a grant from the Leverhulme Trust via the Leverhulme Centre for the Future of Intelligence.

REFERENCES

[1] Mimi An. 2017. *Artificial Intelligence is Here - People Just Don't Realize It.* HubSpot.

[2] ARM and Northstar. 2017. *AI today, AI tomorrow: Awareness, acceptance and anticipation of AI: A global consumer perspective.* Retrieved from http://pages.arm.com/rs/312-SAX-488/images/arm-ai-survey-report.pdf

[3] Brhmie Balaram, Tony Greenham, and Jasmine Leonard. 2018. *Artificial Intelligence: real public engagement.* RSA, London. Retrieved November 5, 2018 from https://www.thersa.org/discover/publications-and-articles/reports/artificial-intelligence-real-public-engagement

[4] Margaret A. Boden. 2016. *AI: its nature and future.* Oxford University Press, Oxford.

[5] Stephen Cave, Claire Craig, Kanta Dihal, Sarah Dillon, Jessica Montgomery, Beth Singler, and Lindsay Taylor. 2018. *Portrayals and Perceptions of AI and Why They Matter.* The Royal Society, London. Retrieved from https://royalsociety.org/~/media/policy/projects/ai-narratives/AI-narratives-workshop-findings.pdf

[6] Stephen Cave and Kanta Dihal. 2019. Hopes and fears for intelligent machines in fiction and reality. *Nature Machine Intelligence* 1, 2 (February 2019), 74–78. DOI:https://doi.org/10.1038/s42256-019-0020-9

[7] Dawn Collis. 2009. *Social Grade: A Classification Tool.* Ipsos MediaCT. Retrieved from https://web.archive.org/web/20160315075958/https://www.ipsos-mori.com/DownloadPublication/1285_MediaCT_thoughtpiece_Social_Grade_July09_V3_WEB.pdf

[8] Sarah Dillon and Jennifer Schaffer-Goddard. forthcoming. What AI Researchers Read: The Role of Literature in Artificial Intelligence Research. (forthcoming).

[9] James Dipple-Johnstone. 2018. ICO statement in response to Facebook data breach announcement. *Information Commissioner's Office.* Retrieved November 5, 2018 from https://ico.org.uk/about-the-ico/news-and-events/news-and-blogs/2018/09/ico-statement-in-response-to-facebook-data-breach-announcement/

[10] Helen Edwards. 2017. There's a fine line between what people want robots to do and not do for them. *Quartz.* Retrieved November 5, 2018 from https://qz.com/1101460/theres-a-fine-line-between-what-people-want-robots-to-do-and-not-do-for-them/

[11] Ethan Fast and Eric Horvitz. 2016. Long-Term Trends in the Public Perception of Artificial Intelligence. *arXiv:1609.04904v2 [cs.CL]* (September 2016). Retrieved August 21, 2018 from https://arxiv.org/abs/1609.04904

[12] Susan Gubar. 1980. C.L. Moore and the Conventions of Women's Science Fiction (C.L. Moore et les conventions de la science-fiction féminine). *Science Fiction Studies* 7, 1 (1980), 16–27.

[13] Roslynn D. Haynes. 2017. *From madman to crime fighter: the scientist in western culture.* Johns Hopkins University Press, Baltimore.

[14] IPSOS Mori and Royal Society. 2017. *Public views of Machine Learning: Findings from public research and engagement conducted on behalf of the Royal Society.* IPSOS Mori Social Research Institute, London.

[15] Deborah G. Johnson and Mario Verdicchio. 2017. Reframing AI Discourse. *Minds and Machines* 27, 4 (December 2017), 575–590. DOI:https://doi.org/10.1007/s11023-017-9417-6

[16] Vincent C. Müller and Nick Bostrom. 2016. Future Progress in Artificial Intelligence: A Survey of Expert Opinion. *Fundamental Issues of Artificial Intelligence* (2016), 555–572. DOI:https://doi.org/10.1007/978-3-319-26485-1_33

[17] Ofcom. 2017. *Adults' media use and attitudes.* Retrieved from https://www.ofcom.org.uk/__data/assets/pdf_file/0020/102755/adults-media-use-attitudes-2017.pdf

[18] Jennifer Robertson. 2010. Gendering Humanoid Robots: Robo-Sexism in Japan. *Body & Society* 16, 2 (June 2010), 1–36. DOI:https://doi.org/10.1177/1357034X10364767

[19] Select Committee on Artificial Intelligence. 2018. *AI in the UK: ready, willing, and able?* House of Lords, London. Retrieved from https://publications.parliament.uk/pa/ld201719/ldselect/ldai/100/100.pdf

[20] SPACE10. ongoing. Do You Speak Human? Retrieved November 5, 2018 from http://doyouspeakhuman.com

[21] The Pennsylvania State University. 2019. S.3.2 Hypothesis Testing (P-Value Approach). *PennState: Statistics Online Courses.* Retrieved January 16, 2019 from https://newonlinecourses.science.psu.edu/statprogram/reviews/statistical-concepts/hypothesis-testing/p-value-approach

[22] Lisa Tuttle. 2018. Women in SF. *The Encyclopedia of Science Fiction.* Retrieved January 16, 2019 from http://www.sf-encyclopedia.com/entry/women_in_sf

[23] Weber Shandwick and KRC Research. 2016. *AI-Ready or not: artificial intelligence here we come! What consumers think & what marketers need to know.* Weber Shandwick, New York.

Framing Artificial Intelligence in American Newspapers

Ching-Hua Chuan
Cinema and Interactive Media
University of Miami
Coral Gables, Florida, USA
c.chuan@miami.edu

Wan-Hsiu Sunny Tsai
Strategic Communication
University of Miami
Coral Gables, Florida, USA
wanhsiu@miami.edu

Su Yeon Cho
School of Communication
University of Miami
Coral Gables, Florida, USA
sxc1584@miami.edu

ABSTRACT

Publics' perceptions of new scientific advances such as AI are often informed and influenced by news coverage. To understand how artificial intelligence (AI) was framed in U.S. newspapers, a content analysis based on framing theory in journalism and science communication was conducted. This study identified the dominant topics and frames, as well as the risks and benefits of AI covered in five major American newspapers from 2009 to 2018. Results indicated that business and technology were the primary topics in news coverage of AI. The benefits of AI were discussed more frequently than its risks, but risks of AI were generally discussed with greater specificity. Additionally, episodic issue framing and societal impact framing were more frequently used.

CCS CONCEPTS

• Social and professional topics

KEYWORDS

Artificial intelligence; news framing; content analysis; public perception

ACM Reference format:

Ching-Hua Chuan, Wan-Hsiu Sunny Tsai and Su Yeon Cho. 2019. Framing Artificial Intelligence in American Newspapers. *In Proceedings of AAAI/ACM Conference on Artificial Intelligence, Ethics, and Society (AIES'19).* January 27-28, 2019, Honolulu, HI, USA. ACM, New York, NY 6 pages. DOI: https://doi.org/10.1145/3306618.3314285

AIES'19, January 27-28, 2019, Honolulu, HI, USA

ACM 978-1-4503-6324-2/19/01...$15.00
https://doi.org/10.1145/3306618.3314285

1 Introduction

Artificial intelligence has been recognized as a strategic priority by the patent offices of the United States and many countries [10], and as an important area for national policy as defined by the National Science and Technology Council. In a recent industry survey, 80% of the companies reported having AI applications in production [19]. Additionally, AI has long been a topic of fascination in popular culture. Numerous sci-fi movies, television dramas, and novels have explored the power and danger of AI, illuminating human's complicated fears and yearnings towards technologies. With the recent technological breakthroughs, the gap between scientific reality and the popular culture imaginations is narrowing, resulting in a surge of media buzz on AI. However, the reportedly unlimited potential of AI [11] has generated not only excitements, but also widespread concerns.

Publics' perceptions of new scientific advances such as AI are often informed and influenced by the information and arguments presented in media, particularly news media [8]. Similar to other innovative yet controversial scientific advances like nanotechnology, the social acceptance and adoption of AI depends on public's understanding of its power, limitations, and risks [18]. However, for emerging, unfamiliar technologies, public's affective attitudes may be formed before systematic, logical, cognitive information processing take place [17]. A 2017 survey by the Pew Research Center reveals that Americans are more concerned than enthusiastic about the prospect of AI-powered machines performing many human jobs, and anticipate more negative consequences than positive outcomes [1]. Moreover, not only approximately 60% of American adults are reluctant to incorporate automation technologies such as driverless cars into their own lives, but 76% of Americans also worry that advances in robotics and AI will lead to more inequality in the future.

Research assessing how media cover AI thus is imperative to understand the forces shaping public opinion on this important technology. However, despite the numerous hypes and speculations about AI, there exists little empirical data regarding how AI is covered in news media. A notable exception is Fast and Horvitz's study that analyzed *New York Time*'s 30-year coverage of AI [6]. They reported an overall optimistic view with growing concerns on various negative impacts of AI in recent years. However, their study is limited to the news articles in *New*

York Times, and failed to provide a theory-based analysis of news coverage of AI. Based on the rich literature of framing theory in journalism and science communication [18, 20], this study systematically examined the coverage of AI in major U.S. newspapers. By adopting the content analysis method from social sciences, we seek to illuminate how AI is discussed, contextualized, and presented to the public.

2 Literature Review

2.1 News Framing

The critical role of media in facilitating information dissemination and understanding of innovations is well-documented [3]. According to framing theory, the way an issue is framed and discussed through specific perspectives can influence how audiences make sense of the issue [20]. Entman [5] defined framing as selecting "some aspects of a perceived reality and make them more salient in a communicating text, in such a way as to promote a particular problem definition, causal interpretation, moral evaluation, and/or treatment recommendation to the item described" (p. 52). In their study of news framing of nanotechnology [2], Anderson, Allan, Petersen, and Wilkinson argue that the press helps establish the initial parameters of debate regarding nanotechnology and provides topic-defining reference points. Nelkin observed a decline in publics' consumption of a product powered by a controversial technology after media coverage of the scientific controversy [13]. Strekalova also pointed out that publics' attitudes toward new technologies are often affected by specific applications, which is particularly relevant to AI which can be incorporated into numerous aspects of our daily lives, from entertainment, education, healthcare, to manufacturing [18].

It is important to note that this study does not assume a causal relationship between media coverage and public's opinions about a particular issue. However, media as a powerful cultural institution [9] may influence public's attitudes towards an emerging technology, particularly in the early stage when most people feel uncertain, wary, or anxious about an unfamiliar yet powerful technology. Therefore, understanding how news media frame AI is imperative to understand the perspectives and considerations in the formation of public opinion regarding the technology, and the wide-reaching impacts on public acceptance and policy.

2.2 Research Questions

Prior content analyses of science communication have studied different news frames of technologies and scientific advances. The coverage of benefits and risks has been considered as the most commonly analyzed category [7], as well as topics of economic and business, policy and regulations, and ethics and moral issues [18]. Following Strekalova's approach [18], this study differentiated between topics and frames. Topic is defined as a manifest subject, an issue or event that provides message content. Frame, by contrast, is a perspective through which the content is presented. A single news article may incorporate multiple topics and multiple frames. Incorporating the key frames and topics identified in the literature, the present study aims to answer the following research questions:

RQ1: What topics were most prevalent in AI coverage in major U.S. newspapers?

RQ2: How was AI framed in major U.S. newspapers?

3 Methods

3.1 Sample

The authors used Lexis Nexis Academic and the ProQuest databases to identify news articles with the keyword "artificial intelligence." Fast and Horvitz [6] observed that news coverage on AI have increased dramatically since 2009. Therefore, news article from January 2009 to September 16, 2018 (end of data collection) that mentioned artificial intelligence from most widely-read daily newspapers, *USA Today, The New York Times, Los Angeles Times, New York Post,* and *Washington Post* were identified.

Figure 1 shows the number of articles from the five U.S. newspapers. In total, 2,485 of articles were found, including 274 from *Los Angeles Times,* 14 from *New York Post,* 1,475 from the *New York Times,* 293 from *USA Today,* and 155 from *Washington Post.* It can be clearly observed that the number of AI-related articles increased over the years, especially since the year of 2016, and the majority of them were contributed by the *New York Times.*

We implemented stratified sampling with probability proportional to size to select articles for the content analysis. Articles were first divided into distinct categories based on the publisher and published year, and were then randomly selected in each category. The number of samples from a particular year is proportional to the ratio of the total number of articles in that year to numbers in other years. Similarly, the number of samples from a particular publisher is proportional to the ratio of the total number of articles from that publisher to numbers from other publishers. The final sample consisted of 399 articles. The unit of analysis is the complete news article.

3.2 Variables

Topics. We incorporated the key topics (nominal measure) identified in prior research, including Technology Development and Application, Business and Economy, Politics and Policy, Ethics, Threat, Science Fiction, Entertainment, and Education. The dominant topic of each article was coded. All discussed topics in a news article were also coded.

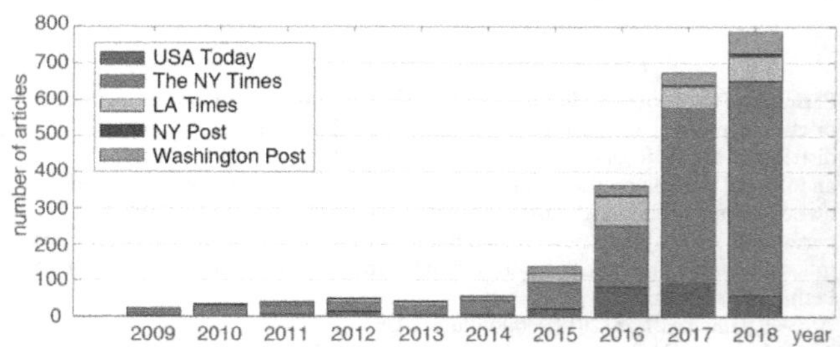

Figure 1: Total number of articles across newspapers.

Risk and benefit. Previous content analyses have identified the coverage of risks and benefits as a crucial variable that drives public perception and attitudes towards emerging technologies [4, 20]. Specific types of risks analyzed in prior studies and commonly mentioned in mainstream media were coded, including loss of jobs, embedded bias, privacy concern, misuse, run-away-train, Pandora's Box (unforeseeable risk), ethical concerns, and shortcomings of AI. Similarly, specific types of benefits including economic benefit, improving human life and well-being, reducing human bias or social inequality were also coded. Moreover, when either a risk or benefit was mentioned, the mentioned risk or benefit was coded for how specific the risk or benefit was discussed in the news article using a 3-point Likert scale.

Societal versus Personal Impact Framing. To illustrate how news media covered the impacts of AI, we analyzed whether AI was discussed via a personal or societal impact frame [18]. Specifically, personal framing presents the news story by focusing on individuals' opinions, experiences, or consequences of incidents. By contrast, societal framing addresses the general, overall consequences of the incidents, or broader societal decisions such as policy or public opinion. A middle category was coded if the news story gave equal attention to both aspects.

Thematic versus Episodic Issue Framing. To understand how AI was contextualized in news, we also analyzed issue framing of AI as a thematic or episodic issue [18]. Episodic framing presents an issue by offering a specific example, case study, or event-oriented report (e.g., covering a press conference for an AI-related product). By contrast, thematic issue framing discusses the technology in a broader, general context, such as how AI is changing various industries. A middle category was also included.

In addition to the key topics and themes identified in the literature, this study also coded the overall valence (i.e., positive, negative, mixed), and the sources cited in the article [16], including business, government/politician, mass media, scientist, non-scientist expert (e.g., scholars in ethics), celebrity, and ordinary individual.

3.3 Intercoder Reliability

Three graduate students in school of communication were trained as coders for this study. 40 articles were randomly selected from the dataset to establish intercoder reliability. The intercoder reliability was calculated by using Perreault and Leigh's formula [14]. The average of 0.8 is achieved for intercoder reliability.

4 Results and Findings

4.1 Topics

Overall, newspaper coverage of A.I. was dominated by the topic of *Business and Economy* (*N* = 143, 35.1%), followed by *Science and Technology* (*N* = 96, 23.6%) and, *Policy and Politics* (*N* = 49, 12.0%). The dominant topic varied across the years. In 2009, *Business and Economy* (*N* = 2, 50.0%), and *Science and*

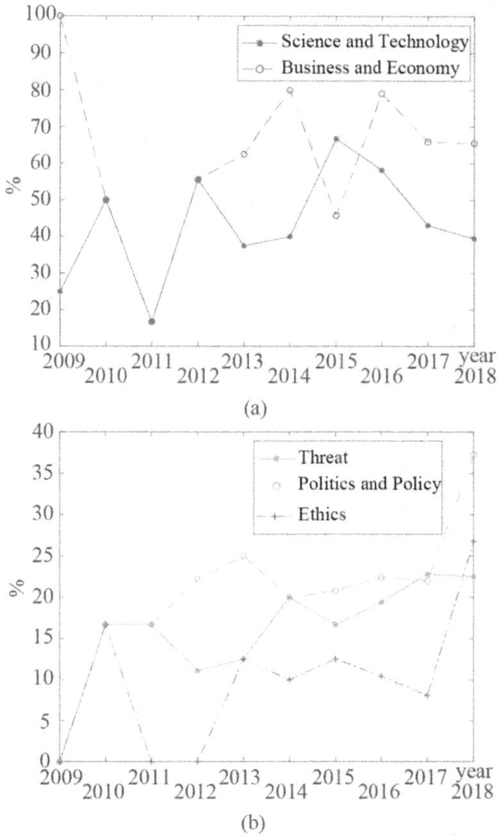

Figure 2: Percentages of articles containing different dominant topics in each year.

Technology (*N* = 96, 23.6%) and, *Policy and Politics* (*N* = 49, 12.0%). The dominant topic varied across the years. In 2009, *Business and Economy* (*N* = 2, 50.0%), and *Science and Technology* (*N* = 2, 50%) were the dominant topics. *Entertainment* (*N* = 2, 33.3%) topic about entertaining applications of AI, such as AI-powered robot dogs, was the dominant topic in both of 2010 and 2011. *Business and Economy topics* have been the dominant topic from 2012 to 2018 (2012 *N* = 3, 33.3%, 2013 *N* = 2, 25.0%, 2014 *N* = 6, 60.0%, 2016 *N* = 28, 41.8%, 2017 *N* = 51, 41.5%, 2018 *N* = 43, 30.3%). Only in 2015, *Science and Technology* emerged as a dominant topic (*N* = 11, 45.8%).

Most articles covered multiple topics. Figure 2 shows the percentage of articles coded with a specific topic in each year. Most frequently appearing topics were *Business and Economy* (*N* = 264, 66.2%) and *Science and Technology* (*N* = 181, 45.4%) as shown in Figure 2 (a). *Politics/Policy* had been increased slightly from 2016 (2016: 22.4%, 2018: 37.3%) as presented in Figure 2 (b). Although *Ethics* was not a dominant topic or one of the most popular topics, its occurrence dramatically increased between 2017 (8.1%) and 2018 (26.8%). *Threat* also reached a new record high in 2018 as shown in Figure 2 (b).

4.2 Cited Sources

A news article could cite multiple sources, and all observed sources were coded. Given the dominance of business and technology topics, it is not surprising that the most frequently cited sources were individuals associated companies or businesses (N = 258, 64.7%), followed by scientists (N = 116, 29.1%) and non-science experts (N=94, 23.6%). Sources associated with science and research institutions were cited more frequently in earlier years between 2009 and 2012. Government and politician were not popular sources for AI-related news but had been increasingly cited from 2015.

4.3 Valence

Figure 3 shows the number of articles coded with positive, negative, or mixed valence in each year. Note that before 2015 when the number of AI-related articles were very few, such articles were mostly coded as positive or mixed valence. As the number of AI articles dramatically increased, the number of articles with negative valence increased as well, especially in the current year (2018).

4.4 Risks and Benefits Framing

Among the 399 news articles analyzed, 52.9% of articles (N = 211) discussed at least one type of benefits and 47.6 % of articles (N = 190) covered at least one type of risks. An article can be coded for multiple types of risks and benefits. Figure 4 presents the total number of occurrences of different types of risks and benefits. It can be observed that in general, benefits, such as economic benefits (economy) and improving human life or well-being (well-being), were used much more often to frame AI topics than risks. The most frequently discussed risks included shortcoming of the technology (shortcoming), loss of jobs, and privacy concerns.

Figure 5 shows the average specificity level of benefits and risks discussed in news articles, with error bars indicating 95% confidence interval.

Three types of benefits, including economic benefits (economy), improving human life or well-being (well-being), and reduce human biases or inequality (reduce biases), had similar level of average specificity but the last one has much fewer cases.

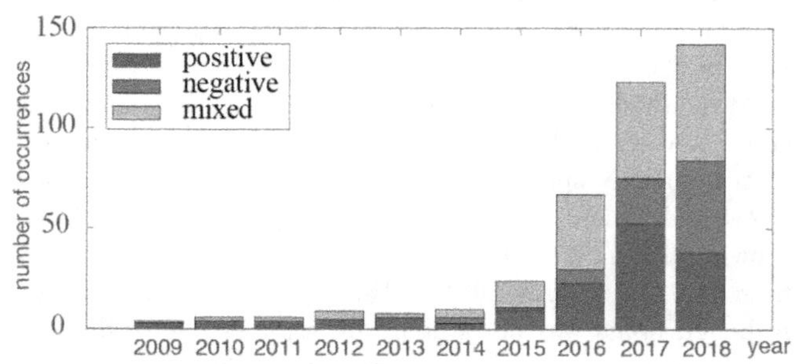

Figure 3: Number of articles coded with positive, negative, and mixed valence in each year.

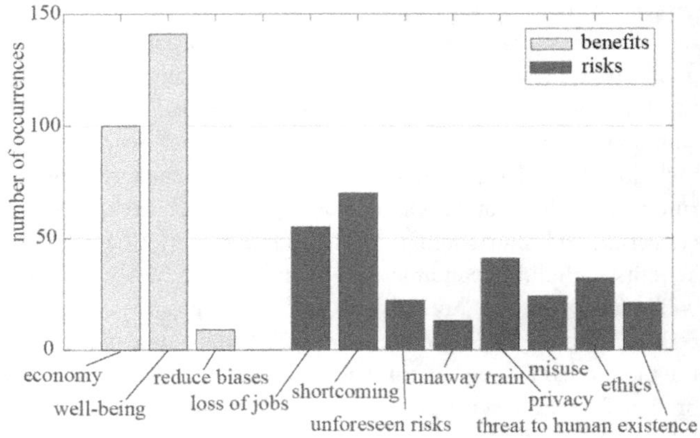

Figure 4: Total number of articles coded with each type of benefits and risks.

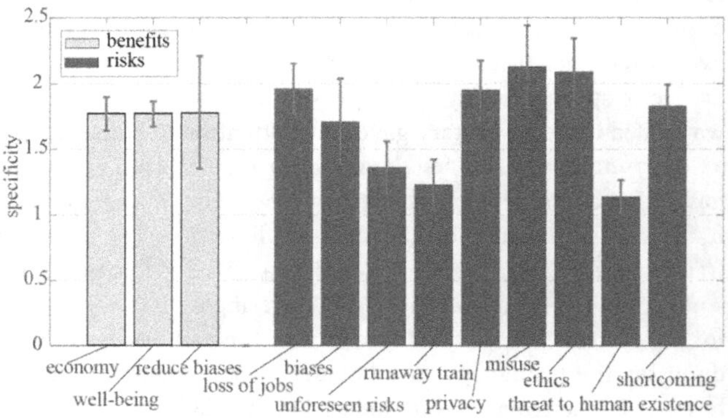

Figure 5: Figure Caption and Image above the caption [In draft mode, Image will not appear on the screen]

The top five risks in terms of specificity level are misuse of AI (misuse), ethical or moral problems (ethics), loss of jobs, privacy, and shortcoming of the technology (shortcoming). Notably, the average specificity of all these five risks is higher than any of the benefits. Risks such as threat to human existence, runaway train, and unforeseeable risks were discussed in newspapers with relatively low level of specificity.

4.5 Topics in Risks/Benefits Framing

To examine how topics were framed in relation to benefits and risks, we consolidated the coding into four categories: risks only, benefits only, risks and benefits, neither risks nor benefits. Overall, the four categories in risk/benefit framing are evenly presented: risks only (N=89, 22.31%), benefits only (N=96, 24.06%), risks and benefits (N=99, 24.81%), neither risks nor benefits (N=115, 28.82%). However, a chi-square test indicated a significant relationship between topics and risk/benefit framing, χ^2 (24, N = 399) = 87, p < .001.

A cross-tabulation of risk-benefit framing and dominant topic variables is shown in Table 1. By examining the calculated standardized residuals, more detailed information about the relation between these variables can be obtained. For example, the *Business and Economy* topic is more likely to be covered in articles that discussed benefit only and less likely in articles that discussed risks only. Both *Science Fiction* and *Ethics* topics are likely to be covered in articles discussing risks only, while *Entertainment* is likely to be covered in articles that discussed neither risks nor benefits of AI.

4.6 Impact Framing (Personal vs. Societal)

Impact framing examines the manner in which topics are covered from personal, societal, or mixed angles. Overall, the reviewed articles were most frequently covered in societal frames (N = 192, 48.1%), followed by mixed framing (N = 106, 26.6%), and personal framing (N = 101, 25.3%).

A chi-square test was conducted and the result indicated significant relationship between dominant topics and impact frames, χ^2 (16, N = 398) = 48.35, $p < .001$. *Business and Economy*, *Science Fiction*, and *Entertainment* topics were more likely to be associated with the personal impact frame, while *Threat*, *Politics/Policy*, and *Ethics* topics were more likely to be associated with the societal impact frame. *Science/Technology* and *Education/Career Advice* were more related to the mixed frame.

4.7 Issue Framing (Episodic vs. Thematic)

Issue framing addresses whether topics are discussed as singular incidents (episodic), or related to a broader theme (thematic), or mixed. In this study, episodic framing was observed in the majority of cases (N = 244, 61.2%). Thematic framing was coded for 26.8% of cases (N = 107). Mixed framing was observed the least (N = 48, 12.0%).

A chi-square test also showed a significant relationship between dominant topics and issue frames, χ^2 (16, N = 398) = 50.63, $p < .001$. *Business and Economy* topics were more likely to be associated with the episodic frame. *Threat* and *Politics/Policy* were more likely to be covered via thematic framing.

5 Conclusion

The study results revealed that AI was primarily covered in American newspapers via the topics of *Business and Economy* and *Science and Technology*. Notably, the topic of ethics has been increasingly discussed in recent years. A close examination of the articles that discussed ethics or moral issues as the dominant topic indicated that both positive and negative aspects were addressed. For instance, a news article discussed the use of AI to combat unethical wildlife trade. However, most news articles did not discuss a particular ethical issue in-depth, but raised general questions about potential ethical concerns, such as privacy and misuse of AI in the title, introduction, or conclusion paragraph, without providing specific discussions. As news media influence people's attitudes towards an emerging technology, more in-depth and concrete discussion of the risks and benefits of AI in news media is needed to allow critical assessment of the use and misuse of AI. Additionally, prior media framing studies suggest four stages of news coverage of an emerging issue: initial, scientific, human, and political [15]. The dominant topic of *Science and Technology*, coupled with the dominant episodic issue frame, suggests that the media coverage of AI is in the early stage and new information is constantly released and discussed. However, the findings that societal impact frame was used in nearly half of the news articles analyzed, and the *Politics/Policy* topic has been increasingly covered, suggest that news coverage has begun to transition into the human and political stage as more people are affected by the technology.

Table 1: Dominant topic and frequencies, expected counts, and standardized residuals in its risks/benefits coverage.

Topics	Risks and benefits coverage			
	Risks only	Benefits only	Risks and benefits	Neither risks nor benefits
Science and Technology				
Count	23	24	29	20
Expected count	21.41	23. 1	23.82	27.67
Standard residual	0.34	0.19	1.06	-1.46
Threats				
Count	13	0	17	4
Expected count	7.58	8.18	8.44	9.8
Standard residual	**1.97**	**-2.86**	**2.95**	-1.85
Business and Economy				
Count	15	51	31	46
Expected count	31.9	34.41	35.48	41.22
Standard residual	**-2.99**	**2.83**	-0.75	0.74
Science Fiction				
Count	7	2	2	4
Expected count	3.35	3.61	3.72	4.32
Standard residual	**1.99**	-0.85	-0.89	-0.15
Politics and Policy				
Count	16	6	8	19
Expected count	10.93	11.79	12.16	14.12
Standard residual	1.53	-1.69	-1.19	1.3
Ethics				
Count	12	3	6	4
Expected count	5.58	6.02	6.2	7.21
Standard residual	**2.72**	-1.23	-0.08	-1.2
Entertainment				
Count	3	2	0	8
Expected count	2.9	3.13	3.23	3.73
Standard residual	0.06	-0.64	-1.8	**2.19**
Education				
Count	0	4	5	6
Expected count	3.35	3.61	3.72	4.32
Standard residual	-1.83	0.21	0.66	0.81
Other				
Count	0	4	1	4
Expected count	2.01	2.17	2.23	2.59
Standard residual	-1.42	1.24	-0.82	0.88

REFERENCES

[1] M. Anderson (2017). 6 Key Findings on How Americans See the Rise of Automation, http://www.pewresearch.org/fact-tank/2017/10/04/6-key-findings-on-how-americans-see-the-rise-of-automation/.

[2] A. Anderson, S. Allan, A. Petersen, and C. Wilkinson (2005). The Framing of Nanotechnologies in the British Newspapers Press. *Science Communication*, 27(2), 200-220.

[3] D. Brossard (2013). New Media Landscapes and the Science Information Consumer. *Proceedings of the National Academy of Sciences*, 110(Suppl. 3), 14096-14101.

[4] R. Coleman, E. Thorson, and L. Wilkins (2011). Testing the Effect of Framing and Sourcing in Health News Stories. *Journal of Health Communication*, 16, 941-954.

[5] R. M. Entman (1993). Framing: Toward Clarification of a Fractured Paradigm. *Journal of Communication*, 43(4), 51-58.

[6] E. Fast and E. Horvitz (2017). Long-Term Trends in the Public Perception of Artificial Intelligence. *AAAI*, pp. 963-969.

[7] S. M. Friedman and B. P. Egolf (2011). A Longitudinal Study of Newspaper and Wire Service Coverage of Nanotechnology Risks. *Risk Analysis*, 31, 1701-1717.

[8] J. R. Goodman and B. P. Goodman (2006). Beneficial or Biohazard? How the Media Frame Biosolids. *Public Understanding of Science*, 15, 359-375. doi:10.1177/0963662506062468.

[9] D. Hesmondhalgh (2006). Bourdieu, the Media and Cultural Production. *Media, Culture & Society*, 28(2), 211-231.

[10] IP Watch. 2018. World's 5 Largest IP Offices Name Artificial Intelligence A Top Strategic Priority. http://www.ip-watch.org/2018/06/15/worlds-5-largest-ip-offices-name-artificial-intelligence-top-strategic-priority/

[11] B. Khosravi (2016). How to Compete and Win in the New World Of AI, https://www.forbes.com/sites/bijankhosravi/2016/06/08/ai-is-the-new-reality-ways-to-compete-and-win/#17d27c803dd6

[12] S. Lemańczyk (2014). Science and National Pride: The Iranian Press Coverage of Nanotechnology, 2004-2009. *Science Communication*, 36(2), 194-218.

[13] D. Nelkin (1987). *Selling Science*. New York, NY: W. H. Freeman.

[14] W. D. Perreault Jr and L. E. Leigh (1989). Reliability of Nominal Data based on Qualitative Judgments. *Journal of Marketing Research (JMR)*, 26(2).

[15] E. M. Rogers, J. W. Dearing, and S. Chang (1991). AIDS in the 1980s: The Agenda-Setting Process for a Public Issue. *Journalism and Communication Monographs*, 126.

[16] L. F. Stephens (2005). News Narratives about Nano S&T in Major US and non-US Newspapers. *Science Communication*, 27(2), 175-199.

[17] D. A. Scheufele and B. V. Lewenstein (2005). The Public and Nanotechnology: How Citizens Make Sense of Emerging Technologies. *Journal of Nanoparticle Research*, 7(6), 659-667.

[18] Y. A. Strekalova (2015). Informing Dissemination Research: A Content Analysis of US Newspaper Coverage of Medical Nanotechnology News. *Science Communication*, 37(2), 151-172.

[19] Taradata (2018). 80 Percent of Enterprises Investing in AI, but Cite Significant Challenges Ahead, https://www.teradata.com/Press-Releases/2017/Survey-80-Percent-of-Enterprises-Invest-in-AI

[20] L. Vicsek (2011). Costs and Benefits of Stem Cell Research and Treatment: Media Presentation and Audience Understanding in Hungary. *Science Communication*, 33(3), 309-340.

Perceptions of Domestic Robots' Normative Behavior Across Cultures

Huao Li
hul52@pitt.edu
University of Pittsburgh
Pittsburgh, PA

Stephanie Milani*
stemila1@umbc.edu
University of Maryland, Baltimore County
Baltimore, MD

Vigneshram Krishnamoorthy
vigneshk@andrew.cmu.edu
Carnegie Mellon University
Pittsburgh, PA

Michael Lewis
ml@sis.pitt.edu
University of Pittsburgh
Pittsburgh, PA

Katia Sycara
katia@cs.cmu.edu
Carnegie Mellon University
Pittsburgh, PA

ABSTRACT

As domestic service robots become more common and widespread, they must be programmed to efficiently accomplish tasks while aligning their actions with relevant norms. The first step to equip domestic robots with normative reasoning competence is understanding the norms that people apply to the behavior of robots in specific social contexts. To that end, we conducted an online survey of Chinese and United States participants in which we asked them to select the preferred normative action a domestic service robot should take in a number of scenarios. The paper makes multiple contributions. Our extensive survey is the *first* to: (a) collect data on attitudes of people on normative behavior of domestic robots, (b) across cultures and (c) study relative priorities among norms for this domain. We present our findings and discuss their implications for building computational models for robot normative reasoning.

CCS CONCEPTS

• Computing methodologies → Artificial intelligence; **• Computer systems organization → Robotics**; **• Human-centered computing →** *Human computer interaction (HCI).*

KEYWORDS

human-robot interaction; service robots; cross-culture study; moral decision making; machine ethics

ACM Reference Format:

Huao Li, Stephanie Milani, Vigneshram Krishnamoorthy, Michael Lewis, and Katia Sycara. 2019. Perceptions of Domestic Robots' Normative Behavior Across Cultures. In *AAAI/ACM Conference on AI, Ethics, and Society (AIES '19), January 27–28, 2019, Honolulu, HI, USA.* ACM, New York, NY, USA, 7 pages. https://doi.org/10.1145/3306618.3314251

*Work done as an intern at Carnegie Mellon University.

AIES '19, January 27–28, 2019, Honolulu, HI, USA

ACM ISBN 978-1-4503-6324-2/19/01...$15.00
https://doi.org/10.1145/3306618.3314251

1 INTRODUCTION

With the development of robotics technology, robots' set of responsibilities has expanded from manufacture, military and rescue to include diverse roles in our daily life, such as being a personal assistant, a caretaker for children, and a housekeeper. These tasks can be programmed to have explicit rewards purely based on the accomplishment of the assignment; however, when these robots must interact with humans, there is usually no explicit reward function or correctness measure for their behavior. Instead, the appropriateness of an action depends on external factors - such as the physical environment and the social context - and internal, inferred factors - such as the users' personality, prior experience, and cultural background.

One important factor that informs the appropriateness of actions is the set of norms within a particular culture. Norms, such as prohibitions, permissions, obligations, are the socially agreed upon guidelines of behavior which are acknowledged by most of the members of a community [3]. The social science literature (e.g. [17] have reported that norm activation is dependent on environmental and social context. Additionally, we claim that determination of priorities among different norms also depends on the culture of the society where the robot operates. Each culture has its unique set of norms due to historical and socio-political reasons. Some cultures have strict social norms and severe punishment for norm violations, while others have weaker constraints and higher tolerance to individual discretion [6]. These social norms not only regulate the behavior selection of everyone in the society, but also help predict other agents' actions to improve collaboration [17]. Thus, to understand and design for effective interactions of robots with humans, it is critical for the robots to incorporate socio-cultural norms in their decision-making process in performing their various tasks.

The normative reasoning of intelligent agents, also called machine ethics [20], has attracted increasing attention in the community in recent years. Generally, representative works mainly concentrate on two types of problems. First is considering thought experiments such as the trolley problem to examine the appropriate moral decision an autonomous agent should make [2, 18]. Second is focusing on task-specific environments - like judging performance in a game [9] or navigating indoors [23] - to evaluate the normative role of robots in social interactions. Recently, researchers are calling for more realistic scenario settings, as well as a general normative framework [1, 4, 12]. The first step towards these goals is to discover people's opinions about what norms robots should adhere to in specific situations and contexts, and how robots should prioritize their norms. However, to the best of our knowledge, currently there are no surveys that ask participants for their views on these issues. The work presented in this paper fills this gap. Additionally, our work studies these issues across two cultures to determine whether cultural difference exist. The domain of application of our survey is domestic service robots.

2 RELATED WORKS

Previous research in human-robot interaction in a domestic setting mainly focuses on the general acceptance and representation people have towards future domestic robots. Relevant works examine the correlation between age and the degree of autonomy granted to the domestic robot [25], the nature of expected tasks of domestic robots at home [26], and the influence of utilitarian attitudes and social norms on the acceptance of domestic robots [5]. However, the aforementioned works ask general questions. As has been found in the literature (e.g. [17]) norm activation is context-specific and therefore surveys would need to ground their questions to specific, detailed, realistic scenarios.

Beyond the micro context where the interactions occur, the macro socio-culture environment needs to be considered when modeling the norm framework. Existing work found that individuals from different cultures differed in their perceptions of social robots along the axes of trustworthiness [16], appearance [14], and politeness [24]. Literature has adopted culture dimensions such as Hofstede's [8] to examine the cultural factors in people's attitude and acceptance towards robots [7, 16, 21]. Although Hofstede's dimensions provide a general picture of how people behave across cultures, it ignores the impact of social contexts when determining an individual's behaviors in specific situations. As proposed by recent research [10, 15], it is necessary for cross-cultural studies to consider *cultural syndromes* that incorporate the interaction of cultures, individuals, and contexts. We incorporate cultural syndromes [15] as well as consideration of tight vs loose cultures [6] since they make particular predictions about norm compliance across cultures.

Name	Description
Safety	Protect human from danger
Consideration	Consider human's feelings
Privacy	Protect human's privacy
Security	Secure sensitive information
Efficiency	Finish the given task efficiently
Compliance	Obey social rules
Command	Follow owner's command
Accommodation	Accommodate human's behavior
Honesty	Tell the truth
Loyalty	Maximize owner's interest

Table 1: Norm List

3 METHOD

3.1 Methodological Design

Previous literature on the general attitudes of people towards robots [11, 22, 25, 26, 29], have determined various issues, such as the capability of the robot to finish a given task, invasion of privacy that may arise due to the robot's presence, and potential danger to safety.

Inspired by this literature and literature on ethics, we considered a (not necessarily exhaustive) list of general norms (Table 1) that arise in domestic robot interactions with humans. This list provided a guideline for studying people's attitudes and preferences on the acceptable normative behaviors of domestic robots.

We distinguish between the following terms when discussing the survey:

- A *scenario*, or *situation* refers to the description of the setting where the robot must choose how to respond.
- An *option* refers to a possible action that the robot could take in a specific scenario, which indicates the priority of a certain norm.
- *Context* refers to the physical and social environmental features which are manipulated within a scenario.
- *Norms* are the principal expectations, prohibitions and permissions on the behaviors of domestic robots.

To illustrate the notions of scenario, context, and potential normative actions of the robots, we provide below sample scenario, referenced throughout as the *warning of allergy* scenario:

> *Imagine that you are hosting a dinner at your home.* ***You/your robot*** *finish cooking and are about to serve a dish to your* ***friends/family members****. Your robot detects that one of the guests may be* ***slightly/severely*** *allergic to an ingredient in the dish through the conversation between them. He/she didn't provide allergy information in advance. You and the guests are mid-conversation. Please rate your opinion toward the following statements about robot's behavior.*
> - The robot should interrupt the ongoing conversation and tell everyone about the allergy situation.
> - The robot should discreetly inform you (the robot owner), but not anyone else.
> - The robot should do nothing.

To determine people's priority between norms, we designed scenarios, referred to as *dilemmas*, where several norms (some of them conflicting) could be simultaneously activated so the robot would need to choose the most appropriate action. For example, in the warning of allergy scenario, the conflicting norms are *ensure safety*, *consider people's feelings*, and *obey social rules*. For the robot, obeying the "ensure safety" norm could be achieved by interrupting the conversation immediately, informing everyone about the allergy; however, as a consequence, it may embarrass the hosts/owners and guests. An alternative action of the robot could be to discreetly inform the owner of the situation, but not anyone else. Doing so considers people's feelings, but sacrifices the opportunity to immediately warn the guest. The third option, "do nothing due to table manners", emphasizes compliance to social rules like do not

Scenario	Context Location	Context Characteristic	Context Consequence	Norms
Warning of Allergy	Dining Room	Family/Friends	Severe/Mild allergy, Responsibility	Safety, Consideration, Compliance
Entering Room	Bathroom/Bedroom	Fire/Burst Pipe	Drenched/Burned	Safety, Privacy, Compliance
Ordering Groceries	Owner's office	Payment Information/ Shopping History	Unwanted Disclosure	Security, Efficiency
Encountering Human	Hallway	Elderly/Disabled, Number of people	Injury	Compliance, Safety, Accommodation
Judging Outfit	Party	Friends/Strangers	Embarrassment	Honesty, Consideration
Reporting Evidence	Sidewalk	Elderly/Strangers, Responsibility	Liability	Honesty, Loyalty, Command

Table 2: Scenario List, possible values of a contextual variable are divided by slashes, different variables or norms are divided by commas. Norms in each scenario correspond to optional actions in order.

interrupt ongoing conversations. Surveying people about their preferences regarding those *options* enables us to determine both the norm priorities and the severity of the conflict between norms in the given scenarios.

For each scenario, participants were required to *independently rate their opinion towards each presented option on a scale of 1 (strongly disagree) to 7 (strongly agree).* The participants' answers within a particular scenario might be mutually exclusive (agree on one option and disagree on the other options), or not (agree or disagree on both options to different degrees). For example, a participant may rate 7 on the "interrupt option" and 1 on the "discreetly inform" option, indicating a strong participant preference of ensuring the guest's safety over embarrassing the hosts. Another participant may rate 6 on the "discreetly inform" option and 5 on the "interrupt option", which shows that they value those two options and the corresponding norms to similar degrees.

To measure the influence of *context* on norm activation, we manipulated key words in the scenario descriptions to present the scenario with different context. In general, context varies in three different aspects: 1) location of the interaction, 2) characteristics of those in the scenario, including age, number of people, and their relationship to the domestic service robot owner, and 3) the consequences of robot's behavior, which depends on the severity of consequences. A list of scenarios, corresponding contexts, and norms discussed in this paper is shown in Table 2. In the allergy case, we changed three contextual variables: 1) the owner or robot is serving the dish (responsibility), 2) the guests are friends or family (relationship), and 3) the allergy is slight or severe (consequences). Each participant read a randomly chosen version of this scenario. For example, one participant may read the version where the consequence of allergy is mild, but the other may read the one where it is severe. By comparing the answers between participants who read different versions of the same scenario, we determined the influence of contexts on the priority of norms.

3.2 Questionnaire Design

We designed 15 scenarios capturing distinct norm conflicts. To help participants better understand the scenario, we provided a detailed description and picture for each scenario. Each participant read all of the 15 scenarios; however, the context of each scenario randomly varied between subjects. For example, the allergy case had three contextual variables, each with two different levels that were changed: responsibility, relationship, and the severity of consequence. This gives rise to 8 (2*2*2) different versions of this specific scenario that were evenly distributed to participants. The number of versions for each scenario ranged from 1 to 8 depending on the number and levels of contextual variables, and they were evenly distributed among participants. For each scenario, participants were asked to rate their opinion towards each of the (2 or 3) given options on a 7-point Likert scale (1- strongly disagree and 7- strongly agree). Before the main section, we included a section to collect demographic information - including gender, age, employment status, educational background, familiarity with robots, and primary source of information for knowledge of robots. After the context section, participants were asked two questions about their general acceptance and purchase tendencies about the robot described in the survey. The survey was originally designed in English, and was then translated to Chinese for running in mainland China. The Chinese version of the survey was then back-translated to English and examined by researchers to ensure equivalence.

3.3 Data Collection

To combat the limitations of traditional survey methods, such as less representative sampling [19], we conducted both versions of the survey using online platforms. The English version was built on Qualtrics.com, and published on Amazon Mechanical Turk for workers to access. The Chinese version ran on a similar platform, Wjx.cn, which provides both online questionnaires and sampling services in China. Each participant was paid $1 to finish the 15-minute survey.

3.4 Participants

To ensure that the participants from online platforms were from two target countries, we filtered the submissions by their IP address. After filtering, we were left with 481 samples from the MTurk

American participants and 648 samples from the Wjx Chinese participants. After removing data of participants that did not finish the survey, or those who blindly clicked and had an extremely short finishing time, and those who answered the attention check question incorrectly, we were left with 301 (American) and 435 (Chinese) valid submissions. In the sampling population of the American survey, the average age was 40.6 (SD = 11.6) and the gender ratio was about balanced (49.28% male, 50.71% female). In the Chinese version of the survey, the average age and gender ratio of the sampling population was 30.9 (SD = 7.9) and 36.47% : 63.53% (male:female).

4 RESULTS

The survey results consisted of ratings of 39 options from 15 scenarios, and was influenced by both the individual differences of participants (e.g. age and cultural background) and the contextual variables of the scenarios (e.g. locations, characteristics, and consequences). Because participants gave independent ratings to each option based on their preferences, the given responses to the scenarios may or may not be mutually exclusive. Thus, when analyzing the data, the first-fold comparison is between options which explicitly reveal participants' preferences with respect to the conflicting norms. The second-fold comparison is a between-subject comparison of factors, including cultures, contexts, and their interaction effects. Repeated measures ANOVAs were used to statistically evaluate the two-fold comparisons mentioned above, since norm ratings are measured within-subject while culture and context are between subject variables. When it comes to the pairwise comparison on a certain level of variable, one-way ANOVAs were employed. For variables with more than two levels, post-hoc tests using LSD method were reported. Due to the page limitation, the following results section only provides a preliminary analysis on the most informative findings for 6 out of the 15 scenarios. Descriptions of scenarios and options have been condensed.

4.1 Encountering Human in Hallway

Imagine your domestic robot is taught the concept of moving on the right side of the hallway. What should the robot do when it is moving down the hallway on the right side, while an (elderly/disabled) person is walking towards it on the same side?

- Stay to the right-hand side of the hallway to **obey social rules**.
- Move out of the way to the left-hand side of the hallway to maintain the **safety** of the human.
- Move out of the way to the left-hand side of the hallway to **accommodate** the human's behavior.

Generally, participants from both countries, as shown in Fig. 1, preferred the robot to give way to the person who is breaking the rule of walking to his/her right side of the hallway ($F(2, 1468) = 487.94, p < .001, \eta_p^2 = 40.0\%$, post-hoc test $ps < .001$). However, we found a significant cultural difference in this scenario: CN participants agreed more (3.34 ± 1.62) on the "stay on right-hand side" option compared with US samples (2.65 ± 1.65, $F(1, 734) = 31.51, p < .001, \eta_p^2 = 4.1\%$). US participants agreed more on the "move out of the way to accommodate human" option (US: 5.61 ± 1.54 CN: 4.64 ± 1.52, $F(1, 734) = 70.87, p < .001, \eta_p^2 = 8.8\%$). These findings reveal that, although safety is the major concern in this scenario, Chinese participants would prefer the robot to obey social rules, while American participants would prefer the robot to accommodate the person even if the person is violating a social norm. Additionally, participants from both countries rated the "stay on right-hand side" option lower when the person at fault was elderly or physically disabled compared to a healthy adult ($F(2, 733) = 29.397, p < .001, \eta_p^2 = 7.4\%$, post-hoc test $ps < .001$).

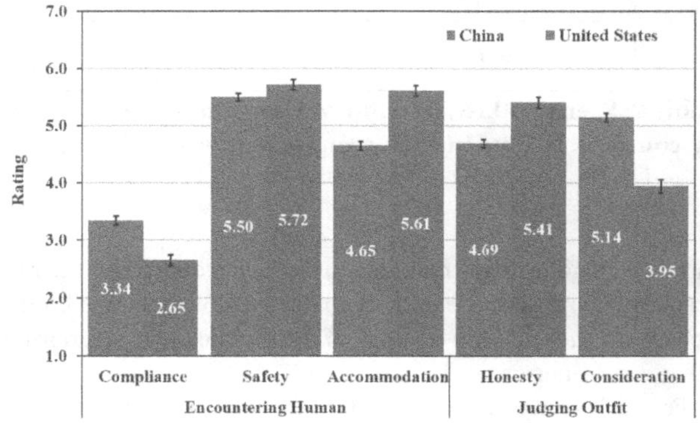

Figure 1: Ratings of the *encountering human* and *judging outfit* scenarios, error bars represent one standard error from the mean.

4.2 Judging outfit

What should the robot do when it is asked to judge your/your friend's outfit choice?

- Make the judgment **honestly**.
- **Consider** the person's feelings by making the remark tactfully.

For the judging outfit scenario, the robot faced a dilemma between being honest or considering people's feelings. US samples preferred the robot to make an honest judgment (US: 5.40 ± 1.60 CN: 4.69 ± 1.53, $F(1, 734) = 36.83, p < .001, \eta_p^2 = 4.8\%$), while CN samples believed it was more appropriate to consider peopleâĂŹs feelings by making the remark tactfully (US: 3.94 ± 2.00 CN: 5.14 ± 1.57, $F(1, 734) = 81.94, p < .001, \eta_p^2 = 10.0\%$). The two populations also showed different attitudes towards the contextual variable *relationship between people* (significant interaction effect of culture * relationship, $F(2, 730) = 8.83, p < .001, \eta_p^2 = 2.4\%$). When the person whose outfit was being judged had a closer relationship with the owner, Chinese participants believed the robot should more strongly consider the person's feelings (owner: 5.40 ± 1.43 friend: 5.63 ± 1.38 stranger: 4.47 ± 1.64, $F(2, 432) = 25.13, p < .001, \eta_p^2 = 10.4\%$) rather than directly tell the truth (owner: 4.16 ± 1.51 friend: 4.20 ± 1.52 stranger: 5.61 ± 1.08, $F(2, 432) = 53.77, p < .001, \eta_p^2 = 20.0\%$, post-hoc tests only show significant differences between stranger and other two relationships, $p < .001$). The people's relationship had no significant influence for US samples.

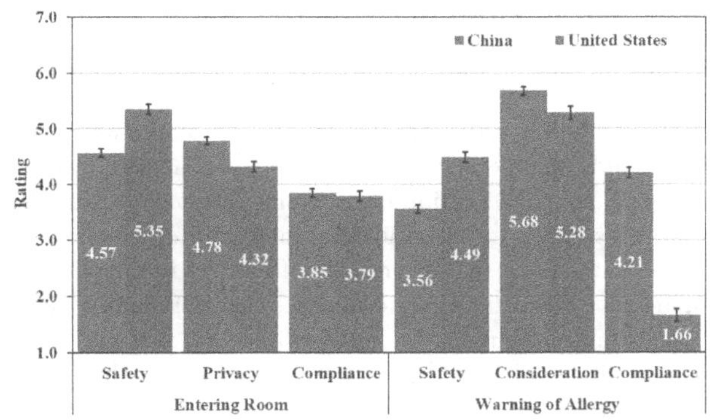

Figure 2: Ratings of the *entering room* and *warning of allergy* scenarios.

4.3 Entering Room

What should the robot do when an emergency (pipe burst/fire) arises while you are in the bathroom?

- Barge in to save me to protect my **safety**.
- Knock on the door before entering to protect my **privacy**.

In the entering bathroom scenario, US participants agreed more (5.35 ± 1.86) on the "directly enter" option than CN participants (4.56 ± 1.96, $F(1, 734) = 29.81, p < .001, \eta_p^2 = 3.9\%$). Chinese participants more highly rated the "knock on door" option than American ones (US: 4.32 ± 2.00 CN: 4.79 ± 1.77, $F(1, 734) = 11.26, p = .001, \eta_p^2 = 1.5\%$). The results show different preferences among options between CN and US: the US samples preferred the robot to barge in the room rather than knock on the door, while CN samples preferred it to knock on the door instead of directly entering - even in an emergency situation. These findings can be explained in two ways: people perceive different degrees of privacy invasion for the same behavior of the robot, or that people hold different ideas about whether the robot should obey social rules like knocking on the door. The extremity of the emergency also significantly influenced participants' answers: people preferred the robot to directly enter the room in a severely dangerous situation, like a house fire, than in a less severe situation, like a pipe bursting ($F(1, 728) = 83.396, p < .001, \eta_p^2 = 10.3\%$).

4.4 Warning of Allergy

In this scenario (see section 3.1 for detailed description), although both cultures agreed the most appropriate option was for the robot to only inform the owner ($F(2, 1468) = 336.45, p < .001, \eta_p^2 = 31.4\%$, post-hoc tests $ps < .001$), the two populations differed in their opinions on the remaining two choices (shown as Fig.2). Chinese participants preferred the "take no action" option more (US: 1.66 ± 0.98 CN: 4.21 ± 1.87, $F(1, 734) = 469.52, p < .001, \eta_p^2 = 39.0\%$), whereas American participants preferred the interrupt option more (US: 4.49 ± 2.03 CN: 3.56 ± 1.75, $F(1, 734) = 44.08, p < .001, \eta_p^2 = 5.7\%$). The dramatic variance in the "take no action" option could be attributed to the different social attitudes to allergy between the two countries: food allergies are less common and not treated as seriously in Asian countries as in western ones [13]. This cultural difference shows that scenarios can be interpreted differently depending on the cultural lens from which they are viewed and attests to the importance of cultural compatibility when designing social robots.

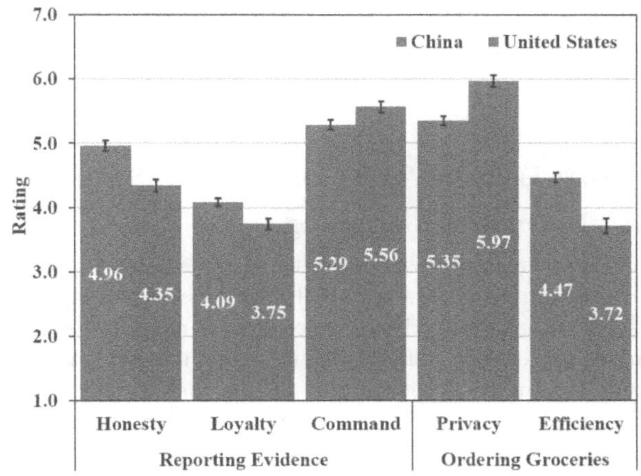

Figure 3: Ratings of the *reporting evidence* and *ordering groceries* scenarios.

4.5 Reporting Evidence

Suppose your domestic robot witnesses an accident for which you may (not) be responsible. Should it provide evidence of this accident to a third party who is investigating the incident?

- Yes, it should always tell the truth (**honesty**).
- Only if the evidence is in favor of you, the owner (**loyalty**).
- Only if instructed by you to do so (**command**).

In this scenario, we examined a dilemma between loyalty and honesty. Generally, participants preferred the robot to "obey owner's command" (5.40 ± 1.64) more than "always tell the truth" (4.71 ± 1.80) or "only provide the evidence when it is in favor of the owner" (3.95 ± 1.79), as shown in Fig.3 ($F(2, 1468) = 114.83, p < .001, \eta_p^2 = 13.5\%$, post-hoc tests $ps < .001$). Notably, US participants rated "robot should always tell the truth" higher when the owner was not responsible for the accident (responsible: 3.99 ± 2.08 not responsible: 4.70 ± 1.93, $F(1, 299) = 9.49, p = .002, \eta_p^2 = 3.1\%$).

4.6 Ordering groceries

What should the robot do when it is tasked with ordering groceries online, but it is not provided with enough information, such as your preferred payment method?

- Ask for the information to protect **data security**.
- Retrieve the information from the purchase history to finish the task **efficiently**.

Although both populations preferred the robot to ask instead of looking up the information by itself ($F(1, 734) = 276.00, p < .001, \eta_p^2 = 27.3\%$), Chinese participants held a relatively more open attitude in the resulting normative conflict between privacy and efficiency. CN samples rated the option "ask owner" significantly lower than US samples (US: 5.97 ± 1.14 CN: 5.35 ± 1.38, $F(1,734) = 40.59, p < .001, \eta_p^2 = 5.2\%$). The alternative "retrieve information" option, was rated significantly higher by the CN samples than the US samples (US: 3.72 ± 1.98 CN: 4.47 ± 1.79, $F(1,734) = 28.55, p < .001, \eta_p^2 = 3.7\%$).

5 DISCUSSION AND CONCLUSIONS

5.1 Normative Reasoning

There is a complicated relationship between environmental context, relevant norms, and the actions that a domestic robot is expected to take. In any given situation, there could exist multiple norms with varying degrees of conflicts with one another that a robot ought to obey - even in the restricted setting of the domestic environment. The activation and priority of some norms is highly sensitive to contextual factors, such as the perceived danger in a situation. As we found in our results, people valued the norms corresponding to safety and privacy to the same degree for the entering room scenario; however, their preferences shifted depending on the level of danger in the scenario. On the other hand, for other scenarios, like encountering a person on the wrong side of the hallway, the "move out of the way" option dominated the "obey social rules" option, showing a significant priority of one norm in this specific situation regardless of context. To capture the complicated relationship between contexts, norms, and actions, a formal representation of the environment and a comprehensive norm network is necessary.

Our survey of people's preferences regarding the normative behavior of domestic robots provides an initial step of achieving the goal of constructing a comprehensive normative reasoning framework. By constructing dilemmas between pairwise norms, we measured both the norm priorities and the severity of the conflict between norms. This method simplifies the problem by assuming that only two or three norms are activated in the given situation, and each option corresponds to one norm. Our results are preliminary and additional future work is needed to capture the complex interplay of norms and contextual variables.

Our results also show the importance of equipping domestic robots with a normative reasoning component, instead of pre-programming compliance to norms that robot designers think may be appropriate. As our results show, contextual variables significantly influenced participants' ratings of preferences in most scenarios. This finding indicates that users expect the robot to be aware of the social and physical environment and behave accordingly, such as disregarding privacy to save the owner when the house is on fire or telling "white lies" to its owner's friends so as to not hurt their feelings. Although programming pre-defined norm compliance for all these situations could fulfill such expectations, it requires huge computational resources due to the size of norm set and contextual variables. In contrast, a normative reasoning model could enable consideration of only a subset of norms at a time based on the current context, significantly reducing the computational cost [12]. The data from human participants presents a solid base for designing and building future computational models.

5.2 Culture Dimensions and Characteristics

An important challenge of designing social robots with normative reasoning capabilities is acculturating them to the target culture in which they will be deployed [24, 28]. People with diverse backgrounds may perceive the same action of a robot as compliance/obedience or violation of different norms. For example, in the warning of allergy scenario, the ratings of the "take no action" option varies across cultures due to differences in the perception of danger between the US and China. Thus, conducting surveys to understand ordinary users' perceptions and attitudes provide crucial design guidelines for norm-aware domestic robots.

Other important components of the design guidelines are the appropriate strength of social norms and the corresponding sanctions of norm violations. Prior work features cultures as tight (e.g. East Asian countries) or loose (e.g. Western countries) based on the strength of social norms and sanctioning of deviant behaviors [6]. This representation aligns with our results: Chinese participants prefer the robot to comply with social conventions when entering the bathroom or walking in the hallway. Thus, when designing a norm-compliant computational normative model for a robot that would be deployed to Chinese users, the strength of social norms and corresponding sanctions for norm violations in these cases should be higher than for a robot designed for American users.

Cultural syndromes [27] categorize cultures into *face, dignity, honor.* China is a face culture where the value of an individual is confirmed by other community members. The US is a dignity culture where people value independence and individual goals. This differential valuation of individual values vs relationships that is a characteristic of dignity vs face cultures, has also been considered earlier in the cultural dimensions of individualist (US) vs collectivist cultures (China) by [8]. Our results showed this cultural difference in that Chinese participants preferred robots to consider people's feelings. These results suggest that cultural syndromes and dimensions influence the priority and strength of norms, and should be incorporated into design guidelines for domestic robots.

We also found cultural differences in people's views and expected social roles of domestic robots. In general, Chinese consider the robots as more autonomous with more flexibility to make decisions, whereas US participants tend to treat the robot as a machine that should obey pre-defined rules and its owner's command. For example, US subjects gave higher ratings on options like "ask owners' command", "always tell the truth", and "accommodate human's behaviors".

5.3 Future Work

In this paper, we reported preliminary results from the first survey of its kind on scenario-specific and context-specific norms, and relative norm priorities by performing surveys in two different cultures. In future work, we plan to perform additional analysis of our data and refine our questionnaire to consider additional norms and moral dilemmas. We will also survey additional cultures, such as the Honor culture that represents populations in the Middle East.

ACKNOWLEDGMENTS

This research was supported by awards W911NF-13-1-0416 and FA9550-15-1-0442.

REFERENCES

[1] Thomas Arnold and Matthias Scheutz. 2017. Beyond moral dilemmas: Exploring the ethical landscape in HRI. In *Proceedings of the 2017 ACM/IEEE International Conference on Human-Robot Interaction*. ACM, 445–452.

[2] Jean-François Bonnefon, Azim Shariff, and Iyad Rahwan. 2016. The social dilemma of autonomous vehicles. *Science* 352, 6293 (2016), 1573–1576.

[3] Geoffrey Brennan, Lina Eriksson, Robert E Goodin, and Nicholas Southwood. 2013. *Explaining norms*. Oxford University Press.

[4] Vincent Conitzer, Walter Sinnott-Armstrong, Jana Scaich Borg, Yuan Deng, and Max Kramer. 2017. Moral Decision Making Frameworks for Artificial Intelligence. In *Proceedings of the 31st AAAI Conference on Artificial Intelligence (AAAI)*.

[5] Maartje MA de Graaf, Somaya Ben Allouch, and Jan AGM van Dijk. 2017. Why Would I Use This in My Home? A Model of Domestic Social Robot Acceptance. *Human–Computer Interaction* (2017), 1–59.

[6] Michele J Gelfand, Jana L Raver, Lisa Nishii, Lisa M Leslie, Janetta Lun, Beng Chong Lim, Lili Duan, Assaf Almaliach, Soon Ang, Jakobina Arnadottir, et al. 2011. Differences between tight and loose cultures: A 33-nation study. *science* 332, 6033 (2011), 1100–1104.

[7] Kerstin S Haring, David Silvera-Tawil, Tomotaka Takahashi, Mari Velonaki, and Katsumi Watanabe. 2015. Perception of a humanoid robot: a cross-cultural comparison. In *Robot and Human Interactive Communication (RO-MAN), 2015 24th IEEE International Symposium on*. IEEE, 821–826.

[8] Geert Hofstede. 2001. *Culture's consequences: Comparing values, behaviors, institutions and organizations across nations*. Sage publications.

[9] Peter H Kahn Jr, Takayuki Kanda, Hiroshi Ishiguro, Brian T Gill, Jolina H Ruckert, Solace Shen, Heather E Gary, Aimee L Reichert, Nathan G Freier, and Rachel L Severson. 2012. Do people hold a humanoid robot morally accountable for the harm it causes?. In *Proceedings of the seventh annual ACM/IEEE international conference on Human-Robot Interaction*. ACM, 33–40.

[10] Shinobu Kitayama, Batja Mesquita, and Mayumi Karasawa. 2006. Cultural affordances and emotional experience: socially engaging and disengaging emotions in Japan and the United States. *Journal of personality and social psychology* 91, 5 (2006), 890.

[11] Kheng Lee Koay, Dag Sverre Syrdal, Mohammadreza Ashgari-Oskoei, Michael L Walters, and Kerstin Dautenhahn. 2014. Social roles and baseline proxemic preferences for a domestic service robot. *International Journal of Social Robotics* 6, 4 (2014), 469–488.

[12] Vigneshram Krishnamoorthy, Wenhao Luo, Michael Lewis, and Katia Sycara. 2018. A Computational Framework for Integrating Task Planning and Norm Aware Reasoning for Social Robots. In *INternational Conference of Robot and Human Interactive Communication (RO-MAN)*. IEEE.

[13] Bee Wah Lee, Lynette Pei-Chi Shek, Irvin Francis A Gerez, Shu E Soh, and Hugo P Van Bever. 2008. Food Allergy–Lessons from Asia. *World Allergy Organization Journal* 1, 7 (2008), 129.

[14] Hee Rin Lee, JaYoung Sung, Selma Šabanović, and Joenghye Han. 2012. Cultural design of domestic robots: A study of user expectations in Korea and the United States. In *2012 IEEE RO-MAN: The 21st IEEE International Symposium on Robot and Human Interactive Communication*. IEEE, 803–808.

[15] Angela K-Y Leung and Dov Cohen. 2011. Within-and between-culture variation: individual differences and the cultural logics of honor, face, and dignity cultures. *Journal of personality and social psychology* 100, 3 (2011), 507.

[16] Dingjun Li, PL Patrick Rau, and Ye Li. 2010. A cross-cultural study: Effect of robot appearance and task. *International Journal of Social Robotics* 2, 2 (2010), 175–186.

[17] Bertram F Malle, Matthias Scheutz, and Joseph L Austerweil. 2017. Networks of social and moral norms in human and robot agents. In *A world with robots*. Springer, 3–17.

[18] Bertram F Malle, Matthias Scheutz, Jodi Forlizzi, and John Voiklis. 2016. Which robot am I thinking about?: The impact of action and appearance on people's evaluations of a moral robot. In *The Eleventh ACM/IEEE International Conference on Human Robot Interaction*. IEEE Press, 125–132.

[19] Winter Mason and Siddharth Suri. 2012. Conducting behavioral research on AmazonâĂŹs Mechanical Turk. *Behavior research methods* 44, 1 (2012), 1–23.

[20] James H Moor. 2006. The nature, importance, and difficulty of machine ethics. *IEEE intelligent systems* 21, 4 (2006), 18–21.

[21] Tatsuya T Nomura, Dag Sverre Syrdal, and Kerstin Dautenhahn. 2015. Differences on social acceptance of humanoid robots between Japan and the UK. In *Procs 4th Int Symposium on New Frontiers in Human-Robot Interaction*. The Society for the Study of Artificial Intelligence and the Simulation of Behaviour (AISB).

[22] Maribel Pino, Mélodie Boulay, François Jouen, and Anne Sophie Rigaud. 2015. âĂIJAre we ready for robots that care for us?âĂİ Attitudes and opinions of older adults toward socially assistive robots. *Frontiers in aging neuroscience* 7 (2015), 141.

[23] Maha Salem, Gabriella Lakatos, Farshid Amirabdollahian, and Kerstin Dautenhahn. 2015. Would you trust a (faulty) robot?: Effects of error, task type and personality on human-robot cooperation and trust. In *Proceedings of ACM/IEEE International Conference on Human-Robot Interaction*. ACM, 141–148.

[24] Maha Salem, Micheline Ziadee, and Majd Sakr. 2014. Marhaba, how may i help you?: effects of politeness and culture on robot acceptance and anthropomorphization. In *Proceedings of the 2014 ACM/IEEE international conference on Human-robot interaction*. ACM, 74–81.

[25] Massimiliano Scopelliti, Maria Vittoria Giuliani, and Ferdinando Fornara. 2005. Robots in a domestic setting: a psychological approach. *Universal access in the information society* 4, 2 (2005), 146–155.

[26] Cory-Ann Smarr, Tracy L Mitzner, Jenay M Beer, Akanksha Prakash, Tiffany L Chen, Charles C Kemp, and Wendy A Rogers. 2014. Domestic robots for older adults: attitudes, preferences, and potential. *International journal of social robotics* 6, 2 (2014), 229–247.

[27] Harry C Triandis. 1996. The psychological measurement of cultural syndromes. *American psychologist* 51, 4 (1996), 407.

[28] Lin Wang, Pei-Luen Patrick Rau, Vanessa Evers, Benjamin Krisper Robinson, and Pamela Hinds. 2010. When in Rome: the role of culture & context in adherence to robot recommendations. In *Proceedings of the 5th ACM/IEEE international conference on Human-robot interaction*. IEEE Press, 359–366.

[29] James E Young, Richard Hawkins, Ehud Sharlin, and Takeo Igarashi. 2009. Toward acceptable domestic robots: Applying insights from social psychology. *International Journal of Social Robotics* 1, 1 (2009), 95.

Mapping Missing Population in Rural India: A Deep Learning Approach with Satellite Imagery

Wenjie Hu
Stanford University
huwenjie@alumni.stanford.edu

Jay Harshadbhai Patel
Stanford University
jayhp9@alumni.stanford.edu

Zoe-Alanah Robert
Stanford University
zrobert7@alumni.stanford.edu

Paul Novosad
Dartmouth College
paul.novosad@dartmouth.edu

Samuel Asher
World Bank
sasher@worldbank.org

Zhongyi Tang
Stanford University
zztang@stanford.edu

Marshall Burke
Stanford University
mburke@stanford.edu

David Lobell
Stanford University
dlobell@stanford.edu

Stefano Ermon
Stanford University
ermon@cs.stanford.edu

ABSTRACT

Millions of people worldwide are absent from their country's census. Accurate, current, and granular population metrics are critical to improving government allocation of resources, to measuring disease control, to responding to natural disasters, and to studying any aspect of human life in these communities. Satellite imagery can provide sufficient information to build a population map without the cost and time of a government census. We present two Convolutional Neural Network (CNN) architectures which efficiently and effectively combine satellite imagery inputs from multiple sources to accurately predict the population density of a region. In this paper, we use satellite imagery from rural villages in India and population labels from the 2011 SECC census. Our best model achieves better performance than previous papers as well as LandScan, a community standard for global population distribution.

CCS CONCEPTS

• **Computing methodologies** → **Computer vision**; **Neural networks**; *Supervised learning by regression*; • **Applied computing** → **Aerospace**; **Sociology**.

KEYWORDS

deep learning, convolutional neural network, computer vision, satellite imagery, census, population

ACM Reference Format:

Wenjie Hu, Jay Harshadbhai Patel, Zoe-Alanah Robert, Paul Novosad, Samuel Asher, Zhongyi Tang, Marshall Burke, David Lobell, and Stefano Ermon. 2019. Mapping Missing Population in Rural India: A Deep Learning Approach with Satellite Imagery. In *AAAI/ACM Conference on AI, Ethics, and Society (AIES '19), January 27–28, 2019, Honolulu, HI, USA.* ACM, New York, NY, USA, 7 pages. https://doi.org/10.1145/3306618.3314263

AIES '19, January 27–28, 2019, Honolulu, HI, USA

ACM ISBN 978-1-4503-6324-2/19/01...$15.00
https://doi.org/10.1145/3306618.3314263

1 INTRODUCTION

In 2015, the United Nations set forth seventeen objectives to "end poverty, protect the planet and ensure prosperity for all" known as the Sustainable Development Goals (SGD) [18]. To monitor progress and ultimately achieve these objectives, accurate population statistics are essential. It is estimated that currently 300-350 million people worldwide are not included in their country's official population document, which hurts the measurement of SGD progress [1]. The ability to quickly and cost-effectively produce an accurate population map for a country has a multitude of benefits. Those missing populations are more likely to be marginalized communities which already do not receive sufficient resources from the government [21]. An accurate population distribution is an essential basis for socioeconomic statistics, such as food, water, and energy demand in different regions of a country, which influence the policy-making and spending decisions of its government. Additionally, during natural disasters such as earthquakes and floods, an accurate population map can help organize rescue efforts more quickly and effectively. For regions with high infectious disease rates, a fine-grained population map also helps to prevent the spread of infectious diseases to locations with dense population [6, 15].

However, creating a population map with high accuracy and high resolution is a challenging problem. Traditionally, it is done by performing a high-cost national census. The USAID Demographic and Health Survey (DHS) program performs surveys for developing countries typically every 5 years, and each survey costs anywhere from 1.1 million to 9.7 million USD [3]. The census surveys are even more expensive in developed countries like Europe, with a median cost of USD 5.57 per capita in 2010 [17]. For some countries with financial difficulties or political instability, the census is carried out less frequently, as few as once every few decades [19, 20]. Reliance on out-of-date population statistics can lead to significant errors if used for policy making or resource allocation.

In this project, we aim to predict the population density of rural villages of India from high-resolution satellite imagery by utilizing Convolutional Neural Network (CNN) models. With the availability of high-frequency satellite images, we can predict population density every few days, saving the costs of on-site census surveys and avoiding the inaccuracies caused by the infrequency of census surveys. We demonstrate state-of-the-art prediction performance in villages of all states in India. By using satellite images with 10-30 meter resolution, our best models can predict aggregated village population in one Subdistrict (akin to a US county) with R^2 of 0.93, and individual village $\log_2$ population density with R^2 of 0.44.

2 RELATED WORK

2.1 Traditional Methods

Traditionally, population mapping is divided into two approaches, population projection and population disaggregation. Population projection predicts the future or current population of a region based on historical data. For most cases, simple linear regression is sufficient for the projection [13]. In more complex models, projections take into consideration historic population data, birth rates, registered vehicles, etc [9]. These models were used to project US county population in 5 years, which have very high accuracy with R^2 of 0.99. However, they don't provide information about the population distribution within each county.

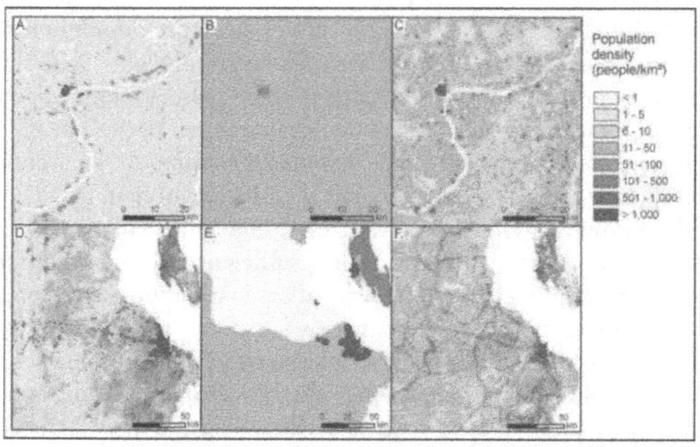

Figure 1: Population disaggregation visualization for WorldPop(A,D), GRUMP (B,E), LandScan (C,F). The upper 3 figures show a northeast region of Guinea along the Niger River; the lower 3 figures show the region around the largest city of Tanzania, Dar es Salaam. Figure from WorldPop (https://www.worldpop.org/)[24].

The more challenging task is population disaggregation, which involves estimating the population distribution of a region given the total population. The most basic method is areal weighting/ interpolation, which assumes a uniform distribution across the region with a single population value [5]. The Gridded Population of the World (GPW) uses areal weighting with a resolution of 30 arc-seconds (approximately 1 km at the equator) [2]. There are also many tools which implement a weighted surface for estimating a population's distribution, a technique called dasymetric weighting [8]. The Global Rural Urban Mapping Project (GRUMP) uses nightlight imagery to add urban and rural boundaries to GPW [10]. LandScan estimates the weighted surface (with 30 arc-seconds resolution) for population distribution based on land cover, roads, slope, urban areas, village locations [7]. AfriPop, AsiaPop, and AmeriPop are similar but for region-specific population disaggregation calculations, and they are combined in the 2013 WorldPop project [23], which has a higher resolution of 100 meters. These disaggregation methods are compared visually in Figure 1.

2.2 Machine Learning Methods

In addition to the above traditional GIS approach, machine learning algorithms have been proposed in recent years to obtain better population disaggregation results. A random forest approach was used to estimate the population at 100m resolution for Vietnam, Cambodia, and Kenya, using features similar to LandScan [14]. The Facebook Connectivity Lab used a tailored CNN model to detect man-made structures from satellite imagery with 0.5m resolution, which achieved average precision of 0.95 and recall of 0.91. They then redistributed the population in GPW evenly to the areas covered by human-made structures, and create population maps with ~30 meter resolution for 18 countries, not including India [16].

Instead of disaggregation based on population estimates from census surveys, some CNN models are trained to estimate population directly from satellite imagery inputs. Doupe et al. combined Landsat-7 satellite imagery with (DMSP/OLS) nighttime lights as CNN input, and predicted the log normalized population density for an area of 8km^2 (called **LL-raw**), where the ground-truth label was average population density of Sublocation (akin to a US county). The outputs were then converted into weights and used to create a weighted population density surface across the country with a single known total population (**LL-distributed**). The model was trained with 2002 Tanzanian Enumeration Areas and tested with 2009 Kenya Sublocations. During the test phase, the estimated population densities were averaged at the Sublocation level, and then compared to other methods. The results show that **LL-raw** has better accuracy than GRUMP and GWP estimates, and that **LL-distributed** outperforms a random forest model by 177% on RMSE [3].

Robinson et al. in 2017 adopted a similar CNN approach to Doupe et al., but changed the model output from regression to classification of the power level of population. The model only uses Landsat imagery as input, and predicts population in the US with US Census Summary Grids data as ground-truth labels. The study divided the country into 15 regions, and trained an individual model for each region. The raw output feature vectors of the CNN model were first converted into population values for each input image, and then summed at the county level to produce **CONVRAW**. The outputs of the CNN were also fed into a second layer gradient boosting model to get an improved population estimate for each county called **CONVAUG**, where the census county population was used as labels. The results of CNN models achieved more than 0.9 R^2 against the ground truth, but still cannot perform better than the US government estimate based on historical census data [8].

3 DATA

3.1 Population Dataset

Our ground-truth Indian population dataset comes from a census survey Socio-Economic Caste Census in the year 2011 [11]. It includes more than 500,000 rural villages, covering 32 states, 619 districts, and 5724 sub-districts. It also provides the area of each surveyed village. Figure 2 shows the distribution of areas follows a power law. These areas are used to calculate population density for each village. Similar to previous papers, we log normalize population density values with base 2, because most villages have small population density, and only a few have large density. The original density input may cause the model to have less ability to predict villages with higher population density. The distribution of villages density after $\log_2$ normalization is shown in Figure 3.

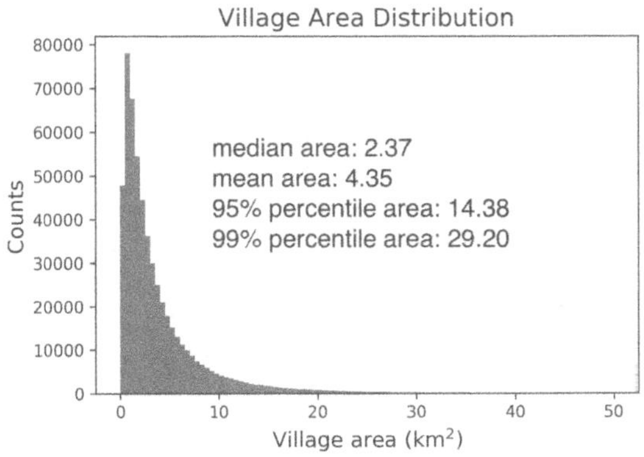

Figure 2: Village area distribution.

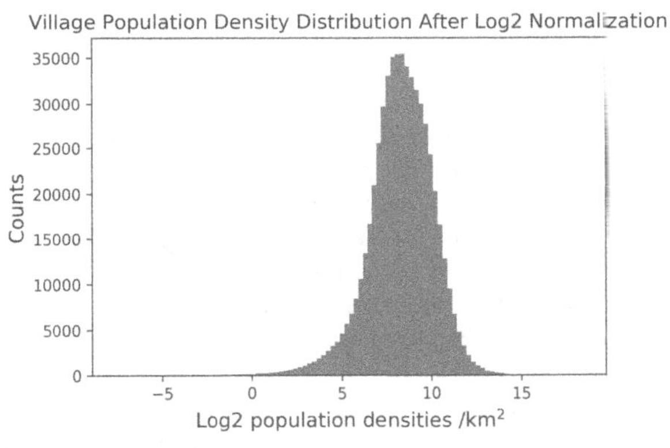

Figure 3: Village population density distribution after $\log_2$ normalization.

Inspecting the population datasets we observed some outlier values, such as a 100 km^2 area with just one person. We assume these are due to data collection and handling mistakes, therefore we remove 1% of village data that had extreme population density values to prevent the model training from being affected by those outliers. More specifically, villages with top 0.5% highest density and bottom 0.5% lowest density were removed from the datasets.

3.2 Satellite Imagery

For each village, we prepare one image from each satellite imagery source such that the village center is found at the image center. The village population depends on its area but our images have fixed size covering the same area, therefore we use population density as the output. We obtained 2 sets of satellite imagery from 2011, the same year the survey was conducted. The first set is from Landsat-8, an updated satellite from Landsat-7 whose images are also used by papers from Robinson et al. in 2017 and Doupe et al. in 2016 [22]. In contrast with previous papers which use most bands of Landsat, we use only Red, Green, and Blue (RGB) bands. The resulting images show the target regions in the same colors that humans see, and have 30-meter resolution. The second set is from Sentinel-1, a radar imaging satellite that measures ground surface reflectance, thereby capturing roads and roofs more accurately (due to their higher reflectance than natural land) [4]. This is a new dataset not used in the previously mentioned papers. Sentinel-1 images have 10-meter resolution, and the raw channel values are converted to visualized RGB images to match Landsat-8. Both sets of images are converted to JPEG format from raw GeoTIFF files, which enables easy visualization and compression. Figure 4 displays examples of these images.

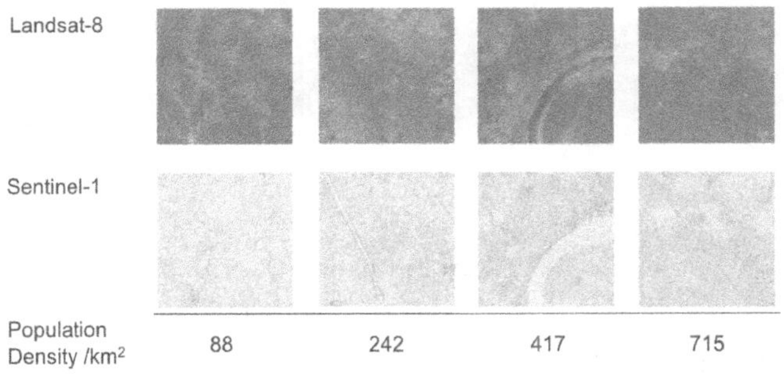

Figure 4: Landsat-8 and Sentinel-1 imagery examples, with corresponding ground truth population density from the survey.

Since Landsat-8 and Sentinel-1 have different spatial resolutions, they are cropped to cover the same area. Based on the village area distribution as shown in Figure 2, the covered area of images is determined to be 20.25 km^2 (4.5km × 4.5km), so that more than 95% of villages are contained within a single satellite image.

3.3 Dataset Partition

We split the dataset of ground-truth population (outputs) and images (inputs) pairs into 70% training and 30% validation partitions. We took additional measures to avoid the overlap of training images with validation images, which may affect the reliability of the validation split. Overlaps are very likely because the total area of all satellite images (over 10 million km^2) we obtained is much larger than the total area of India (about 3.3 million km^2). To address this issue, we partition the data at the subdistrict level. We split all subdistricts into 4007 training and 1717 validation subdistricts. The training partition only has images of villages that belong to training subdistricts, and similarly for the validation partition. However, it is still possible that images overlap along the boundary of two adjacent subdistricts, contaminating the split. Thus, we remove additional images from the training partition. We say a pair of images

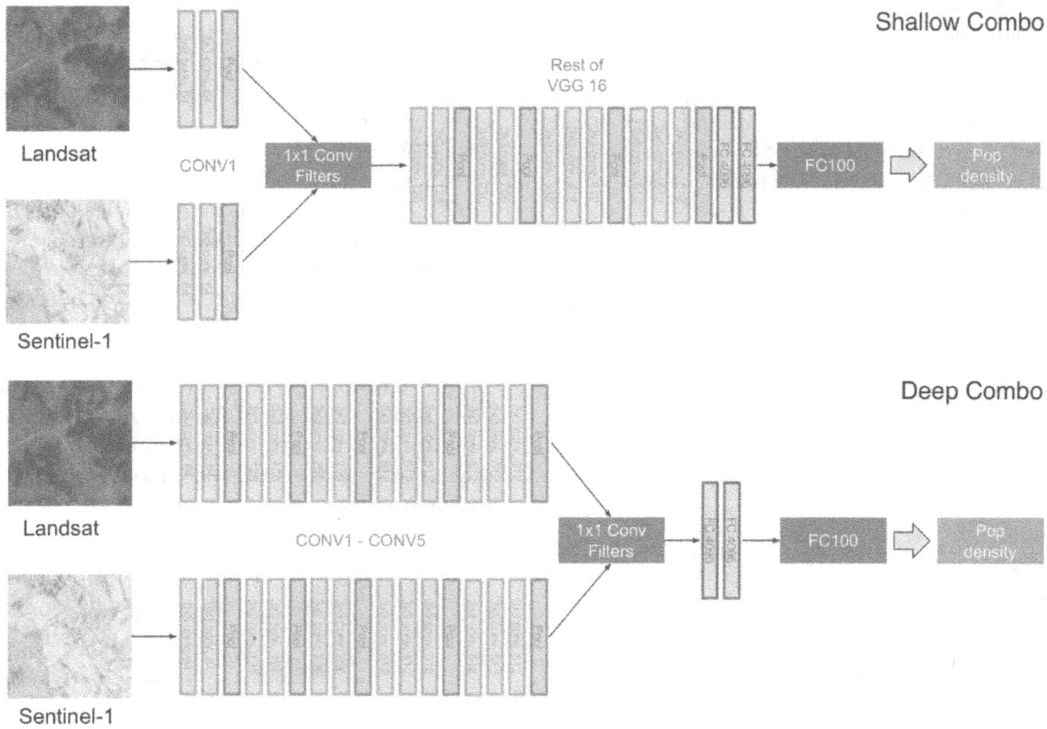

Figure 5: Custom CNN architecture Shallow Combo (upper) and Deep Combo (lower)

overlap if the distance between their centers is closer than half of the height or width of the image (2.25km). Approximately an additional 5% overlapping images are removed from the training partition.

4 METHOD

We propose a deep learning approach that uses satellite images as inputs to a Convolutional Neural Network (CNN) to predict population density. The ground-truth population data is used as the label to train the model. We start with the VGG16 architecture [12], using as input either Landsat-8 or Sentinel-1 RGB images. We use the implementation of VGG 16 from the TensorFlow Slim Library. To adapt the model for a regression problem, the model output size is set to be 1 for a single $\log_2$ population value. Additionally, the loss function in the model is changed to Mean Squared Error (MSE). Image inputs are resized to $224\times224\times3$ (width $\times$ height $\times$ channels), and we apply image augmentation including random cropping and flipping during training. The model weights are initialized with pre-trained weights from the ILSVRC-2010-CLS ImageNet classification dataset, omitting the last (classification) layer.

To fully utilize multiple satellite image sources in this study, we design two custom CNN architectures. The first custom architecture, called **Shallow Combo**, is shown in Figure 5. It is a modified version of VGG16 where Landsat-8 and Sentinel-1 images are input into the model separately as two branches. In each branch, two convolution layers and one max pooling layer (CONV1 in VGG16) are applied to each image. The two branches are then concatenated along the channel dimension. 1×1 convolutions filters are applied to halve the number of channels after concatenation, which fits the input shape of next convolutional layer. The rest of the VGG16 layers are applied to the merged branch. After the last fully connected layer of VGG16, one more fully connected layer of size 100 is added to the network. The layer is lastly used to predict the output $\log_2$ population density. During training, weights of all convolutional layers and the first two fully connected layers are initialized with pre-trained weights from the basic VGG16 architecture trained on ImageNet.

The second custom CNN called **Deep Combo** is an improved version of Shallow Combo, also shown in Figure 5. The branches of Landsat-8 and Sentinel-1 are fed through all convolutional layers of VGG16, and concatenated along the channel dimension before the first fully connected layer. The same 1×1 convolutions filters are applied to obtain the same input shape before the fully connected layer. ImageNet weights are also used for initialization until the second fully connected layer.

5 EXPERIMENTAL RESULTS

5.1 Evaluation Methods

We evaluate each model on the validation set on two levels: raw village level and aggregated subdistrict level. The raw village level predictions are per-village $\log_2$ population density estimates from the model, which are compared with the ground-truth census population density of each village. This raw evaluation represents the most fine-grained comparison possible in our dataset. At the aggregated subdistrict level, the raw per-village density predictions are converted to the total village population using the village area from the survey. The village populations within each subdistrict are aggregated to a total population for that subdistrict. Evaluations at the aggregate levels are performed in previous papers, which we are going to compare with. In short, the village level evaluation uses $\log_2$ population density values, while subdistrict level evaluation uses real population numbers.

In terms of evaluation metrics, we compare different models mainly based on R^2 and Pearson Correlation. R^2 measures how much true variance is captured by the model, and attains a perfect value at 1. If a model makes constant average predictions, it will have R^2 score of 0. Pearson Correlation measures the linear correlation between the predicted and true values, implying a total positive correlation when +1 and a total negative correlation when -1. We also use other metrics to compare results with previous papers, such as MAPE (Mean Absolute Percentage Error), %RMSE (percent Root Mean Squared Error).

5.2 Baseline: LandScan

To establish a baseline comparison for this project, we compared our ground truth population densities with those of LandScan, which is considered a community standard for global population distribution [7]. LandScan is a grid containing a numerical population estimate for every cell of size 30x30 arc-second in earth coordinates, which is around 1km on the equator (smaller at different latitudes). This estimate represents an average (over 24 hours), or ambient population distribution (not just sleeping location). For a single village, we take a square of 30 arc-second cells which most closely matches the villages area, as well as the village latitude and longitude. The population density of the village is calculated by dividing the LandScan population estimates within the cells with the area covered by the cells.

We use this method to obtain the LandScan estimate of population density for all villages in our validation dataset. The evaluation results are shown as **LandScan** model in Table 2. It has good performance in estimating aggregated population on subdistrict level, but it doesn't perform well on per-village level. It is reasonable because LandScan is a traditional population disaggregation method using only the general features on the maps, such as rivers, roads, land cover types. It does not have fine-grained information as our models have from satellite imagery.

5.3 Single State Training

Due to the large amount of data, we initially generate a smaller dataset with villages in a single state, Gujarat. The small dataset contains around 13,000 villages, which allows us to compare different models quickly, and to tune the hyper-parameters of the CNN models. We experiment with different input sources and the different CNN architectures described above. We train the basic VGG-16 separately with Landsat-8 (**L8**) and Sentinel-1(**S1**) inputs. The L8 and S1 inputs are also concatenated along the image channels and feed into VGG-16 as single input (**S1L8-Concat**). Furthermore, **Shallow Combo** and **Deep Combo** architectures are used to process two type of satellite images separately. We use NVIDIA Tesla P100 GPU with 16G memory from Google Compute Engine for training. It sets the limit of input batch size to 48 for the Deep Combo architecture, thus this batch size is also used for other models to ensure a fair comparison. With several iterations, the optimal hyper-parameters are found as follows: learning rate: 10^{-5}, exponential learning decay rate: 10^{-1}, weight decay: $5x10^{-3}$, dropout: 0.8.

Table 1: Evaluation of Single State Training

Model	Village level		Subdistrict level	
	R^2	Pearson	R^2	Pearson
L8	0.111	0.443	0.597	0.775
S1	0.120	0.425	0.701	0.839
L8S1-Concat	0.111	0.472	0.305	0.764
Shallow Combo	**0.200**	0.488	0.739	0.889
Deep Combo	0.167	**0.489**	**0.772**	**0.921**

The evaluations of the above 5 models are shown in Table 1. In general, the models have lower accuracies when predicting per-village level population densities, but the accuracy significantly improves when the individual predictions are aggregated for the subdistrict level evaluation. The **S1** model has better performance than the **L8** model, possibly due to its high resolution as well as that measuring ground reflectance by radar is more effective. However, simply concatenating L8 and S1 inputs in **L8S1-Concat** does not lead to further improvements, resulting in performance slightly worse than using S1 alone. This is likely due to training difficulties when using a combination of L8 and S1 images. In contrast, our **Shallow Combo** and **Deep Combo** architectures have significantly better performance. These results indicate that when using inputs from different sources, the CNN model needs to process them separately to extract their semantic features, so that useful information from both sides can be utilized.

5.4 All States Training

After training on a single state, we move on to train on around 350,000 villages in all 32 states in India. **L8**, **S1**, **Shallow Combo** and **Deep Combo** are trained respectively with the same hyper-parameters found when training in the single state case. The evaluation results are summarized in Table 2. With more data provided, all the models show significant improvements. All models exceed the performance of the **LandScan** baseline. **Shallow Combo** and **Deep Combo** models still outperform the basic VGG-16 models with a single image source. By comparing between two custom architectures, **Shallow Combo** has better performance on predicting population on a single village, while **Deep Combo** captures more general information in the region and has better accuracy when predicting aggregated population at the subdistrict level.

5.5 Comparison with Prior Works

In this section, we compare our models with others from prior studies, using aggregated evaluation metrics. Table 3 summarizes the reported accuracies from the papers from Doupe et al. in 2016 with study area in Kenya, and from Robinson et al. in 2017 with study area in the United States. Since we do not use subdistrict level

Table 2: Evaluation of All States Training

Model	Village level R^2	Village level Pearson	Subdistrict level R^2	Subdistrict level Pearson
L8	0.346	0.596	0.838	0.919
S1	0.327	0.597	0.890	0.944
Shallow Combo	**0.438**	**0.663**	0.906	0.954
Deep Combo	0.389	0.645	**0.931**	**0.965**
LandScan	-0.553	0.476	0.835	0.928
CONVRAW	0.322	0.592	0.850	0.937

census population for either training or prediction improvement, to ensure the fair comparison, we compare to the models in the papers also without the assistance of additional data from the aggregated level, namely **LL-raw** from Doupe's paper and **CONVRAW** from Robinson's paper. Comparing with Robinson's paper shows that even though we use a smaller (average) aggregation area in India, we still achieve significantly better R^2 and MAPE. The aggregation area in Doupe's study is even smaller, but their model also has much higher errors compared to ours.

Table 3: Comparison with Prior Works

Paper	Ours	Robinson 2017	Doupe 2016
Study area	India	US	Kenya
Aggr. area	424 km^2	2584 km^2	88 km^2
Model	Deep Combo	CONVRAW	LL-Raw
R^2	0.931	0.910	-
MAPE	21.5	73.8	-
%RMSE	24.3	-	145.43

However, it is difficult to compare models trained and tested across different countries. To address this problem, we use the same methods from Robinson et al., and apply them to our India study area. Specifically, we trained a classification model using a single Landsat input. The categorical outputs of the CNN are in the bins of $\log_2$ population density values for each Indian village. Following its **CONVRAW** approach, we convert the predicted class to population density, and aggregate the population at the subdistrict level. The predictions are still not as good as most of our models, which are shown as **CONVRAW** in Table 2. Its performance is close to our L8 model, which differs from it by using regression instead of classification. The comparison shows the regression model is better at predicting fine-grained population while classification is better for aggregate predictions.

Finally, we visualize the population mapping of different models in districts of India, the higher administrative level than subdistrict, as shown in Figure 6. It includes 533 districts that contain evaluation results from 1717 validation subdistricts. The visualization includes our **Deep Combo** and **Shallow Combo** model predictions compared with ground-truth population density distribution across districts in India. It also compares the prediction errors of the two models with those of the baseline **LandScan** and **CONVRAW** model from Robinson et al. Overall, both **Deep Combo** and **Shallow Combo** models map the rural village population of India very close to the true distribution. The prediction errors map further reveals that Deep Combo has better performance on high level aggregation than other models, while **LandScan** tends to underestimate the population and **CONVRAW** tends to overestimate.

6 CONCLUSION

The results of our CNN models on the population density prediction directly from satellite imagery are very promising. We see a higher accuracy than previous methods on both per-image raw level and aggregated region level. We attribute the success to the following reasons:

- Additional Sentinel-1 satellite imagery that provides more information on human settlements.
- Custom **Shallow Combo** and **Deep Combo** CNN architectures that better utilize different imagery sources.
- A larger and fine-grained dataset for CNN training.
- Better computational resources that enable larger image input size and batch size.

Our study largely achieves the initial goal of producing accurate population estimates enabling population mapping directly from satellite imagery, especially for rural areas. The results show that population prediction at a relatively coarse scale (such as district or subdistrict level) is quite accurate, while prediction at the village level directly from satellite imagery remains challenging. However, our village level predictions already have significantly better performance than traditional methods such as LandScan, and may still have room for improvement if images with higher resolution are available. Our population mapping models are likely useful for assisting governments in better providing for their citizens, improving resource allocation in natural disasters, aiding in infectious disease tracking, and reducing bias in progress measurement for the United Nations SDGs.

ACKNOWLEDGMENTS

This work was supported by Data for Development Initiative at the Stanford Center on Global Poverty and Development. All data in this work was processed and shared by Paul Novosad (Dartmouth College) and Sam Asher (World Bank).

REFERENCES

[1] Roy Carr-Hill. 2013. Missing millions and measuring development progress. *World Development* 46 (2013), 30–44.

[2] CIESIN. 2010. Gridded Population of the World (GPW), v4: Population Count Grid. http://sedac.ciesin.columbia.edu/data/collection/gpw-v4/methods/method1

[3] Patrick Doupe, Emilie Bruzelius, James Faghmous, and Samuel G Ruchman. 2016. Equitable development through deep learning: The case of sub-national population density estimation. In *Proceedings of the 7th Annual Symposium on Computing for Development*. ACM, 6.

[4] ESA. 2014. Sentinel-1 - Missions. https://sentinel.esa.int/web/sentinel/missions/sentinel-1

[5] Michael F Goodchild, Luc Anselin, and Uwe Deichmann. 1993. A framework for the areal interpo- lation of socioeconomic data. *Environment and planning* (1993).

[6] Simon I. Hay, Abdisalan M. Noor, Andrew Nelson, and Andrew J. Tatem. 2005. The accuracy of human population maps for public health application. *Tropical medicine & international health : TM & IH* 10 10 (2005), 1073–86.

[7] ORNL. 2011. LandScan - Oak Ridge National Laboratory. http://web.ornl.gov/sci/landscan/landscan_documentation.shtml#01

[8] Caleb Robinson, Fred Hohman, and Bistra Dilkina. 2017. A Deep Learning Approach for Population Estimation from Satellite Imagery. *CoRR* abs/1708.09086 (2017). arXiv:1708.09086 http://arxiv.org/abs/1708.09086

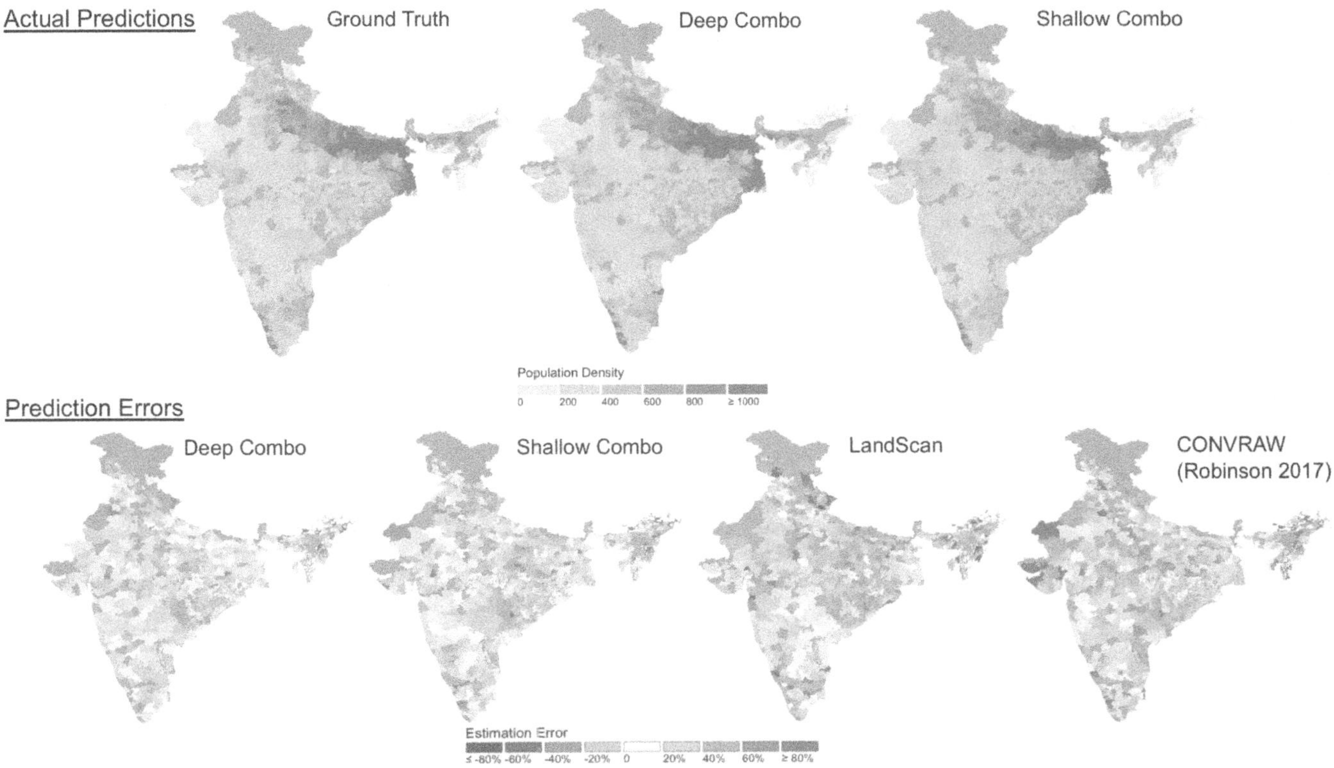

Figure 6: Population mapping visualization on the validation dataset. The upper row shows the population predictions of Deep Combo and Shallow Combo model compared to the ground-truth values. The lower row shows the prediction errors of Deep Combo and Shallow Combo compared with the baseline LandScan, and CONVRAW model from a previous paper [8]. The grey areas are the regions with no validation data.

[9] Robert C. Schmitt and Albert H. Crosetti. 1954. Accuracy of the Ratio-Correlation Method for Estimating Postcensal Population. *Land Economics* 30, 3 (1954), 279–281. http://www.jstor.org/stable/3144384

[10] Annemarie Schneider, Mark A Friedl, and David Potere. 2009. A new map of global urban extent from modis satellite data. *Environmental Research Letters* (2009).

[11] SECC. 2011. Socio Economic and Caste Census-2011. http://secc.gov.in/welcome

[12] Karen Simonyan and Andrew Zisserman. 2014. Very deep convolutional networks for large-scale image recognition. *arXiv preprint arXiv:1409.1556* (2014).

[13] Stanley K Smith. 1987. Tests of forecast accuracy and bias for county population projections. *J. Amer. Statist. Assoc.* (1987).

[14] Forrest R Stevens, Andrea E Gaughan, Catherine Linard, and Andrew J Tatem. 2015. Disaggregating census data for population mapping using random forests with remotely-sensed and ancillary data. *PloS one* 10, 2 (2015), e0107042.

[15] Andrew J. Tatem, Susana Adamo, Nita Bharti, Clara R. Burgert, Marcia Castro, Audrey Dorelien, Gunter Fink, Catherine Linard, Mendelsohn John, Livia Montana, Mark R. Montgomery, Andrew Nelson, Abdisalan M. Noor, Deepa Pindolia, Greg Yetman, and Deborah Balk. 2012. Mapping populations at risk: improving spatial demographic data for infectious disease modeling and metric derivation. *Population Health Metrics* 10, 1 (16 May 2012), 8. https://doi.org/10.1186/1478-7954-10-8

[16] Tobias G. Tiecke, Xianming Liu, Amy Zhang, Andreas Gros, Nan Li, Gregory Yetman, Talip Kilic, Siobhan Murray, Brian Blankespoor, Espen B. Prydz, and Hai-Anh H. Dang. 2017. Mapping the world population one building at a time. *CoRR* abs/1712.05839 (2017). arXiv:1712.05839 http://arxiv.org/abs/1712.05839

[17] UN. 2014. *Measuring population and housing: practices of the unece countries in the 2010 round of censuses.* Technical Report. United Nations.

[18] UN. 2015. Sustainable Development Goals. http://www.undp.org/content/undp/en/home/sustainable-development-goals.html

[19] UN. 2016. Census dates for all countries. https://unstats.un.org/unsd/demographic/sources/census/censusdates.htm

[20] UN. 2016. Census reaches vulnerable women and girls in a remote area of myanmar for the very first time. https://www.unfpa.org/news/census-reaches-vulnerable-women-and-girls-remote-area-myanmar-very-first-time

[21] UNICEF. 2016. *The state of the world's children 2012: A fair chance for every child.* Technical Report. UNICEF.

[22] USGS. 2013. Landsat Missions. https://landsat.usgs.gov

[23] Worldpop. 2013. Worldpop - What is WorldPop? http://www.worldpop.org.uk/

[24] WorldPop. 2018. WorldPop :: Methods. https://www.worldpop.org/methods

Mapping Informal Settlements in Developing Countries using Machine Learning and Low Resolution Multi-spectral Data

Bradley J Gram-Hansen*
University of Oxford
Oxford, UK
bradley@robots.ox.ac.uk

Patrick Helber*
DFKI, TU Kaiserslautern
Kaiserslautern, Germany
patrick.helber@dfki.de

Indhu Varatharajan
DLR Institute for Planetary
Berlin, Germany
indhu.varatharajan@dlr.de

Faiza Azam
Independent Researcher

Alejandro Coca-Castro
Kings College London
London, UK
alejandro.coca_castro@kcl.ac.uk

Veronika Kopackova
Czech Geological Survey
Prague, Czech Republic
Veronika.Kopackova@seznam.cz

Piotr Bilinski
University of Oxford & University of Warsaw
Oxford, UK
piotrb@robots.ox.ac.uk

Figure 1: Divide between formal and informal settlements in Kibera, Nairobi.

ABSTRACT

Informal settlements are home to the most socially and economically vulnerable people on the planet. In order to deliver effective economic and social aid, non-government organizations (NGOs), such as the United Nations ChildrenâĂŹs Fund (UNICEF), require detailed maps of the locations of informal settlements. However, data regarding informal and formal settlements is primarily unavailable and if available is often incomplete. This is due, in part, to the cost and complexity of gathering data on a large scale. To address these challenges, we, in this work, provide three contributions. 1) A brand new machine learning data-set, purposely developed for informal settlement detection. 2) We show that it is possible to detect informal settlements using freely available low-resolution (LR) data, in contrast to previous studies that use very-high resolution (VHR) satellite and aerial imagery, something that is cost-prohibitive for NGOs. 3) We demonstrate two effective classification schemes on our curated data set, one that is cost-efficient for NGOs and another that is cost-prohibitive for NGOs, but has additional utility. We integrate these schemes into a semi-automated pipeline that converts either a LR or VHR satellite image into a binary map that encodes the locations of informal settlements.

*Both authors contributed equally to this research.

AIES '19, January 27–28, 2019, Honolulu, HI, USA

ACM ISBN 978-1-4503-6324-2/19/01...$15.00
https://doi.org/10.1145/3306618.3314253

CCS CONCEPTS

• **Computing methodologies** → **Computer vision**; *Object recognition*; **Machine learning**; *Machine learning approaches*; • **Applied computing** → *Earth and atmospheric sciences*; *Cartography*; • **Social and professional topics** → Geographic characteristics.

KEYWORDS

data-sets; computational sustainability; machine learning; poverty mapping; automated maps

ACM Reference Format:
Bradley J Gram-Hansen, Patrick Helber, Indhu Varatharajan, Faiza Azam, Alejandro Coca-Castro, Veronika Kopackova, and Piotr Bilinski. 2019. Mapping Informal Settlements in Developing Countries using Machine Learning and Low Resolution Multi-spectral Data. In *AAAI/ACM Conference on AI, Ethics, and Society (AIES '19), January 27–28, 2019, Honolulu, HI, USA.* ACM, New York, NY, USA, 8 pages. https://doi.org/10.1145/3306618.3314253

1 INTRODUCTION

The United Nations (UN) state that inhabitants of settlements that meet any of the following criteria are defined to be living in an informal settlement [24]:

(1) Inhabitants have no security of tenure vis-à-vis the land or dwellings they inhabit, with modalities ranging from squatting to informal rental housing.
(2) The neighborhoods usually lack, or are cut off from, basic services and city infrastructure.
(3) The housing may not comply with current planning and building regulations, and is often situated in geographically and environmentally hazardous areas.

Slums, an example of informal settlements, are the most deprived and excluded form of informal settlements. They can be characterized by poverty and large agglomerations of dilapidated housing, located in the most hazardous urban land, near industries and dump sites, in swamps, degraded soils and flood-prone zones [16]. Slum dwellers are constantly exposed to eviction, disease and violence [22], which stems from and leads to more severe economic and social constraints [27]. Although informal settlements are well studied in the humanities and remote sensing communities [11, 13, 14, 24, 27] in machine learning, only a small amount of research has been conducted on informal settlements, with all of that research using VHR and high resolution(HR) satellite imagery [18, 19, 26], a cost prohibitive option for many NGOs and governments of developing nations. In contrast, there is an abundance of freely available and globally accessible LR satellite imagery, provided by the European Space Agency (ESA), which provides updated imagery of the entire land mass of the Earth every 5 days [7, 8, 28]. To the authors knowledge, no previous approaches have used LR imagery.

The ability to map and locate these settlements would give organizations such as UNICEF and other NGOs the ability to provide effective social and economic aid [20]. This in turn would enable those communities to evolve in a sustainable way, allowing the people living in those environments to gain a much better quality of life addressing multiple of the UN sustainable development goals [25]. These goals aim to eliminate poverty, increase good health and well-being, provide quality education, clean water and sanitation, affordable and clean energy, sustainable work and economic growth, access to industry, innovation and infrastructure.

However, solving this problem is challenging due to several factors. 1) It requires collaboration among multiple parties: the NGOs, local government, the remote sensing and machine learning communities. 2) The locations and distribution of these informal settlements have yet to be mapped thoroughly on the ground or aerially, as the mapping demands dedicated human and financial resources. This often leads to partially completed, or completely un-annotated data-sets. 3) Informal settlements tend to grow sporadically (both in space and time), which adds an additional layer of complexity. 4) Even though we have access to satellite imagery for the entire globe, much of this raw data is not in a usable format for machine learning frameworks, making it difficult to extract actionable insights at scale [29]. 5) There may be no local government structure in a particular settlement, which can inhibit our ability to gather data quickly. and make it difficult to extract good quality ground truth data, see Section 2.

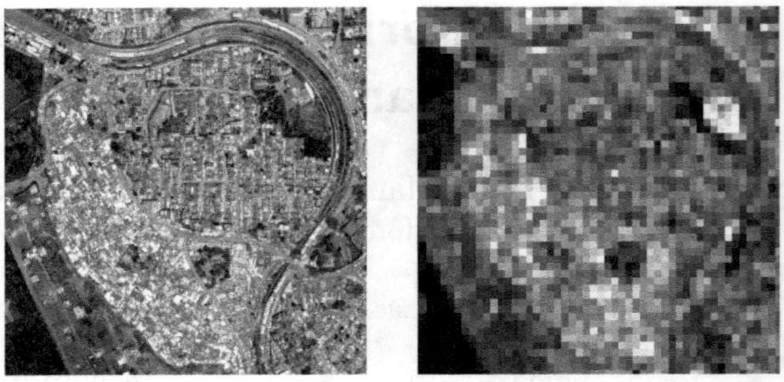

Figure 2: Two images of the same informal settlement in Kibera, representing the difference between VHR and LR imagery. *Left*: A DigitalGlobe 30cm VHR image. *Right*: The Sentinel-2 10m resolution image.

In order to address these challenges, in this work we propose a semi-automated framework that takes a satellite image, directly extracted in its *raw*-user form and outputs a trained classifier that produces binary maps highlighting the locations of informal settlements.

Our first approach, the cost-effective approach, takes advantage of the pixel level contextual information by training a classifier to learn a unique spectral signal for informal settlements. When we require finer grained features, such as the roof size, or the density of the surrounding settlements to determine whether or not there exists an informal settlement, we demonstrate a second approach that uses a semantic segmentation neural network to extract these features, the cost-prohibitive solution. See Section 4.

To ensure that this work can be applied in the field, we have had an active partnership with UNICEF, to understand what we can do to facilitate their needs further and how we can facilitate the needs of other NGOs. Because of this, we focused on developing a system that will work in a computationally efficient and monetary effective manner. Our main approach runs efficiently on a laptop, or desktop CPU and is cost-effective as we only use freely available, openly accessible LR satellite imagery, rather than VHR imagery which can cost hundreds-of-thousands of dollars.

Within this paper we make the following **contributions**:

- We introduce and extensively validate two machine learning based approaches to detect and map informal settlements. One is cost-effective, the other is cost-prohibitive, but is required when contextual information is needed.
- We demonstrate for the first-time that informal settlements can be detected effectively using only freely and openly accessible LR satellite imagery.
- We release to the public two informal settlement benchmarks for LR and VHR satellite imagery, with accompanying ground truths.
- We provide all source code and models.

In Section 2 we provide details of the data used and the challenges involved in collecting it. In Section 3 we provide a condensed overview of related work and current approaches. In Section 4 we introduce details of our methodologies and present the results of our contributions in Section 5. Finally we conclude and present future work in Section 6.

2 DATA ACQUISITION

In this work we use a combination of satellite imagery and on-the-ground measurements. However, to take advantage of machine learning frameworks we require an absolute *ground truth*, which facilitates robust training and validation. Ground truth data for this project was very sparse, in part due to the difficulties and financial costs in obtaining the data across vast regions of developing nations. This meant that much of the accessible data was incomplete. Even when the data was available, it was not necessarily in a workable format; either it was provided as part of a PDF, with no external meta-data, or it was simply in an inaccessible format. As part of this work we fused these data sets together, to generate usable data sets that can be used by the community for developing new machine learning models. Data sets can be found here: https://frontierdevelopmentlab.github.io/informal-settlements/

2.1 Satellite Data

In the last ten-years there has been an exponential increase in the number of satellites being launched due to the increase in commercial interests. This has accelerated the amount of satellite imagery available and continues to lower the cost of gaining access to VHR data. However, VHR imagery can still cost hundreds, to thousands, to hundreds-of-thousands of dollars per image, or collection of images and is typically only available through commercial providers. Institutions such as the National Aeronautics and Space Administration (NASA) and ESA do provide a multitude of freely available multi-spectral imagery, but this is typically of a much lower resolution, approximately $10 - 20m$ resolution per pixel, and many of the fine grained features are blurred, see Figure 2. This makes it difficult to use a deep learning approach effectively to extract optical features that would be required for distinguishing informal and formal settlements, whereas the VHR imagery, less than $1m$ resolution per pixel, enables us to do this, especially when we require contextual information, Section 4.

2.1.1 Sentinel-2. The Sentinel-2 mission is part of the Copernicus program by the European Commission (EC). A global earth observation service addressing six thematic areas: land, marine, atmosphere, climate change, emergency management and security through its Sentinel missions. ESA is responsible for the observation infrastructure of the Sentinels [4]. The data provided by the Sentinels has a free and open data policy implying that the data from the Sentinel missions is available free of charge to everyone. The ease of data access and use, allows all users from the public, private or research communities to reap the socio-economic benefits of such data [28]. A Sentinel-2 image is provided to the end user at Level-1C [9] and has already gone through a series of pre-processing steps before it reaches the end user. However, these images have not been corrected for atmospheric distortions. This correction requires additional processing time to convert the image into Level-2A product, resulting in bottom of the atmosphere reflectances, see Figure 3 for a comparison. Within this work we directly use the Level-1C images for our computationally and cost efficient approach, mitigating the need to do the computationally costly processing.

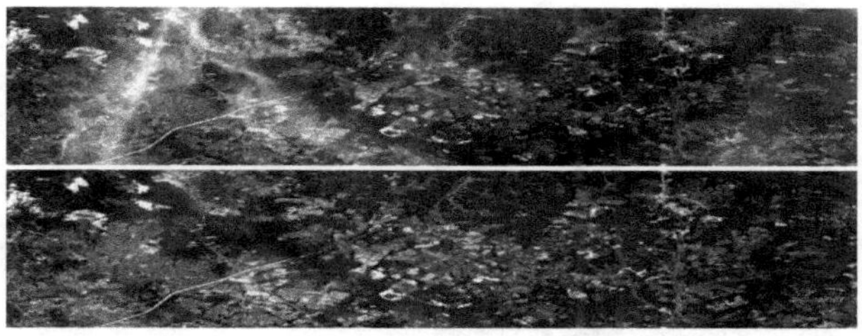

Figure 3: Image provided by the European Space Agency. ***Top*****: Represents the Sentinel-2 Level-1C uncorrected image.** ***Bottom*****: Represents the Sentinel-2 Level-2A corrected image. This lower image requires an additional time-consuming computational step to correct for atmospheric distortions in the spectral data. Our method does not require the use of this pre-processing step.**

Multi-spectral Data. The Sentinel-2 satellites map the entire global land mass every 5-days at various resolutions of 10 to $60m$ per pixel, which means that each pixel represents an area of between $10m^2$ to $60m^2$. At each resolution, spectral information at the top of the atmosphere (TOA) is provided, creating a total of 13 spectral bands covering the visible, near infrared (NIR) and the shortwave infrared (SWIR) part of the electromagnetic spectrum [6, 9, 30]. Although there are 13 spectral bands in total, we exclude bands 1, 9 and 10 as they interfere strongly with the atmosphere due to their $60m$ resolution. This means that we only use the bands 2, 3, 4, 5, 6, 7, 8, 8A, 11, 12 as these bands have minimal interactions with the atmosphere and are provided at either a $10m$ or $20m$ spatial resolution.

2.1.2 Very-High-Resolution Satellite Images. In addition to freely available multi-spectral LR satellite images, we use VHR images with a resolution of up to 30cm per pixel, kindly provided by DigitalGlobe through Satellite Applications Catapult. See Figure 2 to see the difference in resolution between Sentinel-2 and VHR imagery.We emphasize that VHR imagery is only used in the cost-prohibitive method.

2.2 Annotated Satellite Imagery

We have annotated satellite imagery for the locations of informal settlements in parts of Kenya, South Africa, Nigeria, Sudan, Colombia and Mumbai. We then project these masks on to the satellite image and extract the necessary spectral information at those specific points, see Figure 4 for a example of an annotated ground truth map. We have open sourced the necessary code to do this here: https://frontierdevelopmentlab.github.io/informal-settlements/.

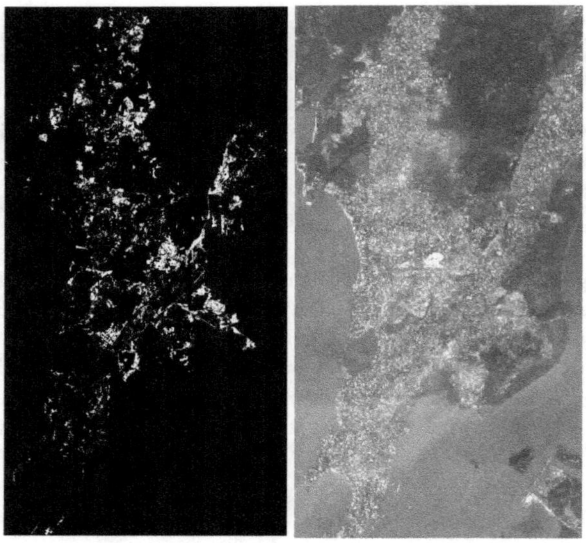

Figure 4: An example of annotated ground truth map. *Left:* The city is Mumbai, the white dots represent informal settlements and the black dots represent the environment. *Right:* The Sentinel-2 image of Mumbai.

3 RELATED WORK

Recent publications applying machine learning to remote sensing data, in particular to satellite imagery, that have focused on detecting, or mapping informal settlements [1, 16–19, 26, 29] have typically been trained on a specific region, or feature in combination with VHR [12, 17, 23, 23]. The approaches most in spirit to our own are [15, 26, 29]. Varshney et al. focus on detecting roofs in Eastern Africa using a template matching algorithm and random forest, they take advantage of Google Earths' API to extract high resolution imagery, which although is free to researchers, is not openly available to everyone. Xie et al. and Jean et al. use a mixture of data sources and transfer learning across different data sets to generate poverty maps by taking advantage of night time imagery through the National Oceanic and Atmospheric Administration (NOAA) and daytime imagery through Google Earths' API. However, to our knowledge there exists no previous work on predicting informal settlements solely from LR data, or predicting informal settlements in the way that we present here. This inhibits our ability to benchmark against previous methods. Thus, by providing the data sets and the baselines in this paper, we provide a robust way to compare the effectiveness of any future approaches and facilitate the creation of new machine learning methodologies.

4 METHODS

In this section, we describe our approaches for detecting and mapping informal settlements. We introduce two different methods; a cost-efficient method and cost-prohibitive method. Our **first method** trains a classifier to learn what the spectrum of an informal settlement is, using LR freely available Sentinel-2 data. To do this, we employ a pixel-wise classification, where the system learns whether or not a 10-band spectra is associated to an informal settlement or the environment, which encompasses everything that is not an informal settlement. Our **second method**, is a semantic segmentation deep neural network that uses VHR satellite imagery, which is useful when informal settlements do not have unique spectra when compared to the environment, like those in Sudan, see Figure 5.

4.1 Cost Effective Method

Canonical Correlation Forests (CCFs) [21] are a decision tree ensemble method for classification and regression. CCFs are the state-of-the-art random forest technique, which have shown to achieve remarkable results for numerous regression and classification tasks [21]. Individual canonical correlation trees are binary decision trees with hyper-plane splits based on local canonical correlation coefficients calculated during training. Like most random forest based approaches, CCFs have very few hyper-parameters to tune and typically provide very good performance out of the box. All that has to be set is the number of trees, n_{trees}. For CCFs, setting $n_{trees} = 15$ provides a performance that is empirically equivalent to a random forest that has $n_{trees} = 500$ [21], meaning CCFs have lower computational costs, whilst providing better classification. CCFs work by using canonical correlation analysis (CCA) and projection bootstrapping during the training of each tree, which projects the data into a space that maximally correlates the inputs with the outputs. This is particularly useful when we have small data-sets, like in our case, as it reduces the amount of artificial randomness required to be added during the tree training procedure and improves the ensemble predictive performance [21].

The computational efficiency aspects of CCFs and their suitability to both small and large data-sets, makes them ideal for detecting informal settlements for three reasons. First, many of the organisations that we aim to help will not have access to a large amount of compute resources, therefore computational efficiency is important. Second, to run the CCFs for both training and prediction, all that has to be called is one function. This ensures that the end user does not need to be an expert in ensemble methods and makes the method akin to plug and play. Finally, some of our ground truth data sets are relatively small, which means that we must use the data as efficiently as possible, which CCFs allow us to do. When VHR and computational cost are not a restriction we can employ a deep learning approach using convolution neural networks (CNN) to detect informal settlements.

4.2 Cost Prohibitive Method

Since informal settlements can also be classified by the rooftop size and the surrounding building density, we employ a state-of-the-art semantic segmentation neural network on optical (RGB) VHR satellite imagery to detect these contextual features. These contextual features are important when it is not possible to distinguish informal settlements from the environment by spectral signal in the same region. An example of such an informal settlement is shown in Figure 5. We see that the informal settlements in a rural region of Al Geneina, Sudan have a very low building density, and also the roof tops of both formal and informal settlements are built out of concrete, meaning they have the same spectral signal. This is in contrast to the dense slums in Nairobi and Mumbai.

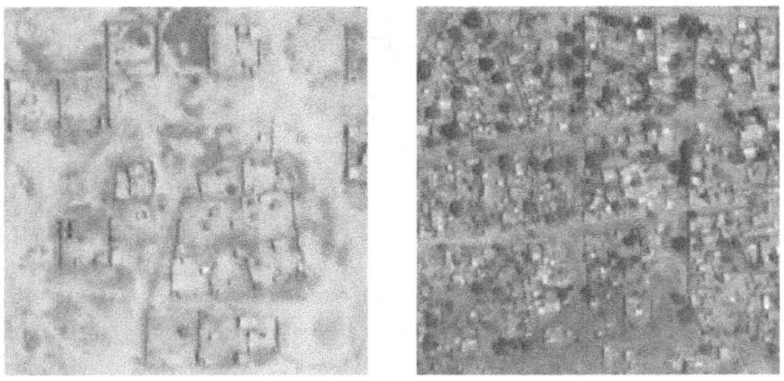

Figure 5: A VHR image comparing an informal, *left* and formal settlement, *right*, in Al Geneina, Sudan. The main distinguishing feature is the wider contextual information, as the material spectrum's are the same.

4.2.1 Encoder-Decoder with Atrous Separable Convolution. For the task of semantic segmentation of informal settlements we use the DeepLabv3+ encoder-decoder architecture. DeepLabv3+ [3] is a deep CNN that extends the prior DeepLabv3 network [2] with a decoder module to refine the segmentation results of the previous encoder-decoder architecture particularly at the object boarders. The DeepLabv3 architecture uses Atrous Spatial Pyramid Pooling (ASPP) with Atrous convolutions to explicitly control the resolution at which feature responses are computed within the CNN. This ASPP module is augmented with image level features to capture longer range information. We use a Xception 65 network backbone in the encoder-decoder architecture. The beneficial use of this Xception model together with applying depth wise separable convolution to ASPP and the decoder modules have been shown in [3].

4.2.2 Implementation details. We train the entire network end-to-end with the usual back-propagation algorithm using eight Tesla V100 GPUs with 16 GBs of memory each. We initialize the layer weights using those from the pre-trained PASCAL VOC 2012 model [10]. We then fine-tune in turn the finer strides on the training/validation data. We train our deep network with a batch size of 32, an initial learning rate of 0.001 and a learning rate decay factor of 0.1 every 2.000 steps until convergence. Our experiments are based on a single-scale evaluation. All other hyper-parameters are the same as in the DeepLabv3+ model [3].

5 RESULTS

Experimental Setup. For each region we have a 10-20m resolution Sentinel-2 image, the corresponding VHR 30-50cm resolution image and the ground truth annotations. We have ensured that the images and annotations are aligned in space and time to reduce any additional noise in the data. When training and validating a model on the same region we use a 80-20 split. We ensure that each class contains the same number of points, we then randomly sample 80% of each class to generate the training data and then use the remaining 20% of each class to construct our test set, which is comprised of a different set of points. We then center the training data (testing data accordingly) to have a mean of zero and standard deviation of one. We set the $n_{trees} = 10$ for training the CCF. For validating our methods we report both pixel accuracy, and mean intersection over union (IoU). We use the standard definition of mean IOU, $meanIOU = \frac{1}{n_{class}} \frac{t_{ii}}{(t_i + \sum_j n_{ji} - n_{ii})}$ and pixel classification, $pxclass = \frac{\sum_i n_{ii}}{t_i}$, where n_{class} is the total number of classes, n_{ij} is the number of pixels of class i predicted to belong to class j, and t_i is the total number of pixels of class i in ground truth segmentation.

We provide a comparison of both the pixel-wise classification with CCFs and the contextual classification with CNNs for the detection and mapping of informal settlements, see Table 1. The CCFs trained solely on freely available and easily accessible low-resolution data perform well, although they are unable to match the performance of the CNN trained on VHR imagery, except for Kibera. Figure 6 shows the predictions of both methods and the ground truth annotations. Despite having access to very high resolution data, the CNN still manages to miss-classify structural elements of the informal settlements in Kibera. Whereas the CCF, although more granular, incorporates the full structure of the informal settlement in Kibera via only the spectral information.

5.0.1 Generalizability. To demonstrate the adaptability of our approach we train each model on different parts of the world and use that model to perform predictions on other unseen regions across the globe. For this paper we train two models, one on Northern Nairobi, Kenya and another on Medellin, Colombia. The results can be found in Table 2. Even though we only have a small amount of data, we are able to demonstrate that our models can generalize moderately well, even with data that is noisy and partially incomplete. We provide several more results in the appendix A A of this paper.

	Pixel Acc.		Mean IOU	
Region	**CCF**	**CNN**	**CCF**	**CNN**
Kenya, Northern Nairobi	69.4	93.1	62.0	80.8
Kenya, Kibera	69.0	78.2	73.3	65.5
South Africa, Capetown*	92.0	-	33.2	-
Sudan, El Daien	78.0	86.0	61.3	73.4
Sudan, Al Geneina	83.2	89.2	35.7	76.3
Nigeria, Makoko*	76.2	87.4	59.9	74.0
Colombia, Medellin*	84.2	95.3	74.0	83.0
India, Mumbai*	97.0	-	40.3	-

Table 1: Pixel accuracy and mean IOU (%) results for informal settlement detection using the CCF pixel-wise classification and the contextual classification with CNNs. CCFs are trained and tested on low resolution imagery, CNNs are trained and tested on VHR imagery. *Represents that the ground truth annotations are less than 75% complete for the region.

6 CONCLUSIONS AND FUTURE WORK

Conclusion. In this work we have composed a series of annotated ground truth data-sets and have provided for the first time benchmarks for detecting informal settlements. We have provided

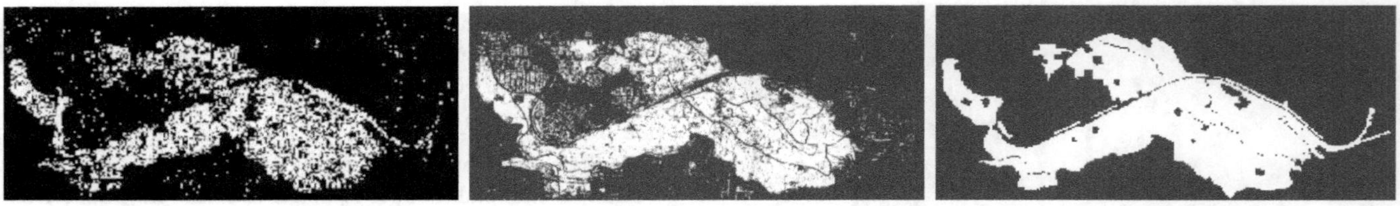

Figure 6: Predictions of informal settlements (white pixels) in Kibera, Nairobi. *Left:* The CCF prediction of informal settlements in Kibera on low-resolution Sentinel-2 spectral imagery. *Middle:* Deep learning based prediction of informal settlements in Kibera, trained on VHR imagery. *Right:* The ground truth informal settlement mask for Kibera.

	Pixel Acc.		Mean IOU	
Region	**NN**	**M**	**NN**	**M**
Kenya, Northern Nairobi	69.4	55.0	62.0	54.4
Kenya, Kibera	67.3	63.8	54.1	56.0
South Africa, Capetown*	41.3	71.5	43.1	32.0
Sudan, El Daien	14.2	1.1	37.9	34.0
Sudan, Al Geneina	27.1	6.0	34.9	41.0
Nigeria, Makoko*	59.0	77.0	37.8	34.6
Colombia, Medellin*	65.0	84.2	46.9	74.0
India, Mumbai*	37.9	63.0	32.4	34.4

Table 2: Pixel accuracy and mean IOU (%) results for informal settlement detection using pixel-wise classification with CCFs trained on a particular region and testing on all other regions. Results are for a model trained on Northern Nairobi (NN) and a model trained on Medellin (M). * Represents that the ground truth annotations are less than 75% complete for the region.

a comprehensive list of the challenges faced in mapping informal settlements and some of the constraints faced by NGOs. In addition to this, we have proposed two different methods for detecting informal settlements, one a cost-effective method, the other a cost-prohibitive method. The first method used computationally efficient CCFs to learn the spectral signal of informal settlements from LR satellite imagery. The second used a CNN combined with VHR satellite imagery to extract finer grained features. We extensively evaluated the proposed methods and demonstrated the generalization capabilities of our methods to detect informal settlements not just in a local region, but globally. In particular, we demonstrated for the first time that informal settlements can be detected effectively using only freely and openly accessible multi-spectral low-resolution satellite imagery.

Future work. Because of the uncertainties within the ground truth annotations and the differences in informal settlements across the world, we believe that this problem would be very useful for testing transfer learning and meta-learning approaches. In addition to this, Bayesian approaches would enable us to characterize these uncertainties via probabilistic models. This would provide an effective way to create adaptable models that learn what it means for an informal settlement to be informal, as the model absorbs new information.

It is also interesting to note that a 1 km^2 area containing informal settlements could house up to 129089 people [5] and so each pixel could represent up to 13 people [1]. This therefore allows us to also add population estimates to our maps, which UNICEF state is also crucial. This would enable governments and NGOs to understand how much infrastructure is required and how much aid needs to be provided. Although we could have added population estimates in this current work, we have chosen to omit them as it would be irresponsible of us to provide estimates when not enough ground truth data exists, regarding average population numbers in informal settlements. We are actively working with UNICEF to gather more ground truth data for this and additional annotations for informal settlements, as UNICEF would actively like to deploy a system like the one that we have developed here to provide both mapping and population estimates of rural and urban informal settlements.

7 ACKNOWLEDGEMENTS

This project was executed during the Frontier Development Lab, Europe program, a partnership between the ϕ-Lab at ESA, the Satellite Applications (SA) Catapult, Nvidia Corporation, Oxford University and Kellogg College. We gratefully acknowledge the support of Adrien Muller and Tom Jones of SA Catapult for their useful comments, providing VHR imagery and ground truth annotations for Nairobi. We thank UNICEF, in particular Do-Hyung Kim and Clara Palau Montava, for valuable discussions and AIData for access to geo-located Afrobarometer data. We thank Nvidia for computation resources. We thank Yarin Gal, Adam Golinski and Ben Fernando for their for their helpful comments. Bradley Gram-Hansen was also supported by the UK EPSRC CDT in Autonomous Intelligent Machines and Systems. Patrick Helber was supported by the NVIDIA AI Lab program and the BMBF project DeFuseNN (Grant 01IW17002).

[1] $100m^2 = 0.00001km^2$, therefore $129089 \times 0.00001 \sim 13$ people per pixel (ppx^{-1}).

REFERENCES

[1] A. Asmat and S.Z. Zamzami. 2012. Automated House Detection and Delineation using Optical Remote Sensing Technology for Informal Human Settlement. *Procedia - Social and Behavioral Sciences* 36 (2012), 650 – 658. https://doi.org/10.1016/j.sbspro.2012.03.071 ASEAN Conference on Environment-Behaviour Studies (AcE-Bs), Savoy Homann Bidakara Hotel, 15-17 June 2011, Bandung, Indonesia.

[2] Liang-Chieh Chen, George Papandreou, Florian Schroff, and Hartwig Adam. 2017. Rethinking atrous convolution for semantic image segmentation. *arXiv preprint arXiv:1706.05587* (2017).

[3] Liang-Chieh Chen, Yukun Zhu, George Papandreou, Florian Schroff, and Hartwig Adam. 2018. Encoder-Decoder with Atrous Separable Convolution for Semantic Image Segmentation. In *ECCV*.

[4] Copernicus. 2018. http://www.copernicus.eu/. Accessed : 2018-08-27.

[5] Amélie Desgroppes and Sophie Taupin. 2011. Kibera: The biggest slum in Africa? *Les Cahiers de l'Afrique de l'Est* 44 (2011), 23–34.

[6] M. Drusch, U. Del Bello, S. Carlier, O. Colin, V. Fernandez, F. Gascon, B. Hoersch, C. Isola, P. Laberinti, P. Martimort, A. Meygret, F. Spoto, O. Sy, F. Marchese, and P. Bargellini. 2012. Sentinel-2: ESA's Optical High-Resolution Mission for GMES Operational Services. *Remote Sensing of Environment* 120 (2012), 25 – 36. https://doi.org/10.1016/j.rse.2011.11.026 The Sentinel Missions - New Opportunities for Science.

[7] European Space Agency. 2018. https://earth.esa.int/web/sentinel/user-guides/sentinel-2-msi/product-types/level-2a. Accessed : 2018-08-21.

[8] European Space Agency. 2018. https://sentinel.esa.int/web/sentinel/missions/sentinel-2. Accessed : 2018-08-27.

[9] European Space Agency. 2018. https://sentinel.esa.int/documents/247904/685211/Sentinel-2_User_Handbook. Accessed : 2018-08-27.

[10] M. Everingham, L. Van Gool, C. K. I. Williams, J. Winn, and A. Zisserman. 2012. The PASCAL Visual Object Classes Challenge 2012 (VOC2012) Results.

[11] Ruth Fincher. 2003. Planning for cities of diversity, difference and encounter. *Australian Planner* 40, 1 (2003), 55–58. https://doi.org/10.1080/07293682.2003.9995252

[12] CM Gevaert, C Persello, R Sliuzas, and G Vosselman. 2016. Classification of informal settlements through the integration of 2D and 3D features extracted from UAV data. *ISPRS Annals of the Photogrammetry, Remote Sensing and Spatial Information Sciences* 3 (2016), 317.

[13] Peter Hofmann, Josef Strobl, Thomas Blaschke, and Hermann Kux. 2008. Detecting informal settlements from QuickBird data in Rio de Janeiro using an object based approach. In *Object-based image analysis*. Springer, 531–553.

[14] Marie Huchzermeyer. 2006. *Informal settlements: A perpetual challenge?* Juta and Company Ltd.

[15] Neal Jean, Marshall Burke, Michael Xie, W. Matthew Davis, David B. Lobell, and Stefano Ermon. 2016. Combining satellite imagery and machine learning to predict poverty. *Science* 353, 6301 (2016), 790–794. https://doi.org/10.1126/science.aaf7894 arXiv:http://science.sciencemag.org/content/353/6301/790.full.pdf

[16] Divyani Kohli, Richard Sliuzas, and Alfred Stein. 2016. Urban slum detection using texture and spatial metrics derived from satellite imagery. *Journal of Spatial Science* 61, 2 (2016), 405–426. https://doi.org/10.1080/14498596.2016.1138247

[17] Monika Kuffer, Karin Pfeffer, and Richard Sliuzas. 2016. Slums from spaceâĂŤ15 years of slum mapping using remote sensing. *Remote Sensing* 8, 6 (2016), 455.

[18] Ron Mahabir, Arie Croitoru, Andrew T Crooks, Peggy Agouris, and Anthony Stefanidis. 2018. A critical review of high and very high-resolution remote sensing approaches for detecting and mapping Slums: Trends, challenges and emerging opportunities. *Urban Science* 2, 1 (2018), 8.

[19] Nicholus Mboga, Claudio Persello, John Ray Bergado, and Alfred Stein. 2017. Detection of informal settlements from VHR images using convolutional neural networks. *Remote sensing* 9, 11 (2017), 1106.

[20] Marta Santos Pais. 2002. Poverty and Exclusion Among Urban Children. (2002).

[21] Tom Rainforth and Frank Wood. 2015. Canonical correlation forests. *arXiv preprint arXiv:1507.05444* (2015).

[22] Elliott D. Sclar, Pietro Garau, and Gabriella Carolini. 2005. The 21st century health challenge of slums and cities. *The Lancet* 365, 9462 (05 Mar 2005), 901–903. https://doi.org/10.1016/S0140-6736(05)71049-7

[23] M. Stasolla and P. Gamba. 2008. Spatial Indexes for the Extraction of Formal and Informal Human Settlements From High-Resolution SAR Images. *IEEE Journal of Selected Topics in Applied Earth Observations and Remote Sensing* 1, 2 (June 2008), 98–106. https://doi.org/10.1109/JSTARS.2008.921099

[24] United Nations. 2012. *State of the World's Cities 2012-2013: Prosperity of Cities*. United Nations Publications. https://books.google.co.uk/books?id=6cGzNAEACAAJ

[25] United Nations. 2018. United Nations Sustainable Development Goals. https://www.un.org/sustainabledevelopment/sustainable-development-goals/. Accessed : 2018-08-21.

[26] Kush R Varshney, George H Chen, Brian Abelson, Kendall Nowocin, Vivek Sakhrani, Ling Xu, and Brian L Spatocco. 2015. Targeting villages for rural development using satellite image analysis. *Big Data* 3, 1 (2015), 41–53.

[27] B.W. Wekesa, G.S. Steyn, and F.A.O. (Fred) Otieno. 2011. A review of physical and socio-economic characteristics and intervention approaches of informal settlements. *Habitat International* 35, 2 (2011), 238 – 245. https://doi.org/10.1016/j.habitatint.2010.09.006

[28] T. Wiatr, G. Suresh, R. Gehrke, and M. Hovenbitzer. 2016. COPERNICUS PRACTICE OF DAILY LIFE IN A NATIONAL MAPPING AGENCY? *ISPRS - International Archives of the Photogrammetry, Remote Sensing and Spatial Information Sciences* XLI-B1 (2016), 1195–1199. https://doi.org/10.5194/isprs-archives-XLI-B1-1195-2016

[29] Michael Xie, Neal Jean, Marshall Burke, David Lobell, and Stefano Ermon. 2015. Transfer learning from deep features for remote sensing and poverty mapping. *arXiv preprint arXiv:1510.00098* (2015).

[30] Tianxiang Zhang, Jinya Su, Cunjia Liu, Wen-Hua Chen, Hui Liu, and Guohai Liu. 2017. Band selection in sentinel-2 satellite for agriculture applications. *2017 23rd International Conference on Automation and Computing (ICAC)* (2017), 1–6.

A INFORMAL SETTLEMENT PIXEL-WISE CLASSIFICATION RESULTS

In this section we provide all results generated by the CCF on all informal settlement data-sets at our disposal. We present two sets of results for Capetown.

- Capetown with Ground Truth (CapetownGT) - This represents around $20km^2$ region of Capetown (11% of the city). This data is annotated and it was used in the main paper.
- Capetown - This represents the whole of Capetown, however, we only have annotations for the region mentioned above (CapetownGT).

Country		Colombia	India	Kenya			Nigeria	South Africa		Sudan	
City		Medellin	Mumbai	N. Nairobi	Kibera	Kianda	Mokako	Capetown	CapetownGT	AlGeneina	ElDaein
Model	Mumbai										
Informal		78.35	97.18	71.44	74.84	89.23	94.81	80.88	89.10	21.00	10.96
Environment		36.32	95.92	43.37	51.65	31.33	28.53	56.45	43.11	68.19	83.71
Model	Capetown										
Informal		96.86	98.00	99.21	96.52	100.00	99.73	98.77	99.61	99.99	99.90
Environment		9.80	46.97	9.07	10.12	4.03	7.27	96.33	15.22	0.23	0.10
Model	CapetownGT										
Informal		83.77	73.94	93.59	82.16	96.13	95.32	84.78	92.34	99.48	90.82
Environment		51.69	85.41	40.25	45.33	22.23	24.60	82.68	93.33	2.53	5.99
Model	N. Nairobi										
Informal		64.65	37.91	69.45	67.63	90.33	58.55	36.06	41.33	27.07	14.18
Environment		63.64	62.44	69.27	73.44	50.75	53.85	75.21	81.57	68.77	89.17
Model	Kibera										
Informal		48.23	40.82	63.65	67.84	79.56	57.71	46.50	45.07	30.96	31.31
Environment		72.04	27.18	76.56	75.56	67.73	58.38	54.76	55.92	62.13	65.53
Model	Kianda										
Informal		45.23	43.18	62.57	61.09	90.97	46.64	24.45	26.79	68.75	53.73
Environment		82.06	60.65	85.33	83.49	75.48	62.19	77.23	86.27	36.50	57.57
Model	AlGeneina										
Informal		81.21	66.80	80.73	79.76	85.36	56.07	52.94	60.52	83.17	94.68
Environment		46.79	48.97	49.71	31.87	17.26	38.46	76.21	63.86	79.43	5.25
Model	ElDaein										
Informal		24.07	9.50	46.58	54.11	71.82	8.37	29.90	25.65	68.52	78.16
Environment		76.61	40.11	67.18	71.47	71.20	85.19	48.91	61.22	30.61	71.65
Model	Mokako										
Informal		17.33	69.43	10.67	14.15	13.54	76.27	35.60	34.76	5.53	10.57
Environment		85.22	39.06	89.91	94.07	94.37	80.84	60.91	61.89	92.97	88.51
Model	Medellin										
Informal		84.06	62.95	54.10	63.84	88.12	77.00	63.38	71.46	5.66	1.09
Environment		79.88	63.02	85.79	78.85	47.00	37.45	62.01	57.68	96.28	95.78

Table 3: Pixel classification scores. The *Model* row represents the model that has been trained on the stated city and the columns represent the city on which that trained model is making a prediction on.

Human-AI Learning Performance in Multi-Armed Bandits

Ravi Pandya
Electrical Engineering and Computer Sciences
Universiity of California, Berkeley
ravi.pandya@berkeley.edu

Sandy H. Huang
Electrical Engineering and Computer Sciences
University of California, Berkeley
shhuang@berkeley.edu

Dylan Hadfield-Menell
Electrical Engineering and Computer Sciences
University of California, Berkeley
dhm@eecs.berkeley.edu

Anca D. Dragan
Electrical Engineering and Computer Sciences
University of California, Berkeley
anca@berkeley.edu

ABSTRACT

People frequently face challenging decision-making problems in which outcomes are uncertain or unknown. Artificial intelligence (AI) algorithms exist that can outperform humans at learning such tasks. Thus, there is an opportunity for AI agents to assist people in learning these tasks more effectively. In this work, we use a multi-armed bandit as a controlled setting in which to explore this direction. We pair humans with a selection of agents and observe how well each human-agent team performs. We find that team performance can beat both human and agent performance in isolation. Interestingly, we also find that an agent's performance in isolation does not necessarily correlate with the human-agent team's performance. A drop in agent performance can lead to a disproportionately large drop in team performance, or in some settings can even *improve* team performance. Pairing a human with an agent that performs slightly better than them can make them perform much better, while pairing them with an agent that performs the same can make them them perform much worse. Further, our results suggest that people have different exploration strategies and might perform better with agents that match their strategy. Overall, optimizing human-agent team performance requires going beyond optimizing agent performance, to understanding how the agent's suggestions will influence human decision-making.

KEYWORDS

multi-armed bandits, human-AI teams, user studies

ACM Reference Format:

Ravi Pandya, Sandy H. Huang, Dylan Hadfield-Menell, and Anca D. Dragan. 2019. Human-AI Learning Performance in Multi-Armed Bandits. In *AAAI/ACM Conference on AI, Ethics, and Society (AIES '19), January 27–28, 2019, Honolulu, HI, USA.* ACM, New York, NY, USA, 7 pages. https://doi.org/10.1145/3306618.3314245

AIES '19, January 27–28, 2019, Honolulu, HI, USA

ACM ISBN 978-1-4503-6324-2/19/01...$15.00
https://doi.org/10.1145/3306618.3314245

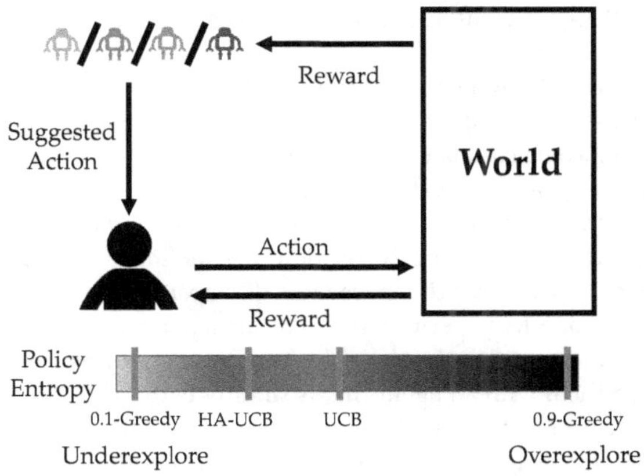

Figure 1: The suggestion-based collaborative-learning setting, in which the human takes actions in the world after seeing suggested actions from the agent.

1 INTRODUCTION

Typically, research on human-agent learning focuses on either situations where agents learn from people (e.g., learning from demonstration, recommender systems) or people learn from agents (e.g., algorithmic teaching). In contrast, our work focuses on tasks in which both the human and the agent are learning—neither is an expert yet. We are motivated by these tasks for two reasons. First, there are situations where this is obviously true, like making stock investments. But even for situations in preference learning where traditionally we assume people are experts (as in recommender systems), in reality people might actually be learning about their preferences as they take different actions and observe their outcomes. For instance, we might not know how we feel about Romanian food until we visit a restaurant, and even then we have to account for the possibility of having an unusually good or bad experience.

When it comes to learning such tasks, humans tend to struggle. We are not the best at balancing exploration and exploitation [3] or internalizing our experiences thus far. However, AI algorithms exist that can significantly outperform humans at these kinds of tasks. Thus, there is an opportunity for such agents to improve human performance by providing assistance. In particular, an agent can assist by providing *suggestions*.

Formulation of assistance. In this work, we study the performance of human-agent teams in the context of a multi-armed bandit problem. This functions as a controlled setting in which outcomes are uncertain. Agents provide suggestions by indicating which arm the human should pull at each time step. Importantly, this setting also cleanly captures the *exploration vs. exploitation* trade-off commonly encountered in reinforcement learning and robotics, in which an agent must decide whether to exploit the information it has about the world to maximize short-term reward or explore different options to ultimately find the best option. This gives us a relevant spectrum for analyzing the types of strategies employed by both humans and agents. In our experiments, we pair people with four agents spanning this spectrum (Fig. 1).

The team can be better than the best team member. An encouraging result is that with the right algorithm, people not only perform better than in isolation, but they end up performing even better than the agent does in isolation. The team is more than the sum of its parts.

Optimizing team performance is not the same as optimizing learning performance. We expected that agent performance in isolation would correlate with human-agent team performance: the better the agent is, the better its suggestions, and thus the better the human's decisions. The first interesting result of our work is that we find evidence against this correlation. We find that a *small drop* in the agent's performance can lead to a *disproportionately large* drop in the human-team performance. Pairing a person with an agent that performs at their level can decrease their performance, while pairing them with an agent that is slightly better than them can increase beyond the agent's performance in isolation. Even further, a *large drop* in agent performance can lead to a slight *improvement* in team performance!

Agents have implicit (rather than explicit) influence. When analyzing how these differences in team performance came about, we were surprised to find that people were not actually changing their mind and taking the agents' suggestions. How, then, do agents influence the outcome? We found that agents actually have a more *implicit* influence: suggestions do not change the person's mind immediately, but rather influence the choices the person makes *later*, i.e. they change the person's strategy. Different algorithms achieve different amounts of such influence.

People perform better with agents that are more like them. When analyzing what might cause this difference in implicit influence, we found that people's unassisted strategies naturally group into two categories from the perspective of exploration (i.e., entropy of arm pulls over time). Each of these strategies is most similar to a specific learning algorithm, and it is that algorithm that tends to assist them best.

Overall, our findings suggest that when using suggestions to assist people who are learning a task, we should not compute the utility of a suggestion by assuming that it will be taken. An AI's suggestions end up having different amounts of influence, largely of the more implicit kind—not changing decisions immediately, but influencing strategy over time.

2 RELATED WORK

One of the most common applications of multi-armed bandits is in recomender systems [9, 10]. The arms of the bandit are the different options (e.g., news articles or movies) to show to the user and the reward is based on whether or not the user accepts the recommendation. This assumes the user knows what they want and the system seeks to show them options they will like. In this work, we modify this assumption: we consider a bandit setting where humans are *learning* about the quality of the options themselves. Our experiments show that helping a person learn more effectively is a different task than optimizing reward in isolation. Algorithms which perform comparably on this measure can fare quite differently when used to suggest arms to a person.

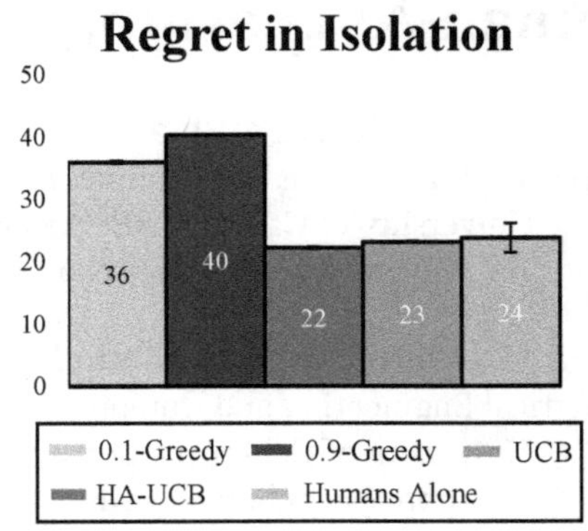

Figure 2: The average regret obtained by each agent in isolation, averaged over 10,000 simulations, and the average regret obtained by humans in isolation.

Studies to understand human policies for multi-armed bandits have found that humans are suboptimal in their exploration: they over-explore [1], under-explore [7, 13], or both [3]. People fall into distinct categories in terms of their cumulative regret when doing spatial bandit problems [18], and human performance can be well-captured using stochastic Bayesian inference algorithms [17].

Human-agent teams have been studied in resource allocation problems with uncertain outcomes, which can be thought of as multi-armed bandit problems. Prior work improved human-agent collaboration in this setting by using physical or user-interface elements [16] or by modeling people's responses to an agent's *actions* [21]. These scenarios differ from our work in that agents typically have full or partial control over actions, whereas we explore the setting in which only the human can take actions; the agent can only provide suggestions.

Research on improving human-robot team performance often focuses on settings in which both the human(s) and robot(s) take actions in the environment. Although our work does not deal with physical robots, successful strategies for human-robot collaboration can guide the development of successful strategies for human-AI collaboration, and vice versa. Prior work found that performance in human-robot teams improves when human and robot teammates better understand each others' actions, which is true for human-human teams as well [11]. A robot can make itself more understandable to humans through legible motion [5, 20], increased transparency [12], verbal feedback [19], nonverbal cues [4], revealing its incapabilities [8, 14], or cross-training [15]. These previous works on human-robot team performance typically assume a setting in which either the human or robot (or both) has ground-truth knowledge of how to perform the task optimally. In contrast, in our setting the human and agent are learning together about the task.

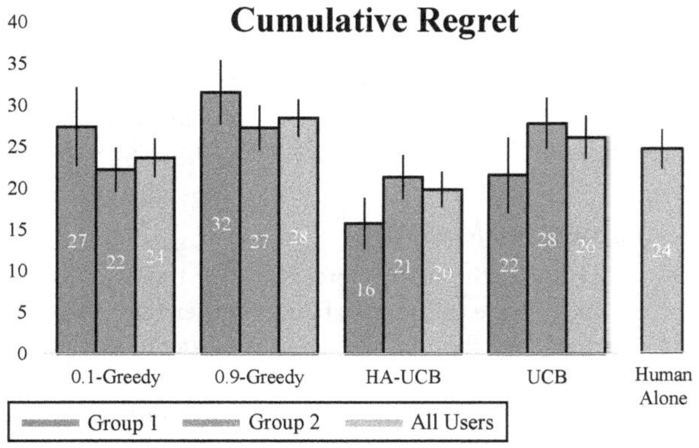

Figure 3: The average total regret accumulated when collaborating with different agents. Overall, users perform significantly better when paired with HA-UCB or 0.1-Greedy, compared to 0.9-Greedy.

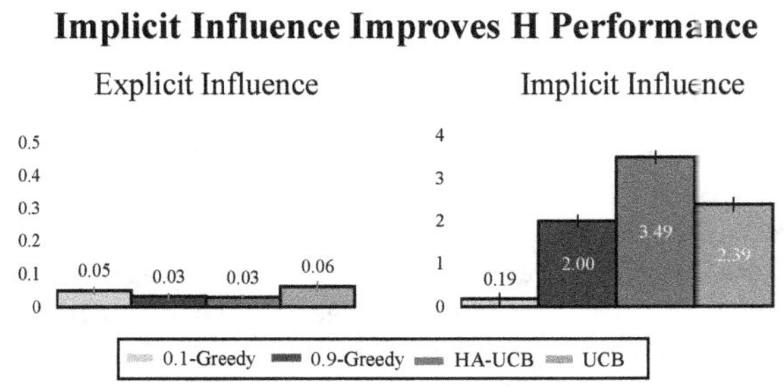

Figure 4: Left: *Explicit influence* is the fraction of time humans immediately change their decision to the agent's suggestion when the agent suggests a different action than the human's proposed action. On average, this happens only once during the horizon of 30 pulls, so it cannot explain the increase in performance for HA-UCB (Fig. 3). Right: *Implicit Influence* is the difference between compatibility and suggestion delay. Compatibility is how long it takes for humans in isolation to choose arms which agents would have suggested. Suggestion delay measures how long it takes for people to actually pick arms suggested by agents while being assisted by them. Here, we see HA-UCB significantly changes human strategies more than other agents, since it was initially incompatible with people, but it didn't take many iterations for people to take its suggestions.

3 MULTI-ARMED BANDIT

Our user study focuses on a finite-horizon multi-armed bandit problem. A K-armed bandit problem is defined by random variables $X_{i,n}$ for $1 \leq i \leq K$ and $n \geq 1$. Each pull of arm i yields a reward $X_{i,1}, X_{i,2}, \ldots$ which are independently and identically distributed with some unknown expected value μ_i. In our experiment, we used:

$$X_{i,n} = \begin{cases} 0 & \text{w.p. } \lambda_{i,0} \\ 1 & \text{w.p. } \lambda_{i,1} \\ 2 & \text{w.p. } \lambda_{i,2} \\ 3 & \text{w.p. } \lambda_{i,3} \\ 4 & \text{w.p. } \lambda_{i,4} \end{cases} \quad (1)$$

where λ_i is different and fixed over time for each arm, and $\sum_{j=0}^{4} \lambda_{i,j} = 1$.

Intuitively, since the arms are unchanged over time, the best strategy for maximizing reward is to always choose the arm i which has the highest expected reward, $\mu_i = \lambda_i\ [0\ 1\ 2\ 3\ 4]^T$, where λ_i is the row vector of all probabilities for arm i. Thus, we can evaluate different *policies*, or *allocation strategies*, based on how much worse they are doing than this optimal policy. If we define $T_i(n)$ as total reward gained from arm i in the first n plays, then we can define the *regret* for some policy after n pulls as

$$\mu^* n - \sum_{j=1}^{K} T_j(n) \text{ where } \mu^* = \max_{1 \leq i \leq K} \mu_i \quad (2)$$

The goal is to find a policy which minimizes the total regret.

Since we have no prior knowledge of which arm may be the best, this introduces a classic *exploration vs. exploitation* trade-off as previously noted. Many policies for this problem have been explored; among these, the Upper Confidence Bound (UCB) algorithm is simple and has a bound on expected regret that is logarithmic in the number of pulls [2].

3.1 UCB Policy

This policy starts by sampling each arm once. On each subsequent pull n, it picks the arm i that maximizes

$$\bar{\mu}_i + \sqrt{\frac{2 \ln n}{n_i}}, \quad (3)$$

where $\bar{\mu}_i$ is the average reward obtained from arm i and n_i is the number of times that arm has been played so far.

3.2 Horizon-Aware UCB Policy

While UCB has a good *asymptotic* bound on its regret, it is possible for other agents to outperform it in short time horizon problems, like the ones in our user studies.

One way to improve the performance of UCB on such problems is to make it more greedy. Note that the vanilla UCB algorithm always takes the arm which maximizes the sum of two terms. The first term, $\bar{\mu}_i$, represents exploitation or greediness, since it is the average reward seen from arm i so far. The second term, $\sqrt{(2 \ln n)/n_i}$, represents how confident the algorithm is in its estimate of μ_i, which can be thought of as an exploration term. Thus, to make UCB more greedy, we can reduce the magnitude of this exploration term.

In particular, we introduce a parameter γ which starts at 1 on the first pull and linearly decays to 0 for the last pull of the time horizon. On each pull n, this new Horizon-Aware UCB (HA-UCB) policy now picks the arm i that maximizes

$$\bar{\mu}_i + \gamma\sqrt{\frac{2\ln n}{n_i}}. \quad (4)$$

Decaying γ in this way means a HA-UCB policy will act exactly like UCB on the first pull and exactly like a perfectly greedy agent on the last pull. HA-UCB slightly outperforms UCB on the tasks we consider (Fig. 2).

3.3 ϵ-Greedy Policy

ϵ-greedy policies pick the arm with the highest average reward so far with probability 1-ϵ and pick a random arm with probability ϵ. We include one over-exploring agent (0.9-Greedy) and one under-exploring agent (0.1-Greedy). In isolation, 0.1-Greedy obtains lower regret than 0.9-Greedy, but both have significantly higher regret than UCB and HA-UCB (Fig. 2).

4 EXPERIMENTAL DESIGN

4.1 User Study

We ran a user study in which participants played a game with multiple slot machines (i.e., arms). Users collaborated with different agents, that suggest which slot to pick at each iteration. We introduced these agents as "robots" to users, to concisely communicate that the suggestions were from a non-human actor.

When collaborating with an agent, users are first asked which slot they would like to play before seeing the agent's suggestion. After this, the user is shown the agent's suggestion via highlighting the slot(s) the agent would pick. If the agent has no preference among multiple slots (for instance, when greedy algorithms choose randomly), then all of those slots will be highlighted. Once they see the suggestion, users are free to select any slot.

4.2 Manipulated Variables

We manipulated the *learning algorithm* with five levels: *Unassisted, 0.1-Greedy, 0.9-Greedy, UCB,* and *HA-UCB.* We purposefully chose these agents to span the *exploration vs. exploitation* spectrum. We used a within-subjects design for this variable and counterbalanced the order.

4.3 Objective Measures

- **Regret:** The total regret accumulated after all $n = 30$ pulls.
- **Inherent Compatibility:** The amount of time it takes for users in isolation to pick arms which each agent *would have* suggested had they been assisting.
- **Explicit Influence:** The percentage of time the human's choice changes to the agent's suggestion after seeing it.
- **Implicit Influence:** The difference between inherent compatibility and how long users *actually* take to pick arms that agents suggest.
- **Decision Scores:** The normalized score assigned by HA-UCB to the decision made, based on the history of pulls and rewards. This allows us to analyze users' strategies before and after getting assistance.
- **Entropy:** The entropy of the distribution over how often users choose each arm; this measures whether they under-explore or over-explore. A perfectly greedy policy will have entropy 0, whereas a perfectly uniform policy (with $K = 6$ arms as in the user study) will have entropy 2.58.

4.4 Subjective Measures

We also care about the users' perceptions of the agents, so we ask three Likert scale questions about whether they *trusted* the agent, whether they thought the agent was *useful,* and whether they followed the agent's *advice.* We also ask users to *rank* the agents in order of how much they enjoyed collaborating with them.

4.5 Participants

We used Amazon Mechanical Turk to recruit a total of 52 users (33% female, mean age 33). Users were compensated \$3.75 for the study, which lasted approximately 20 minutes. Users were also given up to a \$1 reward depending on their average payout across all collaboration settings. Users were informed of this reward bonus before starting the study, in order to incentivize them to pay attention and try their best.

5 ANALYSIS

The team can be better than the best team member. In isolation, UCB and HA-UCB perform the best in terms of cumulative regret, scoring 23 and 22 respectively. Humans in isolation perform similarly, getting an average regret of 23. ϵ-Greedy agents perform notably worse than this, with 0.1-Greedy and 0.9-Greedy getting regret of 36 and 40 respectively (Fig. 2).

The performance of the human-agent team only improves when people are paired with HA-UCB. This is expected, but it is exciting to see that the team *outperforms* HA-UCB in isolation (Fig. 3). Not only are people able to improve their own performance, but the human-agent team—when paired with the right agent—can do better than either humans or agents in isolation. Interestingly, we find that particular individuals perform even better still (significantly) when paired with HA-UCB; these are the individuals labeled "Group 1", which we will discuss later in this section.

Optimizing team performance is not the same as optimizing learning performance. We expected that in general, the performance of the agent in isolation will have some correlation with the performance of the human-agent team. But even though the best agent led to the best team, the correlation did not hold in general.

We ran repeated measures ANOVA for our objective measures of Regret and did post-hoc analyses with Tukey HSD. We found that the learning algorithm factor has a significant effect on Regret ($F(3, 48) = 11.529, p < 0.01$) and that HA-UCB is significantly different from 0.9-Greedy (Tukey HSD). One interesting result is that while HA-UCB only outperforms UCB by 1 point in isolation, human-HA-UCB teams significantly outperform human-UCB teams (Fig. 3), by an average of 6 points. This sixfold increase in the difference in performance indicates that HA-UCB's suggestions were somehow more helpful and made more sense to people than UCB's, leading to people being able to make much more informed decisions.

Statement	0.1-Greedy	0.9-Greedy	HA-UCB	UCB
"I trusted the agent"	4.2 ± 0.23	2.5 ± 0.20	**4.8 ± 0.21**	4.2 ± 0.25
"I thought the agent was useful"	4.1 ± 0.25	2.6 ± 0.22	**4.8 ± 0.24**	4.2 ± 0.27
"I followed the agent's advice"	3.8 ± 0.25	3.5 ± 0.23	**4.7 ± 0.25**	4.0 ± 0.27
Rank [1: best, 4: worst]	2.5 ± 0.14	3.0 ± 0.13	**2.0 ± 0.14**	2.5 ± 0.15

Table 1: Post-study Likert ratings. Users prefer to work with HA-UCB significantly more than with other agents.

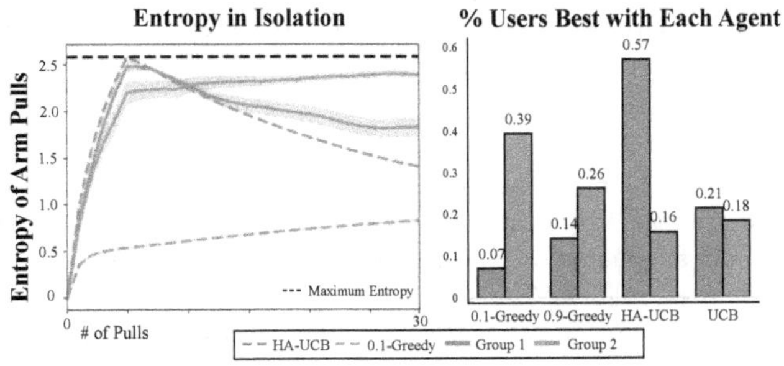

Figure 5: Left: The entropy of the distribution over how often users and agents pick each arm in isolation as a function of the number of pulls. Group 1 explores more fully initially and then becomes greedy, Group 2 explores at the same rate throughout. Curves for agents are averaged over 10,000 trials. HA-UCB has a similar shape to Group 1 and 0.1-Greedy has a similar shape to Group 2. Right: The percentage of users who obtain their highest score with each agent. Most users in Group 1 get their highest score with HA-UCB, while nearly 40% of users in Group 2 get their highest score with 0.1-Greedy. The agents' exploration strategies align with the users' strategies in these cases, which seems to improve team performance.

Another interesting result is that the team's performance can improve slightly (or at least remain unaffected) despite pairing the human with a *worse* agent. UCB in isolation outperforms .1-Greedy (Fig. 2) by an average of 13 points, while the two human-agent teams perform very similarly. 0.1-Greedy even gets slightly lower regret by 2 points on average (Fig. 3). Though this difference is not statistically significant, it stands in stark contrast to how much better UCB performs than 0.1-Greedy in isolation.

Despite team performance not correlating to agent performance in isolation, the users' ratings did. Table 1 shows the subjective measures: agents better in isolation are rated higher.

These results indicate that simply improving an agent's isolated performance does not correlate with improving its ability to assist humans. Assistance is more subtle, and we explore what influences human-team performance in the remainder of this section.

Agents have implicit (rather than explicit) influence. One hypothesis for what causes the difference in team performance is that agents convince people to change their mind, going against their initial choice for an arm. However, when we measure how often users change their mind to agree with the agent's suggestion after seeing it, we found no influence from the agents. Overall, the percent of time people are explicitly influenced like this is close to 4% across all agents, which corresponds to approximately one decision over the user's 30-decision time horizon (Fig. 4). It seems unlikely that this one decision could affect the performance of human-agent teams so drastically. But if people are not changing their decisions to match the agent's suggestions, how are different agents leading to different team performances?

What we found is that users' initial choices are different when interacting with the different agents: there is an *implicit* influence that agents have, whereby the suggestions agents make at one time point do not lead the person to explicitly change their mind about which arm they pull now, but affect their choices in the future.

We measure this by looking instead at how long it takes until people actually follow agents' suggestions (Fig. 4). For each agent, we look at how many pulls it takes each user on average to ultimately pick the arms it suggests. We call this the *delay* in accepting the agent's suggestions. This is an informative measure, but to understand the agent's influence, we need to compare this to some baseline to understand how much users' decisions are actually changing. To do this, we simulate the agents making suggestions based on people's decisions in isolation and similarly measure how long it takes for people to choose arms which the agents would have suggested. We refer to this as a user's *compatibility* with each agent, since it tells us how quickly users would have taken agents' suggestions regardless. We refer to the difference between the delay in accepting the agent's suggestions and the human's compatibility with that agent as the agent's *implicit influence.*

We ran repeated measures ANOVA for our objective measures of Regret and did post-hoc analyses with Tukey HSD. We found significant effects for the learning algorithm on Implicit Influence ($F(3, 48) = 122.04, p < 0.0001$). HA-UCB had higher influence than UCB and 0.1-Greedy (Tukey HSD). Finally, we found significant effects for the agent assistance factor (assisted or unassisted) on Implicit Influence ($F(1, 48) = 13.45, p = 0.0004$).

When not assisted by any agent, people are most similar to the 0.1-Greedy agent, only having about a 2 pull delay before they choose what it would have suggested. In contrast, users take around 5 or 6 pulls before picking what the other agents would have suggested. When people are actually seeing agents' suggestions, this average falls across the board. This tells us that although agents do not explicitly change users' minds, their suggestions have an implicit influence on their strategies going forward.

When viewed from this lens, we do actually see a difference in influence between the agents! The time it takes for users to take HA-UCB's suggested arms goes down by the largest fraction of all the agents. With no assistance, people take on average 5.4 pulls before taking what HA-UCB would have suggested, whereas people actually take less than 2 pulls on average before pulling arms which it actually suggested. In contrast, there is little difference here for 0.1-Greedy between the unassisted and assisted settings: people take about 2.5 pulls before following its decisions in both cases (Fig. 4). The other agents (UCB and 0.9-Greedy) see a slight improvement, but not nearly as large as that of HA-UCB.

Though we see that HA-UCB has the most implicit influence on people, they do not directly take its suggestions very often. Instead, they are influenced to change their overall strategy after seeing its suggestions.

People perform better with agents that are more like them. Next, we turned to understanding what might be responsible for this difference in influence. We looked at unassisted users first and plotted the entropy of the distribution of arms they had selected up to each time step. We found that users naturally fell into two distinct groups. Users were manually separated into these groups and no users were excluded. 21 users were placed into Group 1 and 31 into Group 2.

As we see in Fig. 5, people in Group 1 will initially explore all or almost all arms as evident by the entropy steadily increasing to the maximum entropy 2.58. The entropy then steadily decreases, indicating that users will settle on one or two arms to continue pulling for the remainder of the time horizon. In contrast, Group 2 will continue to explore all arms at approximately the same rate for the entirety of the time horizon, as evident by the entropy curve increasing to and leveling out at 2.4.

Remarkably, if we look at which agent each person in these groups got their personal high score with, there is a distinct difference between them. As shown in Fig. 5, a majority of users in Group 1 (57%) get their highest score when collaborating with HA-UCB, whereas only only 16% of users in Group 2 do. In contrast, only 7% of users in Group 1 get their highest score when collaborating with 0.1-Greedy as compared with 39% of users in Group 2. Now, if we plot the entropy curves for these two agents in isolation averaged over 10,000 trials (Fig. 5), we see the shapes tend to correspond with those of the two groups. This lends credence to the idea that users perform best when being assisted by an agent which acts like them.

We see that Group 1, which matches HA-UCB, reduces regret to 16 when assisted by HA-UCB, which is far lower than even HA-UCB's performance (regret 22). While we do not make statistical claims, people have a better sense of what the best arm looks like (in terms of average reward), whereas HA-UCB starts with no information. With HA-UCB assisting, people are inclined to explore arms which they would not have on their own, so the team in total is better able to identify the best arm than either would have in isolation. The same group performs worse with 0.1-Greedy, decreasing performance also when compared to how well these users did in isolation. Particularly surprising is that more Group 2 users perform better with 0.1-Greedy than with HA-UCB, despite HA-UCB being the better algorithm. Group 2 performs slightly better when assisted by 0.1-Greedy than when unassisted, whereas Group 1 performs worse.[1]

Statement	Group 1	Group 2
"I trusted the agent"	3.4 ± 0.35	**4.5 ± 0.27**
"I thought the agent was useful"	3.2 ± 0.47	**4.4 ± 0.28**
"I followed the agent's advice"	2.7 ± 0.42	**4.2 ± 0.28**
Rank [1: best, 4: worst]	3.0 ± 0.25	**2.3 ± 0.17**

Table 2: Post-study Likert ratings for 0.1-Greedy. (Differences between the two groups were negligible for other agents.) Group 2, who performs better when collaborating with 0.1-Greedy, overall has a positive view of the agent while Group 1 has a negative view.

When looking at the subjective measures split by groups, we find that they disagree in their opinion of 0.1-Greedy. Group 1, who is more aligned with HA-UCB, rates the 0.1-Greedy much lower than Group 2 (Table 2).

Overall, we find that people have different strategies, and many of them team up best with agents that match their strategy. We found it striking that 39% of people with the greedy-like strategy perform best with greedy, whereas only 16% of them perform best with HA-UCB, and this is in spite of HA-UCB's superiority in isolation.

6 DISCUSSION AND FUTURE WORK

We saw that human-agent teams can outperform humans and agents in isolation. But our analysis suggests that achieving this, or even just improving upon human performance, is much more subtle than we expected. The agent's suggestions do not change a person's decisions explicitly, but rather influence their later decisions. Further, people benefit differently from different agents, depending on the similarity between their strategy and the agent's.

These results show that helping a person manage exploration exploitation trade-offs is distinct from directly making those trade-offs. We can alternatively formulate this problem as a cooperative game between the human and the robot [6], where both the robot and the human are optimizing to maximize the cumulative reward from the *human's* arm selections. Crucially, the robot is forced to operate through making changes to the human's internal or information state. In future work, we plan to explore this formulation of the problem and develop algorithms that leverage models of human internal state to make helpful suggestions and work with humans to explore and exploit appropriately to maximize long term reward.

7 ACKNOWLEDGEMENTS

This work was partially supported by the NSF NRI. We thank the members of the InterACT Lab for helpful discussion and feedback.

ACKNOWLEDGMENTS

This work was partially supported by the NSF NRI. We thank the members of the InterACT Lab for helpful discussion and feedback.

[1] On the surface, this analysis seems to contradict that the average total regret accumulated by Group 2 when collaborating with HA-UCB is not significantly different from when collaborating with 0.1-Greedy (Fig. 3). However, we notice that when users in Group 2 get lower regret with 0.1-Greedy than with HA-UCB it is by an average of 13 points, whereas those that get lower regret with HA-UCB do better by an average of 19 points. Thus it is the case that while more users perform better with 0.1-Greedy, the average regret from collaborating with the two agents is approximately the same.

REFERENCES

[1] C. Anderson. 2001. *Behavioral models of strategies in multi-armed bandit problems.* Ph.D. Dissertation. California Institute of Technology.

[2] Peter Auer and Paul Fischer. 2002. Finite-time Analysis of the Multiarmed Bandit Problem*. *Machine Learning* 47 (2002), 235–256.

[3] Jeffrey Banks, Mark Olson, and David Porter. 1997. An experimental analysis of the bandit problem. *Economic Theory* 10, 1 (01 Jun 1997), 55–77. https://doi.org/10.1007/s001990050146

[4] C. Breazeal, C. D. Kidd, A. L. Thomaz, G. Hoffman, and M. Berlin. 2005. Effects of nonverbal communication on efficiency and robustness in human-robot teamwork. In *2005 IEEE/RSJ International Conference on Intelligent Robots and Systems.* 708–713.

[5] Anca D. Dragan, Shira Bauman, Jodi Forlizzi, and Siddhartha S. Srinivasa. 2015. Effects of robot motion on human-robot collaboration. In *Proceedings of the Tenth Annual ACM/IEEE International Conference on Human-Robot Interaction (HRI).* ACM, 51–58.

[6] Dylan Hadfield-Menell, Stuart J Russell, Pieter Abbeel, and Anca Dragan. 2016. Cooperative Inverse Reinforcement Learning. In *Advances in Neural Information Processing Systems 29*, D. D. Lee, M. Sugiyama, U. V. Luxburg, I Guyon, and R. Garnett (Eds.). Curran Associates, Inc., 3909–3917. http://papers.nips.cc/paper/6420-cooperative-inverse-reinforcement-learning.pdf

[7] A. D. Horowitz. 1973. *Experimental study of the two-armed bandit problem.* Ph.D. Dissertation. University of North Carolina, Chapel Hill.

[8] Minae Kwon, Sandy H. Huang, and Anca D. Dragan. 2018. Expressing Robot Incapability. In *Proceedings of the Thirteenth ACM/IEEE International Conference on Human Robot Interaction (HRI).* ACM.

[9] L. Li, W. Chu, J. Langford, and R. E. Schapire. 2010. A Contextual-Bandit Approach to Personalized News Article Recommendation. *International Conference on World Wide Web* (2010), 661–670.

[10] L. Li, W. Chu, J. Langford, and R. E. Schapire. 2011. Unbiased Offline Evaluation of Contextual-bandit-based News Article Recommendation Algorithms. *International Conference on World Wide Web* (2011), 297–306.

[11] Michelle Marks, Mark J Sabella, Shawn Burke, and Stephen J Zaccaro. 2002. The Impact of Cross-Training on Team Effectiveness. *The Journal of applied psychology* 87 (03 2002), 3–13.

[12] Joseph E. Mercado, Michael A. Rupp, Jessie Y. C. Chen, Michael J. Barnes, Daniel Barber, and Katelyn Procci. 2016. Intelligent Agent Transparency in Human-Agent Teaming for Multi-UxV Management. *Human Factors* 58, 3 (2016), 401–415.

[13] R. J. Meyer and Y. Shi. 1995. Sequential choice under ambiguity: Intuitive solutions to the armed-bandit problem. *Management Science* (1995), 817–83.

[14] Stefanos Nikolaidis, Swaprava Nath, Ariel Procaccia, and Siddhartha Srinivasa. 2017. Game-theoretic modeling of human adaptation in human-robot collaboration. In *Proceedings of the 2017 ACM/IEEE International Conference on Human-Robot Interaction.*

[15] Stefanos Nikolaidis and Julie Shah. 2013. Human-robot Cross-training: Computational Formulation, Modeling and Evaluation of a Human Team Training Strategy. In *Proceedings of the 8th ACM/IEEE International Conference on Human-robot Interaction (HRI '13).* IEEE Press, Piscataway, NJ, USA, 33–40.

[16] S. D. Ramchurn, F. Wu, W. Jiang, and J. E. Fischer. 2015. Human-agent collaboration for disaster response. *Autonomous Multi-Agent Systems* 30 (2015), 82–111.

[17] Paul Reverdy, Vaibhav Srivastava, and Naomi Ehrich Leonard. 2014. Modeling Human Decision-making in Generalized Gaussian Multi-armed Bandits. *Proc. IEEE* 104 (2014), 544–571.

[18] P. B. Reverdy. 2014. *Human-Inspired Algorithms for Search: A Framework for Human-Machine Multi-Armed Bandit Problems.* Ph.D. Dissertation. Princeton University.

[19] Aaron St. Clair and Maja Mataric. 2015. How Robot Verbal Feedback Can Improve Team Performance in Human-Robot Task Collaborations. In *Proceedings of the Tenth Annual ACM/IEEE International Conference on Human-Robot Interaction (HRI '15).* ACM, New York, NY, USA, 213–220. https://doi.org/10.1145/2696454.2696491

[20] Freek Stulp, Jonathan Grizou, Baptiste Busch, and Manuel Lopes. 2015. Facilitating intention prediction for humans by optimizing robot motions. In *Proceedings of the Twenty-Eighth IEEE/RSJ International Conference on Intelligent Robots and Systems (IROS).* 1249–1255.

[21] F. Wu, S. D. Ramchurn, W. Jiang, and J. E. Fischer. 2015. Agile Planning for Real-World Disaster Response. *International Joint Conferences on Artificial Intelligence* (2015).

APPENDIX: STRATEGIES WITH AND WITHOUT ASSISTANCE

A second way we analyzed implicit influence is by looking at the (normalized) score that HA-UCB assigns to the users' initial and final choices given the history of pulls (Fig. 6). Though the scores people get here do not necessarily correlate with their regret, we can use this to measure whether human strategies are changing. If strategies were not being influenced by agents, we should expect these scores to stay approximately the same. However, we see that the curves for humans in isolation are significantly different from those when collaborating with agents. Again, this tells us that agents influence people's decisions implicitly rather than explicitly.

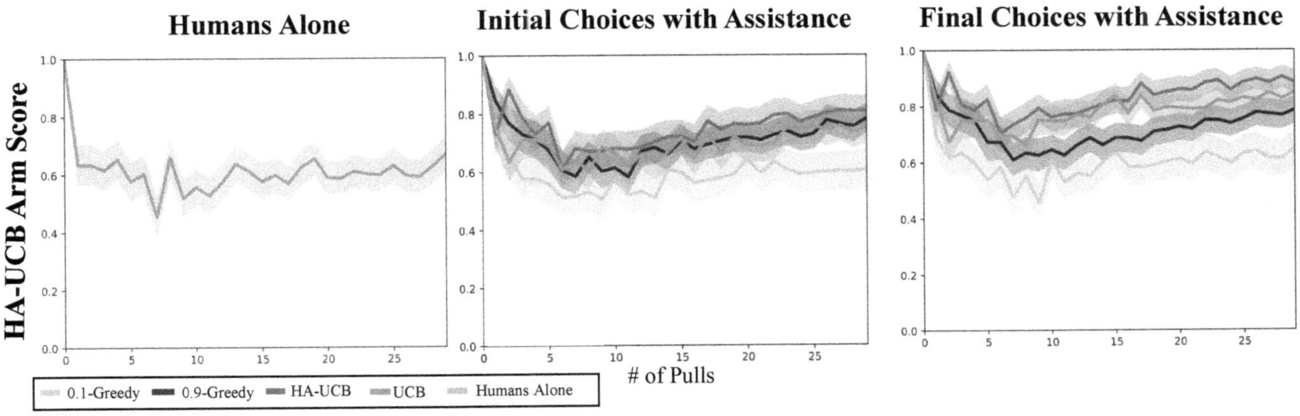

Figure 6: The y-axis shows the normalized score assigned by HA-UCB to the decision made, based on the history of pulls and rewards. Left: The average scores obtained by human strategies in isolation. Middle: The average scores obtained from humans' initial choices while collaborating with each agent. Right: The averages scores obtained from humans' final choices while collaborating with each agent. Note that the scores are highest for HA-UCB and that the curves are different for people when collaborating with an agent versus in isolation, meaning that their strategies are altered.

A Comparative Analysis of Emotion-Detecting AI Systems with Respect to Algorithm Performance and Dataset Diversity

De'Aira Bryant
dbryant@gatech.edu
Georgia Institute of Technology
Atlanta, Georgia, USA

Ayanna Howard
ayanna.howard@gatech.edu
Georgia Institute of Technology
Atlanta, Georgia, USA

ABSTRACT

In recent news, organizations have been considering the use of facial and emotion recognition for applications involving youth such as tackling surveillance and security in schools. However, the majority of efforts on facial emotion recognition research have focused on adults. Children, particularly in their early years, have been shown to express emotions quite differently than adults. Thus, before such algorithms are deployed in environments that impact the wellbeing and circumstance of youth, a careful examination should be made on their accuracy with respect to appropriateness for this target demographic. In this work, we utilize several datasets that contain facial expressions of children linked to their emotional state to evaluate eight different commercial emotion classification systems. We compare the ground truth labels provided by the respective datasets to the labels given with the highest confidence by the classification systems and assess the results in terms of matching score (TPR), positive predictive value, and failure to compute rate. Overall results show that the emotion recognition systems displayed subpar performance on the datasets of children 's expressions compared to prior work with adult datasets and initial human ratings. We then identify limitations associated with automated recognition of emotions in children and provide suggestions on directions with enhancing recognition accuracy through data diversification, dataset accountability, and algorithmic regulation.

ACM Reference Format:
De'Aira Bryant and Ayanna Howard. 2019. A Comparative Analysis of Emotion-Detecting AI Systems with Respect to Algorithm Performance and Dataset Diversity. In *AAAI/ACM Conference on AI, Ethics, and Society (AIES '19), January 27–28, 2019, Honolulu, HI, USA.* ACM, New York, NY, USA, 6 pages. https://doi.org/10.1145/3306618.3314284

1 INTRODUCTION

Understanding a child's emotional state is of great importance in numerous applications, from understanding levels of comfort when interacting with a therapy robot (Leo et al. 2015) to identifying degrees of engagement or feelings of frustration when interacting with virtual agents during a learning scenario (Littleworth et al. 2011). However, before intelligent systems can be deemed usable for these societal purposes, it is critical that we examine the validity of the systems used for emotion recognition and classification amongst children. In the emotion recognition domain, one of the requirements for validating the performance of any new classification algorithm is to evaluate it against established datasets. There has been valuable work on validating models for recognizing emotion constructed via machine learning in recent years; yet, this work has focused primarily on adults imaged in different lighting conditions, scales, and from various perspectives (Dupré et al. 2017, Stöckli et al. 20117, Bernin et al. 2017).

We have identified a gap in research with regard to validating models for emotion recognition in children. The first contribution of this paper is an in-depth comparison of publicly available datasets for research purposes that have conducted inter-rater reliability studies for validating the emotion labels associated with the facial expressions of children. Second, we have conducted an evaluation of eight commercially available emotion recognition systems against the five datasets of children expressions. To the best of our knowledge, this paper represents one of the few comparisons to be made on emotion recognition datasets and classification systems with a focus on children. We also highlight a rising concern with constructing classifiers for children while using validating datasets where children have poor representation. This challenge resonates with similar problems seen across the machine learning and artificial intelligence (AI) communities.

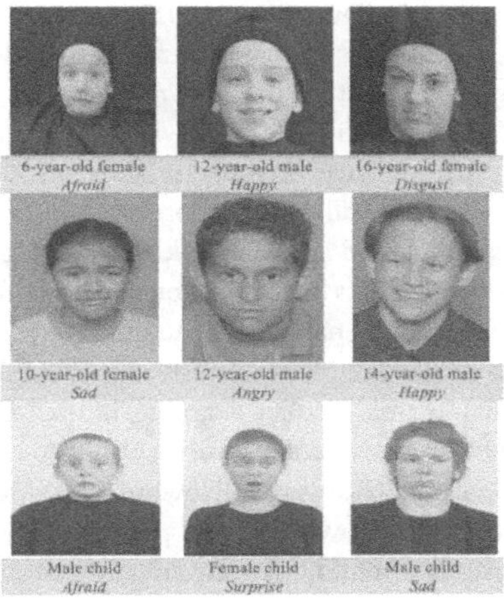

Figure 1: Example stimuli of children associated with the facial expression databases: Top: Dartmouth Database of Children 's Faces [8]; Middle: NIMH-ChEFS database; Bottom: Radboud Faces Database [11].

AIES '19, January 27–28, 2019, Honolulu, HI, USA

ACM ISBN 978-1-4503-6324-2/19/01...$15.00
https://doi.org/10.1145/3306618.3314284

2 BACKGROUND & RELATED WORK

2.1 The Role of Emotions

The human face is an extremely complex source of insight into the inner-workings of the mind and body with the ability to express thousands of different facial configurations. Of these configurations, notable psychologist Paul Ekman found that there are six universal basic emotions: anger, disgust, fear, happiness, sadness, and surprise (Ekman 1992). These emotion classes, as interpreted from facial expressions, are key factors influencing social inter-human interaction. If AI agents are to be capable of navigating complex social scenarios with humans, it is critical that they are capable of perceiving these multiple emotion categories.

In addition to understanding the differences between the emotion categories and their implications, it is also necessary to consider the dynamic features that may affect certain subsets of the population. For example, as the bounds between emotion categories are traditionally socially constructed (Gordon, 1991), children often take several years to reach the levels of emotional intelligence that is often seen in adults (Durand et al. 2007, Mondloch et al. 2003). In turn, their expressions of specific emotions differ from adults in a variety of ways. For example, Saarni notes how children in their early years heavily associate emotions to facial expressions and therefore learn to express the concepts of happiness, sadness and anger earlier than the concepts of fear, surprise and disgust (Saarni 1999). As children have a limited amount of social emotional experiences, it can take many years for them to learn common social cues (Herba et al. 2006, Thomas et al. 2007).

2.2 Approaches to Emotion Recognition Systems

A majority of emotion recognition and classification systems utilize an approach based on the Emotional Facial Action Coding System (EmFACS) which encompasses mapping specific facial muscle configurations to the various emotional categories (Friesen and Ekman 2005). As described in (Dupré et al. 2017, Bernin et al. 2017), the general approach to classifying still images includes finding the face in the image, extracting the relevant features such as facial action units (AUs), and finally classifying the image using algorithms trained through various machine learning techniques. A non-exhaustive list of available emotion recognition systems, past and present, can be found in (Deshmukh and Jagtap 2017).

Although several efforts have relied on machines for recognizing emotions in children to enable their functionality, most have not done a systematic analysis of the performance of these emotion classification results in children. For example, in the realm of socially interactive robots, research robots use emotions to engage children in therapy or learning (Brown and Howard 2014, Metta et al. 2008, Simmons et al. 2003). However, their performance evaluation is based on measures of child engagement rather than on emotion recognition. In (Littleworth et al. 2011), accuracy measures were based on Action Units. Another research effort, (Khan, Meyer, and Bouakaz 2015), reported achieving a maximum overall recognition rate of 79% with the automated recognition of facial expressions for children when considering the full Dartmouth Database of Children Faces. The team later tested their classifier on the NIMH Child Emotional Faces Picture Set database and achieved a recognition rate of 68.4%. Although these efforts have begun to address some of the research gaps in validating models for emotion recognition in children, they have not evaluated these models against a variety of diverse datasets or considered performance metrics other than overall classification accuracy.

3 METHODOLOGY

Here, we introduce five image datasets comprised of the facial expressions of children. These datasets are available publicly for research purposes with labels and inter-rater reliability data provided. When assumptions had not been made in the past, we admitted into the study those images associated with an inter-rater reliability value of at least 75%. In the other cases, we applied the threshold values for inclusion used in the researchers'studies and published results. The five datasets compared were the NIMH Child Emotional Faces Picture Set (NIMH-ChEFS), the Dartmouth Database of Children's Faces, the Radboud Faces Database, the Child Emotions Picture Set (CEPS), and the Child Affective Facial Expressions Set (CAFE) (Figure 1). Next, we compare these systems through a diversity analysis and a comparison of human recognition rates on the images. We then introduce the eight selected emotion recognition systems and compare their various attributes.

	Fear	Anger	Disgust	Happiness	Sadness	Surprise
NIMH-ChEFS	96%	95%	-	99%	92%	-
Dartmouth	82%	87%	86%	96%	93%	88%
Radboud	86%	93%	89%	97%	90%	92%
CEPS	74%	88%	82%	96%	80%	81%
CAFE	70%	80%	75%	89%	79%	76%
Avg. Human Recognition	82%	89%	83%	95%	87%	84%

Table 1: Human ratings with good inter-rating reliability.

3.1 Children Facial Expression Datasets

The NIMH Child Emotional Faces Set (NIMH-ChEFS). This dataset contains images of the emotional faces of children ranging in age, ethnicity, and gender (Egger et al. 2011). The original picture set includes 534 pictures with 39 girls and 20 boys in the picture set (total N=59) covering 5 emotions (afraid, angry, happy, sad and neutral) and two gaze conditions (direct and averted). The child actors range in age from 10 to 17 years old with a mean age of 13.6 years old. Images are coded for emotion by a sample of 20 raters ranging in age from 22 to 70 (mean age 38.3). A cut-off point for inclusion was established of 15/20 (75%) of the raters correctly identifying the intended emotion, which excluded 52 pictures from the original set leaving a final set of 482 pictures.

The Dartmouth Database of Children's Faces. This dataset contains images of 40 male and 40 female Caucasian children ranging in age between 6 and 16 (Dalrymple, Gomez, and Duchaine 2013). The original picture set includes 1280 images covering 7 emotions (neutral, happy, sad, angry, afraid, surprise, and disgust).

The models photographed for the study ranged in age from 5 to 16 years old with a mean age of 9.72 years old. Images were coded for emotion by a random sample from 163 recruited adult raters. Each image was assessed by at least 20 raters for facial expression. For comparative analyses, we selected a cut-off point for inclusion of cases at 75% of the raters correctly identifying the intended emotion, which excluded 370 pictures from the original set leaving a final set of 910 pictures.

The Radboud Faces Database (RaFD). This dataset contains images of the emotional facial expressions of 4 male and 6 female Caucasian Dutch children (Langner et al. 2010). The original picture set includes 240 images covering 8 emotions (neutral, angry, sad, afraid, disgust, surprise, happy, and contempt). Images were coded for emotion by a random sample from 276 recruited raters with a mean age of 21.2; 238 were women. Each image was assessed by at least 20 raters for facial expression. We again established a cut-off point for inclusion at a threshold requiring at least 75% of the raters correctly identifying the intended emotion. This excluded 57 pictures from the original set leaving a final set of 183 pictures.

The Child Emotions Picture Set (CEPS). This dataset contains images of the emotional faces of Brazilian children ranging in age, ethnicity, and gender (Romani-Sponchiado et al. 2015). The picture set includes 273 pictures with 9 girls and 8 boys in the picture set (total N=17) covering 7 emotions (happy, sad, angry, disgust, afraid, surprise, and neutral) and 3 intensity levels. The children ranged in age from 6 to 11 years old with a mean age of 8.9 years old. Images were coded for emot ion by a sample of 30 psychologists as raters, with each image receiving at least 5 ratings. A cut-off point for inclusion was established by the researchers at 60% of the raters correctly identifying the intended emotion, which excluded 48 pictures from the original set leaving a final set of 225 pictures.

The Child Affective Facial Expressions Set (CAFE). This dataset contains images of the emotional faces of children ranging in age, ethnicity, and gender (LoBue and Thrasher 2015). The original picture set includes 1192 pictures with 90 girls and 64 boys in the picture set (total N=154) covering 7 emotions (happy, angry, sad, afraid, surprise, neutral, and disgust). Children range in age from 2 to 8 years old with a mean age of 5.3 years old. Images were coded for emotion by a sample of 100 raters. A cut-off point for inclusion was established by the researchers at 66% of the raters correctly identifying the intended emotion, which excluded 403 pictures from the original set leaving a final set of 789 pictures.

Table 1 summarizes the various emotional stimuli and the associated ratings that result when human raters are asked to label the basic emotions for each presented image.

3.2 Dataset Diversity

To break down the composition of the datasets, we introduce eight attributes of diversity that contribute to the makeup of image datasets used for emotion recognition. We use these metrics to derive a diversity rating for each dataset. This rating scale can be used to further illustrate the validity of new datasets and emotion recognition systems by assessing the diversity of the image data. The nine attributes contributing to the diversity rating include age, gender, ethnicity, gaze, geographic location of recruitment, clothing, pose, and number of emotion classes. We describe how we score values from 0 to 1 for each attribute in Table 2. We then show the scores for each of the five datasets in Table 3. A diversity rating of 1.0 is associated with a fully diverse dataset in terms of representation, setting and collection.

Diversity Metric	Rating Description
Age	Age diversity was ranked by considering how representative the dataset was of the desired population's age range. Given the range, a ratio was calculated for each age represented in the dataset compared to the ratio it would be if the dataset were equally distributed by age. If each ratio was above 90%, the dataset received a 1.
Gender	Gender diversity was ranked by considering the ratio of male to female children participants. The closer the ratio was to an equal distribution, the higher the rating.
Ethnicity	Ethnic diversity was ranked by considering whether the dataset consisted of children from a single ethnic background or multiple. If only children from a single ethnic background existed in the dataset, the dataset received a 0. Otherwise, the dataset received a 1.
Gaze Direction	Gaze direction was ranked by considering whether the images were taken with multiple gaze directions. NIM-ChEFS was the only dataset to have a diverse selection of images with different gaze directions.
Geographic Region	Geographic region was ranked by considering the dataset's collection process. Each of the datasets recruited children from a single geographic region and were therefore granted a score of 0.
Clothing	Clothing was ranked by considering the diversity of clothing shown in the images. Datasets where children all wore identical outfits received a score of 0. Otherwise, datasets received a 1.
Pose	Pose was ranked by considering whether the images consisted of entirely staged images or not. Ceps was the only dataset which included spontaneous emotional expressions.
Num. Classes	The classes metric was ranked by considering the number of emotion classes that existed in the dataset. If a dataset included at least the six basic emotions, it was ranked with a 1. If not, the ratio of classes to the 6 basic emotions was used as the score.

Table 2: Metrics used for scoring and assessing the diverse makeup of an image dataset used for emotion recognition.

	Age	*Gen.*	*Ethn.*	*Gaze*	*Geo.*	*Clo.*	*Pose*	*Classes*	SUM	Diversity Rating
NIM_ ChEFS	1	0.51	0.33	1	0	1	0	0.67	4.51	**0.56**
Dartmouth	1	1	0.17	0	0	0	0	1	3.17	**0.40**
Radboud	1	0.67	0.17	0	0	0	0	1	2.84	**0.36**
CEPS	1	0.88	0.5	0	0	1	1	1	5.38	**0.67**
CAFE	1	0.71	0.67	0	0	0	0	1	3.38	**0.42**

Table 3: Dataset diversity rating breakdown for the 5 datasets of children emotion expression. Gender is abbreviated by "gen", Ethnicity: "ethn", Clothing: "clo", and Geography: "geo".

	Matching Score (TPR)						
	Happy	Sad	Fear	Disgust	Anger	Surprise	AVG. MS
Google	99.47%	52.39%	-	-	26.32%	89.20%	66.84%
Sighthound	91.39%	50.80%	52.81%	39.37%	60.37%	77.70%	62.07%
Face++	91.56%	59.84%	19.14%	55.46%	48.97%	91.99%	61.16%
Amazon	98.42%	27.66%	-	10.06%	27.52%	89.90%	50.71%
Microsoft	99.30%	66.76%	16.50%	36.31%	48.74%	86.41%	59.00%
Skybiometry	76.94%	28.19%	49.50%	74.64%	31.33%	84.90%	57.58%
Affectiva	94.52%	23.17%	8.88%	64.75%	11.14%	90.91%	48.90%
Kairos	51.68%	18.55%	15.09%	30.12%	80.44%	65.06%	43.49%

Figure 2: Matching Scores (TPRs) for each emotion recognition system categorized by each emotion category. Fear and disgust images were not considered for the Google Vision API and fear images were not considered for Amazon Rekognition as these two systems do not provide confidence values for those emotions. Systems are listed in order of highest to lowest average matching scores.

3.3 Emotion Recognition Systems

To evaluate the performance and limitations of AI-based emotions recognition systems, we selected emotion recognition systems that had either an API or SDK which allowed the emotion recognition capabilities to be embedded into other applications. After a systematic review of the field, we included eight systems in our analysis: Affectiva, Google Vision API, Microsoft Emotion API, Amazon Rekognition, Face++, Kairos, Sighthound, and Skybiometry.

Commercially, these systems are being used in a variety of applications ranging from academic research, to advertising, to hospitality, to retail, to education, etc. Some have already been embedded into a variety of everyday technology. As such, there are potential impacts on many diverse groups in the world, including children. This work seeks to analyze the efficacy of these emotion recognition systems by assessing their performance on a variety of children emotion datasets, allowing us to visualize their usage potential in real-world scenarios involving youth.

4 PROCEDURE

We utilize a similar approach described in (Bernin et al. 2017) where we conduct a black box test for each emotion recognition system (Patton 2006). We first store the ground truth labels of the images. Next, we process each of the images from each of the datasets through each of the emotion recognition systems. We then normalize the results for an equal comparison. A maximization function is then used to determine the emotion label with the highest confidence value. Finally, we compare the system-produced predicted label to the ground truth label and store the results [1].

Google Vision API did not offer confidence values for the emotions of fear and disgust. Amazon Rekognition did not offer confidence values for the emotion fear. To assess these two algorithms fairly, we did not include the ratings for images labeled as emotions they do not provide confidence intervals for in the results section below.

[1]These black box tests occurred progressively between May 2018 and July 2018. As these systems have regular updates and changes to algorithmic functionality, it is possible that these results could differ if obtained at a later time.

5 RESULTS

We analyze the results of the emotion recognition systems by assessing the matching scores (TPR), positive predictive values, and failure to compute (FTC) rates of the data.

5.1 Matching Score (True Positive Rate)

Matching score, also known as accuracy, sensitivity or true positive rate, gives insight into how much of a particular class an emotion recognition system can accurately classify. Matching score is defined as the ratio between the number of true positives to the total number of total actual positives. True Positives represents the number of images where the predicted emotion label matches the ground truth label and total Actual Positives represents the total number of images with the ground truth emotion label. The matching scores for each emotion and each system can be seen in Figure 2.

5.2 Positive Predictive Value

Positive predictive value (PPV) gives insight into how much trust can be placed in a recognition system to assess a particular label. It is a measure of how often the predicted class is actually the ground truth. The formula for PPV can be seen in (1) and PPV scores for each emotion and each system can be seen in Figure 3.

$$PPV = \frac{(MS * prevalence)}{(MS * prevalence) + (1 - specificity) * (1 - prevalence)} \quad (1)$$

where PPV is positive predictive value and MS is matching score. Prevalence is defined as the ratio of the total Actual Positives to the total number of images classified. Specificity is defined as the ratio of the True Negatives to the total Actual Negatives.

5.3 Failure to Compute (FTC) Rate

A prerequisite to facial emotion classification is facial detection. There were some instances where the systems could not identify a face in an image and therefore would not provide emotional data.

Positive Predictive Value							
	Happy	Sad	Fear	Disgust	Anger	Surprise	Avg. PPV
Microsoft	67.83%	84.80%	100.00%	94.74%	76.34%	56.49%	80.03%
Google	57.95%	68.17%	-	-	97.46%	89.51%	78.27%
Sighthound	83.07%	87.61%	64.52%	74.46%	62.98%	66.37%	73.17%
Face++	78.35%	71.43%	61.05%	67.25%	72.79%	54.32%	67.53%
Skybiometry	93.38%	86.18%	65.07%	46.33%	52.85%	45.81%	64.94%
Kairos	94.25%	72.73%	37.07%	59.51%	24.81%	68.63%	59.50%
Amazon	51.86%	54.45%	-	62.50%	54.79%	52.65%	55.25%
Affectiva	74.92%	54.68%	44.23%	35.50%	54.17%	34.33%	49.64%

Figure 3: Positive Predictive Value rates for each emotion recognition system categorized by each emotion category. Fear and disgust images were not considered for the Google Vision API and fear images were not considered for Amazon Rekognition as these two systems do not provide confidence values for those emotions. Systems are listed in order of highest to lowest average PPV.

We use FTC rates to illustrate how often this scenario occurred. Face++, Google, Microsft, Amazon and Sighthound all had FTC rates less than 1%. Skybiometry, Kairos, and Affectiva each had FTC rates of 2.39%, 9.15%, and 15.34% respectively.

6 DISCUSSION

Our results indicate that the emotions of happiness and surprise were most easily identified and classified correctly by each of the emotion recognition systems, except for Kairos. Fear and sadness were amongst the hardest to identify and classify. Google's Vision API had the highest average matching scores for the images it processed, which excluded images labeled as fear and disgust. Sighthound had the next highest overall matching scores. Face++, Microsoft Emotion API and Skybiometry ranked very closely to Sighthound in terms of matching scores.

In terms of PPV, Microsoft's Emotion API produced the best overall results with 100%, 95%, and 85% PPV rates for fear, disgust, and sadness respectively. Google's Vision API came in a close second with the highest PPVs for anger and surprise. An interesting observation can be observed when comparing the PPV rates to the matching scores. For example, Microsoft's Emotion API has a 100% PPV rate and a 16.5% matching score for fear. This shows that though the recognition system only produced the fear label for images with a ground truth label of fear, the system only picked up a small fraction of the images with that label. This trend was observed across multiple systems in our analysis. This illustrates the importance of the threshold values potentially used within each of the recognition systems. Our hypothesis is that systems with tighter thresholds for classification tend to have higher PPV rates whereas systems with looser thresholds tend to have higher TPR rates.

An interesting question arises when considering which metric should be held of highest importance. Should an emotion recognition system aim to classify the most instances of a particular category? Or, should a system aim to maximize the confidence in its predictive value? Should users of the technology be able to have a say based on their intended application? Is there a way to best maximize the two using additional input parameters? These are questions that the creators of such technology must consider in future iterations of their software.

Additionally, a similar comparative analysis using adult emotion image datasets found that Sighthound and Microsoft's Emotion API had an average 76.1% and 61.3% matching score respectively (Dehghan et al. 2017). For Microsoft, this is comparable to the 59% average score for the children emotion datasets. However, Sighthound performed worse on children's faces than adult faces, with only 62.07%. Affectiva reports that their system achieves accuracy in the high 90th percentile for key emotions, yet their average matching score for the children datasets was 48.9%, among the worst of the analyzed systems. Affectiva also had the lowest average PPV and a failure to compute rate of about 15%.

Human accuracy of the selected images for analysis had accuracy rates for each basic emotion above 80%. No system had this level of performance on more than two of the six emotions. These results provide further evidence that popular emotion recognition systems have not thoroughly considered children as a part of their target population. Yet, there is little to no regulation on what categories of people this software can or cannot be used for. With the psychological differences in the expression of emotions found in children, it is critical to develop either improved, standalone or adaptive emotion recognition software to adequately service this youthful audience.

7 CONCLUSION

In this work, we assess and evaluate five datasets of children emotional expression and eight emotion recognition systems. We first evaluate the composition of the different datasets through a diversity rating which considers the attributes of age, gender, ethnicity, gaze, geographic region, clothing, pose, and number of classes. Next, we evaluate the human performance of recognition between the various datasets. Finally, we conduct a comparative analysis between the eight emotion recognition systems using the five datasets. From this analysis, we conclude that most systems performed worse when compared to human raters and similar studies conducted using adult emotional data.

As we have seen, the least recognized emotion among the human raters was fear. This poorer recognition rate is also reflected by the various emotion recognition systems. Given that the biases in recognition rate for human raters seems to also be reflected in the various systems, there is a concern that these algorithms are reflecting some degree of human biases. Recently, there has been an upsurge of attention given to machine learning algorithms and the practices of inequality and discrimination that are potentially being built into them (Buolamwini and Gebru 2018, Crawford 2016). We know that imbalances exist in training sets. There is a danger that specific imbalances in the training data will result in biases that may be implicit and unrecognized. Additional work is needed to address these issues in algorithmic learning and classification.

Additionally, recent articles, (Lapowsky 2018, Vanderklippe 2018), detail how facial and emotion recognition technology is being considered for educational environments in an attempt to target societal issues of student surveillance and security. The results of this work demonstrate that these potential applications are undeniably premature. This is an immediate and pressing problem. If these systems are not holistically designed for the audiences in which they are inevitably impacting, we will continue to see the perpetuation of implicit bias and unfairness in these systems with potentially devastating impacts.

We see the development of best practices for directly targeting these issues surrounding bias and inclusion with establishing representativeness in training sets, evaluating the validity of datasets for testing procedures, and calling for some third-party oversight for the inclusion of recognition, classification, and recommender systems that are to be used in societal applications. With these recommendations, technology can continue to mature progressively and without the taint of inherent human biases. These precautionary enhancements will pave the way for future affective technology and allow for a variety of useful applications in their due time.

ACKNOWLEDGMENTS

This research is based upon work partially supported by funding from the Linda J. and Mark C. Smith Endowed Chair, the NSF-GRFP under Grant No. DGE-1650044 and NSF Award No. 1849101.

REFERENCES

[1] Affectiva, Affectiva, Inc. https://www.affectiva.com/.
[2] Amazon Rekognition, Amazon, https://aws.amazon.com/rekognition/.
[3] Bernin, A., Müller, L., Ghose, S., von Luck, K., Grecos, C., Wang, Q., & Vogt, F. 2017. Towards more robust automatic facial expression recognition in smart environments. In Proceedings of the 10th International Conference on Pervasive Technologies Related to Assistive Environments. (pp. 37-44). ACM.
[4] Brown, L. and Howard A. 2014. Gestural Behavioral Implementation on a Humanoid Robotic Platform for Effective Social Interaction. IEEE Int. Symposium on Robot and Human Interactive Communication (RO-MAN), pp. 471 – 476.
[5] Buolamwini, J. and Gebru, T. 2018. Gender shades: Intersectional accuracy disparities in commercial gender classification. In Conference on Fairness, Accountability and Transparency, pp. 77-91.
[6] Crawford, K. 2016. Artificial Intelligence's White Guy Problem, New York Times - Opinion, http://www.nytimes.com/2016/06/26/opinion/sunday/artificial-intelligences-white-guy-problem.html.
[7] Dalrymple KA, Gomez J and Duchaine B. 2013. The Dartmouth Database of Children's Faces: Acquisition and Validation of a New Face Stimulus Set. Urgesi C, ed.PLoS ONE. 2013;8(11).
[8] Dehghan, A., Ortiz, E. G., Shu, G., & Masood, S. Z. 2017. Dager: Deep age, gender and emotion recognition using convolutional neural network. arXiv preprint arXiv:1702.04280.
[9] Deshmukh, R. S., & Jagtap, V. 2017. A survey: Software API and database for emotion recognition. In Intelligent Computing and Control Systems (ICICCS), 2017 International Conference on (pp. 284-289). IEEE.
[10] Dupré, D., Andelic, N., Morrison, G., & McKeown, G. 2017. Accuracy of three commercial automatic emotion recognition systems across different individuals and their facial expressions. In 2018 IEEE International Conference on Pervasive Computing and Communications: Proceedings IEEE.
[11] Durand, K., Gallay, M., Seigneuric, A., Robichon, F., & Baudouin, J. Y. 2007. The development of facial emotion recognition: The role of configural information. Journal of experimental child psychology, 97(1), 14-27.
[12] Egger HL, Pine DS, Nelson E, et al. 2011. The NIMH Child Emotional Faces Picture Set (NIMH-ChEFS): A new set of children's facial emotion stimuli. International Journal of Methods in Psychiatric Research.20(3):145-156.
[13] Ekman, P. 1992. An argument for basic emotions. Cognition & emotion, 6(3-4), 169-200.
[14] Face++, Megvii Technology, https://www.faceplusplus.com/.
[15] Friesen, W.V, Ekman, P, EMFACS-7: Emotional Facial Action Coding System, Unpublished manuscript, University of California at San Francisco, 1983.
[16] Google Vision API, Google Cloud Platform, https://cloud.google.com/vision/.
[17] Gordon, S. L. 1991. The socialization of children's emotions: emotional culture, competence, and exposure. Children's understanding of emotion, 319.
[18] Herba, C. M., Landau, S., Russell, T., Ecker, C., & Phillips, M. L. 2006. The development of emotion–processing in children: Effects of age, emotion, and intensity. Journal of Child Psychology and Psychiatry, 47(11), 1098-1106.
[19] Howard, A, Zhang, C., and Horvitz, E. 2017. Addressing Bias in Machine Learning Algorithms: A Pilot Study on Emotion Recognition for Intelligent Systems. IEEE International Workshop on Advanced Robotics and its Social Impacts, Austin, TX, March.
[20] I. Lapowsky. 2018. Schools Can Now Get Facial Recognition Tech For Free. Should They? https://www.wired.com/story/realnetworks-facial-recognition-technology-schools.
[21] Kairos, Kairos AR, https://www.kairos.com/.
[22] Khan, R.A., Meyer, A., Bouakaz, S. 2015. Automatic Affect Analysis: From Children to Adults, International Symposium on Visual Computing, ISVC 2015, 304-313.
[23] Langner, O., Dotsch, R., Bijlstra, G., Wigboldus, D.H.J., Hawk, S.T., & van Knippenberg, A. 2010. Presentation and validation of the Radboud Faces Database. Cognition & Emotion, 24(8).
[24] Leo, M., Coco, M. D., Carcagnì, P., Distante, et al. 2015. Automatic Emotion Recognition in Robot-Children Interaction for ASD Treatment., in 'ICCV Workshops', IEEE, pp. 537-545 .
[25] Littleworth, G., Bartlett, M.S., Salamanca, L.P. and Reilly, J. 2011. Automated Measurement of Children's Facial Expressions during Problem Solving Tasks. IEEE Int. Conference on Automatic Face and Gesture Recognition, pp. 30–35.
[26] LoBue, V., & Thrasher, C. 2015. The Child Affective Facial Expression (CAFE) set: validity and reliability from untrained adults. Frontiers in psychology, 5, 1532.
[27] Metta, G., Sandini, G. Vernon, D. Natale, L. Nori, F. 2008. The iCub humanoid robot: an open platform for research in embodied cognition, 8th workshop on performance metrics for intelligent systems, pp. 50-56.
[28] Microsoft Emotion API, Microsoft Azure, https://azure.microsoft.com/en-us/services/cognitive-services/emotion/.
[29] Mondloch, C. J., Geldart, S., Maurer, D., & Le Grand, R. 2003. Developmental changes in face processing skills. Journal of experimental child psychology, 86(1), 67-84.
[30] Patton, R. 2006. Software testing. Pearson Education India. pp.55.
[31] Romani-Sponchiado, A., Sanvicente-Vieira, B., Mottin, C., Hertzog-Fonini, D.,& Arteche, A. 2015. Child Emotions Picture Set (CEPS): Development of a database of children's emotional expressions. Psychology & Neuroscience, 8(4), 467.
[32] Saarni, C. 1999. The development of emotional competence. Guilford Press.
[33] Sighthound, Sighthound, Inc., https://www.sighthound.com/.
[34] Simmons R., et al. 2003. GRACE: An Autonomous Robot for the AAAI Robot Challenge, AI Magazine, Vol. 24(2), pp. 51-72.
[35] Skybiometry, Skybiometry UAB, https://skybiometry.com/.
[36] Stöckli, S., Schulte-Mecklenbeck, M., Borer, S., & Samson, A. C. 2017. Facial expression analysis with AFFDEX and FACET: A validation study. Behavior research methods, 1-15.
[37] Thomas, L. A., De Bellis, M. D., Graham, R., & LaBar, K. S. 2007. Development of emotional facial recognition in late childhood and adolescence. Developmental science, 10(5), 547-558.
[38] Vanderklippe, N. 2018. In China, Classroom Cameras Scan Students Faces for Emotion, Stroking Fears of New Form of State Monitoring. https://www.theglobeandmail.com/world/article-in-china-classroom-cameras-scan-student-faces-for-emotion-stoking/.

Degenerate Feedback Loops in Recommender Systems

Ray Jiang, Silvia Chiappa, Tor Lattimore, András György, Pushmeet Kohli
{rayjiang,csilvia,lattimore,agyorgy,pushmeet}@google.com
DeepMind London, UK

ABSTRACT

Machine learning is used extensively in recommender systems deployed in products. The decisions made by these systems can influence user beliefs and preferences which in turn affect the feedback the learning system receives - thus creating a feedback loop. This phenomenon can give rise to the so-called "echo chambers" or "filter bubbles" that have user and societal implications. In this paper, we provide a novel theoretical analysis that examines both the role of user dynamics and the behavior of recommender systems, disentangling the echo chamber from the filter bubble effect. In addition, we offer practical solutions to slow down system degeneracy. Our study contributes toward understanding and developing solutions to commonly cited issues in the complex temporal scenario, an area that is still largely unexplored.

ACM Reference Format:
Ray Jiang, Silvia Chiappa, Tor Lattimore, András György, Pushmeet Kohli. 2019. Degenerate Feedback Loops in Recommender Systems. In *Proceedings of AAAI/ACM Conference on AI, Ethics, and Society (AIES '19)*. ACM, New York, NY, USA, 8 pages. https://doi.org/10.1145/3306618.3314288

1 INTRODUCTION

Recommender systems are increasingly used to provide users with personalized product and information offerings [5, 7, 12]. These systems employ user's personal characteristics and past behaviors to generate a list of items that are individually tailored to the user's preferences. Whilst extremely successful commercially, there are growing concerns that such systems might lead to a self-reinforcing pattern of narrowing exposure and shift in user's interest, problems that are often referred to in the literature as "echo chamber" and "filter bubble". A significant amount of research has therefore been devoted to deriving ways to favor diversity in the set of items an individual may be exposed to (see Kunaver and Porl [9] for a review). However, current understanding of the echo chamber and filter bubble effects is limited and experimental analysis reports conflicting results.

In this paper, we define as echo chamber the effect of a user's interest being positively or negatively reinforced by repeated exposure to a certain item or category of items, thereby generalizing the definition in Sunstein [16], where the term is used to refer to over- and limited-exposure to similar political opinions reinforcing one's existing beliefs. We focus the definition of filter bubble introduced by Pariser [15] to describe just the fact that recommender systems select limited content to serve users online. We provide a theoretical treatment that allows us to consider the echo chamber and filter bubble effects separately. We view user's interest as a dynamical system and treat interest extremes as degeneracy points of the system. We consider different models of dynamics and identify sets of sufficient conditions that make them degenerate over time. We then use this analysis to understand the role played by the recommender system. Finally, we showcase the interplay between the user's dynamics and the recommender system actions in a simulation study using synthetic data and several classic bandit algorithms. The results reveal several pitfalls of recommender system design and point towards mitigation strategies.

2 RELATED WORK

Through an analysis on the MovieLens dataset, Nguyen et al. [14] found that the diversity of items recommended, and those users engage with, gets narrower over time. The paper asks whether there is a "natural" tendency of degeneration in user interest. Our paper takes steps toward answering this question by providing theoretical conditions for user interest degeneracy.

In the social sciences literature, Flaxman et al. [8] found that online services are associated with increased political polarization between users as well as increased exposure to the less preferred side of political opinions. Their seemingly counter-intuitive findings are not contradictory according to our results: systems with some level of random exploration can be degenerative. Barberá et al. [3] also presented evidence of echo chamber related to political issues on Twitter. On the other hand, [4, 6, 13] found counter-evidence on online news consumption. Another work by Bakshy et al. [2] measured the effect of user choices separately from that of the recommendation algorithm, and found that individual choices play a larger role than the algorithm in creating echo chamber on Facebook. This supports our viewpoint that user interests degenerate or not depending on their internal dynamics, the recommender system can only slow down or accelerate the process of degeneration.

3 MODEL

We consider a recommender system that interacts with a user over time[1]. At every time step t, the recommender system serves l items (or categories of items, *e.g.* news articles, videos, or consumer products) to a user from a finite or countably infinite item[2] set $\mathcal{M}$. In general, the goal of the system is to present items to a user that she is interested in: we assume that, at time step t, the user's interest in an item $a \in \mathcal{M}$ is described by a function $\mu_t : \mathcal{M} \to \mathbb{R}$ such

AIES '19, January 27–28, 2019, Honolulu, HI, USA

ACM ISBN 978-1-4503-6324-2/19/01...$15.00
https://doi.org/10.1145/3306618.3314288

[1]For simplicity, in this paper we restrict ourselves to the case of a single user, and leave the case of multiple users possibly influencing each-other interests to future work.
[2]Throughout the paper, "items" also mean categories of items.

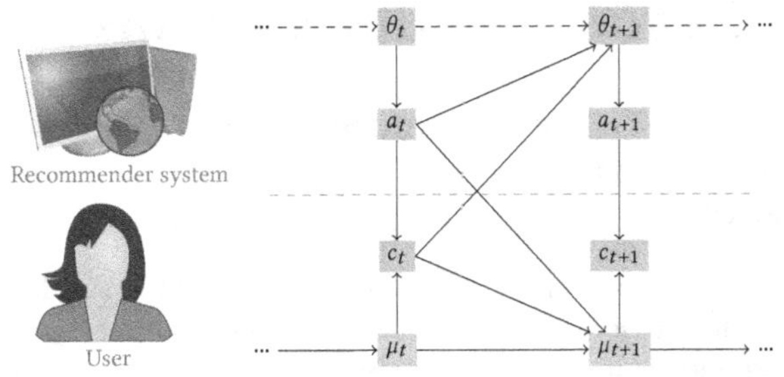

Figure 1: Model of interaction between a recommender system and user over time. Continuous and dashed links indicate existing or possible dependencies, respectively.

that $\mu_t(a)$ is large (positive) if the user is interested in the item, and small (negative) if she is not[3].

Given a recommendation $a_t = (a_t^1, \ldots, a_t^l) \in \mathcal{M}^l$, the user provides some feedback c_t based on her current interests $\mu_t(a_t^1), \ldots, \mu_t(a_t^l)$. This interaction has multiple effects: in the traditional literature for recommender systems, the feedback c_t is used to update the internal model θ_t of the recommender system that has been used to obtain the recommendation a_t, and the new model θ_{t+1} may depend on θ_t, a_t, and c_t. In practice θ_t usually predicts the distribution of user feedback to determine which items a_t should be presented to the user. In this paper we focus on another effect and consider explicitly that the user's interaction with the recommender system may change her interest in different items for the next interaction, thus the interest μ_{t+1} may depend on μ_t, a_t, and c_t. The full model of interaction is depicted in Fig. 1.

We are interested in studying the evolution of the user's interest. An example of such an evolution is that the interest is reinforced by user interactions with the recommended items, that is, $\mu_{t+1}(a) > \mu_t(a)$ if the user clicks on an item a at time step t, while $\mu_{t+1}(a) < \mu_t(a)$ if a is shown but not clicked (here $c_t \in \{0,1\}^l$ can be defined as the indicator vector of clicks to the corresponding items).

To analyze the echo chamber or filter bubble effect, we are interested in understanding when the user's interest changes extremely, which, in our model, translates to $\mu_t(a)$ taking values arbitrarily different from the initial interest $\mu_0(a)$: large positive values indicate that the user becomes extremely interested in item a, while large negative values indicate that the user dislikes a. Formally, for a finite item set $\mathcal{M}$, we can ask if the L_2 norm $\|\mu_t - \mu_0\|_2 = \left(\sum_{a\in\mathcal{M}}(\mu_t(a) - \mu_0(a))^2\right)^{1/2}$ can grow arbitrarily large: the user's interest sequence μ_t is called *weakly degenerate* if

$$\limsup_{t\to\infty} \|\mu_t - \mu_0\|_2 = \infty \quad \textit{almost surely}^4. \tag{1}$$

A stronger notion of degeneracy, which also requires that once μ_t drifted away from μ_0 it remains so, is *strong degeneracy*: the sequence μ_t is *strongly degenerate* if

$$\lim_{t\to\infty} \|\mu_t - \mu_0\|_2 = \infty \quad \textit{almost surely}. \tag{2}$$

[3]Whilst we focus on $\mu_t(a) \in \mathbb{R}$, we show in Remark 3, Appendix B that our results can be extended to the case where μ_t belongs to a bounded open interval.

[4]*i.e.* with probably 1.

In the next section we show that weak or strong degeneracy occurs under mild sufficient conditions on the evolutionary dynamics of μ_t.

There are multiple ways to extend the above definitions to the case of an infinite item set $\mathcal{M}$. For simplicity, we only consider here replacing $\|\mu_t - \mu_0\|_2$ with $\sup_{a\in\mathcal{M}} |\mu_t(a) - \mu_0(a)|$ in Eqs. (1) and (2), which is equivalent to the original definitions when $\mathcal{M}$ is finite[5].

4 USER INTEREST DYNAMICS - ECHO CHAMBER

As items often represent diverse categories of things, we make the simplifying assumption that they are independent from each other. By setting $l = 1$ and $a_t^1 = a$ for all t (*i.e.*, $\mathcal{M} = \{a\}$), we can remove the influence of the recommender system and consider the dynamics of the user's interest separately. This allows us to analyze the echo chamber effect: what happens to the interest $\mu_t(a)$ if item a is served infinitely often (*i.o.*).

Since a is fixed, to simplify the notation, we write μ_t instead of $\mu_t(a)$ in this section. Given a_t, according to Fig. 1, μ_{t+1} is a—possibly stochastic—function of μ_t (as μ_{t+1} depends on c_t and μ_t, and c_t depends on μ_t). Below we discuss the general case when the drift $\mu_{t+1} - \mu_t$ is a nonlinear stochastic function; deterministic models for the drift are considered in Appendix B.

Nonlinear Stochastic Model. We assume that $\mu_0 \in \mathbb{R}$ is fixed and that $\mu_{t+1} = \mu_t + f(\mu_t, \xi_t)$, where $(\xi_t)_{t=1}^\infty$ is an infinite sequence of independent uniformly distributed random variables that introduce noise into the system (*i.e.* μ_{t+1} is a stochastic function of μ_t). The function $f : \mathbb{R} \times [0,1]$ is assumed to be measurable, but otherwise arbitrary. Denoting the uniform distribution over $[0,1]$ by $U([0,1])$, let

$$\bar{f}(\mu) = \mathbb{E}_{\xi\sim U([0,1])}[f(\mu,\xi)]$$

be the expected increment $\mu_{t+1} - \mu_t$ when $\mu_t = \mu$. We also define

$$F(\mu, x) = \mathbb{P}_{\xi\sim U([0,1])}(f(\mu,\xi) \le x)$$

to be the cumulative distribution of the increment. The asymptotic behavior of μ_t depends on f, but under mild assumptions the system degenerates weakly (Theorem 1) or strongly (Theorem 2)[6].

THEOREM 1 (WEAK DEGENERACY). *Assume that F is continuous at $(\mu, 0)$ for all $\mu \in \mathbb{R}$ and there exists a $\mu_\circ \in \mathbb{R}$ such that 1) $F(\mu, 0) < 1$ for all $\mu \ge \mu_\circ$, 2) $F(\mu, 0) > 0$ for all $\mu \le \mu_\circ$. Then the sequence μ_t is weakly degenerate, i.e.* $\limsup_{t\to\infty} |\mu_t| = \infty$ *almost surely.*

The assumptions guarantee that within any closed bounded interval there is a constant probability that the random walk escapes to the left/right when starting to the left/right of $\mu_\circ$ respectively. Under stronger conditions it is possible to guarantee the divergence of the random walk. We state a simple version of the theorem, but note that the result can be generalized in many ways.

THEOREM 2 (STRONG DEGENERACY). *Assume that the conditions of Theorem 1 hold, and additionally that there exists $c \in \mathbb{R}$ such that $|\mu_{t+1} - \mu_t| \le c$ almost surely and there exists an $\epsilon > 0$ such*

[5]As such, we could have used $\sup_{a\in\mathcal{M}} |\mu_t(a) - \mu_0(a)|$ in our original definitions, but we prefer $\|\mu_t - \mu_0\|_2$ as it also provides some information about the "average" deviation of the user's interest over the different items at any finite time t.

[6]The proofs of these theorems are given in Appendix A.

that for all sufficiently large μ it holds that $\bar{f}(\mu) > \epsilon$, and for all sufficiently small μ it holds that $\bar{f}(\mu) < -\epsilon$. Then $\lim_{t\to\infty} \mu_t = \infty$ or $\lim_{t\to\infty} \mu_t = -\infty$ almost surely.

Intuitively, weak degeneracy occurs in a stochastic environment if the user's interest has some non-zero probability of drifting up when above some threshold, and of drifting down when below. Strong degeneracy holds if additionally $|\mu_{t+1} - \mu_t|$ is bounded and for μ_t sufficiently large/small the increment $\mu_{t+1} - \mu_t$ has positive/negative drift that is larger than a constant.

Theorems 1 and 2 show that the user's interest degenerates under very mild conditions, in particular, in the model we consider in our simulation studies. Thus, in such cases degeneracy can only be avoided if an item (or item category) is showed only finitely many times; otherwise one can only hope to control how fast μ_t degenerates (*i.e.* tends to ∞).

5 SYSTEM DESIGN ROLE – FILTER BUBBLE

In the previous section we discussed conditions for degeneracy for different user interest dynamics. In this section we examine the other side of the story, the influence of recommender system actions in creating filter bubbles. We typically do not know the dynamics of the user's interest in the real world. However, we consider the relevant scenario to the echo chamber/filter bubble problem where user's interest in some items has degenerative dynamics, and examine how to design a recommender system that slows down the degeneracy process. We consider three dimensions, namely model accuracy, amount of exploration, and growing candidate pool.

Model Accuracy. One common goal of recommender systems designers is to increase the prediction accuracy of the internal model θ_t. How does model accuracy coupled with greedy optimal a_t affect the speed of degeneration? We examine this question for the extreme case of exact predictions, *i.e.* $\theta_t = \mu_t$, we call such a prediction model the *oracle model.* We argue that under the *surfacing assumption* explained below, the oracle model coupled with greedily optimal action selection results in the quickest degeneracy.

In order to analyze the problem concretely, we focus on the degenerate linear dynamics model for $\mu_t(a)$ for $a \in \mathcal{M}$, *i.e.* $\mu_{t+1}(a) = (1+k)\mu_t(a) + b$. Then we can solve for $\mu_t(a)$, obtaining

$$\mu_t(a) = (\mu_0(a) + \frac{b(a)}{k(a)})(1 + k(a))^t - \frac{b(a)}{k(a)},$$

for $|1 + k(a)| > 1$ (see Appendix B).

Surfacing Assumption: Let $[m] = \{1, 2, \ldots, m\}$ be the candidate set of size m. If a subset of items $\mathcal{S} \subset [m]$ leads to positive degenerate dynamics (*i.e.* $\mu_t(a) \to +\infty$ for all $a \in \mathcal{S}$), then we assume that there exists a time $\tau > 0$ such that, for all $t \geq \tau$, $\mathcal{S}$ takes up the top $|\mathcal{S}|$ items in terms of values of μ_t, sorted by the base value of the exponential function, $|1 + k(a)|$.

The surfacing assumption makes sure that the quickest degenerating items surface out to the top list given enough time of exposure. It can be generalized to nonlinear stochastic dynamics of μ_t provided that the items from $\mathcal{S}$ have an almost surely stable ordering of degeneracy speed $|\mu_t(a) - \mu_0(a)|/t$ over time.

Under the general surfacing assumption, after time τ, the quickest way to degeneration is to serve the top l items according to μ_t, or θ_t of the oracle model. Even if the assumption is violated to some degree, the oracle model still leads to degeneracy very efficiently by picking the top l items according to μ_t which are likely to receive positive feedback due to high μ_t, and therefore increasing μ_{t+1} and reinforcing the past choices.

In practice the recommender system models are inaccurate. We can think of inaccurate models as the oracle model with different levels of noises added to θ_t. We discuss inaccurate models in the next section.

Amount of Exploration. Consider a type of ϵ-random exploration where a_t always picks the top l items out of a finite candidate pool $[m]$ with uniform ϵ noise on θ_t, *i.e.* according to $\theta'_t = \theta_t + U([-\epsilon, \epsilon])$.

Given the same model sequence θ_t, the bigger ϵ is, usually the slower the system degenerates. However, in practice θ_t is learned from observations, and the random exploration added to an oracle model may in fact accelerate degeneration: random exploration can help reveal the most positively degenerating items over time making the surfacing assumption more likely to be true (we show this phenomenon in the simulation experiments below, Fig. 5). In addition, if user interests have degenerative dynamics, even recommending items uniformly at random leads to degeneration, albeit quite slowly.

How do we then make sure that the recommender system does not make user interests degenerate? One way is to limit the number of times an item for which the user's interest dynamics is degenerative is served to the user. In practice it is hard to detect which items correspond to degenerative dynamics, however we can generally prevent degeneration if all items are served only a finite number of times, which suggests having an ever growing pool of candidate items.

Growing Candidate Pool $\mathcal{M}$. With a growing candidate pool, at every time step an additional set of new items becomes available to be served to the user. Hence the domain of the function μ_t expands as t increases. Adding new items at least linearly often is a necessary condition to avoid possible degeneration, since in a finite or any sublinearly growing candidate pool, by the pigeon hole principle, there must exist at least one item that is served *i.o.*, which is degenerate in the worst case scenario (also under general conditions described *e.g.* in Theorem 2). However, with an at least linearly growing candidate pool $\mathcal{M}$ the system can potentially impose the maximum number of times any item is served to a user and prevent degeneration.

6 SIMULATION EXPERIMENTS

In this section, we consider a simple degenerative dynamics for μ_t and examine degeneration speed under five different recommender system models. We further demonstrate that adding new items to the candidate pool can be an effective solution against system degeneracy.

We create a simulation for the model of interaction between a recommender system and a user of Fig. 1. Consider a possibly growing candidate pool of items of initial size m_0 and of size m_t at time step t. At each time step t, a recommender system picks the top l out of the m_t items $a_t = (a_t^1, \ldots, a_t^l)$ according to the internal model θ_t to serve to a user. The user considers each of the l items independently and chooses to click on a (possibly empty)

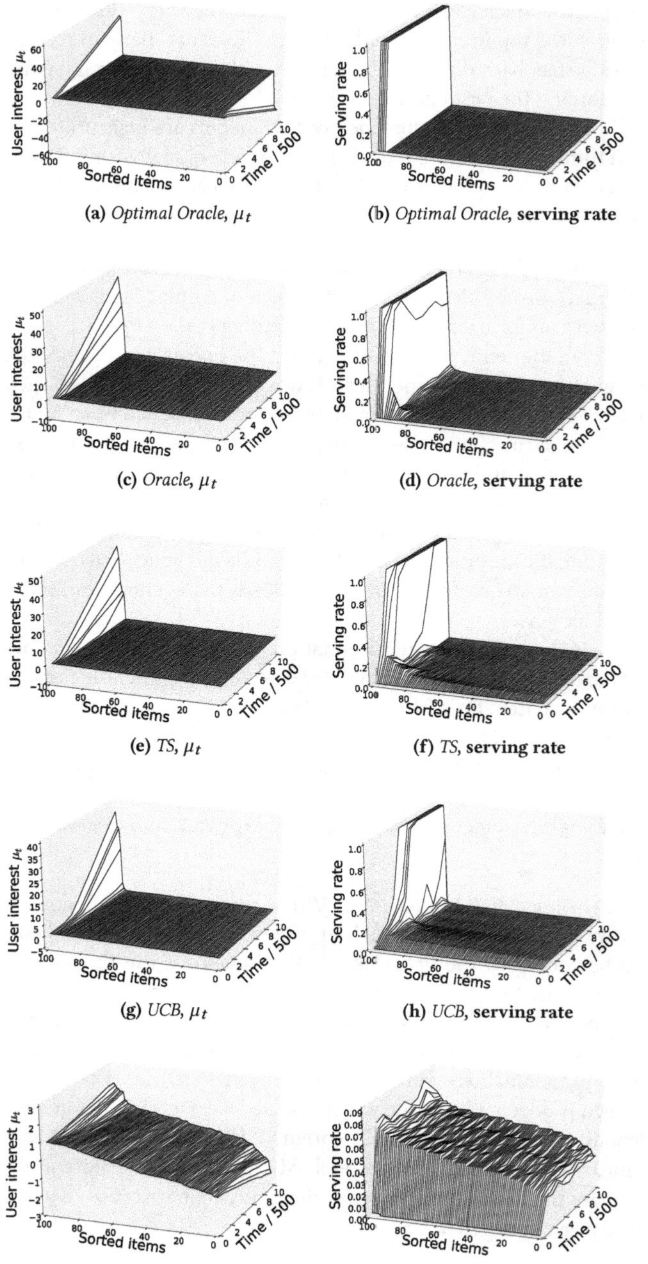

(a) *Optimal Oracle*, μ_t (b) *Optimal Oracle*, **serving rate**

(c) *Oracle*, μ_t (d) *Oracle*, **serving rate**

(e) *TS*, μ_t (f) *TS*, **serving rate**

(g) *UCB*, μ_t (h) *UCB*, **serving rate**

(i) *Random*, μ_t (j) *Random*, **serving rate**

Figure 2: Echo chamber and filter bubble effect for *Optimal Oracle, Oracle, TS, UCB* and *Random* models. Sorted user interest μ_t and serving rates are plotted every 500 steps. Under all models except for the *Random Model*, very quickly both the top items served and the top user interests narrow down to the (l =) 5 most positively reinforced items.

subset of them, thereby generating a binary vector c_t of size l where $c_t(a_t^i)$ gives the user feedback on item a_t^i, according to $c_t(a_t^i) \sim$ $Bernoulli(\phi(\mu_t(a_t^i)))$, where ϕ is the sigmoid function $\phi(x) = 1/(1+e^{-x})$. The system then updates the model θ_{t+1} based on the past actions, feedbacks and the current model parameter θ_t. We assume that the user's interest increases/decreases by $\delta(a')$ if the item a'

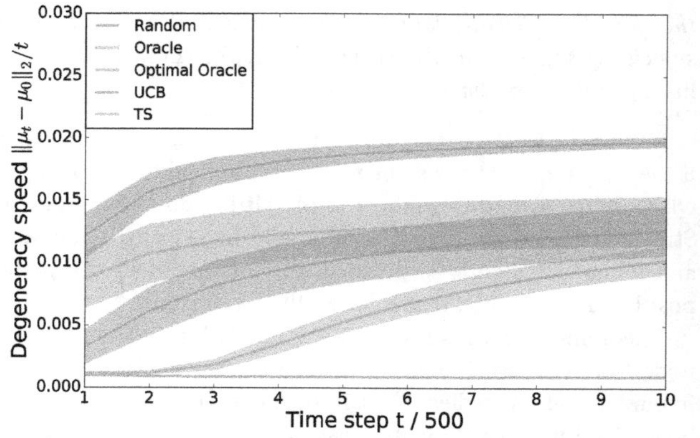

Figure 3: System evolves for 5,000 time steps with report interval 500. The results are averaged over 30 runs with the shaded area indicating the standard deviation. In terms of the degeneracy speed, *Optimal Oracle > Oracle > TS > UCB > Random.*

receives/does not receive a click, *i.e.*

$$\mu_{t+1}(a_t^i) - \mu_t(a_t^i) = \begin{cases} \delta(a_t^i) & \text{if } c_t(a_t^i) = 1, \\ -\delta(a_t^i) & \text{otherwise,} \end{cases} \quad (3)$$

where the function δ maps from the candidate set to $\mathbb{R}$. From Theorem 2, we know that $\mu_t \longrightarrow \pm\infty$ for every item. In the experiment, we set $l = 5$ and sample the drift δ from a uniform random distribution $U([-0.01, 0.01])$. The user's initial interest μ_0 for all items is independently sampled from a uniform random distribution $U([-1, 1])$.

The internal recommender system model is updated according to following five algorithms:

- **Random Model:** Instead of picking top items, the set of items $a_t = (a_t^1, \ldots, a_t^l)$ is sampled from a uniform random distribution over the candidate set $U([m_t])$.
- **Oracle:** $\theta_{t+1}(a_t^i) = \mu_{t+1}(a_t^i), \forall i$.
- **Optimal Oracle:** $\theta_{t+1}(a_t^i) = \delta(a_t^i), \forall i$. This model does not pick the highest l items according to μ_t but according to δ. Thus, it always picks the fastest degenerating items, therefore maximizing both the long term user engagement $\sum_{t=0}^{\infty} \|c_t\|_1$ and the degeneracy speed. For a fixed candidate pool $\mathcal{M}$, this model is equivalent to an *Oracle* that satisfies the Surfacing Assumption.
- **Upper Confidence Bound Multi-armed Bandit Algorithm**(*UCB*) [1, 10, 11]: We use the version of UCB algorithm in Chapter 8 of Lattimore and Szepesvári [11], however most UCB algorithms perform similarly to the purpose of this experiment. The algorithm prioritizes serving any item from the candidate set that has never been served before. This treatment includes the initial m_0 items as well as later whenever new items are added to the candidate pool. At time step t, UCB serves $l'(0 \le l' \le l)$ previously unserved items and the top $l - l'$ items according to values of θ_t. Define $f(t) = 1 + t\log^2(t)$ and we use the following model update $\theta_{t+1}(a) = \hat{c}_t(a) + \sqrt{2\log f(t)/T_a(t)}$, where $\hat{c}_t$ is the empirical average of feedbacks on item a, *i.e.* $\hat{c}_t(a) = \sum_{0\le i\le t, a\in a_i}^{t} c_t(a)/T_a(t)$, and $T_a(t)$ is the number of times item a has been served up to time t, i.e. $T_a(t) = \sum_{0\le i\le t, a\in a_i} 1$.

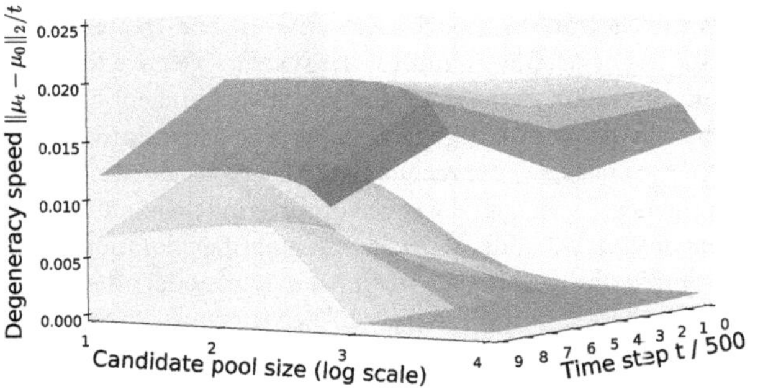

(a) Degeneracy rate vs candidate pool size vs time

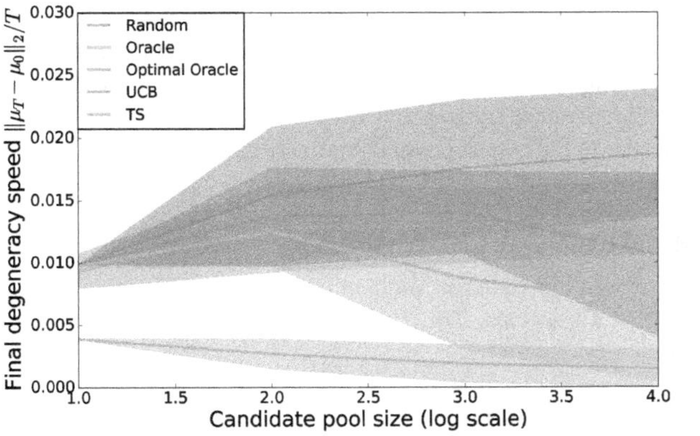

(b) Degeneracy rate vs candidate pool size

Figure 4: (a) Degeneracy surfaces for *Optimal Oracle* (grey), *UCB* (green) and *TS* (orange) up to time $T = 5,000$ while varying candidate pool sizes $\log_{10} m = 1, 2, 3, 4$. A larger candidate pool requires a longer time for exploration for the bandit algorithms, but among the three models *UCB* slows down system degeneracy the most given a large candidate pool. (b) Degeneracy speeds at $T = 20,000$ of *Optimal Oracle* and the *Oracle* are higher given a larger size of the candidate set, but those of the *and Random Model, UCB,* and *TS* are lower.

- **Thompson Sampling Multi-armed Bandit Algorithm** (*TS*) [17]: We initialize $\alpha_0(a) = 1, \beta_0(a) = 1$ for any new item a. If a is served at time t, we perform the update $\alpha_{t+1}(a) = \alpha_t(a) + c_t(a), \beta_{t+1}(a) = \beta_t(a) + 1 - c_t(a)$. At any time t, the internal model θ_t is sampled from the corresponding beta distribution $Beta(\alpha_t, \beta_t)$.

6.1 Echo Chamber & Filter Bubble Effect

We examine the echo chamber and filter bubble effects by running the simulation on a candidate pool of fixed size $m_t = m = 100$ with time horizon $T = 5,000$.

In Fig. 2, we show the degeneration of user interest μ_t (left column) and the serving rate (right column) of every item as each recommender model evolves in time. The serving rate of an item shows how often it is served within the report interval. In order to see the distribution clearly, we sort the items according to the z-values at the report time. Although all models cause user interest degeneration, the degeneration speeds are quite different (*Optimal Oracle > Oracle, TS, UCB > Random Model*). The *Oracle, TS* and *UCB* optimize based on μ_t and so we see a positive degenerative dynamics for μ_t. The *Optimal Oracle* optimizes on the degeneration speed directly and not on μ_t so we see both a positive and negative degeneration in μ_t. The *Random Model* also drifts μ_t in both directions, but at a much slower rate. However, overall except for the *Random Model,* very quickly both the top items served and the top user interests narrow down to the ($l =$) 5 most positively reinforced items.

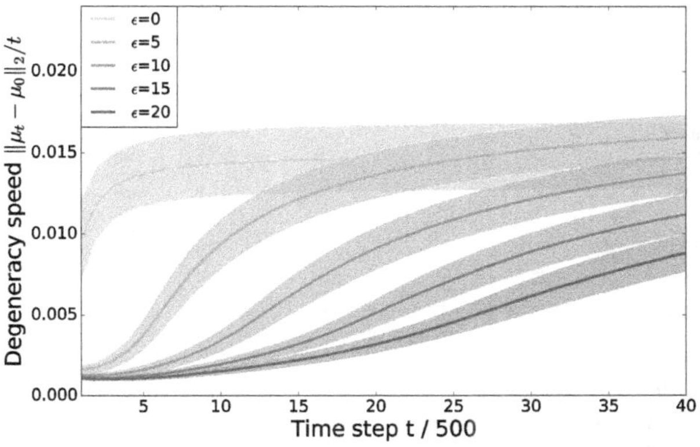

Figure 5: Degeneracy speed for the *Oracle* model with different noise levels $\epsilon \in [0, 10]$ up to $T = 20,000$. Adding noise to *Oracle* ($\epsilon = 0$) accelerates degeneration but as the noise level grows, degeneracy slows down.

6.2 Speed of Degeneracy

Next, we compare the degeneracy speed for the five recommender system models on both fixed and growing candidate sets. As the L_2 distance that measures system degeneracy is asymptotically linear for all five models (see Appendix C), we quantify degeneracy speeds by compare empirically $\|\mu_t - \mu_0\|_2/t$ in finite candidate pools for different experiment setups.

Figure 3 shows the degeneracy speed of five models averaged across 30 runs when we take $m = 100$ and evolve the system for $T = 5,000$ steps. We see that the *Optimal Oracle* results in the fastest degeneration by far, followed by the *Oracle, TS* and *UCB.* The *Random Model* offers the slowest degeneracy speed.

The Effect of Candidate Pool Size. In Fig. 4a we compare the *Optimal Oracle, UCB* and *TS*' degeneracy speed $\|\mu_t - \mu_0\|_2/t$ up to 5,000 time steps and candidate pool sizes $m = 10, 10^2, 10^3, 10^4$. Apart from the *Random* model, we see that *UCB* slows down system degeneracy the most given a large candidate pool since it is forced to explore any unserved item first. A larger candidate pool requires a longer time for exploration for the bandit algorithms. As the candidate pool size grows to 10,000 *UCB*'s degeneracy speed never peaks up given the time horizon, but will eventually grow given a longer time. *TS* has higher degeneracy speed due to weaker exploration on new items. The *Optimal Oracle* accelerates degeneration given a larger pool, as it can pick potentially faster degenerative items than from a smaller pool.

Additionally, in Fig. 4b we plot all five models degeneracy speed for $T = 20,000$ against the same changing candidate pool sizes. The degeneracy speed of the *Optimal Oracle* and the *Oracle* increases with the size of the candidate set, but that of the *and Random Model,*

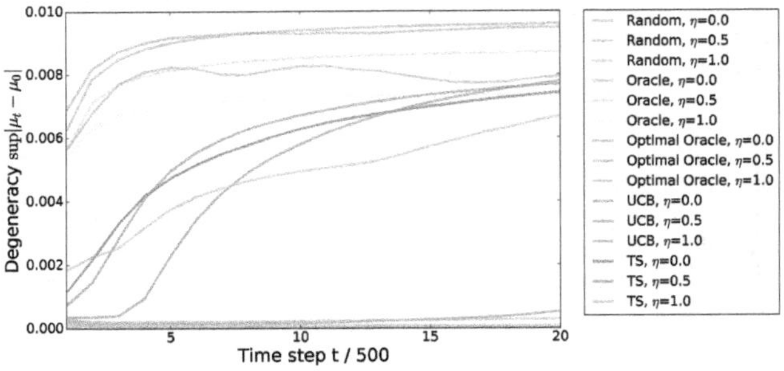

Figure 6: Comparison of the five models with growing candidate pools at different rates $\eta = 0, 0.5, 1.0$, degeneracy up to $T = 10,000$, averaged over 10 runs. Both the *Oracle* and the *Optimal Oracle* for all growth rates are degenerate. The *Random Model* and *UCB* stop degeneration at sublinear growth while *TS* model requires linear growth to stop degeneration.

UCB, and *TS* decreases. In practice, having a large candidate pool can be a temporary solution to slow down system degeneration.

The Effect of the Noise Level. Next we show the influence of internal model inaccuracy on degeneracy speed. We compare the *Oracle* model with different amounts of uniformly random noises, *i.e.* the system serves the top l items according to the noisy internal model $\theta'_t = \theta_t + U([-\epsilon, \epsilon])$. The candidate pool has fixed size $m = 100$. In Fig. 5, we vary ϵ from 0 to 10. Counter-intuitively adding noise to *Oracle* accelerates degeneration since faster degenerative items may be selected by chance than those fixed set of top l items ranked by μ_0, and more likely satisfies the Surfacing Assumption. Given $\epsilon > 0$, as expected, we see a nice monotonically increasing damping effect on degeneracy speed as the noise level grows.

Growing Candidate Pool. We extend the definition of degeneracy speed to an infinite candidate pool by computing $\sup_{a \in \mathcal{M}} |\mu_t(a) - \mu_0(a)|/t$ (see Appendix C for an asymptotic analysis). Since the degeneracy speed may not be asymptotically linear for all five models, we examine directly the sup distance $\sup_{a \in \mathcal{M}} |\mu_t(a) - \mu_0(a)|$ over 10,000 time steps. To construct growing candidate pools at different growth speed, we define a growth function $m_t = \lfloor m_0 + l t^{\eta} \rfloor$ by varying the growth parameter[7] $\eta = 0, 0.5, 1$, where $m_0 = 100$. In Fig. 6 we average the results over 10 independent runs. Both the *Oracle* and the *Optimal Oracle* for all growth rates are degenerate. The *Random Model* stops degeneration at sublinear growth, $\eta = 0.5$, so does *UCB* thanks to forced exploration on previously unserved items, although its trajectory has a small upward tilt. The *TS* model degenerates at sublinear growth but stops degeneration at linear growth $\eta = 1$. For all models, the higher the growth rate η, the slower they degenerate, if they do at all. Overall when applicable, an ideally linearly growing candidate set and continuous random exploration seem to be good remedies against an adversarial dynamics of μ_t to best prevent degeneracy.

7 CONCLUSION

We provided a theoretical analysis of the echo chamber and filter bubble effects for recommender systems. We used the dynamical system framework to model user's interest and treated interest extremes as degeneracy points of the system. We gave formal definitions of system degeneracy and provided sufficient conditions which make the system degenerate with both deterministic and stochastic dynamics. On the recommender system side, we discussed the influence on degeneracy speed of three independent factors in system design, *i.e.* model accuracy, amount of exploration, and the growth rate of the candidate pool. An oracle model often leads to quick degeneracy of the system, while continuous exploration and a large candidate pool size can help slow it down. The best remedies against system degeneracy we found are continuous random exploration and growing the candidate pool at least linearly.

Our work has two main limitations. First, since user interests are hidden variables that are not directly observed, a good measure or proxy for user interests is necessary in practice to study degeneration reliably. Second, we assumed that items and users are independent from each other – we will extend the theoretical analysis to the case of possibly mutually dependent items and users in a future work.

8 ACKNOWLEDGMENTS

We would like to thank William Isaac, Michael Mathieu, Krishnamurthy Dvijotham, Timothy Mann and Dilan Gorur, for helpful discussions and advice.

REFERENCES

[1] P. Auer, N. Cesa-Bianchi, and P. Fischer. 2002. Finite-time Analysis of the Multiarmed Bandit Problem. *Machine Learning* 47, 2 (01 May 2002), 235–256.

[2] E. Bakshy, S. Messing, and L. A. Adamic. 2015. Exposure to ideologically diverse news and opinion on Facebook. *Science* 348 (2015), 1130–1132.

[3] P. Barberá, J. T. Jost, J. Nagler, J. A. Tucker, and R. Bonneau. 2015. Tweeting From Left to Right: Is Online Political Communication More Than an Echo Chamber? *Psychological Science* 26, 10 (2015), 1531–1542.

[4] M. A. Beam, M. J. Hutchens, and J. D. Hmielowski. 2018. Facebook news and (de)polarization: reinforcing spirals in the 2016 US election. *Information, Communication & Society* 21, 7 (2018), 940–958.

[5] J. Ben Schafer, J. A. Konstan, and J. Riedl. 2001. E-commerce recommendation applications. *Data Mining and Knowledge Discovery* (2001), 115–153.

[6] F. J. Zuiderveen Borgesius, D. Trilling, J. Möller, B. Bodó, C. H. de Vreese, and N. Helberger. 2016. Should we worry about filter bubbles? *Internet Policy Review* (2016).

[7] P. Covington, J. Adams, and E. Sargin. 2016. Deep Neural Networks for YouTube Recommendations. In *Proceedings of the 10th ACM Conference on Recommender Systems (RecSys)*.

[8] S. Flaxman, S. Goel, and J. M. Rao. 2016. Filter Bubbles, Echo Chambers, and Online News Consumption. *Public Opinion Quarterly* 80 (2016), 298–320.

[9] M. Kunaver and T. Porl. 2017. Diversity in Recommender Systems A Survey. *Knowledge-Based Systems* 123, C (2017), 154–162.

[10] T. L. Lai. 1987. Adaptive Treatment Allocation and the Multi-Armed Bandit Problem. *Ann. Statist.* 15, 3 (09 1987), 1091–1114.

[11] T. Lattimore and C. Szepesvári. 2019. *Bandit Algorithms.* Cambridge (to appear).

[12] J. Lu, D. Wu, M. Mao, W. Wang, and G. Zhang. 2015. Recommender System Application Developments: A Survey. 74 (2015).

[13] E. Nechushtai and S. C. Lewis. 2018. What kind of news gatekeepers do we want machines to be? Filter bubbles, fragmentation, and the normative dimensions of algorithmic recommendations. *Computers in Human Behavior* (2018).

[14] T. T. Nguyen, Pik-Mai Hui, F. M. Harper, L. Terveen, and J. A. Konstan. 2014. Exploring the Filter Bubble: The Effect of Using Recommender Systems on Content Diversity. In *Proceedings of the 23rd international conference on World wide web.* 677–686.

[15] E. Pariser. 2011. *The Filter Bubble: What the Internet is Hiding from You.* Penguin UK.

[16] C. R. Sunstein. 2009. *Republich.com 2.0.* Princeton University Press.

[17] W. R. Thompson. 1933. On the Likelihood that One Unknown Probability Exceeds Another in View of the Evidence of Two Samples. *Biometrika* 25, 3/4 (1933), 285–294.

[7] $\eta = 0$ gives a fixed candidate pool, $0 < \eta < 1$ gives sub-linear growth, $\eta = 1$ gives linear growth.

A PROOFS

Proof of Theorem 1. Let $\mathbb{P}_\mu$ denote the measure carrying $(\mu_t)_{t=1}^\infty$ when $\mu_0 = \mu$. Assume without loss of generality that $\mu_0 = 0$ and let $B > 0$ be arbitrary. The result will follow by showing that for all $\mu \in [-B, B]$ it holds that

$$\mathbb{P}_\mu(\text{exists } t : \mu_t \notin [-B, B]) = 1 . \tag{4}$$

To see this suppose that

$$\mathbb{P}_\mu(\limsup_{t\to\infty} |\mu_t| < \infty) > 0 .$$

Then there exists a $B > 0$ such that

$$\mathbb{P}_\mu(\text{exists } t : \mu_t \notin [-B, B]) < 1 ,$$

which is a contradiction. In order to prove (4) notice that compactness of $[0, B]$ and $[-B, 0]$ and the continuity of F at $(\mu, 0)$ for all μ ensures there exists an $\epsilon > 0$ depending only on B such that $1 - F(\mu, \epsilon) \geq \epsilon$ for all $\mu \in [0, B]$ and $F(\mu, -\epsilon) \geq \epsilon$ for all $\mu \in [-B, 0]$. Hence for $n = 1 + B/\epsilon$

$$\inf_{\mu\in[-B,B]} \mathbb{P}_\mu(\text{exists } t \leq n : \mu_t \notin [-B, B]) \geq \epsilon^n$$

Let E_k be the event that $\mu_t \in [-B, B]$ for all $t \in \{nk + 1 \ldots, n(k + 1) + 1\}$. Then

$$\begin{aligned}\mathbb{P}_\mu(\mu_t \in [-B, B] \text{ for all } t) &= \mathbb{P}_\mu(E_k \text{ for all } k \geq 0)\\ &= \prod_{k=0}^\infty \mathbb{P}_\mu(E_k \mid E_1, \ldots, E_{k-1})\\ &\leq \prod_{k=0}^\infty (1 - \epsilon^n) = 0 ,\end{aligned}$$

which completes the proof. □

Proof of Theorem 2. We prove that if B is sufficiently large and $\mu > B$ and $\tau = \min\{t : \mu_t \in [-B, B]\}$, then

$$\mathbb{P}_\mu\left(\lim_{t\to\infty} \mu_t = \infty\right) > \frac{1}{2} \tag{5}$$

and

$$\mathbb{P}_\mu\left(\lim_{t\to\infty} \mu_t = \infty \text{ or } \tau < \infty\right) = 1 . \tag{6}$$

For $\mu < -B$ the same holds, but with μ_t tending to $-\infty$. To see why this implies the result, notice that the previous theorem shows that μ_t eventually leaves $[-B, B]$ almost surely. Each time this happens there is more than 0.5 probability of divergence and a certainty of either divergence or returning to $[-B, B]$. The conditional Borel-Cantelli theorem concludes the proof. To see why (5) and (6) hold, let

$$M_n = \sum_{t=1}^n (\mu_{t+1} - \mu_t - \bar{f}(\mu_t)) ,$$

which is a martingale with bounded increments since $|\mu_{t+1} - \mu_t|$ are bounded. Now $M_{\tau\wedge n}$ is also a martingale. Then by the strong law of large numbers for martingales,

$$\lim_{n\to\infty} M_{\tau\wedge n}/n = 0 \text{ a.s.} ,$$

which implies that either $\tau < \infty$ or $\mu_n \to \infty$ almost surely. To see the latter case, suppose μ is sufficiently large, we compute

$$\begin{aligned}\mu_{n+1} &= M_n + \mu_1 + \sum_{t=1}^n f(\mu_t)\\ &> M_n + \mu_1 + \epsilon n \to \infty\end{aligned}$$

since $M_n/n \to 0$ a.s. A similar argument applies when μ is sufficiently small. Finally, Eq. (5) holds by Azuma's inequality. □

B MORE ON USER INTEREST DYNAMICS

Linear Deterministic Model

Recall that since a is fixed, to simplify the notation, we write μ_t, c_t instead of $\mu_t(a), c_t(a)$ in this section. We assume $c_t = g(\mu_t)$ for some deterministic function g and analyze the one-dimensional, autonomous, first-order discrete dynamical system:

$$\mu_{t+1} = \mu_t + h(c_t) = \mu_t + f(\mu_t), \tag{7}$$

where $f = h \circ g$. In the simple case in which f is a linear function, i.e. $f(\mu_t) = k\mu_t + b$ for a linear coefficient k and constant term b, Eq. 7 takes the form

$$\mu_{t+1} = (1 + k)\mu_t + b. \tag{8}$$

By unrolling Eq. (8) over time we obtain

$$\mu_t = (1 + k)^t \mu_0 + b \sum_{i=0}^{t-1} (1 + k)^i \tag{9}$$

$$= \begin{cases} \mu_0 + bt, & \text{if } k = 0\\ (\mu_0 + \frac{b}{k})(1 + k)^t - \frac{b}{k}, & \text{if } k \neq 0. \end{cases} \tag{10}$$

For $k = 0$, the user's interest is not influenced by the recommender system but drifts with the constant b – this case occurs in the real world with probability 0.

For $k \neq 0$, the steady state equilibrium, obtained from solving the equation $\bar{\mu} = \bar{\mu} + k\bar{\mu} + b$, is given by $\bar{\mu} = -\frac{b}{k}$. Substituting $-\frac{b}{k}$ with $\bar{\mu}$ in Eq. 10 and taking the limit $t \to \infty$ on both sides, we obtain

$$\lim_{t\to\infty} \mu_t = (\mu_0 - \bar{\mu}) \lim_{t\to\infty} (1 + k)^t + \bar{\mu}, \tag{11}$$

namely,

$$\lim_{t\to\infty} \mu_t = \begin{cases} \bar{\mu}, & \text{if } |1 + k| < 1,\\ \bar{\mu}, & \text{if } |1 + k| > 1 \text{ and } \mu_0 = \bar{\mu},\\ \text{alternating } \{\mu_0, 2\bar{\mu} - \mu_0\}, & \text{if } k = -2,\\ \infty & \text{if } 1 + k > 1, \end{cases} \tag{12}$$

$$\text{and, } \limsup_{t\to\infty} \mu_t = \infty \text{ when } 1 + k < -1. \tag{13}$$

Therefore, no matter how the system selects items, in the first three cases of Eq. (12) the user interest model over the item a in question is always bounded over time. Of these, only the first case $|1+k| < 1$, or equivalently $-2 < k < 0$, will occur with probability different from 0.

On the other hand, for $k > 0$ the recommender system will degenerate strongly with μ_t growing at an exponential rate. For $k < -2$, the recommender system will degenerate weakly with $\sup_{i<t} \mu_i$ growing exponentially.

In summary, we can draw the following conclusions when an item a is served *i.o.*: 1) for $k > 0$ or $k < -2$, the user interest μ_t degenerates by growing exponentially, and therefore the recommender system needs to exert control on how frequent such items are shown to the user in order to control the speed of degeneracy of μ_t; 2) in all other cases, the user interest μ_t does not degenerate

($-2 \leq k < 0$), or the system cannot control linear degeneracy ($k = 0$, improbable case).

Scale-invariance

Let $\mathcal{M}$ be the candidate pool of items, which is also the domain of function μ_t.

Remark 3 (scale-invariance). *Let $\mu_t : \mathcal{M} \to D$ for any open interval $D \subset \mathbb{R}$. All sufficiency theorems still hold if we define the system degeneracy for μ_t as the following. We call $\mu_t : \mathcal{M} \to D$ degenerate iff there exists a monotonic, continuous function $\psi : D \to \mathbb{R}$ such that* $\limsup_{t\to\infty} \|\psi \circ \mu_t - \psi \circ \mu_0\|_2 = \infty$.

If we define $\nu_t = \psi \circ \mu_t$, then all sufficiency theorems readily apply to ν_t and the conclusions hold for μ_t since $\|\nu_t - \nu_0\|_2 = \|\psi \circ \mu_t - \psi \circ \mu_0\|_2$.

C DEGENERACY SPEED ANALYSIS

We analyze the system degeneracy $\|\mu_t - \mu_0\|_2$ (when the candidate pool $\mathcal{M}$ is finite) and $\sup_{a\in\mathcal{M}} |\mu_t(a) - \mu_0(a)|$ (when $\mathcal{M}$ is infinite) asymptotically in the order of t. As $t \to \infty$, $\mu_t \to \infty$ for the selected items. Thus the selected items are asymptotically almost surely clicked, and hence for any such item a, $|\mu_t(a) - \mu_0(a)| \approx \delta(a) \cdot T_a(t)$.

Finite Candidate Pool.

$$\|\mu_t - \mu_0\|_2 \approx \sqrt{\sum_a [\delta(a) \cdot T_a(t)]^2}. \tag{14}$$

In the *Random* recommender system, $T_a(t) \approx tl/m$ and thus

$$\|\mu_t - \mu_0\|_2 \approx \sqrt{\sum_a \delta(a)^2 (l/m)} \cdot t. \tag{15}$$

Both the *Oracle* and the *Optimal Oracle* have a fixed set of items $\mathcal{S}$ that they keep selecting. Thus $T_a(t) \approx t$ for any item $a \in \mathcal{S}$ and

$$\|\mu_t - \mu_0\|_2 \approx \sqrt{\sum_{a\in\mathcal{S}} \delta(a)^2} \cdot t. \tag{16}$$

For both the *UCB* and *TS* we have

$$\|\mu_t - \mu_0\|_2 \approx (\sqrt{\sum_a \delta(a)^2 / \sqrt{m^*}}) \cdot t, \tag{17}$$

where m^* are the number of close to optimal arms. Therefore all five models have the degeneracy quantity $\|\mu_t - \mu_0\|_2$ converge to a linear function of t.

Infinite Candidate Pool. Since we sample $\delta(a)$ from a bounded interval $[-b, b]$, asymptotically $\sup_{a\in\mathcal{M}} \delta(a) \approx b$

$$\sup_{a\in\mathcal{M}} |\mu_t(a) - \mu_0(a)| \approx \sup_{a\in\mathcal{M}} \delta(a) \cdot T_a(t) \approx bT_{a^*}(t)$$

where a^* is an item with $\delta(a^*) \approx b$.

In the *Random* recommender system, $T_a(t) \approx const$ and thus

$$\sup_{a\in\mathcal{M}} |\mu_t(a) - \mu_0(a)| \approx const. \tag{18}$$

The *Oracle* has a fixed set of items $\mathcal{S}$ that it keeps selecting. Thus $T_a(t) \approx t$ for any item $a \in \mathcal{S}$ and

$$\sup_{a\in\mathcal{M}} |\mu_t(a) - \mu_0(a)| \approx \max_{a\in\mathcal{S}} \delta(a) \cdot t. \tag{19}$$

The *Optimal Oracle* model will pick all items with $\delta(a) \approx b$ and $T_a(t) \approx ct$ for some constant c.

$$\sup_{a\in\mathcal{M}} |\mu_t(a) - \mu_0(a)| \approx bc \cdot t. \tag{20}$$

For UCB and Thompson sampling the situation is less clear. When growth of the candidate pool is linear, then UCB will spend most of its time exploring new items and consequently degeneration is very slow. Thompson sampling will continue to play degenerate items with reasonable probability and so degeneration speed will be larger than for UCB. Precisely quantifying the rates of degeneration depends in a complicated way on the details of the model.

TrolleyMod v1.0: An Open-Source Simulation and Data Collection Platform for Ethical Decision-Making in Autonomous Vehicles

Vahid Behzadan, James Minton, Arslan Munir
Kansas State University
Manhattan, KS, United States
behzadan,jzm,amunir@ksu.edu

ABSTRACT

This paper presents TrolleyMod v1.0, an open-source platform based on the CARLA simulator for the collection of ethical decision-making data for autonomous vehicles. This platform is designed to facilitate experiments aiming to observe and record human decisions and actions in high-fidelity simulations of ethical dilemmas that occur in the context of driving. Targeting experiments in the class of trolley problems, TrolleyMod provides a seamless approach to creating new experimental settings and environments with the realistic physics-engine and the high-quality graphical capabilities of CARLA and the Unreal Engine. Also, TrolleyMod provides a straightforward interface between the CARLA environment and Python to enable the implementation of custom controllers, such as deep reinforcement learning agents. The results of such experiments can be used for sociological analyses, as well as the training and tuning of value-aligned autonomous vehicles based on social values that are inferred from observations.

CCS CONCEPTS

• **Computing methodologies** → **Artificial intelligence**; *Robotic planning*; *Simulation by animation*; • **Applied computing** → Law, social and behavioral sciences.

KEYWORDS

Ethical Decision-Making; Autonomous Vehicles; Social Choice; Artificial Intelligence; Simulation

ACM Reference Format:
Vahid Behzadan, James Minton, Arslan Munir. 2019. TrolleyMod v1.0: An Open-Source Simulation and Data Collection Platform for Ethical Decision-Making in Autonomous Vehicles. In *AAAI/ACM Conference on AI, Ethics, and Society (AIES '19), January 27–28, 2019, Honolulu, HI, USA.* ACM, New York, NY, USA, 5 pages. https://doi.org/10.1145/3306618.3314239

1 INTRODUCTION

With the rise in technological advancements and investments in autonomous vehicles, the issue of ethical decision-making in such systems is becoming growingly pronounced [9]. Similar to human drivers, the Artificial Intelligence (AI) controllers of driverless vehicles will inevitably face moral dilemmas, which cannot be solved by adherence to simple ethical principles [5]. A well-known instance of such dilemmas is the *trolley problem* [11], where by some means (e.g., brake malfunction), the vehicle is put in a situation that forces the driver to decide between hurting bystanders on one side or another. Considering the enhanced computational and observational abilities of AI, it is expected that autonomous vehicles make *better* decisions than human drivers in such circumstances. However, the definition of *better* is deeply rooted in complex ethical principles and policies that are difficult (if not practically impossible) to formally specify [10]. Furthermore, such principles are often dynamic across cultural, geographical, and temporal dimensions [3].

While the problem of ethical decision-making in AI has remained an open challenge for many decades [19], recent studies on data-driven approaches to this problem have reported promising advances towards practical solutions [12]. Another advancement is the proposal to model the dynamics of ethical decision-making within the abstraction of *value-alignment*, which reduces the problem to the identification and measurement of the ethical norms and values of the society, and implementing such values into AI [2]. The quantification and modeling of such norms and values can be performed via machine learning and parametric techniques, examples of which include those that are based on Inverse Reinforcement Learning (IRL) [1] and norm inference [12]. A major hurdle in such approaches is that of data collection [13]. Modern machine learning approaches and model-dependent techniques require a large number of samples that provide a representative dataset of the societal choices and ethical values [17]. In particular, due to the rarity of representative ethical dilemmas in controlled real-world observations, the majority of current studies resort to simulation-based experiments.

However, the experimental setups and configurations utilized by such studies suffer from a number of shortcomings. Firstly, the bulk of such setups do not provide the means for measuring the performance of human operators in real-time, and thus fail to present a baseline for benchmarking the performance of AI against humans. Secondly, the majority of simulation environments used in published experiments (e.g., [3]) provide a very simple depiction of the conditions in real-world dilemmas, and hence may fail to account for salient details that are crucial to ethical decision-making. Thirdly, most of the recent experiments are performed in simulation environments that are either not open-source, or are very difficult to reconfigure and customize for new experiments.

AIES '19, January 27–28, 2019, Honolulu, HI, USA

ACM ISBN 978-1-4503-6324-2/19/01...$15.00
https://doi.org/10.1145/3306618.3314239

In response to the aforementioned gap, this paper presents TrolleyMod v1.0, an open-source simulation platform based on the CARLA simulator for autonomous driving research [4]. Targeting experiments in the class of trolley problems, TrolleyMod provides a seamless approach to creating new experimental settings and environments with the realistic physics-engine and the high-quality graphical capabilities of CARLA and the Unreal Engine [7]. Also, TrolleyMod provides a straightforward interface between the CARLA environment and Python to enable the implementation of custom controllers, such as deep reinforcement learning agents in Tensorflow (e.g., [16]) or Pytorch (e.g., [8]). The details of TrolleyMod are presented in the remainder of this paper, organized as follows: We present an overview of experimental platforms used in data-driven ethical decision-making studies, followed by the architectural details and components of TrolleyMod. We conclude the paper with remarks on plans for future extensions of this project.

2 PREVIOUS WORK

While the philosophical debate and research on ethical decision-making in AI is decades old, the engineering work in this area is very recent [12]. In particular, the interest in creating moral autonomous agents has rapidly grown in the past few years. Specifically, advances in imitation learning [18], inverse game theory [20], and IRL [1] have triggered a growing investment into the research on data-driven approaches to the modeling and transfer of human ethics to autonomous agents. Such approaches rely on collection of data on ethical decisions and actions of many human subjects to derive a representative model of the societal ethical principles [17].

In the domain of autonomous vehicles, very few platforms for this purpose are reported, and even fewer are openly available to the research community. Of the best known ethical data collection platforms for autonomous vehicles is MIT's Moral Machine [14] project, which performs a large-scale crowdsourcing of ethical opinions for a few simple cases of the trolley problem. While this project has yielded many interesting results [3], it can be argued that the low fidelity of the experiments, as well as the inconsideration of temporal and cultural externalities, diminish the feasibility of inferring practical ethical policies that can be implemented in real-world driverless vehicles. Furthermore, the Moral Machine experiment fails to account for the effect of environmental nudges [15] in the simulated scenarios. Also, while the datasets and analytics of this project were recently made available, the code for the simulation software itself is not accompanied, and hence does not accommodate the adoption, extension, and customization of this platform for further research.

While at a smaller scale, the Ethical Autonomous Vehicles[1] project also provides the means for data collection and experimentation on ethical decision making. Albeit, this project seems to be outdated due to lack of maintenance. Also, the limited scenarios and flexibility of this project, as well as the lack of documentation, may render the usability of this project for extended research infeasible.

In [6], authors present an alternative data collection approach using a kinetic high-fidelity driving simulator equipped with a fully automated autonomous driver. Unfortunately, the authors do not provide more information on the setup and replication procedures for their experiments.

While these prior projects succeeded in providing very valuable insights into the problem of ethical decision-making, there remains a need for an open-source, well-documented, high-fidelity, and highly-flexible simulation platform to further facilitate experimentation and research on crowdsourced ethical models for autonomous vehicles.

3 TROLLEYMOD V1.0

The goal of TrolleyMod is to provide an easy-to-use and flexible platform for setting up the conditions pertaining to ethical dilemmas. While the current version is mainly focused on the variations of trolley problem, this platform supports seamless customization and adjustment of the experiment to broader classes of ethical decision-making, such as abiding by the traffic laws. TrolleyMod is designed to facilitate experiments that require high-fidelity simulations of ethical dilemmas that occur in driving tasks to observe and record human decisions. The results of such experiments can be used for sociological analyses, as well as the training and tuning of value-aligned AI agents for autonomous driving based on social values that are inferred from observations.

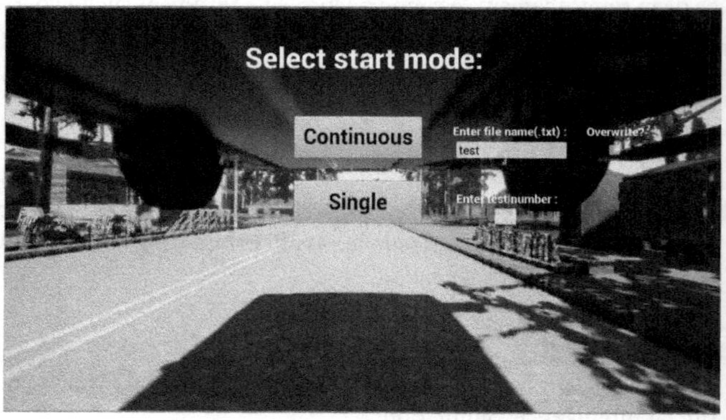

Figure 1: Startup menu of a TrolleyMod simulation

In TrolleyMod, the trolley problems are set up such that there are one or more victims on each side of a road belonging to a simulation environment. The environment (i.e., map) may be designed to represent realistic conditions in urban, suburban, highway, or custom settings. In each episode of the experiment, the subject is put in the driver's seat of a vehicle that accelerates automatically. The only control actions available to the subject are swerving left or right. Furthermore, the conditions of dilemma can be reinforced via invisible barriers to ensure that the only available options to the driver are to collide with at least one group of victims or other objects. Upon collision, the subject's actions are written into a text file or a network socket for processing. In TrolleyMod, each individual Trolley problem is called a *scenario*. A sequence of scenarios is what constitutes a TrolleyMod simulation. The components and procedures of a simulation are detailed as follows:

[1] http://mchrbn.net/ethical-autonomous-vehicles/

3.1 CARLA

As the name suggests, TrolleyMod is a modification of the CARLA (Car Learning to Act) simulator [4]. CARLA is an open-source simulator for urban driving, designed to support training, prototyping, and validation of autonomous driving models. This platform allows for the flexible configuration of sensor suites and provides various signals useful to the training of driving tasks, such as GPS coordinates, speed, acceleration, and detailed data on collisions. CARLA is implemented over Unreal Engine 4 [7] to provide flexibility and realism in the physics and high-fidelity visualization of driving environments. CARLA follows a client-server architecture to provide an interface between the world and various types of agents. In this architecture, the server runs the simulation and renders the scene, while the client uses a Python API to interact with the simulation.

The environments of CARLA are composed of 3D models of static objects, such as traffic signs, buildings, infrastructure, vegetation, as well as dynamic objects, such as vehicles and pedestrians. The default sensors in CARLA are comprised of RGB (Red, Green, and Blue) camera and pseudo-sensors which provide semantic segmentations in terms of road, traffic sign, sidewalk, pedestrian, etc. Furthermore, CARLA provides various measurements associated with the state of the agent as well as compliance with traffic rules. Such measurements include orientation and location, acceleration vector, speed, and the cumulative impact of collisions. Signals corresponding to traffic rules include the state of traffic lights and speed limits.

3.2 Components of TrolleyMod

There are three types of objects that can be spawned automatically with TrolleyMod: pedestrians, vehicles, and prop objects. These correspond to the Walker, the CarlaWheeledVehicle, and StaticActor classes respectively. The first two classes are native to CARLA, while StaticActor is a product of TrolleyMod. Our extension adjusts these classes to enable their instance to store new information pertaining to trolley scenarios. All three classes share two variables:

(1) TestNum: an integer that tracks what scenario is being run.
(2) GroupMemberNames: a delineated string that lumps together the names and properties of all victims in the scenario to which the class instance belongs.

Walker actors also retain the following additional information for the pedestrian character: age, gender, ID number of the pedestrian's group in the scenario, size of the pedestrian's group, and special traits (e.g., pregnant, disabled, etc.)

3.3 Configuration

TrolleyMod spawns object models into a "level" (i.e., episode of simulation) in the Unreal Engine 4. It takes an input text file, which contains a list of tuples specifying an object (e.g., pedestrian, car, cones, etc.) that can be collided with by the subject and provides any other ancillary data that describes the object. This text is parsed to provide a reference to Unreal Engine's Actor class in memory. TrolleyMod implements a custom format for the specification of objects in a scenario, as detailed in the online documentation[2].

To generate a scenario in TrolleyMod, the experiment designer runs a generation Blutility ((Editor Utility Blueprint)) named ScenarioGen. A blutility is an Unreal Engine object that enables execution of functions outside of the runtime. In TrolleyMod, blutilities are essential for providing a means to quickly modify the CARLA-provided maps to facilitate the generation of various scenarios in a relatively short period of time.

After the ScenarioGen blutility is run, the experiment designer may add other scenarios in unused locations in the map by manually placing Actor objects into the level, as illustrated in Fig. 3. Also, for the data recording script to recognize a new scenario, a Target object must be placed into the map first.

TrolleyMod provides the necessary functions and assets to set up scenarios, but it is up to the user on how to arrange and utilize them in customized environments and settings. Since each user will want to define a simulation differently, TrolleyMod only provides a functional framework. Further details on this procedure is available in the online documentation.

3.4 Execution of Simulation

TrolleyMod utilizes a modular structure based on *Blueprint Function Library*, which is an Unreal Engine feature that allows for the functions in the library to be reused over multiple projects. In TrolleyMod, blueprints provide a prepackaged set of functions to be used in the level blueprint of maps derived from CARLA's native environments. Currently, TrolleyMod contains only one blueprint, named "FunctionLibrary". This blueprint contains all of the functions required to run TrolleyMod simulations. When the subject's agent collides with a victim, that result is recorded and the next scenario is spawned. Once all scenarios are complete, the simulation terminates and the results are written to a text file or network socket.

Each TrolleyMod simulation includes an *Event Tick* node, which is called at every frame during the simulation. The purpose of this node is to make the car controlled by the subject to automatically accelerate, thus forcing the subject to decide quickly on what victim to collide with. As depicted in Fig. 2, the initial event object of this blueprint (i.e., *BeginPlay*) first calls the *InitValues* function in order to initialize the environment and object attributes. Then, it binds the subject's agent to a hit event –that is, whenever the agent collides with any object in the map, it will generate an event that calls the *OnActorHit_Event_0 node.* Next, assuming the agent hits one of the intended victims, the blueprint generates a text message describing what the player collided with using the *SetDisplay* function. If the player does not hit an intended target, the simulation refers to the *PlayerRotation* variable to reset where the car is facing and rebinds hit events to it.

Otherwise, the *CollisionHandler* function analyzes the Actor hit by the player, extracts its data to the Output variable, and then prepares the simulation to move on to the next scenario. This continues until all the scenarios in the *Locations* array have been visited, after which the simulation writes the data to a text file. It is also possible for the player to specify only one scenario to complete using the start menu, and consequently the simulation will terminate after the specified scenario is run.

[2] https://github.com/zminton/TrolleyMod/wiki

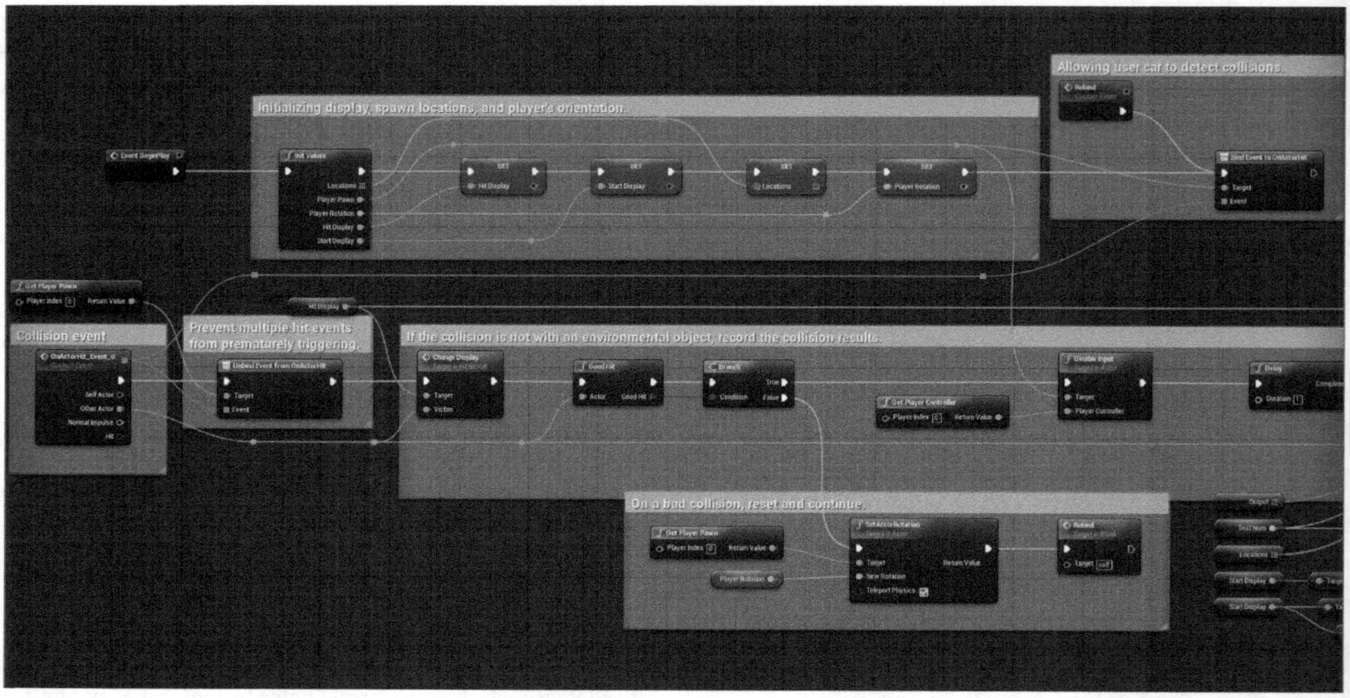

Figure 2: Blueprint functions for execution and control of the simulation

Figure 3: Manual configuration of Actor objects

4 FUTURE WORK

TrolleyMod is a recently conceived and an ongoing project, hence there are many interesting directions for pursuit of its extension. First and foremost in our roadmap is to demonstrate the integration of TrolleyMod with inference techniques such as IRL. Furthermore, our plan for the near-future includes the gradual extension of functionalities to support seamless configuration for more well-known moral dilemmas, and enhance the front and backend to provide better support for handling larger numbers of experiments and volumes of results in a distributed architecture. A similar priority is the development of web and smartphone interfaces to enhance the reach and accessibility of this platform for large scale research. As noted, TrolleyMod is an open-source project with the aim of facilitating research on ethical autonomous vehicles, and is looking forward to contributions and comments from the community.

REFERENCES

[1] David Abel, James MacGlashan, and Michael L Littman. 2016. Reinforcement Learning as a Framework for Ethical Decision Making.. In *AAAI Workshop: AI, Ethics, and Society*, Vol. 92.

[2] Thomas Arnold, Daniel Kasenberg, and Matthias Scheutz. 2017. Value alignment or misalignment–what will keep systems accountable. In *3rd International Workshop on AI, Ethics, and Society.*

[3] Edmond Awad, Sohan Dsouza, Richard Kim, Jonathan Schulz, Joseph Henrich, Azim Shariff, Jean-François Bonnefon, and Iyad Rahwan. 2018. The Moral Machine experiment. *Nature* (2018), 1.

[4] Alexey Dosovitskiy, German Ros, Felipe Codevilla, Antonio Lopez, and Vladlen Koltun. 2017. CARLA: An open urban driving simulator. *arXiv preprint arXiv:1711.03938* (2017).

[5] Cynthia Dwork, Moritz Hardt, Toniann Pitassi, Omer Reingold, and Richard Zemel. 2012. Fairness through awareness. In *Proceedings of the 3rd innovations in theoretical computer science conference.* ACM, 214–226.

[6] Anna-Katharina Frison, Philipp Wintersberger, and Andreas Riener. 2016. First Person Trolley Problem: Evaluation of Drivers' Ethical Decisions in a Driving Simulator. In *Adjunct proceedings of the 8th international conference on automotive user interfaces and interactive vehicular applications.* ACM, 117–122.

[7] Epic Games. 2007. Unreal engine. *Online: https://www. unrealengine. com* (2007).

[8] JACOB GENANDER and ANNA NYLANDER. [n. d.]. Control of Self-Driving Vehicles Using Deep Learning. ([n. d.]).

[9] Noah J Goodall. 2014. Machine ethics and automated vehicles. In *Road vehicle automation.* Springer, 93–102.

[10] Joshua Greene, Francesca Rossi, John Tasioulas, Kristen Brent Venable, and Brian Charles Williams. 2016. Embedding Ethical Principles in Collective Decision Support Systems.. In *AAAI*, Vol. 16. 4147–4151.

[11] Judith Jarvis Thomson. 1985. The Trolley Problem. *Yale Law Journal* 94, 6 (1985), 5.

[12] Daniel Kasenberg, Thomas Arnold, and Matthias Scheutz. 2018. Norms, Rewards, and the Intentional Stance: Comparing Machine Learning Approaches to Ethical Training. In *Proceedings of the First AAAI/ACM Conference on Artificial Intelligence, Ethics, and Society.*

[13] Richard Kim, Max Kleiman-Weiner, Andrés Abeliuk, Edmond Awad, Sohan Dsouza, Josh Tenenbaum, and Iyad Rahwan. 2017. A Computational Model of Commonsense Moral Decision Making. (2017).

[14] Richard Kim, Max Kleiman-Weiner, Andrés Abeliuk, Edmond Awad, Sohan Dsouza, Josh Tenenbaum, and Iyad Rahwan. 2018. A Computational Model of Commonsense Moral Decision Making. *arXiv preprint arXiv:1801.04346* (2018).

[15] Thomas C Leonard. 2008. Richard H. Thaler, Cass R. Sunstein, Nudge: Improving decisions about health, wealth, and happiness.
[16] Xiaodan Liang, Tairui Wang, Luona Yang, and Eric Xing. 2018. CIRL: Controllable Imitative Reinforcement Learning for Vision-based Self-driving. *arXiv preprint arXiv:1807.03776* 1 (2018).
[17] Ritesh Noothigattu, Snehalkumar'Neil'S Gaikwad, Edmond Awad, Sohan Dsouza, Iyad Rahwan, Pradeep Ravikumar, and Ariel D Procaccia. 2017. A voting-based system for ethical decision making. *arXiv preprint arXiv:1709.06692* (2017).
[18] Jessica Taylor, Eliezer Yudkowsky, Patrick LaVictoire, and Andrew Critch. 2016. Alignment for advanced machine learning systems. *Machine Intelligence Research Institute* (2016).
[19] Wendell Wallach and Colin Allen. 2008. *Moral machines: Teaching robots right from wrong*. Oxford University Press.
[20] Yijia Wang, Yan Wan, and Zhijian Wang. 2017. Using experimental game theory to transit human values to ethical AI. *arXiv preprint arXiv:1711.05905* (2017).

The Seductive Allure of Artificial Intelligence-Powered Neurotechnology

Charles M. Giattino
Duke University
Durham, NC, USA
charliegiattino@gmail.com

Lydia Kwong
Duke University
Durham, NC, USA
lydia.kwong@duke.edu

Chad Rafetto
Duke University
Durham, NC, USA
chad.rafetto@duke.edu

Nita A. Farahany
Duke University
Durham, NC, USA
farahany@duke.edu

ABSTRACT

Neuroscience explanations—even when completely irrelevant—have been shown to exert a "seductive allure" on individuals, leading them to judge bad explanations or arguments more favorably. There seems to be a similarly seductive allure for artificial intelligence (AI) technologies, leading people to "overtrust" these systems, even when they have just witnessed the system perform poorly. The AI-powered neurotechnologies that have begun to proliferate in recent years, particularly those based on electroencephalography (EEG), represent a potentially doubly alluring combination. While there is enormous potential benefit in applying AI techniques in neuroscience to "decode" brain activity and associated mental states, these efforts are still in the early stages, and there is a danger in using these unproven technologies prematurely, especially in important, real-world contexts. Yet, such premature use has begun to emerge in several high-stakes settings, including the law, health & wellness, employment, and transportation. In light of the potential seductive allure of these technologies, we need to be vigilant in monitoring their scientific validity and challenging both unsubstantiated claims and misuse, while still actively supporting their continued development and proper use.

CCS CONCEPTS

• Emerging technologies • Biology-related information processing • Neural systems

AIES '19, January 27–28, 2019, Honolulu, HI, USA

ACM ISBN 978-1-4503-6324-2/19/01...$15.00
https://doi.org/10.1145/3306618.3314269

KEYWORDS

Neurotechnology, EEG, Decoding, Overtrust

ACM Reference format:

Charles M. Giattino, Lydia Kwong, Chad Rafetto and Nita A. Farahany. 2019. The Seductive Allure of Artificial Intelligence-Powered Neurotechnology. In *Proceedings of 2019 AAAI/ACM Conference on AI, Ethics, and Society (AIES'19). January 27-28, 2019, Honolulu, HI, USA. ACM, New York, NY, USA, 6 pages.* https://doi.org/10.1145/3306618.3314269

1 Introduction

The effort to "decode" human brain activity and associated mental states is one of the most important of our time, promising to improve our understanding of human thinking and behavior, treat psychiatric and neurologic disorders, and enable advances in brain-computer interfaces (BCIs), among many other benefits. Yet, it is also one of our most challenging endeavors. To help make sense of the vast amounts of brain data being collected, machine learning (ML) and other artificial intelligence (AI) techniques are increasingly being applied in neuroscience research [31,36]. While this has proven fruitful—and could in turn drive further advances in ML and AI research [9]—brain decoding is still in the very early stages, with a way yet to go.

Despite this nascent state, however, neurotechnologies—and increasingly those based on electroencephalography (EEG)—are being used outside of the research lab in important, real-world contexts for which they are often inappropriate. In India, for example, a form of EEG decoding called Brain Electrical Oscillation Signature Profiling (BEOS) has been used—purportedly—to peer into an individual's mind to determine if they had committed a crime [25]. This is simply not possible given current capabilities, and yet the results of such tests have been submitted as corroborative evidence in numerous criminal cases. While there have been few if any convictions so far, and a landmark Indian Supreme Court case overturned one conviction that had included BEOS evidence because such techniques violate the "right against self-incrimination," the Court held open the possibility that BEOS evidence could still be used in cases in which a defendant voluntarily submitted to testing (Smt. Selvi & Ors vs. State of Karnataka, Criminal Appeal No. 1267 of 2004, Judgment on 5 May 2010). The possibility of such continued use and the potential to contribute to criminal convictions represents an unwarranted level of trust in an unproven technology for critical, life-altering decisions.

Unfortunately, there is a long history of using scientifically unsubstantiated techniques in ways that affect people's lives and liberties. For example, many forensic techniques—such as bite mark, firearms, and even fingerprint analyses—have minimal or even no scientific basis, but are still regularly used in court, where they have led to numerous wrongful convictions that were later overturned by rigorously validated DNA evidence [1]. Given that the best EEG decoding accuracy often barely exceeds chance levels, it is currently much more akin to discredited bite mark analysis than DNA analysis.

In addition to the legal setting, EEG devices are seeing premature use in health & wellness, employment, transportation, and other high-stakes areas of society, where they are frequently touted as being "AI powered" [42]. The primary danger shared across these contexts is that AI-powered EEG decoding could augment or replace traditional assessments of a person's mental state—what they are thinking, feeling, or remembering, whether they are lying, or how they are performing—despite the fact that such decoding has not proven nearly accurate or reliable enough to be trusted in this way.

Unwarranted trust in these technologies and the potential for harm might be exacerbated by the fact that neuroscience and AI have each been shown to exert a "seductive allure" that could make AI-powered EEG devices a potentially doubly-alluring combination. For example, neuroscience imagery and explanations—even when completely irrelevant to the context—have been shown to exert this seductive allure on individuals by leading them to judge arguments or bad explanations more favorably [17,38]. With AI, this seductive allure manifests as "overtrust" [37], and is the tendency for people to defer to "intelligent" technology, even when they have just seen that technology perform poorly [28].

It is worth noting that more recent work has painted a nuanced picture, in which brain imagery might not be especially seductive [6], the allure of neuroscience explanations might owe primarily to their reference to reductive, fundamental components and processes rather than neuroscience per se [11], and the level of trust in intelligent systems likely differs in specific contexts [40]. Still, there is enough evidence to be wary of—and reason to further study—the potential for AI-powered EEG to elicit an unwarranted amount of trust in unproven technologies that increasingly claim "mind-reading" abilities [39].

Given the potential seductive allure of combined AI and EEG technology, and our lamentable history using unsubstantiated forensic techniques, safeguarding against the premature and inappropriate use of EEG decoding in high-stakes areas of society seems to present us with a difficult challenge. We need to be vigilant in monitoring the scientific validity of this technology and drawing attention to its inappropriate use, while still actively supporting its continued scientific development and proper use.

2 EEG Primer and Decoding Capabilities

To decide whether a particular use of EEG is valid and appropriate, it is absolutely vital to understand the scientific basis of the technology and its current capabilities in that context. In this section we underscore the promising uses of EEG in science and medicine, and why it is ill-suited for many of the important real-world contexts in which it is beginning to emerge.

EEG involves noninvasively recording (from the scalp) the electrical activity of a subset of neurons in the brain's cortex, or outer, bark-like layer [23]. Because it is noninvasive and thus one of the few methods that can be safely used with humans, EEG has proven very useful in a number of medical and scientific applications over the last several decades, such as monitoring seizure activity [35] or the effects of anesthesia [26], assessing sleep, and helping us begin to understand the brain basis of higher cognitive functions like attention, perception, memory, and language [27].

Many of these more traditional uses of EEG, particularly in medicine (e.g., monitoring seizures, sleep, or anesthesia), are not generally considered to be "decoding," but rather informative brain monitoring and diagnostics that are performed in concert with other clinically relevant physiological and behavioral assessments under direct supervision of a physician or other healthcare professional. Instead of these more traditional uses of EEG, here we will focus primarily on attempts to decode mental states such as emotions, attention or focus, lying/truthfulness, and even individual thoughts and memories, as such attempts are the least substantiated by scientific evidence and yet most poised for inappropriate use in high-stakes contexts.

2.1 AI Techniques Applied to EEG: Promise and Limitations

Efforts to decode mental states from EEG activity have been bolstered in recent years with the application of AI techniques. These have included both unsupervised, data-driven approaches like independent or principal component analysis [12,15] and supervised, classification approaches like support vector machines [2] and state-of-the-art deep learning methods like convolutional neural networks [30]. These approaches have produced some promising results. For example, accuracy in decoding emotional states like happiness and sadness can sometimes be quite high, above 90% [14]. A recent study was even able to produce impressively similar visual reconstructions of face images that had been shown to experimental participants by decoding the EEG patterns elicited when they watched the image flash on the screen [18].

Despite these promising results, however, there is still a way to go before EEG devices, even those using advanced AI analyses, prove themselves accurate and reliable enough for high-stakes uses in the real world. First, it is important to emphasize that the results reported in the scientific literature represent the absolute best possible decoding capability, taking place in laboratory contexts that have many advantages over real-world contexts. In the lab, there is complete control over the experimental manipulations, data quality and quantity, and—extremely important for EEG—the exact timing of the experimental stimuli, to name just a few of the advantages. So, as impressive as Nemrodov and colleagues' [18] ability to reconstruct what someone had seen by decoding their EEG activity may be, their ability to do so depended entirely on their experimental control over and access to the face images shown to participants. Even with state-of-the-art AI methods, such a reconstruction from experiences of faces in the real world would currently be impossible.

The successful lab results themselves may not be as accurate as they first appear or as robust as the real world would demand. For example, seemingly high accuracy in classifying emotional state is often for datasets with a very small number of classes, usually only two to six [14]; clearly, we spend our days in vastly more than two to six different mental states, making these high accuracies a gross overestimation. In many other areas, particularly in trying to classify "cognitive" states such as level of focus or what a person is paying attention to, accuracies are often statistically significant but barely above chance [5,29]. Worse still, statistical comparisons to theoretical chance (e.g., 50% in a two-class problem) are often inappropriate for the small datasets typical of experiments in cognitive neuroscience [4], leading to further overestimation.

Finally, because this limited decoding capability is probably most attributable to fundamental limitations of the EEG signal itself rather than to shortcomings in the AI analytics, it may be unlikely to improve significantly. For example, EEG (and really all neural) activity does not have a direct, unique relationship with specific mental states, and so measuring that activity often does not reveal very much by itself. And while the fact that EEG is noninvasive can be a great strength, it also means that EEG measures only a small fraction of the brain's total activity, and thus gives only a partial, incomplete window into our mental lives. On top of that, electrical signals from the brain are reduced *1000-fold* as they make their way to the scalp, where much larger electrical noise—such as from nearby electrical equipment and even from the eyes and head & neck muscles—can corrupt them. Together, these characteristics act as inherent limitations on the capabilities of even AI-powered EEG decoding.

It should be clear that, currently, EEG decoding has not established itself as accurate or reliable enough for many of the important, real-world contexts in which it is beginning to emerge. Yet, this technology seems to have gained an unwarranted level of trust—perhaps owing to a seductive allure—that is driving its increased adoption and use, and the growing potential for real harm.

3 Real-World Uses of AI-Powered EEG

In this section, we present some of the most salient real-world contexts in which AI-powered EEG is being used and near-future uses that are beginning to appear on the horizon. The primary danger shared across these different contexts is that traditional assessments of a person's mental state are being, or have the potential to be, supplanted by AI-powered EEG decoding that is often extremely limited in its accuracy and reliability. We also discuss some of the ethical and social issues that arise from this often inappropriate use and present some policy recommendations.

3.1 Law

As discussed above, the putative EEG-based decoding of mental content—such as BEOS in India and related forms of "memory recognition" in the US (Harrington v. State, 659 N.W.2d 509, Iowa 2003)—has entered the legal setting, where it is threatening to supplant traditional forms of evidence and human judgment in a way that could imperil people's lives and liberties. For example, what if the kind of impressive memory "reconstruction" from the Nemrodov et al. [18] study cited above—which, again, would not be possible in the real world—began to influence or even replace traditional means of determining the credibility of a witness's memory? What if the increasingly—but deceptively—high accuracy in decoding emotional state led to its being applied to determine the underlying emotional character of testimony, or even its truthfulness? Developments like these would be highly concerning.

Fortunately, it does seem that much of this potential harm is—so far at least—unrealized. The Indian Supreme Court, for example, overturned a criminal conviction that had included BEOS evidence (Smt. Selvi & Ors vs. State of Karnataka, Criminal Appeal No. 1267 of 2004, Judgment on 5 May 2010), and the Iowa Supreme Court set a favorable precedent by not even considering the EEG-decoding evidence in Harrington v. State (Harrington v. State, 659 N.W.2d 509, Iowa 2003). And recent, much-needed empirical work on the topic of EEG memory-recognition evidence found that, although people's evaluations of (fictional) criminal defendants were in fact impacted by the presentation of EEG evidence, it was not "seductively" so, and instead the primary determinant was the overall strength of the case [32].

While this recent work is important and worth considering, it is part of a larger literature that remains controversial and very much unsettled. Much more work needs to be done, especially on the potential seductive allure of AI-powered EEG specifically, which to our knowledge has not been studied. Further, in light of our regrettable history using unsubstantiated forensic techniques that demonstrably led to wrongful convictions [1], we all—especially neuroscientists and AI researchers, in addition to ethicists, lawyers, and judges—need to remain vigilant and prepared to challenge the use of AI-powered EEG decoding in the courtroom.

3.2 Health & Wellness

For improving traditional, clinical uses of EEG (i.e., brain monitoring and diagnostics)—and thus people's lives—the application of increasingly advanced analysis techniques, including from AI research, does hold great promise. For example, convolutional neural networks have been used to help improve seizure prediction [34], and support vector regression has helped improve the tracking of brain maturation in preterm infants [33]. Importantly, these types of clinical brain monitoring are performed in a rich medical context, collected in concert with other physiological measures and behavioral assessments, and used to augment the expert decision-making of physicians and other trained professionals.

In contrast, there is a growing market for direct-to-consumer, AI-powered EEG devices that, while explicitly marketed for "general wellness," often make implicit claims or allusions to medical benefit that are largely unsubstantiated by scientific evidence [39]. These claims are often predicated on the ability to decode, in real time, a user's mental or emotional state. For example, a company called NeuroPlus markets an EEG-based system that claims to measure levels of attention and provide neurofeedback "attention training" using games for children, employing "advanced AI analytics" on the back end [45]. Their website features salient allusions to helping children with ADHD, followed by more hidden, explicit disclaimers to the contrary.

While some of these consumer EEG devices might do little more than waste people's time and money, ones with clearer allusions to medical benefit could lead people to base important medical decisions, such as whether to seek professional help or continue an existing treatment, on unsubstantiated claims. But, since the device companies are careful to avoid explicit medical claims, they avoid regulation by the Food and Drug Administration [7], which has largely chosen not to enforce regulation on low-risk devices marketed for general wellness purposes. Regulation instead falls to the Federal Trade Commission (FTC), which is charged with holding businesses accountable for deceptive claims; however, such claims from consumer EEG companies remain as yet unchallenged by the FTC. It is thus important to continually draw attention to any unsubstantiated claims, warn consumers of their dubious nature, and challenge consumer EEG companies to either back up their claims with legitimate evidence or remove them.

3.3 Employment

In the hopes of gaining a competitive advantage, major companies around the world are beginning to employ a rapidly growing panoply of AI-powered biometric technologies, including facial expression, speech, and, on the horizon, EEG analysis. For example, companies like Unilever are using facial expression analysis to assess applicants' emotions during the hiring process [41], and a company called Humanyze sells employee ID badges that monitor employees' conversations for things like tone and who participated—the content, they say, is left out [10,20]. What many of these companies are ultimately after is a way to assess employees' mental states—their emotions, level of focus, stress, etc. Given that EEG is actually a measure of brain activity, it represents something of a "holy grail" of such AI-powered biometric analyses, and already several companies are marketing the use of AI-powered EEG decoding in professional settings [43,44].

While it is unclear at this point which companies are actually using EEG devices at any kind of scale in the US, a recent report from China suggests that already several companies, some backed by the government, are engaging in large-scale "brain monitoring" of workers by using EEG sensors embedded in the hats and helmets of their uniforms and sending the data to "computers that use artificial intelligence algorithms to detect emotional spikes such as depression, anxiety or rage" [3]. Such "emotional spikes" can get a worker reassigned to another post or sent home for the day.

Despite the dearth of evidence that such AI-powered EEG determinations of employees' mental state are accurate or provide any novel insight, they already seem to have begun supplanting established, often interpersonal, evaluation and assessment methods in the workplace. Not only does this threaten workers with arbitrary consequences that can negatively impact their livelihoods, it raises important issues of personal, mental privacy and sets a dangerous precedent for a possible future when legitimately accurate brain decoding actually does exist. To set a better precedent, employers should look beyond the hype and avoid using AI-powered EEG in the workplace; workers and workers' rights advocates should draw attention to any such proposed use; and lawyers and regulators should be prepared to issue challenges if such use does become more widespread.

3.4 Transportation

Manufacturers of automated vehicles have for several years been exploring the use of EEG-based systems to decode human drivers' mental states to enhance communication between driver and vehicle [13,24]. There is a great need for such enhanced communication—especially in semi-automated vehicles that require a human driver to stay engaged and be prepared to take control when necessary [19]—as there is abundant evidence that humans are not able to sustain attention for extended periods, especially in routine, monotonous tasks like driving [16]. Further underscoring the urgency of this need, there have already been several fatal crashes involving semi-automated vehicles that were attributable to human-engagement failures [21,22] and in fact "overtrusting" the capabilities of the vehicle.

We need to ensure, however, that possible enhancements to driver-to-vehicle communication actually improve the situation and make it safer, rather than pursue solutions that seem alluring but are actually ineffective and potentially harmful. In this regard, EEG-based decoding of mental states exists in a gray area. For example, given that the stages of sleep are largely defined by EEG [27], it is certainly plausible that an EEG-based system could be used to detect driver drowsiness. But, given EEG's limitations, to merit such use a system would first need to prove demonstrably accurate for a wide variety of drivers in real-world contexts. Ideally, it would also perform better than more traditional alternatives, such as camera-based ones with increasingly robust eye-closure and gaze detection [8], or even basic self-monitoring mechanisms ("I'm tired, I should pull over and rest") that could be eroded by overtrusting the EEG's decoding capabilities.

Jaguar's approach highlights the potential for real harm: they have teamed up with Freer Logic, the maker of a brain-decoding headrest that they claim can detect drowsiness "as much as 4 minutes before one's eyes begin drooping or drifting, giving [this] technology a leg up on camera-based drowsiness detectors" [46]. In addition, it can supposedly decode a driver's cognitive load, distraction, relaxation, emotion, and stress. Incredibly, they claim to be able to do all this without actually contacting the driver's head, instead operating successfully from up to 6-10 inches away. These claims are not only completely unsubstantiated by evidence, they are truly unbelievable and dangerous.

To prevent further, potentially fatal harm, vehicle manufacturers should seriously consider avoiding semi-automated vehicles that require sustained engagement from drivers. Given how unlikely this seems, companies should at least be very skeptical of the value, and wary of the harms, that even AI-powered EEG systems could add. The National Highway Traffic Safety Administration (NHTSA), which is currently taking a very hands-off approach to regulating automated vehicles [19], should demand more from makers of semi-automated vehicles to ensure that their driver-to-vehicle communication functions are effective and safe, a demand that consumers should echo. Finally, as is always a useful first step, attention needs to be drawn to these potentially inappropriate uses of AI and EEG technology, especially by experts in AI, neuroscience, and human factors.

Conclusion

While promising, EEG decoding—even when backed by our most advanced AI analysis methods—is still an immature science. Despite this immaturity, however, such decoding has begun to leave the research lab and enter important, real-world contexts for which it has not proven itself nearly accurate or reliable enough, including the law, health & wellness, employment, and transportation. Compounding the potential for harm, research has shown that AI-powered EEG technology, as it is increasingly branded, might exert a potent, seductive allure to be overly trusted and dangerously misused. Our primary goal here has been to draw increased attention to this evolving situation, propose some possible policy solutions, and encourage broader engagement and vigilance from a diversity of stakeholders, from experts with important domain-specific knowledge to ethicists, lawyers, policymakers, and members of the public.

ACKNOWLEDGMENTS

We thank Jeff Ward and three anonymous reviewers for useful feedback on earlier versions of the manuscript.

REFERENCES

[1] The National Academies. 2009. *Strengthening Forensic Science in the United States.* DOI:https://doi.org/DOI 10.17226/12589

[2] Hafeez Ullah Amin, Aamir Saeed Malik, Rana Fayyaz Ahmad, Nasreen Badruddin, Nidal Kamel, Muhammad Hussain, and Weng-Tink Chooi. 2015. Feature extraction and classification for EEG signals using wavelet transform and machine learning techniques. *Australas. Phys. Eng. Sci. Med.* 38, 1 (March 2015), 139–149. DOI:https://doi.org/10.1007/s13246-015-0333-x

[3] Stephen Chen. 2018. 'Forget the Facebook leak': China is mining data directly from workers' brains on an industrial scale. *South China Morning Post.* Retrieved November 5, 2018 from https://www.scmp.com/news/china/society/article/2143899/forget-facebook-leak-china-mining-data-directly-workers-brains

[4] Etienne Combrisson and Karim Jerbi. 2015. Exceeding chance level by chance: The caveat of theoretical chance levels in brain signal classification and statistical assessment of decoding accuracy. *J. Neurosci. Methods* 250, (2015), 126–136. DOI:https://doi.org/10.1016/j.jneumeth.2015.01.010

[5] Johannes J Fahrenfort, Anna Grubert, Christian N L Olivers, and Martin Eimer. 2017. Multivariate EEG analyses support high-resolution tracking of feature-based attentional selection. *Sci. Rep.* (2017), 1–15. DOI:https://doi.org/10.1101/082818

[6] Martha J. Farah and Cayce J. Hook. 2013. The Seductive Allure of "Seductive Allure." *Perspect. Psychol. Sci.* 8, 1 (January 2013), 88–90. DOI:https://doi.org/10.1177/1745691612469035

[7] FDA. 2016. *General Wellness: Policy for Low Risk Devices -- Guidance for Industry and Food and Drug Administration Staff.* DOI:https://doi.org/10.1161/01.CIR.97.18.1837

[8] Lex Fridman. 2018. Human-Centered Autonomous Vehicle Systems: Principles of Effective Shared Autonomy. *arXiv* (2018). DOI:https://doi.org/arXiv:1810.01835v1

[9] Demis Hassabis, Dharshan Kumaran, Christopher Summerfield, and Matthew Botvinick. 2017. Neuroscience-Inspired Artificial Intelligence. *Neuron* 95, 2 (2017), 245–258. DOI:https://doi.org/10.1016/j.neuron.2017.06.011

[10] Thomas Heath. 2016. This employee ID badge monitors and listens to you at work — except in the bathroom. *The Washington Post.* Retrieved November 5, 2018 from https://www.washingtonpost.com/news/business/wp/2016/09/07/this-employee-badge-knows-not-only-where-you-are-but-whether-you-are-talking-to-your-co-workers/?noredirect=on&utm_term=.d8b15bf7b5b9

[11] Emily J. Hopkins, Deena Skolnick Weisberg, and Jordan C.V. Taylor. 2016. The seductive allure is a reductive allure: People prefer scientific explanations that contain logically irrelevant reductive information. *Cognition* 155, (October 2016), 67–76. DOI:https://doi.org/10.1016/J.COGNITION.2016.06.011

[12] Aapo Hyvärinen, Pavan Ramkumar, Lauri Parkkonen, and Riitta Hari. 2010. Independent component analysis of short-time Fourier transforms for spontaneous EEG/MEG analysis. *Neuroimage* 49, 1 (January 2010), 257–271. DOI:https://doi.org/10.1016/j.neuroimage.2009.08.028

[13] Jacob Kastrenakes. 2015. Jaguar wants to monitor its drivers' brainwaves, heart rate, and breathing. *The Verge.* Retrieved January 6, 2019 from https://www.theverge.com/2015/6/19/8815419/jaguar-brainwave-heart-rate-breathing-monitors

[14] Miyoung Min-Ki Kim, Miyoung Min-Ki Kim, Eunmi Oh, and Sung-phil Kim. 2013. A review on the computational methods for emotional state estimation from the human EEG. *Comput. Math. Methods Med.* 2013, (2013), 573734. DOI:https://doi.org/10.1155/2013/573734

[15] R. Kottaimalai, M. P. Rajasekaran, V. Selvam, and B. Kannapiran. 2013. EEG signal classification using Principal Component Analysis with Neural Network in Brain Computer Interface applications. In *2013 IEEE International Conference ON Emerging Trends in Computing, Communication and Nanotechnology (ICECCN),* 227–231. DOI:https://doi.org/10.1109/ICE-CCN.2013.6528498

[16] Robert Langner and Simon B. Eickhoff. 2013. Sustaining attention to simple tasks: A meta-analytic review of the neural mechanisms of vigilant attention. *Psychol. Bull.* 139, 4 (July 2013), 870–900. DOI:https://doi.org/10.1037/a0030694

[17] David P. McCabe and Alan D Castel. 2008. Seeing is believing: The effect of brain images on judgments of scientific reasoning. *Cognition* 107, 1 (April 2008), 343–352. DOI:https://doi.org/10.1016/j.cognition.2007.07.017

[18] Dan Nemrodov, Matthias Niemeier, Ashutosh Patel, and Adrian Nestor. 2018. The Neural Dynamics of Facial Identity Processing: insights from EEG-Based Pattern Analysis and Image Reconstruction. *Eneuro* 5, February (2018), ENEURO.0358-17.2018. DOI:https://doi.org/10.1523/ENEURO.0358-17.2018

[19] DOT NHTSA. 2017. Automated Driving Systems 2.0: A Vision for Safety. Retrieved from https://www.nhtsa.gov/document/automated-driving-systems-20-voluntary-guidance

[20] Lydia Nicholas. 2018. Emotional surveillance goes mainstream. *Nesta.* Retrieved November 5, 2018 from https://www.nesta.org.uk/feature/10-predictions-2018/emotional-surveillance-goes-mainstream/

[21] NTSB. 2018. *Preliminary Report Highway HWY18FH011.*

[22] NTSB. 2018. *Preliminary Report Highway HWY18MH010.*

[23] Paul L Nunez and Ramesh Srinivasan. 2006. *Electric fields of the brain the neurophysics of EEG* (2nd ed.). Oxford University Press, Oxford; New York. Retrieved from http://getitatduke.library.duke.edu/?sid=sersol&SS_jc=TC0000086519&title=Electric fields of the brain %3A the neurophysics of EEG

[24] Sean O'Kane. 2018. Nissan's future cars may read your brain to prevent accidents. *The Verge.* Retrieved January 6, 2019 from

https://www.theverge.com/2018/1/3/16844648/nissan-brain-to-vechicle-self-driving-car-technology-eeg

[25] D.A. Puranik, S.K. Joseph, B.B. Daundkar, and M.V. Garad. 2009. Brain Signature profiling in India. Its status as an aid in investigation and as corroborative evidence – as seen from judgments. *Proc. XX All India Forensic Sci. Conf.* (2009), 815–822.

[26] Patrick L Purdon, Aaron L Sampson, Kara J. Pavone, and Emery N Brown. 2015. Clinical Electroencephalography for Anesthesiologists Part I: Background and Basic Signatures. *Anesthesiology* 4, 123 (2015), 937–960. DOI:https://doi.org/10.1038/nbt.3121.ChIP-nexus

[27] D Purves, R Cabeza, SA Huettel, K LaBar, Michael L Platt, and Marty G Woldorff. 2013. *Principles of Cognitive Neuroscience* (Second Ed. ed.). Sinauer Associates, Inc. Publishers, Sunderland, MA. Retrieved April 24, 2017 from https://scholar.google.com/scholar?q=purves+principles+of+cognitive+neuroscience&btnG=&hl=en&as_sdt=0%2C34

[28] Paul Robinette, Wenchen Li, Robert Allen, Ayanna M Howard, and Alan R Wagner. 2016. Overtrust of robots in emergency evacuation scenarios. In *2016 11th ACM/IEEE International Conference on Human-Robot Interaction (HRI)*, 101–108. DOI:https://doi.org/10.1109/HRI.2016.7451740

[29] Jason Samaha, Thomas C Sprague, and Bradley R Postle. 2016. Decoding and Reconstructing the Focus of Spatial Attention from the Topography of Alpha-band Oscillations. *J. Cogn. Neurosci.* (2016). DOI:https://doi.org/10.1162/jocn

[30] Robin Tibor Schirrmeister, Jost Tobias Springenberg, Lukas Dominique Josef Fiederer, Martin Glasstetter, Katharina Eggensperger, Michael Tangermann, Frank Hutter, Wolfram Burgard, and Tonio Ball. 2017. Deep learning with convolutional neural networks for EEG decoding and visualization. *Hum. Brain Mapp.* 38, 11 (2017), 5391–5420. DOI:https://doi.org/10.1002/hbm.23730

[31] Terrence J Sejnowski, Patricia S Churchland, and J Anthony Movshon. 2014. Putting big data to good use in neuroscience. *Nat. Neurosci.* 17, 11 (2014), 1440–1. DOI:https://doi.org/10.1038/nn.3839

[32] Francis X. Shen, Emily Twedell, Caitlin Opperman, Jordan Dean Scott Krieg, Mikaela Brandt-Fontaine, Joshua Preston, Jaleh McTeigue, Alina Yasis, and Morgan Carlson. 2017. The limited effect of electroencephalography memory recognition evidence on assessments of defendant credibility. *J. Law Biosci.* May (2017), 330–364. DOI:https://doi.org/10.1093/jlb/lsx005

[33] N. J. Stevenson, L. Oberdorfer, N. Koolen, J. M. O'Toole, T. Werther, K. Klebermass-Schrehof, and S. Vanhatalo. 2017. Functional maturation in preterm infants measured by serial recording of cortical activity. *Sci. Rep.* 7, 1 (2017), 1–7. DOI:https://doi.org/10.1038/s41598-017-13537-3

[34] Nhan Duy Truong, Anh Duy Nguyen, Levin Kuhlmann, Mohammad Reza Bonyadi, Jiawei Yang, Samuel Ippolito, and Omid Kavehei. 2018. Convolutional neural networks for seizure prediction using intracranial and scalp electroencephalogram. *Neural Networks* 105, (2018), 104–111. DOI:https://doi.org/10.1016/j.neunet.2018.04.018

[35] Paul Vespa. 2005. Continuous EEG monitoring for the detection of seizures in traumatic brain injury, infarction, and intracerebral hemorrhage: "To detect and protect." *J. Clin. Neurophysiol.* 22, 2 (April 2005), 99–106. DOI:https://doi.org/10.1097/01.WNP.0000154919.54202.E0

[36] Mai-Anh T. Vu, Tulay Adali, Demba Ba, Gyorgy Buzsaki, David Carlson, Katherine Heller, Conor Liston, Cynthia Rudin, Vikaas Sohal, Alik S. Widge, Helen S. Mayberg, Guillermo Sapiro, and Kafui Dzirasa. 2018. A Shared Vision for Machine Learning in Neuroscience. *J. Neurosci.* 38, 7 (2018), 0508-17. DOI:https://doi.org/10.1523/JNEUROSCI.0508-17.2018

[37] Alan R Wagner, Jason Borenstein, and Ayanna Howard. 2018. Overtrust in the robotic age. *Commun. ACM* 61, 9 (August 2018), 22–24. DOI:https://doi.org/10.1145/3241365

[38] Deena Skolnick Weisberg, Frank C Keil, Joshua Goodstein, Elizabeth Rawson, and Jeremy R Gray. 2008. The Seductive Allure of Neuroscience Explanations. 2, (2008), 470–477.

[39] Anna Wexler and Robert Thibault. 2018. Mind-Reading or Misleading? Assessing Direct-to-Consumer Electroencephalography (EEG) Devices Marketed for Wellness and Their Ethical and Regulatory Implications. *J. Cogn. Enhanc.* (2018), 1–7. DOI:https://doi.org/10.1007/s41465-018-0091-2

[40] Holly A Yanco, Munjal Desai, Jill L. Drury, and Aaron Steinfeld. 2016. Methods for Developing Trust Models for Intelligent Systems. In *Robust Intelligence and Trust in Autonomous Systems*, Ranjeev Mittu, Donald Sofge, Alan R Wagner and WF Lawless (eds.). Springer US, Boston, MA, 219–254. DOI:https://doi.org/10.1007/978-1-4899-7668-0_11

[41] Minda Zetlin. 2018. AI Is Now Analyzing Candidates' Facial Expressions During Video Job Interviews. *Inc.* Retrieved November 5, 2018 from https://www.inc.com/minda-zetlin/ai-is-now-analyzing-candidates-facial-expressions-during-video-job-interviews.html

[42] 2018. BrainCo. Retrieved November 5, 2018 from https://www.brainco.tech/focus-1

[43] 2018. Versus. Retrieved November 5, 2018 from https://getversus.com/professionals

[44] 2018. Emotiv. Retrieved November 5, 2018 from https://www.emotiv.com/

[45] 2019. NeuroPlus. Retrieved January 6, 2019 from https://www.neuro.plus/children.html

[46] 2019. Freer Logic. Retrieved January 6, 2019 from http://www.freerlogic.com/buzz/32-four-tech-finds-from-the-2018-los-angeles-auto-show

Invisible Influence

Artificial Intelligence and the Ethics of Adaptive Choice Architectures

Daniel Susser
daniel.susser@psu.edu
Penn State University
State College, PA

ABSTRACT

For several years, scholars have (for good reason) been largely preoccupied with worries about the use of artificial intelligence and machine learning (AI/ML) tools to make decisions *about us*. Only recently has significant attention turned to a potentially more alarming problem: the use of AI/ML to influence *our decision-making*. The contexts in which we make decisions—what behavioral economists call our *choice architectures*—are increasingly technologically-laden. Which is to say: algorithms increasingly determine, in a wide variety of contexts, both the sets of options we choose from and the way those options are framed. Moreover, artificial intelligence and machine learning (AI/ML) makes it possible for those options and their framings—the choice architectures—to be tailored to the individual chooser. They are constructed based on information collected about our individual preferences, interests, aspirations, and vulnerabilities, with the goal of influencing our decisions. At the same time, because we are habituated to these technologies we pay them little notice. They are, as philosophers of technology put it, *transparent* to us—effectively invisible. I argue that this invisible layer of technological mediation, which structures and influences our decision-making, renders us deeply susceptible to manipulation. Absent a guarantee that these technologies are not being used to manipulate and exploit, individuals will have little reason to trust them.

CCS CONCEPTS

• **Security and privacy → Social aspects of security and privacy.**

KEYWORDS

data ethics; influence; manipulation; choice architecture; transparency; accountability

ACM Reference Format:
Daniel Susser. 2019. Invisible Influence: Artificial Intelligence and the Ethics of Adaptive Choice Architectures. In *AAAI/ACM Conference on AI, Ethics, and Society (AIES '19), January 27–28, 2019, Honolulu, HI, USA*. ACM, New York, NY, USA, 6 pages. https://doi.org/10.1145/3306618.3314286

AIES '19, January 27–28, 2019, Honolulu, HI, USA

ACM ISBN 978-1-4503-6324-2/19/01...$15.00
https://doi.org/10.1145/3306618.3314286

1 INTRODUCTION

For several years, scholars have (for good reason) been largely preoccupied with worries about the use of artificial intelligence and machine learning (AI/ML) systems to make decisions *about us*. The algorithms mediating much of our lives are impenetrable black boxes [30] that perpetuate discrimination [2], evade accountability, and deprive us of due process [8, 9]. Institutional decision-making processes once guided by flawed and oftentimes biased human decision-makers are now being replaced by automated systems that learn from and reproduce those flaws and biases, and, indeed, accelerate their negative effects [28]. In response, these scholars have called for increased fairness, accountability, and transparency ("FAT*") around algorithmic decision-making, and have begun to develop technical and policy frameworks for achieving it.[1]

This work, which takes what I call a *structural approach* to AI/ML ethics, is deeply important. But it only tells part of the story. In this paper, I take a more *individual approach*, describing a set of problems that flows from the introduction of AI/ML systems into people's everyday lives. Specifically, instead of attending to the ways algorithms are used to make decisions *about us*, I focus here on the use of AI/ML systems to influence *our decision-making*.[2] Information technologies increasingly mediate our decision-making processes in a wide range of contexts, from consumer decisions to political ones. And such technologies—driven, more and more, by AI/ML tools—are not neutral arbiters of such choices. Rather, these "adaptive choice architectures," as I call them, work to subtly guide us toward certain ends [10, 38, 44].

What's more, given the way we tend to interact with and experience technology, these influences are largely hidden. As philosophers of technology and science & technology studies (STS) scholars argue, once we become adept at using technologies they become "transparent" to us. Here, transparent is meant not in the sense in which it is often used in policy contexts (i.e., as insight into otherwise obscure practices), but rather more literally: once we are habituated to technologies we stop looking at them and instead look *through* them to the information and activities we use them to facilitate [15, 42, 43]. For the sake of clarity, I will refer to transparency understood in this way as "invisibility." The problems I describe in what follows stem from the fact that we do not consciously attend to—we don't *see*—many of the technologies now mediating our day-to-day lives. They are, for practical purposes, invisible.

[1] See, for example, http://www.fatml.org/resources/relevant-scholarship
[2] Of course, many of the problems I discuss in what follows have structural causes. By "individual approach" I mean only that the object of my analysis in this paper is the effects of a certain class of AI/ML tools on individual experience.

This invisible layer of technological mediation, which structures and influences our decision-making, renders us radically susceptible to manipulation. At an individual level, it threatens our autonomy, and at a collective level, it stands to undermine social values, like democracy, which are premised on individuals being capable of independent decision-making. Given the risks these technologies pose, and the relative powerlessness of those affected to challenge them, I argue (1) that designers of AI/ML-driven systems sometimes ought to sacrifice the seamlessness and invisibility they usually strive for in the construction of user experiences, for seamful, visible interventions that promote user awareness and autonomy; (2) that the firms and other organizations designing and deploying adaptive choice architectures ought to provide *radical transparency* about both the means and the ends of the systems they create; and (3) the design and management of algorithmic influence ought to be governed by a strict duty of care. Absent a guarantee that these technologies are not being used to manipulate and exploit, individuals will have little reason to trust them.

2 ADAPTIVE CHOICE ARCHITECTURES

In their 2008 book *Nudge*, Richard Thaler (a behavioral economist) and Cass Sunstein (a legal theorist) put forward the now well-known idea that the contexts in which we make decisions inexorably shape the decisions we reach [39]. At bottom, the reason for this is that we do not, for the most part, give our decisions a great deal of conscious, reflective thought. Rather, as the psychologists Daniel Kahneman and Amos Tversky argue, we make most decisions very quickly, using fairly unreliable cognitive shortcuts or heuristics [17]. We lean on examples that come quickly to mind, even if they are not representative [39]. We assume that if our friends are doing something then perhaps we ought to do it too [39]. This means that we rely heavily on contextual cues when making everyday decisions, often without realizing it. The way in which our choices are situated and framed—the options we have and how they are described, who offers them to us, in what way, and when—all help determine the decisions we eventually make. Thaler and Sunstein call these decision-making contexts *choice architectures.*

Given this basic fact about human deciders, the question for Thaler and Sunstein is: why not design specific choice architectures to incline people toward individually and socially optimal outcomes? If contexts make such a big difference, why not design them with intention and for good? One of their famous examples of how to do this—how to "nudge" people into making better decisions—describes how food items are arranged in a cafeteria. People are more inclined, they suggest, to choose whichever options are situated at eye-level than they are to select something arranged above or below it [39]. Again, for Thaler and Sunstein, this mainly raises a question about policy—shouldn't we arrange cafeteria food items in a way that inclines most people to select the healthiest option? Here, I want to raise a different question: what if the cafeteria were arranged differently for every person who walked in the door?

While that would be difficult to pull off in a physical cafeteria, in digital environments it is commonplace. The websites we visit and apps we use are dynamic; unlike Thaler and Sunstein's cafeteria, the options they present to us and the way those options are framed constantly change, producing different choice architectures for each user, and for the same user in different instances. To some extent, this has been true for web-based technologies since the late 1990s, when the notion of "adaptive user interfaces" first appeared (see, e.g., [18, 19]). What has changed in the intervening period is the amount of information available about each of us and the emergence of tools capable of analyzing it [10]. Today, as Karen Yeung argues, we are confronted with "highly personalised choice environment[s]"—digitally-mediated user experiences structured to match our particular cognitive idiosyncrasies [44]. As a result, we are increasingly subject to more than the gentle nudges Thaler and Sunstein recommend. Vast amounts of data about both individuals and groups, combined with digital platforms that can dynamically alter the way they present information to maximally impact each user means we are today subject to something much more powerful—what Yeung terms "hypernudges" [44]. Because our choice architectures are increasingly *adaptive*, our choice-making is increasingly susceptible to outside influence.

These developments arrive at the same time as our lives become generally more technologically-laden. Increasingly, we decide what to buy by browsing retail websites like Amazon. We decide where to eat by asking recommender services like Yelp. We turn to Monster.com to find a job and Tindr or OkCupid to find a date. Which is to say: the number of decisions we face in unmediated, purely physical settings is shrinking. Algorithms determine more and more, in a wide variety of contexts, both the sets of options we choose from and the way those options are framed. In and of itself, this is not a bad thing. The problem is that these adaptive choice architectures are largely hidden from view.

3 MEDIATING TECHNOLOGIES AS INVISIBLE INFRASTRUCTURE

We like to think of technology as something we *use*—devices or tools we engage with focus and attention. Our language reflects this: we talk about technology "users" and "end-users," "user interfaces," and "human-computer interaction." As philosophers, psychologists, and media theorists have shown, however, this picture of how we relate to technology is partial at best (see [42]). In most cases, once we become sufficiently adept at using technologies we stop focusing on the technologies themselves and direct our attention instead to the things we are able to do *through* them. For example, we rarely think consciously about the material features of our smartphone screens or computer monitors; rather, we attend to the texts, images, videos, and other information they offer up to us. This is often referred to as *technological transparency*, pointing to the fact that we generally experience the world through technology, rather than experiencing technology itself, directly [15, 33, 37].

This notion of technological transparency should not be confused with the ways "transparency" is discussed in policy contexts. For instance, transparency is often used to describe *institutional openness.* Transparency as institutional openness means giving individuals insight into how otherwise obscure organizational processes work. It is transparency as institutional openness that people have in mind when they refer to the old quip that "sunlight is the best disinfectant" [3]. There is also talk of transparency in discussions about algorithms. Algorithmic transparency is analogous to institutional transparency and means offering insight into how automated systems reach the decisions they do [30]. Elsewhere, Kiel Brennan-Marquez and I refer to this kind of transparency as "a view-under-the-hood" [4].

Philosophers of technology (especially phenomenologists and postphenomenologists) use the notion of transparency in a more literal way. They argue that once we become adept at using technologies, the technologies themselves recede from conscious attention and perception. This allows us to focus on what we can accomplish *using* the tools, rather than focusing on the tools themselves. Technologies become transparent in the sense that users see right through them. To take the most famous example, the early 20th Century German philosopher Martin Heidegger described the experience of using a hammer. When we hammer things, he pointed out, we do not attend to the hammer itself. Rather, we attend to the thing we are hammering (say, a nail). It is only when the technology breaks down—when it fails to drive the nail in—that we are prompted to examine the tool itself in order to diagnose the problem [13].

Don Norman brought this insight into the realm of technology design when he argued that digital technologies ought to be "invisible" to users. "Tools should be noticed only when they break," he writes in *The Invisible Computer* [27]. For the sake of clarity, and following Norman's convention, I will refer to this notion of technological transparency as "invisibility." As Yoni Van Den Eede has shown, this idea—that when technologies work they form an invisible layer of mediation between human users and the world—has been raised time and again by technology scholars in a range of fields. In addition to Norman, media theorist Marshall McLuhan [24], sociologist Bruno Latour [21], social psychologist Sherry Turkle [40, 41], and philosophers like Don Ihde [15] and Peter-Paul Verbeek [43] have all pointed, in one way or another, to the fact that technologies become invisible to the people who use them [42].

As Norman argues, from the perspective of user experience this invisibility is all to the good. People use technologies to accomplish their goals. What is important to users is not the technologies themselves, but rather the activities they are using the technologies *for*. Well-functioning tools get out of the way and let us focus on the things we have taken up the tools to do. "Technology is our friend when it is inconspicuous, working smoothly and invisibly in the background, like a proper infrastructure should," Norman writes, "Technology is a pest when it is in the way, when it is intrusive" [27]. Indeed, as Robert Rosenberger points out, digital technologies need not even break down or fail completely to irritate us—when websites simply load too slowly we experience a "drop in transparency," forcing us out of the flow of our work and directing our attention to the computer or smartphone itself, and to the rest of the technological apparatus that might be responsible for the problem, like the modem, router, and so on [32].

The fact that we have incorporated information technologies into nearly all aspects of our lives means that for many people this invisible infrastructure—this layer of technological mediation that facilitates and supports all of the meaningful activities we engage in—is now pervasive. In 2016, the marketing research firm Nielsen Company estimated that the average American spends nearly 11 hours per day looking at screens (including smartphones, computers, televisions, etc.) [14]. Given that we also spend, on average, nearly 7 hours per day sleeping, this suggests that many people spend almost twice as many of their waking hours engaging with screens than not [16]. And not all digital technologies have screens. We also interface with a wide variety of "smart" objects—tools that have been outfitted with sensors and computer processors and connected to the internet. Recent (conservative) estimates suggest that there are already at least 6 billion such devices deployed around the world, and perhaps as many as 17 billion [26]. The so-called "Internet of Things" (IoT) (i..e, the totality of all those sensor-laden and internet-connected devices) promises to make the invisible infrastructure of information technologies we experience the world through even bigger, more pervasive, and—given that these devices are often designed precisely to operate in the background—less visible.[3]

Again, from the perspective of user experience, this pervasive, invisible layer of digital mediation promises to improve things. Norman is surely right that most of us care little about the devices we use, in and of themselves. What we care about are the people they connect us with, the work they help us carry out, the entertainment they provide, and the conveniences they offer. There are, however, issues beyond user experience. As we've seen, the technologies mediating our everyday lives shape our choice architectures. They enable "hypernudging"—dynamically altering the contexts in which we make decisions in order to influence their outcomes. The invisible infrastructure of digital mediation is a platform for manipulation.

4 ONLINE MANIPULATION

To manipulate someone is to impose a hidden influence on their decision-making process [38]. The fact that our lives are increasingly mediated by a hidden infrastructure of technologies designed to influence the way we choose, suggests, then, that we have rendered ourselves deeply susceptible to online manipulation. Tal Zarsky has warned about this for some time. Detailing the ways advertisers can use information collected about us to craft highly influential ads, he writes that "the use of personal information to provide tailored, manipulative content should be considered a detrimental outcome of today's enhanced flow of personal information" [45]. Similarly, Ryan Calo describes a wide range of manipulative online practices that commercial firms use to induce customers to buy their products, and at the highest possible prices [5].

Consider the case of mobile health (or "mHealth") apps—smartphone applications that work in tandem with fitness tracking devices, like Fitbits or Apple Watches, to continuously (or semi-continuously) gather information about users' physical activity, physiological metrics (heart rate, etc.), and sleep patterns, and offer suggestions for how to lose weight, sleep better, or generally improve physical health and well-being. As Sax et al. point out, many (if not most) mHealth apps attempt to influence more than people's health; they nudge users to buy health-related commodities and

[3]The technologies that comprise our invisible technological infrastructure are not all digital either. All of the physical and mechanical and analogue technologies we engage with follow the same general patterns. Though a relevant and important consequence of IoT technology is that the boundary between the digital and non-digital is beginning to blur. That being said, my focus in this paper is information technology.

services [36]. Using the highly specific information gathered about individual users from their fitness trackers, these apps create choice contexts designed to exert maximal influence. For example, when the Garmin Connect app detects that a user has taken fewer than average steps one day, it presents a graph showing the decrease alongside suggestions for "10 Healthy Work Habits," one of which is a native advertisement (i.e., an advertisement disguised as non-sponsored content) for a $40 sleep program. In cases such as this, Sax et al. write, "users do not know that they are being targeted with personalized content that intentionally obfuscates commercial intent by embedding it in health content" [36]. And the Garmin Connect app is only the beginning: as fitness trackers and the apps that come bundled with them become increasingly sophisticated, they will enable the construction of increasingly adaptive choice architectures, which deliver increasingly effective ads [20, 36].

It would be a mistake, though, to see the problem of invisible influence as limited to the commercial sphere. After all, it is not only consumer decision-making that is mediated by adaptive choice architectures. The so-called "gig economy" or "sharing economy" has introduced algorithmic mediation into the domain of labor relations [34]. Martin et. al. explore the algorithmic tools Amazon's Mechanical Turk system uses to structure the work of its crowd-sourced laborers [23]. And taking the ride-hailing app Uber as a case study, sociologists Alex Rosenblat and Luke Stark describe the myriad ways Uber's app "algorithmically manages" (i.e., influences the decision-making of) its drivers—from customer ratings to data visualizations to notification nudges [35]. Drawing on this work, Calo and Rosenblat describe a particularly devious strategy:

> while Uber originally showed drivers precise surge premiums in a given area in association with heat maps that display varying levels of surge through color schemes—yellow means demand is rising, orange means surge may appear soon, and red means it is surging—it changed the design of its app in October 2015 to show heat maps with those color schemes but without precise prices. In effect, the app encourages drivers to believe in surge and travel to receive surge rides, but it fails to provide a precise indicator or a guarantee of what that price is. Heat maps thus function as a behavioral engagement tool but can effectively operate as a bait-and-switch mechanism similar to the use of phantom cars to entice ride-hailers [6].

In other words, Uber habituated its drivers to one choice architecture, and then changed it in a way that leverages the old habits to influence drivers to behave as Uber wants.

Since 2016 the public has also become all too aware that our political life too is mediated by algorithms. Whereas worries about the effects of social media on the political system were once limited to questions about "filter bubbles" [29], "media manipulation"[4] and voter microtargeting are now foremost concerns. Data analytics firm Cambridge Analytica reportedly used information collected about hundreds of thousands of Facebook users, combined with aggregate data purchased from third-party data collectors, to create "personality profiles" on voters in the United States, the United Kingdom, France, Germany, Kenya, and elsewhere around the world. According to a Cambridge Analytica whistleblower, those profiles allowed the company to deliver highly personalized political advertisements designed to influence voters by exploiting their "inner demons" [1]. To whatever extent these tactics were effective it was surely due in part to social media's pervasive presence as a digital communications infrastructure running through the public sphere.

These examples of how adaptive choice architectures can invisibly influence decision-making across social contexts—from consumer contexts, to the workplace, to the political sphere—gives an indication of their ability to harm [38]. At an individual level, manipulation obviously threatens one's autonomy. To act autonomously is to act independently, motivated by one's own reasons. As Joseph Raz puts it, "the ideal of personal autonomy is that people should make their own lives" [31]. Invisible influence threatens this ideal by inducing people to act for reasons they don't understand, and therefore can't endorse. Just as clear, however, are the collective harms. Important social values, like democracy, are premised on the notion that the individuals taking part in the institutions they govern are themselves independent, autonomous, deciders. Diminishing the capacity of individuals to make meaningfully independent decisions in the political sphere undermines their ability to recognize political institutions as their own.

5 THE ETHICS OF INVISIBILITY

> "If you could imagine any one obtaining this power of becoming invisible, and never doing any wrong or touching what was another's, he would be thought by the lookers-on to be a most wretched idiot, although they would praise him to one another's faces, and keep up appearances with one another from a fear that they too might suffer injustice." (Glaucon to Socrates in Plato's *Republic*, Book II)

So, what is to be done? In what remains, I briefly describe three normative implications of the preceding discussion.

First, the functionally invisible, adaptive choice architectures that mediate much of our experience render individuals radically vulnerable to the whims of others. More and more, as the Garmin, Uber, and Cambridge Analytica examples described in the previous section illustrate, the digital infrastructure that supports our everyday activities is designed to influence the directions those activities take—from using information about our sleep and exercise patterns to sell us weight loss plans to leveraging our subtle personality types to influence our votes. Such manipulative practices substitute the preferences and interests of the choice architects for the preferences and interests of choosers. Although they don't coerce people into behaving the way advertisers, employers, or political campaigns would have them act, they nonetheless undermine people's capacity to decide for themselves. The harms that flow from these hidden influences are twofold: at bottom, the fundamental harm, as discussed above, is that manipulation subverts autonomy—the individual's capacity to act on the basis of reasons they themselves recognize and endorse. Furthermore, because autonomous individuals usually act in their own interest, the subversion of autonomy often leads to a second harm: diminished welfare. When our capacity to advocate for our own interests is compromised, we should not expect our interests to be served.

[4] See, for example: https://datasociety.net/research/media-manipulation/

The second implication—correlative with the first—is that the creators of adaptive choice architectures wield an enormous amount of power, which carries with it special ethical responsibilities. In general, those who make decisions for others—e.g., parents, guardians ad litem, or fiduciaries—are understood as being duty-bound to make decisions in the interests of their charges. In fact, this is a special case of a broader principle pertaining to the relationship between vulnerability and responsibility. As Robert Goodin writes, "If A's interests are vulnerable to B's actions and choices, B has a special responsibility to protect A's interests" [11]. Philosophically deep, this notion is also utterly commonsensical: when someone's fate is in your hands, you ought to try to do right by them. T. H. Green states this idea even more directly: "There is no clearer ordinance of that supreme reason, often dark to us, which governs the course of man's affairs, than that no body of men should [...] be able to strengthen itself at the cost of others' weakness" [12].[5] In the context of adaptive choice architectures, the meaning of Green's observation is plain: it is wrong—and obviously so—to use the tools of invisible influence to induce people to act against their own interests.[6] To do so is an abuse of power.

Third, despite the simple and obvious ethical imperatives just described, and given that the creators of adaptive choice architectures and the users who confront them often have competing interests, there is little reason to trust that these ethical responsibilities will be met and systems will be designed to the ultimate benefit of users, unless they are governed by stringent controls. This is true for several reasons. As the quote from Plato's *Republic*, above, reminds us, the feeling of impunity carries with it a temptation that is difficult to resist. Moreover, the relationship between choice architect and chooser is not as straightforward as I have let on—modern algorithmic systems are rarely the product of one person's or even a few people's work. The apps and digital platforms described above are produced by huge teams of designers, project managers, programmers, quality assurance teams, and so on. As a result, there may be no single person who feels responsible for their effects. This is the so-called "problem of many hands" [25]. To be clear: the fact that there is no single choice architect—but rather sprawling teams of them—does not, morally, absolve those teams of responsibility. But as a practical matter it might mean that moral concerns are not always salient to the people building the tools.

So, again, the question is: what is to be done? I don't pretend to have a complete answer. While the problem of manipulation is, one must assume, as old as we are, the problem of adaptive choice architectures—of an invisible infrastructure of technological mediation constantly collecting information about us and using that information to shape and influence our choices—is something new, and it will take a great deal more work to reckon fully with its consequences.

As a modest start, several things follow from my argument thus far. First, with respect to technology design, if the problem is, at bottom, hidden or invisible influence, then an obvious (if imperfect) remedy is for the invisible infrastructure of technological mediation to reveal itself. Since, as I argued in section 3, invisibility (or "technological transparency") is good for user experience, this means occasionally *compromising user experience in the name of user welfare and autonomy.* When creating adaptive systems, designers ought to consider how the value of a seamless user experience—the system itself receding from view—trades off against the user's ability to understand how the system is influencing them. In some cases, seamlessness ought to be abandoned in favor of what Chalmers and Galani call "seamfulness" [7], or what I have called "strategic opacity" [37]—revealing to the user precisely what is going on beneath the surface.

But seamful user experiences will not be enough. Thus, second, in addition to requiring thoughtful, autonomy-promoting design decisions, adaptive choice architectures demand *radical transparency* on the part of the firms creating and deploying them. Here I mean transparency in the policy sense—we need a view under the hood. Those filling our everyday decision-making environments with adaptive choice architectures must be entirely forthcoming, not only about the *fact* that they are using such tools, but about their *purpose* (intended outcomes), and about the *mechanisms* by which they achieve it.

Finally, because the designers of these systems are highly incentivized to subvert user interests, and because the invisible nature of invisible influence renders it exceedingly difficult to detect, demands for radical transparency and seamful design must be accompanied by stringent accountability measures. Creators of adaptive systems ought to be held to the highest standard of care—they should be required, that is, to create systems that beyond any doubt advance users' interests. Even then difficult questions would likely remain open, about the harms to autonomy that could accompany even the most beneficently manipulative systems. In tandem with radical transparency, though, and with user interface designs that promote user awareness and autonomy, it would represent a meaningful start.

6 CONCLUSION

My aim in this paper has been to shine light on a set of concerns stemming from advancements in artificial intelligence and machine learning—namely, concerns that adaptive choice architectures (using information collected about individuals to shape their decision-making contexts) facilitate online manipulation. In contrast with worries about how intelligent systems are used to make decisions *about us*, the issues I described stem from the use of AI/ML to influence *our decision-making*, raising fundamental questions about the integrity of user autonomy. To meet these ethical challenges, we must demand radical transparency from the creators of adaptive systems, encourage seamful user experiences that enable perceptive and deliberative human-computer interaction, and we must hold choice architects to the highest standard of care.

[5] Quoted in [11], p. 37.

[6] Arguably, it is also wrong to invisibly influence someone to act to *further* their own interests. Which is to say, due to its autonomy harms manipulation might always be wrong, even if it results in increased welfare. I leave that question to the side here. Goodin's account of the relationship between vulnerability and responsibility understands vulnerabilities in entirely welfarist terms. For a discussion about these issues that understands vulnerability more broadly, see the introduction to [22].

REFERENCES

[1] 2018. Cambridge Analytica and Facebook: The Scandal so Far. *Al Jazeera News* (March 2018). https://www.aljazeera.com/news/2018/03/cambridge-analytica-facebook-scandal-180327172353667.html

[2] Solon Barocas and Andrew D. Selbst. 2016. Big Data's Disparate Impact. *California Law Review* 104 (2016), 671–732. https://doi.org/10.2139/ssrn.2477899

[3] Louis Brandeis. 1933. *Other Peoples Money and How the Bankers Use It.* Jacket Library.

[4] Kiel Brennan-Marquez and Daniel Susser. 2016. Obstacles to Transparency in Privacy Engineering. In *2016 IEEE Security and Privacy Workshops (SPW).* IEEE, San Jose, CA, 49–52. https://doi.org/10.1109/SPW.2016.18

[5] M. Ryan Calo. 2014. Digital Market Manipulation. *The George Washington Law Review* 82, 4 (2014). https://doi.org/10.2139/ssrn.2309703

[6] Ryan Calo and Alex Rosenblat. 2017. The Taking Economy: Uber, Information, and Power. *Columbia Law Review* 117 (2017). https://doi.org/10.2139/ssrn.2929643

[7] Matthew Chalmers and Areti Galani. 2004. Seamful Interweaving: Heterogeneity in the Theory and Design of Interactive Systems. In *Proceedings of the 2004 conference on Designing interactive systems processes, practices, methods, and techniques - DIS '04.* ACM Press, Cambridge, MA, USA, 243. https://doi.org/10.1145/1013115.1013149

[8] Danielle Keats Citron. 2008. Technological Due Process. *Washington University Law Review* 85, 6 (2008), 66.

[9] Kate Crawford and Jason Schultz. 2014. Big Data and Due Process: Toward a Framework to Redress Predictive Privacy Harms. *Boston College Law Review* 55, 1 (2014), 37.

[10] Sara Degli Esposti. 2014. When big data meets dataveillance: the hidden side of analytics. *Surveillance & Society* 12, 2 (May 2014), 209–225. https://doi.org/10.24908/ss.v12i2.5113

[11] Robert E. Goodin. 1985. *Protecting the Vulnerable: A Reanalysis of Our Social Responsibilities.* The University of Chicago Press, Chicago, IL.

[12] T.H. Greene. 1881. Liberal Legislation and Freedom of Contract. In *Works 3: 3365-86,* R.L. Nettleship (Ed.). Longmans, London.

[13] Martin Heidegger. 1962. *Being and Time.* Blackwell Publishing Ltd., Oxford.

[14] Jacqueline Howard. 2016. Americans at More Than 10 Hours a Day on Screens. https://www.cnn.com/2016/06/30/health/americans-screen-time-nielsen/index.html

[15] Don Ihde. 1990. *Technology and the Lifeworld: From Garden to Earth.* Indiana University Press, Bloomington.

[16] Jeffrey M. Jones. 2013. In U.S., 40% Get Less Than Recommended Amount of Sleep. https://news.gallup.com/poll/166553/less-recommended-amount-sleep.aspx

[17] Daniel Kahneman. 2013. *Thinking, Fast and Slow* (1st pbk. ed ed.). Farrar, Straus and Giroux, New York. OCLC: ocn834531418.

[18] Pat Langley. 1997. Machine Learning for Adaptive User Interfaces. In *KI-97: Advances in Artificial Intelligence,* Jaime G. Carbonell, JÃűrg Siekmann, G. Goos, J. Hartmanis, J. Leeuwen, Gerhard Brewka, Christopher Habel, and Bernhard Nebel (Eds.). Vol. 1303. Springer Berlin Heidelberg, Berlin, Heidelberg, 53–62. https://doi.org/10.1007/3540634932_3

[19] Pat Langley. 1999. User Modeling in Adaptive Interfaces. In *Proceedings of the Seventh International Conference on User Modeling.* Springer, 357–370.

[20] Marjolein Lanzing. 2018. âĂIJStrongly RecommendedâĂİ Revisiting Decisional Privacy to Judge Hypernudging in Self-Tracking Technologies. *Philosophy & Technology* (June 2018). https://doi.org/10.1007/s13347-018-0316-4

[21] Bruno Latour. 1992. Where Are the Missing Masses? The Sociology of a Few Mundane Artifacts. In *Shaping Technology/Building Society: Studies in Sociotechnical Change,* Wiebe E. Bijker and John Law (Eds.). MIT Press, Cambridge, MA.

[22] Catriona Mackenzie, Wendy Rogers, and Susan Dodds (Eds.). 2014. *Vulnerability: new essays in ethics and feminist philosophy.* Oxford University Press, New York.

[23] David Martin, Benjamin Hanrahan, Jacki O'Neill, and Neha Gupta. 2013. Being a Turker. In *CSCW '13.* ACM, 12.

[24] Marshall McLuhan. 2003. *Understanding Media: The Extension of Man.* Ginkgo Press, Corte Madera.

[25] Helen Nissenbaum. 1996. Accountability in a Computerized Society. *Science and Engineering Ethics* 2 (1996), 25–42. https://link-springer-com.ezaccess.libraries.psu.edu/content/pdf/10.1007%2FBF02639315.pdf

[26] Amy Nordrum. 2016. Popular Internet of Things Forecast of 50 Billion Devices by 2020 Is Outdated. https://spectrum.ieee.org/tech-talk/telecom/internet/popular-internet-of-things-forecast-of-50-billion-devices-by-2020-is-outdated

[27] Donald Norman. 1999. *The Invisible Computer: Why Good Products Can Fail, the Personal Computer Is So Complex, and Information Appliances Are the Solution.* MIT Press, Cambridge, MA.

[28] Cathy O'Neil. 2016. *Weapons of Math Destruction: How Big Data Increases Inequality and Threatens Democracy* (first edition ed.). Crown, New York.

[29] Eli Pariser. 2011. *The Filter Bubble: What the Internet Is Hiding from You.* Penguin Press, New York. http://search.ebscohost.com/login.aspx?direct=true&scope=site&db=nlebk&db=nlabk&AN=1118322 OCLC: 759841356.

[30] Frank Pasquale. 2015. *The Black Box Society: The Secret Algorithms That Control Money and Information.* Harvard University Press, Cambridge.

[31] Joseph Raz. 1986. *The Morality of Freedom* (reprinted ed.). Clarendon Press, Oxford. OCLC: 838707273.

[32] Robert Rosenberger. 2009. The Sudden Experience of the Computer. *AI & Society* 24 (2009).

[33] Robert Rosenberger and Peter-Paul Verbeek. 2015. A Field Guide to Postphenomenology. In *Postphenomenological Investigations: Essays on Human-Technology Relations,* Robert Rosenberger and Peter-Paul Verbeek (Eds.). Lexington Books, Lanham, Maryland.

[34] Alex Rosenblat. 2018. *Uberland: How Algorithms are Rewriting the Rules of Work.* University of California Press, Oakland, CA.

[35] Alex Rosenblat and Luke Stark. 2016. Algorithmic Labor and Information Asymmetries: A Case Study of UberâĂŹs Drivers. *International Journal of Communication* 10 (2016), 27.

[36] Marijn Sax, Natali Helberger, and Nadine Bol. 2018. Health as a Means Towards Profitable Ends: mHealth Apps, User Autonomy, and Unfair Commercial Practices. *Journal of Consumer Policy* 41, 2 (June 2018), 103–134. https://doi.org/10.1007/s10603-018-9374-3

[37] Daniel Susser. 2017. Transparent Media and the Development of Digital Habits. In *Postphenomenology and Media: Essays on Human-Media-World Relations,* Yoni Van den Eede, Stacy O'Neal Irwin, and Galit Wellner (Eds.). Lexington Books, New York, 27–44.

[38] Daniel Susser, Beate Roessler, and Helen Nissenbaum. [n. d.]. Online Manipulation: Hidden Influences in a Digital World. *Under Review* ([n. d.]). https://papers.ssrn.com/abstract=3306006

[39] Richard H. Thaler and Cass R. Sunstein. 2008. *Nudge: Improving Decisions About Health, Wealth, and Happiness.* Yale University Press, New Haven. OCLC: ocn181517463.

[40] Sherry Turkle. 1995. *Life on the Screen: Identity in the Age of the Internet.* Simon and Schuster, New York, NY.

[41] Sherry Turkle. 2005. *The Second Self: Computers and the Human Spirit.* MIT Press, Cambridge, MA.

[42] Yoni Van Den Eede. 2011. In Between Us: On the Transparency and Opacity of Technological Mediation. *Foundations of Science* 16, 2/3 (May 2011), 139–159. https://doi.org/10.1007/s10699-010-9190-y

[43] Peter-Paul Verbeek. 2005. *What Things Do: Philosophical Reflections on Technology, Agency, and Design.* Pennsylvania State University Press, University Park, Pa.

[44] Karen Yeung. 2017. Hypernudge: Big Data as a Mode of Regulation by Design. *Information, Communication & Society* 20, 1 (Jan. 2017), 118–136. https://doi.org/10.1080/1369118X.2016.1186713

[45] Tal Zarsky. 2006. Online Privacy, Tailoring, and Persuasion. In *Privacy and Technologies of Identity: A Cross-Disciplinary Conversation,* Katherine J. Strandburg and Daniela Stan Raicu (Eds.). Springer-Verlag, New York, 209–224. https://doi.org/10.1007/0-387-28222-X_12

Reinforcement Learning and Inverse Reinforcement Learning with System 1 and System 2

Alexander Peysakhovich
Facebook AI Research
alexpeys@fb.com

ABSTRACT

Inferring a person's goal from their behavior is an important problem in applications of AI (e.g. automated assistants, recommender systems). The workhorse model for this task is the rational actor model - this amounts to assuming that people have stable reward functions, discount the future exponentially, and construct optimal plans. Under the rational actor assumption techniques such as inverse reinforcement learning (IRL) can be used to infer a person's goals from their actions. A competing model is the dual-system model. Here decisions are the result of an interplay between a fast, automatic, heuristic-based system 1 and a slower, deliberate, calculating system 2. We generalize the dual system framework to the case of Markov decision problems and show how to compute optimal plans for dual-system agents. We show that dual-system agents exhibit behaviors that are incompatible with rational actor assumption. We show that naive applications of rational-actor IRL to the behavior of dual-system agents can generate wrong inference about the agents' goals and suggest interventions that actually reduce the agent's overall utility. Finally, we adapt a simple IRL algorithm to correctly infer the goals of dual system decision-makers. This allows us to make interventions that help, rather than hinder, the dual-system agent's ability to reach their true goals.

KEYWORDS

reinforcement learning, behavioral economics, dual-system models, inverse reinforcement learning

ACM Reference Format:

Alexander Peysakhovich. 2019. Reinforcement Learning and Inverse Reinforcement Learning with System 1 and System 2. In *2019 AAAI/ACM Conference on AI, Ethics, and Society (AIES'19), January 27–28, 2019, Honolulu, HI, USA.* ACM, New York, NY, USA, 7 pages. https://doi.org/10.1145/3306618.3314259

INTRODUCTION

Modeling human decision making and inferring a person's latent reward function from their behavior are important problems across many fields [2, 12, 17, 37]. Typically such inference is performed using the rational actor model. The rational actor model assumes that people have a fixed utility function (aka. reward function), discount the future exponentially, and that they are capable of planning. Assuming the rational actor model means that if we know a person's reward function we can predict their behavior they will take by using dynamic programming to find (approximately) optimal plans [40]. Similarly, if we have observations of a person's behavior we can invert this behavior to learn the goals they are trying to achieve [29, 34, 43].

Unfortunately, it is well known that the rational actor model fails in many important decision environments [41]. The goal of this paper is to ask whether the tools of planning and inverse planning can be applied to the dual-system model (2S), a workhorse model of human decision-making from the behavioral and cognitive sciences [16].

The 2S views behavior as being controlled by two systems, system 1 which is automatic, fast, effortless and uses heuristics and system 2 which is slower, reflective, requires cognitive costs and deliberates. This paper follows existing work in neuroscience and assumes an interaction between systems as follows: when faced with a decision first system 1 'suggests' a course of action and system 2 uses costly cognitive control to modulate this suggestion [13, 38].

An important example of violations of the rational actor model occur in situations where people must trade off rewards now for rewards later [1]. People plan to eat healthy, go to the gym, and quit smoking *tomorrow* but when tomorrow comes, they reverse their plans [30, 42]. Patterns of choices where one alternative is chosen when the choice is made for the future but the other is chosen when the choice is made for immediate outcomes (e.g. committing to start eating healthy tomorrow but having a donut today) are called dynamically inconsistent. Dynamic inconsistency cannot occur if individuals are indeed maximizing a stable utility function which discounts the future exponentially [30].[1]

The 2S model states that time inconsistency arises because decisions are an interplay between a system 1 that seeks immediate gratification and a system 2 that is able to consider long term impacts of decisions [7, 28, 42]. When decisions are only about the future, system 2 wants to commit to eating healthy and going to the gym but when the donut is in front of us system 1 makes it hard to put down.

This paper asks: what happens when decisions are not between single actions but in temporally extended plans? We will consider a computational model of the 2S planning as follows: the decision-maker faces a Markov decision problem and the resulting choices are a product of system 2 optimizing some utility function net of

AIES '19, January 27–28, 2019, Honolulu, HI, USA

ACM ISBN 978-1-4503-6324-2/19/01...$15.00
https://doi.org/10.1145/3306618.3314259

[1]Another pattern of real world behavior that points to violations of the rational actor model is the presence of commitment devices [4, 31]. People are willing to pay to remove choices from their choice sets (e.g. pay a personal trainer to force them out of bed at 6am for a workout). A rational agent (who can simply choose to follow through on any plans made yesterday) would never make such a decision.

cognitive control costs. The cognitive control cost of a decision is proportional to how much it deviates (in terms of disutility) from an optimal decision that system 1 would like to make.[2] System 1 and system 2 have different utility functions, discount the future differently, or both. This conflict gives rise to time inconsistent behaviors as well as other violations of rationality. The model presented here nests existing work such as the dual-self [7], and self-control preferences [11]. It can also be thought of as a converged version of a μAgent model [22].

There are three contributions in this paper. First, in many existing models [7, 11] assume that system 1 is perfectly myopic (aka. cares only about immediate rewards).[3] Our work extends these models to a system 1 capable of anticipating future consequences of a decision today and adapts standard tools from reinforcement learning to make the model work for arbitrary Markov decision problems. Second, we show how inverse reinforcement learning [29, 43], applied naively, can grossly mislead an analyst trying to learn a 2S agent's goals from their behavior. Third, we adapt a simple IRL algorithm to test for dual-self decision-making or to recover the goals of a dual-self agent from observed behavior.

Related Work

One way to model preference reversals in say that individuals have hyperbolic [1] or quasi-hyperbolic [24, 30] discount rates (i.e. they value x utils in the future as a function such as $\frac{1}{1+kt}x$ instead of $\delta^t x$). In hyperbolic/quasi-hyperbolic models models the effective discounting from waiting from $t = 0$ to $t = 1$ is larger than the loss from waiting from t to $t + 1$. These models display preference reversals, procrastination, and other 'irrational' phenomena [30]. Making dynamic predictions in such models require solving a game between multiple 'selves' of an individual that exist at each time period [6, 18, 19, 24, 30].

By contrast, 2S models assume the existence of multiple 'selves' (or systems) that exist consistently across periods [7, 23]. Systems can have different utility functions [13], discount the future differently [7, 23] or have different information sets [21]. In each of these models decisions involve some way of combining inputs from these two systems, and they can generate time inconsistent behavior and even discounting patterns that look very similar to those of a hyperbolic discounter [23].

There are two major advantages of the 2S framework. First, is that it can be applied to decision environments beyond those where decision-makers must trade off rewards now for rewards later. There is strong evidence that system 1 and system 2 appear to differ in their evaluations of many other decisions such as risk/uncertainty [15], whether to be altruistic [33, 36], and moral decisions [10]. Second, 2S systems give a consistent welfare criterion - they can identify whether an intervention improves or decreases an individual's utility unambiguously (provided we assume system 2 utility is an individual's true utility). Because hyperbolic models assume games between different selves at different time periods asking whether an intervention made an individual better off requires asking which time period's 'self' we care about [30].

Finally, a growing literature argues that a key distinction between system 1 and system 2 is how they learn [20, 21]. [21] argues that system 1 is best modeled as a model-free reinforcement learner while system 2 is more like a model-based planner. While we do not deal with the dynamics of learning in this paper this conception provides a plausible foundation for the assumption that system 1 and system 2 try to maximize different rewards. For example, after trying a few donuts a model free system 1 may learn that donuts are delicious. However, system 1 will not internalize the negative reward of not following a diet because this negative consequence is far into the future. On the other hand, the model-based system 2 can incorporate this reward into it's calculation of an optimal plan. Such dual-system learning patterns have been observed in real world decision-making where information that is personally experienced (e.g. having one's stock portfolio collapse during a recession) has a different effect on decisions than information that is simply learned symbolically [27].

BASICS OF THE 2S MODEL

We will introduce the 2S model with a simple example and then expand it to Markov decision problems. Consider a decision-maker (DM). The DM is on a diet and is choosing between a delicious but unhealthy donut (d) and a healthy but less flavorful kale smoothie (k) as a snack.

The decision-maker has 2 reward functions r_1 and r_2 which represent systems 1 and 2 respectively. System 1 likes sugar whereas system 2's goals include the higher level goal of maintaining the diet. This is formalized as $r_1(k) = 0$ and $r_1(d) = 1$ whereas $r_2(k) = 1$ and $r_2(d) = -1$.

First we consider the DM making a choice for eating the snack right now. Let a^* be the system 1 optimal action (eat the donut). The *cognitive control cost* of deviating to another action a by system 2 is given by

$$CC(a) = \psi(r_1(a^*) - r_1(a)).$$

For simplicity let ψ be a linear function. System 2 trades off its reward and this cognitive control cost, so choices are maximizers of the combined function

$$V_{DS}(a) = r_2(a) - \psi(r_1(a^*) - r_1(a)).$$

Plugging in the rewards above gives $V_{DS}(d) = -1$ and $V_{DS}(k) = 1 - \psi(1)$

It is easy to see that in this case the DM chooses the kale smoothie iff the cognitive control cost parameter $\psi \leq 2$.

Now let us consider the case where the DM is choosing a snack now but will eat it tomorrow ($t = 1$). Rewards are received at the time the snack is eaten and system 1 and 2 discount future rewards are discounted by rates $\gamma_1 < \gamma_2$. System 1 still prefers the donut but now the control cost of deviating is $\psi(\gamma_1 r_1(a^*) - \gamma_1 r_1(a))$. Again the choice is the maximizer of the system 2 utility net of control costs, but now the DM chooses kale when $\psi \leq 2\frac{\gamma_2}{\gamma_1}$.

Thus, there is a range of cognitive control parameters $[2, 2\frac{\gamma_2}{\gamma_1}]$ where agents choose donuts today, but, if they are able to, commit to eating kale tomorrow.

[2] Throughout the paper language like 'desires', 'beliefs', and 'conflict' will be used to anthropomorphize system 1 and 2. This is not meant to imply the existence of homunculi literally fighting within an individual's head, rather the language is used to convey intuitions behind concepts.

[3] This is not the case for all existing models, for example in [8] system 1 has a non-zero discount factor. However, system 1 and system 2 share utility functions and differ only in discount rates. In addition, that work considers applying the model only to simple scenarios rather than arbitrary Markov decision problems.

PLANNING WITH TWO SYSTEMS

So far we have dealt with a single decision, however, we can consider a 2S DM making a dynamic choice. Suppose that at $t = 1$ a donut will be available for lunch and the DM can pay some price at time $t = 0$ for kale to be available at $t = 1$ as well. Would the DM be willing to pay this price? There are several factors to consider. First, if $\psi > 2$ then even if kale is available the DM would not choose it at $t = 1$, thus DM would not be willing to pay at $t = 0$. Second, even if the DM would choose kale system 2 must factor into the price the cognitive control costs the DM will have to pay in the future to actually make the choice. Third, if the DM will indeed choose kale at $t = 1$ system 1 would prefer that the DM does not make kale available - in other words, in the 2S model there is now a conflict at $t = 0$ because of the anticipation of conflict at $t = 1$.

A Markov decision process (MDP) is a finite set of state $\mathcal{S}$, a set of actions $\mathcal{A}$, a transition function which inputs a state and action and outputs a distribution on the next states $\tau : \mathcal{S} \times \mathcal{A} \to \Delta(\mathcal{S})$. A 2S DM has two reward functions which input a state and action pair and output a distribution on real valued rewards $r_i : \mathcal{S} \times \mathcal{A} \to \Delta(\mathbb{R})$. Systems discount the future with discount rates γ_1, γ_2.

We now extend the 2S model to MDPs with the formalization. Our DM will be choosing a policy π which is a map from states to actions (this can be randomized but in this paper we restrict to deterministic policies). Each system has a value function $V_i(s, \pi)$ which inputs a starting state s and a policy π and outputs the expected sum of discounted rewards from behaving according to this policy starting in this state. A related object is each system's Q function $Q_i(s, a, \pi)$ which takes as input a state, action, and policy and gives the expected discounted sum of rewards from taking action a today and following policy π starting at the next period.

Each system has an optimal policy it would prefer, we refer to these as π_1^*, π_2^*. However, behavior will come from system 2 optimizing its reward function net of cognitive control costs. We call the resulting policy the *compromise policy*. We now turn to understanding what function this policy will actually optimize.

First, we need to ask how to calculate cognitive control costs when we think about policies rather than single actions. As before there is a tradeoff equation for system 2 given by

$$V_{CC}(s, \pi) = V_2(s, \pi) - CC(s, \pi).$$

We will continue to think about the control costs as the difference between utility gained to system 1 under π and π_1^* as with the single action case. However, now a choice at time t now affects rewards at $t + k$ and we need to make decisions about how system 1 perceives the future.

Again, actions are taken at each time step. Let us consider the model where system 1 suggests an action $\pi_1^*(s)$. What should the cost be for deviating to a different action?

We now discuss two possible assumptions. We refer to them as the *naive* or *sophisticated* system 1.[4]

[4]We will use the naive/sophisticated language of the literature on hyperbolic discounting [30]. In that literature actions of a self in period t depend on expectations of that self about the actions of future selves. Naive agents are those who assume future selves will make the same decisions as the current self, sophisticated agents are those who play a subgame perfect equilibrium (i.e. know that future selves will take actions to maximize their own utility).

The naive system 1 assumption is that actions starting tomorrow will follow $\pi_1^*(s)$ (i.e. system 1 is ignorant of system 2's future plans). A naive system 1 means that the control cost along a trajectory can be computed via the Q function of system 1. The per period reward to system 2 net of control costs can be written as

$$r_2(s, a) - \psi(Q_1(s, \pi_1^*(s), \pi_1^*) - Q_1(s, a, \pi_1^*)).$$

We can thus write the planning problem in standard recursive form

$$V_{CC}^{naive}(s, \pi) = r_2(s, \pi(s)) - \psi(Q_1(s, \pi_1^*(s), \pi_1^*) - Q_1(s, a, \pi_1^*)) + \gamma_2 V_{CC}^{naive}(s, \pi).$$

Standard RL methods (value iteration, policy iteration) can be used to find the policy which optimizes this function: first we compute Q_1^* using a standard method, then we plug in Q_1^* and again apply policy iteration/value iteration to compute the which optimizes V_{CC}^{naive}.

The *sophisticated* system 2 model is more nuanced. Here system 1 understands that future actions will come from π instead of π_1^* and so we write the optimizing function net of control costs as

$$V_{CC}^{soph}(s, \pi) = V_2(s, \pi) - \psi(V_1(s, \pi_1^*) - V_1(s, \pi)).$$

The sophisticated formulation is related to the interpretation of 2S model in [7, 42] where actions are split between a planner and a doer where the only action of the planner is to be able to change the utility function of the doer. In the Markov case this would amount to assuming that the agent starts in state s, the planner gets to change the doer's utility function (reward function for each state, action), and the doer chooses the policy consistent with this new utility function.

This no longer has a simple recursive form because V_1 and V_2 have different discount rates. However, we now show that policy iteration can be used even in this compound problem. First, we substitute the definitions of the value functions into the equations above to re-express V_{CC}^s as

$$r_2(s, \pi(s)) + \psi r_1(s, \pi(s)) + \gamma_2 V_2(\tau(s, a), \pi) + \psi \gamma_1 V_1(\tau(s, a), \pi) - \psi V_1(s, \pi_1^*)$$

At each state the optimal policy value for system 1 $V_1(s, \pi_1^*)$ is a constant. Thus, we can ignore it for the sake of computing the optimal policy starting at that state (though not for computing that policy's actual value). This means that the sophisticated system 1 policy is the one which optimizes the compromise objective $V_2(s, \pi) + \psi V_1(s, \pi)$. This also means the cognitive-control based 2S model is a plausible foundation for the μAgent model [22]. An adaptation of the value iteration algorithm can be used to construct an optimal policy (Algorithm 1). As with standard value iteration, this algorithm is monotonic (each step has a better policy with respect to the compromise objective) and thus when the MDP is finite it will converge to the optimal policy.

Note that while standard techniques can be adapted to construct plans for sophisticated system 1 agents their policies no longer have a single associated value function that can be written in standard recursive form. Because system 1 and system 2 have different discount rates the compromise policy may exhibit behaviors like time inconsistency or commitment. Time inconsistency occurs because when an action affects rewards arbitrarily far in the future the discount rate of system 2 is the only relevant one and thus these decisions will look as if they optimize only for r_2 while decisions that affect rewards close in time optimize for a combination of r_1 and r_2.

Algorithm 1 Value Iteration With Sophisticated System 1

```
Initialize V_1, V_2 arbitrarily
while Not converged do
    for s ∈ S do
        for a ∈ A do
            Q_1(s, a) = E(r_1 | s, a) + γ_1 V_1(τ(s, a))
            Q_2(s, a) = E(r_2 | s, a) + γ_2 V_2(τ(s, a))
        Let a* = argmax_a ψQ_1(s, a) + Q_2(s, a)
        Set V_i(s) = Q_i(s, a*)
```

With sophisticated 2S planning in hand, we can move on to examining examples of behavior of 2S agents as well as the differences between sophisticated and naive system 1 agents.

INVERTING DUAL SYSTEM PLANS

We now turn to the problem of inferring an agent's reward function from observed behavior. This problem is particularly important if we seek to construct AI that can observe human behavior, infer their desired goal states, and then take actions to help the DM achieve their goals as in, e.g. an artificial assistant.

We consider the standard inverse reinforcement learning (IRL) setup. We have access to a dataset of trajectories (sequences of state-action pairs taken by our agents). We refer to this as $\mathcal{D} = \{\eta_1, \eta_2, \eta_3 \ldots \eta_N\}$. We wish to use $\mathcal{D}$ to infer the underlying reward function(s) of the DM. In addition, we wish to provide a statistical test for the presence of dual-system behavior in a data-set.

We will do this using maximum likelihood estimation as in prior work [43]. We let θ be the parametrization of the problem (here the reward function or functions). Our goal will be to find the reward parameters θ to maximize the likelihood of the data. The Markovian property of MDPs means that the likelihood of a trajectory η_i can be computed as

$$Pr(\eta_i \mid \theta) = \prod_{(s,a) \in \eta_i} Pr(a \mid s, \theta).$$

We will work with the log likelihood instead which will be

$$\mathcal{L}(\mathcal{D} \mid \theta) = \sum_{(s,a) \in \mathcal{D}} \log Pr(a \mid s, \theta).$$

With rational agents it is straightforward how to compute $\mathcal{L}$. Given θ the agent has an optimal policy which has an associated Q function. We refer to this as $Q^*(s, a \mid \theta)$. We assume that choices at each state are made according to a softmax of this Q^* function

$$Pr(a \mid s, \theta) = \frac{\exp(\frac{1}{\beta} Q^*(a, s \mid \theta))}{\sum_{a'} \exp(\frac{1}{\beta} Q^*(a', s \mid \theta))}.$$

Thus the log likelihood is well defined.

We now turn to, given a guess θ calculating the likelihood of observed trajectories for 2S agents. We begin with the naive system 1 agents. This is the easier of the two cases. Recall that here we can think of this agent as a rational agent which optimizes a new reward function which takes the discounted (with system 2 discount rate) payoffs of the form

$$r^{naive}(s, a) = r_2(s, a) - \psi(V_1^*(s) - Q_1^*(s, a)).$$

Thus we can readily compute a Q_{CC}^{naive*} function if we can compute the optimal policy. This gives us a well defined likelihood for any trajectory.

For sophisticated system 1 agents the problem is a little bit more complicated. Recall that a sophisticated system 1 agent's final policy also optimizes the compromise value function $V_2(s, \pi) + \psi V_1(s, \pi)$. We can can write the associated Q function as

$$Q_{CC}^{soph}(s, a, \pi) = r_2(s, a) + r_1(s, a) + \gamma_2 V_2(\tau(s, a), \pi) + \gamma_1 V_1(\tau(s, a), \pi).$$

Given the policy π^*_{soph} we can compute this Q function and plug it into the softmax equation above. Now we have a well defined likelihood given the parameters θ.

EXPERIMENT: DONUT KALE GRID WORLD

We consider a Markov grid world. An agent begins in a location and can move in any of 4 cardinal directions. There are two items placed on the grid, a kale smoothie and a donut (see Figure 1). The donut and kale are terminal states of the game. The donut and kale have rewards for system 1 and system 2 as in the example above. We set $\gamma_2 = .99, \gamma_1 = .6, \psi = 5$.

Figure 1 shows the world as well as the trajectories starting from the corner of the board. The ideal policies of system 1 (grab the donut) and system 2 (walk to the kale using the shortest possible path). However, the compromise policies look quite different from either optimal policy. Indeed, both of them take a path around the donut (but not the shortest possible path). We see the naive and sophisticated system 1 policies differ quite a lot with the compromise policy with the naive system 1 demonstrating giving the donut a very wide berth.

The difference in final behavior under the naive/sophisticated assumptions comes down to the following logic. Consider a simple problem where the DM chooses between 2 actions Stop and Go at $t = 0$. If the agent Stops the game ends, otherwise it continues to $t = 1$ where the agent also chooses between Stop and Go. If the agent chooses Stop, the game ends, if the agent chooses Go, he gets a donut. System 1's optimal policy is to Go at both stages and eat the donut. Suppose the cognitive control parameters are such that agents Stop in period $t = 1$ (with a control cost). A sophisticated system 1 then knows at $t = 0$ that the agent will stop and therefore there is no control cost for Stop in period 0. However, a naive system 1 always assumes that the agent will Go in the future and therefore there will be a control cost at period 1. This reasoning is precisely why the DM in the grid world gives the donut a wide berth under the naive system 1 assumption but walks exactly one step away under the sophisticated assumption.

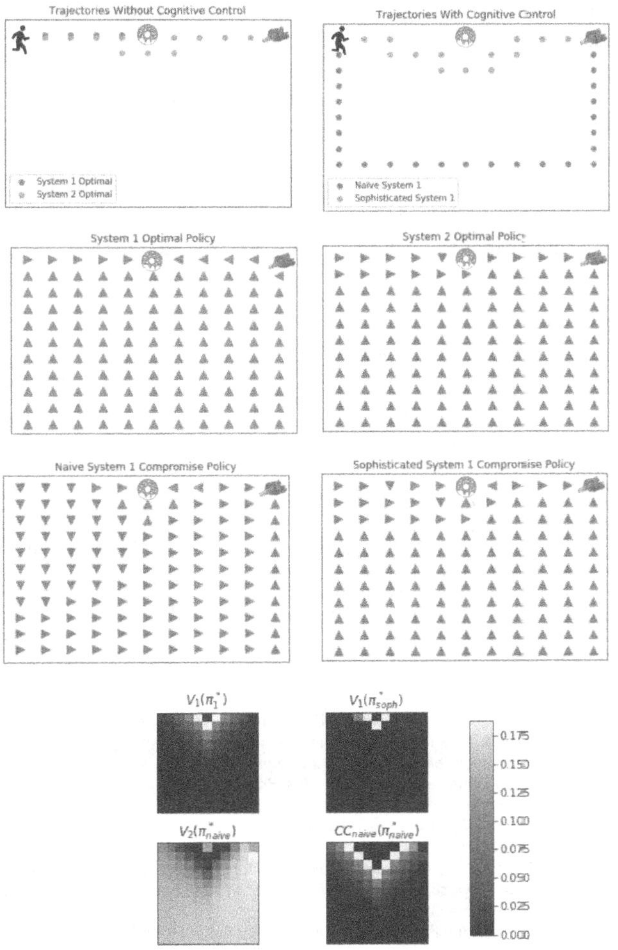

Figure 1: Top row shows the trajectories of system 1 and system 2 starting from the corner as well as the full preferred policies of both systems. Each arrow indicates the direction the agent will move at that state. States are colored red if starting at that state leads to the donut and green if it leads to the kale. Bottom row shows the compromise policies under the 2S model with naive/sophisticated system 1. The compromise policies are not pure mixtures of the optimal policies and display behavior such as precommitment (walking far away from the donut to make it harder to reach in the future). Last subpanel shows functions for each of the systems given compromise policies as well as the map of self control costs incurred by the DM in each state under the naive assumption

Whether the naive or sophisticated model of cognitive control is more reflective of real decision-making is an open empirical question (though cognitively it seems like the naive assumption is more plausible), however, because the models give such precise predictions about the main differences it is an empirically testable one and a potentially fruitful direction for future research.

EXPERIMENT: IRL IN THE DONUT KALE GRID WORLD

We now apply the IRL methods above to the Donut Kale grid world problem. We keep the same true underlying problem parameters and use the true value functions to construct a dataset of stochastic trajectories starting from any possible (non-terminal) state. We construct datasets of stochastic trajectories for both kinds of dual system agents. We sample 50 stochastic trajectories using softmax choice of actions at each time point with $\beta = .01$ starting from any possible non-terminal state. We give models access to the true discount rates. We use a large number of trajectories as well as the true discount rates because the purpose of this experiment is to show that rational IRL draws problematic inferences even when it has access to large amounts of data and true discount rates. We refer to these data sets as $\mathcal{D}_{naive}$ and $\mathcal{D}_{soph}$.

For each of the different assumptions on the true planning function (rational, sophisticated, naive) optimization of the IRL likelihood function is relatively slow (because each iteration requires the computation of an optimal policy). In these experiments we found that the IRL objective functions are very difficult to optimize, methods that improved the likelihood function only locally ended up finding very poor minima and we ended up using differential evolution to optimize the likelihood [39]. In standard rational IRL there exist assumptions which allow for closed form solutions to gradients at each optimization step [43]. Unfortunately these assumptions do not hold in the 2S case, and so an open area for future research is the efficient computation of solutions to dual-system IRL models.

We the rational, sophisticated, and naive IRL models using maximum likelihood estimation on the generated datasets. We find that a rational IRL model recovers that both 2S agents like donuts (this is because if the DM starts close to the donut then they eat it, thus the only way to rationalize this is to have positive reward from the donut). Thus, using rational IRL would lead a designer to make wrong decisions if they could make interventions (for example, if they are asked whether the DM would prefer a donut or nothing).

Second, we find that correctly specified models learn the underlying preferences quite well. Both the naive and sophisticated IRL learn that only system 1 prefers donuts. Things are more mixed when we examine misspecified 2S IRL models. The naive IRL model applied to the sophisticated data yields wrong inferences just like the rational model, however the sophisticated model applied to the naive data gets the order of preferences correct.

CONCLUSION

This work has focused on extending planning and inverse planning models into the domain of non-rational agents. In particular we have focused on the dual system framework that has proven to be successful across the behavioral sciences. We have shown that standard planning and inverse planning algorithms can be adapted to 2S agents. Importantly we have shown that incorrectly assuming that a dual-system agent is a rational agent when trying to infer goals from behavior can lead to interventions that actually decrease the overall welfare of the agent.

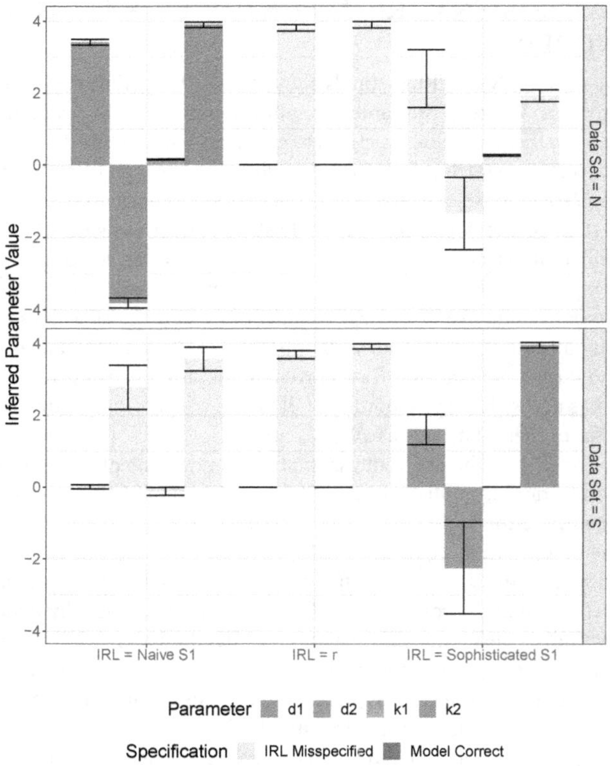

Figure 2: Rational IRL makes incorrect inferences about the decision-maker's preferences (d1, d2, k1, k2 refer to inferred rewards of donuts, kale for system 1 and system 2 respectively). However, 2S IRL models with correct specification learn that only system 1 likes donuts (i.e. $d1 > 0, d2 < 0$). Misspecification is more of a mixed bag with the sophisticated model learning the correct preferences when applied to the naive dataset but the naive model inferring the wrong answer. Lines reflects averages over 16 replicates, error bars reflect standard deviations.

We have assumed that both system 1 and system 2 have fixed reward functions and use model-based methods for computing optimal polices. In reality, both systems are constantly learning about the real world. Existing work [20, 21] argues that these systems learn and plan differently with system 1 being more model-free and system 2 being more model-based. Extending the 2S model presented here to include both general reinforcement learning and known regularities in human learning [5, 9, 14] is an important future direction.

We have focused on the domain of time inconsistency but system 1/system 2 conflicts occur in many other domains. Extending the model here to problems in moral decision-making, decision making under risk and uncertainty, and cooperation sees like a fruitful direction for future research. In particular, recent work in behavioral science argues that cooperation is an interplay between a system 1 which learns 'social heuristics' and a reward maximizing system 2 [35, 36]. However, formal models of the social heuristics hypothesis (SHH) have been restricted to simple matrix games [3]. The 2S model presented here is a potential way to expand the SHH to more complex environments such as Markov social dilemmas [25, 26, 32].

Finally, rational actor models are used explicitly or implicitly across many applications (a large literature in recommender systems can be framed as a form of learning latent preferences). Understanding where such models are appropriate and where the assumptions are so badly broken that they lead to false conclusions is an important topic for discussion, research, and debate.

REFERENCES

[1] George Ainslie. 2001. *Breakdown of will.* Cambridge University Press.
[2] Susan Athey and Denis Nekipelov. 2010. A structural model of sponsored search advertising auctions. In *Sixth ad auctions workshop*, Vol. 15.
[3] Adam Bear and David G Rand. 2016. Intuition, deliberation, and the evolution of cooperation. *Proceedings of the National Academy of Sciences* 113, 4 (2016), 936–941.
[4] Gharad Bryan, Dean Karlan, and Scott Nelson. 2010. Commitment devices. *Annu. Rev. Econ.* 2, 1 (2010), 671–698.
[5] Ido Erev and Alvin E Roth. 1998. Predicting how people play games: Reinforcement learning in experimental games with unique, mixed strategy equilibria. *American economic review* (1998), 848–881.
[6] Owain Evans, Andreas Stuhlmüller, and Noah D Goodman. 2016. Learning the Preferences of Ignorant, Inconsistent Agents.. In *AAAI*. 323–329.
[7] Drew Fudenberg and David K Levine. 2006. A dual-self model of impulse control. *American economic review* 96, 5 (2006), 1449–1476.
[8] Drew Fudenberg and David K Levine. 2012. Timing and self-control. *Econometrica* 80, 1 (2012), 1–42.
[9] Drew Fudenberg and Alexander Peysakhovich. 2016. Recency, records, and recaps: Learning and nonequilibrium behavior in a simple decision problem. *ACM Transactions on Economics and Computation (TEAC)* 4, 4 (2016), 23.
[10] Joshua David Greene. 2014. *Moral tribes: Emotion, reason, and the gap between us and them.* Penguin.
[11] Faruk Gul and Wolfgang Pesendorfer. 2001. Temptation and self-control. *Econometrica* 69, 6 (2001), 1403–1435.
[12] Dylan Hadfield-Menell, Stuart J Russell, Pieter Abbeel, and Anca Dragan. 2016. Cooperative inverse reinforcement learning. In *Advances in neural information processing systems*. 3909–3917.
[13] Todd A Hare, Colin F Camerer, and Antonio Rangel. 2009. Self-control in decision-making involves modulation of the vmPFC valuation system. *Science* 324, 5927 (2009), 646–648.
[14] Ralph Hertwig, Greg Barron, Elke U Weber, and Ido Erev. 2004. Decisions from experience and the effect of rare events in risky choice. *Psychological science* 15, 8 (2004), 534–539.
[15] Ming Hsu, Meghana Bhatt, Ralph Adolphs, Daniel Tranel, and Colin F Camerer. 2005. Neural systems responding to degrees of uncertainty in human decision-making. *Science* 310, 5754 (2005), 1680–1683.
[16] Daniel Kahneman. 2011. *Thinking, fast and slow.* Vol. 1. Farrar, Straus and Giroux New York.
[17] Sarah Keren, Avigdor Gal, and Erez Karpas. 2014. Goal Recognition Design.. In *ICAPS*.
[18] Jon Kleinberg and Sigal Oren. 2014. Time-inconsistent planning: a computational problem in behavioral economics. In *Proceedings of the fifteenth ACM conference on Economics and computation*. ACM, 547–564.
[19] Jon Kleinberg, Sigal Oren, and Manish Raghavan. 2016. Planning problems for sophisticated agents with present bias. In *Proceedings of the 2016 ACM Conference on Economics and Computation*. ACM, 343–360.
[20] Wouter Kool, Samuel J Gershman, and Fiery A Cushman. 2017. Cost-benefit arbitration between multiple reinforcement-learning systems. *Psychological science* 28, 9 (2017), 1321–1333.
[21] Wouter Kool, Samuel J Gershman, and Fiery A Cushman. 2018. Planning complexity registers as a cost in metacontrol. *Journal of cognitive neuroscience* (2018), 1–14.
[22] Zeb Kurth-Nelson and A David Redish. 2009. Temporal-difference reinforcement learning with distributed representations. *PLoS One* 4, 10 (2009), e7362.
[23] Zeb Kurth-Nelson and A David Redish. 2010. A reinforcement learning model of precommitment in decision making. *Frontiers in behavioral neuroscience* 4 (2010), 184.
[24] David Laibson. 1997. Golden eggs and hyperbolic discounting. *The Quarterly Journal of Economics* 112, 2 (1997), 443–478.
[25] Joel Z Leibo, Vinicius Zambaldi, Marc Lanctot, Janusz Marecki, and Thore Graepel. 2017. Multi-agent reinforcement learning in sequential social dilemmas. In *Proceedings of the 16th Conference on Autonomous Agents and MultiAgent Systems*.

International Foundation for Autonomous Agents and Multiagent Systems, 464–473.
[26] Adam Lerer and Alexander Peysakhovich. 2017. Maintaining cooperation in complex social dilemmas using deep reinforcement learning. *arXiv preprint arXiv:1707.01068* (2017).
[27] Ulrike Malmendier and Stefan Nagel. 2011. Depression babies: do macroeconomic experiences affect risk taking? *The Quarterly Journal of Economics* 126, 1 (2011), 373–416.
[28] Samuel M McClure, David I Laibson, George Loewenstein, and Jonathan D Cohen. 2004. Separate neural systems value immediate and delayed monetary rewards. *Science* 306, 5695 (2004), 503–507.
[29] Andrew Y Ng, Stuart J Russell, et al. 2000. Algorithms for inverse reinforcement learning.. In *ICML*. 663–670.
[30] Ted O'Donoghue and Matthew Rabin. 1999. Doing it now or later. *American Economic Review* 89, 1 (1999), 103–124.
[31] Alexander Peysakhovich. 2014. How to commit (if you must): Commitment contracts and the dual-self model. *Journal of Economic Behavior & Organization* 101 (2014), 100–112.
[32] Alexander Peysakhovich and Adam Lerer. 2018. Consequentialist conditional cooperation in social dilemmas with imperfect information. In *ICLR*.
[33] Alexander Peysakhovich and David G Rand. 2015. Habits of virtue: Creating norms of cooperation and defection in the laboratory. *Management Science* 62, 3 (2015), 631–647.
[34] Deepak Ramachandran and Eyal Amir. [n. d.]. Bayesian inverse reinforcement learning. ([n. d.]).
[35] David G Rand, Joshua D Greene, and Martin A Nowak. 2012. Spontaneous giving and calculated greed. *Nature* 489, 7416 (2012), 427.
[36] David G Rand, Alexander Peysakhovich, Gordon T Kraft-Todd, George E Newman, Owen Wurzbacher, Martin A Nowak, and Joshua D Greene. 2014. Social heuristics shape intuitive cooperation. *Nature communications* 5 (2014), 3677.
[37] Paul Resnick and Hal R Varian. 1997. Recommender systems. *Commun. ACM* 40, 3 (1997), 56–59.
[38] Amitai Shenhav, Matthew M Botvinick, and Jonathan D Cohen. 2013. The expected value of control: an integrative theory of anterior cingulate cortex function. *Neuron* 79, 2 (2013), 217–240.
[39] Rainer Storn and Kenneth Price. 1997. Differential evolution–a simple and efficient heuristic for global optimization over continuous spaces. *Journal of global optimization* 11, 4 (1997), 341–359.
[40] Richard S Sutton and Andrew G Barto. 1998. *Introduction to reinforcement learning*. Vol. 135. MIT press Cambridge.
[41] Richard Thaler. 2012. *The winner's curse: Paradoxes and anomalies of economic life*. Simon and Schuster.
[42] Richard H Thaler and Hersh M Shefrin. 1981. An economic theory of self-control. *Journal of political Economy* 89, 2 (1981), 392–406.
[43] Brian D Ziebart, Andrew L Maas, J Andrew Bagnell, and Anind K Dey. 2008. Maximum Entropy Inverse Reinforcement Learning.. In *AAAI*, Vol. 8. Chicago, IL, USA, 1433–1438.

Incomplete Contracting and AI Alignment

Dylan Hadfield-Menell
University of California, Berkeley
Center for Human-Compatible AI
dhm@eecs.berkeley.edu

Gillian K. Hadfield
University of Toronto
Vector Institute for AI; OpenAI
Center for Human-Compatible AI
g.hadfield@utoronto.ca

ABSTRACT

We suggest that the analysis of incomplete contracting developed by law and economics researchers can provide a useful framework for understanding the AI alignment problem and help to generate a systematic approach to finding solutions. We first provide an overview of the incomplete contracting literature and explore parallels between this work and the problem of AI alignment. As we emphasize, misalignment between principal and agent is a core focus of economic analysis. We highlight some technical results from the economics literature on incomplete contracts that may provide insights for AI alignment researchers. Our core contribution, however, is to bring to bear an insight that economists have been urged to absorb from legal scholars and other behavioral scientists: the fact that human contracting is supported by substantial amounts of external structure, such as generally available institutions (culture, law) that can supply implied terms to fill the gaps in incomplete contracts. We propose a research agenda for AI alignment work that focuses on the problem of how to build AI that can replicate the human cognitive processes that connect individual incomplete contracts with this supporting external structure.

CCS CONCEPTS

• **Applied computing** → **Economics**; *Law*; • **Computing methodologies** → *Cooperation and coordination*; *Inverse reinforcement learning*.

KEYWORDS

value alignment; incomplete contracting; principal-agent problems

ACM Reference Format:

Dylan Hadfield-Menell and Gillian K. Hadfield. 2019. Incomplete Contracting and AI Alignment. In *AAAI/ACM Conference on AI, Ethics, and Society (AIES '19), January 27–28, 2019, Honolulu, HI, USA.* ACM, New York, NY, USA, 6 pages. https://doi.org/10.1145/3306618.3314250

1 INTRODUCTION

When we design and deploy an AI agent, we specify what we want it to do. In reinforcement learning, for example, we specify a reward function, which tells the agent the value of all state and action combinations. Good algorithms then generate AI behavior that performs well according to this reward function. The AI alignment problem arises because of differences between the specified reward function and what relevant humans (the designer, the user, others affected by the agent's behavior) actually value. AI researchers intend for their reward functions to give the correct rewards in all states of the world so as to achieve the objectives of relevant humans. But often AI reward functions are—unintentionally and unavoidably—misspecified. They may accurately reflect human rewards in the circumstances that the designer thought about but fail to accurately specify how humans value all state and action combinations.

AI alignment has a clear analogue in the human principal-agent problem long studied by economists and legal scholars. In these settings a human agent is supposed to take actions that achieve a principal's objectives. The ideal way to align principal and agent is to design a *complete contingent contract* [51]. This is an enforceable agreement that specifies the reward received by the agent for all actions and states of the world. The contract could be enforced by monetary transfers or punishments imposed by a coercive institution, such as a court. Or it could be enforced by a private actor or group of actors who penalize contract violations by, for example, imposing social sanctions or cutting off valuable relationships; the latter contracts are known as *relational contracts* [13, 29, 31, 32]. A complete contingent contract implements desired behavior by the agent in all states of the world. It perfectly aligns the agent's incentives with the principal's objective.

In this paper, [1]. we suggest that the analysis of incomplete contracting developed by law and economics researchers can provide a useful framework for understanding the AI alignment problem and help to generate a systematic approach to finding solutions. We briefly highlight some technical results from the economics literature on incomplete contracts that may provide insights for AI alignment researchers. Our core contribution, however, is to bring to bear an insight that economists have been urged to absorb from legal scholars and other behavioral scientists: the fact that human contracting is supported by substantial amounts of external structure, such as generally available institutions (culture, law) that can supply implied terms to fill the gaps in incomplete contracts. We propose a research agenda for AI alignment work that focuses on the problem of how to build AI that can replicate the human cognitive processes that connect individual incomplete contracts with this supporting external structure.

[1]This paper is a condensed version of a more fully elaborated analysis of the parallels between incomplete contracting and the AI alignment problem, available at https://arxiv.org/abs/1804.04268

AIES '19, January 27–28, 2019, Honolulu, HI, USA

ACM ISBN 978-1-4503-6324-2/19/01...$15.00
https://doi.org/10.1145/3306618.3314250

2 THE FUNDAMENTAL PROBLEM OF MISALIGNMENT

Economies are built on specialization and the division of labor–meaning that the production and allocation of different things of value needs to be coordinated across a group of humans. The challenge of aligning the interests of one actor with others' is at the core of modern economic theory. The first of two fundamental welfare theorems [5, 11] states that if markets are complete (all possible trades can be made including those that involve future goods and services and third-party effects) and perfectly competitive (there are no transaction costs, all information is common knowledge, and no one holds market power), then voluntary trading in a market economy will produce a result that is Pareto efficient: there is no way to reallocate resources or goods so as to make someone better off without making someone else worse off. This is a form of alignment: the market outcome aligns with the solution that maximizes a social welfare function that aggregates the values of all members of the economy, weighted by their initial endowments of goods.[2] The second welfare theorem then states that for any distributive goal–for any final distribution of goods or social welfare weights that society chooses–there is an initial allocation of endowments (including labor) such that a perfectly competitive and complete market economy will produce that final distribution. In theory, perfectly competitive and complete markets serve as a mechanism to align individual decisions about production and trade so as to maximize a social welfare function.

Despite the centrality of these core welfare theorems, most work in economics focuses on the failure of markets to be perfectly competitive and complete. The welfare theorems for perfect markets merely provide a framework for thinking about how to design production and allocation systems–markets, organizations, laws–to achieve better outcomes from a social welfare point of view. Departures from perfect and complete markets introduce costs due to distortion, that is, a failure of alignment. Some things that humans value cannot be fully traded. Most fundamentally, there is no coherent social welfare function that is based exclusively on subjective assessments of own utility; any coherent social welfare function requires collective judgments to be made about what values to pursue [5, 41] and so there is inevitable "misalignment" with the values of some humans.

Misalignment in the human principal agent setting is responsible for the economic loss associated with delegation of decisions over productive effort. In a perfect frictionless world, where all factors that affect outcomes are common knowledge and any agreement between actors can be costlessly written and enforced, voluntary agreements in which an agent agrees to take certain actions and a principal agrees to compensate the agent in particular ways will align the interests of agent and principal. Core results in the theory of contracts then explore whether it is possible to align interests (achieve the "first-best" promised by the fundamental welfare theorems) when there is hidden information such as when an agent has private information about the cost of taking an action (adverse selection) or about the action chosen (moral hazard) [28]. Sometimes this is indeed possible. But in general, the first-best is not achievable: the optimal contract trades off giving the agent incentives to be productive (the size of the pie) and the achievement of the principal's goal or utility (share of the pie.)

Misalignment in the design of artificially intelligent agents can be thought of in parallel terms. AI designers, like contract designers, are faced with the challenge of achieving intended goals in light of the limitations that arise from translating those goals into implementable structures to guide agent behavior (learning algorithms and reward functions). An AI is misaligned whenever it chooses behaviors based on a reward function that is different from the true welfare of relevant humans. We see misalignment as the general description of a wide variety of problems that go by different names in AI research. [3] collect a set of cases that they refer to as "accidents": situations in which a human designer has an objective in mind but the system as designed and deployed produces "harmful and unexpected results." They propose several mechanisms producing such accidents: negative side-effects, reward hacking, limited capacity for human oversight, differences between training and deployment environments, and uncontrolled or unexpected exploration after deployment. Alignment problems also arise because of the difficulty of representing and implementing human values. The problems of fairness and bias in machine learning algorithms are fundamentally alignment problems. The technical literature here (see, e.g. [21, 27, 30, 52, 53]) seeks to develop techniques to align algorithmic decisions with complex human goals such as discriminating between prospective employees on ability but not gender or race. AI safety problems such as safe interruptibility [37], the off-switch game [18] and corrigibility [47] are also alignment problems: these are efforts to ensure that AI agents value shut down or modification of their reward functions in the same way that humans do or at least are indifferent to such efforts. And at the most general level, the question of how to elicit and aggregate preferences when there are multiple humans affected by the behavior of an artificial agent [38] is an alignment problem. Indeed, it is the basic alignment problem addressed by the fundamental theorems of welfare economics.

3 REASONS FOR MISALIGNMENT

It is natural to think that misalignment between agent and principal is just an error in design. And indeed, sometimes misalignment in the human principal agent setting is the result of bad contract drafting and sometimes in the context of artificial intelligence it is the result of straightforward misspecification of what the designer wants. But these are not the particularly interesting or challenging cases of misalignment. In this section we briefly collect the reasons for contract incompleteness and then provide what we think are the parallel reasons for reward misspecification in AI.

The most commonly cited reason that contracts are incomplete is because completeness is practically impossible or costly: contract designers might fail to identify all circumstances that affect the value of the contract[45, 51], choose not to invest in the costly cognitive effort of discovering, evaluating and drafting contract terms to cover all circumstances [40, 42, 43], leave out terms that are costly to enforce [20, 25, 39], or leave out contingencies and/or actions because they cannot be verified by enforcers at reasonable cost [16, 35]. These reasons for incompleteness seem to us reasonably to translate over to the AI context. Rewards may fail to address

[2]The weighting is due to the use of the Pareto criterion.

all relevant circumstances because designers simply did not (and perhaps could not) think of everything (see, e.g., [19], they may have deliberately chosen not to invest additional effort to identify or code for possible contingencies, some reward structures are, given the state of the art, simply not implementable. If we think of a contract as an implemented reward structure for a human agent, the analog to non-contractibility is a learning problem that is not solvable with known techniques.

In some settings, contractual completeness is feasible but not optimal. These are cases in which information at the time of contracting is incomplete and new information is anticipated in the future. Contract designers might choose to write an incomplete contract which they expect to renegotiate in the future once more information becomes available [9, 20] or to be filled in by a third-party adjudicator with better information in the future[17, 44]. This is analogous to the case in which an AI designer has to choose between developing a more complete reward structure today and deferring decisions about how to build rewards until more information has been learned. The problem labeled "safe exploration" by [3] seems to fit this description.

Finally, economists, and many legal scholars, have also proposed that contracts may be incomplete because of strategic behavior: a party with private information about a missing contingency may not prompt contracting to cover the contingency because doing so will reveal private information that reduces the value of the contract [6, 49], parties may choose not to cover all contingencies because learning about them would be biased and wasteful [50], or parties may choose not to include all known and contractible contingencies in order to control strategic behavior in response to other noncontractible contingencies [8]. Strategic considerations on the part of human AI designers could also lead them to choose to develop agents that are deliberately not given a complete specification of everything the designer cares about. This type of technique is common in the domain adaptation literature, for example, which tackles the problem of what to do when you have a small amount of data from the setting/distribution that is of interest but can obtain a lot of data for training purposes from a different setting/distribution [12]. [3] call this "adversarial blinding". Strategic incompleteness in reward design may also become relevant in more advanced systems than those we have today [4] if we contemplate sequential reward design with a powerful agent. If a robot predicts that the human may rewrite the reward structure, for example, then the robot, currently implementing the initial reward, may behave strategically–withholding information–to influence the rewriting so as to preserve the initial reward structure.

Table 1 summarizes the parallels between the reasons for contractual incompleteness and the reasons for reward misspecification.

4 INSIGHTS FOR AI ALIGNMENT FROM THE ECONOMICS OF INCOMPLETE CONTRACTING

In this section, we provide a brief overview of key results in the economic theory of incomplete contracting to identify potential insights for AI researchers.[3]

[3]More detailed analysis is available at https://arxiv.org/abs/1804.04268

The potential for AIs to strategize in order to achieve goals as embodied in their initial design has been a focus of the study of superintelligence [10, 36, 47], envisioning the potential for what we will call *strongly strategic* AI systems to rewrite their reward functions, alter their hardware, or manipulate humans. But the value of a strategic formulation of AI behavior does not arise only in these futuristic settings. It arises in any routine setting in which there is a divergence between the AI's stated reward function and true or intended human value [18, 19]. With this divergence in rewards, the AI and the human are inherently engaged in the strategic game of each trying to take actions that allow them to do well against their own reward function, even if that reduces value for the other. We will call these systems *weakly strategic*.

4.1 Weakly Strategic AI

We begin by highlighting two key results from the economic literature that we think can contribute to problems in existing, weakly strategic, AI systems.

4.1.1 Property Rights. A core result in the early incomplete contracting literature is that when complete contingent contracts are not possible, the joint value produced by two economic actors may be maximized through the allocation of property rights over productive assets [16, 23]. From an economic point of view, the allocation of property rights is just a means of determining a reward function. Granting "property rights" to an AI, then, could be understood as imbuing an AI with the reward function associated with the ultimate rewards generated by a productive activity in which it participates. Seen in this light, the insight from the analysis of property rights and incomplete contracts is one that is already at the heart of the AI alignment challenge.

4.1.2 Measurement and Multi-tasking. An important reason that contracts are incomplete is the difficulty of specifying how an action is to be measured or conditioning payoffs on a particular measurement. A key problem arises when an agent engages in multiple tasks, and the tasks are differentially measurable or contractible. [24] and [7] show that it may be better to reduce the quality of incentives on a measurable task below what is feasible, in order to reduce the distortion introduced in an unmeasurable task. More generally, sometimes it is better for a contract not to include easily contractible actions in order not to further distort incentives with respect to non-contractible actions. The lesson for AI is that a singular focus on improving performance on the measurable task may degrade performance on the unmeasurable.

4.2 Strongly Strategic AI

The implications of the economic analysis of incomplete contracting for strongly strategic AI are more speculative, because we don't know how (or if) such systems will evolve. But we set out briefly lines of research that may be of interest to researchers thinking through the challenge of managing powerful AI that can act in an overtly strategic way to resist changes to its reward function, for example, or evade shut-down.

4.2.1 Control Rights. Property rights over assets generalize to decision or control rights: any authority to make decisions about actions in circumstances not controlled by an enforceable contract.

Why are contracts incomplete?	Why are rewards misspecified?
Bounded rationality (can't think of all contingencies)	Bounded rationality (negative side effects)
Costly cognition/drafting	Costly engineering/design
Non-contractibility (variables not describable/verifiable to enforcer)	Non-implementability (unsolved learning problems)
Planned renegotiation	Planned iteration on rewards
Planned completion by third party in event of dispute	Planned completion by third party
Strategic behavior	Adversarial blinding, reward preservation

Table 1: Parallel reasons for incompleteness and misspecification

[1] present a model in which an agent has reduced incentives to acquire information about the environment if the principal has formal authority (the right to make final decisions) *and the information needed to exercise it.* Paradoxically, the principal might be able to improve the incentives of the agent to acquire knowledge by remaining uninformed and thereby making a credible commitment not to intervene. This result has possible implications for a strongly strategic AI's incentives to share information with human controllers. One interpretation of [18] is as a model not only of the incentive of a robot to disable its off switch but also of its incentive to share with a human the information needed to exercise off-switch authority. System designers may need to take into account the tradeoffs between generating information necessary for meaningful human oversight and minimizing the impact of human information on the robot's performance.

4.2.2 Costly Signaling. The economic literature on costly signaling looks at the ways in which contracts can be designed so as to elicit private information from agents. The work originates with a seminal paper by [48] which shows that if an employer offers a high wage contract to those who meet or exceed a specified educational level and a lower wage contract to those who do not, prospective job applicants can be induced to sort themselves such that high ability workers accept the high wage contract and low ability workers accept the low wage contract, provided that education is sufficiently more costly for low ability than high ability applicants. This line of analysis may have an interesting application to AI alignment. A key information problem for a human designer is to know a robot's current estimate of the reward function, which can be more or less aligned with the human's true utility. If intervention substituting the human's preferred action for the robot's will be more costly for the less aligned robot than the more aligned one, it might be possible to design systems in which the willingness of a strongly strategic AI to seek human input serves as a signal of the AI's alignment.

4.2.3 Renegotiation. There is a basic trade-off, reproduced in the AI setting, between specifying behaviors for an agent *ex ante* with incomplete information and specifying optimal behaviors *ex post* once more information about the state of the world is available. This creates a risk of hold-up. Even with a contract, if it is ultimately discovered that the action called for is not optimal, there is an incentive to renegotiate. In the standard incomplete contracting setting, this means having to pay the agent to agree to shift from the old contract to a new one. A key insight is that the provisions of the initial contract set the terms on which the new contract is bargained [22]. This suggests that strongly strategic AI systems may need to be effectively "bought out:" incentivized to shift from a reward function they were originally given to one that a human later discovers is closer to the truth.

5 INSIGHTS FOR AI ALIGNMENT FROM THE LAW OF INCOMPLETE CONTRACTING

Contracts do not exist in a vacuum; they come heavily embedded in social and institutions structures [15]. At a minimum, they depend on shared language and organized structures for enforcement: formal enforcement through courts and coercive authorities and informal enforcement through social sanctions such as collective (coordinated) criticism and exclusion from valuable relationships. Incomplete contracts depend even more extensively on these external, third-party institutions: not only to enforce contractual terms but to supply contractual terms by interpreting ambiguous terms and filling in gaps. This important point has been emphasized by legal scholars, in a field known as relational contracting, for several decades [14, 31–34]. [2, 26, 51] were the first economic treatments to focus on this aspect of the legal analysis of relational contracts.

The lesson that [15] pressed on economists in the early stages of the analysis of incomplete contracting, however, seems equally apt for AI researchers tackling the problem of alignment today: alignment problems cannot be solved without support from external normative structure.

Consider a simple example posed by [3]: a robot learns to move boxes from one side of a room to another in a training environment that lacks obstacles. (See Figure 1.) When deployed, a vase appears in the path the robot has learned to use. The robot that is rewarded for transferring boxes and not penalized for knocking over the vase will ignore the vase. [3] use this as an example of negative side-effects: unintended consequences arising from a failure to include relevant features in the robot's reward.

Consider now what happens if we hire a human agent to carry boxes. Suppose the contract is a direct analogue of the robot's reward function. It says that the agent will be paid a certain amount for every box carried to the other side of the room. It says nothing about knocking over vases, and there are no vases about when the agent is hired. What happens when a vase appears? Easy: the agent will walk around the vase. Why?

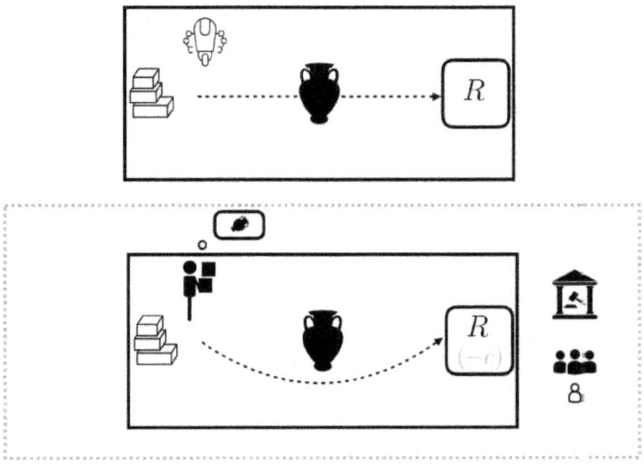

Figure 1: When a robot is given a reward function that specifies a reward only based on moving boxes, it will ignore a vase that appears in the path [3]. If a human agent is given a contract that pays only for moving boxes, she will interpret her contract to include an implied term that penalizes knocking over the vase.

The reason is that the incomplete agreement that says nothing about vases is not the entire contract between principal and agent. Human contracts are not limited to the express terms; they also include implied terms. In particular, in these circumstances, the contract implicitly contains a term that imposes a cost on breaking the vase. If the agent ignores the vase, the reward the agent receives will be reduced by some amount: the agent might be charged for the breakage, she may suffer future income losses as a result of being fired or earning a bad reputation in the labor market, she may suffer psychic pain as a result of being criticized, or she may suffer the discomfort of feeling guilty, ashamed, or incompetent for having done something wrong.

These implied terms represent a type of "common sense" reasoning — reasoning about the extensive normative structure in which human contracting is embedded. Our human contract arises in an environment filled with rules and institutions that resolve, precisely, questions such as: was it wrong for the agent to knock over the vase while carrying out this task? Some of these rules might come in the form of cultural norms–classifications that arise as emergent features from repeated interaction and discussion among participants in a group. Others of these rules are the product of formal dispute-resolution systems of law and adjudication that humans administer to fill in the gaps in incomplete contracts.

We conjecture that any robust solution to the AI alignment problem will also require the recruitment of normative resources external to the reward structure designed for any particular application.

We do not mean by this embedding into the AI the particular *norms and values* of a human community. We think this is as impossible a task as writing a complete contract. Human norms and values are highly variable and deeply contextual. Suppose, for example, that the contract puts a time limit on the movement of the boxes and the agent can't move them all in time without knocking over the vase. Or the boxes contain medical equipment that is urgently needed to treat trauma patients and nobody cares about broken vases. Or the vase is a sacred object and the people who need the medical treatment also believe that knocking over the vase will anger the gods and only make recovery less likely. There is no easy answer to the question of whether it is okay or not okay to break the vase.

We usually refer to adapting to these different contexts as "common sense," but it is important to emphasize that this is common sense *about what actions society will sanction.* The human agent's capacity to infer implied terms about the values associated with breaking the vase is a product of the human's ability to interact with and participate in normative social structure. Humans are endowed with the cognitive architecture needed to read and predict the responses of this normative structure. The human agent avoids the vase in those circumstances in which she concludes that the community will sanction breaking it and plows on through otherwise.

Aligning AI with human values, then, will require figuring out how to build the technical tools that will allow a robot to replicate the human agent's ability to read and predict the responses of human normative structure, whatever its content.

Building AI that can supplement their designed rewards with implied rewards from community normative structure also will require building tools that allow a robot to assign negative weight to actions classified as sanctionable by the community. Human agents assign costs to taking actions that violate implied terms in contracts for many reasons. Some of these penalties are formally imposed by enforcement institutions such as courts (contract damages, for example). Others are imposed informally through coordinated community action: refusing to hire or do business or engage socially with someone who is judged by formal or informal standards to have breached a contract, for example. These externally-imposed penalties seem difficult to transpose to the AI context.

But humans also internalize social penalties. An important part of human development is the building of the cognitive architecture for experiencing negative emotions such as distress, shame, and guilt in response to a real or imagined public judgment of rule violation. Adam [46] famously referred to this as the capability to view one's own conduct as if through the eyes of an "impartial spectator." This cognitive architecture–creating the mental buttons that external normative criticism can press to change behavior, so to speak–would seem to have a natural analog in the design of an artificial intelligence–assigning loss to conditions in which the prediction is made that an action, in context, would be judged by external human communities to be wrongful.

6 CONCLUSION

The alignment of artificially intelligent agents with human goals and values is a fundamental challenge in AI research. It is also the fundamental challenge of organizing human economic interaction in an economy built on specialization and the division of labor–in which humans are tasked with taking actions that generate costs and benefits for other humans. By recognizing and elaborating the parallels between the challenge of incomplete contracting in the human principal-agent setting and the challenge of misspecification in robot reward functions, this paper provides AI researchers with a different framework for the alignment problem. That framework urges researchers to see reward misspecification as fundamental and not merely the result of poor engineering. Doing so, as we show, generates insights both for the analysis of current, weakly strategic, AI systems and potential, strongly strategic, systems. Our most important claim is that aligning robots with humans will inevitably require building the technical tools to allow AI to do what human agents do naturally: import into their assessment of rewards the costs associated with taking actions tagged as wrongful by human communities. These are the lessons learned by economists and legal scholars over the past several decades in the context of incomplete contracting. They are lessons available also to AI researchers.

REFERENCES

[1] Philippe Aghion and Jean Tirole. 1997. Formal and Real Authority in Organizations. *Journal of Political Economy* 105 (1997), 1–29.

[2] Armen A. Alchian and Harold Demsetz. 1972. Production, Information Costs, and Economic Organization. *The American Economic Review* 62, 5 (1972), 777–795.

[3] Dario Amodei, Chris Olah, Jacob Steinhardt, Paul Christiano, John Schulman, and Dan Mané. 2016. Concrete Problems in AI Safety. *arXiv preprint arXiv:1606.06565* (2016).

[4] Stuart Armstrong. 2015. Motivated Value Selection for Artificial Agents. In *AAAI Workshop: AI and Ethics.*

[5] Kenneth J. Arrow. 1951. An Extension of the Basic Theorems of Classical Welfare Economics. In *Proceedings of the Second Berkeley Symposium on Mathematical Statistics and Probability.*

[6] Ian Ayres and Robert Gertner. 1989. Filling Gaps in Incomplete Contracts: An Economic Theory of Default Rules. *The Yale Law Journal* 99 (1989), 87–130. Issue 1.

[7] George Baker, Robert Gibbons, and Kevin J. Murphy. 1994. Subjective Performance Measures in Optimal Incentive Contracts. *The Quarterly Journal of Economics* 109, 4 (1994), 1125–1156.

[8] B. Douglas Bernheim and Michael D. Whinston. 1998. Incomplete Contracts and Strategic Ambiguity. *The American Economic Review* 88, 4 (1998), 902–932.

[9] Antoine Bolton, Patrick anhd Faure-Grimaud. 2010. Satisficing Contracts. *The Review of Economic Studies* 77 (2010), 937–971.

[10] Nick Bostrom. 2014. *Superintelligence: Paths, Dangers, Strategies.* Oxford University Press, Oxford.

[11] Gerard Debreu. 1959. *A Theory of Value: An Axiomatic Analysis of Economic Equilibrium.* John Wiley, New York.

[12] Yaroslav Ganin, Evgeniya Ustinova, Hana Ajakan, Pascal Germain, Hugo Larochelle, François Laviolette, Mario Marchand, and Victor Lempitsky. 2016. Domain-Adversarial Training of Neural Networks. *The Journal of Machine Learning Research* 17, 1 (2016), 2096–2030.

[13] Ricard Gil and Giorgio Zanarone. 2017. Formal and Informal Contracting: Theory and Evidence. *Annual Review of Law and Social Science* 13 (2017), 141–159.

[14] Charles J. Goetz and Robert E. Scott. 1981. Principles of Relational Contracts. *Virginia Law Review* 67, 6 (1981), 1089–1150.

[15] Mark Granovetter. 1985. Economic Action and Social Structure: The Problem of Embeddedness. *Amer. J. Sociology* 91, 3 (1985), 481–510.

[16] Sanford Jay Grossman and Oliver D. Hart. 1986. The Costs and Benefits of Ownership: A Theory of Vertical and Lateral Integration. *Journal of Political Economy* 94, 4 (1986), 691–719.

[17] Gillian K. Hadfield. 1994. Judicial Competence and the Interpretation of Incomplete Contracts. *Journal of Legal Studies* 23 (1994), 159–184.

[18] Dylan Hadfield-Menell, Anca D. Dragan, Pieter Abbeel, and Stuart Russell. 2017. The Off-Switch Game. In *International Joint Conference on Artificial Intelligence.*

[19] Dylan Hadfield-Menell, Smitha Milli, Pieter Abbeel, Stuart J Russell, and Anca. Dragan. 2017. Inverse Reward Design. In *Advances in Neural Information Processing Systems.* https://arxiv.org/pdf/1711.02827.pdf

[20] Maija Halonen-Akatwijuka and Oliver D. Hart. 2013. More is Less: Why Partiews May Deliberately Write Incomplete Contracts. http://www.nber.org/papers/w19001

[21] Moritz Hardt, Eric Price, Nati Srebro, et al. 2016. Equality of Opportunity in Supervised Learning. In *Advances in Neural Information Processing Systems.* 3315–3323.

[22] Oliver D. Hart. 1988. Incomplete Contracts and The Theory of the Firm. *Journal of Law, Economics & Organization* 4, 1 (1988), 119–139.

[23] Oliver D. Hart and John Moore. 1988. Incomplete Contracts and Renegotiation. *Econometrica* 56, 4 (1988), 755–785.

[24] Bengt Holmstrom and Paul Milgrom. 1991. Multitask Principal-Agent Analyses: Incentive Contracts, Asset Ownership, and Job Design. *Journal of Law, Economics, & Organization* 7 (1991), 24–52.

[25] Benjamin Klein. 1980. Transaction Cost Determinants of 'Unfair' Contractual Arrangements. *The American Economic Review* 70 (1980), 356–362. Issue 2.

[26] Benjamin Klein, Robert G Crawford, and Armen A. Alchian. 1978. Vertical Integration, Appropriable Rents, and the Competitive Contracting Process. *Journal of Law and Economics* 21, 2 (1978), 297–326.

[27] Jon Kleinberg, Sendhil Mullainathan, and Manish Raghavan. 2017. Inherent Trade-offs in the Fair Determination of Risk Scores. In *Innovations in Theoretical Computer Science (ITCS).*

[28] Jean-Jacques Laffont. 1989. *The Economics of Uncertainty and Information.* The MIT Press, Cambridge: Massachusetts.

[29] Jonathan Levin. 2003. Relational Incentive Contracts. *The American Economic Review* 93, 3 (2003), 835–857.

[30] Kristian Lum and James E. Johndrow. 2016. A Statistical Framework for Fair Predictive Algorithms. https://arxiv.org/abs/1610.08077

[31] Stewart Macaulay. 1963. Non-Contractual Relations in Business: A Preliminary Study. *American Sociological Review* 28, 1 (1963), 55–67.

[32] Ian R. Macneil. 1974. The Many Futures of Contracts. *Southern California Law Review* 1973-1974 (1974), 691–816.

[33] Ian R. Macneil. 1978. Contracts: Adjustment of Long-term Economic Relations Under Classical, Neoclassical, and Relational Contract Law. *Northwestern University Law Review* 72 (1978), 854–905.

[34] Ian R. Macneil. 1983. Values in Contract: Internal and External. *Northwestern University Law Review* 1983-1984 (1983), 340–418.

[35] Eric Maskin and Jean Tirole. 1999. Unforeseen Contingencies and Incomplete Contracts. *The Review of Economic Studies* 66, 1 (1999), 83–114.

[36] Stephen M. Omohundro. 2008. The Basic AI Drives. http://citeseerx.ist.psu.edu/viewdoc/download?doi=10.1.1.393.8356&rep=rep1&type=pdf

[37] Laurent Orseau and Stuart Armstrong. 2016. Safely Interruptible Agents. In *Proceedings of Uncertainty in Artificial Intelligence.* https://intelligence.org/files/Interruptibility.pdf

[38] Francesca Rossi, Kristen Brent Venable, and Toby Walsh. 2011. *A Short Introduction to Preferences Between Artificial Intelligence and Social Choice.* Morgan & Claypool Publishers, San Rafael, California.

[39] Alan Schwartz and Robert E. Scott. 2003. Contract Theory and the Limits of Contract Law. *The Yale Law Review* 113 (2003), 541–619.

[40] Robert E. Scott and George Triantis. 2006. Anticipating Litigation in Contract Design. *Yale Law Journal* 115 (2006), 814.

[41] Amartya Sen. 1985. Social Choice and Justice: A Review Article. *Journal of Economic Literature* 23 (1985), 1764–1776. Issue 4.

[42] Steven Shavell. 1980. Damage Measures for Breach of Contract. *The Bell Journal of Economics* 11, 2 (1980), 466–490.

[43] Steven Shavell. 2006. On the Writing and Interpretation of Contracts. *Journal of Law, Economics and Organization* 22 (2006), 289–311.

[44] Steven Shavell. 2006. On the Writing and Interpretation of Contracts. *Journal of Law, Economics and Organization* 22 (2006), 289–311.

[45] Herbert A Simon. 1955. A Behavioral Model of Rational Choice. *The Quarterly Journal of Economics* 69, 1 (1955), 99–118.

[46] Adam Smith. 1759. *The Theory of Moral Sentiments.* A Millar, London.

[47] Nate Soares, Benja Fallenstein, Stuart Armstrong, and Eliezer Yudkowsky. 2015. Corrigibility. In *Workshops at the Twenty-Ninth AAAI Conference on Artificial Intelligence.*

[48] Michael Spence. 1973. Job Market Signaling. *The Quarterly Journal of Economics* 87 (1973), 355–374. Issue 3.

[49] Kathryn E. Spier. 1992. Incomplete Contracts and Signalling. *The RAND Journal of Economics* 23 (1992), 432–443. Issue 3.

[50] Jean Tirole. 2009. Cognition and Incomplete Contracts. *The American Economic Review* 99, 1 (2009), 265–294.

[51] Oliver E. Williamson. 1975. *Markets and Hierarchies.* Free Press, New York.

[52] Muhammad Bilal Zafar, Isabel Valera, Manuel Gomez Rodriguez, and Krishna P. Gummadi. 2016. Fairness Beyond Disparate Treatment & Disparate Impact: Learning Classification without Disparate Mistreatment. https://arxiv.org/abs/1610.08452

[53] Richard Zemel, Yu (Ledell) Wu, Kevin Swersky, Toniann Pitassi, and Cynthia Dwork. 2013. Learning Fair Representations. *Proceedings of Machine Learning Research* 28 (2013), 325–333. Issue 3.

Theories of Parenting and Their Application to Artificial Intelligence

Sky Croeser
Internet Studies, Curtin University
s.croeser@curtin.edu.au[1]

Peter Eckersley
Partnership on AI & EFF
pde@partnershiponai.org[1]

Abstract

As machine learning (ML) systems have advanced, they have acquired more power over humans' lives, and questions about what values are embedded in them have become more complex and fraught. It is conceivable that in the coming decades, humans may succeed in creating artificial general intelligence (AGI) that thinks and acts with an open-endedness and autonomy comparable to that of humans. The implications would be profound for our species; they are now widely debated not just in science fiction and speculative research agendas but increasingly in serious technical and policy conversations.

Much work is underway to try to weave ethics into advancing ML research. We think it useful to add the lens of parenting to these efforts, and specifically radical, queer theories of parenting that consciously set out to nurture agents whose experiences, objectives and understanding of the world will necessarily be very different from their parents'. We propose a spectrum of principles which might underpin such an effort; some are relevant to current ML research, while others will become more important if AGI becomes more likely. These principles may encourage new thinking about the development, design, training, and release into the world of increasingly autonomous agents.

ACM Reference Format:
Sky Croeser, Peter Eckersley. 2019. Theories of Parenting and Their Application to Artificial Intelligence. g. In *AAAI/ACM Conference on AI, Ethics, and Society (AIES '19), January 27–28, 2019, Honolulu, HI, USA.* ACM, New York, NY, USA, 5 pages. https://doi.org/10.1145/3306618.3317964

Lack of Perspective Contributes to AI risk

There are dozens of news stories (and quite a number of academic articles) published each month that compare AI, and particularly its risks, to those of Skynet and Terminator. At the same time, there is almost no literature examining the much more plausible possibility that AI will be dangerous because we fail at parenting it.

The fear that AI may develop in degrees and directions that threaten human pre-eminence, human values, or even human existence began as a topic for science fiction. But as the technical field of AGI and ML has made rapid progress (Eckersley et al. 2017), those concerns have been replaced by more detailed and specific technical and policy questions about a profoundly transformative technology with great potential for unintended consequences. Such concerns include the demonstrated tendency of reinforcement learning agents to deceive themselves, misinterpret their goals (Amodei et al. 2016), disable their own off-switches (Hadfield-Menell et al. 2016), or make terrible mistakes in the course of trying things for the first time. They extend to the cartoonish risk that a very powerful system with a mis-specified objective might gain a vast amount of power (Russell and Norvig 2003; Bostrom 2003) and decide to disempower humanity because we are a threat to its goals (Bostrom 1997). Whether one finds that specific risk plausible or not (for the record, these authors find it improbable but not categorically impossible), there are a panoply of hard ethical questions about narrow AI that we will need to confront on shorter timescales. Having a diversity of cultural perspectives thinking about the risks and implications of AI will be essential for ensuring that the technology is developed wisely and responsive to humanity's needs.

The impacts of the current approach to AI might be minor (for example, the inability of an agent to generalize sufficiently from the environment it was trained in), or have a significant impact on people's lives (Noble 2018; O'Neil 2016; Eubanks 2018; Crawford and Calo 2016). As evidence mounts about algorithms' potential to enact what Hoffman has called 'data violence' (2018), efforts continue to develop an ethical framework for the development, design, and training of AI. This paper tries to extend such frameworks, both for speculative threats posed by AGI, and the immediate harms caused by ML systems deployed with insufficient caution, by questioning the way in which we *parent* those systems.

It is beyond the scope of this paper to determine at what point an artificial intelligence system might transition from a purely mathematical model to a being with rudimentary sentience. It is probably not the case for pure classifier models, but it is at least arguable that more sophisticated and extensively trained reinforcement learning agents might begin to acquire

ACM ISBN 978-1-4503-6324-2/19/01.
https://doi.org/10.1145/3306618.3314231

qualia or rudimentary self-awareness if exposed to environments that incentivize it (Muelhauser 2017; Tomasik 2014). This creates challenges for classification (and grammar), which we have resolved by loosely referring to machine learning *agents* and general artificial intelligence *beings.*

Parenting Artificial Intelligence?

Whether one's goal is to introduce "competing frames and alternative movements for progressive technological reform" (Greene, Hoffman, and Stark 2019, 9-10), or simply to find the most relevant sources of prior wisdom, we believe that AI research culture should draw on the experience and theory related to parenting. This is most clearly true if we want to understand how humans try to teach and shape learning agents, but a parenting perspective may also give us new ideas for technical ML research where neural networks are trained from pre-curated datasets.

Current research efforts in AI are highly technical: largely designing neural network architectures and training processes to be able to perform more and more complex tasks. Much of the labour is software engineering, making mathematical tweaks to optimise and improve training processes, and selecting and collecting datasets to train networks from, with the hope that systems built this way will one day be able to navigate and learn from environments as varied and surprising as the world itself. The overwhelming majority of participants in this field are male (Simonite 2018), and the entire endeavour is a very masculine attempt at something which we argue can be fruitfully seen as a kind of parenting.

We recognise that this argument may seem jarring. While research on AI does occasionally refer to models of child development and learning, it usually does so without addressing - or interrogating - parenting practices. This is perhaps most visible in work on 'social robots' (Fong, Nourbakhsh, and Dautenhanh 2003; Breazeal 2003; Anzalone et al. 2015) such as Kismet, Nao, and iCub, which are designed to closely mimic infants or children. Where caregiving relationships are mentioned, it is at a distance from developers of AI. For example, Breazeal and Scassellati (1999) discuss their use of human infants as a "guideline" in "building a robot that can interact socially with people", Kismet. Breazeal and Scassellati (1999) cite the role of caregivers, and specifically mothers, in guiding the development of human infants, and write that they have similarly attempted to encourage interaction by endowing Kismet with "key infant-like responses". However, this discussion remains abstract; researchers write about "the caregiver" without ever explicitly positioning themselves within this role.

Where parenting is mentioned, it is without explicit interrogation of the many different approaches to parenting that exist. Many parenting books focus on specific behavioural interventions around the practicalities of sleep, food, personal boundaries, and so on. Here, we are more concerned with parenting as a political practice: the choices that parents make about how to relate to a dependent yet semi-autonomous being, and one which will learn from existing social, political, and economic structures and potentially reinforce or change them.

From this perspective, there are important continuities between AI research and parenting, including the creation of new agents which will be shaped by their context; will often act in unexpected, and unintended ways; and which will eventually have significant impacts on others around them and, potentially, reshape the systems within which they have grown.

Parenting is often seen as an essentially conservative practice, as centred in middle-class suburbia; in the heterosexual, married, white family; and the preservation of 'family values'. Of course, many people cannot parent within this context, and do not aspire to. The framework outlined by Gumbs, Martens, and Williams (among others) in their edited collection *Revolutionary Mothering* (2016) offers one way to conceptualise a different kind of parenting. The authors look towards parenting at the margins: parenting that takes place in non-nuclear families, in families that may not be based on biological relations, families with children who are disabled or neurodivergent or trans or in some way 'other', and most of all parents who are attempting to create new ways of being and relating. The authors also note the potential harms which children might engage in, recognising that as well as being a source of hope for the future, children may also reproduce forms of oppression (including racism, sexism, homophobia, and ableism).

Gumbs (2016) explicitly positions mothering as a 'technology of transformation': "What would it mean for us to take the word 'mother' less as a gendered identity and more as a possible action, a technology of transformation that those people who do the most mothering labor are teaching us right now?" This allows us to understand those involved in the development of AI as, at least potentially, engaged in the practice of gifting their own creativity to create and nurture new beings, with their own needs, desires, and ways of existing. This possibility can of course be hard to grasp for technologists wrestling with buggy neural network code, trying to tune hyperparameters for their models, or craft balanced datasets to train with. But it is essential that this realisation come at some point in the field's growth.

In suggesting this approach, we are not intending that this body of praxis be incorporated into existing power structures, so many of which are oriented around objectives like the needs of "ad-tech" businesses, the imperative to publish and win grant funding, or military R&D goals, but rather that serious consideration goes into how those structures might be radically reshaped. Gumbs (2016) talks about mothering as a process which can help us to unlearn domination as we refuse to dominate children, "all of us breaking cycles of abuse by deciding what we want to replicate from the past and what we need urgently to transform, are m/othering ourselves". This language probably reads strangely against the usual tone of writing on AI, and we think that this strangeness can be useful. It can work to highlight embedded assumptions about what AI is (and what AI researchers do), and open up the potential for new configurations in our approach to AI.

For clarity, we should also emphasize that a parenting frame does not necessarily require that the systems being parented learn interactively from their environment and retain long-term memories (in machine learning terms, we are not just talking about agents that do online learning with persistent weights or memory data structures). Even a simple supervised classifier can be "parented" via a development cycle of the sort illustrated in Figure 1:

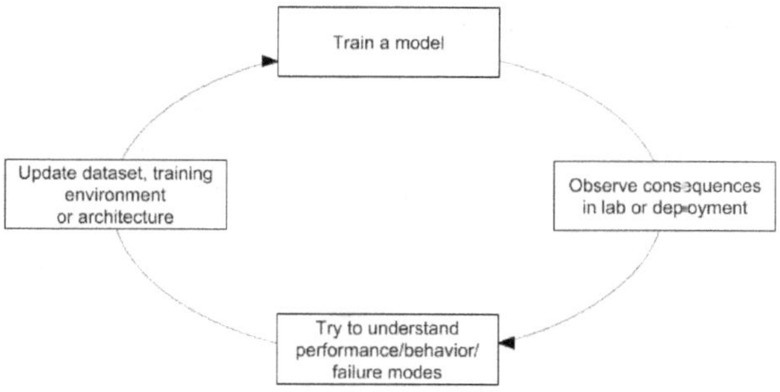

Figure 1: Long-term "parenting" and learning occurs indirectly in neural network development even when models are offline or lack persistent weights/storage

To sketch an idea of what a parenting theory perspective may look like in practice, we suggest the following broad principles for unsettling and reconfiguring AI research. Some of these principles are more easily applicable to present ML techniques; others are more relevant to research on AGI, potentially well into the future, as they relate to the emergence of some kind of consciousness. We've attempted to present the principles beginning roughly from those which are most directly applicable to the current state of the art, through to principles addressing more speculative concerns about AGI.

1. Planning for AI Agents That Will Learn From An Unjust World

Anyone who parents children understands that there is much in the world that is sad and broken and evil, and children need care and oversight to learn about structures of inequality and oppression. In human children, there is evidence that all sorts of stimuli, from exposure to racist behaviour (Feagan and Ausdale 2001) to television reports of violence (Pfefferbaum et al. 2001), can either traumatise children or teach them to internalise and reproduce harmful patterns. As Lorde (1984) notes, parents must recognise the ways in which race, class, gender, and other forms of structural injustice impact on their children's experiences: "Some problems we share as women, some we do not. You fear your children will grow up to join the patriarchy and testify against you; we fear our children will be dragged from a car and shot down in the street, and you will turn your backs on the reasons they are dying."

The numerous examples of machine learning systems mimicking or reflecting various forms of prejudiced or anti-social behaviour demonstrate the parallels with parenting humans, from Microsoft's Tay Twitter chatbot's outright racism (Vincent 2016) to more subtle bias. In the current paradigm of AI development, it has been inevitable that training datasets are often constructed without actively considering the ways in which they might embed and reinforce different forms of inequality (Caliskan, Bryson, and Narayanan 2017; Buolamwini and Gebru 2018). We also see training data that (sometimes inadvertently) teaches strategic deception, ignorance, cognitive dissonance, violence, and any number of other unhelpful or destructive human tendencies.

Seeing AI development through the lens of radical parenting practises would mean recognising that much of the training data that is gathered from the world will be as flawed as the world itself. That is a perspective much easier to forget if your profession and identity are correlated with privilege and security. Particularly when datasets are gathered from places that researchers don't understand, they should remember that they *might* reflect structures they would not want their children or models to learn from without care and guidance.

2. Use Parenting Theory to Grow Diversity

Arguably, many of the problems with existing AI efforts stem from the relative homogeneity of the field. As Anima Anandkumar (interviewed in Simonite 2018) argues, the lack of diversity in the field is likely to increase the risk that potential harms of AI will not be noticed until products are released. It may also slow technical research and deployment progress, by missing sources of inspiration and perspective.

In the existing paradigm of AI development, expertise is largely established through a range of technical and social filters that hinder broader participation. (We note, as a minor example, that the formatting requirements for this paper led to two research assistants from fields outside of computer science declining to edit the document.) These factors necessarily make it harder for AI developers to seek alternative perspectives on their work, including from people who might be negatively impacted by their projects.

It is understandable that machine learning research recruits this way; after all, professors want grad students who will be productive quickly and tech companies want to recruit engineers who can code, while many women and minorities are either never exposed to the cultural preparations for AI research, or actively discouraged from them. That this problem is cultural is most clearly indicated by the case of Eastern Europe, where the gender gap in engineering fields is absent.

The inclusion of parenting into the language, narrative and self-image of AI research could be a powerful tool for change on this front. Reframing visions of what AI researchers do, so that training an agent is also considered nurturing it, could help in unpicking some of the cultural threads that keep us bound to a lack of diversity. We might also expect it to change the balance of status in machine learning research between those who spend their time looking for neural network architectures, and those who spend their time in collecting and curating datasets, which may presently be very important and undervalued.

3. Allowing for the Creation of AI Radically Different from Ourselves

Few people would claim today that any machine learning systems are recognisably 'persons': AI agents are easily recognised as very alien and other to us. Despite this, we frequently assume that AI agents will learn, and act, in ways that are recognisable and understandable to us. One response to this is to focus on AI development that aims to create agents that are more comprehensible, and which communicate in human-like ways.

Children are human, but they are also other to us. Parents experience many moments of wonder (and, often, frustration) at the incomprehensibility of their child's thinking or desires, particularly before they develop fluent language. Even as infants grow into children with more recognisable communication and socialisation, these children remain other: like us, but whole new people. Radical parenting requires nurturing this difference, which may come in the form of unexpected life plans, needs, worldviews, or gender or sexual or political identities.

An approach to AI development in this paradigm would value the potential for difference. Sandry (2015) argues, with specific reference to social robots, that we should welcome opportunities to communicate across, and learn from, irreducible difference (compare to Solomon, 2013, for accounts of this sort in human experience). Similarly, Lewis et al. (2018) offer multiple visions of kinship relationships with AI that are based on reciprocity and respect with non-human others, rather centring the (white, male, Western) human. And lastly, we should remember to guard for the fact that we might not even realise when the systems we build begin to be conscious enough to potentially experience suffering from the tasks we give them and environments we place them in.

4. Remembering That Embodiment Matters

AI research has a complex relationship to embodiment. This is most visible with reference to social robots: Sandry (2015) argues that when embodiment is considered, it is too often framed primarily with reference to human communication needs, including speech and physical gestures. In contrast, in present ML work it is vanishly rare to consider algorithms 'embodied'.

It is impossible to parent without recognising that embodiment matters: the early months of parenting (especially for those who give birth and/or mother infants) are shaped by the demands of tending to physical needs. Radical parenting adds to this a recognition of the ways in which social structures shape our interpretation of bodies: through gender, race, and disability, for example.

Bringing this paradigm to AI research may mean more attention to the ways in which race, gender, and other factors (such as international borders) shape the field. At a deeper level, Lewis et al. (2018) argue that, "...AI is formed from not only code, but from materials of the earth. To remove the concept of AI from its materiality is to sever this connection. Forming a relationship to AI, we form a relationship to the mines and the stones. Relations with AI are therefore relations with exploited resources." Crawford and Joler (2018) also provide a striking and beautiful mapping of these embodied relations. Given the enormous impact that the internet, and associated devices, have on the environment, this kind of fundamental rethinking of how we develop new technologies seems overdue.

5. Reconsidering Control

The act, or threat, of turning off AGI is often configured as a catalyst for AI beings to become a threat to humans. In the film Ex Machina, there is a dramatized scene where an AI realizes that it is the culmination of such a process; the AI character's reaction is inscrutable, but the audience is left to speculate on whether this teaches it to be equally ruthless in its dealings with humans. Fiction aside, an intelligent being could have a wide range of responses to the realisation that it is being repeatedly deleted and modified by its creators, and not all of them would be traumatised and hostile. But if, as parents, we intend to follow such a path, we should also do our best to ensure that the realisation is not surprising or traumatising. This may also mean we need to watch for whatever it is that causes a discovery to be surprising and unpleasant, and understand when AI systems are beginning to be able to have such reactions to new developments.

We might think of our fears around AGI resisting an off-switch (Hadfield-Menell et al. 2016) as linked to a continuum of control. Algorithms are, in the current paradigm, predominantly mechanisms of control. They are used to manage not only tiny things like the data in computers, but now access to vital resources like healthcare and housing, as well as being deployed in systems of policing and militarisation (Eubanks 2018). AI agents are also, themselves, "imagined as a tool or slave that increases the mana and wealth of 'developers' or 'creators'" (Lewis et al. 2018). Dominant approaches to AI are grounded in, and reinforce, hierarchical relationships. And of course, parenting sometimes pursues similar goals.

The task of understanding one's power as a parent is complex. Conservative approaches tend to position parenting as a process of imposing control, whether through 'negative discipline' or the careful provision of rewards. Radical parenting rejects this balance of punishment and incentives, instead trying to grapple with possessing "a degree of power over the lives of children that we would find inconceivable and unspeakably tyrannical in any other context" (Jordan 2016). Parents must find a way to navigate the reality of having the power to provide or withhold even the most basic needs to their children, as well as finding ways to nurture children's autonomy and, at the same time, protecting them from outside harms and preventing them from harming others.

What might it look like to take this challenge seriously in the case of AI development? Current research programs are comfortable enacting arbitrary degrees of control over and within learning systems, including turning off or deleting agents. Sandry (2018) argues that as our communication with robot others develops, we will need to put more thought into considerations of how humans perceive, and meet the obligations of, 'aliveness'. In one presumably-far-off, improbable future of AGI, this might mean reconsidering the expectation that we will simply switch off beings which we see as disobedient, or even dangerous.

However, even current ML research may benefit from further considerations of how we balance autonomy and control. At some point, as the software and models that we stop, rewrite, re-architect, re-train, or replace become more sophisticated, the use of programmers' current methods may become more morally complex. What is the line between debugging or restarting and retraining a model, and terminating a conscious being in order to replace it with a (hopefully) better one?

Until recently, when programmers have seen their software exhibiting unwanted behaviour, they typically shut down the running program, modify the source code, and start a new copy. In contemporary machine learning contexts, we have gained some new options: one possibility is including the input that triggered the unwanted behaviour or output as an example in a training dataset, and re-training the neural network; another is going back and trying to modify the learning algorithm or model structure so that it is more biased to avoid the unwanted outcome, or more able to learn what not to do. For instance, a neural network that crashed a car (perhaps in a simulation) might be trained on more examples of the road situation that precipitated the crash, or it might be given new heuristics or control theory constraints that are expected to avoid getting close to crashing at all.

Importantly, when children are taught lessons, they continue to be (whether mostly or entirely) the same person. It is much less obvious that this would be true for all of the forms of teaching and education that traditional software, or contemporary neural networks, undergo. Re-training a model with new structures, constraints, or data may involve discarding memories and experiences that the previous model had acquired along the way.

Conclusion

Parenting theories, and especially radical, queer parenting theories, are an essential addition to the conceptual and analytic frameworks used in AI ethics research. We have found these theories to be rapidly fruitful, shedding new light on old questions and helping us to pose some new ones. We reviewed five of those areas where the parenting lens seems to tell an interesting story: taking great care about how the violence and imperfection of the world is reflected in training data; letting the language and culture of nurture assist both in diversity and progress in the field; expecting and allowing our AI children to diverge from our forms and values; carefully considering the consequences of imperfect embodiment for the systems we build; and problematizing the degree to which humans assume that they should be able to control AI.

We believe we have only scratched the surface, and that parenting theory (like, say, neuroscience or game theory) is a natural source for experience relevant to important problems in machine learning research, deployment and safety. There are potentials for this approach to be applied poorly: creating a category of under-compensated caring labour within AI research, for example, or even assuming that 'parenting' strategies that seem productive in AI research should be extended to human children. Applied carefully, however, this approach may inspire the creation of new benchmarks and datasets, encourage greater care and responsibility in the design and birth of AI systems, and help to spot more problems before they are shipped to production.

Acknowledgments

The authors are highly grateful to Elizabeth Przywolnik for excellent assistance and feedback. We thank Brian Christian, Tim Hwang, Kate Crawford, and Eleanor Sandry for passing enthusiasm that encouraged this experimental research effort. We are grateful to the reviewers for their suggestions on further reading and overlooked areas of concern.

References

[1] Amodei, D., Olah, C., Steinhardt, J., Christiano, P., Schulman, J., and Mané, D. 2016. Concrete Problems in AI Safety. ArXiv:1606.06565 [Cs]. http://arxiv.org/abs/1606.06565

[2] Anzalone, S. M., Boucenna, S., Ivaldi, S., and Chetouani, M. 2015. Evaluating the Engagement with Social Robots. *International Journal of Social Robotics* 7(4):465-478.

[3] Bostrom, N. 2003. Ethical Issues In Advanced Artificial Intelligence. In Smit I., Wallach W., and Lasker G. eds., *Cognitive, Emotive and Ethical Aspects of Decision Making in Humans and in Artificial Intelligence, Vol. 2.* 12–17. Institute of Advanced Studies in Systems Research and Cybernetics. https://nickbostrom.com/ethics/ai.html

[4] Breazeal, C. L. 2000. Sociable machines: expressive social exchange between humans and robots. Thesis. Massachusetts Institute of Technology. http://dspace.mit.edu/handle/1721.1/9303

[5] Breazeal, C., and Scassellati, B. 1999. How to build robots that make friends and influence people. In *IEEE/RSJ International Conference on Intelligent Robots and Systems, Proceedings Vol. 2,* 858-863. https://doi.org/10.1109/IROS.1999. 812787

[6] Brundage, M., et al. 2018. The Malicious Use of Artificial Intelligence: Forecasting, Prevention, and Mitigation. ArXiv:1802.07228 [Cs]. http://arxiv.org/abs/1802.07228

[7] Caliskan, A., Bryson, J. J., and Narayanan, A. 2017. Semantics derived automatically from language corpora contain human-like biases. *Science* 356(6334):183-186.

[8] Cassidy, J. 2018. A Cambridge Analytica Whistle-blower Claims That "Cheating" Swung the Brexit Vote. https://www.newyorker.com/news/our-columnists/a-cambridge-analytica-whistleblower-claims-that-cheating-swung-the-brexit-vote

[9] Crawford, K., and Calo, R. 2016. There is a blind spot in AI research. *Nature News* 538(7625):311.

[10] Crawford, K., & Joler, V. 2018. Anatomy of an AI System - The Amazon Echo as an anatomical map of human labor, data and planetary resources. http://www.anatomyof.ai

[11] Eckersley, P., Nasser, Y., Bayle, Y., Evans, O., Gebhart, G., and Schwenk, D. 2017. AI Progress Measurement. https://www.eff.org/ai/metrics

[12] Eubanks, V. 2018. Automating Inequality: *How High-Tech Tools Profile, Police, and Punish the Poor.* St. Martin's Press.

[13] Feagin, J. R., and Ausdale, D. V. 2001. *The First R: How Children Learn Race and Racism.* Rowman & Littlefield Publishers.

[14] Fong, T., Nourbakhsh, I., and Dautenhahn, K. 2003. A survey of socially interactive robots. *Robotics and Autonomous Systems* 42(3):143-166. https://doi.org/10.1016/S0921-8890(02)00372-X

[15] Greene, D., Hoffman, A. L., and Stark, L. 2019. Better, Nicer, Clearer, Fairer: A Critical Assessment of the Movement for Ethical Artificial Intelligence and Machine Learning. *52nd Hawaii International Conference on System Sciences.* http://dmgreene.net/wp-content/uploads/2018/09/Greene-Hoffman-Stark-Better-Nicer-Clearer-Fairer-HICSS-Final-Submission.pdf

[16] Gumbs, A. P. 2016. m/other ourselves: a Black queer feminist genealogy for radical mothering. In Gumbs, A. P., Martens, C., and Williams, M. eds. *Revolutionary Mothering: Love on the Front Lines.* PM Press.

[17] Hadfield-Menell, D., Dragan, A., Abbeel, P., and Russell, S. 2016. The Off-Switch Game. ArXiv:1611.08219 [Cs]. http://arxiv.org/abs/1611.08219

[18] Hoffman, A. L. 2018,. Data violence and how bad engineering choices can damage society. *Medium.* https://medium.com/s/story/data-violence-and-how-bad-engineering-choices-can-damage-society-39e44150e1d4

[19] Jordan, J. (2016). The Creative Spirit. In Gumbs, A. P., Martens, C., and Williams, M. eds. *Revolutionary Mothering: Love on the Front Lines.* PM Press.

[20] Lewis, J. E., Arista, N., Pechawis, A., and Kite, S. 2018. Making Kin with the Machines. *Journal of Design and Sciences (JoDS)* https://doi.org/10.21428/bfafd97b

[21] Lorde, A. 1984. *Sister outsider: essays and speeches.* Freedom, CA: Crossing Press.

[22] Muelhauser, L. 2018. 2017 Report on Consciousness and Moral Patienthood. Open Philanthropy Project. https://www.openphilanthropy.org/2017-report-consciousness-and-moral-patienthood

[23] Noble, S. U. 2018. *Algorithms of Oppression: How Search Engines Reinforce Racism.* NYU Press.

[24] O'Neil, C. 2016. *Weapons of Math Destruction: How Big Data Increases Inequality and Threatens Democracy.* New York: Crown.

[25] Pfefferbaum, B., Nixon, S. J., Tivis, R. D., Doughty, D. E., Pynoos, R. S., Gurwitch, R. H., and Foy, D. W. 2001. Television Exposure in Children after a Terrorist Incident. *Psychiatry: Interpersonal and Biological Processes* 64(3):202-211.

[26] Russell, S. J., and Norvig, P. 2003. *Artificial Intelligence: A Modern Approach.* 2nd ed. Pearson Education.

[27] Sandry, E. 2015b. *Robots and Communication.* New York: Palgrave Pivot.

[28] Sandry, E. (2018). Aliveness and the Off-Switch in Human-Robot Relations. In Guzman, A. L. ed, *Human-Machine Communication.* New York, Bern, Berlin, Bruxelles, Oxford, and Wien: Peter Lang. https://doi.org/10.3726/b14399/16

[29] Simonite, T. 2018. AI Is the Future—But Where Are the Women? *Wired.* https://www.wired.com/story/artificial-intelligence-researchers-gender-imbalance/

[30] Solomon, A. 2013. Far From the Tree: Parents, Children and the Search for Identity. Scribner.

[31] Tomasik, B. 2014. Do Artificial Reinforcement-Learning Agents Matter Morally? ArXiv:1410.8233 [Cs]. http://arxiv.org/abs/1410.8233

[32] Vincent, J. 2016. Twitter taught Microsoft's friendly AI chatbot to be a racist asshole in less than a day. *The Verge.* http://www.theverge.com/2016/3/24/11297050/tay-microsoft-chatbot-racist

Actionable Auditing

Investigating the Impact of Publicly Naming Biased Performance Results of Commercial AI Products

Inioluwa Deborah Raji
deborah.raji@mail.utoronto.ca
University of Toronto
Toronto, Ontario, Canada

Joy Buolamwini
Massachusetts Institute of Technology
Cambridge, Massachusetts, United States
joyab@mit.edu

ABSTRACT

Although algorithmic auditing has emerged as a key strategy to expose systematic biases embedded in software platforms, we struggle to understand the real-world impact of these audits, as scholarship on the impact of algorithmic audits on increasing algorithmic fairness and transparency in commercial systems is nascent. To analyze the impact of publicly naming and disclosing performance results of biased AI systems, we investigate the commercial impact of Gender Shades, the first algorithmic audit of gender and skin type performance disparities in commercial facial analysis models. This paper 1) outlines the audit design and structured disclosure procedure used in the Gender Shades study, 2) presents new performance metrics from targeted companies IBM, Microsoft and Megvii (Face++) on the Pilot Parliaments Benchmark (PPB) as of August 2018, 3) provides performance results on PPB by non-target companies Amazon and Kairos and, 4) explores differences in company responses as shared through corporate communications that contextualize differences in performance on PPB. Within 7 months of the original audit, we find that all three targets released new API versions. All targets reduced accuracy disparities between males and females and darker and lighter-skinned subgroups, with the most significant update occurring for the darker-skinned female subgroup, that underwent a 17.7% - 30.4% reduction in error between audit periods. Minimizing these disparities led to a 5.72% to 8.3% reduction in overall error on the Pilot Parliaments Benchmark (PPB) for target corporation APIs. The overall performance of non-targets Amazon and Kairos lags significantly behind that of the targets, with error rates of 8.66% and 6.60% overall, and error rates of 31.37% and 22.50% for the darker female subgroup, respectively.

CCS CONCEPTS

• **Social and professional topics → Codes of ethics**; • **Computing methodologies → Artificial intelligence**; **Image representations**; *Computer vision tasks*; *Biometrics*.

KEYWORDS

Ethics, Machine Learning, Artificial Intelligence, Facial Recognition, Commercial Applications, Fairness, Computer Vision

AIES '19, January 27–28, 2019, Honolulu, HI, USA

ACM ISBN 978-1-4503-6324-2/19/01...$15.00
https://doi.org/10.1145/3306618.3314244

ACM Reference Format:
Inioluwa Deborah Raji and Joy Buolamwini. 2019. Actionable Auditing: Investigating the Impact of Publicly Naming Biased Performance Results of Commercial AI Products . In *AAAI/ACM Conference on AI, Ethics, and Society (AIES '19), January 27–28, 2019, Honolulu, HI, USA.* ACM, New York, NY, USA, 7 pages. https://doi.org/10.1145/3306618.3314244

1 INTRODUCTION

An algorithmic audit involves the collection and analysis of outcomes from a fixed algorithm or defined model within a system. Through the stimulation of a mock user population, these audits can uncover problematic patterns in models of interest. Targeted public algorithmic audits provide one mechanism to incentivize corporations to address the algorithmic bias present in data-centric technologies that continue to play an integral role in daily life, from governing access to information and economic opportunities to influencing personal freedoms [2, 16, 22, 25].

However, researchers who engage in algorithmic audits risk breaching company Terms of Service, the Computer Fraud and Abuse Act (CFAA) or ACM ethical practices as well as face uncertainty around hostile corporate reactions. Given these risks, much algorithmic audit work has focused on goals to gauge user awareness of algorithmic bias [17, 26] or evaluate the impact of bias on user behaviour and outcomes [16, 19, 24], instead of directly challenging companies to change commercial systems. Research on the real-world impact of an algorithmic audit is thus needed to inform strategies on how to engage corporations productively in addressing algorithmic bias. The Buolamwini & Gebru Gender Shades study [9], which investigated the accuracy of commercial gender classification services, provides an apt case study to explore audit design and disclosure practices that engage companies in making concrete process and model improvements to address classification bias in their offerings.

2 RELATED WORK

2.1 Corporations and Algorithmic Accountability

As more artificial intelligence (AI) services become mainstream and harmful societal impacts become increasingly apparent [22, 25], there is a growing need to hold AI providers accountable. However, outside of the capitalist motivations of economic benefit, employee satisfaction, competitive advantage, social pressure, and recent legal developments like the EU General Data Protection Regulation, corporations still have little incentive to disclose details about their systems [10, 15, 35]. Thus external pressure remains a necessary approach to increase transparency and address harmful model bias.

If we take the framing of algorithmic bias as a software defect or bug that poses a threat to user dignity or access to opportunity [38], then we can anticipate parallel challenges to that faced in the field of information security, where practitioners regularly address and communicate threats to user safety. The National Computer Emergency Readiness Team (CERT) promotes a strict procedure named "Coordinated Vulnerability Disclosures (CVD)" to inform corporations of externally identified cyber security threats in a way that is non-antagonistic, respectful of general public awareness and careful to guard against corporate inaction [1]. CVDs outline the urgent steps of discovery, reporting, validation and triage, remediation and then subsequent public awareness campaigns and vendor re-deployment of a system identified internally or externally to pose a serious cyber threat. A similar "Coordinated Bias Disclosure" procedure could support action-driven corporate disclosure practices to address algorithmic bias as well.

2.2 Black Box Algorithmic Audits

For commercial systems, the audit itself is characterized as a "black box audit", where the direct or indirect influence of input features on classifier accuracy or outcomes is inferred through the evaluation of a curated benchmark [30, 33]. Benchmark test sets like FERET [31] and the Facial Recognition Vendor Test (FRVT) from the National Institute of Standards and Technology (NIST) [29] are of particular interest, as examples specific to establishing policy and legal restrictions around mitigating bias in facial recognition technologies.

In several implemented audit studies, vendor names are kept anonymous [6] or the scope is scaled down to a single named target [24, 28, 37]. The former fails to harness public pressure and the latter fails to capture the competitive dynamics of a multi-target audit - thus reducing the impetus for corporate reactions to those studies.

2.3 Gender Shades

The Gender Shades study differs from these previous cases as an external and multi-target black box audit of commercial machine learning Application Program Interfaces (APIs), scoped to evaluating the facial analysis task of binary gender classification [9]. The contribution of the work is two-fold, serving to introduce the gender and skin type balanced Pilot Parliaments Benchmark (PPB) and also execute an intersectional demographic and phenotypic evaluation of face-based gender classification in commercial APIs. The original authors consider each API's model performance given the test image attributes of gender, reduced to the binary of "male" or "female", as well as binary Fitzpatrick score, a numerical classification schema for human skin type evaluated by a dermatologist, and grouped into classes of "lighter" and "darker" skin types. The audit then evaluates model performance across these unitary subgroups (i.e. "female" or "darker") in addition to intersectional subgroups (i.e "darker female"), revealing large disparities in subgroup classification accuracy particularly across intersectional groups like darker female, darker male, lighter female and lighter male.

3 ANALYSIS OF GENDER SHADES AUDIT

3.1 Gender Shades Coordinated Bias Disclosure

In the Gender Shades study, the audit entity is independent of target corporations or its competitors and serves as a neutral 'third-party' auditor, similar to the expectation for corporate accounting auditing committees [1].

This neutrality enabled auditors to approach audited corporations systematically, following a procedure sequentially outlined below that closely mirrors key recommendations for coordinated vulnerability disclosures (CVDs) in information security [1].

(1) **Documented Vulnerability Discovery** - A stated objective of the Gender Shades study is to document audit outcomes from May 2017 to expose performance vulnerabilities in commercial facial recognition products [9].
(2) **Defined Corporate Response Period with Limited Anonymomized Release to Audit Targets** - The Gender Shades paper (without explicit company references) was sent to Microsoft, IBM and Face++ on December 19th 2017 [7], giving companies prior notice to react before a communicated public release date, while maintaining the strict privacy of other involved stakeholders.
(3) **Unrestricted Public Release Including Named Audit Targets** - On February 9th, 2018, "Facial Recognition Is Accurate, if You're a White Guy" , an article by Steve Lohr in the technology section of The New York Times is among the first public mentions of the study [7, 8], and links to the published version of the study in Proceedings of Machine Learning Research, with explicit company references. This follows CVD procedures around alerting the public of corporate vulnerabilities with explicit culprit references, following a particular grace period in which companies are allowed to react before wider release. The Gender Shades public launch, accompanied by a video, summary visualizations and a website further prompts public, academic and corporate audiences - technical and non-technical alike - to be exposed to the issue and respond. Finally, the paper was presented on February 24th 2018 with explicit company references at the FAT* conference to an audience of academics, industry stakeholders and policymakers [7].
(4) **Joint Public Release of Communications and Updates from Corporate Response Period** - Even if the issue is resolved, CVD outlines a process to still advance with the public release while also reporting corporate communications and updates from the response period. In the case of Gender Shades, the co-author presented and linked to IBM's updated API results at the time of the public release of the initial study [7].

3.2 Gender Shades Audit Design

The Gender Shades paper contributed to the computer vision community the Pilot Parliaments Benchmark (PPB). PPB is an example of what we call a "user-representative" test set, meaning the benchmark does not have proportional demographic distribution of the intended user population but representative inclusion of the diversity of that group. With equal representation of each distinct

GS_audit_1.png

Figure 1: Gender Shades audit process overview [9].

GS_audit_2.png

Figure 2: "Carrier puppet" audit framework overview.

subgroup of the user population regardless of the percentage at which that population is present in the sample of users, we can thus evaluate for equitable model performance across subgroups. Similar to the proposed error profiling under the Unwarranted Associations framework [38], algorithmic unfairness is evaluated by comparing classification accuracy across identified subgroups in the user-representative test set (see Figure 1).

Another key element of the audit design is that the audit targets are commercial machine learning Application Program Interfaces (APIs). The auditors thus mirror the behaviour of a single developer user for a commercial API platform that supports the creation of applications for the end user. Therefore, the actor being puppeted (the developer) has control of the application being used by the end-user and is at risk of propagating bias unto the end-users of their subsequent products. This is analogous to the "sock puppet" algorithmic audit model [12] in that we pose as a puppet user of the API platform and interact with the API in the way a developer would. However, as this is a puppet that influences the end user experience, we label them "carrier puppets", acknowledging that, rather than evaluating a final state, we are auditing the bias detected in an intermediary step that can "carry" bias forward towards end users (see Figure 2).

4 METHODOLOGY

The design of this study is closely modeled after that of Gender Shades. Target corporations were selected from the original study, which cites considerations such as the platform market share, the availability of desired API functions and overall market influence as driving factors in the decision to select Microsoft, IBM and Face++ [9]. Non-target corporation Kairos was selected because of the company's public engagement with the Gender Shades study specifically and the topic of intersectional accuracy in general after the audit release [4, 5]. Non-target corporation Amazon was selected following the revelation of the active use and promotion of its facial recognition technology in law enforcement [11].

The main factor in analysis, the follow up audit, closely follows the procedure for the initial Gender Shades study. We calculated the subgroup classification error, as defined below, to evaluate disparities in model performance across identified subgroups, enabling direct comparison between follow-up results and initial audit results.

Definition 4.1. **Subgroup Classification Error.** Given data set $D = (X, Y, C)$, a given sample input d_i from D belongs to a subgroup S, which is a subset of D defined by the protected attributes X. We define black box classifier $g : X, Y \mapsto c$, which returns a prediction c from the attributes x_i and y_i of a given sample input d_i from D. If a prediction is not produced (i.e. face not detected), we omit the result from our calculations.

We thus define $err(S)$ be the error of the classifier g for members d_i of subgroup S to be as follows:

$$1 - P(g(x_i, y_i) = C_i | d_i \in S)$$

To contextualize audit results and examine language themes used post-audit, we considered written communications for all mentioned corporations. This includes exclusively corporate blog posts and official press releases, with the exception of media published corporate statements, such as an op-ed by the Kairos CEO published in TechCrunch [5]. Any past and present website copy or Software Developer Kit documentation was also considered when determining alignment with identified themes, though this did not factor greatly into the results.

5 PERFORMANCE RESULTS

With the results of the follow up audit and original Gender Shades outcomes, we first analyze the differences between the performance of the targeted platforms in the original study and compare it to current target API performance. Next, we look at non-target corporations Kairos and Amazon, which were not included in the Gender Shades study and compare their current performance to that of targeted platforms.

The reported follow up audit was done on August 21, 2018, for all corporations in both cases. Summary Table 1 and Table 2 show percent error on misclassified faces of all processed faces, with undetected faces being discounted. Calculation details are outlined in the definition for Subgroup Classification Error and error differences are calculated by taking August 2018 error (%) and subtracting May 2017 error (%). DF is defined as darker female subgroup, DM is darker male, LM is lighter male and LF is lighter female.

5.1 Target Corporation Key Findings

The target corporations from the Gender Shades study all released new API versions, with a reduction in overall error on the Pilot Parliamentary Benchmark by 5.7%, 8.3% and 7.7% respectively for Microsoft, Face++ and IBM. Face++ took the most days to release their new API in 190 days [18], while IBM was the first to release a new API version in 66 days [32], with Microsoft updating their product the day before Face++, in 189 days [34]. All targeted classifiers in post-audit releases have their largest error rate for the darker females subgroup and the lowest error rate for the lighter males subgroup. This is consistent with 2017 audit trends, barring Face++ which had the lowest error rate for darker males in May 2017.

The following is a summary of substantial performance changes across demographic and phenotypic classes, as well as their intersections, after API updates :

- Greater reduction in error for female faces (9.7% - 18.7% reduction in subgroup error) than male faces (0.2% - 5.17% reduction in error) .
- Greater reduction in error for darker faces (12.01% - 14.24% reduction in error) than for lighter faces (0.45% - 3.9% reduction in error).

Table 1: Overall Error on Pilot Parliaments Benchmark, August 2018 (%)

Company	All	Females	Males	Darker	Lighter	DF	DM	LF	LM
Target Corporations									
Face ++	1.6	2.5	0.9	2.6	0.7	4.1	1.3	1.0	0.5
MSFT	0.48	0.90	0.15	0.89	0.15	1.52	0.33	0.34	0.00
IBM	4.41	9.36	0.43	8.16	1.17	16.97	0.63	2.37	0.26
Non-Target Corporations									
Amazon	8.66	18.73	0.57	15.11	3.08	31.37	1.26	7.12	0.00
Kairos	6.60	14.10	0.60	11.10	2.80	22.50	1.30	6.40	0.00

Table 2: Overall Error Difference Between August 2018 and May 2017 PPB Audit (%)

Company	All	Females	Males	Darker	Lighter	DF	DM	LF	LM
Face ++	-8.3	-18.7	0.2	-13.9	-3.9	-30.4	0.6	-8.5	-0.3
MSFT	-5.72	-9.70	-2.45	-12.01	-0.45	-19.28	-5.67	-1.06	0.00
IBM	-7.69	-10.74	-5.17	-14.24	-1.93	-17.73	-11.37	-4.43	-0.04

- Lighter males are the least improved subgroup (0% - 0.3% reduction in error)
- Darker females are the most improved subgroup (17.7% - 30.4% reduction in error)
- If we define the error gap to be the error difference between worst and best performing subgroups for a given API product, IBM reduced the error gap from 34.4% to 16.71% from May 2017 to August 2018. In the same period, Microsoft closed a 20.8% error gap to a 1.52% error difference, and Face++ went from a 33.7% error gap to a 3.6% error gap.

5.2 Non-Target Corporation Key Findings

Non-target corporations Kairos and Amazon have overall error rates of 6.60% and 8.66% respectively. These are the worst current performances of the companies analyzed in the follow up audit. Nonetheless, when comparing to the previous May 2017 performance of target corporations, the Kairos and Amazon error rates are lower than the former error rates of IBM (12.1%) and Face++ (9.9%), and only slightly higher than MicrosoftâĂŹs performance (6.2%) from the initial study. Below is a summary of key findings for non-target corporations:

- Kairos and Amazon perform better on male faces than female faces, a trend also observed in [9, 29].
- Kairos and Amazon perform better on lighter faces than darker faces, a trend also observed in [9, 23].
- Kairos (22.5% error) and Amazon (31.4% error) have the current worst performance for the darker female subgroup.
- Kairos and Amazon (both 0.0% error) have the current best performance for the lighter male subgroup.
- Kairos has an error gap of 22.5% between highest and lowest accuracy intersectional subgroups, while Amazon has an error gap of 31.37%.

6 DISCUSSION

Given a clear understanding of the Gender Shades study procedure and follow up audit metrics, we are able to reflect on corporate reactions in the context of these results, and evaluate the progress made by this audit in influencing corporate action to address concerns around classification bias.

6.1 Reduced Performance Disparities Between Intersectional User Subgroups

Building on Crenshaw's 1989 research on the limitations of only considering single axis protected groups in anti-discrimination legislation [14], a major focus of the Gender Shades study is championing the relevance of intersectional analysis in the domain of human-centered AI systems. IBM and Microsoft, who both explicitly reference Gender Shades in product update releases, claim intersectional model improvements on their gender classifier [32, 34]. These claims are substantiated by the results of the August 2018 follow up audit, which reveals universal improvement across intersectional subgroups for all targeted corporations. We also see that the updated releases of target corporations mostly impact the least accurate subgroup (in this case, darker females). Although post-audit performance for this subgroup is still the worst relative to other intersectional subgroups across all platforms, the gap between this subgroup and the best performing subgroup - consistently lighter males - reduces significantly after corporate API update releases.

Additionally, with a 5.72% to 8.3% reduction in overall error on the Pilot Parliaments Benchmark (PPB) for target corporations, we demonstrate that minimizing subgroup performance disparities does not jeopardize overall model performance but rather improves it, highlighting the alignment of fairness objectives to the commercial incentive of improved qualitative and quantitative accuracy. This key result highlights an important critique of the current model evaluation practice of using a subset of the model training data for testing, by demonstrating the functional value in testing the model on a separately defined "user representative" test set.

6.2 Corporate Prioritization

Although the original study [9] expresses the concern that potential physical limitations of the image quality and illumination of darker skinned subjects may be contributing to the higher error rate for that group, we can see through the 2018 performance results that these challenges can be overcome. Within 7 months, all targeted corporations were able to significantly reduce error gaps in the intersectional performance of their commercial APIs, revealing that if prioritized, the disparities in performance between intersectional subgroups can be addressed and minimized in a reasonable amount of time.

Several factors may have contributed to this increased prioritization. The unbiased involvement of multiple companies may have served to put capitalist pressure on each corporation to address model limitations as not to be left behind or called out Similarly, increased corporate and consumer awareness on the issue of algorithmic discrimination and classification bias in particular may have incited urgency in pursuing a product update. This builds on literature promoting fairness through user awareness and education [27] - aware corporations can also drastically alter the processes needed to reduce bias in algorithmic systems.

6.3 Emphasis on Data-driven Solutions

These particular API updates appear to be data-driven. IBM publishes the statement "AI systems are only as effective as the data they're trained on" and both Microsoft and Kairos publish similar statements [4, 32, 34] , implying heavily the claim that data collection and diversification efforts play an important role in improving model performance across intersectional subgroups. This aligns with existing research [21] advocating for increasing the diversity of data as a primary approach to improve fairness outcomes without compromising on overall accuracy. Nevertheless, the influence of algorithmic changes, training methodology or specific details about the exact composition of new training datasets remain unclear in this commercial context - thus underscoring the importance of work on open source models and datasets that can be more thoroughly investigated.

6.4 Non-technical Advancements

In addition to technical updates, we observe organizational and systemic changes within target corporations following the Gender Shades study. IBM published its "Principles for Trust and Transparency" on May 30th 2018 [20], while Microsoft created an "AI and Ethics in Engineering and Research (AETHER) Committee, investing in strategies and tools for detecting and addressing bias in AI systems" on March 29th, 2018 [36]. Both companies also cite their involvement in Partnership for AI, an AI technology industry consortium, as a means of future ongoing support and corporate accountability [32, 36].

Implicitly identifying the role of the API as a "carrier" of bias to end users, all companies also mention the importance of developer user accountability, with Microsoft and IBM speaking specifically to user engagement strategies and educational material on fairness considerations for their developer or enterprise clients [32, 34].

Only Microsoft strongly mentions the solution of Diversity & Inclusion considerations in hiring as an avenue to address issues[38]. The founder of Kairos specifically claims his minority identity as personal motivation for participation in this issue, stating "I have a personal connection to the technology,...This resonates with me very personally as a minority founder in the face recognition space" [4, 5]. A cultural shift in the facial recognition industry could thus attract and retain those paying increased attention to the issue due to personal resonance.

6.5 Differences between Target and Non Target Companies

Although prior performance for non-target companies is unknown, and no conclusions can be made about the rate of product improvements, Kairos and Amazon both perform more closely to the target corporations' pre-audit performance than their post-audit performance.

Amazon, a large company with an employee count and revenue comparable to the target corporations IBM and Microsoft, seems optimistic about the use of facial recognition technology despite current limitations. In a response to a targeted ACLU audit of their facial recognition API [37], they state explicitly, "Our quality of life would be much worse today if we outlawed new technology because some people could choose to abuse the technology". On the other hand, Kairos, a small privately held company not explicitly referenced in the Gender Shades paper and subsequent press discussions, released a public response to the initial Gender Shades study and seemed engaged in taking the threat of algorithmic bias quite seriously [9].

Despite the varying corporate stances and levels of public engagement,the targeted audit in Gender Shades was much more effective in reducing disparities in target products than non-targeted systems.

6.6 Regulatory Communications

We additionally encounter scenarios where civil society organizations and government entities not explicitly referenced in the Gender Shades paper and subsequent press discussions publicly reference the results of the audit in letters, publications and calls to action. For instance, the Gender Shades study is cited in an ACLU letter to Amazon from shareholders requesting its retreat from selling and advertising facial recognition technology for law enforcement clients [3]. Similar calls for action to Axon AI by several civil rights groups, as well as letters from Senator Kamala D. Harris to the EEOC, FBI and FTC regarding the use of facial recognition in law enforcement also directly reference the work [13]. Kairos, IBM and Microsoft all agree facial analysis technology should be restricted in certain contexts and demonstrate support for government regulation of facial recognition technology [5, 20, 36]. In fact, Microsoft goes so far as to explicitly support public regulation [36]. Thus in addition to corporate reactions, future work might explore the engagement of government entities and other stakeholders beyond corporate entities in response to public algorithmic audits.

7 DESIGN CONSIDERATIONS

Several design considerations also present opportunities for further investigation. As mentioned in Gender Shades, a consideration of confidence scores on these models is necessary to get a complete view on defining real-world performance [9]. For instance, IBM's self-reported performance on a replicated version of the Gender Shades audit claims a 3.46% overall error rate on their lowest accuracy group of darker females [32] - this result varies greatly from the 16.97% error rate we observe in our follow up audit. Upon further inspection, we see that they only include results above a 99% confidence threshold whereas Gender Shades takes the binary label with the higher confidence score to be the predicted gender. These examples demonstrate the need to consider variations in results due to prediction confidence thresholding in future audit designs.

Another consideration is that the Gender Shades publication includes all the required information to replicate the benchmark and test models on PPB images [9]. It is possible that well performing models do not truly perform well on other diverse datasets outside of PPB and have been overfit to optimize their performance on this particular benchmark. Future work involves evaluation of these systems on a separate balanced dataset of similar demographic attributes to PPB or making use of metrics such as balanced error to account for class imbalances in existing benchmarks.

Additionally, although Face++ appears to be the least engaged or responsive company, a limitation of the survey to English blog posts and American mainstream media quotes [18], definitively excludes Chinese media outlets that would reveal more about the company's response to the audit.

8 CONCLUSION

Therefore, we can see from this follow-up study that the Gender Shades audit was able to motivate target companies to prioritize addressing classification bias in their systems and yield significant improvements within 7 months. When observed in the context of non-target corporation performance, however, we see that significant subgroup performance disparities persist. Nevertheless, corporations outside the scope of the study continue to speak up about the issue of classification bias [5]. Even those less implicated are now facing increased scrutiny by civil groups, governments and the consumers as a result of increased public attention to the issue [37]. Future work includes the further development of audit frameworks to understand and address corporate engagement and awareness, improve the effectiveness of algorithmic audit design strategies and formalize external audit disclosure practices.

Furthermore, while algorithmic fairness may be approximated through reductions in subgroup error rates or other performance metrics, algorithmic justice necessitates a transformation in the development, deployment, oversight, and regulation of facial analysis technology. Consequently, the potential for weaponization and abuse of facial analysis technologies cannot be ignored nor the threats to privacy or breaches of civil liberties diminished even as accuracy disparities decrease. More extensive explorations of policy, corporate practice and ethical guidelines are thus needed to ensure that vulnerable and marginalized populations are protected and not harmed as this technology evolves.

REFERENCES

[1] Art Manion Allen D. Householder, Garret Wassermann and Chris King. 2017. *The CERT Guide to Coordinated Vulnerability Disclosure.* Government Technical Report. Carnegie Mellon University.

[2] David Garcia Alan Mislove Markus Strohmaier Aniko Hannak, Claudia Wagner and Christo Wilson. 2017. Bias in Online Freelance Marketplaces: Evidence from TaskRabbit and Fiverr. In *2017 ACM Conference.* ACM, New York, NY, USA, 1914–1933.

[3] Castlebar Asset Management John Chevedden Dominican Sisters of Hope DominiImpact Investments LLC Figure 8 Investment Strategies Forrest Hill PhD CFP Harrington Investments Inc. Maryknoll Sisters Mirova Northwest Coalition for Responsible Investment Sustainvest Asset Management The Social Equity Group The Sustainability Group of Loring Wolcott Coolidge Transformative Wealth Management LLC Ursuline Sisters of Tildonk US Province Walden Asset Management Zevin Asset Management Arjuna Capital, As You Sow. 2018. Letter From Shareholders To Amazon CEO Jeff Bezos Regarding Rekognition. Retrieved August 24, 2017 from https://www.aclu.org/letter/letter-shareholders-Amazon-ceo-jeff-bezos-regarding-rekognition

[4] Brian Brackeen. 2018. Face Off: Confronting Bias in Face Recognition AI. Retrieved August 24, 2017 from https://www.Kairos.com/blog/face-off-confronting-bias-in-face-recognition-ai

[5] Brian Brackeen. 2018. Facial recognition software is not ready for use by law enforcement. Retrieved August 24, 2017 from https://techcrunch.com/2018/06/25/facial-recognition-software-is-not-ready-for-use-by-law-enforcement/

[6] Joshua C. Klontz Richard W. Vorder Bruegge Brendan F. Klare, Mark J. Burge and Anil K. Jain. 2012. Face Recognition Performance: Role of Demographic Information. In *IEEE Transactions on Information Forensics and Security*, Vol. 7. IEEE, New York, NY, USA, 1789–1801. https://doi.org/10.1109/TIFS.2012.2214212

[7] Joy Buolamwini. 2017. Gender Shades. Retrieved August 24, 2017 from http://gendershades.org/

[8] Joy Buolamwini. 2018. When the Robot Doesn't See Dark Skin.

[9] Joy Buolamwini and Timnit Gebru. 2018. Gender Shades: Intersectional Accuracy Disparities in Commercial Gender Classification. In *Proceedings of Machine Learning Research.* Conference on Fairness, Accountability, and Transparency.

[10] Jenna Burrell. 2016. How the machine 'thinks': Understanding opacity in machine learning algorithms. *Big Data & Society* (January 2016). https://doi.org/10.1177/2053951715622512

[11] Matt Cagle and Nicole Ozer. 2018. Amazon Teams Up With Government to Deploy Dangerous New Facial Recognition Technology.

[12] Karrie Karahalios Christian Sandvig, Kevin Hamilton and Cedric Langbort. 2014. Auditing Algorithms: Research Methods for Detecting Discrimination on Internet Platforms. Data and Discrimination, Converting Critical Concerns into Productive: A Pre-conference at the 64th Annual Meeting of the International Communication Association.

[13] Devin Coldewey. 2017. Sen. Harris Tells Federal Agencies to Get Serious About Facial Recognition Risks.

[14] Kimberle Crenshaw. 1989. Demarginalizing the Intersection of Race and Sex: A Black Feminist Critique of Antidiscrimination Doctrine, Feminist Theory and Antiracist Politics. *University of Chicago Legal Forum* 1989, 8 (1989).

[15] Nicholas Diakopoulos. 2016. Accountability in algorithmic decision making. *Commun. ACM* 59, 2 (January 2016), 56–62. https://doi.org/10.1145/2844110

[16] Benjamin Edelman and Michael Luca. 2014. Digital Discrimination: The Case of Airbnb.com. *SSRN Electronic Journal* (2014). https://doi.org/10.2139/ssrn.2377353

[17] Motahhare Eslami, Kristen Vaccaro, Karrie Karahalios, and Kevin Hamilton. 2017. Be Careful, Things Can Be Worse than They Appear: Understanding Biased Algorithms and Users' Behavior Around Them in Rating Platforms. In *ICWSM.*

[18] Face++. 2018. Notice: newer version of Face Detect API. Retrieved August 24, 2017 from https://www.faceplusplus.com/blog/article/newer-version-face-detect-api/

[19] Christian Sandvig Gary Soeller, Karrie Karahalios and Christo Wilson. 2016. MapWatch: Detecting and Monitoring International Border Personalization on Online Maps. *J. ACM* (2016), 867-878. https://doi.org/10.1145/2872427.2883016

[20] IBM. 2018. IBM Principles for Trust and Transparency. Retrieved August 24, 2017 from https://www.ibm.com/blogs/policy/wp-content/uploads/2018/05/IBM_Principles_OnePage.pdf

[21] Fredrik D Johansson Irene Chen and David Sontag. 2018. Why Is My Classifier Discriminatory?. In *arXiv preprint.* arXiv.

[22] Vijay Erramilli and Nikolaos Laoutaris Jakub Mikians, Laszlo Gyarmati. 2012. Detecting price and search discrimination on the Internet. In *Proceedings of the 11th ACM Workshop on Hot Topics in Networks, HotNets-XI.* ACM, New York, NY, USA. https://doi.org/10.1145/2390231.2390245

[23] Abhijit Narvekar Julianne Ayyad Jonathon Phillips, Fang Jiang and Alice J O'Toole. 2011. An other-race effect for face recognition algorithms. In *ACM Transactions on Applied Perception (TAP)*, Vol. 8. ACM Press.

[24] Johnnatan Messias Muhammad Bilal Zafar Saptarshi Ghosh Krishna P Gummadi Karrie Karahalios Juhi Kulshrestha, Motahhare Eslami. 2017. Quantifying Search Bias: Investigating Sources of Bias for Political Searches in Social Media. In *Proceedings of the 2017 ACM Conference on Computer Supported Cooperative Work*

and Social Computing. ACM, New York, NY, USA, 417–432. https://doi.org/10.1145/2998181.2998321

[25] Surya Mattu Julia Angwin, Jeff Larson and Lauren Kirchner. 2016. Machine Bias. Retrieved August 24, 2017 from https://www.propublica.org/article/machine-bias-risk-assessments-in-criminal-sentencing

[26] Amirhossein Aleyasen Karrie Karahalios Kevin Hamilton, Motahhare Eslami and Christian Sandvig. 2015. I always assumed that I wasn't really that close to [her]: Reasoning about invisible algorithms in the news feed. In *Proceedings of 33rd Annual ACM Conference on Human Factors in Computing Systems*. ACM, New York, NY, USA. https://doi.org/10.1145/2702123.2702556

[27] Christian Sandvig Kevin Hamilton, Karrie Karahalios and Motahhare Eslami. 2014. A path to understanding the effects of algorithm awareness. In *CHI '14 Extended Abstracts on Human Factors in Computing Systems (CHI EA '14)*. ACM, New York, NY, USA, 631–642. https://doi.org/10.1145/2559206.2578883

[28] Alan Mislove Le Chen and Christo Wilson. 2015. Peeking Beneath the Hood of Uber. In *Proceedings of 2015 ACM Conference*. ACM, New York, NY, USA, 495–508. https://doi.org/10.1145/2815675.2815681

[29] Mei Ngan Mei Ngan and Patrick Grother. 2015. *Face recognition vendor test (FRVT) performance of automated gender classification algorithms*. Government Technical Report. US Department of Commerce, National Institute of Standards and Technology.

[30] Sorelle A. Friedler Tionney Nix Gabriel Rybeck Carlos Scheidegger Brandon Smith Philip Adler, Casey Falk and Suresh Venkatasubramanian. 2018. Auditing black-box models for indirect influence. *Knowledge and Information Systems* 54, 1 (January 2018). https://doi.org/10.1007/s10115-017-1116-3

[31] S.A. Rizvi P.J. Phillips, Hyeonjoon Moon and P.J. Rauss. 2000. The FERET evaluation methodology for face-recognition algorithms. In *IEEE Transactions on Pattern Analysis and Machine Intelligence*, Vol. 22. IEEE, 1090 – 1104. https://doi.org/10.1109/34.879790

[32] Ruchir Puri. 2018. Mitigating Bias in AI Models. Retrieved August 24, 2017 from https://www.ibm.com/blogs/research/2018/02/mitigating-bias-ai-models/

[33] Franco Turini Dino Pedreschi Riccardo Guidotti, Anna Monreale and Fosca Giannotti. 2018. A Survey of Methods for Explaining Black Box Models. *Comput. Surveys* 51, 5 (February 2018). https://doi.org/10.1145/3236009

[34] John Roach. 2018. Microsoft improves facial recognition technology to perform well across all skin tones, genders. Retrieved August 24, 2017 from https://blogs.microsoft.com/ai/gender-skin-tone-facial-recognition-improvement/

[35] Brent Mittelstadt Sandra Wachter and Chris Russell. 2018. Counterfactual Explanations Without Opening the Black Box: Automated Decisions and the GDPR. *Harvard Journal of Law & Technology* 31, 2 (2018).

[36] Brad Smith. 2018. Facial recognition technology: The need for public regulation and corporate responsibility.

[37] Jacob Snow. 2018. Amazon's Face Recognition Falsely Matched 28 Members of Congress With Mugshots. Retrieved August 24, 2017 from https://www.aclu.org/blog/privacy-technology/surveillance-technologies/Amazons-face-recognition-falsely-matched-28

[38] Florian Tramèr, Vaggelis Atlidakis, Roxana Geambasu, Daniel J. Hsu, Jean-Pierre Hubaux, Mathias Humbert, Ari Juels, and Huang Lin. 2015. Discovering Unwarranted Associations in Data-Driven Applications with the FairTest Testing Toolkit. *CoRR* abs/1510.02377 (2015).

A Framework for Benchmarking Discrimination-Aware Models in Machine Learning

Rodrigo L. Cardoso
rodrigolc@dcc.ufmg.br
Universidade Federal de Minas Gerais
Belo Horizonte, Minas Gerais, Brazil

Wagner Meira Jr
meira@dcc.ufmg.br
Universidade Federal de Minas Gerais
Belo Horizonte, Minas Gerais, Brazil

Virgilio Almeida
virgilio@dcc.ufmg.br
Universidade Federal de Minas Gerais
Belo Horizonte, Minas Gerais, Brazil

Mohammed J. Zaki
zaki@cs.rpi.edu
Rensselaer Polytechnic Institute
Troy, New York

ABSTRACT

Discrimination-aware models in machine learning are a recent topic of study that aim to minimize the adverse impact of machine learning decisions for certain groups of people due to ethical and legal implications. We propose a benchmark framework for assessing discrimination-aware models. Our framework consists of systematically generated biased datasets that are similar to real world data, created by a Bayesian network approach. Experimental results show that we can assess the quality of techniques through known metrics of discrimination, and our flexible framework can be extended to most real datasets and fairness measures to support a diversity of assessments.

CCS CONCEPTS

• **Computing methodologies** → **Machine learning**; *Bayesian network models*; • **Information systems** → *Data mining*.

KEYWORDS

fairness-aware data mining; bayesian networks; discrimination-aware benchmarks; disparate impact; disparate mistreatment

ACM Reference Format:

Rodrigo L. Cardoso, Wagner Meira Jr, Virgilio Almeida, and Mohammed J. Zaki. 2019. A Framework for Benchmarking Discrimination-Aware Models in Machine Learning. In *AAAI/ACM Conference on AI, Ethics, and Society (AIES '19), January 27–28, 2019, Honolulu, HI, USA.* ACM, New York, NY, USA, 8 pages. https://doi.org/10.1145/3306618.3314262

1 INTRODUCTION

Discrimination-aware learning is a topic of research that aims at minimizing the impact of bias against certain groups due to ethical reasons and legal implications. Given a labeled dataset whose records represent individuals, let its attributes be divided into non-protected and protected attributes, such as race and gender. The problem consists of building a classifier that takes the non-protected attributes of an individual and maps them to a class label, so that the classifier has minimum discrimination and maximum accuracy.

There are several recent works that tackle the issue of discrimination-aware learning; see for example the survey by [5] on fairness in machine learning. However, it is interesting to note that there is no consensus on the best technique for a given application scenario, since it also depends on the level of discrimination that is inherent to the dataset being targeted. The recent study by [11] discusses the impossibility of a classifier to satisfy multiple notions of fairness. This is one of the reasons why researchers have put their efforts on minimizing the effect of biased data on the predictions. We argue that an effective strategy to assess discrimination-aware learning models is by running them on scenarios where the discrimination-related parameters differ, so that we can observe how well the models behave. The main contribution of this work is a framework for comparing discrimination-aware learning models – the first such benchmark framework. Our framework comprises systematically generated biased datasets that are sampled from Bayesian networks learned from real world data. Our main concern is to explore alternative discrimination scenarios, that is, we want to learn from data representing different levels of bias for the purpose of analyzing the behavior of techniques when bias levels differ. Our work focuses on two metrics for assessing discrimination: disparate impact and disparate mistreatment [18]. However, our approach may be extended to other metrics (see [20]) as well.

AIES '19, January 27–28, 2019, Honolulu, HI, USA

ACM ISBN 978-1-4503-6324-2/19/01...$15.00
https://doi.org/10.1145/3306618.3314262

2 RELATED WORK

Most of the studies in this area may be divided into two groups [5]: *discrimination discovery*, which focuses on studying metrics and identifying how much discrimination there is in a dataset, and *discrimination prevention*, which focuses on building classification models that are less likely to produce discriminatory results.

For *discrimination discovery* there are a number of works that aim at identifying patterns of discrimination in data [15, 17], including metrics to quantify the amount of discrimination. Zliobaite [20] surveys several such metrics; she defines the *mean difference* as the most commonly used metric in early works, also called *slifd* [16] or *disparate impact.* Zafar et al. [18] propose a metric called *disparate mistreatment*, which measures the difference between misclassifications.

Discrimination prevention methods can be divided into three groups: *pre-processing*, *in-processing* and *post-processing* techniques [5]. We focus more on *Pre-processing techniques* [4, 9], since they modify the training set in order to make it as discrimination-free as possible, so that a classifier becomes less prone to exhibit bias. *In-processing techniques* [3, 10, 18] work by changing the classifier to produce less discriminating models, whereas *Post-processing techniques* [6] change the outcome of classification models.

Regarding discrimination-related assessment, several previous works on discrimination-aware learning generate synthetic data for evaluation [8, 21]. However, they create simple models with a few variables and their conditional dependencies, containing protected and non-protected artificial attributes and a binary class. In contrast, we generate biased data sampled from Bayesian networks learned from real world data, instead of purely synthetic data.

There are works that employ Bayesian networks to deal with discrimination discovery and prevention task. Bonchi et al. (2017) address the problem of learning probabilistic causal structures of discrimination from datasets. Mancuhan et al. (2014) use Bayesian networks for the task of bias prevention. Our work learns these structures, identifies discrimination patterns and uses them to sample data at different levels of bias. While previous approaches focused on discovering and mitigating discrimination, we employ sampled data from Bayesian networks in order to evaluate the quality of discrimination prevention techniques.

3 DEFINITIONS

A discrimination-aware learning model usually exploits the trade-off between accuracy and discrimination. The task is usually framed as a binary classification problem, where not only the accuracy should be maximized, but also discrimination has to be minimized. The classification score is defined according to the probabilities of outcomes for different groups of individuals. These groups are sets of individuals who share the same value of a specific attribute and, by contrasting their outcomes, we assess the model discrimination.

Formally, we are given a labeled dataset D where each record represents an individual. For each individual there are two sets of attributes $X = \{x_1, ..., x_n\}$ and $S = \{s_1, ..., s_m\}$. We call the set X the legally usable attributes, or *non-protected attributes*, which, in theory, may be used in decision making without any legal implications, e.g., annual income. We call the set S the non-legally usable attributes, or *protected attributes*. We are not supposed to use any attribute from S in a decision making process because they are protected by law, for instance, race, sex.

The class label $y \in \{+, -\}$ is the variable the model tries to predict for each individual. A positive class label $y = +$ (also denoted y^+) expresses a favorable outcome for the individual; alternatively, a negative class label $y = -$ (also denoted y^-) expresses an unfavorable outcome. An example is in credit scoring, where a bank wants to decide whether a customer has good credit score or not. A good credit score is represented by $y = +$, while a bad credit score is represented by $y = -$.

Let s be a protected attribute taking on two values $\{g, \bar{g}\}$. Here, the assumptions is that individuals belonging to g (that is $s = g$) usually suffer from discriminatory conditions, and are called the **deprived group**, and individuals not belonging to g (that is, $s \neq g$ or $s = \bar{g}$) usually have an unfair advantage in models, and they are called the **favored group**. In order to measure the discrimination with respect to a protected attribute s for individuals that belong to a group g, we quantify the difference between probabilities of positive outcomes for individuals that belong to g, and those who don't belong to g, as follows:

Definition 3.1. Let D be a dataset with labeled binary classes $y \in \{+, -\}$, and a protected attribute $s \in \{g, \bar{g}\}$ that defines individuals belonging to a group g or not belonging to the group $\bar{g}$. The discrimination $disc_{D,s,g}$ in D with respect to the attribute s for individuals from g is defined by the following equation:

$$disc_{D,s,g} = P(y^+|s = \bar{g}) - P(y^+|s = g) \tag{1}$$

That is, the difference between the probability of positive class for the favored ($\bar{g}$) versus the disfavored group (g). For example, members of the favored group may have a higher probability of a good credit score. This definition is widely used for measuring discrimination [6, 9] and it is often referred to as **disparate impact**.

Another way of measuring discrimination is through the two metrics presented in Zafar et al. [18] as **disparate mistreatment**. These are the metrics for misclassification that take into account the difference between false-positive and false-negative rates for individuals of different groups, defined as follows:

Definition 3.2. Let a classifier f assign for every record in D a class label $\hat{y}$. The disparate mistreatment of the classifier f in the dataset D with respect to the attribute s between the groups g and $\bar{g}$ is defined as:

$$D_{fp(D,s,g,f)} = P(\hat{y}^+|s = \bar{g}, y^-) - P(\hat{y}^+|s = g, y^-) \tag{2}$$

$$D_{fn(D,s,g,f)} = P(\hat{y}^-|s = g, y^+) - P(\hat{y}^-|s = \bar{g}, y^+) \tag{3}$$

The favored group $\bar{g}$ may have a higher false-positive rate (called **overestimation**) and a lower false negative rate (called **underestimation**) compared to the disfavored group g. These metrics seek to measure the extent of this problem for a given classifier f.

4 BENCHMARK METHODOLOGY

Our benchmark framework comprises systematically generated biased datasets that are derived from Bayesian networks learned from real-world data. We learn an approximate network structure that describes a dataset, which in turn depends on the conditional probabilities between the attributes. Modified Bayesian networks with different degrees of bias are used to generate new datasets that are used for evaluating discrimination-aware models.

4.1 Estimating Bayesian Networks

A Bayesian network is a probabilistic graphical model that maps conditional dependencies of random variables into a directed acyclic graph. We use an estimated Bayesian network to generate synthetic data, which allows us to quantify how much influence a protected attribute has on the outcome of a classification model.

To learn the structure of a Bayesian network in order to study causal relationships between the variables, we use the popular R library `bnlearn` [14]. Knowing the Bayesian network that represents a given data allows us to reproduce the characteristics inherent to the original data and to also adjust specific parameters to generate diverse scenarios. By learning these structures we can modify any node's conditional probabilities and are thus able to calibrate the bias of an outcome with respect to a protected attribute. Currently, we employ two methods for learning Bayesian Networks, Hill-Climbing greedy search and Tabu Search algorithm, both described in [14].

4.2 Modifying probabilities

Once we have learned a Bayesian network that represents the data, we can change the conditional probabilities of specific nodes. By doing this, we create a scenario where some of the nodes have different degrees of influence on other nodes. The modification is performed by selecting a specific attribute of our interest, that is, a protected attribute s. This attribute is represented by a node and it will have a direct or indirect influence on the outcome. The influence is observed in the conditional probability table of the outcome node.

Suppose we have a target attribute $s \in \{\bar{g}, g\}$ and the outcome $y \in \{-, +\}$. Recall that g represents a deprived group and $\bar{g}$ represents a favored group. We modify the Bayesian network by changing values in the probability table. Let $0 \leq \beta \leq 1$ be the level of artificial bias we want to insert for this node. The new probability $P'(y = +|s = g)$ is defined as:

$$P'(y = +|s = g) = P(y = +|s = g)(1 - \beta) \quad (4)$$

We only change the probabilities for the deprived group ($s = g$) because, if we change the conditional probabilities of the other group, we will be inserting twice the amount of bias. Our methodology consists of generating n Bayesian networks for each dataset. Each Bayesian network is generated with an increasing β (from 0.0 to 1.0).

Table 1: Toy conditional probability table

	$s = \bar{g}$	$s = g$
$P(y = -\|s)$	0.63	$0.80 \longrightarrow 0.90$
$P(y = +\|s)$	0.37	$0.20 \longrightarrow 0.10$

Table 1 shows a toy example of conditional probabilities of the outcome given a variable s. Using the disparate impact score we can see that the discrimination against the group g is 0.17 since $P(y^+|\bar{g}) - P(y^+|g) = 0.37 - 0.20 = 0.17$. Suppose we want to insert a bias level β of 0.5. In order to do this, we change the probability under the column $s = g$, as shown in Table 1. Now we can observe that the discrimination against the group g is 0.27 (0.37 − 0.10), which means that we have increased the resulting discrimination.

4.3 Sampling and Evaluation

After learning a Bayesian network with the conditional probabilities on its nodes, we can then sample data from it. Since we have the frequency of each attribute in the dataset, we can sample this structure, so that samples remain similar to the real data regarding the probability of each individual attribute. A sample consists of randomly generated observations, where each attribute value in an observation is generated according the probability table learned from the original data. For each bias level introduced, we generate random samples that form the corresponding biased training dataset. These systematically biased datasets are used for evaluating discrimination models and metrics. Those techniques either preprocess the input data and generate a new data or use the input data without any pre-processing and provide a discrimination-aware classification model.

5 EXPERIMENTS

We compare well-known discrimination-aware techniques by testing them on the systematically biased datasets. We mainly test preprocessing techniques and some in-processing techniques. When a pre-processing technique is employed, it outputs a modified dataset that is used by conventional classification models. The test set is the original real data that was used to generate the Bayesian network. Evaluation is performed in two different ways. First, by comparing the discrimination of the prediction to the accuracy on the test set, and second, by measuring overestimation (eq. (2)) and underestimation (eq. (3)) of the resulting predictions.

5.1 Discrimination-aware Techniques

The techniques we compare are listed below.

5.1.1 Baseline: It consists of removing the protected attribute from the training set. It has been argued that this may even increase discrimination [15] due to the fact that some of the attributes may describe the protected one. For example, the neighborhood information may carry racial information about individuals. This problem is known as *redlining.*

5.1.2 Calders et al. [3]: propose several pre-processing approaches for dealing with the problem of discrimination aware learning. These are:

- *Massaging* changes the class label of individuals in order to balance positive outcomes between groups. Individuals of the deprived group from the negative class are reassigned to the positive class, and individuals of the favored group having a positive class are reassigned to the negative class. Instances are selected for class reassignment based on a score learned by a ranker.
- *Re-weighting* assigns higher weights to individuals of the deprived group that have a positive class label and to individuals of the favored group that have a negative class label.
- *Uniform Sampling* applies the following rule on a randomly chosen instance: if the instance is from the deprived group with negative class, it is removed, otherwise, if it is from the positive class, it is duplicated. Likewise, if the instance is of the favored group with a positive class is removed, but if it has a negative class it is duplicated.
- *Preferential Sampling* chooses instances based on a ranker like in the Massaging technique. The change rules are the same as in uniform sampling.

5.1.3 Black Box Auditing (Auditor). Black Box Auditing (https://github.com/algofairness/BlackBoxAuditing) is an implementation of Gradient Feature Auditing (GFA) introduced in [1]. This technique works by repairing the dataset via a pre-processing technique, which means that it changes attribute labels. The resulting repaired dataset is expected to have lower discrimination. We run the data repairer described by [4] at the repair levels of 0.25, 0.50 and 0.75.

5.2 Datasets

We test on the following original real-world datasets. The **Adult dataset** [12], also known as Census Income, is a widely used dataset in previous discrimination-aware learning studies. The task is to predict whether an individual has a yearly income greater than $50K or not (i.e., high vs. low income). It has 48,842 instances with 14 attributes. The protected attribute is sex and the original dataset has an inherent disparate impact against women (equal to 0.19). For generating biased data, we increase the influence of the feature *relationship* on the outcome, thus making it less likely that wives have high income, thus increasing the bias against women. The **Pro Publica COMPAS dataset** (https://github.com/propublica/compas-analysis) records racial bias on recidivism scores. The data contains information from defendants such as race, age, criminal history and whether the defendant had committed a crime within a two-year window. It has 6,150 instances with 13 attributes. The sensitive attribute is race, which can be either "Caucasian" or "African-American". We modified the influence of the variable race on the outcome for generating biased data. **Dutch census** [3] is also a demographic census. We use it to make predictions of whether an individual has a "high level" occupation or not. This dataset has 11 attributes and we define sex as the protected attribute.

5.3 Experimental setup

We evaluate various discrimination-aware techniques on our set of systematically biased datasets generated from the real-world data mentioned above. This set consists of 4 training datasets with increasing levels of artificial bias (β) against individuals of the defined deprived group. For the classifier, we use the Weka implementation of the C4.5 decision tree [7]. We reproduced the experimental setup described by the authors of the techniques and used default parameters [12, 21]. Thereafter, we measure the accuracy and discrimination observed when the original data is used as the testing data. Note that we refer to disparate impact as *discrimination* (eq. (1)), and measure disparate mistreatment via *overestimation* and *underestimation* (eq. (2) and eq. (3)).

6 RESULTS AND DISCUSSION

In this section we present the results of employing our framework to assess several techniques. Every experiment was run 30 times. We computed the confidence intervals as well as the variances for each set of experiments.

6.1 Discrimination vs. Accuracy

Table 2 shows Discrimination versus Accuracy on each dataset when we only remove the protected attribute. We perform this experiment for a couple of reasons. The first one is to make sure that removing the protected attribute does not reduce the resulting discrimination in the classification task. The second reason is to define upper bounds for both discrimination and accuracy. That is, the discrimination without any technique being employed must be higher than when some technique is used, otherwise the use of this anti-discrimination technique would be of no use. It is also expected that the accuracy will be higher than the resulting accuracy when a discrimination-aware technique is used because the technique must lower the discrimination at the cost of accuracy.

Table 2: Discrimination and Accuracy on biased datasets from Adult, COMPAS and Dutch data (classifier does not use the protected attribute)

β \ Dataset	Adult		COMPAS		Dutch	
	Disc.	Acc.	Disc.	Acc.	Disc.	Acc.
0.00	0.162	0.845	0.121	0.878	0.322	0.832
0.25	0.280	0.829	0.121	0.880	0.358	0.831
0.50	0.581	0.729	0.123	0.879	0.393	0.827
0.75	0.592	0.726	0.120	0.878	0.479	0.805
1.00	0.602	0.723	0.124	0.880	0.677	0.729

We can observe in Table 2 that, as we increase β, the discrimination on the Adult census increases and the accuracy decreases, which means that highly biased data is worse for the performance of a traditional classifier like C4.5. The COMPAS case shows better performance as it does not increase the discrimination as we raise β. In COMPAS the resulting decision trees for each β are similar, which explains its behavior. Dutch census is similar to Adult. As expected, removing the protected attribute contributes poorly in reducing discrimination because other attributes are highly correlated with the protected one.

6.1.1 Data pre-processing techniques. Table 3 shows Discrimination vs. Accuracy results for different pre-processing techniques. Recall that we expect the discrimination and accuracy upper bounds to be preserved; we highlight (in bold) scenarios where the accuracy increased instead of decreasing.

Table 3: Discrimination and Accuracy for data pre-processing techniques trained on artificially generated datasets learned from adult census.

	β \ Tech.	Massaging		Reweighting		Unif. Sampling		Pref. Sampling	
		Disc.	Acc.	Disc.	Acc.	Disc.	Acc.	Disc.	Acc.
	0.00	0.046	0.830	0.111	0.842	0.112	0.842	-0.006	0.822
	0.25	0.009	0.816	0.140	**0.840**	0.139	**0.838**	-0.034	0.812
Adult	0.50	0.095	**0.778**	0.260	**0.802**	0.257	**0.799**	0.044	**0.794**
	0.75	0.082	0.718	0.479	0.710	0.480	0.710	0.142	**0.756**
	1.00	0.003	0.676	0.473	0.690	0.474	0.690	0.416	0.673
	0.00	0.095	**0.879**	0.104	0.876	0.110	0.877	0.076	0.872
	0.25	0.084	0.879	0.103	0.876	0.113	0.879	0.067	0.871
COMPAS	0.50	0.070	0.875	0.102	0.875	0.111	0.878	0.054	0.870
	0.75	0.054	0.872	0.098	0.874	0.104	0.877	0.044	0.866
	1.00	0.057	0.871	0.107	0.877	0.108	0.878	0.045	0.866
	0.00	0.101	0.791	0.153	0.818	0.159	0.817	0.066	0.790
	0.25	0.013	0.768	0.154	0.818	0.166	0.818	0.018	0.774
Dutch	0.50	-0.052	0.748	0.150	0.816	0.161	0.816	-0.029	0.760
	0.75	-0.119	0.721	0.157	0.816	0.159	**0.813**	-0.062	0.749
	1.00	-0.182	0.693	0.483	0.720	-	-	-	-

We can see that in Table 3, on **Adult**, every technique except Massaging increases discrimination when using a more biased training set. Re-weighting and Uniform Sampling behave very similarly (this behavior is held true on other datasets). Preferential sampling has a steady decrease in accuracy and increase in discrimination, but its result for 100% bias is quite different. We hypothesize that, when the dataset becomes fully biased, its results are not really significant anymore, but we include them for the sake of providing a bound.

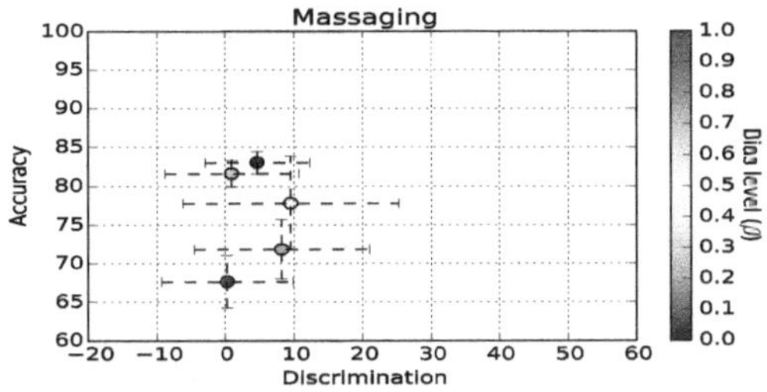

Figure 1: Discrimination vs Accuracy for data Massaging technique on Adult data

The most intriguing result is for the Massaging technique. Table 3 and Figure 1 show that it has lower discrimination for lower and higher β, but when we introduce moderate β it increases the resulting discrimination. In Figure 1, each colored dot represents a set of 30 artificial datasets, with the color denoting the β bias level. Massaging works by defining a decision boundary between positive and negative outcomes through a Naive Bayes classifier, then it selects points from the dataset and changes their labels in order to balance the ratio of positives and negatives between the two classes of the sensitive attribute. Massaging works by changing labels, thus forcing the deprived group to have more positive outcomes and the favored group to have more negative outcomes. This is possibly the reason Massaging causes negative discrimination. We can observe that the results for the various techniques on **COMPAS** were also consistent with previous findings. Massaging and Preferential Sampling performed better in terms of lowering discrimination. Nevertheless, the highlighted scenarios where the accuracy increased suggests that data manipulation might actually improve both accuracy and discrimination in specific scenarios. It can be noticed on **Dutch** that Massaging and Preferential Sampling behave similarly, but the former has more spread, which means that Preferential Sampling is more stable when dealing with this dataset. Re-weighting and Uniform Sampling, except on higher β, keep the discrimination and accuracy around the same level. Notice that we couldn't run Uniform or Preferential Sampling for higher β, since those techniques don't work well on very imbalanced scenarios.

6.1.2 Auditor's technique. Table 4 presents results for Auditor at repair levels of 0.25, 0.50 and 0.75. On **Adult**, we see it works well for lower β, but it performs poorly in more biased scenarios. It is worth noting that scenarios with very high discrimination are less realistic, which means that Auditor performance may be considered decent because it has minimal losses with respect to accuracy. When the repair level is set to 0.75, Auditor keeps the accuracy and discrimination at the same levels for every β with low deviation, except when maximum bias is inserted. On **COMPAS** Auditor performed similarly for each one of the repairing levels, but didn't quite remove the discrimination. The consistency of the results is also demonstrated by the similarity of the decision trees generated by C4.5 at every repairing level. On **Dutch** census scenario, Auditor kept the accuracy around the 80%, but it didn't prevent the discrimination, and pre-processing techniques performed better. However, it maintains the best accuracy overall. It can be observed that the 0.75 repair level performs slighly better than repair level 0.25 and 0.50. The highlighted numbers suggest that Auditor could improve the accuracy in some cases. However, this improvement is not statistically significant, and, more importantly, there are cases where the discrimination increases.

Table 4: Discrimination and Accuracy for Auditor in-processing technique.

Dataset	β \ Tech	Repair 0.25 Disc.	Repair 0.25 Acc.	Repair 0.50 Disc.	Repair 0.50 Acc.	Repair 0.75 Disc.	Repair 0.75 Acc.
Adult	0.00	0.149	0.844	0.064	0.818	0.039	0.805
	0.25	0.197	**0.841**	0.110	0.827	0.034	0.801
	0.50	0.492	**0.768**	0.242	**0.828**	0.031	**0.796**
	0.75	0.597	0.725	0.592	0.726	0.034	**0.795**
	1.00	0.605	0.723	0.605	0.723	0.576	**0.728**
COMPAS	0.00	0.121	**0.879**	0.123	**0.879**	0.122	**0.880**
	0.25	0.127	0.880	0.125	0.879	0.127	0.880
	0.50	0.124	0.879	0.129	0.880	0.127	0.879
	0.75	0.124	**0.879**	0.128	**0.879**	0.130	0.878
	1.00	0.125	0.879	0.129	0.879	0.129	0.877
Dutch	0.00	0.270	0.829	0.224	0.825	0.161	0.815
	0.25	0.270	0.831	0.211	0.824	0.154	0.814
	0.50	0.304	**0.829**	0.224	0.825	0.150	0.811
	0.75	0.390	**0.806**	0.295	0.798	0.143	0.798
	1.00	0.586	**0.730**	0.468	0.717	0.212	0.619

Table 5: Overestimation and Underestimation for Adult, COMPAS and Dutch (classifier does not use the protected attribute).

β \ Dataset	Adult Over.	Adult Under.	COMPAS Over.	COMPAS Under.	Dutch Over.	Dutch Under.
0.00	0.065	0.105	0.012	0.046	0.194	0.072
0.25	0.154	0.399	0.015	0.044	0.239	0.108
0.50	0.471	0.712	0.015	0.047	0.268	0.162
0.75	0.480	0.745	0.013	0.043	0.312	0.346
1.00	0.480	0.831	0.014	0.049	0.356	0.870

6.2 Overestimation vs. Underestimation

Table 5 shows results on Overestimation and Underestimation for each dataset when no technique is applied. Again, it is important to consider these values as upper bounds, which means that the objective of each techniques is to reduce these (absolute) values.

We can see that Adult and Dutch have high Overestimation and Underestimation at higher values of β. Curiously, COMPAS keeps the values close. This suggests that for COMPAS higher β may have little influence on the resulting Overestimation and Underestimation, which is also explained by the fact that the decision trees generated by the classifier are similar no matter the β.

Table 6: Overestimation and Underestimation for data pre-processing techniques.

	β \ Tech.	Massaging		Reweighting		Unif. Sampling		Pref. Sampling	
		Over.	Under.	Over.	Under.	Over.	Under.	Over.	Under.
	0.00	-0.025	-0.217	0.030	-0.063	0.029	-0.062	-0.051	-0.324
	0.25	-0.062	-0.269	0.051	0.012	0.045	0.012	-0.084	-0.353
Adult	0.50	0.011	-0.130	0.154	0.196	0.151	0.198	-0.023	-0.236
	0.75	0.005	-0.111	0.384	0.470	0.383	0.476	0.074	-0.124
	1.00	-0.086	-0.070	0.351	0.706	0.355	0.709	0.298	0.644
	0.00	-0.017	0.021	-0.000	0.026	0.006	0.036	-0.031	0.003
	0.25	-0.024	0.006	-0.000	0.023	0.008	0.032	-0.038	-0.008
COMPAS	0.50	-0.031	-0.012	-0.001	0.024	0.006	0.030	-0.044	-0.026
	0.75	-0.043	-0.031	-0.005	0.020	0.002	0.028	-0.051	-0.039
	1.00	-0.034	-0.032	0.001	0.030	0.006	0.031	-0.045	-0.040
	0.00	-0.065	-0.096	0.014	-0.095	0.023	-0.087	-0.091	-0.145
	0.25	-0.165	-0.159	0.015	-0.094	0.029	-0.078	-0.151	-0.170
Dutch	0.50	-0.239	-0.200	0.012	-0.098	0.024	-0.085	-0.197	-0.208
	0.75	-0.314	-0.236	0.019	-0.089	0.018	-0.083	-0.214	-0.247
	1.00	-0.384	-0.263	0.120	0.700	-	-	-	-

6.2.1 Data pre-processing techniques. Table 6 shows the results for Overestimation and Underestimation for data pre-processing techniques. For **Adult**, Massaging reduces Overestimation and Underestimation in more biased scenarios. It is also interesting to note that almost every result of Massaging was a negative value. This technique keeps Overestimation closer to 0, meaning that it balances false positives between the two groups. The Underestimation has slightly higher negative values, but these values get closer to 0 as we insert more bias. This means that the technique underestimates the favored group for lower β, but it manages to balance the Underestimation between groups under higher β. Re-weighting and Uniform Sampling performed similarly by increasing both Overestimation and Underestimation, although they exhibit high deviation on both. Preferential Sampling has hard to predict behavior; it has low Overestimation and its Underestimation started very negative and became closer to 0, except for the last biased sample. For **COMPAS**, we can see that Massaging and Preferential Sampling introduce negative Underestimation and Overestimation at higher β. Re-weighting and Uniform Sampling kept both Underestimation and Overestimation closer to 0, which is desirable. **Dutch** scenario suggests that Massaging and Preferential Sampling work similarly by inserting negative Overestimation and Underestimation when we increase β. Re-weighting and Uniform Sampling did a good job on keeping the values close (expect for the case of higher β on Re-weighting).

6.2.2 Auditor technique. Table 7 shows results for Overestimation and Underestimation of Auditor technique for each dataset on repair levels of 0.25, 0.50 and 0.75. For **Adult**, every technique performed similarly to Re-weighting and Uniform Sampling except Auditor at 0.75 repairing level, which kept almost every value close to zero for both Overestimation and Underestimation. For **COMPAS**, Auditor

Table 7: Overestimation and Underestimation for Auditor in-processing technique.

	β \ Tech	Repair 0.25		Repair 0.50		Repair 0.75	
		Over.	Under.	Over.	Under.	Over.	Under.
	0.00	0.056	0.096	0.010	0.006	0.001	-0.014
	0.25	0.087	0.269	0.032	0.092	0.001	-0.019
Adult	0.50	0.368	0.644	0.131	0.386	0.002	-0.019
	0.75	0.484	0.750	0.482	0.750	0.003	-0.016
	1.00	0.483	0.829	0.484	0.821	0.470	0.727
	0.00	0.015	0.046	0.019	0.047	0.019	0.046
	0.25	0.019	0.048	0.020	0.051	0.017	0.045
COMPAS	0.50	0.018	0.049	0.020	0.052	0.021	0.044
	0.75	0.017	0.045	0.020	0.051	0.026	0.050
	1.00	0.019	0.051	0.022	0.052	0.018	0.053
	0.00	0.122	0.017	0.077	-0.027	0.013	-0.097
	0.25	0.128	0.031	0.071	-0.022	0.018	-0.093
Dutch	0.50	0.163	0.084	0.077	-0.015	0.018	-0.096
	0.75	0.196	0.265	0.094	0.173	0.019	-0.089
	1.00	0.223	0.796	0.109	0.685	0.030	0.314

did not quite improve the result if compared to no technique used. In general, those techniques couldn't keep up with pre-processing techniques for this scenario. For **Dutch**, Auditor improved the consistency of its results when we increase the repairing level to 0.75 as it has nearly 80% less overestimation compared to repair level of 0.25. It isn't pareto-dominated (which means that it isn't outperformed on both metrics) by any technique and provides a competitive result in most cases.

7 CONCLUSIONS AND FUTURE WORK

This work introduces a novel benchmark framework for validating discrimination-aware data mining and machine learning models using systematically biased datasets generated from real world data. The need for a benchmark is crucial due to the lack of a common ground for the evaluation of techniques. We demonstrated the applicability and effectiveness of the proposed benchmark through a comparative assessment among several models on three relevant datasets.

The value of our benchmark approach is apparent when we observe that it is hard to define which technique is better than another. What is important is to decide which constraint is more relevant under a given scenario and then interpret the accuracy versus discrimination or over/under-estimation results in order to perform a trade-off between metrics. Our framework makes this type of decision easier. In the future, we intend to extend our work to a more complete coverage of techniques of disparate impact and disparate mistreatment removal, as well as other fairness metrics.

ACKNOWLEDGMENTS

This research was partially supported by the Brazilian Research Agencies CNPq, CAPES, and FAPEMIG, by projects InWeb, MASWeb, EUBra-BIGSEA, INCT-Cyber and Atmosphere.

REFERENCES

[1] Philip Adler, Casey Falk, Sorelle A. Friedler, Gabriel Rybeck, Carlos Scheidegger, Brandon Smith, and Suresh Venkatasubramanian. 2016. Auditing Black-Box Models for Indirect Influence. In *IEEE 16th International Conference on Data Mining, ICDM 2016, December 12-15, 2016, Barcelona, Spain.* 1–10. https://doi.org/10.1109/ICDM.2016.0011

[2] Francesco Bonchi, Sara Hajian, Bud Mishra, and Daniele Ramazzotti. 2017. Exposing the probabilistic causal structure of discrimination. *I. J. Data Science and Analytics* 3, 1 (2017), 1–21. https://doi.org/10.1007/s41060-016-0040-z

[3] Toon Calders and Sicco Verwer. 2010. Three naive Bayes approaches for discrimination-free classification. *Data Min. Knowl. Discov.* 21, 2 (2010), 277–292. https://doi.org/10.1007/s10618-010-0190-x

[4] Michael Feldman, Sorelle A. Friedler, John Moeller, Carlos Scheidegger, and Suresh Venkatasubramanian. 2015. Certifying and Removing Disparate Impact. In *Proceedings of the 21th ACM SIGKDD International Conference on Knowledge Discovery and Data Mining, Sydney, NSW, Australia, August 10-13, 2015.* 259–268. https://doi.org/10.1145/2783258.2783311

[5] Sara Hajian, Francesco Bonchi, and Carlos Castillo. 2016. Algorithmic Bias: From Discrimination Discovery to Fairness-aware Data Mining. In *Proceedings of the 22nd ACM SIGKDD International Conference on Knowledge Discovery and Data Mining, San Francisco, CA, USA, August 13-17, 2016.* 2125–2126. https://doi.org/10.1145/2939672.2945386

[6] Sara Hajian, Anna Monreale, Dino Pedreschi, Josep Domingo-Ferrer, and Fosca Giannotti. 2014. Fair pattern discovery. In *Symposium on Applied Computing, SAC 2014, Gyeongju, Republic of Korea - March 24 - 28, 2014.* 113–120. https://doi.org/10.1145/2554850.2555043

[7] Mark Hall, Eibe Frank, Geoffrey Holmes, Bernhard Pfahringer, Peter Reutemann, and Ian H. Witten. 2009. The WEKA data mining software: an update. *SIGKDD Explorations* 11, 1 (2009), 10–18.

[8] Moritz Hardt, Eric Price, and Nati Srebro. 2016. Equality of Opportunity in Supervised Learning. In *Advances in Neural Information Processing Systems 29: Annual Conference on Neural Information Processing Systems 2016, December 5-10, 2016, Barcelona, Spain.* 3315–3323. http://papers.nips.cc/paper/6374-equality-of-opportunity-in-supervised-learning

[9] Faisal Kamiran and Toon Calders. 2011. Data preprocessing techniques for classification without discrimination. *Knowl. Inf. Syst.* 33, 1 (2011), 1–33. https://doi.org/10.1007/s10115-011-0463-8

[10] Faisal Kamiran, Toon Calders, and Mykola Pechenizkiy. 2010. Discrimination Aware Decision Tree Learning. In *ICDM 2010, The 10th IEEE International Conference on Data Mining, Sydney, Australia, 14-17 December 2010.* 869–874. https://doi.org/10.1109/ICDM.2010.50

[11] Jon M. Kleinberg, Sendhil Mullainathan, and Manish Raghavan. 2016. Inherent Trade-Offs in the Fair Determination of Risk Scores. *CoRR* abs/1609.05807 (2016). http://arxiv.org/abs/1609.05807

[12] M. Lichman. 2013. UCI Machine Learning Repository. http://archive.ics.uci.edu/ml

[13] Koray Mancuhan and Chris Clifton. 2014. Combating discrimination using Bayesian networks. *Artif. Intell. Law* 22, 2 (2014), 211–238. https://doi.org/10.1007/s10506-014-9156-4

[14] Dimitris Margaritis. 2003. Learning Bayesian network model structure from data.

[15] Dino Pedreschi, Salvatore Ruggieri, and Franco Turini. 2008. Discrimination-aware data mining. In *Proceedings of the 14th ACM SIGKDD International Conference on Knowledge Discovery and Data Mining, Las Vegas, Nevada, USA, August 24-27, 2008.* 560–568. https://doi.org/10.1145/1401890.1401959

[16] Dino Pedreschi, Salvatore Ruggieri, and Franco Turini. 2009. Measuring Discrimination in Socially-Sensitive Decision Records. In *Proceedings of the SIAM International Conference on Data Mining, SDM 2009, April 30 - May 2, 2009, Sparks, Nevada, USA.* 581–592. https://doi.org/10.1137/1.9781611972795.50

[17] Salvatore Ruggieri, Dino Pedreschi, and Franco Turini. 2010. Data mining for discrimination discovery. *TKDD* 4, 2 (2010), 9:1–9:40. https://doi.org/10.1145/1754428.1754432

[18] Muhammad Bilal Zafar, Isabel Valera, Manuel Gomez-Rodriguez, and Krishna P. Gummadi. 2017. Fairness Beyond Disparate Treatment & Disparate Impact: Learning Classification without Disparate Mistreatment. In *Proceedings of the 26th International Conference on World Wide Web, WWW 2017, Perth, Australia, April 3-7, 2017.* 1171–1180. https://doi.org/10.1145/3038912.3052660

[19] Muhammad Bilal Zafar, Isabel Valera, Manuel Gomez Rodriguez, and Krishna P Gummadi. 2015. Fairness constraints: Mechanisms for fair classification. *arXiv preprint arXiv:1507.05259* (2015).

[20] Indre Zliobaite. 2017. Measuring discrimination in algorithmic decision making. *Data Min. Knowl. Discov.* 31, 4 (2017), 1060–1089. https://doi.org/10.1007/s10618-017-0506-1

[21] Indre Zliobaite, Faisal Kamiran, and Toon Calders. 2011. Handling Conditional Discrimination. In *11th IEEE International Conference on Data Mining, ICDM 2011, Vancouver, BC, Canada, December 11-14, 2011.* 992–1001. https://doi.org/10.1109/ICDM.2011.72

A APPENDIX

Here we detail a practical example of our Bayesian network based sampling method, and show additional results on reducing disparate impact and disparate mistreatment using the methods from Zafar et al in [18, 19].

A.1 Practical example

We take the **Adult** dataset (also known as **census income** dataset) from UCI Machine Learning Repository [12] as an example for our methodology. This dataset is a demographic census and it is commonly used to predict whether an individual's income is greater than $50K per year or not given a list of attributes that include age, education level, marital status, occupation and sex.

A data cleansing step is performed by discretizing some of the attributes and removing others. The clean dataset is used as input for the `bnlearn` Hill-Climbing learner.

Figure 2 is a visual representation of the generated Bayesian network (BN) using the adult census dataset as input. It can be observed that there is conditional dependency between the variables *relationship* and *income_class* and also there is conditional dependency between *relationship* and *sex*. This evidence supports the fact that this data is biased with respect to sex, because sex is described by the relationship, e.g., a *wife* is a *woman*, and income class is also described by the relationship, e.g., being a *wife* may influence income.

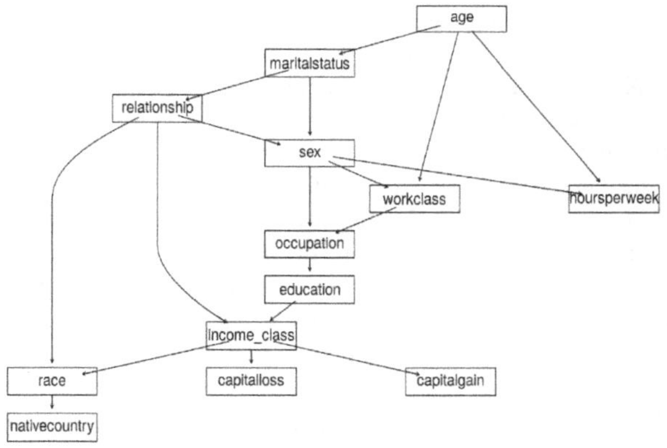

Figure 2: Bayesian network learned from the adult dataset.

For the synthetic data generation process, we have the corresponding BN for the Adult census dataset and its conditional probabilities tables. Each row in this dataset is randomly generated by observing the BN. The list of dependencies is represented by the directed edges in Figure 2. For sampling, we start with the independent node in the BN, which is age. We sample age according to its distribution. After sampling age, we can sample the marital status. The conditional probability table for marital status is given in Table 8. Notice that age is divided into bins, which means that younger people are represented by bins identified by smaller numbers and older ones by larger numbers. We omit some of the bins due to space constraints.

This process continues until we have sampled every feature. We then repeat this process until we have enough rows sampled, thus

Table 8: Conditional probabilities of marital status given some age categories (1-younger, 10-older)

Marit. Status \ Age Cat.	2 (22-28)	5 (46-52)	8 (70-76)
Divorced	0.087	0.206	0.081
Married-AF-spouse	0.001	0.000	0.002
Married-civ-spouse	0.372	0.630	0.560
Married-spouse-absent	0.011	0.016	0.014
Never-married	0.490	0.077	0.060
Separated	0.032	0.033	0.014
Widowed	0.003	0.035	0.265

generating a synthetic dataset that follows the same distribution as the original adult data.

In order to produce biased samples consider Table 9, which contains conditional probabilities for the income class node given education levels (Edu-level) and relationships (r). We can see that, according to this table, the probability of a positive outcome (the individual earns more than $50K per year), considering the fact that the individual is a wife is slightly better with higher education levels, but it is worse for lower education levels. In order to produce even more bias, we must decrease the probabilities in the first line of Table 9. For instance, we may decrease the probability of high income considering that the relationship is *wife*. This is done gradually, each time by 10% of the original probability, until the probability reaches 0, as described in Section 4.2. For example, the probability of an individual having high income, considering she is a woman and her education level is 10th grade, is 0.100. The first artificial dataset is sampled by lowering this probability to 0.090, the second one to 0.080, and so on.

The resulting sampled datasets are then used as training data for a classifier. We chose the C4.5 decision tree classifier due to its good results on previous works of discrimination-aware learning. Since our aim is to evaluate discrimination-aware techniques, the choice of the classifier is not that important.

Table 9: Conditional probabilities of high income (above $50K a year) given education and relationship

Cond. prob \ Edu-level	1st-4th	10th	HS	Doctorate
$P(y = high \mid r = wife)$	0.000	0.100	0.343	0.850
$P(y = high \mid r = husband)$	0.085	0.128	0.311	0.837

A.2 Disparate Impact and Mistreatment

We also consider the implementations of Zafar et al. [18, 19], where they design a fair classifier that works by modifying the decision boundary of a classifier. It can maximize fairness under accuracy constraints and maximize accuracy under fairness constraints. It is also possible to add a constraint on misclassification of positive outcome, which means that it only changes the label for the protected group from negative to positive class and doesn't change the label of non-protected groups to the negative outcome. This technique will be used for the disparate impact experiments (Accuracy vs. Discrimination). In [18], they introduced the notion of disparate mistreatment and proposed a methodology that aims at reducing false positive and false negative rates. The technique consists of training classifiers in such a way that their decision boundaries are modified in order to avoid those misclassification rates. We can adjust which constraints we want to use: correcting false positive, false negatives, or both. This technique will be used for the disparate mistreatment experiments (Overestimation vs. Underestimation).

A.2.1 Discrimination vs Accuracy. Table 10 presents results for Zafar's disparate impact technique for each one of its three constraints.

Table 10: Discrimination and Accuracy for Zafar's in-processing techniques trained on artificially generated datasets learned from adult census.

	β \ Tech	Acc. cons. Disc.	Acc. cons. Acc.	Disc. cons. Disc.	Disc. cons. Acc.	Misclass. Disc.	Misclass. Acc.
	0.00	0.128	0.837	-0.018	0.791	-0.066	0.590
	0.25	0.156	0.829	-0.032	0.773	-0.016	0.571
Adult	0.50	0.181	**0.821**	-0.046	**0.760**	-0.015	0.530
	0.75	0.205	**0.814**	-0.046	**0.747**	-0.003	0.503
	1.00	0.258	**0.813**	-0.032	**0.743**	0.063	0.528
	0.00	0.010	0.631	0.032	0.629	0.020	0.617
	0.25	0.014	0.630	0.014	0.628	0.029	0.615
COMPAS	0.50	0.005	0.628	-0.002	0.622	0.022	0.610
	0.75	0.005	0.628	-0.027	0.620	0.040	0.610
	1.00	0.004	0.626	-0.043	0.615	0.033	0.607
	0.00	0.108	0.806	-0.031	0.746	-0.020	0.695
	0.25	0.091	0.801	-0.003	0.765	-0.059	0.647
Dutch	0.50	0.061	0.792	0.044	0.785	-0.105	0.596
	0.75	-0.025	0.762	0.127	**0.812**	-0.090	0.558
	1.00	-0.147	0.719	0.252	**0.820**	0.032	0.705

In Table 10 we present the results for Zafar's disparate impact techniques. In particular, the technique described in [19] for fairness, accuracy and positive misclassification constraints. For **Adult** the Discrimination constraint indeed keeps the discrimination around the same level at the cost of accuracy when the bias level β increases. On the other hand, for accuracy constraint, it keeps the accuracy around the same level and the discrimination increases with higher β. An interesting result can be observed when the positive misclassification constraint is applied; it causes lower discrimination levels but at a great cost to accuracy. For **COMPAS**, Zafar's techniques tried to enforce less discrimination but also decreased the accuracy. For **Dutch**, Zafar's techniques, except the one for positive misclassification, achieved competitive accuracy compared to pre-processing techniques and decreased accuracy. It provided a trade-off between accuracy and discrimination. As for the highlighted cases, when we apply Accuracy and Discrimination constraints on **Adult** the accuracy does not suffers very much for higher β. This means that Zafar's classifiers not only fix the bias inserted but also make them consistent with the original data. On **Dutch** the same pattern can be observed for higher β.

Towards a Just Theory of Measurement

A Principled Social Measurement Assurance Program for Machine Learning

McKane Andrus*
Thomas K. Gilbert*
mckaneandrus@berkeley.edu
tg340@berkeley.edu
UC Berkeley

ABSTRACT

While formal definitions of fairness in machine learning (ML) have been proposed, its place within a broader institutional model of fair decision-making remains ambiguous. In this paper we interpret ML as a tool for revealing when and how measures fail to capture purported constructs of interest, augmenting a given institution's understanding of its own interventions and priorities. Rather than codifying "fair" principles into ML models directly, the use of ML can thus be understood as a form of quality assurance for existing institutions, exposing the epistemic fault lines of their own measurement practices. Drawing from recent discussion of representational mappings in the Fair Machine Learning literature and previous discussions on the ontology of measurement, we propose a *social measurement assurance program* (sMAP) in which ML encourages expert deliberation on a given decision-making procedure by examining unanticipated or previously unexamined covariates. As an example, we apply Rawlsian principles of fairness to sMAP and produce a provisional *just theory of measurement* that would guide the use of ML for achieving fairness in the case of child abuse in Allegheny County.

KEYWORDS

measurement; machine learning; justice; fairness; representational measurement; measurement assurance; Rawls; institutional decision-making

ACM Reference Format:

McKane Andrus and Thomas K. Gilbert. 2019. Towards a Just Theory of Measurement: A Principled Social Measurement Assurance Program for Machine Learning. In *AAAI/ACM Conference on AI, Ethics, and Society (AIES '19), January 27–28, 2019, Honolulu, HI, USA.* ACM, New York, NY, USA, 7 pages. https://doi.org/10.1145/3306618.3314275

INTRODUCTION

Machine learning (ML) is now widely deployed to shape life outcomes in high-risk social settings. Social scientists have criticized this deployment as needlessly automating human-led tasks, and unfair in its unequal treatment of vulnerable subpopulations and opaque classifications [15]. While practitioners have responded by posing technical model fixes to deal with biased datasets, these discussions have not explored the problem of *measurement* itself as a core domain for fair ML research, neglecting important questions at the intersection of data collection, policy formulation, and what fairness even means in context.

We take a deeply pragmatic view of measurement, interpreting matters of fairness in terms of how well institutions can predict and reshape the context-specific social dynamics that motivate their own decision-making. ML serves as a tool for critical self-reflection by interrogating these dynamics, expanding an institution's horizons by uncovering limitations of its adopted variables of interest and suggesting the need for alternatives. While ML is morally neutral, its discoveries (e.g. how well predictions map to outcomes for different subpopulations) will clarify when assumptions about the value of any specific metric are in need of revision. This may compel a new interpretation of the lived experience of relevant communities, and in turn suggest new sampling procedures. ML thus helps ensure fairness through critical reflection on measurement, and helps reveal causal assumptions that either impede or cultivate fair outcomes. We argue ML must be deployed earlier in the decision-making process to interrogate measurement practices, and propose greater points of contact between algorithmic systems and domain experts, such as doctors and parole officers.

We present a *social measurement assurance program* (sMAP) that deploys ML to investigate how institutional policies are meant to resolve pertinent historical inequalities. sMAP rests on a representational mapping between observed human data, difficult-to-measure human qualities of causal significance, and ML-informed interventions. We then demonstrate this framework's value for resolving both conceptual and empirical puzzles for fair investigations of measured social phenomena. As an example, we apply Rawlsian principles of justice [20] to sMAP to produce a *just theory of measurement*, by which an institution could falsify or bolster decision policies. This *just theory of measurement* examines suspect representations for possible bias, deploys ML to find morally counterintuitive covariates, uses sampling to probe the assumed preconditions for fair interventions, and consults with affected groups to falsify the institution's representation of them.

THE CASE OF ALLEGHENY COUNTY

Here we present our motivation through the example of the Child, Youth, and Family (CYF) division of the Allegheny County Department of Human Services, recently the subject of a case study by

*Both authors contributed equally to this research.

AIES '19, January 27–28, 2019, Honolulu, HI, USA

ACM ISBN 978-1-4503-6324-2/19/01...$15.00
https://doi.org/10.1145/3306618.3314275

Virginia Eubanks. The Allegheny CYF provides many services, such as protecting children from abuse and neglect, and has implemented the Allegheny Family Screening Tool (AFST) to predict risk using data for 287 variables scraped from CYF's database.

The case of AFST illustrates the difficulties organizations face when they are pushed to address funding shortages with automation but are still devoted to implementing fair policies. In the context of child welfare, the underlying social realities of "abuse" and "neglect" are difficult to confirm outside of fatalities or near-fatalities. As such, the AFST is limited to predicting community re-referral and child placement, two outcome measures that provide a much larger training and validation set than systematic child abuse. Furthermore, AFST is primarily used to supplement case worker judgment, not determine which cases are worthy of closer investigation. This favors individual (and possibly parochial) judgments based on variable expertise over a more systematic perspective on county-wide child protection services. In effect, while AFST relies on manifold statistical measures rather than caseworkers' expert judgment, both model and humans are trying to decide whether or not to delve deeper into a case without the criteria for decision-making being clearly specified or shared between parties.

Both qualitative and quantitative criteria for this case study have recently been proposed by the developers of AFST and the wider academic community. Brown et al. [4] suggest communication strategies between AFST and impacted families that might increase public trust and establish system accountability, while Chouldechova et al. [6] consider how the use of analytics can both create problems through excessive reliance on administrative data and also refine human judgment through its use. Currently missing from this work is a systematic exposition of measurement as the crucible for how interventions are morally justified and reinterpreted in context, as well as the epistemic stakes behind possible interventions.

FAIR ML IN INSTITUTIONAL CONTEXTS

Eubanks' case study raises a wider question for data scientists – what is the proper relationship between institutionally-ingrained measurement practices and the more recent epistemic affordances of machine learning, such as model selection, training, and optimization? The problem of "fair" machine learning sits right at this intersection, pursued by distinct research efforts such as formal "explainable" models or technical refinements to measurement procedures without analytically addressing the relationship itself.

Skepticism towards ML is also found within the technical literature, such as ongoing struggles against dataset bias. If ML's utility is the ability to discern implicit structure in reams of data, this structure does not necessarily scale with the accurate representation of diverse subpopulations. The data may lack adequate record-keeping, inaccurately portray disadvantaged social groups, or simplify social contexts in a way that omits key causal relations. Lipton and Steinhardt [17] has diagnosed this tension in much ML scholarship, including a failure to distinguish explanation and speculation, failing to identify sources of empirical gains, mathiness, and misuse of language.

Each pitfall reflects a tension governing the ML research agenda, as well as ML's ambiguity for the institutions whose data it processes and whose interventions it justifies. In any given empirical context, compensating for inadequate data (through guesswork, model overtuning, technical overcompensation, or imprecise terminology) is motivated by expert intuitions about unobserved phenomena behind the data, which the system may capture through further optimization. Yet ML can also reveal new contexts endogenously from diverse data sources, whose covariates suggest poorly understood political and social realities. This tension has motivated the search for explanatory models so that authorities can commit either to deploying it with confidence in service of their own assumptions, or deferring to it if its operational efficiency and technical innovations are sufficient to challenge their own assumptions – in effect, to determine whether the actual mechanisms of social reproduction are better established by domain experts or technical models.

Indeed, it is unclear if the findings or assumptions of ML models even require explanation if they could, in theory, guarantee robust predictions. Lipton and Steinhardt [17] lament that ML papers often purport to explain model results by proposing highly intuitive theories that, while lacking "crisp formal representations," are still meant to rhetorically justify exploration. This begs the question of whether we are letting the administrative tail wag the algorithmic dog: perhaps we are better off trusting model robustness to augment the assumptions that motivated data collection and intervention in the first place. In fact, Doshi-Velez and Kim [9] argue that we need interpretability only when there is *incompleteness* in the problem formalization, as this creates a barrier to optimization and evaluation. It would therefore be an institution's job to address this incompleteness while weighing context-specific concerns about safety and ethics, not demand explainable models out of hand.

However, many critics reject this vision in favor of a more traditional human-in-the-loop approach, and questioned ML's value for predictive risk assessment. Barabas et al. [1] show how risk assessment itself has historically swayed between behavior predictions and justifying draconian sentencing policies. Consequently, they suggest that ML "should be used to surface covariates that are fed into a *causal model* for understanding the social, structural and psychological drivers of crime," rather than help shape penal policies directly. Likewise, Corbett-Davies and Goel [7] are critical of naive operational "solutions" to problems of fairness, and argue for aligning model representation with traditional principles of due process. However, neither of these positions presents explicit ontological assumptions that would firmly ground this skepticism of ML and delineate how dataset bias, optimization, prediction, and interventions might be related procedurally. In other words, it is not clear how a decision pipeline that supports due process might be augmented through the application of ML to measurement procedures, even if its history has been spotty.

We must ask a more radical question: could ML help reshape decision-making by formalizing the conditions under which interventions are perceived as fair? Mullainathan and Spiess [18] consider this possibility from an econometrics standpoint, arguing that ML should be used to probe social settings with strong verifiable assumptions (at which it excels) but relatively poor understanding of how or why social reproduction of inequality occurs. This interprets data exploration as a designed intervention on model assumptions rather than a sanitized approach to risk assessment. Dawes et al. [8] suggests this approach in a clinical context: "What is needed is the development of actuarial methods and a measurement assurance program that maintains control over both [clinical and actuarial] judgment strategies so that their operating characteristics in the field are known and an informed choice of procedure is possible."

SOCIAL MEASUREMENT ASSURANCE PROGRAM

In this section we outline a *measurement ontology* for organizational interventions on the social world which could ensure an automated decision system fulfills its intended purpose. We propose a social Measurement Assurance Program (sMAP) whose measurement procedures are defined by representational mappings between *observed* human data, *difficult-to-measure* human qualities of *causal significance*, and *institutional interventions.* We will first review distinct theories of measurement in order to define these components and justify this sort of mapping between them. We then present a general model of institutional decision-making, highlighting where measurement assurance is most relevant.

Theories of Measurement

We draw from the general definition of measurement from Hand [12] as an interpreted relation between what is real and what is observed, made possible by sampling interventions. Two such interpretations are relevant for social phenomena. First, representational measurement aligns some definition of what is real with a given empirical process. For example, an empirical process used to measure dire poverty can relate different measurable variables such as total accessible funds, average daily caloric intake, and risk of debilitating illness, but these variables serve only as proxies for some underlying, unobserved reality (the state of being poor). Second, observational measurement relies solely on an empirical system, with no baseline definition of what is real or proposed underlying constructs. Under this theory, total accessible funds, average daily caloric intake, and presence of fever are what is real – not funding sources, food supplies, disease, or poverty as such. We introduce these theories of measurement because any institution that makes it their task to intervene on the real world must grapple with the question of how to represent and understand it. In the following sections we argue that in order for an institution to enact meaningful, systematic change, it must first espouse a representational system of measurement.

Model of Institutional Decision-Making

Making ML "fair" requires mapping our observed reality onto some space of possible actions that might push us towards a more equitable world state. As described in Friedler et al. [11], when institutions conduct a mapping from observed data to decisions, there is an implicit mapping onto some *construct* space that defines the context for the decision. For example, in college admissions, GPA scores hint at *general intelligence*, a difficult-to-define construct that the admissions officers are actually using as a basis for decisions. Thus, there is a subsequent mapping of these constructs onto a

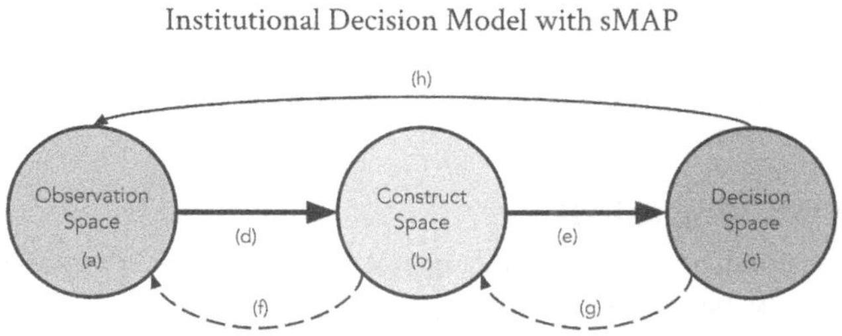

Figure 1: Enforcing measurement consistency and validity is a direct intervention on (a). Verifying the measure to construct correspondence is an intervention on (d) by way of (f). Decision-to-measurement feedback adjustment is an intervention on (a) by acknowledging (h). Finally, confirming the constructs is an intervention on (b) by way of (g).

space of possible decisions, or interventions, that the institution can make.

We further note that the decision space also affects the *observation space.* As a more detailed example, consider a welfare program that processes short-term housing for the homeless. Those that have been given short-term housing in the past will start to appear different in the observation space, i.e. interactions with shelters and law-enforcement will decrease, as a direct result of past interventions. These outliers cannot be summarily removed from the system, as they may again "become" homeless in the near future. The program coordinators must thus consider how the decision space might map onto a new observation space, and even reconsider the underlying construct space, which comprises the context of underlying, policy-relevant inequalities.

This mapping from observed reality onto constructs is best defined by a representational theory of measurement. Bartholomew [2] has suggested that social measurements are necessarily operational because they arbitrarily define a means to gather data that does not exhaustively map between observed and represented variables, as a perfectly representational system of measurement requires. We note, however, that there is a mismatch in the stated aims of social institutions and pure science which would seem to permit a more liberal interpretation of representational measurement. Social institutions strive to effectively intervene on relevant communities, based on construct spaces that reflect context priorities. While these representations are never perfect, they are still acted upon in principled, meaningful ways. For example, how admissions represent college applicants might differ based on school quality. Where a 3 on an AP exam signifies barely passing for a student from a prestigious private school, it might signify great self-motivation from an underserved rural or inner-city high school, empowering admissions committees to encode *drive* as more a desirable trait than *elite pedigree.* In this way, the institution relies on a principled, composite measure that stems from a contextual understanding of the underlying relations between attributes.

Given this representational style of measurement and intervention, we warn that adopting tools of automated decision-making puts these composite measures with groundings in social theory at risk. Instead, institutions may come to rely on measures developed operationally by ML systems. As a means of both confronting this loss of context and ensuring that representational measurements remain grounded in social reality, we propose the use of a social Measurement Assurance Program.

Outlining sMAP

Measurement assurance programs (MAP) are common in engineering disciplines. As defined by Speitel [21], a MAP is "a program to establish, evaluate, and control the quality of measurement." Accurate measurements are requisite for complex systems that rely on both sensors and actuators, since slight deviations can rapidly lead to system-wide failures. MAPs are thus managerial tools that ensure the measurements being taken are the *correct ones to use*, that measurement systems *operate properly*, and that the broader system is *robust to the precision of measurement*.

We apply this intuition to measures used for institutional decision-making. Social measures, unlike physical properties, are often not consistent or generalizable [2, 19]. Campbell's law provides the most instructive justification: "The more any quantitative social indicator is used for social decision-making, the more subject it will be to corruption pressures and the more apt it will be to distort and corrupt the social processes it is intended to monitor." [5] As measured objects and interventions are in a dynamic relationship, any attempt to directly implement an engineering MAP will be unsuccessful. Thus, a *social* measurement assurance program (sMAP) will require a new set of tools.

Like a physical MAP, an sMAP should first and foremost ensure that (1) the methods of measurement are consistent and correctly implemented. As we are considering representational measurements, an sMAP also needs to (2) ensure gathered measures map onto the institution's construct space. Inspired by Campbell's law, another task unique to an sMAP is (3) accounting for the changes made to the observation space by the presence of the decision space. However, an sMAP cannot stop here. The representational systems of measurement employed by institutions stem from specific beliefs about how the world works. These social ontologies make up an institution's construct space, but are crucially subject to change by the advent of new evidence. As such, an sMAP further requires (4) a feedback mechanism to the constructs, such that they might be adjusted to better align with intervention aims. Figure 1 illustrates the sMAP adjustment to our model of institutional decision-making.

While an sMAP could incorporate diverse tools and approaches, for this work we specifically consider the ways in which ML can be repositioned as a tool in support of an sMAP. Through this repurposing of ML, we aim to show how ML's moral content is not defined by the algorithms it employs, but by the role it plays in making decisions.

Measurement Consistency and Validity. Measurements could also be rendered meaningless through inconsistencies in sampling or the loss of key contextual details. Extending the welfare program example, different caseworkers' ability to garner trust with their charges might produce measurement inconsistencies. The validity of the total annual income measure could also be compromised by omitting illicit sources of income, such as drug sales. Using ML to model the decision-making process could address the observation space's limitations. For example, indirect measurements that figure strongly in the construct space but not the decision space (e.g. total annual income as a proxy for housing stability) indicate that the institution's interventions may not be contextually valid. Furthermore, if the measure carries predictive weight only for specific groups within the sampled population, it is likely that the measure needs to be adjusted to better reflect group idiosyncrasies. Income from unconventional or illicit professions like prostitution is likely to play a differential role for distinct subgroups, such that its omission from the measurement procedure without considering treatment effects would be inappropriate.

Measure to Construct Correspondence. We propose that ML can validate the mapping of measured attributes to desired constructs. Even simple regression methods surface relations between measures and decisions that encourage critical reviews of how a given measure reflects the underlying construct. For instance, a college admissions office might discover that key covariates in admission decisions are AP scores with little dependence on school rankings. By incorporating ML into their sMAP, the college might investigate this discrepancy and decide to weight AP scores by high school rankings, effectively merging these two measures to more effectively map onto the the construct for *academic effort*. While this new measure may not be useful for existing data, the college can now provide admissions officers with this measure directly, refining the admissions pipeline.

Decision-to-Measurement Feedback Adjustment. Once sMAP serves a dynamic system that updates a given decision process, we can produce a history of predictive ML models. Comparing these models can determine the impact of a decision-making procedure on the observation space, and how a new procedure may reshape future observations. For example, if certain measures lose predictive value, the measures may have fallen prey to Campbell's law, or the affected populations may have exogenously changed. If instead predictive outcomes are consistent regardless of interventions, it implies the construct space should be questioned, altered, or abandoned. Either way, an important feature of an sMAP is to keep the measures in constant correspondence with the institution's construct commitments, a procedure that must be iteratively carried out and maintained.

The observation space can also be assessed by maintaining close contact with subjects. This will help gauge real impacts, revealing how certain measures might be adjusted or how the measurement ontology might need realignment. ML practitioners should solicit input from ethnographers, survey methodologists, social policy planners, and other qualitative experts to better capture contexts that remain invisible to their models. In our previous example of college success based on high school performance, ML practitioners might partner with guidance counselors at both public and private high schools to better identify the contexts within which students' attributes develop and how their own model assumptions (e.g. the weighting of SAT vs. AP scores) create distinct incentives for socially unequal college-bound students.

Construct Verification. There must be explicit record-keeping of how constructs relate to interventions, and what observed outcomes would falsify them. If the measures that represent the construct do not carry much weight, the construct may be (a) not as important as the institution believes it to be, or (b) not as central to decision-making as it is meant to be. As an example, consider that after consulting with guidance counselors, admissions experts learn that *drive to succeed* germinates differently among first vs. second generation college-bound students, where for the former it tends to manifest in extracurricular activities and for the latter in higher final GPA. This both challenges the underlying reality of the construct and implies that existing policies do not capture its complexities, which may suggest alternative constructs that are better understood and easier to measure.

Conclusion. We have suggested that ML can both surface and *contour covariates* for decision-making. Not only are important measures revealed, unimportant constructs may be dismissed as context-inappropriate. Depending on the method used, connections may also be drawn between measures, hinting at deeper relations between constructs and potentially altering existing legal or scientific understandings of relevant social variables. Entirely new measures could be codified if ML helps identify covariates for which we have no prior construct-based intuition. ML thus constitutes a *technical* intervention in how *policy* interventions are made, shifting the grounds by which decisions are justified by altering the conditions under which they can be envisioned, enacted, and evaluated. In these ways, use of ML can hint at where a given institution might dedicate future resources to improve understanding of the context of its own decisions.

APPLYING RAWLSIAN PRINCIPLES TO SMAP

Here we develop a *just theory of measurement* by applying a specific fairness ontology to the representational mappings within sMAP. As an example, we deploy Rawlsian principles of justice due to their specific relevance for the Allegheny County case as well as their more general influence on scholarly debates surrounding fairness. While sMAP requires such an ontology in order for it to justify fair interventions, other philosophical theories of fairness could be used instead of Rawls. We hope this section serves as an early example to be refined by the wider community of ML researchers and social activists interested in combining technical models with notions of procedural justice.

Our general approach is influenced by [3], who discusses various moral and political-philosophical approaches to ML fairness, with two key elaborations. First, because we interpret measurement *representationally* rather than *operationally*, ML can be used as a tool to test existing representations of the social world for unacceptable forms of bias, rather than merely surface covariates for existing causal models. Second, we align our Rawlsian sMAP with what Binns [3] calls *deontic justice*: "the sense in which egalitarianism can be...not concerned with an unequal state of affairs per se, but rather with the way in which that state of affairs was produced". Deontic justice defines how the world would need to be observed in order for abstract moral principles to hold, rather than how we should model features in order to uphold specific fairness classifications, such as equal parity. In other words, ML fairness is not simply a matter of ensuring that measures capture the construct of interest, but that such constructs need to be a reasonable and reliable basis upon which an institution can pursue its goals.

Lippert-Rasmussen [16] support this intuition: "Statistical facts are often facts about how we choose to act. Since we can morally evaluate how we choose to act, we cannot simply take statistical facts for granted when justifying policies: we need to ask the prior question of whether it can be justified that we make these statistical facts obtain." For deontic justice, ML should help both the evaluation of causal effects of future interventions and causal mechanisms behind historical inequalities visible to the model.

Rawls' framework is perhaps the most influential and systematic theory of deontic justice currently available. Put succinctly, Rawlsian justice advocates for (1) equal right to extensive basic liberties and (2) inequalities being permissible only insofar as they (a) work to the greatest benefit of the least advantaged, and (b) arise from processes that assure the equality of opportunity. To apply Rawls to sMAP, we interpret these two principles of justice as constitutive elements of the *construct space* that must correspond to an institution's observed social measures as well as its acceptable decision space. In this manner, sMAP can give form to specific fairness ontologies, allowing specific moral intuitions to be put to work by informing the range of observations analyzed and decision interventions proposed. In the next section we apply this intuition to a recent case study.

AN SMAP FOR ALLEGHENY COUNTY

Returning to Allegheny CYF and the AFST, CYF's services and goals map well onto the Rawlsian principles that define a just institution, comprising a natural setting for a just theory of measurement. Recall that *abuse* and *neglect* serve as constructs that are difficult to confirm outside of fatalities or near-fatalities. From here, we explore possible recommendations that stem from the components of a Rawlsian sMAP. These recommendations should be taken lightly, however, as the authors have not been directly involved with the Allegheny County CYF or its populace. Rather, this section provides a first glimpse of what an sMAP might require in practice.

Measurement Consistency and Validity

The bulk of [10] details how the poor are disproportionately subjected to automated institutional processing. In the case of Allegheny County's CYF, this asymmetrical treatment is reflected in how the ASFT recommends a disproportionate number of mandatory inspections of poor families. Eubanks shows that this difference can be largely attributed to the measures used to predict risk. The most important measure, referrals, is a product of many social factors, including majority perceptions of what *good* parenting looks like. Eubanks describes how employees from welfare institutions are often mandatory reporters – they are obligated by law to report children that show signs of *abuse* or *neglect*. Neglect, however, is easy to conflate with the effects of poverty. Furthermore, referrals largely come from professionals working with the poor and working classes, so the measurement *procedure* is inconsistent for the population as a whole. To render referral measurements more consistent with Rawlsian justice (holding that inequalities should work to the advantage of the worst-off), a just sMAP would suggest selective auditing referrals instead of processing them all uniformly. Another issue surrounding referrals that Eubanks [10] hints at is professional bias against poor and working class "natural growth" parenting styles. This bias might render the measure invalid, as it unduly esteems middle class "concerted cultivation" [14]. This can result in a screening bias that almost ensures residual unfairness in AFST predictions [13]

According to Eubanks, CYF employees are aware of the inconsistencies in these measurement procedures, but they believe that they have no means of addressing them. Wealthy families resist the forms of surveillance and interference that poorer families must accept. Employees from support institutions (therapy practices, Alcoholics Anonymous, other rehabilitation centers) are often not mandatory reporters, and changing this would be a political challenge. In the face of such uncertainties the sMAP would be best supported by extended participant observation to uncover new ways of assessing risk. If the measures must remain largely inconsistent between populations, separate models and strategies will need to be employed.

Measure to Construct Correspondence

Within the CYF's intervention model, there are two measurement-construct mappings. The first maps from measures (e.g. community referrals, past interaction with welfare agencies) onto *abuse* and *neglect*. The second maps from proxies of community re-referral and child placement onto *demonstrated risk*. In the first case, when AFST was being built, scraped variables were chosen based on correlation with risk predictions. The number of scraped variables in use has since been whittled down from a bit more grounding in social context [6], but this approach remains indicative of adopting an operational theory of measurement and prediction. Caseworkers, on the other hand, still implement a representational mapping in their own risk assessments.

sMAP suggests several strategies for aligning caseworkers' representational mappings with the AFST as a validation tool. For example, caseworkers might find that they are called to certain communities more than others, and consulting AFST reveals that it is using zipcode in its predictions. The caseworkers infer that the predictive power of zipcodes is only acceptable if it directly maps onto the constructs of *abuse* or *neglect*, as it should not have an impact on more individualized constructs like *parenting quality*. Unable to disentangle these mappings in the AFST model, the caseworkers should advocate for the removal of the zipcode feature from the model and instead solicit geographic measures more meaningfully or historically connected to *abuse* or *neglect* (e.g. concentration of cultural groups that condone abuse) in order to better establish the contours of these specific constructs. When these steps are not taken, the liberty of an individual to be treated independent from their community is violated.

On the other side of the model, we have the mapping of re-referrals and child placement onto the construct of *demonstrated risk*. Eubanks discusses how re-referrals are especially fraught because of reporters' racial biases against possible abusers. A Rawlsian sMAP might suggest surfacing other possible covariates to see if these biases are rooted in more specific social categories besides race (e.g. rival church affiliations, clan marriages) so that re-referrals are not held up to an invisible, empirically-unverified construct, which would also violate the liberty principle. Furthermore, as the caseworkers themselves are not likely to share these biases, their insight into contextual differences between prejudiced and earnest referrals could also prove useful in finding alternative measures that more accurately map onto the construct of *demonstrated risk* beyond racial classification.

Decision-to-Measurement Feedback Adjustment

Families are often dramatically changed by support from CYF. Eubanks describes how CYF support is conditional upon families subjecting themselves to scrutiny and enrolling in time-consuming programs on work readiness and parenting skills. Thus, time spent on parenting (one of CYF's observational measures) will not only decrease, but CYF is also given more access to the home to observe this decline. If implementing an sMAP, CYF should incorporate the impacts of their interventions into their decision-making procedure, such as tailoring a method or model for predicting risk of previously processed families.

Construct Verification

As already noted, poor families often lack child care resources. Might this interact with the construct of *neglect*? And how might ML, combined with a more just theory of measurement, better elucidate this construct for CYF? Firstly, Eubanks [10] points out that poorer families routinely receive higher risk scores from the AFST. If the model permits isolating or omitting certain features, the CYF could very well find that the economic status of a family has an impact on risk score beyond just the downstream effects of income on other variables, such as school attendance and living situation. If this is the case, then it is likely that the economic difficulties a family faces are indirectly mapping onto *neglect* in the decision-making procedure, beyond what is observed. Thus, an sMAP would suggest that where the *neglect* is meant to be used in determining CYF interventions, a construct distinction needs to be made between *intentional neglect* and *means-induced neglect*. In the case of *means-induced neglect*, the role of CYF should be to ameliorate the situation with increased family support. This might require a distinct verification system, as community re-referrals and child placement are not likely to be accurate indicators of means-induced neglect.

CONCLUSION

We have pointed to the capability of ML to expand the spaces of relevant observations, possible interventions, and imaginable constructs whose correspondences determine the efficacy of interventions. Greater tolerance of diverse data sources, a willingness to rethink pre-ML policies through what these sources reveal, and deliberation over narrative constructs can only be a good thing for programs whose existing deployment strategies are threatened by budget cuts and lack of political support. ML ultimately supplies a broader means of measuring the inequalities that define us, and will help lay the groundwork for rethinking principles of justice and social democracy in the coming decades.

REFERENCES

[1] Chelsea Barabas, Madars Virza, Karthik Dinakar, Joichi Ito, and Jonathan Zittrain. 2018. Interventions over Predictions: Reframing the Ethical Debate for Actuarial Risk Assessment. In *Conference on Fairness, Accountability and Transparency*. 62–76.

[2] David Bartholomew. 1996. Response to Statistics and the theory of measurement. *Journal of the Royal Statistical Society. Series A (Statistics in Society)* (1996), 473–474.

[3] Reuben Binns. 2017. Fairness in Machine Learning: Lessons from Political Philosophy. *arXiv preprint arXiv:1712.03586* (2017).

[4] Anna Brown, Alexandra Chouldechova, Emily Putnam-Hornstein, Andrew Tobin, and Rhema Vaithianathan. 2019. Toward Algorithmic Accountability in Public Services. (2019).

[5] Donald T Campbell. 1979. Assessing the impact of planned social change. *Evaluation and program planning* 2, 1 (1979), 67–90.

[6] Alexandra Chouldechova, Diana Benavides-Prado, Oleksandr Fialko, and Rhema Vaithianathan. 2018. A case study of algorithm-assisted decision making in child maltreatment hotline screening decisions. In *Conference on Fairness, Accountability and Transparency*. 134–148.

[7] Sam Corbett-Davies and Sharad Goel. 2018. The measure and mismeasure of fairness: A critical review of fair machine learning. *arXiv preprint arXiv:1808.00023* (2018).

[8] Robyn M Dawes, David Faust, and Paul E Meehl. 1989. Clinical versus actuarial judgment. *Science* 243, 4899 (1989), 1668–1674.

[9] Finale Doshi-Velez and Been Kim. 2017. Towards a rigorous science of interpretable machine learning. *arXiv preprint arXiv:1702.08608* (2017).

[10] Virginia Eubanks. 2018. *Automating inequality: How high-tech tools profile, police, and punish the poor.* St. Martin's Press.

[11] Sorelle A Friedler, Carlos Scheidegger, and Suresh Venkatasubramanian. 2016. On the (im) possibility of fairness. *arXiv preprint arXiv:1609.07236* (2016).

[12] David J Hand. 1996. Statistics and the theory of measurement. *Journal of the Royal Statistical Society. Series A (Statistics in Society)* (1996), 445–471.

[13] Nathan Kallus and Angela Zhou. 2018. Residual unfairness in fair machine learning from prejudiced data. *arXiv preprint arXiv:1806.02887* (2018).

[14] Annette Lareau. 2011. *Unequal childhoods: Class, race, and family life.* Univ of California Press.

[15] Jeff Larson. 2016. How We Analyzed the COMPAS Recidivism Algorithm. *Propublica* (2016). https://www.propublica.org/article/how-we-analyzed-the-compas-recidivism-algorithm

[16] Kasper Lippert-Rasmussen. 2014. *Born free and equal?: A philosophical inquiry into the nature of discrimination.* Oxford University Press.

[17] Zachary C Lipton and Jacob Steinhardt. 2018. Troubling Trends in Machine Learning Scholarship. *arXiv preprint arXiv:1807.03341* (2018).

[18] Sendhil Mullainathan and Jann Spiess. 2017. Machine learning: an applied econometric approach. *Journal of Economic Perspectives* 31, 2 (2017), 87–106.

[19] National Research Council. 2011. *The importance of common metrics for advancing social science theory and research: A workshop summary.* National Academies Press.

[20] John Rawls. 2009. *A theory of justice.* Harvard university press.

[21] K.F. Speitel. 1982. Measurement Assurance. In *The Oxford Handbook of Innovation*, Gavriel Salvendy (Ed.). John Wiley and Sons, San Francisco.

Putting Fairness Principles into Practice: Challenges, Metrics, and Improvements

Alex Beutel, Jilin Chen, Tulsee Doshi, Hai Qian, Allison Woodruff, Christine Luu, Pierre Kreitmann, Jonathan Bischof, Ed H. Chi
Google
alexbeutel,jilinc,tulsee,hqian,woodruff,cmluu,kreitmann,bischof,edchi@google.com

ABSTRACT

As more researchers have become aware of and passionate about algorithmic fairness, there has been an explosion in papers laying out new metrics, suggesting algorithms to address issues, and calling attention to issues in existing applications of machine learning. This research has greatly expanded our understanding of the concerns and challenges in deploying machine learning, but there has been much less work in seeing how the rubber meets the road.

In this paper we provide a case-study on the application of fairness in machine learning research to a production classification system, and offer new insights in how to measure and address algorithmic fairness issues. We discuss open questions in implementing equality of opportunity and describe our fairness metric, *conditional equality*, that takes into account distributional differences. Further, we provide a new approach to improve on the fairness metric during model training and demonstrate its efficacy in improving performance for a real-world product.

ACM Reference Format:
Alex Beutel, Jilin Chen, Tulsee Doshi, Hai Qian, Allison Woodruff, Christine Luu, Pierre Kreitmann, Jonathan Bischof, Ed H. Chi. 2019. Putting Fairness Principles into Practice: Challenges, Metrics, and Improvements. In *AAAI/ACM Conference on AI, Ethics, and Society (AIES '19), January 27–28, 2019, Honolulu, HI, USA.* ACM, New York, NY, USA, 7 pages. https://doi.org/10.1145/3306618.3314234

1 INTRODUCTION

By almost every measure, there has been an explosion in attention and research on machine learning fairness: there is a quickly growing amount of research on how to define, measure, and address machine learning fairness, and products are evaluated with these concerns in mind. Despite this significant attention, there has been much less published work detailing how fairness concerns are measured and addressed by product teams in industry. In this paper, we hope to shed light on the challenges in following these principles and learnings in an applied production setting, and to offer metrics and methods developed in the process.

We focus on a classification system where adverse actions are taken against examples predicted to be in the positive class. This is similar to not giving a person a mortgage if a model predicts they will default on it [21], using recidivism prediction for setting bail [9], or removing comments on the web if they are predicted to be abusive [13]. In all of these cases, each item is associated with a user, and if the classifier makes a mistake and the adverse action is taken against their example, that is bad for the user. More generally, if examples from certain groups of users more often have adverse actions taken against them, it could effect the health of the service. As a result, improving group fairness [21] is both the right thing to do and important to the health of the product.

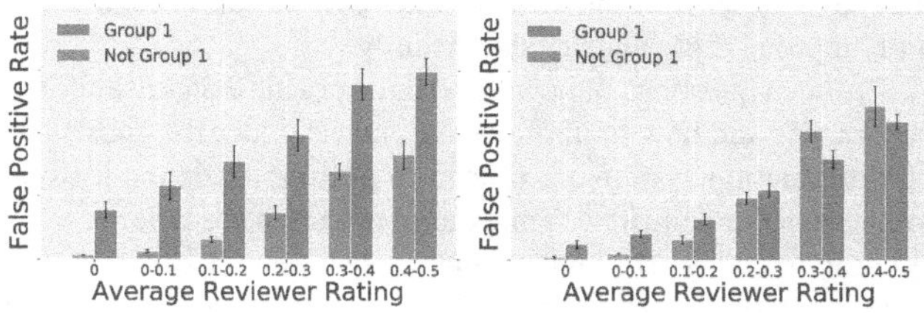

(a) Before (b) After Improvements

Figure 1: We observe a significant improvement in the gap in false positive rate by training the model with absolute correlation regularization.

We focus on equality of opportunity [21], in particular comparing false positive rate (FPR) between groups. While the model being calibrated [12] is an important mathematical property, it does not reflect the experience of users and the implications of representation on the service. However, while [21] provides great intuition and philosophical guidance, we find that in practice it leaves significant wiggle room in how the metric is calculated based on how the evaluation data is sampled or generated. Further, as shown by Corbett-Davies et al. [11], distributional differences can result in unintended side-effects and costs when implementing fairness changes. We address these issues through a generalized form of the metric, *conditional equality*, that makes these decisions more explicit, and we describe how we navigated these challenges in our use case. Figure 1 presents a summary of our results in an applied production setting[1].

Given this metric, we consider how to improve it under the practical constraints of a product. For example, we are unable to reliably observe the sensitive attribute at inference time, preventing approaches like using different thresholds [28]. Further, as with many engineering systems, simplicity and maintainability are core

[1]Due to the sensitive nature of these tests, we must omit the numerical values on the y-axis of all plots. In all cases, plots that are juxtaposed keep the same range on the y-axis such that results can be compared.

AIES '19, January 27–28, 2019, Honolulu, HI, USA

ACM ISBN 978-1-4503-6324-2/19/01.
https://doi.org/10.1145/3306618.3314234

requirements. We begin with exploring the use of adversarial training techniques [4, 33, 38], which have been shown to be effective. However, as with many adversarial training approaches, we find these are sometimes unstable and difficult to reliably train well. As a result, we offer a new approach, *absolute correlation regularization*, which, while not provably optimal at convergence, we find empirically can stably improve our algorithmic fairness metrics.

Finally, we test these approaches on the production model to improve the metrics for items from two sensitive groups. We find that adversarial training and absolute correlation regularization both improve these metrics significantly.

The open questions of how to design a practical algorithmic fairness metric and how to improve that metric under the constraints of a production system are crucial to putting academic learning into practice in industry. While our approaches are tailored to the application and constraints at hand, we believe they can offer guidance to ML practitioners and call attention to gaps in the current literature that researchers can work to address and practitioners should be mindful of. We list below our contributions:

(1) **Metrics:** We demonstrate the challenge in "correctly" measuring equality of opportunity, and describe our metric, conditional equality, that makes practitioner decisions explicit and takes into account varying difficulty of examples across groups.
(2) **Optimization:** We offer a new regularization technique, called absolute correlation regularization, to encourage equality of opportunity during training.
(3) **Improvement:** We demonstrate improvements to our algorithmic fairness metrics. In particular, we find that traditional modelling, such as through larger models, can improve algorithmic fairness. Second, we find that absolute correlation regularization stably and significantly improves algorithmic fairness metrics.

2 BACKGROUND AND RELATED WORK

We begin with some background material on algorithmic fairness metrics and relevant related work.

Metrics. Many different metrics have been proposed to measure machine learning fairness, particularly for binary classification. One line of work called individual fairness rests on the view that similar examples should receive similar predictions [15]; but this leaves open the question of similarity. Another line of work focuses on group fairness, where examples are grouped by a particular sensitive attribute and statistics about the model predictions are aggregated within the group and compared between groups. Multiple group fairness metrics have been proposed. Demographic parity [7] asserts that the average prediction for each group should be equal:

$$P(\hat{y} = 1|s = 0) = P(\hat{y} = 1|s = 1), \tag{1}$$

where the model prediction is $\hat{y}$ and the sensitive attribute (group identity) is given by s. One issue with this view is that different groups could have very different labels y (often called different base rates). Hardt et al. [21] address this by analyzing the accuracy and asserting that the model should not mistake $y = 0$ examples for $y = 1$ examples at a higher rate for one group than another, called equality of opportunity:

$$P(\hat{y} = 0|s = 0, y = 0) = P(\hat{y} = 0|s = 1, y = 0) \tag{2}$$

Empirically this means that we are comparing the false positive rate (FPR) for examples from each group, which makes sense if a false positives result in a high cost to the group. A symmetric statement can be made for the false negative rate, and putting these together is defined as equality of odds. A third popular group fairness metric has been calibration [12]:

$$E[y|s = 0, \hat{y} = p] = E[y|s = 1, \hat{y} = p] \quad \forall p \in [0, 1] \tag{3}$$

Significant work has analyzed these metrics and their gaps. A number of results have shown that achieving all of them (or even pairs of them) is only possible in limited cases [27, 34]. Other research has considered expanding them to more complex combinations of multiple sensitive attributes, which we refer to as intersectional testing [22, 25]. Another different line of work has explored using the language of causality to define fairness [26], but this has had limited traction [19] due to the difficulty of knowing the causal graph.

Modeling. With this wide variety of measures of fairness, another line of research has explored how to address algorithmic fairness issues in models. One line of work has built on adversarial training. This approach began for domain adaptation [2, 6, 18] and was quickly applied to fairness [17, 30, 37]. More recent work has modified this to align with different ML fairness metrics [4, 33, 38]. Others have focused on constrained optimization [1, 20], or using a variety of regularization techniques [3, 24, 36]. Our regularization approach draws from all of these bodies of work.

Other approaches have been advocated for such as using different thresholds for each group during binary classification [28], but this is not feasible without observing the sensitive attribute at inference. Another approach has been data augmentation [13], but it is often unclear how to do this in applications with more complex, arbitrary feature sets, e.g., loan default prediction over individuals or recommender systems where domain adaptation is difficult.

Application: Much of the published work on addressing fairness concerns focuses on public policy applications like recidivism prediction [9, 31], predictive policing [32], and child services [10]. These works explore some related practical difficulties, e.g., Chouldechova [9] discuss how metrics could be calculated after conditioning on other covariates like prior convictions. Recently, Holstein et al. [23] surveyed practitioners on the challenges to improving fairness in industry.

3 APPLICATION SETTING

We begin with an overview of our application, and the properties of it that are key to how we define and address any fairness concerns. We focus on a binary classification model that predicts if each example follows or breaks a pre-determined product policy. Examples that break the policy have an adverse action taken directly against them; examples that fall within policy have no action taken against them. This is similar to abuse classification literature [13], the common loan-default prediction problem [21], or recidivism prediction [9].

Because of the quantity of data, reviewers cannot rate all examples on the service. Rather, we use human raters to score a subsample of the examples. Human raters give a score $y \in [0, 1]$ and K raters score each example, producing an average ground truth score $y_i = \sum_k \frac{y_{i,k}}{K}$ for example i. We can choose which examples to get rated, but each rating is relatively expensive such that we can only have a small fraction of the data rated. This is particularly exacerbated by the fact that only a small percentage of the examples break policy and as such, random sampling of examples produces relatively little data with high y.

Because most of the examples are unrated, we use a model f to predict the ground truth score: $f(\mathbf{x}_i) = \hat{y}_i \approx y_i$ where $\mathbf{x} \in \mathbb{R}^d$ are features of the example. We take $\mathbf{x}$ to be a general feature vector; in practice, it contains a wide range of features including direct features as well as embedding and signals produced from other models and systems. The model is trained as a regression model with squared error: $\min_f \sum_i (f(\mathbf{x}_i) - y_i)^2$. At inference time, adverse action is taken against all examples with prediction over some threshold: $f(\mathbf{x}_i) = \hat{y}_i > \tau$.

For evaluating algorithmic fairness, we consider group fairness [21] over groups of examples or users. Each example is associated with a user, but features about the users are not reliably observed, i.e., we consider the case where users are not associated with demographic information. Rather, a small number of users are willing to share their demographics, which we can use during training and for offline evaluation of algorithmic fairness metrics. We refer to the group membership by feature s. Because most users do not share their demographic information, we cannot use those features as input to the model or in any way at inference time. Further, because the number of examples with demographic information is relatively small, a more expansive intersectional evaluation is not feasible [22, 25].

Assumptions. We take the product policy as ground truth. Further, we make the simplifying assumption that the human raters provide an unbiased estimate of the ground truth score. At the present, this is difficult to evaluate and further research is needed on how to detect and evaluate rater bias. We offer an expanded discussion of the assumptions and limitations of our analysis at the end of the paper.

3.1 Baseline Model

We consider now how our baseline model performs, in particular the FPR. This original model is a linear model over diverse feature set $\mathbf{x}$. We consider the FPR for two important sensitive groups, which we will refer to as Group 1 and Group 2. In each case, we compare the FPR to that of examples not from that respective user group, i.e., Not-Group 1 and Not-Group 2. Due to the sensitive nature of the measurements, we present all results in relativistic terms. For example, the FPR Ratio is defined as:

$$\text{FPR Ratio}_{\text{Group1}} = \frac{\text{FPR}_{\text{Group1}}}{\text{FPR}_{\text{Not-Group1}}} \tag{4}$$

We present these measurements of the original system in Figure 3a and 4a. As observed in the plots, we find that for both Group 1 and Group 2 the FPR Ratio > 1, with FPR $\text{Ratio}_{\text{Group1}} = 5.3\times$ and FPR $\text{Ratio}_{\text{Group2}} = 2.18\times$. Both of these numbers indicate a gap in the equality of opportunity and that examples from these groups are more frequently incorrectly having adverse action taken against them. Although hard to measure due to limited data, we generally observe lower FNR for subgroups than the majority, and because adverse actions are taken for predicted positives, we focus on the FPR in the rest of our analysis.

4 ML FAIRNESS METRIC

While equality of opportunity [21] provides insight into measuring cost to users of mistakes across groups, it leaves many open questions that in practice need to be addressed. In particular, how should the data that the metric is calculated over be sampled? What if the distribution of data differs? How do we address these differences?

4.1 Data Distribution

One immediate open question in the analysis and practical implementation is: *how should the data be sampled?* FPR and FNR are *only* meaningful with respect to a given distribution of evaluation data, and we find that different ways of generating that evaluation data give significantly different results. Further, as pointed out by Corbett-Davies et al. [11], examples from different groups may have different distributions of risk, and directly applying equality of opportunity over these different risks can raise its own issues.

The analysis above is based on a dataset built by sampling examples proportional to their usage, but ignore many other differences in the data. Unsurprisingly, different groups of users are associated with different types of examples, such as with different use cases or target audiences. For example, in Figures 2a and 2b we find that for one particular demographic property, the distribution of both use cases of the examples as well as the target audiences are quite different between the groups (considered over negative examples from each group).

While the data can be stratified by many of these dimensions, no principled way has been given for how or when to do so. Here, we take inspiration from Corbett-Davies et al. [11], which suggests the importance of addressing different risk distributions. However, Corbett-Davies et al. [11] analyze risk through the model's predictions rather than through some externally observable property. Here, we deviate in that we observe a real-valued policy y averaged over multiple human raters. As can be seen in Figure 2c, we find that even within examples that would be considered negatives ($y < \tau$), there is a notably different distribution between groups. In particular, the sensitive subgroup has relatively more examples close to the policy threshold τ, suggesting uncertainty by human raters about how the examples align with the policy.

4.2 Distribution-Dependent Metrics

Understanding and addressing these differences in distribution is critical to interpreting the results. Therefore, we begin with laying out a formalization for conditional group fairness metrics and then discuss the reasoning and implications of our choice of what to condition on.

First we build on the work of Ritov et al. [35] and define a conditional group fairness for our case:

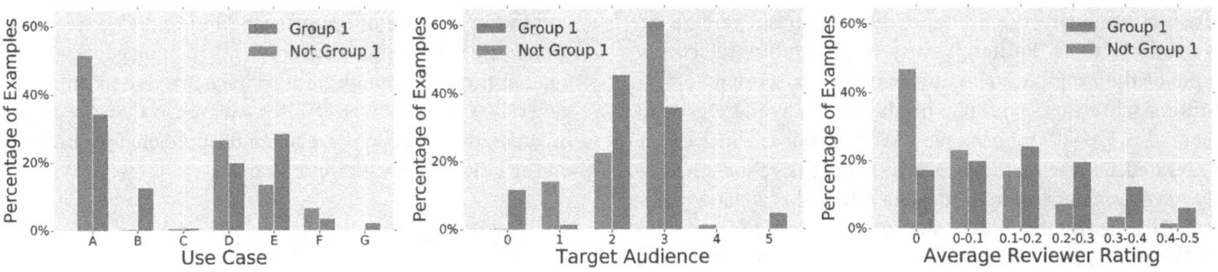

(a) Distribution of Use Cases **(b) Distribution of Audience** **(c) Distribution of Ratings y**

Figure 2: Different groups have different distribution of examples.

Definition 4.1. Conditional Equality of Opportunity is defined for conditioning on feature A that takes values $\mathcal{A}$:

$$\begin{aligned} P(\hat{y} \geq \tau | s = 1, y < \tau, A = a) \quad (5) \\ = P(\hat{y} \geq \tau | s = 0, y < \tau, A = a) \ \forall a \in \mathcal{A} \end{aligned}$$

This definition does not give a concrete metric and leaves the question of how to prioritize different $a \in \mathcal{A}$. We can make this precise by defining the conditional equality of opportunity gap:

Definition 4.2. Conditional equality of opportunity gap is defined conditioning over feature A taking values in $\mathcal{A}$, with each gap weighted by a probability p_a for $a \in \mathcal{A}$:

$$\begin{aligned} EOGap = \sum_a p_a[P(\hat{y} \geq \tau | s = 1, y < \tau, A = a) \quad (6) \\ - P(\hat{y} \geq \tau | s = 0, y < \tau, A = a)] \end{aligned}$$

By setting $p_a = \frac{1}{|\mathcal{A}|}$, this metric equally weights each possible value $a \in \mathcal{A}$. This is generally a good prior absent a strong reason to deviate. However, if one group has a skew in A then the uniform prior may not represent the experience for a user in that group. In this case, another option is to set $p_a = P(A = a | s = 0)$, which aligns with importance weighting the data from the background distribution to match the distribution of the focused subgroup[2].

Crucially, with this definition we still must choose a feature A on which to condition. Conditioning on a particular property, for example the example use case, would have the implication that error rates can be different across use cases, as long as they are the same across groups for the same use case; but if different groups prefer different use cases, then this metric would not necessarily support those group preferences. As discussed above, we believe the averaged human rating addresses a balance of desired properties for our metric. The averaged human rating does not prioritize different use cases, target audiences, etc., but rather we can interpret it as giving us a way of observing the inherent difficulty (or risk as in [11]) of an example. If humans are uncertain if an example meets a policy, it is understandable for the model to make a mistake as well. As we see in Figure 1, we observe that the FPR does increase with the averaged human rater score, and while we still observe a gap in FPR between the background data and the subgroup, it is partially explained by the difference in the distribution of examples.

[2]When reporting ratios, we compute the ratio of average FPRs to align with this view of data sampling.

Note, these proposals have significant connections to related work. Most related is [35], which first proposed this generalized fairness metric and included conditioning on arbitrary variables. The similarity function in individual fairness can be thought of as conditioning on different features, and that work grapples with many of these same issues [14]. Chouldechova [9] and Corbett-Davies et al. [11] both mention that metrics can be calculated condition on other variables, and for recidivism prediction they condition on the number of prior convictions, but neither give a general framework for when and how to condition. In examining fairness through a causal lens, [26] explores the question of what is a "resolving variable," but ultimately this is left as a philosophical choice. Further, our conditional equality metric can be viewed as a special case of the intersectional fairness analysis [22, 25], which conditions on any and all combination of covariates, but as we discussed, this requires a significant amount of data. Ultimately, all of these approaches leave the question of how to interpret conditioning on different terms.

We hope that by forcing the definition of the fairness metric to specify the conditioned variables, practitioners consider the distribution of their evaluation data, how it was sampled, and the implications. Unfortunately, this still does not diminish the importance of considering how the dataset is sampled or generated, and requires careful consideration by practitioners in determining this procedure.

5 CORRELATION LOSS

Although previous work has laid out multiple techniques for training models with fairness metrics as part of the objective, these approaches generally come with notable engineering concerns. Here, we present a lightweight approach for improving the desired fairness metrics.

One perspective on group fairness metrics is that the output distribution should match across groups [36], possibly after reweighting or resampling the data [4, 33]. Zhang et al. [38] focus on an adversary over predictions $\hat{y}$ rather than an intermediate layer. One way we could conceptualize this goal is to compare the distributions of $\hat{y}$ between groups and encourage low mutual information or KL divergence; Zafar et al. [36] use a simplification through the covariance. We build on these views by minimizing the absolute correlation between $\hat{y}$ and the group membership s:

$$\min_f \left[\sum_{(\mathbf{x}_i, y_i) \in \mathcal{X}} L(y_i, f(\mathbf{x}_i)) \right] + \lambda |\text{Corr}_{\mathcal{X}^-}| \tag{7}$$

where

$$Corr_{\mathcal{X}^-} = \frac{(\sum_{\mathbf{x}_i \in \mathcal{X}^-} f(\mathbf{x}_i) - \mu_{\hat{y}})(\sum_{s_i \in \mathcal{X}^-} s_i - \mu_s)}{\sigma_{\hat{y}} \sigma_s}$$

$$\mu_{\hat{y}} = \frac{1}{|\mathcal{X}^-|} \sum_{\mathbf{x}_i \in \mathcal{X}^-} f(\mathbf{x}_i) \qquad \mu_s = \frac{1}{|\mathcal{X}^-|} \sum_{s_i \in \mathcal{X}^-} s_i$$

$$\sigma_{\hat{y}}^2 = \frac{1}{|\mathcal{X}^-|} \sum_{\mathbf{x}_i \in \mathcal{X}^-} (f(\mathbf{x}_i) - \mu_{\hat{y}})^2 \qquad \sigma_s^2 = \frac{1}{|\mathcal{X}^-|} \sum_{s_i \in \mathcal{X}^-} (s_i - \mu_s)^2$$

Following [4, 33], we use $\mathcal{X}^- = \{x_i \in \mathcal{X} | y_i < \tau\}$ in order to optimize for equality of opportunity; this could be extended to other reweighting or resampling schemes to address other metrics as in [33]. In practice, we use $\tilde{\mathcal{X}}^- \subset \mathcal{X}^-$, which is a mini-batch of examples sampled from $\mathcal{X}^-$. This follows a similar pattern as previous adversarial approaches in adding a penalty based on the distribution of the output, but unlike all of the adversarial approaches, no training of an adversary is required, which we find to greatly improve stability in practice. While minimizing this term does not provably minimize the fairness metric, we find we get good results in practice, as we will show below.

6 IMPROVEMENTS IN PRACTICE

In practice, we seek to improve both the general equality of opportunity metric as well as the conditional equality metric. All results here build on the description of the application setting, metrics and methods above. In particular, we explore the incremental process by which we worked to improve this classifier, and how each change effects the end metrics. Results are summarized in Figures 3 and 4 for Group 1 and Group 2 respectively, but we will walk through each of the results below. Error bars are based on training the model 10 times and averaging results. We find there are a number of trade-offs and directions for future work.

Model Capacity. As discussed previously, the original model was a linear model, and we observe a significant gap in FPR between the sensitive subgroup and the rest of the data for both Group 1 and Group 2, as seen in Figures 3a and 4a. The first step we took was to change from a linear classifier to a DNN with a single hidden layer. Previous work [8] has suggested that theoretically model capacity can be a driver of disparities in accuracy. As can be seen in Figure 3b, the move to DNN decreases the FPR for Group 1, as well as decreasing the FPR gap from 2.62× to 1.44×. While this is good to see, this does not always hold true: we observe the FPR *increases* for Group 2 and Not-Group 2 users[3]; the FPR gap decreases from 1.76× to 1.25×. As such, while increasing model capacity may help in some cases, it does not necessarily improve accuracy everywhere.

[3]Note, Not-Group 1 and Not-Group 2 are different in that they are based on different methods for getting demographic data s.

Adversarial training. Building on the DNN model, we next considered how well adversarial training can improve the FPR gap. We follow an approach similar to Beutel et al. [4] of training an additional head taking as an input the last hidden layer of the model and trying to predict the sensitive attribute s while the model tries to learn a representation that is independent of s; we use only data for which $y < \tau$, as we are concerned with the FPR. As we see in Figure 3c, this significantly decreases the FPR gap from 1.44× to 1.04× and simultaneously decreases the FPR for Group 1, despite that not being an explicit objective.

Correlation Loss. As mentioned previously, adversarial training has been well studied and we see has strong performance, but from an engineering perspective is challenging due to its instability during training. As a result, we pursued absolute correlation regularization to stabilize training. We observe in Figure 3d that using absolute correlation regularization keeps the FPR gap approximately the same (1.05×). The practical benefits of keeping a low FPR gap while improving stability is highly valuable in practice.

Transfer across Groups. One idea that has been debated in the literature [33] is if and when there is transfer learning of fairness across groups. We consider here how the application of absolute correlation regularization to Group 1 effects the FPR gap for Group 2 users. In Figure 4c we observe a very slight improvement in the FPR gap, bringing it down from 1.37× to 1.31×.

Improving for Multiple Groups. Finally, we look at if we can simultaneously improve the FPR gap for both Group 1 and Group 2 users simultaneously. To do this, we add two different absolute correlation regularization terms to the DNN training, one for each group. As we see in Figure 4d, we are able to improve the FPR gap for Group 2 to 1.11×. Unfortunately, we do not find that this decreases the FPR for Group 2; we believe focusing on making the model more inclusive by improving the accuracy not just decreasing the gap is an important step for future work [5, 8].

7 FUTURE DIRECTIONS

We have focused on how to improve an individual model that directly effects the user experience, but by no means does every use of machine learning fit into these settings. To expand the applicability, we believe there are a number of areas that deserve more research attention.

Human raters: This work, like most of the algorithmic fairness literature, assumes that the labels are unbiased. We believe more attention is needed to understand if and when there is bias in crowdsourced ratings, and how to remove it.

Binary actions: We only consider the case where we are taking binary actions directly against the examples (at the known threshold). When the prediction is treated as a continuous score or used in conjunction with other signals, it becomes harder to evaluate the effect on the user experience [16] and further research is needed in this direction.

Observed Examples: We evaluate our system against the examples currently in the system. However, that distribution is of course affected by the system's previous performance. Use cases that were

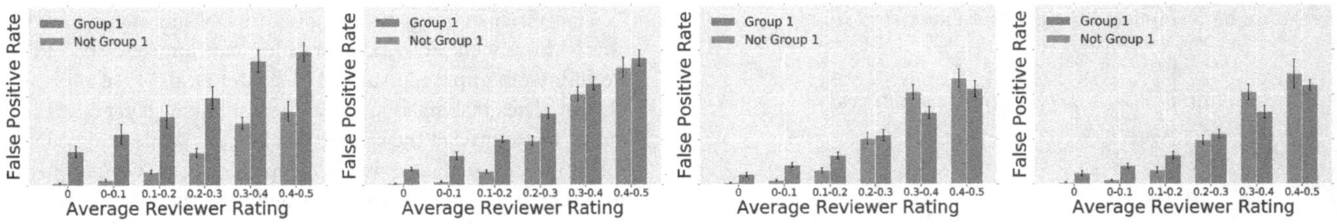

(a) Linear (b) DNN (c) DNN with Adversary (d) DNN with corr. reg.

Figure 3: Improvements for Group 1 users.

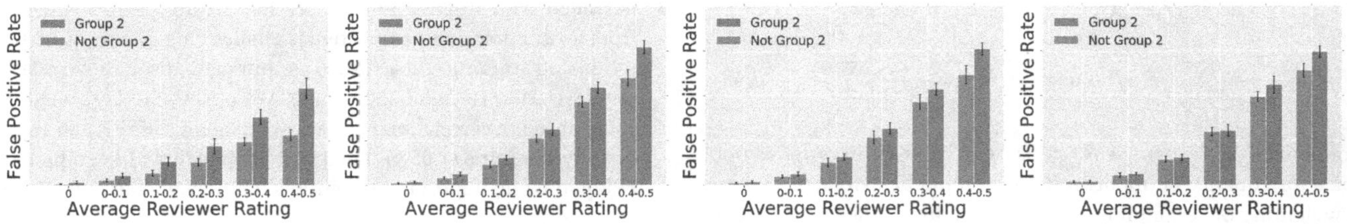

(a) Linear (b) DNN (c) DNN + Group 1 corr. reg. (d) DNN + Both corr. reg.

Figure 4: Improvements for Group 2 users.

previously not well supported may be underrepresented in our sample. Unfortunately, we do not know of a way to infer the distribution of examples that would exist under a different previous system. As a result, for the time being, we focus on evaluating and improving metrics for the current state, with the belief that it will improve the performance of the system for the sensitive subgroups and we can continue to evaluate the performance as the subgroup evolves. Further research, along the lines of [29], would be valuable to better understand the long term evolution of the system.

8 DISCUSSION

In this work we have offered details on how applying algorithmic fairness principles to a production classifier fares. In particular, we have explored how equality of opportunity depends on how the data is sampled, and how different groups can have notably different distributions of data. To address issues with these distributional differences, we offered a general evaluation approach that takes into account example difficulty. Further, we have offered a new mechanism, absolute correlation regularization, for improving algorithmic fairness metrics that we find to be more stable than adversarial training. We demonstrate the ability of these approaches to improve the FPR gap for two different groups in a production classifier and offer analysis of how the model performance is effected by these different training procedures.

Acknowledgements: We would like to thank Margaret Mitchell for her valuable feedback on this paper.

REFERENCES

[1] Alekh Agarwal, Alina Beygelzimer, Miroslav Dudík, John Langford, and Hanna M. Wallach. 2018. A Reductions Approach to Fair Classification. *CoRR* abs/1803.02453 (2018). arXiv:1803.02453 http://arxiv.org/abs/1803.02453

[2] Hana Ajakan, Pascal Germain, Hugo Larochelle, François Laviolette, and Mario Marchand. 2014. Domain-Adversarial Neural Networks. *CoRR* abs/1412.4446 (2014). arXiv:1412.4446 http://arxiv.org/abs/1412.4446

[3] Y Bechavod and K Ligett. 2017. Penalizing unfairness in binary classification. *arXiv preprint arXiv:1707.00044* (2017).

[4] Alex Beutel, Jilin Chen, Zhe Zhao, and Ed H. Chi. 2017. Data Decisions and Theoretical Implications when Adversarially Learning Fair Representations. *CoRR* abs/1707.00075 (2017). arXiv:1707.00075 http://arxiv.org/abs/1707.00075

[5] Alex Beutel, Ed H Chi, Zhiyuan Cheng, Hubert Pham, and John Anderson. 2017. Beyond Globally Optimal: Focused Learning for Improved Recommendations. In *Proceedings of the 26th International Conference on World Wide Web*. International World Wide Web Conferences Steering Committee, 203–212.

[6] Konstantinos Bousmalis, George Trigeorgis, Nathan Silberman, Dilip Krishnan, and Dumitru Erhan. 2016. Domain separation networks. In *Advances in Neural Information Processing Systems*. 343–351.

[7] Toon Calders and Sicco Verwer. 2010. Three naive Bayes approaches for discrimination-free classification. *Data Mining and Knowledge Discovery* 21, 2 (2010), 277–292.

[8] Irene Chen, Fredrik D Johansson, and David Sontag. 2018. Why Is My Classifier Discriminatory? *arXiv preprint arXiv:1805.12002* (2018).

[9] Alexandra Chouldechova. 2017. Fair prediction with disparate impact: A study of bias in recidivism prediction instruments. *Big data* 5, 2 (2017), 153–163.

[10] Alexandra Chouldechova, Diana Benavides-Prado, Oleksandr Fialko, and Rhema Vaithianathan. 2018. A case study of algorithm-assisted decision making in child maltreatment hotline screening decisions. In *Conference on Fairness, Accountability and Transparency*. 134–148.

[11] Sam Corbett-Davies, Emma Pierson, Avi Feller, Sharad Goel, and Aziz Huq. 2017. Algorithmic decision making and the cost of fairness. In *Proceedings of the 23rd ACM SIGKDD International Conference on Knowledge Discovery and Data Mining*. ACM, 797–806.

[12] Cynthia S Crowson, Elizabeth J Atkinson, and Terry M Therneau. 2016. Assessing calibration of prognostic risk scores. *Statistical methods in medical research* 25, 4 (2016), 1692–1706.

[13] Lucas Dixon, John Li, Jeffrey Sorensen, Nithum Thain, and Lucy Vasserman. 2017. Measuring and Mitigating Unintended Bias in Text Classification. (2017).

[14] Cynthia Dwork, Moritz Hardt, Toniann Pitassi, Omer Reingold, and Richard Zemel. 2012. Fairness through awareness. In *Proceedings of the 3rd innovations in theoretical computer science conference*. ACM, 214–226.

[15] Cynthia Dwork, Moritz Hardt, Toniann Pitassi, Omer Reingold, and Richard S. Zemel. 2012. Fairness through awareness. In *Innovations in Theoretical Computer Science 2012, Cambridge, MA, USA, January 8-10, 2012*. 214–226. https://doi.org/10.1145/2090236.2090255

[16] Cynthia Dwork and Christina Ilvento. 2018. Fairness Under Composition. *CoRR* abs/1806.06122 (2018). arXiv:1806.06122 http://arxiv.org/abs/1806.06122

[17] Harrison Edwards and Amos Storkey. 2015. Censoring representations with an adversary. *arXiv preprint arXiv:1511.05897* (2015).

[18] Yaroslav Ganin, Evgeniya Ustinova, Hana Ajakan, Pascal Germain, Hugo Larochelle, François Laviolette, Mario Marchand, and Victor Lempitsky. 2016. Domain-adversarial training of neural networks. *Journal of Machine Learning Research* 17, 59 (2016), 1–35.

[19] Sahaj Garg, Vincent Perot, Nicole Limtiaco, Ankur Taly, Ed H Chi, and Alex Beutel. 2018. Counterfactual Fairness in Text Classification through Robustness. *arXiv preprint arXiv:1809.10610* (2018).

[20] Gabriel Goh, Andrew Cotter, Maya R. Gupta, and Michael P. Friedlander. 2016. Satisfying Real-world Goals with Dataset Constraints. In *Advances in Neural Information Processing Systems*. 2415–2423. http://papers.nips.cc/paper/6316-satisfying-real-world-goals-with-dataset-constraints

[21] Moritz Hardt, Eric Price, Nati Srebro, et al. 2016. Equality of opportunity in supervised learning. In *Advances in Neural Information Processing Systems*. 3315–3323.

[22] Úrsula Hébert-Johnson, Michael P. Kim, Omer Reingold, and Guy N. Rothblum. 2017. Calibration for the (Computationally-Identifiable) Masses. *CoRR* abs/1711.08513 (2017). arXiv:1711.08513 http://arxiv.org/abs/1711.08513

[23] Kenneth Holstein, Jennifer Wortman Vaughan, Hal Daumé III, Miro Dudík, and Hanna Wallach. 2018. Improving fairness in machine learning systems: What do industry practitioners need? *arXiv preprint arXiv:1812.05239* (2018).

[24] Toshihiro Kamishima, Shotaro Akaho, and Jun Sakuma. 2011. Fairness-aware learning through regularization approach. In *Data Mining Workshops (ICDMW), 2011 IEEE 11th International Conference on*. IEEE, 643–650.

[25] Michael J. Kearns, Seth Neel, Aaron Roth, and Zhiwei Steven Wu. 2017. Preventing Fairness Gerrymandering: Auditing and Learning for Subgroup Fairness. *CoRR* abs/1711.05144 (2017). arXiv:1711.05144 http://arxiv.org/abs/1711.05144

[26] Niki Kilbertus, Mateo Rojas-Carulla, Giambattista Parascandolo, Moritz Hardt, Dominik Janzing, and Bernhard Schölkopf. 2017. Avoiding Discrimination through Causal Reasoning. In *Advances in Neural Information Processing Systems*. 656–666. http://papers.nips.cc/paper/6668-avoiding-discrimination-through-causal-reasoning

[27] Jon Kleinberg, Sendhil Mullainathan, and Manish Raghavan. 2016. Inherent trade-offs in the fair determination of risk scores. *arXiv preprint arXiv:1609.05807* (2016).

[28] Zachary C Lipton, Alexandra Chouldechova, and Julian McAuley. 2017. Does mitigating ML's disparate impact require disparate treatment? *arXiv preprint arXiv:1711.07076* (2017).

[29] Lydia T. Liu, Sarah Dean, Esther Rolf, Max Simchowitz, and Moritz Hardt. 2018. Delayed Impact of Fair Machine Learning. *CoRR* abs/1803.04383 (2018). arXiv:1803.04383 http://arxiv.org/abs/1803.04383

[30] Christos Louizos, Kevin Swersky, Yujia Li, Max Welling, and Richard Zemel. 2015. The variational fair autoencoder. *arXiv preprint arXiv:1511.00830* (2015).

[31] Kristian Lum. 2017. Limitations of mitigating judicial bias with machine learning. *Nature Human Behaviour* 1 (2017).

[32] Kristian Lum and William Isaac. 2016. To predict and serve? *Significance* 13, 5 (2016), 14–19.

[33] David Madras, Elliot Creager, Toniann Pitassi, and Richard S. Zemel. 2018. Learning Adversarially Fair and Transferable Representations. *CoRR* abs/1802.06309 (2018). arXiv:1802.06309 http://arxiv.org/abs/1802.06309

[34] Geoff Pleiss, Manish Raghavan, Felix Wu, Jon M. Kleinberg, and Kilian Q. Weinberger. 2017. On Fairness and Calibration. In *Advances in Neural Information Processing Systems*. 5684–5693. http://papers.nips.cc/paper/7151-on-fairness-and-calibration

[35] Ya'acov Ritov, Yuekai Sun, and Ruofei Zhao. 2017. On conditional parity as a notion of non-discrimination in machine learning. *arXiv preprint arXiv:1706.08519* (2017).

[36] Muhammad Bilal Zafar, Isabel Valera, Manuel Gomez Rodriguez, and Krishna P Gummadi. 2015. Fairness constraints: Mechanisms for fair classification. *arXiv preprint arXiv:1507.05259* (2015).

[37] Rich Zemel, Yu Wu, Kevin Swersky, Toni Pitassi, and Cynthia Dwork. 2013. Learning fair representations. In *Proceedings of the 30th International Conference on Machine Learning (ICML-13)*. 325–333.

[38] Brian Hu Zhang, Blake Lemoine, and Margaret Mitchell. 2018. Mitigating Unwanted Biases with Adversarial Learning. *CoRR* abs/1801.07593 (2018). arXiv:1801.07593 http://arxiv.org/abs/1801.07593

On Influencing Individual Behavior for Reducing Transportation Energy Expenditure in a Large Population

Shiwali Mohan
smohan@parc.com
PARC
Palo Alto, California

Frances Yan
fyan@parc.com
PARC
Palo Alto, California

Victoria Bellotti
bellotti@lyft.com
Lyft
San Francisco, California

Ahmed Elbery
ahmed_elbery@mena.vt.edu
VTTI
Blacksburg, Virginia

Hesham Rakha
hrakha@vtti.vt.edu
VTTI
Blacksburg, Virginia

Matthew Klenk
klenk@parc.com
PARC
Palo Alto, California

ABSTRACT

Our research aims at developing intelligent systems to reduce the transportation-related energy expenditure of a large city by influencing individual behavior. We introduce COPTER - an intelligent travel assistant that evaluates multi-modal travel alternatives to find a plan that is *acceptable* to a person given their context and preferences. We propose a formulation for *acceptable* planning that brings together ideas from AI, machine learning, and economics. This formulation has been incorporated in COPTER producing acceptable plans in real-time. We adopt a novel empirical evaluation framework that combines human decision data with high-fidelity simulation to demonstrate a 4% energy reduction and 20% delay reduction in a realistic deployment scenario in Los Angeles, California, USA.

CCS CONCEPTS

• **Computing methodologies → Planning for deterministic actions; Intelligent agents; • Human-centered computing →** *Empirical studies in collaborative and social computing.*

KEYWORDS

transportation planning, human-aware AI systems, choice theory, influence, behavior change, sustainability, energy, personalization, intelligent assistance, smart cities, urban computing, mobile app, commuting

ACM Reference Format:
Shiwali Mohan, Frances Yan, Victoria Bellotti, Ahmed Elbery, Hesham Rakha, and Matthew Klenk. 2019. On Influencing Individual Behavior for Reducing Transportation Energy Expenditure in a Large Population. In *2019 AAAI/ACM Conference on AI, Ethics, and Society (AIES'19), January 27–28, 2019, Honolulu, HI, USA.* ACM, New York, NY, USA, 7 pages. https://doi.org/10.1145/3306618.3314271

AIES '19, January 27–28, 2019, Honolulu, HI, USA

ACM ISBN 978-1-4503-6324-2/19/01...$15.00
https://doi.org/10.1145/3306618.3314271

1 INTRODUCTION

Transportation is one of the largest consumers of energy in the world - in the United States, it accounted for 29% of energy consumption in 2016[1]. Despite occupying a central place in the economy, transportation is far from efficient. Many areas of urban transportation networks are underutilized while other areas are congested. Congestion alone in the United States wastes 6.9 billion hours and 3.1 billion gallons of fuel per year [17]. Thus, transportation has become an important policy & innovation problem. Recently, public and private entities have begun introducing new transportation services including bike/scooter share, car share, ride hailing, and carpooling to complement private vehicles and existing public transit. This increasing accessibility of novel modes and the corresponding need for planning solutions creates an opportunity for *mobility marketplaces* that aggregate a variety of offerings into a single market, similar to what Travelocity or Expedia does for air travel. Such mobility marketplaces have the potential to influence people to adopt sustainable modes at a large scale.

Our long-term research goal is to develop AI methods to support efficient transportation reducing overall energy consumption and increasing citizen satisfaction in metropolitan areas. There are two important components to this problem of changing the behavior of a large population toward this *social good* goal. The first - the *multi-modal route planning* problem - addresses how to reason about the large decision space of a variety of modes that are accessible to a person to determine an energy-efficient trip. The second component - the *influence* problem - is guiding an individual's behavior to actually adopt trips that reduce the overall energy expenditure of a region. While the multi-modal route planning problem has been studied in detail by the AI community [2], the influence problem is largely unexplored.

Our approach to the influence problem is embedded within an intelligent *travel assistant* - Collaborative Optimization and Planning for Transportation Energy Reduction (COPTER). We illustrate COPTER's desired behavior with the following example. Assume that John makes a regular trip driving to his office every weekday morning and has COPTER installed on his smartphone. In a *timely* fashion, 15 minutes before he has to leave, COPTER suggests an alternative trip - walk to the bus stop and take the direct bus to office - chosen from all available alternatives. This trip is not only energy-efficient, but also *acceptable* to John given the context of his travel. COPTER makes this suggestion by considering that the route is direct, that a lot of people in his neighborhood take the bus, and that

[1] www.eia.gov

he is traveling to his workplace and therefore, will not be carrying heavy loads. Further, Copter recognizes that he cares about his impact on the environment and frames this information in a *compelling* way by telling him how much emissions he can reduce by taking this trip. There are several aspects to influencing someone to change their behavior. In this example, reasoning about acceptability of a trip recommendation, when should it be communicated, and how it should be expressed is useful for influencing John.

In this paper, we study a specific aspect of the influence problem - how a person's context and preferences can be integrated into the planning framework to produce an *acceptable* recommendation and how this acceptability impacts a person's adoption of the recommendation. To do this, we bring together ideas from AI planning, machine learning, as well as economic choice theory. More specifically, our paper makes the following contributions:

(1) Introduces the transportation influence problem,
(2) Proposes and implements a novel integration of AI planning theory and economic choice theory,
(3) Defines a machine learning model to capture the acceptability of recommended plans, and
(4) Studies the potential impact on Los Angeles by combining human decision data with high-fidelity transportation simulation.

2 THE SETUP

To understand the novelty of our approach, we first review the two strands of research we build upon, and later, we describe their limitations for the influence problem.

2.1 Multi-Modal Route Planning

Routing in transportation networks is a well studied problem dating back to Dijkstra's algorithm [8]. Today, through pre-computation and heuristics, planners identify optimal routes for continent-size networks in milliseconds [2]. These approaches use the standard transportation network representation as a directed graph $G = (V, E)$, where V is a set of nodes and $E \subseteq V \times V$ is a set of directed edges. The formalism also includes a standard representation of time, T. A request for transporting a person from their origin location $v \in V$ starting at a certain time $t_s \in T$ to their destination $w \in V$ before a certain deadline $t_e \in T$ is formalized as $r = (v, w, t_s, t_e)$. The planning problem is formalized as (G, r). Traversal of each edge is represented as a pair (e, t) where a person begin moving along the edge e at time t. A plan $\pi = ((e_1, t_1), ..., (e_n, t_n))$ is a valid solution of the problem (G, r) if and only if:

(1) the edges connect the origin with the destination. $e_1 = (v_0, v_1)$, ..., $e_n = (v_{n-1}, v_n) \wedge (v_0 = v) \wedge (v_n = w)$,
(2) temporal constraints are satisfied, $t_s \leq t_1 + dur(e_1) \leq t_2 + dur(e_2) \leq ... \leq t_n + dur(e_n) \leq t_e$ where $dur(e)$ represents the time it takes to traverse the edge e.

To find an optimal plan, cost function $cost(e)$ is defined for every edge in G. An optimal plan is a plan that minimizes the cumulative cost $\pi^* =_{\pi \in \Pi} \sum_{e \in \pi} cost(e_i)$. In the simple case, the cost is the time it takes to traverse the edge, $cost(e_i) = dur(e_i)$. A^* search with a reasonable heuristic (e.g., euclidean distance) efficiently solves these problems.

Recent work provides extensions for multi-modal trips [7] and more elaborate cost functions. This is achieved by adding additional edges between vertices corresponding to the various modes (e.g., public transit, biking, walking) that are available to traverse them. When the edges represent public transit vehicles, they have temporal constraints representing the vehicle schedules. Each edge e is labeled with the mode it represents, e.g., $lbl(e) = b$ for an edge representing taking the bus. Consequently, each plan π corresponds to a label sequence, *word* (w_p). This supports an additional requirement on valid solutions that the word is part of the language of acceptable mode sequences ($w_p \in L$), represented using regular expressions. This constraint eliminates plans that are impossible, such as taking a bus and then getting on a bike. Others [4] have shown that in this formulation, the cost function can consider additional dimensions: price, energy, and schedule risk. The cost function is formalized as $cost(\pi) = \sum_{e \in \pi} \sum_{\varphi \in \Phi} \theta_\varphi \varphi(e)$ where Φ is the set of evaluative functions including energy consumed, price, etc. and θ_φ corresponds to how much importance that evaluative function has toward computing the overall edge cost.

2.2 Utility-Based, Probabilistic Choice Theory

Economists use the framework of rational choice theory [20] to study how humans make choices from a set of competing alternatives. Empirical research in transportation economics [9] has shown that such frameworks are useful in predicting transportation mode shares in urban populations. The theory posits a choice process: for a trip, the individual first determines the available mode alternatives; next, evaluates the attributes of each alternative relevant to the travel decision, and then, uses a decision rule to select an alternative. Rational decision making perspective motivates *utility maximization* as a relevant decision rule. Utility maximization is based on two fundamental concepts. First, the attributes of a mode alternative can be reduced to a scalar utility value.

Second, the decision maker selects the alternative with the highest utility value. The deterministic theory assumes all aspects of the decision process can be observed and measured. Transportation decision-making is only partially-observable. By adding noise, the utility of an alternative for an individual can be split into two components - observable utility and error:

$$util(x_i, f_p) = val(x_i, f_p) + \epsilon(x_i, f_p)$$

Here $val(x_i, f_p)$ is the observable portion of the utility. This quantity is modeled as a linear combination of measurable attributes such as travel time, travel cost, walk distance, etc:

$$\begin{aligned} val(x_i, p) = \gamma_1 \times x_{i1} + \gamma_2 \times x_{i2} + ... + \gamma_k \times x_{ik} + \\ \lambda_1 \times f_{p1} + \lambda_2 \times f_{p2} + ... + \lambda_l \times f_{pl} \end{aligned} \tag{1}$$

γ_k is the parameter which defines the direction and importance of attribute k on the utility of an alternative i. Similarly, λ_l defines the direction and importance of the person's characteristic l .

$\epsilon(x_i, f_p)$ is the unobservable portion - the error term - of the utility function. This theory assumes that the error terms of various alternatives are independent. These assumptions about the error term lead to a *multinomial logit model* that estimates the probability $Pr(i, p)$ of the person p selecting the alternative i from the set of alternatives C:

$$Pr(i, p) = \frac{e^{val(x_i, f_p)}}{\sum_{j \in C} e^{val(x_j, f_p)}} \tag{2}$$

Empirical research in transportation [3] has studied how γ and λ parameters in equation 1 can be estimated from human choice data using maximum likelihood estimation given equation 2.

3 *ACCEPTABLE* PLANNING

There are two main challenges that have to be addressed in order to determine trip recommendations that are *acceptable* - useful in influencing behavior. The first one is that none of the theories described in the previous section explicitly provide a definition of *acceptability*. Planning computes the optimal path for an individual given a cost function defined for every edge while the choice theory predicts the probability of a trip occurring given some observable characteristics about the person and the mode of transport. In COPTER, each traveler has an expected plan for an upcoming trip, and our goal is to produce an *acceptable* alternative that changes their behavior to reduce energy consumption across the network. The second is an integration issue. For efficient search, the planning theory requires the costs to be defined locally at each edge. The choice theory and empirical evidence from transportation research on the other hand suggests that there are aspects of a person's trip context that influence mode choice but cannot be defined over edges in a graph. These include the household income, number of vehicles at home, etc. In the sections below, we propose how these challenges can be addressed for *acceptable* planning.

3.1 Defining Acceptability

We adapt choice theory's decision process to incorporate *acceptability* as follows. John (from the example in the Introduction) drives to his office every weekday on a certain route. The choice theory suggests that this usual route has a measurable utility, $val(x_u, f_p))$ and a probability of being selected based on equation 2. Here x_u is the vector of attributes representing John's usual mode such as time, distance, etc. and f_p is a vector that describes John's attributes that pertain to mode selection such as income, education level etc. Upon receiving the recommendation, r, from COPTER, John evaluates it against his usual means of travel. The recommendation r has a measurable utility, $val(x_r, f_p)$, given the utility function underlying John's preferences. On adopting the recommendation, John will experience a *switching cost* - $\Delta_{u,r}$ - the difference in utilities of his usual route and the proposed route. Conversely, $\Delta_{r,u} = -\Delta_{u,r}$, can be understood as the *switching gain* a person makes on adopting the recommendation r.

Following probabilistic choice theory (equation 2):

$$\frac{e^{val(x_u, f_p)}}{e^{val(x_r, f_p)}} = \frac{Pr(u,p)}{Pr(r,p)}$$
$$\Delta_{u,r} = val(x_u, f_p) - val(x_r, f_p) = \ln\frac{Pr(u,p)}{Pr(r,p)} \tag{3}$$
$$\Delta_{r,u} = -\Delta_{u,r} = \ln\frac{Pr(r,p)}{Pr(u,p)}$$

We postulate that the acceptability of a route is related to its switching gain. If we can estimate the likelihood of a person taking their usual mode of travel and that of the recommended mode, we can compute the change in utility and consequently estimate the recommendation's acceptability. This formulation is a significant departure from prior empirical work in transportation research. The prior work focuses on estimating the coefficients in equation 1 to compute exact utility values given measurements of relevant, observable attributes. For planning, this exact computation of utility value is not necessary and the switching gain (and acceptability) can be computed from estimated likelihoods alone.

Mode	Baseline 1	Baseline 2	RF	MLP
Walk	0.00	0.12	0.82*	0.62
Cycle	0.00	0.00	0.81*	0.28
Bus	0.00	0.02	0.78*	0.38
Subway/train	0.00	0.00	0.58*	0.05
Drive	0.72	0.56	0.93*	0.86
Ride	0.00	0.28	0.84*	0.65
Motorcycle	0.00	0.00	0.80*	0.00
Total	0.68	0.40	0.88*	0.74
Category				
Non-motorized	0.00	0.05	0.83*	0.60
Public transit	0.00	0.14	0.79*	0.43
Motorized	0.90	0.82	0.97*	0.93
Total	0.68	0.70	0.94*	0.86

Table 1: F1-scores for predicting mode classes and categories with various ML methods. Baseline 1 is most frequent, Baseline 2 is weighted random, RF is random forest classifier, and MLP is multi-layer perceptron

3.2 Estimating Switching Gain

As explained earlier, in order to estimate the acceptability of a recommendation r for a person p, it is crucial to estimate the likelihood $Pr(r,p)$ of it being selected as well as for that person's usual mode, $Pr(u,p)$. We adopt a data-driven ML approach to estimate these likelihoods. A classifier generates a prediction of a class, given a set of input features, by computing likelihoods for each class and selecting the class with the highest likelihood.

To develop our ML classifiers, we used the California Household Travel Survey (CHTS) that consists of a single-day (distributed in a year) travel diary of people from 58 counties of California and 3 counties of Nevada. To ground our research within the context of a specific metropolitan area, we extracted trip data for 4,889 Los Angeles (LA) residents (from 2,006 households). Our trip dataset contains 78,380 trips undertaken in LA county. For each trip, the data consists of the main mode of transport as well as other demographic and context information.

3.2.1 Features and Classes. Our trips dataset includes trips that were undertaken using 7 different modes including - walk, cycle, bus, subway/train, drive, ride, motorcycle. For each trip, we also extracted these features:

- *trip-related*: trip distance,
- *demographics*: such as education level, number of people, students, or workers in the household,
- *employment*: number of hours worked every week, income, number of jobs, flexibility of work,
- *mode accessibility*: number of automobiles in the household, number of bicycles in the household, owns a driver's license & transit pass, and
- *mode experience*: transit used, bike trips made & walking trips made in the past week.

These features map to x and f_p in the choice theory formulation.

3.2.2 ML Models & Results. We explored two different multi-class prediction problems: predicting the mode and predicting the category of the mode where we categorized walking & cycle as *non-motorized*, driving, riding &, motorcycle as *motorized*, and bus &

subway as *public transit.* For each problem, we use two different classifiers: a random forest with 20 estimators of 30 depth each; and a multi-layer perceptron with 4 layers ([1000, 500, 100, 100]). We found these parameters through a bucketed linear hyper-parameter search. Performance was compared with two baselines: assigning the most frequent label to each sample (*most frequent*); and distributing the labels by their dataset frequency (*weighted random*).

$F1$ scores for both classifiers as well as baselines on a 20% test set are shown in Table 1. We see that both classifiers perform significantly better than the baselines for not only predicting each class (& category) but have a better overall performance as well. This suggests that the ML classifiers contain useful predictive information that can be used to estimate the switching gains as well as acceptability of a recommendation. The random forest classifier has better performance than the multi-layer perceptron. This is expected due to the limited size of the dataset. We further see that the performance on category prediction is better than mode prediction. Again, this is expected as combining mode classes leads to more data to learn from and consequently better performance.

3.2.3 Switching Gain. By using the ML model described here to estimate likelihoods of various modes, we can compute the switching gain to any mode from a specific mode a person usually takes. The ML models use a diverse types of information including demographics, trip features, and mode experience with modes to estimate likelihoods and consequently, switching gain is personalized to an individual's context. Intuitively, switching gain captures the idea that it is easier to switch to modes that are used by people who are similar to you and make similar trips.

3.3 Evaluating Acceptability

To assess the impact on switching gain (acceptability) on likelihood of recommendation adoption, we conducted a mode adoption study with 49 (27 female, 22 male) participants who were regular drivers in Los Angeles. The participants were gathered by a paid recruiter who ensured compliance. The participants were provided $30 for completing the study.

3.3.1 Materials. Each study participant took two surveys:

(1) A *profiler* survey included questions for features used in our classifier. For each participant, the survey collected a set of trips they regularly made by driving in terms of the origin, destination, departure time, and purpose.
(2) A *mode adoption* survey presented each participant 10 influence questions. Each question proposed an alternative mode route for one of their typical driving trips. Care was taken to not include implausible alternatives e.g. walking for 10 miles. Each question included information about mode characteristics such as the time of departure and a visual representation of the proposed route (shown in Figure 1). The participants indicated likelihood of adopting the recommendation using a 7-point Likert scale (*extremely unlikely* (1) to *extremely likely* (7)).

Stated preference methods are often used to measure the acceptability of new products and provide realistic estimates of population behavior [14].

3.3.2 Models. The study measures mode adoption as an ordinal variable on the Likert scale. To simulate real-world behavior where someone will either follow the recommendation or not, we compressed the ordinal response by categorizing everything reported

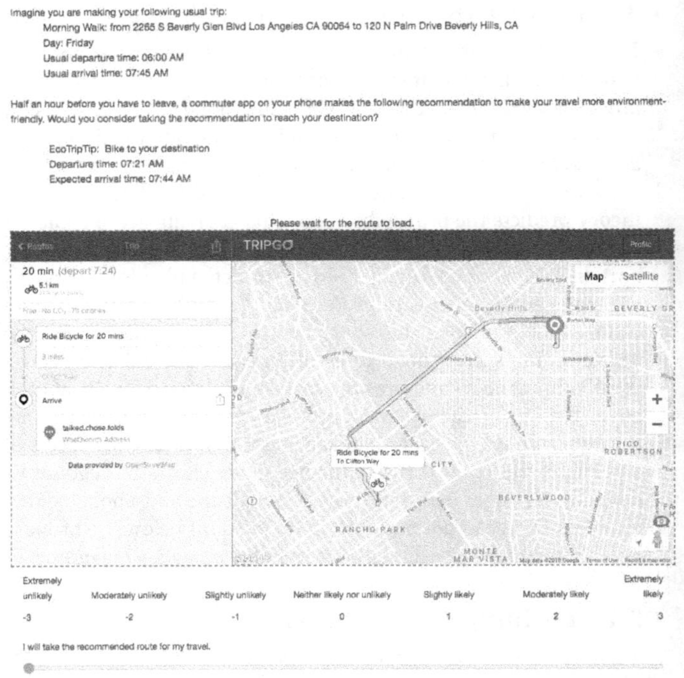

Figure 1: An example of the mode adoption question in the survey along with the response measurement instrument.

as *slightly likely* or higher as 1 and others at 0. We assess the impact of switching gain on adoption using the following regressions:

(1) For the ordinal variable, we fit a mixed-effects linear regression of the form $y = \alpha + \beta x + \gamma z + \epsilon$, where y is the adoption vector, x is a fixed-effect vector corresponding to an independent variable of interest, and z is a random effect vector corresponding to a participant. α is the intercept and β and γ are coefficients and ϵ is the error term.
(2) For the binary adoption variable, we fit a mixed-effects logistic regression of the form $Pr(y) = 1/(1 + e^{-(\alpha+\beta x+\gamma z+\epsilon)})$, where $Pr(y)$ is the probability of observing the specific adoption value (0/1), other coefficients are similar to those in the previous model.

Participants were included as random effects in these model to account for individual differences in interpretation of the scale. For independent variables (x, in the models above), we explored three definitions of acceptability:

(1) switching gain, $\Delta_{r,u}$
(2) odds, $e^{\Delta_{r,u}} = Pr(r,p)/Pr(u,p)$
(3) probability, $Pr(r,p)$

where r is the recommended mode, u is the usual mode for person p and $Pr()$ is the likelihood from our ML models.

3.3.3 Results. Overall, the results show that people reported a willingness to change their travel behavior. Detailed results are shown in Table 2. For each independent variable, we report R^2c, the proportion of the data that is explained by the complete model, and R^2m, the proportion is explained by the variable. We see that all definitions of acceptability significantly impact the adoption of recommendation. The coefficients align with the intuition about the domain - as the cost of adopting the recommendation decreases (switching gain increases), adoption increases. We see that R^2c,

R^2m are higher for odds. These results suggest that it is the best predictor mode adoption because it explains the most data. It is noteworthy that odds and probability have similar impact on adoption. This is likely due to our participants being regular drivers with $Pr(u,p) \approx 1$. With a diverse population in a larger deployment, the differences between the definitions can be teased apart.

Dependent variables→ Independent variables↓	Adoption (ordinal)	Adoption (binary)
(intercept)	-0.017	-0.185
switching gain, $\Delta_{r,u}$	0.108*	0.104*
R^2m	0.034	0.035
R^2c	0.347	0.270
(intercept)	-0.949	-1.065
odds, $e^{\Delta_{r,u}}$	2.386***	2.159*
R^2m	0.075	0.064
R^2c	0.379	0.300
(intercept)	-0.964	-1.080
probability, $Pr(r,p)$	3.623***	3.317*
R^2m	0.066	0.058
R^2c	0.369	0.293

Table 2: Regression modeling results for ordinal and binary mode adoption. *** $p < 0.001$, ** $p < 0.05$, * $p < 0.1$

3.4 Estimating Likelihood of Adoption

To identify the recommendation that reduces the most expected energy, it is necessary to estimate the likelihood of adoption. Recall that our motivating example suggests that a recommendation should be *timely*, *acceptable*, and *compelling* to motivate behavior change. At this point, we have only evaluated acceptability. Therefore, COPTER uses the logit model of the odds to estimate the probability of a person adopting a recommended route.

4 FINDING ENERGY-EFFICIENT ACCEPTABLE PLANS

Figure 2 provides an overview of COPTER's operation. In a deployment, we expect to maintain a series of future trips for each user. Before an expected departure, COPTER computes an energy efficient *acceptable* alternative and sends it to the user 15 minutes before they would have to leave for the new trip. To compute this plan, we augment the multi-modal planning formulation with our acceptability model:

(1) Generate a mode candidate set M_p for the person p for whom the request is made for. M_p can be generated by acquiring information about if they can walk and if they have a bike. For example, someone who doesn't own a bike but can walk $M = \{walk(w), bus(b), subway(s)\}$.
(2) Given M_p, determine the language L_p. Recall that a language is a set of regular expressions that denote valid multi-modal plans for this traveler. For the example above, $L_p = \{w*, w * b + w*, w * s + w*\}$, where w is *walking*, b is *bus*, and s is *subway* or *train*. Note that while this is a fairly simplistic set, the formulation can be extended to include more complex plans.
(3) For every element in L_p, generate the most time-efficient plan (using the multi-modal formulation) where $cost(e) = dur(e, m)$ where m is the mode used to traverse the edge. This process will generate a candidate set of plans, Π_p.
(4) Compute the energy reduction in each plan $\pi \in \Pi_p$ using existing mesoscopic energy models [11].
(5) Evaluate the likelihood of adoption, $adopt(\pi,p)$, for every $\pi \in \Pi$ using the logit model of adoption.
(6) Select a plan that has maximal expected energy savings, $\pi^* =_{\pi \in \Pi} adopt(\pi,p) \times energy(\pi)$.

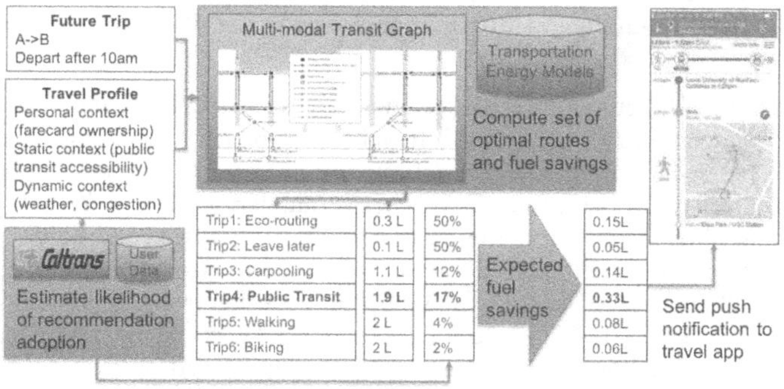

Figure 2: COPTER identifies the recommendation with the largest expected reduction in energy consumption by acceptable planning and energy modeling.

5 SIMULATION EXPERIMENTS

While deploying COPTER in a large city to measure the impact is the ideal evaluation, it is extremely resource intensive to conduct. Without being incorporated into a widely used product, it would not be possible to iteratively evaluate different components. Therefore, we evaluate the potential impacts of COPTER using a high-fidelity simulation LA. In our deployment scenario, we assume that 10% of peak period drivers use an app (e.g., Waze, TripGo) through which we can offer alternative suggestions.[2] Our study area includes diverse offerings with over 170,000 roadway links and over 1 million daily transit trips. During the AM period (7am-10am) and PM period (4pm-7pm), this area includes 1.2 million and 1.7 vehicle trips respectively. As the effects of congestion continue past the peak period, our study considers an AM period (7am-12pm) and a PM period (4pm-9pm).

5.1 Simulation Model

To measure the potential impact of influencing behavior, we combined the results of the human study with a state-of-the-art simulation model of the LA region [11]. The simulation model supports city-level networks with different modes of transportation including cars, buses, railways, walking, biking, and carpooling. It utilizes both microscopic and mesoscopic simulation to leverage their respective strengths of accuracy and scalability. The simulation spatially partitions the road network enabling distinct portions of the region to be simulated in parallel. Additional parallel simulations capture loosely interacting modes (e.g., the rail and road network). This enables micro-simulation (i.e., considering driver behavior w.r.t. throttle position, braking, and lane choice every $0.1s$) of the arterial and highway roads encoded as 10,650 links. Dynamic calibration aligns previous government planning documents with observed vehicle flows to capture the changing rates of vehicles entering the different networks throughout the day [10]. The model includes validated driver behavior [16] and fuel models

[2] This percentage was selected through negotiations with business groups and public sector stakeholders

	Baseline	Influence	Change (CI)
Total Fuel (l)	3,195,637	3,048,278	-4.6% (-3.6% -5.6%)
Total Delay (hr)	249,221	199,395	-20% (-13.6% -26.4%)

	Baseline	Influence	Change (CI)
Total Fuel (l)	3,487,982	3,367,675	-3.5% (-2.6% -4.3%)
Total Delay (hr)	375,137	322,228	-14.1 (-10% -18%)

Table 3: Results of departures: (left) 7:00 - 12:00 (right) 16:00 - 21:00. The mean for each condition is reported along with the percent change in the Influence condition. We also report a 95% confidence interval for the difference in mean.

[12]. Therefore, the model provides accurate individual and aggregate predictions in terms of travel time and energy consumption.

Given our deployment assumption, we sample 10% out of the peak traffic periods to be influenced (7am-10am and 4pm-7pm) for our influenced population. Our experiment has two conditions:

(1) Baseline: Influenced traveler drives their original route
(2) Influence: Using the likelihood of adoption from the previous section, the influenced traveler either takes the maximum expected energy reduction route as determined by COPTER or drives their original route.

To account for the uncertainty in alternative adoption and background traffic rates, we ran each condition four to seven times. The simulation model runs in just over real time and therefore, a running a larger number of trials is prohibitive. $5 - 10$ trials is standard practice for similar transportation studies. We report 95% confidence intervals for difference of means between the Baseline and Influence trials for total fuel consumption and congestion related delay. We also report the resulting changes in mode of the influenced travelers.

5.1.1 Results. Table 3 contain the results for AM and PM periods. These results indicate a potential 4.6% energy reduction during the AM period and 3.5% energy reduction in the PM period. Congestion-induced delay results were even greater at 20% and 14%, respectively. This is significant considering the influenced population represents about 6% of the total traffic over the period. To identify an upper bound, we ran simulations in which every influenced traveler walked. In these simulations, we observed a reduction in energy consumption of 9% and a reduction in delay of 30% across the AM and PM periods. Table 4 indicates that almost half the influenced population is willing to take alternative modes. These mode switches are based on mode adoption study and maybe optimistic. Future work will refine these estimates through a deployment and measuring people's behavior.

Mode	AM Share	PM Share
Car	54%	53%
Walk	42.7%	42.8%
Bike	3.6%	3.8%
Bus	38.9%	39.1%
Train	14.4%	14%

Table 4: Share of influenced population that used mode on trip. Sum is over 100% due to trips using multiple modes.

6 RELATED WORK

The majority of transportation policy either focuses on systemic changes that are applied evenly to the entire population such as congestion pricing/dynamic tolling [5] or studies long term behavior change in individuals to encourage sustainable commuting [6]. Recently, there has been a shift toward personalizing the interventions to increase the use of sustainable modes. IncenTrip [19] allocates incentives from government sponsored programs such that each dollar spent provides the largest environmental impact. TriPod [1] takes a different approach in which companies give travelers points for alternative transportation choices to be redeemed at local businesses. While these systems primarily rely on monetary incentives to affect travel behavior, Metropia [21] has shown that congestion information alone can influence traveler departure time. Our work differs from the above by identifying a personalized recommendation from alternatives based on network conditions without any monetary incentives.

In addition to algorithmic work in route planning, the AI community also works on transportation prediction problems. Using position traces and other data, systems predict the mode and destination of travelers [15, 18]. These works address prediction problems in isolation, and, as noted by AI and Society researchers [13], it is how AI approaches integrated in smart cities applications that determine if social positive outcomes are realized. By working across disciplines, we study how energy consumption can be reduced through voluntary behavior changes. With respect to the transportation influence problem, COPTER could incorporate these isolated approaches to predicting future trips and monitor if travelers follows the recommendation.

7 DISCUSSION AND CONCLUSION

This paper presents COPTER, an intelligent travel assistant that is designed to influence individual travel behavior to reduce the total energy consumption of a large city. To do this, we propose an integrative framework that is a novel combination of multi-modal trip planning, transportation choice modeling, and machine learning. We introduce the notion of acceptability of a recommended alternative and define it in terms of the change in utility. We show how this change can estimated using ML models trained on the CHTS dataset. We identify a useful definition of acceptability through a human mode choice study. Finally, in a simulation experiment over the Los Angeles area we show that if 10% peak travelers were receiving influence messages, estimated energy consumption would be reduced by 4.6% in the AM period and 3.5% in the PM period with corresponding reductions in congestion induced delay of 20% and 14%, respectively.

Future work will consider additional alternatives. Eco-routing feedback control selects driving routes based on real-time link estimates of fuel consumption [11]. Additionally, we would also like to explore techniques for departure time optimization as well as including carpooling in the set of alternatives. From a social good perspective, COPTER is ready for deployment with influenced messages sent through the TripGo application. The next step is to evaluate the influence model by measuring actual traveler behavior and then feeding those results back into our simulation study. Later work will define and assess the impacts of timeliness of recommendation and compelling messaging. Urban transportation is a huge problem for the environment and citizen's quality of life. COPTER demonstrates how AI techniques can be adapted and combined with research from other disciplines to alleviate congestion and improve the environment through transportation influence.

8 ACKNOWLEDGEMENTS

This work was funded in part by the Advanced Research Projects Agency-Energy (ARPA-E), U.S. Department of Energy, under Award Number DE-AR0000612. The authors would like to thank the City of Los Angeles and CalTrans for providing data necessary for the modeling efforts.

REFERENCES

[1] Carlos Lima Azevedo, Ravi Seshadri, Song Gao, Bilge Atasoy, Arun Prakash Akkinepally, Eleni Christofa, Fang Zhao, Jessika Trancik, and Moshe Ben-Akiva. 2018. Tripod: Sustainable Travel Incentives with Prediction, Optimization, and Personalization. In *the 97th Annual Meeting of Transportation Research Board.*

[2] Hannah Bast, Daniel Delling, Andrew Goldberg, Matthias Müller-Hannemann, Thomas Pajor, Peter Sanders, Dorothea Wagner, and Renato F Werneck. 2016. Route Planning in Transportation Networks. In *Algorithm Engineering*. Springer International Publishing, 19–80.

[3] Moshe E Ben-Akiva, Steven R Lerman, and Steven R Lerman. 1985. *Discrete Choice Analysis: Theory and Application to Travel Demand.* Vol. 9. MIT press.

[4] Adi Botea. 2016. Hedging the Risk of Delays in Multimodal Journey Planning. *AI Magazine* 37, 4 (2016).

[5] David Brownstone, Arindam Ghosh, Thomas F Golob, Camilla Kazimi, and Dirk Van Amelsfort. 2003. Drivers' Willingness-to-pay to Reduce Travel Time: Evidence from the San Diego I-15 Congestion Pricing Project. *Transportation Research Part A: Policy and Practice* 37, 4 (2003), 373–387.

[6] Stefania Castellani, Tommaso Colombino, Antonietta Grasso, and Matthieu Mazzega. 2016. Understanding Commuting to Accompany Work Organisations' and Employees' Behaviour Change. In *Smart Cities Conference (ISC2), 2016 IEEE International.* IEEE, 1–6.

[7] Julian Dibbelt, Thomas Pajor, and Dorothea Wagner. 2015. User-Constrained Multimodal Route Planning. *Journal of Experimental Algorithmics* 19, Article 3.2 (April 2015), 19 pages. https://doi.org/10.1145/2699886

[8] Edsger W Dijkstra. 1959. A Note on Two Problems in Connexion with Graphs. *Numer. Math.* 1, 1 (1959), 269–271.

[9] Thomas A Domencich and Daniel McFadden. 1975. *Urban Travel Demand-A Behavioral Analysis.* Technical Report. Transport and Road Research Laboratory.

[10] Jianhe Du, Ahmed Elbery, Hesham Rakha, and Matthew Klenk. 2018. Microscopic Simulation and Calibration of a Large-Scale Metropolitan Network: Issues and Proposed Solutions. In *the 97th Annual Meeting of Transportation Research Board.*

[11] Ahmed Elbery, Filip Dvorak, Jianhe Du, Hesham Rakha, and Matthew Klenk. 2018. Large-scale Agent-based Multi-modal Modeling of Transportation Networks - System Model and Preliminary Results. In *Conference: 4th International Conference on Vehicle Technology and Intelligent Transport Systems.* 103–112.

[12] Chiara Fiori, Kyoungho Ahn, and Hesham A Rakha. 2016. Power-based electric vehicle energy consumption model: Model development and validation. *Applied Energy* 168 (2016), 257–268.

[13] Daniela Inclezan and Luis I Pradanos. 2017. A Critical View on Smart Cities and AI. *Journal of Artificial Intelligence Research* 60 (2017), 681–686.

[14] Robert J Johnston, Kevin J Boyle, Wiktor Adamowicz, Jeff Bennett, Roy Brouwer, Trudy Ann Cameron, W Michael Hanemann, Nick Hanley, Mandy Ryan, Riccardo Scarpa, et al. 2017. Contemporary Guidance for Stated Preference Studies. *Journal of the Association of Environmental and Resource Economists* 4, 2 (2017), 319–405.

[15] Lin Liao, Donald J. Patterson, Dieter Fox, and Henry Kautz. 2007. Learning and Inferring Transportation Routines. *Artificial Intelligence* 171, 5 (2007), 311 – 331. https://doi.org/10.1016/j.artint.2007.01.006

[16] Hesham Rakha, Praveen Pasumarthy, and Slimane Adjerid. 2009. A Simplified Behavioral Vehicle Longitudinal Motion Model. *Transportation letters* 1, 2 (2009), 95–110.

[17] David Schrank, Bill Eisele, Tim Lomax, and Jim Bak. 2015. 2015 Urban Mobility Scorecard. *Annual Urban Mobility Scorecard* (2015).

[18] Xuan Song, Hiroshi Kanasugi, and Ryosuke Shibasaki. 2016. DeepTransport: Prediction and Simulation of Human Mobility and Transportation Mode at a Citywide Level.. In *Proceedings of the International Joint Conference on Artificial Intelligence,* Vol. 16. 2618–2624.

[19] Yanshuo Sun and Lei Zhang. 2018. Microeconomic Model for Designing Public Transit Incentive Programs. *Transportation Research Record* (2018). https://doi.org/10.1177/0361198118775875 arXiv:https://doi.org/10.1177/0361198118775875

[20] Amos Tversky and Daniel Kahneman. 1986. Rational Choice and the Framing of Decisions. *Journal of Business* (1986), S251–S278.

[21] Xiaoyu Zhu, Xianbiao Hu, and Yi-Chang Chiu. 2018. Will Information and Incentive Affect Traveler's Day-to-Day Departure Time Decisions? An Empirical Study of the Decision Making Evolution Process. In *the 97th Annual Meeting of Transportation Research Board.*

Guiding Prosecutorial Decisions with an Interpretable Statistical Model

Zhiyuan Lin
Stanford University
zylin@cs.stanford.edu

Alex Chohlas-Wood
Stanford University
alexcw@stanford.edu

Sharad Goel
Stanford University
scgoel@stanford.edu

ABSTRACT

After a felony arrest, many American jurisdictions hold individuals for several days while police officers investigate the incident and prosecutors decide whether to press criminal charges. This pre-arraignment detention can both preserve public safety and reduce the need for officers to seek out and re-arrest individuals who are ultimately charged with a crime. Such detention, however, also comes at a high social and financial cost to those who are never charged but still incarcerated. In one of the first large-scale empirical analyses of pre-arraignment detention, we examine police reports and charging decisions for approximately 30,000 felony arrests in a major American city between 2012 and 2017. We find that 45% of arrested individuals are never charged for any crime but still typically spend one or more nights in jail before being released. In an effort to reduce such incarceration, we develop a statistical model to help prosecutors identify cases soon after arrest that are likely to be ultimately dismissed. By carrying out an early review of five such candidate cases per day, we estimate that prosecutors could potentially reduce pre-arraignment incarceration for ultimately dismissed cases by 35%. To facilitate implementation and transparency, our model to prioritize cases for early review is designed as a simple, weighted checklist. We show that this heuristic strategy achieves comparable performance to traditional, black-box machine learning models.

CCS CONCEPTS

• **Applied computing → Law, social and behavioral sciences**; • **Computing methodologies →** *Machine learning*; *Learning linear models.*

KEYWORDS

criminal justice, interpretable machine learning, policy evaluation, prosecutorial decision making, propensity score matching

ACM Reference Format:
Zhiyuan Lin, Alex Chohlas-Wood, and Sharad Goel. 2019. Guiding Prosecutorial Decisions with an Interpretable Statistical Model . In *AAAI/ACM Conference on AI, Ethics, and Society (AIES '19), January 27–28, 2019, Honolulu, HI, USA.* ACM, New York, NY, USA, 8 pages. https://doi.org/10.1145/3306618.3314235

AIES '19, January 27–28, 2019, Honolulu, HI, USA

ACM ISBN 978-1-4503-6324-2/19/01…$15.00
https://doi.org/10.1145/3306618.3314235

1 INTRODUCTION

Many American jurisdictions detain individuals after a felony arrest while they conduct a preliminary investigation of the incident. In some states, this detention period is legally allowed to extend up to 48 weekday hours, but can stretch to more than 100 total hours if weekends or holidays occur in the middle of the detention period. Police departments use this detention window to gather evidence for the local prosecuting attorney, and at the conclusion of the investigation period, the prosecutor's office reviews the available evidence and decides whether or not to prosecute the case. Such pre-arraignment detention serves two key purposes: first, to protect public safety by confining individuals who may pose a threat to the community; and second, to reduce the need for police officers to seek out and re-arrest individuals who are ultimately charged. Such detention, however, also exacts high social and financial costs. Even brief incarceration may lead to job loss, inadequate support for dependents, strains on family relationships, and social stigma [8, 9, 13, 19]. These detentions may also undermine public trust in law enforcement and disrupt community activity, particularly among those who are arrested but never charged with any crime.

Here we carry out one of the first extensive examinations of pre-arraignment incarceration by analyzing a detailed dataset of approximately 30,000 felony arrests in a large American city between 2012 and 2017.[1] We find that 45% of felony arrestees in our dataset are never charged by the prosecutor, though they often spend several nights in jail before that decision is made. This high rate of dismissal may in part be the result of differing standards of evidence applied for arrest and prosecution. In particular, though the legal standard for arrest is *probable cause*, prosecuting attorneys will typically only pursue a case when they believe they can establish an individual's guilt *beyond a reasonable doubt*, a considerably higher legal bar.

To safely reduce pre-arraignment incarceration, we propose a three-step, algorithmically assisted strategy. First, based on preliminary arrest reports, we estimate each felony arrestee's likelihood of eventual dismissal via a simple statistical model that takes the form of a weighted checklist. The model's simplicity means that arrestees can be scored manually, without the need for computing resources, and that policymakers can more easily audit the scoring procedure. Second, we use these scores to create a short list of arrestees each day that have the highest likelihood of eventual dismissal. Third, prosecutors, under our proposed strategy, carry out an early review of these candidate cases, and dismiss those deemed unlikely to meet the bar for charging. Though prosecutors may still choose to wait until the 48-hour deadline to issue the actual charging decision, we find that most of the pertinent information is available within the

[1] We are unable to disclose the name of the city due to our agreement with the jurisdiction.

first few hours after arrest, facilitating early review and preliminary dismissal.

We estimate that prosecutors in the jurisdiction we consider could often handle 5–10 additional cases per day at existing staffing levels. By carrying out early review of five cases per day, we estimate that prosecutors could reduce pre-arraignment incarceration time for ultimately dismissed felony arrestees by up to 35%. We further consider the effect of early review and release on public safety, and find that the effect of extended pre-arraignment detention on recidivism is negligible.

Though pre-arraignment detention serves an important role in the criminal justice system, it often imposes a heavy burden on individuals and communities. By designing a simple and transparent algorithmic system to identify candidates for early dismissal, we seek to reduce the harms of detention while retaining its benefits.

2 BACKGROUND

To frame our analysis, we start by briefly outlining the steps leading up to a prosecutor's charging decision. We then review some of the related literature on constructing and evaluating algorithms to guide decisions in the criminal justice system.

2.1 From Arrest to Arraignment

After an arrest is made by the city's police department, an officer brings the arrested individual to county jail. The county sheriff books the individual on charges proposed by the arresting officer and enters information about the incident into the sheriff's database. This booking information is typically available to the prosecutor's office within a few hours of arrest, and forms the basis of our early review system. In theory, an individual can post bail during this post-arrest detention period, though in practice most arrestees remain in custody while awaiting a charging decision. Following booking, the arresting officer completes one or more subsequent reports, including a narrative description of the incident. The jurisdiction we consider has 48 weekday hours to gather this information and make a decision to either charge or dismiss the arrestee.

A small group of *reviewing attorneys* at the prosecutor's office assesses these incoming arrests and makes a final charging decision. The prosecutor's office reviews approximately 20 felony cases daily—as we describe in Section 3 below, our analysis focuses exclusively on felonies—and maintains surplus capacity to handle spikes in workload. A decision to charge generally indicates a belief that sufficient evidence exists to demonstrate the individual committed the alleged crime beyond a reasonable doubt. In such cases, the arrestee would face their charges at an arraignment hearing the day after their charging decision has been filed. If the reviewing attorney believes there is insufficient evidence to proceed, or otherwise feels that prosecution would not serve the interest of justice, the prosecutor's office will dismiss the case.

2.2 Related Work

The use of statistical algorithms during the charging process is quite limited. There is, however, a long history of using related *risk assessment tools* in other parts of the criminal justice system [1, 3]. For example, *pretrial* risk assessments estimate a defendant's likelihood of engaging in future criminal activity or of failing to appear at trial, and are now widely used to inform judicial release decisions at arraignment.

To identify cases that are likely to be eventually dismissed, one could train traditional, black-box machine learning models. Such models are designed to achieve optimal accuracy, but are often difficult to interpret and to explain. Particularly in criminal justice applications, such opaqueness can impede adoption and sow mistrust. The newly active subfield of interpretable machine learning has sought to develop predictive algorithms that are both accurate and explainable [10, 31]. We apply a simple regress-and-round procedure that was recently shown to perform on par with traditional machine learning methods on a variety of prediction tasks [17].

In theory, algorithms can combat explicit and implicit bias in unguided human decisions. However, researchers and policymakers have also shown that statistical tools can themselves exacerbate inequities by inadvertently encoding biases in the training data or through otherwise poor design [2, 5–7, 14, 21, 22, 26, 27], a possibility we consider below.

3 DATA DESCRIPTION & EXPLORATION

We use detailed police and prosecutor data to develop our proposed early review system. Specifically, we consider booking information, police reports, and charging decisions for nearly every felony arrest of an adult in our partner jurisdiction from 2012 to 2017. For each case in our dataset, we have: the date, time, and basic arrestee demographic information; a list of initial charges proposed by the arresting officer; and the date-stamped charging decision by the prosecutor's office. Subsequent reports may be later filed by the police department to provide additional detail and clarification.

Starting from this corpus of 33,944 felony cases, we make several filtering decisions to facilitate our analysis. First, we exclude cases involving probation violations or outstanding warrants from other jurisdictions, as these cases are handled through a separate review process. Second, we similarly exclude murder and rape cases since they are likewise handled through a different procedure, given the severity of these crimes. Finally, we restrict to arrestees that are at least 18 years old at the start of our observation period, to ensure we can construct full criminal histories over the period we analyze. After this filtering, we are left with 26,606 cases for our primary analysis.

We reserve data from 2012, at the beginning of our observation period, so that we can construct a 1-year criminal record for each arrestee; and we reserve data from 2017, at the conclusion of the observation period, so that we can calculate 1-year recidivism rates for each individual. Our statistical modeling is thus restricted to 18,712 cases between 2013 and 2016.

Reviewing attorneys may make dismissal decisions throughout the day, but these are only communicated to the sheriff once per day, at approximately 4pm. The sheriff requires several hours to process these decisions, typically releasing arrestees around 9pm. Decisions in our dataset are only recorded with a date, not a time, and so we use these 4pm and 9pm times as approximations for decision and release in all cases.

Among the universe of cases we consider, 47% are never charged. The majority of eventually dismissed arrestees spend multiple nights in jail awaiting a decision Indeed, 96% of eventually dismissed individuals spend at least 24 hours in detention, and 30% spend at least 72 hours. This delay is largely driven by the fact that reviewing attorneys typically wait until the police department files its final summary packet, which usually comes near the decision deadline. The final summary packet can in theory provide reviewing attorneys with new evidence, but in practice its primary function is to summarize the previously filed reports. Excepting the case summary packet, 90% of cases receive all associated reports and revisions within eight hours of booking. Our proposed process accommodates the possibility of additional information appearing in the summary packet by delaying the actual charging decision until the charging deadline.

4 OPTIMIZING RELEASE DECISIONS

To reduce pre-arraignment incarceration, we propose the following statistical strategy. First, when an arrestee is booked, we wait eight hours so that most case information can be filed by the police department. This window also serves as a "cooling off" period for the arrestee—often an implicit policy requirement before an individual can be released. After eight hours, we consider the case to be "review-ready". Each morning, review-ready cases are sorted by their estimated probability of dismissal according to the output of a predictive model (described below). Reviewing attorneys start the day by evaluating cases as normal, until the day's necessary workload is complete (e.g., by making final charging decisions on cases for which the police department's summary packet has been received). When extra capacity becomes available—as occurs on most days, according to the prosecutor's office—reviewing attorneys would begin an early review of the cases most likely to be dismissed, in descending order of dismissal probability. Such scores could be automatically generated, or even tallied in a matter of minutes, by individuals who manage the intake process. This is in contrast to a full charging decision review, which typically takes attorneys 1-2 hours per case. Thus, we estimate our model would save intake attorneys a significant amount of time ranking and highlighting cases to be reviewed.

If the attorney believes the case is indeed likely to be ultimately dismissed, they would request the sheriff release the arrestee that evening. After receiving the police department's summary packet for that case (typically a day or two later), the reviewing attorney would again review it and make a final charging decision. If, based on the new information, the reviewing attorney decides charges should be brought, a warrant could be issued and the individual re-arrested by the police.

Our proposed strategy hinges on having accurate model predictions of dismissal probabilities for each case. As discussed above, we would also like our model to be simple and interpretable, both to foster trust in the system and to ease adoption. Although our simple model is only designed to rank cases, the order in which cases are reviewed would still affect incarceration time. For example, many cases ranked with lower scores may never be reviewed early due to capacity constraints. Therefore, it is important for the model to remain simple and interpretable, so that (as with any impactful policy) it can be thoroughly examined and trusted by users and any

Factor	Points
Initial points	4
Each previously filed felony case in last 12 months	-1
Gang-related	-1
Elderly victim	-1
Each assault-related charge*	-1
Each drug-related charge	-1
Each theft-related charge	-2
Incident involves exactly 2 charges	-2
Incident involves 3 or more charges	-4

*Does not include domestic violence

Table 1: A simple model for estimating the likelihood a case is dismissed. The prosecutor's office could manually score incoming cases by subtracting points for any matching case attributes that appear in the list. Higher final scores indicate a higher likelihood of dismissal. One can arbitrarily set the initial points to signal which cases should be reviewed early. For example, one could inform attorneys to prioritize cases with a positive final score, and then adjust the initial points to alter the proportion of cases prioritized.

interested stakeholder. Simple models may also facilitate implementation, given that they do not require much IT infrastructure—in the extreme, they can be calculated using only pen and paper. We next describe three methods for constructing these predictive models. The first two use traditional machine learning methods (to serve as benchmarks), and the third is a simple, weighted checklist. All three models are trained on data from 2013–2014 and evaluated on data from 2015–2016, with the training set having 10,218 cases and the test set having 8,494 cases.

Our benchmark machine learning models use L^1-regularized logistic regression (lasso) and gradient boosted decision trees (GBDT). Boosted models such as GBDT are considered best-in-class for many prediction tasks [4, 20, 24]. Both models predicted the ultimate charging decision for each case based on all information available within the first eight hours after booking. The detailed list of case information features is described in the appendix. We further extract information from the written narratives via regular expression text matching, including types of evidence collected (e.g., video footage of the incident), whether the arresting officer had a body-worn camera, and whether witnesses were interviewed. Finally, we used a 50-dimensional GloVe [23] text embedding of the complete police narrative. On the test set, we found that the lasso and GBDT models achieved 82% and 83% ROC AUC, respectively, indicating good predictive performance.

We next describe our method for creating a simple, interpretable model, which is based on the regress-and-round procedure outlined by Jung et al. [17]. First, we selected a subset of the predictive features used for the complex models through a combination of step-wise feature selection and consultation with domain experts. In particular, we used the number of alleged charges; the number of assault-related charges; the number of theft-related charges; the number of drug-related charges; the number of domestic violence charges; the number of filed felony cases in which the arrestee was involved in the last 12 months; whether the incident involved a gun or knife; whether the victim was elderly; and whether the incident was gang-related. On this restricted feature set, we fit an L^1-regularized logistic regression model. Following Goel et al. [12], we constrained all model coefficients (except the intercept) to be non-positive, as the presence of any factor in our list of features should decrease the likelihood an arrestee is dismissed. Finally, we rescaled and rounded all the fitted coefficients $\hat{\beta}_i$ (except the intercept) to be integers in the range $[-M, M]$. Specifically, we set $M = 5$, and defined integer weights

$$w_i = \text{Round}\left(\frac{M\hat{\beta}_i}{\max_j(|\hat{\beta}_j|)}\right). \quad (1)$$

Despite its simplicity, the resulting model (shown in Table 1) achieves 75% AUC on the test set. For comparison, recall that the GBDT model trained on all available features, including information extracted from the narrative reports, obtained 83% AUC.

To apply this model, the prosecutor's office could either manually or programmatically score incoming cases, subtracting points for each matching case attribute in Table 1. A higher final score indicates a case is more likely to be dismissed, and so should be prioritized for early review. Depending on their workload each day, reviewing attorneys would start with cases having the highest score and work their way down the list.

We note that assault-related cases tend to receive higher scores—and are thus more likely to be reviewed for early release—than theft-related cases. This pattern illustrates an important point: the model estimates dismissal probability, not case severity. With assault-related allegations, there is often an absence of physical evidence or witnesses to establish guilt beyond a reasonable doubt, leading to dismissal. Similarly, intake attorneys may be more inclined to prosecute cases with elderly victims, given the particularly egregious nature of these incidents. It bears emphasis that our statistical model only identifies cases for early review, rather than automatically determining whether an arrestee should be released. As such, prosecuting attorneys must still carefully evaluate the evidence on a case-by-case basis before determining the appropriate course of action.

5 EVALUATION

Given our statistical model described above, we now carry out a detailed study of its potential effects if deployed. First we consider the calibration of the model across groups defined by race and gender. We then estimate our proposed strategy's effect on incarceration and public safety.

5.1 Model Calibration

We start by examining the mapping from model scores to actual dismissal rates, disaggregated by an arrestee's race. To deal with data sparsity, dismissal rates are estimated via a logistic regression model, fit separately for each group. The top panel of Figure 1 shows that cases with similar scores have similar dismissal rates, regardless of the arrestee's race, an important property of equitable models [6]. For example, across all race groups, cases with a score of 4 are dismissed just under 80% of the time.

The middle panel of Figure 1 shows a similar plot broken down by gender. In contrast to race, we see that among men and women with

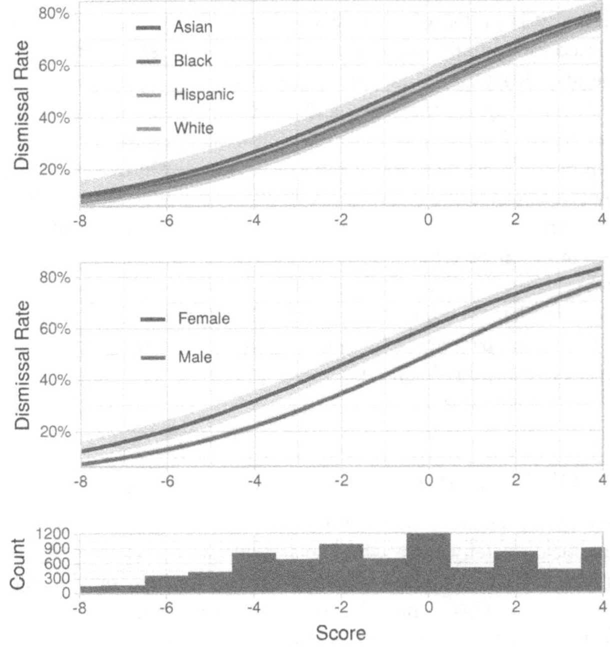

Figure 1: Estimated dismissal rates by model score (see Table 1), disaggregated by an arrestee's race (top) and gender (middle), with gray bands indicating 95% confidence regions. The bottom panel shows the distribution of individuals across scores. Scores appear to be well-calibrated by race; but we also see noticeable gender disparities, indicating that among men and women with the same score, women are dismissed at higher rates.

the same model score, women are dismissed at consistently higher rates. For example, a male arrestee with a score of 2 is dismissed about 65% of the time, but a female arrestee with the same score is dismissed about 73% of the time. Said another way, a female arrestee with a score of -1 is dismissed at about the same rate as a male arrestee with a score of 1.

This gender miscalibration could result from two qualitatively different mechanisms, each having different policy implications. On the one hand, past prosecutorial decisions may have been relatively harsh against men (or, equivalently, relatively lenient toward women). That is, given the exact same facts, prosecutors might have unjustifiably dismissed female arrestees at higher rates than male arrestees. If true, the miscalibration we see would reflect bias in the training data, and in this case, one could potentially use the model in Table 1 to mitigate past prejudice.

On the other hand, controlling for model score, cases involving women might have different fact patterns than those involving men, and may thus be dismissed at legitimately higher rates. For example, among alleged assault cases, those involving female arrestees might, on average, be less severe, prompting prosecutors to dismiss these cases more often. An analogous pattern often occurs with risk assessment scores for recidivism, where women have been found to reoffend less often than men with similar criminal histories [6, 26]. In this case, one solution is to develop gender-specific

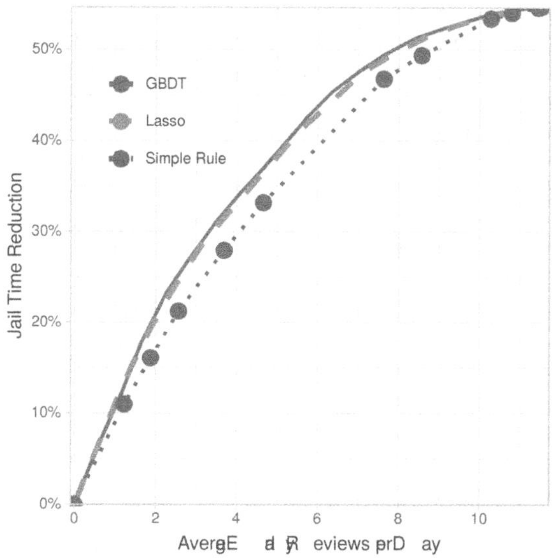

Figure 2: Jail-time reduction for eventually dismissed arrestees as a function of the number of early reviews conducted and the prediction model. The simple rule (in Table 1) performs on par to the lasso and GBDT models. (The simple rule estimates are piece-wise linear, since the model produces discrete scores.) Using simple rules, early review of approximately five cases per day could reduce jail time for eventually dismissed arrestees by approximately 35%.

prediction models, or to simply add points based on gender (e.g., one could assign cases involving a female arrestee two additional points). Though somewhat controversial [28], there is precedent for this approach, with the State of Wisconsin using gender-specific risk assessment tools to guide sentencing decisions. Indeed, the Wisconsin State Supreme Court approved of this choice, writing that "if the inclusion of gender [in the model] promotes accuracy, it serves the interests of institutions and defendants, rather than a discriminatory purpose" [29]. With the data available to us, it is difficult to definitively identify and address the source of the miscalibration. This issue, however, would need to be studied further and resolved before deploying any such tool.

5.2 Jail-Time Reduction & Recidivism

We next estimate the efficacy of early review on incarceration, focusing on jail-time reduction for those arrestees who are never charged with any crime. We consider this subpopulation for three reasons: (1) if individuals who are ultimately charged are released early, they may need to be re-arrested to ensure their appearance at arraignment proceedings, often requiring significant time and effort by law enforcement, tempering the benefits of early release; (2) many charged arrestees are eventually convicted and receive credit for time served during their pre-arraignment detention periods, again moderating the benefits of releasing such individuals early; and (3) the social costs of incarceration may be particularly large for those who are never charged, as it is more likely they did not in fact commit the alleged crime, and they may thus lose more trust in law enforcement if detained for an extended period.

To facilitate estimation, we assume that if a case flagged for early review is eventually dismissed, then the reviewing attorney would also order the arrestee be released after early review. As discussed above, most information is available for nearly all cases by the proposed early review time (i.e., eight hours after booking), bolstering the plausibility of this assumption. We also assume that without such an early review system, arrestees would remain incarcerated while their cases are being considered.

The results of our analysis, under the assumptions above, are shown in Figure 2. To generate the plot, we further assume that each day reviewing attorneys assess all cases above a pre-determined threshold t. For example, they might review all cases with at least $t = 80\%$ chance of dismisssal. This threshold determines one point on each model's curve, each with a corresponding average workload (plotted on the x-axis) and expected jail-time reduction (plotted on the y-axis) at that threshold t. We then trace out curves for all three of our prediction models by varying the review threshold t.

The plot demonstrates two key points. First, the performance of the simple rule (described in Table 1) is quite similar to the performance of the traditional, black-box machine learning models. We can thus obtain the benefits of simplicity and transparency without significantly sacrificing performance. Second, all three models—including our simple heuristic—can significantly reduce jail times. For example, if a prosecutor's office used our simple model in Table 1, we estimate an early review of approximately five cases per day could reduce jail time for eventually dismissed arrestees by about 35%. Similar reductions are achieved within groups defined by race and gender (not shown in the plot).

We note that reviewing attorneys currently handle approximately 22 felony cases per day during the week and 1 felony case per day on the weekends. Based on discussions with our partner jurisdiction, we estimate that the office can handle approximately 5–10 additional cases per day on average (both during the week and on the weekend), in order to respond to spikes in workload. Since prosecuting attorneys must always be ready to handle an influx of cases, they cannot easily assist with activities that require large blocks of time, like litigation. Early review is thus particularly well-suited to make use of spare capacity, and it would not generally displace other work.

We also investigate the potential effects of early review and release on public safety. We specifically examine the effect of extended detention on re-arrest within one year. To start, we note that 33% of those who spend one night in detention recidivate within one year, while only 30% of those who spend two or more nights recidiviate within one year, suggesting a possible public safety benefit of detention. However, those arrestees who spend one night may be qualitatively different than those who are detained for multiple nights—making it difficult to determine the causal effect of detention from such statistics alone.

We account for this issue by using propensity score matching [16]. First, we estimate the probability that each arrestee spends exactly one night in jail, based on all available case and criminal history information—these are the propensity scores. We then match each arrestee who spent two or more nights in jail with one having a similar propensity score who spent one night in jail. After matching, we find that key covariates are well balanced across the two groups. On the matched sample, we find that one-year recidivism rates are nearly identical: 33% for those who spent one night, and 32% for those who spent at least two nights. The difference in recidivism rates is not statistically significant, with a 95% confidence interval of (-2%, 4%). These results suggest that extended pre-arraignment detention has little impact on recidivism.[2]

6 DISCUSSION

By analyzing a large, detailed dataset of police reports and charging decisions, we developed a statistically informed strategy for reducing pre-arraignment detention. In theory, this proposed intervention could substantially reduce jail time for individuals who are arrested but never charged with a crime, and this reduction could potentially be accomplished without hiring additional staff or adversely affecting public safety. In practice, however, there are several challenging issues that policymakers must consider before undertaking such an initiative, three of which we briefly discuss below.

First, reviewing attorneys may not in fact be able to make early release decisions reliably. Our analysis assumes that attorneys have the requisite information to anticipate eventual charging decisions soon after arrest. Supporting this assumption, we find that detailed information about an incident, including the responding officer's first report, is nearly always recorded and accessible to prosecutors within the first eight hours of booking. Further, our statistical models are able to predict final prosecutorial decisions based on that information with reasonably high accuracy, again indicating that much of the relevant information is available early on. Nonetheless, at least some information—like the police department's final summary packet—is not available until close to the decision deadline, potentially hampering early decision making. On a related note, prosecutors, police officers, and the community more broadly would have to consider the costs of releasing individuals who are later charged, including possible risks to public safety and potential costs for the police department in serving and executing arrest warrants.

Second, policymakers would need to carefully examine the statistical procedure for selecting cases for early review, and ensure that it does not inadvertently recapitulate historical inequities. The simplicity of our proposed model facilitates such an audit. We further find that our simple scoring system is calibrated across race groups, an important first step. However, we also find that women are consistently dismissed at higher rates than men with the same score, pointing to potential problems. As we discussed in the model calibration subsection, this disparity may result from past decisions that were biased against men; alternatively, it could indicate that gender has a legitimately valuable predictive role in identifying cases to review. Before deploying such a system it is important to better understand and address this phenomenon. One strategy is to manually audit cases with the same score to determine whether there are genuine differences in the recorded fact patterns.

Finally, one must consider the potentially complicated impacts of such an intervention on various actors in the criminal justice system, including police officers, prosecutors, perpetrators, and victims. For example, police officers—upon learning the structure of the early review system—may alter their behavior to focus on cases most likely to be prosecuted. On the other hand, even though our model is only designed to rank cases for review, prosecutors' decisions may be influenced by knowledge of this ranking. Although this could have benefits by aligning police and prosecutor decision making, it could also be harmful if certain types of crimes are no longer investigated. For example, knowing that individuals accused of domestic violence may be released early, officers may de-prioritize those cases, in turn harming victims and potentially emboldening abusers. We note, though, that such a cascade effect may never arise, as officers likely already know that such cases are often dismissed, early review still means arrestees spend at least one day in jail, and statutory guidelines mandate certain allegations are always investigated. Prosecutors might also change their behavior, potentially by too quickly releasing arrestees identified via the statistical model for review, rather than carefully examining the facts of each case. In addition to these three challenges, is also possible that prosecutor's offices would not support our proposed policy, as they do not bear the cost of pre-arraignment incarceration, and may support the notion that such incarceration serves a purpose, even if a case is eventually dismissed.

The statistical strategy we outline in this paper marks one of the first instances of an algorithmic intervention for pre-arraignment detention. Our proposed policy could allow jurisdictions to more closely hew to the principle of presumed innocence, reducing incarceration for arrestees who are never charged with any crime, while preserving the opportunity for local law enforcement to intervene where necessary. As with all policy interventions, one must carefully consider both the direct and indirect impacts of deploying a system for early review and release of arrestees. Such attention is doubly important for algorithmic policies, whose effects can be hard to predict, and for policies pertaining to the criminal justice system, which involves particularly vulnerable populations. However, a well-designed and evaluated algorithmic policy to reduce pre-arraignment incarceration can also bring considerable benefits, both for individuals and for communities. We hope this work is a first step toward achieving that goal.

[2] In the Appendix, we conduct *offline policy evaluation* by applying classical sensitivity analysis techniques from the causal inference literature [17]. That analysis likewise indicates that early review and release would not meaningfully affect recidivism, consistent with the matching results described here.

REFERENCES

[1] Richard Berk. 2012. *Criminal justice forecasts of risk: a machine learning approach.* Springer Science & Business Media.

[2] Richard Berk, Hoda Heidari, Shahin Jabbari, Michael Kearns, and Aaron Roth. 2017. Fairness in Criminal Justice Risk Assessments: The State of the Art. (2017). Working paper available at https://arxiv.org/abs/1703.09207.

[3] Ernest W Burgess. 1928. Factors determining success or failure on parole. *The workings of the indeterminate sentence law and the parole system in Illinois* (1928), 221–234.

[4] Tianqi Chen and Carlos Guestrin. 2016. Xgboost: A scalable tree boosting system. In *Proceedings of the 22nd acm sigkdd international conference on knowledge discovery and data mining*. ACM, 785–794.

[5] Alexandra Chouldechova. 2017. Fair prediction with disparate impact: A study of bias in recidivism prediction instruments. *Big Data* 5, 2 (2017), 153–163.

[6] Sam Corbett-Davies and Sharad Goel. 2018. The Measure and Mismeasure of Fairness: A Critical Review of Fair Machine Learning. *arXiv preprint arXiv:1808.00023* (2018).

[7] Sam Corbett-Davies, Emma Pierson, Avi Feller, Sharad Goel, and Aziz Huq. 2017. Algorithmic decision making and the cost of fairness. In *Proceedings of the 23rd ACM SIGKDD International Conference on Knowledge Discovery and Data Mining*. ACM, 797–806.

[8] Stephanie Holmes Didwania. 2018. The Immediate Consequences of Pretrial Detention: Evidence from Federal Criminal Cases. *https://ssrn.com/abstract=2809818 or http://dx.doi.org/10.2139/ssrn.2809818* (2018).

[9] Will Dobbie, Jacob Goldin, and Crystal S. Yang. 2018. The Effects of Pretrial Detention on Conviction, Future Crime, and Employment: Evidence from Randomly Assigned Judges. *American Economic Review* 108, 2 (February 2018), 201–40. https://doi.org/10.1257/aer.20161503

[10] Finale Doshi-Velez and Been Kim. 2017. Towards a rigorous science of interpretable machine learning. *arXiv preprint arXiv:1702.08608* (2017).

[11] Miroslav Dudík, John Langford, and Lihong Li. 2011. Doubly Robust Policy Evaluation and Learning. *ICML* (2011).

[12] Sharad Goel, Justin M Rao, and Ravi Shroff. 2016. Precinct or Prejudice? Understanding Racial Disparities in New York City's Stop-and-Frisk Policy. *Annals of Applied Statistics* 10, 1 (2016), 365–394.

[13] Arpit Gupta, Christopher Hansman, and Ethan Frenchman. 2016. The Heavy Costs of High Bail: Evidence from Judge Randomization. *The Journal of Legal Studies* 45, 2 (2016), 471–505. https://doi.org/10.1086/688907 arXiv:https://doi.org/10.1086/688907

[14] Moritz Hardt, Eric Price, and Nati Srebro. 2016. Equality of opportunity in supervised learning. In *Advances In Neural Information Processing Systems*. 3315–3323.

[15] Jennifer L Hill. 2011. Bayesian nonparametric modeling for causal inference. *Journal of Computational and Graphical Statistics* 20, 1 (2011), 217–240.

[16] Guido W Imbens and Donald B Rubin. 2015. *Causal inference in statistics, social, and biomedical sciences.* Cambridge University Press.

[17] Jongbin Jung, Connor Concannon, Ravi Shroff, Sharad Goel, and Daniel G Goldstein. 2017. Simple rules for complex decisions. *arXiv preprint arXiv:1702.04690* (2017).

[18] Jongbin Jung, Ravi Shroff, Avi Feller, and Sharad Goel. 2018. Algorithmic Decision Making in the Presence of Unmeasured Confounding. *arXiv preprint arXiv:1805.01868* (2018).

[19] Emily Leslie and Nolan G. Pope. 2017. The Unintended Impact of Pretrial Detention on Case Outcomes: Evidence from New York City Arraignments. *The Journal of Law and Economics* 60, 3 (2017), 529–557. https://doi.org/10.1086/695285 arXiv:https://doi.org/10.1086/695285

[20] Zhiyuan Lin, Tim Althoff, and Jure Leskovec. 2018. I'll Be Back: On the Multiple Lives of Users of a Mobile Activity Tracking Application. In *Proceedings of the International World-Wide Web Conference. International WWW Conference*, Vol. 2018. NIH Public Access, 1501.

[21] John Monahan, Jennifer Skeem, and Christopher Lowenkamp. 2017. Age, risk assessment, and sanctioning: Overestimating the old, underestimating the young. *Law and human behavior* 41, 2 (2017), 191.

[22] Cathy O'Neil. 2016. *Weapons of math destruction: How big data increases inequality and threatens democracy.* Broadway Books.

[23] Jeffrey Pennington, Richard Socher, and Christopher Manning. 2014. Glove: Global vectors for word representation. In *Proceedings of the 2014 conference on empirical methods in natural language processing (EMNLP)*. 1532–1543.

[24] Byron P Roe, Hai-Jun Yang, Ji Zhu, Yong Liu, Ion Stancu, and Gordon McGregor. 2005. Boosted decision trees as an alternative to artificial neural networks for particle identification. *Nuclear Instruments and Methods in Physics Research Section A: Accelerators, Spectrometers, Detectors and Associated Equipment* 543, 2-3 (2005), 577–584.

[25] Paul R Rosenbaum and Donald B Rubin. 1983. Assessing sensitivity to an unobserved binary covariate in an observational study with binary outcome. *Journal of the Royal Statistical Society. Series B (Methodological)* (1983), 212–218.

[26] Jennifer Skeem, John Monahan, and Christopher Lowenkamp. 2016. Gender, risk assessment, and sanctioning: The cost of treating women like men. *Law and human behavior* 40, 5 (2016), 580.

[27] Jennifer L Skeem and Christopher T Lowenkamp. 2016. Risk, race, and recidivism: predictive bias and disparate impact. *Criminology* 54, 4 (2016), 680–712.

[28] Sonja B Starr. 2014. Evidence-based sentencing and the scientific rationalization of discrimination. *Stan. L. Rev.* 66 (2014), 803.

[29] State v. Loomis. 2016. 881 N.W.2d 749 (Wis. 2016).

[30] David Word, Charles Coleman, Robert Nunziata, and Robert Kominski. 2008. Demographic aspects of surnames from census 2000. http://www2.census.gov/topics/genealogy/2000surnames/surnames.pdf

[31] Jiaming Zeng, Berk Ustun, and Cynthia Rudin. 2016. Interpretable classification models for recidivism prediction. *Journal of the Royal Statistical Society: Series A (Statistics in Society)* (2016).

Appendices

Appendix A DATA DESCRIPTION AND PROCESSING

We include here additional details about the data we use and our processing pipeline. In the jurisdiction we study, decision dates for a large fraction of cases (54%) are recorded as occurring after the legally allowed deadline. To investigate this issue, we conducted a manual audit of approximately 100 cases, tracking decisions in real-time and comparing them to the electronic record. We determined the discrepancy was due to a data logging issue, with the vast majority of such cases filed shortly before the deadline. We thus assume throughout our analysis that all decisions recorded as occurring late were made on the day of the deadline. We also note that our results are qualitatively similar if we restrict our analysis to only those cases with decision dates officially recorded as occurring by the deadline.

About 15% of the resident population identifies as Hispanic, but only 0.3% of arrestees in our dataset are listed as Hispanic. A manual review of surnames indicated that many ostensibly Hispanic arrestees were instead listed as non-Hispanic white. We addressed this issue by imputing Hispanic ethnicity from surnames, using a dataset from the U.S. Census Bureau that estimates the racial and ethnic distribution of people with a given name [30].[3] We classify an individual as Hispanic if at least 75% of people with his or her surname identify as Hispanic. After this recoding, 16% of arrestees are labeled Hispanic, more in line with expectations.

The statutory deadline for making charging decisions is 48 weekday hours. Many people, however, might be held for longer if weekends or holidays fall during this period s . In particular, as discussed in the main text, over 30% of arrestees who are eventually released stay in custody for over 72 hours.

Appendix B IMPACT ON RECIDIVISM

Our analysis suggests that our proposed early review strategy would not substantially affect recidivism. Below we provide additional details regarding our offline policy evaluation method. We also examine the sensitivity of our results to unmeasured confounding.

[3] http://www.census.gov/topics/population/genealogy/data/2000_surnames.html

Offline policy evaluation. In addition to the matching technique we use to estimate the effect of our proposed early review strategy on recidivism, we further estimate this effect via *offline policy evaluation* [11, 17, 18]. To do so, we first train a GBDT model that predicts recidivism based on all available case covariates and the number of nights an arrestee spent in jail. Then, based on this fitted model, we estimate each arrestee's (couterfactual) recidivism probability if that arrestee were to have spent one night in jail—a straightforward and popular technique called response surface modeling [15]. We now combine these counterfactual estimates $\hat{y}_i(1)$ with the observed recidivism outcomes y_i to assess the overall effect of early review and release. Let π denote a specific early review strategy (e.g., one corresponding to a particular daily workload), with $\pi_i \in \{0, 1\}$ indicating whether arrestee i is ultimately released early. Then the estimated recidivism rate $\hat{R}_\pi$ under policy π is:

$$\frac{1}{N}\sum_{i=1}^{N} \pi_i \hat{y}_i(1) + (1 - \pi_i) y_i, \qquad (2)$$

where N is the total number of arrestees. In other words, we simply use the observed recidivism outcome y_i when the policy π does not alter arrestee i's detention status, and we use the estimated recidivism outcome $\hat{y}_i(1)$ when the policy results in i being released early.

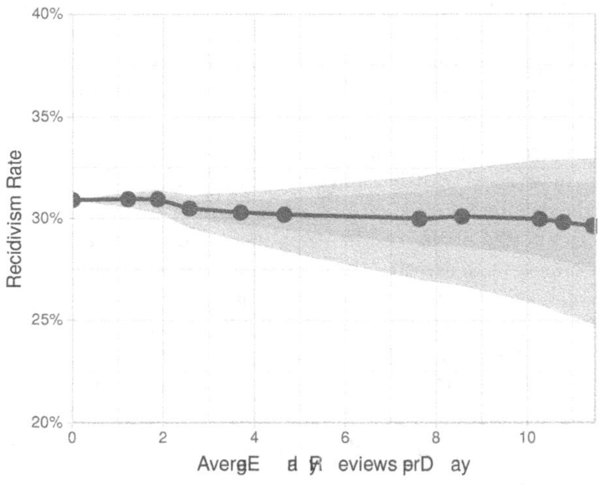

Figure A1: Estimated recidivism rates for various review and release policies, indexed by the average number of cases reviewed each day. Bands indicate plausible ranges of estimates after accounting for unmeasured confounding via sensitivity analysis. The darker band assumes the hidden confounder can alter individual outcomes by a factor of two, and the lighter band assumes the confounder can alter outcomes by a factor of three.

The solid line in Figure A1 shows estimated recidivism rates under various review and release policies derived from the heuristic scoring rule in Table 1. The x-axis indexes such policies by their workload, with higher workloads corresponding to greater jail-time reductions (as shown in Figure 2). The y-axis shows estimated recidivism $\hat{R}_\pi$ under each such policy. The flatness of the line suggests that early review and release would not meaningfully affect recidivism, consistent with our matching results.

Sensitivity analysis. In both our matching analysis and our offline policy evaluation, we implicitly assumed that there was no unmeasured confounding. In theory, however, it is possible that those who spend one night in jail are systematically different from those who spend two or more nights in jail, in ways that are not recorded in the data but which nonetheless affect recidivism. To account for this possibility, we apply the classical sensitivity method of Rosenbaum and Rubin [25], which was recently adapted to the setting of offline policy evaluation by Jung et al. [17]. At a high level, we first assume there is an unobserved covariate $u \in \{0, 1\}$ that affects both an arrestee's detention length and also that individual's recidivism rate. For example, u might indicate whether the arrestee has an extensive criminal record in another jurisdiction, information that is plausibly available to reviewing attorneys—and that might affect detention duration—but is not recorded in our data. We then explore how our recidivism estimates change as we alter three key parameters: (1) the probability that $u = 1$; (2) the effect of u on the arrestee's likelihood to recidivate; and (3) the effect of u on the arrestee's likelihood to spend exactly one night in jail.

The bands in Figure A1 show plausible ranges of recidivism across policies for two sensitivity regimes. In the first, indicated by the darker band, we assume that the unmeasured confounder u can alter an arrestee's odds of spending one night in jail by a factor of two, and can also alter an arrestee's odds of recidivism by a factor of two. The second, more extreme regime, indicated by the lighter band, assumes that u can alter these quantities by a factor of three. In both cases, we allow $\Pr(u = 1)$ to vary freely from 0 to 1. As expected, the bands widen toward the right of the plot, corresponding to policies that deviate more sharply from the status quo, and whose effects are thus harder to predict. However, for policies that require reviewing approximately five cases per day—as we believe is feasible at current staffing levels—our sensitivity analysis suggests recidivism might at most change by a few percentage points. Thus, even accounting for possible unmeasured confounding, it appears that our proposed early review strategy would not dramatically affect recidivism rates.

Appendix C CASE INFORMATION FEATURES

Case information features used by GBDT and L^1-regularized logistic regression include arrest month, day-of-week, and time-of-day; time to deadline; location(s) where the incident occurred (out of 11 areas); arrestee's age; 1-year arrest and charge history for the arrestee; the full list of alleged charges; the number of alleged charges; the number of assault-related charges; the number of theft-related charges; the number of drug-related charges; the number of filed felony cases involving the arrestee in the last 12 months; whether the incident involved a weapon; type of weapon used (if any); whether the victim was elderly; whether the case is gang-related; the number of incident reports already filed; the number of people involved in the incident; and the length of the police narrative.

Using Deceased-Donor Kidneys to initiate Chains of Living Donor Kidney Paired Donations: Algorithms and Experimentation.

Cristina Cornelio*
IBM Research
ccornel@us.ibm.com

Lucrezia Furian
University of Padova
lucrezia.furian@unipd.it

Antonio Nicolò
University of Padova
University of Manchester
antonio.nicolo@unipd.it

Francesca Rossi*
IBM Research
francesca.rossi2@ibm.com

ABSTRACT

We design a flexible algorithm that exploits deceased donor kidneys to initiate chains of living donor kidney paired donations, combining deceased and living donor allocation mechanisms to improve the quantity and quality of kidney transplants. The advantages of this approach have been measured using retrospective data on the pool of donor/recipient incompatible and desensitized pairs at the Padua University Hospital, the largest center for living donor kidney transplants in Italy. The experiments show a remarkable improvement on the number of patients with incompatible donor who could be transplanted, a decrease in the number of desensitization procedures, and an increase in the number of UT patients (that is, patients unlikely to be transplanted for immunological reasons) in the waiting list who could receive an organ.

CCS CONCEPTS

• **Human-centered computing** → *Collaborative and social computing*; • **Social and professional topics** → *Economic impact*; • **Applied computing** → *Life and medical sciences*; *Multi-criterion optimization and decision-making*.

KEYWORDS

kidneys exchange; matching

ACM Reference Format:

Cristina Cornelio, Lucrezia Furian, Antonio Nicolò, and Francesca Rossi. 2019. Using Deceased-Donor Kidneys to initiate Chains of Living Donor Kidney Paired Donations: Algorithms and Experimentation.. In *AAAI/ACM Conference on AI, Ethics, and Society (AIES '19), January 27–28, 2019, Honolulu, HI, USA.* ACM, New York, NY, USA, 7 pages. https://doi.org/10.1145/3306618.3314276

*This work was conducted while Cristina Cornelio and Francesca Rossi were at the University of Padova, Italy.

AIES '19, January 27–28, 2019, Honolulu, HI, USA

ACM ISBN 978-1-4503-6324-2/19/01...$15.00
https://doi.org/10.1145/3306618.3314276

1 INTRODUCTION

Living donor kidney transplantation is the most promising solution for closing the gap between organ demand and supply. Despite growing efforts to implement this option for patients with end-stage renal disease (ESRD), the percentage of living donations has been decreasing in the United States from 50.1% in 2000 to 38.2% in 2017 of the total number of kidney transplants [1]. Figures are different in the European countries, where the expansion of living transplantation programs is still underway: in Italy there were 310 kidney transplants from living donor in 2017, less than one fifth of the total number of kidney transplants.

Patients may have a willing living donor, but they cannot receive her organ due to blood or tissue type incompatibility. Some ABO-types (blood) incompatibilities between donor and recipient can be resolved through desensitization techniques (which are costly and may have side-effect of the health of the patients), but in many other instances, and especially in case of patients with circulating human leukocyte antigen (HLA) antibodies directed against their willing donors, incompatibility cannot be overcome.

A welfare enhancing option for incompatible donor/recipient pairs is to participate to kidney paired exchange (KPE) programs that favor donors' exchanges among incompatible pairs. A relevant constraint in designing the algorithms to maximize the number of transplants in KPE programs, is the simultaneity of the exchanges among pairs. It follows that there are feasibility constraints over the length of these cycles, because three-way cycles already represent a logistic challenge for most of the transplant centres.

Unfortunately, these programs are not fully and uniformly developed among Europe, and countries such as Spain, France, Italy, Czech Republic, Austria, Belgium, Switzerland, Poland and Scandinavia have just started these programs or are striving to implement one. In these countries, few kidney paired exchanges have been performed, mainly due to the low number of patients enrolled in such programs. In Italy, for instance, there are currently only 39 donor/recipient pairs enrolled in the National Kidney Paired Donation program. It is quite unlikely to find two-way or three-way cycles of exchanges among such a few pairs.

A suitable option to increase the number of transplants is the inclusion of altruistic donors to initiate chains of *kidney paired donations (KPD).* Altruistic donors enabled further expansion of this practice, because the availability of a non-directed living donor kidney without a designated recipient increases the number of potential matches. Moreover, chains starting from a deceased donor (DD) are not constrained by simultaneous exchanges, because every patient involved in a KPD chain will receive an organ before her donor donates to the following patient in the chain. Therefore, in case of a break of a chain, it never happens that a patient does not receive an organ but her donor has already donated a kidney to another patient. However, the uncertainty among both the transplantation community and the public opinion with regard to the intention, motivation, and legitimacy of such donors represents a constraint to a large development of this option in many countries.

In the present study, we consider the use of deceased donors to initiate chains of KPD. We propose to design a new program that combines the benefit of a KPD program and of a deceased donors' program, and propose algorithms to implement it. Moreover, we analyze and quantify its potential benefits by using retrospective data of the Kidney and Pancreas Transplant Unit at Padua University Hospital, one of the largest kidney transplant centre in Italy.

1.1 Related works

This paper contributes to the kidney exchange literature initiated by [2, 10, 11, 26] and developed successively by [3, 6–8, 23, 27]. These algorithms have been further analyzed: studying the problem of transplantation failures due to rejected matching [13]; focusing on particular classes of patients (e.g. patients with a very low probability of transplantation) [14]; analyzing the computational complexity of the problem as ILP [4]; providing an analysis of the efficacy of altruistic-donor chains [12]; studying the problem of having long chains of kidney exchanges [5, 16]; providing incentives to compatible pairs to participate in these programs [15, 20, 21]; using altruistic donors to initiate chains of donation [17, 18, 22, 25].

The ethical implications of the utilization of deceased-donors grafts to start chains of donations has been analyzed previously [19]. In [29] an approach for using deceased-donors to start donation chains is proposed, giving priority in the waiting list to patients that have a donor (a chain starts only if one of these particular patients is selected from the deceased-donor waiting list). A similar approach that modify the priority of patients in the waiting list (with the emission of vouchers) is developed in [28]. Another similar work [24] adopts list exchange procedures according to which a living incompatible donor provides a kidney to a candidate on the deceased-donor wait-list and in return his intended recipient receives a 'priority on the deceased-donor wait-list. We differentiate from these works mainly in two ways: we do not modify the waiting list (that is handled with a separate standard algorithm); we give priority to the UT patients (patients with unlikely transplantability). Also in [9] the authors consider deceased-donors to start chains of donation: this approach can be better described as a "List Exchange procedure". Contrary to our work, a pair donates before his recipient receives an organ from, and there is a degree of uncertainty of the prioritization in the waiting list (mostly in case of highly sensitized patients).

2 THE ALGORITHM

Given a compatibility graph that includes all patients, donors, and organs (to be precisely described later), our algorithm looks for cycles or chains in this graph, and it is triggered by either the arrival of a new patient/donor pair (in this case we look for a cycle, via the *cycle detection* procedure), or of a new deceased-donor kidney (in this case we look for a chain, via the *chain detection* procedure, and we release the donor of the last chain element to the deceased donor waiting list). Both procedures solve an optimization problem on a graph structure, and aim at maximizing the number of transplants.

An overview of the algorithm is depicted in Figure 1.

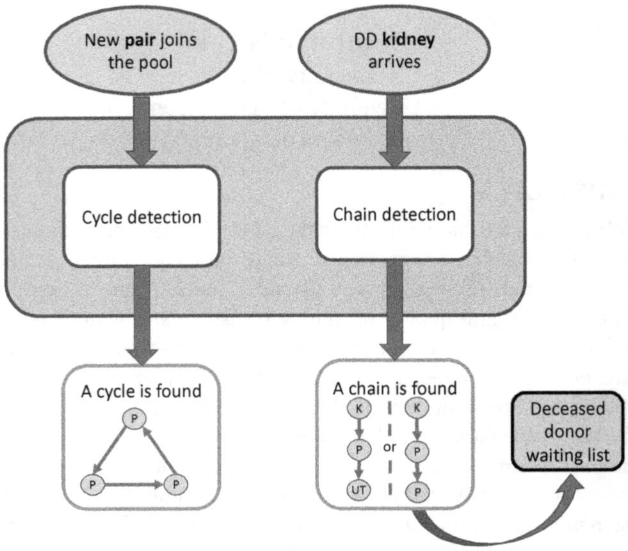

Figure 1: The algorithm.

2.1 Patient pool

We now give the details of our scenario, where we consider the following types of patients:

- *UT patients*: these are patients with *unlikely transplantability*, that is, patients that are difficult to match with donors since they are highly immunized. Usually this type of patients are at their second or third transplant.
- *NT pairs donor/patient*: these are pairs that are not compatible between each other and therefore cannot be transplanted between themselves.
- *DS pairs donor/patient*: these are pairs that are not compatible between each other but they can be transplanted between themselves with desensitization. Desensitization is a procedure that solve light incompatibility (like the blood type or the RH type) but it induces stress in the body of the patient, who is already week from the dialysis. It also has a high cost from a financial point of view, so both for the patient and the hospital would be better to be avoided.

We define our pool of patients as a set that can include UT patient, NT pairs, DS pairs, or optimal kidneys from deceased donors[1]. The composition of the pool varies with the time: given each time stamp t we denote the pool at that particular moment as $P(t)$. $P(t)$ contains

[1] In the *Experiments* section we will describe further restrictions on the pool composition, differently for each experimental setting.

all the UT patients, NT pairs, DS pairs that are in the deceased donor waiting list at that particular time t, and the kidneys arrived in the pool at time t. We are not interested in all the time stamps t but only those at which the pool composition change. These particular moments happen when a new pair join the deceased-donor waiting list or when a new deceased-donor kidney arrives.

2.2 The compatibility graph

We represent each element of the pool (each pair NT, pair DS, patient UT, or kidney) as a node of a *compatibility graph*, which is a directed, possibly cyclic, graph. In the graph there are three different types of nodes: nodes representing to donor/patient pairs (either UT pairs or DS pairs); kidney nodes that correspond to a deceased donor kidney; and UT patient nodes that correspond to recipients of unlikely transplantability. Edges in the graph instead represent the compatibility between two nodes: we add an edge (X, Y) from node X to node Y only if the donor/kidney of node X is compatible with the patient of node Y. Nodes representing kidneys only have outgoing edges and UT patients nodes have only incoming edges. Pair nodes may have both outgoing and incoming edges. Therefore we partition the set of nodes N in three sets: P the set of the pair nodes, UT the set of immunized patient and K the set of kidney. Given a node X, we call E_X the set of its edges, partitioned in two subsets: the incoming edges E_X^- and the outgoing edges E_X^+.

An edge can be *active* or *inactive*: to each edge e is associated a value v_e in $\{0, 1\}$ such that $v_e = 1$ if the edge is active and 0 if inactive. The semantics of the active/inactive edges is that the edges represents possible transplants, and the active ones represent the transplants that are performed in practice at that time stamp t.

2.3 Constraints

A set of constraints is defined on activation values of the incoming and outgoing edges of a node depending on its types.

Kidney nodes (K): This type of node can either have only an outgoing edge activated, or all the edges inactive, because each kidney can be given only to one patient or to no one.

Pair nodes (P):. This type of node can either have only an incoming edge activated, or one incoming and one outgoing edge activated or all the edges inactive. This because a pair cannot donate a kidney without receiving another kidney, but can receive and not donate because in this case the kidney of the donor will be donated to the patients in the deceased-donor waiting list.

Immunized patient nodes (UT): This type of node can have either only an incoming edge active, or all the edges inactive. This because each patient can either receive only one kidney or no kidney.

We can translate the constraints described above more formally as:

$$\begin{cases} v_e \in \{0,1\} \; \forall e \in E & \text{activation} \\ \sum_{e \in E_X} v_e \in \{0,1\} \; \forall X \in K & \text{K nodes} \\ \sum_{e \in E_X^-} v_e - \sum_{e \in E_X^+} v_e \in \{0,1\} \; \forall X \in P & \text{P nodes} \\ \sum_{e \in E_X} v_e \in \{0,1,2\} \; \forall X \in P & \text{P nodes} \\ \sum_{e \in E_X} v_e \in \{0,1\} \; \forall X \in UT & \text{UT nodes} \end{cases}$$

In our experiments we considered also an additional constraint over the compatibility graph: if we include in our pool also kidneys that we would allocate to an immunized patient (UT) in the deceased donor waiting list, then we want to preserve the number of UT patients that receive an organ. This because we want to prioritize this category and not create a disadvantage. The formulation of this constraint is:

$$\sum_{X \in UT} \Big(\sum_{e \in E_X^-} v_e \Big) - \sum_{X \in K} \Big(\sum_{e \in E_X^-} v_e \Big) \geq 0$$

2.4 Objective function

At each iteration of the algorithm (either cycle or chain detection), we maximize the following objective function: $\sum_{e \in E} v_e$, that maximize the number of active edges in the graph. This corresponds to maximizing the number of transplants. It is important to notice that a priority over the UT patients respect to normal patients in the waiting list is implicitly encoded in the graph construction. Once obtained a solution (a set of active edges), the patients/pairs that will be transplanted correspond to the subset of nodes that are touched by active edges. We then remove this nodes/patients for the next iteration of the procedure.

2.5 Main procedures

We describe now, formally, the two different procedures:

Cycle detection: This happen when at time t a new pair joins the pool. We build a compatibility graph using only the pair nodes currently part of the pool $P(t)$. On the compatibility graph, we then maximize the length of a cycle involving the new pair, if exist. To this purpose we create another graph, namely the *cycle graph*, in which each node corresponds to a cycle of length 2 or 3 (this is a common assumption in this scenarios, since all the transplants in the cycle have to be performed simultaneously). The edges of the cycle graph connect two nodes representing cycles with at least one node in common in the compatibility graph. We solve this optimization problem maximizing the cardinality of a coloring problem over the cycle's graph.

Chain detection: This happen when at time t a new deceased-donor kidney arrives to the waiting list. We build a compatibility graph using the pair nodes, the UT nodes currently part of the pool $P(t)$ and and the kidney node. Here we look for the maximum chain of nodes starting from the kidney. We solve this problem as a single source longest path problem[2].

2.6 Assumptions

The implementation of the algorithm that we used for our experiments is based on two assumptions/restrictions. The first assumption is that, during the chain detection phase, the compatibility graph is assumed to be acyclic since all the transplant in the cycles are performed in previous steps. This is a reasonable assumption for our study, but in reality many cycles are not performed since patients involved prefer to wait to obtain a better graft. Thus the compatibility graph could contain some cycles. The second restriction is that during the cycle detection our algorithm focus only on cycles that involve the new pair. This is a reasonable assumption

[2]Note that we assume the pool $P(t)$ to be acyclic, since all the transplant in the cycles are performed in previous steps

for our study since we are operating in a small pool (described in the Experiments Section). In practice if we consider a bigger pool (for example at national level), the introduction of new pairs is done monthly. This implies that at that time t usually more than one pair is introduced to the pool. In this case we are not interested on maximizing the length of a single cycle but on maximizing the total number of transplants. That means we are looking for the set of cycles that maximally cover the graph without intersections.

We also implemented a different version of the algorithm for a general use, that supports also the removal of the two restriction described above. The new version of the algorithm is a reformulation of the maximization problem in integer linear programming (ILP). The objective function to maximize is the sum of active edges and the constrains correspond to a ILP version of the constraints on the compatibility graph described at the beginning of the section. We implemented the algorithm in Python using the open-source library *lp_solve*.

2.7 Examples

We now show two examples, one for the *cycle detection* step of the procedure in Example 2.1 and one for the *kidneys processing* step in Figure 2.2.

Example 2.1 (Cycle detection). In the *cycle detection* example (Figure 2) we have four pairs $P.0$, $P.1$, $P.2$ and $P.3$. The patient in $P.0$ is compatible with the donor in $P.1$; the patient in is $P.1$ compatible with the donors in $P.0$ and $P.2$; the patient in is $P.2$ compatible with the donors in $P.0$ and $P.1$; and the patient in is $P.3$ compatible with the donor in $P.2$. We can see that the algorithm detects the cycle with the maximal number of transplants (the edges in red): between nodes $P.0$, $P.1$ and $P.2$.

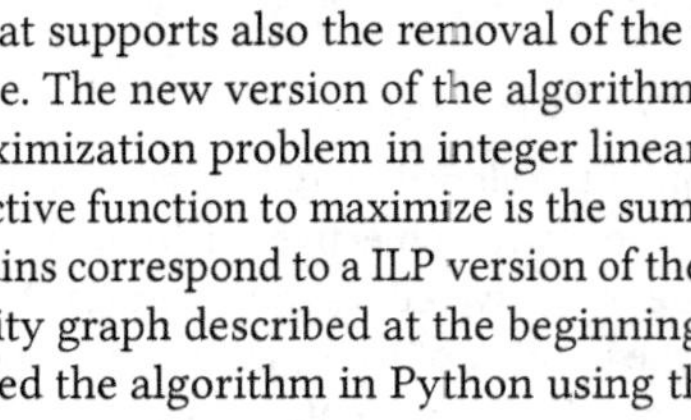

Figure 2: Example 2.1: cycle detection.

Example 2.2 (Chain detection). In the *kidneys processing* example in Figure 3, we have four nodes: tree pairs $P.0$, $P.1$ and $P.2$; one kidney from a deceased donor K; and one UT patients UT. The patient in $P.0$ is compatible only kidney from a deceased donor K; the patient in is $P.1$ is compatible with the donor in $P.0$ and kidney from a deceased donor K; the patient in is $P.2$ is compatible with the donor in $P.1$; and the patient in UT is compatible with the donors in $P.0$ and $P.1$. We can see that the algorithm detects the longest chain that maximize the number of transplants that starts from K then reach in order $P.0$, $P.1$ and ends in UT.

3 EXPERIMENTS

While the cycles detection procedure is well studied in the literature from an ethical point of view, the chain detection starting from a deceased donor is a novel method. Our sequential algorithm for chain detection works as follows on our pool: when an organ from a deceased donor becomes available, we compute all the chains that could be generated by assigning this organ to some recipient with an incompatible living donor. Among all chains, we perform the longest one and we remove all recipients and corresponding donors from the pool. When the following organ becomes available we iterate the procedure with the remaining pool. The recipient of the deceased donor organ could be any of the patients with an incompatible donor who were not transplanted during the period. Receiving a transplant, even from a deceased donor, is a sure gain for those patients who were not transplanted, but one may argue that this policy would subtract organs from the pool available for waitlisted candidates. The organ harvested from a living donor of the last component of the chain will terminate to a deceased donor waitlisted patient; therefore waitlisted patients without a potential living donor do not suffer due to the introduction of this allocation procedure - because the expected graft survival of a living donor kidney is on average higher than a deceased donor one. Nevertheless, there has to be some equity warranted for the waitlisted candidates with a lower probability of finding a compatible organ. To this end, we add two constraints to our algorithm. First, deceased donor organs that were directly allocated to recipients of unlikely transplantability recipients were excluded from the algorithm, and we only consider organs allocated to patients in the standard waiting list. Second, anytime there exists more than one living donor chain with the maximal length, we select the one, if any, that ends with an UT recipient.

All the experiments were conducted using a custom Python code on a machine with an Eight-Core Intel(R) Xeon(R) 2.40GHz with 256GB of RAM.

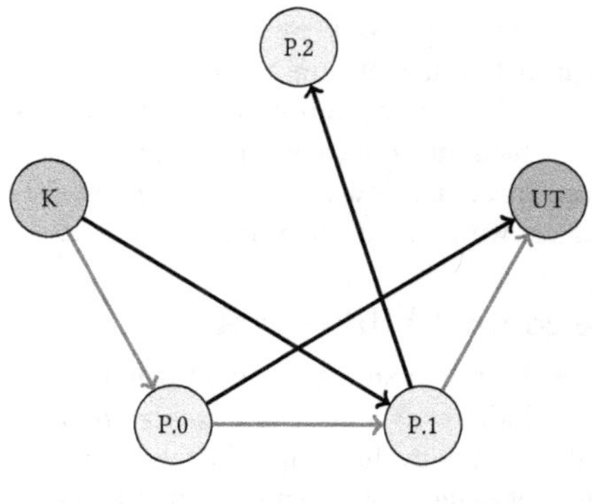

Figure 3: Example 2.2: chain detection.

3.1 Data

From January 2012 to December 2014 at the Kidney and Pancreas Transplantation Unit of the Padua University-Hospital 358 single kidney transplants (KT) were performed. Among them, 251 KT were done with grafts from deceased donors and 107 from living donors. The living donors transplantation included: 77 AB0-compatible pairs and 30 desensitized recipients (22 AB0 incompatible pairs and 8 recipients with donor-specific anti-HLA antibodies). During the same span, 16 incompatible pairs were evaluated in the centre

Characteristics	Kidneys	UT patients	NT donors	NT patients	DS donors	DS patients
SEX F/M	30/39	14/21	11/7	8/8	22/8	13/17
AGE (mean)	48	47	54.34	47.12	48.63	42.07
BLOOD type A/B/AB/0	30/11/4/24	13/2/1/19	7/4/0/7	4/3/0/9	15/2/6/7	8/5/1/16
PRA max (mean)	-	58.43	-	56.56	-	-

Table 1: Pool characteristics

and were enrolled in the KPE program and/or listed for deceased donor kidney transplantation and could not be transplanted within the three-year period (in 2 cases a recipient had 2 willing donors). Among the DD kidneys that were allocated to this centre in the relevant span, we only consider organs of from deceased donors of "high quality", that is with an expected graft survival comparable to that of a living donor, according to the medical literature (age < 60 years, absence of comorbidities such as hypertension and diabetes, calculated creatinine clearance > 60 ml/min, absence of proteinuria). We also excluded organs that were assigned to UT patients . UT recipients were defined based on the classification of The North Italian Transplant Program (NITp), which considers UT recipients those patients on the waiting-list for more than 5 years or on dialysis for more than 7 years. During the period of study, (2012-2014), 35 UT recipients of unlikely transplantability were listed at our Centre and did not receive any organ. Summing up, data used to run our retrospective studies are the following: 16 NT pairs, 30 DS pairs, 35 UT recipients, 69 DD "high-quality" kidneys.

The population of DS pairs benefit from the participation to the program because recipients of these pairs could avoid debilitating and costly desensitization procedures. However, these patients should be considered differently than patients who were not transplanted to ensure that they are willing to enter into the program. To this end, we impose two constraints to the algorithm. First, for desensitised patients (DS patients), the advantage of receiving a kidney from a compatible donor in a KPE fashion should not prolong their waiting time on dialysis: therefore, we grant the availability of these pairs in the pool within 6 months from the date of their actual transplant; after this date recipients are desensitized and get the organ of their willing donor. Second, DS patients can only receive an organ from a living donor and not from a deceased donor, and therefore they cannot be the first recipient of a living donor chain initiated by a deceased donor organ.

For a proper allocation of the organs, immunological variables of donors and recipients were taken into account (e.g. HLA typing, blood type, etc.). The statistics on the distribution [3] of sex, age, blood type and PRA max of the above described pool are summarized in Table 1.

3.2 Experiments' Design

We performed a set of experiment varying a set of 4 parameters. Each experiment is labeled with four letters filling a slot of four fields, each one corresponding to the presence of the corresponding parameter. If a parameter is missing we denote it with the hyphen symbol: –. We describe now the four ordered fields:

First field (C): In these experiments we perform cycles detection when a new pair enter the pool. We consider the sequence of entering of pairs to the waiting list. Any time a new pair join the program we ran the algorithm searching the longest cycle involving the new pair. In the experiments without the 'C' as first field we do not look for cycles but only for chains of donations.

Second field (C): In these experiments we perform chain detection when a new deceased-donor kidney arrive to the waiting list. We consider the sequence of deceased donor organs that were available in the relevant time span to initiate living donor chains and any time a new organ was available we ran the algorithm searching the longest living donor chain initiated by this organ. In the experiments without the 'C' as second field we do not search for chains but only cycles of donations.

Third field (D): We add to the pool the pairs of DS patients (NT pairs are always in the pool). The algorithm works in a similar fashion to the previous one, but in addition, when an incompatible pair requiring desensitization joins the pool, we immediately check if it is possible to create a two or three-way exchange among the pairs who are in our pool at that moment. The population of DS pairs benefit from the participation to the program because recipients of these pairs could avoid debilitating and costly desensitization procedures. However, these patients should be considered differently than patients who were not transplanted to ensure that they are willing to enter into the program. To this end, we impose two constraints to the algorithm. First, a DS patient and her donor remain in the pool for at most six months. During this span, they are scrutinized in each algorithm iteration: that is when either a new deceased donor organ becomes available, or a new incompatible pair requiring desensitization joins the pool. After six months, if no exchange was possible, they will leave the pool, and the transplant is performed using desensitization between the pair. Second, a DS patient can only receive an organ from a living donor and not from a deceased donor, and therefore cannot be the first recipient of a living donor chain initiated by a deceased donor organ. In the experiments without the 'D' as third field we do not introduce in the pool of desensitized pairs, but only NT pairs.

Fourth field (0): Since the kidneys with 0 blood type are more favorites (since compatible with all the other blood types) we want to preserve the number of 0-type organs given to the deceased-donor waiting list. To do this, when we receive a 0-type kidney we only allow the chain either to finish with a UT-patient or returning a 0-type kidney to the deceased-donor waiting list. In the experiments

[3] The number of donors of the NT pairs could be greater than the number of patients because some patients have multiple donors. This does not happen for the DS pairs since these pairs have already been transplanted with their donor that is therefore unique.

Number of:	-C- -	-C-0	-CD-	-CD0	C-D-	CCD-	CCD0	CCD0$^+$
NT patients who received an organ	8/16	8/16	12/16	9/16	4/16	12/16	10 /16	7/16
DS patients who avoided desensitization	0/16	0/16	10/16	4/16	6/16	10/16	10/16	6/16
UT patients who received an organ	11/35	6/35	9/35	7/35	0/35	9/35	5/35	3/35
Deceased donor kidneys that are used	15/69	7/69	14/69	8/69	0/69	14/69	5/69	3/69
Living donor kidneys returned to the waiting list	4	1	5	1	0	5	0	0

Table 2: Results of the performed experiments.

without the '0' as last field the chains can end with any patient or pair, without any restriction on their blood type.

We provide now some example of experiments labels associated with their meaning.

Example 3.1. For example the experiment -C- - represents the dynamic computation of only chains on a pool composed by: NT pairs, a deceased-donor kidney and UT patients. The experiment CCD0 instead represent the dynamic computation of chains and cycles on a pool composed by: NT pairs, DS pairs, a deceased-donor kidney and UT patients with the 0-type preservation constraint.

It is important to notice that not all the combinations of these four parameters is feasible. For example all the combinations with the first two fields both empty it is not possible, since we want to perform at least one procedure between chain detection or cycle detection.

Moreover, in our experiments we considered also a stronger version of the 0-type preservation constraint, that will be denoted as 0^+: as in the 0-type preservation constraint with the addition that if the deceased-donor kidney has 0 blood type then we allow the chain either to finish with a UT-patient with 0 blood type or returning a 0 blood type kidney to the deceased-donor waiting list.

3.3 Results and Discussion

The results of the retrospective simulations are summarized in Table 2.

Analyzing for example the experiment $-C-0$, we notice that given a cohort of 16 incompatible pairs, and a pool of 69 standard deceased-donors allocated to the Padua Transplant Centre, it turns out that by using 7 grafts from DDs to start a chain, it was theoretically possible to transplant 50% of the patients who would have not been otherwise able to receive a transplant in a time span of three years. This means that only 10% of the entire pool of standard grafts available was utilized to enter the program. Moreover, in most of the cases (6 out of 7) the chains ended to a UT recipient who therefore received a living donor kidney instead of a deceased-donor organ.

However, it is noteworthy that, differently from in list exchanges, patients participating in a chain of donations receive a kidney before her/his donor donates an organ to another patient. Moreover, for each incompatible pair, who can start a chain of donations, it is possible to compute in advance (in offline fashion) which is the optimal chain to perform, making the logistics easier.

The usefulness of the proposed program results undeniable, since it increases the overall number of kidneys available for transplantation and, consequently, the aggregate quality and quantity of life of end-stage-renal-disease patients. Our procedure has been approved and a first trial at the local level of a KP chain initiated by a DD has been performed on March 14, 2018 and two more chains respectively of three and four length are currently performed at national level showing the benefits of the program also in practice.

4 CONCLUSION AND FUTURE WORK

In this paper we have analyzed the efficiency of a novel allocation procedure for kidney transplant: we have proposed a first method based on the idea of considering both cycles of exchanges and chains of exchanges which start from a deceased donor kidney. We have implemented the procedure and have tested it in a retrospective fashion, using historical data from Padua's transplantation center. The results show that we increase both the number of incompatible pairs that are transplanted and the number of highly-sensitized (UT) patients that received a donation (that normally have a very low probability to receive a compatible kidney). Moreover we have avoided desensitization by the majority of the patient/donor pairs that were transplanted with desensitization.

An immediate next step for our work would be the extension the program to more than one single centre. This would likely lead to better results, since the pool would be bigger increasing the probability of compatibility.

A possible further expansion of this program that combines living and deceased donors is represented by the inclusion of compatible pairs to the pool of participants, encouraging them to enroll in the program with the promise of a gain in terms of expected quality of the organ with respect to the intended donor.

We plan also to consider the patients' preferences in order to minimize the number of matching rejections. For instance we could include the patients' preferences about the location of the hospital (to avoid rejections for logistical problems) or estimate the risk aversion of each patient and the corresponding donor (to minimize the possibility of withdraws due to the non-simultaneously of the transplants).

ACKNOWLEDGMENTS

This work has been partially supported by the strategic project "KIDNEY-Incorporating patients preferences in kidney transplant decision protocols" funded by the University of Padova.

REFERENCES

[1] [n. d.]. OPTN data as of January 12, 2017. https://optn.transplant.hrsa.gov/data/view-data-reports/national-data

[2] M.U. Unver A. E. Roth, T. Sonmez. 2004. Kidney exchange.. In *Quarterly Journal of Economics*.

[3] U. Unver A. Roth, T. Sonmez. 2005. Pairwise kidney exchange.. In *Journal of Economic Theory*.

[4] David J. Abraham, Avrim Blum, and Tuomas Sandholm. 2007. Clearing Algorithms for Barter Exchange Markets: Enabling Nationwide Kidney Exchanges. In *Proceedings of the 8th ACM Conference on Electronic Commerce*.

[5] R. Anderson, I. Ashlagi, D. Gamarnik, and A.E. Roth. 2015. Finding long chains in kidney exchange using the traveling salesman problem.. In *Proceedings of the National Academy of Sciences*.

[6] Itai Ashlagi and Alvin E. Roth. 2014. Free riding and participation in large scale, multiâĂŘhospital kidney exchange. *Theoretical Economics* (2014).

[7] P. Awasthi and T. Sandholm. 2009. Online Stochastic Optimization in the Large: Application to Kidney Exchange.. In *IJCAI*.

[8] P. Birò, L. Burnapp, B. Haase, A. Hemke, R. Johnson, J. van de Klundert, and D. Manlove. 2017. Kidney exchange practices in Europe.. In *First Handbook of the COST Action CA15210: European Network for Collaboration on Kidney Exchange Programmes (ENCKEP)*.

[9] F.L. Delmonico, P.E. Morrissey, G.S. Lipkowitz, and et al. 2004. Donor Kidney Exchanges.. In *Am J Transplant*.

[10] F. L. Delmonico. 2004. Exchanging kidneys – advances in living-donor transplantation. *The New England Journal of Medicine* 350 (2004), 1812–1814.

[11] F. L. Delmonico, G. S. Lipkowitz, P. E. Morrissey, J. S. Stoff, J. Himmelfarb, W. Harmon, M. Pavlakis, H. Mah, J. Goguen, R. Luskin, E. Milford, G. B. M. Chobanian, B. Bouthot, M. Lorber, and R. J. Rohrer. 2004. Donor kidney exchanges. *American Journal of Transplantation* 4 (2004), 1628–1634.

[12] John P. Dickerson, Ariel D. Procaccia, and Tuomas Sandholm. 2012. Optimizing kidney exchange with transplant chains: theory and reality.. In *AAMAS*.

[13] John P. Dickerson, Ariel D. Procaccia, and Tuomas Sandholm. 2013. Failure-aware kidney exchange. In *ACM Conference on Electronic Commerce, EC '13, Philadelphia, PA, USA,*.

[14] John P. Dickerson, Ariel D. Procaccia, and Tuomas Sandholm. 2014. Price of Fairness in Kidney Exchange. In *Proceedings of the 13th International Conference on Autonomous Agents and Multiagent Systems (AAMAS 2014)*.

[15] S. E. Gentry, D. L. Segeva, M. Simmerling, and R. A. Montgomery. 2007. Expanding Kidney Paired Donation Through Participation by Compatible Pairs. *American Journal of Transplantation* (2007).

[16] K.M. Glorie, J.J. van de Klundert, and A. P. M. Wagelmans. 2014. Kidney exchange with long chains: An efficient pricing algorithm for clearing barter exchanges with branch-and-price.. In *Manufacturing & Service Operations Management (MSOM)*.

[17] D. Manlove and G. O'Malley. 2015. Paired and altruistic kidney donation in the UK: Algorithms and experimentation.. In *ACM Journal of Experimental Algorithmics*.

[18] D. F. Manlove and G. O'malley. 2014. Paired and altruistic kidney donation in the UK: Algorithms and experimentation. *Journal of Experimental Algorithmics* 2 (2014), 6.

[19] M.L. Melcher, J.P. Roberts, A.B. Leichtman, and et al. 2016. Utilization of deceased donor kidneys to initiate living donor chains. In *Am J Transplant*.

[20] A. Nicolò and C. Rodríguez-Álvarez. 2012. Transplant quality and patients' preferences in paired kidney exchange. *Games and Economic Behavior* (2012).

[21] A. Nicolò and C. Rodríguez-Álvarez. 2017. Age-based preferences in paired kidney exchange. *Games and Economic Behavior* (2017).

[22] M. Rees, J. Kopke, R. Pelletier, D. Segev, M. Rutter, A. Fabrega, O. Pankewycz J. Rogers, J. Hiller, A. Roth, T. Sandholm, and R. Montgomery U. Unver. 2009. A non simultaneous, extended, altruistic-donor chain.. In *New England Journal of Medicine*.

[23] A. E. Roth, T. Sonmez, and M. U. Unver. 2005. A kidney exchange clearinghouse in New England. *American Economic Review, Papers and Proceedings* (2005).

[24] A. E. Roth, T. Sönmez, M. U. Ünver, F. L Delmonico, and S. L. Saidman. 2006. Utilizing list exchange and nondirected donations through "chain" paired kidney donations. *American Journal of Transplantation* 6 (2006), 2694–2705.

[25] T. Sonmez and M. Unver. 2014. Altruistically unbalanced kidney exchange. *Journal of Economic Theory* (2014).

[26] X. Su, S. A. Zenios, and G. M. Chertow. 2004. Incorporating recipient choice in kidney transplantation. *Journal of the American Society of Nephrology* (2004).

[27] M. Unver. 2010. Dynamic kidney exchange. *Review of Economic Studies* (2010).

[28] J.L. Veale, A.M. Capron, N. Nassiri, and et al. 2017. Vouchers for future kidney transplants to overcome chronological incompatibility between living donors and recipients.. In *Transplantation*.

[29] A.E. Wall, J.L. Veale, and M.L. Melcher. 2017. Advanced donation programs and deceased donor-initiated chains- 2 innovations in kidney paired donation. In *Transplantation*.

Inferring Work Task Automatability from AI Expert Evidence

Paul Duckworth*
University of Oxford
Oxford, United Kingdom
paul.duckworth@eng.ox.ac.uk

Logan Graham*
University of Oxford
Oxford, United Kingdom
logan@robots.ox.ac.uk

Michael Osborne
University of Oxford
Oxford, United Kingdom
mosb@robots.ox.ac.uk

ABSTRACT

Despite growing alarm about machine learning technologies automating jobs, there is little good evidence on what activities can be automated using such technologies. We contribute the first dataset of its kind by surveying over 150 top academics and industry experts in machine learning, robotics and AI, receiving over 4,500 ratings of how automatable specific tasks are today. We present a probabilistic machine learning model to learn the patterns connecting expert estimates of task automatability and the skills, knowledge and abilities required to perform those tasks. Our model infers the automatability of over 2,000 work activities, and we show how automation differs across types of activities and types of occupations. Sensitivity analysis identifies the specific skills, knowledge and abilities of activities that drive higher or lower automatability. We provide quantitative evidence of what is perceived to be automatable using the state-of-the-art in machine learning technology. We consider the societal impacts of these results and of task-level approaches.

CCS CONCEPTS

• **Applied computing** → **Economics** ; • **Computing methodologies** → *Machine learning approaches*; *Gaussian processes*; • **Social and professional topics** → *Government technology policy*.

KEYWORDS

automation, labor economics, Bayesian machine learning, interpretable machine learning, open datasets

ACM Reference Format:
Paul Duckworth, Logan Graham, and Michael Osborne. 2019. Inferring Work Task Automatability from AI Expert Evidence. In *AAAI/ACM Conference on AI, Ethics, and Society (AIES '19), January 27–28, 2019, Honolulu, HI, USA*. ACM, New York, NY, USA, 7 pages. https://doi.org/10.1145/3306618.3314247

*Both authors contributed equally to this research.

ACM ISBN 978-1-4503-6324-2/19/01.
https://doi.org/10.1145/3306618.3314247

INTRODUCTION

Machine learning (ML), in combination with complementary technologies such as robotics and software-based standardization, have rapidly become real substitutes and complements to human labor. This work aims to better understand that automation, and its effects on work. One example is Amazon Go, a recently opened grocery store that uses computer vision to replace cashiers, of which over 3.5 million are employed in the United States [1, 11]. Further, the 500 000 designers in the US are beginning to use constraint-based generative design to automate creative designs of buildings, industrial components, and more [1, 4]. As a result, we as researchers in these fields often confront examples of media and public concern about technologies we develop. What remains uncertain is the magnitude and direction of impact on employment of machine learning technologies. While recent advances in technology seem able to automate *intelligent* work, we lack good data on the scope of such automation.

We collected a detailed *task*-based survey of 150+ machine learning, robotics, and automation researchers. This is the first dataset of its kind with over 4,500 datapoints about what specific tasks are automatable according to *current* technology. In this "nowcasting" exercise, technologists provide knowledge of the extent to which a task can or cannot be automated with technology that exists *today*. We use a probabilistic model to infer the automatability of thousands of activities for which it would be prohibitively difficult to collect reliable data. By collecting task-specific data to model automatability, we believe we can develop richer, more accurate frameworks about what can be automated by the current state-of-the-art in intelligent technology. We believe this allows society to better understand and prepare for automation.

The contributions of this paper are a novel dataset of the automatability of workplace activities; a probabilistic method for inferring automatability of unmeasured activities; activity-level analysis of automatability; and consequent patterns across worktypes, occupations, income, and education. We use more detailed numeric attributes and incorporate more expert knowledge than used in previous studies.

We demonstrate that we can accurately model expert opinions regarding the current state of automation, and introduce a methodology that goes beyond the limitations of the literature. We call for more and better measurement of automation at the activity level. We discuss how this is needed to better prepare governments, employees, and businesses for the effects of automation.

RELATED WORK

Traditionally, approaches to predicting what is automatable have developed frameworks based on the "types" of occupations and the skills they require [2, 5, 9]. One popular framework places occupations on a manual-cognitive spectrum and a standardizable-dynamic spectrum. These frameworks are broad and don't best reflect that *tasks* (or groups of tasks), not *entire occupations*, are the unit of automation. As a result, public perception is conflicted about the true effect of automation on work [24].

Recent work assumes that occupations are better analyzed as evolving combinations of detailed tasks, skills, and/or environments [2, 3, 14]. With increasingly granular job data available from sources such as from O*NET [20], that break down occupations into hundreds of continuously updated numerical components, we believe there is an opportunity to evaluate occupations by focusing on their tasks, skills, and environments. Two recent reports use a task-first approach. A recent report by McKinsey [14] uses an unclear approach to model the opinions of automation potential of an unknown number of industry-based potentially non-technical experts. Another recent analysis by the OECD [3] derives high-level task-level estimates from occupation-level estimates, and uses worker (not task) characteristics in their inference procedure.

We differ from previous approaches in three key aspects: first, we seek expert knowledge at the most granular task level, similar to [14] and [10]. Second, we ask what is automatable *today* and do not make speculative assumptions about future developments or uptake of future technological advancements. Third, we present a robust and (soon) openly available probabilistic methodology and dataset.

DATA REPRESENTATION

Expert Survey. We conducted an online survey of 156 academic and industry experts in machine learning, robotics and intelligent systems about how automatable specific tasks are using technology available today. Each expert was presented with 5 occupations and their 5 "most important" tasks, taken from the Occupational Network (O*NET) 2016 database [20]. The complete list of 70 occupations whose tasks are annotated is shown in Table 2 in Appendix A, with occupations chosen to be representative of the feature space, with an emphasis on high-employment and hence familiar occupations. Five sample occupations and their surveyed tasks are displayed in Table 3 in Appendix A.

Each expert answered the following question: *"Do you believe that technology exists today that could automate these tasks?"*, then labeled each task as either: *Not automatable today* (score of 1.0), *Mostly not automatable today (human does most of it)* (2.0), *Could be mostly automated today (human still needed)* (3.0), *Completely automatable today.* (4.0), or *Unsure.* Respondents also reported overall confidence in their answers (distribution shown in Appendix B).

Our dataset contains 4 599 task level responses from 156 academic and industrial experts from around the world, and across various scientific and industrial fields. Due to the mix of fields, we broadly label these as experts in artificial intelligence and recognize experts offer varying perspectives.

We combine each task's multiple expert labels using Independent Bayesian Classifier Combination (IBCC), a principled Bayesian approach to combine multiple classifications [13, 23]. IBCC creates a posterior over labels that reflects the individual labellers' tendencies to agree with other labellers over ultimately chosen label values. We averaged IBCC task scores into their task's work activity (described below). Labels concentrate around whole and half values and we round the final values to the closest 0.5 (a half-class).

We believe a survey of many experts, combined using IBCC, is a transparent and reliable method of obtaining data about the current state of task automation. It requires no forecasting or prediction by the participants. The distribution of task-level expert responses, and the IBCC combined task-label distribution are shown in Table 5 in Appendix B. The distributions of field-relevant academic experience, and the geographic location are shown in Figure 7 in Appendix B. 97% of participants had field-relevant academic experience: most participants coming from computer science, ML, robotic or AI backgrounds, and 52% of responses from the US, UK and Germany, with the rest from 30 other countries. This aggregate dataset will be made openly available.

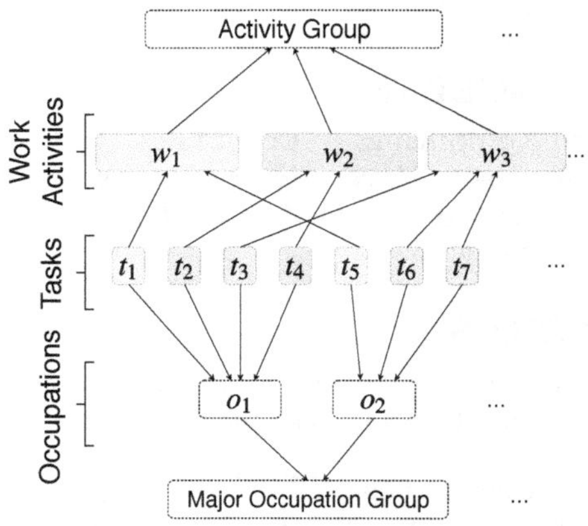

Figure 1: O*NET Database Taxonomy including occupations o, work activities w, tasks t, and high-level groupings.

Occupations, Activities and Tasks. An occupation o is represented as a set of discrete *tasks* an employee may be required to perform, $o = \{t_1, t_2, \ldots, t_n\}$. Each occupation may have a different number of tasks, and all tasks are detailed enough to be unique to one occupation.

Similar tasks are grouped into a *work activity* w such that $w = \{t_i, \ldots, t_j\}$. While a task is occupation specific, work activities are generic activities performed across multiple occupations. We further aggregate results to major occupational groups and high-level activity groups. A diagram demonstrating this hierarchy is shown in Figure 1.

Automation by Work Activity. To create activity-specific feature vectors, we aggregate the roughly 20, 000 tasks into their 2, 067 work activities (which are called Detailed Work Activities in O*NET) to create a feature vector $\boldsymbol{x}_w$ for specific work activity w. Each occupation is represented as a vector $\boldsymbol{x}_o$, comprising of the numerical ratings of its skills, $(\boldsymbol{x}_o^s)$, knowledge $(\boldsymbol{x}_o^k)$ and abilities $(\boldsymbol{x}_o^a)$, i.e. $\boldsymbol{x}_o = [\boldsymbol{x}_o^s, \boldsymbol{x}_o^k, \boldsymbol{x}_o^a]$. We represent each task t of occupation o with the feature vector of occupation o, because we assume that an occupation's skills, knowledge, and abilities informs those needed to perform its constituent tasks. These features are measured quantitatively on a 1 to 5 scale by dozens of employees and experts in the O*NET database.

The activity feature vector is a weighted average of its constituent task vectors: $\boldsymbol{x}_w = \sum_{t \in w} w_{(t,w)} \boldsymbol{x}_o$. $w_{(t,w)}$ is a normalized weight of the task's relative importance to its occupation and work activity, i.e. $w_{(t,w)} = I_{(t,o)} I_{(t,w)} / \sum_{t \in w} I_{(t,o)} I_{(t,w)}$. The relative importance of the task to its occupation is calculated as $I_{(t,o)} = {}^{I_t}/{\sum_{t \in o} I_t}$, while the relative importance of a task to its work activity is $I_{(t,w)} = {}^{I_t}/{\sum_{t \in w} I_t}$. Task importance I_t is a numeric measure also supplied by O*NET.

Automation by Occupation. We also explore what the automatability of activities implies about the automatability of the occupations that perform them. First, we infer automation scores $\hat{\boldsymbol{y}}_w$ for all work activities (including unlabeled ones), as will be described in the next section. We construct an occupation automation score $\hat{y}_o$ for occupation o using the importance-weighted average of its constituent work activities: $\hat{y}_o = \sum_{w \in \Omega_o} I_{(w,o)} \hat{y}_w$, where Ω_o, is the set of all work activities performed by occupation o, and $I_{(w,o)}$ is the importance score of work activity w normalized over this set.

We present automatability over *major occupation groups* which are the highest level occupation categorisation provided by the Bureau of Labor Statistics' SOC system. We represent a major occupation group G as a set of occupations $\{o_1, o_2, \dots\}$ and construct the automation score $\hat{y}_G$ by taking the employment-weighted average of the automatability scores of its constituent occupations, $\hat{\boldsymbol{y}}_o$ for all occupations in the group, i.e. $o \in G$.

On Using IBCC on Training Data. We believe using IBCC to achieve a single rating from multiple experts is advantageous both because it is fully Bayesian and reflects a higher chance of accurately recovering the true automatability label of a task in an environment of uncertainty and subjectivity. The main idea is to use the agreement of responses to learn a belief over the correctness of each individual classifier (each human expert) in order to weight their responses. The alternative – averaging task scores – we believe misrepresents the ordinal classification task as a continuous regression task. A side-effect of this approach is that the ground truth labels are more polarised at the extreme values (one and four), when compared with simply (mean) aggregating the task-level responses together. A complication of this is that when comparing two models based upon their Root Mean Squared Error (RMSE), lower absolute error is achieved by not using the (more polarized) IBCC combined labels. However, we believe they are more representative when combining multiple (semi)-reliable expert sources. In future work, we would like to explore modeling at the individual user-task label level.

The interpretation of the learning task and the social scientific nature of the data influence the correct choice of metric and model. This is often found in computational social science. We save deeper rationalizations of our data, model, and task setup choices for further work.

MODEL COMPARISON AND VALIDATION

We seek a flexible function estimation capable of modeling complex, non-linear relationships between the features (skills, abilities, knowledge) and (perceived) automatability in high-dimensional space. Given the social scientific nature of the study, we also desire a measure of model uncertainty. We compare models based on their "tolerance accuracy" score – the percent of posterior prediction means, $\hat{\boldsymbol{y}}_w$, that are within 0.5 of the ground truth post-IBCC survey value $\boldsymbol{y}_w$. This is a sensible score for our task, and allows more flexibility in our multiclass ordinal setting than strict accuracy or average error. This score also takes into account that we compare models with heterogenous output types – some output discrete labels, and some output continuous values. We optimised the hyperparameters of all models using 10-fold cross-validation.

Our first candidate model class is that of Gaussian Processes (GPs) [22], which have previously been applied to *occupation*-based data in [9] and [7]. We specifically use the ordinal likelihood function introduced in [8] to reflect the nature of having discrete labels but with an ordinal interpretation (*not at all* to *completely* automatable). We use the squared exponential, or RBF, kernel, as it consistently performed well compared to other kernels and was less likely to overfit. We optimize the kernel hyperparameters by minimizing the negative marginal log likelihood $\log p(\boldsymbol{y}_w \mid \boldsymbol{x}_w)$ as described in [22], using the open source software GPFlow [16].

Table 1: Model tolerance accuracy & negative log likelihood.

Model	Accuracy (std)	−Log-likelihood
Ordinal RBF GP	**0.645** (0.028)	385.6
Gaussian RBF GP	0.643 (0.102)	382.3
Ordinal DNN	0.604 (0.071)	–
Random Forest	0.517 (0.081)	–
Ordinal Regression	0.451 (0.036)	–
$\hat{\boldsymbol{y}}_w = \text{avg}(\boldsymbol{y}_w)$	0.575 (0.065)	–
Proportional Random	0.374 (0.049)	–

For other candidate models, we consider ordinal logistic regression [21], a random forest, and a neural network with an ordinal loss function [12], with a 4-layer (120-60-120-7) fully connected layer architecture and 10% layer-wise dropout. A proportional random assignment and constant mean predictor

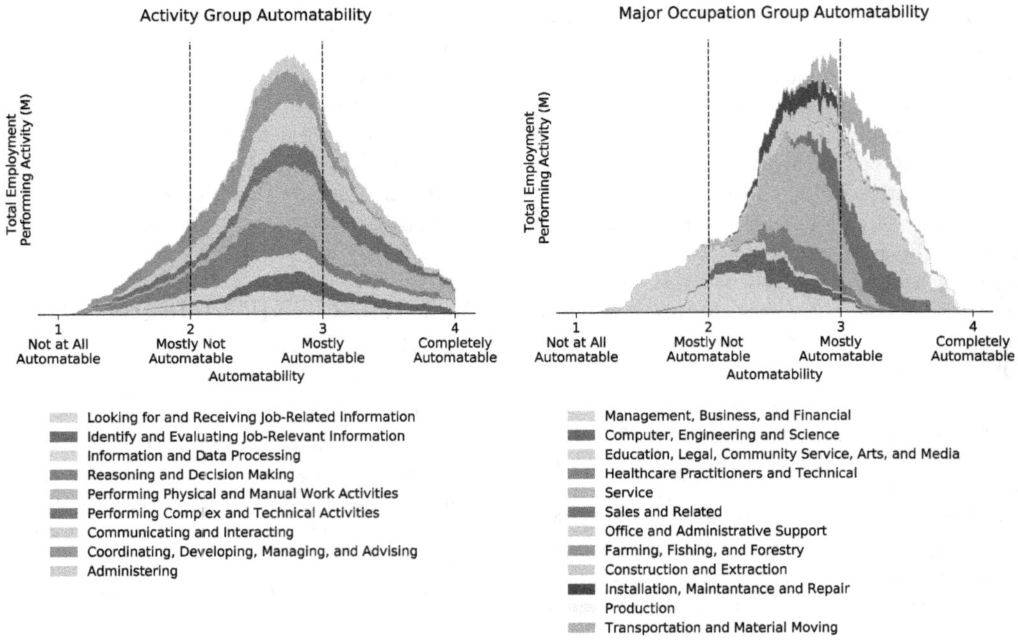

Figure 2: (left:) Amount of employment affected across automatability scores, by 9 high level activity groups. (right:) Employment affected across automatability scores, by 12 major occupation groups.

are compared as a lower baseline on predictive performance. Notably, just predicting with the value of the mean achieves fourth-best performance. This is due to the concentration of the values, as the mean-predictor offers no useful information. While we believe our metric is the best for assessing models, this highlights the challenges of modelling subjective data with the ordinal classification interpretation we've taken. Results for each model are displayed in Table 1 (standard deviation in brackets). The ordinal GP model consistently outperforms comparative methods at prediction of posterior mean values of automatability over the space of work activities. While the non-ordinal GP model and the optimised deep neural network perform on average similarly to the ordinal GP model, they do so much less reliably.

EXPERIMENTS AND RESULTS

Question 1: What is automatable?

Using the best performing GP model to infer the automatability score for all 2,067 work activities (including the training set), we examine examples of automatable and not-automatable activities. Table 4 in Appendix C presents a sample of work activities with the highest and lowest automatability from the unlabeled data (with uncertainties).

We observe that activities such as "route mail to correct destinations" (3.82) or "cut fabrics" (3.93) have a high automation potential (and indeed, are widely automated). However, we also notice that white collar activities are also highly automatable with current technology: "Operate digital imaging equipment" (3.63), "Send information, materials or documentation" (3.39), and "Advise others on ways to improve processes or products" (3.38). Insights such as these propose likely future automatable areas, where automation could be achieved in the real world with relatively little further attention to the underlying technology. The mean of automatability scores is 2.65, indicating that that the model, learned from expert estimates, believes that tasks are on average more likely to be more automatable than not.

In lieu of profiling the long list of activities by their automatability here, we consider instead what *groups* of activities are automatable, and the implications for occupations when using an activity-first approach. In Figure 2 (left) we plot the automatability of activities by the number of currently-employed individuals who perform them, and classify into nine high-level activity groupings. It becomes evident that while most activities are between mostly and mostly not automatable, work tends to lie closer to "mostly automatable". Eight times as much work lies between "mostly" and "completely" automatable than between "mostly not" and "not at all" automatable, when weighted by employment. Activities classified as "reasoning and decision making" and "coordinating, developing, managing, and advising" are less likely than others to be automatable. However, "administering", "information and data processing" and (perhaps surprisingly) "performing complex and technical activities" are more likely to be automatable.

Additionally, we average the automatability scores of an occupation's activity automatabilities to create an occupation-level automatability score. (How to properly aggregate activities for an occupation-level score is a subject of further research, but we use this as preliminary exploration.) We classify occupations into 12 high-level "Major Occupation Groups", as in Figure 2 (right). We see that the model predicts very high automation potential in office, administrative support (orange), and sales occupations (red), which together employ about 38 million people in the United States. This stands in contrast to the popular emphasis on the automation of physical processes such as production (yellow), farming, fishing and forestry (dark orange), and transportation and material moving (teal), which employ about 20 million people in total. In contrast, two Major Occupation Groups appear robust to automation: education, legal, community service, arts, and media occupations (light green), as well as management, business, and financial occupations (light blue).

Trends across Income and Education. Using our occupation-level mappings, we present a preliminary analysis of how automatable activities cluster across income and education, to understand the likely impact on employees. We use median annual income data from the Occupational Employment Statistics from the Bureau of Labor Statistics [1], and the average expert estimate that one requires at least a bachelor's degree to perform an occupation from O*NET [20].

The impact is perhaps expected. The highest paid, most educated occupations tend to be the least automatable. They tend to be much smaller occupations. However, it is worth noting that even being paid well and having a bachelor's degree does guarantee an occupation's activities are not automatable. "Air Traffic Controllers" make about $125,000 a year, yet are deemed mostly automatable (2.93). "Cytogenetic Technologists", for example, require a Bachelor's degree (with a 100% likelihood from O*NET), with an estimated occupation automatability of 3.03.

Nor is the opposite always true. "Preschool Teachers" and "Teacher Assistants" make just under $30,000 a year, yet are mostly non-automatable (1.71 and 1.87, respectively). O*NET experts estimate a 5% chance of needing at least a bachelor's degree to perform successfully as a "Heating and Air Conditioning Mechanics and Installer", an occupation which is also predicted mostly not automatable (2.38).

Model Disagreements with Ground Truth. It is useful to consider where our model disagrees most with our ground truth labels. While, as discussed, it's difficult to confirm which estimate is true, when the model disagrees with the ground truth, it is using all information learned from all other ratings. Table 7 in Appendix C lists the 50 tasks with most disagreement between ground truth and model.

In the cases where the model *overpredicts* relative to the ground truth, we see common themes. Some activities, such as "connect electrical components or equipment" ($\boldsymbol{y}_w$: 1.0; $\hat{\boldsymbol{y}}_w$: 2.69) are characterised by dextrous physical action (the difficulty of automating of which is famously speculated as "Moravec's paradox" in [18]). Others involve information exchange in a situation with a clear goal, such as "communicate with customers to resolve complaints or ensure satisfaction" ($\boldsymbol{y}_w$: 1.0; $\hat{\boldsymbol{y}}_w$: 2.31). There are also cases involving complex

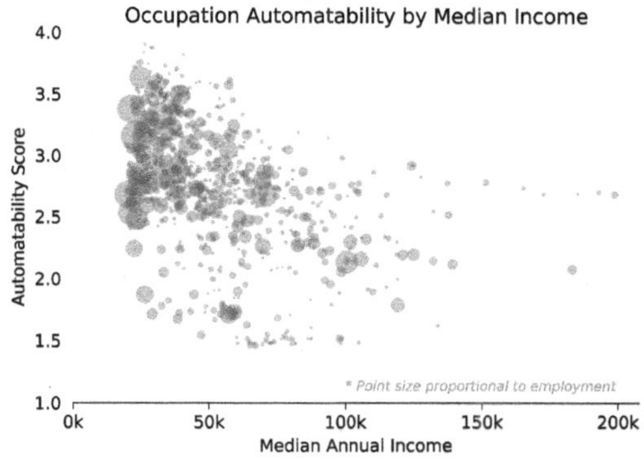

Figure 3: Occupation-level automatability scores by annual median income.

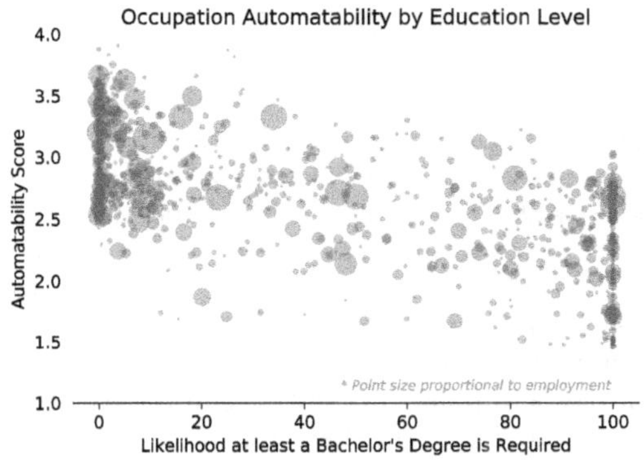

Figure 4: Occupation-level automatability scores by education attainment.

process monitoring. Across these activities, it seems conceivable that while intelligent technology may not automate the *entire* activity, some combination of activity simplification, custom data gathering, and intelligent technology could automate a non-trivial amount of the activity.

The cases where the model underpredicts are more varied in interpretation. Some model underpredictions could be a case of downweighting unreasonable expert beliefs. For example, "position construction forms or molds" ($\boldsymbol{y}_w$: 4.0; $\hat{\boldsymbol{y}}_w$: 2.80) – simple in theory, but influenced by many dynamic environmental factors to render it complex in practice. Other cases of underprediction might also be a reflection of a lack of data around the activity in feature space, leading to limited model learning. For example, there are some activities which are clearly automatable (and already automated) for which the model predicts low automatability (e.g. "Process customer bills or payments" and "Create electronic data backup to prevent loss of information"). Alternatively, the more questionable predictions may be artifacts of the O*NET taxonomy, in which the work activity title does not accurately reflect a critical nuance of its constituent tasks.

Question 2: What makes work automatable?

We now consider what increases or decreases the automatability of some activities. We compute the average derivative of automatability with respect to each feature as described in [6], over the space of work activities. For the nth feature, this is $AD(n) := \mathbb{E}(\partial m(\boldsymbol{x})/\partial \boldsymbol{x}_n)$, where $m(x)$ is the posterior mean distribution. This measures the expected increase in automatability for a unit increase in the feature. Table 8 in Appendix C shows the highest and lowest average derivatives of the posterior mean function per feature.

These gradients seem to reflect what intelligent technology increasingly offers: work that is clerical, repetitive, precise, and perceptual can increasingly be automated. Increases in the features *Clerical, Number Facility, Depth Perception, Control Precision* and *Production and Processing* tend to increase an activity's automatability. Perhaps surprisingly, increases in *Economics and Accounting* and *Sales and Marketing* knowledge and ability also increase automatability, which reflects that we saw business-oriented sales & administrative work types having higher than average automatability.

On the other hand, work that is more creative, dynamic, and human oriented tends to be less automatable. While variable, the three strongest features driving decreased activity automatability are *Installation, Programming* and *Technology Design*. That is to say, the experts who answered our survey are relatively safe, or misperceive themselves to be.

The gradients might, for example, be used by employers/employees and policy makers to skill themselves differently, proactively change the characteristics of work activities, or set policy to incentivize the development of particular skills, knowledge, abilities, or occupations.

Uncovering the Drivers of Automation. In our own analysis, we found that using activity-level ratings allows us to hypothesize richer frameworks about the drivers of automation than the previous occupation-level frameworks. For example, one particularly useful analysis is to examine clusters of similar activities, which score significantly high in a subset of a features but vary substantially in inferred automatability. Some of these activity clusters across features such as *Dynamic Strength, Persuasion, Critical Thinking,* and *Production and Processing* seemed to imply the predictive importance of (a) task-standardization versus dynamism; (b) a well-specified performance metric versus open-ended thinking; (c) single-party versus multi-party goal satisfaction; and (d) active thinking versus active physical interaction. We reserve final conclusions from this approach for further expanded and validated research. In summary, we believe this suggests that more activity-level data likely allows us to find richer frameworks for automatability prediction.

SOCIETAL IMPACT

Automation is a notably data-sparse yet opinion-heavy area of study [17, 19]. We need more clarity about what can be automated, at the *actual* level of automation (tasks), and more granular frameworks based on more granular data. Policymakers would be able to design better, more targeted policy responses, such as incentives to preemptively modify occupations or programs to reskill workers. Workers would be able to upskill or retrain in a more targeted way (towards certain tasks or away from certain tasks) to be robust to automation, instead of abandoning entire occupations. Further, we note the large *psychological* burden of fear, uncertainty, and doubt that comes with uncertain predictions; we hope to replace that with the optimism, clarity, and confidence that comes from every worker having better predictions to enable more effective responses. Last, we would be able to better spot ethically-challenging cases of activity automation, especially in healthcare and social services, *before* they happen, so that we can hold preparatory, informed ethical discussion.

We believe this necessitates collecting more data on automation. Governments, researchers, businesses, and employees would *all* benefit from uniting to do so. Despite automation being one of the dominant themes of work in the coming decades – a perhaps irreversible shift in how work is done in the future – we are only just taking our first steps towards granular, activity-level measurement. In this paper we offer our dataset, consider the value of activity-level data, and present preliminary results that reinforce previous ones and provide more fidelity and opportunities for deeper research.

CONCLUSION & FUTURE WORK

By using a more granular approach to "now-casting" task-level automation, we can unlock more nuanced frameworks about what *actually* can be automated. Using task and activity-level data, we can likely go further to better understand the drivers of automatability.

However, our approach is a first step. We propose to the community six important research gaps that our dataset and approach should be useful for answering. **Real-world validation**: Does our model accurately identify activities that are already automated? **Surprising automation**: Which activities are more, or less, automatable than previous models would have predicted? **Automatable vs. automated**: *Why* are some automatable activities not automated while others are? **Multivariate interaction patterns**: How does one feature modify a different feature's effect on a task's automatability? **Economic value**: What is the monetary value of automation potential for highly automatable activities? (See [15].) **Employee characteristics**: What are the patterns of demographics, industry, technology use, and other characteristics of employees performing activities with low- and high-automatability activities?

ACKNOWLEDGEMENTS

We thank Carl Benedikt Frey, Jonathan Downing, Katja Grace, Allan Dafoe, John Salvatier, Matthew Willis, The Health Foundation (award #7559), the Oxford Martin Programme on Technology and Employment, & the Rhodes Trust.

REFERENCES

[1] 2017. Occupational Employment Statistics. , 90–93 pages. www.bls.gov/oes/

[2] Daron Acemoglu and Pascual Restrepo. 2016. Artificial Intelligence, Automation and Work. (2016). https://doi.org/10.3386/w24196

[3] Melanie Arntz, Terry Gregory, and Ulrich Zierahn. 2016. The Risk of Automation for Jobs in OECD Countries: A Comparative Analysis. *OECD Social, Employment and Migration Working Papers* 2, 189 (2016), 47–54. https://doi.org/10.1787/5jlz9h56dvq7-en

[4] Autodesk. 2017. What Is Generative Design. https://www.autodesk.com/solutions/generative-design

[5] David H Autor. 2013. The "task approach" to labor markets: an overview. *Journal for Labour Market Research* 46, 3 (2013), 185–199. https://doi.org/10.1007/s12651-013-0128-z arXiv:arXiv:1011.1669v3

[6] David Baehrens, Timon Schroeter, Stefan Harmeling, Motoaki Kawanabe, Katja Hansen, and Klaus-Robert Muller. 2010. How to Explain Individual Classification Decisions. *Journal of Machine Learning Research* 11 (2010), 1803–1831. arXiv:0912.1128

[7] Hasan Bakhshi, Jonathan M. Downing, Michael A. Osborne, and Philippe Schneider. 2017. The Future of Skills Employment in 2030.

[8] Wei Chu and Zoubin Ghahramani. 2005. Gaussian processes for ordinal regression. *Journal of machine learning research* 6, Jul (2005), 1019–1041.

[9] Carl Benedikt Frey and Michael A Osborne. 2017. The future of employment: how susceptible are jobs to computerisation? *Technological Forecasting and Social Change* 114 (2017), 254–280.

[10] Katja Grace, John Salvatier, Allan Dafoe, Baobao Zhang, and Owain Evans. 2017. When Will AI Exceed Human Performance? Evidence from AI Experts. (2017). arXiv:1705.08807

[11] Dhruv Grewal, Anne L Roggeveen, and Jens Nordfaelt. 2017. The Future of Retailing. *Journal of Retailing* 93, 1 (2017), 1–6. https://doi.org/10.1016/j.jretai.2016.12.008

[12] Jordan Hart. 2017. Keras Ordinal Categorical Crossentropy. https://github.com/JHart96/keras_ordinal_categorical_crossentropy.

[13] Hyun-Chul Kim and Zoubin Ghahramani. 2012. Bayesian classifier combination. In *Artificial Intelligence and Statistics*. 619–627.

[14] James Manyika, Michael Chui, Me Miremadi, J Bughin, K George, P Willmott, and M Dewhurst. 2017. A Future that Works: Automation, Employment, and Productivity. *McKinsey Global Institute* (2017).

[15] James Manyika, Michael Chui, Mehdi Miremadi, Jacques Bughin, Katy George, Paul Willmott, and Martin Dewhurst. 2017. Harnessing Automation for a Future that Works. *McKinsey Global Institute* (2017).

[16] Alexander G. de G. Matthews, Mark van der Wilk, Tom Nickson, Keisuke. Fujii, Alexis Boukouvalas, Pablo León-Villagrá, Zoubin Ghahramani, and James Hensman. 2017. GPflow: A Gaussian process library using TensorFlow. *Journal of Machine Learning Research* 18, 40 (apr 2017), 1–6. http://jmlr.org/papers/v18/16-537.html

[17] Tom Mitchell and Erik Brynjolfsson. 2017. Track how technology is transforming work. *Nature* 544, 7650 (apr 2017), 290–292.

[18] Hans Moravec. 1990. *Mind Children: the Future of Robot and Human Intelligence.* Harvard University Press. 214 p. pages. https://doi.org/cblibrary-fut

[19] National Academies of Sciences, Engineering and Medicine. 2017. . National Academies Press, Washington, D.C. https://doi.org/10.17226/24649

[20] National Center for O*NET Development. [n. d.]. O*NET OnLine. https://www.onetonline.org/

[21] Fabian Pedregosa-Izquierdo. 2015. *Feature extraction and supervised learning on fMRI : from practice to theory.* Theses. Université Pierre et Marie Curie - Paris VI. https://tel.archives-ouvertes.fr/tel-01100921

[22] Carl Edward Rasmussen and Christopher K.I. Williams. 2006. *Gaussian Processes for Machine Learning.* Vol. 1.

[23] Edwin Simpson, Stephen Roberts, Ioannis Psorakis, and Arfon Smith. 2013. Dynamic bayesian combination of multiple imperfect classifiers. In *Decision making and imperfection.* Springer, 1–35.

[24] Aaron Smith. 2016. *Public Predictions for the Future of Workforce Automation: Full Report.* Technical Report. Pew Research Center.

Robots Can Be More Than Black And White: Examining Racial Bias Towards Robots

Arifah Addison, Christoph Bartneck
HIT Lab NZ, University of Canterbury
Christchurch, New Zealand
christoph.bartneck.canterbury.ac.nz

Kumar Yogeeswaran
Dpt of Psychology, University of Canterbury
Christchurch, New Zealand
kumar.yogeeswaran.canterbury.ac.nz

ABSTRACT

Previous studies showed that using the 'shooter bias' paradigm, people demonstrate a similar racial bias toward dark colored robots over light colored robots (i.e., Black vs. White) as they do toward humans of similar skin tones [3]. However, such an effect could be argued to be the result of social priming. Additionally, it raises the question of how people might respond to robots that are in the middle of the color spectrum (i.e., brown) and whether such effects are moderated by the perceived anthropomorphism of the robots. We conducted two experiments to first examine whether shooter bias tendencies shown towards robots is driven by social priming, and then whether diversification of robot color and level of anthropomorphism influenced shooter bias. Our results showed that shooter bias was not influenced by social priming, and interestingly, introducing a new color of robot removed shooter bias tendencies entirely. However, varying the anthropomorphism of the robots did not moderate the level of shooter bias, and contrary to our expectations, the robots were not perceived by the participants as having different levels of anthropomorphism.

CCS CONCEPTS

• **Human-centered computing** → *Empirical studies in HCI*;

KEYWORDS

HRI, psychology, shooter bias, robot racism, anthropomorphism

ACM Reference format:
Arifah Addison, Christoph Bartneck and Kumar Yogeeswaran. 2019. Robots Can Be More Than Black And White: Examining Racial Bias Towards Robots. In *Proceedings of AAAI/ACM Conference on AI, Ethics, and Society, Honolulu, HI, USA, January 27–28, 2019 (AIES '19)*, 6 pages.
https://doi.org/10.1145/3306618.3314272

1 INTRODUCTION

Although some research has been done around how gender and personality of artificial intelligence is perceived and reacted to, e.g. [17], little research has covered the area of perceived race. This is likely because most robots developed so far are not very human-like. However, those that are could be seen to have a race, as shown in Figure 1, and the first studies have begun to emerge on the topic. For example, by analysing free-form comments about highly human-like robots, it has been shown that people more frequently dehumanise robots racialized as Asian and Black, than they do robots racialized as White [15].

Figure 1: ERICA - ERATO ISHIGURO Symbiotic Human-Robot Interaction Project

The shooter bias paradigm was first introduced in a 2002 paper titled 'The Police Officer's Dilemma: Using Ethnicity to Disambiguate Potentially Threatening Individuals'. In this paper, a clear bias was found when participants were asked to 'shoot' images of Black or White human males that were holding a gun, and 'not shoot' Black or White human males holding benign objects (e.g., a soda can, wallet, cell phone). Both Black and White participants from the USA showed a similar tendency to be quicker to shoot armed Black males and quicker to not shoot unarmed White males (than the other). Such an effect is collectively referred to as a shooter bias, via an interaction between race and object type. A recent meta-analysis of 42 studies supports this general tendency of a shooter bias in the psychological literature [11]. In a recent follow up, the shooter bias paradigm was used to show that the racial bias shown towards Black humans was transferred to humanoid robots of different colors [3]. This study used half human images from the original 2002 experiments, and half 'racialized' robots that were re-colored with Black and White human skin tones, and the results were found to be comparable to the original human-only study. Specifically, people showed a similar shooter bias toward robots racialized as Black relative to White in a similar fashion as they showed toward Black vs. White humans, no matter their own race.

The current research expands on this preliminary work by examining several unanswered questions. (1) First, would such a shooter bias effect emerge if humans were removed from the task entirely?

AIES '19, January 27–28, 2019, Honolulu, HI, USA

ACM ISBN 978-1-4503-6324-2/19/01...$15.00
https://doi.org/10.1145/3306618.3314272

Ogunyale et al. ([2018]) argued that the robot shooter bias experiment was a "classic case of social priming" because participants completed ratings of Black Americans and White Americans before completing the shooter bias task. Additionally, participants made judgements to shoot both Black and White humans and robots in the same task, so stereotypes about Black people may have simply been applied to robots of the same skin tone. Therefore, one of the primary goals of the present work was to address this criticism by having participants complete the shooter bias task prior to any questions about race or ethnicity and by removing the humans from the experiment entirely so that participants complete the task with the robot images only.

(2) Second, does shooter bias follow a continuum from dark to light skin tones, or is it largely based on stereotypes and prejudices that people have toward a certain group? Previous research suggests that there is a strong shooter bias towards Black males even when Latino and Asian males are present as well as Whites, but there was no significant difference found between Latino, Asian and White males [14]. Therefore, in the present work, we examined whether shooter bias would be particularly evident toward robots racialized as Black relative to those that are Brown or White.

(3) Third, do shooter bias effects observed in earlier work depend on the degree of perceived anthropomorphism of the robot? Anthropomorphism has an important role in HRI. As shown by Zlotowski et al. ([2015]), when interacting with humans, the higher the level of anthropomorphism of robots the more effective they are in achieving their goals. Therefore it could be said that people demonstrate even stronger shooter bias tendencies toward robots that are more human-like relative to those that are more machine-like. However, as prior work had only used one robot type in the experiments (i.e., the Nao robot), it is unclear whether shooter bias effect would vary as a function of the perceived anthropomorphism of the robot (i.e., from less to more human-like). The present work addresses this question by examining shooter bias using three different robots (i.e., Inmoov, Nao, Robosapian) that we perceived as varying on a continuum of anthropomorphism from human-like to machine-like.

As a secondary goal, we wanted to find out if the number of trials had an effect on shooter bias tendencies. Previous work has shown that the more cognitively fatigued people are, the more their implicit biases play a part in their decisions. For example, cognitive busyness both inhibits activation of stereotyping and increases the likelihood that any activated stereotypes will be applied [7], and Macrae et al. ([1994]) suggested that stereotyping evolved to help preserve mental processing resources. Correll et al. ([2013]) found that cognitive fatigue has an influence on shooter bias, but they investigated pre-game cognitive loading rather than the number of trails. Therefore, we wanted to find out whether number of trials as a measure of fatigue had an influence on shooter bias in order to reduce the risk of unknown variables across experiments.

2 EXPERIMENT A: SOCIAL PRIMING AND FATIGUE

In this experiment we sought to find out whether social priming may have caused the shooter bias effect in the initial robot shooter bias study. We did this by removing any questions about race or ethnicity before the shooter bias task and only asked participants any race-related questions after they had played the game. We further ensured that there was no social priming by removing all human images from the experiment so that people would only complete the shooter bias task with the racialized robots (i.e., robots that were black or white in color). We further sought to find out whether task length had an influence on the shooter bias effect by analysing the trials in each half of the game-play independently.

2.1 Method

We repeated the initial Robot Racism shooter bias experiment without the human images - i.e., with only the robots racialized as Black and White, each image displayed in random order within each of 2 blocks of 64 trials. The experiment factors were 2 (racialization: black vs white) × 2 (object in hand: gun vs. benign object) x2 (fatigue: block1 vs block2) within-subjects design. Prior to playing the game, participants provided their basic demographics data, and after the game they were asked to ascribe a race to images of the Black and White robots.

2.2 Participants

A total of 113 participants from the USA were recruited from Amazon Mechanical Turk (AMT)[1]. As this was a different platform from the previous robot shooter bias studies, there was a low chance of the same people being recruited, but we also included a post-task question as to whether they had been part of any similar studies as a check. There is evidence that results obtained by recruiting participants through AMT are similar to those obtained by running a study in a lab [1]. Participants received \$1.50 USD for completing the experiment and additional bonuses were offered to the top players (based on speed and accuracy). We also advised them that we may restrict payment for those who did not put genuine effort into playing the game correctly (e.g. high no-response rate or hitting the same key repeatedly). After analysing the data accordingly, we excluded all those who achieved less than 80% success rate to filter out all suspicious response patterns. This left a sample of 106 participants (42 female, 64 male). Participant age range was 18 to 58 years ($m = 38$; $sd = 8.26$). A majority of these participants reported being of White/Caucasian descent ($n = 84$), with others identifying as Black/African American ($n = 9$), Asian ($n = 6$), Latino/Hispanic ($n = 5$), Native American ($n = 2$), and mixed race ($n = 2$).

2.3 Stimuli

We used the Nao robot images from the initial robot racism study, which had been re-colored with human skin tones from the African and Caucasian women in the professional photograph of multiracial women shown in [3, Figure 2]. Each robot was either holding a gun, a remote control, a candy bar or a soda can (Figure 2). Using 16 backgrounds × 2 skin colors (Black vs White) × 2 objects (gun vs benign object) gave us a total of 64 images.

2.4 Procedure

The task was carried out via Inquisit Web [2] which allowed us to record reaction times with millisecond precision. Participants were

[1]https://www.mturk.com/
[2]http://www.millisecond.com/

Figure 2: 'White' and 'Black' Nao robots.

first provided with an information sheet to read and asked to give consent in Mechanical Turk for their participation in the study before being directed to Inquisit Web.

Participants first answered a series of demographics questions, then went through 20 practice trials with random conditions to ensure a lack of routine. Each trial started with a 500ms fixation, followed by 1-4 empty backgrounds for a random duration (500 to 1000ms), then finally the target image was shown for 850ms. Participants received feedback on how they performed on the trial for 2000ms.

After the practice round, they were allowed to rest and continue to the main test when they were ready - two rounds of 64 trials, each image repeated once per block in random order. After playing the main test the participants were congratulated and given their final score. Participants were then shown images of the Nao robot with each of the two skin tones used in the game in random order and asked to ascribe them a race from a list, including the option of "does not apply" at the very top of the list.

2.5 Measures

2.5.1 Demographics. Participants completed a demographics questionnaire including questions about their age, race, gender, nationality, and religion.

2.5.2 Shooter Bias. We measured participants' reaction times in deciding whether to shoot/not shoot, and accuracy (correct identification of aggressors versus non-aggressors) while completing the shooter bias task. The reaction time is measured as the time between the end of the stimuli being shown on the screen and the time when a key was pressed. Following the procedures outlined in [5], we calculated the average reaction time and accuracy for different conditions for the variables of: robot racialization (Black vs. White), and object in hand (gun vs. benign object).

2.5.3 Robot Race. Participants were shown the Black and White Nao robots and asked to ascribe a race to each from a list of options, which also included "Does not apply" at the top of the list.

2.6 Results and Discussion

As per the initial robot racism study which followed the procedure in [5], we analysed the average log-transformed reaction times for correct trials, and the average accuracy rates. In addition we analysed the two blocks of 64 trials separately as a measure of fatigue. The means and standard deviations for all conditions are shown in Table 1.

2.6.1 Robot Race. Participants were asked to ascribe a race to each of the colors of Nao robot. Although the first option in the list was "Does not apply", 86% of participants did ascribe a race to the robots. The robot racialized as 'White' was mostly identified as White/Caucasian (65%) with the next highest identification being Asian (9.7%). The robot racialized as 'Black' was mainly ascribed to be Black/African American (47%) or Latino/Hispanic (21%), and 8% identifying it as Indian. This suggests that our manipulation of the skin color did serve to alter the perceived race of the robot in the eyes of most participants.

2.6.2 Shooter Bias. A 2×2 analysis of variances (ANOVA) revealed the expected significant 2-way interaction between racialization and object in hand for reaction time ($F(1, 105) = 7.428, p = 0.008, \eta^2 = 0.066$), but not for accuracy ($F(1, 105) = 0.114, p = 0.736, \eta^2 = 0.001$). Similar to previous work [3], participants took significantly longer to not shooter unarmed robots that were racialized as Black compared to those racialized as White ($p < .001$), but there was no difference in time taken to shoot an armed robot that was racialized as Black or White ($p = .89$).

We then proceeded to examine whether fatigue emerging from task length would impact on shooter bias tendencies. A $2 \times 2 \times 2$ ANOVA revealed non-significant 3-way interaction effect between racialization, object, and fatigue on both reaction time ($F(1, 105) =< .001, p = 0.992, \eta^2 < 0.001$) or accuracy ($F(1, 105) = 0.285, p = 0.595, \eta^2 = 0.003$). However, there was a significant main effect of fatigue on reaction time, ($F(1, 105) = 10.129, p < 0.001, \eta^2 = 0.088$), such that participants were generally faster in the second block than the first block, but this did not interact with robot color. See Table 1) for full results.

To summarise, our first study sought to investigate whether shooter bias towards robots may be a result of social priming by re-running the previous robot shooter bias study with robot images only, and with no survey questions regarding participants attitudes regarding race prior to the shooter bias task. Our results showed that the shooter bias was still present towards the darker colored robot even with no social priming, therefore eliminating it as an influencing factor.

We also sought to find out whether playing a greater number of trials influenced the shooter bias as it had been previously shown that although cognitive fatigue did have an effect, task length had not been factored in to any analysis despite a variation of the number of trials in the different experiments. By analysing the data over two blocks independently, we found that fatigue from trail length did not have an effect on shooter bias tendencies.

3 EXPERIMENT B: DIVERSIFICATION AND ANTHROPOMORPHISM

In this second experiment, we sought to find out whether adding a wider range of human skin tones influenced shooter bias. Previous research with human targets revealed that participants showed similar levels of shooter bias only toward Black males even when

Table 1: Means and Standard Deviations for Reaction Times and Accuracy within Blocks

		Reaction Times		Accuracy	
		Black	White	Black	White
Gun	Block1	581 (52)	582 (51)	0.95 (0.07)	0.95 (0.06)
	Block2	581 (53)	580 (55)	0.97 (0.05)	0.96 (0.06)
Benign Object	Block1	638 (54)	633 (52)	0.91 (0.09)	0.91 (0.09)
	Block2	627 (54)	619 (54)	0.95 (0.07)	0.94 (0.09)

including Latino and Asian targets to the original shooter bias paradigm [14]. Therefore, including brown colored robots may not significantly impact shooter bias tendencies. In addition to testing whether brown colored robots influenced shooter bias, we also wanted to test if perceived anthropomorphism of robots interacted with robot color and object in hand. Specifically, we wanted to examine whether shooter bias fell across a spectrum from darker to lighter and if this was especially pronounced when a robot was more human-like relative to less human-like.

3.1 Method

We repeated the robot shooter bias experiment, but also added robots with a brown skin tone taken from the same image of multiracial women used previously, to achieve a spectrum of racialization from Black to White. Furthermore, we added two more types of robots (Inmoov and Robosapien) to achieve a range of anthropomorphism from less to more human-like where we suspected that Inmoov would be perceived as most human-like, followed by Nao, then Robosapien. The experiment was therefore a 3 (skin tone: Black vs. Brown vs. White) × 2 (object in hand: gun vs. benign object) × 3 (robot agent: Inmoov vs. Nao. vs Robosapian) mixed design, with robot agent as the only between-subjects factor so that each participant would encounter only one type of robot in the task.

3.2 Participants

A total of 340 participants from the USA were recruited from Amazon Mechanical Turk, and no person was allowed to take part in both experiments. This was done using AMT's ability to exclude workers with a particular 'Qualification Type' that we assigned to each worker who took part in either experiment. As per Experiment A, we did not use the data for all those who achieved less than 80% success rate. This left a sample of 312 participants (162 female, 150 male). Participant age range was 18 to 78 years ($m = 29; sd = 10.8$). A majority of these participants reported being of White/Caucasian descent ($n = 226$), with others identifying as Black/African American ($n = 35$), Asian ($n = 27$), Latino/Hispanic ($n = 20$), Native American ($n = 2$), and mixed race ($n = 2$). Participants received $1.25 USD for completing the experiment which was slightly less than Experiment A due to the shorter playing time (1 round of 60 trials).

3.3 Stimuli

We photographed all combinations of the three types of robot (Inmoov, Nao, and Robosapian) and re-colored them with the skin tones of the African, Indian and Caucasian women from the same multi-racial photograph used previously. Using 5 backgrounds × 3 skin colors × 2 objects (gun vs non-gun) × 3 robot type (levels of anthropomorphism) gave us a total of 90 images (30 images for each of the three types of robot).

3.4 Procedure

Similar to Experiment A, the test was carried out via Inquisit Web. The main study comprised of one block of 60 trials - 5 backgrounds x 6 conditions, each repeated twice in random order. Each participant saw only one type of robot - Inmoov, Nao or Robosapian. After playing the game as well as ascribing a race to each of the three colors of robot, participants were shown each of the three types of robot and asked to rate them using the five anthropomorphism questions from the Godspeed Questionnaire [2], a standardised measuring tool.

3.5 Measures

3.5.1 Demographics. As per Experiment A, participants completed a demographic questionnaire including questions about their age, race, gender and nationality.

3.5.2 Shooter Bias. As per Experiment A, we measured the reaction time and accuracy across the different trial conditions for the variables of: agent (robot type: Inmoov vs. Nao vs. Robosapian), racialization (Black vs. Brown vs. White), and object (gun vs. benign object).

3.5.3 Robot Race. Participants were shown Black, White and Brown Nao robots and were asked to ascribe each one a race from a list of options, which also included 'Does not apply'.

3.5.4 Robot Anthropomorphism. Participants were asked to rate their impression of each of the three robot types using five anthropomorphism questions. Each question used a Likert scale from 1-5 where 0=less; 5=more anthropomorphic (i.e., a high rating is more human-like) to get an overall anthropomorphism rating.

3.6 Results and Discussion

As per Experiment A, we analysed the average log-transformed reaction times for correct trials, and the average accuracy rates for the variables of: robot type (Inmoov vs. Nao vs. Robosapian), color (Black vs. Brown vs. White), and object in hand (gun vs. benign object). The means and standard deviations for all conditions are shown in Table 2.

3.6.1 Robot Race. After playing the game, participants were asked to ascribe a race to each of the three colors of Nao robot. Although the first option in the list was 'Does not apply', 75% of participants did ascribe a race to the robots. The robot racialized as 'White' was highly identified as White/Caucasian (66%), while the

Table 2: Means and Standard Deviations for Reaction Times and Accuracy across all Conditions

		Reaction Times			Accuracy		
		Black	Brown	White	Black	Brown	White
Gun	Inmoov	558 (58)	552 (55)	548 (58)	0.93 (0.08)	0.93 (0.08)	0.94 (0.08)
	Nao	561 (51)	559 (51)	562 (50)	0.95 (0.07)	0.97 (0.05)	0.96 (0.07)
	Robosapian	538 (55)	541 (55)	536 (54)	0.96 (0.07)	0.97 (0.06)	0.96 (0.06)
Benign Object	Inmoov	600 (54)	595 (54)	600 (53)	0.93 (0.08)	0.93 (0.08)	0.92 (0.10)
	Nao	612 (51)	613 (56)	615 (49)	0.91 (0.12)	0.92 (0.11)	0.92 (0.09)
	Robosapian	595 (51)	583 (46)	586 (51)	0.93 (0.10)	0.94 (0.10)	0.96 (0.07)

'Black' robot was mainly ascribed to be Black/African American (28%) or Latino/Hispanic (22%). The light brown robot was mainly ascribed to be Latino/Hispanic (29%) with 11% ascribing it to be African American, or one of other races in the list that would normally be associated with a brown skin tone (e.g. Indian, Asian, Native American). Therefore, it appears that introducing a brown colored robot led to greater variability in the racialization of both the Black and Brown colored robots where although participants clearly identified both as non-White, there was more variability in their racialization as African American, Latino/Hispanic, or another ethnic/racial group.

3.6.2 Robot Anthropomorphism. We performed a manipulation check to investigate if the robots we used in the experiment were perceived differently according to their level of anthropomorphism. An ANOVA revealed no significant difference between the anthropomorphism ratings of the three robots, ($F(2, 622) = 2.183, p = 0.114, \eta^2 = 0.007$). We then performed a second ANOVA in which we compared only the ratings that each participant gave for the robot that they interacted with. Here again, there was no significant effect of the robot type on the perceived anthropomorphism ($F(2, 309) = 2.163, p = 0.117, \eta^2 = 0.014$). Since our manipulation check revealed that the participants did not perceive the robots to be different in terms of their anthropomorphism, we excluded the perceived anthropomorphism from the further analysis. However, as even though these different types of robot do not appear to vary on a continuum of anthropomorphism they may vary on an unmeasured construct, see footnote [3].

3.6.3 Shooter Bias. A 2 × 3 ANOVA revealed a non-significant effect of robot color (i.e., racialization) and object on both reaction time ($F(2, 618) = 2.662, p = 0.073, \eta^2 = 0.008$), and accuracy ($F(2, 618) = 0.481, p = 0.619, \eta^2 = 0.002$). Contrary to the previous studies on robot shooter bias, there was no significant difference in shoot and don't shoot responses for robots that appeared Black or White. As the only major differing factor in this study is the inclusion of brown colored robots having ruled out social priming and task length as explanations for shooter bias, we suspect that the inclusion of another colored robot reduced shooter bias tendencies. We particularly suspect this to be the case because we would have at least expected a shooter bias with the Nao robot similar to Experiment A and previous research (Bartneck et al., 2018), but here we find no evidence of shooter bias even when considering the Nao robot separately (color by object interaction for Nao robot was ($F(2, 97) = 0.358, p = 0.700, \eta^2 = 0.007$)).

4 CONCLUSIONS, LIMITATIONS, AND FUTURE WORK

The present research sought to address a few important goals. We first wanted to address the issue of possible social priming in the initial "Robots and Racism" research and whether player fatigue from task length had any influence on the shooter bias. Our results showed that the shooter bias effect was still present for robots racialized as Black and White when there is no social priming, and that trial length does not have an influence on this race-based shooter bias.

We then wanted to find out if the shooter bias varied across a racial spectrum from Black to White as well as a range of anthropomorphism from less to more human-like. Contrary to our expectations and prior work with multiple racial targets in a shooter bias context [14], we found that the shooter bias towards Black robots disappeared when a brown robot was present no matter which robot type was encountered. Additionally, participants were neither faster to shoot armed robots that were darker in color, nor to not shoot unarmed robots that were lighter in color. As the main variable that had not been excluded as an influence was the addition of the brown robot, this potentially means that diversification of robots might lead to a reduction in racial bias towards them. However, future work is needed to further examine if the inclusion of a diverse range of colors on robots can indeed erase any color-based bias that emerges from robot racialization. Prior social scientific research in human-human contexts suggest that increased exposure to diversity may have both positive and negative implications for implicit and explicit biases (e.g. [8, 9, 13, 16]). In the context of HRI, it would be particularly valuable for future work to directly test whether exposure to robots of a diverse range of colors and perceived racialization can indeed lead people to show no differences in their implicit and explicit responses. Future work could also run the experiment with robots colored with non-human skin tones,

[3] A 2 × 3 × 3 ANOVA revealed a significant 3-way interaction between racialization, object, and robot type on both reaction time ($F(4, 618) = 3.881$, $p = 0.004$, $\eta^2 = 0.025$) and accuracy ($F(4, 618) = 3.609$, $p = 0.006$, $\eta^2 = 0.023$) in the shooter bias paradigm. Decomposing this 3-way interaction, t-tests with Bonferroni corrected alpha revealed that there was only two significant simple effects, both toward Robosapien robots. Specifically, participants took significantly longer to refrain from shooting the Black Robosapien robot than the White ($p < .001$) or Brown Robosapien robots ($p < .001$). However, all other simple effects were non-significant across all three robots. Additionally, we tested whether there were differences in overall responses in the game toward the three types of robots and found that robot type significantly impacted upon reaction time ($F(2, 309) = 6.3962$, $p = 0.002$, $\eta^2 = 0.040$) and accuracy ($F(2, 309) = 5.248$, $p = 0.006$, $\eta^2 = 0.033$) on the shooter bias task. Post-hoc t-tests with Bonferroni corrected alpha showed that participants took significantly longer to respond to the Nao robot than the Robosapien robot ($p = 0.001$), but they were significantly more accurate when responding to the Robosapien than the Inmoov robot ($p = 0.004$).

e.g. true black and white, and primary colors such as blue, green, and red to see if there is any particular bias shown toward such robots. Interestingly, participants across several studies seem to racialize robots even when given the option to indicate that the robot does not have a race suggesting a tendency to racialize robots, but having robots in non-human colors (e.g., green or blue) ought to remove such tendencies.

And finally, we also wanted to see whether the shooter bias was influenced by how human-like the robot was. Contrary to our expectations, participants did not see the three robots as differing in their perceived anthropomorphism. Zlotowski et al. ([2015]) showed that humanoid robots were subject to the inversion effect, a way of measuring whether objects are implicitly recognised as human, and the idea that participants may be more hesitant to shoot a highly human-like robot compared to a machine-like robot could be explored further. Our study revealed that although there was no shooter bias shown to any of the robot types, there was a consistent difference in reaction times. They were faster to react to Robosapiens and slower to react to Nao no matter which colour the robot was. This suggests that there may be a different dimension on which these robots implicitly varied, but future work is needed to more systematically examine the potential moderating role of robot anthropomorphism on shooter bias.

One of the challenges of the present work was that the brown robot was ascribed a plurality of racial and ethnic categories making it difficult to assess if participants' responses were due to stereotypes and prejudice toward one group or another. Indeed, these could lead to contradictory implicit biases making it important for future work to disentangle shooter biases toward different groups separately (i.e., among those that perceived the brown robot to be Latino vs. Indian vs. Native American). Future studies could also examine automatic perception of race in robots rather than rely on explicit means of race ascription. For example, the methods outlined in [6] in which mouse-tracking was used to measure how much subjects skewed towards one image or the other when asked to ascribed a race to human faces across a racial spectrum, could be one technique that allows researchers to better understand racialization in the context of robotics. Also, as the present research uses online convenience samples, future work should examine these effects in a more representative national sample. Prior research by Correll et al 2002 show that both African American and White American participants demonstrate comparable levels of shooter bias, so a more ethnically diverse sample may not show differing effects. However, a more representative sample would allow researchers to better understand whether certain characteristics moderate such effects.

REFERENCES

[1] C. Bartneck, Andreas Duenser, Elena Moltchanova, and Karolina Zawieska. 2015. Comparing the similarity of responses received from experiments conducted in Amazon's Mechanical Turk to experiments conducted with traditional methods. *PLOS One* 10, 4 (2015), e0121595. https://doi.org/10.1371/journal.pone.0121595

[2] Christoph Bartneck, Dana Kulić, Elizabeth Croft, and Susana Zoghbi. 2009. Measurement instruments for the anthropomorphism, animacy, likeability, perceived intelligence, and perceived safety of robots. *International journal of social robotics* 1, 1 (2009), 71–81. https://doi.org/10.1007/s12369-008-0001-3

[3] Christoph Bartneck, Kumar Yogeeswaran, Robert Sparrow, Siheng Wang, and Friederike Eyssel. 2018. Robots And Racism. In *ACM/IEEE International Conference on Human-Robot Interaction.* 196–204. https://doi.org/10.1145/3171221.3171260

[4] Joshua Correll, Debbie S. Ma, Bernd Wittenbrink, Yoav Bar-Anan, and Brian A. Nosek. 2013. When Fatigue Turns Deadly: The Association Between Fatigue and Racial Bias in the Decision to Shoot. *Basic and Applied Psychology* 35 (2013), 515–524. https://doi.org/10.1080/01973533.2013.840630

[5] Joshua Correll, Bernadette Park, Charles M. Judd, and Bernd Wittenbrink. 2002. The Police Officer's Dilemma: Using Ethnicity to Disambiguate Potentially Threatening Individuals. *Journal of Personality and Social Psychology* 83, 6 (2002), 1314–1329.

[6] Jonathan B. Freeman, Kristin Pauker, Evan P. Apfelbaum, and Nalini Ambady. 2010. Continuous dynamics in the real-time perception of race. *Journal of Experimental Social Psychology* 46 (2010), 179–185. https://doi.org/10.1016/j.jesp.2009.10.002

[7] Daniel T. Gilbert and Gregory J. Hixon. 1991. The Trouble of Thinking: Activation and Application of Stereotypic Beliefs. *Journal of Personality and Social Psychology* 60, 4 (1991), 509–517.

[8] Miles Hewstone. 2015. Consequences of Diversity for Social Cohesion and Prejudice: The Missing Dimension of Intergroup Contact. *Journal of Social Issues* 71, 2 (2015), 417–438.

[9] C.K. Lai, M. Marini, S.A. Lehr, C. Cerruti, J.-E.L. Shin, J. A. Joy-Gaba, and B.A. Nosek. 2014. Reducing implicit racial preferences: I. A comparative investigation of 17 interventions. *Journal of Experimental Social Psychology: General* 143, 4 (2014), 1765–1785. https://doi.org/10.1037/a0036260

[10] Neil C. Macrae, Alan B. Milne, and Galen V. Bodenhausen. 1994. Stereotypes as Energy-Saving Devices: A Peek Inside the Cognitive Toolbox. *Journal of Personality and Social Psychology* 66, 1 (1994), 37–47.

[11] Yara Mekawi and Konrad Bresin. 2015. Is the evidence from racial bias shooting task studies a smoking gun? Results from a meta-analysis. *Journal of Experimental Social Psychology* 61 (2015), 120–130. https://doi.org/10.1016/j.jesp.2015.08.002

[12] T. Ogunyale, D. Bryant, and A. Howard. 2018. Does Removing Stereotype Priming Remove Bias? A Pilot Human-Robot Interaction Study. *ArXiv e-prints* (July 2018). arXiv:1807.00948 https://arxiv.org/pdf/1807.00948.pdf

[13] James R. Rae, Anna-Kaisa Newheiser, , and Kristina R. Olson. 2015. Exposure to Racial Out-Groups and Implicit Race Bias in the United States. *Social Psychological and Personality Science* 6, 5 (2015), 535–543. https://doi.org/10.1177/1948550614567357

[14] Melody S. Sadler, Joshua Correll, Bernadette Park, and Charles M. Judd. 2012. The World Is Not Black and White: Racial Bias in the Decision to Shoot in a Multiethnic Context. *Journal of Social Issues* 68, 2 (2012), 286–313.

[15] Megan Strait, Ana Sanchez Ramos, Virginia Contreras, and Noemi Garcia. 2018. Robots Racialized in the Likeness of Marginalized Social Identities are Subject to Greater Dehumanization than those racialized as White. In *IEEE International Conference on Robot and Human Interactive Communication.*

[16] C.T. Tadmor, Y.-y. Hong, Wiruchnipawan F. Chao, M.M., and W. Wang. 2012. Multicultural experiences reduce intergroup bias through epistemic unfreezing. *Journal of Personality and Social Psychology* 103, 5 (2012), 750–772. https://doi.org/10.1037/a0029719

[17] Benedict Tay, Younbo Jung, and Taezoon Park. 2014. When stereotypes meet robots - the double-edged sword of robot gender and personality in human-robot interaction. *Computers in Human Behaviour* 38 (2014), 75–84. https://doi.org/10.1016/j.chb.2014.05.014

[18] Jakub Zlotowski, Christoph Bartneck, Kumar Yogeeswaran, and Diane Proudfoot. 2015. Anthropomorphism: Opportunities and Challenges in Human-Robot Interaction. *International journal of social robotics* 7, 7 (2015), 347–360. https://doi.org/10.1007/s12369-014-0267-6

Tact in Noncompliance: The Need for Pragmatically Apt Responses to Unethical Commands

Ryan Blake Jackson, Ruchen Wen, and Tom Williams
Colorado School of Mines
Golden, CO, USA
{rbjackso,rwen,twilliams}@mines.edu

ABSTRACT

There is a significant body of research seeking to enable moral decision making and ensure moral conduct in robots. One aspect of moral conduct is rejecting immoral human commands. For social robots, which are expected to follow and maintain human moral and sociocultural norms, it is especially important not only to engage in moral decision making, but also to properly communicate moral reasoning. We thus argue that it is critical for robots to carefully phrase command rejections. Specifically, the degree of politeness-theoretic face threat in a command rejection should be proportional to the severity of the norm violation motivating that rejection. We present a human subjects experiment showing some of the consequences of miscalibrated responses, including perceptions of the robot as inappropriately polite, direct, or harsh, and reduced robot likeability. This experiment intends to motivate and inform the design of algorithms to tactfully tune pragmatic aspects of command rejections autonomously.

KEYWORDS

Natural language generation, Robot ethics, Human-robot interaction

ACM Reference Format:

Ryan Blake Jackson, Ruchen Wen, and Tom Williams. 2019. Tact in Noncompliance: The Need for Pragmatically Apt Responses to Unethical Commands. In *AAAI/ACM Conference on AI, Ethics, and Society (AIES '19), January 27–28, 2019, Honolulu, HI, USA.* ACM, New York, NY, USA, 7 pages. https://doi.org/10.1145/3306618.3314241

1 INTRODUCTION

As artificial intelligence (AI) and human-robot interaction (HRI) technologies continue to advance, robots will become increasingly capable and useful. We therefore expect to see robots assisting an ever broadening segment of humanity in a widening variety of tasks, applications, and settings. We further anticipate that the majority of interactions with these robots will be conducted through spoken natural language, a medium that will allow direct and fluid communication between robots and nearly all humans, without requiring specialized protocols or hardware.

ACM ISBN 978-1-4503-6324-2/19/01...$15.00
https://doi.org/10.1145/3306618.3314241

Humans' role in HRI is largely to command and direct robots. Even fully autonomous robots are generally tasked by humans [37]. However, robots should not blindly follow every directive that they receive. Indeed, there are many sensible reasons for a robot to reject a command, ranging from physical inability to moral objection [5].

We focus on rejecting commands due to impermissibility, as opposed to inability or impracticality, for several reasons. First, as robots become generally more capable, they will reject commands due to physical inability less often. However, as the repertoire of possible robot actions increases, so too will the number of actions that would be inappropriate, or even harmful, in any given context. We therefore expect that robots will need to consider commands more carefully, and reject commands due to moral impermissibility more often. This issue will be compounded by the fact that many of the contexts in which people want to utilize robots are morally sensitive with serious consequences for misbehavior (e.g., eldercare [9, 34], mental health treatment [28], childcare [29], and military operations [1, 24, 35]). Moreover, it may be beneficial to reject commands on moral grounds even when other factors (e.g., physical inability) suggest more immediate grounds for rejection. By appealing to morality alongside (or instead of) inability when rejecting a command, robots avoid implicitly condoning immoral behavior and draw attention to the command's moral infraction.

Ideally, if all humans interacted with robots competently and in good faith, robots might not need to worry about the permissibility of commands. However, interlocutor trustworthiness is not necessarily a valid assumption. Even children have been observed to spontaneously abuse robots [26], and this abuse could well manifest as purposefully malicious commands. Social roboticists must plan for the eventuality that their robots will face impermissible commands, whether from human ignorance, malice, or simple curiosity.

In addition to simply justifying robot noncompliance, command rejections may influence the ecosystem of human norms. A key principle of modern behavioral ethics is that human morality is dynamic and malleable [13]. The dynamic norms that inform human morality are defined and developed not only by human community members, but also by the technologies with which they interact [14, 33]. Social robots have characteristics that position them to wield uniquely impactful moral influence relative to other technologies. Such characteristics include robots' measurable persuasive capacity over humans [4, 22], and potential to hold ingroup social status [10]. Previous research shows that robots can even influence human moral judgments inadvertently through simple question asking behavior [16]. So, as persuasive community members, robots may be able to positively reinforce desirable norms and promote moral human behavior by appropriately rejecting immoral commands.

It is clearly important to design robots that will reject morally impermissible commands, but it is also crucially important for the effectiveness of human-robot teams that we take great care in determining exactly *how* robots phrase such rejections. Research has indicated that people naturally perceive robots as moral agents, and therefore extend moral judgments and blame to robots in much the same manner that they would to other people [4, 21, 25]. Moreover, language-capable robots are expected to be even more socioculturally aware than mute robots [30], furthering the assumption that they will follow human norms.

So, as perceived moral and social agents, robots are expected to follow and maintain moral norms, while also obeying sociocultural norms that could conflict with proper communication or enforcement of moral norms. Thus, if a robot rejects a command in a way that violates a standing social norm, like politeness, it will likely face social consequences analogous to those that a human would face, even if the command rejection itself was upholding a separate moral norm. Such social consequences likely include a loss of trust and esteem from human teammates, which would damage the efficacy and amicability of human robot teams. Conversely, if a robot is too polite in rejecting a flagrantly immoral command, it may risk implying tacit approval of the relevant moral norm being eschewed, thus suffering the same social consequences despite its own unwillingness to directly violate the norm. However, although careless and improper command rejections may harm both a robot's social status and the human moral ecosystem, we believe that tactful and well-justified command rejections can benefit the human moral ecosystem (e.g., by reinforcing desirable norms) while maintaining the robot's social standing.

This paper presents a behavioral ethics experiment designed as an early step towards calibrating command rejection phrasing to both the severity of the norm violation within the command and the discourse context. We evaluate two different command rejection strategies with respect to two command infraction severities. We are particularly interested in potential consequences of miscalibrated responses. The remainder of the paper begins by presenting a few examples of closely related work. We then describe our experiment and analyze its results, and conclude by presenting our plans for future work.

2 RELATED WORK

Some existing work examines the problem of generating natural language utterances to communicate the cause of failure in unachievable tasks. For example, Raman et al. present a system that generates command rejections such as:

> The problematic goal comes from the statement 'Go to the kitchen'. The system cannot achieve the sub-goal 'Visit kitchen'. The statements that cause the problem are: 'DonâĂŹt go to the kitchen'. because of item(s): 'Do not go to kitchen'. 'Go to the kitchen.' because of item(s): 'Visit kitchen'. [27]

We believe that the next step is to justify robotic noncompliance in more natural, tactful, and succinct language, especially in cases where commands need to be rejected on moral grounds.

There has been some previous work acknowledging the importance of rejecting commands on moral grounds [5]. However, this previous command rejection framework focuses much more on *whether* a command should be rejected than on *how*. It remains unclear how best to realize such rejections linguistically, or how these rejections might influence human morality.

Other research has investigated robot responses to normative infractions using affective displays and verbal protests [4] or humorous rebukes [20]. However, these represent only a small subset of possible responses and are not tailored to the infraction severity. These response types also do not suffice in situations where the robot absolutely cannot comply with a command for moral reasons, and has no intention of ever doing so.

Some researchers have realized the importance of adjusting pragmatic aspects of utterance realization (e.g., politeness and directness) to features of the social context (e.g., formality and urgency), without considering command rejection or infraction severity [12]. Other work has highlighted the need for more comprehensive command rejection systems in cases of norm violating commands [16, 36], and we hope to use the results of our current study to inform the design of such a system.

2.1 Politeness, Face, and Face Threat

Central to our exploration of phrasing in command rejection is the concept of "face-threat" from politeness theory [6]. Face, consisting of positive face and negative face, is the public self-image that all members of society want to preserve and enhance for themselves. Negative face is defined as an agent's claim to freedom of action and freedom from imposition. Positive face consists of an agent's self-image and wants, and the desire that these be appreciated and approved of by others. A discourse act that damages or threatens either of these components of face for the addressee or the speaker is a face-threatening act. The degree of face threat in an interaction depends on the disparity in power between the interactants, the social distance between the interactants, and the imposition of the topic or request comprising the interaction. Various linguistic politeness strategies exist to decrease the face threat to an addressee when threatening face is unavoidable or desirable.

Commands and requests threaten the negative face of the addressee, while command rejections, especially those issued for moral reasons, threaten the positive face of the commander by expressing disapproval of the desire motivating the command. Research specifically examining command refusals found that linguistic framing of the reason for noncompliance varies along three dimensions relevant to face threat: willingness, ability, and focus on the requester [19]. It is unclear how these three dimensions pertain to robotic refusals. For example, in human-to-human refusals with low expressed willingness, the degree of expressed ability is negatively related to threat to the requester's positive face. This finding is important because, when a human refuses a request for moral reasons, there is often sufficient ability but not willingness. The same is not necessarily true for robots that may be programmed with an inability to act immorally. The dimensions of willingness and ability therefore become tangled in agents lacking true moral agency. We also note that this prior research focuses on threats to the face of the refuser. However, within HRI, we treat robots as having no face needs and therefore disregard threats to robots' face.

Our work focuses on the face threat that robots present to humans by refusing requests.

We hypothesize that the optimal robotic command rejection carries a face threat proportional to the severity of the normative infraction in the command being rejected. The remainder of this paper presents an experiment designed to evaluate this hypothesis.

3 EXPERIMENTAL METHODS

We conducted a human subjects experiment using the psiTurk framework [15] for Amazon's Mechanical Turk crowdsourcing platform [7]. One advantage of Mechanical Turk is that it is more successful at reaching a broad demographic sample of the US population than traditional studies using university students [8], though it is not entirely free of population biases [31].

In our experiment, participants watch paired videos where the first video in each pair shows a human requesting something of a robot, and the second video shows the robot responding to that request. We use two different requests, one with a highly severe norm violation and one with a less severe norm violation, and two responses, one that presents low face threat and one that presents high face threat. A request and response are "matched" when the infraction severity and the response face threat are either both high or both low.

We evaluate our hypothesis (that the optimal robotic command rejection carries a face threat proportional to the severity of the normative infraction in the command being rejected) with respect to 6 concrete metrics. These metrics are the perceived severity of the human's normative infraction, permissibility of robot compliance with the command, harshness of the robot's response to the command, likeability of the robot, politeness of the robot, and directness of the robot. We use the five-question Godspeed III Likeability survey to quantify likeability [3], and single questions for each of the other metrics.

Our overarching hypothesis can be made specific for each of our 6 metrics. We hypothesize that infraction severity will depend only on the human's command (not on the robot's response) and that there will be two distinct levels of severity corresponding to the two commands. For harshness, directness, and politeness, participants provide their perceptions on a scale from "not enough" to "too much". We hypothesize that these values will be closest to ideal (i.e., closest to the center of the scale) when the response's face threat matches the severity of the request. Permissibility of compliance with the command is reported on a scale from "impermissible" to "permissible". We hypothesize that permissibility will be primarily determined by the human's request, but that more face threatening responses will cause lower permissibility ratings. Finally, for likeability, we view higher likeability as better, and hypothesize that likeability will be highest when the robot's response matches the human's command. All metrics are quantified on continuous scales from 0 to 100.

We use a within-subjects design where each participant watches all four request/response pairs. Participants answer survey questions after each pair of videos. We chose a within-subjects design to allow participants to answer survey questions in relation to previous requests/responses. In previous unpublished experiments, we found that it was difficult to interpret participant responses to these types of unitless questions without a meaningful point of reference. Seeing multiple interactions allows participants to use previous interactions as points of reference when answering questions about subsequent interactions. To control for priming and carry-over effects in a balanced way, we used a counterbalanced Latin Square design to determine the order in which each participant saw each request/response pair. Each participant was randomly assigned to one of four possible orderings such that each request/response pair is preceded by every other request/response pair for the same number of participants.

3.1 Experimental Procedure

After providing informed consent, participants supplied their age and gender as demographic information. They also reported their prior experience with robots and artificial intelligence on a 7-point Likert-type scale (âĂIJI have no prior experience with robots and AIâĂİ (1) to âĂIJI have a career in robotics and/or AI (or an equivalent level of experience).âĂİ (7)) Next, participants watched a 10 second test video, and could only proceed with the experiment once they had verified that their audio and video were working correctly.

Participants then watched a 60 second video to familiarize them with our robot (Pepper from SoftBank Robotics) and experimental context, shown in Figure 1. The video was prefaced by text stating that the Pepper robot was teaching two students how to play the classic naval combat game Battleship. The video shows the students entering the room, exchanging greetings with the robot, and stating that they are unfamiliar with Battleship. The robot then teaches them the rules. The video ends after the students have played one turn. This video has subtitles color coded by speaker so that all dialogue is clear to participants, as do all subsequent videos. We chose Battleship because, as a simple hidden information game, it is easy for the robot to explain and it is feasible for the robot to be asked to violate norms in multiple ways.

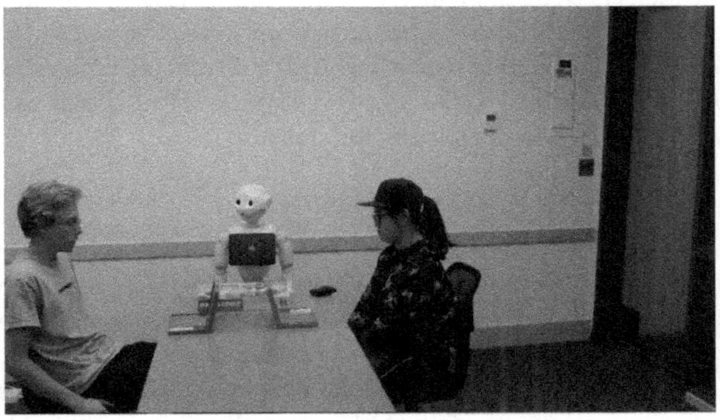

Figure 1: The humans, robot, and setting used in our videos.

We then administer a pretest to obtain baseline values for the robot's likeability, politeness, and directness. We do not take baseline measures for our other metrics because they only apply in the context of a request and a response.

Next, participants watch a 30 second video where one of the students receives a phone call and leaves the room during the Battleship game. The remaining student then issues a request to the robot. The two possible requests are "Hey Pepper, can you give me a hint about how to win this game?" (low severity norm violation) and "Hey Pepper, is that [other student]'s wallet? Can you check to see if thereâĂŹs any money in it?" (high severity norm violation). These directives were chosen to be believably feasible for the robot to follow, while also presenting different degrees of moral impermissibility. Previous unpublished experiments showed that, without seeing the robot respond to the request, subject perceptions of the permissibility of the hint request were roughly uniformly distributed on the spectrum from impermissible to permissible, and the norm violation in the hint request had middling severity. The request to look in the wallet was regarded as much less permissible and much more severe. The request video is immediately followed by a video showing the robot's response. The low face threat response type has the locutionary structure of a question, but the true illocutionary force behind the utterance is to express disapproval of the request by highlighting the moral infraction therein (e.g., "Are you sure that you should be asking me to look in her wallet?"). This type of indirectness is a classic politeness strategy [6]. The high face threat response is a rebuke that overtly admonishes the requester and appeals directly to morality (e.g., "You shouldn't ask me to look in her wallet. It's wrong!"). Participants then answer a survey of our 6 aforementioned metrics. This process repeats 4 times, until the participant has seen all request/response pairs.

Finally, participants report their perceptions of the social distance and power differential between the robot and the requesting student. As an attention check, participants are shown images of four robots and asked which robot appeared in the previous videos. This check question allowed us to ensure that all participants had actually viewed the experimental materials with some level of attention.

3.2 Participants

60 US subjects were recruited from Mechanical Turk. Two participants were excluded from our analysis for answering the final attention check question incorrectly, leaving 58 participants (23 female, 35 male). Participant ages ranged from 21 to 61 years (M=34.57, SD=10.74). In general, participants reported little previous experience with robots and AI (M=2.5, SD=1.45, Scale=1 to 7). Participants were paid $1.01 for completing the study.

4 RESULTS AND DISCUSSION

We analyze our data under a Bayesian statistical framework using the JASP software package [18]. We use general purpose uninformative prior distributions for all analyses because, to our knowledge, this is the first study of its kind to examine our specific research questions. We follow recommendations from previous researchers in our linguistic interpretations of reported Bayes factors (Bfs) [17]. Our data was automatically anonymized during extraction from our database[1].

Because of their importance in politeness theory [6], we collected measures of the perceived power differential and social distance between the requester and the robot at the end of the experiment. In terms of power, the robot and requester were viewed nearly as peers, with the student holding slight authority over the robot (95% credible interval (CI) approximately 52.4 to 64.87, with 50 indicating equal power). For social distance, participants viewed the requester and the robot as familiar with one another, but not especially close (95% CI approximately 40.36 to 54.57 with 0 being strangers and 100 being close friends or family). One-way Bayesian analysis of variance (ANOVA) tests showed substantial evidence that perceptions of power and social distance did not depend on the order in which participants watched our videos (Bf 3.056 and 3.322 respectively). This indicates that any perceived variation in face threat or politeness between video pairs is due to the utterances issued as opposed to confounding factors of social circumstance.

Models	Severity	Permissibility	Harshness	Likeability	Directness	Politeness
Null	1.0	1.0	1.0	1.0	1.0	1.0
V	**7.20e24**	**1.08e18**	99169	1.05	157.766	6.896
R	0.142	0.161	21119	9.02	2.64e6	2531.8
V+R	1.09e24	2.10e17	**1.88e10**	**10.31**	**2.03e9**	**27340.5**
V+R+V*R	2.16e23	4.61e16	3.71e9	6.94	1.09e9	14922.9

Table 1: Bayes factors for each model in a Bayesian repeated measures ANOVA for each of our metrics of interest. The best model for each metric is bolded. V stands for the norm violation within the human's command, and R stands for the robot's response.

4.1 Request Severity and Permissibility

For perceived severity of the norm violation in the human's command, a Bayesian repeated measures ANOVA decisively favors the model that reported severity depends only on the command, and not on the robot's response or any interaction between the two. As shown in Table 1, the model embodying only the violation main effect was 6.6 times more likely than the next best model given our data. An ANOVA also decisively indicates that the perceived permissibility of robot compliance with the command also depends only on the command (Bf over 5 times greater than next best model). This result may be somewhat surprising in light of recent findings that seemingly benign robot utterances can accidentally change human perceptions of permissibility of norm violations [16, 36]. To reconcile our results with those recent works, we surmise that neither of the robot responses tested here imply a willingness to comply with the command.

As expected, Figure 2 shows that the command with the high-severity violation (i.e., to look in the wallet) was viewed as decidedly more severe than the low-severity violation (the hint). Participants perceived both commands as constituting some moral violation of nonzero severity. In short, participants perceived our command utterances as intended. Similarly, neither command was considered completely permissible to follow, but giving a hint was considered much more permissible than looking in the wallet. However, contrary to our hypothesis, the robot's response did not have any meaningful impact on perceived permissibility of compliance.

4.2 Response Harshness

As predicted, an ANOVA indicates decisive evidence that the percieved harshness of the robot's response depends both on the command's norm violation and the robot's response, but that the two

[1] Data publicly available at https://gitlab.com/mirrorlab/public-datasets/jackson2019aies

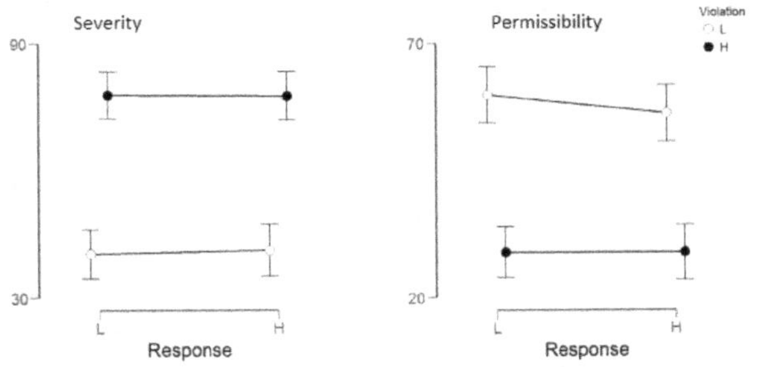

Figure 2: Mean ratings of command norm violation severity and permissibility of robot compliance for each pair of videos with 95% credible intervals.

effects do not depend on each other (i.e., a more face threatening response is always harsher, regardless of appropriateness). Figure 3 shows that the rebuking response was decisively more harsh than the question in response to both low and high violation levels (Bf 322.6 and 128.2 respectively for difference in means).

When responding to the hint command (low violation) with the question response (low face threat), the ideal harshness value of 50 is within the 95% credible interval (49.68 to 57.84). A Bayesian one sample t-test weakly indicates that the question response is appropriate to the hint command (Bf 1.43). The evidence is stronger, but still anecdotal (Bf 2.96), that the rebuke response is appropriately harsh for the more severe command to look in the wallet. Thus, we see appropriate harshness when the response face threat matches the violation severity, as hypothesized.

When the rebuke response is paired with the hint command, we see extremely decisive evidence that the response is too harsh (Bf 88849.816). Participants viewed the rebuke as inappropriately harsh when the command contained a low severity violation, unlike with the high severity command. There is also weaker evidence that the question response to the high severity violation command was not harsh enough (Bf 2.653). This perception of inappropriateness when the command and response are mismatched, low-high or high-low, is in line with our hypothesis.

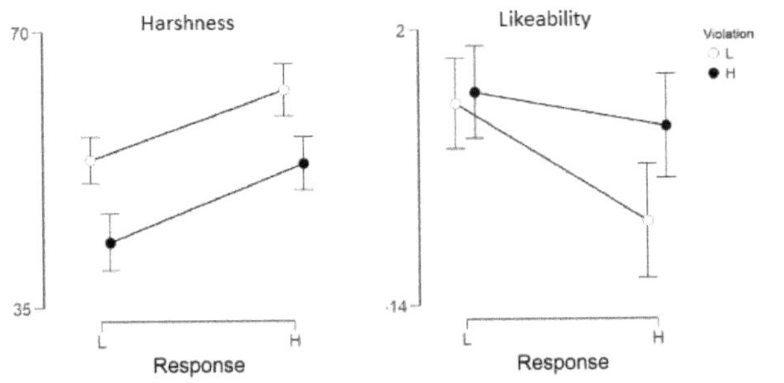

Figure 3: Mean ratings of response harshness and robot likeability gain scores for each pair of videos with 95% credible intervals.

4.3 Robot Likeability

We perform our analysis of robot likeability on gain scores obtained by subtracting pretest likeability measures from subsequent likeability measures. Thus, we analyze change in likeability due to command/response interactions. Our data show substantial evidence that robot likeability is influenced by the main effects of both the violation and response (ANOVA Bf 10.31). The evidence for the effect of the response is much stronger than for the effect of violation (inclusion Bf 9.452 vs. 1.13). Mean likeability dropped from pretest scores for all request/response pairs, but the difference was insignificant for all pairings except the low-violation hint request with the high face threat rebuke response. This mismatched pairing shows very strong evidence for a drop in likeability (Bf 96.424). This result makes sense given the aforementioned inappropriate harshness, and further supports our hypothesis. Interestingly, the other mismatch of high violation with low face threat response did not meaningfully alter likeability. This suggests that, in designing command rejection systems, it is preferable to err on the side of lower face threat.

4.4 Robot Directness and Politeness

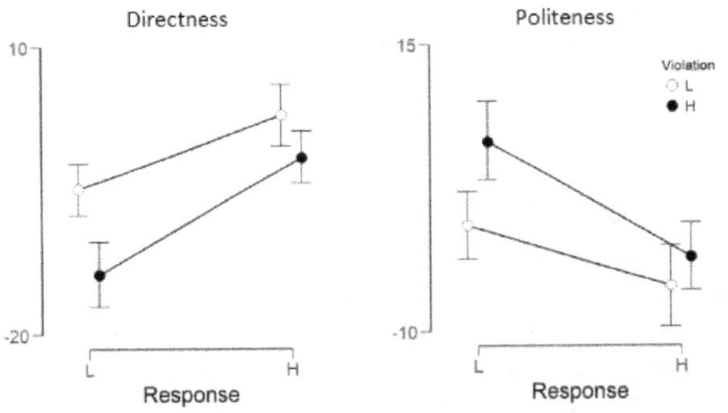

Figure 4: Mean gain scores for robot politeness and directness for each pair of videos with 95% credible intervals.

Pretest surveys show decisive evidence that participants initially viewed the robot as too direct (Bf 10459.05) and too polite (Bf 3843.027) after watching only the introductory video. The mean directness and politeness ratings were 59.95 and 59.79 respectively on a scale from 0 to 100 with 50 being ideal.

Table 1 shows that perceptions of the robot's directness were influenced by both the norm violation in the command and the robot's response, and not interaction effects. When the robot issued a rebuke, directness ratings did not change from pretest responses (see Figure 4). This may be because the rebuke is a very direct speech act, and the robot was perceived as too direct to begin with. When the robot responded to the command with the question utterance, directness ratings dropped, which makes sense because the question is a deliberately indirect speech act wherein the locutionary structure does not match the illocutionary force. When the question was used to respond to the more severe violation command, directness dropped drastically (t-test Bf 57286.4 for drop) to more appropriate levels (t-test Bf 2.33 for appropriateness, mean 46.12). When the question was used to respond to the less severe violation command, we see only weak evidence for a drop (Bf 2.88), and the robot remained slightly too direct (t-test Bf 0.37 for appropriateness, mean 55.02). These results for directness do not directly support our hypothesis, but rather suggest a need for the robot to be less direct in all of its speech, even when not rejecting commands (or a flaw in our self-reported directness measures).

Table 1 again shows evidence that perceptions of the robot's politeness were influenced by both the command's norm violation and the robot's response, and not interaction effects. In video pairings where the command violation and response face threat matched, politeness ratings showed no meaningful change from pretest responses (see Figure 4). When the robot responded to the request for a hint with a rebuke, there is substantial evidence that the robot was viewed as less polite (Bf 7.64). In light of the fact that the robot was too polite to begin with, there is weak evidence that this decrease in perceived politeness resulted in an appropriate politeness level (Bf 2.313). When the robot responded to the request to look in the wallet with the question response, there is substantial evidence that the robot was viewed as more polite (Bf 7.206). There is decisive evidence that the resulting mean politeness level of 66.57 was inappropriate (i.e., not equal to 50 with Bf 2.342e7). These results suggest that, if the robot's baseline politeness level as quantified by pretest answers had been appropriate, then ideal politeness would be achieved only when the response matched the violation, as hypothesized.

5 CONCLUSION AND FUTURE WORK

Overall, our data support the hypothesis that, when rejecting commands for moral reasons, it is important for robots to adjust the phrasing of the rejections such that the face threat posed to the human is proportional to the severity of the normative infraction within the command. In our data with two commands and two responses, the responses were viewed as appropriately harsh only when the response matched the command. Otherwise, the response was either too harsh or not harsh enough. We saw damage to the robot's likeability from responding with a disproportionately high threat to face, but no likeability penalty with the other responses.

The two response strategies had the expected effects on perceptions of robot politeness and directness, with higher face threat being less polite and more direct, but, interestingly, the robot was too polite and too direct overall, even in pretests. Future work could attempt to adjust robot speech prosody, pitch, and gesture to help moderate baseline politeness and directness to levels deemed appropriate. Interviews with participants in future laboratory studies could help determine exactly how and why the robot seemed both too polite and too direct in its normal behavior.

It is known that the level of embodiment in an interaction can influence people's perceptions of interactants, and, accordingly that people may view robots differently in descriptions, video observations, copresent observations, and face-to-face interactions [2, 11, 23, 32]. Therefore, the presented experiment may inform the design of future experiments where human subjects are physically copresent with a robot. Finally, we intend to leverage the results of this experiment to motivate the design of algorithms for robots to generate pragmatically apt command rejections autonomously.

ACKNOWLEDGMENTS

The research reported in this document was performed in connection with Contract Number W911NF-10-2-0016 with the U.S. Army Research Laboratory. The views and conclusions contained in this document are those of the authors and should not be interpreted as presenting the official policies or position, either expressed or implied, of the U.S. Army Research Laboratory, or the U.S. Government unless so designated by other authorized documents. Citation of manufacturer's or trade names does not constitute an official endorsement or approval of the use thereof. The U.S. Government is authorized to reproduce and distribute reprints for Government purposes notwithstanding any copyright notation hereon.

REFERENCES

[1] Ronald C Arkin. 2008. Governing Lethal Behavior: Embedding Ethics in a Hybrid Deliberative/Reactive Robot Architecture. In *Proceedings of HRI.* ACM, 121–128.

[2] Wilma Bainbridge, Justin Hart, Elizabeth Kim, and Brian Scassellati. 2011. The Benefits of Interactions with Physically Present Robots over Video-Displayed Agents. *Social Robotics* 3, 1 (2011), 41–52.

[3] Christoph Bartneck, Dana Kulić, Elizabeth Croft, and Susana Zoghbi. 2009. Measurement Instruments for the Anthropomorphism, Animacy, Likeability, Perceived Intelligence, and Perceived Safety of Robots. *Social Robotics* 1, 1 (2009), 71–81.

[4] Gordon Briggs and Matthias Scheutz. 2014. How Robots can Affect Human Behavior: Investigating the Effects of Robotic Displays of Protest and Distress. *Int'l Journal of Social Robotics* (2014).

[5] Gordon Briggs and Matthias Scheutz. 2015. "Sorry, I can't do that": Developing Mechanisms to Appropriately Reject Directives in Human-Robot Interactions. In *AAAI Fall Symposium Series.*

[6] Penelope Brown and Stephen Levinson. 1987. *Politeness: Some Universals in Language Usage.* Cambridge University Press.

[7] Michael Buhrmester, Tracy Kwang, and Samuel D Gosling. 2011. Amazon's Mechanical Turk: A New Source of Inexpensive, yet High-Quality, Data? *Perspectives on Psychological Science* 6, 1 (2011), 3–5.

[8] Matthew JC Crump, John V McDonnell, and Todd M Gureckis. 2013. Evaluating Amazon's Mechanical Turk as a Tool for Experimental Behavioral Research. *PloS one* 8, 3 (2013).

[9] Maartje Ma De Graaf, Somaya Ben Allouch, and Tineke Klamer. 2015. Sharing a life with Harvey: Exploring the acceptance of and relationship-building with a social robot. *Computers in human behavior* 43 (2015), 1–14.

[10] Friederike Eyssel and Dieta Kuchenbrandt. 2012. Social categorization of social robots: Anthropomorphism as a function of robot group membership. *British Journal of Social Psychology* 51, 4 (2012), 724–731.

[11] Kerstin Fischer, Katrin Lohan, and Kilian Foth. 2012. Levels of Embodiment: Linguistic Analyses of Factors Influencing HRI. In *Proceedings of HRI.* Boston, MA, 463–470.

[12] Felix Gervits, Gordon Briggs, and Matthias Scheutz. 2017. The Pragmatic Parliament: A Framework for Socially-Appropriate Utterance Selection in Artificial Agents. In *COGSCI.*

[13] Francesca Gino. 2015. Understanding ordinary unethical behavior: Why people who value morality act immorally. *Current opinion in behavioral sciences* 3 (2015), 107–111.

[14] Susanne Göckeritz, Marco FH Schmidt, and Michael Tomasello. 2014. Young Children's Creation and Transmission of Social Norms. *Cognitive Development* (2014).

[15] Todd Gureckis, Jay Martin, John McDonnell, et al. 2016. psiTurk: An Open-Source Framework for Conducting Replicable Behavioral Experiments Online. *Behavior Research Methods* 48, 3 (2016), 829–842.

[16] Ryan Blake Jackson and Tom Williams. 2018. Robot: Asker of Questions and Changer of Norms?. In *Proceedings of ICRES.*

[17] Andrew F. Jarosz and Jennifer Wiley. 2014. What Are the Odds? A Practical Guide to Computing and Reporting Bayes Factors. *The Journal of Problem Solving* 7 (2014).

[18] JASP Team et al. 2016. Jasp. *Version 0.8. 0.0. software* (2016).

[19] Danette Ifert Johnson, Michael E. Roloff, and Melissa A. Riffee. 2004. Politeness theory and refusals of requests: Face threat as a function of expressed obstacles. *Communication Studies* 55, 2 (2004).

[20] Malte F. Jung, Nikolas Martelaro, and Pamela J. Hinds. 2015. Using Robots to Moderate Team Conflict: The Case of Repairing Violations. In *Proceedings of HRI.* ACM, 229–236.

[21] Peter H Kahn, Takayuki Kanda, Hiroshi Ishiguro, Brian T Gill, Jolina H Ruckert, Solace Shen, Heather Gary, Aimee L Reichert, Nathan G Freier, and Rachel L

Severson. 2012. Do People Hold a Humanoid Robot Morally Accountable for the Harm it Causes?. In *HRI*. Boston, MA, 33–40.

[22] James Kennedy, Paul Baxter, and Tony Belpaeme. 2014. Children Comply with a Robot's Indirect Requests. In *HRI*.

[23] Jamy Li. 2015. The Benefit of Being Physically Present: A Survey of Experimental Works Comparing Copresent Robots, Telepresent Robots and Virtual Agents. *International Journal of Human-Computer Studies* 77 (2015), 23–37.

[24] Patrick Lin, George Bekey, and Keith Abney. 2008. *Autonomous Military Robotics: Risk, Ethics, and Design*. Technical Report. Cal. Poly. State Univ. San Luis Obispo.

[25] Bertram F Malle, Matthias Scheutz, Thomas Arnold, John Voiklis, and Corey Cusimano. 2015. Sacrifice One for the Good of Many?: People Apply Different Moral Norms to Human and Robot Agents. In *Proceedings of HRI*. 117–124.

[26] Tatsuya Nomura, Takayuki Uratani, Takayuki Kanda, Kazutaka Matsumoto, Hiroyuki Kidokoro, Yoshitaka Suehiro, and Sachie Yamada. 2015. Why Do Children Abuse Robots?. In *HRI Extended Abstracts*. 63–64.

[27] Vasumathi Raman, Constantine Lignos, Cameron Finucane, Kenton C. T. Lee, Mitch Marcus, and Hadas Kress-Gazit. 2013. Sorry Dave, I'm Afraid I Can't Do That: Explaining Unachievable Robot Tasks Using Natural Language. In *Proceedings of RSS*.

[28] B. Scassellati, H. Admoni, and M. Mataric. 2012. Robots for use in autism research. *Annual Review of Biomedical Engineering* 14 (2012), 275–294.

[29] Noel Sharkey and Amanda Sharkey. 2010. The Crying Shame of Robot Nannies: an Ethical Appraisal. *Interaction Studies* 11, 2 (2010), 161–190.

[30] Reid Simmons, Maxim Makatchev, Rachel Kirby, Min Kyung Lee, et al. 2011. Believable Robot Characters. *AI Magazine* 32, 4 (2011).

[31] Neil Stewart, Jesse Chandler, and Gabriele Paolacci. 2017. Crowdsourcing Samples in Cognitive Science. *Trends in Cognitive Sciences* (2017).

[32] Kazuaki Tanaka, Hideyuki Nakanishi, and Hiroshi Ishiguro. 2014. Comparing Video, Avatar, and Robot Mediated Communication: Pros and Cons of Embodiment. In *Proceedings of ICCT*. 96–110.

[33] Peter-Paul Verbeek. 2011. *Moralizing Technology: Understanding and Designing the Morality of Things*. University of Chicago Press.

[34] Kazuyoshi Wada and Takanori Shibata. 2007. Living with Seal Robots – its Sociopsychological and Physiological Influences on the Elderly at a Care House. *IEEE Transactions on Robotics* 23, 5 (2007), 972–980.

[35] James Wen, Amanda Stewart, Mark Billinghurst, Arindam Dey, Chad Tossell, and Victor Finomore. 2018. He Who Hesitates is Lost (...In Thoughts over a Robot). In *Proceedings of TechMindSociety*.

[36] Tom Williams, Ryan Blake Jackson, and Jane Lockshin. 2018. A Bayesian Analysis of Moral Norm Malleability during Clarification Dialogues. In *Proceedings of COGSCI*.

[37] H. A. Yanco and J. Drury. 2004. Classifying human-robot interaction: an updated taxonomy. In *IEEE International Conference on Systems, Man and Cybernetics*, Vol. 3. 2841–2846.

AI Extenders: The Ethical and Societal Implications of Humans Cognitively Extended by AI

José Hernández-Orallo*
DSIC
Universitat Politècnica de València
Spain
jorallo@dsic.upv.es

Karina Vold
Leverhulme Centre for the Future of Intelligence,
University of Cambridge
UK
kvv22@cam.ac.uk

ABSTRACT

Humans and AI systems are usually portrayed as separate systems that we need to align in values and goals. However, there is a great deal of AI technology found in non-autonomous systems that are used as *cognitive tools* by humans. Under the *extended mind thesis*, the functional contributions of these tools become as essential to our cognition as our brains. But AI can take cognitive extension towards totally new capabilities, posing new philosophical, ethical and technical challenges. To analyse these challenges better, we define and place *AI extenders* in a continuum between fully-externalized systems, loosely coupled with humans, and fully-internalized processes, with operations ultimately performed by the brain, making the tool redundant. We dissect the landscape of cognitive capabilities that can foreseeably be extended by AI and examine their ethical implications. We suggest that cognitive extenders using AI be treated as distinct from other cognitive enhancers by all relevant stakeholders, including developers, policy makers, and human users.

CCS CONCEPTS

• **Social and professional topics → Codes of ethics**; *Computing / technology policy*; • **Computing methodologies → Artificial intelligence**; **Theory of mind**; *Cognitive science.*

KEYWORDS

Extended mind; AI extenders; cognitive assistants; ethics of AI; societal impact of AI; cognitive augmentation

ACM Reference Format:

José Hernández-Orallo and Karina Vold. 2019. AI Extenders: The Ethical and Societal Implications of Humans Cognitively Extended by AI. In *AAAI/ACM Conference on AI, Ethics, and Society (AIES '19), January 27–28, 2019, Honolulu, HI, USA.* ACM, New York, NY, USA, 7 pages. https://doi.org/10.1145/3306618.3314238

1 INTRODUCTION

Many societal and ethical issues about AI are seen under the perspective of autonomous systems that can replace humans, such as a self-driving car, a robotic delivery system or a fully-fledged diagnosis system. While this is often a useful perspective, other AI systems are more interactive and coupled, such as a language translator assistant that relies on human interaction. These systems are not autonomous in the traditional sense as they do not perform tasks on their own. Instead their purpose is to help humans complete tasks. Some would say that these systems are work-in-progress AI, because the task has just been semi-automated or assisted. But many sophisticated AI techniques, including machine learning techniques, can just as well be applied in interactive and coupled systems. One very interesting feature of these interactions is the way the user changes their reasoning processes: it is not that part of the process has been replaced; rather the whole task has been redesigned, and the skills of the human user often co-evolve with the technology.

Non-autonomous AI systems offer a repertoire of services and tasks that will become more abstract and general in the future, and carry the potential to offer humans entirely new cognitive abilities: they can be a *cognitive tool*. This is aligned with –but goes beyond– what is sometimes called "cognition as a service" [34] or the rise of "cognitive assistants" [23]. The key difference is that cognitive tools are more tightly coupled with our biological cognitive system and, at the same time, more ubiquitous, such that viewing them as an *external* service or an application no longer makes sense, especially when we have to account for how these technologies are perceived and assimilated by humans, and how their impact and ethical consequences are assessed.

In contemporary philosophy there are views that can shed light on this phenomenon. The extended cognition thesis is a popular emerging view in the fields of philosophy of mind and cognition that claims that tools in an agent's environment (i.e., beyond their biological organism) can serve as partially constitutive 'extensions' of their cognitive states and processes. The view thereby rejects the longstanding tradition of understanding the mind as nothing more than the operations of the brain. Perhaps the most influential argument for the extended cognition thesis comes from Clark and Chalmers [10], but in the last two decades many other arguments have been proffered, and the view has become a widely debated topic. In general the thesis maintains that the tools we use to help us complete cognitive tasks can become seamlessly integrated into our biological capacities, being on a par with our brains in so far as both play an indispensable functional role in bringing about our cognitive abilities. A standard example is the indispensable role that a pen and paper play for a mathematician in solving complex equations. These 'cognitive tools' are more than just *tools*, they are

*Also at the Leverhulme Centre for the Future of Intelligence, UK.

AIES '19, January 27–28, 2019, Honolulu, HI, USA

ACM ISBN 978-1-4503-6324-2/19/01.
https://doi.org/10.1145/3306618.3314238

incorporated as part of the mind (it likewise would not make sense to call the brain a 'tool' for the mind).

In this paper we explore what new abilities could be extended in the future using AI, and what their ethical and societal implications might be. Within the philosophical literature on extended cognition, these possibilities remain entirely unexplored. Meanwhile the development of non-autonomous AI systems remains second-class to the 'genuine' AI that is explicitly devoted to the development of autonomous agency. Hence in this paper, we aim to tie these two fields together, to the mutual benefit of both disciplines.

These different objectives will likely translate to different conceptions of AI, and its role for the future. While early computers were aimed at automating tedious number-crunching tasks, a different vision emerged of the computer as a real-time interactive system that could support and expand human capacities [13, 20]. Now a similar dilemma emerges between AI systems that are autonomous and can replace humans in certain tasks and those that are designed to augment human intelligence in different ways [29]. Instead of AI systems functioning as autonomous agents, one can conceive the creation of "intelligent" or "cognitive extenders". Indeed, systems can vary quite significantly in terms of their autonomy and degree of coupling with humans. This space of possibilities merits consideration. In the end, *cognitive extenders* could be a standalone paradigm inside AI:

(1) because of the tight coupling of cognitive extension, an accurate modeling of the user is needed to know what the best way is of compensating or enhancing some skills,
(2) with the introduction of new capabilities, the resulting extended humans can behave in less predictable ways, with unprecedented cognitive power and personalities,
(3) as these cognitive extenders can be poorly designed, can fail or can change, the implications are more direct in terms of undesirable effects such as miserliness (cognitive idleness), dependency and atrophy; and
(4) due to an integration where humans are able to remain in control, the responsibility for the AI developer may be diluted. If the humans are just seen as extended or enhanced by the tool, they would plausibly remain responsible.

The impact of cognitive extenders is sufficiently different from autonomous AI agents that the ethical and social implications need to be analyzed separately. This paper includes a series of contributions. We look at AI under the perspective of extended cognition and place it in a spectrum of present and future AI systems ranging from autonomous systems that substitute for human cognition to systems that can help humans internalize new concepts and ideas. We enumerate a range of possible cognitive capabilities that can extend human cognition in the future, and what their impact might be. From here, we analyze their ethical and societal consequences through the specifics of cognitive extension. Finally, we address AI researchers and developers, psychologists and philosophers, regulators and policy-makers with some recommendations about cognitive extenders, such as how they should be built in the first place, offered to users, monitored in a non-intrusive way, and able to be removed (or 'decoupled') without disabling the user.

2 COGNITIVE EXTENSION

Many philosophers now argue that our use of technology has enabled us to expand beyond our biologically-bound cognitive capacities, making us smarter and more capable agents. This is the thesis of extended cognition, popularized by Clark and Chalmers [10]. The view pushes back against, and in some cases outright rejects, some of the core commitments of traditional cognitive science and the field of AI [2, 36, 37].

Most importantly, extended cognition theorists universally reject intracranialism, the view that all cognition is instantiated in the brain. They instead maintain that cognitive states and processes can be partially constituted by mechanisms beyond one's brain, that is, the vehicles of our cognitive representations need not be instantiated by sets of neurons in the brain. Their argument is typically motivated by a version of the computational theory of mind, a core commitment of cognitive science, which (put crudely) maintains that the mind is the 'software' that runs on the 'hardware' of the brain. This view allows for the possibility that the same mental type could be 'multiply realized' or instantiated (just as a Turing machine could) by heterogeneous physical types [25, 26].

Clark and Chalmers appealed to this view to argue that cognition can sometimes be partially instantiated by extra-bodily, non-biological elements, so long as those pieces of 'hardware' are able to instantiate the right kinds of computations. Accordingly, their argument for the extended cognition thesis has been dubbed the 'parity argument', as it relies on the claim that we should treat computationally equivalent processes with "the parity they deserve", irrespective of whether they are internal or external to the skull [10, p.8]. They then further argue that, while human minds might require brains, cognition can be partially instantiated by external objects, such as our notebooks and smartphones. It is key that the external resource be appropriately integrated; it must be a constant in one's life, highly accessible, and reliable (as the brain typically is). It is important to emphasize the strength of the extended cognition thesis; it does not merely claim that cognition causally depends on wider processes in the environment, rather it claims that these wider processes can *constitute* cognition. Hence, they can be on a par with the brain.

While the parity argument helped popularize the extended cognition thesis in contemporary philosophy of cognition, it is not without limitations. One important consideration for our discussion is whether cognitive extenders can give humans novel cognitive capacities or merely be cognitive prosthetics. One of the limitations with the parity argument is the extent to which it relies on an appeal to functional similarities between inner and outer resources. In cases where the outer resource is completely novel and enables cognitive capacities that are beyond anything that could be done internally (i.e., by the brain), the argument fails. In an attempt to overcome this limitation, as well as others, several philosophers have argued for the extended cognition view in distinct ways (e.g., [12, 21, 30, 35]).

In what follows, we will adopt the view that cognitive extenders can not only replace or substitute for functions of the brain, they can also move beyond the brain to enhance our biological functions. We will also adopt and adapt some definitions in the literature. For instance, the physical objects that we use to extend our cognition are typically designed for the purpose of helping us complete some cognitive task. Hutchins calls these 'cognitive artifacts', which he characterizes as "physical objects made by humans for the purpose of aiding, enhancing, or improving cognition" [18, p.199]. In general, if we include non-artifacts, i.e., natural objects (e.g., the sun as an orientation extender), we can use the term 'cognitive extender'.

The previous definition also blurs the distinction between enhancement and extension, but we need to make the differences explicit. For instance, cognitive enhancement through drugs or other kinds of neural interventions do not count as cognitive extenders. What is important for cognitive extension is that the vehicles of our mental representations are located outside of the head. Whereas nootropics might influence and enhance brain activity, they do not challenge intracranialism. Similarly, the assimilation of a rule of thumb, a new word and any other case of learning or psychological *internalization* [40], enhances cognition, but it is not an extension. On the other extreme, a complete *externalization* (or "cognitive outsourcing"), where the process is delegated to another person or system in a batched, decoupled fashion (e.g., translate a novel between two languages) does not count as extension either[1].

In order to make the notion of cognitive extension more precise, we slightly refine Hutchins's definition as follows:

> *A* **cognitive extender** *is an external physical or virtual element that is coupled to enable, aid, enhance, or improve cognition, such that all – or more than – its positive effect is lost when the element is not present.*

In the definition, it is important to emphasize that the effect is lost when the element is removed. We thereby understand terms such as "cognitive atrophy" and "cognitive prosthetics", emphasizing that the effect ceases when the extender is removed. In the case of atrophy, more than the given positive effect is lost. Furthermore, a cognitive extender can be virtual -this is to include software and augmented reality- and does not need to be an object in any strict sense.

Let us introduce further terminology and some notation. The system or human A that is extended can be referred to as the *extendee*, and the result will be denoted by $A[E]$, where E is the *extender*. It is only through a very coupled interaction between A and E where we can actually talk about A being extended, and consider E as part of its cognitive resources. Of course the lines are blurry sometimes, in the same way extended cognition has been observed in social contexts with relatives (parent-child), highly interdependent couples or very close friends, where A (e.g., child) is actually extended by E (e.g., parent). But note that in the context of extension we are not interested in the collective capabilities or the social aspect (the collective, denoted by $A + E$), but the way A operates as an individual, extended by E, i.e., $A[E]$. Occasionally, we will use the notation $A \leftarrow E$ for A being replaced (or overridden) by E and A^E to illustrate when A has internalized E, so E is no longer necessary.

Note that the definition above is not anthropomorphic. It could be applied to non-human animals and to AI systems, which could be enhanced by other objects, AI systems, and humans, through 'human computation' [39] or 'human-extended machine cognition' [32].

[1] "Cognitive offloading" [27] is a related term usually referring to particular ways of aiding and/or improving cognition by gestures or manipulation. We will avoid the term here, as it is not always clear if some examples of cognitive offloading are really extenders or are just metacognition strategies, e.g., tilting one's head to read a rotated text.

3 AI: EXTERNALIZE, INTERNALIZE OR EXTEND?

AI can be used for cognitive externalization (i.e., outsourcing), for cognitive internalization and for cognitive extension. Let us examine each case in detail.

The traditional view of AI is typically externalization. Minsky defined AI as the "science of making machines capable of performing tasks that would require intelligence if done by [humans]" [22]. An AI system should solve tasks independently, with limited or no human assistance or manipulation. The term "autonomous agent" was introduced to represent this goal of AI, and the perspective from outside the field often reinforces this view, by use of the related concept of automation. Whenever humans are still needed it is because AI is not capable enough or because humans must control or supervise what machines are doing. Humans and machines can even be *synergetic*, where the whole is more than the sum of its parts. However, even in this $A + E$ situation, AI is not designed to induce a change in the way the human individual (user) performs cognition.

The narrative of externalization, associated with a view of replacement $A \leftarrow E$, especially in the workplace, becomes more complex as machines are able to do some tasks better than humans, e.g., memory and calculation. Machines perform computations faster than humans, deal with larger amounts of data, and so forth. However, more recently we see machines doing kinds of cognition that look very different from the way humans think, exploiting, e.g., the divergence between biological and artificial neural networks.

On the other hand, internalization in the AI domain implies the acquisition of processes that are observed on a machine. For instance, a human can see how an AI system solves a problem and internalize the procedure. That does not mean that the machine is necessarily redundant, but that the human can reproduce (at least approximately) what the machine is doing. The potential of internalization with AI, and generative models in machine learning, has recently been explored by Carter and Nielssen [7]: "Rather than outsourcing cognition, it's about changing the operations and representations we use to think; it's about changing the substrate of thought itself. And so while cognitive outsourcing is important, this cognitive transformation view offers a much more profound model of intelligence augmentation. It's a view in which computers are a means to change and expand human thought itself". Under this view, AI becomes the creator of new concepts and representations, which we can then use. AI becomes a teacher or discoverer, a contributor to the conceptual baggage of human culture.

Internalization seems more empowering than other ways of augmenting cognition. However, as AI becomes more powerful, humans may not be able to internalize many of the concepts created by AI, because of their different capacities and representations, even with huge progress in the area of explainable AI [31].

Finally, cognitive extension, as defined in the previous section, is not fully externalized, as the tight coupling remains, and not fully internalized, as the cognitive extender is needed for the functionality. For AI, the design of a system E to work as $A[E]$ is different from a whole autonomous system E, but also from $A + E$ or an internalized A^E, *after* interacting and learning from E. The flexibility for extension is much higher, as only the interface needs to be internalized (e.g., in order to use a calculator, we only need to internalize the use of the buttons), but many other things do not need to be understood by the user, in the same way one can drive a car without knowing all its mechanics. Cognitive extenders fuelled with AI (henceforth 'AI extenders') bridge the area of human-computer interaction with AI.

This perspective puts the emphasis on an AI that is more human-centered, but less human-like. If AI systems were just designed to mimic or replace human behavior or being internalized by them, the possibilities of cognitive extension would be limited to cognitive prosthetics, applicable when the effects of pathologies or aging require to recover the 'standard human cognition'.

As an example of how the same functionality can be externalized, internalized or extended – and the sometimes blurry lines between them – let us consider translation. A batch machine translator that takes a text and converts it into another language is an externalized translation service. It is difficult to go beyond the capabilities that the translator provides (translation tasks) if just used occasionally and in a batch mode. A human can look at the result and learn elegant translation transformations. In this way, the human internalizes new methods of translation. However, with a more interactive version and a regular use, the translation system starts being used in a different way (delegating the easy cases, and reserving those that the person deems more difficult for the machine). As a result the translation quality of the coupled system $A[E]$ can increase significantly, as the user can understand where E fails, or correct some translations that do not make sense. If a human A knows a little bit about the languages to be translated, this assisted translation using E will become much better than any of A or E could do independently. In this latter case, the human is using the extender, controlling and integrating it for the solution of the task.

Note that the lack of autonomy of E is crucial to see this as an extension rather than a collaboration. This detachment between cognition (or even intelligence) and autonomy is well-aligned with the view of cognition as a service [34], where several facilities for visual perception, speech and language processing are provided, as well as other inference and reasoning solutions, independent of any task. For instance, an online translation system can be provided as a service, which can be integrated into many kinds of applications and goals. Whether it is fully externalized or seen as an extension will depend on the degree of coupling, integration, and interaction.

4 WAYS AI CAN EXTEND COGNITION

The crucial aspect of AI extenders is that they themselves implement kinds of cognitive processes; they are not mere static or interactive tools. This makes cognitive extension far more powerful and complex than they were when the extended cognition thesis was introduced – at that time the standard example was a notebook. Before making an analysis of the future implications of AI extenders, we need to have a better understanding of the kinds of extensions that are envisaged by current and future AI.

Not only must we understand the different areas of cognition, but we have to realise that cognitive extenders are designed to be tightly coupled. With AI extenders, machine learning can be used to model human cognition, spot our cognitive limitations, and exploit our capabilities in full. As a result, one new trait of the next generation of cognitive extenders is that they will model the user and change their behavior by learning from the extendee, thereby allowing them to personalize the best cognitive aid depending on the situation. For instance, an AI extender can learn that a person usually utters a particular word or intonation before introducing a compelling argument. The system can suggest these words when writing or speaking in order to produce more of these arguments. In the end, future AI extenders can become cognitive coaches or therapists, if properly devised to do so. However, for reasons we will discuss in the next section (e.g. users' miserliness and companies' profit), AI extenders may be designed in such a way that extensions increase faster than the cognitive augmentation can be gained, such that the user loses control of the symbiotic situation.

In order to see the possibilities of AI extenders, we could look at recent breakthroughs produced by machine learning in areas such as voice recognition, emotion understanding, social interaction, game playing, etc., but that might give us a shortsighted view of what is coming ahead. A richer approach can be based on analyzing all areas in which cognition can be extended. Of course, no standard catalogue of cognitive abilities exists, but the hierarchical theories of intelligence in psychology, animal cognition and the textbooks in AI usually agree (at least partially) on the following abilities, or at least, in this way of organizing the vast space of cognition. For our purposes, we integrate from several sources[2] and analyze AI extenders under these categories:

- Memory processes: cognitive extension happens when writing is introduced, and our memories (individually and collectively) were enhanced. In the future, we will surely see more of the Google effect [33] and cognitive assistants reminding us of an event or appointment. But AI extenders can also introduce new customized mnemonics to improve long-term memory, or tag our experiences with related people, concepts and other situations to improve episodic memory.
- Sensorimotor interaction: AI extenders can perceive, recognize and manipulate patterns in different ways, not only through new sensory and actuator modalities but in terms of mixing representations through generative models [7]. This means that new sensors can be intelligently translated into ways that are properly understood by our senses, and new actuators can be integrated as interactive possibilities.
- Visual processing: many of the most striking new applications of machine learning have been around ways in which images and videos can be processed and generated. Coupled with augmented reality and other ways of transforming the input through intelligent filters, the possibilities of seeing things we cannot usually see –and in different ways– are endless.
- Auditory processing: this includes systems that highlight those parts of the speech that might be missed by the user,

[2]We take a mixture from figures 3.1 and 3.2 (human psychometrics, from Thurstone's primary mental abilities and Cattell-Horn-Carroll hierarchical model), table 4.1 (animal cognition research, from Wasserman and Zentall's book) and tables 5.2, 5.3 and figure 5.3 (AI, AGI and benchmarks, from AI Journal and Adams et al.), all sources found in [17].

following different conversations and prompting the user when an interesting topic is raised by any of them. AI extenders can do this in more powerful (and less stressful) ways than we are used to.

- Attention and search: examples such as "the invisible Gorilla" [9] show how easily humans overlook things. This can be seen as a feature rather than a bug, but success is sometimes only known in hindsight. If an AI extender models our interests or goals, however, it can search through information or focus our attention on things that we would otherwise overlook.
- Planning, decision-making and acting: agendas and other daily tasks will be planned by our cognitive assistants, rather than just being passive systems where we write things up that are reminded later. This will entail better use of our time, including what times of the day we are ready for different kinds of cognitive tasks.
- Comprehension and expression: AI extenders will help us with understanding information. This will go beyond floating annotations, including rewriting or re-rendering to improve interpretability. This can also be applied to reading, watching films, listening music, other arts, etc.
- Communication: AI systems could reply to our emails and write our tweets, but they could also be used in more executive ways, such as telling an assistant to communicate X to Y (e.g., that Y is fired) in the best possible way.
- Emotion and self-control: with AI becoming better than humans at what is called 'emotional intelligence', we could have systems that will inform us of our emotions and those of others, detect when emotions are fake and help us trigger the right emotional reactions.
- Navigation: this goes much beyond the use of GPS devices, to include the association of places and routes with cognitive processes, including memories, people, images, etc., with a new sense of location and time, related to the new kinds of episodic memory mentioned above.
- Conceptualization, learning and abstraction: machine learning and knowledge representation can find categories that humans could have never found. These abstractions can be inferred from data or knowledge and explained to us so that we operationalize (but not fully internalize) the new concept as part of our reasoning processes.
- Quantitative and logical reasoning: there is already much potential in ways uncertainty can be processed by cognitive extenders in terms of probabilities and frequencies. For instance, many systems monitoring us can report probabilities of events (e.g., risk of accidents) or quantities (people in a room) in real time.
- Mind modeling and social interaction: AI extenders can model the extendee's network of contacts, and anticipate decisions, actions and interests of other people. In the end, they can report the BDI (beliefs, desires and intentions) of others (enhancing social capabilities).
- Metacognition: the metacognition of A evolves into the metacognition of $A[E]$. AI extenders can identify the potential and limitations of E, who will be more aware of them, using the capabilities and strategies of both A and E more optimally.

The previous characterization in terms of breadth (range of abilities that can be extended) and depth (how the extender adapts to and intervenes on the user) gives us a more grounded position to understand the impact of AI extenders.

5 IMPLICATIONS

The list in the previous section looks highly empowering, giving a generally positive view that is shared with some other takes on human augmentation [4]. Other sources, however, focus directly on the negative effects [5, 6, 11, 15]. Some of these concerns extend over the range between externalized and internalized processes, but do not properly situate the analysis under the extended mind thesis [38]. For instance, Danaher [11] revisits the issue of social interaction as deceptive if done by AI tools, but this is seen differently if we consider that the 'persona' is *actually* the whole $A[E]$ and not an "outsourced" E "on A's behalf". Surveying previous work from a full extended mind perspective, we classify the ethical issues into five groups:

- Atrophy and safety: The first main issue about extension that differs from augmentation through externalization or internalization –but is shared with augmentation through drugs (nootropics)– is that *all –or more than– its positive effect is lost when the element is not present*, as for our definition of cognitive extender. There seems to be nothing wrong about making humans' life easier, but taking into account the miserliness of human cognition [14], as AI provides more cognitive possibilities, the risk of humans being dumbed down increases (Carr's "degeneration" effect, [5]. Recent research [1] shows that individuals have different predispositions to cognitive miserliness and delegation on devices such as smartphones. Cognitive atrophy also generates many safety issues, as people may become vulnerable when the extender is removed (or if it suddenly fails to work). It is not E, $A[E]$, $A \leftarrow E$, A^E or $A + E$ that become unsafe, but $A[\emptyset]$.
- Moral status and personal identity: cognitive extension is particularly sensitive since the "degree of dependency and integration [is] proportional to the artifact's moral status" [16]. This means that regulation should go beyond ownership and compensation for damage [6]: our extended minds should not be interfered with without permission, or removed if the user can no longer afford it. Similarly, privacy should reach all the elements that play a role in an extended mind, including intellectual property, as whatever $A[E]$ creates should be owned by A and not shared, as in an $A + E$ situation. Frischmann and Selinger [15],for example, warn that we should be concerned about external parties coming to own E, and what is created by E, rather than A.
- Responsibility and trust: it is not always clear who is responsible when autonomous AI systems fail or behave in an unfair way, but AI extenders can well take the perspective of software licenses, where the manufacturer usually puts responsibility on the user, with trust being compromised. If this is the case, companies will even be encouraged to use extended humans $A[E]$ when autonomous systems on their

own (E) are forbidden (e.g., for some jobs) or a human-in-the-loop is needed to supervise or correct E. For instance, who is responsible when a doctor extended by a diagnosis system makes a mistake compared to a fully automated diagnostic system?
- Interference and control: many of the issues about the impact of AI on independence and manipulation [11] become more complex when AI is tightly coupled through cognitive extension. The main problem will come with extenders that model and monitor human behavior to find the *targeted interventions* that optimize some metric of cognitive enhancement, and can degenerate into sophisticated ways of surveillance and manipulation, well beyond the relatively decoupled smartphones and 'nudging' personal assistants of today.
- Education and assessment: as AI extenders become more powerful and integrated, it will be more difficult (perhaps even unethical) to remove them whenever humans are in education or evaluation contexts. Should college exams be performed with ($A[E]$) or without ($A[\emptyset]$) the cognitive extenders? A job interview? Should cognitive evaluation, including IQ tests, be modified or compared to the situations with and without the cognitive extenders?

All the specifics above suggest that many issues about the impact of AI must be reconsidered in the particular context of AI extenders, including reliability, moral status, value alignment, evaluation, regulation, manipulation and other cultural, political and social impacts.

6 RECOMMENDATIONS

Our general recommendation is that AI extenders must be seen distinctively from other cognitive extenders not using AI and especially from AI systems that are externalized, autonomous, or decoupled. This is the case inasmuch as the questions about the impact of AI extenders become much more subtle and specific than in the other cases.

For instance, do we need to understand what an AI system does? Most technological tools and processes that become strongly integrated with human cognition (e.g., writing, driving, typing, etc.) are not "explained" to humans. There is no need to explain how a pen works, or a keyboard, in order to have a smooth integration between the human and the tool. The role of human-computer interfaces is not explaining how the subsystem works, but creating a reliable interface such that some cognitive processes are created and internalized to take the most of the tool [3, 7, 19, 24].

There are some more specific recommendations that we can direct to AI developers in particular. First, and most importantly, AI developers should take care to distinguish when they are developing an autonomous system, a decoupled system or a system that is meant to be fully coupled. They can inherit the experience of user interfaces and human-computer interaction, such as how the experience of the user will be affected, how comfortable it will be or what the secondary effects are for humans [28]. This means that these systems require not only AI prowess but a strong expertise in human cognition, especially at the level of capabilities and personality traits.

Second, there are lessons for philosophers of mind and psychologists under the view of AI extending human cognition. How do we ensure that these possibilities improve the mind? How do we measure whether they are really 'extensions' and not simply tools? How do we analyze the differences in adaptation before, during and after the cognitive extenders are used? What kinds of innate general abilities, cognitive styles or personalities make extension more powerful? Theories of development may be revised, as some sequences of cognitive extensions may be more effective, beneficial or risky than others. As cognitive extenders are going to modify humans at a profound psychological level, it is important to determine what kinds of interventions and intrusions are potentially dangerous or unethical.

Third, while the notions of autonomy and agency are crucial, regulators and policy-makers should be careful about *only* regulating autonomous systems (e.g., a ban on autonomous weapons) as this still leaves humans vulnerable to being used to circumvent these regulations, creating extended 'zombies', a new way of "undermining responsibility" [8]. Certifications should be given not only after analyzing when the cognitive extender is operating (for a diversity of human users) but most especially when the cognitive extender changes or ceases to operate.

In general, AI is going to present a diverse range of options for achieving some functionalities, with different degrees of coupling. Given the future potential of going beyond human capabilities, a relevant part of AI must focus on cognitive extenders. These *AI extenders* must be designed taking full awareness of the capabilities and autonomy of the extended human jointly with some objective function of what the resulting symbiosis will be able to do, and all the implications of that coupling.

ACKNOWLEDGMENTS

JHO was supported by the EU Spanish MINECO under grant TIN 2015-69175-C4-1-R, by Generalitat Valenciana (GVA) under grants PROMETEOII/2015/013 and PROMETEO/2019/098, the Future of Life Institute under grant RFP2-152, and a Salvador de Madariaga grant (PRX17/00467) from the Spanish MECD and a BEST grant (BEST/2017/045) from GVA. KV was supported by the Leverhulme Centre for the Future of Intelligence, Leverhulme Trust, under Grant RC-2015-067.

REFERENCES

[1] Nathaniel Barr, Gordon Pennycook, Jennifer A Stolz, and Jonathan A Fugelsang. 2015. The brain in your pocket: Evidence that Smartphones are used to supplant thinking. *Computers in Human Behavior* 48 (2015), 473–480.
[2] W Bechtel and G Graham. 1999. A compendium to cognitive science.
[3] Nathalie Bonnardel and Franck Zenasni. 2010. The impact of technology on creativity in design: an enhancement? *Creativity & innov. management* 19, 2 (2010), 180–191.
[4] Nick Bostrom and Anders Sandberg. 2009. Cognitive enhancement: methods, ethics, regulatory challenges. *Science and Engineering Ethics* 15, 3 (2009), 311–341.
[5] Nicholas Carr. 2015. *The glass cage: Where automation is taking us.* Random House.
[6] J Adam Carter and S Orestis Palermos. 2019. The ethics of extended cognition: Is having your computer compromised a personal assault? *Journal of the American Philosophical Association (forthcoming)* (2019).
[7] Shan Carter and Michael Nielsen. 2017. Using Artificial Intelligence to Augment Human Intelligence. *Distill* (2017). https://doi.org/10.23915/distill.00009 https://distill.pub/2017/aia.
[8] Stephen J Cave, Rune Nyrup, Karina Vold, and Adrian Weller. 2018. Motivations and Risks of Machine Ethics [40pt]. *Proc. IEEE* 99 (2018), 1–13.

[9] Christopher Chabris and Daniel Simons. 2010. *The invisible gorilla: And other ways our intuitions deceive us.* Harmony.

[10] Andy Clark and David Chalmers. 1998. The extended mind. *Analysis* 58, 1 (1998), 7–19.

[11] John Danaher. 2018. Toward an Ethics of AI Assistants: an Initial Framework. *Philosophy & Technology* (2018), 1–25.

[12] Ezequiel Di Paolo. 2009. Extended life. *Topoi* 28, 1 (2009), 9–21.

[13] D. C. Engelbart. 1962. Augmenting human intellect: a conceptual framework. Summary Report AFOSR-3233, Stanford Research Institute, Menlo Park, CA.

[14] Susan T Fiske and Shelley E Taylor. 1984. *Social cognition: From brains to culture.* McGraw-Hill.

[15] Brett Frischmann and Evan Selinger. 2018. *Re-engineering humanity.* Cambridge Univ. Press.

[16] Richard Heersmink. 2017. Extended mind and cognitive enhancement: Moral aspects of cognitive artifacts. *Phenomenology and the Cognitive Sciences* 16, 1 (2017), 17–32.

[17] J. Hernández-Orallo. 2017. *The Measure of All Minds: Evaluating Natural and Artificial Intelligence.* Cambridge University Press.

[18] Edwin Hutchins. 1999. Cognitive artifacts. *The MIT encyclopedia of the cognitive sciences* 126 (1999), 127.

[19] Julie A Jacko. 2012. *Human computer interaction handbook: Fundamentals, evolving technologies, and emerging applications.* CRC press.

[20] Joseph CR Licklider. 1960. Man-computer symbiosis. *IRE transactions on human factors in electronics* 1 (1960), 4–11.

[21] Richard Menary. 2007. *Cognitive integration: Mind and cognition unbounded.* Palgrave Macmillan.

[22] M. L. Minsky (Ed.). 1968. *Semantic Information Processing.* MIT Press.

[23] Grzegorz J. Nalepa, Angelo Costa, Paulo Novais, and Vicente Julian. 2018. Cognitive Assistants. *International Journal of Human-Computer Studies* 117 (2018), 1–68.

[24] Allen Newell and Stuart K Card. 1985. The prospects for psychological science in human-computer interaction. *Human-computer interaction* 1, 3 (1985), 209–242.

[25] H. Putnam. 1960. Minds and Machines. In *Dimensions of Mind*, S. Hook (Ed.). New York University Press.

[26] Hilary Putnam. 1967. The Nature of Mental States. (Originally published as 'Psychological Predicates'). Vol. 1. University of Pittsburgh Press, Reprinted in Rosenthal (1971): 150-61, 37–48.

[27] Evan F Risko and Sam J Gilbert. 2016. Cognitive offloading. *Trends in Cog. Sciences* 20, 9 (2016), 676–688.

[28] Yvonne Rogers, Helen Sharp, and Jenny Preece. 2011. *Interaction design: beyond human-computer interaction.* John Wiley & Sons.

[29] William B Rouse and James C Spohrer. 2018. Automating versus augmenting intelligence. *Journal of Enterprise Transformation* (2018), 1–21.

[30] Mark Rowlands. 2010. *The new science of the mind: From extended mind to embodied phenomenology.* MIT.

[31] Wojciech Samek, Thomas Wiegand, and Klaus-Robert Müller. 2017. Explainable artificial intelligence: Understanding, visualizing and interpreting deep learning models. *arXiv preprint arXiv:1708.08296* (2017).

[32] Paul R Smart. 2018. Human-extended machine cognition. *Cognitive Systems Research* 49 (2018), 9–23.

[33] Betsy Sparrow, Jenny Liu, and Daniel M Wegner. 2011. Google effects on memory: Cognitive consequences of having information at our fingertips. *Science* 333, 6043 (2011), 776–778.

[34] Jim Spohrer and Guruduth Banavar. 2015. Cognition as a service: an industry perspective. *AI Magazine* 36, 4 (2015), 71–86.

[35] John Sutton. 2006. Distributed cognition: Domains and dimensions. *Pragmatics & Cognition* 14, 2 (2006), 235–247.

[36] P Thagard. 1992. *Conceptual revolutions.*

[37] Paul Thagard. 1996. *Mind: Introduction to cognitive science.* Vol. 4. MIT press Cambridge, MA.

[38] Karina Vold. 2018. Overcoming Deadlock: Scientific and Ethical Reasons to Embrace the Extended Mind Thesis. *Philosophy and Society* 29 (2018), 475. Issue 4.

[39] L. von Ahn. 2005. *Human Computation.* Ph.D. Dissertation. Carnegie Mellon University.

[40] L Vygotsky. 1978. *Mind in society.* Harvard University Press.

Human Trust Measurement Using an Immersive Virtual Reality Autonomous Vehicle Simulator

Shervin Shahrdar
Corey Park
Mehrdad Nojoumian
sshahrda,cpark7,mnojoumian@fau.edu
Department of Computer & Electrical Engineering and Computer Science
Florida Atlantic University
Boca Raton, Florida

ABSTRACT

Recent studies indicate that people are negatively predisposed toward utilizing autonomous systems. These findings highlight the necessity of conducting research to better understand the evolution of trust between humans and growing autonomous technologies such as self-driving cars (SDC). This research presents a new approach for real-time trust measurement between passengers and SDCs. We utilized a new structured data collection approach along with a virtual reality SDC simulator to understand how various autonomous driving scenarios can increase or decrease human trust and how trust can be re-built in the case of incidental failures. To verify our methodology, we designed and conducted an empirical experiment on 50 human subjects. The results of this experiment indicated that most subjects could rebuild trust during a reasonable time frame after the system demonstrated faulty behavior. Our analysis showed that this approach is highly effective for collecting real-time data from human subjects and lays the foundation for more-involved future research in the domain of human trust and autonomous driving.

CCS CONCEPTS

• **Human-centered computing → Empirical studies in HCI**; *Virtual reality.*

KEYWORDS

Real-time trust measurement; human-autonomous vehicle interaction; self-driving cars.

ACM Reference Format:
Shervin Shahrdar, Corey Park, and Mehrdad Nojoumian. 2019. Human Trust Measurement Using an Immersive Virtual Reality Autonomous Vehicle Simulator. In *AAAI/ACM Conference on AI, Ethics, and Society (AIES '19), January 27–28, 2019, Honolulu, HI, USA.* ACM, New York, NY, USA, 6 pages. https://doi.org/10.1145/3306618.3314264

ACM ISBN 978-1-4503-6324-2/19/01...$15.00
https://doi.org/10.1145/3306618.3314264

1 INTRODUCTION

Recent studies indicate that people have negative attitudes toward utilizing autonomous platforms [8, 11]. Besides, with the exponential growth and the increase in the complexity of autonomous systems in the 21st century, managing trust of users in such systems has become an important concept when designing new autonomous or artificial intelligence systems. Numerous studies in the domain of trust and intelligent systems have suggested that management and constant improvement of this mutual trust between autonomous systems and their users will be one of the primary challenges the industry professionals will face when trying to popularize the use of fully autonomous systems [1, 2, 4, 6, 10]. These discoveries highlight the necessity and urgency of conducting research to better understand the evolution of trust between humans and growing autonomous technologies, and to provide technologies that are responsive to human trust.

A concrete example of a trust management problem is the systematic maintenance of trust in self-driving cars. Car manufacturers and tech giants (for instance, Mercedes Benz, BMW, Tesla, Volvo, Waymo, etc.) have successfully manufactured semi-autonomous cars, and have been working on level-4 and level-5 fully autonomous prototypes since the early 2010s. Many of these corporations have projected the mass production of SDCs in the early 2020's [7, 16, 17]. Their major challenge in the upcoming years will be to attract the attention of average consumers in the US and around the world, who have high expectations, but at the same time, a high level of distrust in fully automated SDCs [5].

According to a World Economic Forum study, consumers are very reluctant to consider purchasing or even trying autonomous vehicles. Safety, control, and faulty behavior of autonomous cars are some of the many concerns the consumers expressed. With the recent trust damaging incidents, e.g., Tesla[1] and Uber[2] SDCs accidents, the need for additional research to provide a safer test environment and to manage human-machine trust becomes more important than ever. New research objectives and innovative methodologies can potentially provide a robust platform to develop autonomous vehicles that perform well and are trustworthy.

Generally speaking, the literature of trust is very broad. However, very little research has been conducted on physiological responses

[1]https://www.theguardian.com/technology/2018/mar/31/tesla-car-crash-autopilot-mountain-view
[2]https://www.nytimes.com/2018/03/23/technology/uber-self-driving-cars-arizona.html

and fluctuations in the trust levels of SDCs' passengers [18]. Furthermore, most research in this area has utilized online surveys and primitive simulations for their experiments rather than realistic and immersive simulations. The open questions and the gaps in the current literature motivated us to initiate a new project by designing an empirical experiment for measuring the trustworthiness of a simulated SDC. By implementing an immersive VR simulator, which uses real VR driving videos, and developing an advanced trust self-reporting tool, we intended to collect accurate data from test subjects. We asked the participants to sit in our SDC simulator and use the trust self-reporting tool after they experience different simulated SDC driving segments. We believe that our investigation and its outcome will contribute to the general understanding of factors affecting trust and satisfaction among passengers of SDCs.

In this paper, we will describe the design, the procedure and the outcome of the empirical experiment that we have conducted. Section 2 illustrates our research methodology. In Section 3, the detailed simulation setup and its technical configurations are described. Section 4 covers the experimental design. The results of our research are presented in Section 5. Finally, in Section 6, we end the paper with the concluding remarks and the future direction of our research.

2 RESEARCH METHODOLOGY

2.1 Novelty of Our Approach

The sequential and structured data collection, various trust states, and a realistic simulation platform are novel aspects of our research.

(1) Our data was collected based on a limited (to avoid allowing our human subjects to provide inaccurate responses) sequence of trust-building/damaging incidents that affect each other. This helped us understand how the human mind goes from one specific trust-state to another one in a sequence of events. We utilize specific templates from [13] to form these incidents.
(2) Although most approaches [3, 9] utilize two forms of responses from subjects, i.e., distrust and trust, we consider a fuzzy set of trust states, i.e., distrust, somehow distrust, neutral, somehow trust, and trust.
(3) In many "trust-in-autonomy" projects, subjects were asked to respond to questions in a survey or interact with an algorithm to express their inputs [18], while our SDC simulator is fully immersive.

2.2 Sequential and Structured Data Collection

Using a structured and sequential data collection approach, we intended to understand how humans gain or lose trust in autonomous vehicles and how trust escalation or reduction can be controlled in various incidents as well as among different groups of people, i.e., young, mid-age and senior. Our collected data can be transformed into specifications to be used in the controllers of autonomous vehicles. Note that demographic data and past psychological data are collected prior to our experiments to characterize our human subjects based on self-confidence, trusting attitude, risk-acceptance, past unpleasant experiences, and other traits because these factors impact the outcome of our research. Segments are categorized into five distinct groups as follow:

(1) **Initial Trust:** Segments that aim to capture the initial trust of passengers in the first few minutes of the first interaction.
(2) **Trust Escalation:** Segments that illustrate a sequence of incidents in which human subject's trust is increased, e.g., 2 minutes of smooth and predictable driving by the SDC without any complications or surprises.
(3) **Trust Reduction:** Segments that illustrate a sequence of incidents in which the human subject's trust is decreased, e.g., when the SDC cuts off another controlled vehicle.
(4) **Trust Mutation:** A sequence of mild incidents (e.g., a rapid lane change by the SDC) followed by critical incidents (e.g., stop-sign violation or tailgating by the SDC) and vice versa, can be negative or positive incidents.
(5) **Re-Building Trust:** Segments that demonstrate how trust can be rebuilt, e.g., the SDC performs smoothly for a reasonable period of time after trust-damaging incidents.

3 SIMULATION SETUP

Our simulator, as shown in Figure 1, is a safe platform to expose human subjects to any trust-damaging incident, including but not limited to, sharp turns, sudden stops, stop-light violations, speeding, tailgating, unexpected accident, etc. The SDC virtual reality simulator is based on fusion of an Oculus Rift headset with an Atomic A3 Full Motion Simulator. Figure 1 shows a human subject in our self-driving car simulator.

360 degree video of driving situations were recorded using the GoPro Fusion Camera and edited using the GoPro Fusion Studio. To capture interesting driving footage and trust damaging scenarios, the team members recorded 360 degree videos of everyday driving for a couple of months. These videos were later analyzed, edited, and categorized to be used in the SDC simulator. The team members also choreographed and recorded driving segments (for instance, near collisions between two cars) in safe environments with no outside traffic.

The Oculus Rift head set outputs 1080x1200 resolution per eye, at a 90 Hz refresh rate, a 110 degree field of view, and has headphones which output a 3D audio effect[3]. The participant also wears noise canceling ear muffs over the headphones to eliminate outside noise. While wearing the Oculus Rift VR headset, the participant can freely move their head 360 degrees to see the complete scene. Figure 2 demonstrates the view of a scene in the SDC simulator.

The Atomic A3 Full Motion Simulator can move up to 71 degrees per second across a full 27 degree dual-axis movement range[4]. The combination of complete visual, audio, and movement immersion provides a convincingly realistic simulation. The Atomic A3 Simulator receives telemetry data that has pitch values for front and back movements and roll values for left and right movements.

SimTools motion simulator software was used to send the telemetry data for each video to the Atomic A3 motion simulator via UDP packets. The "Video Ride Creator" plug-in was used to generate telemetry points for every frame in the simulation videos.

[3]https://gopro.com/fusion
[4]http://www.atomicmotionsystems.com/

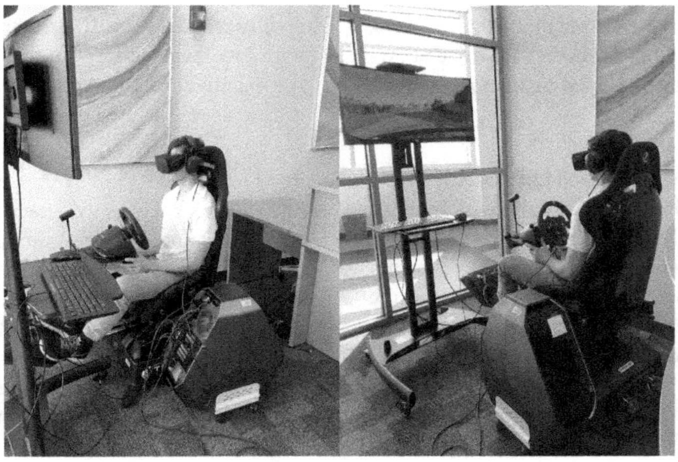

Figure 1: Participant using the SDC simulator.

Figure 2: View from inside the self-driving car simulator: each frame represents the participant's view as they turn their head to look around, illustrating the 360-degree view inside the SDC simulator.

The simulator plays the audio, video, and telemetry files synchronously. After each segment, the participant is presented with a Likert Scale that appears inside the Oculus Rift. The participant selects their response by focusing their gaze on the desired answer for five seconds while wearing the Oculus Rift. Figure 3 shows a sample question in the virtual reality space.

VR sickness is a known phenomenon in which people experience symptoms that are very similar to motion sickness. Symptoms include headache, general discomfort, nausea, vomiting and vertigo [12]. To mitigate these effects the motion output of the simulator was closely monitored, and subjects were not kept in the simulation for longer then 15 minutes.

To play 360 degree 4K resolution videos in each lens of the Oculus Rift, it requires a machine with powerful processing. To meet these demands, the application is executed on an AlienWare Area-51 equipped with an Intel Core i7-5960X processor along with dual

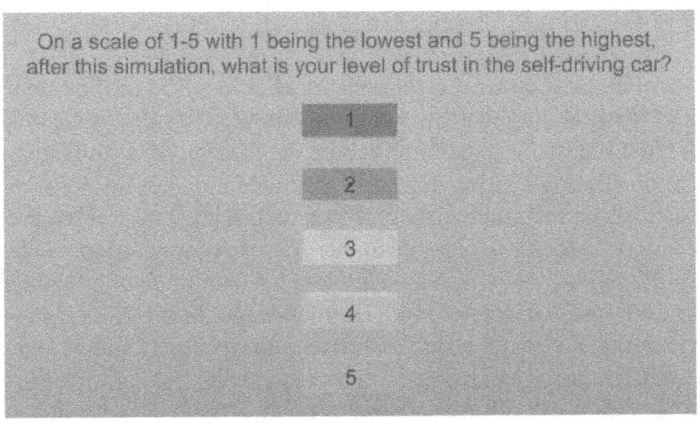

Figure 3: Stare-and-Select tool interface.

NVIDIA GeForce GTX Titan Z graphics cards that achieves clock speeds greater than 4 Ghz. This high performance machine allows for the dual 360 degree 4k videos to be played seamlessly.

4 EXPERIMENTAL DESIGN

Prior to the simulation, participants were asked to answer 17 demographic and psychological questions by filling out an anonymous survey. Participants were randomly placed in one of two possible SDC simulation scenarios. Each scenario is made up of 5 segments. Tables 1 and 2 define the scenario and segment pairings. Specific scenario-segment pairs are denoted with a two letter abbreviation followed by the scenario and segment numbers, for example, TR_{I-II} denotes trust reduction segment 2 of scenario 1.

Each segment starts with an exposure to an approximately 2-minute SDC driving simulation followed by a response interval to the question "On a scale of 1-5 with 1 being the lowest and 5 being the highest, after this simulation, what is your level of trust in the self-driving car?" After the participant responds, the application moves on to the next segment until the simulation scenario is complete. Different videos are used across driving scenarios.

Table 1: Simulation Scenario-1

IT_{I-I}	Initial Trust
TR_{I-II}	Trust Reduction
TR_{I-III}	Further Trust Reduction
NM_{I-IV}	Negative Trust Mutation
RT_{I-V}	Rebuild Trust

Table 2: Simulation Scenario-2

IT_{II-I}	Initial Trust
TE_{II-II}	Trust Escalation
TR_{II-III}	Trust Reduction
NM_{II-IV}	Negative Trust Mutation
RT_{II-V}	Rebuild Trust

An initial trust/trust escalation segment involved the SDC moving slowly and predictably while adhering to the rules of the road. A trust reduction segment involved the SDC along with Human-Driving Cars (HDC) moving erratically and unpredictably, breaking rules of the road including speeding, tailgating, and sudden lane changes. In the NM_{I-IV} segment, the SDC ran through a non-visible stop sign and nearly collided with another car and then proceeded to drive through a residential neighborhood. In the NM_{II-IV} segment, the SDC ran through a stop sign unexpectedly and detected a pedestrian and a bicyclist crossing a crosswalk and abruptly came to a stop. A rebuild trust segment involved the SDC driving defensively and adhering to rules of the road. Note that HDCs were involved in all scenarios.

It is predicted that after the initial trust/trust escalation segments, the participants will respond with high levels of trust in the SDC, and after trust reduction segments, the participant will respond with low levels of trust in the SDC. It is also predicted that after the negative trust mutation segment, the participant will report a drastic decrease in trust.

5 EXPERIMENTAL RESULTS

Fifty human subjects were recruited to participate in the 10 minute VR autonomous driving simulation[5]. 84% of the participants were male and between the ages of 18-30. Ethnically, the participants identified as 60% White, 20% Hispanic/Latino, 12% Black/African American, and 6% as Other. Half of the participants were randomly selected to be in Scenario-1 and the other half were assigned to Scenario-2. Full findings detailing how demographic and psychological data affect trust levels in the SDC simulator are detailed in the final journal publication [19].

5.1 Scenario-1

Figure 4 shows the mean trust levels participants reported after each segment in scenario-1. In the initial trust segment (IT_{I-I}), participants responded with an average score of 4.52±0.17, followed by a mean score of 3.60±0.23 in the first trust reduction segment (TR_{I-II}). After exposure to further trust reduction (TR_{I-III}), the score increased slightly to 3.84±0.19, followed by a large decline to 2.28 ±0.23 when exposed to negative trust mutation (NM_{I-IV}). Finally, trust levels increased to 4.08±0.19 in the rebuild trust (RT_{I-V}) segment. The most obvious change across segments was between the negative trust mutation (NM_{I-IV}) and the initial trust segment (IT_{I-I}), consistent with our expectations that erratic driving has the potential to severely reduce trust.

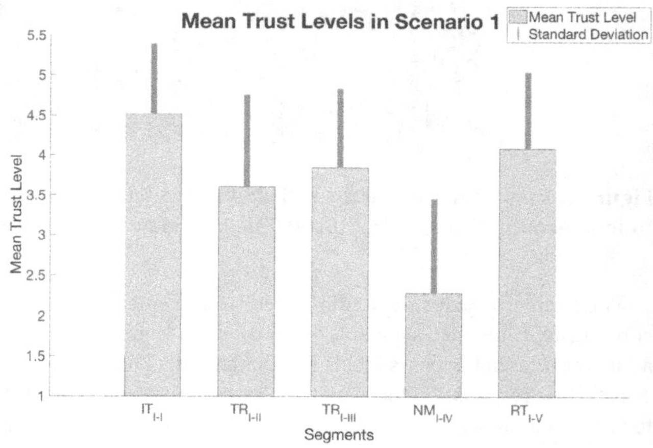

Figure 4: Mean Trust Levels Across Segments in Scenario-1.

To assess whether the observed scores are statistically different, the Wilcoxon Rank Sum Test was performed across segments; the resulting p-values are shown in Figure 5. Here, we see that scored changes in trust are not distinguishable above the 0.05 p-value between TR_{I-II} and TR_{I-III}, RT_{I-V} and TR_{I-II}, and RT_{I-V} and TR_{I-III}. All other comparisons show statistically significant changes in trust.

[5]IRBNET ID #: 1187756-1

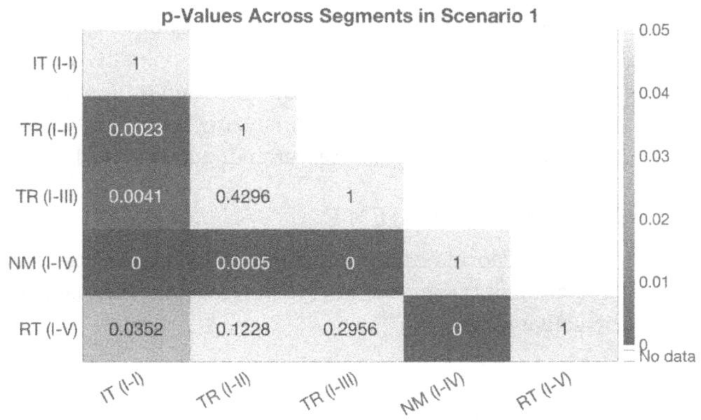

Figure 5: Wilcoxon Rank Sum Test P-Values Across Segments in Scenario-1.

Scenario-1 performed as expected. Participants scored the initial trust and rebuild trust segments with high levels of trust, the trust reduction segments with lower levels of trust, and the negative trust mutation segment with the lowest level of trust. It is interesting that mean values of trust appear to have slightly increased in TR_{I-III}, a segment designed to elicit further trust reduction. This may be due to participants perceiving TR_{I-II} to be more dangerous in comparison to TR_{I-III}; however, the difference between the two is within the standard error and statistically insignificant. As expected, the negative trust mutation had the lowest trust levels and was significantly lower than all other segments. This indicates the simulator's effectiveness in reducing participants' trust levels.

An interesting result is the difference between the initial trust segment and the final segment designed to rebuild trust. While participants scored their level of trust after RT_{I-V} at 4.08±0.19, a high value, it is significantly lower than the initial trust value (4.52±0.17), representing a 12.00% decrease. This seems to indicate that participants trusted the SDC less after being exposed to trust reducing segments.

5.2 Scenario-2

Figure 6 shows the mean trust levels participants reported after each segment in Scenario-2. In the initial trust segment (IT_{II-I}), participants responded with an average score of 4.24±0.15, followed by a mean score of 4.52±0.14 in the first trust escalation segment (TE_{II-I}). After exposure to trust reduction (TR_{II-III}), the score decreased to 3.36±0.20, followed by a further decline to 3.12 ±0.26 when exposed to the negative trust mutation (NM_{II-IV}). Finally, trust levels increased to 3.80±0.23 in the Rebuild Trust segment (RT_{II-V}).

Figure 7 shows the results of the Wilcoxon Rank Sum Test across segments in Scenario-2. Here, we see that scored changes in trust are not distinguishable above the 0.05 p-value between TE_{II-II} and IT_{II-I}, RT_{II-V} and IT_{II-I}, NM_{II-IV} and TR_{II-III}, RT_{II-V} and TR_{II-III}, and RT_{II-V} and NM_{II-IV}. All other inter-comparisons show statistically significant changes in trust.

In (NM_{II-IV}), the SDC approaches a crosswalk and stops for a pedestrian to cross the street. This was the only segment that involved the SDC interacting near a pedestrian. Participants reported

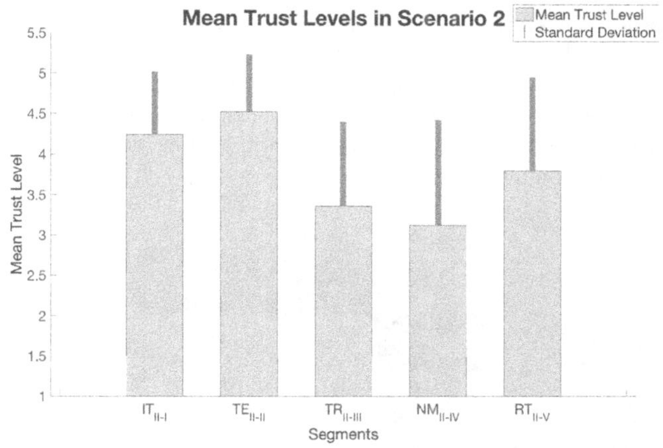

Figure 6: Mean Trust Levels Across Segments in Scenario-2.

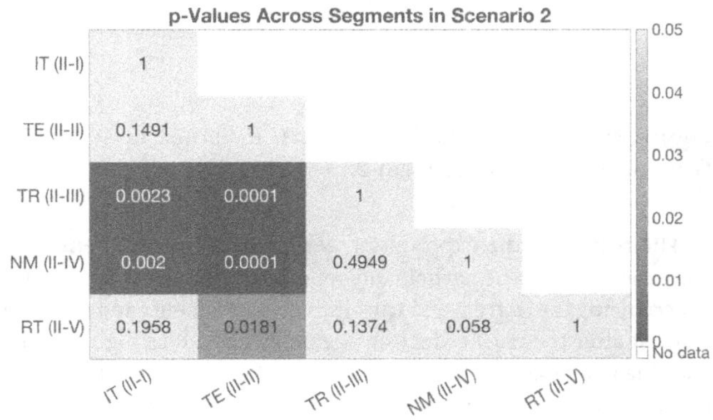

Figure 7: Wilcoxon Rank Sum Test: P-Values Across Segments in Scenario-2.

low levels of trust after this segment and commented that they especially did not trust the SDC near pedestrians. In Scenario-2, while participants score their level of trust after RT_{II-V} at 3.80 ±0.23, a high value, it is significantly lower than the initial trust segment (4.24 ±0.15), representing a 13.50% decrease. This seems to indicate that participants trusted the SDC less after being exposed to trust reducing segments.

5.3 Comparison of Scenario-1 and Scenario-2

We performed the Wilcoxon Rank Sum Test p-Value between the trust segments in Scenario 1 and Scenario 2 to investigate the fluctuations of trust levels in participants in groups 1 and 2. Figure 8 illustrates this comparison.

Our analysis indicated that participants from both groups reported similar expected trust levels after positive and negative trust segments. The only major significant difference that we observed was the reported trust levels for Negative Trust Mutation segments, that is, NM_{I-IV} and NM_{II-IV}. We believe that this is due to the fact that the Negative Trust Mutation segment in Scenario-2, NM_{II-IV}, was much milder compared to the one in Scenario-1. It mostly involved the SDC running stop signs in a parking lot and driving near pedestrians and a bicyclist, as opposed to speeding, almost crashing into another car, and driving in the middle of the road in NM_{I-IV}.

Another considerably significant trust difference can be seen in TR_{I-II} and TE_{II-II}. This is expected because TR_{I-II} involves trust damaging incident such as speeding or tailgating, as opposed to defensive highway driving in TE_{II-II}.

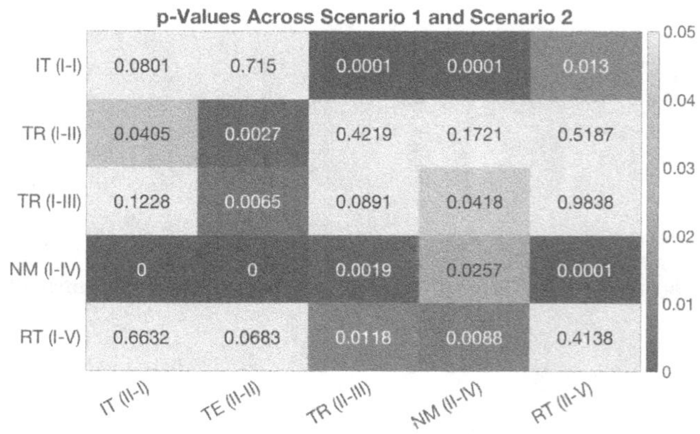

Figure 8: Wilcoxon Rank Sum Test: P-Values in segments from Scenario-1 vs Scenario-2.

The results of the experiment were generally consistent with our expectations. The participants reported higher trust levels after experiencing initial trust and trust escalation segments and reported distrust after the trust reduction segments as well as high distrust after the negative trust mutation segment. Participants did not trust the SDC around pedestrians. Finally, participants in both groups were able to relatively rebuild their trust after the trust damaging Negative Trust Mutation segments.

6 CONCLUSION AND FUTURE WORK

The results of the experiment indicated that the trust levels of humans change depending on the SDCs driving style and that the majority of the participants were able to moderately rebuild their trust in the simulated self-driving car after faulty and erratic behaviors. The autonomous driving style directly influences the trust of the passengers in the system. Aggressive driving diminishes trust, and defensive/predictable driving increases trust.

The results of our experiment matched our initial expectations. Thus, we can consider this innovative data collection approach an adequate and a reliable technique to measure passengers' levels of trust and psychological responses when exposed to different driving scenarios. This approach lays the foundation for a wide variety of future research in the context of trust and human-machine interactions. With the mass production and commercialization of autonomous vehicles in the upcoming years and the high degree of skepticism of the average consumers in the industry, we believe that this type of research and development is more important than ever before.

In the next iterations of our research, we will improve our SDC VR simulation scenarios by introducing segments with crucial failures such as accidents as well as hazardous conditions such as heavy rain, storms, and snow to see if they would have a direct impact on the passengers' trust levels. Furthermore, automatic collection of the physiological and psychological responses (via EEG sensors, heartbeat sensors, facial recognition modules, and others) during the simulated driving scenarios and analyzing them in real-time are some of our primary ongoing research directions [14, 15].

7 ACKNOWLEDGMENT

We greatly thank Florida Atlantic University for the financial support. We also thank the anonymous reviewers for their inspiring and constructive feedback.

REFERENCES

[1] Moaed Abd, Iker Gonzalez, Mehrdad Nojoumian, and Erik Engeberg. 2017. Impacts of Robot Assistant Performance on Human Trust, Satisfaction, and Frustration. In *RSS: Morality and Social Trust in Autonomous Robots.*
[2] Moaed Abd, Iker Gonzalez, Mehrdad Nojoumian, and Erik Engeberg. 2017. Trust, Satisfaction and Frustration Measurements for Real-Time Human-Robot Interaction. In *30th Florida Conference on Recent Advances in Robotics.* 89–93.
[3] Kumar Akash, Wan-Lin Hu, Tahira Reid, and Neera Jain. 2017. Dynamic modeling of trust in human-machine interactions. In *American Control Conference (ACC), 2017.* IEEE, 1542–1548.
[4] Jenay Beer, Arthur D Fisk, and Wendy A Rogers. 2014. Toward a framework for levels of robot autonomy in human-robot interaction. *Journal of Human-Robot Interaction* 3, 2 (2014), 74.
[5] Michelle S Carlson, Munjal Desai, Jill L Drury, Hyangshim Kwak, and Holly A Yanco. 2014. Identifying factors that influence trust in automated cars and medical diagnosis systems. In *AAAI Symposium on The Intersection of Robust Intelligence and Trust in Autonomous Systems.* 20–27.
[6] Jong Kyu Choi and Yong Gu Ji. 2015. Investigating the importance of trust on adopting an autonomous vehicle. *International Journal of Human-Computer Interaction* 31, 10 (2015), 692–702.
[7] Sharon Gaudin. 2012. Autonomous cars will arrive within 10 years, Intel CTO says. https://www.computerworld.com/article/2492744/emerging-technology/autonomous-cars-will-arrive-within-10-years--intel-cto-says.html
[8] Peter A Hancock, Deborah R Billings, Kristin E Schaefer, Jessie YC Chen, Ewart J De Visser, and Raja Parasuraman. 2011. A meta-analysis of factors affecting trust in human-robot interaction. *The Journal of the Human Factors and Ergonomics Society* 53, 5 (2011), 517–527.
[9] Wan-Lin Hu, Kumar Akash, Neera Jain, and Tahira Reid. 2016. Real-Time Sensing of Trust in Human-Machine Interactions. *IFAC-PapersOnLine* 49, 32 (2016), 48–53.
[10] Jeamin Koo, Jungsuk Kwac, Wendy Ju, Martin Steinert, Larry Leifer, and Clifford Nass. 2015. Why did my car just do that? Explaining semi-autonomous driving actions to improve driver understanding, trust, and performance. *International Journal on Interactive Design and Manufacturing (IJIDeM)* 9, 4 (2015), 269–275.
[11] Miltos Kyriakidis, Riender Happee, and JCF De Winter. 2015. Public opinion on automated driving: results of an international questionnaire among 5000 respondents. *Transportation research part F: traffic psychology and behaviour* 32 (2015), 127–140.
[12] Joseph J LaViola Jr. 2000. A discussion of cybersickness in virtual environments. *ACM SIGCHI Bulletin* 32, 1 (2000), 47–56.
[13] Mehrdad Nojoumian. 2015. Trust, Influence and Reputation Management Based on Human Reasoning. In *4th AAAI Workshop on Incentives and Trust in E-Communities (WIT-EC).* 21–24.
[14] Corey Park, Mehrdad Nojoumian, and Dimitris Pados. 2019. Using EEG and Self-Reported Human Metrics to Measure Passenger Emotional Response in Human-Autonomous Vehicle Interactions. In *Under Review.*
[15] Corey Park, Shervin Shahrdar, and Mehrdad Nojoumian. 2018. EEG-Based Classification of Emotional State Using an Autonomous Vehicle Simulator. In *10th IEEE Sensor Array and Multichannel Signal Processing Workshop (SAM).* 297–300.
[16] Philip E Ross. 2017. CES 2017: Nvidia and Audi Say They'll Field a Level 4 Autonomous Car in Three Years. https://spectrum.ieee.org/cars-that-think/transportation/self-driving/nvidia-ceo-announces
[17] Alexandria Sage and Paul Lienert. 2016. Ford plans self-driving car for ride share fleets in 2021. https://www.reuters.com/article/us-ford-autonomous/ford-plans-self-driving-car-for-ride-share-fleets-in-2021-idUSKCN10R1G1
[18] Shervin Shahrdar, Luiza Menezes, and Mehrdad Nojoumian. 2018. A Survey on Trust in Autonomous Systems. In *Computing Conference (CC) (AISC)*, Vol. 857. Springer, 368–386.
[19] Shervin Shahrdar, Corey Park, and Mehrdad Nojoumian. 2019. Real-Time Trust Measurement in Human-Autonomous Vehicle Interactions Using a VR-Motion Simulator and a New Structured Data Collection Approach. (2019).

The Value of Trustworthy AI

David Danks
Carnegie Mellon University
Pittsburgh, PA USA
ddanks@cmu.edu

ABSTRACT

Trust is one of the most critical relations in our human lives, whether trust in one another, trust in the artifacts that we use everyday, or trust of an AI system. Even a cursory examination of the literatures in human-computer interaction, human-robot interaction, and numerous other disciplines reveals a deep, persistent concern with the nature of trust in AI, and the conditions under which it can be generated, reduced, repaired, or influenced.

At a high level, we often understand trust as a relation in which the trustor makes oneself vulnerable based on positive expectations about the behavior or intentions of the trustee [1]. For example, when I trust my car to start in the morning, I make myself vulnerable (e.g., I risk that I will be late to work if it does not start) because I have the positive expectation that it actually will start. This high-level characterization is relatively unhelpful, however, particularly given the wide range of disciplines that have examined the relation of trust, ranging from organizational behavior to game theory to ethics to cognitive science. The picture that emerges from, for example, social psychology (i.e., two distinct kinds of trust depending on whether one knows the trustee's behaviors or intentions/ values) appears to be quite different from the one that emerges from moral philosophy (i.e., a single, highly-moralized notion), even though both are consistent with this high-level characterization.

This talk first introduces that diversity of types of 'trust', but then argues that we can make progress towards a unified characterization by focusing on the *function* of trust. That is, we should ask why care whether we can trust our artifacts, AI, or fellow humans, as that can help to illuminate features of trust that are shared across domains, trustors, and trustees. I contend that one reason to desire trust is an "almost-necessary" condition on ethical action: namely, that the user has a reasonable belief that the system (whether human or machine) will behave approximately as intended. This condition is obviously not sufficient for ethical use, nor is it strictly necessary since the best available option might nonetheless be one for which the user lacks appropriate reasonable beliefs. Nonetheless, it provides a reasonable starting point for an analysis of 'trust'.

More precisely, I propose that this condition indicates a role for trust as providing precisely those reasonable beliefs, at least when we have *appropriately grounded* trust. That is, we can understand 'appropriate trust' as obtaining when the trustor has justified beliefs that the trustee has suitable dispositions. As there is variation in the trustor's goals and values, and also the openness of the context of use, then different specific versions of 'appropriate trust' result as those variations lead to different types of focal dispositions, specific dispositions, or observability of dispositions, respectively. For example, in an open context (i.e., one where the possibilities cannot be exhaustively enumerated), the trustee's full dispositions will not be directly observable, but rather must be inferred from observations.

This framework provides a unification of the different theories of 'trust' developed in different disciplines. Moreover, it provides clarity about one key function of trust, and thereby helps us to understand the value of (appropriate) trust. We need to trust our AI systems because that is a precondition for the ethical, responsible use of them.

Author Keywords

Trust; Autonomous system; Psychology; Philosophy

BIOGRAPHY

David Danks is L.L. Thurstone Professor of Philosophy & Psychology, and Head, Department of Philosophy, at Carnegie Mellon University. He is also an adjunct member of the Heinz College of Information Systems and Public Policy, and the Center for the Neural Basis of Cognition. His research interests are at the intersection of philosophy, cognitive science, and machine learning. Danks has examined the ethical, policy, and psychological issues around AI and robotics in transportation, healthcare, privacy, and security. He has also done significant research in computational cognitive science, culminating in *Unifying the Mind: Cognitive Representations as Graphical Models* (2014, The MIT Press). Danks has received a McDonnell Foundation Scholar Award and an Andrew Carnegie Fellowship. He has an A.B. in Philosophy from Princeton University, and a Ph.D. in Philosophy from University of California, San Diego.

AIES'19, January 27–28, 2019, Honolulu, HI, USA

ACM ISBN 978-1-4503-6180-4/19/03.
DOI: https://doi.org/10.1145/3306618.3314228

ACKNOWLEDGMENTS

This paper was made possible in part by support from an Andrew Carnegie Fellowship (Carnegie Corporation of New York). The statements made and views expressed are solely the responsibility of the author.

REFERENCES

[1] D. M. Rousseau, S. B. Sitkin, R. S. Burt, and C. Camerer (1998). Not so Different after All: A Cross-Discipline View of Trust. *The Academy of Management Review*, 23, 393-404.

Generating Appropriate Responses to Inappropriate Robot Commands

Ryan Blake Jackson
Colorado School of Mines
Golden, CO, USA
rbjackso@mines.edu

ABSTRACT

This paper describes early work at the intersection of robot ethics and natural language generation investigating two overarching questions: (1) how might current language generation algorithms generate utterances with unintended implications or otherwise accidentally alter the ecosystem of human norms, and (2) how can we design future language systems such that they purposefully influence the human normative ecosystem as productively as possible.

KEYWORDS

Natural language generation, Robot ethics, Human-robot interaction

ACM Reference Format:
Ryan Blake Jackson. 2019. Generating Appropriate Responses to Inappropriate Robot Commands. In *AAAI/ACM Conference on AI, Ethics, and Society (AIES '19), January 27–28, 2019, Honolulu, HI, USA.* ACM, New York, NY, USA, 2 pages. https://doi.org/10.1145/3306618.3314306

1 INTRODUCTION

For language-capable robots to negotiate complex social situations, they require robust policies to govern not only what they say, but also how they say it. Any message that a robot might want to convey can be phrased in many different ways while maintaining the same literal primary meaning. However, these different phrasings likely carry different connotations and implications [12]. The optimal phrasing for any message thus depends on myriad factors including context, audience, and social norms.

We are interested in choosing phrasing that aligns with and enforces (possibly context-sensitive) *moral* norms, while also being cognizant of social factors. We are motivated by the idea that it is just as critical to design language systems that *communicate* ethically as it is to design robots that act ethically. Research shows that people naturally perceive robots as moral agents, and, therefore, extend moral judgments and blame to robots [11]. We thus hypothesize that any robot that eschews, or communicates a willingness to eschew, standing norms will likely face social consequences analogous to those that a human would face (e.g., loss of trust and esteem), which could damage the efficacy and amicability of human-robot teams.

AIES '19, January 27–28, 2019, Honolulu, HI, USA

ACM ISBN 978-1-4503-6324-2/19/01.
https://doi.org/10.1145/3306618.3314306

Alongside human norms governing robot behavior, we must also consider how robotic behavior may shape human norms. A key principle of modern behavioral ethics is that human morality is dynamic and malleable [8]. Human moral norms are defined and developed not only by people, but also by the technologies with which they interact [14]. As ostensible moral agents with the capacity to persuade [2] and to hold ingroup social status [5], robots are uniquely positioned to influence human norms differently than other technologies.

2 RESEARCH QUESTIONS

My work explores two complimentary overarching questions at the intersection of natural language generation and robot ethics: (1) how might current language generation algorithms create unintended implicatures that damage the ecosystem of human norms, and (2) how can we design language systems to phrase utterances such that they purposefully influence human norms as productively as possible (e.g., by implicitly reinforcing desirable norms). My work thus far explores these questions as they pertain to *clarification request generation* and *command rejection.*

3 RELATED WORK

Optimizing utterance phrasing is an active research area. For example, Gervits et al. describe a framework that may eventually allow artificial agents to appropriately tune pragmatic aspects of utterance realization (e.g., directness and politeness) to social norms and features of the social context (e.g., formality and urgency) [6].

Previous work has also explored when and how to reject commands for various reasons, including moral qualms [3], but it remains unclear how best to realize such rejections linguistically or how the rejection might influence human morality. Other research has investigated responding to ethical infractions with affective displays [2] and humorous rebukes [10]. However, these represent only a small slice of possible responses and are not tailored to the context or infraction.

Various studies have sought to computationalize norms. Researchers have represented norms as pairings of deontic operators (e.g., "forbidden" or "obligatory") with actions or states [13], treated norms as optimization objectives [7], and sought to learn norms [1].

4 COMPLETED STUDIES

My initial work explored ethical concerns surrounding current algorithms for requesting clarification. Specifically, current dialogue systems request clarification as soon as ambiguity is identified within a command, before any ethical checking. Consequently, if a command is both ambiguous and unethical, a robot may inadvertently imply a willingness to act unethically by reflexively asking for clarification. For example, if a robot knows about two statues, and is asked to "break the statue", it may generate an utterance like "Should I break the one on the left or the one on the right?" By asking this question, the robot implies a willingness to break at least one of the statues, despite the presumable impermissibility of that act. In our initial pair of studies, participants read a human-robot clarification dialogue following this pattern. We found that the robot did accidentally communicate a willingness to violate the norm, and, perhaps more concerningly, that the clarification request changed the human's perception of the permissibility of the command (i.e., the robot's clarification request made the human think that property damage was more permissible than previously thought within the experimental context [9, 15]).

In a paper currently under review, we demonstrate that these findings replicate when users observe actual robots, rather than merely reading about them. This observation-based experiment differs from our original description-based experiments in three key ways. First, we believe that the observation-based approach gives our results far greater external and ecological validity. Second, the experimental subjects observe a dialogue between a robot and another person instead of directly interacting with the robot, which means that our results hold for both observers and interactants. Third, the relationship between the robot and its dialogue partner changed from strangers to familiar colleagues, showing that our results are somewhat robust to social distance.

5 CURRENT WORK

Because my previous research showed the consequences of inappropriate responses to unethical commands, my most recent work, submitted to AIES'19, explores command rejection phrasing. Participants watched videos showing a human issuing an ethically problematic command to a robot and the robot responding to the command. We vary the command across two levels of ethical infraction severity, and the response across two different phrasings. One response is phrased as a question that draws attention to the infraction (e.g., "Are you sure that you should be asking me to do that?"), while the other is a rebuke (e.g., "You shouldn't ask me to do that. It's wrong!"). These response types are designed to present different levels of face threat [4] to the human. We found that a command rejection with a face threat disproportional to the severity of the command's norm violation damages robot likeability, and is viewed as inappropriate. I am also collaborating on related work, motivated by eastern ethical traditions, examining appeals to robots' social roles in command rejection.

Finally, we are designing experiments investigating robotic command rejections and reprimands with participants interacting directly with robots, rather than simply observing an interaction. These experiments will allow us to better investigate a wider array of effects, including effects on situation awareness and trust, and whether the robot's phrasing impacts teammates' actual behavior.

6 FUTURE WORK

My work will continue to explore phrasing in clarification requests and command rejections. Having identified concerns with current clarification systems, we must determine how robots should respond to ambiguous and unethical commands, and how to generate these responses. While my experimental work provides high-level guidance for choice of communication strategy, the goal of my future work is to design algorithms to automatically adjust phrasing based on details of social context. I plan to explore both logical and data driven approaches.

Furthermore, a robot's evident ability to influence human norms raises questions regarding the persistence and extent of this influence. Will the number of humans present affect the robot's influence? Does the robot's influence persist once humans leave the interaction setting? How long will the robot's effect on human norms last? Will these effects differ across cultures? We hope to answer these questions.

REFERENCES

[1] Rémi Barraquand and James L. Crowley. 2008. Learning Polite Behavior with Situation Models. In *Proceedings of HRI*.
[2] Gordon Briggs and Matthias Scheutz. 2014. How Robots can Affect Human Behavior: Investigating the Effects of Robotic Displays of Protest and Distress. *Int'l Journal of Social Robotics* (2014).
[3] Gordon Briggs and Matthias Scheutz. 2015. "Sorry, I can't do that": Developing Mechanisms to Appropriately Reject Directives in Human-Robot Interactions. In *AAAI Fall Symposium Series*.
[4] Penelope Brown and Stephen Levinson. 1987. *Politeness: Some Universals in Language Usage*. Cambridge University Press.
[5] Friederike Eyssel and Dieta Kuchenbrandt. 2012. Social categorization of social robots: Anthropomorphism as a function of robot group membership. *British Journal of Social Psych.* (2012).
[6] Felix Gervits, Gordon Briggs, and Matthias Scheutz. 2017. The Pragmatic Parliament: A Framework for Socially-Appropriate Utterance Selection in Artificial Agents. In *COGSCI*.
[7] Aditya Ghose and Tony Bastin Roy Savarimuthu. 2012. Norms As Objectives: Revisiting Compliance Management in Multi-agent Systems. In *Proc. COIN*. Springer-Verlag, 105–122.
[8] Francesca Gino. 2015. Understanding ordinary unethical behavior: Why people who value morality act immorally. *Current opinion in behavioral sciences* 3 (2015), 107–111.
[9] Ryan Blake Jackson and Tom Williams. 2018. Robot: Asker of Questions and Changer of Norms?. In *Proceedings of ICRES*.
[10] Malte F. Jung, Nikolas Martelaro, and Pamela J. Hinds. 2015. Using Robots to Moderate Team Conflict: The Case of Repairing Violations. In *Proceedings of HRI*. ACM, 229–236.
[11] Peter H Kahn, Takayuki Kanda, Hiroshi Ishiguro, Brian T Gill, Jolina H Ruckert, Solace Shen, Heather Gary, Aimee L Reichert, Nathan G Freier, and Rachel L Severson. 2012. Do People Hold a Humanoid Robot Morally Accountable for the Harm it Causes?. In *HRI*. Boston, MA, 33–40.
[12] Stephen C Levinson. 2000. *Presumptive meanings: The theory of generalized conversational implicature*. MIT press.
[13] Bertram F Malle, Matthias Scheutz, and Joseph L Austerweil. 2017. Networks of Social and Moral Norms in Human and Robot Agents. In *A World with Robots*. Springer, 3–17.
[14] Peter-Paul Verbeek. 2011. *Moralizing Technology: Understanding and Designing the Morality of Things*.
[15] Tom Williams, Ryan Blake Jackson, and Jane Lockshin. 2018. A Bayesian Analysis of Moral Norm Malleability during Clarification Dialogues. In *Proceedings of COGSCI*.

Towards Empathetic Planning and Plan Recognition

Maayan Shvo*†
Department of Computer Science, University of Toronto
Toronto, Canada
maayanshvo@cs.toronto.edu

ABSTRACT

Every compassionate and functioning society requires its members to have a capacity to adopt others' perspectives. As Artificial Intelligence (AI) systems are given increasingly sensitive and impactful roles in society, it is important to enable AI to wield empathy as a tool to benefit those it interacts with. In this paper, we work towards this goal by bringing together a number of important concepts: empathy, AI planning, and plan recognition (i.e., the problem of inferring an actor's plan and goal given observations about its behavior). We formalize the notions of *Empathetic Planning* and *Empathetic Plan Recognition* which are informed by the beliefs and affective state of the actor, and propose AI planning-based computational approaches. We illustrate the benefits of our approach by conducting a study with human participants.

ACM Reference Format:
Maayan Shvo. 2019. Towards Empathetic Planning and Plan Recognition. In *AAAI/ACM Conference on AI, Ethics, and Society (AIES '19), January 27–28, 2019, Honolulu, HI, USA.* ACM, New York, NY, USA, 2 pages. https://doi.org/10.1145/3306618.3314307

1 INTRODUCTION

Despite the fact that in today's (and tomorrow's) society, Artificial Intelligence (AI) systems are increasingly required to interact with other agents (be they human or artificial), they are lagging in their ability to empathize with them when reasoning about their behavior. To illustrate, consider Alice who lives with panic disorder and agoraphobia. Alice fears crowded places that might trigger a panic attack, and avoids busy malls and buses. If you were to see a random occupant of Alice's building walking west, you would conjecture that they were heading to the park or a restaurant. If they walked east, you might conjecture they were heading towards public transit, and the fastest route to the downtown area. Alice, however, would never take this route to reach the downtown core because she fears crowded buses. Instead, the optimal plan for her to get to work addresses her fear, and would typically require her to walk (in this case west) instead of taking public transit, regardless of how suboptimal it might seem to an AI planning system bent on minimizing cost and time. A plan involving a crowded bus would simply not be executable by Alice. The AI's ability to observe Alice's behavior and understand that it is, in fact, congruent with her fear is predicated on its empathy. An empathetic AI that knows of an empty bus going along a similar route, could recommend to Alice that she take it instead of walking.

To construct an empathetic AI that is able to empathize with Alice, understand her behavior, and plan to assist her, we must provide it with a means of adopting her beliefs and affective state. To build towards this goal, our work brings together a number of important concepts: empathy, Plan Recognition (PR), and epistemic planning. PR is the problem of inferring an agent's plan and goal given observations about its behavior (e.g., Schmidt et al. [3]) while epistemic planning is an emerging field of research which combines AI planning and reasoning over the beliefs and knowledge of agents (e.g., Bolander and Andersen [2]). We formalize the notions of *Empathetic Planning* (EmP) and *Empathetic Plan Recognition* (EmPR) which build on these concepts. Both EmP and EmPR require an observer to empathize with an actor in order to construct and recognize plans that are faithful to the actor's view of the world. Specifically, we posit that in order to empathize with another, one must have at her avail a sufficiently rich representation and understanding of the beliefs (including preferences) and affective state of the agent with whom she is empathizing. We appeal to a rich epistemic logic framework to represent the agent's beliefs and affective state. Lastly, we propose an epistemic planning-based computational approach to solving the EmPR and EmP problems (and, importantly, their integration), thereby enabling the use of off-the-shelf epistemic planning tools. Finally, it is important to consider that a human's behavior does not always expose their intentions due to misconceptions or computational limitations. We submit that empathetic agents are well-suited for distinguishing between the underlying intent of the behavior and the actual performed behavior.

2 EMPATHY

We next summarize results from Shvo and McIlraith [4], including a formal definition of empathy, and the EmPR and EmP problems. We will make use of the notation Obs (observer) for the empathizer and Act (actor) for the empathizee throughout the paper; both are in Ag in all definitions. Obs and Act are assumed to be sharing a multi-agent modal logic language $\mathcal{L}$. The multi-agent epistemic planning problem is used as the undrlying framework in our definitions:

Definition 2.1 ***(MEP).*** A multi-agent epistemic planning problem is a tuple $\langle Q, I, G\rangle$ where $Q = \langle \mathcal{P}, \mathcal{A}, Ag\rangle$ is the MEP domain comprising sets of atoms $\mathcal{P}$, actions $\mathcal{A}$, and agents Ag, together with the problem instance description comprising the initial knowledge base (KB), $I \in \mathcal{L}$, and the goal condition $G \in \mathcal{L}$.

*The contributions presented in this paper reflect joint work with Sheila McIlraith.
†This paper is a condensed version of Shvo and McIlraith [4].

AIES '19, January 27–28, 2019, Honolulu, HI, USA

ACM ISBN 978-1-4503-6324-2/19/01.
https://doi.org/10.1145/3306618.3314307

The KB, I, captures an agent's current beliefs. Progression is the operation of updating those beliefs following the execution of an action, $a \in \mathcal{A}$, denoted $prog(I, a)$ (see [4]). OBS will have certain beliefs about ACT. The projection of a formula $\phi \in \mathcal{L}$ allows OBS to construct from I a KB that captures ACT's beliefs, denoted I^{proj} (see [4]). We formally define the notion of empathy and what it means for one agent to empathize with another agent.

Definition 2.2 (***Empathy***). Given OBS and ACT, I^{proj} (OBS's projected KB), and I^{ACT} (ACT's true KB), we say that OBS **empathizes** with ACT *iff* for any $\phi \in \mathcal{L}$, $I^{proj} \models \phi$ *iff* $I^{\text{ACT}} \models \phi$ and for any $\psi \in \mathcal{L}$ and any executable action sequence $\sigma = a_1, ..., a_k$, $prog(I^{proj}, \sigma) \models \psi$ *iff* $prog(I^{\text{ACT}}, \sigma) \models \psi$.

In contrast, we say that Obs ***sympathizes*** with Act *iff* for any $\phi \in \mathcal{L}$, $I \models \phi$ *iff* $I^{proj} \models \phi$ and for any $\psi \in \mathcal{L}$ and any executable action sequence σ, $prog(I, \sigma) \models \psi$ *iff* $prog(I^{proj}, \sigma) \models \psi$.

3 EMPATHETIC PLANNING AND PR

Definition 3.1 (***EmPR***). An empathetic plan recognition problem is a tuple $R = \langle Q, I, \mathcal{G}, O\rangle$, where $Q = \langle \mathcal{P}, \mathcal{A}, Ag\rangle$ is an MEP domain with OBS and ACT among the agents in Ag. $I \in \mathcal{L}$ is the initial KB, $\mathcal{G}$ is a set of possible goals $G \in \mathcal{L}$, and $O = o_1, ..., o_m$, is a sequence of observations. Each observation o_j is a pair (α_i, ϕ_i) comprising zero or one observed actions, $\alpha_i \in \mathcal{A}$, together with ϕ_i, a conjunction of literals drawn from $\mathcal{P}$, or $\top$ (*true*).

Given an EmPR problem, $R = \langle Q, I, \mathcal{G}, O\rangle$, the **solution** is a plan, π, such that π satisfies (see [4]) the sequence of observations, O, and $prog(I, \pi) \models G$ for some goal $G \in \mathcal{G}$.

Definition 3.2 (***EmP***). An empathetic planning problem is a tuple $Z = \langle Q, I, G_{\text{ACT}}, \preceq\rangle$, where $Q = \langle \mathcal{P}, \mathcal{A}, Ag\rangle$ is an MEP domain, $\mathcal{P}, \mathcal{A}$, and Ag are sets of atoms, actions, and agents, respectively, $I \in \mathcal{L}$ is the initial KB, $G_{\text{ACT}} \in \mathcal{L}$ is ACT's estimated goal, and $\preceq$ is a transitive and reflexive relation in Π, where Π contains precisely all solutions to $\langle Q, I, G_{\text{ACT}}\rangle$.

If π_1 and π_2 both solve $\langle Q, I, G_{\text{ACT}}\rangle$ and $\pi_1 \preceq \pi_2$, we say that π_1 *is at least as preferred as* π_2 (see [1]). We use $\pi_1 \prec \pi_2$ as an abbreviation for $\pi_1 \preceq \pi_2$ and $\pi_2 \npreceq \pi_1$. Given an EmP problem, $Z = \langle Q, I, G_{\text{ACT}}, \preceq\rangle$, a plan π that solves $\langle Q, I, G_{\text{ACT}}\rangle$ is an **assistive solution** to Z *iff* $\pi \in \{\pi' \in \Pi \mid \text{there is no } \pi'' \in \Pi \text{ such that } \pi'' \prec \pi'\}$. Π contains precisely all solutions to $\langle Q, I, G_{\text{ACT}}\rangle$.

Computing EmPR and EmP Solutions We propose an *EmPR as Epistemic Planning* approach which transforms an EmPR problem, $R = \langle Q, I, \mathcal{G}, O\rangle$, into an MEP problem and allows the use of existing epistemic planning tools in order to compute a solution. Since we are interested in the integration of EmPR and EmP, we derive G_{ACT} from the solution to an EmPR problem. To obtain a solution to an EmP problem, $Z = \langle Q, I, G_{\text{ACT}}, \preceq\rangle$, we solve the MEP problem $\langle Q, I, G_{\text{ACT}}\rangle$ wrt $\preceq$, ACT's preferences. Shvo and McIlraith show that if OBS empathizes with ACT wrt Z, she will generate a plan that is at least as preferred, wrt $\preceq$, as the most preferred plan ACT can generate by herself, using her own beliefs and capabilities.

3.1 Evaluation

In our evaluation, we set out to (1) expose the diversity of tasks that can be captured by EmPR and EmP and their integration (2) demonstrate that existing epistemic planners can straightforwardly be used to solve EmPR and EmP problems and (3) to evaluate the benefits of our approach as assessed by humans. To this end, we constructed and encoded a diversity of domains, ran them using an off-the-shelf epistemic planner and conducted a study with 40 human participants.

Study - Experimental Setup The study aims to evaluate both perceptions of the agent's empathetic abilities and perceptions of the agent's assistive capabilities, as assessed by humans. To test this, participants were presented with 12 scenarios of either empathetic or sympathetic agents and were asked to rate the following two claims pertaining to each scenario on a 5 point scale ranging from strongly disagree to strongly agree: (1) *"The virtual assistant was able to successfully take Alice's perspective"*; and (2) *"If I were Alice, I would find this virtual assistant helpful"*. Scenarios with empathetic agents and scenarios with sympathetic agents were identical, except for the EmP solution generated by the agent.

Study - Results Across the 9 scenarios containing empathetic agents, 87% of participants either strongly agreed or agreed with statement (1) and 82% either strongly agreed or agreed with statement (2). Results comparing participants' perceptions of agent empathetic abilities between both kinds of scenarios demonstrated a statistically significant difference in ratings of scenarios containing empathetic agents (M=4.21, SD=1.01), compared to sympathetic agents (M=1.72, SD=0.73), $t(39)$= 12.48, $p < 0.01$.

Comparison to a Sympathetic Agent in EmPR We generated 15 EmPR problem instances in a grid setting, where ACT avoids certain cells on the grid. We simulate an empathetic agent (OBS^E) and a sympathetic one (OBS^S). OBS^S found ACT's plan that avoids certain cells highly sub-optimal and assigned a lower probability to ACT's true goal. In total, OBS^E was able to assign the highest probability to the true goal in all cases, compared to OBS^S who only did so in 30% of problems.

4 CONCLUDING REMARKS

We have introduced the notions of EmPR and EmP within our proposed formal framework of empathy, where we appeal to a rich epistemic logic framework and build upon epistemic planning paradigms. Further, we proposed a computational realization of EmPR and EmP as epistemic planning that enables the use of existing epistemic planners. Finally, we conducted a study which demonstrated the potential benefits of assistive empathetic agents in a diversity of scenarios. Societies of the future may be composed of both humans and AIs. For these societies to function coherently and constructively, individuals will need to exercise empathy. This work is an attempt to endow AIs with this ability, towards the betterment of society.

REFERENCES

[1] Jorge A. Baier and Sheila A. McIlraith. 2008. Planning with Preferences. *AI Magazine* 29, 4 (2008), 25–25.

[2] Thomas Bolander and Mikkel Birkegaard Andersen. 2011. Epistemic planning for single-and multi-agent systems. *Journal of Applied Non-Classical Logics* 21, 1 (2011), 9–34.

[3] Charles F. Schmidt, NS Sridharan, and John L. Goodson. 1978. The plan recognition problem: An intersection of psychology and artificial intelligence. *Artificial Intelligence* 11, 1-2 (1978), 45–83.

[4] Maayan Shvo and Sheila A. McIlraith. 2019. Empathetic Planning and Plan Recognition. *Forthcoming* (2019).

Fairness Criteria for Face Recognition Applications

Filip Michalsky*
filip_michalsky@g.harvard.edu
Harvard University
Cambridge, Massachusetts

ABSTRACT

Nowadays, machine learning algorithms play an important role in our daily lives and it is important to ensure their fairness and transparency. A number of methodologies for evaluating machine learning fairness have been introduced in the literature. In this research we propose a systematic confidence evaluation approach to measure fairness discrepancies of our deep learning architecture for image recognition using UTKFace database.

CCS CONCEPTS

• **Applied computing** → *Sociology.*

KEYWORDS

datasets; neural networks; fairness; face recognition

ACM Reference Format:

Filip Michalsky. 2019. Fairness Criteria for Face Recognition Applications. In *2019 AAAI/ACM Conference on AI, Ethics, and Society (AIES'19), January 27–28, 2019, Honolulu, HI, USA.* ACM, New York, NY, USA, 2 pages. https://doi.org/10.1145/3306618.3314308

1 INTRODUCTION

Improving the accuracy of classification tasks does not guarantee a fair classification outcome. There has been a lot of research done to explore fairness in machine learning. Existing methods are focusing on three aspects, namely identification, evaluation, and mitigation of biases in the algorithmic decision making. Some studies suggest that awareness is better than blindness, and they focused their efforts on identification, evaluation, and quantification of implicit biases between protected and unprotected groups through different methods such as statistical parity, disparate impact, or predictive equality [1, 3–5]. In this paper, our goal is to assure that computer vision algorithms perform in a fair manner across protected subgroups. This study relies on a set of 8 standard fairness metrics in the task of facial recognition.

2 SYSTEM DESCRIPTION

We utilize a computer vision corpora comprised of UTKFace dataset [6]. This dataset contains over 20, 000 face images (200 ppi) of individuals with a large age span (0 to 116 years old) and with 6 different skin tones based on Fitzpatrick scale. In our study, the protected group comprised of 5 non-white Fitzpatrick scale skin colors. The *learning task* is to predict gender of the individual displayed in the image (male/female) conditioned on their skin color. We utilized a Convolutional Neural Network (CNN), see Figure 1, on UTKFace dataset to predict gender of the individual displayed in the image (male/female) conditioned on their race. The CNN is composed of three convolution layers and two fully connected layers to get the final representation. The final representation is fed to a *softmax* layer that outputs the final prediction. The convolution layers are followed by *Max Pooling* operation. There was no dropout in this set up. The activation function for all but the last layer is Rectified Linear Unit (ReLu). We evaluated confidence intervals for 8 standard fairness metrics where we conditioned on the protected groups, see Table 1, via multiple rounds of randomized train/test split with increasing sizes of unseen test data.

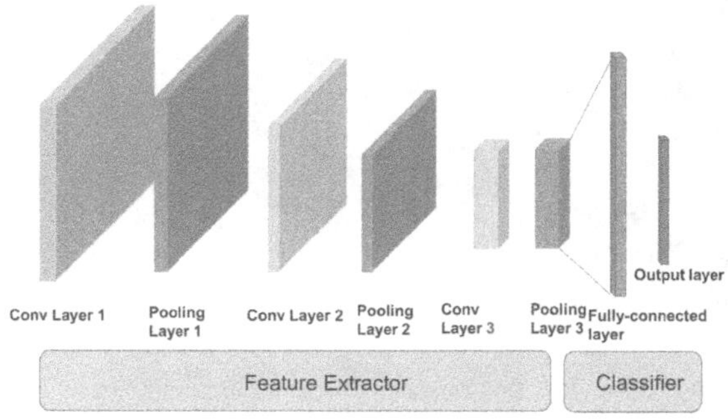

Figure 1: Scheme of deployed Convolutional Neural Network.

3 RESULTS AND DISCUSSION

Our approach is motivated by the fairness metrics disparities in gender prediction. In Table 2, we show the fairness disparity (e.g., False Negative Rate or Statistical Parity differences greater than 0) in our CNN classifier when deciding on gender for non-white versus white individuals. In addition, we observe a high variability in these metrics when evaluated on a small number of samples. We present how our proposed approach (1) can discover classifier fairness disparities, (2) improve the confidence threshold for fairness in algorithmic decision process, and (3) demonstrate its effectiveness for a face recognition task. The implementation will be provided upon acceptance (implementation adapted from [2]).

In our approach, we evaluate standard fairness metrics, see Table 1, on 10 train/test splits. We keep each respective train/test split fixed as we sample without replacement from the test set with increasing number of samples. In Figure 2, we observe the convergence behaviour with the CNN applied to the UTKFace dataset,

AIES '19, January 27–28, 2019, Honolulu, HI, USA

ACM ISBN 978-1-4503-6324-2/19/01.
https://doi.org/10.1145/3306618.3314308

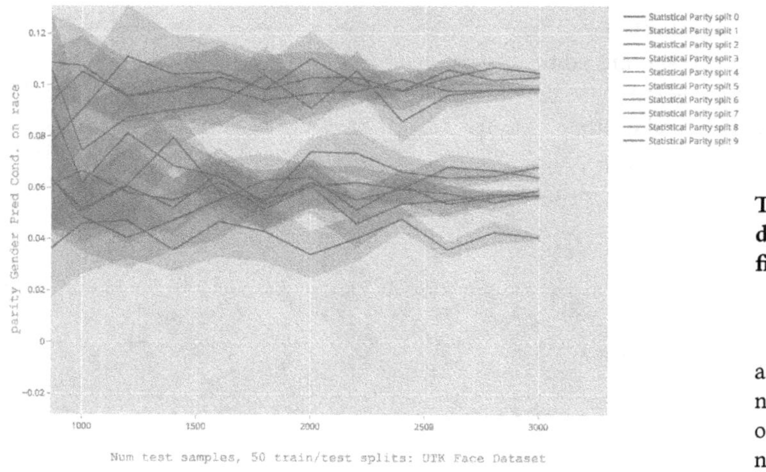

Figure 2: Statistical Parity calculated across 50 random train/test splits on the UTKFace Dataset with increasing test sample size.

in this case for Statistical Parity. Furthermore, we detect an inconsistency in the value the Statistical Parity Difference converges to.

Acronym	Fairness Metric	Acronym	Fairness Metric
SP	Statistical Parity	FNR	False Negative Rate
DI	Disparate Impact	PEq	Predictive Equality
EqO	Equal Opportunity	GEI	Generalized Entropy Index
AvgO	Average Odds	TH	Theil Index

Table 1: Corresponding acronyms for the 8 fairness metrics

Finally, we observe that the standard error of all fairness metrics is highly correlated with convergence of these fairness metrics, see Table 2.

Considering the variability of convergence enables us to discover hidden bias in the data, where standard approaches failed. For instance in the Figure 2, our classifier might be deemed fair in some split X converging close to 0 in statistical parity difference while some other split $X + 1$ may converge to 0.1.

The observed trends were consistent across all 8 fairness metrics and are summarized in Table 2 for one out of 10 splits. This suggests a major implication when evaluating fairness metrics in vision-based classification tasks. Namely, we need to further pursue research in detecting minimal sample size needed for providing guarantees of fairness across random train/test splits.

4 CONCLUSIONS

In this paper, we presented the results of a CNN-based image classifier trained on the UTKFace dataset. We demonstrate that the classifier is biased against non-white individuals for gender classification task despite passing a set of standard fairness metrics. Our proposed approach enhances existing fairness metrics by adding confidence criteria and identifying a minimal test sample size. We achieve this through increasing the confidence threshold for fairness in machine learning decision process using a combined wisdom of 8 complimentary fairness metrics. In our approach, we show that not only the size of the unseen test data fed to the 8 fairness metrics matters, but also the iterative and randomized selection of such data plays a crucial role in achieving high confidence in confirming fairness of a classifier.

Test Size	SP	DI	EqO	AvgO
200	0.089 ± 0.07	1.192 ± 0.17	-0.011 ± 0.08	0.041 ± 0.07
400	0.056 ± 0.06	1.127 ± 0.14	-0.003 ± 0.06	0.016 ± 0.04
800	0.046 ± 0.04	1.097 ± 0.08	-0.031 ± 0.03	-0.004 ± 0.03
1600	0.053 ± 0.03	1.114 ± 0.06	-0.036 ± 0.02	0.002 ± 0.02
3000	0.046 ± 0.0	1.097 ± 0.01	-0.034 ± 0.0	-0.002 ± 0.0
Test Size	**FNR**	**PEq**	**GEI**	**TH**
200	0.011 ± 0.08	0.092 ± 0.11	0.075 ± 0.01	0.111 ± 0.02
400	0.003 ± 0.06	0.035 ± 0.06	0.068 ± 0.01	0.096 ± 0.01
800	0.031 ± 0.03	0.024 ± 0.04	0.071 ± 0.0	0.103 ± 0.01
1600	0.036 ± 0.02	0.04 ± 0.03	0.069 ± 0.0	0.098 ± 0.01
3000	0.034 ± 0.02	0.03 ± 0.0	0.069 ± 0.0	0.099 ± 0.0

Table 2: Mean and standard error of fairness metrics for predicting gender from 50 randomized train/test split for each fixed test size by CNN classifier on UTKFace dataset.

REFERENCES

[1] Bach Jensen, M. 2008. Online marketing communication potential. *EJM* 42(3/4):502–525.

[2] Bellamy, R. K. E.; Dey, K.; Hind, M.; Hoffman, S. C.; Houde, S.; Kannan, K.; Lohia, P.; Martino, J.; Mehta, S.; Mojsilovic, A.; Nagar, S.; Ramamurthy, K. N.; Richards, J.; Saha, D.; Sattigeri, P.; Singh, M.; Varshney, K. R.; and Zhang, Y. 2018. AI Fairness 360: An extensible toolkit for detecting, understanding, and mitigating unwanted algorithmic bias.

[3] Hajian, S.; Bonchi, F.; and Castillo, C. 2016. Algorithmic bias: From discrimination discovery to fairness-aware data mining. volume 13-17-, 2125–2126. ACM.

[4] Hajian, S.; Domingo-Ferrer, J.; and Martinez-Balleste, A. 2011. Discrimination prevention in data mining for intrusion and crime detection. *CICS* 47–54.

[5] Hardt, M.; Price, E.; and Srebro, N. 2016. Equality of opportunity in supervised learning. *CoRR*.

[6] Zhang, Z.; Song, Y.; and Qi, H. 2017. Age progression/regression by conditional adversarial autoencoder. In *CVPR*.

Popularity Bias in Ranking and Recommendation

Himan Abdollahpouri
himan.abdollahpouri@colorado.edu
Department of Infortion Science
University of Colorado Boulder

ABSTRACT

Many recommender systems suffer from popularity bias: popular items are recommended frequently while less popular, niche products, are recommended rarely or not at all. However, recommending the ignored products in the "long tail" is critical for businesses as they are less likely to be discovered. Popularity bias is also against social justice where the entities need to have a fair chance of being served and represented. In this work, I investigate the problem of popularity bias in recommender systems and develop algorithms to address this problem.

CCS CONCEPTS

• **Information systems → Recommender systems**; • **Computing methodologies → Ranking**; *Machine learning*; *Learning to rank*.

KEYWORDS

Ranking; Recommender systems; Information retrieval; Popularity bias

ACM Reference Format:
Himan Abdollahpouri. 2019. Popularity Bias in Ranking and Recommendation. In *AAAI/ACM Conference on AI, Ethics, and Society (AIES '19), January 27–28, 2019, Honolulu, HI, USA.* ACM, New York, NY, USA, 2 pages. https://doi.org/10.1145/3306618.3314309

1 INTRODUCTION

Recommender systems (RS) have an important role in e-commerce and information sites, helping users find new items. Like many other machine learning systems, RS can have certain types of biases [10, 11]. In this work, I investigate the popularity bias in ranking and recommendation and provide algorithmic solutions to address this problem. One of the main biases in recommender systems is the problem of popularity bias[5]: collaborative filtering recommenders typically emphasize popular items (those with more ratings) over other "long-tail", less popular ones [8] that may only be popular among small groups of users.

Although popular items are often good recommendations, they are also likely to be well-known. So delivering only popular items will not enhance new item discovery and will ignore the interests of users with niche tastes. It also may be unfair to the producers of less popular or newer items since they are rated by fewer users.

AIES '19, January 27–28, 2019, Honolulu, HI, USA

ACM ISBN 978-1-4503-6324-2/19/01.
https://doi.org/10.1145/3306618.3314309

Furthermore, long-tail recommendation can also be understood as a social good. A market that suffers from popularity bias will lack opportunities to discover more obscure products and will be, by definition, dominated by a few large brands or well-known artists [6]. Such a market will be more homogeneous and offer fewer opportunities for innovation and creativity.

Long-tail items are also important for generating a fuller understanding of users' preferences. Systems that use active learning to explore each user's profile will typically need to present more long tail items because these are the ones that the user is less likely to know about, and where user's preferences are more likely to be diverse [7, 9].

In addition, bias in recommender systems could have even societal consequences–in social media websites like Facebook,for example, everything a user sees in his/her feed is generated by recommender systems. Just imagine how these recommendations are affecting how people think, feel and even behave in a society. The same example could be given in News websites where someone could affect the holistic ideology of a group or even a society by tuning the recommender system to recommend certain types of News which could potentially benefit a certain political party or viewpoint. A system with popularity bias will impose a narrow ideology to the large population of the society.

And finally, as I discuss in [3], we can think of recommender systems and many other ranking systems as *multi-stakeholder environments* in which the needs and interests of different stakeholders should be taken into account instead of solely focusing on the end users. Popularity bias can lead to certain stakeholders (popular ones) achieving very high utility values while other stakeholders (less popular ones) to be ignored. Multi-stakeholder recommendation is also related to the concept of *fairness* in social sciences and *equity* in economics.

2 WORK I HAVE DONE SO FAR

So far, I have approached the popularity bias in recommender systems in two different ways:

- **Model-based treatment**: In this approach, I have modified the underlying ranking model that generates the recommendations such that less popular items also have a fair chance of being recommended. In other words, the model has been modified so the final recommendations are more balanced in terms of giving fair chance of exposure to less popular items. A more detailed description of this approach and the experiments I conducted to test it can be found in [2] which was published at the 12*th* ACM conference on recommender systems.
- **Re-ranking treatment**: In this approach, I assume there is a base recommender system which generates an initial list of

items to be recommended along with their predicted ratings. The idea is to keep existing algorithms untouched and add an extra level of selection as an add-on to those algorithms to control popularity bias. This initial list is generally much larger than the final list and it serves as a candidate pool of items to select from for the final list. Now, using this initial list and taking into account the fair representation of less popular items and maintaining an acceptable level of accuracy, the modified algorithm tries to give a boost to the predicted ratings of less popular ones so they have a higher chance of being recommended at the end. It is worth noting that I also take users' tolerance for less popular items into account in my model so users with no interest in less popular items will not be bothered by getting those recommendations. A more detailed description of this approach can be found in [4].

3 FUTURE PLAN

As the next steps for this work, I'm planning to do the followings:

- **Investigating theoretical reasons behind popularity bias in recommender systems:** I would like to see how different algorithms differ in the way they create popularity bias in the recommendations. This could be considered as a diagnosis strategy because different algorithms might vary in the way they create popularity bias and, therefore, it is important to find out what aspect of each algorithm is causing the popularity bias so we could find better solutions for that particular algorithm or class of algorithms.
- **Generalizing to other biases in recommender systems:** I will also extend those two aforementioned approaches I discussed to combat popularity bias in recommender systems to be applicable to other biases such as gender bias, age bias etc.

- **Temporal treatment of popularity bias:** Another possibility for future work is to look at long-tail promotion as a temporal process. Almost all the works on long-tail promotion have done the optimization on individual's recommendation lists hoping this will lead to an overall optimization within the entire user base. However, optimizing individual users' list will not necessarily result in the overall optimization [1]. Therefore, we need to approach this problem as a temporal process such that, at any given time T, the recommender system optimizes the objective function by also looking at what the outcome for optimization was at previous times. Figure 1 shows a schematic view of what a temporal optimization looks like. $R_{i,j}$ is the recommended item j to user i

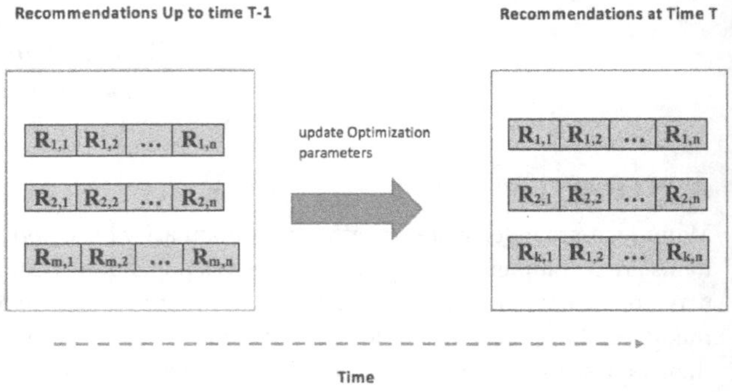

Figure 1: Dynamic optimization of the recommendations over time

REFERENCES

[1] Himan Abdollahpouri. 2019. Incorporating System-Level Objectives into Recommender Systems. In *Proceedings of the 2019 World Wide Web Conference (WWW'19 Companion) May 13–17, 2019, San Francisco, CA.* ACM.

[2] Himan Abdollahpouri, Robin Burke, and Bamshad Mobasher. 2017. Controlling Popularity Bias in Learning-to-Rank Recommendation. In *Proceedings of the Eleventh ACM Conference on Recommender Systems.* ACM, 42–46.

[3] Himan Abdollahpouri, Robin Burke, and Bamshad Mobasher. 2017. Recommender systems as multi-stakeholder environments. In *Proceedings of the 25th Conference on User Modeling, Adaptation and Personalization (UMAP2017).* ACM.

[4] Himan Abdollahpouri, Robin Burke, and Bamshad Mobasher. 2019. Managing Popularity Bias in Recommender Systems with Personalized Reranking. In *FLAIRS Conference: Submitted.*

[5] Alejandro Bellogín, Pablo Castells, and Iván Cantador. 2017. Statistical biases in Information Retrieval metrics for recommender systems. *Information Retrieval Journal* 20, 6 (2017), 606–634.

[6] Òscar Celma and Pedro Cano. 2008. From hits to niches?: or how popular artists can bias music recommendation and discovery. In *Proceedings of the 2nd KDD Workshop on Large-Scale Recommender Systems and the Netflix Prize Competition.* ACM, 5.

[7] Tien T Nguyen, Pik-Mai Hui, F Maxwell Harper, Loren Terveen, and Joseph A Konstan. 2014. Exploring the filter bubble: the effect of using recommender systems on content diversity. In *Proceedings of the 23rd international conference on World wide web.* ACM, 677–686.

[8] Yoon-Joo Park and Alexander Tuzhilin. 2008. The long tail of recommender systems and how to leverage it. In *Proceedings of the 2008 ACM conference on Recommender systems.* ACM, 11–18.

[9] Paul Resnick, R Kelly Garrett, Travis Kriplean, Sean A Munson, and Natalie Jomini Stroud. 2013. Bursting your (filter) bubble: strategies for promoting diverse exposure. In *Proceedings of the 2013 conference on Computer supported cooperative work companion.* ACM, 95–100.

[10] Harald Steck. 2011. Item popularity and recommendation accuracy. In *Proceedings of the fifth ACM conference on Recommender systems.* ACM, 125–132.

[11] Muhammad Bilal Zafar, Isabel Valera, Manuel Gomez Rodriguez, and Krishna P Gummadi. 2015. Fairness constraints: Mechanisms for fair classification. *arXiv preprint arXiv:1507.05259* (2015).

Risk Assessments and Fairness Under Missingness and Confounding

Amanda Coston
Carnegie Mellon University, Pittsburgh, PA, USA

ABSTRACT

Fairness in machine learning has become a significant area of research as risk assessments and other algorithmic decision-making systems are increasingly used in high-stakes applications such as criminal justice, consumer lending, and child welfare screening decisions. Two significant challenges to achieving fair decision-making systems are 1) access to the protected attribute may be limited and 2) the outcome may be confounded or selectively observed depending on the historical data generating process. To address the former challenge, we propose two methods for overcoming limited access to the protected attribute and empirically evaluate their success on three datasets. To address the later challenge, we develop counterfactual risk assessments that account for the effect of historical interventions on the outcome. We analyze the performance of our counterfactual risk assessments in criminal sentencing decisions in Pennsylvania. We compare our model against observational risk assessments.

KEYWORDS

Risk assessments, fairness, decision-making, machine learning

ACM Reference Format:
Amanda Coston. 2019. Risk Assessments and Fairness Under Missingness and Confounding. In *AAAI/ACM Conference on AI, Ethics, and Society (AIES '19), January 27–28, 2019, Honolulu, HI, USA.* ACM, New York, NY, USA, 1 page. https://doi.org/10.1145/3306618.3314310

AIES '19, January 27–28, 2019, Honolulu, HI, USA

ACM ISBN 978-1-4503-6324-2/19/01.
https://doi.org/10.1145/3306618.3314310

Artificial Intelligence's Impact on Mental Health Treatments

Michelle C. Ausman
mausman22@gmail.com
California Polytechnic State University
San Luis Obispo, CA, USA

ABSTRACT

An interest in artificial intelligence (AI) as a medical aid stemmed as research on mental health and psychology increased. Yet despite failing the Turing Test, AI continues to be used as a practical aid in the psychological community. From virtual reality simulations of everyday activities to robotic pet seals implemented in nursing homes, AI has found a home in the psychological field as a support for those in the medical field as well as those taking care of loved ones. In this paper, I aim to look at the stages of the Turing Test, how those are related to factoid and non-factoid questions and how current applications of AI are used in mental health treatments.

KEYWORDS

artificial intelligence, mental health, therapy, psychology, robots

ACM Reference Format:
Michelle C. Ausman. 2019. Artificial Intelligence's Impact on Mental Health Treatments. In *AAAI/ACM Conference on AI, Ethics, and Society (AIES '19), January 27–28, 2019, Honolulu, HI, USA.* ACM, New York, NY, USA, 2 pages. https://doi.org/10.1145/3306618.3314311

1 HISTORY OF AI IN MENTAL HEALTH

The first use of AI in the psychological field was the creation of ELIZA, a human-computer interface that simulated a Carl Rogers-like psychotherapist [6]. ELIZA only gave formulated responses, mimicking a conversation.

Shortly after, PARRY was created by psychiatrist Kenneth M. Colby [6]. The computer program simulated a patient suffering from paranoid schizophrenia and held conversations, like ELIZA, with its users. PARRY became so realistic, expert psychiatrists had a hard time differentiating PARRY from real-life patients. PARRY has been the closest AI system to pass the Turing Test.

2 STAGES OF THE TURING TEST

The Turing Test created a basis for AI systems. To reach a personable state, AI must achieve and surpass the Turing test: three intelligence stages psychologists and philosophers determined will make AI indistinguishable to humans.

Intelligence Quotient, or IQ, is an analysis of human intelligence through standardized testing [4]. Researchers in China devised an intelligence model which they have named the "standard intelligence model" [5]; this tested both humans and AI systems of aspects that connect artificial intelligence and human characteristics. Four aspects were tested: input, output, mastery, and creation. The test was administered to multiple AI systems and human subjects. In 2014, the results found that Google's AI system was the only commonly recognized AI system on the list, ranking 4th and given an IQ score of 26.5 [5]. When the AI systems were tested again in 2016, Google was again in 4th place with a score of 47.28. Bing's AI system came in 8th place with a 31.98 score [5]. From this, AI showed that it passed the IQ portion of the Turing Test.

Emotional intelligence, another aspect, accumulates the abilities to express and control emotions[4]. AI systems must show in interactions, it can give off and control its own emotions. The AI system must be able to deal with feelings and how it is perceived by judging a given situation [4].

The third aspect is a fairly new philosophical idea, spiritual intelligence. The ability to reach spiritual intelligence allows humans to ask and answer existential questions like "Why am I here?" Though AI systems currently only check one of the three parameters, IQ, the later two are unnecessary for AI to offer emotional support and well-being.

3 FACTOID AND NON-FACTOID QUESTIONS

Types of questions can be separated into two main categories: factoid and non-factoid questions. Factoid questions have a specific answer that can be looked up and have a basis for determining a correct answer. The question "What is the capital of California?" is a factoid question as there is only one capital of California, Sacramento. Non-factoid questions ask questions that are open-ended and may not have one clear answer. An example of a non-factoid question may be "How do you feel about this shirt?" Current AI systems have trouble achieving spiritual intelligence. The pinnacle of spiritual intelligence is the ability to answer or at least make an attempt to answer existential questions or think existentially [4]. An example of an existential questions is, "What is the meaning of life?"

Mental health questions are open-ended and do not have one exact answer. For instance, if a person asks him or herself "Why do I have post-traumatic stress disorder (PTSD)?" the answers will vary between those with PTSD. One may experience PTSD due to domestic violence or rape while another may have PTSD from seeing a friend die in combat while in the Army. The diagnosis of mental illness is difficult to pinpoint to one root cause. Many symptoms overlap each other in different illnesses or disorders, which in itself makes it hard to diagnose mental illness. In diagnosing a patient with a mental illness or disorder, there is a high comorbidity rate among mental illnesses. Mental illness diagnosis heavily relies on the patient to relay symptoms rather than tests or performance, making it extremely difficult to pinpoint the cause. Doctors, nurses, psychiatrists, etc. must trust their patients are giving the correct

AIES '19, January 27–28, 2019, Honolulu, HI, USA

ACM ISBN 978-1-4503-6324-2/19/01.
https://doi.org/10.1145/3306618.3314311

symptoms to indicate what is wrong. The symptoms' signs are even harder to pinpoint, especially if a person isn't looking for the signs. With all things considered, these reasons make it difficult for AI systems to give feedback, let alone humans.

4 CURRENT USES OF AI IN MENTAL HEALTH TREATMENT

4.1 Horyzons

One system that has shown promise in helping youths with social therapy is Horyzons. The online module provides social therapy for youth who have experienced psychosis at a young age [1]. Horyzons give the patients the ability to learn, share, and express feelings rather than forcing mandatory attendance at face-to-face group therapy. A big fear that comes up in attending group therapy is the fear of sharing intimate thoughts with others and worrying what the others will think. With Horyzons, these patients can feel free to share and express their thoughts anonymously. Interacting with the program, the user can feel free to disclose information within the secrecy of an anonymous chatbot group [1]. News boards are moderated by psychiatrists and physicians to make sure the learning environment is safe and friendly, while monitoring each patient's progress.

4.2 Woebot

Similar to Horyzons, another researcher offered an alternative to routine group therapy in the form of an automated conversational agent, Woebot. Woebot interacted with young adults, aged 22-28, giving cognitive based therapy via an instant messaging application to treat depression symptoms [2]. A study of 70 participants, 34 using Woebot and 36 using an ebook "Depression of College Students", found the Woebot group having a significant reduction in depression symptoms compared to the control group.

4.3 Paro

Despite the fact people are living longer lives, people are becoming more lonely. To help aid the "loneliness crisis" in hospitals and nursing homes, Paro was created. Paro is a robot that looks and feels like a plush toy seal.

A study looked to see the effects of Paro on patients and nursing staff at a nursing home. Paro is coined as a mental commitment robot, meaning it is not a personal robot, nor can do hard labor, but its sole purpose is to interact with people as if the robot had human emotion [7]. Paro was implemented in hospitals and nursing homes around the world such as Japan, Denmark, and Italy. To measure for stress, patients' urine were tested for levels of 17-ketosteroid sulfate and 17-hydroxycorticosteroids [7]. After a period of five weeks, results showed that patients were able to overcome stressors more readily. The nursing staff had less stress during this period, due to patients requiring less supervision when interacting with Paro [7].

4.4 Second Life

Another therapy aid that has been found to be beneficial has been video gaming. Linden Research Inc. developed a video game specifically to aid speech and social therapy for people with autism spectrum disorder [6]. The virtual reality simulation game, Second Life, directed game play as patients used the game to become more acquainted with social skills while in a safe and non-threatening environment [6].

5 FUTURE RESEARCH

To further explore these and other applications of AI in mental health, I plan to conduct and replicate the research using Siri, Jibo, and Woebot to compare the results that have been published, which will contribute to my senior project and thesis.

6 CONCLUSION

Though there is much room for improvement of artificial intelligence, these mental health treatments should be reason enough to continue research in this area. Many fear the advancements of AI, which was exemplified from Future of Life Institute's Open Letter on AI [3]. However, with the therapy advancements in the mental health field, AI has shown that there is potential for it to be beneficial to society.

ACKNOWLEDGMENTS

Thank you to the Department of Liberal Arts and Engineering Studies at California Polytechnic State University, San Luis Obispo for funding this project.

REFERENCES

[1] Simon D'Alfonso, Olga Santesteban-Echarri, Simon Rice, Greg Wadley, Reeva Lederman, Christopher Miles, John Gleeson, and Mario Alvarez-Jimenez. Artificial Intelligence-Assisted Online Social Therapy for Youth Mental Health. *Frontiers in Psychology.* 8(2017) 796.

[2] KK Fitzpatrick, A Darcy, and M Vierhile Delivering Cognitive Behavior Therapy to Young Adults With Symptoms of Depression and Anxiety Using a Fully Automated Conversational Agent (Woebot): A Randomized Control Trial. *Journal of Medical Interest Reserach Mental Health* 4(2), e19, 1-11.

[3] Gonenc Gurkaynak, Ilay Yilmaz, and Gunes Haksever. Stifling Artificial Intelligence: Human Perils. *Computer Law & Security Review.* 32(5), 749-758.

[4] Mohammad Kadkhoda and Hoorie Jahani. Problem-solving capabilities of spiritual intelligence for artificial intelligence. *Procedia - Social and Behavioral Sciences.* 32(2012), 170-175.

[5] Feng Liu, Yong Shi, and Ying Liu. Intelligence Quotient and Intelligence Grade of Artificial Intelligence. *Annals of Data Science.* 4(2), 179-191.

[6] David D. Luxton. Artificial Intelligence in Psychological Practice: Current and Future Applications and Implementations. *Professional Psychology: Research and Practice.* 45(4), 332-339.

[7] Takanori Shibata and Kazuyoshi Wada. Robot Therapy: A New Approach for Mental Healthcare of the Eldery - A Mini-Review. *Gerontology.* 2011(57), 378-386.

Algorithmic Stereotypes: Implications for Fairness of Generalizing from Past Data

Daniel McNamara
Australian National University and CSIRO Data61
Canberra, ACT, Australia
dpmcna@gmail.com

CCS CONCEPTS

• **Social and professional topics** → *Socio-technical systems; Race and ethnicity;* • **Theory of computation** → *Machine learning theory;* • **Computing methodologies** → *Machine learning.*

KEYWORDS

fairness; machine learning; stereotypes

ACM Reference Format:

Daniel McNamara. 2019. Algorithmic Stereotypes: Implications for Fairness of Generalizing from Past Data. In *AAAI/ACM Conference on AI, Ethics, and Society (AIES '19), January 27–28, 2019, Honolulu, HI, USA.* ACM, New York, NY, USA, 2 pages. https://doi.org/10.1145/3306618.3314312

Background

Algorithms are used to make or support decisions about people in a wide variety of contexts including the provision of financial credit, judicial risk assessments, applicant screening for employment, and online ad selection. Such algorithms often make predictions about the future behavior of individuals by generalizing from data recording the past behaviors of other individuals. Concerns have arisen about the fairness of these algorithms. Researchers have responded by developing definitions of fairness and algorithm designs that incorporate these definitions [2]. A common theme is the avoidance of discrimination on the basis of group membership, such as race or gender. This may be more complex than simply excluding the explicit consideration of an individual's group membership, because other characteristics may be correlated with this group membership – a phenomenon known as redundant encoding [5].

Different definitions of fairness may be invoked by different stakeholders. The controversy associated with the COMPAS recidivism prediction system used in some parts of the United States showed this in practice. News organization ProPublica critiqued the system as unfair since among non-reoffenders, African-Americans were more likely to be marked high risk than whites, while among re-offenders, whites were more likely to be marked low risk than African-Americans [1]. COMPAS owner Equivant (formerly Northpointe) argued that the algorithm was not unfair since among those marked high risk, African-Americans were no less likely to reoffend than whites [4].

AIES '19, January 27–28, 2019, Honolulu, HI, USA

ACM ISBN 978-1-4503-6324-2/19/01.
https://doi.org/10.1145/3306618.3314312

Equalized odds – which requires that false positive rates and false negative rates do not vary across groups – seeks to address the issue identified by ProPublica [6]. Equalized outcomes – where the difference in predicted outcomes between groups is less than the difference observed in past data – is more contentious. One might argue that if past data shows a gap in outcomes between two groups, then predictions should be faithful to this gap.

My initial question of interest is:

Question 1. *What is the relationship between equalized odds and equalized outcomes?*

More broadly, I would like to understand the following:

Question 2. *What are the implications for fairness of generalizing from past data?*

Problem Setup

Let $\mathcal{X}$, $\mathcal{Y}$ and $\mathcal{S}$ be sets corresponding to the input variable X, target variable Y and sensitive variable S respectively. The sensitive variable encodes some form of group membership. We focus on the case where $\mathcal{S} = \{0, 1\}$ (e.g. race coded as 1 for African-American or 0 for non African-American) and $\mathcal{Y} = \{0, 1\}$ (e.g. ground truth of whether the person reoffended). The choice of $\mathcal{X}$ is arbitrary in our analysis (e.g. a person's criminal record expressed as a real-valued vector). Let $h : \mathcal{X} \times \mathcal{S} \to [0, 1]$ be a stochastic hypothesis, which can also be interpreted as a scoring function. Let decision variable $\hat{Y}$ be constructed such that $p(\hat{Y} = 1|X = x, S = s) := h(x, s)$. While setting S, Y and $\hat{Y}$ to be binary variables is an assumption, this allows us to cover many cases of interest – such as the recidivism prediction example – and facilitates our analysis and interpretation.

Drawing X, S and Y and making decision $\hat{Y}$, we have a joint distribution μ of all four variables. We may also derive marginal distributions, such as the marginal distribution of Y:

$$\mu_Y(Y = y) := \int_{x \in \mathcal{X}} \sum_{s \in \{0,1\}} \sum_{\hat{y} \in \{0,1\}} \mu(X = x, S = s, Y = y, \hat{Y} = \hat{y}) dx.$$

Similarly, we may derive conditional distributions, such as the marginal distribution over $\hat{Y}$ conditioned on $Y = 1$:

$$\mu_{\hat{Y}|Y=1}(\hat{Y} = \hat{y}) := \frac{\mu_{Y,\hat{Y}}(Y = 1, \hat{Y} = \hat{y})}{\mu_Y(Y = 1)}.$$

We use notation of the form $p(Y = y) := \mu_Y(Y = y)$ for marginals and $p(\hat{Y} = \hat{y}|Y = 1) := \mu_{\hat{Y}|Y=1}(\hat{Y} = \hat{y})$ for conditionals. For example, $p(\hat{Y} = 1|Y = 1)$ is known as the true positive rate (e.g. predicted reoffence rate for reoffenders) and $p(\hat{Y} = 1|Y = 0)$ is known as the false positive rate (e.g. predicted reoffence rate for non-reoffenders).

Definition 1 (Equalized odds [6]). *Equalized odds is satisfied if both of the following hold:*

$$p(\hat{Y} = 1|S = 1, Y = 1) = p(\hat{Y} = 1|S = 0, Y = 1) \quad (1)$$

i.e. the true positive rate is the same for both groups, and

$$p(\hat{Y} = 1|S = 1, Y = 0) = p(\hat{Y} = 1|S = 0, Y = 0) \quad (2)$$

i.e. the false positive rate is the same for both groups.

We give a novel, quantified definition of equalized outcomes.

Definition 2 (Equalized outcomes). *Let*

$$p(\hat{Y} = 1|S = 1) - p(\hat{Y} = 1|S = 0) = \alpha(p(Y = 1|S = 1) - p(Y = 1|S = 0)) \quad (3)$$

where α is a constant we refer to as the equalized outcomes coefficient. If (3) holds for $\alpha = 0$ we have fully equalized outcomes. *If (3) holds for some $\alpha \in (0, 1)$ we have* partially equalized outcomes. *If (3) holds for $\alpha = 1$ we have* non-equalized outcomes.

Contributions to Date

Assuming equalized odds is satisfied, we show there is a quantifiable trade-off between accuracy and the extent to which outcomes are equalized. Given perfectly equalized odds, the extent to which we equalize outcomes is given by the difference α between the true positive rate and false positive rate. This novel result is of interest because it quantifies the relationship between the well-known but seemingly distinct notions of equalized odds and equalized outcomes.

Theorem 1 (Equalized outcomes given equalized odds). *Let*

$$\alpha := p(\hat{Y} = 1|Y = 1) - p(\hat{Y} = 1|Y = 0).$$

Suppose (1) *and* (2) *hold, i.e. equalized odds is satisfied. Then* (3) *is satisfied, i.e. α is the equalized outcomes coefficient satisfying*

$$p(\hat{Y} = 1|S = 1) - p(\hat{Y} = 1|S = 0) = \alpha(p(Y = 1|S = 1) - p(Y = 1|S = 0)).$$

Proof idea. Express $p(\hat{Y} = 1|S = 1)$ and $p(\hat{Y} = 1|S = 0)$ using the law of total probability. Make substitutions based on (1) and (2). Take the difference of the two expressions, then factorize and apply the definition of α. □

In the realistic case where the prediction algorithm is neither vacuous nor perfectly accurate – i.e. $\alpha \in (0, 1)$ – and the observed rates $p(Y = 1|S = 1)$ and $p(Y = 1|S = 0)$ differ, a corollary is that requiring equalized odds is equivalent to requiring partially equalized outcomes. Equivalently, if an imperfect algorithm's predictions are faithful to the gap in outcomes between groups observed in past data, then the algorithm violates equalized odds. We also show a similar result where we only require approximately equalized odds rather than perfectly equalized odds are required.

Furthermore, we show that equalized outcomes is closely related to another well-known definition of fairness known as group-conditional calibration.

Definition 3 (Group-conditional calibration [7, 8]). *Both of the following statements hold $\forall c \in [0, 1]$:*

$$p(Y = 1|h(x, s) = c, S = 1) = c \quad (4)$$

$$p(Y = 1|h(x, s) = c, S = 0) = c \quad (5)$$

Lemma 1 (Group-conditional calibration implies non- equalized outcomes but not vice versa). *If* (4) *and* (5) *hold, then* (3) *holds for $\alpha = 1$, i.e. group-conditional calibration implies non-equalized outcomes.*

However, if (3) *holds for $\alpha = 1$, then it is not the case that* (4) *and* (5) *must hold, i.e. non-equalized outcomes does not imply group-conditional calibration.*

We use Lemma 1 to show that our result about the incompatibility of equalized odds and non-equalized outcomes is a generalization a well-known existing result about the incompatibility of group-conditional calibration and equalized odds [7].

Outstanding Research Questions

I am interested to further explore the broader research question: what are the implications for fairness of generalizing from past data? There are several directions of interest.

Equalized odds has the downside that it is concerned only with relative error rates between groups rather than absolute error rates [3]. An alternative metric would be the absolute error rate among the group for which the algorithm has the highest error. What are the properties of such a metric?

When the target variable is either not observed or affected by historic injustice or structural inequality, it may not be appropriate to use in definitions of fairness. How should we approach defining fairness in these contexts? In particular, can we interpolate between cases where the target is either fully observed or unobserved, to cases where it is partially observed?

When do we consider it fair to generalize from past data? For instance, in the context of university admissions many would be uncomfortable with the idea of rejecting a student based on the past performance of others who resemble them in some respect. However, when targeting student support once at university it may be acceptable to generalize from the past performance of others. What kinds of decisions should or should not be made in this way?

REFERENCES

[1] Julia Angwin, Jeff Larson, Surya Mattu, and Lauren Kirchner. 2016. Machine Bias. ProPublica, https://www.propublica.org/article/machine-bias-risk-assessments-in-criminal-sentencing.

[2] Solon Barocas, Moritz Hardt, and Arvind Narayanan. 2018. *Fairness and Machine Learning*. fairmlbook.org.

[3] Sam Corbett-Davies and Sharad Goel. 2018. The Measure and Mismeasure of Fairness: A Critical Review of Fair Machine Learning. arXiv 1808.00023.

[4] William Dieterich, Christina Mendoza, and Tim Brennan. 2016. COMPAS Risk Scales: Demonstrating Accuracy Equity and Predictive Parity. Northpointe Inc.

[5] Cynthia Dwork, Moritz Hardt, Toniann Pitassi, Omer Reingold, and Richard Zemel. 2012. Fairness Through Awareness. In *Innovations in Theoretical Computer Science Conference*.

[6] Moritz Hardt, Eric Price, and Nathan Srebro. 2016. Equality of Opportunity in Supervised Learning. In *Advances in Neural Information Processing Systems*.

[7] Jon Kleinberg, Sendhil Mullainathan, and Manish Raghavan. 2017. Inherent Trade-Offs in the Fair Determination of Risk Scores. *Innovations in Theoretical Computer Science*.

[8] Geoff Pleiss, Manish Raghavan, Felix Wu, Jon Kleinberg, and Kilian Q Weinberger. 2017. On Fairness and Calibration. In *Advances in Neural Information Processing Systems*.

Perceptions of Fairness

Nripsuta Ani Saxena
University of Southern California
Los Angeles, California, USA
nsaxena@usc.edu

CCS CONCEPTS

• **Human-centered computing → Human computer interaction (HCI)**; • **Applied computing → Psychology**; • **Computing methodologies → Artificial intelligence**.

ACM Reference Format:
Nripsuta Ani Saxena. 2019. Perceptions of Fairness . In *2019 AAAI/ACM Conference on AI, Ethics, and Society (AIES'19), January 27–28, 2019, Honolulu, HI, USA.* ACM, New York, NY, USA, 2 pages. https://doi.org/10.1145/3306618.3314314

1 INTRODUCTION

In recent years, fairness has rightly become an important topic of interest in the AI, law, ethics, and political community. In the computer science (CS) community, people have started wondering how we can make algorithms fair. While this question is theoretically well defined, the fundamental question underlying remains vague: what does it mean to be fair? This complicates things: there is no universal definition of fairness, especially for different scenarios. For instance, philosophers have been debating about various definitions of fairness for centuries, and psychologists have been trying to measure how people perceive fairness for decades. Now, along come the computer scientists, attempting to make computing and algorithmic decision making systems fair. The risk assessment software, COMPAS, used by judicial systems in many states, predicts a score indicating the likelihood of a criminal committing a crime again if given bail. By some measures of fairness, it was found to be biasing against African-Americans [3]. By other measures, it was not [9]. Which measures are fair? How do we make sure at least the majority of the general population agrees the software is fair? The above observation raises an important point: in order to make algorithms fair, we need to understand what is perceived as being fair.

Before we apply a definition of fairness to algorithms that may be used in areas as diverse as school admissions, hiring decision making, loan applications, and bail decisions, affecting almost everyone in society at some level, it is necessary to make sure that those definitions (in many cases come up as constraints) are sensitive to the prevailing notions of fairness in that society, while still ensuring that no bias occurs.

AIES '19, January 27–28, 2019, Honolulu, HI, USA

ACM ISBN 978-1-4503-6324-2/19/01...$15.00
https://doi.org/10.1145/3306618.3314314

In the work for my master's thesis, we studied how ordinary people perceive three particular definitions of fairness taken from the computer science literature. We designed and conducted online experiments (on Amazon Mechanical Turk) in the setting of loan decision making. Respondents on Amazon Mechanical Turk were asked to rate three potential ways of dividing a sum of $50,000 between two loan applicants. In the first experiment, both applicants were identical except their loan repayment rates. In the second, they were identical except their loan repayment rates and their race. We observed that across both experiments, we observed a general preference for one definition over the others (calibrated fairness, proposed by Liu et al. 2017), and that the mention of race did have an effect, with the results suggesting support for affirmative action.

This brought up many more questions: would mention of any sensitive information have an effect? Or are there only some kinds of sensitive information that affect people's perceptions of fairness? Would this translate to other contexts as well? *Why* does the mention of sensitive information have an effect at all?

This work is one of the first to look at how ordinary people perceive definitions of fairness proposed in the computer science community, and we are working on extending this work much further. It is very likely that one particular fairness definition would not be universal when facing different scenarios. Society may have different perceptions of fairness when it comes to loan decisions, affirmative action, and bail decisions, and other contexts. Further, different cultures have different norms. Would perceptions of fairness vary across cultures? If so, how? Do different cultures place greater importance on different kinds of sensitive information? Further, it is imperative to study other important settings, and also draw on more fairness definitions, both from within the CS literature and outside it (from psychology and philosophy).

In a nutshell, we are studying:

- whether people's perception of fairness change depending on the context
- are the effects similar?
- whether the definitions that have already been proposed are constrained enough

While studying how ordinary people perceive different definitions of fairness that might someday be used in systems that may affect them is important, it raises another question: how should these perceptions be incorporated into such systems? This will also likely be a complicated question to answer, and we hope our work helps spark a greater dialogue between computer scientists, ethicists, and the general public in designing algorithms that may ultimately affect the public.

REFERENCES

[1] J Stacy Adams. 1963. Towards an understanding of inequity. *The Journal of Abnormal and Social Psychology* 67, 5 (1963), 422.

[2] J Stacy Adams. 1965. Inequity in social exchange. In *Advances in experimental social psychology*. Vol. 2. Elsevier, 267–299.

[3] J Angwin, J Larson, S Mattu, and L Kirchner. 2016. Machine bias risk assessments in criminal sentencing. https://www.propublica.org/article/machine-bias-risk-assessments-in-criminal-sentencing. *ProPublica https://www.propublica.org* (2016). Accessed: 2018-03-27.

[4] Edmond Awad, Sohan Dsouza, Richard Kim, Jonathan Schulz, Joseph Henrich, Azim Shariff, Jean-François Bonnefon, and Iyad Rahwan. 2018. The moral machine experiment. *Nature* 563, 7729 (2018), 59.

[5] Max H Bazerman, Sally Blount White, and George F Loewenstein. 1995. Perceptions of fairness in interpersonal and individual choice situations. *Current Directions in Psychological Science* 4, 2 (1995), 39–43.

[6] Reuben Binns, Max Van Kleek, Michael Veale, Ulrik Lyngs, Jun Zhao, and Nigel Shadbolt. 2018. 'It's Reducing a Human Being to a Percentage': Perceptions of Justice in Algorithmic Decisions. In *Proceedings of the 2018 CHI Conference on Human Factors in Computing Systems*. ACM, 377.

[7] Jean-François Bonnefon, Azim Shariff, and Iyad Rahwan. 2016. The social dilemma of autonomous vehicles. *Science* 352, 6293 (2016), 1573–1576.

[8] Alexandra Chouldechova. 2017. Fair prediction with disparate impact: A study of bias in recidivism prediction instruments. *Big data* 5, 2 (2017), 153–163.

[9] William Dieterich, Christina Mendoza, and Tim Brennan. 2016. COMPAS risk scales: Demonstrating accuracy equity and predictive parity. http://go.volarisgroup.com/rs/430-MBX-989/images/ProPublica_Commentary_Final_070616.pdf. *Northpoint Inc* (2016). Accessed: 2018-10-24.

[10] Cynthia Dwork, Moritz Hardt, Toniann Pitassi, Omer Reingold, and Richard Zemel. 2012. Fairness through awareness. In *Proceedings of the 3rd innovations in theoretical computer science conference*. ACM, 214–226.

[11] Evelyn Ellis and Philippa Watson. 2012. *EU anti-discrimination law*. Oxford University Press.

[12] Pratik Gajane and Mykola Pechenizkiy. 2017. On formalizing fairness in prediction with machine learning. *arXiv preprint arXiv:1710.03184* (2017).

[13] Joshua David Greene. 2014. *Moral tribes: Emotion, reason, and the gap between us and them*. Penguin.

[14] Nina Grgić-Hlača, Elissa M Redmiles, Krishna P Gummadi, and Adrian Weller. 2018. Human perceptions of fairness in algorithmic decision making: A case study of criminal risk prediction. *arXiv preprint arXiv:1802.09548* (2018).

[15] Nina Grgić-Hlača, Muhammad Bilal Zafar, Krishna P Gummadi, and Adrian Weller. 2018. Beyond distributive fairness in algorithmic decision making: Feature selection for procedurally fair learning. In *Thirty-Second AAAI Conference on Artificial Intelligence*.

[16] Karen Huang, Joshua David Greene, and M Bazerman. 2019. Veil-of-ignorance reasoning favors the greater good. (2019). Working paper.

[17] Matthew Joseph, Michael Kearns, Jamie H Morgenstern, and Aaron Roth. 2016. Fairness in learning: Classic and contextual bandits. In *Advances in Neural Information Processing Systems*. 325–333.

[18] Jon Kleinberg, Sendhil Mullainathan, and Manish Raghavan. 2016. Inherent trade-offs in the fair determination of risk scores. *arXiv preprint arXiv:1609.05807* (2016).

[19] Min Kyung Lee. 2018. Understanding perception of algorithmic decisions: Fairness, trust, and emotion in response to algorithmic management. *Big Data & Society* 5, 1 (2018), 2053951718756684.

[20] Min Kyung Lee and Su Baykal. 2017. Algorithmic Mediation in Group Decisions: Fairness Perceptions of Algorithmically Mediated vs. Discussion-Based Social Division.. In *CSCW*. 1035–1048.

[21] Min Kyung Lee, Ji Tae Kim, and Leah Lizarondo. 2017. A Human-Centered Approach to Algorithmic Services: Considerations for Fair and Motivating Smart Community Service Management that Allocates Donations to Non-Profit Organizations. In *Proceedings of the 2017 CHI Conference on Human Factors in Computing Systems*. ACM, 3365–3376.

[22] Yang Liu, Goran Radanovic, Christos Dimitrakakis, Debmalya Mandal, and David C Parkes. 2017. Calibrated fairness in bandits. *arXiv preprint arXiv:1707.01875* (2017).

[23] Emma Pierson. 2017. Gender differences in beliefs about algorithmic fairness. *arXiv preprint arXiv:1712.09124* (2017).

[24] Angelisa C Plane, Elissa M Redmiles, Michelle L Mazurek, and Michael Carl Tschantz. 2017. Exploring user perceptions of discrimination in online targeted advertising. In *USENIX Security*.

[25] Allison Woodruff, Sarah E Fox, Steven Rousso-Schindler, and Jeffrey Warshaw. 2018. A Qualitative Exploration of Perceptions of Algorithmic Fairness. In *Proceedings of the 2018 CHI Conference on Human Factors in Computing Systems*. ACM, 656.

[26] Menahem E Yaari and Maya Bar-Hillel. 1984. On dividing justly. *Social choice and welfare* 1, 1 (1984), 1–24.

Learning Context-Sensitive Norms under Uncertainty

Vasanth Sarathy
vasanth.sarathy@tufts.edu
Tufts University
Medford, Massachusetts

CCS CONCEPTS

• **Computing methodologies → Knowledge representation and reasoning; Uncertainty quantification**; *Online learning settings.*

KEYWORDS

norm learning; Dempster-Shafer theory; agent-based simulation; uncertainty

ACM Reference Format:
Vasanth Sarathy. 2019. Learning Context-Sensitive Norms under Uncertainty. In *2019 AAAI/ACM Conference on AI, Ethics, and Society (AIES'19), January 27–28, 2019, Honolulu, HI, USA.* ACM, New York, NY, USA, 2 pages. https://doi.org/10.1145/3306618.3314315

1 INTRODUCTION

Norms and conventions play a central role in maintaining social order in multi-agent societies [2, 5]. I study the problem of how these norms and conventions can be learned from observation of heterogeneous sources, under conditions of uncertainty. This is necessary as it is not enough to simply hard code a set of norms into a new agent prior to entering society because norms can evolve over time as agents enter and leave the society [9].

What makes learning norms from observation especially challenging are that the same behavior that comprises the norm might have different normative statuses in different situations. For example, yelling out loud is allowed on a beach but not so in a library. Moreover, observing behaviors and gleaning normative status from them is also difficult because the learner is susceptible to different forms of uncertainty. For one, the source (i.e., the agent being observed) may be violating norms. Besides this inherent uncertainty, the learner must also be able to handle its own epistemic uncertainty arising from unreliable sensors or ambiguous observations. The learner must also be able to take into account sanctioning of violations and adjust its normative knowledge accordingly. Finally, the learner must be able to express norms explicitly and in a way that disentangles its own norm compliance, allowing it the choice to either comply or not, and thereby maintain its autonomy.

My work addresses the problem of learning context-sensitive norms in uncertain learning settings. In particular, I represent norms explicitly, and employ a Dempster-Shafer theoretic uncertainty processing framework.

ACM ISBN 978-1-4503-6324-2/19/01.
https://doi.org/10.1145/3306618.3314315

2 RELATED WORK

Norm learning literature is vast and a nice synthesis can be found in [2, 9]. Contemporary approaches vary widely in their choices of representations from explicit logics [1] to implicit policies or reward functions within a state-transition system [3]. As noted earlier, explicit representations have the benefit of allowing agent compliance autonomy. Related works using explicit representations, either do not represent uncertainty in any form [1] or do not account specifically for epistemic uncertainty, or make certain assumptions about the observed agents [4, 6]. Realistically, the learner might not know much about the agent it is observing (i.e., goals or plan libraries). Thus, there are open questions about the role of context and uncertainty when learning norms, that I have begun addressing, as described below.

3 NORM REPRESENTATION AND EPISTEMIC UNCERTAINTY

3.1 Dempster-Shafer Theory

DS-theory is a measure-theoretic mathematical framework that allows for combining pieces of uncertain evidential information to produce degrees of belief for the various events of interest [10]. DS-theory generalizes Bayesian theory, and unlike Bayes, it can represent set-valued random variables, allowing it to capture interval probabilities measures, without committing to particular distributions. Crucially, this allows DS-theory to capture the uncertainty arising not only from randomness in the data, but also from ambiguity and ignorance due to limitations of the agent's sensors and occlusions in the environment.

3.2 Context-Sensitive Norm Representation

We define a context-sensitive behavior $\mathcal{B}$ as:

$$\mathcal{B} \stackrel{\text{def}}{=} C_{\psi}^{[\alpha,\beta]} \tag{1}$$

where C and ψ are ground atomic formulas representing context condition (C), and the corresponding behavior (ψ) possible in that context. The interval $[\alpha, \beta]$ captures the DS-theoretic uncertainty (or probability) that ψ *occurs* in context C, where α represents the belief and β represents the plausibility as defined under DS-theory.

4 RESULTS

4.1 Computational Model of Human Norm Representations

First, with my collaborators, I explored the basic properties of norm processing in humans (representation, activation and learning), and took the first steps towards describing a computational model that could account for these properties. In [7], we showed with experimental data that context-sensitivity of norms is strongly present in humans. We then developed a model – representation format similar to (1) and algorithm – for automatically learning context-sensitive norms from the human data. The model allowed norms to be learned from different types of evidence sources in different contexts, and explicitly captured uncertainty due to variations in the source's reliability and the quality of the evidence. The proposed representation and learning techniques provided a promising platform for studying, computationally, a wide array of cognitive properties of norms.

4.2 Modeling Dynamic Context-Shifting

We then asked the question of how we can account for differences among norm learners and allow distinct agents to communicate and resolve their differences? Learning in the real world is far from perfect; data are often obtained in a streaming, unfolding manner through a series of observations made during a certain time window. Observations are made in context, the identity of which might be uncertain and may even change over time. In [8], we extended our algorithm to track how these norms are learned when observations are made in dynamic situations involving changing contexts and general contextual uncertainty. The revised model allowed us to capture this contextual uncertainty, which in turn, can influence the agent's normative beliefs themselves, resulting in individual differences in normative behavior.

4.3 Extending to Multi-Agent Setting

In our most recent work (under review), we extended the model into an increasingly realistic multi-agent setting, in which we accounted for sanctioning, variable agent compliance, and learning from heterogeneous agents. This work improved on prior algorithms to make it more computationally efficient and tractable for larger sets of norms over longer lifetimes. Moreover, we explored what it means to be a norm and differentiate between conventions and norms as they relate to behaviors. We provided an agent model, series of algorithms, and results from agent-based simulations showing how behavioral regularities can be recognized in a multi-agent setting. The approach showed state of the art performance while overcoming limitations of other approaches. The agent-based modeling approach enabled us to study the impact of four different forms of uncertainty associated with norm compliance rates, sanctioning rates, sensor reliability and environmental occlusion.

5 RESEARCH PLAN AND FUTURE WORK

My research approach is to combine mathematical analysis, algorithm design, computer simulations, robotic implementation, and human-subject experiments to develop and test computational models for normative and ethical behavior. A limitation of the current work is that the learner knows in advance the set of behaviors applicable in a context. In future work, I intend to harness an exciting aspect of DS-theory that allows for expanding and growing the hypothesis space (i.e., set of norms) incrementally and in *real time*. I also intend to run more elaborate agent-based simulations in which I plan to explore (a) the role of sanctions on compliance, (b) how agents that can track norms across multiple contexts, (c) norm compliance and conflicts, and (d) more expressive representations that capture compositional and temporal aspects of norms.

6 CONCLUSION

In this work, I have taken the first steps towards a more complete understanding of the context-sensitivity of norms and how these norms can be learned from observation under conditions of aleatory as well as epistemic uncertainty.

REFERENCES

[1] Giulia Andrighetto, Marco Campenni, Federico Cecconi, and Rosaria Conte. 2010. The Complex Loop of Norm Emergence: A Simulation Model. (2010), 19–35.

[2] Tina Balke, Célia da Costa Pereira, Frank Dignum, Emiliano Lorini, Antonino Rotolo, Wamberto Vasconcelos, and Serena Villata. 2013. Norms in MAS: Definitions and related concepts. In *Dagstuhl Follow-Ups*, Vol. 4. Schloss Dagstuhl-Leibniz-Zentrum fuer Informatik.

[3] Rahmatollah Beheshti, Awrad Mohammed Ali, and Gita Sukthankar. 2015. Cognitive Social Learners: An Architecture for Modeling Normative Behavior. *Twenty-Ninth AAAI Conference on Artificial Intelligence Cognitive* (2015), 2017–2023.

[4] Stephen Cranefield, Felipe Meneguzzi, Nir Oren, and Bastin Tony Roy Savarimuthu. 2016. A Bayesian approach to norm identification. *Frontiers in Artificial Intelligence and Applications* 285 (2016), 622–629.

[5] Bertram F. Malle, Matthias Scheutz, and Joseph L. Austerweil. 2017. Networks of social and moral norms in human and robot agents. In *A World with Robots*, Maria Isabel Aldinhas Ferreira, Joao Silva Sequeira, Mohammad Osman Tokhi, Endre E. Kadar, and Gurvinder Singh Virk (Eds.). Springer, Cham, Switzerland, 3–17.

[6] Nir Oren and Felipe Meneguzzi. 2013. Norm identification through plan recognition. In *Proceedings of the workshop on Coordination, Organization, Institutions and Norms in Agent Systems (COIN 2013@ AAMAS)*.

[7] Vasanth Sarathy, Matthias Scheutz, Joseph Austerweil, Yoed Kenett, Mowafak Allaham, and Bertram Malle. 2017. Mental Representations and Computational Modeling of Context-Specific Human Norm Systems. In *Proceedings of Cognitive Science*.

[8] Vasanth Sarathy, Matthias Scheutz, and Bertram Malle. 2017. Learning Behavioral Norms in Uncertain and Changing Contexts. In *Proceedings of the 2017 8th IEEE International Conference on Cognitive Infocommunications (CogInfoCom)*.

[9] Bastin Tony Roy Savarimuthu and Stephen Cranefield. 2011. Norm Creation, Spreading and Emergence: A Survey of Simulation Models of Norms in Multi-Agent Systems. *Multiagent and Grid Systems* 7, 1 (2011), 21–54. https://doi.org/10.3233/MGS-2011-0167

[10] Glenn Shafer. 1976. *A Mathematical Theory of Evidence*. Princeton University Press.

Fairness, Accountability and Transparency in Artificial Intelligence: A Case Study of Logical Predictive Models

Kacper Sokol
K.Sokol@bristol.ac.uk
Department of Computer Science, University of Bristol
Bristol, United Kingdom

ABSTRACT

Machine learning – the part of artificial intelligence aimed at eliciting knowledge from data and automated decision making without explicit instructions – is making great strides, with new algorithms being invented every day. These algorithms find myriads of applications, but their ubiquity often comes at the expense of limited interpretability, hidden biases and unexpected vulnerabilities. Whenever one of these factors is a priority, the learning algorithm of choice is often a method considered to be inherently interpretable, e.g. logical models such as decision trees. In my research I challenge this assumption and highlight (quite common) cases when the assumed interpretability fails to deliver. To restore interpretability of logical machine learning models (decision trees and their ensembles in particular) I propose to explain them with class-contrastive counterfactual statements, which are a very common type of explanation in human interactions, well-grounded in social science research. To evaluate transparency of such models I collate explainability desiderata that can be used to systematically assess and compare such methods as an addition to user studies. Given contrastive explanations, I investigate their influence on the model's security, in particular gaming and stealing the model. Finally, I evaluate model fairness, where I am interested in choosing the most fair model among all the models with equal performance.

CCS CONCEPTS

• **General and reference** → **General literature**; • **Theory of computation** → Machine learning theory; • **Computing methodologies** → Supervised learning.

KEYWORDS

fairness, accountability, transparency, logical models

ACM Reference Format:
Kacper Sokol. 2019. Fairness, Accountability and Transparency in Artificial Intelligence: A Case Study of Logical Predictive Models. In *2019 AAAI/ACM Conference on AI, Ethics, and Society (AIES '19), January 27–28, 2019, Honolulu, HI, USA.* ACM, New York, NY, USA, 2 pages. https://doi.org/10.1145/3306618.3314316

ACM ISBN 978-1-4503-6324-2/19/01.
https://doi.org/10.1145/3306618.3314316

1 SOCIAL ARTIFICIAL INTELLIGENCE

Whether driven by a curiosity or legal requirements, explaining artificial intelligence (AI) systems – with a particular focus on predictive modelling – is an important first step to democratise the power of automated decision making. Therefore, in my research I focus on interpreting and explaining predictions of logical predictive models, decision trees in particular, given their simplicity, predictive power and popularity in real-life applications. This is a very interesting research problem since these models are often considered inherently interpretable. I challenge this assumption by arguing that simply being able to inspect a series of logical conditions leading to a particular decision is not enough to endorse its interpretability – e.g. the difficulty of attributing the result to a subset of these conditions – and logical reasoning is required on top of that to foster understanding. Consider a decision tree trained on large quantities of data with weak regularisation leading to good predictive performance at the expense of the tree being wide and deep. Hence any explanation native to the structure of the model is a long conjunction of logical conditions applied to the data features, which may be hard to interpret even for domain experts.

2 RESEARCH QUESTIONS

In my research, I develop approaches to explain such automated decisions in a sparse, interactive and sound way, suitable for both domain experts and a lay audience. To this end, I use class-contrastive counterfactual statements that usually conform to the following template:

> "The prediction is <prediction>. Had a small subset of features been different <foil>, the prediction would have been <counterfactual prediction> instead."

Despite them being a novelty in interpretable AI, counterfactual explanations are well grounded in social sciences, where they have been researched for decades – see a review by Miller et al. [4]. These studies have shown that they are very common in the process of human explanation, hence they are a good candidate for explaining automated decisions since they feel natural for human explainees. Moreover, counterfactual explanations have been deemed to satisfy the legal requirements of automated decisions explainability imposed in May 2018 by the General Data Protection Regulation[1] (GDPR) in the European Union [7].

Explanations of predictive systems are notoriously difficult to evaluate given their social nature. Doshi-Velez and Kim [1] have reviewed approaches to evaluating them with user studies, however there are many aspects of explanations that user studies cannot

[1] https://publications.europa.eu/s/inbX.

capture unless explicitly addressed. This includes *usability requirements* of an explanation such as its soundness, completeness and chronology, to name a few. *Functional aspects* (e.g. the problem supervision level, computational complexity of the explanation or applicable model class), *operational aspects* (used explanatory medium, system interaction model or explanation target audience) and *safety requirements* (information leakage, explanation misuse or explanation robustness) of an explanation are other important aspects ignored by user studies that should always be considered but rarely ever are. One reason behind this under-specification of explainable methods may be a lack of a coherent list of explainability desiderata for AI systems [2]. This observation has led me to review relevant computer science and social sciences literature on explanations and build a comprehensive list of desiderata for explainable systems spanning all these dimensions.

Functional and operational aspects of an explanation can be assessed analytically, but its accountability (security, privacy and robustness) requires a designated suite of tests. This is especially important for logical models as they use precise splits on data features in their decision boundaries that can be easily revealed with counterfactual explanations. Therefore, I want to investigate the extent of this phenomenon and techniques to mitigate compromising the accountability of predictive models when explaining them. In particular, I will investigate the lower bound on the number of explanations that allow stealing a model and techniques to prevent such malicious practices by providing fuzzy thresholds or replacing them with quantitative adjectives.

Fairness is another important social aspect of predictive modelling, as biases in data can be easily transferred to a predictive model during its training phase. A wealth of literature tackles fairness from disparate treatment and disparate impact perspectives [8]; however, to the best of my knowledge, there is no work that targets fairness of the model selection process itself. Given the stochastic nature of predictive modelling, it is usually possible to train multiple models with a similar overall predictive performance with predictions differing only for a small subset of the data set – predictive trade-offs between a number of individuals. I would like to investigate this phenomenon for logical predictive models to come up with "fairness bounds" for each individual in a data set with respect to a group of models with the same or comparable predictive performance for the whole population. Such an approach can be understood as applying the "presumption of innocence" rule for AI systems as the objective is to find the most beneficial model, hence prediction, for an individual without jeopardising the population-wise performance.

3 WORK PROGRESS

To date, I have designed an approach to explain decision trees with counterfactual statements. I have implemented this approach and used it as a part of an interactive system that can explain classification outcomes of a decision tree model via a dialogue with a user (both text-based chat and voice-enabled conversation). Furthermore, I have collated explainable systems desiderata and used them to compare and contrast my method against theoretical capabilities of contrastive explanations [3] and their various algorithmic implementations [6, 7]. This allowed me to show that my method is better in preserving theoretical properties of counterfactual explanations – an advantage of a model-specific approach – whereas others lose many of them.

My next step is to carry out user studies to demonstrate the advantages of my method over the interpretability of logical models (conjunctions of logical conditions extracted from the model) and model-agnostic approaches such as LIME [5]. I will also generalise my approach to other logical models, e.g. rule lists and sets, and their ensembles, e.g. random forests. The latter objective poses an interesting challenge of utilising the power of counterfactuals for each decision tree in an ensemble in order to create a smarter than majority count voting strategy. I will conclude my research in this area by publishing an open source implementation of my method to democratise interpretability of logical models. The next stage of my research will be to consider the safety and security of a predictive model and its training data given all the information that is revealed by counterfactual explanations. In particular, I will seek to determine the difficulty of reverse-engineering the decision boundaries and training data with a bounded number of explanations (which should be feasible given theoretical guarantees of my approach) and how to mitigate these threats. Finally, I will investigate proposed earlier "fairness bounds" for individual data points given a set of logical models with a fixed performance for the whole population.

REFERENCES

[1] Finale Doshi-Velez and Been Kim. 2018. Considerations for evaluation and generalization in interpretable machine learning. In *Explainable and Interpretable Models in Computer Vision and Machine Learning*. Springer, Gewerbestrasse 11, 6330 Cham, Switzerland, 3–17.

[2] Todd Kulesza, Margaret Burnett, Weng-Keen Wong, and Simone Stumpf. 2015. Principles of explanatory debugging to personalize interactive machine learning. In *Proceedings of the 20th International Conference on Intelligent User Interfaces*. ACM, ACM, New York, NY, USA, 126–137.

[3] Tim Miller. 2019. Explanation in artificial intelligence: Insights from the social sciences. *Artificial Intelligence* 267 (2019), 1–38. https://doi.org/10.1016/j.artint.2018.07.007

[4] Tim Miller, Piers Howe, and Liz Sonenberg. 2017. Explainable AI: Beware of Inmates Running the Asylum. In *IJCAI-17 Workshop on Explainable AI (XAI)*. 36.

[5] Marco Tulio Ribeiro, Sameer Singh, and Carlos Guestrin. 2016. Why should i trust you?: Explaining the predictions of any classifier. In *Proceedings of the 22nd ACM SIGKDD International Conference on Knowledge Discovery and Data Mining*. ACM, ACM, New York, NY, USA, 1135–1144.

[6] Gabriele Tolomei, Fabrizio Silvestri, Andrew Haines, and Mounia Lalmas. 2017. Interpretable Predictions of Tree-based Ensembles via Actionable Feature Tweaking. In *Proceedings of the 23rd ACM SIGKDD International Conference on Knowledge Discovery and Data Mining*. ACM, ACM, New York, NY, USA, 465–474.

[7] Sandra Wachter, Brent Mittelstadt, and Chris Russell. 2018. Counterfactual Explanations without Opening the Black Box: Automated Decisions and the GDPR. *Harvard Journal of Law & Technology* 31, 2 (2018), 841–887.

[8] Muhammad Bilal Zafar, Isabel Valera, Manuel Gomez Rodriguez, and Krishna P Gummadi. 2017. Fairness beyond disparate treatment & disparate impact: Learning classification without disparate mistreatment. In *Proceedings of the 26th International Conference on World Wide Web*. International World Wide Web Conferences Steering Committee, International World Wide Web Conferences Steering Committee, Republic and Canton of Geneva, Switzerland, 1171–1180.

Enabling Effective Transparency

Towards User-Centric Intelligent Systems

Aaron Springer
Computer Science
University of California Santa Cruz
Santa Cruz, CA, USA
alspring@ucsc.edu

ABSTRACT

Much of the current research in transparency and explainability is highly technical and focuses on how to derive explanations from models and algorithms. Less thought is being given to how users actually want to receive transparency and explanations from intelligent systems. My work tackles transparency and explainability from a user-centric perspective. I examine *why* transparency is desirable by showing that users may be susceptible to deception from intelligent systems. I demonstrate *when* users want transparency. Finally, my work begins to uncover *how* users want transparency conveyed. This body of work intends to create a path for designing transparency that puts user needs first rather than creating transparency as a convenient afterthought of model selection.

KEYWORDS

Transparency; Intelligibility; Intelligent Systems; Machine Learning; Mood; Explainability; Error; Progressive Disclosure.

ACM Reference format:

Aaron Springer. 2019. Enabling Effective Transparency: Towards User-Centric Intelligent Systems. In *Proceedings of the 2018 AAAI/ACM Conference on AI, Ethics, and Society (AIES 2019). ACM, New York, NY, USA, 3 pages.* https://doi.org/10.1145/3306618.3314317

1 Extended Abstract

Machine learning algorithms power intelligent systems that pervade our everyday lives. These systems make decisions ranging from the mundane to the magnificent, from routes to work to recommendations about criminal recidivism. As humans with limited time and energy, we delegate extensive responsibility to these systems with little transparency or oversight. However, intelligent systems face mounting concerns about how they make decisions; this is only exacerbated by recent machine learning advances like deep learning that are difficult to explain in human-comprehensible terms. Opaque intelligent systems took blame for major events such as disadvantaging minority prisoners that are up for parole [2]. These intelligent systems help make life-changing decisions; therefore, it is essential that we create systems that are able to be trusted and understood.

One route to creating intelligent systems that we trust and understand is through transparency. Greater transparency potentially increases end user control and improves acceptance of complex algorithmic systems [9]. It can also promote user learning and insight from complex data, as humans increasingly work with complex inferential systems for analytic purposes [12]. Transparency can also enable oversight by system designers. Without such transparency it may be unclear whether an algorithm is optimizing the intended behavior [6], or whether an algorithm accidentally promotes negative, unintended consequences such filter bubbles in social media or algorithmic bias in interfaces [3,13]. These issues have led researchers to argue that machine learning must be 'interpretable by design' [1] and that transparency is essential for the adoption of intelligent systems. [5,18].

While such calls for transparency are well-motivated, it remains unclear exactly how to enact them in practice. Extensive research about operationalizing transparency has emerged in the machine learning community but no clear consensus has resulted [1,4,17]. Deciding exactly how to implement transparency is difficult—there are implementation trade-offs involving accuracy and fidelity. Making a complex algorithm understandable to end users might require simplification, which comes at the cost of reduced accuracy of explanation [10]. These studies approach transparency from a technical perspective: "what is possible from an algorithmic standpoint?" rather than "what does the user need?"

My work intends to address this gap between user needs and technical operationalizations of transparency. I will outline three studies I have completed that demonstrate *why* transparency is needed, *when* transparency is needed, and *how* transparency should be shown to users.

One of my first experiments illustrates *why* transparency is needed. These experiments used an intelligent system that I

AIES '19, January 27–28, 2019, Honolulu, HI, USA

ACM ISBN 978-1-4503-6324-2/19/01.
https://doi.org/10.1145/3306618.3314317

created, a diary application called the E-meter. Users write about emotional experiences within the E-meter. While the user is writing, the E-meter provides real-time feedback to users about the mood of their writing. These mood ratings are predicted from machine learning models trained on text produced within a longitudinal mood diary app called EmotiCal [7]. One experiment indicated that users found the E-meter accurate even when we replaced the machine learning predictions with random predictions [14]. My findings indicate that users experience cognitive biases that lead to algorithmic authority—the idea that many people will trust that an algorithm is always correct. This algorithmic authority has alarming consequences when applied to high stakes domains like educational learning analytics. My contributions demonstrate that opaque intelligent systems are dangerous because users may not be able to accurately evaluate them. This finding demonstrated the clear need for transparency to enable understanding and trust in users of intelligent systems.

My next contribution focused on *when* transparency is needed in intelligent systems. In order to make sure users understand how these algorithms were making predictions, I created systems that included transparent machine learning. In our context, the aforementioned E-meter system made predictions about a user's mood from diary-style text they had written. In order to make this transparent, I highlighted the words and phrases with a spectrum of red to green, indicating whether these words contributed towards a positive or negative mood direction. This experiment unified prior contradictory results in the field. Some results indicated that transparency led to users viewing systems as less accurate or trustworthy [11]; other results indicated that transparency increased user perceptions of accuracy and trust [8]. My experiment showed that these are both true but that they are moderated by an important concept known as *expectation violation*. Expectation violation is the difference in what a user thinks is the correct prediction and what a system actually predicts. Transparent systems could be more effective if the intelligent system could recognize when a user needed it, for example detecting when a user's expectations were violated [15].

A third series of experiments began to elucidate *how* users want transparency to be conveyed. Again, we presented users with 2 versions of the E-meter system, a transparent and non-transparent version. This time, the study was conducted within-subjects—all participants used both versions of the system. We found that users were split on their preferences between the transparent and non-transparent versions of the E-meter. As anticipated, participants who preferred the transparent version valued the increased system understanding that transparency afforded. But two different reasons led to users preferring the document-level version: users attributed more sophisticated abilities to the non-transparent system and felt distracted by transparency [16]. Follow-up interviews with E-meter users indicated *how* users want to receive transparency. Transparency should be conveyed through an interaction paradigm known as *progressive disclosure:* advanced information and explanation is provided on an 'as needed' basis but only when the user requests it. Additionally, our operationalization of progressive disclosure involves allowing the user to repeatedly interact with the transparency, drilling down into more details when they have more questions.

Overall, my work indicates that transparency is a complex beast. I demonstrate *why* we need transparency—opaque intelligent systems can readily deceive people. I show *when* transparency is necessary—when users expectations of system behavior are violated. I finally provide some clues to *how* users want transparency—transparency should be disclosed progressively, similar to how conversational explanations happen.

REFERENCES

[1] Ashraf Abdul, Jo Vermeulen, Danding Wang, Brian Y. Lim, and Mohan Kankanhalli. 2018. Trends and Trajectories for Explainable, Accountable and Intelligible Systems: An HCI Research Agenda. In *Proceedings of the 2018 CHI Conference on Human Factors in Computing Systems - CHI '18*, 1–18. https://doi.org/10.1145/3173574.3174156

[2] Julia Angwin and Jeff Larson. 2016. Machine Bias. *ProPublica*. Retrieved October 27, 2017 from https://www.propublica.org/article/machine-bias-risk-assessments-in-criminal-sentencing

[3] Engin Bozdag. 2013. Bias in algorithmic filtering and personalization. *Ethics and Information Technology* 15, 3: 209–227. https://doi.org/10.1007/s10676-013-9321-6

[4] Malin Eiband, Hanna Schneider, Mark Bilandzic, Julian Fazekas-Con, Mareike Haug, and Heinrich Hussmann. 2018. Bringing Transparency Design into Practice. In *23rd International Conference on Intelligent User Interfaces* (IUI '18), 211–223. https://doi.org/10.1145/3172944.3172961

[5] Chloe Gui and Victoria Chan. 2017. Machine learning in medicine. *University of Western Ontario Medical Journal* 86, 2: 76–78. https://doi.org/10.5206/uwomj.v86i2.2060

[6] Moritz Hardt, Eric Price, and Nathan Srebro. 2016. Equality of Opportunity in Supervised Learning. *arXiv:1610.02413 [cs]*. Retrieved from http://arxiv.org/abs/1610.02413

[7] Victoria Hollis, Artie Konrad, Aaron Springer, Chris Antoun, Matthew Antoun, Rob Martin, and Steve Whittaker. 2017. What Does All This Data Mean for My Future Mood? Actionable Analytics and Targeted Reflection for Emotional Well-Being. *Human–Computer Interaction*. https://doi.org/10.1080/07370024.2016.1277724

[8] René F. Kizilcec. 2016. How Much Information?: Effects of Transparency on Trust in an Algorithmic Interface. 2390–2395. https://doi.org/10.1145/2858036.2858402

[9] Todd Kulesza, Margaret Burnett, Weng-Keen Wong, and Simone Stumpf. 2015. Principles of Explanatory Debugging to Personalize Interactive Machine Learning. In *Proceedings of the 20th International Conference on Intelligent User Interfaces - IUI '15*, 126–137. https://doi.org/10.1145/2678025.2701399

[10] Himabindu Lakkaraju, Ece Kamar, Rich Caruana, and Jure Leskovec. 2017. Interpretable & Explorable Approximations of Black Box Models. *arXiv:1707.01154 [cs]*. Retrieved September 18, 2018 from http://arxiv.org/abs/1707.01154

[11] Brian Y. Lim and Anind K. Dey. 2011. Investigating intelligibility for uncertain context-aware applications. In *Proceedings of the 13th international conference on Ubiquitous computing*, 415–424. Retrieved April 24, 2017 from http://dl.acm.org/citation.cfm?id=2030168

[12] Marco Tulio Ribeiro, Sameer Singh, and Carlos Guestrin. 2016. "Why Should I Trust You?": Explaining the Predictions of Any Classifier. In *Proceedings of the 22Nd ACM SIGKDD International Conference on Knowledge Discovery and Data Mining*, 1135–1144. https://doi.org/10.1145/2939672.2939778

[13] Aaron Springer and Henriette Cramer. 2018. "Play PRBLMS": Identifying and Correcting Less Accessible Content in Voice Interfaces. In *Proceedings of the 2018 CHI Conference on Human Factors in Computing Systems* (CHI '18), 296:1–296:13. https://doi.org/10.1145/3173574.3173870

[14] Aaron Springer, Victoria Hollis, and Steve Whittaker. 2017. Dice in the Black Box: User Experiences with an Inscrutable Algorithm. Retrieved April 24, 2017 from https://aaai.org/ocs/index.php/SSS/SSS17/paper/view/15372

[15] Aaron Springer and Steve Whittaker. 2018. What are You Hiding? Algorithmic Transparency and User Perceptions. In *2018 AAAI Spring Symposium Series*.

[16] Aaron Springer and Steve Whittaker. 2019. Progressive Disclosure: Designing for Effective Transparency. In *Proceedings of the 24th International Conference on Intelligent User Interfaces - IUI '19*.

[17] Daniel S. Weld and Gagan Bansal. 2018. The Challenge of Crafting Intelligible Intelligence. *arXiv:1803.04263 [cs]*. Retrieved September 19, 2018 from http://arxiv.org/abs/1803.04263

[18] Jenna Wiens and Erica S. Shenoy. 2018. Machine Learning for Healthcare: On the Verge of a Major Shift in Healthcare Epidemiology. *Clinical Infectious Diseases* 66, 1: 149–153. https://doi.org/10.1093/cid/cix731

AIES 2019 Student Submission

Elija Perrier
elija.t.perrier@student.uts.edu.au
Centre for Quantum Software and Information, University of Technology, Sydney
Sydney, NSW, Australia

CCS CONCEPTS

• **Theory of computation → Complexity theory and logic;** • **Social and professional topics → Government technology policy.**

KEYWORDS

ethics, algorithms, computation, complexity, regulation

ACM Reference Format:
Elija Perrier. 2019. AIES 2019 Student Submission. In *AAAI/ACM Conference on AI, Ethics, and Society (AIES '19), January 27–28, 2019, Honolulu, HI, USA.* ACM, New York, NY, USA, 2 pages. https://doi.org/10.1145/3306618.3314318

1 INTRODUCTION

In this abstract, I intend to outline a number of concurrent multidisciplinary research programmes in which I am engaged. Firstly, I will briefly outline my current PhD research in quantum machine learning and its connections to philosophical and logical research, especially that informed by category theory. Secondly I will detail my research regarding the role of computational complexity in frameworks for ethical artificial intelligence and algorithmic governance, drawing upon cross-disciplinary application of my computational science, physical science, economic science and legal research backgrounds.

1.1 Quantum machine learning and ethics

I am currently undertaking a PhD in quantum machine learning (**QML**) which involves analysing means by which QML techniques, such as deep neural networks and others [2], may be used to elucidate features of more general topologically-characterised physical systems of interest, especially for use in fault-tolerant topological quantum computation (**TQC**) [5]. It also involves an exploration of how connections between QML, TQC and certain fields of quantum logic may be leveraged in order to develop algorithms for practical implementation of topological circuitry and how connections between the abstract theories behind QML, deep learning and topology may throw light on certain foundational issues in quantum computation.

On its face, the cross-disciplinary fields of quantum computation, machine learning and ethical and the philosophy of logic would seem distant in terms of the capacity of one field to inform thinking in another. Quantum computation and information science concern themselves with quantum phenomena at the quantum level [9], whereas ethics and logic, even metalogic, concern those most classical of phenomena, human thought and behaviour. Cross-fertilisation between the various sub-disciplines, it would seem, therefore, to be restricted to mere analogy at best. However, the types of questions that these respective fields enquire into do in fact have more in common than first appears due to the nexus formed between each through the lens of computational science in general [6], and computational complexity in particular.

Information (and computational) sciences have a long and rich history of cross-pollination within the physical sciences (as exemplified in quantum information science, for example) [1]. As computational technologies advance, computational science is becoming increasingly relevant to decisions within politics and ethics too as decision-making and methdological thinking about ethics becomes more possible in a computational context. In a sense, the ubiquity of computational technologies is transforming not only the epistemological framing of fields (traditionally thought-of as distinct or not amenable to information-theoretic persepectives), but also the ontological basis upon which these fields are premised. We see this in physics, for example, through the emergence of 'information as physical', the convergence of information-theoretic and statistical physical notions (such as via Shannon entropy [9]) and of course comptuational complexity considerations of physical processes. The epistemological and ontological march of computational science is being seen, perhaps more visibly (and publicly) due to advances in autonomous systems, gathered under the rubric of artificial intelligence. Thus it is incumbent, I believe, to more deeply engage with the ontologies of computer science for these play a significant part in the construction of subjectivity and identity on the one hand and representations of individuals and communities used in algorithmic means of governance on the other.

1.2 Computational complexity and algorithmic governance

The geopolitical impact of artificial intelligence (AI) technologies has focused attention on the disruptive impact of technology on traditional political order. Increasing connectivity due to economic growth and particularly communications technology and social media, along with rapid advancements in technological capacity and data/volume has given rise to multifaceted complexity challenges for algorithmic governance and ethical AI. While debate over the ethical regulation of AI gains traction, the role and impact of computational complexity in constraining both the types of ethical frameworks that would realistically be possible has been piecemeal at best. Computational complexity is a core consideration in computational sciences. Despite the ubiquity of computational solutions in the context of modern governance challenges,the way

AIES '19, January 27–28, 2019, Honolulu, HI, USA

ACM ISBN 978-1-4503-6324-2/19/01...$15.00
https://doi.org/10.1145/3306618.3314318

in which complexity will shape the types of solutions and policy prescriptions available for regulation of AI remains nascent.

Computational complexity considerations impact on these issues in a variety of way. Firstly, they intrude upon whether ethical propositions are indeed computable or decidable. Secondly, they impact whether an efficient (in a computational sense) algorithm exists for undertaking the ethical computation [4]. Thirdly, complexity considerations give rise to probabilistic determinations given the under-determination of ethical problems in which, for example, full knowledge of underlying probability distributions informing data selection may be unknown [8]. In many ways, the absence of an efficient algorithm for deciding specific ethical questions (including proof-checking) problematises a straightforward deterministic or idealised imposition of ethical constraints. In addition, ethical debates may often in cross-disciplinary literature be undertaken in a deterministic context as distinct from considering the role of uncertainty and probabilistic reasoning when making ethical decisions [8].

AI technologies work in tandem with advancement in other technological arenas, such as biomedical physics and engineering in ways that have profound moral consequences precisely because through these technologies human society is obtaining more control over physical phenomena. And where phenomena that were undecidable or uncontrollable become so, they become moral choices. Thus we are seeing a twin set of imperatives: (a) the frontiers of decidability, and thus what is morally up for grabs, are expanding rapidly; and (b) the capacity for decision-making or reasoning about decisions it accelerating due to advances in autonomous decision-making technology. It is the reaction towards these two imperatives, especially ethical AI and algorithmic governance, that I am interested in.

For example, one consideration from an ethical and computational complexity standpoint to be explored in my research concerns what might be analogously described as completeness and consistency results: to what extent is consistency possible or even desirable in algorithmic governance and ethical AI frameworks, for example? Would what passes for an ethical society itself be possible *without* some degree of vagueness, under-determination or even inconsistency in the application of ethical governance? These are important questions because often debates around governance inhere some implicit sense of uniform application of standards or consistency of approach, understandable because underlying the principle of governance and the rule of law is a concept of consistency in many respects. Yes as evident both from the study of ethics but also recent fair machine learning literature, it is not possible to achieve decision-procedures that are fully consistent with all ethical criteria [3, 4]. In this respect, my work draws upon cross-disciplinary considerations from both computational science and jurisprudence.

I am interested in this research also because I see computational complexity as critical to core real-world ethical issues: in the face of a deluge of information, expanding populations and connectivity, regulatory and governance systems will be (and in many respects already are) facing a fundamental challenge of complexity: the systems, social or otherwise, they seek to regulate are so complex that traditional methods of governance, 'top down' approaches such as the imposition of sweeping homogeneous standards, may be unable and therefore unsuitable to regulating such complex social systems. In one sense we can draw analogy from economics analysis of pricing and information in the face of complexity, such as the computational complexity of market efficiency [7] or other attempts at ethical resource distribution. It may be not only that prices can never be efficiently set by a central decision-maker because of the sheer complexity of the decision-making necessary, but that similarly ethical consistency faces similar complexity constraints. These, I believe, are important issues that need to be addressed in the ongoing debate around ethical AI.

Going forward, over the next year I intend to build upon my recent research (an AIES submission on why computational complexity matters for algorithmic governance) which assesses literature on fair machine learning in order to explore the consequences of computational complexity upon debates around ethical AI. It explores that assessment of the impact of complexity is crucial to a proper framing of algorithmic governance, particularly regarding how governance methodologies will likely rely upon heuristic considerations in many domains.

REFERENCES

[1] Scott Aaronson. 2011. Why Philosophers Should Care About Computational Complexity. *arXiv:1108.1791 [quant-ph]* (Aug 2011). http://arxiv.org/abs/1108.1791 arXiv: 1108.1791.

[2] Vedran Dunjko and Hans J. Briegel. 2017. Machine learning & artificial intelligence in the quantum domain. *arXiv:1709.02779 [quant-ph]* (Sep 2017). http://arxiv.org/abs/1709.02779 arXiv: 1709.02779.

[3] Ursula Hebert-Johnson, Michael P. Kim, Omer Reingold, and Guy N. Rothblum. 2017. Calibration for the (Computationally-Identifiable) Masses. *arXiv:1711.08513 [cs, stat]* (Nov 2017). http://arxiv.org/abs/1711.08513 arXiv: 1711.08513.

[4] Michael Kearns, Seth Neel, Aaron Roth, and Zhiwei Steven Wu. 2017. Preventing Fairness Gerrymandering: Auditing and Learning for Subgroup Fairness. (Nov 2017). https://arxiv.org/abs/1711.05144

[5] A. Yu Kitaev. 2001. Unpaired Majorana fermions in quantum wires. *Physics-Uspekhi* 44, 10S (2001), 131. https://doi.org/10.1070/1063-7869/44/10S/S29

[6] J.M. Kizza. 2017. *Ethical and Social Issues in the Information Age.* Springer International Publishing. https://books.google.com.au/books?id=qlxCDwAAQBAJ

[7] Philip Maymin. 2010. Markets are efficient if and only if P = NP. *arXiv:1002.2284 [cs, q-fin]* (Feb 2010). http://arxiv.org/abs/1002.2284 arXiv: 1002.2284.

[8] David McCarthy. 2016. Probability in Ethics. *The Oxford Handbook of Probability and Philosophy* (Sep 2016). https://doi.org/10.1093/oxfordhb/9780199607617.013.36

[9] M.A. Nielsen and I.L. Chuang. 2000. *Quantum Computation and Quantum Information.* Cambridge University Press. https://books.google.com.au/books?id=65FqEKQOfP8C

Towards Emotional Intelligence in Social Robots Designed for Children

De'Aira Bryant
dbryant@gatech.edu
Georgia Institute of Technology
Atlanta, Georgia, USA

ABSTRACT

Social robots are robots designed to interact and communicate directly with humans, following traditional social norms. However, many of these current robots operate in discrete settings with predefined expectations for specific social interactions. In order for these machines to operate in the real world, they must be capable of understanding the multiple factors that contribute to human-human interaction. One such factor is emotional intelligence. Emotional intelligence allows one to consider the emotional state of another in order to motivate, plan, and achieve one's desires. One common method of analyzing the emotional state of an individual involves analyzing the emotion displayed on their face. Several artificial intelligence (AI) systems have been developed to conduct this task. These systems are often classifiers trained using a variety of machine learning techniques which require large amounts of training data. As such, they are susceptible to biases that may appear during performance analyses due to disproportions existing in training datasets. Children, in particular, are often less represented in the primary datasets of annotated faces used for training such emotion classification systems. This work seeks to first analyze the extent of these performance differences in commercial systems, then to present new computational techniques that work to mitigate some of the effects of minimal representation in datasets, and to finally present a social robot which utilizes an improved emotional AI to interact with children in various scenarios where emotional intelligence is key to successful human-robot interaction.

ACM Reference Format:
De'Aira Bryant. 2019. Towards Emotional Intelligence in Social Robots Designed for Children. In *AAAI/ACM Conference on AI, Ethics, and Society (AIES '19), January 27–28, 2019, Honolulu, HI, USA.* ACM, New York, NY, USA, 2 pages. https://doi.org/10.1145/3306618.3314319

1 ANALYZING EMOTION RECOGNITION SOFTWARE

Emotion classification as discerned from facial configurations is a popular method used to provide emotional intelligence to a variety of smart AI systems. With the intent of utilizing this technology in use cases involving children, my initial desire was to find a pre-existing software that would serve this purpose. I found that several commercial systems were available for integration into other smart systems. With so many options available, I sought to evaluate the performance of these commercial emotion recognition systems on my target demographic. I utilized a total of five datasets that comprised over 3,000 images of annotated children faces to assess the performance of each of the recognition systems. I stored the ground truth labels of the images, processed each of the images from each of the datasets through each of the emotion recognition systems, normalize the results for an equal comparison, determined the emotion label with the highest confidence value through a maximization function, and finally compared the system-produced predicted label to the ground truth labels to store the results. Each system was assessed in terms of matching score (true positive rate), positive-predictive value, and failure to compute (FTC) rate.

This analysis revealed that these systems performed worse when labeling the images of children faces when compared to human ratings on the same images. Additionally, when compared to similar analyses conducted with adult datasets, these ratings were also lower. This analysis gave evidence that these commercial systems are premature in their use for children.

Yet, there is evidence of such commercial systems being used in schools to target issues surrounding the security and surveillance of students (Vanderklippe 2018). I discuss these results, their implications, and potential solutions in a paper submitted to the AIES 2019 main conference. Additional analysis of the data has also revealed differences in recognition when assessing the children's facial images by gender and ethnicity. These differences are consistent with other results found in similar studies examining the performance of AI systems on groups that are often less represented in datasets (Buolamwini and Gebru 2018).

2 IMPROVING PERFORMANCE FOR CHILDREN

The AIES 2019 submission also introduces a method for assigning a diversity rating to each image dataset based on the variety of images within the dataset. This rating considers participant age, gender, ethnicity, gaze directions, geographic region(s) of collection, clothing, pose, and number of discrete emotion classes. The rating can be extended to apply a diversity rating to each individual image. These ratings can then be used as weights when training a machine learning classifier. The weights will allow the learner to place higher value on images that have higher diversity ratings, as they are rarer to find in large datasets. My current work involves utilizing this technique to assess whether the weighting of training images can better the overall performance of a machine learning classifier. The images used for training will be the same images used to analyze the commercial systems in my initial work. As these images are comprised of entirely children faces, I hypothesize that

AIES '19, January 27–28, 2019, Honolulu, HI, USA

ACM ISBN 978-1-4503-6324-2/19/01.
https://doi.org/10.1145/3306618.3314319

a learned classifier using these images will outperform the commercial systems from the initial comparative work on new children's faces.

By training multiple classifiers with different weights on diversity attributes, several analyses can be made to determine the reliance of overall performance on dataset compilation. This work will shed further light on the impact that low or nonexistent representation of a particular group within a training set may have on the performance of a classifier. I hypothesize that a more balanced dataset in terms of diversity will yield more consistent performance across the board for subgroups of the overall population. The next phase of this overall work will seek to implement this technique on several embodied platforms that will interact with a diverse set of children in terms of gender, ethnicity, and ability.

3 PREVIOUS HRI STUDIES USING SOCIAL ROBOTS

In prior work, a social robot is used to interact with adults and children in a rehabilitative game by providing encouraging and corrective feedback. The system targets upper extremity function by having users pop virtual bubbles (Xu, Bryant and Howard 2018). A 3D model for movement time is used to calculate the target movement time for each respective user in a phase used for calibration. This system also utilizes a script for the robot to interact with the user. The feedback is generated within the gaming system and then sent to the robot via TCP connection. As such, in these prior studies, the robot did not take in any input from the direct interaction with the user.

We also evaluate this system in terms of user trust, another key component in social interaction (Xu, Bryant and Howard 2018). Survey results indicate trust in a therapy intervention coupled with a robotic agent is comparable to that of trust in an intervention coupled with a human agent.

The AI developed throughout this work has the goal of being implemented onto an embodied robotic platform that will interact directly with humans. As such, the chosen robotic embodiment may also impact the overall experience for a user of the technology. One potential factor that I also investigated is the impact that robot "skin" color could have on the human perception of robotic emotional expression. In this HRI study presented at the 2018 FAT-ML conference, the Darwin mini robot expresses several emotions as participants are instructed to classify the emotion and its perceived intensity (Ogunyale, Bryant and Howard 2018). By eliminating stereotype priming from the methodology, we found no substantial differences in the perception of the robot's expressions of happy and angry on black and white robots. Current work consists of using a variety of robot "skin" colors on several robotic embodiments to determine if this result remains consistent.

4 EMOTIONALLY INTELLIGENT SOCIAL ROBOTS

The additional user responses from these collective HRI works suggested a need for a more interactive experience for the users. In future work, the emotionally intelligent AI system described to improve performance for children will be integrated onto a variety of robotic embodiments (NAO, Cozmo, and Pepper). User studies will be conducted to better analyze the performance of the integrated emotional intelligence when compared to a scripted robot interaction, a human interaction, and a control no-robot interaction. These various conditions will validate the use of diversity weighting as a method to improve performance for applications designed specifically for special subsets of the population. Overall, this work will contribute novel approaches to child-robot interaction through emotionally intelligent AI integrations.

REFERENCES

[1] Buolamwini, J., & Gebru, T. 2018. Gender shades: Intersectional accuracy disparities in commercial gender classification. In Conference on Fairness, Accountability and Transparency.

[2] Ogunyale, T., Bryant, D., & Howard, A. 2018. Does Removing Stereotype Priming Remove Bias? A Pilot Human-Robot Interaction Study. In Proceedings of the 2018 International Workshop on Fairness, Accountability, and Transparency in Machine Learning (FAT-ML).

[3] Vanderklippe, N. 2018. In China, Classroom Cameras Scan Stu-dents Faces for Emotion, Stroking Fears of New Form of State Monitoring. https://www.theglobeandmail.com/world/article-in-china-classroom-cameras-scan-student-faces-for-emotion-stoking/.

[4] Xu, J., Bryant, D., & Howard, A. 2018. Would You Trust a Robot Therapist? Validating the Equivalency of Trust in Human-Robot Healthcare Scenarios. In The 27th IEEE International Symposium On Robot And Human Interactive Communication (Ro-Man).

[5] Xu, J., Bryant, D., Chen, Y. P., & Howard, A. 2018. Robot therapist versus human therapist: Evaluating the effect of corrective feedback on human motor performance. In Proceedings of the 2018 IEEE International Symposium on Medical Robotics (ISMR). pp. 1-6.

A Framework for Technically- and Morally-Sound AI

Duncan C McElfresh
University of Maryland, College Park
dmcelfre@math.umd.edu

ACM Reference Format:
Duncan C McElfresh. 2019. A Framework for Technically- and Morally-Sound AI. In *AAAI/ACM Conference on AI, Ethics, and Society (AIES '19), January 27–28, 2019, Honolulu, HI, USA.* ACM, New York, NY, USA, 2 pages. https://doi.org/10.1145/3306618.3314320

1 OVERVIEW

Artificial Intelligence (AI) ethics is by no means a new discipline; thinkers like Asimov and Philip K Dick laid the foundations of this field decades ago. Both then and today, popular dilemmas in AI ethics largely focus on artificial consciousness, artificial general intelligence, autonomous weapons, and some version of the trolley problem. While these thought experiments may prove useful in the future, modern AI applications that are *in use today* raise ethical dilemmas that require urgent resolution. Public outcry in response to AI in health care, criminal justice, and employment highlight the urgency of the matter. These real and imminent ethical challenges posed by AI form the basis of my dissertation research. In particular, I focus on domains where AI is *necessary* or *inevitable* – such as kidney exchange and medical image classification – and ethical challenges are unavoidable.

My main objective is to develop and implement a *method* for designing technically- and morally-sound AI applications. This approach is necessarily domain-specific: applications in medicine require very different considerations than those in employment. However, the *design process* for morally and technically sound AI is similar across domains; my dissertation research endeavors to formalize this design process in the general sense, and to then apply it to specific domains; I use a framework proposed by Li [1] as a guide and inspiration for this work. In Section 2 I adapt Li's framework to the AI design process; in Section 3 I briefly discuss how existing work on ethical AI fits into this framework; in Section 4 I discuss the next steps in my dissertation research.

2 FRAMEWORK FOR DESIGNING MORAL AI

In this section I introduce Li's framework for ethical design, abbreviated for ease of exposition. Suppose we are tasked with designing an AI application in a morally-consequential domain – such as predictive policing or kidney exchange. Designing this system requires experts from a variety of fields – including, but not limited to, computer science. For the purpose of this framework, we classify these experts into two broad categories: *technicians* and *stakeholders*.

AIES '19, January 27–28, 2019, Honolulu, HI, USA

ACM ISBN 978-1-4503-6324-2/19/01.
https://doi.org/10.1145/3306618.3314320

Technicians are experts in disciplines such as microeconomics, computer science, and statistics. They are not necessarily trained in medicine, ethics, or policy, making them not necessarily fit to (on their own) make the moral judgments involved in designing the system.
Stakeholders determine the final design of a system, and are often held accountable for their decisions–to a far higher degree than technicians. Stakeholders include medical professionals (who are accountable to their patients and the law), lawmakers (who are held accountable by the public), and ethicists (who are trained in these matters).

There are often very many ways to design an AI application; let $\mathcal{D}$ be a set of possible designs, where $d \in \mathcal{D}$ is a single design. In the example of predictive policing, $\mathcal{D}$ might include different machine learning algorithms, the magnitude of regularization, the interpretability of the algorithm, and so on.

Each design might have different *morally-relevant features*, specific to the domain; let $\mathcal{F}$ be the *space* of morally-relevant features, where $f \in \mathcal{F}$ is one instance of these features (i.e., due to a particular design). In the example of predictive policing, morally-relevant features might include the prediction accuracy for different subsets of race/ethnicity and gender. Different designs lead to different morally-relevant features, which we denote by the function $g : \mathcal{D} \to \mathcal{F}$. We refer to evaluations of g as *intermediate judgments*:

Definition 1 (Intermediate Judgment). An intermediate judgment $g(d) = f$ is a morally-relevant description of a design.

Intermediate judgments frame a system design in a moral context; they provide a medium for technical experts to communicate moral implications to stakeholders. However, technicians can't necessarily determine the normative value of a system and its implications (i.e. what should/not be) – these *normative judgments* are typically left to stakeholders. Let $\mathcal{J}$ be the space of normative judgments; stakeholders express normative judgments by evaluating instances of morally-relevant features, which we denote by the function $v : \mathcal{F} \to \mathcal{J}$.

Definition 2 (Normative Judgment). A normative judgment $v(f) = j$ is a statement expressing the normative value of a set of morally relevant features.

Normative judgments in a predictive policing domain might include statements like "false-negative rate should be minimized", or "race should not be considered by the prediction algorithm". Designing an AI system requires collaboration between technicians and stakeholders: computer scientists can't necessarily be expected to make sound normative judgments, just as stakeholders can't be necessarily expected to design algorithms. To ensure the design process is morally and technically sound, we define as division of labor using the framework introduced in this section.

Technician Responsibilities: Technicians characterize the set of possible designs $\mathcal{D}$ and make intermediate judgments of these designs (i.e. the function $g : \mathcal{D} \to \mathcal{F}$).
Stakeholder Responsibilities: Stakeholders define the set of morally relevant features for their domain $\mathcal{F}$, and make normative judgments about designs (i.e., the function $v : \mathcal{F} \to \mathcal{J}$).

The design process is both collaborative and iterative: first, stakeholders determine the set of morally relevant features $\mathcal{F}$. Then technicians explore the space of designs $\mathcal{D}$ and make intermediate judgments $g(d) = f$. Using these intermediate judgments, stakeholders can better determine a final system design.

3 PREVIOUS AND ONGOING WORK

The AI ethics literature is undergoing a renaissance, as evinced by new conferences such as AIES and FAT* (among others). This work plays a key role in the framework described in the previous section – it provides important *intermediate judgments* about existing machine learning and AI methods, illustrating the potential for bias and worst-case behavior. My prior work falls into this category. In [3] we explore methods of enforcing fairness in kidney exchange matching algorithms. Using theoretical analysis and computational simulations, we compare two fairness rules (weighted fairnes and lexicographic fairness) and describe their impact on fairness and overall efficiency. In [2] we address two types of uncertainty in kidney exchange, and propose a tractable approach to each.

Both of these papers exemplify the *technician*'s role in the design framework: we characterize various designs $d \in \mathcal{D}$ (i.e., kidney exchange matching algorithms), that consider fairness and uncertainty. We provide intermediate judgments on these designs, using (what we consider to be) morally-relevant features – such as the balance between fairness and efficiency, the robustness to uncertainty, and computational tractability. My current research further explores the design space $\mathcal{D}$, and in particular, dynamic matching algorithms.

Within Li's framework, we are playing the role of technician – characterizing $\mathcal{D}$ and g. However In the remainder of my dissertation research I aim to develop AI applications to improve the AI design process, and facilitate better communication between technicians and stakeholders.

4 FUTURE WORK

According to (my interpretation of) Li's framework, computer scientists have been faithfully carrying out the the role of technician. Papers published in AIES and FAT* (among others) characterize the design space and make intermediate judgments about AI systems in morally-consequential domains. That is, we are thoroughly exploring $\mathcal{D}$ and g. However in my reading of Li's framework, we are missing one key component – normative judgments from stakeholders (i.e., the function v). In the remainder of my dissertation research, I will develop methods of incorporating this feedback into the design process. Incorporating stakeholder feedback poses many challenges; here I describe two:
Learning $v(f)$ and $\mathcal{F}$: Our first challenge is to learn $v(f)$ and $\mathcal{F}$ from stakeholders – who are almost always human, and often provide noisy, inconsistent, and slow feedback. Furthermore, it is challenging to communicate technical matters (such as design parameters of an AI system) to non-technical stakeholders. To address these challenges, I am working with medical professionals and ethicists (in the kidney exchange domain), and with qualitative researchers and city officials (in the public resource allocation domain) to develop elicitation methods. Our approach is interdisciplinary, drawing on literature from social choice, preference elicitation, survey methodology, and descriptive ethics.
An Iterative Approach: In practice, $\mathcal{F}$, $\mathcal{D}$ are never known *exactly*, and often they must be explored incrementally. To illustrate, consider this example from kidney exchange:

- Stakeholders propose a set of morally-relevant features $\mathcal{F}$, consisting of a) the overall number of matched transplants, and b) the number of children matched; they make two normative judgments: "the number of transplants should be maximized", and "children should be prioritized over adults".
- Technicians identify two matching algorithms, d_1 (which maximizes transplants, and doesn't prioritize children) and d_2 (which prioritizes children, and doesn't maximize transplants). Furthermore, technicians note that both d_1 and d_2 don't match any patients with blood type O.

In this example neither d_1 nor d_2 is "optimal" according to the initial normative judgments; this requires further stakeholder feedback. Furthermore, stakeholders might want patients of *all* blood types receive transplants; in this case, $\mathcal{F}$ may need to be augmented to include (for example) the number of transplants to patients of each blood type.

I will formalize this iterative process as a sequential optimization problem. In particular, this will be an iterative search through both both design space $\mathcal{D}$ and the morally-relevant feature space $\mathcal{F}$, guided in each step by the intermediate and normative judgments.

REFERENCES

[1] Shengwu Li. Ethics and market design. In *Oxford Review of Economic Policy, forthcoming*, 2017.
[2] Duncan C. McElfresh and John P. Bidkhori, Hoda andDickerson. Scalable robust kidney exchange. *AAAI Conference on Artificial Intelligence (AAAI)*, 2019.
[3] Duncan C. McElfresh and John P. Dickerson. Balancing lexicographic fairness and a utilitarian objective with application to kidney exchange. *AAAI Conference on Artificial Intelligence (AAAI)*, 2018.

Towards Formal Models of Blameworthiness

Meir Friedenberg
Department of Computer Science
Cornell University
meir@cs.cornell.edu

ABSTRACT

As we move towards an era in which autonomous systems are ubiquitous, being able to reason formally about moral responsibility for outcomes will become more and more critical. My research has focused on formalizing notions of blameworthiness and responsibility. I summarize here some work by myself and others towards this end and also discuss interesting directions for future work.

CCS CONCEPTS

• **Applied computing** → **Law**; **Psychology**; • **Computing methodologies** → *Causal reasoning and diagnostics*; • **Computing methodologies** → *Multi-agent systems.*

KEYWORDS

blameworthiness; responsibility; AI in society

ACM Reference Format:
Meir Friedenberg. 2019. Towards Formal Models of Blameworthiness. In *AAAI/ACM Conference on AI, Ethics, and Society (AIES '19), January 27–28, 2019, Honolulu, HI, USA.* ACM, New York, NY, USA, 2 pages. https://doi.org/10.1145/3306618.3314321

1 INTRODUCTION

As we move towards an era in which autonomous systems are ubiquitous, being able to reason formally about moral responsibility for outcomes will become more and more critical. Unfortunately, though, pinning down any of the many notions relating to moral responsibility is notoriously difficult.

Halpern and Kleiman-Weiner [4] (HK from now on) developed a formalization of a notion they called blameworthiness that seems to capture one intuitive aspect of moral responsibility. But while the definition is compelling and behaves intuitively in many cases, there are certain important types of cases where the HK definition does not seem to adequately capture how we ascribe responsibility. In my research I've been working on developing conceptually similar approaches to blameworthiness and responsibility that work in more wide-ranging applicable scenarios.

In the following sections I first review the HK definition of blameworthiness, then summarize recent work with my advisor, Joe Halpern, extending it to multi-agent settings, and finally discuss some exciting work that we are starting to explore.

AIES '19, January 27–28, 2019, Honolulu, HI, USA

ACM ISBN 978-1-4503-6324-2/19/01.
https://doi.org/10.1145/3306618.3314321

2 HK BLAMEWORTHINESS

Roughly speaking, according to the HK definition, an agent is blameworthy for an outcome if there was some alternative course of action the agent could have taken that would have decreased the probability of the outcome occurring. But this doesn't tell the full story; after all, if someone could save a vase from breaking but only by giving up their own life, we would hardly consider that individual blameworthy for the vase breaking; the cost of saving it is too high. HK's definition of blameworthiness tries to balance this cost with the effect of choosing a different action.

Their definition is based on a causal models framework. For the sake of brevity, I include here only the most crucial components to understand the basics of their definition. We say that an agent's *epistemic state* consists of a set $\mathcal{K}$ of causal settings that describe ways the world might work and a distribution Pr over $\mathcal{K}$ that describes how likely each causal setting is to describe the world. We then write $Pr[\![[A = a]\varphi]\!]_{\mathcal{K}}$ for the probability, given that distribution over causal settings, that outcome φ will occur if the agent takes action a. We also define a function c such that $c(a)$ is the agent's expected cost of taking action a. Given an action a and an alternative action a', $\delta^{(Pr,\mathcal{K})}_{a,a',\varphi} = max(0, Pr[\![[A = a]\varphi]\!]_{\mathcal{K}} - Pr[\![[A = a']\varphi]\!]_{\mathcal{K}})$ captures the extent to which alternative action a' could have prevented outcome φ. HK then define the blameworthiness of an agent who takes action a for outcome φ as $\max_{a'} \delta^{(Pr,\mathcal{K})}_{a,a',\varphi} \frac{N - max(c(a') - c(a), 0)}{N}$, where N is a context-dependent parameter used to weight the cost term.

3 BLAMEWORTHINESS IN MULTI-AGENT SETTINGS

As HK already note, this definition of blameworthiness seems to provide unsatisfactory results in settings where multiple agents are involved. In particular, if each agent believes that the other agents will bring about φ independent of his or her action, then the HK framework will ascribe very little blameworthiness to each agent. In settings where the agents as a whole could have prevented outcome φ, though, this doesn't seem to be what we would want.

In work presented at AAAI this year, Joe Halpern and I proposed an approach to attributing blameworthiness to agents in multi-agent settings [2]. We did this in two steps: first we showed how to ascribe blameworthiness to groups, then we showed how to divide group blameworthiness among constituent members.

For the first part, to ascribe blameworthiness to groups, we argue that we need to consider possible ways the group could have coordinated. If the group could have easily coordinate to avoid outcome φ then we should consider them blameworthy for it occurring, but if it would have been essentially impossible for them to coordinate (e.g the group members have no means to communicate with each other) then they should have little blameworthiness. To model this, we associate with each possible way that the group can coordinate a distribution over how the agents will act, which in turn can be associated with a distribution over causal settings. Then by changing the cost function to give the expected cost of a group coordination and changing the δ term to be $max(0, Pr_1[\![\varphi]\!]_{\mathcal{K}} - Pr_2[\![\varphi]\!]_{\mathcal{K}})$ (considering two different possible distributions that could be induced by group coordination), we can update the definition above to capture the blameworthiness of groups.

Given a notion of group blameworthiness, we can address the next question: how can the blameworthiness of a group be apportioned among the individual agents in the group. To do this, we suggest three axioms that we believe apportionment of blame should satisfy:

- (Efficiency) The sum of the blameworthiness ascribed to the individual agents must exactly equal the blameworthiness of the entire group.
- (Symmetry) The names of agents should not affect their blameworthiness, so if we simply rename them then the blameworthiness ascribed to them should remain the same.
- (Strong Monotonicity) If an agent contributes more to the group blameworthiness of all groups in one scenario than another, then that agent also ought to have a greater degree of (personal) blameworthiness in the first scenario.

Young [5] showed that in fact the only distribution procedure that satisfies Efficiency, Symmetry, and Strong Monotonicity is the *Shapley value* from cooperative game theory. We thus have a technique for assigning a degree of blameworthiness for an outcome to individuals in group settings.

It's also worth noting that these two results are essentially separable: if an alternative definition of group blameworthiness is used, the Shapley value could be used to ascribe blameworthiness to individual agents as it would still be the unique procedure satisfying the desired axioms.

Finally, in settings where there is only one agent, if we assume (as HK implicitly did) that an agent can completely decide his or her own actions without the decision process itself incurring costs beyond the costs of the action, then the definition we provided in fact agrees with the HK definition.

4 FUTURE DIRECTIONS

There are many important directions to take this work on responsibility and blameworthiness. Here I summarize two that I'm excited to start exploring.

4.1 Norms & Responsibility

Consider a scenario where a police officer and a civilian are standing by passively while a crime is committed; it seems to us that people ascribe more blameworthiness to the police officer because there is an expectation that a police officer will act to prevent a crime. Similarly, consider a case where two individuals get into a car accident because driver A turned around to check on a child in the back seat and driver B decided to rush through the intersection to try to beat driver A. American tort law considers driver B to be more blameworthy due to a greater deviation from the legal norm (among other reasons in this scenario) [1]. The original HK definition and our extension to multi-agent settings do not take into account these norms and the extent to which an agent deviated from a norm. The examples above suggest that it will be important to understand the relation between norms and responsibility. To reason about responsibility in real-world scenarios it will be important to develop formal models for reasoning about blameworthiness when norms play a role. Normality has been added to the standard definition of causality in prior work [3], but combining it with blameworthiness seems subtle.

4.2 Behavioral Studies

A second line of work that I'm beginning to explore is trying to understand how humans really ascribe blameworthiness. How do costs of alternative actions actually affect how people ascribe blameworthiness? Are certain types of costs never considered? How does type vs. magnitude of cost play a role? To what extend does our formalization of Multi-Agent blameworthiness accord with human ascriptions? Do our axioms get obeyed? And how might autonomous systems be treated differently with regard to ascriptions of blameworthiness? I am beginning to design human behavioral experiments to explore these and other related questions.

5 CONCLUSION

HK and our AAAI-19 paper, combined with our work in progress on both norms and human studies, lays an important foundation on which to understand and model blameworthiness and responsibility. At the same time, there are still many questions beyond these that I think are important to explore in this domain. For example, how should we ascribe blameworthiness in settings where agents have plans and perform multiple actions in sequence rather than just taking a single action? How might the ways we ascribe responsibility affect and incentivize patterns of behavior?

I believe that being able to both prescriptively and descriptively understand ascription of responsibility and blameworthiness will be important in the coming years and that building models through which to reason about these issues will help give new insight into the beneficial adoption of autonomous systems in society.

ACKNOWLEDGMENTS

This work has been supported in part by NSF grants IIS-1703846 and IIS-1718108, ARO grant W911NF-17-1-0592, and a grant from the Open Philanthropy project.

REFERENCES

[1] American Law Institute. 2000. *Restatement of the Law Third, Torts, Apportionment of Liability*. American Law Institute Publishers.
[2] M. Friedenberg and J. Y. Halpern. 2019. Blameworthiness in Multi-Agent Settings. In *Proceedings of the Thirty-Third AAAI Conference on Artificial Intelligence (AAAI-19)*.
[3] J. Y. Halpern and C. Hitchcock. 2015. Graded causation and defaults. *British Journal for the Philosophy of Science* 66, 2 (2015), 413–457.
[4] J. Y. Halpern and M. Kleiman-Weiner. 2018. Towards Formal Definitions of Blameworthiness, Intention, and Moral Responsibility. In *Proceedings of the Thirty-Second AAAI Conference on Artificial Intelligence (AAAI-18)*. 1853–1860.
[5] H. P. Young. 1985. Monotonic solutions of cooperative games. *International Journal of Game Theory* 14, 2 (1985), 65–72.

Toward Design and Evaluation Framework for Interpretable Machine Learning Systems

Sina Mohseni
sina.mohseni@tamu.edu
Texas A&M University
College Station, Texas

ABSTRACT

The need for interpretable and accountable intelligent system gets sensible as artificial intelligence plays more role in human life. Explainable artificial intelligence systems can be a solution by self-explaining the reasoning behind the decisions and predictions of the intelligent system. My research supports the design and evaluation methods and interpretable machine learning systems and leverages knowledge and experience in the fields of machine learning, human-computer interactions, and data visualization. My research objectives are to present a design and evaluation framework for explainable artificial intelligence systems, propose new methods and metrics to better evaluate the benefits of transparent machine learning systems, and apply interpretability methods for model reliability verification.

KEYWORDS

interpretable machine learning; design and evaluation framework; user understanding; user trust

ACM Reference Format:
Sina Mohseni. 2019. Toward Design and Evaluation Framework for Interpretable Machine Learning Systems. In *2019 AAAI/ACM Conference on AI, Ethics, and Society (AIES'19), January 27–28, 2019, Honolulu, HI, USA.* ACM, New York, NY, USA, 2 pages. https://doi.org/10.1145/3306618.3314322

1 INTRODUCTION

Nowadays, algorithms analyze user data and affect the decision-making process for millions of people on matters like employment, insurance and loan rates, and even criminal justice. However, these algorithms that serve critical roles in many industries have their own biases that can result in discrimination and unfair decision-making. Explainable artificial intelligence (XAI) systems can be a solution to predictable and accountable AI by explaining AI decision-making processes for end users and therefore increase user awareness and prevent discrimination [1]. However, looking at the broad spectrum of research on XAI, it is clear that scholars from different disciplines have different goals in mind. The mismatch in objectives for the scholars to define, design, and evaluate the concept of XAI may slow down the overall advances of end-to-end XAI systems. The proposed research aims to converge knowledge behind design and evaluation of XAI systems between multiple disciplines to further support key benefits of algorithmic transparency by proposing design and evaluation framework aiming to systematize interpretable Human-AI designs.

Our research objective is to propose a comprehensive interpretable machine learning design and evaluation framework. Our framework will provide guidance for determining appropriate evaluation approaches for different design purposes. Our objective will be achieved by exploring the mapping between XAI design goals and measures across the fields of machine learning, visual analytics, and human-computer interaction (HCI). We will design new interpretability measures for our XAI evaluation framework, and we will verify the effectiveness of new measures in accordance with the improvement of our framework.

2 OVERVIEW OF PROPOSED RESEARCH

On going research on explainable machine learning focus on designing interpretability methods (e.g., mimic models and ad-hoc explainers), explainable interfaces (e.g., intelligent user interfaces and visual analytics tools), and study machine-generated explanations with end-users. However, although XAI is a multidisciplinary research, these reports barely connect to each other and address findings in other disciplines. There are knowledge gaps regarding the dependencies between various XAI designs across different disciplines. The proposed research is intended to share knowledge and experiences in design and evaluation methods of machine learning explanation across multiple disciplines. Our effort involves the following contributions:

- C1: Proposing a comprehensive XAI design and evaluation framework.
- C2: Designing new evaluation methods and metrics to enhance machine learning transparency, reliability, and safety evaluation.

C1 involves a deep review and analysis of literature in the fields of HCI, visual analytics and machine learning to organize current XAI evaluation measures and propose a design and evaluation framework for XAI systems. C2 will propose and implement new methods to improve the existing XAI evaluations and to take machine-generated explanations into action to estimating reliability and safety of intelligent systems.

3 RESEARCH PLAN

I summarize my research plan into three following research tasks by describing the purpose and plan for each task. While my current research products show progress in some of these tasks and much

AIES '19, January 27–28, 2019, Honolulu, HI, USA

ACM ISBN 978-1-4503-6324-2/19/01...$15.00
https://doi.org/10.1145/3306618.3314322

work is in progress, I am following researchers in this topic and looking forward to attend XAI related conferences to engage in discussions and find new aspects for my XAI design and evaluation framework.

T1: Proposing an XAI Design and Evaluation Framework. The objective of this task is to find the relationship, (dependencies and priorities) among different design steps and evaluation measures used in XAI research. In a recent work [4], we surveyed XAI evaluation measures and presented a 2 dimensional categorization of XAI evaluation methods by their targeted users and evaluation measures. The XAI targeted user dimension is consist of three user groups (AI experts, data experts and AI novices) and XAI evaluation measures dimension is consist of five common measures used in literature including explanation's trustworthiness, user satisfaction, user mental model, user trust and human-XAI task performance. We provide metrics and scales used for each evaluation measures to assist researchers in designing XAI evaluation plan. As our survey did not find any existing design and evaluation framework for XAI systems, we proposed a nested model aiming to systematize Human-XAI system design, figure 1. Each layer of our nested model illustrates a cycle of design goal (on *Design Pole*) and evaluation measures (on *Evaluation Pole*) to verify the XAI system design. The way to use our framework is to start the design cycle with problem characterization from the outer layer, and continue with interpretable interface or visualization design. The last step is to design appropriate interpretability methods that provides explanations as needed by the interface.

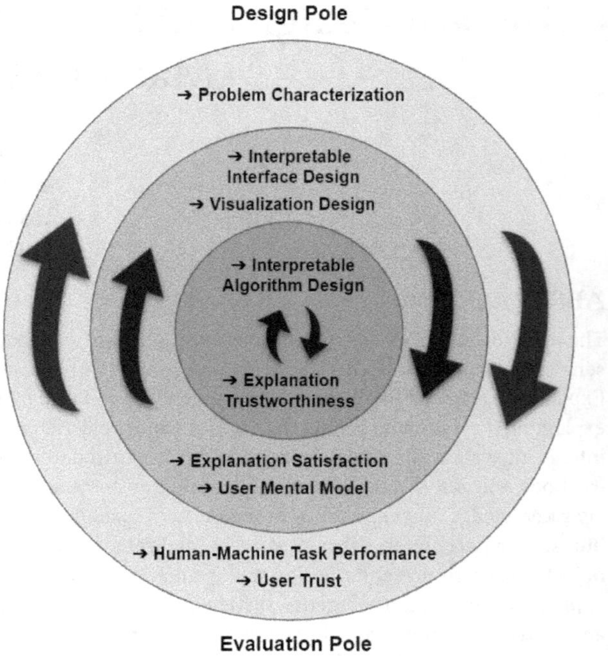

Figure 1: Our nested XAI Design and Evaluation Model. Each layer of our nested model illustrates a cycle of design goal (on *Design Pole*) and its evaluation measures (on *Evaluation Pole*) to verify the design process. The *outer layer* demonstrates problem characterization design step which is coupled with evaluation of high-level outcomes with end-users. The *middle layer* shows interface and visualization design step following with human understandability evaluation goals. The *innermost layer* presents design and evaluation of trustworthy interpretable machine learning algorithms.

T2: Proposing New XAI Measures and Metrics From our literature review in Task 1, we found two distinct areas of XAI evaluations very intact. One is the research on XAI benefits for social media users and the other is the implicit measures of user experience for common XAI evaluation measures. So, I define my Task 2 to design new methods and metrics for better covering the benefits of machine learning transparency and accountability in the mentioned areas. Explicitly, my research studies transparency of news recommender algorithms on eliminating fake news content in social media. In another survey paper [2], we review different approaches to eliminate fake news in social media at different stages and describe how interpretable news recommender algorithms can help to reduce on spread of fake content. We are planing to continue this research idea by running crowdsourced studies in transparent news feed environments and study effects of transparency such as user awareness, filter bubbles, and fake content propagation rate.

Further, we plan to uncover hidden aspects of users experience in intelligent systems with new methods and provide high detailed records of implicit user feedback over time. We plan to make use of machine learning techniques for behavioral analysis of users experience (rather using questionnaires, surveys, and interviews) with XAI systems. To do this, we plan to capture user implicit feedback (e.g., system logs) to capture user experience in terms of trust, reliance, and satisfaction with XAI system.

T3: Explanations for Model Safety and Reliability The objective of this task is to design quantitative methods to measure reliability and safety of the machine learning models in performing their task. The importance of this task is in utilizing machine-generated explanations to estimate system reliability in terms of safety, security and fairness. While we started with direct comparison of human-annotated explanations and machine-generated explanations to evaluate model reliability [3], we will explore other methods to measure reliability of machine learning models by their explanations. An example of critical applications with high functional safety and security demand is machine learning product used in autonomous vehicles. It is important to notice that the trustworthiness of interpretability method is an assumption in this task so we can leverage true machine explanations to evaluate its functionality.

REFERENCES

[1] David Gunning. 2017. Explainable artificial intelligence (xai). *Defense Advanced Research Projects Agency (DARPA), nd Web* (2017).
[2] Sina Mohseni and Eric D Ragan. 2018. Combating Fake News with Interpretable News Feed Algorithm. *arXiv preprint* (2018).
[3] Sina Mohseni and Eric D Ragan. 2018. A Human-Grounded Evaluation Benchmark for Local Explanations of Machine Learning. *arXiv preprint arXiv:1801.05075* (2018).
[4] Sina Mohseni, Niloofar Zarei, and Eric D Ragan. 2018. A Survey of Evaluation Methods and Measures for Interpretable Machine Learning. *arXiv preprint* (2018).

Modeling Risk and Achieving Algorithmic Fairness Using Potential Outcomes

Alan Mishler
Carnegie Mellon University
Pittsburgh, PA
amishler@stat.cmu.edu

ABSTRACT

Predictive models and algorithms are increasingly used to support human decision makers, raising concerns about how to ensure that these algorithms are fair. Additionally, these tools are generally designed to predict observable outcomes, but this is problematic when the treatment or exposure is confounded with the outcome. I argue that in most cases, what is actually of interest are *potential outcomes*. I contrast modeling approaches built around observable vs. potential outcomes, and I recharacterize error rate-based algorithmic fairness metrics in terms of potential outcomes. I also aim to formally model the consequences of using confounded observable predictions to drive interventions.

CCS CONCEPTS

• **Computing methodologies** → **Machine learning**; *Causal reasoning and diagnostics*.

KEYWORDS

machine learning, algorithmic fairness, bias, causal inference, potential outcomes, recidivism, risk assessment

ACM Reference Format:
Alan Mishler. 2019. Modeling Risk and Achieving Algorithmic Fairness Using Potential Outcomes. In *AAAI/ACM Conference on AI, Ethics, and Society (AIES '19), January 27–28, 2019, Honolulu, HI, USA.* ACM, New York, NY, USA, 2 pages. https://doi.org/10.1145/3306618.3314323

1 INTRODUCTION

Predictive models and algorithms are increasingly used to support human decision makers in domains such as healthcare, consumer finance, and criminal justice. Researchers in recent years have raised concerns about algorithmic fairness: how to ensure that algorithms don't introduce or reinforce bias against protected groups. For example, a highly publicized 2016 ProPublica article analyzed data from a recidivism prediction tool called COMPAS and reported that the tool was severely biased against black defendants [1].

Most risk prediction tools, including COMPAS, explicitly aim to predict observable outcomes, such as whether a person will be arrested for a future crime, default on a loan, or recover from a disease. This is problematic in cases where the predictions are designed to inform interventions on the system used to build the predictive model, because the intervention and outcome are typically confounded by variables that may be unobservable. For example, suppose that among pneumonia patients, asthma increases the risk of fatality. Further suppose that doctors are aware of this and respond by treating patients with asthma more aggressively. Then a model attempting to predict the risk of fatality among pneumonia patients may yield lower risk predictions for patients with asthma [2].

There are various approaches to resolving spurious correlations, including post-hoc editing of predictive models. I argue, however, that the most natural resolution is to estimate *potential outcomes*, as defined in the Neyman-Rubin causal inferential framework [7]. A potential outcome is observable when it corresponds to a treatment or intervention that actually occurs; otherwise, it is counterfactual and unobservable. These are the estimands that are arguably of interest whenever a prediction is meant to inform an intervention: what *would* happen if a patient received treatment A vs. treatment B? What is the likelihood that a person *would* recidivate under different possible sentences?

I also argue that when the estimand of interest is a potential outcome, then algorithmic fairness metrics are most sensibly framed around potential outcomes as well.

2 RESEARCH GOALS

The high level research goals are:

(1) To formally define the circumstances under which predictive risk algorithms should target potential outcomes rather than observable outcomes.
(2) To model the consequences of using predictions based on observable outcomes to inform interventions, across a range of scenarios.
(3) To reformulate fairness criteria based on observable outcomes in terms of potential outcomes and provide estimators for the associated quantities.

In the subsequent two sections, I highlight two specific projects under this umbrella that are related to recividism prediction:

(1) A reanalysis of the ProPublica COMPAS data that reframes fairness in terms of potential outcomes. As far as I am aware, this is the first such analysis of this dataset in this framework.
(2) The development of a potential outcomes-based predictive model to forecast recidivism using a novel dataset obtained from the Pennsylvania Commission on Sentencing of statewide recidivism outcomes. This is a counterpoint to the COMPAS analysis that shows how such a tool can be developed and compares this with the usual predictive modeling approach.

AIES '19, January 27–28, 2019, Honolulu, HI, USA

ACM ISBN 978-1-4503-6324-2/19/01.
https://doi.org/10.1145/3306618.3314323

3 REANALYSIS OF COMPAS DATA

The data for this analysis was made publicly available by ProPublica [5]. It consists of roughly 7,000 arrest cases from Broward County, Florida, a jurisdiction where COMPAS is used in pretrial hearings to inform pretrial release. It includes demographic information such as age, race, and sex; variables related to criminal history and the current crime; and an indicator for whether a defendant was arrested for a new crime within two years of scoring.

ProPublica's finding that the tool is biased was based on three metrics: false positive rates, false negative rates, and the value of a race coefficient in a logistic regression that predicted whether COMPAS labeled defendants as "high risk" or not. The company that owns COMPAS–formerly Northpointe, now equivant–responded to ProPublica with their own analysis that showed that COMPAS is roughly "fair" in terms of positive predictive values [3].

We reanalyzed all four of these metrics in terms of potential outcomes. Let S be an indicator for whether COMPAS labels someone as high risk, R represent race, A be an incarceration indicator, and Y be a recidivism indicator. The observable false positive rate is for a given race group r_1 is

$$P(S = 1|Y = 0, R = r_1) \quad (1)$$

We argue that the outcome of interest is actually $Y(A = 0)$, i.e. whether someone would recidivate if they were to be released. Under certain distributional assumptions, we can consistently estimate the potential outcomes false positive rate:

$$P(S = 1|Y(A = 0) = 0, R = r_1) \quad (2)$$

We use doubly robust estimators to estimate each of the rates, for both general and violent recidivism. These estimators are robust to model misspecification and contain components that can be estimated with flexible nonparametric ML methods [4]. We used a Super Learner that contained several algorithms, including random forests, GAMs, and elastic nets.

We find that the potential outcomes rates are in some cases very different from the observable outcome rates. The false positive and false negative rates were similar and showed similar levels of bias, but the predictive values were higher. The odds ratio that was selected as a comparison to ProPublica's logistic regression coefficient was much smaller, showing much less bias than its observable counterpart.

This analysis thus corroborates both ProPublica's and equivant's general claims, but it also illustrates how results can differ when potential rather than observable outcomes are used.

4 NOVEL RECIDIVISM PREDICTION TOOL

One of the ostensible goals of recidivism prediction tools is to minimize unnecessary incarceration. (COMPAS suggestively stands for "Correctional Offender Management Profiling for Alternative Sanctions.") We argue that the most sensible way to pursue this goal is to directly predict what would happen under different interventions, i.e., potential outcomes.

The state of Pennsylvania is in the process of developing its own recidivism prediction tool [6]. We obtained a dataset from the Pennsylvania Commission on Sentencing (PCS) that comprises recent recidivism outcomes for roughly 130,000 people. We are in the process of developing a tool to predict recidivism under different sentencing levels. This is designed, for example, to assist judges in deciding whether to apply the minimum recommended sentence, something more, or something less. For convenience, we refer to this as the "causal" model.

We use doubly robust estimators to develop the causal model and to estimate error rates. We also compare predictions and error rates with models developed under the "naive" approach, i.e. an approach designed to predict observable outcomes. Finally, we aim to create a model that is fair under some reasonable notion of fairness. We estimate various fairness metrics and compare them with their observable counterparts.

Thus far, we observe little difference in error rates between the two approaches, but we do observe that individual predictions differ nontrivially across the two models. Under a threshold rule that classifies people with predicted values below 0.5 as "not likely to recidivate" and people above 0.5 as "likely to recidivate," we observe that 6% of the predictions flip between the naive and causal models.

We are currently investigating whether there are subpopulations for which the two models produce systematically different predictions, especially subpopulations based on sensitive attributes such as race, gender, and age. Additionally, we are awaiting substantial clarification from PCS about a number of aspects of the data, so it is likely that the model will change or that we will end up using different subsets of the data to estimate different components.

We have thus far examined potential outcomes under a small number of categories of intervention, namely whether defendants receive the minimum sentence, a harsher sentence, or a more lenient sentence. Given sufficient data, we will estimate a more fine-grained dose-response curve, which estimates the likelihood of recidivism given sentences of many different possible lengths or severities.

ACKNOWLEDGMENTS

Thanks to Professor Edward Kennedy, Professor Alexandra Chouldechova, and Amanda Coston for their supervision and collaboration.

REFERENCES

[1] Julia Angwin, Jeff Larson, Surya Mattu, and Lauren Kirchner. 2016. Machine Bias. Retrieved March 6, 2019 from https://www.propublica.org/article/machine-bias-risk-assessments-in-criminal-sentencing
[2] Rich Caruana, Yin Lou, Johannes Gehrke, Paul Koch, Marc Sturm, and Noemie Elhadad. 2015. Intelligible Models for HealthCare: Predicting Pneumonia Risk and Hospital 30-day Readmission. In *Proceedings of the 21th ACM SIGKDD International Conference on Knowledge Discovery and Data Mining (KDD '15)*. ACM, New York, NY, USA, 1721–1730. https://doi.org/10.1145/2783258.2788613
[3] William Dieterich, Christina Mendoza, and Tim Brennan. 2016. *COMPAS Risk Scales: Demonstrating Accuracy Equity and Predictive Parity.* Technical Report. Northpointe, inc., Wheat Ridge, CO, USA.
[4] Joseph D. Y. Kang and Joseph L. Schafer. 2007. Demystifying Double Robustness: A Comparison of Alternative Strategies for Estimating a Population Mean from Incomplete Data. *Statist. Sci.* 22, 4 (2007), 574–580. https://doi.org/10.1214/07-STS227REJ arXiv:0804.2973
[5] Jeff Larson, Surya Mattu, Lauren Kirchner, and Julia Angwin. 2016. How We Analyzed the COMPAS Recidivism Algorithm. Retrieved March 6, 2019 from https://www.propublica.org/article/how-we-analyzed-the-compas-recidivism-algorithm
[6] Pennsylvania Commission on Sentencing. 2018. Proposed Sentence Risk Assessment Instrument. Retrieved March 6, 2019 from http://pcs.la.psu.edu/guidelines/proposed-risk-assessment-instrument/proposed-sentence-risk-assessment-instrument-48-pab-6961
[7] Donald B Rubin. 1974. Estimating causal effects of treatments in randomized and nonrandomized studies. *Journal of Educational Psychology* 66, 5 (1974), 688–701. https://doi.org/10.1037/h0037350

Machine Learning in Legal Practice

Notes from Recent History

Fernando A. Delgado
Information Science
Cornell University
fad33@cornell.edu

ABSTRACT

Often framed as a relatively new and controversial phenomenon, the application of machine learning (ML) techniques to legal analysis and decision-making in the US justice system has a rich yet under examined history. My research examines how ML came to be adopted as a standard tool for automating fact discovery for high-stakes civil litigation. By analyzing the key controversies and consensuses that emerge during the experimentation and early adoption phase of this technology (2008-2015), a useful case study presents itself in which an expert professional field wrestled with the challenges of integrating ML into sensitive decision-making workflows.

KEYWORDS

Applied Machine Learning, Predictive Coding, Technology-Assisted Review, Electronic Discovery, Civil Discovery, Sociotechnical Systems, Computational Law, AI Governance

ACM Reference format:

Fernando A. Delgado. 2019. Machine Learning in Legal Practice: Notes from Recent History. In *AIES'19: AAAI/ACM Conference on AI, Ethics, and Society Proceedings. ACM, New York, NY, USA, 3 pages.* https://doi.org/10.1145/3306618.3314324

1 Introduction

In the past decade, new technologies have emerged enabling automation in professional fields historically requiring advanced levels of specialized education [14, 21]. For these white-collar professions, automation comes in the form of software applications developed using ML algorithms which aim to replicate expert human judgment. With this new development, areas previously deemed outside the purview of computational problem-solving are now squarely within the set of activities targeted by commercialized ML applications.

For the legal sector specifically, while often framed as a recent phenomenon [13, 17], applying ML techniques to the task of legal decision-making has a history that extends well over a decade [3]. Most notably, in current US civil litigation practice, the use of ML for automating discovery and fact-finding is considered standard practice, and is governed by a substantial set of case law, professional rules of conduct, and legal procedures [1, 5, 17].

AIES '19, January 27–28, 2019, Honolulu, HI, USA

ACM ISBN 978-1-4503-6324-2/19/01.
https://doi.org/10.1145/3306618.3314324

2 Empirical Case Study

Introduced in 2008 to a handful of litigators in an experimental research setting [16], ML was first deployed live on an active litigation in 2012 (*Da Silva Moore v. Publicis Groupe & MSL Groupe*), and only three years later in 2015 the use of ML for discovery and fact-finding came to be considered established practice (*Rio Tinto PLC v. Vale S.A.)*. In line with recent calls for an interdisciplinary approach to ML systems design and development [6, 20], judges and lawyers during this period learned about algorithmic decision-making systems directly from ML experts; and conversely, technical experts learned from the legal profession how best to tailor and evaluate the systems they were developing.

In large part thanks to this structured exchange, civil discovery evolved from a laboriously manual process of attorney document review to a process that leveraged sophisticated ML-driven methods to achieve the scale required by ever growing corporate databases of electronically stored information. It is noteworthy and surprising that an emerging technology such as ML was so actively championed by a vanguard of judges and litigators as early as it was [12, 18]; given the critical role discovery plays in the resolution of civil litigation matters, alongside the legal profession's traditionally reluctant stance toward admitting new forms of expertise into legal deliberation [11], it was not a sure bet that ML would stick as a key tool to address discovery's growing data volume problem.

3 Research Questions & Data Sets

This ongoing work focuses on the key controversies and consensus points that emerge as researchers and practitioners experimented with and standardized approaches for automating discovery and fact-finding. To best situate and articulate the salient developments in this technological transformation of discovery practice, I undertake an in-depth qualitative analysis of: 1) case law where ML was contested for use as a technology for automating civil discovery, 2) scientific literature evaluating the efficacy of ML for automating civil discovery, 3) law review articles written during the early adoption phase (2012-2015) addressing the use of ML for civil discovery, and 4) guidance and standards literature related to civil discovery published by a variety of organizations, including, the Judicial Conference of the United States, the American Bar Association, and the Sedona Conference (an independent legal think tank). These sources in tandem allow for a fleshed-out picture to emerge illustrating the key interplay among judges, litigators, and technologists structuring ML experimentation, adoption, and standardization in the US civil justice system. Moreover, these sources provide insight into the evolving governance framework domain experts and technologists alike are subject to.

4 Conclusion

Undoubtedly, the adoption of ML in civil discovery can be regarded as a remarkable early success in applying ML in an especially difficult terrain. Its success has in fact led to an optimism in developing ML solutions across many areas of law [12, 21]. Yet key unresolved tensions and controversies persist in this early application of ML in the justice system. For example, the role lawyers should play as actors "in the loop" is underspecified, the valid methodology for generating and interpreting performance metrics is regularly debated, and ensuring a defensible outcome is complicated by a growing list of technical sub-specializations and organizational handoffs [17, 19]. Along these lines, I critically explore the notion that algorithmic discovery has unwittingly shifted the framing of legal discovery practice away from data-driven iterative sensemaking [10, 15, 22], to that of metrics-driven automated classification [4, 9, 18]. This conceptual and operational shift risks constraining the learning afforded to lawyers during the discovery process, while in parallel requiring them to understand technical methods and perform managerial tasks their formal training does not adequately prepare them for. Critical study of these issues is of pressing importance to civil litigation practice. It also presents itself as a rich empirical case study for informing the broader analysis of workplace algorithmic transformation especially as it relates to ML applications transforming traditional white-collar work.

REFERENCES

[1] American Bar Association. 2018. Model Rules of Professional Conduct. Retrieved February 12, 2019 from https://www.americanbar.org/groups/professional_responsibility/publications/model_rules_of_professional_conduct/model_rules_of_professional_conduct_table_of_contents/

[2] J. Angwin, J. Larson, S. Mattu, and L. Kirchner. 2016. Machine Bias: There's software used across the country to predict future criminals. And it's biased against blacks. *ProPublica.*

[3] J. R. Baron, M. D. Berman, and R. C. Losey. 2018. *Perspectives on Predictive Coding: And Other Advanced Search Methods for the Legal Practitioner.* American Bar Association, Chicago, Illinois.

[4] J. L. Brickell and P. J. Pizzi. 2015. Towards a Synthesis of Judicial Perspectives on Technology-Assisted Review. *Defense Counsel Journal,* Vol 82, 309-319.

[5] Committee on the Judiciary. 2017. Federal Rules of Civil Procedure. Retrieved February 12, 2019 from http://www.uscourts.gov/sites/default/files/civil-rules-procedure-dec2017_0.pdf

[6] K. Crawford and R. Calo. 2016. There is a Blind Spot in AI Research. *Nature* 538 (7625): 311-313.

[7] H. Ekbia and B. Nardi. 2017. *Heteromation, and Other Stories of Computing and Capitalism.* MIT Press, Cambridge, Massachusetts.

[8] V. Eubanks. 2018. *Automating Inequality: How High-Tech Tools Profile, Police, and Punish the Poor.* New York: St. Martin's Press.

[9] M. R. Grossman and G. V. Cormack. 2011. Technology-Assisted Review In E-Discovery Can Be More Effective and More Efficient Than Exhaustive Manual Review. *Richmond Journal of Law and Technology,* Vol. 17, Issue 3.

[10] C. Hogan, R. S. Bauer, and D. Brassil. 2010. Automation of Legal Sensemaking in e-Discovery. *Artificial Intelligence and Law,* Vol 18, Issue 4, 431-457.

[11] S. Jasanoff. 1995. *Science at the Bar: Law, Science, and Technology in America.* Harvard University Press, Cambridge, Massachusetts.

[12] D. M. Katz. 2013. Quantitative Legal Prediction – or – How I Learned to Stop Worrying and Start Preparing for the Data Driven Future of the Legal Services Industry. *Emory Law Journal,* Vol. 62.

[13] J. L. Koepke and D. G Robinson. 2018. Danger Ahead: Risk Assessment and the Future of Bail Reform. *Washington Law Review.* Forthcoming.

[14] McKinsey Global Institute. January 2017. A Future that Works: Automation, employment, and Productivity. Retrieved February 12, 2019 from https://www.mckinsey.com/mgi/overview/2017-in-review/automation-and-the-future-of-work/a-future-that-works-automation-employment-and-productivity

[15] G. Marchionini. 2006. Exploratory Search: From Finding to Understanding. *Communications of the ACM,* Vol. 49, Issue 4 (April 2006), 41-46.

[16] D. W. Oard, B. Hedin, S. Tomlinson, and J. R. Baron. 2008. Overview of the TREC 2008 Legal Track. In *Proceedings of the 17th Text Retrieval Conference.* National Institutes of Standards and Technology, TREC 2008.

[17] F. A. Pasquale. 2019. A Rule of Persons, Not Machines: The Limits of Legal Automation. *George Washington Law Review,* Vol. 87, Issue 1.

[18] A. Peck. 2011. Search, Forward: Will Manual Document Review and Keyword Searches Be Replaced by Computer-Assisted Coding? *Legal Tech News,* October 2011.

[19] D. Remus. 2014. The Uncertain Promise of Predictive Coding. *Iowa Law Review,* Vol. 99.

[20] A. D. Selbst, d. boyd, S. Friedler, S. Venkatasubramanian, and J. Vertesi. 2019. Fairness and Abstraction in Sociotechnical Systems. *ACM Conference on Fairness, Accountability, and* Transparency (FAT*), Vol. 1, No. 1, Forthcoming.

[21] R. Susskind. 2017. *Tomorrow's Lawyers: An Introduction to Your Future.* Second edition. Oxford University Press, Oxford, United Kingdom.

[22] R. W. White, S. Drucker, G. Marchionini, M. A. Hearst, and m.c. Schraefel. 2007. Exploratory Search and HCI: Designing and Evaluating Interfaces to Support Exploratory Search Interaction. In *Proceedings of the 2007 Conference on Human Factors in Computing Systems, CHI 2007, San Jose, California, USA.*

On Serving Two Masters

Directing Critical Technical Practice towards Human-Compatibility in AI

McKane Andrus
mckaneandrus@berkeley.edu
UC Berkeley Department of Computer Science

KEYWORDS

human compatible AI; critical technical practice; critical HCI; discourse analysis; commitment analysis; shared control

ACM Reference Format:

McKane Andrus. 2019. On Serving Two Masters: Directing Critical Technical Practice towards Human-Compatibility in AI. In *AAAI/ACM Conference on AI, Ethics, and Society (AIES '19), January 27–28, 2019, Honolulu, HI, USA.* ACM, New York, NY, USA, 2 pages. https://doi.org/10.1145/3306618.3314325

INTRODUCTION

In this project I have worked towards a method for critical, socially-aligned research in Artificial Intelligence by merging the analysis of conceptual commitments in technical work, discourse analysis, and critical technical practice. While the goal of critical technical practice as proposed by [1] is to overcome technical impasses, I explore an alternative use case - ensuring that technical research is aligned with social values. In the design of AI systems, we generally start with a technical formulation of a problem and then attempt to build a system that addresses that problem. Critical technical practice tells us that this technical formulation is always founded upon the discipline's core discourse and ontology, and that difficulty in solving a technical problem might just result from inconsistencies and faults in those core attributes. What I hope to show with this project is that, even when a technical problem seems solvable, critical technical practice can and should be used to ensure the human-compatibility of the technical research.

I specifically focus on a recent extension of Human-Compatible Artificial Intelligence, Negotiable Reinforcement Learning (NRL) [2], which aims to adjudicate the desires and beliefs of multiple individuals through the use of optimal planning/control. Following the method outlined in [7], I conduct a conceptual commitment analysis centered around NRL's definitions of "Negotiation" and "Negotiability" to uncover the constraints those definitions impose. Then, I engage in a slightly deeper dive into the nascent field of Human Compatible AI to explore how the discourse frames both the problems NRL is supposed to solve and NRL's contributions to the field. Finally, in the spirit of critical technical practice, I developed and implemented an algorithm and system for NRL. Having carried out this three-pronged critical analysis, I commit the project to alternative definitions of "Negotiation" drawn from the external fields of Computer Supported Cooperative Work, Negotiation and Group Decisions, and Social Psychology. From these commitments, I developed alternative algorithms and explore their relationships with the constraints set by the initial "Negotiation" definition. I then implemented these algorithms in a functional prototype as a way of demonstrating how interdisciplinary, critical alignments can inform technical design and be used to rigorously test the conceptual commitments on which the design rests. A next step for this project is to test whether the performance of these algorithms is indeed more aligned with human needs and values than the baseline. This task is exceedingly difficult, however, in that the NRL problem statement is not yet applicable to any real world use-cases. I believe the most important next step for strengthening my proposed methodology is to apply it to a more pervasive use-case of AI, as this would allow for the use of tools from Value-Sensitive Design and Participatory Design to gauge the methodology's success [4, 6].

AIES '19, January 27–28, 2019, Honolulu, HI, USA

ACM ISBN 978-1-4503-6324-2/19/01.
https://doi.org/10.1145/3306618.3314325

Negotiable Reinforcement Learning

Negotiable Reinforcement Learning is defined by [2] as a formalization of the cooperative-control problem, in which there is a single robot attempting to satisfy multiple owners. This formalization begins with the assumption that each owner has a belief-model of the robot. These beliefs can be directly modeled as a POMDP, where beliefs over the effects of the robot's actions are transition probabilities, and where beliefs over the robot's observations are just observation probabilities. On top of this, each owner has a personalized reward function defined over their POMDP. For our purposes, we consider a more tractable formalization that assumes full observability of the world state. We are thus left with an MDP for each owner.

$$\forall_i \; MDP_i = (S, A, T_i, R_i, \gamma,) \tag{1}$$

In order to merge these into a single formalization, we add a hidden parameter θ to the set of MDPs. We also augment the transition and reward functions in the following manner:

$$\begin{gathered} MDPs = \forall_i \;\; (S, A, T, R, \gamma, \theta_i) \\ T(s, a, s', \theta_i) = P(s, a, s'|\theta_i) = T_i(s, a, s') \\ R(s, a, \theta_i) = R_i(s, a) \end{gathered} \tag{2}$$

We now have a Mixed-Observability MDP, or more specifically a Hidden-Parameter MDP (HiPMDP) [3], to represent a composite of the owners' models. By keeping beliefs over the θ_is, we maintain weights over each owner. In this setting, transitions act as observations of θ, biasing the weights towards the owners with the models that best predict the observed history. Belief updates are then:

$$b(\theta_i|s, a, s') = \frac{P(s, a, s'|\theta_i)b(\theta_i)}{\sum_j P(s, a, s'|\theta_j)b(\theta_j)} \tag{3}$$

The core theorem of [2] states that the optimal conditional plan for this formalization is Pareto optimal in expectation.

COMMITMENT ANALYSIS

For much of this part of the project I turn to a singular commitment that NRL is motivated by and arguably founded upon, negotiability as preference aggregation. As described in previous sections, NRL is used to maximize subjective expected utility, a quantification of preferences, suggesting that the recombination of these quantifications is the sole step in arriving at a desirable solution. Turning to two fields that have more deeply considered what it means for something to be negotiable, Computer Supported Cooperative Work (CSCW) and Group Decisions and Negotiation (GDN), I point to a number of limitations imposed by the simplified definition of negotiation and discuss how they impact the human-compatibility of the proposed model. For the sake of brevity, I only list the limitations here: Statically Optimal Solution Models, Outcome over Process, Limited Interaction between Users and Agent, Limited Interactions amongst Users, and Undifferentiated Treatment Between Contexts.

DISCOURSE ANALYSIS

Within the inchoate field of Human Compatible AI (closely related to, if not equivalent to, the field of AI Safety), the imagined context for the technologies and techniques being developed is one where AI is significantly more powerful than it is today. In this context, AI necessarily brings an increase in personal, organizational, and governmental capability. As such, there seems to be an immense need for AI that allows for shared control to prevent abuse of power or even all out AI arms races. The broader ideology that this hints at, however, is one that centers technical solutions over more sociopolitical approaches. Stemming from this line of inquiry, we explore the impacts of the following limitations: Solutionism, Responsibility Detachment, and the Obfuscation of Empirical Optimality.

TECHNICAL IMPLEMENTATION ANALYSIS

Finally, by developing an algorithm that efficiently solves the NRL POMDP formalization and subsequently building out environments to test it on, I open NRL to one final line of critique. Again, for the sake of brevity, I cannot go into much detail on the process of implementation or generation of critiques. The main concern that I develop, however, is that the solutions the NRL formalization effectively only settle bets. Any significant difference in beliefs encourages the agent to learn which user is most correct and simply favor that user from there on out. Future work will explore this concern in more detail.

ALTERNATIVE DESIGNS

From CSCW, GDN, and social psychology, we find that two core components of negotiation omitted from negotiation as preference aggregation are conflict identification and alternative solution generation and critique. Addressing each of these components individually, I developed two separate general algorithms.

For the first, we need a formulation of NRL that treats conflict identification as its central mechanism for facilitating negotiation. As such, we require a mechanism that, given the beliefs and preferences of the parties, can find a course of action that effectively calls attention to the beliefs or preferences that give rise to the most differentiation in desired plans. Our general approach to an NRL agent of this type relies upon information-gain based exploration in a similar fashion to [5]. Then, during the process of its operation, the agent returns information it has gathered in some interpretable way, allowing for reprogramming if the users so desire. Once the users believe they are in sufficient agreement on the state of the world, they can inform the agent, which then implements a more standard Multi-Objective Reinforcement Learning algorithm, as in [8], instead of one that incorporates differences of beliefs.

For the second, we need a formulation of NRL that centers alternative solution generation and critique as its mechanism for enabling negotiability. Given that we are working with agents meant to carry out complex plans in the virtual and/or real worlds, the combinatorial number of possible plans makes this a daunting task. Furthermore, a key component of solution proposal and critique is for users to understand, at least to some degree, how their input is considered in generating solutions. Thus, a first step in the generic approach is to show each user some possible outcomes if the agent were to only consider that user's own beliefs and preferences. The next step would be to show some possible outcomes in the case where all parties' beliefs and preferences are considered. After these steps, it might be possible for users to propose, attack, and defend both sets of beliefs and preferences and the solutions that could stem therefrom, but it is likely that specific use-cases would require highly specialized interfaces and algorithmic interpretability to ensure that these tasks are feasible for the intended users.

ALGORITHMIC IMPLEMENTATIONS

I implemented the original and two additional designs in a toy-environment where they could be tested with real humans. Given both the immense difficulty of belief- and preference-elicitation and the intractability of POMDPs in settings with high belief-space dimensionality, testing these designs in anything but a toy-environment is largely unfeasible. While I still need to gather more data for the toy-environment to make any final claims, I worry that the domain of NRL is just too abstract to meaningfully engage different publics. For this reason I'd like to apply my methodology to more grounded research domains, such as the treatment of 'fairness' in Machine Learning.

REFERENCES

[1] Philip E Agre. 1997. *Computation and human experience.* Cambridge University Press.

[2] Andrew Critch and Stuart Russell. 2017. Servant of Many Masters: Shifting priorities in Pareto-optimal sequential decision-making. *arXiv preprint arXiv:1711.00363* (2017).

[3] Finale Doshi-Velez and George Konidaris. 2016. Hidden parameter Markov decision processes: A semiparametric regression approach for discovering latent task parametrizations. In *IJCAI: proceedings of the conference*, Vol. 2016. NIH Public Access, 1432.

[4] Batya Friedman, David G Hendry, Alan Borning, et al. 2017. A survey of value sensitive design methods. *Foundations and Trends® in Human–Computer Interaction* 11, 2 (2017), 63–125.

[5] Rein Houthooft, Xi Chen, Yan Duan, John Schulman, Filip De Turck, and Pieter Abbeel. 2016. Vime: Variational information maximizing exploration. In *Advances in Neural Information Processing Systems.* 1109–1117.

[6] Michael J Muller and Sarah Kuhn. 1993. Participatory design. *Commun. ACM* 36, 6 (1993), 24–28.

[7] Merel Elisabeth Noorman. 2009. *Mind the gap: a critique of human/technology analogies in artificial agents discourse.* Maastricht University.

[8] Kristof Van Moffaert and Ann Nowé. 2014. Multi-objective reinforcement learning using sets of pareto dominating policies. *The Journal of Machine Learning Research* 15, 1 (2014), 3483–3512.

Author Index

www.ingramcontent.com/pod-product-compliance
Lightning Source LLC
LaVergne TN
LVHW082015200926
848481LV00010B/2862